THE CAMBRIDGE
HISTORY OF JUDAISM

VOLUME TWO

THE CAMBRIDGE HISTORY OF JUDAISM

THE CAMBRIDGE HISTORY OF JUDAISM

EDITED BY

W. D. DAVIES, D.D., F.B.A.
LOUIS FINKELSTEIN, D.Litt., D.H.L.

ASSISTANT EDITOR

John Sturdy
Fellow, Gonville and Caius College, Cambridge

VOLUME TWO

THE HELLENISTIC AGE

PUBLISHED BY THE PRESS SYNDICATE OF THE UNIVERSITY OF CAMBRIDGE
The Pitt Building, Trumpington Street, Cambridge, United Kingdom

CAMBRIDGE UNIVERSITY PRESS
The Edinburgh Building, Cambridge CB2 2RU, UK
40 West 20th Street, New York NY 10011–4211, USA
477 Williamstown Road, Port Melbourne, VIC 3207, Australia
Ruiz de Alarcón 13, 28014 Madrid, Spain
Dock House, The Waterfront, Cape Town 8001, South Africa

http://www.cambridge.org

First published 1989
Third printing 2005

Printed in the United Kingdom at the
University Press, Cambridge

British Library cataloguing in publication data

The Cambridge history of Judaism.
Vol. 2: The Hellenistic Age
1. Judaism–History
296′.09 BM155.2 I. Davies, W. D. II. Finkelstein, Louis

Library of Congress catalogue card number: 77–85704

ISBN 0 521 21929 9

CONTENTS

PREFACE

This is the second of four volumes in this history of Judaism designed to cover the changes of the religion from the Persian period (roughly 539–332 B.C.E.) to the codification of the Mishnah (about 250 C.E.), points of departure and of closure which will be readily recognized as appropriate, the one having seen the emergence of Judaism and the other the definitive legal formulation of the rabbinism which developed after the fall of Jerusalem in 70 C.E. The history of Judaism in the Amoraic, Talmudic and later periods is not touched upon in these four volumes.

Volume One dealt with the Persian period, when many of the Jews taken captive to Babylon in 587 B.C.E. were enabled by Cyrus to return to Palestine some fifty years later, and when other Jews had settled throughout Egypt, especially at Elephantine. It examined the experiences of these Jews in their respective Persian, Egyptian and Palestinian milieux. Within Palestine, those returning to Judah confronted Jews who had not been in exile, a situation which helps to explain the Samaritan schism described by Dr J. D. Purvis. Outside Palestine they had to come to terms with Persian and Egyptian cultures.

Whether history repeats itself is a familiar subject of debate; yet this first volume offers evidence of what seem to be proven – albeit intermittent – constants in the history of the Jews: their continual assertion of their link with Israel, their particular land; and their recurring engagement with alien cultures menacing it, within and without. Certain fundamental factors help to explain these constants: the geographic location of Palestine between lands which were 'foreign' to it, and the Jewish faith which demanded allegiance to the one God of Israel, all others being excluded. The history of Judaism in this Persian period was thus one of exile and restoration: it was also a struggle between the rejection of alien cultures and their assimilation.

In the Hellenistic period these constants emerge in an even more emphatic form. The theme of this second volume is threefold: (1) the encounter of Judaism with the Hellenism disseminated throughout the Land of Israel by the activity and influence of Alexander the Great and those who succeeded him; (2) the efforts of Jews led by the Maccabees to counter this influence and to establish their own state in their own land; (3) the resulting Jewish ideologies and literary activities. The archeology of Hellenistic Palestine described by Dr Marie-Christine Halpern-Zylberstein, the political and social history dealt with by Professor Martin Hengel and the linguistic multiplicity of Palestine revealed by Professor James Barr all witness to the very extensive Hellenization of Jewish life in the period. But if Jews in Palestine were exposed to Hellenistic influences, how much more so were those who either from choice or necessity lived outside that land. The evidence for the mutual interpenetration of Judaism and Hellenism inside Palestine and in the Diaspora, described by Professor H. Hegermann, has been gathered by Professor Hengel. It is evidence for an almost ubiquitous interpenetration which is now increasingly cogent. The traditional neat distinction made between Jerusalem and Athens, between Palestinian and Hellenistic Judaism, has had to be radically modified even if it cannot be wholly abandoned. Hellenistic culture encroached intrusively and effectively on Judaism.

At times and for the majority of Jews perhaps, Hellenism was insidiously attractive: at other times many Jews succumbed to its enticements. Yet for these same Jews, it was a smiling tiger: an enemy to be resisted as a threat to their religion and very existence. Acceptance and even assimilation, rejection and even opposition, were characteristic of Jews in the Hellenistic as in the Persian period. But the challenge of the Hellenistic world probably became more pointed and direct than had been that of the Persian. The chapters on 'The men of the Great Synagogue' and 'The Pharisaic leadership' enable us to enter into the minds of the leaders for whom Hellenism was a threat. But before there could be open revolt against the alien occupying power there had to come a deadly and inescapable challenge. This came through Antiochus IV, described by Dr O. Mørkholm. Religious Jews could not ignore his activity. The causes of the Maccabean revolt which followed upon Antiochus' sacrilege, dealt with by Professor Jonathan A. Goldstein, are not easily disentangled. Religious, economic, social and political factors were all involved. Whatever the assessment of these various factors, the Maccabean revolt resulted in the creation of an independent Jewish state under the Hasmoneans. This independent state in Palestine lasted from 142 to 63 B.C.E. After it ceased to exist, there was to be no independent Jewish state in Palestine until the creation of the State of Israel in 1948.

A Jewish-Greek literature, described by Professor N. Walter, arose which borrowed from the Hellenistic world even when that world was being rejected. Jews took over the literary forms, methods of argumentation and theological usages of the Hellenistic world. Above all, there emerged the translation of the Torah into the Greek of the Septuagint, the purpose and character of which are treated by Professor H. M. Orlinsky. Even Pharisaism was later to be described as the acute Hellenization of Judaism and Aristotle deemed to be the father of Akiba.

But there was also a literature in Hebrew and Aramaic in the Hellenistic period. The decline in the use of Hebrew among Jews themselves created the need for the Targumim discussed by Father R. Le Déaut. This need has also been connected with the coming into being of the Septuagint. Finally, under the impact of the totality of the forces impinging on the religious, intellectual, social and political life of Jews in the Hellenistic period, came the apocalyptic thinking revealed in the Apocryphal and Pseudepigraphical literature. In the past this was often regarded as outside the main stream of Judaism. But the chapters by Professors Delcor, Ginsberg, Hanson and Rowland in this volume and in Volume Three (forthcoming) present Apocalyptic not as a bizarre, fringe element in Judaism, but as a significant aspect of it, illuminating the ways in which Jews regarded the Gentile world which surrounded and invaded their own. In the final chapter of this volume Dr Emilio Gabba examines an opposite theme – the attitude of non-Jews to Jews and Judaism in the Hellenistic period: the Maccabean struggle profoundly influenced this.

This second volume, then, puts in question the validity of long-standing dichotomies often made in scholarship and in literature between Judaism and Hellenism, Pharisaism and Apocalyptic, the Hebraic and the Hellenic. In the Hellenistic Age the Hebraic and the Hellenic so interpenetrated that Judaism survived only by adopting much from Hellenism and using it in its own interests. Athens and Jerusalem remained distinct but not isolated: there was often a taste for Hellenism among Jews, and for Judaism among Gentiles.

It is a pleasure to recognize the help of the Mary Duke Biddle Foundation, Ms S. Freedman, Duke University, Ms L. Bacus, Texas Christian University and Dr Menahem Mor, Haifa University. Nor can we fail to thank Dr and Mrs L. H. Barnett of Fort Worth, Texas, and Professor David Daube and Dr J. S. Whale for their constant encouragement. The editors particularly wish to acknowledge the meticulous work of Dean John Sturdy in the preparation of this volume during its final stages of production for the press.

W. D. D.

L. F.

ABBREVIATIONS

AASOR	*Annual of the American Schools of Oriental Research*
AB	Anchor Bible
AcOr	*Acta orientalia* (Copenhagen)
AfO	*Archiv für Orientforschung*
AGG	Abhandlungen der Gesellschaft der Wissenschaften, philologisch-historische Klasse, Göttingen
AGJU	Arbeiten zur Geschichte des antiken Judentums und des Urchristentums
AGSU	Arbeiten zur Geschichte des Spätjudentums und Urchristentums
AHHI	*Alon ha- ḥevra ha-numismaṭith l^{e}Yiśra'el*
AJA	*American Journal of Archaeology*
AJP	*American Journal of Philology*
AJT	*American Journal of Theology*
ALGHJ	Arbeiten zur Literatur und Geschichte des hellenistischen Judentums
AnBib	Analecta Biblica
ANET	J. B. Pritchard (ed.), *Ancient Near Eastern Texts*
APAT	E. Kautzsche (ed.), *Die Apokryphen und Pseudepigraphen des Alten Testaments* 2 vols. (Tübingen, 1900)
APOT	R. H. Charles (ed.), *The Apocrypha and Pseudepigrapha of the Old Testament in English* 2 vols. (Oxford, 1913)
ARW	*Archiv für Religionswissenschaft*
ASOR	American Schools of Oriental Research
ASTI	*Annual of the Swedish Theological Institute*
ATD	Das Alte Testament Deutsch
BA	*Biblical Archaeologist*
BASOR	*Bulletin of the American Schools of Oriental Research*
BBB	Bonner biblische Beiträge
Bib	*Biblica*
BIFAO	*Bulletin de l'institut français d'archéologie orientale*
BJ	Bible de Jerusalem
BJRL	*Bulletin of the John Rylands University Library*

BLE	*Bulletin de littérature ecclésiastique*
BPC	L. Pirot and A. Clamer, *La Sainte Bible* (Paris, 1951)
BWANT	Beiträge zur Wissenschaft vom Alten und Neuen Testament
BZ	*Biblische Zeitschrift*
BZAW	Beihefte zur Zeitschrift für die alttestamentliche Wissenschaft
BZNW	Beihefte zur Zeitschrift für die neutestamentliche Wissenschaft
CAH	*Cambridge Ancient History*
CAT	Commentaire de l'Ancien Testament
CBQ	*Catholic Biblical Quarterly*
CCHS	*Catholic Commentary on Holy Scripture*, 1953 (2nd edn. 1969)
CD	Cairo (Genizah text of the) Damascus (Document)
ChE	*Chronique d'Egypte*
CIG	*Corpus inscriptionum graecarum*
CIJ	J. B. Frey (ed.), *Corpus Inscriptionum Judaicarum*
CPJ	V. Tcherikover and A. Fuks (eds.), *Corpus Papyrorum Judaicarum*
CRAIBL	*Comptes rendus de l'Académie des inscriptions et belles-lettres*
CSCO	Corpus Scriptorum Christianorum Orientalium
CTM	*Concordia Theological Monthly*
DBSup	*Dictionnaire de la Bible, Supplément*
DJD	P. Benoit et al. (eds.), Discoveries in the Judaean Desert of Jordan
DTC	*Dictionnaire de théologie catholique*
EB	Echter Bibel
EBib	Etudes bibliques
EncJud	C. Roth and J. Wigoder (eds.), *Encyclopedia Judaica* (Jerusalem, 1971)
EnşMiq	*Enşiklopedia Miqra'it* (Jerusalem, 1950)
EstBib	*Estudios bíblicos*
ET	English translation
ETL	*Ephemerides theologicae lovanienses*
FRLANT	Forschungen zur Religion und Literatur des Alten und Neuen Testaments
FGrHist	*Fragmente der Griechischen Historiker*, ed. F. Jacoby (Leiden, 1923ff.)
GCS	Die griechischen christlichen Schriftsteller der ersten drei Jahrhunderte
GRBS	*Greek, Roman and Byzantine Studies*
HAT	Handbuch zum Alten Testament
HAW	Handbuch der Altertumswissenschaft
HKAT	Handkommentar zum Alten Testament

HSAT	Die heilige Schrift des alten Testaments, ed. F. Feldmann and H. Herkenne (Bonn, 1923ff.)
HSM	Harvard Semitic Monographs
HTR	*Harvard Theological Review*
HTS	Harvard Theological Studies
HUCA	*Hebrew Union College Annual*
IB	Interpreter's Bible
ICC	International Critical Commentary
IDBSup	Supplementary volume to the *Interpreter's Dictionary of the Bible*, ed. K. Crim
IEJ	*Israel Exploration Journal*
IG	*Inscriptiones Graecae*, ed. Preussische Akademie der Wissenschaften (Berlin, 1873ff.)
Int	*Interpretation*
JAC	*Jahrbuch für Antike und Christentum*
JAOS	*Journal of the American Oriental Society*
JBC	R. E. Brown, J. Fitzmyer and R. E. Murphy (eds.), *The Jerome Biblical Commentary* (Englewood Cliffs, N.J., 1968)
JBL	*Journal of Biblical Literature*
JEA	*Journal of Egyptian Archaeology*
JHS	*Journal of Hellenic Studies*
JJS	*Journal of Jewish Studies*
JNES	*Journal of Near Eastern Studies*
JQR	*Jewish Quarterly Review*
JR	*Journal of Religion*
JRAS	*Journal of the Royal Asiatic Society*
JRS	*Journal of Roman Studies*
JSJ	*Journal for the Study of Judaism in the Persian, Hellenistic and Roman Period*
JSS	*Journal of Semitic Studies*
JTC	*Journal for Theology and the Church*
JTS	*Journal of Theological Studies*
KAT	Kommentar zum Alten Testament
Leš	*Lešonénu*
LD	Lectio divina
MBPAR	Münchener Beiträge zur Papyrusforschung und antiken Rechtsgeschichte
MGWJ	*Monatsschrift für Geschichte und Wissenschaft des Judenthums*
NEB	New English Bible
NJV	New Jewish Version
NovTSup	Novum Testamentum Supplements
NRT	*Nouvelle revue théologique*

NTS	*New Testament Studies*
OBO	Orbis Biblicus et Orientalis
OGIS	*Orientis Graecae Inscriptiones Selectae*, ed. W. Dittenberger, (Leipzig, 1903–5, repr. Hildesheim, 1970)
OTL	Old Testament Library
OTS	Oudtestamentische Studiën
PAAJR	*Proceedings of the American Academy of Jewish Research*
Pap. Giss.	*Griechische Papyri zu Giessen*, ed. O. Eger, E. Kornemann and P. M. Meyer
PCZ	C. C. Edgar (ed.), *Zenon Papyri* 4 vols. (Catalogue général des antiquités Egyptiennes du Musée de Caire, Cairo 1925–31)
PEFA	*Palestine Exploration Fund Annual*
PEQ	*Palestine Exploration Quarterly*
PER	Papyrus Erzherzog Rainer
PG	J. P. Migne (ed.), *Patrologiae cursus completus, series graeca* (Paris, 1875ff)
PL	J. P. Migne (ed.), *Patrologiae cursus completus, series latina* (Paris, 1844ff)
PJ	*Palästina-Jahrbuch des deutschen Evangelischen Instituts*
P. Lond.	F. G. Kenyon et al. (eds.), *Greek Papyri in the British Museum* (London, 1893ff)
P. Petrie	J. P. Mahaffy and J. G. Smyly (eds.), *The Flinders Petrie Papyri* (Dublin, 1891ff)
PSI	*Pubblicazioni della Società italiana per la Ricerca dei Papiri greci e latini in Egitto: Papiri greci e latini* ed. G. Vitelli *et al.* (Florence, 1912ff.)
PVTG	Pseudepigrapha Veteris Testamenti graece
PW	Pauly-Wissowa (eds.), *Real-Encyclopädie der classischen Altertumswissenschaft* (Stuttgart, 1894ff)
PWSup	Supplement to Pauly-Wissowa, *Real-Encyclopädie der classischen Altertumswissenschaft* (Stuttgart, 1903ff)
QDAP	*Quarterly of the Department of Antiquities in Palestine*
1*QH*	*Hodayot (Thanksgiving Hymns)* from Qumran Cave 1
1*QM*	*Milḥāmāh* (War Scroll)
1*QS*	*Serek ha-yaḥad* (Rule of the Community, Manual of Discipline)
RAC	*Reallexikon für Antike und Christentum* (Stuttgart, 1950ff)
RB	*Revue biblique*
RechBib	*Recherches bibliques*
REG	*Revue des études grecques*
REJ	*Revue des études juives*
RevQ	*Revue de Qumran*

RGVV	Religionsgeschichtiche Versuche und Vorarbeiten
RHPR	*Revue d'histoire et de philosophie religieuses*
RHR	*Revue de l'histoire des religions*
RPh	*Revue de philologie, d'histoire et de littérature anciennes*
RSR	*Recherches de science religieuse*
SAH	Sitzungsberichte der Heidelberger Akademie der Wissenschaften, Philosophisch-historische Klasse
SAW	Sitzungsberichte, Oesterreichische Akademie der Wissenschaften in Wien, Philosophisch-historische Klasse
SB	Sources bibliques
SB	*Sammelbuch griechischer Urkunden aus Ägypten*, ed. F. Preisigke *et al.* (Strasbourg etc., 1913ff.)
SBLASP	*Society of Biblical Literature Abstracts and Seminar Papers*
SBLMS	Society of Biblical Literature Monograph Series
SBLSCS	Society of Biblical Literature Septuagint and Cognate Studies
SBS	Stuttgarter Bibelstudien
SBT	Studies in Biblical Theology
SC	Sources chrétiennes
SCO	*Studi classici e orientali*
SD	Studies and Documents
SEG	J. J. E. Hondius *et al.* (eds.), *Supplementum Epigraphicum Graecum*
SJLA	Studies in Judaism in Late Antiquity
SPB	Studia postbiblica
SUNT	Studien zur Umwelt des Neuen Testaments
SVF	*Stoicorum Veterum Fragmenta*
SVTP	Studia in Veteris Testamenti Pseudepigrapha
TAPA	Transactions of the American Philological Association
TDNT	G. Kittel and G. Friedrich (eds.), *Theological Dictionary of the New Testament* (Grand Rapids, 1964ff.); ET of *TWNT*
TextsS	Texts and Studies
Textus	*Textus, Annual of the Hebrew University Bible Project*
TF	*Theologische Forschung*
TLZ	*Theologische Literaturzeitung*
TRev	*Theologische Revue*
TRu	*Theologische Rundschau*
TSU	*Theologische Studien and Kritiken*
TU	Texte und Untersuchungen zur Geschichte der altchristlichen Literatur
TWNT	G. Kittel and G. Friedrich (eds.), *Theologisches Wörterbuch zum Neuen Testament* (Stuttgart, 1933ff)
VS	Verbum salutis

VT	*Vetus Testamentum*
VTSup	Vetus Testamentum Supplements
WMANT	Wissenschaftliche Monographien zum Alten und Neuen Testament
WUNT	Wissenschaftliche Untersuchungen zum Neuen Testament
ZAW	*Zeitschrift für die alttestamentliche Wissenschaft*
ZDMG	*Zeitschrift der deutschen morgenländischen Gesellschaft*
ZDPV	*Zeitschrift des deutschen Palästina-Vereins*
ZNW	*Zeitschrift für die neutestamentliche Wissenschaft*
ZTK	*Zeitschrift für Theologie und Kirche*

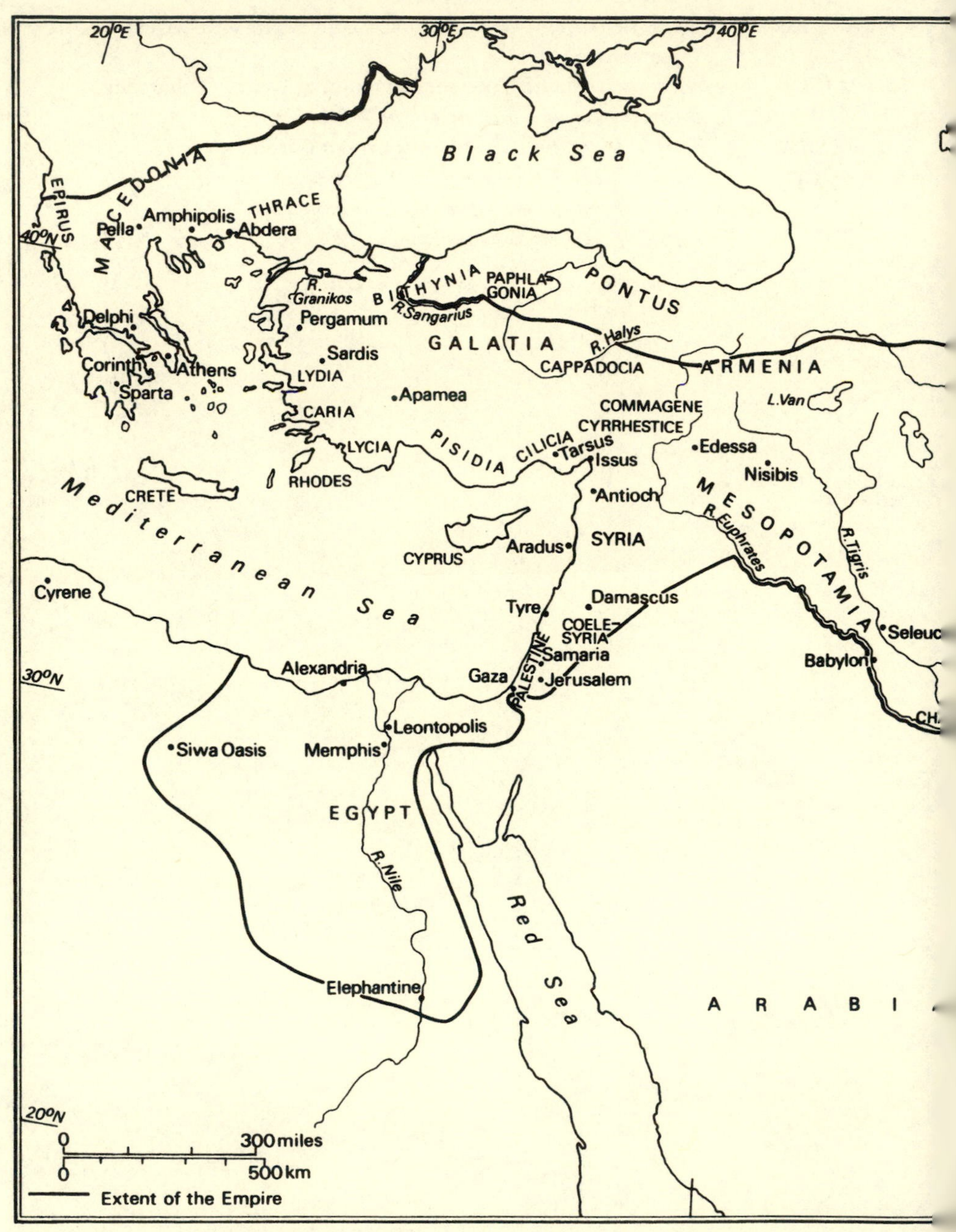
20°E
30°E
40°E
40°N
30°N
20°N
Black Sea
EPIRUS
MACEDONIA
THRACE
Pella
Amphipolis
Abdera
R. Granikos
BITHYNIA
PAPHLAGONIA
PONTUS
R.Sangarius
Delphi
Pergamum
GALATIA
R. Halys
Corinth
Athens
Sardis
LYDIA
CAPPADOCIA
ARMENIA
Sparta
Apamea
L.Van
CARIA
COMMAGENE
CYRRHESTICE
PISIDIA
CILICIA
Tarsus
LYCIA
Edessa
Issus
Nisibis
RHODES
CRETE
Antioch
MESOPOTAMIA
R.Euphrates
R.Tigris
Mediterranean Sea
SYRIA
Aradus
CYPRUS
Cyrene
Tyre
Damascus
COELE-SYRIA
Seleuc
Babylon
Samaria
Alexandria
Gaza
Jerusalem
PALESTINE
Leontopolis
Siwa Oasis
Memphis
EGYPT
R.Nile
Red Sea
Elephantine
ARABI
0
300 miles
0
500 km
Extent of the Empire

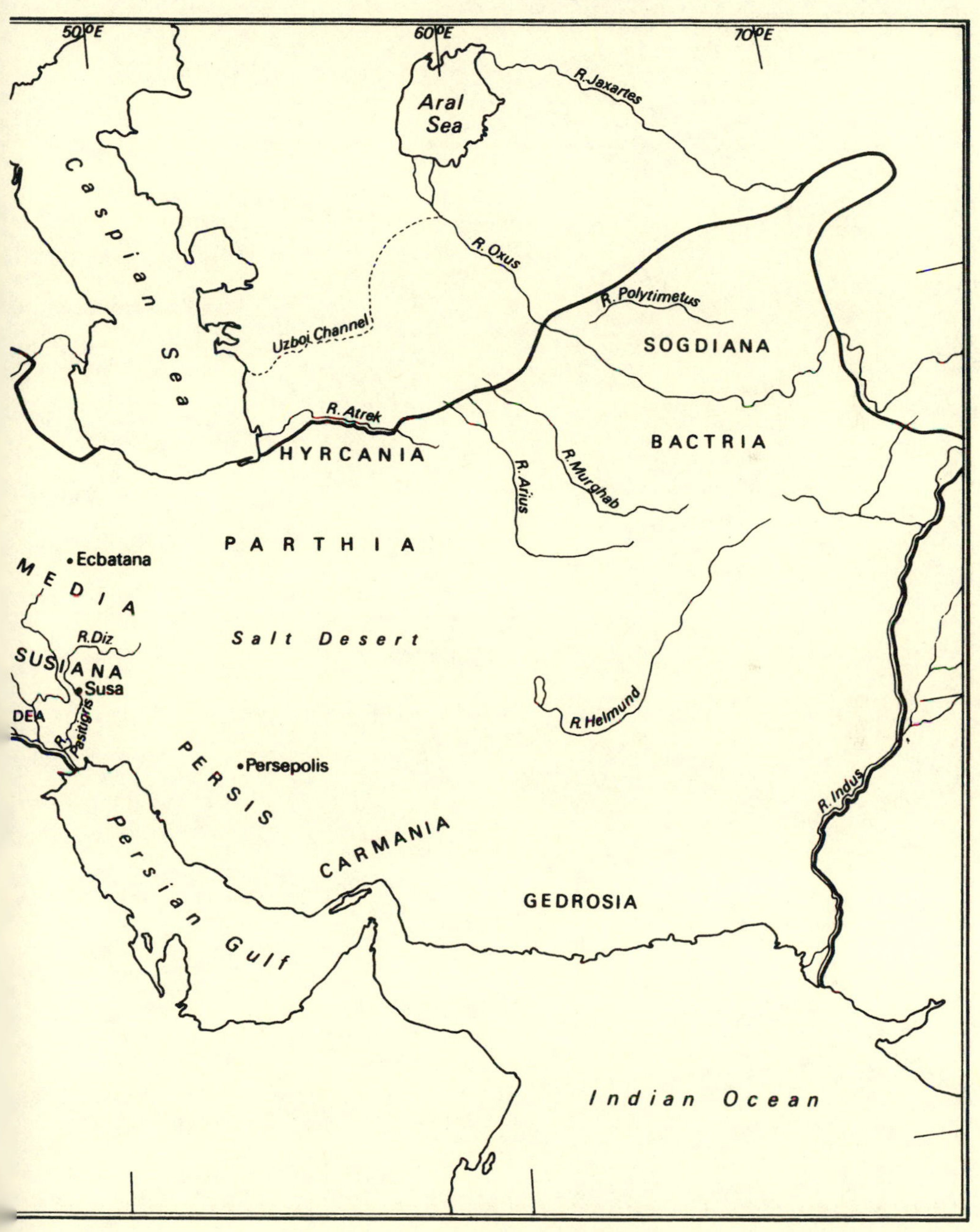
50°E
60°E
70°E
Aral Sea
R. Jaxartes
Caspian Sea
R. Oxus
R. Polytimetus
Uzboi Channel
SOGDIANA
R. Atrek
BACTRIA
HYRCANIA
R. Ariius
R. Murghab
PARTHIA
Ecbatana
MEDIA
Salt Desert
R. Diz
SUSIANA
Susa
R. Pasitigris
R. Helmund
PERSIS
Persepolis
R. Indus
Persian Gulf
CARMANIA
GEDROSIA
Indian Ocean

CHAPTER I

THE ARCHEOLOGY OF HELLENISTIC PALESTINE

In Palestine, as in the whole Near East, it was not that the curtain rose abruptly on the new world of Hellenism at the time of Alexander's expedition. The Macedonian soldiers only overturned barriers which were already offering only feeble resistance to the interpenetration of the Greek and Jewish worlds. In some respects there was in the cultural life of Israel no break in continuity between the Persian period and the Hellenistic age. It was just that what previously was only an incipient influence was to become a major force.

From this time on the new ways of life introduced by the Greeks broke upon the Orient. In Palestine, under the favourable auspices of the long period of peace – almost a whole century – which followed the advent of the Ptolemies, the new ways were to flourish. By means of all kinds of contacts, and particularly thanks to the development of commerce, Hellenism infiltrated on all sides in varying degrees.

From an archeological point of view, the penetration of Hellenism was evident everywhere. First in military installations: the immense superiority of Greco-Macedonian martial techniques necessitated the perfecting and extension of the defensive system. Similarly in dwelling places: the settlement of Greek colonists, who brought with them their standards of comfort and the refined tastes of ruling classes who had known the ostentation of Alexandria and the oriental capitals, was at the root of the development of domestic architecture and of the expansion of decorative refinements. The latter used artistic themes of the Hellenistic *koinē*, like those to be found on funerary monuments.

It was in religion that the situation was most complex; around Judea the Greek gods were superimposed on the old Semitic divinities, whilst in Judea itself strange forces making for decentralization were apparent throughout the whole pre-Maccabean period.

Lastly, in the field of pottery, the local production was very little different from that of the rest of the Greek world.

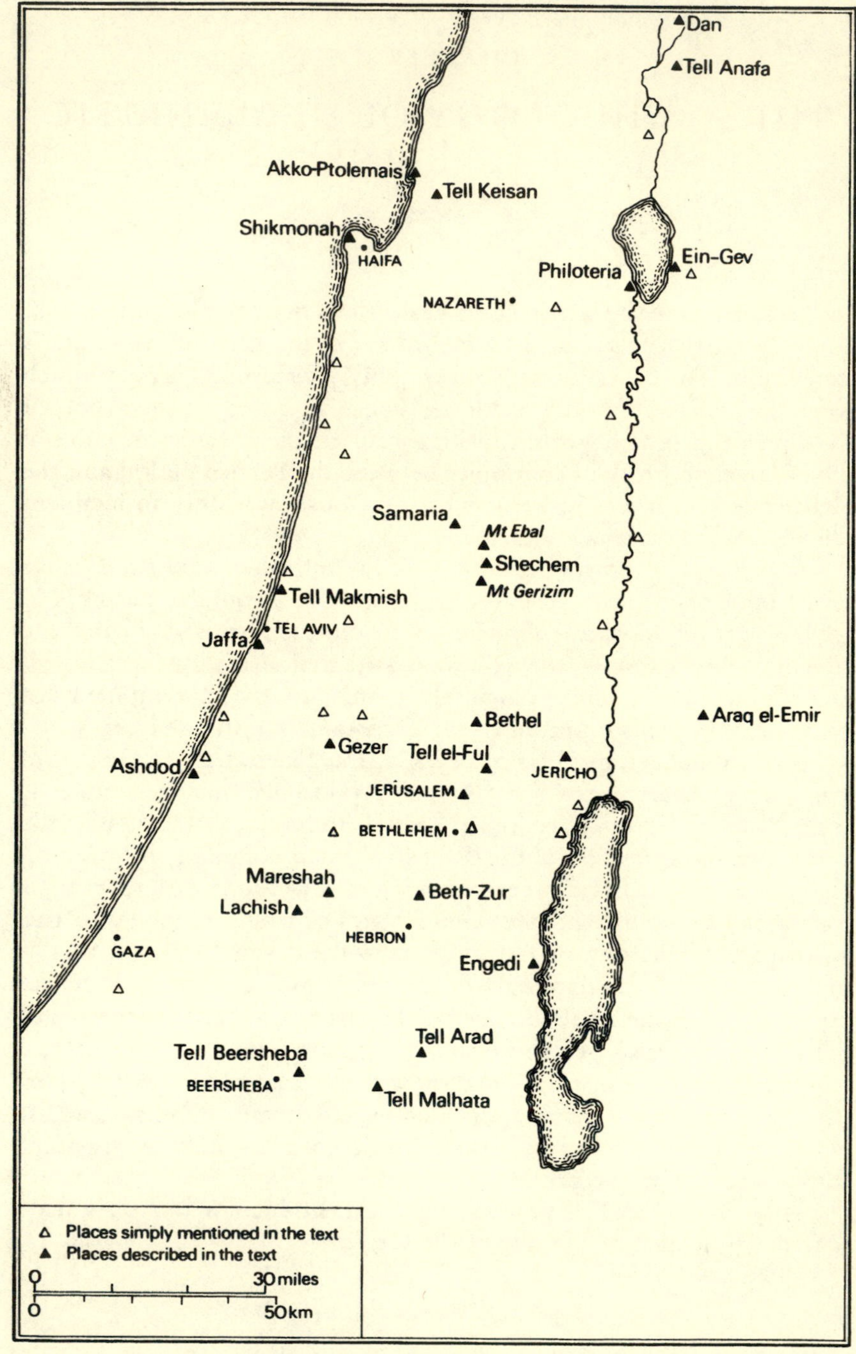

Fig. 1 Hellenistic archeological remains in Palestine.

Fig. 2 Stones of the Samaria round tower. (Plate XXXVI, 2, from J. W. Crowfoot *et al., Samaria–Sebaste,* 1*: The Buildings* (London, 1942), reproduced by permission of the publishers, The Palestine Exploration Fund.)

FORTIFICATIONS

In the twenty-two years which separated the death of Alexander from the battle of Ipsus, Palestine changed masters seven times. This was the period when the first military colonists settled in the country.

At *Samaria*, the settling of these Macedonian colonists was marked by the repairing of the system of defences of the town. The Israelite rampart of the upper city, five centuries old, was restored. On the corners, it was flanked by very strong round towers, of excellent bonding (see Fig. 2). Three of them have been excavated, two at the south-west corner and one – 'the finest monument of the Hellenistic age in Palestine'[1] – at the north-east corner of the enclosure (see Fig. 3). These fortifications were restored towards 200 B.C.E. But in the middle of the second century B.C.E., under the Maccabean threat, the Samaritans had to replace the old Israelite rampart by a new wall with many salients, four metres thick, with stone facings, which reused a good part of the material from the Israelite wall. At first the round towers strengthened this wall. Later on they were replaced by

[1] J. W. Crowfoot, K. M. Kenyon and E. L. Sukenik, *Samaria-Sebaste, Reports of the Joint Expedition in 1931–33,* 1: *The Buildings* (London, 1942), p. 27.

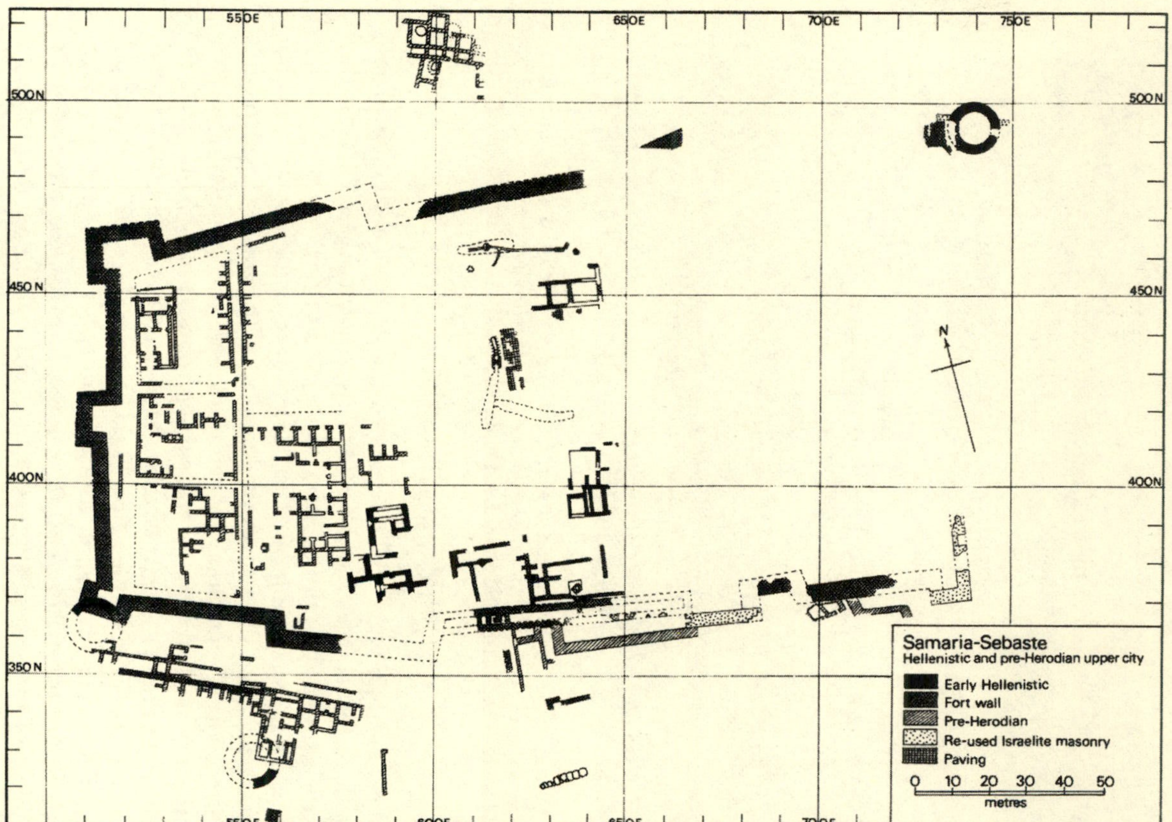

Fig. 3 Remains of the Hellenistic period in Samaria. (Plan IV from J. W. Crowfoot *et al.*, *Samaria–Sebaste*, 1: *The Buildings* (London, 1942), reproduced by permission of the publishers, The Palestine Exploration Fund.)

protruding quadrangular bastions, which were added to the numerous salients of the curtain wall.

About three hundred metres below this acropolis ran the huge rampart which enclosed the lower town. Only the western part of this wall has been excavated. It too was made up of Israelite elements which had been re-utilized and strengthened in the Hellenistic period.

The inhabitants of Samaria, thus driven out by the Macedonian colonists, settled on the nearby and long abandoned site of *Shechem*. In order to protect themselves they restored the ruins of one of the massive walls of the Middle Bronze period, capping it with a superstructure of bricks; a glacis was built on the collapsed debris of the Bronze Age.

Subsequently the defences of Shechem were damaged and rebuilt four times, before finally being buried under a pile of earth – no doubt by John Hyrcanus at the end of the second century B.C.E. – so that they could never be used again.

The ports of the Mediterranean coast were indispensable to commerce and, from the very beginning of the Hellenistic period, underwent great development, particularly *Ptolemais* (Akko), which profited greatly from the decline of Tyre. Recent excavations have brought to light at Akko-Ptolemais a defensive round tower, very like those of Samaria, which also dates from the end of the fourth century B.C.E.[1] Above it was a rampart from the end of the third century, a period of transition between Ptolemaic and Seleucid rule.

At the foot of Mount Carmel, at *Shikmona* (Sycaminus), a fortress, dating from the last third of the fourth century, was reoccupied by the Seleucid army in the second century B.C.E. Further south, at *Joppa* (Jaffa), a fortress made of well bonded blocks of masonry was built in the Ptolemaic period.

The chain of fortifications built by the Ptolemies in Palestine passed close to the lake of Gennesaret: at *Ein-Gev* they built a fort; in particular, at the southern end of the lake, Ptolemy II Philadelphus founded, in honour of his sister, the principal town of the region, *Philoteria*. The town, which nestles between the old bed of the Jordan and the lake of Gennesaret, was protected, on the side nearest the river (that is, on its southern and western fronts) by a wall 1,600 metres long (see Fig. 4). On a high footing of basalt blocks rose a brick wall. Its flexible and winding course, embracing and utilizing the undulations of the terrain, showed numerous indented salients recessed by round or square towers.

[1] Cf. M. Dothan, 'Akko 1976' and 'Akko 1978', *IEJ*, 26 (1976), 207; 28 (1978), 264–6.

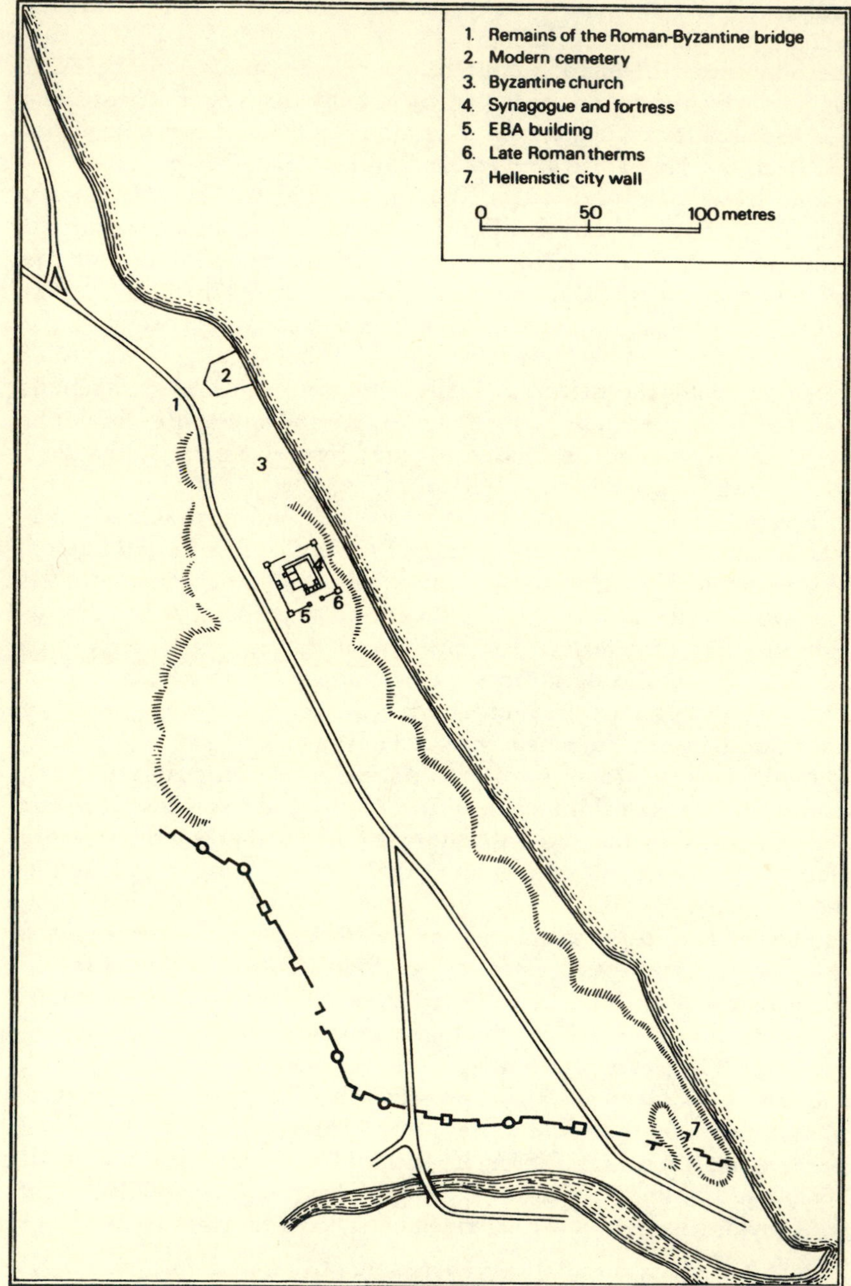

Fig. 4 The Hellenistic fortifications in Philoteria.

Fig. 5 Map of Hellenistic Mareshah. (Fig. 51 from W. F. Albright, *The Archaeology of Palestine* (Pelican Books, 1954), p. 153, copyright © W. F. Albright, 1949; reproduced by permission of Penguin Books Ltd.)

The south of the country had to be defended against pillaging Arabs. In Idumea, Sidonian colonists founded, towards the middle of the third century, the town of *Mareshah*. The enclosure which protected it (150 by 160 metres approximately) had a ground plan which was in the main reminiscent of the one at Samaria, although very much less well conceived (see Fig. 5). Its quadrangular bastions, sometimes only slightly protruding, had to be multiplied to produce true flanking defences. They were very unevenly distributed. The construction material was poor: stones of soft limestone the size of a brick; the wall was of no great thickness, only about a metre and a half. In order to strengthen it, a defensive outer wall ran parallel to it, 4.5 metres down the slope.

Further south, a chain of small forts protecting the region ran through *Beersheba, Tell Malḥata, Arad*, where a square tower with sides 18 metres long has been found, and *Engedi*, where a small fort guarded the royal domain. In fact, the oases around the Dead Sea represented an important source of wealth for the economy of the Ptolemies, on account of their production of balsam, perfume, dates and spices. Later on the Hasmoneans were equally anxious to protect this region and make it prosperous.

This southern frontier was also guarded by a military colony established on the other side of the Jordan, in Ammanitis, under the command of a Jewish chief, Tobias the Ammonite, whose ancestors had already settled there in the time of Nehemiah.

In spite of the defences which the Ptolemies had built, the Seleucids conquered Palestine at the very beginning of the second century. Three decades later, the revolt of the Maccabees broke out in Judea. The rebels seized the localities surrounding Jerusalem.

From then onwards, throughout the region, fortifications were built, either by the Seleucid generals, or by the Maccabees. The defence of the towns consisted as much in the building of small forts on a suitable undulation of the terrain as in the actual erecting of ramparts.

Beth-Zur was one of the most important Hellenistic strongholds in Palestine, being on the border of Idumea on the Hebron–Jerusalem road and mentioned several times in the books of the Maccabees (1 Macc. 4:29, 61; 6:26, 31, 49, 50; 9:52; 11:65; 14:7; 2 Macc. 11:5 etc.). The built-up area was surrounded by a city wall dating from the Bronze Age which was rebuilt in the Ptolemaic period; the site was chiefly protected by a strong citadel at the foot of which houses were clustered.

A first citadel, more or less square, was built in the Persian period or in the Ptolemaic period. Only a few fragments of it remain. It was rebuilt, no doubt by Judas Maccabeus, when he took the fortress in 165 B.C.E.[1] Its plan then was oriental in character (very long narrow rooms, arranged in several rows, etc. (see Fig. 6)).

Soon after its construction, this citadel was burnt down by soldiers of the Syrian general Bacchides (about 160 B.C.E.) and he then rebuilt it, strengthening and stiffening several walls and adding a peristyle to the courtyard, an arrangement which points forward to the big Herodian fortresses.

Simon Maccabeus took the fortress again about 142 B.C.E., and peace was re-established throughout the region. In Beth-Zur the dwellings spread outside the old rampart. But when John Hyrcanus had completed the conquest and Judaization of Idumea, Beth-Zur, formerly a frontier fortress, lost its *raison d'être*, and was gradually abandoned in the early decades of the first century B.C.E.

[1] 1 Macc. 4:61. However the date of this second citadel is not absolutely certain: Watzinger placed it in the third century B.C.E., under the autonomous high priests of Judah: cf. *Denkmäler Palästinas*, vol. 2 (Leipzig, 1935), p. 25.

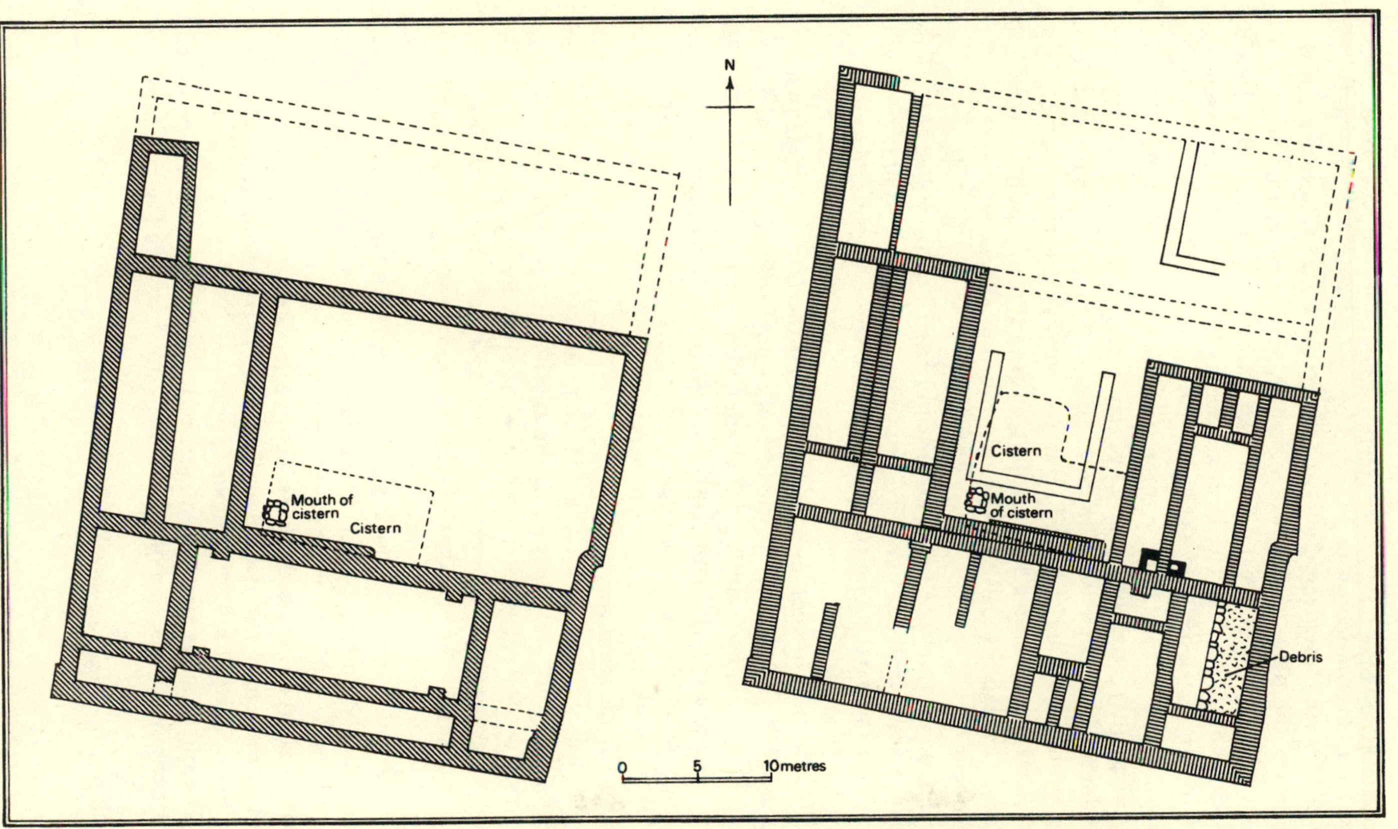

Fig. 6 The Hellenistic fortresses of Beth-Zur. (Based on Tafel 3, Abb. 20–21 in K. Watzinger, *Denkmäler Palästinas*, vol. 2. (Leipzig, 1935)).

It is one of the towers which Bacchides built at *Jericho* that was found at the entrance to the Wadi Qelt. We know, in fact, from Strabo (XVI.2.4) that Jericho was defended by two towers, Threx and Taurus, which were destroyed by Pompey in 63 B.C.E. These two towers guarded the plain of the Jordan valley, at the eastern opening of the mountainous gorges of the Wadi Qelt, on the site of Herodian Jericho, Tulul Abu el-Alayiq. The twin towers were subsequently covered by Herodian constructions. The base of one of them, to the south of the wadi, was perhaps used for the foundation of the Herodian structure subsequently erected there. Close to a large piscina, this Herodian building had a circular interior and it has not been possible to determine how it was used. But its massive sub-foundation on an artificial mound raises a compelling suggestion of a military construction of an exceptionally solid kind, in a region where earthquakes are frequent.

There are traces of other defences erected by Bacchides (Josephus, *Antiquitates Judaicae* XIII.5–8), for example, the rebuilding of the 'exterior rampart' dating from the Bronze Age at *Gezer*, and a small fort not far from *Bethel*.

Further south, another fortress guarded the northern approaches to Jerusalem: *Tell el-Fûl* (Gibeah of Benjamin). A little north of Jerusalem, King Saul had built a great citadel, the south-west tower of which was used again in the seventh century B.C.E. It then became an isolated corner-tower, more or less square, 20 metres long, and protected by a thick embankment. A casemate wall surrounded the little town which had grown around this citadel.

At the beginning of the Hellenistic period Tell el-Fûl was occupied again, and the wall of the town was brought back into use. In the second century B.C.E., the citadel was also repaired: its filled-in lower part served as a solid and very strong base for the upper storeys. At the end of the second century, Tell el-Fûl was abandoned.

In *Jerusalem*, reconstruction was very important at this time. Indeed, since the beginning of the Hellenistic period, the city had grown considerably and had expanded westwards, going beyond the rocky spur situated to the south of the Temple, or 'Lower City'. The built-up area spread into the central valley, the Tyropoeon, and on to the immense western hill, or 'Upper City'.

The old Israelite and Nehemianic ramparts were therefore no longer sufficient and a new line of defence was erected[1] (see Fig. 7). This wall

[1] Sir. 50:1–4; 1 Macc. 4:60; 10:10–11; 12:35–6; 14:37, etc.

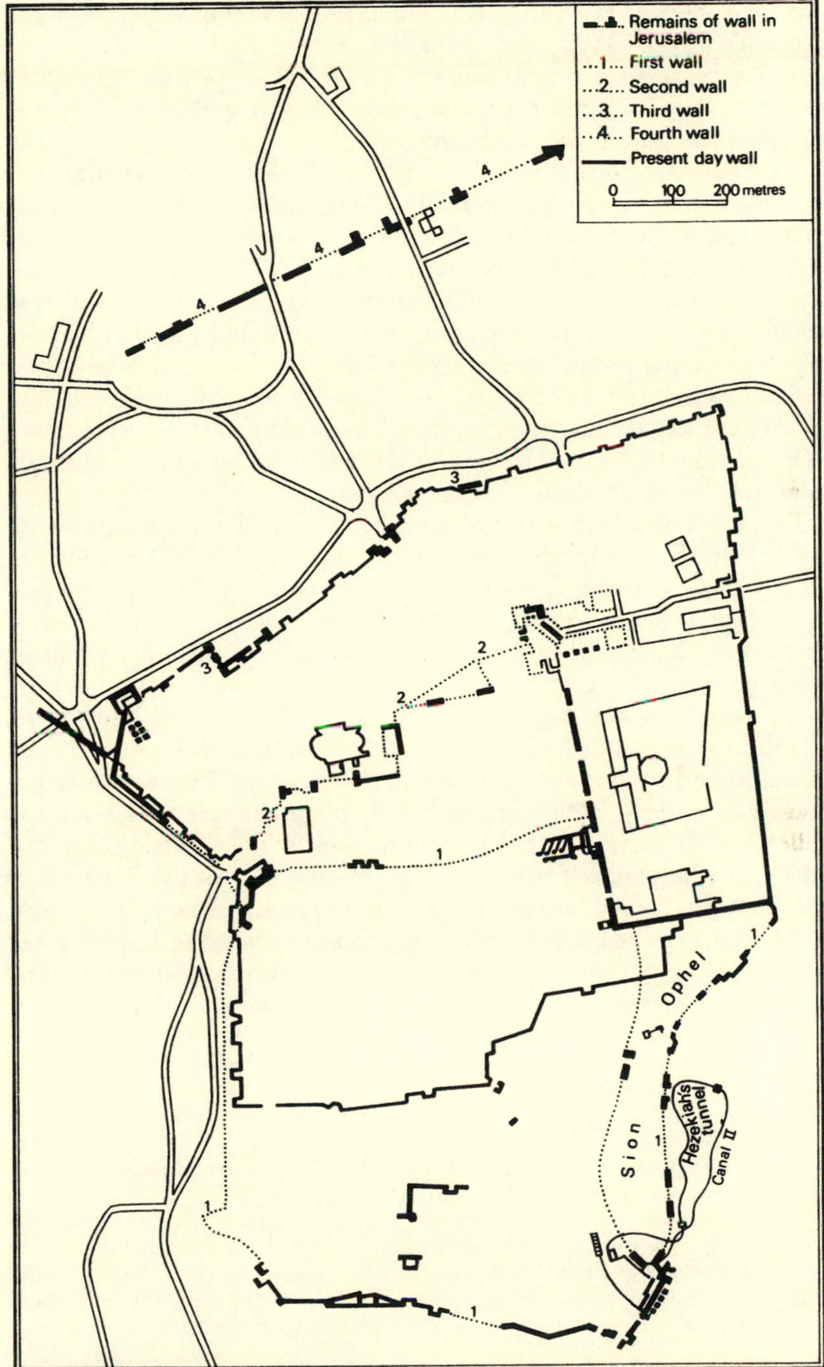

Fig. 7 Map of archeological Jerusalem. (Plan IX in P. Lemaire and Donato Baldi, *Atlas Biblique* (Louvain, 1960), reproduced by permission of Marietti editori, Turin.)

was for the most part brought to light, on its south front at least, by Frederick J. Bliss at the end of the last century.[1]

At the north-west, it began on the well-chosen site of the 'Citadel' to the north-west of the 'Upper City', over which the Phasael Tower of the Palace of Herod was later built.

At that spot, under the Herodian and Mameluke remains, the archeologist C. N. Johns succeeded in detecting a length of wall dating at the very latest to the middle of the second century B.C.E., attributed to Jonathan or Judas Maccabeus and destroyed soon after its construction.[2] This defence of large rough masonry consisted of a simple wall winding along the ridge of the hill, reinforced only by a solid bastion, which protected its most vulnerable side.

Some years after its construction, this wall was damaged – perhaps by Antiochus VII in 134 B.C.E. – and rebuilding was necessary. Not only was the wall rebuilt in well-faced, well-bonded stone, but it was reinforced by three strong, rectangular towers.

From this western fortress, the wall ran straight towards the south, much further than the present wall of the Old City. The wall then turned obliquely and continued west to east for about 500 metres,[3] strengthened here and there by large square towers, one of which is particularly strong, since it is 40 metres long and included six inner casemate rooms.

This southern wall ended at the junction of the valleys of the Kidron and the Tyropoeon on the site of the *Pool of Siloam*, where a thick wall of the second century B.C.E. blocked the bed of the Tyropoeon. From there the wall ran from south to north along the side of the Kidron valley and finally joined the enclosure wall of the Temple. The wall which was originally constructed by Nehemiah was used again and greatly strengthened in the second century B.C.E. by the Hasmoneans.

The northern line of this wall began on the west of the Temple at the site of 'Wilson's Arch' and followed a straight course from east to west as far as the Citadel, doubtless passing by the famous 'Akra'[4] built by

[1] Cf. F. J. Bliss, *Excavations at Jerusalem, 1894–1897*; plans and illustrations by A. C. Dickie (London, 1898).

[2] Cf. C. N. Johns, 'The Citadel, Jerusalem. A summary of work since 1934', *QDAP*, 14 (1950), 121–90 and pl. 64.

[3] This part of the circuit of the rampart is disputed by some archeologists, who think the wall turned northwards earlier.

[4] The placing of the citadel of the Akra – no archeological trace of it has been found – at this spot is the most probable topographically. However, it contradicts some of the statements of Josephus (*Ant.* XII.252) who situated the citadel in the 'Lower City'. For the state of the question, see Y. Tsafrir, 'The Location of the Seleucid Akra in Jerusalem', *Jerusalem Revealed*, ed. Y. Yadin (Jerusalem, 1975), pp. 85–6.

Antiochus IV Epiphanes. Along the whole of this line, remains cannot be identified since they are buried under modern buildings.

The construction of the wall which Josephus calls the 'Second Wall' has also often been attributed to the Hasmoneans. We only know that it ran from the 'Gennath Gate' (see Josephus, *Jewish War* v.146) somewhere on the 'First Wall' and that it ended at the Antonia fortress, enclosing the northern part of Jerusalem. The very controversial line of this wall today represents one of the chief mysteries concerning the topography of the city.

Viewed as a whole, the ground-plan of the enclosing walls, following a pattern already begun at the time of the kings, was polygonal, flexible and winding, following the natural features of the terrain. The curtain walls were very thick, sometimes strengthened by buttresses, embankments or outer walls, in order to resist the newer and much heavier offensive batteries.

Arrangements for flanking fire were quite numerous, often simple quadrangular salients of the rampart. Occasionally these bastions protected the corners. When they were simply connected by one corner to the rampart (as at Samaria and Mareshah), and placed obliquely, projectiles hit them aslant, ricocheted and thus lost some of their force. These bastions, which projected almost in their entirety clear of the curtain wall, played more or less the same protective role as, and at less cost than, a round tower (for example, at Samaria).

In Palestine the system of defences met the same demands as in the rest of the Greek world: they had to adapt to new military techniques, and in particular to the introduction of offensive and defensive artillery at the beginning of the Hellenistic period. Consequently it is not surprising that the solutions adopted here were more or less identical to those chosen elsewhere at the same time.

DWELLING PLACES

In the Iron Age the Palestinian house had its own distinctive plan: the dwelling was quadripartite, made up of three long parallel rooms and a transverse room (the 'four-room house' type). Often the room in the middle was used as a courtyard with access from the street. In the post-exilic period the Palestinian house or palace, under Mesopotamian influence, began to have a larger courtyard, but true to the plan of the preceding period it remained open on its fourth side.

Hellenistic influences were to add new elements to this basic local pattern. The well-ordered Greek house, with an inner courtyard and sometimes a peristyle, usually included a side entrance and a vestibule: the courtyard was thus moved back into the centre of the dwelling. It brought light and air into all the rooms, which were set around it in a row. When necessary, rather than having two adjacent rows of rooms, of which some had neither light nor air, a second courtyard would be added adjoining the main one.

The ruins of houses discovered at Gezer, Mareshah and Samaria respectively show in this connection an interesting evolution from the informal plan of indigenous origin to that of a perfectly structured Hellenistic house.

At *Gezer*, in Judea, Macalister excavated a dwelling of Hellenistic origin, the house of 'Abd Allah's Cairn'.[1] An entrance opened on to a courtyard around which a labyrinth of twelve small rooms was scattered. A secondary building housed an installation for collecting water, with a basin for decanting it, a stepped cistern and a tank.

Mareshah, a mercantile city and stopping place on the road from Hebron to the coast, contained both small, badly-constructed houses in which small rooms were placed irregularly in several rows, sometimes without a courtyard, and fine dwellings with a central court. Judging by their particularly large dimensions (their courtyards measure not less than 400 square metres), some of them were no doubt used as caravanserais. The merchandise, which was later put into the warehouses and shops round about, was unloaded in the big courtyards, whilst the master's dwelling, which also served at times as a lodging for travelling traders, had an upper floor.

In the eastern part of the city was a large U-shaped building for public or administrative use, which housed little square shops. In front of this building was a spacious public square.

At *Samaria*, the plan of the upper city has been partially uncovered. It was simple and systematic: a main street from north to south divided the built-up area into two, and secondary streets marked off rectangular *insulae* usually occupied by four connected houses. The streets were sometimes lined with small shops.

One of the houses, which was particularly rich and spacious (more than 350 square metres), contained eleven rooms and two interior courtyards, one of which had a portico. Under the second one was a cistern.

Stepped cisterns are very frequently to be found under the courtyards of Hellenistic houses. Moreover, various domestic installations (grape-presses, oil presses, dyeing installations, stores, pottery kilns)

[1] Cf. R. A. S. Macalister, *The Excavation of Gezer*, I (London, 1912), pp. 173–5.

Fig. 8 Tell Anafa: imitation marble panel. (Photo by courtesy of University of Missouri Excavations in Israel.)

bear witness to the multiplicity of activities which were practised intensively almost everywhere in the country.

The sense of comfort was often in evidence: the walls have niches hollowed out which served as cupboards and the houses were often provided with latrines and baths resembling our modern 'slipper-baths' (Beth-Zur). The floors of the courtyards were usually paved and those of the bedrooms were plastered or in some cases covered with seashells (Jaffa).

In some dwellings the décor could even be called luxurious: the floors were covered with mosaics and the walls were stuccoed and painted with multi-coloured geometric designs or in imitation of marble.

The finest example of a Hellenistic house with rich interior decoration discovered in Palestine to date is undoubtedly that at *Tell Anafa* in Upper Galilee. The site, which in ancient times was situated near the road which linked the Phoenician coast with Damascus, was continuously inhabited, it seems, from the Persian epoch up to the end of the Hellenistic period. The rich remains of stuccoed decoration and of mosaics which were found there belonged to a dwelling built in about 150 B.C.E. and destroyed half a century later.

Since numerous fragments of stucco have been found above the remains of walls still standing, they undoubtedly decorated the upper storey of the building. The walls were painted in panels of black, red, yellow, green, white or in imitation marble (see Fig. 8).

The doors and windows were framed with engaged columns in stucco, the walls were decorated with pilasters having multi-coloured Doric, Ionic or Corinthian capitals. Some fragments of mouldings, which perhaps belonged to a coffered ceiling, were gilded.

A fine mosaic covered the floor of this room. The tesserae, which were very small (5 mm square), were of all colours and, apart from some white panels, were arranged in geometric and floral motifs, with animals and perhaps even human figures. A number of glass tesserae occur in these mosaics; their colour has become very faint. Together with the thousands of glass fragments and numerous objects made completely of glass which have been found on the site, these testify to glass production locally or in the region.

An important centre of Greek culture, the little town of Tell Anafa was destroyed around 80 B.C.E., probably after the campaigns of Alexander Janneus against the pagan cities of Gaulanitis which he incorporated into his kingdom.

At Jericho the winter palace, built for the kings beside the Wadi Qelt in a particularly attractive and climatically favourable position, demonstrates clearly their preoccupation with comfort and their luxurious tastes.

This was an important complex constructed on the northern bank of the Wadi Qelt and comprised a piscina, a large palatial building and a small annexe. The rectangular and very large piscina (34 × 20 × 4 metres) was fed by an aqueduct leading from 'Ein Nureima, six kilometres to the north. A broad path went round three sides of it, while on the fourth side stood a building twenty metres long, of which only the foundations have been found – a bathing pavilion, summer-house or 'folly'?

About twenty metres from the pool stood the great winter palace; fifty metres long, it was a two-storey building with a central courtyard. Its brick walls carried rich, typically Hellenistic, decoration of stucco, painted or in relief. Josephus (*Ant.* xv.53 ff.) recounts how the young Aristobulus III was drowned, one very hot day, in one of the pools of Jericho. Perhaps the deep basin recently uncovered was the scene of this incident?

In *Jerusalem*, the palace of the Hasmonean kings compares favourably – as far as richness of decoration is concerned – with the dwellings of other Hellenistic sovereigns. The recent excavations to the south-west of the Temple Mount[1] have brought about the discovery of a very large Ionic capital, several column drums and an Attic column base. The capital is of remarkable workmanship, in a perfect Hellenistic style. It has been calculated that the column to which it belonged was at least ten metres high. This capital has parallels in the great Hellenistic temples of Asia Minor. In the Herodian era, it was imitated in the sculptured capitals which surmounted the engaged columns of the 'Tomb of Zachariah' in the Kidron Valley.

The feeling for comfort and the conveniences of life which was apparent in the dwellings was also beginning to be noticeable in the conception of the cities. The paved streets were often wide (two to eight metres) and on a rectilinear plan, delimiting blocks of more or less regular rectangular shape in chequerboard fashion, according to the principles of town-planning introduced by the geometrician–philosopher Hippodamos of Miletus. It was at *Samaria*, an extremely Hellenized city, that this regular planning was most in evidence.

On the other hand, at *Mareshah* the social structure was more complex: merchants of oriental origin, but influenced by Hellenism, were often allied by marriage with local families. This composite character was reflected not only, as we have seen, in the disparity of types of dwelling, but also in the plan of the city.

One main street certainly ran straight across it from east to west, ending at a great public square, but the secondary streets were irregularly laid out, in a loose, wide-meshed pattern of squares (see Fig. 5). They often ended in culs-de-sac instead of leading right up to the city wall. The blocks of houses formed amorphous clusters rather than well-proportioned rectangles.

At the end of the Hellenistic period, the Maccabean wars in many cases meant the end of the cities and centres which had multiplied in Palestine. Almost everywhere evidence can be seen of the destruction which marked a depopulation and a serious impoverishment of the country. To see the region recover, it is necessary to wait for the reign of Herod in the last third of the first century B.C.E.

TOMBS

Funerary customs are often the ones which are perpetuated in the most tenacious way in the history of a people. Hence it is not surprising that

[1] Excavations of N. Avigad in the 'Jewish Quarter' site H. See M. Avi-Yonah, 'Excavations of Jerusalem. Review and Evaluation', *Jerusalem Revealed* (Jerusalem, 1975), map, p. 23.

the funerary practices of Hellenistic Palestine should be inherited from the Iron Age.

Caves were numerous in Palestine. Originally they were used as burial-places. When their capacity was seen to be insufficient, artificial hypogea were added to them by digging into the soft rock; these were the shaft-tombs. A vertical shaft gave access to the funerary chamber which contained one or several bodies.

In the Iron Age the shaft-tomb type continued to be used, but underwent some changes. It was often a simple oval pit covered by a stone slab. However, the shaft with vertical sides gradually gave way to a sloping one or to one with rough steps. At this period too the multi-chambered hypogeum began to appear: around a room or atrium open to the sky, several funeral chambers were arranged. Stone benches sometimes ran along the walls, whilst circular pits were dug in the floor to take the accumulated funerary deposits when room was needed for new burials.

The Hellenistic period witnessed a major development in this type of Iron Age tomb. Of course, there also existed at this time almost everywhere in the country burial places of an extremely simple sort, mere pits dug out of the soil or rock, which could be covered by a slab. Usually these tombs can only be dated by examining the funerary objects which accompanied the body (Beth-Zur).[1]

But pre-eminently the multi-chambered hypogea became more numerous and bigger as the towns developed. The atrium opening on to the funeral chambers, the benches and often the ossuary-pits dug in the ground survived from the preceding period. However, these arrangements, which did not allow for many bodies to be buried, became inadequate; this explains why, from the Ptolemaic period, *kokim* tombs, which made possible a relatively large number of burials in a vault of fairly restricted size, became popular. These *kokim* are deep and narrow niches dug perpendicularly in the wall of the funeral chamber (see Fig. 9). After the body had been deposited there, this loculus was sealed by a stone slab.

It was in the very populous city of Alexandria that the loculi or *kokim* tombs attained their maximum development and complication. Although tombs of this type were frequent in Palestine in Hellenistic times, they always remained relatively simple in design.

The most important funerary group of Hellenistic times so far discovered in Palestine is the one in *Mareshah*. These seven tombs, known from the beginning of the twentieth century, are cut out of the

[1] Cf. O. R. Sellers, R. W. Funk, J. L. McKenzie, P. Lapp and N. Lapp, 'The 1957 excavations at Beth-Zur', *AASOR*, 38 (1968).

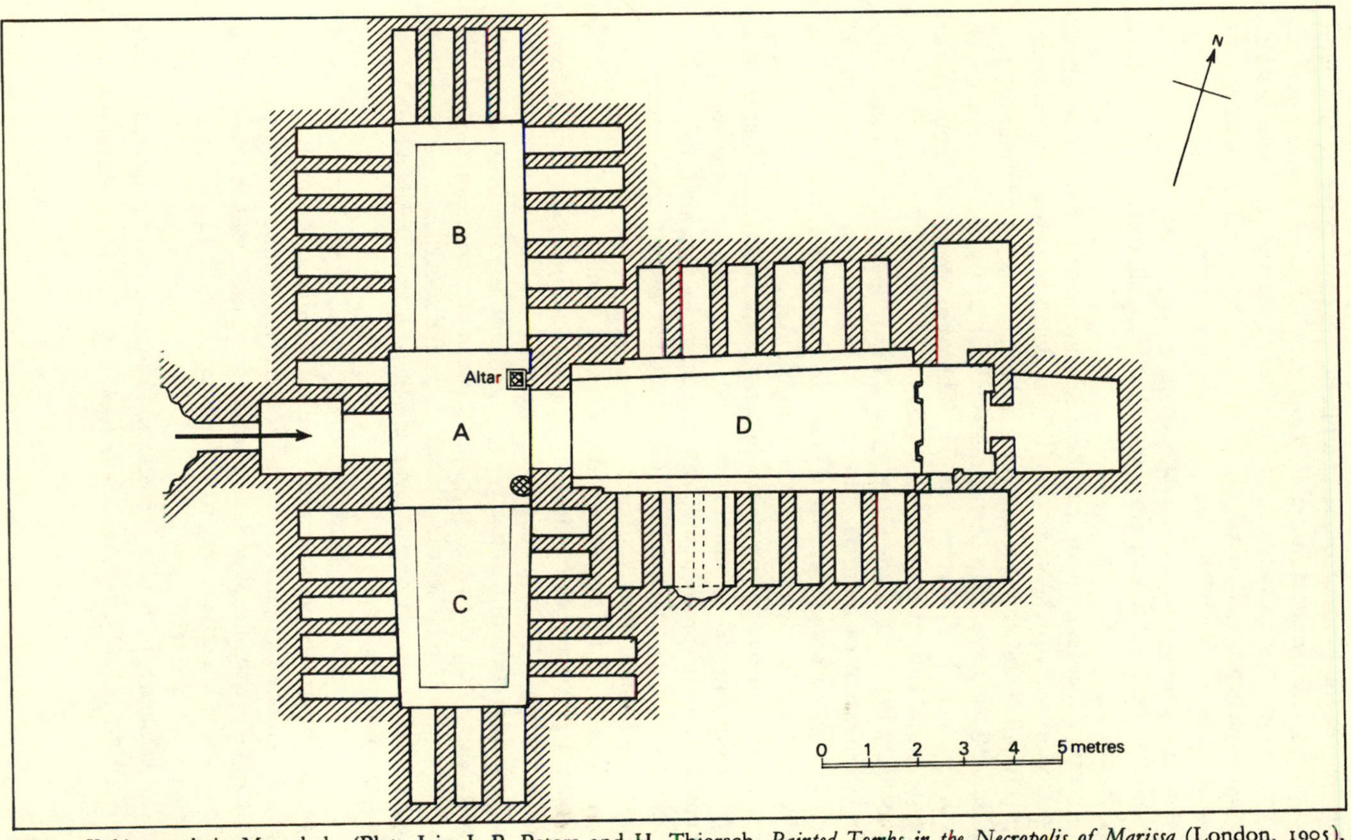

Fig. 9 *Kokim* tomb in Mareshah. (Plate I in J. P. Peters and H. Thiersch, *Painted Tombs in the Necropolis of Marissa* (London, 1905), published by the Palestine Exploration Fund.)

soft limestone of the region and are all of the same type: a flight of steps leading to a hypogeum, the *kokim* of which were hewn in the sides of one or several underground chambers. Two of these tombs were decorated with frescoes, notably *Tomb I*, which had a rather complicated design: the entrance corridor opened into a vestibule, leading to an antechamber, flanked on either side by a room pierced with *kokim*. The main room lay opposite the entrance to the antechamber. Apart from the *kokim*, this main room also included three small chambers which contained sarcophagi. In all, this tomb contained 44 burials.

It was in the main room that the most noteworthy murals occurred. Their colours, which were very bright when they were discovered, quickly faded and scarcely anything is visible today. For the most part these frescoes have only been preserved for us by the surveys which two scholars, J. P. Peters and H. Thiersch, made of them at the beginning of the century, in very difficult conditions.[1]

Below a big floral frieze made up of a winding garland was painted a long procession of animals. This directly surmounted the loculi, the tops of which were gable-shaped in accordance with a custom inherited long ago from vaulted construction in the tombs of Mesopotamia.

The animal frieze began with a hunting scene of oriental inspiration. Then came, in no specific order, the long line of animals, some imaginary, some real (giraffe, rhinoceros, hippopotamus, fish and so on), most of them African. Over each animal was a Greek inscription giving its name.

At the end, this room opened through a gabled entrance on to a rectangular niche which led to three chambers for sarcophagi, obviously reserved, as places of honour, for the heads of family. The painted decoration of this niche, remarkable on the inside as well as on the outside, comprised two big Panathenean amphorae surmounting a funeral couch, whilst on the outside the niche was decorated with two eagles with wings outspread over sacrificial vessels from which came tongues of flame.

Another hypogeum (Tomb II) of the same type, but smaller and more simply decorated, was found a few metres from Tomb I. Its mural decoration may be much less rich but it has been done with great care. Here again are the floral garland and the amphorae. But in this case the animal frieze has given way to a banqueting scene in which a harpist and a flautist are seen.

The *kokim* of the tombs were surmounted by inscriptions in Greek

[1] Cf. J. P. Peters and H. Thiersch, *Painted Tombs in the Necropolis of Marissa* (London, 1905).

which usually named the occupant of each niche. The longest of the inscriptions is found in Tomb I, above one of the sarcophagus chambers. It indicates a particularly important individual, possibly the founder of the hypogeum: 'Apollophanes, son of Sesmaios, who was for thirty-three years archon of the Sidonians of Marisa, and considered the most virtuous and the most devoted to his family of all the men of his time, is dead, having lived for seventy-four years'.

Apollophanes – whose name is Greek, though that of his father is Phoenician – was, at the end of the third century B.C.E., the head of a large family, four successive generations of which were buried there over the whole of the second century. Within that same family names might be Idumean, Phoenician, Macedonian, but predominantly Greek.

This tendency towards the Hellenization of the onomasticon and the fact that all the inscriptions are in Greek confirm the very Hellenistic character of the paintings. In particular the animal frieze was directly inspired either by the zoological garden in Alexandria or by its collections of natural history compilations. Perhaps the artist or artists who painted these frescoes had themselves been trained in the great metropolis.

The necropolis which surrounded *Jerusalem* during the time of the Second Temple was vast. Hundreds of underground rooms were hewn out of the rock. Usually only their very discreet entrances were visible. In the Hellenistic period, however, the custom of building ornamented façades for these tombs was introduced. Commemorative or symbolic monuments of the deceased (*nefesh*) were even set up. Simon Maccabeus thus put up a funerary monument topped by pyramids for his brothers and his parents at Modein.[1]

In Jerusalem a remarkable funerary monument surmounted by a pyramid, of a slightly later period, has recently been discovered: the *Tomb of Jason* (see Fig. 10). This monument of Doric order, reached by a triple courtyard, had on one of its walls an inscription in Aramaic commemorating a certain Jason. The name of this first occupant was then given to the tomb, which it has been possible to date through the coins and pottery which it contained as belonging to the period of Alexander Janneus.

The complex comprised, in succession and on a north–south axis, a forecourt separated by an arch from an exterior courtyard, an interior courtyard, and then the monument proper, hewn out in the rock; the wide hall with its single Doric column, *in antis* façade and a pyramidal

[1] Macc. 13: 27–30.

Fig. 10 The Tomb of Jason. (Photograph by courtesy of Israel Department of Antiquities and Museums.)

coping, and the funerary chambers. One of them (B) stood on the axis and had been used as an ossuary depository; the other (A) opened on to the west wall of the porch. It was provided with ten *kokim*, two of which, at a level about two metres lower, opened on to a central pit.

The porch, with this triple courtyard, its monumental columned façade and its pyramidal coping, was particularly highlighted. On its plaster-covered walls numerous graffiti were to be seen: two funerary inscriptions and several drawings. Apart from the one in Aramaic, a Greek inscription was written in the style of a Hellenistic epitaph, on the theme 'enjoy life'. It is at present the earliest Greek inscription in Jerusalem. There were also chalk drawings on the walls, the biggest and most important of which is one depicting a naval battle: two warships, one of them with a single bank of oars, surround a fishing boat. A deer and a palm had also been drawn in chalk, whilst five graffiti representing seven-branched menorahs had been incised with a sharp point in a style completely different from the rest. The drawing of the naval battle referred no doubt to the personal history of the man first buried in the monument: it is reasonable to think that he was one of those Jews who were engaged in those maritime ventures which developed at the beginning of the first century B.C.E. on the coast of Palestine. Jason, a rich man, influenced by Hellenism, and who had himself buried in the Greek tradition with his game of dice, was perhaps a member of the Sadducean aristocracy of Jerusalem. Indeed, his tomb was pillaged in the time of Herod soon after its first utilization and we do know that Herod avenged himself for the support which the Sadducees had given to the Hasmoneans, by organizing a massacre and pillaging their property when he entered Jerusalem in 37 B.C.E. Soon after this devastation, the monument caved in because of an earthquake (in 31 B.C.E.). Then, at the beginning of the first century C.E., the tomb was reused, and it was perhaps at this time that the menorahs were engraved under the porch.

In its general form, its proportions, its pyramidal roof and the emphasis placed on its columned façade–porch in the Greek order, the Tomb of Jason foreshadows the great monuments of Herodian Jerusalem. Of these, it is above all the Tomb of Zachariah[1] in the valley of the Kidron[2] which shows the closest resemblance to this Maccabean monument. This pyramid on a cube, cut entirely out of the rock, was seen to have not only the same coping, the same square plan and the same compact proportions, but even the same very restrained decoration as the Tomb of Jason. In this last detail, these two monuments contrast sharply with another Herodian monument in the valley of the Kidron, the 'Tomb of Absalom', which, by the extravagance and exuberance of its decoration, resembles more directly the very ornate grand façades of Petra.

[1] This attribution is purely fanciful.

[2] The tombs of the valley of the Kidron, especially the tombs of the Bene-Hezir, have sometimes been dated as being from the Hellenistic period (cf. N. Avigad, 'The Architecture of Jerusalem in the Second Temple Period', *Jerusalem Revealed*, ed. Y. Yadin (Jerusalem, 1975), p. 18; and L. H. Vincent, *Jérusalem de l'Ancien Testament* (Paris, 1954), I, p. 342). But these monuments are more usually attributed to the Herodian period, and this is most probable if one considers stylistic details.

CULTIC MONUMENTS

The Yahwistic Temple of *Jerusalem*, the national monument and the spiritual centre of the Jewish people, was, in Hellenistic times, the one which had been rebuilt in the sixth century, at the time of the return from Exile. Nothing has been recovered of this Second Temple: when, later, the Herodian temple was built, the Herodian builders covered everything that could have survived from previous times. We know that it followed the same general arrangement as Solomon's Sanctuary, using similar materials and techniques. But, although in the main they remained true to the past, the builders were not able to reproduce the richness and luxury which the First Temple had possessed.

The only pre-Herodian remains which could date from Hellenistic times are a fragment of wall about thirty metres to the north of the south-east corner of the esplanade. There the wall of the Herodian enclosure is connected by a vertical joint to an older stretch of rustic masonry[1] (see Fig. 11).

Antiochus IV Epiphanes was anxious to encourage a tendency towards unity of worship in order to give a common outward form to the local deities, and it was this desire which made him place the Temple under the dedication of Zeus Olympius. In fact the Temple was not arranged as a Greek sanctuary, but as a Syrian one to the heavenly deity Baal Šamem who, like Zeus Olympius, seemed to be more or less identical with the God of the Jews. If however this tendency towards syncretism aroused resistance from the Jews in Jerusalem, in *Shechem* on the other hand it was forestalled by the Samaritans. According to Jewish tradition, they proposed on their own account to place their sanctuary on Mount Gerizim under the dedication of Zeus Xenios. The schismatic Samaritans on the return from Exile had not been allowed to take part in the reconstruction of the Temple of Jerusalem on account of their mixed origins – or else they had refused to take part in it. They had then built a sanctuary on Gerizim, their sacred mountain. Their temple was built on *Tell er-Ras*, the northern spur of Mount Gerizim, and here they finally adopted a free monotheism which horrified the purists of Judah. Their equivocal attitude made them ready to admit that their supreme god might be identical with a pagan deity. Accord-

[1] This dating is the one most commonly agreed upon now. However, this piece of wall is sometimes attributed to the time of Solomon (cf. E. M. Laperrousaz, 'A-t-on dégagé l'angle sud-est du "Temple de Salomon"?', *Syria*, 50 (1973), 378–84 or, more often, to the Persian period (cf. M. Dunand, 'Byblos, Sidon, Jérusalem. Monuments apparentés des temps achéménides', *Congress Volume Rome 1968*, VTSup 17 (Leiden, 1969), p. 69).

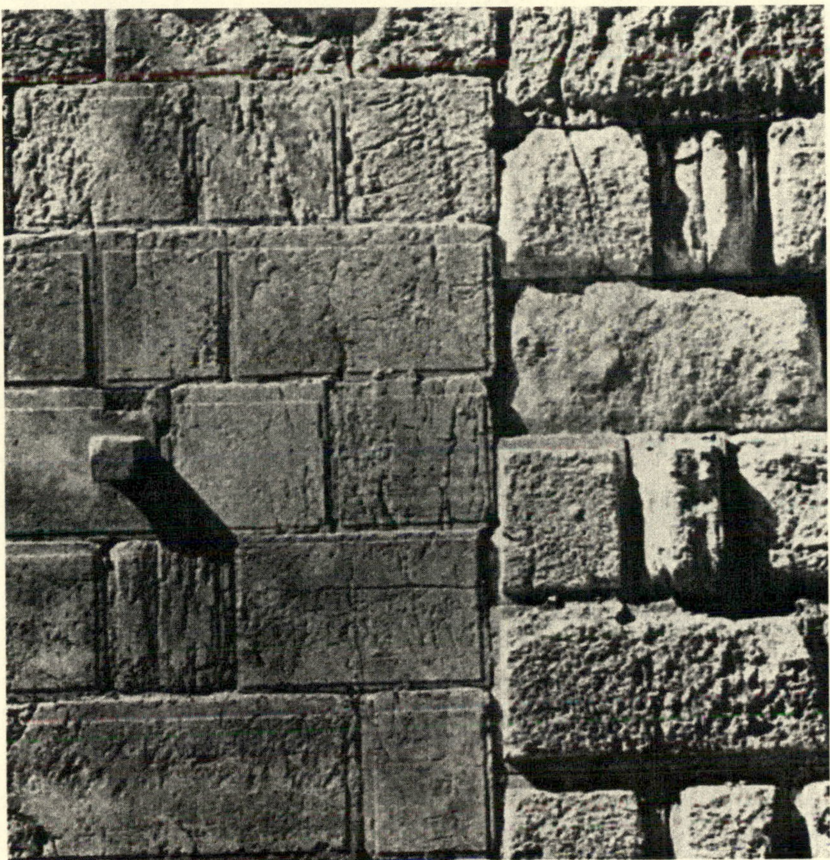

Fig. 11 Vertical joint in Jerusalem Temple wall. (From an article by Y. Tsafrir in *Jerusalem Revealed*, ed. Y. Yadin (Jerusalem, 1975), p. 85, published by the Israel Exploration Society.)

ing to tradition it was at the time of Alexander the Great that the temple of Gerizim, which was meant to be a reproduction of the Temple of Jerusalem, was founded. The plan of this sanctuary, which was later destroyed by John Hyrcanus (*circa* 128 B.C.E.), has been rediscovered in the course of recent excavations on Tell er-Ras.[1] The Hellenistic ruins were covered by a temple in Greek style which was constructed in 130 C.E. and dedicated to Zeus Hypsistos. The Hellenistic temple of the Samaritans, built of large crudely cut stones, was

[1] Cf. R. J. Bull, 'The two Temples at Tell er-Ras on Mount Gerizim in occupied Jordan', *AJA*, 74 (1970), 189–90; and *IEJ*, 18 (1968), 192–3.

almost square in shape (18 × 21 metres). It has not been possible to define its plan or any architectural details more precisely, since the Hellenistic remains were used again in the construction of the podium of the Roman temple.

Lachish in Idumea, which has been identified as Tell ed-Duweir, was in an equally remote position. Lachish is mentioned in Nehemiah (11:30) in the list of 'remains of Israel' (which means that there was there a Jewish settlement at the time of return from Exile). It flourished in the Persian period but declined in the Hellenistic period, when it was supplanted in the region by Mareshah. However, in the second century B.C.E. an edifice of a religious nature was built. The 'Solar Shrine', discovered in 1935, was a structure measuring 27 × 17 metres, orientated east–west and built of small stones set into mortar. The plan consisted of a spacious square courtyard occupying half the total area, bordered on the east by a row of four small rooms, whilst the sanctuary proper was situated in the western part. This comprised, over practically the whole width of the building, a raised antechamber which was reached by five steps, and, beyond that, three small square rooms. The central room, in line with the entrance, was approached by a flight of three stairs. In its southern wall was a niche where a drainpipe ran. On the steps leading to the ante-room, a stone altar was discovered at the time of excavations. Even apart from the presence of the altar, the east–west axis, the fact that the sanctuary was two metres higher than the rest of the building, the existence of a drain in the cella, all led to the conclusion that the building was a place of worship. This fact was confirmed at the time of recent excavations led by Y. Aharoni between 1966 and 1968: the Hellenistic building had been constructed above a temple of the tenth century B.C.E. Basing his theory on the resemblance of plan, dimensions and orientation between the 'Solar shrine' and the Israelite temple of Arad, dating from the tenth century B.C.E., Y. Aharoni concluded that the temple of Lachish could have been built by Jews, and that it was a traditional Israelite altar.[1]

The Hellenistic temple of *Beersheba* also occupied the site of a former Israelite sanctuary destroyed in the time of King Hezekiah. The plan of this temple, which dated from the third or second century B.C.E., was of the same type as the one at Lachish: the centre of a courtyard was taken up by an altar for offerings and from there one moved eastwards up two steps into a wide room. A little cella was fitted into the western wall of the room. The *favissae* (rubbish pits), set in the courtyard and round about, were filled with pagan votive objects made of bronze, ivory,

[1] Cf. 'Excavations at Tel-Arad', *IEJ*, 17 (1967), 233–49.

glass or stone and among them were numerous statuettes, amulets, small incense altars and so on.

It was at *Samaria*, the city of the Macedonian colonists, that the worship of the Greek gods must have been most widely practised. But unfortunately there only remain faint indications of it: on the northern slope of the Tell, to the north-east of a Roman temple to Kore, two reliefs bearing the emblems of the Dioscuri, as well as a dedication to Isis and Serapis, were associated with remains dating from the third century B.C.E. In the third century, in fact, the worship of Isis together with Serapis was to develop greatly in the empire of the Ptolemies. Palestine did not escape this trend and the worship of Isis, identified with the indigenous goddess Astarte, is to be found at *Ashkelon, Gaza* and possibly even in *Jerusalem*.

At *Ptolemais*, a Greek inscription tells us it was under her old Syrian name of Atargatis[1] that the deity – linked with her consort Hadad – received a dedication made by a Greek. On the other hand another Greek inscription dating from the second half of the second century B.C.E. testifies to a cult of Zeus Soter at this period in this same city.

Although they were easily confused with Zeus, the *Baalim* none the less continued to be honoured in Hellenistic times according to the old Canaanite and Phoenician traditions. In places of worship in the open air, surrounded only by a wall, sacrifices were made on a simple altar among the trees and groves. Throughout Hellenistic times the most venerable Palestinian sanctuaries preserved this form: so it was at Mamre near Hebron, so too especially at Carmel, where the archaic rites which were practised were described by Tacitus (*Histories* II.78). At the foot of Mount Hermon, *Dan*, where one of the sources of the Jordan rose, was a religious centre which was already long-established in the period of the kings. Jeroboam set up a high place there. This spacious esplanade remained in use during the Hellenistic period. It was even enlarged and renovated at that time.

On the Mediterranean coast, some fifteen kilometres north of Tel Aviv, very near *Tell Makmish*, a sanctuary of the Persian period was reused in the third century B.C.E. as an open-air platform on which an altar was built, to perform a cult of the Phoenician type to Astarte.

Hyrcanus tried to build in Transjordan a temple to rival the one in Jerusalem; at Lachish Jews built a Yahwistic temple; and we are

[1] Cf. M. Avi-Yonah, 'Syrian Gods at Ptolemais-Accho', *IEJ*, 9 (1959), 2, where the inscription is dated to the second century B.C.E., but against this cf. J. and L. Robert, 'Bulletin Epigraphique', *REG*, 73 (1960), 200, who would put it back, presumably to the third century B.C.E.

compelled to admit that the Deuteronomic law to centralize worship was not yet strictly enforced in Palestine itself in Hellenistic times. In the period which followed the Maccabean rebellion, this state of affairs was radically changed: after the destruction of the Temple of Jerusalem in 70 C.E., there was no further attempt to put up another temple.

In non-Jewish circles, Greek religion, rather than replacing the old Canaanite traditions, developed alongside them. And so the new masters gave Greek names to the old Semitic deities, and the old Canaanite practice of worshipping in the open air could not have seemed to them very different from their own custom of honouring Zeus on a simple altar on top of Mount Ida or Olympus.

POTTERY

For the archeologist dealing with Palestine, pottery is not only the most valuable chronological evidence, but also a reflection of the evolution of material culture. In the Hellenistic period, the evidence provided by pottery reflects the situation of the country in the Mediterranean world at that time. Palestine was a small province which had its position in the Hellenistic *koiné*, but it was the modest position of a country somewhat removed from the great cultural and commercial movements, a country which was often ravaged by wars and preserved a strong indigenous tradition. Local production reflected this position. Sometimes forms would reproduce in a mediocre fashion pieces made in the Greek world, sometimes old forms were adapted with hardly any changes, forms which had been traditional in the country, some for many centuries (as for example cooking-pots, which scarcely underwent any development between the Iron Age and the Byzantine period). Forms from sites in the north and the south were very much alike. There seems to have been no local variation for geographical reasons. However, pottery production in Hellenistic times was never industrialized. It is true that the workshops began to use more mechanical and more rapid methods, but the processes remained those of the craftsman. Manufacture was to a large extent individual and though forms were in the main standardized, complete uniformity did not occur, since each piece differed from the others in some detail and kept the mark of the hand which had fashioned or painted it.

In the whole of the Hellenistic world, the manufacture of pottery was decentralized and the shapes produced originally in Greece were swiftly copied in the Orient, which in turn became an exporter. The great centres of production like Tarsus or Antioch were counterbalanced by workshops in small localities. In Palestine every centre of any importance developed its own production. There were not really many imported vessels, except in the big urban centres like Ptolemais (Akko) or Samaria, which were greatly influenced by Hellenism. These pieces are vessels easily distinguishable from the local pottery both on account of the superior quality of their paste and by their glaze, when there is any. Apart from vessels which had been used for carrying wine (amphorae) or imported perfumes (unguentaria), most of these imports were fine table vessels with a black glaze.

Palestinian potters in Hellenistic times used a cream-coloured, pink or light brown paste, which was particularly well-refined and well-fired. When it was painted, the local pottery was covered with characteristic paint of a mediocre quality, which was often matt and clumsily applied; the colour varied from black to brown and particularly red (Hellenistic Decorated Ware).

Apart from a general tendency towards elongation and lightening, the shapes in everyday use evolved relatively little during the period. *Jars* were cylindrical, ovoid or bell-shaped, with a rounded base and vertical handles, and had, at the beginning of the Hellenistic period, a low neck which became much higher in the second and first centuries B.C.E. The rim, curved or angular, was formed either by flaring out or by turning back the neck. *Jugs*, often of very great capacity, were ovoid or pearshaped. Right at the beginning of the Hellenistic period, their base was rounded as in Persian times. Later, they always had a ring base on which they could stand upright. In the second and first centuries B.C.E., very narrow necks appeared. *Flasks*, with two vertical handles and elongated neck, *oil-bottles* and spherical *juglets* were also frequent. The *unguentaria* were little phials to hold expensive oils and perfumes. The spindle-shaped unguentarium appeared in Greece in the fourth century B.C.E. and replaced the lekythos. In Palestine it was made from the third century B.C.E. onwards and was replaced in the Herodian period by the pearshaped unguentarium. The spindle-shaped unguentarium changed very little. However, one can distinguish the earlier very bulbous bodies and the later shapes which were on the contrary very slim with an elongated base. The main characteristic of the spindle-shaped unguentaria of the third and second centuries B.C.E. was the very thick material of which they were made; in the first century on the other hand it was very thin. These vessels, which were common everywhere in the Hellenistic world, were occasionally decorated either with rough circular bands or by a glaze on the upper two-thirds of their bodies.

Cooking pots. Numerous fragments of these are always to be found on the Hellenistic sites in Palestine. The cooking-pots of the Hellenistic period were scarcely any different from those of the Iron Age or the Persian period, nor yet from those which were to be made in the Roman period. Their paste was red in colour, about 3 mm thick and usually ribbed; it was fine and hard and much purer than that made in the Israelite period. After 150 B.C.E. the paste became extremely delicate and fragile. The belly of the pot was generally spherical, but tended to become more squat in the first century B.C.E. The short neck surrounding the narrow opening was less and less distinguishable from the body. Its rim was either flat, rounded or folded back, or alternatively, when it was to have a lid, it was grooved. Another type of cooking-pot is to be found; this has a belly which is not spherical but shorter and more shallow: the stewing-pan. Thick *mortars* can be recognized by their paste which has many large grits; these were particularly common at the beginning of the Hellenistic period. *Bowls, plates* and *dishes* are the pieces which are found in the greatest numbers. Obviously they are of varying sizes and used for different purposes, and range from the large dish with a 40 cm diameter to tiny beakers measuring only a few centimetres wide. Their edges are vertical, turned either in or out. These pieces, which in some cases have small vertical handles, are often painted: the painting would cover the whole of the inside of the vessel and the top third of the exterior. A variant of these plates, which is characteristic of the Hellenistic levels, is the *fish plate*. This was a plate at the base of which was a little hollow. In certain later forms another refinement was added, when a small ring was set around the hollow. In Athens, the fish plate was in use from the end of the fifth to the beginning of the third century B.C.E. Later, this form was manufactured in the Eastern Mediterranean where it was found over a wide area. Although fish plates were found in Tarsus from the fourth century B.C.E., the form achieved its *floruit* around 200 B.C.E. and then almost completely disappeared after the end of the second century. *Bowls with relief decoration* were till recently still incorrectly called 'Megarian Bowls'. They were covered in a black or red glaze and decorated with plant motifs or scenes depicted in relief. They appeared in Athens at the beginning of the third century B.C.E. and in Tarsus at the end of the same century. They appear to have been introduced and then produced in Palestine from 150 B.C.E. Exact dating is difficult due to the fact that the repertoire of moulded decorative motifs was relatively limited and was repeated indefinitely up to the first century B.C.E.

Lamps. Wheel-made lamps, of Greek type, without decoration or handles and with a thick, flat nozzle, are found frequently on all sites, even more than the folded saucer lamp, the heritage of an old local

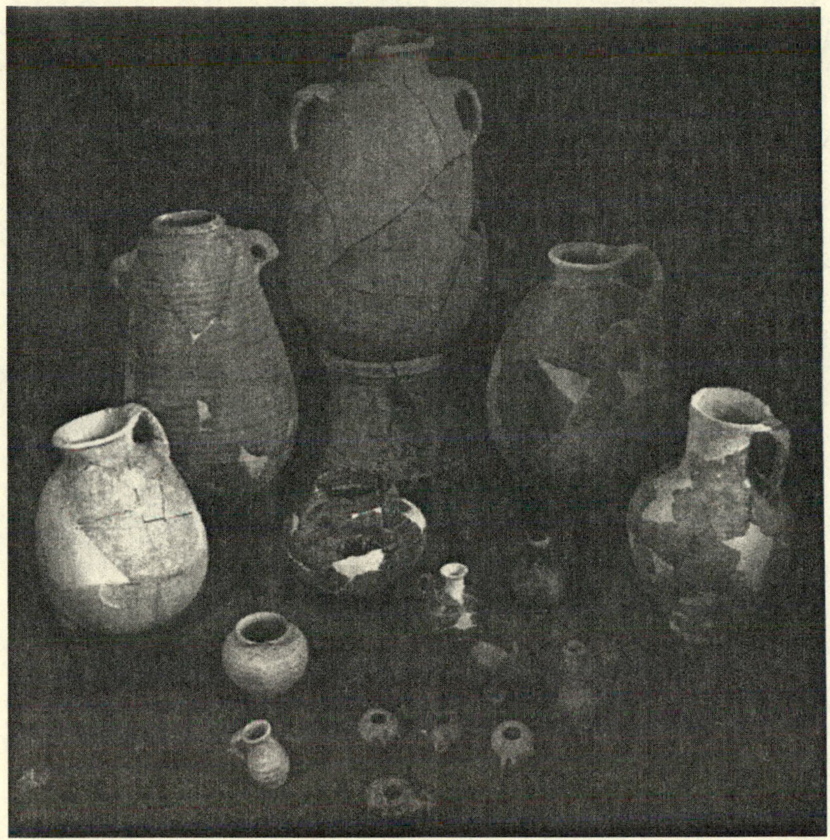

Fig. 12 Hellenistic pottery. (Tell Keisan.) (By permission.)

tradition. The wheel-made lamps usually had very little decoration, but sometimes had a small lateral protruberance for holding them by, rather like a dolphin's fin ('delphiniform' lamps). But from the end of the third century B.C.E., when the use of relief pottery was so widespread in the Hellenistic Orient, the wheel-made lamps seemed too sober. It was at that time that the practice of moulding lamps was introduced. This technique indeed allowed rapid and cheap production of the lamps decorated in relief, which became particularly common after 150 B.C.E. The most frequent decorative motifs for this type of lamp – even more elaborate in the Orient than in Greece itself – were rays, scrolls, or sometimes little cupids, which flanked the oil-hole (see Fig. 12).

Fig. 13 Amphora with stamped handles from Rhodes. (Tell Keisan.) (By permission of the Ecole Biblique et archéologique française, Jerusalem.)

Amphorae with stamped handles. One of the main exports from the Greek world (particularly from Rhodes, Cnidos and Thasos) to Palestine was wine. It travelled in large pot-bellied amphorae with narrow corked necks, two vertical handles, and an onion-shaped base which was used for gripping when the contents were poured out. The thick vertical handles of the amphorae, which were practically indestructible, are found on all the Hellenistic sites, and the stamp which they bear on their upper surface is an important indication of their source and date. These stamps were in fact usually marked with a symbol of the town where the amphorae were made (for example, Rhodes had a rose or the head of the god Helios, Cnidos had the bucranium), with the name of the contractor who had arranged the transportation, together with that of the eponymous magistrate, and even – in the case of Rhodes – with the name of the month during which the amphora was sent off. Thanks to these pieces of information, the handles can often be dated to within twenty years. They were used everywhere from the beginning of the Hellenistic period and then ceased being used in the first century B.C.E. In Palestine the great majority of these stamped handles (nearly 90 per cent) came from Rhodes. The rest were imports from Cos, Thasos, Cnidos, Paros, etc. (see Fig. 13).

Pottery decorated in the *West Slope* technique (so called because it was first found on the west slopes of the Acropolis) was often imported into Palestine before local copies began to be made. They were usually amphorae, jugs or juglets. The special decorative technique consisted of using the clay in its natural pink or yellow colour to paint on the black glaze plant or geometrical motifs (palm-leaves, vine scrolls, garlands, and so on). The motifs could be cut beforehand on the black glazed base and the paint was sometimes so thick that it looked like an *appliqué* bas-relief.

As with the relief bowls, the West Slope ware was a direct copy of the very expensive metal vases. The fine pottery with red glaze (*vernis rouge*), which appeared towards the end of the Hellenistic period in Palestine[1] and was to become widespread in the Herodian period, had the same source of inspiration. Ordinary pottery (cooking ware and kitchen ware), which represented 80 per cent of local production, retained on the whole the forms which had been known since Israelite times. As far as tableware was concerned, until the introduction of red glazed ware (*vernis rouge*), Greek models were copied, but the vessels seem to have been carelessly made, they were drab in colour, their shape was very ordinary, and they were crudely decorated. However, this pottery does not give the impression of lack of technique, but rather of an absence of interest due to the fact that, in the Hellenistic period in Palestine as elsewhere in the Greek world, the search for elegance was hardly ever pursued any more as far as pottery was concerned.

With the penetration of Hellenism, Palestine began to open up greatly to the West. In spite of wars, vigorous economic progress and the social changes created by the arrival of the new masters favoured the emergence of well-to-do classes. The priestly aristocracy, then the Hasmonean dynasts of Jerusalem and the rich commercial middle-classes of Idumea, of Samaria or of Galilee, brought about the development and flowering of a domestic architecture directly inspired

[1] The appearance of this type of pottery (especially dishes and bowls) has often been placed in the second quarter of the first century B.C.E. However, according to S. S. Weinberg, at Tell Anafa this pottery appeared in about 150 B.C.E. Cf. S. S. Weinberg, 'Tel Anafa: the Hellenistic town', *IEJ*, 21 (1971), 101.

by Hellenistic models. The cemeteries and the monumental tombs continued and developed this decorative richness.

However, local conservative traditions continued, and beneath the new outward forms the traditional structures persisted in such a way that Hellenistic features often appeared in association with the old local substructure. Sometimes ill-understood, disparate elements could be brought together on the same monument, giving it a heterogeneous appearance.

Still, in general, Hellenistic schemata were freely integrated into the indigenous tradition, without ever taking its place. Thus assimilated, they ended by producing an art peculiar to the country, a very free syncretistic aesthetic which the Herodian period, rich in so many respects, was to use to the full.

CHAPTER 2

THE POLITICAL AND SOCIAL HISTORY OF PALESTINE FROM ALEXANDER TO ANTIOCHUS III (333–187 B.C.E.)

Considerable darkness shrouds the political and social history of Palestine in the early Hellenistic period between the rise of Alexander and the death of Antiochus III a few years after his defeat by Rome, a defeat which began the downfall of the Hellenistic monarchies. The very fragmentary ancient sources available mention the area of interest to us only sporadically in the context of wider politico-military developments. We are, therefore, forced to begin our reconstruction from these broader contexts. We gain insight into social conditions only through combining fortuitous discoveries in the field of archeology and papyri which, as in the case of the Zenon papyri, partially lighten the darkness at particular points. Information about the Jews is still more scanty, since legend and history are so closely interwoven in our primary source, Josephus. In some areas, therefore, we can only hope to draw a sketchy and to some extent a hypothetical picture, which may at any time have to be revised in the light of new discoveries. Nevertheless, there can be no doubt that within this period, which for us is so obscure, there occurred the first intensive encounter between ancient Palestinian Judaism and the superior Hellenistic culture. This clash left a decisive stamp on later development, and constitutes the significant factor of this epoch.

ALEXANDER'S CAMPAIGN AND PALESTINE (333–331 B.C.E.)

The last decades of the Persian empire had already brought for Palestine and the Jews the troubles of war. The revolt of King Tennes of Sidon (*circa* 354–346 B.C.E.) had affected Palestine too, for a large part of the coastal plain belonged to Sidon; and it is likely that Judah too suffered during the Persian counter-attack.[1] A few years later Artaxerxes III Ochus setting out from Palestine managed to win back Egypt, which two generations earlier had, with Greek help, shaken off the Persian yoke. For a long time the western districts of the empire,

[1] Diodorus XVI.41–5.

especially Phoenicia, had been oriented in economic, cultural and military affairs towards Greece and the Aegean. In the struggles mentioned above, Greek mercenaries were employed and won military victories for both sides. No well-to-do household in Palestine would have lacked Greek pottery, terracottas and other luxury items; Greek coins and their local imitations had long been an important medium of exchange.[1] This means that when the Greeks, in the guise of the Macedonians, came into power they had long since ceased to be strangers. Nevertheless, the campaign of the young Macedonian king gave the Semitic populations of Syria and Palestine a deep shock. Hitherto they had known the Greeks only as guests, but now they became acquainted with the kindred Macedonians as harsh overlords. The victory at Issus in November 333 B.C.E. demonstrated the military superiority of Alexander and his small army against the multinational troops of the Great King; even the Greek mercenaries of Darius could no longer save the ageing World empire. After the victory, Parmenion pushed on to Damascus, conquered the Syrian hinterland and captured the immensely rich Persian baggage-train with its war treasury.[2] The king, who was marching along the coast, received the willing submission of the Phoenician cities of Arados, Marathos, Byblos and Sidon, the latter remembering only too well the terrible vengeance of the Persians. Only Tyre, basing its confidence on its insular situation, believed that it could remain neutral and free. The king, who wished to offer sacrifice in the temple of the god of the city Heracles-Melkart, his mythical ancestor, was refused entry into the city.[3] In a seven-month siege, from January to August 332, with the help of his celebrated mole and his fleet, augmented from the other Phoenician cities, Alexander laid low this proud sea-fortress, which was regarded as impregnable and which had previously succeeded in resisting Sennacherib for five and Nebuchadrezzar for thirteen years.[4] The

[1] D. Auscher, 'Les relations entre la Grèce et la Palestine avant la conquête d'Alexandre', *VT*, 17 (1967), 8–30; S. S. Weinberg, 'Post-exilic Palestine – an archaeological report', *Proceedings of the Israel Academy of Sciences and Humanities* 4, (1971), pp. 78–97; M. Hengel, *Judentum und Hellenismus*, WUNT 10 (2nd edn., Tübingen, 1973), pp. 61–7; ET *Judaism and Hellenism*, London 1974, 1, pp. 32–5.

[2] Arrian II.11.10; Curtius Rufus III.13.1ff, IV.1.4; Plutarch, *Alexander* 24. For what follows see F.-M. Abel, 'Alexandre le Grand en Syrie et en Palestine', *RB*, 43 (1934), 528–45 and 44 (1935), 42–61; and his *Histoire de la Palestine depuis la conquête d'Alexandre jusqu'à l'invasion Arabe*, 1 (Paris, 1952), pp. 1–22; F. Schachermeyr, *Alexander der Grosse* (Vienna, 1973), pp. 206ff, 211ff.

[3] Diod. XVII.40.2f; Arr. II.16.7f; Curt. Ruf. IV.2.2f.

[4] O. Eissfeldt, 'Tyros', *PW*, 2nd series, 7 (1948), cols. 1887, 1890.

astounded orientals witnessed, not only the superiority of Greek military technique and strategy, but also the severity of the foreign conquerors. 30,000 survivors, mostly women and children, went off to the slave markets, and Alexander crucified 2,000 of those capable of bearing arms.[1] The burnt-down city was rebuilt as a Macedonian fortress, and was repopulated with both country people and colonists.[2]

From Tyre the king hastened south along the Phoenician and Palestinian coastal road without encountering any opposition. But in Gaza, the most important trading centre for Arabian wares and the only coastal city not under Phoenician rule,[3] the Persian governor Batis refused to surrender and with his garrison of Persians and Arabs desperately resisted Alexander's troops for two months. The king himself was injured in an attempted sortie. The machines, which had already mastered the walls of Tyre, had here again to prove their power. With their help the city was finally stormed at the fourth assault, the male population massacred, and the women and children sold.[4] The gallant Batis fell wounded into the hands of the conqueror who, as Achilles once did to the dead Hector, caused him to be dragged behind a war-chariot around the city.[5] Like Tyre, the city was resettled with inhabitants from the neighbourhood and converted into a Macedonian fortress.[6] The stubborn opposition of Tyre and Gaza to Alexander, as indeed that of Sidon previously to Artaxerxes III, shows the strong political self-consciousness of these rich cities, which was no weaker than that of a Greek *polis*.[7] This later facilitated

[1] Diod, XVII.46.4; Arr. II.24.5f; Curt. Ruf. IV.4.17; H. Volkmann, *Die Massenversklavungen der Einwohner eroberter Städte in der hellenistisch-römischen Zeit*, Abhandlungen der Akademie der Wissenschaften und der Literatur in Mainz: Geistes- und Sozialwiss. Klasse 1961, no. 3, pp. 62, 112.

[2] Justin, *Epitome* XVIII.3.19; see V. Tcherikover, *Die hellenistischen Städtegründungen von Alexander dem Grossen bis auf die Römerzeit*, Philologus Suppl. 19, 1 (Leipzig, 1927), pp. 68f; Eissfeldt, *PW*, 2nd ser. 7 (1948), col. 1895.

[3] U. Rappaport, 'Gaza and Ascalon in the Persian and Hellenistic periods in relation to their coins', *IEJ*, 20 (1970), 75f.

[4] Arr. II.25.4–27.7; Curt. Ruf. IV.6.7–30; Diod. XVII.48; Plut. *Alex*. 25.

[5] Hegesias, *FGrHist* 142, F5 cited by Dionysius Halicarnassensis, *De Compositione Verborum* 18; Curt. Ruf. IV.6.26–9. W. W. Tarn, *Alexander the Great*, 2 (Cambridge, 1948), pp. 265–70, because of his tendency to idealize Alexander, doubts the historicity of this act. Against this cf. Abel, *RB*, 44 (1935), 47f. For Batis' origin see E. Merkel in F. Altheim and R. Stiehl, *Die Araber in der Alten Welt*, 1 (Berlin, 1964), pp. 171ff.

[6] Arr. II.27.7; see Abel, *RB*, 44 (1935), 48.

[7] A. H. M. Jones, *The Cities of the Eastern Roman Provinces* (2nd edn., Oxford, 1971), p. 234; see below, p. 56.

an outward, political Hellenization whilst still retaining their Semitic individuality.

Those who wrote the history of Alexander in ancient times had little interest in the fate of the Syrian and Palestinian hinterland; they concentrated their accounts on the great military exploits of the king. After narrating the conquest of Tyre, Arrian sums up the subjugation of these areas in a single sentence: 'the remainder of Syria known as Palestine had already come over to him'. This means that at the time of the siege of Tyre the majority of the Palestinian peoples and cities had already declared their loyalty to him and aided him with the laborious siege-works at Tyre. Only one example is described in more detail. At the beginning of the siege of Tyre, Alexander himself undertook an expedition against 'the Arabs living in the Anti-Lebanon,' who had killed 30 Macedonians felling trees. 'Some of the inhabitants he overcame with violence, the others by submission. Within ten days he was able to return.'[1] The remark of Curtius Rufus after the advance of Parmenion to Damascus and his appointment as commander-in-chief of Coele-Syria is not entirely clear: 'The Syrians, not yet humiliated by defeat, rejected the new rule, but they were quickly subjugated and then obediently complied with his orders'.[2] It remains unclear whether the reference is to the subjugation of the Syrian and Palestinian hinterland by Parmenion, or whether the campaigns of Alexander himself are meant. A note by Pliny the elder[3] mentioning Alexander in connection with the balsam plantations in Jericho is also ambiguous, and is historically uncertain, as are the late Roman or Byzantine reports of the alleged foundation of cities by Alexander in East Jordan.[4] A large number of ancient cities sought to establish a connection with the most renowned sovereign of the ancient world in order to enhance their own prestige. Local legends grew without limits.

This critical assessment must also be applied to Josephus' account of Alexander's visit to Jerusalem and the associated clashes with the Samaritans. There are parallels in Rabbinic literature and, from the opposite viewpoint, in the Samaritan tradition.[5] Büchler had already

[1] Arr. II.25.4; 20.4f; Curt. Ruf. IV.2.24; Plut. *Alex.* 24; cf. Abel, *RB*, 43 (1934), 543f.

[2] IV.1.5.

[3] *Naturalis Historia* XII.25, 117; see V. Tcherikover, *Hellenistic Civilization and the Jews* (Philadelphia, 1959), p. 422 n. 31: 'The sentence *Alexandro Magno res ibi gerente* may be interpreted as referring to Alexander's stay in Syria as a whole.'

[4] Tcherikover, *Städtegründungen*, pp. 75f, 143; Jones, *Cities*, pp. 237f, cf. p. 50 n. 5.

[5] *Antiquitates Judaicae* XI.302–47. Older literature, including Rabbinic parallels, is given by R. Marcus in *Josephus*, Loeb Classical Library, 6 (1937), appendix C, pp. 512–32 and by J. Seibert, *Alexander der Grosse*, Erträge der Forschung 10,

recognized that Josephus' account is not homogeneous, but is a combination of Jewish and Samaritan accounts.[1] The legend of Alexander's visit to the Holy City and his sacrifice in the Temple after the conquest of Gaza has the least historical value. Tcherikover's judgement is unquestionably correct: 'It is a historical myth designed to bring the king into direct contact with the Jews, and to speak of both in laudatory terms.' His view is that it is based on 'a Palestinian folk-story', which found its way also into the Talmudic tradition; the literary version known to Josephus originated in Alexandria in the first century C.E.[2] A version of the Greek Alexander romance by Pseudo-Callisthenes also has elements of the Jewish Alexander legend obtained from Alexandrian circles.[3] Historical traces are most likely to be found in Josephus' account of the building of the Samaritan temple on Mount Gerizim. According to this, Manasseh, a brother of the Jewish High Priest Jaddus, had fled to Samaria, because his marriage to Nicaso (the Greek name is to be noted[4]), the daughter of Sanballat governor of Samaria, could not be tolerated in Jerusalem, and his father-in-law had promised to him 'to build on Mount Gerizim a temple like the one in Jerusalem'.[5] When Alexander commenced the siege of Tyre, he demanded aid from the Jewish high priest and also the tribute previously paid to Darius. The high priest, however, turned down the king's demand on the ground of his oath of fidelity to Darius. Sanballat, on the other hand, hurried to Alexander's help with 8,000 Samaritans, acknowledged him as sovereign and received permission to build a temple. A few months later he died.[6] Hitherto the accepted interpretation was that the reference to Sanballat, governor of Samaria, was due to a secondary confusion with the similarly named opponent of Nehemiah.[7] But the discovery of Samaritan papyri in a cave in Wadi Daliyeh, north of Jericho, which include many documents down to the year 335 B.C.E., suggests the probability that a third bearer of the name

(Darmstadt, 1972), pp. 103–7, 271–4; cf. also Tcherikover, *Hellenistic Civilization*, pp. 41–50; H. G. Kippenberg, *Garizim und Synagoge*, RGVV 30 (Berlin–New York, 1971), pp. 44–57.

[1] A. Büchler, 'La relation de Josèphe concernant Alexandre le Grand', *REJ*, 36 (1898), 1–26.

[2] *Hellenistic Civilization*, pp. 45, 420 n. 17.

[3] Pseudo-Callisthenes, *Der griechische Alexanderroman, Rezension* Γ, book 2, ed. H. Engelmann, Beiträge zur klassischen Philologie 12 (Meisenheim am Glan, 1963), pp. 216–30, chs. 24–8.

[4] Hengel, *Hellenismus*, p. 114; ET I, p. 61.

[5] Jos. *Ant.* XI.310.

[6] *Ant.* XI.325.

[7] So Tcherikover, *Hellenistic Civilization*, pp. 44, 419 n. 12.

Sanballat was governor in Samaria at the time of Alexander's campaign.[1] It is not unlikely that Sanballat, like other peoples and cities in Syria and Palestine, submitted to Alexander and provided auxiliaries for the siege of Tyre. Even if Alexander relied militarily on his trustworthy Macedonian fighting forces, he could not do without the help of foreign peoples. The remark of Curtius Rufus adduced against this, that 'less confidence was felt in soldiers enlisted from among the conquered tribes than in native troops', does confirm that barbarian mercenaries were used.[2] One need be no more suspicious of the information about these Samaritan troops which Alexander is supposed to have taken with him to Egypt,[3] than about the note by Pseudo-Hecateus and Josephus that Jewish mercenaries served Alexander in Babylon and Egypt.[4] On the other hand, it must be assumed, contrary to the report of Josephus, that the Jewish high priest too yielded to the new ruler without dramatic incident. It remains open whether this recognition of Alexander occurred before the conquest of Tyre, as with the Samaritans, or whether, in accordance with Talmudic tradition, it happened during his march along the coast at Kephar Saba, the later Antipatris, or somewhere else.[5] It is certain that the Jews, at this change of sovereignty, would have requested from Alexander, as they had previously done under Persian kings and later under Hellenistic kings, the right 'to live according to the laws of their fathers', and that this was granted to them. Alexander also granted the right to their 'own laws' to the cities of Ionia, to the Lydians, Indians and Arabians.[6]

There is also an historical kernel in Josephus' suggestion of a conflict between Alexander and the Samaritans, which the Talmudic tradition represents as being still more acute.[7] According to Curtius Rufus the Samaritans rebelled against the Macedonians at the beginning of 331, while Alexander stayed in Egypt, and they burned alive the new satrap

[1] F. M. Cross, Jr. 'The discovery of the Samaria papyri', *BA*, 26 (1963), 110–21; see also his 'Aspects of Samaritan and Jewish history in late Persian and Hellenistic times', *HTR*, 59 (1966), 201–11; Kippenberg, *Garizim*, p. 44.

[2] IV.6.31. Cf. Abel, *Histoire*, 1, 2 and Hengel, *Hellenismus*, p. 27, ET I p. 15, II p. 11, against Tcherikover, *Hellenistic Civilization*, p. 420 n. 13.

[3] Jos. *Ant.* XI.321, 345.

[4] Josephus, *Contra Apionem* 1.192, 200; cf. *Ant.* XI.339.

[5] *b. Yoma* 69a and in the scholion on *Megillat Ta'anith*, see H. Lichtenstein, 'Die Fastenrolle', *HUCA*, 8/9 (1931/2), 339; cf. Tcherikover, *Hellenistic Civilization*, p. 48: 'the town's mention in the tale is purely a matter of convention'.

[6] Jos. *Ant.* XI.338; cf. Antiochus III: *Ant.* XII.142, 150; for this cf. below, p. 72. Arr. 1.17.4; 18.2; VII.20.1; Strabo XVI.1.11 (C 741).

[7] *Ant.* XI.340ff.; cf. n. 5 above. for the Rabbinic versions.

of Coele-Syria, Andromachus, who had succeeded Parmenion. Alexander hurried to Samaria, had the men responsible for the crime, who had been handed over to him, executed, and appointed Menon as the successor to Andromachus.[1] This information is supplemented by the *Chronicle* of Eusebius, which states that Alexander destroyed Samaria and colonized it with Macedonians, which means that it became a Macedonian military colony. According to a second reference in the same course the refounding of the city was in fact carried out by Perdiccas.[2] There is now confirmation of these fragmentary statements in the previously mentioned documents discovered at Wadi Daliyeh. Evidently eminent Samaritans had fled there. Their hiding place was betrayed and the cave, in which the excavators found the bones of 205 persons, was smoked out by the Macedonian pursuers.[3] It is very possible that the Jewish cult community in Jerusalem sought some advantage of its own from this catastrophe of its own tribal and religious kindred in the north, and gained some increase of territory.[4] Perhaps the late apocalypse in Isaiah 24 to 27, with its frequent allusions to the destruction of 'the city of chaos', reflects the catastrophe of Samaria.[5] Alexander's coming from the north and his success in war against Tyre and other cities has elsewhere, too, inspired later prophets, as is shown by the threat in Zechariah 9:1–8.[6] A series of coin hoards and destroyed sites in the coastal region of Palestine from the period around 332 show that, in addition to the devastation of Tyre and Gaza, smaller places had become victims of the Macedonian invasion. The onslaught of the victorious conqueror was felt to be

[1] Curt. Ruf. IV.8, 9ff.

[2] For a German translation of the *Chronicle* preserved in Armenian, see J. Karst, GCS 20 (Leipzig, 1911), p. 197; cf. however p. 199 on 296/5 B.C.E.: 'it was settled by Perdiccas' (cf. below pp. 45f, 53). Cf. the version of Jerome, ed. R. Helm, GCS 47 (Berlin, 1956), pp. 123, 128, and ibid. p. 365, also passages from Byzantine historians.

[3] Cf. p. 40 n. 1; cf. also P. W. Lapp, 'Wâdi ed-Dâliyeh', *RB*, 72 (1965), 405–9 on a new exploration of the cave.

[4] Ps-Hecateus, as reported in Jos. *C.Ap.* II.43, exaggerated: 'In recognition of the consideration and loyalty shown to him by the Jews, he added to their territory the district of Samaria free of tribute.' According to 1 Macc. 11:34 the Jews received three Samaritan districts from Demetrius *c.* 145 B.C.E., and it is possible that Demetrius was only confirming an older frontier. It is noteworthy that the wadi ed Daliyeh near Jericho, with its cave, was in Jewish territory. Alexander had possibly already put it under Jerusalem.

[5] Isa. 24:10; 25:2; 26:5f; 27:10; cf. on the other hand, the extension of all the boundaries in 26:15.

[6] K. Elliger, 'Ein Zeugnis aus der jüdischen Gemeinde im Alexanderjahr 332 v. Chr.', *ZAW*, 62 (1949–50), 63–115; M. Delcor, 'Les allusions à Alexandre le Grand dans Zach. IX, 1–8', *VT*, 1 (1951), 110–24.

simply a catastrophe.[1] Apart from the repopulation of the destroyed cities of Tyre and Gaza, Alexander himself could hardly have undertaken the 'founding of cities' in the area with which we are concerned. On the return march from Egypt in the spring of 331 he could not delay longer in Palestine than for a quick settlement of the Samaritan tragedy. After magnificent games celebrated in Tyre he pressed on to Mesopotamia, where on 1 October 331, at Gaugamela, his victory in the decisive battle between him and Darius III opened a completely new era for Asia and for Europe.

The foundation of the cities of Samaria and Gaza, ascribed sometimes to Alexander and sometimes to Perdiccas, was perhaps planned by Alexander but completed by the regent Perdiccas (323–320) after the king's death. Other cities beyond the Jordan, too, such as Dion, Pella and the Capitolias of imperial times later claimed Alexander as their founder.[2] The slightly later resettlement of Shechem and the building of a temple on Mount Gerizim are also probably linked with the catastrophe and refoundation of Samaria. It is not impossible that this building of a temple was instigated by the secession of a priestly group from Jerusalem under the leadership of a brother of the high priest and that it had already been planned before Alexander's campaign; but the execution may have followed later. The Samaritan source behind Josephus' account attempts to legitimize the erection of this schismatic sanctuary by connecting it with the person of Alexander.[3] According to excavations at Shechem the site was unoccupied between 480 and 330 B.C.E., but there followed a period of intensive building with a new *floruit* around 330 B.C.E. G. E. Wright connects this with the fate of Samaria: after its colonization by Macedonian military settlers, the Samaritans needed a new centre, and established one on the old site of Shechem at the foot of the holy mountain Gerizim,[4] where under the foundations of the Hadrianic temple of Jupiter older remains have been discovered which perhaps are those of the Samaritan sanctuary.[5] The

[1] According to E. Stern, 'The dating of Stratum II at Tell Abu Hawam', *IEJ*, 18 (1968), 213–19, the second phase of the settlement of Tell Abu Hawam near Haifa, as also ancient Akko, Shikmona and Stratum I Megiddo, was devastated in connection with the siege of Tyre.

[2] For Gerasa see H. Seyrig, 'Alexandre le Grand, fondateur de Gérasa', *Syria*, 42 (1965), 25–8. A coin from Capitolias (Beit Ras) north of Gerasa calls Alexander the 'genarchēs' of the city: H. Seyrig, *Syria*, 36 (1959), 66.

[3] Kippenberg, *Garizim*, p. 56.

[4] G. E. Wright, *Shechem* (New York–Toronto, 1965), pp. 170–84; cf. O. R. Sellers, 'Coins of the 1960 excavation at Shechem', *BA*, 25 (1962), 87–96.

[5] R. J. Bull and G. E. Wright, 'Newly discovered temples on Mt Gerizim in Jordan', *HTR*, 58 (1965), 234–7; R. J. Bull and E. F. Campbell, Jr., 'The sixth campaign at

demarcation between the new Macedonian Hellenistic city and the Samaritans with their new centre at Shechem remains unclear. It is quite possible that, after cutting off certain Judean districts, the remainder of Samaria became the territory of the new *polis* and did not, as did the Jews and the Idumeans, receive the status of an independent *ethnos*. This would explain the fact that Strabo speaks of only the four *ethnē* of the Judeans, Idumeans, Gazeans and Azotians; the fact that the Samaritans in situations of crisis did not refer to themselves as an *ethnos* but as 'Sidonians in Shechem'; and the fact that Sirach could, in dependence on Deut. 32:21, mock them as 'not a people'.[1]

We know hardly anything about the form of administration introduced by Alexander in Syria and Coele-Syria, except for the names of the frequently changing satraps. The capital of the province, which was identical with the previous Persian satrapy of Abar Nahara, was Damascus. It is striking also that from 329–325 the satrap was a Persian, Bessos.[2] All this indicates that the king had hardly interfered with the internal structure of the country with its numerous cities and peoples. The Phoenician city-kings continued in office, as did the Jewish high priest.[3] Only in one thing did he introduce a fundamental change. He introduced restrictions on the very mixed types of local coinages in Syria and Phoenicia, and took the first steps towards a relatively uniform coinage. Since these new coins of Alexander, unlike the Persian darics, were paid out directly to the garrisons, they entered circulation among the populace and prospered commercial activity.[4] The king also turned his attention to a better registration of economic resources. He already regarded the conquered districts as his personal property, as 'land won with the spear'.[5] As had happened in Egypt through the organizational genius of Cleomenes of Naucratis, in Syria and Palestine also he no doubt tightened the screw of dues and taxes, as

Balâṭah (Shechem)', *BASOR*, 190 (1968), 17f and the short note of E. F. Campbell, Jr., *BASOR*, 204 (1971), 4.

1 Strabo XVI.2.2 (C 749); Jos. *Ant.* XI.344; XII.260; Sirach 50:25f; see Hengel, *Hellenismus*, p. 44 n. 153; ET II, p. 18 n. 156.

2 So Abel, *Histoire*, I, p. 13; otherwise H. Berve, *Das Alexanderreich auf prosopographischer Grundlage* (Munich, 1926), 2, pp. 108f.

3 Jones, *Cities*, pp. 236f.

4 M. Rostovtzeff, *The Social and Economic History of the Hellenistic World* (Oxford, 1941), I, pp. 129f; see also, for the hoards of coins of Alexander in Byblos and Galilee, A. R. Bellinger, 'An Alexander hoard from Byblos', *Berytus*, 10 (1952/53), 37–49 and J. Baramki, 'Coin hoards from Palestine. II', *QDAP*, 11 (1945), 86–90; Abel, *Histoire*, I, pp. 15ff.

5 W. Schmitthenner, 'Über eine Formveränderung der Monarchie seit Alexander d.Gr.', *Saeculum*, 19 (1968), 31–46.

compared with Persian times. The frequent and rapid change of satraps in Syria suggests that the king was not content with their financial achievements. Menon and his successor Arimmas were both dismissed in quick succession, the latter because he had not adequately supplied the troops for the campaign east of the Euphrates in the summer of 331.[1] As far as his monetary system and financial policy are concerned, Alexander adopted the principles that were also advocated in the pseudo-Aristotelian *Oeconomica* which were later the foundations of the economic power of the Hellenistic monarchies, especially the Ptolemaic kingdom. All this was only a beginning: a real consolidation of the kingdom was not possible for him. Little more than a year after his return from India, the 33-year-old king died in Babylon, on 10 June 323.

The after-effects of Alexander's reign are almost beyond measure. In Alexandria the Hellenistic Jewish legend about Alexander, like later Talmudic and Christian legends, makes him a worshipper of the God of Israel and so a monotheist.[2] Critical judgements of him cannot however be overlooked, and this applies especially to the Jewish tradition. Apocalyptic such as that of the Book of Daniel or of the Book of Dream Visions in Ethiopic Enoch, saw Alexander's campaign as introducing the final change of world-history: 'Then a mightly king (*melek gibbōr*) shall arise, who shall rule with great dominion and do according to his will.'[3] His kingdom will indeed soon be broken up and divided, and what comes after will not be 'according to the dominion with which he ruled',[4] yet it is indicated that the 'fourth kingdom' introduced by him, of Macedonians and Greeks, is the ultimate climax of violence and ungodliness: 'behold, a fourth beast, terrible and dreadful and exceedingly strong; and it had great iron teeth; it devoured and broke in pieces, and stamped the residue with its feet.'[5]

The first book of Maccabees too begins its account with a negative characterization of the world conqueror: 'he fought many battles, conquered strongholds and slew the kings of the earth, and advanced

[1] Abel, *Histoire*, 1, p. 13; a different view in H. Berve, *Alexanderreich*, 2, pp. 60, 259.

[2] F. Pfister, *Eine jüdische Gründungsgeschichte Alexandrias*, SAH 1914, 11 (Heidelberg, 1914) and his *Alexander der Grosse in den Offenbarungen der Griechen, Juden, Mohammedaner und Christen*, Abhandlungen der Deutschen Akademie d.Wiss.zu Berlin 1956, 3 (Berlin, 1956); M. Simon, 'Alexandre le Grand, Juif et Chrétien', *RHPR*, 21 (1941), 177–91; I. J. Kazis (ed.), *The Book of the Gests of Alexander of Macedon* (Cambridge, Mass., 1962).

[3] Dan. 11:3; cf. 8:5–21; 1 *Enoch* 90:2; *Sib*.4. 88–96; Justin, *Epit*. XII.16.9–11.

[4] Dan. 11:4; cf. 8:8, 22f.

[5] Dan. 7:7.

to the ends of the earth, and took spoils of a multitude of nations. And when the earth was quiet before him, he was exalted and his heart was lifted up.'[1] This last sentence is closely linked with the taunt song on the prince of Tyre in Ezek. 28:1: 'Because your heart is proud, and you have said, "I am a god" '. Behind the Jewish criticism of Alexander and his successors is the condemnation of their claim to divine honours. The Jews could never acquiesce in such a demand.[2]

PALESTINE DURING THE STRUGGLES OF THE DIADOCHI (323–301 B.C.E.)

In the struggles for the succession after Alexander's death, Palestine quickly became once more a focal point of political and military events. It fell to the army assembled at Babylon to decide the fate of the empire and it agreed on a compromise. The unity of the World empire was to be retained under the nominal sovereignty of Philip Arrhidaeus, the imbecile brother of Alexander. Perdiccas became 'chiliarch' of the Asiatic part of the kingdom, and thus simultaneously the champion of the empire's unity. The more important satrapies, too, got new incumbents. Ptolemy son of Lagus secured for himself Egypt, which was rich and geographically difficult to reach. Together with Lysimachus of Thrace he became a successful champion of the formation of separate states. The satrapy of Syria was taken by Laomedon, who spoke two languages[3] – meaning no doubt Aramaic and Greek.

In November 322, the 44-year-old Ptolemy arrived in Egypt and skillfully took possession of Cyrenaica. A little later, at Damascus, despite resistance from Perdiccas's supporters, he took possession of Alexander's body. This precious relic, escorted by his troops, he carried right across the foreign satrapy to Memphis, whilst Laomedon did not dare to oppose him. Diodorus describes how the glistening gold chariot of state was gazed upon with astonishment in each city by the thronging onlookers.[4] In May–June 320, Perdiccas, having marched

[1] 1 Macc. 1:2f.

[2] Cf. Dan. 8:10 and 2 Macc. 9:10 concerning Antiochus Epiphanes. For the deification of Alexander see Seibert, *Alexander*, pp. 192ff; Schachermeyr, *Alexander*, pp. 242ff, 525ff, 595ff. For Jewish conflict with the ruler cult, see M. Hengel, *Die Zeloten*, AGJU 1 (Leiden, 1961), pp. 103ff.

[3] Arr. III.6.6: he was on this account commander over captives under Alexander. Cf. further J. Seibert, *Untersuchungen zur Geschichte Ptolemaios' I*, MBPAR 56, (1969), pp. 27ff, and R. M. Errington, 'From Babylon to Triparadeisos: 323–320 B.C.', *JHS*, 90 (1970), 49–77.

[4] Arr. *De reb. succ. Alex.*, in *FGrHist* 156, F9, 25; Diod. XVIII.28.1; Abel, *Histoire*, 1, p. 24: 'ce...véritable temple ambiant'.

from Damascus to Egypt in order to break the increasing power of Ptolemy, was murdered at Memphis by mutinying officers, amongst them Seleucus. In the consequent redistribution of power at Triparadeisos in Syria on the upper course of the Orontes, Ptolemy's sphere was confirmed, but not expanded as he wished.[1] In the words of Diodorus, he, like the ancient pharaohs before him, saw 'in Phoenicia and the so-called Coele-Syria a ready base for attack against Egypt, and therefore did all he could to bring these districts under his sovereignty'. It appeared to him that it was necessary to control this buffer zone in order to make secure his sovereignty in Egypt. Only by controlling the Phoenician ports and fleets could he achieve the desired military predominance in the Eastern Mediterranean. Under the command of his friend Nicanor he despatched troops and a fleet which, 'in a short and successful campaign', took Laomedon prisoner and secured the most important 'Phoenician cities' – which included the coastal towns of Palestine – by means of garrisons.[2] Two years later (318 B.C.E.) Eumenes, the former secretary of Alexander and a partisan of the king's family, attempted to win Phoenicia and Coele-Syria, but was driven back to the east by Antigonus Monophthalmus, 'the commander of Asia'.[3] The imprisonment and execution of Eumenes by Antigonus in 317/16 destroyed finally all hopes for the dynasty of Alexander, and the idea of 'national unity' was transferred to this 'One-eyed' who now possessed the greatest power in Asia. Before the threat of his wrath the young satrap Seleucus of Babylon fled to Ptolemy. Antigonus himself marched into Syria, and repulsed a deputation of his united rivals who sought the recognition of Ptolemy's claim to the disputed province. Open war became inevitable. An army of workmen was sent to fell trees for Antigonus in Lebanon and the Taurus mountains, so that he could build up a fleet from scratch in four dockyards. Ptolemy's forces were driven out of the Phoenician ports, Jaffa and Gaza were taken by storm, and the garrison of Tyre surrendered after a fifteen-month siege.[4]

Summoned back to Asia Minor, Antigonus handed over the command in Palestine to his twenty-year-old son Demetrius, later nicknamed 'city-besieger'. On the advice of Seleucus, who had taken refuge with him, Ptolemy now advanced into the area he had lost. In the spring of 312, at a point south from Gaza, battle was joined, and

[1] E. Will, *Histoire politique du monde hellénistique (323–30 av. J.-C.)*, I (Nancy, 1966), pp. 35ff.

[2] Diod. XVIII.43; cf. Appian, *Syr.* 52; Seibert, *Untersuchungen*, p. 129.

[3] Diod. XVIII.73.2

[4] Diod. XIX.57–9.

Alexander's two battle-trained officers wrought upon the youthful Demetrius a crushing defeat.[1] So for the second time in a few years Ptolemy became master of Palestine, and once again the Phoenician cities he desired fell into his hands. After the conquest of Tyre he sent off his friend and comrade in arms Seleucus with an army to go to Babylon to regain his lost satrapy. His return to Babylon in the early autumn of 312 (October 1 in the Julian calendar) marks the beginning of the Seleucid era, an era that in the Orient has remained significant and been much imitated down to modern times.[2] Ptolemy did not remain master of his newly-won territory for long. Six months after his victory, his general, Cilles, with 7,000 men, was taken unawares by Demetrius in a marshy area of central Syria and taken prisoner.[3] When Demetrius' father Antigonus himself marched into Syria, the cautious Ptolemy avoided another encounter and retreated to the safety of Egypt after destroying the fortresses of Akko, Jaffa, Samaria and Gaza.[4] For the next few years both father and son occupied themselves with consolidating this regained and strategically important southern province, which also provided a base for attacking Ptolemy son of Lagus in Egypt. They attempted, but with little success, to subjugate the Nabatean Arabs, who for the first time enter the arena of history as a political power. The Nabateans played a key role in the caravan trade with Gerrha on the Persian Gulf and with South Arabia, which supplied the Hellenistic world with highly prized perfumes, spices and other luxuries. A surprise attack by Demetrius on the Nabatean rock fortress, later known as Petra, was a miserable failure.[5] Hieronymus of Cardia, 'the authoritative historian of the first fifty years after Alexander's death', and an officer of Eumenes and later of Antigonus, gives us a graphic account both of this campaign and of the Dead Sea. His attempt to get bitumen there failed because of Arabian attacks.[6] These conflicts with the Nabateans are to be understood as part of their attempt to maintain their independence. Of greater significance, however, are the accomplishments of Antigonus in founding cities in

[1] Diod. xix.80; Justin. xv.1.6–9; Plut. *Demetrius* 6. On the place of the battle, see F.-M. Abel, 'La Syrie et la Palestine au temps de Ptolémée Ier Soter', *RB*, 44 (1935), 567–75; cf. Seibert, *Untersuchungen*, pp. 162ff.

[2] E. J. Bickerman, *Chronology of the Ancient World* (London, 1968), pp. 71ff.

[3] Diod. xix.93.2; Plut. *Demetr.* 6.3. The place called 'Myus' cannot be identified. It is to be sought along the upper course of the Orontes or in the northern end of the Beqaʿ.

[4] Diod. xix.93.5–7.

[5] F.-M. Abel, 'L'expédition des Grecs à Pétra en 312 avant J.-C.', *RB*, 46 (1937), 373–91; R. Dussaud, *La pénétration des Arabes en Syrie avant l'Islam* (Paris, 1955), pp. 21ff.

[6] F. Jacoby, *PW*, 8 (1913), cols 1540ff; *FGrHist* 154, Diod. xix.100.1–3 = T6.

Palestine. In the decade between the reconquest of Palestine and the battle of Ipsus, the land had enjoyed for the first time since the death of Alexander a relatively quiet period of development. During this time the first actions of a new administration became evident, and colonies of Macedonian veterans were established. In Northern Syria Antigonus founded Antigoneia as the first genuine city (*polis*), intended to be the capital of his empire. The cities in Palestine which bear typical Macedonian or Northern Greek names no doubt go back to his initiative. In contrast, those founded later by the Ptolemies and Seleucids nearly always have dynastic names. Examples of the former are Apollonia, Arethusa and Anthedon in the coastal region, and Pella, Dion, Hippos and Gadara in East Jordan. In the case of Pella (Pehal), named after the birthplace of Alexander, and Apollonia (present day Arṣūf) it may be that older Semitic placenames have been Hellenized.[1] The settlements along the coast, where Phoenician cities already clustered thickly, were meant to reinforce the military presence of the Macedonians. On the other hand, because of the relative lack of cities in East Jordan, here the military colonies served as a protection against the Arabs.[2] As already under Alexander, great significance was attached to monetary policy and financial administration. Constant conflict between rival contenders for Alexander's empire devoured vast amounts of money, and this had to be squeezed out of the subjugated districts in order to pay the armies. It was probably Antigonus who developed the division into 'toparchies' of Syria and Palestine which had already been planned by Alexander. From now until the time of Herod, the 'toparchy' formed the basic unit for administration and taxation,[3] and above it came the 'hyparchy', called 'nomos' in Egypt. It is successor to the small satrapy of the Persian kingdom and often formed a political–tribal entity. It is in the time of Antigonus or of Ptolemy I that we can place the origin of those Hellenized names for administrative units which end in -itis, such as Ammanitis, Esbonitis, Gaulanitis, Galaaditis and so on. The designations for the 'nomoi' in Egypt were Hellenized in much the same way. Other 'hyparchies' acquired the ending -ia, such as Ioudaia, Samareia (also Samareitis), Idoumaia and Galilaia.[4]

Demetrius destroyed Ptolemy's fleet before Salamis in Cyprus in the spring of 306. This encouraged both father and son to use once again

[1] Tcherikover, *Städtegründungen*, pp. 69–81, also his *Hellenistic Civilization*, pp. 90–116, esp. 105f; Jones, *Cities*, pp. 237f.

[2] Hengel, *Hellenismus*, pp. 24f.; ET I, p. 14.

[3] A. Schalit, *König Herodes*, Studia Judaica 4 (Berlin, 1969), pp. 186f.

[4] Hengel, *Hellenismus*, pp. 36ff; ET I, pp. 20f; Jones, *Cities*, p. 240.

their Palestinian base for an attack on Egypt. Their fleet put out to sea from the port of Gaza but was driven back by a sudden northerly storm on to the coast near Raphia and decimated. The whole enterprise failed eventually because of the invincibility of the Ptolemaic fortifications at Pelusium and the inclemency of the weather.[1] After his victory at Salamis, Antigonus had already adorned himself and his son with the title of king. Ptolemy, after his success in warding off their attack on Egypt in 305, followed suit. The other Diadochi joined in, and so Alexander's empire finally became legally broken up into five smaller kingdoms. The final encounter between Antigonus and his rivals occurred, not on the Egyptian border, but at Ipsus in Phrygia in the summer of 301 B.C.E. The 80-year-old 'One-eyed' lost both the battle and his own life in an engagement with the united army of Seleucus and Lysimachus. His most tenacious opponent, Ptolemy Soter, as he now called himself, did not participate. He left the risk to the allies, and instead occupied Palestine himself. Because of a rumour of the defeat of his friends, and although engaged at the time in besieging Sidon, he quickly left the province again, leaving garrisons behind. Contrary to previous agreements, the victors gave Coele-Syria totally to Seleucus. Ptolemy anticipated him by occupying the country speedily again. The new master of Asia did not wish to wage war against his one-time friend to whom he owed so much; yet he was unwilling to renounce his claim. The struggle for Phoenicia and Palestine was for the next 150 years a decisive factor in the policies of both kingdoms.[2]

As with the historians of Alexander, so too in the history of the Diadochi the Greek writers scarcely refer to the Jews. Even Josephus takes exception to the fact that Hieronymus of Cardia 'although he had lived almost within our borders, has nowhere mentioned us in his history'. According to him he was 'through an ill-natured disposition, totally blind to the truth'.[3] It can be concluded from this that as a matter of fact the small Jewish temple state in the highlands between the Dead Sea and the coastal region was not of sufficient importance politically or economically to attract the attention of historians. The exceptions are those writers who are interested in foreign religious customs, such as Theophrastus[4] or Megasthenes[5] or Hecateus of

[1] Diod. xx.73,74,76; F.-M. Abel, 'Les confins de la Palestine et de l'Egypte sous les Ptolémées', *RB*, 48 (1939), 219–23.

[2] Hengel, *Hellenismus*, p. 8; ET 1, p. 6.

[3] *C.Ap.* 1.214.

[4] In Porphyry, *De Abstinentia* 11.26 (Nauck p. 155); see also T. Reinach, *Textes d'auteurs grecs et romains relatifs au Judaïsme* (Paris, 1895, repr. Hildesheim, 1963), pp. 7f.

[5] In Clement of Alexandria, *Stromateis* 1.72.4 = *FGrHist* 715 F3; Reinach, *Textes*, p. 13.

Abdera, who in his Egyptian history mentions the Exodus under Moses and the founding of Jerusalem.[1] Josephus in his *Contra Apionem* quotes further extracts from a composition attributed to him, written 'about the Jews', which may however have originated from a Jewish forger of the middle of the second century B.C.E.[2] It reports that after the victory of Ptolemy at Gaza many of the inhabitants of Syria followed him to Egypt because of the 'friendliness and kindness' of the ruler. Among them was the 66-year-old Jewish High Priest Hezekiah, a man of exceptional abilities not least in economic matters. He also urged many of his friends to emigrate to Egypt in view of the favourable political status of the Jews there.[3] It is not improbable that we are dealing here with an historical report that must be taken seriously, even if the full story also contains clear allusions to the high priest Onias IV settling in Leontopolis around 160 B.C.E. As happened later, the Jewish followers of Ptolemy presumably left Jerusalem with him at the approach of the attackers and went with him to Egypt (see below, page 190). This Hezekiah is often connected with the Hizkia whose name appears on the earliest Jewish coins, bearing the inscription '*yḥzqy(h) hpḥh*' (Hezekiah the governor).[4] It is well within the realm of possibility that the last governor of Judah at the end of the Persian period was of high-priestly descent and went to Egypt as an adherent of Ptolemy in 312. There appear to have been the same conflicts here as are found again later, towards the end of the third century. We can do no more here than make conjectures.

A further account is found in the work of the geographer and historian Agatharchides of Cnidus (second century B.C.E.).[5] According to him, Ptolemy son of Lagus conquered the inaccessible city of Jerusalem on a Sabbath, when the inhabitants, because of their 'superstition', would not take up arms. In him they found a 'cruel master'. The *Letter of Aristeas* confirms that harsh actions were taken by Ptolemy I against the Jews: after his conquest of Jerusalem this founder of the dynasty deported 100,000 Jews to Egypt, of whom 30,000 were picked as soldiers, and the remainder, the elderly, women and children became slaves. Although the figures are exaggerated, the

[1] Diod. XL.3 = *FGrHist* 264 F6; cf. Reinach, *Textes*, pp. 14ff.

[2] Cf. M. Hengel, in *Pseudepigrapha I*, Entretiens sur L'Antiquité Classique 18 (Geneva, 1972), pp. 301ff.

[3] *C.Ap.*1.186–9.

[4] L. Y. Rahmani, 'Silver coins of the fourth century B.C. from Tel Gamma', *IEJ*, 21 (1971), 158–60. The replacement of the older reading *yhd* by *hpḥh* does not exclude the identification with the High Priest Hezekiah mentioned by Hecateus.

[5] Jos. *C.Ap.* 1.208–11; *Ant.* XII.5f.; cf. also Appian, *Syr.* 50.

event is historical. His son, Ptolemy II Philadelphus, later ordered the release of the enslaved Jews.[1] With Tcherikover[2] this attack on Jerusalem is hardly to be taken as a consequence of the victory at Gaza in 312 B.C.E. Ptolemy then advanced quickly into Phoenicia; rather it happened on the final conquest of the land in 302 B.C.E. The Jews seem to have come down at that time much more strongly on the side of their overlords until then, the Antigonids. In the period that followed, Jewish slaves and mercenaries formed the main basis of the Jewish Diaspora in wide areas of the Hellenistic world. It is to be noted however that a considerable Jewish minority had existed in Egypt ever since the period of Persian rule.[3]

The whole of Coele-Syria was hotly contested during the wars of the Diadochi, and suffered as a consequence; so too did Judah. It is only to be expected therefore that this time of trouble left its mark on Jewish tradition. 1 Macc. 1:9 says of the successors of Alexander that 'they caused many evils on the earth'. There may be an echo of the capture of Jerusalem by Ptolemy I in Zech. 14:1ff: 'the city shall be taken and the houses plundered and the women ravished; half of the city shall go into exile, but the rest of the people shall not be cut off from the city'. In Joel 3:4ff (Heb. 4:4ff), a passage perhaps as early as Persian times, the Phoenicians and the inhabitants of the coastal plain are rebuked for selling Jewish slaves to the Greeks; and the threat against them is that, conversely, their own children will be sold by the Jews to the South Arabians.[4] Again in the books of Chronicles the numerous references to Jewish troops equipped 'with shield and spear' remind us of the Greek phalanx, which was familiar in Palestine since Persian times.[5] The proud description of the fortifications, army organization and elaborate siege engines of King Uzziah may have in mind Greco-Macedonian models. The command of the prophet that the Jews were not to fight alongside mercenaries from the Northern Kingdom and the pillaging march of the rejected mercenaries point to tension in relation to the Samaritans. It also illustrates the problem of mercenaries in the Hellenistic period. Hatred towards the military superiority of foreign conquerors is visible in Zech. 9:13f:

[1] *Letter of Aristeas* 4, 12ff, 23.

[2] *Hellenistic Civilization*, pp. 56ff, against Abel, *Histoire*, I, p. 31.

[3] Hengel, *Hellenismus*, pp. 27ff, 79ff.; ET I, pp. 17ff., 41f.

[4] *Ibid.* p. 81; ET 42.

[5] Cf. 1 Chron. 12:8, 24; 2 Chron. 11:12; 12:3; 14:8; 25:5; fortifications and war machines: 2 Chron. 26:9, 14ff. Cf. also the economy of the royal estates in verse 10; for the rejection of mercenaries from the Northern Kingdom in the war against the men of Seir from Sela (Petra), see 25:6ff. for Hellenistic influence on the books of Chronicles see P. Welten, *Geschichte und Geschichtsdarstellung in den Chronikbüchern*, WMANT 42 (Neukirchen-Vluyn, 1973), pp. 106ff, 110ff, 199ff.

For I have bent Judah as my bow;
I have made Ephraim its arrow.
I will brandish your sons, O Zion,
over your sons, O Greece,
and wield you like a warrior's sword.

Israel itself becomes the weapon of God against the Macedonians and Greeks. Here we find the introduction of an attitude which reaches its final development in the War Scroll of Qumran. The 'world-war dimension'[1] of Holy War which can be discerned in Chronicles and in the apocalyptic prophetic tradition is strikingly at variance with the slight political significance of the contemporary small Jewish state.

PALESTINE UNDER THE PTOLEMIES UP TO THE BEGINNING OF THE RULE OF THE SELEUCID ANTIOCHUS III (301–223 B.C.E.)

For the next hundred years after Ptolemy I's definitive oddupation of Palestine after the battle of Ipsus (301 B.C.E.), Ptolemaic rule left its mark in a new way on Palestine, and changed it. With the exception of the fourth Syrian war (219–217) it was for most of the land a time of peace; indeed Palestinian Jews were not to experience another such period of peace for the next 350 years. Polybius' report of the sympathy felt by the inhabitants of Coele-Syria towards the Lagids may well have this as its background.[2] Unfortunately our sources are worse than scanty, and the little that we have is so accidental that only a fragmentary picture of this important period can be projected. This means that the situation in Palestine and Coele-Syria can only be seen within the general framework of the history of the Hellenistic monarchies.

To begin with, Ptolemy was not yet in undisputed possession of the whole province of 'Syria and Phoenicia', as the official Ptolemaic title ran.[3] Demetrius Poliorcetes, the 'sea king', still held the Phoenician cities of Tyre and Sidon even after his defeat at Ipsus. In the year 296 he undertook once again an advance into Palestine during which, according to the *Chronicle* of Eusebius, he destroyed Samaria. However, Ptolemy brought the sea empire of the Seleucids step by step into his own hands. Within ten years, at the most, he controlled the Phoenician

[1] Welten, *Geschichte*, p. 201; Hengel, *Hellenismus*, pp. 31f.; ET I, pp. 17f.
[2] Polybius v.86.10.
[3] Hengel, *Hellenismus*, p. 10 n. 4; ET II, p. 3 n. 4.

coastal cities.[1] The boundary with the Seleucid kingdom remained fairly stable, although these did not abandon their claims.[2] The frontier ran from the small river Eleutherus, the present-day Nahr el Kabir, through the Beqa‘ north of Baalbek to the disputed city of Damascus.[3] Thus the district under Ptolemaic rule contained Coele-Syria proper,[4] that is, Palestine and the Beqa‘, and also the Phoenician cities, except Aradus which remained independent.[5] Together with Cyprus, the southern coast of Asia Minor and the forests of Lebanon, these cities were the basis for the sea power of the Ptolemies.

Will characterizes the relation between the two empires in the period between the murder of Seleucus I and the accession of Antiochus III as ‘l’impossible stabilité’.[6] Due to the internal weakness of the Seleucid empire, the Ptolemies, who controlled the Eastern Mediterranean, were at first at an advantage. The highly gifted and energetic Ptolemy II Philadelphus (285/3–246) brought Egypt to the zenith of its power. The first clash, the so-called Syrian war of succession (280/279), began with a mutiny of Seleucid troops in Seleucis in northern Syria, especially at the military base of Apamea. It can be assumed that Ptolemy II was behind it. Nevertheless this did not lead to any movement of the Ptolemaic frontier further north; on the other hand Egypt was able to extend its possessions on the coast of Asia Minor.[7] Two years later, in a successful campaign, Ptolemy II subjugated the Nabateans and so gained control over the perfume trade with Gerrha and South Arabia. From now on this trade was mainly routed through the Ptolemaic fortress of Gaza, and thus the trade routes from Petra to Northern Syria were cut off. In order to keep a further check on the Arabian tribes, the southern and eastern boundaries of Palestine received military strengthening.[8] The so-called first (but really second) Syrian war was set off

[1] Eusebius, *Chron. des Hieronymus*, ed. Helm, GCS 47, pp. 127f, cf. p. 369; see Hengel, *Hellenismus*, p. 9 n. 2; ET II, p. 3 n. 2; E. Will, *Histoire*, 1, pp. 73, 79f.

[2] Diod. XXI.1 fr. 5; Polyb. V.67.4–10; Hengel, *Hellenismus*, p. 8 n. 1; ET II, p. 3 n. 1.

[3] M. Hengel, *Hellenismus*, p. 11 n. 12; ET II p. 4 n. 12.

[4] For the concept, see E. J. Bickerman, ‘La Coelé-Syrie. Notes de géographie historique’, *RB*, 54 (1947), 256–68; Tcherikover, *Hellenistic Civilization*, p. 423 n. 36.

[5] H. Seyrig, ‘Aradus et sa pérée sous les rois Séleucides’, *Syria*, 28 (1951), 206–20; Jones, *Cities*, pp. 238f.

[6] Will, *Histoire*, 1, p. 115.

[7] H. Volkmann, ‘Ptolemaios II’, *PW* 23, 2 (1959), cols. 1646ff.; Will, *Histoire*, 1, pp. 121ff.

[8] W. W. Tarn, ‘Ptolemy II and Arabia’, *JEA*, 15 (1929), 9–25; H. Kortenbeutel, *Der ägyptische Süd- und Osthandel in der Politik der Ptolemäer und römischen Kaiser*, phil. Diss. (Berlin, 1931); for Palestine, see Hengel, *Hellenismus*, pp. 25, 27, 71f.; ET I pp. 14, 15, 37.

by what turned out to be an unsuccessful attack on Egypt from Cyrenaica by Magas, who was an ally of Antiochus I. The events that followed can only be reconstructed hypothetically. In order to forestall a Seleucid advance into Coele-Syria, Ptolemy II advanced to the region of Hamath in Syria;[1] at the same time Antiochus conquered Damascus through a military ruse. Nevertheless, his attack, viewed as a whole, seems to have failed, and so in 271/0 victory was extravagantly celebrated in Alexandria. According to the Zenon papyri, Damascus was by 259 B.C.E. again firmly in the hands of the Ptolemies. But it is probable that, due to the diversion of the Arabian trade, the city had lost much of its significance.[2] The so-called second Syrian war (260–53) was conducted almost exclusively in Asia Minor and the Aegean and hardly touched Palestine. The suggestion that Antiochus II succeeded in moving the boundary as far south as a line between Berytus and Sidon is very dubious.[3]

Some detailed information about Palestine in this period is obtained through the Zenon archive. Of the 2,000 or so documents surviving in it, about 40 refer to Syria and Phoenicia.[4] Practically no trace is found in them of military clashes, but they reflect intensive political and economic activity.[5] On the orders of the finance minister, Apollonius, Zenon travelled to and fro throughout the land between January 259 and February 258 B.C.E. The first and longest of his journeys lasted for five months, and he was accompanied by a retinue of high officials and officers. He travelled from Strato's Tower on the coast, through Jerusalem and Jericho and into East Jordan, to the fort of the Jewish magnate Tobias in Ammanitis, before turning northwards to the

[1] D. Lorton, 'The supposed expedition of Ptolemy II to Persia', *JEA*, 57 (1971), 160–4. Theognis XVII.86 says that Ptolemy had 'cut off' a section of 'Phoenicia, Arabia and Syria'.

[2] Polyaenus IV.15; *PCZ* 59006; cf. M. Rostovtzeff, *Caravan Cities* (Oxford, 1932), pp. 95ff and Will, *Histoire*, I, pp. 128f.

[3] Against U. Kahrstedt, *Syrische Territorien in hellenistischer Zeit*, AGG, NF 19, ii (Berlin, 1926), pp. 23f and Will, *Histoire*, I, pp. 209, 215. It is not implied by *PCZ* 59251 that Sidon was the first city south of the (new) frontier. *PSI* 495 mentions, for example, a Ptolemaic garrison in Tripolis.

[4] V. Tcherikover, 'Palestine under the Ptolemies', *Mizraim*, 4/5 (1937), 7–90 and also his *Hellenistic Civilization*, pp. 60ff. The papyri relating to the Jews are collected in V. Tcherikover and A. Fuks, *Corpus Papyrorum Judaicarum* (Cambridge, Mass., 1957), I, pp. 115–46. Cf. Abel, *Histoire*, I, pp. 60–71; Hengel, *Hellenismus*, pp. 10, 38f, 76ff, 92f, 486ff.; ET I, pp. 7, 21, 39ff, 47f, 267f.

[5] W. W. Tarn, 'The first Syrian war', *JHS*, 46 (1926), 162: 'The Zeno papyri exhibit a country which might never have heard of battles, with its finance minister seemingly anxious only about his new apple trees.'

Hauran and as far as the sources of the Jordan. From there he proceeded to Galilee, where Apollonius had an immense vineyard in Beth-anath, and finally back again to the coast at Akko-Ptolemais.[1] After this there followed excursions to the Phoenician cities, to Gaza and the chief Idumean cities, Mareshah and Adora. Moreover, his own agents were active in the various districts of the land. This widespread activity of Zeno as plenipotentiary of Apollonius, who was himself the king's right-hand man, shows the lively interest taken at Alexandria in this border province in the north-east. The aim was clearly to mould its political administration and economic development as strictly and as effectively as had already been done in Egypt itself. Behind this stood the concept, which was fundamental for the Hellenistic monarchies, that the whole area under their rule was the king's possession and that he had as sovereign a control over it as did a Macedonian landlord over his estate. This concept reached its fullest consummation in Egypt. In the areas under Ptolemaic rule there was a strict monopoly of coinage which had its own standard, which was quite different from the usual Attic one. There was also a state monopoly in the production of and trade in the most important economic goods such as especially grain, oil, linen. Agricultural production on the 'king's land' was strictly pre-planned; through a complicated system of leasing and state supervision they took in practically every branch of production and trade so that the royal exchequer constantly received a great flow of financial resources. Especially stringent measures were used for controlling foreign trade. Such intensive utilization of the riches of Egypt gave a firm basis for the politico-military domination of the Ptolemies in the Eastern Mediterranean region in the third century. Alexandria became the largest economic centre of the Hellenistic world, and Egyptian gold played the same role with the Macedonian leadership in third-century Greece as had previously been the case with Persian gold.[2] Ptolemaic Egypt became, in the words of Tarn, 'a money-making machine'.[3]

Attempts were made to introduce this Egyptian 'state capitalism'

[1] For his route, see S. Mittmann, 'Zenon im Ostjordanland', *Archäologie und Altes Testament*, Festschrift für K. Galling (Tübingen, 1970), pp. 199–210.

[2] For Ptolemaic economic policy see C. Préaux, *L'économie royale des Lagides* (Brussels, 1939); Rostovtzeff, *History* (Oxford, 1941), 1, pp. 255–422. On its external monetary political aspects see Will, *Histoire*, 1, pp. 148–78 and p. 155 for their policy. For the economic role of Alexandria see P. M. Fraser, *Ptolemaic Alexandria* (Oxford, 1972), 1, pp. 132–88.

[3] W. W. Tarn and G. T. Griffith, *Hellenistic Civilization* (3rd edn., London, 1952), p. 179.

into this province too.[1] Barely a year before Zenon's tour two royal decrees concerning a tax-census of cattle and of native slaves in 'Syria and Phoenicia' were issued. They were recorded in even the remotest hamlet by 'village tax farmers' or 'village mayors', and false declarations were punished with heavy fines.[2] Zenon's tour may have been concerned with supervising the implementation of these decrees. The contacts with East Jordan and Gaza suggest that there was also a move to control the perfume trade. An increase in productiveness is also indicated by the great increase in the number of coins found in Palestine and dating from the time of Ptolemy II. Among them copper coins, the currency of the lesser folk, appear for the first time. It was now that minted money replaced the traditional barter. It can be concluded from this that the king and his minister succeeded in developing considerably the productive capacity of 'Syria and Phoenicia' as well as that of Egypt. We hear of the export – of course under strict supervision – of slaves, corn, oil and wine; the world-famous balsam plantations at Jericho and Engedi had become 'royal property', and were much more intensively exploited than previously under the Persians. Imports from Egypt included papyrus, linen, glass and luxury goods. In Palestine, as in Egypt, technical improvements were introduced, and new plants and breeds were cultivated. For example, in the vineyard of Apollonius in Galilee 80,000 quality vines from the island of Cos were planted, whose product could no longer be differentiated from the popular imports from the Aegean. Further improvements were brought by the introduction of irrigation, water-wheels, sowing-ploughs, screw-presses and so on.[3] The ostraca from Khirbet el-Kom, which are to be dated probably in the sixth year of Ptolemy II (that is, in 277 B.C.E., about eighteen years before Zenon's tour) and which come from the archives of an Idumean money-lender 'Qos-yada' bin Hanna'', confirm that Hellenistic influence in Palestine was manifested at first primarily in the economic sphere. Four of these ostraca are in Edomite, one in Greek and one bilingual. From this it appears that basically this milieu was one of mixed culture, a feature that is encountered again slightly later, with the addition of Phoenician influence, in the Idumean capital Mareshah.[4]

[1] Hengel, *Hellenismus*, pp. 35ff, 67ff, 76ff; ET I, pp. 20ff, 35ff, 39ff.

[2] PER 24.552 gr (= *SB* 8008). Text with bibliography and commentary in M.-T. Lenger, *Corpus des Ordonnances des Ptolémées*, Académie Royale de Belgique, Classe des lettres, Mémoires 57.1 (Brussels, 1964), pp. 37ff, nos. 21–22.

[3] Rostovtzeff, *History*, 1, pp. 351ff; Hengel, *Hellenismus*, 76f, 84ff, 91ff; ET I pp. 39f, 42f, 46f.

[4] L. A. Geraty, *Third Century B.C. Ostraca from Khirbet el Kom*, Phil. Diss. Harvard Divinity School, 1972, with summary in *HTR*, 65 (1972), 595f.

Inseparably bound up with economic development was the development of the administration. The capital of the province was probably Akko-Ptolemais, which had received its new name in 261 B.C.E. shortly before Zenon's tour.[1] The royal decree mentioned above refers to a 'financial officer' responsible for Syria and Phoenicia, but it may be supposed, with H. Bengtson, that there was in addition to him a 'governor' responsible for politico-military administration and that he was the highest official. Further development was made of the subdivision into 'hyparchies' and 'toparchies' already established in the time of Alexander or Antigonus. This enabled the administration, as in Egypt, to register each individual village as its smallest fiscal unit. The 'hyparchies', like the districts in Egypt, each had a politico-military 'governor' and an *oikonomos* for financial administration. In a letter of Zenon we meet five different Ptolemaic officials in Mareshah, the capital of the hyparchy of Idumea. Thus Hellenistic administrative bureaucracy gained entry into the province, and Greek merchants and officials penetrated to the remotest of Palestinian farmsteads.[2]

Abundant archeological traces testify to an intensive building of fortresses aimed at military security against the Seleucids in the north, and the Arabs in the east and south, which was also served by the foundation of military colonies and cities. One of these was Philoteria on the sea of Chinnereth, formerly Beth Yeraḥ, which was renamed after a sister of Philadelphus. Again at Scythopolis, the old Beth-shean, there was a settlement probably of mercenaries from the Bosporus.[3] Damascus was possibly refounded as Arsinoe, while a second settlement of this name possibly lay in the Beqa'.[4] Pella received the name Berenice, the old fortress of Rabbath-Ammon became Philadelphia, and Baalbek became Heliopolis. A whole range of smaller Phoenician towns along the coast must have got their typically Greco-Egyptian names in Ptolemaic times, such as Leonton polis, Ornithon polis, Sycaminon polis, Boucolon polis, Krokodeilon polis and Porphyreon polis.[5] Excavations at Tell Anafa on Lake Huleh have revealed a purely Hellenistic settlement, for which no name is yet known. It was a

1 Hengel, *Hellenismus*, pp. 36f.; ET I, pp. 20f.

2 H. Bengtson, *Die Strategie in der hellenistischen Zeit*, 3 (2nd edn., Munich, 1967), pp. 166ff; Hengel, *Hellenismus*, pp. 36ff; ET I, pp. 20ff. For Mareshah see *PCZ* 59015 and Tcherikover, *Mizraim*, 4/5 (1937), 40ff and his *Hellenistic Civilization*, pp. 65f. A detailed commentary is given by F.-M. Abel, 'Marisa dans le Papyrus 76 de Zénon', *RB*, 33 (1924), 566–74.

3 M. Avi-Yonah, 'Scythopolis', *IEJ*, 12 (1962), 123–34.

4 Tcherikover, *Städtegründungen*, pp. 65ff.

5 Pseudo-Scylax 87; Strabo XVI.2.27 (C 758); see G. Hölscher, *PW*, 22 (1953–4), cols 271ff.

centre of great economic activity and of considerable wealth. Although the results of excavations have hitherto mainly concerned the Seleucid era of the second century B.C.E., older strata from Ptolemaic times have been discovered.[1] Even the Phoenician cities of the coast for all their rich traditions in part took over Hellenistic constitutional forms. Thus Sidon, after the death of its last king, the Ptolemaic admiral Philocles, assumed a democratic constitution. On the other hand, its rival Tyre in 274 B.C.E. chose an aristocratic constitution under Suffetes. Some similar 'Hellenizing' changes of city constitutions can be assumed in the case of other coastal cities as far south as Gaza.[2] From the end of the third century Tyrians and Sidonians appear as participants in contests which were held in Greece and were open only to 'Hellenic' contestants.[3] In some cities such as Dura Europos, Damascus, Gerasa, Samaria, Philoteria and Mareshah we find remains of a typically early Hellenistic, rectangular, Hippodamian city-plan.[4]

Despite Ptolemaic efforts, a province of such variety was difficult to unify politically. The relatively autonomous cities along the coast stood in contrast to the 'peoples' of the interior, who were organized as *ethnē*.[5] Moreover, there were the military colonies established mainly on royal territory which possessed only limited 'city status'. In Egypt the sharp difference between the natives and the Greeks and Macedonians was deliberately maintained, but it seems that in 'Syria and Palestine' the distinction was not so clearly retained. Taking natives as concubines was relatively frequent.[6] In the East Jordan fortress of the Jewish magnate Tobias there was harmonious co-operation between Macedonian and Jewish soldiers. Tobias himself employed a Greek secretary, and his correspondence with Apollonius and the king shows him to be a very self-assertive man. According to Josephus he was the brother-in-law of the High Priest Onias II, and was the first Jew to hold an influential position in Hellenistic times.[7] In contrast with Egypt, the Ptolemaic administration could not dispense

[1] S. S. Weinberg, 'Tel Anafa: The Hellenistic town', *IEJ*, 21 (1971), 86–109.

[2] Jones, *Cities*, pp. 239ff; Abel, *Histoire*, 1, pp. 51ff; Tcherikover, *Hellenistic Civilization*, pp. 90ff.

[3] Hengel, *Hellenismus*, pp. 131f.; ET, I, p. 71.

[4] Hengel, *Hellenismus*, p. 91 n. 362, ET II pp. 37f n 373; cf. A. Kriesis, *Greek Town Building* (Athens, 1965), pp. 71ff.

[5] For the distinction betwen *polis* and *ethnos* see E. J. Bickerman, *Institutions des Séleucides* (Paris, 1938), pp. 141ff, 164ff and above p. 43 n. 1.

[6] See the decree of Ptolemy II on the registration of native-born slaves (see p. 56 n. 3); M.-T. Lenger, *Corpus*, p. 43, no. 22 ll 17ff for soldiers and other settlers living with native women.

[7] *PCZ* 59003; 59076; 59075 = *CPJ*, 1, pp. 118ff, 125ff, nos. 1, 2, 4, 5; Hengel, *Hellenismus*, pp. 27, 41, 92f, 488ff; ET I, pp. 15, 22, 47f., 268f.

with the co-operation of the native aristocracy on a basis of equality. The Zenon papyri reflect clearly the difficulties of the new masters face to face with the self-confident native population. One village elder expelled with physical force from his village the agents of Zenon together with the representatives of the Ptolemaic administration who had come to collect a debt. Two Idumean sheikhs had sold some slaves to Zenon; but when two of the slaves fled back to them they did not return them and demanded an additional payment.[1] Wine-growers on Apollonius' large estate at Beth-anath protested strongly against too high taxation, and appealed to the minister.[2] The royal administration on the other hand, in the interest of orderly agriculture and taxation, had to protect the half-bond peasants (*sōmata laïka eleuthera*) against Greek adventurers and freebooters; therefore arbitrary enslavement of the natives was forbidden. Social conditions in Palestine were therefore complex under the rule of the first Ptolemies. The native aristocracy improved their position under their new overlords, for they participated in the economic upturn and were at least partly prepared to assimilate to the Hellenistic governing classes in both life-style and language. On the other hand, the lower social classes were further exploited owing to the more intensive methods of state and private production. Because the king wished to maintain the productivity of the land, he in turn had to pay heed to certain basic rights of the population. The possibility of presenting petitions and complaints within the ascending hierarchy of the royal bureaucracy also provided a measure of relief.[3]

The Phoenicians formed an important link in the transmission of Hellenistic culture in Palestine. For a long time previously they had been involved in economic and cultural interchanges with the Greeks, and received from them more respect than other barbarians. In Persian times they were in control of the whole coastal region, and their influence still seems to have been strong under the Ptolemies. The Sidonian colony in Mareshah demonstrates this; it was established about the middle of the third century, and its culture was a mixture of Hellenistic, Phoenician and Idumean elements. This colony of 'the Sidonians in Mareshah' was under the leadership of an *Archōn*. Greek was the predominant language and its tombs show Alexandrian

1 *PCZ* 59015, see p. 57 n. 3; *PCZ* 59018 = *CPJ*, I, pp. 129f, no. 6.

2 *P. Lond.* 1948 and *PSI* 554; see M. Hengel, 'Das Gleichnis von den Weingärtnern Mc. 12, 1–12 im Lichte der Zenonpapyri und der rabbinischen Gleichnisse', *ZNW*, 59 (1968), 11–16, 23ff.

3 Hengel, *Hellenismus*, pp. 74f, 79ff, 93ff; ET I, pp. 38f., 41f., 48ff.

influence. It is probable that similar Sidonian colonies existed in Shechem and in Rabbath-Ammon-Philadelphia.[1]

The second Ptolemy had ability less in waging war than in the field of economics and administration, and not least in diplomacy. Conditions in Egypt and Palestine as portrayed in the Zenon papyri give some indication of this, as also the development of relations with the Seleucid empire after the second Syrian war. Through the success of the Macedonian King Antigonus Gonatas, that war had destroyed the hegemony of the Ptolemies in the Aegean. In 253 Philadelphus induced his opponent until then, Antiochus II, to make peace and to ally himself by marriage. The Seleucid king parted with his wife until then, Laodice, and their sons, and declared himself ready to marry Ptolemy's daughter Berenice. The minister Apollonius escorted the princess from Pelusium along the coast of Palestine and Phoenicia to the frontier.[2] This 'diplomatic masterstroke'[3] ended in tragedy, however, seven years later after Philadelphus died (246 B.C.E.). Immediately before his death Antiochus II acknowledged again the legal status of his first wife Laodice and made their son, Seleucus II, his heir. In the interest of her young son, Berenice opposed this solution, and it was the intervention of her brother Ptolemy III Euergetes that led to the third Syrian war (246–241 B.C.E.). But just before Euergetes entered Antioch, Berenice and her son became victims of an assassination plot. Ptolemy III was initially successful, and after receiving homage from Northern Syria and Cilicia pressed on, it is thought, as far as Babylonia. However, serious set-backs followed. A rebellion called Ptolemy III back to Egypt.[4] In a counter-attack Seleucus II Callinicus succeeded in conquering Damascus and Orthosia, which the Egyptians besieged in vain in 242/1 B.C.E.[5] The attempt to conquer all Coele-Syria, however, was a complete failure, and the struggle with his brother, Antiochus Hierax, forced Seleucus eventually to conclude a peace treaty. From this Ptolemy III gained a considerable amount of territory mostly in southern Asia Minor and also, as an enclave, Seleucia in Pieria, the port

[1] J. P. Peters and H. Thiersch, *Painted Tombs in the Necropolis of Marissa* (London, 1905); Hengel, *Hellenismus*, pp. 84, 115ff, 535f, n. 215; ET I, pp. 43, 61f, II p. 195 n. 233.

[2] A. Pridik, *Berenike, die Schwester des Königs Ptolemaios III. Euergetes*, Acta et commentationes Universitatis Tartuensis B. Humaniora 35/36 (Tartu, 1935); Will, *Histoire*, I, pp. 213ff.

[3] H. Volkmann, *PW*, 23 (1959), col. 1655.

[4] The main source is P. Petrie II no. 45 and III no. 144 = *FGrHist* 160. The author of this report was Ptolemy III or his brother Lysimachus. See also the inscription of Adulis *OGIS* 54 and Polyaen. VIII.50. On this see Will, *Histoire*, I, pp. 223ff; a different view in H. Volkmann, *PW*, 23 (1959), cols. 1669ff.

[5] Euseb. *Chron.* (Armenian version, ed. Karst, GCS 20), p. 118 for 242/1 B.C.E. (according to *FGrHist* 260 F32, from Porphyry).

of Antioch.[1] At the conclusion of this campaign Ptolemy toured through the province and, as reported by Josephus in *Contra Apionem*, may have visited Jerusalem and offered sacrifice there to celebrate his victory.[2] The book of Daniel in its *vaticinium ex eventu* in chapter 11 follows with great interest the fate of Berenice and the success of Ptolemy III, a sign of how deeply involved Jewish apocalyptic circles were in the clash between Ptolemy and Seleucus as it affected the fate of Syria.[3]

The dismissal of the procurator Apollonius, like the attempt to simplify the administration by introducing district governors and abolishing the distinction between military and economic executives, clearly led to a decline in economic returns. The king was forced to resort to a debasement of the currency, which gradually brought about an inflation of the copper coinage.[4] It is probable that the first part of the story of Tobias, which has been heavily elaborated with fiction, belongs to the time of Euergetes. This narrative has been preserved for us by Josephus, though he puts it at the wrong period.[5] It throws light on the change of conditions in Palestine under Ptolemy III. It tells that the High Priest Onias II, the brother-in-law of the feudal lord Tobias known from the Zenon papyri, refused to pay the annual tribute to the king. The reason for this was probably not senile obstinacy, as stated in the Tobiad romance, but rather that he was tired of being domineered by the Ptolemaic administration and possibly also that he expected a change of power in favour of Seleucus II Callinicus. The king promptly threatened to expropriate Jewish territory and resettle it with military colonists. This threat was averted through the intervention of Joseph, the high priest's nephew and son of the feudal lord Tobias. Joseph received in return the office of *prostasia*, that is, the political representation of the Jewish *ethnos vis-à-vis* the Ptolemaic administration. His position in Judea was now similar to that of the former *peḥāh* under the Persians. In return for doubling the tax tender, he obtained in Alexandria the right to farm the taxes throughout 'Syria and Phoenicia'. He found the way successfully to break down the opposition of individual Hellenized cities like Ashkelon and Scythopolis to increased

[1] Justin XXVII.2.9; cf. Dan. 11:9.

[2] *C.Ap.* II.48.

[3] Dan. 11:5–9, cf. Jerome's commentary, Migne, *PL* 25 (1845), cols. 559ff, which is based on Porphyry (*FGrHist* 260 F33–61).

[4] A. Segrè, 'The Ptolemaic copper inflation, *ca.* 230–140 B.C.', *AJP*, 63 (1942), 174ff; O. R. Sellers, 'Coins of the 1960 excavation at Shechem', *BA*, 25 (1962), 92; Hengel, *Hellenismus*, pp. 52f, 84f, ET I, pp. 27f, 43f, and coin statistics, p. 573, ET II, pp. 208f.

[5] Jos. *Ant.* XII.158–236.

taxes and he retained the office of tax farmer for twenty-two years, probably until the outbreak of the fourth Syrian war, that is, from *circa* 240 to 218 B.C.E.[1] In this capacity he was the first Jewish 'merchant banker', and maintained a permanent agent in Alexandria and deposited large sums there. These events fit in well with the administrative reforms of the king. For, after the removal of the financial genius Apollonius, he attempted to simplify the complicated bureaucracy of the administration and to increase income from taxation. However, coin finds in Palestine indicate that the additional exploitation reduced the circulation of money and the gradual economic decline of the Ptolemaic empire began (see p. 42 n. 4). The rise of the Tobiad Joseph, on the other hand, was no disadvantage for the Jews, for it gained for the hitherto unimportant Jerusalem a new economic and political status. Polybius still knew of Jerusalem primarily as a sanctuary, for he speaks of the Jews 'who live around the temple called Jerusalem'.[2] Whereas the feudal lord Tobias had his residence in East Jordan, Joseph and the later Tobiads lived in the city. More and more of the nobility came to live in the capital itself, which also means that it was more and more open to Hellenistic influence. Like his father Tobias before him, Joseph seems to have regarded the regulations of the Torah with great laxity. After giving a portrayal of his life, the Tobiad romance commends him as 'an excellent and high-minded man' who 'had brought the Jewish people from poverty and a state of weakness to more splendid opportunities of life'.[3] The concept behind this judgement is clear; it is that which was later embodied in the programme of the Jewish Hellenists in the time of Antiochus IV and which is formulated in 1 Macc. 1:11, namely that the condition of Jews in Palestine could only be improved through closer economic, political and cultural contact with the non-Jewish, Hellenized (or as we today would say, 'progressive') environment.

Another writing that throws light on the situation in Jewish Palestine under Ptolemaic rule is the book of Ecclesiastes. We cannot indeed trace in it the direct influence of Greek philosophical schools, but it does convey well the spirit of the early Hellenistic period and shows acquaintance with Greek proverbial wisdom.[4] Of interest for us here are its allusions to political and social conditions: 'If you see in a

[1] *Ant.* XII.224. For this see Rostovtzeff, *History*, 1, p. 349; 3, p. 1400 n. 132; Tcherikover, *Hellenistic Civilization*, pp. 130ff; Hengel, *Hellenismus*, pp. 51f, 489ff; ET I pp. 27f, 268ff.

[2] Cited by Jos. *Ant.* XII.136; cf. *Sib.* 3. 213f.

[3] Jos. *Ant.* XII.224.

[4] Rainer Braun, *Kohelet und die frühhellenistische Popularphilosophie*, BZAW 130 (Berlin, 1973); Hengel, *Hellenismus*, pp. 210–37; ET I, pp. 115–28.

province the poor oppressed and justice and right violently taken away, do not be amazed at the matter; for the high official is watched by a higher, and there are yet higher ones over them' (5:8). Here we find an allusion to the bureaucracy of the Ptolemaic administration, which we have already encountered in the Zenon papyri. Ecclesiastes 10:20 refers to the prevalence of informers in the Hellenistic kingdoms.[1] The avarice of the new Hellenistic–oriental 'managers' is exposed and criticized by the sages who themselves stand 'in the shadow of money' in these words: 'He who loves money will not be satisfied with money; nor he who loves wealth, with gain: this also is vanity. When goods increase, they increase who eat them' (5:10f). A postscript to 5:8 clearly refers to the interest of the Ptolemies in increasing the return in agriculture: 'The best thing for a country is a king whose lands are well tilled'.[2] Similarly the work of the Chronicler, which belongs to the same early Hellenistic period, mentions the interest of King Uzziah in the agriculture of large estates. Not only did he build fortresses and provide them with war machines (see above, p. 51) but 'he had large herds, both in the Shephelah and in the plain, and he had farmers and vinedressers in the hills and in the fertile lands, for he loved the soil'.[3] Against this background, it is understandable that the old prophetic critique of the wealth, luxury and oppression of the rulers received a new actuality. In such circumstances the anti-Hellenists could interpret the sociological concept 'poor' in the sense of 'pious'. The piety of the poor as developed above all in apocalyptic circles contained an unmistakable protest against the transformation of the social structure by the foreign Hellenistic rulers and their aristocratic accomplices.[4]

PALESTINE DOWN TO THE CONQUEST BY ANTIOCHUS III (223–200 B.C.E.)

The first 80 years of the third century were characterized by the constant flaring up of dynastic struggles, by the irruption of the Gauls into Asia Minor and by the rivalry of the expanding Pergamene kingdom, as well as by the premature and violent death of the most able

[1] Rostovtzeff, *History*, 1, p. 350.

[2] NEB translation. The verse is textually uncertain. Generally see E. Bickerman, *Four Strange Books of the Bible* (New York, 1967), pp. 141–67; Hengel, *Hellenismus*, pp. 98ff.; ET I, pp. 50f.

[3] 2 Chron. 26:10 and cf. also the list of royal officials in 1 Chron. 27:25ff.

[4] E. Bammel, '*ptōchos*', *TWNT*, 6 (1959), pp. 889–902; ET *TDNT*, 6 (1968), pp. 889–902.

rulers.[1] Consequently the Seleucids, although they had a very much larger empire with inexhaustible resources, were prevented on more than one occasion from taking possession of disputed Coele-Syria. Ptolemaic diplomacy combined with an offensive form of defence tactics was stronger than all Seleucid attempts at conquest. In 223 Antiochus III, who was scarcely twenty years old,[2] was made king to succeed his brother Seleucus III Ceraunus, who had been assassinated, and the old plans for conquest were immediately revived. Although Molon, the satrap of Media, had rebelled, the young king, on the advice of his vizier Hermias, opened his first campaign in the summer of 221 and crossed the northern frontier of Ptolemaic territory in Syria.[3] The time appeared opportune, for Ptolemy III had died at the end of 222 B.C.E., and his eldest son, Ptolemy IV Philopator, who was only seventeen years old and had been educated by Eratosthenes, showed more inclination for intellectual and artistic pursuits than for the hard realities of politics and administration. Polybius describes him as a spoilt *rex otiosus* who, shielded by a coterie of court favourites, devoted himself to exquisite amusements without bothering about the national interest.[4]

Antiochus occupied the plain of Marsyas, the present-day Beqa', but his attack became bogged down at its narrow southern end between the fortresses of Gerrha and Brochoi where the Ptolemaic commander Theodotus had erected his defence line.[5] After several abortive attacks, Antiochus was forced to withdraw. In the following year he suppressed the rebellion in the eastern satrapies, and prepared for a new attack. Despite the defection of his kinsman Achaeus, who made himself king of Asia Minor, he concentrated all his plans on conquering Coele-Syria. Badly advised by his ministers, Sosibius and Agathocles, Philopator had neglected to prepare for a renewed attack from the north and had also annoyed his able commander Theodotus. Antiochus began the fourth Syrian war (which was actually the sixth clash) in the spring of 219 by conquering the Ptolemaic enclave of Seleucia in Pieria at the

1 Seleucus I was assassinated in 281 and Seleucus III Ceraunus in 223; Antiochus II Theos died in uncertain circumstances when 40 years old in 246.

2 H. H. Schmitt, *Untersuchungen zur Geschichte Antiochos' des Grossen und seiner Zeit*, Historia Einzelschriften 6 (Wiesbaden, 1964), pp. 2ff.

3 Polyb. v.42.5–9. On the passages from Polybius cited here see F. W. Walbank, *A Historical Commentary on Polybius*, 1 (Oxford, 1957).

4 v.34; H. Volkmann, 'Ptolemaios IV Philopator', *PW* 230 (1959), cols. 1679ff; for the date see A. E. Samuel, *Ptolemaic Chronology*, MBPAR 43 (1962), pp. 106ff.

5 Polyb. v.45.5 to 46.5.

gates of Antioch.[1] There he received a written invitation to invade Coele-Syria from the commander Theodotus, who had risen in revolt against Philopator in Akko-Ptolemais. Polybius gives us the first detailed description of a Seleucid campaign in Phoenicia and Palestine. Once more Antiochus marched into the Beqa', bypassed the fortresses of Brochoi and Gerrha and captured the passes near Berytus; at this the Ptolemaic troops abandoned their siege of the rebel-held provincial capital Ptolemais and withdrew. A large quantity of supplies together with 40 ships fell into the king's hands on the seizure of Tyre and Ptolemais.[2] However, he gave up the plan to make a direct attack on Pelusium, before which so many previous attacks on Egypt had failed; the reason was that he had heard of the massive defence preparations being made by the Egyptians. Instead he proceeded to occupy the smaller towns of Phoenicia and Palestine, which readily surrendered. It was only larger fortresses, such as Dor on the coast, that dared to resist. The excellent Ptolemaic system of defence in depth was shattered by treachery. Philopator and his adviser Sosibius were taken by surprise by the rebellion of Theodotus and the quick successes of Antiochus, and by now felt too weak to intervene in Palestine at once. They therefore sought time to acquire armaments and entered into negotiations with the Seleucid king. Antiochus, who was engaged in the siege of Dor, agreed to an armistice for four months for the winter season. He left the conquered districts in the control of garrisons under the command of the turncoat Theodotus, and himself set out with the main body of his army to Seleucia in the hope, which was encouraged by his Egyptian partner in the negotiations, that Ptolemy would not try to regain the area, and that, therefore, the province was in practice already conquered.[3] The negotiations in Memphis came to a natural breakdown owing to deft handling by the Egyptians, who even succeeded in concealing Egyptian rearmament from the Seleucid delegation. Therefore in the spring of 218 Antiochus set out to conquer the rest of Palestine. In the meantime, the Egyptian general Nicolaus, himself an Aetolian like Theodotus, marched to Phoenicia and occupied the 'Plane Tree pass', as well as Porphyreonpolis between Berytus and Sidon.[4] In a combined land and sea battle Antiochus forced him to retreat to Sidon. The victor refrained from undertaking a siege, but instead marched into Galilee and there occupied Philoteria, where the Jordan flows out from the sea of Chinnereth, and the strategically important Scythopolis; through a stratagem he also captured the mountain

[1] Polyb. v.58.1–61.2; cf. Abel, *Histoire*, 1, pp. 74ff.

[2] Polyb. v.40.1–3; 61.3 to 62.6. [3] Polyb. v.66–67; Will, *Histoire*, 2, pp. 25ff.

[4] Polyb. v.68.6; cf. Jos. *Ant.* xvi.361 = *BJ* 1.539 and B. Spuler, 'Platanos 3', *PW* 20 (1950), cols. 2338ff.

fortress of Atabyrion, i.e. Mount Tabor. A good number of Ptolemaic officers, some with their troops, went over to him, and this was a sure sign that Ptolemaic domination in Palestine was declining. Antiochus owed a good deal of his success to these deserters.[1] He crossed the Jordan, and took Pella in the Jordan valley, and both Kamon and Ephron (Gephrus) in the highlands of Gilead. The point of this incursion into East Jordan was to make an alliance with the Arabian tribes, who promptly and unanimously came over to his side. We may surmise that the Nabateans are the ones mainly referred to here, who had not forgotten their humiliation at the hands of Philadelphus.[2] He was considerably strengthened by their support and, abundantly provided for, consequently conquered Abila, to which Nicias, the friend and kinsman of a local dynast Menneos, had given aid in vain. The Ptolemies had obviously entrusted the defence of their eastern boundary against the Arabs and other enemies to the natives.[3] After this Antiochus took the particularly strong fortress of Gadara after a short siege. There he heard that a strong force had been assembled in Rabbath-Ammon and was plundering the territory of the Arabs who had gone over to Antiochus; these were probably units of the Ptolemaic 'frontier guard' in Ammanitis, the Tobiad military colony.[4] He put off his other plans in order to surround this almost inaccessible fortress. All assaults failed, until a prisoner betrayed its secret water supply and he forced the besieged to surrender from lack of water. Following this Antiochus sent two of the Ptolemaic officers who had recently come over to him, with 5,000 men, 'into the territories near Samaria'; these may well have included Judea and Jerusalem, though they are not actually mentioned.[5] For Polybius, mainly concerned with the fate of the great Ptolemaic fortresses, the Jews in Palestine evidently carried no independent military significance. Towards the end of the year 218 Antiochus retired to winter quarters in Ptolemais.

By the spring of the following year Philopator had completed his preparations and so marched eastwards from Pelusium. Antiochus then

[1] Polyb. v.70.1–11; Hengel, *Hellenismus*, p. 12; ET I, p. 8.

[2] Polyb. v.70.12. Kamous = Kamon Judg. 10, 5. Jdt. 4. 4(?); Jos. *Ant.* v.254; F.-M. Abel, *Géographie de la Palestine*, 3rd edn., 2, (Paris, 1967), p. 412. Gephrous = Ephron 1 Macc. 5:46; 2 Macc. 12:27; Abel, *Géographie*, 1, pp. 318f. In v.71.2 Polybius speaks of the district of Galatis, i.e. the biblical Gilead.

[3] Polyb. v.71.1–3; B. Niese, *Geschichte der griechischen und makedonischen Staaten*, 2, p. 378.

[4] Polyb. v.71.4–10; cf. S. Mittmann, 'Zenon im Ostjordanland', *Archäologie und Altes Testament*, pp. 208f.

[5] Polyb. v.71.11; cf. the same term in 2 Macc. 15:1.

moved southwards along the coast, and on 22 June 217 B.C.E. the two armies met at Raphia on the southern boundary of Palestine. An attempt on the life of Ptolemy IV by the deserter Theodotus failed, the king being saved by a Jewish apostate, Dositheos son of Drimylus.[1] Among the very mixed Seleucid troops there were around 10,000 Arabs under the command of one Zabdibelus and also elite Syrian troops.[2] Moreover, the Indian elephants and the cavalry of Antiochus were superior to those on the Egyptian side. Nevertheless, the steadfastness of the Ptolemaic phalanx, made up of Greek mercenaries and Egyptians trained in the Macedonian method, was decisive. Whilst the young king was pursuing the fleeing cavalry of his opponents, his own troops suffered a crushing defeat.[3] The decisive effect in battle of native Egyptians stimulated the self-awareness of the fellahin in the years that followed and led to constant disturbances in Egypt. Antiochus fled to Gaza with the remains of his army, and arranged a short truce in order to bury the dead. His losses amounted to 10,000 infantrymen and 300 cavalrymen; Ptolemy lost only 1,500 foot and 700 horse. The Seleucid king had to withdraw very quickly from the conquered province, and the Phoenician cities vied with one another in paying compliments to their legitimate ruler. Polybius specifically stresses that the sympathies of the Palestinians had always been with the royal house of Alexandria.[4]

As soon as he reached Antioch, the Seleucid king opened peace negotiations, for he was afraid of being caught in a pincer movement between Achaeus in Asia Minor and Ptolemy in the south. Delighted with his unexpected success and having no political and military ambition, Ptolemy, after some hesitation, was quite happy to agree. He had not obstructed the rapid retreat of his opponent, and only, according to the decree of Raphia, advanced into Seleucid territory for three weeks when the negotiations dragged on much too long.[5] He had no plans for conquest; he did not even claim the return of Seleucia in Pieria, which he had lost; he was content with simply re-establishing by and large the old border. Perhaps his readiness to make peace was encouraged by disturbances among the Egyptian troops.[6] However he

1 3 Macc. 1:3, see *CPJ* 1, pp. 230ff., no. 127; cf. Polyb. v.81.

2 Polyb. v.79.9, 12; 85.4. The 'Syrians' of 85.10 are no doubt to be identified with 'those selected from the whole empire, equipped in the Macedonian way, in 79.4.

3 Polyb. v. 82–6; W. Peremans, 'Notes sur la bataille de Raphia', *Aegyptus*, 31 (1951), 214ff.

4 Polyb. v.86.9.

5 Polyb. v.87; H.-J. Thissen, *Studien zum Raphiadekret*, Beiträge zur klassischen Philologie 23 (Meisenheim am Glan, 1966), pp. 19, 60ff, §23–5.

6 Polyb. v.107.1–3; cf. Thissen, *Studien*, p. 62 on the basis of §25 of the Raphia decree.

and his sister and wife Arsinoe allowed themselves to be the more warmly fêted by the cities of the regained province. He visited their sanctuaries in order to demonstrate his reverence for the gods of the land and to receive varied acts of homage from the populace.[1] Honorific inscriptions from Mareshah, Jaffa and from the area around Tyre[2] bear witness of the king's visit to the province which, according to the Raphia decree, lasted four months.[3] Despite its heavy novelistic colouring, the legendary account in 3 Maccabees of the ill-fated visit of Philopator to the Jerusalem Temple may well contain an historical kernel.[4] The book of Daniel too, which describes in more detail the fourth Syrian war, speaks finally of the 'arrogance' of Philopator, who cast down tens of thousands but whose power lacked endurance.[5] Through idleness and indolence, Ptolemy IV let the fruits of his success slip out of his hand; 'he could have robbed Antiochus of his kingdom had he supported his good fortune with bravery.'[6]

In the years that followed, the two empires developed in opposite directions. Antiochus III first of all subdued the usurper Achaeus in Asia Minor (216–213), and thereafter undertook his celebrated 'anabasis' into the eastern provinces, which led to the re-establishment (212–205) of the kingdom of his great-grandfather, Seleucus I. On the other hand, Egypt was plagued by increasing internal disturbances. Incited by their own priesthood, the natives rebelled, partly against increasing taxation by which the king tried to restore finances weakened by warfare. In 207 B.C.E. the Thebais in Upper Egypt withdrew from the united kingdom, and for about twenty years remained independent under native Nubian kings.[7] This marks a fundamental

[1] Polyb. v.86.11; and the Raphia decree in Thissen, *Studien*, p. 15, §15f: 'He passed through the remainder of the towns of his kingdom. He entered into the temples that were there. He offered burnt-offerings and drink-offerings because all the people in the cities received him ...'

[2] Mareshah: F. J. Bliss and R. A. S. Macalister, *Excavations in Palestine 1898–1902* (London, 1902), pp. 62f, supplemented by C. Clermont-Ganneau, 'Séance du 19 Oct. 1900', *CRAIBL* 1900, 536–41. Joppa–Jaffa: B. Lifschitz, 'Beiträge zur palästinischen Epigraphik', *ZDPV*, 78 (1962), 82f. The inscription of the commander Dorymenes from the region of Tyre: *SEG*, no. 325, cf. Polyb. v.61.9.

[3] Thissen, *Studien*, p. 19, §26; Polyb. v.87.6 speaks of three months.

[4] 3 Macc. 1:6 to 2:24; V. Tcherikover, 'The third book of Maccabees as a historical source of Augustus' time', *Scripta Hierosolymitana*, 7 (1961), 1–26. Bibliography in J. Tondriau, 'La Dynastie Ptolémaique et la religion dionysiaque', *ChE*, 50 (1950), 301ff.

[5] Dan. 11:10–12 and on it Jerome *in Dan.*, *PL*, 25 (1845), cols. 561f.

[6] Justin xxx.1.6.

[7] Will, *Histoire*, 2, pp. 32ff.

crisis in the relation between the Hellenistic monarchy and the native population, which worsened still further in the second century. Apocalyptic-sounding texts like the Demotic Chronicle and the Potter's Oracle reflect the mood of the Egyptian people, and dream of the end of foreign rule in Egypt.[1] Forced by circumstances, the king tried to counteract this development by partially giving in to the wishes of the native population. It could be expected that such a crisis in the kingdom would influence conditions in Palestine, but our sources contain only hints of it. The Tobiad romance in Josephus reports how the Tobiad Joseph, whose relations with the royal house had cooled off, sent his youngest son, Hyrcanus, to Alexandria to the celebrations of the birth of an heir to the throne, perhaps the later Ptolemy V Epiphanes in 210 B.C.E. By means of generous presents he won the favour of the king and his friends. On his return to Jerusalem he fell into conflict with his father, and above all with his brothers, and he had to withdraw to the old lands of the Tobiads beyond the Jordan, where 'he waged war upon the Arabs' and 'imposed a tribute on the barbarians'.[2] This probably means that the supreme command over Ptolemaic cleruchy in Ammanitis had been given to him, while his position in Jerusalem had become untenable. This points to a change in the political hierarchy in Jerusalem. Simon II, 'the Just', son of the Onias II who was once humiliated by Joseph, was the new and energetic high priest. He exercised considerable influence, perhaps as a result of the split in the Tobiad family, in which he, like the majority of the aristocracy, took the side of Hyrcanus' brothers. The whole people was divided by this dispute.[3]

It is very likely that this split was more than a family quarrel within the leading family in the land, and that it also had a political and religious background. Hyrcanus, who had acquired a considerable powerbase in East Jordan, remained a supporter of the Ptolemies until he committed suicide in the time of Antiochus IV Epiphanes. The Tobiads of Jerusalem, however, allied with the high Priest Simon in his support of the Seleucid party. When Antiochus III finally conquered Palestine, this pro-Seleucid group in Jerusalem was obviously in the majority, and the High Priest Simon had become the defender of his people's interests: 'He considered how to save his people from ruin,

[1] For the problem see S. K. Eddy, *The King is Dead* (Lincoln, 1961), pp. 290ff. A new edition of the Potter's Oracle is given by L. Koenen, 'Die Prophezeiungen des "Töpfers"', *ZPapEp*, 2 (1968), 178–209.

[2] Jos. *Ant.* XII.186–222, 228–236, quotations from 229 and 222. For this see Hengel, *Hellenismus*, pp. 491–503; ET I, pp. 269–77.

[3] Jos. *Ant.* XII.228f; Tcherikover, *Hellenistic Civilization*, pp. 80f, 154.

and fortified the city to withstand a siege'.[1] Ptolemaic rule was obviously in political decline in Egypt, with increasing financial difficulties, made apparent by, among other things, the inflation in copper coinage.[2] This probably brought about a change of mood in favour of the Seleucids in the province of 'Syria and Phoenicia' also. Certain anti-Jewish policies of Philopator in Egypt, which are reported to us in the admittedly legendary 3 Maccabees, may have assisted in this change among the Jews. The king, it says, who is known to have had an interest in the cult of Dionysus, attempted to convert Jews by force to this cult.[3]

Antiochus III was able to reap the fruits of these developments in the so-called fifth Syrian war (202–200 B.C.E.). His prestige in the west was increased by his successful campaign in the eastern provinces as far as Bactria and 'India', which was seen as an *imitatio Alexandri.* To distinguish himself from the kings of Armenia, Parthia and Bactria, who had become vassals, he took the title 'The Great King'.[4] Josephus has preserved a letter written by the king to Zeuxis, the commander of Asia Minor, probably at the time of this 'anabasis', in which he gives orders for the settlement in Phrygia and Lydia of 2,000 Jewish cleruchs from Babylonia with their families.[5] This means that the Seleucids as well as the Ptolemies relied on Jewish mercenaries. An incidental note in 2 Maccabees reports that 8,000 Jewish soldiers, presumably in the time of Antiochus I, decided the course of a battle against the Galatians.[6] Through his 'anabasis' Antiochus extended considerably the area under his rule; he also carried through an administrative reform by which the power of the great satrapies was not replaced by smaller administrative units. The unity of the kingdom was also strengthened by promoting the ruler cult.[7] His son Antiochus IV Epiphanes sought to continue these policies, but in much less favourable circumstances.

At the end of 205 or beginning of 204 B.C.E. Philopator died in

[1] Sir. 50:4.

[2] T. Reekmans, 'Economic and social repercussions of the Ptolemaic copper inflation', *ChE,* 24 (1949), 324–42; Volkmann, *PW* 23 (1959), col. 1690; and above p. 61 n. 4.

[3] 3 Macc. 2:25ff; Volkmann, *PW* 23 (1959), col. 1689.

[4] H. H. Schmitt, *Untersuchungen zur Geschichte Antiochos des Grossen und seiner Zeit* (Wiesbaden, 1964), pp. 92ff.

[5] Jos. *Ant.* XII.147–53; A. Schalit, 'The letter of Antiochus III to Zeuxis regarding the establishment of Jewish military colonies in Phrygia and Lydia', *JQR*, N.S. 50 (1959–60), 289–318; E. Olshausen, 'Zeuxis', *PW* 2nd series, 10 (1972), cols. 383f. The authenticity of this letter is seldom doubted today.

[6] 2 Macc. 8:20; Hengel, *Hellenismus*, p. 29; ET I, p. 76.

[7] Schmitt, *Untersuchungen*, pp. 104ff; E. Bickerman, *Institutions des Séleucides* (Paris, 1938), pp. 236ff, 247ff; F. Taeger, *Charisma,* 1 (Stuttgart, 1957), pp. 314ff.

Egypt in mysterious circumstances. For some time his death was kept secret by the court party. Ptolemy V Epiphanes, a five-year-old boy, came to the throne. Antiochus took advantage of his opponent's weakness. First of all he took possession of the Ptolemaic possessions in southern Asia Minor, and then, after a secret agreement with Philip V of Macedon[1] (202 B.C.E.), he attacked Coele-Syria. Because the relevant passages in Polybius are now lost, we are substantially less well informed about the fifth Syrian war than about the fourth.[2] The province obviously fell prey to him even more easily than it had eighteen years previously. Only Gaza, which as the terminus for the Arabian trade was most closely bound up with Egypt, could offer longer resistance.[3] When the king withdrew to winter quarters, the Ptolemaic commander Scopas availed himself of the opportunity in the winter of 201/200 to march his troops into Palestine and to reconquer the southern part of the country. Above all it was the Jews in Jerusalem who suffered from Ptolemaic revenge, for they had become predominantly supporters of the Seleucids under the leadership of the High Priest Simon and the Tobiads. Josephus, quoting Polybius, reports that Scopas had 'during the winter subdued the Jewish nation (*ethnos*)'.[4] This is the first full account of the Jews in Polybius. Under the leadership of the High Priest Simon the Just the Jews in Palestine clearly played a greater role than during earlier campaigns. The seer of the book of Daniel describes the revolt against the Ptolemies in negative terms: 'In those times many shall rise against the king of the south; and the men of violence among your own people shall lift themselves up in order to fulfil the vision; but they shall fail.'[5] Jerome, basing himself on Porphyry, saw that this refers to a clash between the pro-Ptolemaic and pro-Seleucid parties.[6] The century-long struggle between the great powers for Coele-Syria had thus led to a schism within the Palestinian community, a schism which broke out again in the time of Antiochus IV Epiphanes. Scopas suffered a crushing defeat by Antiochus a little later at Paneas by the sources of the Jordan.[7] With

1 Will, *Histoire*, 2, pp. 99f; Schmitt, *Untersuchungen*, pp. 237ff. For the dating see A. E. Samuel, *Chronology*, pp. 108ff.

2 Niese, *Geschichte*, 2, pp. 577ff; H. Volkmann, 'Ptolemaios V. Epiphanes', *PW* 23 (1959), col. 1695. For the dating see M. Holleaux, 'La chronologie de la 5e guerre de Syrie', *Etudes d'épigraphie et d'histoire grecques* (Paris, 1942), 3, pp. 318–35.

3 Polyb. XVI.22a; 18.2; Jos. *Ant.* XII.130f; XIII.150f; Justin XXXI.1.1f.

4 Jos. *Ant.* XII.135 = Polyb. XVI.39.1.

5 Dan. 11:14; Tcherikover, *Hellenistic Civilization*, pp. 77ff.

6 *In Dan. PL*, 25 (1845), col. 562.

7 Polyb. XVI.18f following Zenon of Rhodes; on this see F. W. Walbank, *A Historical Commentary on Polybius*, 2 (Oxford, 1967), pp. 523ff.

10,000 men, the remains of his army, he fled to Sidon. After the failure of three further relief attempts, he had to capitulate in 199 B.C.E. in exchange for a safe conduct.[1] As a result of his victory at Paneas, Antiochus occupied Palestine for the second time. Polybius mentions Batanea in East Jordan, and also Samaria, Abila and Gadara, three fortresses which had played a role in 218 as well, and finally the temple city of Jerusalem. According to Josephus and Porphyry (as cited by Jerome), the Jews wholeheartedly helped the king to overcome the Ptolemaic garrison in the citadel and supplied ample provisions for the Seleucid troops and their elephants.[2] Jerome adds further that the Jewish supporters of the Ptolemies were evacuated to Egypt by the Egyptian troops.[3] Thus the 'hundred years' war' for Phoenicia and Palestine was finally concluded in favour of the Seleucids. It appeared at first that the native population, the Jews included, were on the whole very satisfied with the outcome,[4] although they had suffered heavily in the to and fro of the campaigns, and even Jerusalem was partly destroyed.

PALESTINE UNDER SELEUCID RULE DOWN TO THE DEATH OF ANTIOCHUS III (200–187 B.C.E.)

Through skilful policies Antiochus tried to win or to retain the sympathy of his new subjects in Coele-Syria. We have three testimonies to this: two are preserved by Josephus, and the third was discovered some years ago in Hephzibah to the west of Scythopolis. They consist of: (1) a letter from the king to Ptolemy, the commander of Coele-Syria, favourable to the Jews and their temple;[5] (2) extracts from a royal edict,[6] aimed at safeguarding the ritual purity of Jerusalem and its Temple; (3) a correspondence of six letters from the period 201–195 B.C.E. recorded in the form of an inscription and concerning the

[1] Jerome, *in Dan., PL,* 25 (1845), 563. Dan. 11:15 refers to the siege of Sidon and not the siege of Gaza, so Porphyry and Jerome.

[2] Jos. *Ant.* XII.136, 133, 138. Jerome, *In Dan., PL,* 25 (1845): 'quod praesidium Scopae in arce Hierosolymorum, annitentibus Judaeis, multo tempore oppugnarit'.

[3] *In Dan., PL,* 25 (1845): 'et, optimates Ptolemaei partium secum abducens, in Aegyptum reversus est'.

[4] Jos. *Ant.* XII.124f, 139.

[5] *Ant.* XII.138–44; E. J. Bickerman, 'La charte séleucide de Jérusalem', *REJ*, 100 (1935), 4–35, or in German in *Zur Josephus-Forschung*, ed. A. Schalit, Wege der Forschung, 84 (Darmstadt, 1973), pp. 205–40; Abel, *Histoire,* 1, pp. 88–93; R. Marcus in *Josephus*, vol. 7 (Loeb edition, 1943), pp. 743ff, 751ff.

[6] *Ant.* XII.145–6; E. Bickerman, 'Une proclamation séleucide relative au temple de Jérusalem', *Syria*, 25 (1946/48), 67–85; Marcus, *Josephus*, vol. 7, pp. 761ff.

estates of the commander Ptolemy son of Thraseas, in the plain of Megiddo.[1]

The king writes to this commander about the Jews in the form of an edict, in which Antiochus gives thanks for the energetic support of the Jews during the campaigns in their district. As a matter of fact, these 'acts of favour' were not a spontaneous act of the king's, but rather the result of negotiations in which a priest by the name of John had played a decisive role. Later, in the time of Judas Maccabeus, his son Eupolemus was to be the leader of a Jewish delegation to Rome.[2] By its terms the edict does no more than grant what had already been conceded by the king to other cities damaged by war, as in Asia Minor, and what was already common practice, ever since the time of the Persians. The recipient in this case was not the city of Jerusalem, but the Jewish *ethnos*. Jerusalem is spoken of only as 'the city of the Jews'. This means that it did not have city status like a Greek *polis*,[3] but was only the main town of a barbarian *ethnos*. The king promised to support the rebuilding of the Temple and to help the daily offering by gifts in kind. Leaders of the *ethnos* were exempted from personal taxation (poll, crown and salt tax); among them were the members of the *gerousia* which, as the highest political authority, must have developed in Ptolemaic times;[4] then there were the priests, the Temple clerks who were the precursors of the later scribes, and the Temple singers, but not all the Levites. Those returning to the extensively damaged city were to be exempted from taxation for three years,[5] and there was a reduction of a third in the tribute of the Jewish *ethnos* as compensation for war damage. The amount as assessed by the Ptolemaic overlords was probably 300 talents a year, but the amount was afterwards substantially increased again by Antiochus III's successors.'[6] All those illegally enslaved by the soldiers too were to be freed. As was done by the Persians and Alexander, all belonging to the *ethnos*, Jews of the

1 Y. H. Landau, 'A Greek inscription found near Hefzibah', *IEJ*, 16 (1966), 54–70; J. and L. Robert, 'Bulletin Épigraphique', *REG*, 83 (1970), 469ff, no. 627.

2 2 Macc. 4:11; cf. 1 Macc. 8:17. This Eupolemus is possibly identical with the Jewish historian quoted by Alexander Polyhistor: Hengel, *Hellenismus*, pp. 169ff.; ET I, pp. 92ff.

3 V. Tcherikover, 'Was Jerusalem a "Polis"?', *IEJ*, 14 (1964), 61–78; F. W. Walbank, *Polybius*, 2, pp. 546f, on Polyb. XVI.39.4.

4 Hengel, *Hellenismus*, pp. 48ff.; ET I, pp. 25ff.

5 Jos. *Ant*. XII.143 *atelesin einai*: for a three-year tax exemption with the same formula connected with an amalgamation of cities (*synoikismos*), see the letter of Antigonus to Teus in C. B. Welles, *Royal Correspondence in the Hellenistic Period* (New Haven/London, 1934), 18 no. 3, ll. 70/1.

6 Hengel, *Hellenismus*, pp. 53f, ET I, pp. 28f.

Diaspora included, had their right conceded, 'to live according to the laws of their fathers'. In this way the traditional law of Moses was legitimated as 'royal law' for the Jews.[1] Some twenty-five years later, however, Jewish Hellenists from Jerusalem obtained permission from the new king, Antiochus IV Epiphanes, to repeal this 'act of royal favour' and to give Jerusalem a new constitution, namely that of a Greek *polis* with the name of Antiochia.[2] A new parallel to this edict of Antiochus III is to be found in his acts of 'philanthropy' shown towards the city of Teus in Ionia. On account of war damage and previous exploitation by the Attalids, he granted the citizens full tax exemption and the right of asylum.[3]

In the second edict foreigners were forbidden to enter the sanctuary, a concession that was later acknowledged by the Romans too.[4] It was forbidden to breed unclean animals as well as to import meat and hides, and only animals for sacrifice could be kept in the city. Any infringement of these rules was to be punished with heavy fines. Probably the High Priest Simon and the strictly orthodox section of the priesthood were behind these regulations, but they must have reduced considerably Jerusalem's importance as a trading centre. Non-Jewish merchants and their caravans would avoid as far as possible a city with such frustrating regulations. Time and again, right up to the war with Rome in 66–70 C.E.,[5] we come across this tendency to curb by ritual prohibitions that commercial contact with the pagan world which was regarded as dangerous. But in the background of this edict to 'sanctify' the Temple and the city in the interest of strict orthodoxy lay conflicts which were to erupt a little later.[6]

The inscription of Hephzibah near Scythopolis concerns the protection of the village populations in the widespread possessions of Ptolemy son of Thraseas against rioting by Seleucid garrison troops. In 219 B.C.E., at the beginning of the fourth Syrian war, Ptolemy was a troop commander in the service of the Ptolemies, but later he went over to the Seleucid side and under Antiochus III became the governor of the new province of Coele-Syria and chief priest of the ruler cult.[7] The king's letter about 'acts of favour' to the Jews was addressed to

1 E. Bickerman, *Der Gott der Makkabäer* (Berlin, 1937), pp. 50ff.

2 2 Macc. 4:9, 19 and below, p. 77.

3 P. Herrmann, 'Antiochos der Grosse und Teos', *Anadolu,* 9 (1965), 29–160.

4 M. Hengel, *Die Zeloten*, AGJU 1 (Leiden, 1961), pp. 219f.

5 Hengel, *Die Zeloten*, pp. 204ff.

6 Hengel, *Hellenismus*, pp. 100f, 494f; ET I, pp. 52f, 271f.

7 Polyb. v.65.3; *OGIS,* 1, p. 376, no. 230; H. Bengtson, *Die Strategie,* 2, pp. 161ff supposes that he is referred to also in 2 Macc. 3:5.

him. It is not clear whether his estates in the plain of Megiddo had belonged to him during his period in the service of the Ptolemies, or whether they were given to him from the 'king's land' as a reward for his desertion. The inscription mentions both private property and land held as a heritable fief (*eis to patrikon*).[1] In the earliest letter, written during the war in 201, Ptolemy was given permission for his villages to engage in mutual exchange and trading, presumably without the burden of customs duty. But in a further later exchange of letters, the soldiers were forbidden to take up quarters in these villages, or to requisition or to expel the inhabitants from their homes. A tenfold fine was threatened for any damage done.

Antiochus' endeavour to tread carefully during this change of power is seen further in the fact that he left the pro-Ptolemaic Tobiad, Hyrcanus, in control in Ammanitis. It was only in the time of Antiochus IV Epiphanes that his power was broken.[2] In contrast to Ptolemaic Egypt, the administration of the Seleucid empire was 'federal' and not centralized, and even after the administrative reforms of Antiochus III each city, nation and dynasty had considerable independence.[3] The people of Palestine must at first have felt an improvement in their condition under the Seleucid rule, especially in its measures for alleviating the tax burden. A number of cities founded or re-named in the new province gives us an indication of the new rulers' activity in this respect also. They are mostly attributable to Seleucus IV and Antiochus IV Epiphanes, the sons of Antiochus III. Tcherikover suggests that Antiochus III founded only one Antiochia and one Seleucia on Lake Huleh, to celebrate his decisive victory over Scopas in 200 B.C.E.[4]

In the meantime, a new power had appeared on the scene. In the same year as Antiochus III finally conquered Palestine, Rome decided to wage war against Philip V of Macedon. The Roman delegation, which brought the Macedonian king an ultimatum to abandon all his acquisitions in Asia Minor and in the Aegean, visited the Seleucid king next, possibly in Palestine, and secured his neutrality in the coming conflict. They refrained from undertaking the mediation desired by Egypt. The conquest of Coele-Syria scarcely interested Rome, but it is likely that the delegation extracted a promise from Antiochus that he

[1] Landau, *IEJ*, 16 (1966), 66 n. 15.

[2] Jos. *Ant.* XII.234ff with a clearly incorrect date; see Hengel, *Hellenismus*, pp. 496, 500f; ET I, pp. 272f, 275f.

[3] Bickerman, *Institutions*, pp. 170ff for local rulers.

[4] *Städtegründungen*, pp. 70f, 175; *Hellenistic Civilization*, pp. 101f following A. Schlatter, *Zur Topographie und Geschichte Palästinas* (Stuttgart, 1893), pp. 314ff. One of the sites can be identified with the recently excavated Hellenistic settlement of Tel Anafa, see above p. 57.

would not attack Egypt.[1] Rome thus had a free hand against Macedonia, and in 197 B.C.E. Titus Flaminius defeated her at Cynoscephalae in Thessaly. The downfall of the Hellenistic monarchies had now begun. Antiochus must have been conscious of the threat in the west, even if he did underestimate his new opponent. He sent away a Roman delegation which in 196 B.C.E. demanded from him freedom for the Greek cities in Asia Minor, and at the same time offered to negotiate in the Ptolemaic–Seleucid conflict. Instead Antiochus took upon himself the initiative in coming to terms with the old enemy. In 197 B.C.E. the barely fourteen-year-old Ptolemy V Epiphanes had been declared of age and crowned king. The Seleucid king opened peace negotiations with him, which were crowned with success in 194/3 when the young king married Cleopatra, Antiochus' daughter. As dowry it is possible that the king handed over to Ptolemy part of the revenues from Coele-Syria, and thus made it easier for him to renounce his claims on the province. Later Ptolemy VI Philometor tried to base a claim against Antiochus IV Epiphanes on this gift. But political sovereignty and military power remained unreservedly in the hands of the Seleucid King.[2] Having thus cemented his peace treaty with a marraige alliance, so that he had nothing to fear from the rear, Antiochus believed that he could devote himself to his enterprises in western Asia Minor and in Greece; thus war with Rome became inevitable. It came to an end in 190 at Magnesia in Lydia with a catastrophic defeat for the king and the Seleucid monarchy. Antiochus' multinational army, including Medes, Elamites, Syrians and Arabian camel-riders,[3] was destroyed by an army only half as numerous, consisting of the Romans and their allies under the command of the Scipios. The disaster was completed by the peace terms imposed on the king at Apamea in 188 B.C.E.; Seleucid territory in Asia Minor as far as the Taurus was stripped from him and added to the Pergamene Kingdom. He had to cede his war-elephants and fleet except for ten ships. Thus any effective political action in the west became impossible. Furthermore, a war indemnity of 12,000 talents was to be paid to the victors within twelve years.[4] This was a large sum and

[1] Polyb. XVI.27.5; Justin, *Epit.* XXXI.1, 2; M. Holleaux, *CAH*, 8 (1930), pp. 165f.

[2] Livy XXXV.13; Polybius XVIII.51.10; XXVIII.20.9; Appian, *Syr.* 5; Josephus, *Ant.* XII.154f; E. Cuq, 'La condition juridique de la Coelé-Syrie au temps de Ptolémée V Epiphane', *Syria*, 8 (1927), 143–62; against this, H. Bengtson, *Die Strategie in der hellenistischen Zeit*, 2, p. 161 n. 2: 'an invention of Josephus'; Will, *Histoire*, 2, pp. 161ff.

[3] Livy XXXVII.40; App. *Syr.* 32 (following Polybius).

[4] Will, *Histoire*, 2, pp. 185–93; A. H. McDonald, 'The Treaty of Apamea (188 B.C.)', *JRS*, 57 (1967), 1–8.

laid a heavy burden on the kingdom's finances, especially as the king made painstaking endeavours to keep the terms of the treaty. The loss of the silver mines in Asia Minor made future monetary policy more difficult. Thus the king's initial tax relief for Palestine cannot have lasted long.[1] It is against this background that we must understand the reports constantly appearing from now on that the Seleucids were plundering rich sanctuaries in the area under their control. Only a year after the peace treaty, Antiochus III, in attempting to rob the treasures of a temple in Elymais, was killed by the local people 'comme un vulgaire bandit' (187 B.C.E.).[2] Under his son, Seleucus IV, the vizier Heliodorus tried to sieze the Temple treasures of Jerusalem, and Polybius says of Antiochus IV Epiphanes that 'he plundered numerous sanctuaries'. What appeared to the Hellenistic rulers as an obvious right must have appeared to their subjects a sacrilege and a crime.[3] A further result was that Ptolemy V Epiphanes entertained hopes that he could regain Palestine and Phoenicia, and so the conflict that appeared to have been settled smouldered again. Ptolemaic supporters, those in Judea included, received considerable stimulus.[4] The defeat at Magnesia thus provided the basis for new conflicts in Palestine. The prestige of the Hellenistic monarchies had always been linked to the fortune of their kings in war. Defeat by republican Rome was a heavy blow, and movements for national independence in the eastern provinces, as well as in Phoenicia and in Coele-Syria, were thus encouraged. It is one of the contradictions of history that it was now, when the decline of the Hellenistic Kingdoms was evident, that radical reformers in Jerusalem set about changing the holy city into a Seleucid *polis* with a Greek constitution.

The apocalyptic historian of the book of Daniel, who was an alert observer, comments as follows[5] on Antiochus' catastrophic end: 'Afterward he [the king of the north] shall turn his face to the coastlands, and shall take many of them; but a commander [*qaṣîn* here for consul] shall put an end to his insolence; cursing him[6] he shall turn his insolence back upon him. Then he shall turn his face back toward

[1] Hengel, *Hellenismus*, pp. 17, 53f; ET I, pp. 10, 28; O. Mørkholm, *Antiochus IV of Syria*, Classica et Mediaevalia, Diss. 8 (Copenhagen, 1966), pp. 22–37: 'The Seleucid Kingdom after Apamea'.

[2] Will, *Histoire*, 2, pp. 200ff.

[3] 2 Macc. 3; Polyb. XXX.26.9; cf. XXXI.4.9; Hengel, *Hellenismus*, p. 511; ET I, p. 280.

[4] The High Priest Onias III was again in close alliance with the pro-Ptolemaic Hyrcanus, 2 Macc. 3:11; Hengel, *Hellenismus*, p. 495; ET I, p. 272.

[5] Dan. 11:18f.

[6] The text according to A. Bentzen, *Daniel*, HAT, 1, 19 (Tübingen, 2nd edn. 1952), p. 80 and J. A. Montgomery, *A Critical and Exegetical Commentary on the Book of Daniel*, ICC (Edinburgh, 1927), p. 444; *balḥi* = LXX *en horkōi*.

the fortresses of his own land; but he shall stumble and fall, and shall not be found.'

The new situation in Judea at the beginning of Seleucid rule is illustrated in a number of remarks by Ben Sira, who was possibly one of the Temple scribes mentioned in the edict of Antiochus III. In his book, the high esteem felt by the ancient Wisdom teachers for wealth in moderation and unflagging industry is combined with a harsh, prophetic-sounding polemic against the extravagance of wealth and the exploitation of the workers, and also a warning against foreign merchants.[1] In the *Praise of the Fathers* the heroes of the people's own great national and religious past right down to Simon the Just are extolled, but at the same time his sons are exhorted to unity.[2] The warning against despisers of the law, renegades and sceptics cannot be missed.[3] Behind this lies the menacing influence of Hellenistic civilization on the aristocracy. In contrast, Ben Sira identifies the divine wisdom which penetrates the whole world with the Law given to Moses.[4] His political attitude is illustrated in the prayer for an eschatological deliverance from Seleucid rule. It is also characteristic of the Jewish cultic community in general during the early Hellenistic period: 'Save us, O God of all, and cast thy fear upon all the nations. Shake Thy hand against the strange people, and let them see Thy power.' We find a coded reference to the heathen ruler and his cult: 'Make an end of the head of the princes of Moab that says: There is none beside me.'[5] The closing formula, imitating Deutero-Isaiah, shows the universal dimension which is characteristic of Jewish apocalyptic in Hellenistic times: 'that all the ends of the earth may know that Thou art the eternal God.'[6]

(Editors' note: this chapter has also been published in an expanded form as M. Hengel, *Juden, Griechen und Barbaren*, SBS 76 (Stuttgart, 1976), ET *Jews, Greeks and Barbarians* (London, 1980), chs. 1–5.)

[1] Sir. 11:34; 13.2–20; 34:20–22; Hengel, *Hellenismus*, pp. 249ff; ET I, pp. 136ff.

[2] Sir. 50:23f; Hengel, *Hellenismus*, pp. 244f; ET I, p. 133.

[3] Sir. 15:11–17; 16:17–23; 41:8f. Hengel, *Hellenismus*, pp. 256ff, 270ff; ET I, pp. 141ff, 150ff.

[4] Sir. 24:23f; Hengel, *Hellenismus*, 289ff; ET I, pp. 160ff; J. Marböck, *Weisheit im Wandel,* BBB, 37, (1971).

[5] Sir. 36:1f, 10.

[6] Sir. 36:17. The conjecture of T. Middendorp, *Die Stellung Jesu ben Siras zwischen Judentum und Hellenismus* (Leiden, 1973), pp. 125ff, that Sir. 36:1–17 was inserted in the Maccabean period, is not justified. But his survey of the political and social milieu (pp. 137ff) is valuable.

CHAPTER 3

HEBREW, ARAMAIC AND GREEK IN THE HELLENISTIC AGE

HEBREW

Apart from final adjustments, the main body of the Hebrew Bible was already complete before Hellenistic times, and it is easy to forget that the latest portions of it were in fact written within that period. Of such portions, however, it is often hard to decide definitely whether their origin was in the Persian or the early Greek period, especially since the setting and subject matter is often Persian, as in Esther and Daniel. Some parts of the prophets, like Zechariah 9 to 14, and more doubtfully other 'proto-apocalyptic' passages like Isaiah 24 to 27, have been assigned to a Hellenistic date, but even if this is right it may mean the very beginning of that era, a time therefore before its character had yet fully flowered. Some of the biblical psalms may also be Hellenistic; but the dating of psalms is notoriously difficult, and the practice of dating canonical psalms in late (for example, in Maccabean) times is now less widely supported than it once was. Nevertheless it is significant that characteristic 'late' linguistic features are displayed by many of the psalms found at the end of the Psalter: for example, the relative *še* appears only from Ps. 122 on, and then occurs about nineteen times. Since the tradition of psalmody went on and psalms continued to be written after the canonical Psalter was complete, it would not be surprising if some canonical psalms were of Hellenistic date. Finally, one writing which by the main consensus of scholars was written well down within the Hellenistic age is the latest portion of Daniel (8 to 12), coming from the second quarter of the second century B.C.E.

Thus the Bible itself provides evidence of literary activity in Biblical Hebrew right down into the Hellenistic age. But these late sources are themselves also evidence of change, for they belong to a sector of the language which may well be termed 'Late Biblical Hebrew'. This differs in many ways from the Hebrew of the central period, for example, from that of Deuteronomy. Works in Late Biblical Hebrew like Chronicles, Ecclesiastes and Esther show how the character of the language had altered by this time (Persian or Greek periods). For instance, the pronoun *'anoki* 'I', preferred in the earlier documents, in

Chronicles (as in P) is largely replaced by *'ᵃni*. The relative particle *'ᵃšer* similarly comes to be replaced by *še* (Song of Songs, Ecclesiastes, sporadically in Chronicles). The later *šel*, which came to function rather like our 'of', is still entirely marginal within the Bible (three occurrences, and only with pronoun suffixes or a personal name); *bᵉ-šel* 'on account of' also occurs (Jonah, Ecclesiastes). The particle *'et*, a characteristic feature of Biblical Hebrew, acting as marker of the direct object, also shows signs of change: we find a number of cases of *'et* with the subject (three in Nehemiah at 9:19, 32, 34, and compare Dan. 9:13: 'all this evil came upon us', *'et* accompanying the subject). For the marking of an object Late Biblical Hebrew also uses the particle *lᵉ*, here running parallel with Aramaic usage or being influenced by it; this same particle also appears occasionally with the subject of a nominal sentence, in lists, and in other modes novel to Biblical Hebrew. But the late books do not only innovate: sometimes they go back to older patterns. The P source of the Pentateuch had a marked fondness for *'et* + pronoun suffix to express a pronoun object; Chronicles by contrast returns to the older pattern by using a suffix attached to the verb.

Thus patterns long established in Hebrew were changing. The 'waw-consecutive' system, one of the most striking characteristics of Biblical Hebrew, was also breaking down. Even in quite early sources, before the Exile, we meet with occasional places where it is disregarded, and in some books, like Ecclesiastes, it has fallen into almost complete disuse, though other sources at the same time continue to employ it. Thus many of the changes in Late Biblical Hebrew have the character of a statistical shift rather than a drastic alteration of direction; but the effect on particular phenomena and their functions may be quite a drastic change. Lexical changes also take place; some typical words from Late Biblical Hebrew are *qibbel* 'receive' (rare in earlier sources), *zᵉman* 'time', *ḥepeṣ* in the sense 'matter, affair, *kašer* 'be proper, be suitable, succeed' (Esther and Ecclesiastes only), *nᵉkasim* 'possessions' (Ecclesiastes and Chronicles; once in Joshua) and *'inyan* 'task, affair' (Ecclesiastes only). Some of these new terms may be adoptions from Aramaic but not all the lexical changes can be explained in this way.

Loanwords from Akkadian and Persian continued to gain entrance into Late Biblical Hebrew: *'iggeret* 'letter' (only Nehemiah, Esther, Chronicles), of uncertain origin, was widely used in later Akkadian and in the Persian empire; *dat* 'decree, law' (once in Ezra, twenty times in Esther) is certainly Persian. There is, by contrast, little or no influx of Greek words into the Hebrew of the canonical books, unless in international terms like *darkᵉmon* 'drachma'. The word *'appiryon* is often derived from the Greek φορεῖον, but this is only one of the possibilities canvassed by scholars.[1]

Thus there is no simple distinction between 'Biblical' and 'Post-biblical' Hebrew; on the contrary, already within the biblical books the character of Hebrew had begun to display features that were to be characteristic of a later time. The 'Biblical' and 'Post-biblical' stages overlap, in language as in literature and religion. But Late Biblical Hebrew has also some features which, though different from what had been normal in Biblical Hebrew, were not in fact taken up and developed in later times.

Thus, to sum up our argument thus far, the biblical text itself demonstrates a substantial continuum, including both change and identity, running well down into the Hellenistic age. This evidence is strengthened when we consider Ben Sira (Sirach, Ecclesiasticus), a work long known only through the Greek and other versions but now extant in Hebrew text over a considerable part of its length. The study of the Hebrew fragments, once very controversial, has now been placed on a new footing by the find of a scroll at Masada, which is said to confirm in general the text of manuscript B from the Geniza. This book, composed about 190 B.C.E., uses a register of Hebrew which has recognizable continuity with the late canonical books of the Bible. Its general characteristics belong with Biblical Hebrew, taken in the larger sense as opposed to Middle or Mishnaic Hebrew; but, as against earlier biblical usage, it shows the shifts of style and language that we would expect from a work of this time. The waw-consecutive is still in use, but with exceptions (for example 48:7, *wᵉ-hišmia*ʿ 'and he caused to hear'). The relative particle *'ᵃšer* is still fully established, but *šellᵉka* 'yours' is also twice found.

On the lexical side, the words *ṣorek, ṣarik* (Biblical Hebrew only exceptionally, once in Chronicles) suddenly burst forth in frequent use; with the sense of 'requirement, necessity' these are essential features of later diction, for which Biblical Hebrew has no real equivalent. The root of *seder* 'order', a word later to be common, and typically in the War Scroll, has its first real appearance here (earlier in Job 10:22, but there plural); and *mamon* 'possessions, money' also first appears here. As elsewhere in Late Biblical Hebrew, words of Persian origin are still appearing: *zan* 'sort, kind', *pitgam* 'word'. Aramaic too has an influence on vocabulary: *raz* 'secret' is in the near-contemporary Aramaic of Daniel, though this word too is of Persian origin; *zabad* 'give' is

[1] See recently the entry s.v. in W. Baumgartner, *Hebäisches und aramäisches Lexikon zum AT* (3rd edn., Leiden, 1967), p. 78a.

probably a result of the same influence (Biblical Hebrew only in names and in a name explanation, and not used in Middle Hebrew either). Greek influence, on the other hand, in the form of words actually adopted from Greek, remains minimal, and we may contrast the prominence of such borrowings in Middle Hebrew. But Greek influence may lie behind some of the semantic paths in Ben Sira's language;[1] for instance, the common ἀνάγκη, ἀναγκαῖος might have stimulated the use of *ṣorek, ṣarik*. Perhaps the register and style of Ben Sira was already an archaizing one, just as his genre followed in part that of the biblical Wisdom literature. Some signs suggest that his spoken Hebrew was an early form of what we later know as Middle Hebrew; but this had only limited influence on his writing, which basically belongs to Late Biblical Hebrew.[2]

We shall now, therefore, consider the position of Middle Hebrew, the register of Hebrew best known from, and best represented by, the Mishnah. This material generally derives from the first two centuries C.E. Although, as we have seen, Late Biblical Hebrew was in a number of points moving rather in a direction towards what was later realized in Middle Hebrew, the contrast between Biblical Hebrew as a whole and Middle Hebrew as a whole remains very striking. This is so much so that an influential scholarly trend – initiated particularly by A. Geiger[3] – has long supposed Middle Hebrew to be an 'artificial' Hebrew, lacking a basis in actual speech and specially concocted for rabbinical discussion. This artificial language – it was often compared to medieval Latin – was put together from Biblical Hebrew and Aramaic; according to the theory, Hebrew of any kind had ceased to be spoken as far back as perhaps the fourth century, and the only Semitic speech used in actual life was Aramaic. The scholarly jargon was thus pieced together from the surviving evidence of the biblical text, combined with the known facts of Aramaic. The persistence of this view was encouraged by the separation between biblical and post-

1 I am doubtful however of Hengel's suggestion (*Judaism and Hellenism*, 1 (London, 1974), p. 136) that *taḥ*ʳ*lip*, which occurs thrice in Ben Sira, means 'successor' and is, he seems to imply, related to the Greek διάδοχος, διαδοχή; the meaning seems to be rather 'exchange, recompense, reward'. Thus at 44:17 Noah was a compensation (Greek ἀντάλλαγμα) for the general evil of the world, rather than a successor; at 46:12 I think the sense is 'their name is a reward, a recompense, passed on' (ἀντικαταλλασσόμενον), though this comes fairly close to a succession. At 48:8, though the Greek in fact has διαδόχους, the parallel in the Hebrew is *tašlumot* = ἀνταπόδομα, which again suggests a recompense as the Hebrew sense of *taḥ*ʳ*lip*.

2 Cf. C. Rabin in 'The historical background of Qumran Hebrew', *Scripta Hierosolymitana* 4 (Jerusalen, 1958), p. 152.

3 Abraham Geiger, *Lehr- und Lesebuch zur Sprache der Mischnah* (Breslau, 1845).

biblical studies; and it has been particularly influential through its effect upon New Testament studies.

It is therefore important to realize that this older view of Middle Hebrew is no longer held by experts in the field. It was the work of M. H. Segal in particular that altered the prevailing view and gave good evidence from grammar and lexicon, from style of expression and literary character, that Middle Hebrew rests upon a basis of colloquial spoken Hebrew.[1] That this is so is no longer questioned by major workers in the field. It is true that the recognition of a colloquial basis for Middle Hebrew, and the abandonment of the idea that it is an artificial jargon, do not in themselves prove that Hebrew was still generally spoken in the Tannaitic period. Nevertheless, when we consider the language situation of (say) the first century C.E., it can no longer be assumed that the emphasis must lie on Aramaic to the exclusion of Hebrew. On the question, in what language the teaching of Jesus was given, an increasing number of scholars in recent years has considered Hebrew as a responsible hypothesis, though the evidence for Aramaic continues to be rather stronger.[2] In general, the continuing vitality of Hebrew as a medium of communication down to the first century C.E. and the early second has recently been demonstrated by the use of it in the Qumran documents, and that not only in strictly religious texts but in casual documents such as letters. Thus the Qumran evidence has done for Hebrew something that was scarcely accomplished by the scholarship of those who worked on Middle Hebrew itself: it convinced many that Hebrew was still alive and in use as a spoken medium.

It is the more important to observe that the fundamental argument for the colloquial foundation of Mishnaic Hebrew rests not upon Qumran evidence but upon the analysis of Middle Hebrew itself: the range of its vocabulary, the character of its expression, its style and the fact of its very considerable differences from Biblical Hebrew. Thus, on the lexical side, the stock of words for such unlearned matters as shopping or cooking was much greater in Middle Hebrew than in Biblical Hebrew. Negatively, Segal was able to show that the facts of Middle Hebrew contradicted the theory that it was an artificial construct out of Biblical Hebrew and Aramaic. Particularly important

1 M. H. Segal, *A Grammar of Mishnaic Hebrew* (Oxford, 1927).

2 Among some recent surveys, with bibliography of recent literature, see: J. A. Emerton, 'Did Jesus speak Hebrew?', *JTS*, N.S. 12 (1961), 189–202; 24 (1973), 1–23; J. Barr, 'Which language did Jesus speak? – Some remarks of a Semitist', *BJRL*, 53 (1970–71), 9–29; J. A. Fitzmyer, 'The languages of Palestine in the first century A.D.', *CBQ*, 32 (1970), 501–31.

are the following arguments: (*a*) there are elements in Middle Hebrew which are genuinely Semitic but which are not found in either Biblical Hebrew or Aramaic; (*b*) there are elements that are common to Biblical Hebrew and Aramaic but are not taken up into Middle Hebrew; (*c*) perhaps most important – and this argument was not fully used by Segal – there are easily seen continuities between Late Biblical Hebrew in particular and Middle Hebrew; in other words, Middle Hebrew is not a fabric made up from any and every stage of Biblical Hebrew but fits clearly, within the terms of historical linguistics, with the Hebrew of the later books in particular.[1] These arguments are in themselves decisive, and are only reinforced by the use of Hebrew in the Qumran material, which includes both compositions of biblical type and materials, like the letters and the Copper Scroll, which use the register of Middle Hebrew.

How then are we to envisage the origins of Middle Hebrew? It is a reasonable hypothesis that it goes back to a colloquial register of Hebrew which overlapped with the Late Biblical Hebrew of the latest biblical books and which occasionally threw up within their text outcrops of Middle-Hebrew-like features. Hebrew, as found within the biblical text, came even in its Late Biblical Hebrew form to be used less and less as a medium of ordinary speech: solemn documents like religious texts might be written in it, and even this was to some extent an archaism, an exercise that was knowingly carried out in a register different from that of common speech, while common speech used a colloquial register, from which our Middle Hebrew later descended. At some stage this colloquial register of Hebrew began to have some sort of official status. As found in the Mishnah, the materials are striking for the terseness and abbreviation of their expression, and this might well fit with a medium having a basis in popular speech but then recognized, cultivated and developed in an official and legal setting. One hypothesis is that this happened under the Hasmoneans, and that the origins of Middle Hebrew lie in 'the legal and chancery style of the Hasmonean palace'.[2] But against this one has to set the probable great influence of Greek on Hasmonean administration. To the present writer it seems the safest course to recognize that Middle Hebrew reached the form in which we know it in the hands of the rabbis. They took the colloquial Hebrew of their time and accepted it as the medium for their discussions, which fell within a dominantly legal mould. This legal

[1] By contrast, medieval imitation of Biblical Hebrew drew equally on all historical stages as a model; cf. Rabin, *Scripta Hierosolymitana,* 4 (1958), p. 149.

[2] Cf. M. Greenberg, 'The stabilization of the text of the Hebrew Bible', *JAOS*, 76 (1965), 160; Rabin, *Scripta Hierosolymitana,* 4 (1958), pp. 156–8.

setting and use robbed Middle Hebrew of much of the freshness of the colloquial out of which it developed; but the difference is a stylistic one, and does not obscure the colloquial base upon which Middle Hebrew rested.

In any case, whatever the mode of its origin, Middle Hebrew displays marked differences from Biblical Hebrew and even from Late Biblical Hebrew. Some striking differences in syntax and in the use of particles may serve to illustrate this. In Middle Hebrew *še* has completely replaced *'ašer*; the form *šel* has come to function rather like English 'of' and the 'construct state' mechanism dominant in Biblical Hebrew, though still much in evidence, has come to be noticeably restricted in use; another characteristic construction is that with *šel* + anticipatory pronoun suffix: *yado šel 'ani* 'the hand of the poor man'. Again, there are substantial differences in the use of the article; thus *kohen gadol* 'the High Priest' without article, *keneset ha-gedola* 'the Great Synagogue', with article on the adjective but not on the noun (in Biblical Hebrew only in exceptional cases, as with numerals after *yom* 'day'). The waw-consecutive system in the verb, so characteristic of Biblical Hebrew, has completely fallen out of use. The imperfect, which in Biblical Hebrew has a subtle and varied group of functions, including actions lying in the past or present, comes to be basically a modal form denoting intentions, wishes, and prayers. The participle tense, known in Biblical Hebrew but more restricted in functions, has grown enormously in frequency, becoming more or less a present tense but also – and this often in the legal and prescriptive diction of the Mishnah – stating that which is customary and therefore right: 'they do' this or that; that is, this is what ought to be done. This usage is often impersonal: *keṣad maprišin* 'how do they separate...?', that is, 'how is such and such a thing separated?' Again, the combination of the participle with the verb *haya* 'be', though not without precedent in Biblical Hebrew, is greatly extended in Middle Hebrew; an analogous development took place in Aramaic. It is used to mark repeated, usual, or concurrent action: *hu' haya 'omer* 'he used to say'. For explicit expression of the future one has the new formation *'atid* + *le*.

On the lexical side also Middle Hebrew shows many distinctive developments as against Biblical Hebrew. Familiar examples include: *masar* 'give over, deliver' (scarcely attested in Biblical Hebrew) and its reciprocal (for both are used of the process of religious tradition) *qibbel* 'receive' (a few times in Late Biblical Hebrew, as mentioned above, but now very common; meanwhile *laqaḥ*, common in Biblical Hebrew, in part moves into a different semantic field, notably into that of buying).

For 'enter', *niknas* becomes extremely common (compare Biblical Hebrew *kanas* 'collect', and this mainly Late Biblical Hebrew), taking over part of the older function of Biblical Hebrew *bo'*. *Nahag*, in Biblical Hebrew 'to drive, lead (a chariot, a flock)' becomes specialized as 'to behave'. In Biblical Hebrew *'olam* means 'the remotest time, eternity', but in Middle Hebrew it moves also into the more spatial field of 'the world'. Some Middle Hebrew words are new formations, for instance *taram* 'remove ash from the altar, formed on the noun *t^eruma*, itself from the Biblical Hebrew verb *herim* 'lift up'; and similarly *hitḥil* 'begin', formed upon *t^eḥilla*, from the Biblical Hebrew verb *heḥel*. Characteristic particles include *'^abal* 'but', *šemma'* 'perhaps'.

Middle Hebrew includes many loanwords from those sources, like Akkadian and Persian, which had already been drawn upon in Biblical Hebrew; many words from these sources, though first attested in the Mishnah, were very likely made at home in Hebrew earlier. Aramaic also provided many loanwords, although, as we shall see, the influence of Aramaic was more pervasive and more fundamental than this. That a Middle Hebrew word comes from Aramaic, and is not derived from original Semitic ancestry directly, can be shown wherever a word contains one of those consonants which characteristically differ between Aramaic and Hebrew, such as *'era'* or *'ira'* 'occur, happen' (the *'ayin*, from the Proto-Semitic *ḍ*, would have been *ṣ* if the word had been an indigenous Hebrew word). One particle widely used is *'ella'* 'but' (especially after a negative) from Aramaic *'en + la'*.

But the prime source of loanwords in Middle Hebrew is Greek, and it particularly affects the legal and administrative terminology, as in such central terms as *sanhedrin* (συνέδριον), *prozbol* (προσβολή, a legal mechanism,[1] *hedyoṭ* 'common person, private citizen, ignorant person' (ἰδιώτης). More general words taken from Greek are *zug* 'pair' (ζυγόν), *q^etidra* a kind of chair (καθέδρα), *pinqes* 'list, account-book' (πίναξ). Even where the derivation is quite clear we often note that the Greek word, as indigenized in Hebrew, undergoes considerable changes of form as against the Greek form familiar to us, the result no doubt of the phonetic non-homogeneity of the two languages.

Apart from actual loanwords, Aramaic affected Middle Hebrew through the process of calque and through shifts in meaning. Biblical Hebrew *'eṣ* has the range of meaning (*a*) 'tree', (*b*) 'wood' (the material); the borrowing from Aramaic of *'ilan* for the former meant a restriction of the meaning of *'eṣ*, now effectively limited to the latter.

[1] So correctly Hengel, *Judaism and Hellenism*, 1, p. 61; 2, p. 44, n. 25, as against other and erroneous derivations.

Indeed, more must now be said about the Aramaic influence upon Middle Hebrew. As we have seen, Segal argued that Middle Hebrew derived to a very great extent from true Hebrew sources, and he pointed to the quite limited degree of Aramaic influence upon its lexical stock. Recent study, while it has confirmed Segal's main conclusion that Middle Hebrew depended on a truly spoken colloquial, has shown that Aramaic influence on Middle Hebrew was much greater than he supposed.[1] Segal relied on the received text of the Mishnah and other documents, as available in our printed editions; but deeper study of the manuscript tradition has shown that the more reliable manuscripts have a Mishnah text which departs more fully from Biblical Hebrew and which has more Aramaic (or Aramaic-influenced) features than the received text has. In other words, the manuscript tradition of the Mishnah carried out an operation of purification or standardization, following a biblical norm and overlaying with this the original Middle Hebrew diction. This result, however, does not negate Segal's main object, his defence of the base of Middle Hebrew in a popular spoken dialect; on the contrary, while Middle Hebrew was less pure Hebrew than he believed, the degree of Aramaic influence now perceptible in it actually enhances the probability that it should be understood as resting on a spoken colloquial. For the features now seen to have attached to Middle Hebrew are not such as to suggest or to support an artificial creation out of Aramaic. Among features which resulted from Aramaic, or which at least ran to some extent parallel with Aramaic, we may mention: the use of *lᵉ* as direct object marker; the form *'att* for the masculine pronoun 'thou'; the pronoun suffixes *-ak, -ik* (Masoretic *-ᵉka, -ek*). Another striking feature was the tendency for final *-m* to become *-n*, and this not only in familiar cases like the masculine plural ending *-in* but in uninflected words like that for 'man', *'adan*, which writing was later 'corrected' out of existence by the scribes. Similarly the pronoun endings *-m* and *-n* (in Biblical Hebrew masculine and feminine) tended to merge.

Finally, it is probable that there were dialectal differences within Middle Hebrew which our traditional texts do not reflect. The Bar Kochba letters, for instance, write the particle *'t* with *t* alone: *š'ny ntn t kblym* 'that I put the fetters', a practice paralleled in Punic.[2] The Copper Scroll also shows certain peculiarities, and in Milik's judgement

[1] On the following, see especially the writings of the late E. Y. Kutscher, e.g. his article 'Hebrew Language' in *EncJud*, 16, cols. 1593ff, and 'Mišnisches Hebräisch', *Rocznik Orientalistyczny*, 28 (1964–5), 35–48.

[2] See E. Y. Kutscher, 'The language of the Hebrew and Aramaic letters of Bar Kosiba and his contemporaries: 2. The Hebrew letters' (in Hebrew), *Leš*, 26 (1962), 7ff.

is in some respects more developed than the language of the Mishnah but in other features closer to Biblical Hebrew.[1]

Thus we have now looked at those sources for Hebrew which have been longer known: Late Biblical Hebrew, Ben Sira, and Middle Hebrew. To this the Dead Sea Scrolls have added in recent years a volume of new information which greatly increases our knowledge and assists us to fit together the various pieces of information that we previously had. Linguistically, the information coming from the Dead Sea Scrolls can be classified as follows: (*a*) biblical texts, written with orthographies differing from that of the Masoretic text, which may thus reveal something of the linguistic usages of the period – the most important such source is the Isaiah scroll IsA; (*b*) texts previously unknown, written in a register basically akin to the biblical, and which may thus be regarded as a last offshoot of Late Biblical Hebrew – such texts as the Manual of Discipline, the War Scroll, the Hodayoth; (*c*) texts, like the Copper Scroll and the Bar Kochba letters, which are basically Middle Hebrew. Of these last nothing more will be said, since they have already been mentioned under Middle Hebrew.

The general structure and syntactic patterns of Qumran Hebrew are biblical, if we contrast this on the gross scale with Middle Hebrew. Thus for instance the waw-consecutive construction is still in operation; *šel* as a normal marker of possession is not in use; the relative particle is the biblical *'ᵃšer*. On the other hand there are a large number of writings and spellings which are abnormal by traditional standards, and these have suggested to scholars that Qumran Hebrew had many differences in pronunciation, morphology and so on. For example, there are a very large number of *plene* spellings compared with the Masoretic text, and this use is extended to 'short' vowels, which are only exceptionally so spelled in the Masoretic text, thus *kwl* = *kol* 'all'; *lo'* 'not' is commonly written with *waw*, *lw'*. Aleph is very often written at the end of words like *ki, mi* (*ky', my'*). Some of these writings are no doubt only a matter of orthography (for instance, it has been held that *lo'* was written with *waw* to prevent misreading as *la* in Aramaic fashion) but others of them appear to indicate that the morphological structure of words was different from that to which we are accustomed from the Masoretic text. Among verbs, for example, where the Masoretic text would have *dršw* (= *diršu* 'seek'), we find a common writing as *drwšw*, similar to the pause form in the Masoretic text. A noun spelling like

[1] See J. T. Milik, 'Le rouleau de cuivre de Qumrân (3Q15)', *RB*, 66 (1959), 323; Kutscher, *EncJud*, 16, cols. 1606f.

swdm (Masoretic text *sdm* = *sᵉdom*) suggests a pronunciation like *sodom* (Greek Σόδομα) and this may further suggest that the stress lay on the penult rather than on the final syllable. Such writings, where they diverge from the types of the Masoretic text, have excited much comparison with various traditions of Hebrew pronunciation, such as the Samaritan.

In phonology, the laryngals are occasionally confused with one another or omitted in writing, for example, *ybwr* 'he will pass' (= Masoretic text *yaʿᵃbor*). There are, indeed, traditions that this happened in certain areas (Haifa, Beth-Shean), conceivably under the influence of Greek. A few such cases, however, do not count for a great deal, for they are not sufficiently systematic for us to rule out the possibility of mere scribal error: there are no texts with large masses of laryngals systematically confused or omitted. One case that is recurrent and is also readily understandable is that of aleph after a *shewa*: *tntw* 'his fig' (Masoretic text *t'ntw* = *tᵉ'enato*); the aleph was quiescent, and thus failed to be written. The common word (Masoretic text) *nᵉ'um* 'oracle of' is commonly written as *nw'm*: it was probably pronounced simply as *num*.[1] This is done fairly consistently in the Isaiah scroll (but *n'wm* at 37:34, 41:14). As an aleph, traditionally written, may be omitted because it is not pronounced, conversely one may be inserted where traditionally it did not belong: so *b'h* 'in it (fem.)' (IsA. 37:34). The word we know as *ro'š* 'head' is found written variously as *rwš, rw'š, r'wš* and *r'š*. For *goyim* the writing *gw'ym* is found. *Zᵉ'eb* 'wolf' is written once with aleph (11:6) and once as *zb* (65:25) in the Isaiah scroll. Other cases in which phonetic similarities have led to unusual writings are such as *rwknym* (1QS 11:1), probably the same word normally taken as *rogᵉnim* 'rebellious ones', and *'akzari* written as *'gzry* (IsA. 13:9).

In morphology, the following are among the phenomena which deserve mention. The pronouns 'he' and 'she' are very frequently written *hw'h* and *hy'h*; many scholars have interpreted these as signs of a pronunciation *hu'a, hi'a*. The pronoun 'you' (plural masculine) is often written *'tmh* (Masoretic text *'tm* = *'attem*). The suffix of the second singular masculine is very often written with *k* + *h*, in this supporting the Tiberian tradition of pronunciation as *-ᵉka*, but also suggesting that this latter realization lay alongside the *-ak* which we have seen to apply for Middle Hebrew. One very interesting phenomenon is the appear-

[1] Cf. E. Y. Kutscher, *Ha-lašon wᵉ-ha-reqaʿ ha-lᵉšoni šel mᵉgillat Yᵉšaʿyahu ha-šᵉlema mi-mᵉgillot yam ha-melaḥ* (Jerusalem, 1959), p. 42 (ET *The Language and Linguistic Background of the Isaiah Scroll* (*1QIsaᵃ*) (Leiden, 1974), p. 56); this work is basic to the entire section. More briefly, see Kutscher, *EncJud*, 16, cols. 1583–90.

ance of verb forms in the imperfect, with suffix, like *yšwpṭny* (Tiberian would be *yišpᵉṭeni*), *yswmknw, tdwršhw* and *yʿwšqnw*. Such forms have been identified as remains of an old present-future tense, with vowel after the first radical, like the Akkadian tense, and also as parallel to Samaritan forms like *yā'ūkel* from *'kl* 'eat'; but perhaps they most suggest those imperfects with 'o-colouring' in their vowels like *tʿbdm* in Exod. 20:5.[1]

In vocabulary the Scrolls use the familiar lexicon of Late Biblical Hebrew but have many characteristic features of their own: *pešer* 'interpretation'; *serek* 'order'; *goral* 'lot, group', used of the community and its density; *mᵉbeqqer* 'overseer'; *qeṣ* 'period'; *yaḥad* 'community', and also *rabbim* with something of the same sense. Some of these words and senses, clearly witnessed to in the Scrolls, have now also been identified in some places in the Bible.[2] In addition, we find old words of the Bible, probably long archaic, reused with senses which have come to be attached to them through exegetical tradition. Thus the Hodayoth use no less than four times the word *ḥelka'im*, which occurs thrice in the difficult Ps. 10 and is obscure already there. It is hardly to be supposed that this word was still current in conversational Hebrew; rather, its very obscurity lent it to exegetical speculation and reuse in the sense attained by stuch study. Some of the words mentioned above, like *serek* and *seder*, may have been derived under Aramaic influence or with an Aramaic sense; but on the whole it is remarkable how free the language is from Aramaic lexical interference. There are also Akkadian terms, doubtless adopted through Aramaic, like *'wḥzy 'bwt* 'intercessors', and some Persian terms are still appearing in the language for the first time, like *naḥšir* (thrice in the War Scroll), meaning apparently 'hunt, battle'; from Greek, on the other hand, there is little explicit influence.

Finally, something may be learned about the character of Hebrew in our period from the words transcribed in Greek and Latin sources, such as the Second Column of Origen's *Hexapla* and the works of Jerome; such transcriptions are vocalized and the evidence from them can be linked with that of Late Biblical Hebrew, of Middle Hebrew, and of the Scrolls. Due care has to be exercised, of course, in assessing this material.

[1] Cf. M. Goshen-Gottstein, 'Linguistic structure and tradition in the Qumran documents', *Scripta Hierosolymitana*, 4 (1958), p. 126 and n. 174, with literature there cited. On the Samaritan form, see R. Macuch, *Grammatik des samaritanischen Hebräisch*. Studia Samaritana 1 (Berlin, 1969), p. 293, line 15.

[2] E.g. for *yaḥad* as a biblical noun, see S. Talmon, 'The sectarian *yḥd* – a biblical noun', *VT*, 3 (1953), 133–40.

ARAMAIC

The position of Aramaic in our period was long a somewhat ironic one. The central importance of the language was universally recognized, and many scholars, as has been said, supposed it to be the Semitic vernacular of Palestine to the virtual exclusion of Hebrew; yet actual texts in Aramaic from our period have until recently been very scanty. The Aramaic sections of Daniel (2:4 to the end of 7) might be good evidence for a time coming down to about 165 B.C.E. at the latest (much of the material in these chapters may have its origin in late Persian times, even if the final form is later), but comparatively little else remained. Grave inscriptions in Aramaic commonly consisted of little more than personal names. Connected texts were rather late: *Megillath Ta'anith* is from the late first century C.E.; the Aramaic parts of the Palestinian Talmud are third century or later. Extensive texts in the form of Targums have indeed always been available, and these have now been amplified by modern discoveries such as that of the Neofiti text. But there are two great difficulties in the use of Targum texts as evidence for linguistic usage. Firstly, it is difficult to give a precise date to a Targum; and, secondly, even where some relative dating can be achieved through considerations of content, methods of interpretation, and so on, these do not in themselves afford a full guarantee for the dating of the present linguistic form of the text as we have it; for many Targums may have undergone extensive linguistic revision long after their date of origin. Thus Targum texts, though of central importance in themselves, are uncertain as evidence of linguistic change.

Now, however, finds at Qumran have provided us with more solid evidence. Many fragments are in Aramaic, and of these there are two which are of larger size and have received fuller linguistic analysis: the Genesis Apocryphon and the Targum of Job. To these can be added many shorter fragments: portions of the Testament of Levi; the 'Prayer of Nabonidus'; marriage contracts, legal documents and, particularly striking, letters of the Bar Kochba period. Meanwhile, also, and quite apart from Qumran, our knowledge of Targums has greatly expanded beyond what was possible on the basis of those Targums, like Onkelos, which had been traditionally transmitted; for the Cairo Geniza disclosed portions of a Palestinian Targum, and recently there was added the discovery of the important Neofiti text, a complete Targum to the Pentateuch and one previously unknown.

This greatly increased material has, however, left us with many questions and difficulties about the character of Aramaic within our period. There seem to be two main approaches among scholars. The first is to establish a historical relationship, on the basis of diachronic linguistic reconstruction, between the Qumran evidence and the other Aramaic materials already known. This approach is taken, for instance, by scholars like Kutscher and Fitzmyer. When this is done, we can trace a development from the Aramaic of the Persian empire down through Ezra and Daniel to the Job Targum and the Genesis Apocryphon, and from there on to later materials like the Bar Kochba letters. Thus, for instance, the editors of the Job Targum hold that its language is older than that of the Genesis Apocryphon and closer to that of Daniel. As an example we may cite the various forms of the relative–possessive particle: Imperial *zy*, Ezra and Daniel *di*, Job Targum *dy*, but Genesis Apocryphon mixed, with *d* (= *dᵉ*) eight times, *dy* (= *di*) very much more common, Bar Kochba letters also mixed (as cited by Kutscher, *dᵉ* twice, *di* nine times).[1] Onkelos, however, regularly has *dᵉ*. Again, in respect of the verb formation *haphel/aphel*, Biblical Aramaic has overwhelmingly *haphel* (only four cases of *aphel*) and Job Targum is the same; in Genesis Apocryphon no *haphel* is found but only *aphel*, which is, of course, the normal Onkelos form also and that of later Aramaic generally. This approach, then, seeks to establish a clear and strictly linguistic development running from the earliest beginnings of Hellenistic Aramaic down to the Bar Kochba period.

The second approach, prominent in the work of scholars like Kahle, Díez Macho and others, begins rather from the Targum texts, and in particular the Neofiti text. This, it is claimed, comes close to representing the spoken Aramaic of the centre of our period (say, first century C.E.). The dating of Neofiti (and of the original form of the Palestinian Targum texts recovered from the Geniza) is done less on purely linguistic criteria and more on criteria of content, methods of exegesis and the like. In contrast with the diachronic analysis described above, this approach works with a synchronic distinction:[2] works like Genesis Apocryphon and Job Targum belong to a literary stratum of Aramaic, built upon the older Official Aramaic of the Persian empire, while a Targum of the Neofiti type represents actual spoken Aramaic, a text read to the people in the synagogue, where popular comprehension was essential. The spoken idiom of contemporary Aramaic has had some effect on documents like Job Targum and Genesis Apocryphon but their language is basically a literary register, which existed at the same time as the colloquial register known from Neofiti.

[1] See E. Y. Kutscher, 'The language of the Hebrew and Aramaic letters of Bar Kosiba and his contemporaries: 1. The Aramaic letters' (in Hebrew), *Leš*, 25 (1961), 121.

[2] Cf. for instance A. Díez Macho, *El Targum* (Barcelona, 1972), pp. 31–73, and especially p. 47.

This chapter cannot argue out the case between the two approaches; but the one that will be taken as our model will be the first rather than the second. It seems better to work from texts which can be securely dated through the finding of them at Qumran; and the dating of texts on the basis of the exegetical methods, the *halakah* which they presuppose, and so on, seems as yet not sufficiently secure.[1] It is true that texts like Genesis Apocryphon suggest something of a 'literary' air, and this is true of most texts that have been preserved, apart from letters and contracts. But it does not seem sufficiently proven that the Aramaic of Neofiti is a 'popular' or 'spoken' register of the language any more than this is true of the other extant texts. Therefore it seems good that the dating of Neofiti, like the dating of Onkelos and other Targums, apart from the Job Targum, should be left on one side as a yet unproven quantity. The following exposition will therefore be based on the texts the dating of which has a firm anchorage at Qumran, and to these will be added some mention of other texts such as Onkelos, Neofiti, and other kinds of Aramaic.

The Aramaic of our period can be designated, following Fitzmyer, as 'Middle Aramaic', a term that fits happily with 'Middle Hebrew';[2] this phase covers the time from approximately 200 B.C.E. to C.E. 200. In this time, it seems, that certain homogeneity which had earlier applied to Aramaic and which is generally attributed to the standardizing effects of the imperial chancery style seems to break up, and different forms and dialects appear. In the following period ('Late Aramaic') we have the clearer distinction between Eastern Aramaic (as in Syriac, the Aramaic of the Babylonian Talmud, and Mandaic) and the various branches of Western Aramaic (such as Palestinian Christian Aramaic, Palestinian Jewish Aramaic, and Samaritan Aramaic).

We may now exemplify some of the changes from the texts which have been named. The Job Targum, as we have seen, still has the relative–possessive *di* as in Biblical Aramaic, and also the *haphel* rather than an *aphel*.[3] For the demonstrative masculine singular 'this', on the other hand, the Job Targum has *dn (den)* as against the *dn*' *(dᵉna)* of the biblical material. The closeness to Biblical Aramaic is reinforced by the

[1] See A. D. York, 'The dating of Targumic literature', *JSJ*, 5 (1974), 49–62.

[2] Kutscher in his earlier articles e.g., 'The language of the Genesis Apocryphon: A preliminary study', *Scripta Hierosolymitana*, 4 (1958), p. 3, uses 'Middle Aramaic' to designate what Fitzmyer calls Late Aramaic, but in his later and major articles in *Current Trends in Linguistics* (see pp. 347f.) and *EncJud* he falls in with Fitzmyer's classification. The *Current Trends* article remained unfinished and unfortunately did not go much beyond Biblical Aramaic.

[3] See J. P. M. van der Ploeg, A. S. van der Woude and B. Jongeling, *Le Targum de Job* (Leiden, 1971), p. 4, for this and the following.

existence of Old Persian loanwords, such as *dḥšt* 'desert' and *ḥrtk* 'thorn';[1] as we have seen, words of this origin are found also in the Hebrew scrolls from Qumran. It would not be surprising if the editors of the Job Targum are right in placing their text in the second part of the second century B.C.E.

The Aramaic of the Genesis Apocryphon, as has been suggested, lies a little farther away from Biblical Aramaic; *d (dʼ)* has begun to appear, and the *aphel* has taken the place of the *haphel*. The demonstrative pronoun 'this' (masculine singular) is nearly always *dn* (*dn'* only exceptionally). In syntax, some peculiarities of Biblical Aramaic, where the subject commonly precedes the verb, the object may precede the verb, and the object of an infinitive generally precedes it, are not found in this scroll; in this respect it returns to patterns more generally familiar in Semitic. On the other hand, some features are shared with Biblical Aramaic and thus distinguish the language of the scroll from the common usage of the later dialects ('Late Aramaic' in our terms): for instance, there is dissimilation of a geminate consonant, as in *yndʻ* (*yindaʻ* 'he may know'). The direct object marker is still *lʼ-* as in the earlier forms of Aramaic, and *yt* is nowhere found; *yt*, though found once in Daniel and also in Egyptian texts, becomes regular and characteristic in texts which are probably later.

Moreover, there are clear signs that Genesis Apocryphon sometimes either imitates the Aramaic of Daniel or draws from the same fount of usage, for we find idioms almost identical with those of Daniel, even when the expressions are quite unusual ones: decisive examples are *ṣlm 'npyh'* 'the form of her face' (20:2), compare Dan. 3:19 *ṣᵉlem 'anpohi*; and *nšmty lgw ndnh'* 'my breath in the midst of its sheath' (2:10), cf. Dan. 7:15 *ruḥi...bᵉgo' nidneh*. This *ndn*, incidentally, is another word of Persian origin, and we also find *'sprk*, interpreted as 'shield' or as 'spear'.[2] Thus here again we find lexical signs of Iranian influence rather than of Greek; this pattern, repeated in the Hebrew and the Aramaic sources, suggests that loanwords were slow to enter this register of language and that the incidence of them represented a stage of language change that was already well past. There are also Hebrew elements, for instance writings like *mlk kwl ʻlmym* 'the king of all the ages' (2:7), although the Aramaic writing *ʻlmy'* is also found (21:2, 14); in this sort of literature such elements can naturally be interpreted as citations of Hebrew phraseology, rather than as indications that the Aramaic of the writer

[1] See J. C. Greenfield and S. Shaked, 'Three Iranian words in the Targum of Job from Qumran', *ZDMG*, 122 (1972), 37–45.

[2] Greenfield and Shaked, *ZDMG*, 122 (1972), 38 and literature there cited; cf. J. Fitzmyer, *The Genesis Apocryphon of Qumran Cave 1* (2nd edn., Rome, 1971), p. 182.

itself embodied such Hebrew expressions as part of its own idiom.[1] The semantic patterns of Genesis Apocryphon seem also to remain close to those of biblical Aramaic: thus *'olamim* as cited above belongs to the traditional temporal field rather than the later spatial sense 'world', thus paralleling the situation in Qumran Hebrew as against Middle Hebrew. But the addition of the quantifying particle *kwl* 'all', something quite marginal in the Bible (Ps. 145:13), may accord with that other semantic development whereby this plural is taken to indicate a plurality of referents, 'ages'. In the Bible, and still in the Qumran documents in general, the choice between singular and plural of *'olam* marks no difference in the referent but is purely stylistic;[2] and the distinction between one 'age' and another, familiar from rabbinic texts, has not yet become manifest with *'olam*, though the path towards it is indicated by our example and also by locutions like *lkwl qysy 'wlmym* 'for all the ages of eternity' in Qumran Hebrew.[3]

The Aramaic of Genesis Apocryphon can be shown, moreover, to have important contacts with other forms of Aramaic. On the one hand it has been argued by Kutscher that it has significant connections with the language of Targum Onkelos (and Jonathan). This in turn requires us to make brief mention of the controversy over the place of origin of this Targum, which of course eventually became the chief and standard Targum to be transmitted to later ages. While Kahle emphatically asserted that it originated in Babylonia, Nökdeke and Dalman argued for a Palestinian origin, and in this they have been followed in recent times by Kutscher, who thinks of an origin 'perhaps even Judean'.[4] He also classifies the language of Onkelos as Middle Aramaic and thus puts it within the same chronological bracket as the Qumran documents.[5] This side of the argument, however, seems to have been insufficiently worked out as yet; the similarities between the language of Genesis Apocryphon and that of Onkelos are – so far as can be seen from studies at present available – rather minor, and they have to be set against some considerable differences, for example, the consistent use of *yt* as direct object marker in Onkelos. Kutscher's view is that Onkelos originated in Palestine but was transmitted and vocalized in Babylonia. Here again (as we have seen with Mishnaic Hebrew) the

[1] The contrary view is held by Fitzmyer, *Genesis Apocryphon*, p. 25; perhaps it is hard to be sure either way.

[2] See J. Barr, *Biblical Words for Time*. SBT 33 (London, 2nd edition, 1969), p. 70 and note, and pp. 86–134 generally.

[3] Cf. Barr, *Time*, pp. 124f.

[4] In *Scripta Hierosolymitana*, 4 (1958), p. 10.

[5] Kutscher, *EncJud*, 3, cols. 267–8.

printed editions and the manuscripts upon which they have been based are incorrect and give a wrong impression of the grammar.[1] For the present it seems wiser, while recognizing the similarities between the Aramaic of Genesis Apocryphon and that of Onkelos, to consider that the latter is a later form of the language, belonging perhaps to the very end of the period of Middle Aramaic.

In addition, significant contacts have been pointed out between Genesis Apocryphon and two other forms of Aramaic, both belonging (in the form in which we known them) to Late Aramaic: Palestinian Christian and Samaritan Aramaic.

For comparison, a few tentative observations about the Aramaic of the Neofiti Targum may be added here. The relative–possessive particle occurs both as *d* (*dᵉ*) and *dy* (*di*) but the former is much more common; it thus stands between the position we have noted for the Bar Kochba letters and the position of Onkelos. Also *di*, when used, appears often to have the relative function rather than the possessive, the latter very commonly being exercised by *dᵉ*. The demonstrative pronoun 'this' is masculine singular *dyn* (*den*), plural *'lyn* (*'illen*), as in Onkelos. The conjunction *'rwm* (*'ᵃrum*) is extremely common in functions like 'because, when, that' (Onkelos *'ᵃri*, but also often *kᵉdi*, etc.).

Lexically, we note the frequency of *ḥm'* 'to see', a common Christian–Palestinian word (Onkelos generally *ḥẓ'*) and of *šr'* 'to dwell' (Onkelos commonly *ytb*). The word 'blood' is found spelt *'dm*. For 'time' we find, as well as *š'ʿt'* and *ʿdwn* (*ʿiddun*) the word *'šwn* (*'ešwan*), for example, Gen. 29:7, 35:16, this is the normal word in Christian Palestinian. 'Possessions' are *mmwn* (*mamon*) (for instance, Gen. 36:7, Masoretic text *rᵉkuš*, Onkelos *qinyan*). The shift of meaning in *ʿalma'* to 'world' has already taken place; for example, in Gen. 4:3 the generation of the flood is to be removed *mn gw' ʿlm'* 'from the midst of the world'. Words of Greek origin are noticeable, for example, in Gen. 4:3 Cain brought a *dwrwn* (*doron* = δῶρον 'gift', Onkelos *minḥata'*); this word, of course, is already well represented in rabbinic literature. Abraham asked for the welfare of visiting strangers *knymws 'rʿ'* (*kᵉnimus 'arʿa'*), as was the custom (Greek νόμος) of the country (Gen. 18:2). A homely word of the Roman empire is *'spqlṭr* 'guard', Greek, from Latin *speculator* (Gen. 39:1).

In spite of the undoubted importance of the Neofiti text and of other Palestinian Targum texts, it seems at least premature to identify their language as being exactly the spoken Aramaic of (say) the first century

[1] Kutscher, *EncJud*, 3, cols. 267–8.

C.E. A preliminary opinion would suggest that Neofiti represents a written stage later than that of the Qumran Aramaic documents, a written stage the idiom of which has indeed been affected by the spoken Aramaic of the first century or two C.E. For it is reasonable to judge that the language of a text like Genesis Apocryphon was in some measure archaizing when it was composed, in comparison with the idiom then generally spoken, just as was the case with the 'Biblical' Hebrew of the Scrolls. If this is so, it means that the documents of Qumran Aramaic, though definitely to be dated within our period, do not precisely reflect the spoken idiom of their time, just as Qumran Hebrew did not reflect the spoken (Middle Hebrew) idiom of the time. But it is one thing to admit this, and quite another to suppose that a quite different literary text like Neofiti can be identified without more ado with the spoken idiom of the period.

For this spoken idiom there are one or two other directions in which we can look. In the first century C.E. small indications can be derived from such Greek sources as the New Testament, in spite of the difficulties of interpretation. The form cited as ταλιθα κουμ 'maiden, arise' (Mark 5:41) is interesting; a variant reading has the form κουμι, but κουμ is to be preferred, both as having better manuscript authority and as being the stranger reading. The phrase is certainly Aramaic and, if reliable, seems to indicate a dialect in which the feminine ending *-i* had been lost (as later in Syriac). Again, the New Testament gives evidence that at this time the Galilean dialect, most probably meaning the Galilean dialect of Aramaic, was recognizably different.

Somewhat later we can consider a rabbinic document like *Megillath Taʿanith*, usually dated about 100 C.E. but from the nature of its contents (a list of dates on which fasting was forbidden because of joyful events that had taken place on them, many of the events lying in Hasmonean times) probably containing older material to which newer had been added. The Aramaic of this unfortunately very brief document has a distinctly colloquial air, and in this respect its style is markedly parallel with the Mishnaic style in contemporary Hebrew. Among the numerals we find the popular-looking forms *ḥmysr* 'fifteen' and *šybsr* 'seventeen', and there are several straight citations of Greek words, including *ḥqr'* 'the Akra' (the Seleucid fortress of Jerusalem) and *symw't'*, probably 'military standards' (σημεία).

Another important source is the Bar Kochba correspondence from the Dead Sea finds.[1] In these we find interesting variations from historical spelling: *nsy* (with *samekh*) for customary *nśy'* 'prince'; *slm*

[1] See Kutscher in *Leš*, 25 (1961), 117–33.

'peace', also with *samekh*, but also *šlm* with *shin* in the same group of letters. We find also a Greek word like *'sply'* (= ἀσφάλεια, literally 'safety, security'); admixtures with Hebrew, such as *'m* 'if' rather than the Aramaic *'n*; also a form like *htšdr* 'make an effort', with the surprising *h* rather than ' and the still more surprising failure to place the *š* before the *t*; we find *dy* (*di*) functioning as the particle introducing quoted speech (as ὅτι in Greek, and so already in Daniel). We note the idiom *'nḥn' ṣrykyn* 'we need (something)', the form *yhw'* for the imperfect of 'be' and so on. The use of the direct object particle *yt* is particularly interesting.[1] This particle – not necessarily a late phenomenon, since an example from Elephantine is known – occurs along with *l* as object marker in the Western Aramaic dialects, Jewish (Galilean), Christian and Samaritan, but is not used before nouns, only with pronoun suffixes, while *l* is used with both. These letters however use *yt* repeatedly with noun objects, and this is a striking contrast with Onkelos. In general, the Bar Kochba correspondence comes from the end of our period, but in its simple and unceremonious wording it no doubt reflects much of the manner of speech that was customary for some decades before. Incidentally, the fact that the correspondence is in both Aramaic and Hebrew (as well as Greek)[2] seems to put aside the possibility, sometimes urged, that Bar Kochba's use of Hebrew was based on nationalistic ideology; had this been so, he would surely have avoided Aramaic.

GREEK

This section describes the rise and the character of the Greek *koine* and in particular its relations with Jewish life and Judaism.

The *koine* or 'common' Greek of Hellenistic times can be traced back in its origins to the fifth century. Although Greek was markedly split into dialects, with major groupings like Ionic, 'Aeolic' or Achean, and Doric, and further local divisions between individual cities and groups, there were many factors which favoured a transcending of these differences. In a sense this may be said to go back to the beginnings of Greek literature with Homer, for epic poetry did not follow the lines of any one historical dialect but included elements which at least by later analysis belonged to several. In the same tradition Pindar write his poetry not in the dialect of his Boeotian home but in a mixture of Homeric, Aeolic and Doric which was mandatory for the choral lyricist

[1] See the full discussion of Kutscher, *Leš*, 25 (1961), 129–33.

[2] Cf. J. N. Sevenster, *Do You Know Greek?* (Leiden, 1968), pp. 166–72.

of the time; and similarly the Attic tragedians used a Doric colouring in the choral parts of their plays. In other words, the form of dialect used was dictated not purely by the native speech of writer or audience but by certain literary conventions which held good more or less throughout the Greek world. Literary prose grew up in the fifth century on an Ionic linguistic basis, though its greatest practitioner was Herodotus, a Dorian of Halicarnassus.

The political and cultural centrality of Athens led to an increasing importance of Attic throughout the entire Greek world. In Athens oratory and comedy had always belonged particularly to Attic; and gradually Attic took over from Ionic the position of dominance in literary prose. The centrality of Athens in the confederacy allied against Persia, and the colonizing activity of Athens throughout the Aegean world, were important factors in the process. In the fifth and fourth centuries the amphictyonies, organs of inter-state religious life, expressed their decisions in Attic, or in forms modified by Attic;[1] and the activity of the mind, the life of sophists and philosophers, from 400 on was carried on overwhelmingly in Attic, with only limited exceptions. The growing influence of Attic upon public life and administration, a process that can be traced in a multitude of inscriptions, was a force leading towards a common Greek language.

Thus the work of Alexander the Great and the rise of the Macedonian empire accelerated and universalized a process that was already under way. The native Macedonian speech had negligible influence on events. Philip of Macedon already a Greek and Attic chancellery, and Alexander's upbringing was based on Athenian culture. His armies were not purely Macedonian but included Greeks of the most diverse origins, another strong influence toward the attainment of a common speech. By the time of Alexander's death and the establishment of the successor empires the *koine* was already well established. And, just as the *koine* internally gained influence within the Greek world, so the conquest of vast oriental territories and the rise of Greek to the status of official language in the new empires gave an external impetus to the same movement.

Naturally, the old Greek dialects did not disappear overnight; the strength and duration of their survival varied from place to place, from one social stratum to another, from one subject field to another. This diversity can be followed in the inscriptions, private and public, of various localities. For a history of Judaism, however, it is unnecessary to follow this up. Equally is it unnecessary to go in detail into the mode

[1] A. Debrunner, *Geschichte der griechischen Sprache* (Berlin, 1954) 2, p. 32 (§42).

in which various dialect elements found their way into the *koine*. Though we have stressed the way in which Attic influence anticipated the extension of the *koine*, we have to go on to say that *koine* was not identical with Attic. Attic was the strongest element within it, but the second major element came from Ionic, and to these were added some Doric and Aeolic features. Elements which were entirely, or almost entirely, peculiar to Attic were commonly dropped: thus the -ττ- of φυλάττω, θάλαττα is replaced by the -σσ-: φυλάσσω, θάλασσα. The peculiarly Attic forms like λεώς, νεώς were lost in the *koine* and superseded by the forms λαός 'people' and ναός 'temple', both of them, as it happens, significant words in Jewish usage.[1] Yet ἵλεως survives and is much used in Jewish literature, meaning 'gracious, forgiving, merciful' and used in the LXX to translate Hebrew verbs of forgiving.[2]

The *koine*, then, was in principle not differentiated into local dialects: we do not find a Syrian Greek distinct from Cyrenaican Greek, apart from minor lexical features. There is indeed the question of the influence of substrate languages: of Semitic in Palestine–Syria, of Coptic in Egypt, and this will be considered shortly. But in general the *koine* formed a more or less homogeneous medium of communication extending over the entire Greek-speaking world. As with all languages, however, there are differences of degree, gradations of stratum and register. The term *koine* itself is in this respect somewhat ambiguous: it may mean 'common' in the sense of universal, that is, the general Hellenistic Greek as distinct from the particularized local Greek of the old dialects; but it may also mean 'common' in the sense of 'colloquial', as opposed to literary, for literary Greek often sought to avoid those departures from classical usage which seemed to be vulgar to the point of objectionability. Thus Hellenistic literary Greek represents something of a different standard from the speech of the man in the street. This striving for literary distinctness from common usage later took the more explicit form of Atticism, the careful weeding out from the vocabulary of that which failed to meet the 'Attic' norms. This movement had considerable influence in the first two centuries C.E. and affected much Jewish literature, such as parts of Josephus, and this will be mentioned again below. Atticism also had an effect on the transmission of texts like the LXX, since scribes sometimes later revised the texts in order to 'improve' their Greek according to Attic standards. In the LXX text this revision is associated particularly with the work of

[1] But see below, p. 104.

[2] The frequency and extent of the use of this word is understated by Debrunner, *Geschichte*, 2, pp. 109f, §173.

Lucian. In place of *koine* forms like εἶπαν 'they said', the revision put classical forms like εἶπον, thus, from our point of view, distorting the original form of the LXX text.

The conquest of the East (Asia Minor, Syria, Palestine, Egypt, Mesopotamia) by the *koine* was swift and far-reaching. All governmental administration used Greek, and in commerce Greek made the most remote markets accessible, from Bactria on the Indian border to the far west of the Mediterranean – a wider world, in fact, than that which Aramaic had made accessible under the Persians. Because of the centrality of Greek for administration and commerce, and because of the extremely high development of Greek learning, science and culture, Greek was the language of education. In much of the East literacy came to mean literacy in Greek, and the native languages, though still existing, were the languages of those who did not read or write. In Jewish society in Palestine the importance of Hebrew and Aramaic literature, and the close connection of it with the religion, prevented this relation from coming to pass. But even so Greek made rapid strides and its connection with education, with administration and with international commerce made the acquisition of it desirable for persons aspiring to distinction and leadership. In a period during which little is known of the history of Palestine, around 259–257 B.C.E., the Zenon Papyri give a vivid picture of the Jew Tobias, his family and its position, through the Greek correspondence in which they engaged.[1]

But the area in which Jewish life was most completely carried on in Greek was Egypt, and within Egypt Alexandria in particular. As against the numerous references to Jews in voluminous correspondence in Greek, only negligible amounts of written material in Hebrew or Aramaic have survived, out of a period of several centuries.[2] A few Aramaic funerary inscriptions come from an early Ptolemaic cemetery; Aramaic ostraca are found, but only in the *chora*, the Egyptian countryside, as distinct from the city,[3] and sometimes we find an isolated word, like *šalom* 'peace', added to a Greek funerary inscription, very much in the manner of one who knows two or three keywords of Hebrew culture but nothing more. In the earlier period of Ptolemaic rule, the evidence suggests that Jews coming to Egypt were speakers of Aramaic rather than of Hebrew, but the Aramaic quickly dropped away and the permanent language of everyday intercourse was Greek. The

1 On all this see Hengel, *Judaism and Hellenism*, esp. 1, pp. 58ff; and the summary of the linguistic situation in V. A. Tcherikover and A. Fuks, *Corpus Papyrorum Judaicarum*, 1 (Cambridge, Mass., 1957), pp. 30ff.

2 Cf. Hengel *Judaism*, 1, p. 58 and note 4, vol. 2, p. 42.

3 Cf. P. M. Fraser, *Ptolemaic Alexandria* (Oxford, 1972), 2, p. 958.

Greek translation of the Law, and later of the Bible generally, is rightly said to have originated and to have been carried out here, for here in Alexandria it was most needed and there was the greatest motivation for it. It is probable that the entire synagogue worship (the Alexandrian word was not συναγωγή but προσευχή) was carried out in Greek, and there is no reason to suppose that the Bible was normally read in Hebrew.[1] Of Philo, the greatest thinker of the Alexandrian community, it has remained quite uncertain whether he knew any Hebrew at all. Not until the end of Roman times, in the early Byzantine era, when conditions in Egypt had totally altered for Jews, do we find communities corresponding with one another in Hebrew, and this language again functioning as the official tongue.[2]

The advance of Greek, however, was not confined to areas like Egypt, now the most important centre of the Diaspora,[3] but took place also in Palestine. From the third century B.C.E. on, apart from the inscriptions on tombs and ossuaries and in synagogues, inscriptions in Palestine are almost entirely in Greek.[4] Moreover, this importance of the Greek language continued even after the break with the cultural Hellenization policy of the government and after the Maccabean revolt, for the entire life of foreign policy of the new government seems to have been conducted in Greek, and its negotiations with the Seleucid rulers, to say nothing of its contacts with places like Rome and Sparta, depended on Greek. Moreover, the importance of Jerusalem itself was related to the Diaspora: the cultivation of relations with the Diaspora enhanced the status of the city, and these relations were at this time and for most of the Diaspora expressed in Greek. The numerous Greek inscriptions of Jerusalem, dating mostly from the Herodian and Roman period, cannot be ascribed to Diaspora Jews alone but probably indicate the linguistic situation of public life in the capital at this time.[5]

A good index of the place of Greek is provided by the incidence of

[1] Cf. Fraser, *Alexandria*, 1, p. 284, and note 777 on p. 443 of vol. 2.

[2] Tcherikover and Fuks, *CPJ*, I pp. 101f. As they point out (pp. 106ff) by this time not only had the Jews turned away from Hellenism but Hellenism itself was losing ground in Egypt, with the resurgence of Coptic language, Egyptian nationalism and Monophysite Christianity.

[3] The inscriptions of the Jews of Rome are overwhelmingly Greek, to a lesser extent Latin; Hebrew and Aramaic together make less than one per cent. See H. J. Leon, *The Jews of Ancient Rome* (Philadelphia, 1960), p. 76.

[4] Cf. Hengel, *Judaism*, 1, p. 58. It may be, however, that the argument becomes even stronger if the sepulchral inscriptions are included in the reckoning, since they are very often in Greek and often represent a wide stratum of the population; cf. Leon, *Jews*, p. 75.

[5] Hengel, *Judaism*, p. 60.

Greek personal names.[1] In Egypt a very large majority of the names borne by Jews are Greek names. In names including a theophoric element there was a marked preference for names like Theodotus, Dositheus, which included the general term θεός, 'God', rather than the name of a particular deity; yet names including elements like Apollo, Athene, Sarapis and so on are also plentifully evidenced. In certain circles there was a tendency to take a double name, with a Greek form resembling the Hebrew, as in Jeshua-Jason, Eliakim-Alkimus, and most popular of all Simeon-Simon; interestingly, these practices are found in the Jerusalem ruling circles in both the Hellenizing and the anti-Hellenizing factions. Names like Antigonus, Alexander and the like, popular as the names of leading persons in Hellenistic society, were also widely used.

Thus for Jews, as for others whose cultural past had not lain in the Greek language area, entrance into the world of Hellenism was made much easier by the existence of the *koine*. There is no sign that the acquisition of Greek was felt as very difficult, and the competence in Greek attained, though depending on the register of Greek acquired, was very respectable in the sources to which we have access. The cultural movement was overwhelmingly in one direction: orientals learned Greek, but not much was done by native Greek speakers to learn oriental languages or to assimilate oriental culture through their written sources.

But not all Jewish self-expression in Greek took the general *koine* as its medium. A man of letters did not write in the language of the market-place but in the appropriate idiom for his literary genre. Thus the Jewish poet Philo the Elder, because he writes in an epic style and genre, adopts the language of Alexandrian epic, which was learned, artificial and quite remote from common speech: for instance, he repeatedly uses the genitive in -οιο, hallowed as a Homeric and epic form but long disused in speech; it was, incidentally, very helpful to a poet since it enabled him to get his words into the hexameter, hence such startling forms as Ἀβραάμοιο.[2] A similar separation from the spoken language is found in the Jewish or Samaritan poet Theodotus, in whose work (on the city of Shechem) we find such phrases as τέτυκται 'is' or ἀγέμεν ποτὶ δῶμα 'to take home'.[3] The tragic poet Ezekielos followed, similarly, the idiom of tragedy. All these are writers of whom only fragments have survived; but they show how

1 Ibid. pp. 61–5; Tcherikover and Fuks, *CPJ*, I pp. 27–30, cf. p. 109.

2 See F. Jacoby, *Die Fragmente der griechischen Historiker*, part 3, C (Leiden, 1958), p. 691, line 7, and pp. 690f in general.

3 Jacoby, *FGrHist* 3C, p. 693, lines 31–2.

deeply imbued with the Greek language the writers were: they had not only a working knowledge of Greek, such as one must pick up through daily life in a place like Alexandria or any other Hellenistic city, but a scholarly knowledge, which enabled them to follow the learned conventions and use a poetic vocabulary which was far removed from current usage and depended on connections in the remote past history of the literature. The Jewish parts of the Sibylline Oracles, which have survived in larger extent, also follow – at a considerable distance in respect of quality – the epic conventions.

More central and more important is the Atticizing convention of literary Greek prose, which was strong in the first century C.E. when the two major prose writers, Philo and Josephus, were writing. Josephus indeed was a special case, for he used literary assistants, one at least of whom was an active imitator of ancient models like Thucydides. But Philo's style is his own; to him it would have seemed only in keeping with the elevated subject matter of his work that it should use an idiom more lofty and more educated than the average *koine* of his city. Thus we find in him forms like τέτταρες 'four', περιττόν 'odd' (of number), συνταράττων 'causing trouble', with the Attic -ττ-; the optative is in fairly wide use; in the *Legation to Gaius* we find phrases like οἷοί τε ὄντες 'being able' and παντί τῳ δῆλον 'it is clear to anybody at all'. But this is hardly a strict and purist Atticism, and the *koine* forms are also found: τέσσαρες and so on. Even within the Greek Bible we find similar tendencies among the books which were not translated from a Hebrew original. 4 Maccabees is highly Atticistic in many ways, and freely uses the optative, the decline of which was a common mark of the *koine*. 2 Maccabees uses the Attic form νεώς 'temple'.[1]

The central source for *koine* Greek of Jewish authorship is, of course, the Bible; indeed, the Greek Bible, both LXX and New Testament, is one of the main literary monuments of the entire *koine*. Those literary and Atticizing fashions which influenced the writing of free Jewish literature in Greek had much less influence upon the Bible translation; this in the beginning has the air of being controlled by a more *practical* and less literary set of aims and principles.[2] But within the Bible a distinction has to be made between the practices of various LXX translators and various writers of New Testament books. Investigation over the last century has shown how deeply the language of the LXX

[1] 2 Macc. 6:2 etc.; the book uses also the *koine* form ναός. See above, p. 100.

[2] See especially Ch. Rabin, 'The translation process and the character of the Septuagint', *Textus*, 6 (1968), 1–26, and S. P. Brock, 'The phenomenon of the Septuagint', in A. S. van der Woude, ed., *The Witness of Tradition*, OTS 17 (Leiden, 1972), pp. 11–36.

in its central books, which was once regarded as a peculiar and unparalleled sort of Greek, mirrors the contemporary usage of the Ptolemaic papyri and of other 'non-literary' *koine* writers. Thus the papyri and other *koine* sources provide exact parallels to characteristic LXX forms such as εἶπαν 'they said' (Attic εἶπον), ἦλθα 'I came' (Attic ἦλθον), γενηθῆναι (aorist infinitive; Attic γενέσθαι), γογγύζειν 'to mutter rebelliously', λειτουργεῖν 'to serve' (a deity). Even in the expression of central theological concepts, such as that of love or that of the 'people' (of God), the LXX commonly uses the general terminology of its own time.[1] Good examples of fairly colloquial Jewish *koine* can also be found in non-canonical writings like *Joseph and Asenath* or the *Testaments of the Twelve Patriarchs*.

The *koine* was, as we have seen, something of a universal speech, and did not have local dialects. Nevertheless the LXX has something of a local atmosphere belonging to Alexandria. Some terms, especially those representing things and places known in Egypt, are rendered with customary words of the contemporary Egyptian linguistic usage; we notice this in words for flora and fauna, for administration and government, law and social relations. It has been suggested also that Egyptian in its Coptic form, as the substrate language underlying Greek in Egypt, has effected the viability of certain choices of rendering in the LXX;[2] but these are essentially a minor element in the total linguistic structure of the translation and, though their origins were local, they were not such as to affect the general intelligibility of the text to speakers of Greek elsewhere.

Much more important is the Semitic influence upon the Greek of those biblical books which were translated from Hebrew (or Aramaic). The language as thus used contains many collocations, idioms and uses which either were not found, or were abnormal, or were statistically much less common, in the Greek of texts not translated from Semitic. I think of terms like προσέθετο + τοῦ + infinitive 'he added to do something', that is, he did it again; ἄνθρωπος ἄνθρωπος 'man man', that is, each man; καὶ ἐγένετο followed by another verb phrase 'and it came to pass that x took place'; υἱὸς τοῦ ἀνθρώπου 'son of man'; ψυχή

[1] The view, long popular in many trends of religious study, that ἀγαπᾶν/ἀγάπη were specially coined by the LXX in order to give expression in Greek to the peculiar biblical concept of love (or of the love of God) is clearly untrue even on the basis of LXX evidence itself: the same words are used by the LXX indifferently for the love of God for his people and for the pathological love of Amnon for his half-sister Tamar (2 Sam. 13:1, 15).

[2] See Brock, OTS 17 (1972), pp. 33–6. These suggestions, though stimulating, are, however, hard to demonstrate definitely.

'soul' used for 'himself', and so on, reflexively, after Hebrew phrases with *nepeš*. All cases like this can be understood as 'literal' rendition of the Semitic idiom: commonly the translator followed the segmentation of elements in the Hebrew and rendered each element lineally in succession into Greek. In the main parts of the LXX this practice was not carried beyond the point where it led to serious and densely concentrated difficulties of understanding in Greek; the expressions in Greek, though strange when first seen, are often statistically peculiar rather than quite unintelligible or impossible. Often an expression that in *koine* is strange but possible is made more common and normal in LXX and New Testament, that is, the difference is a statistical one.[1]

Literalism may however be pushed farther, and when it goes beyond a certain point intelligibility in Greek is damaged. A historical development in this respect can be traced, and it is largely a result of the religious and interpretative problems felt within Judaism in its use of the Greek versions of the Bible. The original Alexandrian LXX, we may suppose, had been executed without any great theoretical sophistication – it was, after all, the world's first major work of translation to span such a gap of language, culture and religion. In the course of time demands for a Greek version which would more exactly follow the lineaments of the original were heard, and these led to various attempts at revision and fresh translation, which often included a higher degree of 'literalism'. One instance is the systematic use of ἐγώ for Hebrew *'ᵃni* and ἐγώ εἰμι for *'anoki*, which produced such strange combinations, defying all Greek syntax, as Judg. 5:3 (B text): ἐγώ εἰμι τῷ κυρίῳ, ἐγώ εἰμι ᾄσομαι. The meaning intended is 'I to the Lord, I will sing'; but the Greek is highly puzzling unless it is understood that the pronoun + verb combination ἐγώ εἰμι is a code indicator for the longer form of the Hebrew personal pronoun as against the shorter.

Where this sort of policy was pushed far enough, a translation became not an expression in Greek of the meaning of Hebrew, but an index in Greek to the *form* of the Hebrew. It was Aquila (second century C.E.) whose translation went farthest along this line. He is said to have been influenced by R. Aqiba's exegetical methods; and by his time the Jews had somewhat lost confidence in the Alexandrian LXX because of the way in which the Christians had exploited some of its expressions. The most famous example is παρθένος at Isa. 7:14: used quite unthinkingly by the Alexandrian translator in its general sense

[1] On the operation of literal translation see J. Barr, *The Typology of Literalism in Ancient Biblical Translations*, Nachrichten von der Akademie der Wissenschaften in Göttingen, 1. Philologisch–historische Klasse, 1979, nr. 11, pp. 275–325.

'girl', it was later taken within Christianity in the narrower and more specific sense, 'virgin'. The future use of the LXX lay within Christianity; Aquila's rendering, by contrast, was to have high repute and much use in Greek-speaking Jewry right down to Byzantine times.

Aquila's translation technique included among others the following elements. He tried fairly consistently to represent a Hebrew word by the same Greek word throughout and to distinguish between different Hebrew words of similar meaning by using different Greek words, thus ὁρᾶν for *ra'a* 'see' but ὁραματίζεσθαι, a word coined by him, for *ḥaza*; he expressed in Greek 'etymological' relations perceived to exist in the Hebrew, as in κεφάλαιον 'beginning' for Hebrew *re'šit*, intended to display the connection with the word 'head' (Hebrew *ro'š*, Greek κεφαλή): here the sense 'beginning' is not natural to Greek. Thus semantically a word of Aquila's Greek often cannot be understood on one plane, as a word in the Greek language: rather, it has to be understood on two planes, firstly as an item with a sense in Greek and secondly as a coded representation of formal relations existing in the Hebrew original. Under the circumstances, it is remarkable that so much of his translation is intelligible at all; this is partly because the facts of language made it impossible to carry out his intentions with absolute rigour. Aquila's very strange Greek is thus in no way a result of poor knowledge of Greek on his part; it follows entirely from his translation technique, and his Greek, seen apart from that technique, was rather good and sophisticated. No Jews spoke Greek such as the translated books of the LXX evinced, still less did they speak like Aquila's version, nor did Aquila do so himself. There seems to be a connection between the name of Aquila and that of Onkelos, but the exact relation remains obscure. Another second-century translator, Symmachus, working at about the same time as Aquila, did not follow him in his literalism, and employed a rather elevated literary style in his Greek.

Thus the Hebraic aspect of LXX Greek derives, as we have emphasized, above all from the translation technique and the patterns of the original language. Jewish writers, when writing original compositions in Greek, that is, when not translating, wrote a general *koine* (or a literary Greek) and had none of the Hebraizing characteristics of the translations. In other words, there was not a 'Jewish Greek', a Greek with Semitic colouring which was normally spoken by Jews and was quite distinct from other varieties of *koine*. In the New Testament, though no Semitic text has survived, some part of the Hebrew and Aramaic colouring has come, again through translation technique, from originals in these languages, and much of the rest can well be accounted for as literary imitation of the style of the LXX itself: the LXX and especially its Pentateuch (which, it is thought, was taken as a model and lexical source by the translators of some later books) eventually created something approaching a literary sub-language.[1]

Thus Jewish usage made its mark on Greek in several different ways. There were loanwords adopted into the *koine* from Hebrew or Aramaic, like σάββατον 'sabbath, week'. There were also technical terms for essential institutions of Judaism. Some of these, though first found in the LXX, very probably existed in the working vocabulary of the religion before the actual translation of the Bible was made: so προσήλυτος 'proselyte', ἀκροβυστία 'uncircumcision'. Terms may be technical to Jewish Greek but not built upon Hebrew idiom: προσευχή as a house of prayer does not seem to rest on a Hebrew form in particular; there seems to be a clear pre-Jewish instance, and even if the connection of sense and form is Jewish the linguistic basis is Greek. Even if προσήλυτος and similar words are new coinages, in the sense that this precise form is found first in Jewish usage, the neologism is one built upon existing Greek morphemes, by accepted modes of Greek formation, and on established Greek analogies. There are extensions of meaning, the motive for the extension being provided by the Hebrew but the possibility being already present in the semantics of the Greek: for instance, the combination of πνεῦμα 'spirit' into a collocation like πνεῦμα τοῦ θεοῦ, to represent the Jewish religious concept known in Hebrew as *ruaḥ 'elohim*.[2]

Some shifts of this kind eventually affected the semantics of Greek as a whole, but often this was not until much later, that is, after the rise of Christianity had made these shifts more or less indigenous over the general body of Greek speakers, chronologically therefore in late Roman times.

Many other expressions were calques on Hebrew idiom, like ἄνθρωπος ἄνθρωπος for 'each man': this represented a Hebrew syntactic device, was dictated by translation technique and not adopted even in Jewish Greek usage; it never became indigenous or permanent in Greek. And even where we can see a change of sense in a Greek word, like δικαιοσύνη 'righteousness' or δόξα, which in much Greek usage

[1] See Brock, OTS 17 (1972), p. 36, and more generally pp. 31–6; for the existence of a 'Jewish Greek' see H. S. Gehman, 'The Hebraic character of Septuagint Greek', *VT*, 1 (1951), 81–90; more recently cf. D. Hill, *Greek Words and Hebrew Meanings* (Cambridge, 1976), pp. 16–18, and J. Barr, 'Common sense and Biblical language', *Bib*, 49 (1968), 379.

[2] Hill, *Greek Words*, p. 218; Barr, *Bib*, 49 (1968), 381.

meant 'opinion' but in the Greek Bible means 'glory' (for example, the 'glory' of God), this change of meaning cannot be attributed directly to the meaning of the Hebrew words translated, and this for an obvious reason: it was only the actual translators themselves, and not the Jewish Greek-speaking public, who were in real contact with the Hebrew original, and they only transitorily. Thus in so far as a translation like the LXX led eventually to shifts of meaning within Greek, this was only, and could be only, through the effect of the context and content of the Bible in its Greek form, through the syntactic and semantic chains perceptible within Greek in the newly-created Bible text.

In general, then, there were certain special words and special developments of meaning in areas of technical Jewish institution and practice; but this constitutes a distinct department within a language, rather than leading towards the idea of a Jewish form of the Greek language itself.

There were indeed Jews – as there were other non-Greeks – who were not good at Greek and whose competence in it was limited. In such cases we might have to ask about the effect of bilingualism or multilingualism. Josephus himself noted (*Ant.* xx.263) that his native language interfered with his pronunciation of Greek, and similar features may have been found in those with the same personal history; but this is a matter of 'accent' rather than of general command of the language. Such facts do not lead towards any idea of a *standard* of 'Jewish Greek'. The Greek and Latin of the Jews of Rome displays a wide variety of uneducated and erroneous misuses and miswritings, but these do not constitute a special Jewish group of features; rather, they show that the Roman Jews, who did not have enough history of Aramaic or Hebrew to interfere with their Greek or Latin, shared the general patterns of ill-educated users of Greek and Latin throughout the Mediterranean world.[1] Of the totality of Jewish literature in Greek, comparatively little suggests or demands interpretation in terms of bilingual interference in ordinary speech. Thus, in spite of Josephus' difficulties with Greek, there is little Hebraism or Aramaism to be discerned in his pages.[2] The main Jewish writers, as we have seen, were fluent in Greek; and the Hebraisms of the Bible translations derived not from the normal speech of the translators but from their translation technique. The situation was one in which many Jews were completely at home in the *koine* but certain individuals through

[1] Leon, *Jews*, p. 92 and pp. 75–92 generally.

[2] H. St J. Thackeray, *Josephus: the Man and the Historian* (New York 1929), p. 102, with reference to the *Bellum Judaicum*.

personal experience, or through social and religious changes, might find themselves speaking or writing a language in which they were not at home. Among texts known to us, perhaps the most likely cases for bilingual interference might be among those persons who through the religious upsets of the first century C.E. suddenly found themselves writing Christian literature in Greek.[1]

THE INTERRELATION OF HEBREW, ARAMAIC AND GREEK

In order to understand this period we have to free our minds from the picture of the linguistic situation in Jewry which became prevalent in later (Byzantine) times. Then Hebrew became firmly established as the language of liturgy (with some elements in Aramaic) over the entire Jewish world, while common life proceeded in the local language, whatever it was. Religious law and religious study involved some Hebrew and Aramaic. These languages were used by most people on a passive rather than an active basis: that is, there was a certain education in them and a certain knowledge of them, but the command of the languages was passive: people generally could understand what they had been specifically taught to understand, but they did not have the active productive capacity to generate new sentences in a language like Hebrew. Their productive capacity was in the vernacular, but Hebrew was entrenched in the religious core of the culture. But that situation, which in essence remained so down to the dawn of modern times, in Hellenistic times had not yet arrived. It was still not yet clear what the linguistic pattern for Judaism was to be. In particular, the relation to Hebrew was a free one and it was not clear that belonging to the Jewish people or to Judaism involved any living connection with Hebrew. Only after the historical development within our period had unrolled could it be seen that certain possibilities had been closed off and others opened up.

The rabbinic pronouncements about relations between the languages and Jewish practice mostly date from late in the Greco-Roman period (second century C.E.) and they do not give a correct impression of the situation in its fluid state as it was in (say) the second or first centuries B.C.E. or the first century C.E.; in other words, these pronouncements are in large measure a response to the language situation as it had

[1] The best study, well informed with modern linguistic method but confined to the Greek of one writer, the Christian author of the New Testament Book of Revelation, is that of G. Mussies, *The Morphology of Koine Greek as used in the Apocalypse of St John: a Study in Bilingualism*. NT Sup 27 (Leiden, 1971).

developed after the great wars with the Romans, and not a guide to the character of that situation as it had been before.[1]

At the beginning of the Hellenistic age, around 330, Aramaic was gaining ground; the basis for this lay not in the Babylonian Exile itself but in the importance of Aramaic in Persian imperial administration and the commercial contacts which went with it. Already before 400 there were substantial groups of Jews whose entire life was carried on in Aramaic.[2] But in Palestine, though Aramaic had made great inroads, Hebrew was still maintaining itself: it was still possible to write original literature in Late Biblical Hebrew, and it continued so down to the first century C.E. Meanwhile the colloquial form of Hebrew, the basis of Middle Hebrew, was also taking hold in certain quarters. There is at this time little evidence of sensitivity on the language issue, of value judgements between Hebrew and Aramaic, between classical and colloquial Hebrew; probably many did not perceive that the differences were substantial.

Hebrew might have suffered decline earlier but for the help it gained, paradoxically, from Greek. The arrival of Greek, and the total swing in the political balance that accompanied it, substantially reduced the value and attractiveness of Aramaic, especially from the viewpoint of social, cultural and commercial leadership. Even much later, when much of the farther East had been lost to the Greek empires and regained by the Parthians, Greek retained some importance there,[3] and the status of the indigenous Pahlavi limited the possibilities for a renascence of Aramaic. In the Western Diaspora Greek quickly became dominant in Jewish life and little sign remains of profound contact with Hebrew or Aramaic. Of the two, it is probable that Aramaic was much the more prevalent, the Jewish migrants having come from Aramaic-speaking previous homes. As we have seen, the great Alexandrian community lived entirely in Greek; there is no reason to believe that Hebrew found substantial use even in the synagogue service. The Eastern Diaspora, in Mesopotamia, remained as a reservoir of influence for Aramaic.

In Palestine also Greek made enormous headway, but it is clear that Semitic languages retained a strong hold. The distinctions commonly made, which aver that 'the upper classes' spoke this language, the

[1] Works like S. Lieberman's *Greek in Jewish Palestine* (Philadelphia, 1942), which draw basically upon these rabbinic pronouncements, are thus rather limited in value for an impression of the actual linguistic situation before the second century C.E.

[2] The statement occasionally made, that the Jews of Elephantine used Hebrew in their worship, rests on no evidence, cf. B. Porten, *Archives from Elephantine* (London, 1968), p. 33 n. 27.

[3] Debrunner, *Geschichte*, 2, p. 76, §121.

'lower' another, are much too simplistic to be of any use. Language competence probably varied with many variables: with social class, with occupation, with locality, with sex, with position in the family, with past personal history, travel and education; in other words, it varied almost personally, and wide generalizations cannot be made. Partly for this reason, and partly for lack of detailed knowledge, we cannot create an exact language map of Palestine in our period. Probably Greek was strong in Galilee and the North, and also in the coastal towns; but there is also adequate evidence for considerable knowledge of Greek in Judea; the Herodian families, after all, were completely Hellenized. Between the two Semitic languages, Aramaic and Hebrew, boundary lines are equally hard to draw; but most scholars seem to agree that Aramaic was strong in Galilee and the North generally, while the main concentrations of spoken Hebrew were in the Judean countryside; but no doubt there were pockets of Hebrew elsewhere, and a considerable representation of Aramaic even in the South.

There is no indication that the revolt against Hellenization under the Maccabees carried with it any explicit overtone of linguistic nationalism; on the contrary, the external and even the internal policies of the Hasmonean governments involved a continual use of Greek, and this is reflected in the histories of their times. It was, indeed, typical of the anti-Hellenic cultural reaction that it expressed itself linguistically in Greek: it is so with Josephus and other works of Jewish apologetic, and also in the Egyptian reaction as seen in the Hermetic documents, and in a Phoenician writer like Philo of Byblos.[1] For the first century C.E. the Gospels are an interesting document in this respect: they quote a few phrases in Aramaic (or in some cases perhaps in Hebrew) but they lay no emphasis on exact definition of the language used. But if the difference between Hebrew and Aramaic in this context carried no great cultural overtones, the difference between Greek and a Semitic language could be more significant: Paul of Tarsus, faced with an angry crowd in Jerusalem (Acts 22:2), is said to have got a good hearing when they discovered that his speech would be not in Greek but in the 'Hebrew' language (the use of Ἑβραϊστί or ἡ Ἑβραΐς διάλεκτος in the New Testament cannot securely be used to determine between Hebrew and Aramaic, since no term unequivocally meaning Aramaic is found there).[2]

[1] See J. Barr, 'Philo of Byblos and his "Phoenician History"', *BJRL*, 57 (1974–75), 17–68.

[2] Even for Josephus the argument of J. M. Grintz, 'Hebrew as the spoken and written language in the last days of the Second Temple', *JBL*, 79 (1960), 42–5, that these terms must mean Hebrew and not Aramaic in his usage, is not satisfactory.

In a person like Paul, though brought up in the Diaspora and writing an idiomatic *koine* Greek, the knowledge of Aramaic/Hebrew can be naturally related to his rabbinic training. Another personal history known to us is that of Josephus. A man of the Jerusalem priestly aristocracy, he had a thorough training in various types of Judaism; and at an early age he was sent on a mission to Rome, no doubt because of his knowledge of Greek,[1] and on a mission which he could not have performed well without that knowledge. But the first edition of his history of the Jewish wars was written in his 'ancestral' (πάτριος) language to be sent τοῖς ἄνω βαρβάροις 'to the up-country barbarians'; this phrase almost certainly fixes the language as Aramaic, since he probably has in mind the Aramaic-speaking peoples, especially the Jews, within the Parthian kingdom.[2] In spite of his long experience in intercourse with the Roman authorities, he still needed literary assistance with his works in Greek, and the rather simple and crude Greek of the *Life*, his latest work, written without such assistance, may be significant.

Many people, then, were bilingual or trilingual, and the whole linguistic situation of Palestine was characterized by this fact, which had its impact also on Jewry elsewhere in varying degrees. But that there could be a sort of occupational specialization of this or that language is clearly shown by the example of the rabbis themselves. It has been adequately shown that many rabbis knew some Greek, or even a lot of Greek, and could quote this word or that, this proverb or that. But this made no difference to the basic structure of their linguistic behaviour. No rabbi wrote texts in Greek: not necessarily because he could not but because the social definition of a rabbi, at least from the later first century C.E. onward, entailed the corollary that the basic work of such a man is done in a social group that works in Middle Hebrew, or (depending on place and time) in Aramaic. That this choice was practical and socially-based rather than ideological is shown by the ease with which the main rabbinic language switched in the end from Hebrew to Aramaic.

What finally changed the language situation was the wars with the Romans. The war of 66–70 C.E. had enormous effects in all spheres of Jewish life. Linguistically, the wars in Egypt and Cyrene in 115–117

1 See A. Schalit in *EncJud*, 10, col. 251. Thackeray, *Josephus*, p. 102, rather suggests that Josephus was almost devoid of Greek until his coming to Rome (i.e. after the war), but one cannot see how he could have done what he did on his earlier mission to Rome if he had not been able to speak reasonable Greek for practical communicative purposes; cf. Sevenster, *Do You Know Greek?*, pp. 61–76.

2 Schalit, *EncJud* 10, col. 254, rightly, as against Grintz, *JBL*, 79 (1960), 44.

C.E. brought about a greater change, for they destroyed, or at least brought to the beginning of a disastrous decline, those Jewish communities which had most prospered upon a linguistic basis of Greek. In Palestine, by 135 it would seem that the strongest outposts of spoken Hebrew were in Judea, and the destruction of the war was probably the main reason for the decline of colloquial Hebrew, the basis of Mishnaic; by the end of the century the centre of rabbinic activity in Palestine had moved to Galilee and the language of the entire surviving Jewish population of the country was Aramaic. Yet friendly relations with Greek continued to prevail right down into Byzantine times.[1]

[1] M. Avi-Yonah, *Geschichte der Juden im Zeitalter des Talmud*, Studia Judaica 2 (Berlin, 1962), pp. 71–4; ET *The Jews of Palestine* (Oxford 1976), pp. 72–4.

[Apart from minor alterations, this chapter was completed before the end of 1974.]

CHAPTER 4

THE DIASPORA IN THE HELLENISTIC AGE

POLITICAL HISTORY

THE BEGINNINGS: ALEXANDER THE GREAT

Alexander's breath-takingly rapid campaign of conquest, which in the space of a few years made him master of all the most important territories of the huge Persian empire, is commonly held to have ushered in a new historical era, the Hellenistic age. Though this accepted view has recently been hotly disputed, it is still in fact correct.[1] In this particular instance, what we see is not just the replacement of one ancient empire by another, but the introduction of something substantially new and different. Even though to begin with this transformation remained more of a vision than a reality and had not developed beyond the initial stages, the phenomenon is clearly recognizable: a community of nations inwardly united by the intellectual power of a transnational culture, the dawn of the Hellenistic era.

The origins of this development were not without paradox. To the Greeks proper, the Macedonians appeared a semi-barbaric people, for all that the ruling dynasty was acknowledged to be of Greek blood. Only by force of arms did King Philip of Macedonia prevail upon the Greek city states to unite in the Corinthian League (in 338 B.C.E., after his victory over them at Chaeronea). Only with reluctance did they accept him as their commander-in-chief and support his plans for a war of revenge against the Persians, which he saw as a means of forging national unity. When Philip was suddenly assassinated in 336 B.C.E.,

[1] For studies of Alexander, see J. Seibert, *Alexander der Grosse*, Erträge der Forschung, 10 (Darmstadt, 1972), a summary of recent scholarship. Also W. Tarn, *Alexander the Great* (2 vols, Cambridge, 1948; German transl. Darmstadt, 1963); R. L. Fox, *Alexander the Great* (London, 1973; German transl. Düsseldorf, 1974); F. Schachermeyr, *Alexander der Grosse. Das Problem seiner Persönlichkeit und seines Wirkens*, SAW, 285 (Vienna, 1973); M. Hengel, *Juden, Griechen und Barbaren. Aspekte der Hellenisierung des Judentums in vorchristlicher Zeit*, SBS 76 (Stuttgart, 1976), especially §§1, 6; ET *Jews, Greeks and Barbarians*, London 1980, esp. chs. 1 and 6. (Editors' note: most of the material referred to in this chapter in Hengel, *Juden*, also appears in chs. 2 and 5 of the present volume.)

this plan took on new dimensions. The place of the fiftyish Philip who had already attained the summit of his ambition, the unification of Greece, was taken by Alexander, thirty years his junior. Alexander had been given a Greek education and had been schooled in philosophy by his tutor Aristotle. He was surrounded by friends who shared his interest in philosophy, among them Theophrastus, later Aristotle's successor as head of the school. Alexander had made his mark as an energetic ruler and military leader at an early age: when he was only eighteen years old, he had held a command at the battle of Chaeronea. While his entourage consisted of young, ambitious comrades in arms, sons of the Macedonian nobility, he also cultivated the friendship of his father's veteran generals. He had at his disposal a superb force in the form of the Macedonian cavalry and infantry which had been built up by his father. First, in a series of brief, hard-fought and astute campaigns, he 'pacified' (as he regarded it) his northern neighbours and the Greek cities. Then in the spring of 334 he crossed the Dardanelles and embarked on the conquest of Asia Minor. The Persians were caught unprepared and Alexander defeated the Persian army on the Granikos in north-west Asia Minor; though numerically superior, the enemy had been hastily mobilized and were under poor leadership. Darius then mustered a great force but this too suffered defeat at Alexander's hands in a hard-fought battle near Issus on the Syrian border in 333 B.C.E. Before setting off in pursuit of the fleeing Persian king, Alexander first marched south. He seized the important coastal cities of Phoenicia, though it took seven months to capture Tyre and two months to capture Gaza. He thus defeated the Persian fleet without having to fight a single naval engagement, by the simple expedient of depriving it of its last and most important bases.[1] The Greek cities on the western seaboard of Asia Minor had surrendered to him mostly without a struggle, since he restored their erstwhile autonomy and democratic constitutions. This betokened far more than a policy of encouraging Greek nationalism, for even in the case of the Phoenician cities Alexander did not wish to appear as a conqueror.[2] True, he smashed any resistance with utter ruthlessness, but his intentions were different in character.

This emerged more clearly during his invasion of Egypt, whither he rapidly proceeded in the late autumn of 332, after entrusting the occupation of Syria to his generals. In Egypt he did not need to use force. The Persian satrap offered no resistance. The Egyptian leader-

[1] Tarn, *Alexander,* 1, p. 18; Schachermeyr, *Alexander*, pp. 281f.

[2] Tarn, *Alexander,* 1, pp. 31–3, 40f; Schachermeyr, *Alexander*, pp. 220, 258–60; Fox, *Alexander*, pp. 232–6.

ship hailed him as a liberator, the Egyptian priests in Memphis as a new pharaoh. Alexander visited the oracle and shrine of Amon in the oasis of Siwa, and there the priests addressed him by the ancient title of the pharaohs, 'son of Amon-Re'.[1] Alexander's motives and experiences during this expedition will never be completely elucidated.[2] In any case, we glimpse here aspirations which evidently transcend the limitations of power politics. The few short months of his stay in Egypt were enough to determine the whole of his future policy, and in consequence shaped the politics of this realm for centuries to come, in the sense that it was to be at once Hellenistic and Egyptian. Alexander treated the Egyptian gods with respect and sought the co-operation of Egyptian institutions.[3] Yet his rule was based on Macedonian and Greek elements in the population. Drawing on the support of the numerous Greeks who had already settled in Egypt, especially in the Nile delta, Alexander founded a Greek city on the west coast of the delta and named it after himself Alexandria. He obviously planned to make this city the new maritime, mercantile and cultural centre of the Eastern Mediterranean. He set up a mixed Greek–Egyptian administration in Egypt and left behind small garrisons of occupation forces under Macedonian commanders.[4] Then, in the spring of 331, he hastened back to Mesopotamia, where the struggle against the Persians still had to be decided. He defeated the Persian army for the third and final time on 1 October 331 B.C.E. at Gaugamela near Babylon. Babylon itself surrendered without resistance. In a bold, rapid thrust he occupied the heartland of the enemy, Persis, together with its royal capital Persepolis. With the destruction of Xerxes' palace the war of revenge waged by the Hellenic alliance came to an end and Alexander disbanded the troops of his Greek allies.[5] The next goal was to complete the conquest of the Persian empire. Media, along with Ecbatana, was occupied. In the summer of 330 Darius was assassinated by his own officers while fleeing from Alexander, and left no successor. Thereafter Alexander cast himself in the role of the new Great King of the Persians.[6]

1 Tarn, *Alexander,* 1, pp. 42–4; 2, p. 350.

2 Seibert, *Alexander*, pp. 116–25; Tarn, *Alexander,* 2, pp. 346–59; Schachermeyr, *Alexander*, pp. 242–56; Fox, *Alexander*, pp. 255–88.

3 Tarn, *Alexander,* 1, p. 44; Schachermeyr, *Alexander*, pp. 235–8.

4 Schachermeyr, *Alexander*, pp. 237–42.

5 On the subject of Alexander's motives for burning down the palaces, see Seibert, *Alexander*, pp. 132–4. His action probably had a symbolic meaning: Schachermeyr, *Alexander*, pp. 289f; Tarn, *Alexander,* 1, p. 53.

6 Tarn, *Alexander,* 1, p. 59; Schachermeyr, *Alexander*, pp. 321f; Fox, *Alexander*, pp. 371f.

Black Sea
MACEDONIA
BITHYNIA
PONTUS
R. Sangarius
R. Halys
Delphi
Corinth
Athens
Sparta
Paros
Magnesia
Sardis
PHRYGIA
LYDIA
Apamea
Hierapolis
CAPPADOCIA
Miletus
CARIA
Halicarnassus
PISIDIA
LYCIA
CILICIA
Iss
Tarsus
Antioch
Mediterranean Sea
CRETE
CYPRUS
Aradus
PHOENICIA
Cyrene
CYRENAICA
Damascus
Tyre
COEL
SYRI
Samaria
Mt Gerizim
Shech
Jerusalem
Gaza
PALESTINE
Alexandria
Migdol
Raphia
Leontopolis
Berenic
Petra
Memphis
FAYUM
Siwa Oasis
EGYPT
R Nile
Red Sea
Thebes
0
200 miles
0
300 km
Elephantine

Fig. 1

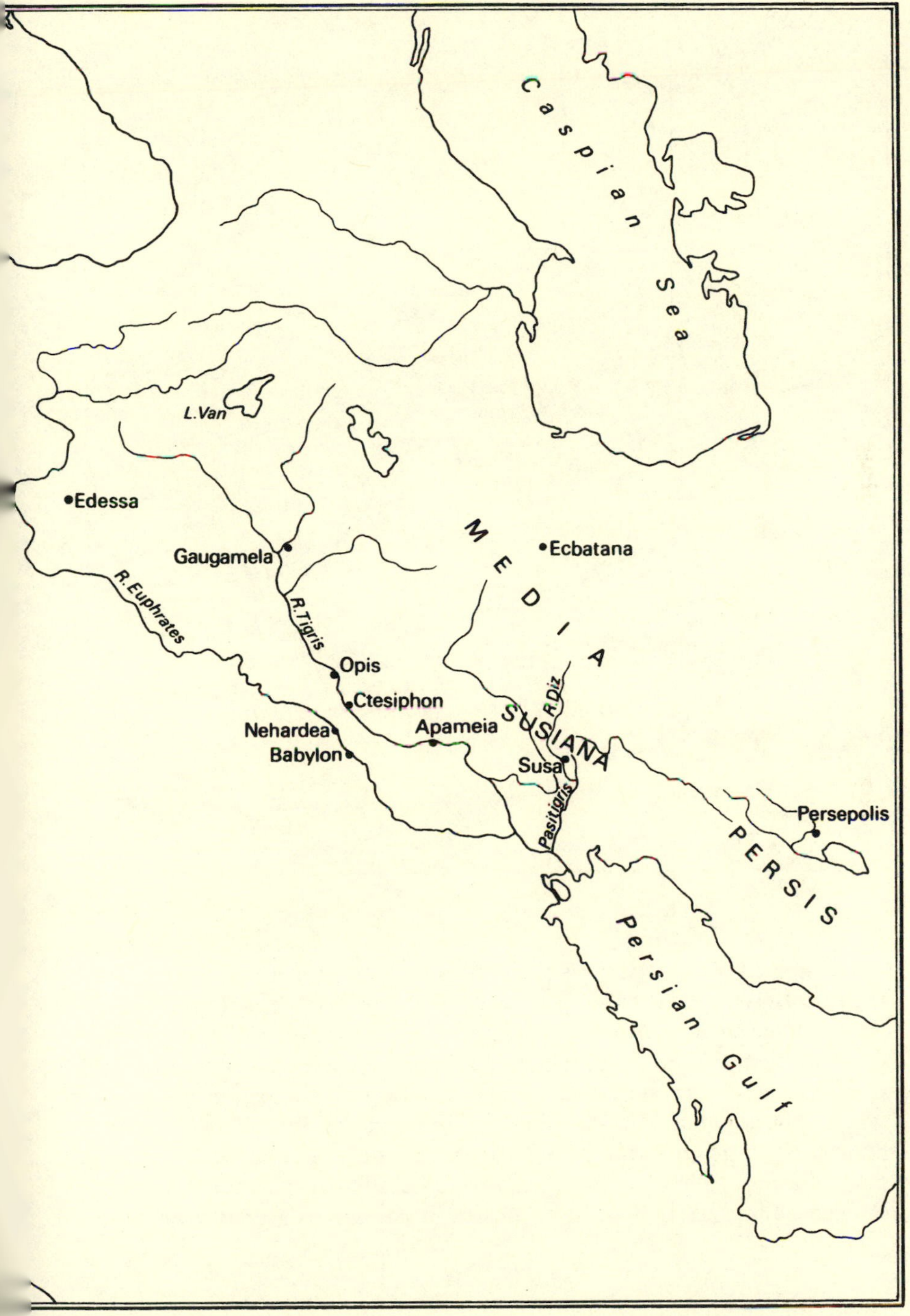
Caspian Sea
L. Van
Edessa
Gaugamela
R. Euphrates
R. Tigris
MEDIA
Ecbatana
Opis
Ctesiphon
Nehardea
Babylon
Apameia
SUSIANA
R. Diz
Susa
Pasitigris
Persepolis
PERSIS
Persian Gulf

Fig. 2 Alexandria in early Christian times.

He spent several laborious and dangerous years in the conquest of the eastern satrapies (330–325; he returned to Susa in the spring of 324). At the same time he made preparations to consolidate his hold on his enormous empire and to give it an appropriate political structure. It is clear that he deliberately chose to work through the existing framework. The kings of the Phoenician cities and the Jewish high priest continued to govern and the Persian administration was for the most part retained. What is more, Alexander obviously planned that the Persian ruling class should participate in the actual government and that Macedonians and Persians should be equal partners in the empire. In pursuit of this objective he made some dramatic gestures. His main opponent in the decisive battle at Gaugamela, Mazaios, former satrap of Syria, who had voluntarily surrendered to Alexander in Babylon, was made satrap of the city. Other satraps who yielded to him were allowed to remain in office. Alexander ordered 30,000 young Persians to be trained for his army and increasingly integrated Iranian cavalry units and archers with his own forces. Even his personal bodyguard opened its ranks to Persian noblemen. He married Roxana, the daughter of an Iranian prince, and forced all his friends along with the Macedonian officers and men to take Persian wives (a mass wedding took place in Susa in 324). He wanted to be king of both the Macedonians and the Persians in Persia.[1] He began to mint a single imperial coinage to replace the myriad local currencies. He constructed new harbours in order to open up better trading routes between the various parts of his empire. He founded many Hellenistic cities, especially in the east, in order to consolidate Hellenistic supremacy. But before such measures could get properly under way, he died unexpectedly on 10 July 323, barely 33 years of age.

Alexander does not seem to have had any close contact with Jews. At all events, there is no mention of it in the important ancient sources.[2] A number of Jewish traditions concerning Alexander need to be examined critically: (1) various reports of a confrontation between Alexander and the Jews in Palestine during his first visit to that land, at the time of the siege of Tyre and subsequently of Gaza in 332;[3] (2) Josephus' testimony that Jewish mercenaries fought with Alexander's auxiliary forces;[4] (3) another statement by Josephus to the effect that Alexander gave Jews equal rights as citizens with Greeks when he founded the city of Alexandria.[5]

Let us deal with this third contention first. There is a widespread consensus of opinion among scholars that Josephus is here acting as the spokesman of a Jewish apologetic fiction which first arose in the early

[1] Tarn, *Alexander,* 2, p. 444.

[2] On this point, see V. Tcherikover, *Hellenistic Civilization and the Jews* (Philadelphia, 1959), pp. 41f; a number of pieces of indirect evidence are discussed by Hengel, *Juden*, pp. 15f.; ET pp. 6f.

[3] Josephus, *Antiquitates Judaicae* XI.302–47; *Contra Apionem* II.43; *b. Yoma* 69a; *Megillat Ta'anit*, ed. Lichtenstein in *HUCA*, 8–9 (1931–32), 339; Tcherikover, *Civilization*, pp. 42–50; Hengel, *Juden*, pp. 15–22; ET pp. 6–10.

[4] Jos. *C.Ap.* I.192, 200; cf. *Ant.* XI.339.

[5] Jos. *Bell.* II.487; *C. Ap.* II.35.

Roman period.[1] It is certain that at that time Jewish circles in Alexandria had recently attempted to gain full citizenship. Claudius in his missive to the Alexandrians expressly commands the Jews 'not to strive constantly for more than they had enjoyed in the past...not to intrude themselves into the games held by the gymnasiarchs and *kosmētai*'.[2] But the Jews were in fact trying to defend themselves against a recent deterioration in their civic status which itself went back to the very origins of the city.[3] Josephus avers that Alexander himself bestowed upon them the title 'Macedonians' as a reward for the services of Jews in the war.[4] A privilege of this nature had probably been enjoyed by some of the Jews of Alexandria for a very long time, though it is open to doubt whether it originated with Alexander himself.[5] Moreover, in the light of reliable evidence that Jewish mercenaries served in Egypt both before and after the Persian conquest,[6] and thereafter under Alexander's successors, we can accept that Jews did indeed fight in Alexander's army too. The fact is, however, that this tells us little about Alexander's relationship with the Jewish people as a whole.

The story which Josephus relates in *Ant.* XI.304–45, indicates that this relationship initially fluctuated but was in the end friendly. This tells first of all of the dangerous tension that prevailed between Alexander and the Jewish high priest. The latter had refused to comply with Alexander's demand for auxiliaries and provisions, on the grounds of his oath of loyalty to Darius. The Samaritan governor, Sanballat, on the other hand, placed 8,000 soldiers at the disposal of the Macedonians. Consequently, after the fall of Gaza, Alexander advanced on Jerusalem to exact retribution. The danger was, however, miraculously averted. The appearance of the high priest reminded Alexander of a vision in which the God of the Jews had promised him that he would rule over Asia. He was also shown a prophecy concerning him in the book of Daniel. Now the second half of this story is clearly

[1] Tcherikover, *Civilization*, pp. 309–26; M. Hengel, *Judentum und Hellenismus*, WUNT 10. 2nd edn. Tübingen, 1973; ET 2 vols, London, 1974; p. 27 n. 82 (ET 2, p. 11 n. 85).

[2] *CPJ*, 2, pp. 36–55, no. 153, in the text p. 41, lines 89f., 92f.

[3] Philo, *Vit. M.*I.34f; *Leg.* 350; *CPJ*, 1, p. 63; Tcherikover, *Civilization*, pp. 315–17. See below, p. 161

[4] Jos. *Bell.* II.488.

[5] Tcherikover, *Civilization*, pp. 323f.

[6] Cf. the evidence of the papyri of Elephantine; E. Schürer, *Geschichte des jüdischen Volkes im Zeitalter Jesu Christi*, 3 (4th edn., Leipzig, 1909), pp. 24–33; Tcherikover, *Civilization*, pp. 269f; Pseudo-Aristeas 13 (Jewish soldiers serving under Psammetichus II, 594–589 B.C.E.); Deut. 17:16.

legendary, a noteworthy Hellenistic Jewish Alexander tradition;[1] interesting though it may be, the text cannot help us to establish the historical truth about Alexander's actions. But it is highly probable that the introductory section of the story, with its account of the differing attitudes of the Samaritans and the Jews towards Alexander, is based on historical fact. It is apparently contradicted by a report in Hecateus, again transmitted by Josephus, which states that Alexander in fact showed hostility to the Samaritans. However, this report must be viewed in connection with the new situation that arose when, as is reliably attested, the Samaritans rebelled against Alexander during his stay in Egypt; they seized the Macedonian governor of Samaria, Andrŏmachus, and burnt him alive. On his return from Egypt Alexander launched a punitive action, razed the city of Samaria and established a Macedonian military colony within its boundaries.[2]

A second report tells, again with legendary accretions, of a Jewish delegation that appeared before Alexander to pay homage to him after the fall of Gaza.[3] That something of the kind should have happened is of course historically quite plausible. The ruling class in Jerusalem doubtless soon abandoned their initial attempt to take a neutral position and tried to win Alexander's favour. By and large the picture is inconsistent, but probably the more historically correct for that. For, to begin with, the Jews had to take care not to antagonize the Persians – Alexander was not yet master of the Persian empire. It was some time before the outcome of the struggle became evident. Therefore it may be presumed that a Jewish delegation did indeed seek to make contact with Alexander even prior to his campaign in Egypt and tender the homage of the Jewish people. It is equally probable that Alexander assured the Jews on one such occasion that they could continue to live according to their traditional laws; this would have been consistent with the policy pursued by him elsewhere.[4] The defection of the Samaritans and the retribution visited upon the city have been confirmed by the discovery of new documents. Moreover, the excavations at Shechem have thrown light on the far-reaching consequences

[1] On this point see F. Pfister, *Eine jüdische Gründungsgeschichte Alexandrias. Mit einem Anhang über Alexanders Besuch in Jerusalem*, SAH, Philos.-hist. Kl., 1914, 11 (Heidelberg, 1914). However, an earlier dating is advisable, roughly contemporary with Ps. Hecateus, at the end of the second century B.C.E. Cf. R. Marcus, in *Josephus*, vol. 6 (Loeb Library, London, 1937), pp. 512–32; Tcherikover, *Civilization*, pp. 41–50; Seibert, *Alexander*, pp. 103–7.

[2] Jos. *Ant.* XI.344; Hengel, *Juden*, pp. 19–22; ET pp. 8–10.

[3] *Meg. Ta'anit*, ed. Lichtenstein, *HUCA*, 8–9 (1931–32), 339; Tcherikover, *Civilization*, p. 46.

[4] Cf. Jos. *Ant.* XI.338; XII.142, 150; Hengel, *Juden*, p. 19; ET p. 8.

of these events. It seems that at this time the former site of Shechem was resettled and the Samaritan temple erected at the foot of Mount Gerizim, symbolizing a rift between Samaritans and Jews which could no longer be healed.

Alexander's sudden death led to serious upheavals in Palestine; two decades of devastating warfare followed (323–301 B.C.E.). There is no need to set out here the details of the conflict between the 'satraps' of the various parts of the empire and Perdiccas, or of the quarrels that then ensued among the former.[1] Alexander's heirs soon had no alternative but to acknowledge the centrifugal tendency of their separate provinces. Ptolemy in particular had quickly started to pursue a definitely Egyptian policy in the Egyptian kingdom which fell to his lot. In the west he annexed Cyrenaica along with five ancient Greek cities; he occupied the southern areas along the Nile as far as the Nubian frontier; and he robustly asserted his sovereignty over the strategically important territory of Palestine. However, not until the final defeat and death of Antigonus in the battle of Ipsus were his efforts crowned with lasting success. In the partitioning of the empire which followed (in 301), Palestine was actually allotted to Seleucus. Ptolemy, who had withdrawn from the campaign against Antigonus and had thus missed the negotiations after the battle of Ipsus, refused to surrender the territory and stationed troops along its borders. Thus the Jewish homeland remained from 300 to 198 under Ptolemaic rule and was politically united with the Jewish Diaspora in Egypt throughout the third century, a factor which contributed decisively to the rapid rise of the Egyptian Jews.

What was Alexander's character and what sort of influence did he have? Was he simply a political and military genius who was retrospectively endowed with a divine mission to reconcile the nations and civilize the barbarians? The problems of the historical Alexander need not be examined here – only those issues associated with the image of Alexander that continued to exert an influence in history, though of course the two are closely intertwined. It is evident that the following centuries though of themselves very much an epoch under Alexander's influence, dynastically, politically, culturally and in religious terms. This notion strongly influences the nature of Hellenism, and so the

[1] Cf. Seibert, *Alexander*, pp. 157–7; E. Kornemann, *Weltgeschichte des Mittelmeerraumes, von Philipp II. von Makedonien bis Muhammed*, ed. H. Bengtson (Munich, 1967), vol. 1, pp. 160–88; Schachermeyr, *Alexander*, pp. 566–78.
For an examination of Alexander's posthumous influence, see Seibert, *Alexander*, pp. 217–19; M. P. Nilsson, *Geschichte der griechischen Religion*, vol. 2: *Die hellenistische und römische Zeit* (HAW, V. Abteilung, 2. Teil; 2nd edn., Munich, 1961), pp. 154–6.

history of Hellenistic Jewry, especially in the Diaspora, is in part conditioned by the interpretation of the figure of Alexander. When in the Hellenistic period Alexander became a symbol of the universal obligation to strive for *homonoia*, the concert of nations, this concerned the Hellenistic Jews as well. When Alexandrian Jews claimed that their civic rights originated with Alexander himself,[1] when the Jewish synagogues were dedicated to successors of Alexander,[2] when the Greek Bible was acquired for the *mouseion* at Alexandria,[3] these could not be merely tactical ploys to mask ambition for power and wealth: it must also have betokened a deeper conviction. The same thing was true when, 150 years after Alexander's death, Jewish Hellenists in Jerusalem proclaimed a programme of *homonoia* and to this end sought to establish a Hellenistic city in Jerusalem.[4] According to Martin Hengel, it was in fact Plutarch who first depicted Alexander as a civilizing and conciliatory force – inspired by the Stoic ideal of world-citizenship and in the context of a Roman world which was increasingly informed by a synthesis of eastern and western influences.[5] The presupposition for all this is the desire of the orientals for assimilation.[6] Hengel refers to the numerous pieces of evidence showing the continuing delimitation by Greeks of non-Greeks in the Hellenistic cities.[7] But should one not bear in mind here the cultural reinterpretation of the very concept 'Greek'?[8] Not only did this change underlie Alexander's whole policy; it was also given its ideological justification from within Alexander's immediate entourage. Theory and practice are both connected with a revised conception of *homonoia* as it affected the ruler, which again was developed in intellectual circles very close to Alexander. We shall now examine some of the main features of the historical image of Alexander from this point of view.[9]

(1) Alexander stood at the centre of a very interesting and lively philosophical debate which originated with his teacher Aristotle. The

[1] See above, pp. 121f.
[2] See below, pp. 151f.
[3] Ps.-Arist. 10f, 29–31, 38.
[4] 1 Macc. 1:11–14, 2 Macc. 4:7–15; behind the polemically slanted account we can discern a constructive programme.
[5] *Juden*, pp. 73–7; ET pp. 51–4, and frequently elsewhere.
[6] *Juden*, pp. 104f.; ET pp. 74f.
[7] *Juden*, pp. 77–90 *passim*; ET pp. 55–63.
[8] *Juden*, pp. 90–3; ET pp. 63–6.
[9] For what follows, see Tarn, *Alexander*, 2, pp. 399–449; Nilsson, *Religion*, 2, pp. 15f; F. Altheim, *Weltgeschichte Asiens im griechischen Zeitalter*, I (Halle, 1947), pp. 182–5, 193–201, 224f; Seibert, *Alexander*, pp. 186–92.

latter's disciple Theophrastus clearly took issue with his master over the crucial question of what the idea of *homonoia* should mean to a ruler. In Theophrastus we find a universalizing reinterpretation of the *homonoia* programme. This is paralleled in Alexander's political conduct. Isocrates had already developed an active political version of the *homonoia* idea and restricted this to the need to forge Greek national unity; he had imparted this to his pupil Philip of Macedonia.[1] The king, as a new Hercules, had the task of leading the Greeks out of a state of disunity and strife, to *homonoia* by means of a war against the Persians. Alexander took over this mission and strove to fulfil it. In doing so, however, he went against Isocrates' stated understanding and the view of his own teacher Aristotle,[2] in that he refused to treat the barbarians as born slaves or as born enemies. On the contrary he extended the *homonoia* mission of the ruler to encompass Persians and Eastern Iranians, and in a rather different sense even the Egyptians.

Theophrastus, like Alexander a pupil of Aristotle, formulated his new conception of the *homonoia* idea in his teaching of οἰκείωσις: all men are related to one another and bound together by φιλία through their common origin. It has been claimed that Thoephrastus derived his new conception from Alexander's new policy.[3] But this cannot be proved – indeed, it is untenable, since we know of two other instances of the new mode of thought which originated in Theophratus' immediate circle but which had definitely no connection with Alexander. The philologist and utopian thinker Alexarchos,[4] son of one of Alexander's generals called Antipater, founded his ideal city Ouranopolis, a 'miniature world state', which had Ouranos as its supreme deity and where all men were called 'children of heaven' and were brothers one of another. The second example is that of Euhemeros,[5] a friend of Cassander and Theophrastus. Euhemeros likewise made Heaven the supreme ruler who unites all mankind in a world-state, joined together by friendship (φιλία).

Thus alongside Alexander stand Theophrastus, Alexarchos and Euhemeros; each of them in his own way took the decisive step towards a vision of universal brotherhood for which the moment was opportune. It was to be further developed through the political legacy left by Alexander and the philosophical influence of Theophrastus and Euhemeros.

[1] Tarn, *Alexander,* 2, pp. 426–8.

[2] Ibid. 1, pp. 146f, 2, pp. 401f; pp. 436f; pp. 439f.

[3] Ibid. 2, pp. 426–8.

[4] Ibid. 2, pp. 429–34.

[5] Ibid. 2, p. 433.

(2) To begin with, Alexander articulated his new interpretation of the *homonoia* concept in his political praxis. There are however traditions which attest that he also couched this new ideal in words heavy with meaning. Though these traditions cannot easily be authenticated, we must not overlook their distinctive claims.[1]

According to Plutarch, an Egyptian philosopher called Psammon told Alexander in the oasis of Siwa that all men were ruled by God (πάντες οἱ ἄνθρωποι βασιλεύονται ὑπὸ θεοῦ); Alexander, yet more philosophically than his interlocutor, concluded that all men had a common father in God, but that the latter chose the best and made them peculiarly his own (ὡς πάντων μὲν ὄντα κοινὸν ἀνθρώπων πατέρα τὸν θεόν, ἰδίους δὲ ποιούμενον ἑαυτοῦ τοὺς ἀρίστους).[2] According to this tradition, then, Alexander without detriment to his own special relationship with the deity (which he enjoyed in common with other members of the élite) owned that all men were sons of God; compare the dream city of Alexarchos mentioned above. Plutarch's source cannot be reliably ascertained and the authenticity of the declaration attributed to Alexander cannot be proved;[3] yet the testimony is striking; and at the very least it shows that Alexander was being interpreted in this light at a very early stage.

A similar tradition concerns Alexander's great feast of reconciliation.[4] After putting down the mutiny in Opis Alexander gave a huge banquet. It ended with Alexander, surrounded by the dignitaries of the Macedonians, Greeks, Persians and other nations seated at his table, offering a prayer which Arrian summarizes in the words: 'He prayed however for general blessings and in particular for concord and partnership in government for both Macedonians and Persians' (εὔχετο δὲ τά τε ἄλλα ἀγαθὰ καὶ ὁμόνοιάν τε καὶ κοινωνίαν τῆς ἀρχῆς ... Μακεδόσι καὶ Πέρσαις).[5] ἀρχή may also mean the territory occupied by the two peoples.[6] Plutarch expands on this: 'his intention was to bring about for all men Homonoia and peace and partnership with one

[1] For a discussion of these, see Seibert, *Alexander*, pp. 186–92.

[2] Plutarch, *Alexander* 27; Tarn, *Alexander*, 2, pp. 435f.

[3] Tarn, *Alexander*, 2, p. 435.

[4] Ibid. 1, pp. 114–17; 2, pp. 434–99; Seibert, *Alexander*, p. 172; Schachermeyr, *Alexander*, pp. 492–500.

[5] Arrian, VII.11.9; Tarn, *Alexander*, 2, p. 443.

[6] Tarn, *Alexander*, 2, p. 444: 'and for partnership in the realm between Macedonians and Persians'. The textual interpretation favoured above substantiates Tarn's point more convincingly; it was precisely by accepting Persians into the ruling class that Alexander showed how deeply committed he was to this idea of partnership.

another' (κοινωνία).[1] Here is a second extremely significant scene involving the figure of Alexander; like the weddings in Susa, it expresses Alexander's *homonoia* programme, again supported by an ancient testimony concerning statements of Alexander. At an important point the tradition interprets Alexander's whole conduct explicitly as the fulfilment of a universal *homonoa* mission entrusted to him by God. Plutarch in the *Alexandri Fortuna* 1.6 cites Eratosthenes to the effect that Alexander, contrary to Aristotle's view, saw the real differences between men to lie not in their race or nationhood but in their moral natures; he believed 'that he had come from God as uniter and reconciler of the whole world (κοινὸς ἥκειν θεοθὲν ἁρμοστὴς καὶ διαλλακτὴς τῶν ὅλων), by bringing together peoples of diverse origin, by blending as though in a cup of friendship their lives and values and marriages and social manners (ὥσπερ ἐν κρατῆρι φιλοτησίῳ μίξας τοὺς βίους καὶ τὰ ἔθη καὶ τοὺς γάμους καὶ τὰς διαιτάς)'. Thus Alexander was taken at a very early stage to be aware of a divine mission to establish a world-wide *homonoia*, and his conduct – for example, the recruiting of Persians for his bodyguard,[2] the adoption of Persian
habits in his dress and court ceremonial,[3] or the marriages with Persian women[4] – was viewed in the light of this awareness. These pronouncements are cited in the oldest sources and even if they are not a verbatim record, they do in all probability convey Alexander's self-understanding accurately, at least as it was perceived by his friends and handed down by them as a solemn trust.

(3) Alexander's conduct clearly shows that he did not consistently pursue power-political aims. There is a strangely experimental quality about it. He tried to put *proskunēsis* into effect, met with resistance and promptly abandoned the attempt.[5] He began to install Persians as satraps, but on his return from India realized that this policy was proving an almost unmitigated disaster; he therefore revoked it, ordered executions to be carried out and installed Macedonians in office instead.[6] In Bactria he stubbornly clung to his faith in the loyalty of the conquered tribes, despite an increasing number of warning signs which pointed to the likelihood of a national uprising; when he finally reversed his policy, it was almost too late.[7] He then took ruthless, at

[1] *De Alexandri fortuna* 1.330E; Tarn, *Alexander*, 2, p. 443.
[2] Tarn, *Alexander*, 1, p. 111; Altheim, *Weltgeschichte*, 1, p. 201.
[3] Altheim, *Weltgeschichte*, 1, pp. 194–200; Schachermeyr, *Alexander*, pp. 321f.
[4] Tarn, *Alexander*, 1, p. 111; Altheim, *Weltgeschichte*, 1, pp. 199f.
[5] Tarn, *Alexander*, 1, p. 80.
[6] Ibid. 1, pp. 109f.
[7] Ibid. 1, pp. 69–71.

times even savage counter-measures. Yet when it was all over he resorted once again to his old policy of *rapprochement*. What we see here is not simply a volatile, tempestuous temperament or a political pragmatism responding merely to the demands of the hour.[1] Rather, his conduct reveals a quite consistent programme which was constantly disrupted or which suffered grave setbacks, usually through external forces. The objective itself agrees with the sense of mission ascribed to him. The courageous manner in which he reinstated his vanquished enemies in positions of power was not without method. If driven to it, he could be hard and relentless: one thinks of the razing of Thebes and the enslavement of all the survivors,[2] or of the destruction of Tyre and Gaza.[3] But on each occasion he returned forthwith to a programme of friendship, peace and reconstruction. No sooner had he laboriously accomplished the defeat of his mortal enemy in Bactria than he commanded Seleucus to marry his daughter. Alexander overcame the resistance of another stubborn opponent by himself becoming his son-in-law.[4]

Of course, it was Alexander's intimidating military power that made the greatest impression on his contemporaries, as is attested by the allusions to him in the book of Daniel and other sources.[5] Nevertheless, the fact is that as in the Roman period powerful political ambition and military ruthlessness went hand in hand with a determined search for peace and a sense of dedication to a humanizing cultural mission. Certainly, the educating of young non-Greeks in the Greek manner was carried out with a view to giving them proper military training; but at the same time it was a means of integrating them into a Hellenistic culture. Alexander's new cities and his Hellenization of native towns were designed to consolidate his political, economic and military hold over the subject peoples, yet at the time they were to serve as places 'to promote the fusion of Europe and Asia on a basis of Greek culture'. Thus Alexander began to unite the peoples of his empire into a great 'community of culture'.[6] In this he was guided by a sense of divine mission. He gave various tokens of his living faith in the gods.[7] He

[1] For a discussion of the problems raised by Alexander's personality, see Seibert, *Alexander*, pp. 24f, 183–211; Kornemann, *Weltgeschichte*, vol. 1, pp. 150–4; Schachermeyr, *Alexander*, pp. 579–97, 609–51.

[2] Tarn, *Alexander*, 1, pp. 7f.

[3] Ibid. 1, pp. 40f; 2, pp. 265–70.

[4] Ibid. 1, pp. 75f.

[5] Dan. 2:40–4; 7:7f, 23; 8:5–8, 21f; 11:3–4.

[6] Tarn, *Alexander*, 1, pp. 134, 138.

[7] Ibid. 2, pp. 354–6, 439, 447f, Nilsson, *Religion*, 2, pp. 12–14; Kornemann, *Weltgeschichte*, vol. 1, pp. 132f, 152; Schachermeyr, *Alexander*, pp. 244, 537, 562.

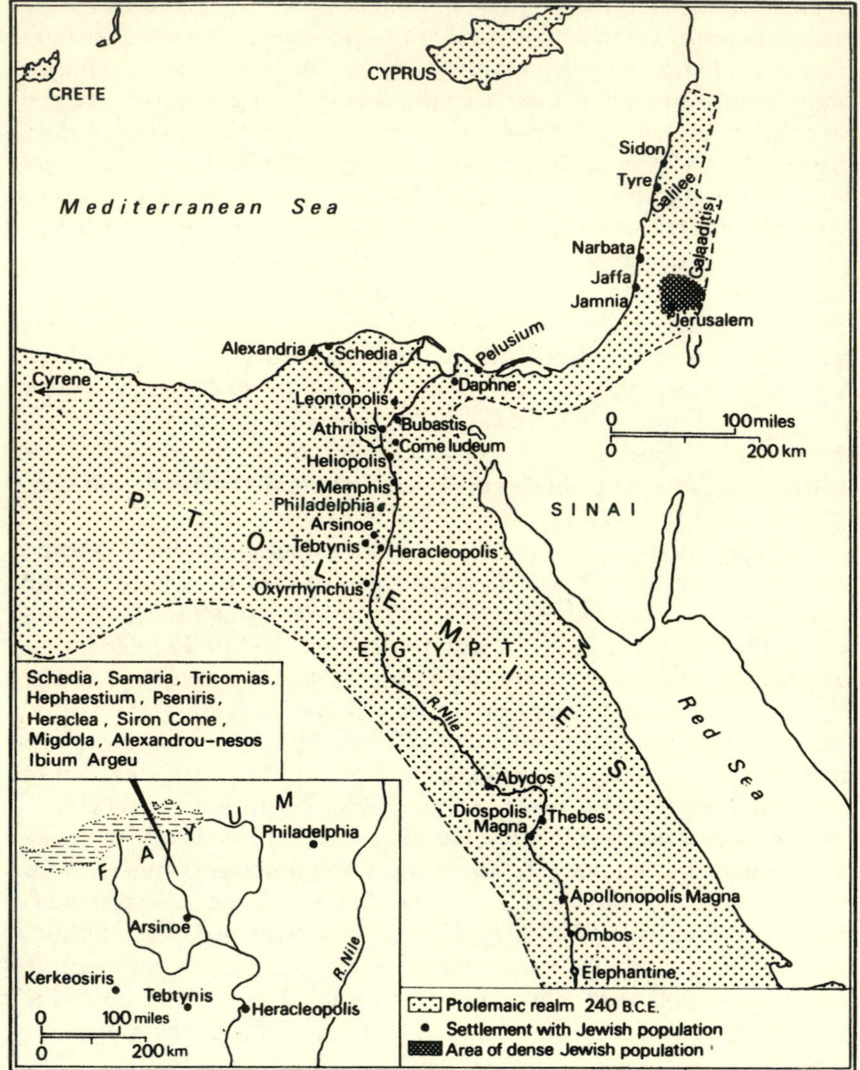

Fig. 3 The Jewish Diaspora in the Ptolemaic kingdom, 3rd to 1st centuries B.C.E.

believed in the significance of his descent from Hercules. He was assiduous in the observation of traditional religious rites and took cognizance of omens, as interpreted for him by seers who accompanied him on his campaigns. Thus too his visits to the oracles at Delphi and in the oasis of Siwa must be seen as having a serious religious motive.

At Siwa in particular his sense of mission appears to have been decisively strengthened. This then is the Alexander who made such an ineradicable impression on his contemporaries and on the following centuries, not least upon certain groups among Hellenistic Judaism who saw him almost as a new Cyrus.[1]

THE JEWISH DIASPORA IN PTOLEMAIC EGYPT

The history of the Jewish Diaspora in the post-Alexander period can in this period be illuminated only with reference to Egypt (and even then not with complete clarity). We shall therefore examine this area in more detail.

The Jewish Diaspora in Egypt was already several centuries old. It was as old as that of the East, but not until the early Hellenistic period did it achieve comparable importance. Thereafter in fact its significance even outstripped that of its counterpart. The meagreness of the sources prevents us from tracing its development in detail, but the main features are discernible. We see that Jews increasingly met with a friendly reception in the land of the Ptolemies as its political and economic power expanded apace.

Our earliest accounts are admittedly ambiguous. On the one hand, Josephus transmits the statement by Hecateus[2] that after the temporary victory of Ptolemy at Gaza in 312 many inhabitants of Syria decided in view of his 'generosity and humanity...to travel to Egypt with him and participate in (his) affairs'. Among them was a high priest called Ezekias, a highly respected man some 66 years of age. The *émigrés* were of course at the same time seeking refuge in the security of Egypt from the impending counter-offensive by Antigonus. A short time later[3] the same source relates: 'After Alexander's death...considerable numbers of people migrated to Egypt and Phoenicia on account of the troubled times.' These reports sound reliable even if the texts themselves are of dubious authenticity. There was indeed a high priest by the name of Ezekias (Hezekiah) at this time.[4] The attraction of Ptolemy was not his warm character but his political friendliness towards his Jewish sympathizers. This in turn resulted from his long-term ambition to bring the Jewish nation and homeland under his sway. In these

1 Cf. Isa. 45:1. See above pp. 122f.

2 Jos. *C.Ap.* 1.186–9.

3 Jos. *C.Ap.* 1.194.

4 Tcherikover, *Civilization*. pp. 56, 273, 300; Hengel, *Juden*, pp. 31f, 123f.; ET pp. 17f, 90f. N. Walter, ed., *Fragmente jüdisch-hellenistischer Historiker*, Jüdische Schriften aus hellenistisch-römischer Zeit 1, 2 (Gütersloh, 1976), pp. 146f, is too cautious.

circumstances a legitimate candidate for the office of high priest in Jerusalem was especially valuable to Ptolemy. He doubtless offered the Jews favourable terms to settle in his realm and perhaps also accepted the services of Jewish auxiliaries. On the other hand, however, we read in the letter of Pseudo-Aristeas[1] that, in the course of a campaign in Coele-Syria and Phoenicia, Ptolemy deported a large number of Jews to Egypt, the majority of them as slaves. The contradiction between these two sources may be resolved if we assume that in the first instance the Jews in question were supporters of Ptolemy, whereas in the second instance the reference is to Jews who had opposed him and been defeated. It is clear that on his third campaign in Syria in 302/301 Ptolemy was compelled to use force for the most part to subjugate territory occupied by the Jews: Jewish auxiliaries fought on the side of his enemy Antigonus, and the Jewish population offered active resistance.[2] They had come to terms with the rule of the Antigonids after so many years. But the inhabitants of Jerusalem itself seem as before to have included many who sympathized with Ptolemy, since the city opened its gates to him voluntarily.[3] The way the report in Pseudo-Aristeas is couched suggests the possibility that in 301 Ptolemy transported not only captives but also large numbers of his Jewish supporters to Egypt, in order to resettle them as military colonists and thus reinforce the defences of his realm.[4] Jewish military colonists had played their part in Egypt even before the time of Alexander, as Pseudo-Aristeas informs us.[5] Clearly the older Jewish colonies continued to exist into the early Hellenistic period. An Aramaic papyrus records that in about 310 B.C.E. there were ten Jewish settlements in the area between Migdol in the north-eastern corner of Egypt and the southern frontier at Syene (Assuan or Elephantine).[6] The Ptolemaic kings built on and extended this Egyptian–Jewish military tradition.

1 Ps-Arist. 12–14.

2 See Jos. *C.Ap.* 1.208–11; *Ant.* XII.5f; Tcherikover, *Civilization*, p. 56; Hengel, *Juden*, pp. 33f.; ET p. 19.

3 This is the probable historical background to the report of Agatharchides; the Sabbath motif attributes to the early Hellenistic period what was in fact the fruit of a later experience.

4 Selected prisoners of war were also resettled as military colonists, though not with the status of slaves, cf. Ps.-Arist. 14; Hengel, *Juden*, pp. 33, 117, 120f.; ET pp. 19, 85, 88f.

5 Ps.-Arist. 13.

6 Cf. P. Cowley 81 in A. Cowley, *Aramaic Papyri of the Fifth Century B.C.* (Oxford, 1923), pp. 190–9. See also J. Harmatta, 'Irano-Aramaica (Zur Geschichte des frühhellenistischen Judentums in Ägypten)', *Acta Antiqua*, 7 (1959), 339–40; Hengel, *Hellenismus*, p. 28 (ET 1, p. 16); *Juden*, pp. 116f.; ET pp. 85f.

On the whole the position of the Jews under Ptolemy I seems to have been quite favourable – not least because the leading Jewish families soon showed themselves receptive to the appeal of Hellenism, doubtless for more than just material advantage. For the first Ptolemy energetically pursued a policy of Hellenization, diligently following in Alexander's footsteps.[1] Besides being a hard-headed political leader, he was in the last analysis guided by the desire to realize Alexander's vision of a commonwealth of nations, tailored to the demands of the situation prevailing in Egypt. Thus he strengthened the role of Alexandria as the centre of Hellenistic culture by attracting Greek luminaries such as Demetrius of Phaleron to his court and paving the way for the subsequent establishment of the famous *mouseion* under his successor.[2] Alexandria's renown during the next few centuries as a metropolis of learning was begun by Ptolemy I. Not only did he choose the Greek city of Alexandria as his new seat of government: he also introduced the cult of Sarapis that united Greeks and Egyptians.[3] Both these measures were born 'of the spirit of Alexander'.[4]

In the reign of the second Ptolemy the importance and influence of the Jewish element in Egypt increased noticeably, while at the same time the broad mass of Jewish settlers rapidly became imbued with the Hellenistic spirit.[5] Evidence of this can be seen in the following developments: (1) the freeing of Jewish slaves under Ptolemy II; (2) the translation of the Pentateuch into Greek; (3) the acquisition of Greek names by Jews during this period; (4) references to Jewish Hellenists in non-Jewish sources of the period.

The details given in Pseudo-Aristeas 12–13, 22–6 about Ptolemy II's freeing of the slaves were usually dismissed without further ado by earlier scholars.[6] Nowadays, however, they are widely believed to be true.[7] It has been plausibly argued that the decree reproduced in

[1] Altheim, *Weltgeschichte,* 1, pp. 224–6.

[2] See Kornemann, *Weltgeschichte*, vol. 1, pp. 196–205; H. Bengtson, *Herrschergestalten des Hellenismus* (Munich, 1975), pp. 27–30. W. Schubart, 'Alexandria', *RAC,* 1 (1950), cols. 271–83; E. A. Parsons, *The Alexandrian Library* (Amsterdam–London, 1952); N. Walter, *Der Thoraausleger Aristobulos*, TU, 86 (Berlin, 1964), p. 41 n. 2.

[3] Altheim, *Weltgeschichte,* 1, pp. 224–8; Nilsson, *Religion,* 2, pp. 156–8; L. Vidmann, *Isis und Sarapis bei den Griechen und Römern*, RGVV 29 (Berlin, 1970), pp. 17–47.

[4] Altheim, *Weltgeschichte,* 1, p. 226.

[5] Kornemann, *Weltgeschichte*, vol. 1, pp. 196–210; Bengtson, *Herrschergestalten*, pp. 111–38.

[6] On the discussion, see A.-M. Denis, *Introduction aux Pseudépigraphes Grecs d'Ancien Testament* (Leiden, 1970), pp. 105–10; Hengel, *Hellenismus*, pp. 55f n. 198 (ET 2, p. 23 n. 206); Tcherikover, *Civilization*, pp. 272–4, 496f.

[7] Tcherikover, *Civilization*, pp. 272–4; Hengel, *Juden*, pp. 33, 117; ET pp. 19, 85.

Pseudo-Aristeas is based on an authentic document with certain unmistakable pro-Jewish revisions.[1] The reported purchase price of twenty drachmas can be verified from contemporary documents.[2] Admittedly, the numbers quoted by Pseudo-Aristeas are exaggerated, but a not inconsiderable number must have been affected by this action, which eloquently attests the political influence of the Jews in Egypt and their friendly relations with the royal house.

The translation of the Pentateuch into Greek, which is known as the translation of 'the seventy', was undertaken in the reign of Ptolemy II, according to Pseudo-Aristeas. The problems surrounding the origins of the Septuagint are discussed elsewhere.[3] When we seek answers to these questions, the details given in the letter of Pseudo-Aristeas must be treated with caution. However, the evidence of Pseudo-Aristeas does serve to support an early dating for the compilation of the Septuagint (Pentateuch). It seems to me unlikely that the letter of Pseudo-Aristeas, which was written at some point during the second century,[4] could have been composed in support of the introduction of a new, authorized translation.[5] The history of the origins of the Septuagint is used by the author simply to illustrate the philosophical standing of the Jews and to confute their detractors. To this end he doubtless had recourse for the most part to familiar material. The period in which he claims it was written, the first half of the third century, is readily compatible with other historical evidence.[6] Recent scholarship rightly considers it possible that Ptolemy II encouraged the idea of a translation and that it was acquired for the *mouseion*.[7] This would demonstrate a notably open attitude towards the Jews. Nor can there be any doubt that the authorities in Jerusalem co-operated in the production and introduction of the Septuagint among the Egyptian Jews.[8] This translation by its very nature is a profession of faith in the truth of the sacred tradition of Judaism, especially in the oldest parts in the Pentateuch. The actual task of translation was probably executed by

[1] Tcherikover, *Civilization*, pp. 274, 498.

[2] Ibid. p. 496.

[3] See below, ch. 15.

[4] On this question of the dating, see Denis, *Introduction*, p. 110; Hengel, *Hellenismus*, pp. 55f n. 198 (ET 2, p. 23 n. 206); N. Meisner, ed., *Aristeasbrief*, Jüdische Schriften aus hellenistisch-römischer Zeit 2, 1 (Gütersloh, 1973), pp. 37–43.

[5] See P. Kahle, *The Cairo Geniza* (2nd edn., Oxford, 1959), pp. 209–14; O. Eissfeldt, *Einleitung in das Alte Testament* (3rd edn., Tübingen, 1964), p. 820, ET p. 605; Meisner, *Aristeasbrief*, pp. 38, 41f.

[6] Cf. the spread of the Greek language among the Egyptian Jews at this time. *CPJ*, 1, pp. 30–2; Tcherikover, *Civilization*, p. 348; Hengel, *Juden*, pp. 127f.; ET pp. 93f.

[7] Hengel, *Juden*, pp. 128f; ET pp. 93f.

[8] Hengel, *Juden*, pp. 131f; ET pp. 95f.

the leading Jews of Alexandria itself, perhaps indeed by a specially commissioned team established on the island of Pharos.[1] From this we may infer that even at this early stage leading orthodox Jews in Alexandria were well versed in the Greek language and culture. The introduction of Greek Bible texts for the use of Jewish congregations shows too the degree of Hellenization which the broad mass of Egyptian Jews had already undergone – a process which was of course given a fresh and decisive impetus by the new translation.

Important confirmation of this view may be derived from the prosopography of this period.[2] Whereas in about 310 B.C.E., in papyrus no. 81 of the Cowley edition, only one Jew bears a Greek name, the papyri of the third century begin to reveal a majority of Jews with Greek names. This is not the case with lower class Jews: there we find mostly Hebrew or even Egyptian names.[3] Significantly the Hellenized Egyptian Jews preferred theophorous Greek names, which they substituted for Hebrew names of a confessional character, for example Theodotos (for Yehonathan) or Dositheos (for Matathyahu).[4] It was still possible that a Jew bearing a name of this kind might in fact become an apostate from the faith of his fathers in order to further his career at court (see below, p. 139, the instance of Dositheos, son of Drimylos).

Finally, it is significant that precisely in this early Hellenistic period Gentile writers judge the Jews to be true Greeks and a nation of philosophers. Thus Clearchus of Soli, a pupil of Aristotle, invents a meeting between his master and a Jewish sage who surpasses him in wisdom; he characterizes the Jew as follows, 'He was a Greek not only in his language but also in his soul.' This judgement is extended in the same context to the whole of the Jewish people: he considers them all to be 'descendants of the philosophers of India' and holds them to be the philosophers among the Syrians.[5] A similar estimation can be found shortly after in Megasthenes.[6] More important, however, is the

1 Ps.-Arist. 301.

2 *CPJ*, 3, pp. 167–96; cf. 1, pp. 27–30; Tcherikover, *Civilization*, p. 346; Hengel, *Hellenismus*, pp. 117f (ET 1, p. 63).

3 A slave with an Egyptian name: *CPJ*, 1, no. 9; peasant farmers and wine growers who leased their vineyards: *CPJ*, 1, nos. 13, 14. Cf. *CPJ*, 1, pp. 43f.

4 *CPJ*, 1, p. 29.

5 In Josephus, *C.Ap.* 1.176–82, esp. 179f; Hengel, *Hellenismus*, pp. 467f (ET 1, p. 257); M. Stern, *Greek and Latin Authors on Jews and Judaism*, vol. 1: *From Herodotus to Plutarch* (Jerusalem, 1974), pp. 49–52.

6 Clemens Alexandrinus, *Stromateis* 1.725. F. Jacoby, ed., *Die Fragmente der Griechischen Historiker* (Leiden, 1935ff), 737 F 8; cf. Hengel, *Hellenismus*, p. 467 (ET 1, pp. 256f); Stern, *Authors*, p. 46.

detailed testimony of Hecateus of Abdera, which was based on first-hand knowledge and included in his book on Egypt, written about 300 B.C.E.[1] Hecateus, working from his knowledge of contemporary Jewish political life where the high priest was the acknowledged leader of the people, presented the Jewish state established by Moses after the Exodus as the perfect realization of the Hellenistic model of the state. In addition, Hecateus provided an unreservedly approving account of Jewish monotheism,[2] such as we also encounter in Theophrastus,[3] to whom several references have already been made. Clearly this represents the influence of Aristotle's philosophical monotheism to which subsequently Hellenistic Jewish philosophers in their turn often hark back.[4] In the second half of the third century Hermippus' testimony is to be added.[5]

These early testimonies to the existence of a truly Hellenistic Jewish population are the more remarkable if they are viewed in conjunction with the continuing fidelity to traditional Judaism which finds expression, for example, in the translation of the Pentateuch into Greek.

It is against this background that we must evaluate the subsequent movement for reform among Jewish Hellenists in Jerusalem.[6] After the failure of this endeavour and after the Maccabees had adopted a critical attitude towards Hellenism, opinions about the Jews underwent a radical change[7] – because, in Posidonius' view, they had abandoned the faith of Moses in favour of superstition, ritualism and political ambition.[8] Yet we should not overlook the fact that certain aspects of the Jewish religion were already felt to give offence even in the early Hellenistic period. The relationship with Judaism was never entirely free from friction and contained latent dangers of one kind or another. Already in the reign of Ptolemy II, Manetho wrote about the Jews in an extremely hostile fashion;[9] in his history of Egypt he offered a counter-

[1] Jacoby, *FGrHist*, 264 F 6 = Diodorus XL.3; cf. Hengel, *Hellenismus*, pp. 465f (ET 1, pp. 255f); Stern, *Authors*, pp. 26–35.

[2] Stern, *Authors*, p. 26, lines 20–3.

[3] Jacoby, *FGrHist*, 737 F 6; Hengel, *Hellenismus*, p. 466 (ET 1, p. 256); Stern, *Authors*, pp. 10–12.

[4] Cf. Ps.-Arist. 15–16; Nilsson, *Religion*, 2, pp. 569; Hengel, *Hellenismus*, pp. 466, 475f (ET 1, pp. 256, 261f); *Juden*, p. 132; ET p. 96.

[5] In Jos. *C.Ap.* 1.162–5; Stern, *Authors*, pp. 95f.

[6] Cf. Hengel, *Hellenismus*, pp. 532–54 (ET 1, pp. 292–303) who there develops arguments first advanced by Bickerman. There is further corroboration in the echoes of the *homonoia* idea to be found in Philo, for example, *Virt.* 119f; *Praem.* 97.

[7] Hengel, *Hellenismus*, p. 469 (ET 1, p. 258).

[8] In Strabo, *Geographica* XVI.2.43 (C 764); Stern, *Authors*, 1, p. 295, lines 40–50. Cf. Hengel, *Hellenismus*, pp. 469–71 (ET 1, pp. 258–60).

[9] In Jos. *C.Ap.* 1.73–91, 93–105, 228–52; Stern, *Authors*, 1, pp. 62–86.

account as it were to the Exodus story as related in the Septuagint, drawing on stories already current in Egypt. These were at first a specifically Egyptian creation, but fell on fruitful soil elsewhere as well.[1] The history of the Jews in Egypt proceeded to develop along similar lines under the later Ptolemaic rulers. Numerous papyri,[2] ostraca[3] and inscriptions[4] attest the steady expansion of the Jewish community in Egypt. Towards the end of the third century the Jewish historian Demetrius became the first of a number of Hellenistic Jewish writers whose work, though preserved only in fragments, illuminates their ever-increasing assimilation to Hellenistic language and culture.[5]

The earliest surviving inscriptions from Jewish houses of prayer (*proseuchai*) date back to the reign of Ptolemy III Euergetes.[6] The fact that they bear a dedication to the ruling monarchs and that conversely Jewish houses of prayer enjoyed rights of sanctuary similar to those of classical temples, shows the good relations that obtained between the congregations and the ruler.[7] Two sets of sources merit particular attention – the Zenon papyri[8] and the story of the Tobiads,[9] both primarily of relevance to the Jewish homeland. Yet the situation in the Egyptian Diaspora too is illuminated by them: witness the close ties, indeed the firm economic integration, of Palestine with the Ptolemaic kingdom ruled from Alexandria, and the friendly relations which existed between the royal court and the leaders of the Jewish community.

In 259 B.C.E., in the twenty-seventh year of Ptolemy II's reign,

[1] Cf. the anti-Jewish remarks in Apollonios Molon, Lysimachos, Apion, Chairemon (Stern, *Authors,* 1, pp. 148–56, 382–8, 389–416, 417–21), even in Tacitus (*Histories* V.3–5).

[2] *CPJ,* 1, pp. 113–93, 227–56.

[3] *CPJ,* 1, pp. 194–226; additions in L. A. Geraty, *Third Century B.C. Ostraca from Khirbet el Kom* (Phil. Diss. Harvard Divinity School, 1972).

[4] *CPJ,* 3, pp. 138–66, in particular pp. 138–43.

[5] A.-M. Denis, *Fragmenta Pseudepigraphorum quae supersunt Graeca una cum historicorum et auctorum Iudaeorum hellenistarum fragmentis*, PVTG 3 b (Leiden, 1970), pp. 175ff. See also Hengel, *Juden*, pp. 134–41; ET pp. 97–101.

[6] *CPJ,* 3, p. 141, no. 1440; p. 164, no. 1532 A.

[7] *CPJ,* 3, p. 144, no. 1449.

[8] *CPJ,* 1, pp. 115–46. cf. Tcherikover, *Civilization*, pp. 60–72; Hengel, *Hellenismus*, pp. 10, 38f, 76–84, 92f, 486–8 (ET 17, 21f, 39–43, 47f, 267f); *Juden*, pp. 38–41, 45; ET pp. 23–5, 27.

[9] Jos. *Ant.* XII.154–222, 224, 228–36; *CPJ,* 1, pp. 115–29, nos. 1, 2b, c, d, 4, 5; cf. J. Goldstein, 'The Tales of the Tobiads', *Christianity, Judaism and other Greco-Roman Cults*, Studies for Morton Smith at Sixty, ed. J. Neusner, SJLA 12 (Leiden, 1975), part three: *Judaism before 70*, pp. 85–123; Tcherikover, *Civilization*, pp. 60ff, 126–42; Hengel, *Hellenismus*, pp. 51f, 489–503 (ET 1, pp. 27f, 268–77); *Juden*, pp. 48–50; ET pp. 29–32.

Zenon, a chief official of the finance minister Apollonius in Alexandria, journeyed throughout Palestine, inspecting at his lord's behest economic enterprises and government officials, strengthening commercial links and forging new ones, and in general seeking ways of increasing the economic exploitation of this province by the royal court at Alexandria. This tour, and the correspondence engendered by it, have left their mark in numerous documents in Zenon's archive. From these numerous documents we get a vivid impression of the zeal with which the Alexandrian court administered the Jewish homeland and fostered its economic development for their own purposes. At the same time we meet a representative of the Jewish upper class who aided them in their efforts, the Jewish landowner Tobias from Eastern Jordan, whose name occurs six times in the Zenon papyri.[1] Josephus recounts the story of this man's family.[2] His two letters to Apollonius show Tobias as a self-confident partner, a man who regarded himself as the minister's equal and who was fully conversant with Hellenistic social and linguistic conventions. He also maintained a friendly though respectful relationship with the king himself, as is revealed by the letter he wrote to accompany a number of precious gifts to the ruler.[3] Tobias was in command of a contingent of Ptolemaic military colonists on the Nabatean border.[4] A brother-in-law of the ruling high priest, Onias II, and the scion of an old, respected family, he was probably the second most important man in the Jewish nation after the high priest.[5] His son Joseph and his grandson Hyrcanus occupied positions of the highest authority under the two succeeding Ptolemies.[6]

Soon after his journey to Palestine, Zenon left the court to take up an important post in the Fayum.[7] His archive furnishes a second, very different set of insights into Jewish life at that time, deriving from his activities in his new office. The Jews whom he now had to deal with were not those at court, nor the relatively prosperous Jewish military colonists, but poor peasants, a shepherd, two leasers of vineyards, and other such people. Clearly in Ptolemaic Egypt Jews were to be found in the lower social strata as well.[8] For Jews of this kind it was essential to

[1] *CPJ*, I, pp. 115f.

[2] Jos. *Ant.* XII.154–236.

[3] *CPJ*, I, nos. 4, 5.

[4] *CPJ*, I, pp. 116f; Tcherikover, *Civilization*, p. 64; Hengel, *Hellenismus*, p. 487 (ET I, p. 267).

[5] Hengel, *Hellenismus*, p. 487 (ET I, p. 267).

[6] For Joseph, see Jos. *Ant.* XII.157–84 (chief tax farmer and *prostatēs* of the Jews); for Hyrcanus and his brothers: *Ant.* XII.186–222, 228–36.

[7] *CPJ*, I, p. 131.

[8] *CPJ*, I, pp. 131–46: Jews of the Fayum.

gain access to the Greek language and culture, if they were not to be swallowed up among the Egyptian peasantry.[1] On the other hand, wholehearted Hellenization inevitably led to the renunciation of Judaism. Even in the case of Tobias and Joseph we can discern signs of a perilous dilution of their Jewish identity.[2] Dositheos, the son of Drimylos, pursued this course consistently. In about 240 B.C.E. he held one of the highest administrative offices. By 222 B.C.E. he appears in documents from the Fayum as chief priest of an Egyptian cult, as a priest of the apotheosized Alexander and the deified Ptolemaic kings.[3]

At this time radical changes occurred in the political sphere.[4] On the one hand, Ptolemaic sovereignty over the Jewish homeland, in which the Seleucids had never really acquiesced, was finally forfeited to the Seleucids under Ptolemy IV and his successor. In the battle of Raphia in 217 B.C.E. Ptolemy IV Philopator managed in dramatic circumstances to defeat the young, energetic Antiochus III. An attempt on his life was foiled by Dositheos, the son of Drimylos,[5] and he owed his victory to the Egyptian infantry, a group recently admitted into his army.[6] Yet he failed to make the most of this opportunity to consolidate his rule by military means. Increasingly too he faced difficulties with his Egyptian subjects who, once they had secured a place in the king's army, began to rebel against their growing economic exploitation and the harsh alien rule of the governing Greeks.[7] In Jerusalem more and more Jews supported the Seleucids. Antiochus III strengthened his position by a successful campaign – similar to Alexander's – in the eastern provinces as far as Bactria and India. When Ptolemy IV died and was succeeded by Ptolemy V, who was a five-year-old boy, Antiochus III again invaded Palestine. Though he was once more driven back by the Ptolemaic general Scopas, he finally defeated the latter in 200 B.C.E. at Paneas by the sources of the Jordan. The inhabitants of Jerusalem had given substantial assistance to the Seleucids, especially during the storming of the Ptolemaic citadel within the city, while many supporters of the Ptolemies fled to Egypt.

Antiochus rewarded the Jewish people by reducing taxes and

[1] Hengel, *Hellenismus*, p. 75 (ET 1, p. 39).
[2] *CPJ*, 1, p. 26; Tcherikover, *Civilization*, pp. 71, 131–4, 139f; Hengel, *Hellenismus*, pp. 488f, 491 (ET 1, pp. 268f).
[3] *CPJ*, 1, pp. 230–6, nos. 127 d, e.
[4] *CPJ*, 1, pp. 19–25; Tcherikover, *Civilization*, pp. 73–7; Hengel, *Hellenismus*, pp. 11–15 (ET 1, pp. 7–9); *Juden*, pp. 51–63; ET pp. 33–41.
[5] 3 Macc. 1:3; *CPJ*, 1, p. 230.
[6] Hengel, *Juden*, p. 56; ET p. 36.
[7] Ibid.

renewing their right to live according to the laws of their fathers.[1] He also complied with the wishes of the priesthood for a ban on strangers entering the temple at Jerusalem and a further ban on the importing of unclean animals and unclean meat into the city.[2] All this demonstrates a policy of *rapprochement* on both sides, although at the same time the leaders of the pro-Seleucid upper class resolutely opposed the ever-increasing influence of Hellenism in favour of a faithful fulfilment of the Law.[3] Then a new situation arose with the intervention of Rome. In 190 Antiochus was defeated by the Romans at Magnesia in Lydia and was permanently weakened by the terms of the dictated peace of Apameia in 188. He was forced to surrender large amounts of territory, for example almost the whole of Asia Minor; he lost his entire fleet and faced enormous reparation payments of 12,000 talents which compelled him to levy heavy taxes in the remainder of his dominions and to confiscate the treasure amassed in the numerous temples. During an attempt to 'plunder' one such temple Antiochus III was slain by the enraged inhabitants (187 B.C.E.).[4] These events led to an undermining of the position of the Seleucids in Jerusalem, and Jewish nationalist tendencies acquired a fresh impetus. Jewish nationalism was not, however, a united force. The new, anti-Hellenist circles among the upper class, who were zealous adherents of the Law, were opposed by the majority of the upper class who were still sympathetic towards Hellenism and were also for the most part pro-Ptolemaic. It was in this situation that Jason, the brother of the ruling high priest, Onias III, attempted to introduce Hellenistic reforms in Jerusalem, an endeavour corrupted by Menelaus and his friends. There followed the looting of the Temple by Antiochus IV, Jason's desperate resort to violence, the ruthless intervention of the Syrian king, the desecration of the Temple in conjunction with the pagan Jewish *polis* in the Akra in Jerusalem, religious persecution and the revolt of the Maccabees. These developments cannot be discussed here,[5] but they form the background to significant events in the Diaspora.

The growth in numbers and influence of the Egyptian Diaspora continued unabated during the reigns of the third, fourth and fifth Ptolemies. Though according to the third book of the Maccabees the Jews were persecuted under Ptolemy IV,[6] this must have occurred at a

[1] Jos. *Ant.* XII.138–44; Tcherikover, *Civilization*, pp. 82–8.

[2] Jos. *Ant.* XII.145f; Hengel, *Juden*, pp. 65f; ET pp. 43f.

[3] Hengel, *Hellenismus*, pp. 235f, 453–5, 493f (ET I, pp. 127f, 247–9, 271f).

[4] Hengel, *Juden*, pp. 69f; ET p. 46.

[5] See *Cambridge History of Judaism*, vol. 2, ch. 8.

[6] 3 Macc. 2:25 to 6:29.

later period, in the reign of Ptolemy VIII Euergetes II, for which there is corresponding evidence in Josephus.[1] Under Ptolemy VI (181–145 B.C.E.) the Jewish influence in Egypt clearly reached a zenith. These decades witnessed the following far-reaching developments: (1) the building of a temple at Leontopolis; (2) the political and military leadership of Onias and his friend Dositheos; (3) the work of the Jewish philosopher Aristobulus.

The story of the founding of the temple at Leontopolis[2] raises many questions. Josephus' information is contradictory. It is best to begin with his later account of events in the *Antiquities*.[3] Here we learn that the temple was the brainchild of the high priest, Onias IV. After the victory of the Maccabees and the reconsecration of the Temple, Onias initially hoped to succeed his father who had been murdered at the instigation of the high priest, Menelaus. When however on Menelaus' death the succession fell instead upon Alcimus, Onias withdrew to Egypt. The temple at Leontopolis was built in part because Onias wanted to make a name for himself, but also 'so that the Jews in Egypt might be able to pray for the prosperity of the king, when they gathered together in this temple with a feeling of mutual harmony'.[4] The temple was thus to serve as a centre for the Egyptian Jews and to be a pledge of their allegiance both to Onias and to the Ptolemaic royal house. Only a limited proportion of the Jewish population could have been drawn to the remote village of Leontopolis. There is not a single reference in Alexandrian Jewish literature to the Leontopolis temple: on the contrary, it is the pilgrimages to the Temple in Jerusalem which are in vogue.[5] According to Josephus, Onias erected a fortification in that same area, which was called Onias' land.[6] Many years previously the region had indeed contained a certain location known as the 'Jewish camp';[7] for it was militarily a very important frontier zone. It is therefore probable that Onias IV built his temple in connection with the establishment of a Jewish military colony at Leontopolis, to cater for the religious needs of these Jewish inhabitants but at the same time to satisfy Onias' aspirations to the office of high priest, which he based upon his high-priestly descent. Behind the royal approval we glimpse the old claims of the Ptolemies to be masters of southern Syria and

[1] Jos. *C.Ap.* II.53–5.

[2] Jos. *Bell.* I.33; VII.423–32; *Ant.* XII.387f; XIII.62–73, 285; XX.236f. Cf. Tcherikover, *Civilization*, pp. 275–81.

[3] Especially XIII.62–73, cf. XII.387f; Tcherikover, *Civilization*, p. 276.

[4] Jos. *Ant.* XIII.67; Tcherikover, *Civilization*, p. 277.

[5] Tcherikover, *Civilization*, p. 278.

[6] Jos. *Bell.* VII.427; *Ant.* XIV.131.

[7] Jos. *Bell.* I.191; *Ant.* XIV.133; Tcherikover, *Civilization*, p. 279.

Palestine. A legitimate claimant to the office of high priest in Jerusalem could even now in certain circumstances be extremely useful to the Ptolemies.

In Egypt a situation had developed which was conducive to a closer relationship between the Jews and the court. The young king, Ptolemy VI Philometor, needed the support of the Jews. He had to struggle against growing hostility on the part of the Egyptian population towards all foreigners, particularly Greeks and Macedonians. His power was further threatened by his brother and his adherents among the Greeks of Alexandria.[1] He had to retreat twice in the face of the advance of Antiochus IV, who in effect conquered Egypt and would have delivered the final blow to the Ptolemaic monarchy, if the Romans had not insisted that he withdraw from Egypt.[2] The Jews represented a third force beside the Egyptians and the Greeks. Their numbers were swollen by the influx of members of the Ptolemaic party from Palestine who sought help and asylum from the king. The Jews were thus his natural allies. Now, for the first time, we come across a purely Jewish military unit in Egypt, under the command of a Jewish general Onias, who is undoubtedly identical with the aforementioned Onias IV. Josephus reports that the king placed Onias and his compatriot Dositheos in supreme command of all his forces; but this must be an exaggeration.[3] On the death of the king, however, Onias did intervene on behalf of the queen in the contest over the succession and entered Alexandria at the head of an army.

This loyalty earned him little reward when Cleopatra was overthrown by her rival Physcon. The new king, Ptolemy VII Euergetes II, seems to have initiated a savage persecution of the Jews in Alexandria and the rest of Egypt. According to Josephus,[4] he ordered all the Jews of Alexandria, together with their wives and children, to be cast before drunken elephants. But the animals, so the story goes, turned away from the Jews and attacked the king's servants instead, trampling many of them to death. Thereupon the king called off the campaign of persecution. Many aspects of this account are doubtless pure fabrication. Yet in later years an annual festival was held in Alexandria to commemorate a deliverance of the Jews in the reign of Euergetes II, from which we may assume that there must have been some historical basis for Josephus' tale.[5] It may, for example, have been a turning-point in the military situation during the hostilities which undoubtedly ensued after Onias' intervention. On the other hand, we can also

[1] Jos. *C.Ap.* 11.49–52; *CPJ*, 1, pp. 19f.

[2] *CPJ*, 1, p. 20.

[3] Jos. *C.Ap.* 11.49.

[4] Jos. *C.Ap.* 1.53–56.

[5] Ibid. 1.55; *CPJ*, 1, pp. 21f.

perceive a political turning-point: the new king made peace with Cleopatra soon after capturing the city and married her. This probably put a rapid end to the newly begun persecution of the Jews.

Apart from its tension-filled beginnings, the reign of the seventh Ptolemy (145–116 B.C.E.) was again a favourable period for the Jews. It was among the Greek citizens of Alexandria that the king's opponents were to be found, and these were dealt with harshly. In addition he had to quell numerous rebellions among the Egyptian population. We have no direct information about the fortunes of the Jews. But it appears that the antagonism which is found in the early Roman period between the Greek citizens of Alexandria and the Jewish inhabitants had its origins in these decades, at a time when the Jews remained loyal to the king, while the Greeks were being treated harshly and without mercy.[1] There must have been many Jews among the large numbers of foreigners who were accorded Alexandrian citizenship during these years.[2]

This interpretation is confirmed by events after the death of the king. Once again Jewish generals, Helkias and Hananias, intervened on the side of the queen in the struggle for the succession. Josephus tells us that the queen held them in high esteem.[3] In the course of her campaign in Palestine some of her advisers suggested that they should annex the aspiring Hasmonean state under the young Alexander Janneus. Hananias prevented this by arguing that such a step would antagonize all the Jews of Egypt towards the queen.[4] At the same time the episode shows that the Jews had influential enemies even at court. However, they were kept in check, thanks to the good relations between the Jews and the ruling house.[5]

The considerable political and military importance of the Jews in Egypt and particularly in Alexandria was matched by their energetic participation in economic activity, in civic administration and in the Greek cultural life of Alexandria. We have already met the leading civil servant Dositheos, the son of Drimylos, and the chief tax farmer, Joseph, as examples of Jews who held high office in the administrative and financial hierarchy of Ptolemaic Egypt.[6] In the reign of Ptolemy VI we encounter the first known Hellenistic Jewish philosopher, Aristobulus, who was descended from the high priestly line.[7] Besides

[1] *CPJ*, I, pp. 23f.

[2] *CPJ*, I, pp. 23f.

[3] Jos. *Ant.* XIII.287; *CPJ*, I, p. 24.

[4] Jos. *Ant.* XIII.354.

[5] *CPJ*, I, pp. 24f.

[6] See above, p. 139.

[7] N. Walter, ed., *Aristobulos*, Jüdische Schriften aus hellenistisch-römischer Zeit, 3 (Gütersloh, 1975), pp. 259–79; cf. N. Walter, *Thoraausleger Aristobulos*, TU 86 (Berlin, 1964); Hengel, *Hellenismus*, pp. 295–309 (ET I, pp. 163–9); *Juden*, pp. 136f.; ET pp. 98f.

the early reference in 2 Macc. 1:10 – where he is indeed described as Philometor's teacher – we have several fragments of a didactic work by Aristobulus written, it is thought, between 175 and 170 B.C.E. and dedicated to the young king Ptolemy VI.[1] The authenticity of these fragments, which are nowadays accepted as genuine, and the main tenets of Aristobulus' philosophy are discussed elsewhere. What needs to be pointed out here is that the case of Aristobulus illustrates the respected status enjoyed in the reign of Ptolemy VI by Alexandrian Jews who had acquired a Greek education; it also reveals the depth of their Hellenism.

As with the Septuagint, we see a remarkable reconciliation of the Jewish religion on the one hand and Hellenistic philosphy on the other, an achievement moreover that is contemporary with Jason's attempt to introduce Hellenistic reforms in Jerusalem and the preceding anti-Hellenistic campaign. Aristobulus attacks both conservative Jews for clinging to the letter of the Torah and rejecting allegorizing, and also Greek critics of Mosaic Law for pouring scorn on the anthropomorphisms and other objectionable details in the text of the Septuagint, even though the Greeks were concerned to interpret the myths of their own religious tradition in an allegorical way.[2] Aristobulus picks up the old Greek notion of the superiority of ancient oriental wisdom;[3] he views Plato's teaching on creation in the *Timaeus* and Pythagoras' number symbolism as having been derived from Moses.[4] The great importance that Aristobulus attaches to the Sabbath as the expression of a cosmic wisdom based on the significance of the number seven[5] shows him to be a practising Jewish believer. The Jewish principle of keeping holy the Sabbath day was after all one of the most familiar aspects of the Jewish way of life. And, as one might expect, Aristobulus' primary philosophical concern is with the purity of the idea of God and the appropriateness of the concepts applied to the divinity.[6] Here he has no choice but to correct the Greek philosophers, but he also seeks to bring a discriminating gaze to bear on his own Jewish traditions. Behind Aristobulus there must have been a whole school of Jewish philosophy, as we see a short time later from the letter of Pseudo-Aristeas and the book entitled 'The Wisdom of Solomon'. A broad tradition of Alexandrian Jewish philosophy and Torah exegesis extends from Aristobulus down to Philo of Alexandria.[7]

[1] Walter, *Thoraausleger Aristobulos*, pp. 13–26, 35–40, 123.
[2] Cf. Walter, *Thoraausleger Aristobulos*, pp. 124–9.
[3] Hengel, *Hellenismus*, p. 166 (ET 1, p. 90).
[4] Ibid, p. 300 (ET 1, pp. 165f).
[5] Ibid. pp. 300–7 (ET 1, pp. 166–9).
[6] Ibid. pp. 483 (ET 1, pp. 265f).
[7] Ibid. pp. 300–7 (ET 1, pp. 165–9), 481–6 (ET 1, pp. 264–7) and frequently elsewhere.

The last decades of Ptolemaic rule were turbulent. Rome, which had already aided the Ptolemies against Antiochus IV, went on supporting them to the end.[1] The Jews too gave assistance. In 55 B.C.E. they allowed Gabinius, the Roman proconsul of Syria, to march through their territory on his way to Alexandria to restore Ptolemy XI Auletes to the throne. Similarly the Jews co-operated with the Romans when Julius Caesar intervened on Cleopatra's behalf in 48 B.C.E.[2] Thus the loyalty shown by the Alexandrian and Egyptian Jews to the Ptolemies found its natural extension in their good relations with the new Roman rulers. Their participation in Hellenistic culture reached its climax in the early Roman period, as the works of Philo of Alexandria testify. The latter's nephew, Tiberius Alexander, even became the Roman prefect of Egypt, albeit after forswearing his Jewish faith.[3] However, the majority of Hellenistic Jews in Alexandria and Egypt remained as always true to the religion of their forefathers.

THE OTHER TERRITORIES

The sparse information that exists about the eastern Diaspora in the Hellenistic age suggests that the situation there was by and large the same as it was in Egypt.[4] As in the west, Jews figured in the armies of the Seleucid empire. We have in addition a noteworthy reference in Josephus to the trouble which Alexander experienced with Jewish auxiliaries in Babylon.[5] The second book of Maccabees (2 Macc. 8:20) contains an inserted reference to 8,000 Jewish soldiers who supposedly in the reign of Antiochus I were instrumental in deciding a battle against the Galatians.[6] In the reign of Antiochus III we know that 2,000 Jewish families from Babylonia were resettled as military colonists in Lydia and Phrygia.[7] All this indicates a long tradition of recruiting Jews into the Seleucid armies, just as in Egypt. This continued under the Parthian empire.

This action of Antiochus III is mentioned in a letter from the king to Zeuxis, the king's friend and *stratēgos* in Babylon and/or Lydia, which is

[1] *CPJ*, 1, pp. 55f.; Bouché-Leclerq, *Histoire des Séleucides*, 2, pp. 129ff, 152ff.

[2] Jos. *Ant.* XIV.99, 131; *Bell.* 1.190.

[3] Jos. *Ant.* XX.100–3. Cf. *Bell.* II.220, 309, 492; IV.616–18; V.45f, 510, cf. 205; VI.237, 242; V. Burr, *Tiverius Julius Alexander*, Antiquitas 1, 1 (Bonn, 1955).

[4] For what follows, see Schürer, *Geschichte*, 3, pp. 2–42, 52–70; Tcherikover, *Civilization*, pp. 287–95.

[5] Jos. *C. Ap.* 1.192, 200; cf. *Ant.* XI.339. See above, pp. 121f.

[6] C. Habicht, ed., *2. Makkabäerbuch*, Jüdische Schriften aus hellenistisch-römischer Zeit, 1, 3 (Gütersloh, 1976), pp. 240f.; Hengel, *Juden*, p. 118; ET pp. 86f.

[7] Jos. *Ant.* XII.148–53.

quoted by Josephus. The letter is nowadays rightly regarded as genuine.[1] Antiochus was in the middle of his great campaign in the eastern provinces when he learnt of disturbances in Lydia and Phrygia, and he commissioned Zeuxis to resettle 2,000 Jewish families there to pacify these areas. The text of the letter reveals the good relations between the Jews and the king, and at the same time their fidelity to their own Judaism; the practice of it is placed under royal protection. We may also infer that the proportion of Jews in the population of Babylon was quite large.[2] Furthermore, the subsequent presence of large numbers of Jews in Lydia and Phrygia shows that the resettlement did indeed occur.[3]

Over the next two or three centuries the Jews spread throughout Asia Minor as far as Bithynia and Pontus on the Black Sea.[4] In Syria, in the time of Josephus, there were more Jews than in any other country.[5] However, these particular numbers probably did not become large until after the annexation of the Jewish homeland to the Seleucid empire – and the increase was doubtless due in part to the civil war that prevailed from time to time in Palestine. In the reign of the High Priest Jonathan, exclusively Jewish military units served in the Seleucid armies (1 Macc. 10:36; 11:43f) and likewise under John Hyrcanus, as Josephus records.[6] We may presume that such Jewish units existed in the pre-Maccabean period as well. Finally, it is worth noting that the Seleucid rulers who succeeded Antiochus IV donated valuable oblations to the main synagogue at Antioch and returned the bronze vessels plundered from the Temple in Jerusalem.[7] This indicates a pro-Jewish policy, in spite of the conflicts of the Maccabean period. The persecution under Antiochus Epiphanes was in any case confined to Palestine.[8]

As far as Cyrenaica is concerned, Ptolemy I is said to have settled Jewish mercenaries there when he conquered the province.[9] Strabo writes of the state of affairs in Cyrene in 88 B.C.E.: 'There were four

[1] Tcherikover, *Civilization*, p. 287; A. Schalit, 'The letter of Antiochus III to Zeuxis regarding the establishment of Jewish military colonies in Phrygia and Lydia', *JQR*, n.s. 50 (1960), 289–318; Hengel, *Juden*, pp. 60, 118, 144; ET pp. 39, 87, 104.

[2] See Schürer, *Geschichte*, 3, pp. 6–10; Tcherikover, *Civilization*, p. 290.

[3] Tcherikover, *Civilization*, p. 288.

[4] J.-B. Frey, ed., *CIJ* (vol. 1, Rome/Paris, 1936; vol. 2, Rome, 1952), 1, no. 690; Schürer, *Geschichte*, 3, pp. 23f.

[5] Jos. *Bell.* VII.43f.

[6] Jos. *Ant.* XIII.249–52; Hengel, *Hellenismus*, p. 29 (ET 1, p. 16).

[7] Jos. *Bell.* VII.44f.

[8] Hengel, *Hellenismus*, p. 537 (ET 1, p. 294); *Juden*, p. 151; ET p. 108.

[9] Jos. *C.Ap.* II.44. Cf. 1 Macc. 15:23; 2 Macc. 2:23.

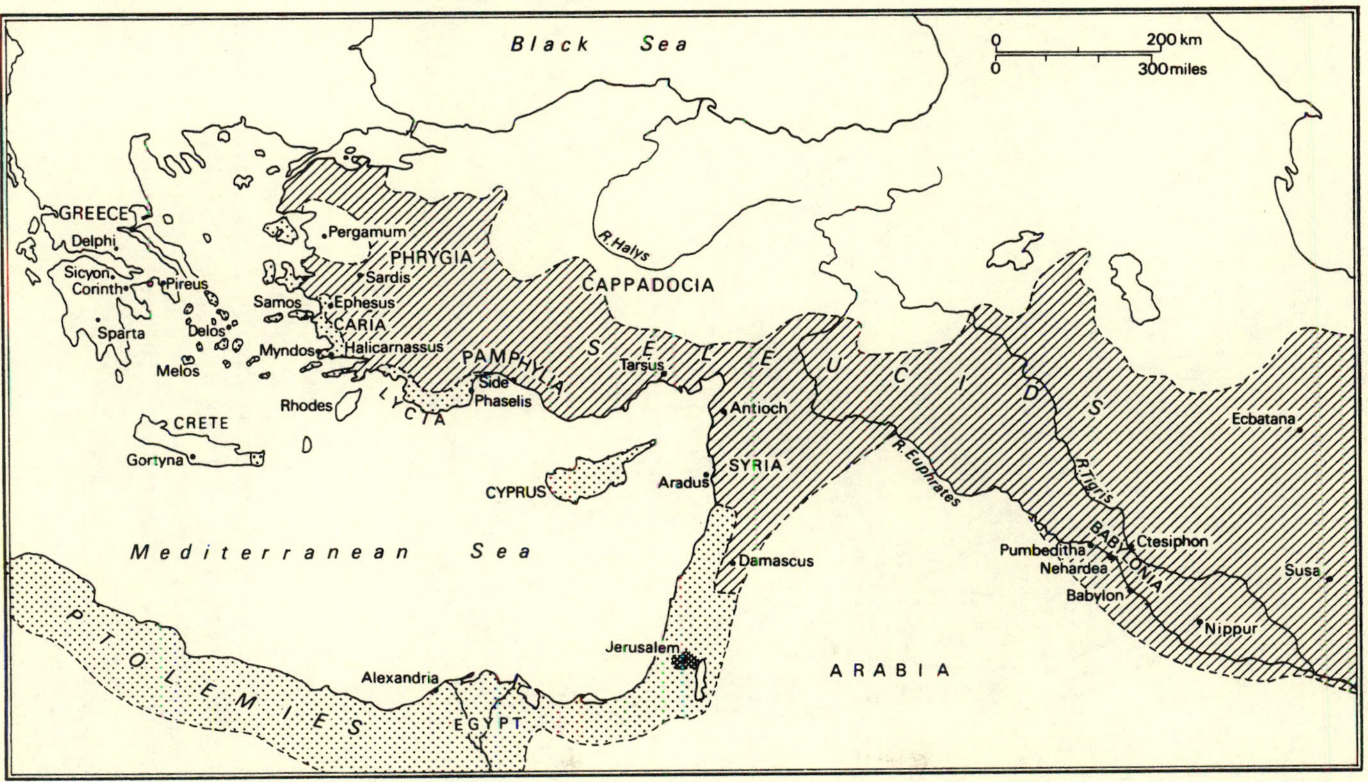

Fig. 4 The Jewish Diaspora in Babylonia, Asia Minor and Greece, 3rd to 1st centuries B.C.E.

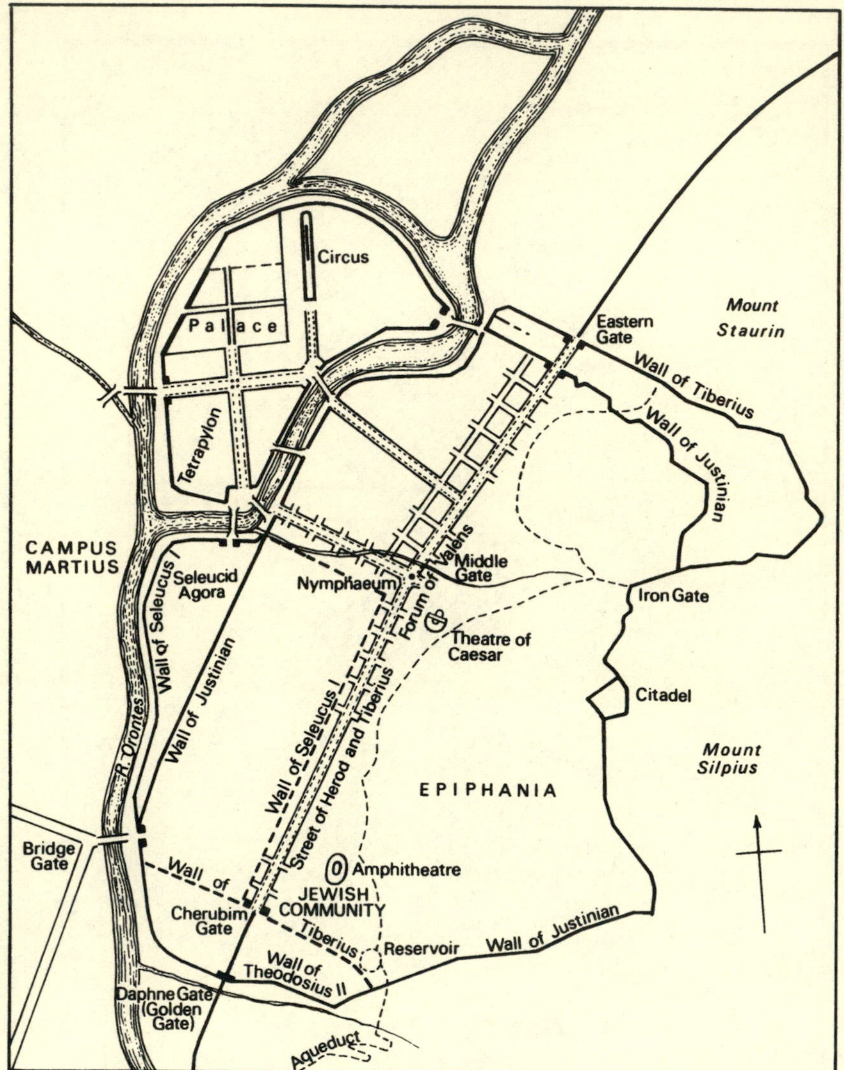

Fig. 5 Plan of ancient Antioch.

(classes) in the city of the Cyreneans – that of citizens, that of husbandmen, the third of *metoikoi* and the fourth of Jews'. He relates too that like Egypt Cyrenaica was the scene of a massive influx of Jewish immigrants.[1] Later, in the reign of Trajan, a Jewish uprising took

[1] In Jos. *Ant.* XIV.110–18.

place here (in 115–117 C.E.) of devastating extent; it was crushed by the Romans in a ferocious campaign and resulted in the complete extermination of the Jewish community in this area.

In Greece the presence of Jews is attested perhaps as far back as the fourth century.[1] There is a third century inscription concerning the manumission of a Jewish slave at Oropos in Attica,[2] and we have several such pieces of evidence dating from the second century B.C.E.[3] In Rome the Jews had already become a strong and influential ethnic group by 62 B.C.E.; this is clearly implied in a speech of that time by Cicero.[4] The same text also records that in preceding years Jews had taken munificent donations of gold to Jerusalem 'from Italy and every province' and that Roman officials had taken steps to prohibit this, or at least Flaccus had done so in Asia Minor.

At the outset of the Roman era there is a prevailing impression that the Jews are to be found all over the world. 'There is no part of the earth that has not admitted this people or been possessed by them' (thus Strabo in Josephus, *Antiquitates Judaicae* XIV.7.2). 'Land and sea are full of them' (*the Sibylline Oracles, circa* 140 B.C.E.).[5] It is impossible to provide precise figures. The various estimates have not produced usable approximate estimates,[6] especially since the data available in the ancient sources are of little value. Philo for example estimates the number of Jews living in the Egypt of his day at a million.[7] Yet it is unlikely that there was ever an official census of the Egyptian Jews.[8] The figure given by Philo is clearly meant as a rough total, with a certain inherent tendency towards exaggeration. The same is true of the figures in Pseudo-Aristeas[9] mentioned above and of the details which Josephus gives of the number of victims of the various pogroms in the early Roman period.[10] What is certain is that in some cities, such as Alexandria and Antioch, Jews made up a considerable proportion of the total population. In Alexandria two out of the five districts of the city were almost entirely inhabited by Jews.[11] The city certainly contained more Jews at this time than Jerusalem itself. The proportion of Jews in the Diaspora in relation to the size of the nation as a whole increased steadily throughout the Hellenistic era and reached astonish-

[1] *Inscriptiones Graecae*, Preussische Akademie der Wissenschaften (Berlin, 1873ff), II[2], 10678; Hengel, *Juden*, p. 121; ET p. 88.

[2] Hengel, *Juden*, p. 121; ET p. 88.

[3] *CIJ*, I, pp. 512f, no. 709–10.

[4] Cicero, *Pro Flacco* 28.

[5] *Die Oracula Sibyllina*, J. Geffcken, ed. GCS 8 (Leipzig, 1902), III.271.

[6] Tcherikover, *Civilization*, pp. 272–94.

[7] Philo, *In Flaccum* 43.

[8] Tcherikover, *Civilization*, p. 286.

[9] Ps.-Arist. 12f, 27. See above, p. 134.

[10] Jos. *Bell.* II.457, 468, 477, 509, 561; VII.368.

[11] Philo, *Flacc.* 55.

Fig. 6 The Jewish Diaspora in the time of Jesus.

ing dimensions in the early Roman period. It was not least for this reason that the Jewish people became a major political factor, especially since the Jews in the diaspora, notwithstanding strong cultural, social and religious tensions, remained firmly united with their homeland.

RELIGIOUS LIFE

THE SYNAGOGUE (προσευχή)[1]

The Jews in the 'dispersion' possessed an excellent unifying bond in the form of their meeting houses, known in the Hellenistic period as προσευχαί or places of prayer.[2] Jewish *proseuchai* are attested in Egypt from the mid-third century onwards: as far as the Delta and Lower Egypt are concerned, not only in Alexandria but also in Schedia, Xenephyris, Athribis and Nitriai, all in the third to the second century B.C.E.; in the Fayum we know of examples in Crocodilopolis-Arsinoe and Alexandrou-Nesos, both of the third century; besides these there is an unnamed location in Upper Egypt and two other sites for which we do not have names. The two oldest inscriptions are the ones in Schedia near Alexandria and in Crocodilopolis-Arsinoe in the Fayum.[3] In Philo's day every district of Alexandria contained numerous *proseuchai*;[4] the same was presumably true of the Hellenistic period. The *proseuchai* fulfilled a double purpose. In the first place, as the name προσευχή (τῶν Ἰουδαίων) implies, they were religious meeting places. In addition, however, they had a socio-political function similar to pagan temples and sacrificial sites. In Alexandrou-Nesos an alleged thief, Dorotheos, fled into a *proseuche* with his spoil, a cloak. The disputed garment was then placed in the safe keeping of the synagogue attendant, Nikomachos, until the affair could be investigated.[5] Perhaps the fleeing thief was seeking sanctuary in the synagogue.[6] The civic status of the *proseuchai* also finds expression in the dedicatory inscriptions. The two earliest inscriptions read: 'to King Ptolemy and Queen

[1] For what follows, see M. Hengel, 'Proseuche und Synagoge. Jüdische Gemeinde, Gotteshaus und Gottesdienst in der Diaspora und in Palästina', in *Tradition und Glaube*, Festgabe K. G. Kuhn, ed. G. Jeremias, H.-W. Kuhn and H. Stegemann (Göttingen, 1971), pp. 157–84; S. Krauss, *Synagogale Altertümer* (Berlin-Vienna, 1922, repr. Hildesheim, 1966); E. R. Goodenough, *Jewish Symbols in the Greco-Roman Period* (New York, 1952–68), 2, pp. 70–100; W. Schrage, 'συναγωγή', *TWNT*, 7 (1964), pp. 798–839; *TDNT*, 7 (1971), pp. 798–841.

[2] On the term, see Hengel, 'Proseuche', pp. 161f; on the ancient evidence for *proseuchai* in Egypt, cf. *CPJ*, 1, pp. 8f.

[3] *CPJ*, 3, p. 141, no. 1440; 3, p. 164, no. 1532A.

[4] Philo, *Legatio ad Gaium* 132.

[5] *CPJ*, 1, pp. 239–241, no. 129.

[6] *CPJ*, 1, pp. 240f.

Berenice the sister and spouse and to the children the Jews (dedicate) the *proseuche*'; 'to King Ptolemy (son) of Ptolemy and Queen Berenice the spouse and sister and to the children the Jews in the city of Crocodilopolis (dedicate) the *proseuche*'.[1] The evidence for Jewish houses of prayer in Egypt is the earliest record we have of such institutions. It documents an important development in Jewish life in which the Diaspora appears to have given the lead.[2] In the Persian period the Jewish military colonists in Elephantine had a temple with sacrificial rituals, not without syncretistic features.[3] It is presumed that several such regional temples existed at that time.[4] In the second century we do indeed find temple buildings both in Leontopolis and in the capital of the Tobiads in Eastern Jordan – but in both instances they are exceptions, established to meet specific local needs.[5] As a rule, from the third century onwards the Jews built a new kind of holy place.

The term προσευχή points to a group of people assembled together primarily for the purpose of prayer, whether spoken or sung – for a service of the word, in other words, whose individual elements had long been known in Jewish worship but which now made an appearance on their own, shorn of any association with sacrificial ceremonies.[6] The language of worship in Egypt from the beginning of the third century was undoubtedly Greek and the same must have been true of other areas of the western Diaspora.[7] It is not possible to reconstruct in detail the history of this service of the word. Information dating from the rabbinical or even from the early Roman period ought not to be read into the earliest beginnings unless this can be substantiated.[8] There is an almost total dearth of ancient literary evidence. The Alexandrian historian Agatharchides of Cnidos, born around 200 B.C.E., writes that the Jews 'pray...in their holy places with outstretched hands until evening'.[9] But whether he is describing the custom in the Diaspora remains uncertain. We can draw more reliable conclusions where features of Diaspora worship contrast sharply with the rabbinical conventions in Palestine. Philo of Alexandria emphasizes the important role of the hymn.[10] A valuable Talmudic testimony concerning the form of service used in the great synagogue of Alexandria shows that prayer was of central significance, with the whole congre-

[1] See p. 151 n. 3.

[2] Hengel, 'Proseuche', pp. 179–82.

[3] See *Cambridge History of Judaism*, vol. 1, chs. 13 and 14.

[4] For example, in Thmouis and Boreion; Hengel, *Hellenismus*, p. 28 (ET 1, pp. 15f).

[5] Tcherikover, *Civilization*, pp. 392–4; Hengel, *Hellenismus*, pp. 496–503 (ET 1, pp. 272–7). But compare Jos. *Ant.* XIII.66.

[6] Hengel, 'Proseuche', pp. 162–5.

[7] Hengel, *Juden*, pp. 126f.; ET p. 93.

[8] Hengel, 'Proseuche', pp. 164f.

[9] According to Josephus, *C. Ap.* 1.209.

[10] Hengel, 'Proseuche', p. 163.

gation joining in the amen; because of the size of the gathering, men were placed on a podium to give a visible signal to the worshippers when it was time to pronounce the amen.[1] It is hard to say when readings from the scriptures and an address were introduced into the form of service used in the Diaspora. Both were firmly established by Philo's day and had been for a long time. Perhaps the assembly of the people referred to in Neh. 7:73 to 9:37 represents a precursor of the new prayer service.[2]

It soon became the practice in the synagogues of the Diaspora to celebrate the Jewish new moons and annual festivals. Above all, the Sabbath was marked everywhere by services of worship.[3] In this connection ceremonial meals were also arranged. At all events, permission to hold religious feasts was one of the privileges granted to the Jews of Paros in the middle of the first century B.C.E.[4] The Jews of Alexandria were expressly committed to commemorating the consecration of the Temple in Jerusalem (2 Macc. 1 to 2). They also observed special Alexandrian festivals, namely, to mark the composition of the Septuagint[5] and their deliverance from persecution under Ptolemy VII.[6]

It is unlikely that these prayer services were inspired by non-Jewish models: rather, we are dealing with an internal Jewish development which derived its impulse from the systematic centralization of worship in the Diaspora along the lines laid down in Deuteronomy. For the new institution of the *proseuchai* is closely connected with the firm orientation of Jews throughout the Diaspora towards the one most holy Temple in Jerusalem, the only place of cultic worship. (It must be said, however, that pilgrimages to the Temple were none too frequent in earlier times.[7]) The *proseuche* is not a cultic place. Anyone can enter it and it is used as much for teaching and legal matters as for prayer and hymnsinging. The original *proseuchai* were probably simple, unsophisticated structures unadorned by any religious symbolism.[8] Later they became splendid edifices. The main synagogues in Antioch and Alexandria were particularly renowned.[9] It is clear that from the outset women sat or stood apart from the men, and from an early date the

1 *b. Sukka* 51a; cf. Tcherikover, *Civilization*, pp. 354f.

2 Hengel, 'Proseuche', pp. 165 n. 30.

3 Philo, *Spec.* II.61–4; Jos., *C. Ap.* II. 280–4; *Ant.* XIV.241f., 244–6. Cf. E. Lohse, 'σάββατον', *TWNT*, 7 (1964), p. 17, *TDNT*; 7 (1971), pp. 16f., Tcherikover, *Civilization*, pp. 354f.

4 Jos. *Ant.* XIV.213–16; cf. 256–8.

5 Philo, *Vita M.* II.41f.

6 Jos. *C. Ap.* II.53–5.

7 For the early Roman period, see Philo, *Spec.* I.169–70; *Provid.* II.107; Jos. *Bell.* VI.422–7.

8 Hengel, 'Proseuche', pp. 166f. Cf. Schrage, *TWNT*, 7 (1964), pp. 813–20, *TDNT*, 7 (1968), pp. 814–21.

9 See above n. 1.

leader of the assembly had a special seat.[1] Perhaps it was not long before vestibules were attached to some of the larger *proseuchai* where votive offerings and inscriptions could be displayed as in the ancient temples. However, this is specifically attested only in the case of the principal cities of Alexandria and Antioch and may in fact have been confined to them.[2]

Philo never uses any other designation save *proseuche*. But from the early Roman period onwards the term συναγωγή begins to occur in the Diaspora, probably under the influence of developments in Palestine. Initially it is applied to the assembly but then it comes to mean the building itself.[3] Its Hebrew equivalent is firmly established in Palestinian Judaism by the first century, as can be seen from the New Testament.[4] At what point exactly houses of assembly and prayer appeared in the Jewish homeland, alongside the Jerusalem Temple, is a contentious issue. It was probably in the second century B.C.E. that Palestinian Jews adopted an institution which had originally developed and proved its worth in the Diaspora.[5]

JERUSALEM AS THE CENTRE

In many respects Jerusalem was the focal point of all Jewish life. Every male Jew, wherever he might be, paid his annual tax of half a shekel to the Jerusalem Temple.[6] This was a question of moral duty and was zealously adhered to. Wealthy Jews often contributed several times the appointed sum.[7] Other dues prescribed by the Torah were also paid in the Diaspora.[8] The right to transfer to Jerusalem the monies owing to the Temple had sometimes to be asserted in the face of strong opposition.[9] Apparently the payments to the Temple were approved from the start by the Ptolemaic and the Seleucid kings. Philo informs us that there were treasuries in almost every town into which the taxes were paid;[10] at certain times the monies thus collected would be transported to Palestine by large delegations headed by leading dignitaries. The Jerusalem Temple attracted tens of thousands of pilgrims each year in the early Roman period.[11] Hellenistic Jewish literature

[1] Hengel, 'Proseuche', pp. 167–72.
[2] Philo, *Flacc.* 49; *Leg.* 133.
[3] Hengel, 'Proseuche', pp. 177–84.
[4] Schrage, *TWNT*, 7 (1964), pp. 828–30, *TDNT*, 7 (1968), pp. 828–31. But compare Acts 16:13; Hengel, 'Proseuche', p. 175.
[5] Hengel, 'Proseuche', pp. 179f.
[6] Philo, *Spec.* I.76–8; IV.98f.; *Leg.* 156, 216, 291, 311–16; Jos. *Ant.* XIV.110; XVI.163; XVIII.312f.
[7] S. W. Baron, *A Social and Religious History of the Jews* (2nd edn., Philadelphia, 1952), I, p. 215.
[8] Schürer, *Geschichte*, 2, p. 312.
[9] Schürer, *Geschichte*, 3, pp. 112f; Jos. *Ant.* XIV.213–16.
[10] Philo, *Spec.* I.78.
[11] See p. 141 n. 5.

shows many traces of the fascination exerted by the Temple.[1] Thus the Temple in Jerusalem united Jews throughout the world into a universal community.

Similarly the high priest was a powerful force for integration, far beyond his political authority and influence.[2] The ceremonial robes of the high priest, repeatedly vaunted in Hellenistic Jewish literature and interpreted in terms of cosmic symbolism, endowed him with transcendent glory.[3] His religious duties in the cult, especially those performed on the great Day of Atonement, were viewed as a universal saving event, particularly by Jews in the Diaspora.[4]

Thirdly, in the Hellenistic period, the Diaspora was perceptibly under the influence of the teaching authorities in Jerusalem.[5] Even for a writer as explicitly sympathetic towards Hellenism as Pseudo-Aristeas, the Jerusalem authorities were the guarantors of the canonical validity of the Greek translation of the Torah.[6] The events of the Maccabean uprising soon became the subject of a committed, pro-Maccabean historical account by Jason of Cyrene and his epitomator, likewise a member of the Hellenistic Jewish community in Egypt.[7] Before that the continuing translation of new prophetic–apocalyptic and Wisdom books from Palestine shows that intensive links were maintained with the homeland.[8] As far as the translation and dissemination of Ecclesiasticus and the book of Esther are concerned, we have some details of the process.[9] They reveal that the authorities in Jerusalem exerted a strong influence over what went on in the Diaspora and that in the post-Maccabean period they even voiced wholesale criticisms of pro-Hellenistic attitudes, as in the additions to the book of Esther.[10]

Despite the fluctuating fortunes and the divisions within Palestinian Judaism up to 70 C.E., Jews in the Diaspora continued to take their bearings from the religious authorities in Jerusalem.

1 Cf. Ps-Arist. 84–91; 2 Macc. 3.12, 24–40; Eupolemus in Eusebius, *Praep. Ev.* IX.30. 1–34, 18; Walter, *Fragmente*, pp. 99–106, Ps.-Hecateus in Jos. *C.Ap.* 196–9; Philo, *Leg.* 188–98, 209–16, 295; *Sib.* 3.265–94, 573–581.

2 Cf. Jos. *Ant.* XI.329–35; XIV.131; Ps.-Arist. 96–9. See also pp. 141f. above.

3 *Wisd. Sol.* 18:24; Philo, *Spec.* 1.84–97; *Vit. M.* II.109–35; *Quaest. Exod.* II.107–24; Jos. *Ant.* III.159–78; *Bell.* V.231–5.

4 Philo, *Spec.* 1.197; II.162, 165f.

5 Cf. Ps.-Arist. 121f, 128–71; 2 Macc. 1:1–9; 1:10 to 2:18; Hengel, *Hellenismus*, pp. 143–8, 186–90, 241–75 (ET 1, pp. 78–81, 100–2, 131–53); *Juden*, pp. 168–71; ET pp. 121–3.

6 Ps.-Arist. 46.301–11.

7 On the subject of their pro-Palestinian attitude, see Hengel, *Hellenismus*, pp. 185–90; ET 1 pp. 100–2.

8 For the history of the origins of the Septuagint, see below, ch. 15.

9 Cf. Hengel, *Hellenismus*, pp. 187f, 189f, 241f (ET 1, pp. 101f, 131).

10 Ibid. p. 188 (ET 1, pp. 101f).

THE MOSAIC LAW IN THE HELLENISTIC DIASPORA

The impression of pious observance and study of the Torah which we gain from the Roman period ought not to colour our reading of the evidence from the Hellenistic epoch without further examination. By and large it is true to say that in the Hellenistic period the figure of Moses as law-giver, wise man and prophet took precedence over the Torah as a sacred text. Moses was considered one of the great sages of ancient times, towering above his rivals. The great Greek philosophers in particular were said to have derived many valuable lessons from him.[1] In thus stressing the link with Moses, the Hellenistic Jews were not retreating into sectarian isolation but rather taking their place in the vanguard of the intellectual and religious life of their age. They tried to justify this claim through the medium of contemporary cultural and philosophical discourse. The Hellenistic Jewish disciples of Moses whom we can identify from Aristobulus onwards did not shrink from trying to convince the Hellenistic world of the superiority, profundity and beauty of Moses' wisdom, and in particular of the pre-eminence and self-evident truth of his legislation which elevated the Jews above all other nations.[2] Conversely they also undertook the task of providing a rationalist interpretation of Moses with the aid, for instance, of allegorical rules first developed for expounding Homer.[3] Anything in the holy scriptures which ostensibly appeared objectionable was given a deeper meaning, sometimes with excessive sophistry.[4] The apparently disordered multiplicity of admonitions was plausibly systematized, in that every Mosaic injunction was shown to be derived from the two basic requirements of pure worship and righteousness. In Pseudo-Aristeas this occurs only occasionally and without any system but in Philo it is carried out systematically according to a preconceived design.[5] The main features of the traditional laws and customs of the Jews are fully preserved. These writers aver that true Judaism is consonant with the best Greek traditions.[6] Pseudo-Aristeas presents the Hellenistic monarch and the Jewish sages in an idealized light and

[1] Thus Aristobulus and Eupolemus: Walter, *Thoraausleger Aristobulos*, pp. 43–51; *Fragmente*, pp. 93–8; Hengel, *Hellenismus*, pp. 297–300 (ET 1, pp. 164–6). However, the same is not true of Artapanus: Walter, *Fragmente*, p. 122.

[2] The apologetic element is overestimated by Walter, *Thoraausleger Aristobulos*, pp. 26–9, 44f. It is a favourite device to have eminent Gentiles singing the praises of the Jews: Ps.-Arist. 31, 174–80, 312–17.

[3] Walter, *Thoraausleger Aristobulos*, pp. 124–48.

[4] Cf. Ps.-Arist. 150–4, 161–6.

[5] Ps.-Arist. 131–3 and frequently elsewhere; Philo, *Decal.* 18–19, 50–2; *Spec.* IV.132.

[6] This is the central theme especially of Ps.-Arist. Cf. Hengel, *Hellenismus*, pp. 275–307, 464–78 (ET 1, pp. 153, 169, 255–63) and frequently elsewhere.

in perfect harmony with one another.[1] Enlightened tolerance towards Hellenistic kingship existed in Palestine too, as is attested by the court tales in the books of Daniel and Esther and in other writings.[2] On the other hand, the critical attitude towards Hellenism which prevailed in the homeland after the failure of the Hellenistic reform movement under Jason and the victory of the Maccabees soon made itself felt in the Diaspora as well, though here it did not become dominant.[3]

Moses was consistently depicted not as a uniquely Jewish figure but as a unique teacher of true wisdom and righteousness who is authoritative for all true disciples of philosophy. The Mosaic teachings which Aristobulus and later Pseudo-Aristeas expounded before the king were directed at all who aspired to true piety, virtue and order, Jews and Gentiles alike.[4] Philo's works addressed themselves explicitly to all those who sought wisdom and godliness.[5]

The reverberations of this universalism, at once Jewish and Hellenistic, can be discerned in the widespread adherence to Moses by non-Jews at this time.[6] Not until the early Roman period can one speak of conversions and proselytes proper. The older form of Gentile commitment to Moses is represented in the Roman period by the 'God-fearers' who embrace Jewish monotheism and adopt the Jewish moral Law, without however accepting circumcision.[7] A worldwide movement to profess the truth of Mosaic teaching is seen by Philo as *the* great opportunity for the nations of the earth.[8] This attitude must have been even more pronounced among his predecessors in the Hellenistic period.

However, the anti-Hellenistic campaign in Palestine, with its zealous

[1] Ps.-Arist. 15–16, 187–292.

[2] Hengel, *Hellenismus*, pp. 55–61 (ET 1, pp. 29–32); W. L. Humphreys, 'A life-style for Diaspora: a study of the tales of Esther and Daniel', *JBL*, 92 (1973), 211–23.

[3] Hengel, *Hellenismus*, pp. 60f, 100, 187f, 306f, 549f, 556–64 (ET 1, pp. 31f, 52, 101f, 169, 299f, 304–9).

[4] Thus Aristobulus in Euseb. *Praep. Ev.* XIII.12. 9–11; Walter, *Aristobulos*, pp. 72f.; Ps.-Arist. 124–7 and frequently elsewhere.

[5] Philo, *Spec.* II.165f; *Virt.* 119f.

[6] Philo, *Vit. M.* II.17–31; Jos. *C.Ap.* II.123, 281ff. Cf. K. G. Kuhn, 'προσήλυτος' *TWNT*, 6 (1959), pp. 730–45, *TDNT* 6 (1968), pp. 730–44; M. Simon, *Verus Israel* (Paris, 1964), pp. 315–55; K. G. Kuhn and H. Stegemann, 'Proselyten', *PWSup* 9 (1962) cols. 1248–83.

[7] H. Hegermann, 'Das hellenistische Judentum', *Umwelt des Urchristentums*, ed. J. Leipoldt and W. Grundmann (Berlin, 1976), 1, pp. 307–11; Idem, 'Das griechischsprechende Judentum', *Literatur und Religion des Frühjudentums*, ed. J. Maier and J. Schreiner (Würzburg, 1973), pp. 349–52; F. Siegert, 'Gottesfürchtige und Sympathisanten', *JSJ*, 4 (1973), 109–64.

[8] Philo, *Virt.* 119f.

emphasis on the Law, had an unmistakable and growing impact in the Diaspora. Initially some of the Jews of Alexandria lived together, while others were scattered at random in every quarter of the city. Later, this freedom to choose one's place of residence is inconceivable, and a systematic segregation of the Jews in the interests of greater solidarity is backdated by Josephus to earlier times.[1] In the middle of the first century B.C.E. this became a definite programme. The Jews of Sardis requested and were granted at that time a residential district to themselves 'in order that they might gather together there with their wives and children and pray and worship God in the traditional manner'.[2] Jewish monotheism had always prevented the complete integration of Jews into Hellenistic society. A dangerous friction was clearly inherent in this situation from the start. In the multinational Hellenistic culture the Jews were the only group who consistently had to refuse to participate in pagan rituals. Yet in the earlier period the offensive sections of the Mosaic Torah were damped down and adapted to a liberal practice acceptable to the Gentile milieu.[3] Direct participation in pagan worship was always out of the question. Anyone who aspired to high office in the state or who simply desired complete cultural assimilation had to pay the price of apostasy (e.g. Dositheos, son of Drimylos). Rules about food and cleanliness, and certain details of Sabbath observance do not appear to have caused any serious problems in the early Hellenistic period. But a new era is indicated when Jewish inhabitants fight successfully for the privilege of not having to attend courts or carry weapons or march or even receive their apportionment of oil on the Sabbath.[4] This step implies an intensified observance of the Torah which, to name only one consequence among several, inevitably led to the permanent debarring of Jews from military service.[5]

LEGAL AND SOCIAL CONDITIONS

QUESTIONS OF CIVIC RIGHTS[6]

The social status of the Jews varied widely. Under the Ptolemies it ranged from the highest ranks of the political, economic and cultural élite down to small tenant farmers, labourers and slaves.[7] And even

1 Jos. *Bell.* II.488.

2 Jos. *Ant.* XIV.259–61.

3 Cf. Ps.-Arist. 182, 184f; Hengel, *Hellenismus*, pp. 126f, 188 (ET 1, pp. 67f, 101).

4 Jos. *Ant.* XII.119f; XVI.162f; Philo, *Leg.* 158.

5 Jos. *Ant.* XIV.223–40.

6 For what follows, see Schürer, *Geschichte,* 3, pp. 71–134; Tcherikover, *Civilization*, pp. 296–332; *CPJ,* 1, pp. 5–10, 39–41, 59–74.

7 See pp. 133–5 above.

within the urban communities there were many different ranks and privileges. If we consider the matter of civic rights, an equally diverse picture emerges. Families who were residents of long-standing might possess civic rights which were denied to more recent arrivals.[1] When a kind of aristocratic upper class developed in the large Jewish communities of the Hellenistic period, it enjoyed civic privileges beyond the reach of ordinary Jews. Yet such matters were of less moment than the freedoms that were essential to the fulfilment of the basic admonitions of the Mosaic Torah and which were thus of vital significance to every Jew.

The Jews were not always organized into a corporation of their own.[2] In Alexandria, and for example in the city of Berenice in Cyrenaica, we find the Jewish inhabitants organized as a πολίτευμα.[3] The Jews of Hierapolis are designated in inscriptions as a κατοικία.[4] This was the normal term for colonies of aliens in a particular locality.[5] Thus there were at an early stage *katoikiai* of Macedonian military settlers.[6] An organization of this kind always involved a measure of self-government but not originally civic rights as a city, even though such communities might develop into cities.[7] Other designations for communities of aliens are λαός, σύνοδος, συναγωγή.[8] What we must not forget is that as far as their civic rights were concerned, the Jews constituted less of an exception in the ancient world than we might assume.[9] The Hellenistic world with its busy international trade and its political openness developed means of integrating foreigners into the social and legal structure of city and country quite independently of the particular problem posed by the Jews.[10]

The term πολίτευμα can denote an ordinary urban settlement or its

1 Tcherikover, *Civilization*, p. 297.

2 For this they needed permission from the state, see p. 160 n. 3. However, various forms of community life always developed on a private basis. Cf. Tcherikover, *CPJ*, 1, pp. 5f.

3 *CIG*, no. 5361f; Ps.-Arist. 310; Jos. *Ant.* XII.108.

4 *CIG*, no. 775.

5 Tcherikover, *Civilization*, pp. 297f.

6 Tcherikover, *Civilization*, p. 25.

7 Towns such as Pella, Edessa or Larissa may have originated thus: cf. Tcherikover, *Civilization*, p. 25.

8 Schürer, *Geschichte*, 3, pp. 73–5. However, the terms σύνοδος, συναγωγή belong to a later period.

9 *CPJ*, 1, p. 6.

10 Thus the basic privilege of Jews living abroad τοῖς πατριοῖς νόμοις χρῆσθαι, *CPJ*, 1, p. 7.

inhabitants,[1] but it more often means a community of aliens who have acquired privileges analogous to civic rights. In Egypt we thus encounter πολιτεύματα of Idumeans, Phrygians and Cilicians, as well as of Jews.[2] Such ethnic groups always possessed their own religious identity as well.

The establishment of πολιτεύματα or κατοικίαι certainly required official permission in each instance. In the case of the settlement under Ptolemy I of the High Priest Hezekiah and the Jews who accompanied him – the earliest known settlement of Jews in Hellenistic Egypt – the appropriate royal warrant is explicitly mentioned:[3] it was probably a short royal decree, the contents of which would be comparable to the letter from Antiochus III to Zeuxis.[4] Apart from the requisite details concerning the founding of the settlement, including an initial tax exemption, we find there above all a guarantee of the right of the Jewish colonists to live according to their traditional laws and to apply their own laws within their community. A similar right extended to other colonists.[5] In view of the highly detailed admonitions of the written Torah together with the interpretations enshrined in the oral tradition, it becomes clear that such guarantees in effect granted the Jews wide-ranging control over their own affairs, naturally within the limits determined by the political sovereignty of the king and the authority of the laws promulgated by him. The measure of autonomy enjoyed by Jewish *politeumata* of this kind could easily stand comparison with that accorded to Greek cities at the time. These Jewish communities had their own law courts and their own schools, they appointed their own civic officials, and so on.[6] Writing of the great Jewish *politeumata* in Alexandria, Strabo apprises us that there an ethnarch 'ruled the people, judged its cases and supervised the implementation of contracts and orders like the ruler of an independent state'.[1] This quasi-monarchical structure did not last for long. Pseudo-Aristeas does not mention an ethnarch but rather a group of leaders of the *politeuma* (§310), in effect probably a *gerousia* such as Augustus was

[1] The term is not unambiguous, cf. Schürer, *Geschichte*, 3, pp. 71f.; H. Strathmann, 'πόλις, πολίτευμα, *TWNT*, 6 (1959), p. 519, *TDNT*, 6 (1968), pp. 519f.; Tcherikover, *Civilization*, pp. 299f.

[2] *CPJ*, 1, p. 6 n. 16.

[3] Jos. *C.Ap.* 1.189, citing Ps.-Hecateus: εἶχε γὰρ τὴν κατοίκησιν αὐτῶν καὶ τὴν πολιτεῖαν γεγραμμένην. Tcherikover translates: 'For he possessed (the conditions) of their settlement and their political constitution (drawn up) in writing' (*Civilization*, p. 300).

[4] Tcherikover, *Civilization*, pp. 300f.

[5] Jos. *Ant.* XII.147–53.

[6] Cf. Tcherikover, *Civilization*, pp. 82–4.

[7] In Jos. *Ant.* XIV.117. Cf. Tcherikover, *Civilization*, p. 302; H. J. Wolff, *Das Justizwesen der Ptolemäer*, MBPAR 44 (2nd edn., Muhich, 1970), p. 21.

later to re-establish.[1] The customary title for the individual leaders of the community was ἄρχων. The name was derived from the terminology of the Greek cities,[2] though no corresponding democratic constitution existed. On the contrary, we must assume a thoroughly oligarchic structure. The question whether the Hellenistic Jews of Alexandria possessed full citizenship has been widely discussed.[3] Tcherikover's detailed examination of this issue has definitively shown that this was not the case as far as the Alexandrian Jews as a whole were concerned.[4]

The Jewish inhabitants of the city were never granted full citizenship as a body. Moreover, to begin with, this did not create any difficulties in view of the generous privileges enjoyed by the Jews of Alexandria in the Hellenistic period, some of which even exceeded those of mere citizenship.[5] However, when the antagonism between the Greeks and the Jews came to a head in the early Roman period and at the same time Augustus introduced a poll-tax on all non-citizens, an acute problem arose.[6] In order to preserve the *status quo* the Jews had to try to acquire Alexandrian citizenship for the whole Jewish community. Their efforts did not meet with success.[7] On the other hand, individual Jewish families and groups had obtained Alexandrian citizenship over the years – of this we have indisputable proof.[8]

THE PARTICIPATION OF THE JEWS IN THE DIASPORA IN THE URBAN CULTURE OF THE HELLENISTIC PERIOD

The fascination with Hellenistic culture which increasingly permeated the Near East in the centuries after Alexander made itself felt among the Jewish ruling class as well, both in Palestine and in the Diaspora. It

1 According to Philo, *Flacc.* 74, Augustus entrusted the administration of Jewish affairs after the death of the 'genarch' to the *gerousia*, which either was now instituted for this porpose or more probably had its former functions restored to it.

2 Schürer, *Geschichte*, 3, pp. 85–8, 90f; Tcherikover, *Civilization*, pp. 302f.

3 Schürer, *Geschichte*, 3, pp. 121–34; *CPJ*, 1, pp. 39–41, 59–74; 2, pp. 25–107; *Civilization*, pp. 309–32; M. Brücklmeier, *Beiträge zur rechtlichen Stellung der Juden im römischen Reich* (Theol. Diss.; Münster, 1939).

4 In particular, Tcherikover, *Civilization*, pp. 309–32.

5 Tcherikover, *Civilization*, pp. 326f. According to Tarn, Alexandria was not a *polis* but comprised a collection of national *politeumata* (W. Tarn and G. T. Griffith, *Hellenistic Civilization*, p. 185 (p. 218)).

6 *CPJ*, 1, p. 41; Tcherikover, *Civilization*, p. 332.

7 Claudius' letter to the Alexandrians was decisive, *CPJ*, 2, pp. 25, 36–55, no. 153, especially lines 88–95.

8 Cf. *CPJ*, 2, pp. 29–33, no. 151; Jos. *Ant.* XIV.236; *CPJ*, 1, pp. 39f, 61f; Tcherikover, *Civilization*, pp. 327f.

had been Alexander's declared aim to bring Greeks and Persians together through the unifying power of a universal culture. To this end Hellenistic cities were founded with their elementary schools and their gymnasia as centres of Greek *paideia*.[1] They exerted a powerful attraction particularly on the younger members of the native upper class, who were inspired as much by down-to-earth political and economic self-interest as by the desire for education, good fellowship and a schooling in the new humanism. Those who mastered the Greek language and adopted the values of Hellenistic urban culture could expect a ready entrance into the service of the Greco-Macedonian rulers and appointment to diverse posts in the army, in business or in the financial administration. So once Jews in Palestine and in the Diaspora learnt Greek – in Palestine, alongside their mother tongue, in Alexandria and Egypt, before long instead of it – many opportunities were open to them. But did they fully participate in Hellenistic culture? Did Jewish youngsters attend the gymnasium, did they take part in the athletic contests like the sons of other citizens? They certainly did so in the Jerusalem of Jason during the brief period of his Hellenistic reforms. But this was a special case, a *polis* composed entirely of Hellenistic Jews.[2] In Alexandria by contrast, and elsewhere, Hellenistic Jews did not as a rule attend the gymnasia or participate in the ephebeia, except where they had renounced their ancestral faith. Philo found it quite natural that Greek culture and philosophy should for so long have been taught and discussed in the *proseuchai*. None the less a small élite, such as the sons of the most distinguished Jews in Alexandria, may well have had access to the city's gymnasia up to the early imperial period.[3] The polytheism that informed life in the gymnasium could be tolerated up to a certain point and in part defused by compromises; Jews in exile were familiar with this sort of problem in every sphere of life. At all events, as late as the Roman period a gymnasium education seems to have been regarded as the normal course for the sons of the leading families even by an observant Hellenistic Jew like Philo.[4] In Seleucid Antioch, Jews were clearly entitled to a share in the official distribution of oil by the gymnasiarchs, which indicates a similar state of affairs.[5] It was a grave setback when in the early Roman period young men from old-established, leading

[1] Hengel, *Hellenismus*, pp. 120–43 (ET I, pp. 65–78).

[2] Ibid., pp. 130, 137–40 (ET I, pp. 70, 74–6). Cf. E. Schürer, *History of the Jewish People in the Age of Jesus Christ*, a new English version revised and edited by Geza Vermes, Fergus Millar, P. Vermes and M. Black (Edinburgh, 1973), I, p. 148.

[3] *CPJ*, I, pp. 38f.

[4] Cf. Philo, *Spec*. II.229f, 246; *Opif*. 78.

[5] Jos. *Ant*. XII.120.

Jewish families, for whom gymnasium and ephebeia had become a tradition, began to be excluded from both.[1]

What sort of relationship prevailed between the small Jewish upper class and the broad mass of Jewish inhabitants? Participation in Hellenistic culture became steadily more widespread, while the quality of the Jewish contribution improved all the time. In the documents of Hellenistic Judaism we find evidence of notable literary and linguistic attainment, side by side with texts of inferior standard, such as the writings of the historian Demetrius (*circa* 200 B.C.E.)[2], the novelist Artapanus[3] and the Jewish dramatist Demetrius.[4] They provide interesting illustrations of various stages in this process of assimilation. Jewish education could not remain élitist. A Jewish teacher like Philo desired to reach all Jews, indeed if possible all men everywhere.[5] Early Hellenistic Christianity was later able to draw on this pedagogic tradition and to benefit from the intellectual resources created by it. The situation is rather different when we look at the economic and social spheres.

SOCIAL CONDITIONS

Information about the social circumstances of the Jews in the dispersion during the Hellenistic period is meagre, and what little evidence we have refers mainly to Egypt. Most of it has already been mentioned briefly: it reveals a complex picture which may be amplified and corroborated if we work back from our knowledge of conditions in the Roman era. On the whole, we can conclude that there existed a small upper class of very wealthy and influential Jews, and a broad mass of people living in much poorer circumstances. There were relatively few Jewish slaves. At certain times, indeed, there must have been large numbers of them, such as in the aftermath of the numerous wars, but this state of affairs did not last long since the Jews always showed commendable solidarity in pressing for the release of their enslaved compatriots. Philo maintains that the majority of Jews in Rome were former captives who were now freedmen.[6]

1 *CPJ*, 2, pp. 29–33, no. 151; p. 41, no. 153, lines 93f.; Tcherikover, *Civilization*, pp. 311–14.

2 See below, ch. 10.

3 Ibid.

4 Ibid.

5 See pp. 156–8 above; against Tcherikover, *Civilization*, pp. 163–5; Hengel, *Hellenismus*, p. 138 (ET 1, p. 73). Cf. the analogous goal of a comprehensive education of the people in post-Maccabean Palestine, Hengel, *Hellenismus*, pp. 143–52, ET 1, pp. 78–83.

6 Philo, *Leg.* 155. On the subject of the social structure as a whole, see *CPJ*, 1, pp. 10–19, who gives a list of sources.

The great majority of the Jewish upper class remained loyal to Moses, as did the Jews of the Diaspora as a whole. Men such as Dositheos, who was discussed earlier, or the Tobiad Joseph or Tiberius Alexander were exceptions. We can see this in the early Roman period from the example of Philo's family: his father was a Roman citizen, his elder brother Gaius Julius Alexander was a very rich man who managed the estates of Claudius' mother Antonia; for all that, Tiberius Alexander was the sole apostate.[1] The family were effortlessly integrated into the culture of their environment and were loyal to the king, yet retained firm roots in the *proseuche* community. Philo reveals that many of the leaders of the Jewish community were very prosperous.[2] Their wealth was primarily derived from great maritime trading enterprises, as we might expect in a commercial capital like Alexandria. This is confirmed when Philo refers to Jewish ship-owners, whom he distinguishes from the mass of small merchants and tradespeople.[3] But Jews also had a significant share in the banking institutions which flourished in Alexandria.[4] In addition they occupied high posts in the state treasury and the customs.[5] It is legitimate to assume that a similar situation existed in Alexandria in the pre-Roman period – there is verification of this in the history of the Tobiads. Of course, conditions in the rich metropolis of Alexandria would have been very different from those in provincial towns, let alone in the countryside.

Even there, however, we find the occasional rich merchant and tax farmer, such as a certain Sabbataios who collected the taxes from the Nile ferries, or Simon, the son of Iazarus, who paid several talents in fishermen's taxes into a royal bank. Both are known to us from ostraka found in Upper Egypt.[6] For the rest, the Jewish military colonists were also relatively well off. These comprised either former mercenaries or active frontier defence troops who were given land, sometimes extensive estates, and who leased it out to tenant farmers.[7] Apart from the colonists, there were also large numbers of Jewish mercenaries,

[1] See above, pp. 135, 139, 145, 158, 162f; *CPJ*, I, pp. 36f.

[2] Philo, *Flacc.* 76. Any inference which one may care to draw from this about the pre-Roman period must be treated with caution: *CPJ*, I, p. 16.

[3] Philo, *Flacc.* 57; *CPJ*, I, pp. 48–50.

[4] Cf. *CPJ*, I, p. 49; for Philo's brother Alexander, cf. Jos. *Ant.* XVIII.159f; *Bell.* V.205.

[5] *CPJ*, I, pp. 17–19. On the problem of the alabarchs ('ἀλαβάρχης') in Jos. *Ant.* XVIII.159, 259; XX.100) cf. *CPJ*, I, p. 49 n. 4.

[6] *CPJ*, I, pp. 194–226; for Sabbataios, pp. 204–7, no. 51–60; for Simon, pp. 207f, 217, 222, no. 61–3, 90, 107. Hengel, *Juden*, p. 123, ET p. 90.

[7] *CPJ*, I, pp. 12f, 15f.

some of them officers, serving in cavalry and infantry units of both the regular army and the auxiliary forces.[1]

The majority of Jews in the Diaspora were farmers, farmworkers and craftsmen, just like the Jews in Palestine. To the above-mentioned evidence from Egyptian papyri[2] can be added two pieces of literary evidence relating to Alexandria in the early Roman period. The rabbinical account of the great *proseuche* in Alexandria mentioned earlier tells us that in the assembly members of the various guilds sat together: 'People did not sit in indiscriminate confusion but the goldsmiths all sat together as did the silversmiths, the blacksmiths and the coppersmiths; and if someone needy arrived, he would recognize his fellow craftsmen and turn to them for help and he would thus find succour both for himself and his household'.[3] Philo confirms the existence of Jewish artisans in Alexandria in his own day when he writes of the pogrom of 38 C.E. under the prefect Flaccus.[4] The anti-Jewish mob broke into and looted the workshops (ἐργαστήρια) of the Jews which happened to be closed because the court was observing a day of mourning. At the end Philo enumerates some of the occupations pursued by the Alexandrian Jews and specifies in addition to shipowners and merchants the craftsmen (τεχνῖται) and farmers.

If we may generalize from this picture, we see that on the one hand the social structure of the Jews of the Diaspora, like their economic circumstances, differed little from that of their non-Jewish neighbours. The marked variations between town and country, the glaring contrast of ostentatious wealth and crushing poverty existed within the Jewish community and in the Gentile milieu alike. However much the Torah of Moses led to the religious segregation of the Jews in the ancient world, it did not give rise to any radical social innovations. But social hardship was considerably alleviated: Jewish slaves quickly had their freedom purchased by their families or even by the community, each local congregation had its poor-relief, the guilds provided protection for their members. Wherever there was a Jewish community, the individual Jew was assured of help and support. There is another factor that deserves mention, a question of social ethics. Philo once emphasizes that it was characteristic of the Jews, with their strong sense of family obligation, to work hard for their living.[5] This was doubtless true of the pre-Roman period as well. Every opportunity

[1] *CPJ*, 1, pp. 12f, 147f.
[2] See above, pp. 135, 151 n. 5.
[3] *b. Sukka* 51b.
[4] Philo, *Flacc.* 56f.
[5] Philo, *Legat.* 230.

was seized to attain material security by hard work. The Roman inscriptions mention not only tradesmen and businessmen but also Jewish tailors, butchers, painters and smiths, and even singers and actors.[1]

[1] Cf. Frey, *CIJ*, 1, pp. lxv; *CPJ*, 1, pp. 50–5; 2, pp. 1–5.

CHAPTER 5

THE INTERPENETRATION OF JUDAISM AND HELLENISM IN THE PRE-MACCABEAN PERIOD

GREEKS, BARBARIANS AND JEWS: THE PROBLEM OF HELLENIZATION IN THE EARLY HELLENISTIC PERIOD

A description of the interpenetration of Judaism and Hellenism in the pre-Maccabean period, that is, in the 158 years between 333 and 175 B.C.E., presents us with a twofold difficulty. Firstly, from this period we have only fragmentary and sporadic reports about the Jews in Palestine and the Diaspora. Non-Jewish literary sources are almost completely silent, and, where they do provide information, they are minimally concerned with the absorption of Hellenistic culture by the Jews. Even epigraphic, papyrological and archeological evidence is in the main sparse and often difficult to assess. Furthermore, Jewish literature of this epoch can often be dated only hypothetically, and most often can be used only as indirect evidence of this penetration or of repulsion. It either (at least apparently) says nothing at all about relationship to its Hellenistic environment or, in the case of polemic or apologetic writings, it presents a biased view. Nearly all the Jewish literature available to us from this period is religiously and nationalistically biased.[1] A complete picture cannot be derived from such sources, and we can at best only describe individual situations and developments as they are fortuitously presented to us in the sources.

Secondly, although we can grasp fairly clearly what 'Judaism' means, i.e. those belonging to the Jewish *ethnos* both in Palestine and the Diaspora, their religion, their way of life and their literature, the much used terms 'Hellenism' and 'Hellenization' are less clear and more subject to dispute. In this connection Hellenism means not only a historical epoch between the rise of Alexander (334 B.C.E.) and the battle of Actium (31 B.C.E.);[2] it is to be understood as meaning an

1 M. Hengel, 'Anonymität, Pseudepigraphie und "literarische Fälschung" in der jüdisch–hellenistischen Literatur', *Pseudepigrapha*, 1, Entretiens sur l'antiquité classique, 18 (Vandoeuvres–Geneva, 1972), pp. 252ff, 304.

2 M. Hengel, *Judentum und Hellenismus*, WUNT 10, 2nd edn. (Tübingen, 1973), p. 4 = ET *Judaism and Hellenism* (London, 1974), 2 vols. 1, p. 9.

apparently firmly delineated culture, which, because of its expansive character, tried to incorporate ancient Judaism too. This portrayal of Hellenism as a world culture, which penetrated the eastern countries conquered by Alexander, goes back to Gustav Droysen, the first great historian of the period, who was influenced by Hegel's philosophy of history. The Greek world appeared to him as the antithesis of the ancient Orient, and Hellenism was the synthesis which reached fulfilment in Christianity.[1] This interpretation had a certain basis in antiquity itself, especially in Plutarch's *De fortuna aut virtute Alexandri Magni*. Here Alexander appears not only as world conqueror but also as one educated in philosophy, who was a 'world-tutor' and 'world-reconciler',[2] who 'civilized barbaric kings', 'founded Greek cities among savage peoples' and 'taught lawless and uneducated tribes law and peace'.[3] Plutarch's idealistic picture is painted under the influence of the Stoic concept of the world-citizen and against the background of the Roman empire which was then at peace and relatively humane,[4] before it was shaken by the crises of the third century C.E. This notion of the political unity of the world in a 'world empire', which was so self-evident for him, was originally foreign to the Greek mind, which was more orientated to the individual *polis*. On the other hand, we do find the notion in the Persian empire[5] and later in Jewish apocalyptic.[6] Alexander began his campaign in reality as a war of revenge. Scholars argue even to this day when and in what way the thought of world empire first occurred to him, if it ever did.[7] We may, therefore, conclude that the idea of a self-contained but expanding Hellenistic culture, behind which lies the political and philosophical concept of a humanitarian amalgamation of peoples, cannot be placed in the early Hellenistic period of Alexander's march, the struggles of the Diadochi and the monarchies of the third century. At first only the upper classes among the Macedonian conquerors were influenced by Greek culture, and so in general they appeared more as destroyers than bearers of

[1] C. Préaux, 'Réflexions sur l'entité hellénistique', *ChE*, 40 (1965), 133ff.; Hengel, *Hellenismus*, pp. 2ff. = ET 1, pp. 2ff.

[2] Ch. 5 (329 C): *diallaktēs tōn holōn*.

[3] Ch. 4 (328 B).

[4] Cf. Trajan in Pliny the younger, *Epistulae* x.97 for the rejection of anonymous denunciation *nec nostri saeculi est*.

[5] V. Martin, 'La politique des Achéménides', *Museum Helveticum*, 22 (1965), 38ff: Ahuramazda had 'given all the kingdoms of the earth into the hand' of the great king; F. Wehrli, review of H. C. Baldry, *The Unity of Mankind in Greek Thought*, in *Gnomon*, 38 (1966), 643 = *Theoria und Humanitas* (Zurich/Munich, 1972), p. 174).

[6] Hengel, *Hellenismus*, pp. 330ff. = ET 1, pp. 181ff.

[7] For a summary of literature see J. Seibert, *Alexander der Grosse*, Erträge der Forschung 10 (Darmstadt, 1972), pp. 207ff.

culture. Both the very anti-macedonian Demosthenes, and Isocrates, who warmly admired Philip II, call them barbarians.[1] If we leave out the exceptional figure of Alexander, the others certainly possessed no missionary zeal for civilizing others. The object of the young king himself, too, was probably no more than the amalgamation of the new governing class of Macedonians with the old Persian aristocracy.[2] The reason for this is to be found more in pragmatic power politics than in the humanitarian field. After the king's death the assembled army immediately abandoned these schemes. It is indeed astonishing how quickly and unconditionally the Macedonians, who had up till then been considered barbarians, now took over the élitist concepts of the Greeks.

The Diadochi and later Hellenistic kings were mainly interested, not in the spreading of Hellenistic culture among their oriental vassals, but in securing and extending their personal power. But this could be better served by separation from the orientals and the more intensive recruitment of Macedonians and Greeks to the army and the administration. Royal power rested on the Macedonian phalanx, and Greek mercenaries, civil servants and technicians. It required assistants who could think rationally and who possessed organizational talent but few moral scruples. For this reason the kings, in order to secure their authority in the conquered colonial districts, established numerous cities and military settlements. The cultural unity of the new and much larger Hellenistic world did not enter their vision. On the contrary they often conducted a narrow mercantile policy of separation (and enticement), and destroyed each other in suicidal fashion in constant wars lasting from the death of Alexander to the final victory of Rome. The Roman power took over their inheritance in the west and forcibly imposed peace; in the east it was taken over by national, oriental rulers, particularly the Parthian empire. A more comprehensive and thorough Hellenization of the lower classes took place in Syria and Palestine for the first time under the patronage of Rome, which could here appear as the saviour of the Greek cultural inheritance. In the east, and as far as the Euphrates boundary, Rome was the first to help 'Hellenism' to real victory.

Thus, the theme of the interpenetration of Judaism and Hellenism presents us with a phenomenon that is complicated, many-sided and often contradictory. To begin with, the controversial and shifting concepts and historical phenomena of Hellenism and Hellenization must be examined.

1 A. Daskalakis, *The Hellenism of the Ancient Macedonians* (Salonica, 1965).

2 Seibert, *Alexander*, pp. 186ff, 300ff.

The starting-point is the traditional Greek distinction between Greeks and barbarians, which reached its full sharpness with the victorious conclusion of the Persian war.[1] Both words are used to convey a collective concept. The barbarians were those of 'foreign speech', a negative, belittling designation by which 'highly cultured, semi-cultured and primitive peoples, who dwelt outside the Greek environment, were curiously lumped together'.[2] Nor were the 'Hellenes' a 'people' in the strict sense, but a community of peoples and cities, as is made clear by the original description *panhellēnes*. The theory of blood-relationship by common descent from a tribal ancestor, Hellen the son of Deucalion, is secondary. It is similar to the Jewish emphasis on Shem the son of Noah, after the great flood.[3] The community of Hellenes was manifested in a particular way of life, a culture shaped by an open concept of man and by associated political institutions, such as common games and supra-regional sanctuaries. The experiences of the struggle for freedom against the Persians strengthened the feeling of solidarity and of superiority, while the picture drawn of the barbarians was distorted. They were considered uneducated, and even brutish, unfriendly to strangers, despotic and slavish, superstitious, cruel, cowardly and treacherous.[4] This negative list could easily be enlarged. When Cicero later describes Syrians and Jews as nations 'which were born for slavery' or when Livy defines the army of Antiochus III as 'Syrians...who on account of their servile minds [*servilia ingenia*] are a people of slaves rather than soldiers', we have here merely the expression of the widespread bias of classical times, that by nature barbarians were slaves and the Greeks masters.[5] Aristotle, who took up this supposition into his political science, is said to have given the young Alexander the advice to treat the Greeks as a leader treats his men, but barbarians, on the other hand, as a master treats his slaves.[6] Since slaves according to him had only the function of tools, he implies that the subjected barbarians were basically merely

[1] J. Jüthner, *Hellenen und Barbaren*, Das Erbe der Alten 8 (Leipzig, 1923); W. Speyer, 'Barbar A,B', *JAC*, 10 (1967), 251–67; H. Schwabl, 'Die Hellenen–Barbaren Antithese im Zeitalter der Perserkriege', *Grecs et barbares*, Entretiens sur l'antiquité classique 8 (Vandoeuvres–Geneva, 1962).

[2] H. E. Stier, *Die geschichtliche Bedeutung des Hellenennamens*, Arbeitsgemeinschaft für Forschung des Landes Nordrhein-Westfalen 159 (Cologne, 1970), p. 20.

[3] Stier, *Bedeutung*, pp. 22ff.

[4] Speyer, *JAC*, 10 (1967), 255f, 263f.

[5] *De Provinciis Consularibus*, 10; Livy xxxv.49.8; cf. Euripides, *Iphigenia Aulidensis* 1400f; *Helena* 276; Jüthner, *Hellenen*, pp. 25ff; Speyer, *JAC*, 10 (1967), 253.

[6] Aristotle, *Politica* 1.1.6 (1252b), quoting Euripides, *Iph. Aul.* 1400; Plutarch, *De fort. aut virt. Alex.* (329 B); Speyer, *JAC*, 10 (1967), 256.

the tools of the conqueror, that is, objects for exploitation.[1] Lysander sold the inhabitants of Cedreae in Caria as slaves, because they were only *mixobarbaroi*, but he granted freedom to the (Greek) inhabitants of Lampsacus in Ionia, which he conquered a little later.[2] Similarly the mingling of Greeks and barbarians was prohibited. According to Plato's *Menexenus*, the Athenians boasted that they, unlike other Greek cities, had no Phoenician or Egyptian ancestors:

> The mind of this city is so noble and free and whole and natural and its hatred of barbarians so strong, because we are totally and purely Hellenes and are not mingled with barbarians. For no Pelops or Kadmos, no Aigyptos or Danaos, nor anyone else who is by nature barbarian and only by law Greek, lives amongst us, but we live here as pure Hellenes and not as mixed barbarians (*ou mixobarbarois*). Therefore the city is a totally dedicated enemy of alien natures.[3]

Again Livy attributes very similar statements to the ambassadors of Macedonia at the Panaetolian Congress of 200 B.C.E.: 'Eternal war exists between the barbarians and all Greeks, and will exist. Because of unchangeable nature ...they are enemies.'[4]

Alexander's campaign seemed to confirm the absolute military and political superiority of the Hellenes, among whom the Macedonian aristocracy, and especially the royal house of the Argeads reckoned themselves[5]. There was an attempt, too, to maintain the distinction between Hellenes and barbarians in the newly established *poleis* and military colonies in the conquered districts. This was achieved through emphasis on Greco-Macedonian ancestry, through restrictions on rights of citizenship in the newly-founded cities, and through the conservative educational upbringing which formed a basis for the typical Greek and aristocratic way of life. For example, in late Ptolemaic and Roman Alexandria, down to the edict of Claudius, granting of citizenship was bound up with graduation from the gymnasium.[6] Though it may have been possible, especially in newly-founded cities in the new colonial districts, for mixed marriages between Greco-Macedonian colonizers and natives to happen, in the main the attempt was made to keep the citizenry 'pure' from mixed

[1] Arist. *Pol.* I.5 (1254a).

[2] Xenophon, *Hellenica* II.1.15, 19, cf. *Agesilaos* VII.6.

[3] 245 c/d.

[4] Livy XXXI.29.15. Cf. Isocrates, *Panegyricus* 184, Plato, *Respublica* V.470c: 'polemious physei einai', *Menexenus* 242d: the Greeks fight among themselves until they achieve victory, but against barbarians until they annihilate them. Cf. E. Schütrumpf, 'Kosmopolitismus oder Panhellenismus?', *Hermes,* 100 (1972), 9ff.

[5] Herodotus V.22; cf. Daskalakes, *Hellenism*, pp. 97ff.

[6] Hengel, *Hellenismus*, pp. 122ff = ET 1, pp. 65ff.

marriages with barbarians.[1] In the speech of the embassy from Rhodes before the Senate in 190 B.C.E. it was stressed that the cities planted in Asia were no less Greek than their mother-cities in Greece itself, 'the change of place brought about no change of descent or custom'.[2] Still in the time of the Parthians and the Roman empire the citizens of Dura Europos, which had been founded by Seleucus I, considered themselves to be genuine Macedonians among whom mixed marriages did occur, but were in no way a matter of course.[3] The many marriages between relatives in the old families must have served to preserve the Greco-Macedonian heritage. Tacitus himself praises the citizens of Seleucia in Babylonia, who were under Parthian dominion, because 'they had not been corrupted into barbarism, but had retained the way of life of their founder Seleucus I'. He must have found this view in his Greek sources, for one of the constant *topoi* in classical Greece was that it was the greatest ill-fortune for a Greek city 'to become barbarian'.[4] Thus, Isocrates, for example, describes how Salamis in Cyprus 'was barbarized' through Phoenician rulers and 'brought under the yoke of the Great King' until Euagoras brought new life politically and economically to both city and island.[5] According to Josephus the inhabitants of the already mentioned Babylonian Seleucia right down to the first century C.E. consisted of three groups, Greeks, Syrians and Jews; and the privileged Greek citizens contended bitterly against the other two groups in order to defend their position and authority in the city.[6] Strabo reports that there was a fourfold division of the population in the Cyrenean Pentapolis,[7] where Greek citizens, Libyan farmers, resident aliens (*metoikoi*) and Jews stood over against one another. Josephus[8] and Polybius[9] too testify to a threefold division of population in Alexandria. In the struggles which used to break out between the different groups, the Jews, who were in the minority,

[1] M. Rostovtzeff, *The Social and Economic History of the Hellenistic World* (Oxford, 1941), vol. 3, index under 'intermarriage'. C. Vatin, *Recherches sur le mariage et la condition de la femme à l'époque hellénistique*, Bibliothèque des écoles françaises d'Athènes et de Rome 217 (Paris, 1970), pp. 132ff.

[2] Livy XXXVII.54.18, following Polybius.

[3] M. Rostovtzeff, *Dura-Europos and its Art* (Oxford, 1938), pp. 21f; Vatin, *Recherches*, pp. 136ff.

[4] *Annals* VI.42.1; cf. Plato, *Epistles* 353a; cf. *Laws* 692c/693a; Polybius III.58.8; Plutarch, *Timoleon* 17.2 (244) and G. Walser, *Rom, das Reich und die fremden Völker*, Basler Beiträge zur Geschichtswissenschaft 37 (Basel, 1951), p. 71.

[5] *Evagoras* 20,47 (Loeb edn, vol. 3, 1945, ed. L. Van Hook, pp. 14, 28f).

[6] *Ant.* XVIII.372ff.

[7] From his historical work, cited by Jos. *Ant.* XIV.115.

[8] *C.Ap.* II.68–72: *Iudaei, Graeci, multitudo Aegyptiorum.*

[9] XXXIV.1.14 = Strabo XVII.1.12 (C 797): Egyptians, mercenaries and citizens; cf. P. M. Fraser, *Ptolemaic Alexandria* (Oxford, 1972), 1, pp. 61–86.

usually suffered most. We see from these examples how attempts were made, with greater or less success, to maintain the ancient barriers at least in part right down to Roman times.

In the early Hellenistic period of the third century B.C.E. the partition wall between the Greco-Macedonian overlords and their subject peoples was largely insurmountable. In the third century native Egyptians required a special permit to live in Alexandria. The statement of place of birth official documents demanded was intended, amongst other things, to prevent Egyptians from assuming the rights of a Greek citizen. Only in the second century through immigration from the countryside, did the Egyptian part of the population greatly increase and form that restless mass described by Polybius, which consisted predominantly of Hellenized Egyptians but which had no political rights.[1] The Jews formed a 'third force' between Greek citizens and natives. Even in Roman times Jews in Syria and Egypt were not, as a rule, admitted into citizenship for political and religious reasons, although they had long since adopted the Greek language and the upper classes had welcomed Greek culture. The biased and misleading account given by Josephus of Jewish *isopoliteia* in Alexandria and Antioch and also the struggles of Jews in Alexandria and Caesarea for citizen rights, which received a negative response from Claudius and Nero,[2] shows how difficult this barrier was to overcome. Jews and Egyptians were not alone in this. We hear of similar situations in other parts of the Greek colonial areas, such as Massilia on the southern coast of Gaul, Asia Minor and Greek cities on the northern coast of the Black Sea.[3] The Hellenes of Greek cities in old and new colonial areas kept struggling – even until Roman times with some success – to prevent the entry of non-Greeks into citizenship. When Polybius, towards the end of the second century, censured the citizens of Alexandria as on account of their mixed origin (*migades*) not suited for the regular organized administration of a *polis*, this 'mixing' might be linked with the fact that Ptolemy VIII Euergetes around 127 B.C.E. had violently decimated the body of citizens and then replenished

[1] H. Braunert, *Binnenwanderung*, Bonner historische Forschungen 26 (Bonn, 1964), pp. 54, 75ff, Fraser, *Alexandria*, 1, pp. 70–3, 82f.

[2] Alexandria: *Ant.* XII.8; XIV.188; XIX.281; *C.Ap.* II.32, 38ff., 69, 71f. Cf. V. Tcherikover, *Corpus Papyrorum Judaicarum*, 1, pp. 41, 61ff; 2, pp. 29ff, 36ff, for the letter of Claudius. Antioch: *Ant.* XII.119ff; Caesarea, *Bell.* II.266ff., 284ff.; cf. A. N. Sherwin-White, *Racial Prejudice in Imperial Rome* (Cambridge, 1967), pp. 86–101; V. Tcherikover, *Hellenistic Civilization and the Jews* (Philadelphia, 1959), pp. 296–332.

[3] Livy XXXVII.54.21 with reference to the inhabitants of Massilia: *mores et leges et ingenium sincerum integrumque a contagione accolarum servarunt*, cf. however also XXXVIII.17.12; the *politeuma mikton* of Emporium is an exception: Strabo III.4.8 (C 160). The 'Mixhellenes' in Olbia were a group separate from the full citizens; see Vatin, *Recherches*, pp. 141ff.

it with foreigners. It remains uncertain whether these were Greeks from the motherland or Greco-Egyptians.[1] We may note that Polybius in the same breath extols the Alexandrians against the two other groups, the Egyptians and mercenaries, 'for they have not forgotten the original way of life common to all Greeks'. Livy, probably following Posidonius, mentions that Macedonians scattered throughout the *coloniae* of the east 'degenerated into Syrians, Parthians and Egyptians', but ascribes this less to mixture of race than to a change of place and climate: 'Everything develops more in accordance with its nature in its place of origin; on being transplanted to a strange soil it changes its nature according to what it absorbs there.'[2]

Therefore in analysing the concept of Hellenization various components have to be distinguished. These are: firstly, purely occupational and business contacts; secondly, the physical mixture of peoples through mixed marriages; thirdly, the adoption by orientals of Greek language and culture; fourthly, the full assimilation of orientalized Greeks and Hellenized orientals. Lack of women was one reason why mixed marriages could not always be avoided in the new military settlements and newly-founded cities. However, full assimilation was a rare exception, at least in the early part of the third century. We most frequently encounter assimilation of orientals, but, viewing the population as a whole, it does not usually affect broad classes of people. A real interpenetration first occurs in the Roman period.

There was considerable resistance on the question of mixed marriages. The marriages made by Alexander between his Macedonian *hetairoi* and Persian princesses were later annulled at the demand of the assemblage of the army – even that of Seleucus. Alexander himself commanded that the 10,000 veterans taken back by Krateros to Macedonia should leave behind their children by barbarian wives, and the king himself would have them brought up in Macedonian fashion.[3] According to a historical novel by Hermesianax (third century B.C.E.), Nicocreon, king of the city-state of Salamis in Cyprus,

[1] See p. 172 n. 8; cf. Justin XXXVIII.8.6f, for this Braunert, *Binnenwanderung*, pp. 77ff; a different view in Fraser, *Alexandria,* I, 86f.

[2] XXXVIII.17.11, 13. Philo attributes the superiority of the Greeks to the excellent climate of their homeland; *de Prov.*, in Euseb. *Praep. Evang.* VIII.14.66, GCS 43, ed. Mras, p. 477. Cf. Speyer, *JAC,* 10 (1967), 256. According to Plato, *Resp.* 435e–436a the Greeks were for that reason greedy for possessions, but the Phoenicians and the Egyptians were greedy to learn, cf. *Timaeus* 24b–c and *Laws*, Book 5, 747c.

[3] Arrian VII.4.4ff; 12.2.

refused to give his daughter in marriage to the wealthy Arceophon 'because of Arceophon's shameful descent, for his ancestors were Phoenicians'.[1] In Ptolemaic Palestine in the middle of the third century we hear of concubinage between garrison troops and native women. But they were not treated as equal to wedded wives; a royal decree was necessary to save them from registration as slave girls.[2] There are isolated examples of mixed marriages between Greeks and Egyptian women in the Egyptian countryside, for example the Fayum;[3] but mixed marriages of Jews were quite rare (see below, p. 194). But even in these exceptional cases the attempt was made to keep the status of Greeks for the children. A full Egyptianization of Greeks is seldom found, for it was always connected with a sharp fall in social status. It affected primarily the Hellenomemphites who had immigrated already in pre-Ptolemaic times, and is associated later with the impoverishment of the countryside in the second and first centuries B.C.E.[4]

Examples of the opposite trend are far more abundant; talented natives were eager to climb the social ladder of Hellenization, to learn the Greek language and in part adopt Greek names, so that it is often difficult to say whether those with Greek names are Egyptians, Jews (see below, p. 188) or real Greeks. Since only the language of the ruling class had official recognition, only bilingual natives could obtain posts as officials in the lower and middle sections of the royal administration. The state, in order to attain the maximum exploitation of agriculture, depended on the positive collaboration of these bilingual Egyptians.[5] In a list of qualities desired in a Ptolemaic official, it is required that he be a *philhellēn*; and this must apply to the non-Greek, Jewish or native,

1 Antoninus Liberalis, *met.* 39 in *Mythographi Graeci* 2, 1, ed. E. Martini (Leipzig, 1896), p. 121; see Rostovtzeff, *History,* 2, pp. 1071f.

2 See the *prostagma* of Ptolemy II concerning the registration of cattle and slaves in Syria and Phoenicia, 260 B.C.E., *SB* 8008. Bibliography in M.-T. Lenger, *Corpus des Ordonnances des Ptolémées*, Académie royale de Belgique, Classe des lettres, Mémoires 57, 1 (Brussels, 1964), pp. 37ff., no. 22, ll. 17ff.

3 Vatin, *Recherches*, pp. 132ff; Fraser, *Alexandria,* 1, pp. 71ff.

4 Braunert, *Binnenwanderung*, pp. 41ff, 72ff; cf. A. Świderek, 'La société indigène en Égypte au IIIe siècle avant notre ère d'après les archives de Zenon', *Journal of Juristic Papyrology,* 7/8 (1953/4), 256. 'Il semble pourtant qu'en général la situation d'un homme pauvre, fut-il Egyptien, Grec, Syrien, Arabe ou d'une autre nationalité encore, était presque la même.' It must be added that among the Egyptians poverty was common, among the Greeks it was the exception.

5 A. E. Samuel, 'The Greek element in the Ptolemaic bureaucracy', *Proceedings of the Twelfth International Congress of Papyrology*, American Studies in Papyrology, 7 (Toronto, 1970), pp. 443–53. For bilingualism see R. Rémondon, 'Problèmes du

officials of the king.[1] The Ptolemaic kings and the Greek upper class certainly did not consider the Egyptians as opponents; there was no fundamental and legally fixed preference for Greeks and Macedonians. Nevertheless, the natives came to be exploited. Tarn writes: 'The Greek came to Egypt to grow rich'. Świderek agrees, and comments that

each document from the third-century Zenon archives confirms this view.[2] From the beginning a political and economic approach characterized the kings in their dealings with the natives. Ptolemy I, before any adequate Greek civil service had been built up, at first brought into his administration high Egyptian officials and counsellors.[3] Later he, and above all his son, employed only Greek talents in the most important positions – presumably in order to achieve greater economic efficiency. The finance minister Apollonius from Caunus in Caria[4] is a prototype, and he brought in further citizens of that city, including Zeno. The Egyptians were thus ousted from the highest positions, though this did not prevent the king, when it appeared advantageous to him, from falling back on them. The best known examples are the Macedonian-trained Egyptian phalanxes with whose help Ptolemy IV Philopator won the battle of Raphia in 217 B.C.E. (see above, p. 67). On the lower level of administering the villages and toparchies their co-operation could never be dispensed with.

A real Hellenization of the native *laoi*, that is, the population working on the land, was never intended by the Hellenistic overlords. The main duty of the natives as *basilikoi geōrgoi*, in an economic system based on a mercantile state capitalism, was to till the land and deliver up the largest possible share of its produce. The foreign and mostly Greco-Macedonian military colonists were economically much better placed, by comparison. The amount they had to deliver was smaller and, in the

bilinguisme dans l'Egypte Lagide (U.P.Z. I, 148)', *ChE* 39 (1964), 126–46 and, in qualification of this, W. Peremans, 'Über die Zweisprachigkeit im ptolemäischen Ägypten', *Studien zur Papyrologie und antiken Wirtschaftsgeschichte, Friedrich Oertel zum 80. Geburtstag gewidmet*, ed. H. Braunert (Bonn, 1964), pp. 49–60.

[1] See the quotation from a Greek writer of comedy in A. S. Hunt and J. G. Smyly, ed. *The Tebtunis Papyri* (London, 1902–37), 3, 703, p. 71; Rostovtzeff, *Social and Economic History*, 3, pp. 1421 n. 212.

[2] W. W. Tarn and G. T. Griffith, *Hellenistic Civilization* (3rd edn., London, 1952), p. 201; Świderek 'La société grecque en Egypte au IIIme siècle av.n.è. d'après les archives de Zenon' *Journal of Juristic Papyrology*, 9/10 (1955–6), 365f.

[3] C. Bradford Welles, 'The Egyptians under the first Ptolemies', *Proceedings of the Twelfth International Congress of Papyrology*, pp. 505–10.

[4] A. Świderek, 'A la cour alexandrine d'Apollonios le dioecète', *Eos*, 50 (1959/60), 81–9.

vast majority of cases, they did not themselves work their huge estates but leased them out to natives.[1] The centralizing administration of the sovereign, which was conducted from the Greek metropolis of Alexandria, prevented the natives from forcibly breaking down these political and social barriers. So, too, did the solidarity of the Greeks with one another, their education in the gymnasia from which Egyptians were normally excluded, and the exclusiveness of the corporations of citizens in those few *poleis* which existed. Even in Roman times, these 'proven' policies were continued for fiscal reasons. The native population reacted by resigning themselves to the situation, but sometimes by passive resistance or open rebellion. The third possibility was the attempt to assimilate and to ascend socially.

The second century brought a measure of change, which was felt as much in Egypt, about which we are best informed, as in the Seleucid kingdom, where the contrasts were perhaps not quite so sharp, but were still present. At that time the influx of new Greek immigrants from the motherland had lessened significantly, so that to a certain extent Hellenized Egyptians and Semites won greater influence. In the Seleucid kingdom, which had a greater variety of peoples, the tendency towards Hellenization and the social 'acceptance' of the native upper classes was stronger than in Ptolemaic Egypt, which, with the exception of priests, lacked a genuine native aristocracy. The priests there, as the leaders of national resistance, supported the natives in the anti-Greek disturbances which broke out mainly in Upper Egypt from the end of the third century. For this reason, the Ptolemies, after the decline of immigration from the motherland, remained dependent on foreign mercenaries, particularly those from their colonial areas. An important role was played here by Semitic and more especially Jewish mercenaries.[2]

After the severe treaty of Apamea in 188 B.C.E., which drove them out of Asia Minor, the Seleucids, on the contrary, attempted to strengthen the Hellenistic element in their kingdom by giving the native aristocracy the option and, on payment of an appropriate sum into the royal treasury, the opportunity to become citizens of a Hellenized *polis*. From the very beginning the Seleucids had done much more to found new cities in their wide-spreading kingdom than the Ptolemies, who founded new cities only in their provinces outside

[1] Rostovtzeff, *Social and Economic History*, 2, pp. 1070ff., C. Préaux, *ChE*, 40 (1965), 129–39 and *Les Grecs en Egypte d'après les archives de Zenon* (Brussels, 1947).

[2] M. Launey, *Recherches sur les armées hellénistiques*, Bibliothèque des écoles françaises d'Athènes et de Rome 169 (Paris, 1949/50) vol. 1, pp. 535ff. The statistics in 1, pp. 89ff. show clearly the growth of the Semitic element.

Egypt. More than any other, Antiochus IV Epiphanes, who was perhaps influenced by Roman practice, adopted this policy, a policy which after a promising start failed disastrously in relation to the Jews.[1]

In the second century there emerged in Egypt, Palestine and Syria, as previously in Asia Minor and on the northern coast of the Black Sea, a new class, which we might call 'Greco-Egyptian' or 'Greco-Syrian';[2] but it was not Greco-Macedonian in origin and did not possess citizens' rights in the old colonial cities of these areas, though it certainly differentiated itself from the 'barbarian' country populace both in language and culture. In education and behaviour, especially in later times, members of this new class could be regarded as Hellenes. This is shown by the criticism levelled by Strabo (*circa* 63 B.C.E.–21 C.E.) at Ephoros (*circa* 405–330 B.C.E.), who made a distinction between three Greek peoples and the barbarian rest of the sixteen peoples of Asia Minor, but qualified this on the ground that some of the latter were 'mixed'. Strabo argues against him: 'We cannot name any...whom we should reckon "mixed"...even if they have become mixed, the dominant element makes them into either Greeks or barbarians. We do not know a third "mixed" people.'[3] It is evident that the collective concept of 'Hellenes' was not always clearly defined ethnically. Aetolians, Acarnaneans, Epirotes and Macedonians all joined the community of the Hellenes at a later stage, and the same may be true of the Hellenized inhabitants of Asia Minor. In Hellenistic times the Romans, after their victory over the Illyrian sea-pirates in 229 B.C.E., were admitted into the Panhellenic Isthmian games.[4] Clearly people did not want to treat this power, which was politically and militarily superior, any longer simply as barbarian. The Phoenician cities, too, which for hundreds of years had been in close contact with the Greeks and had given them their alphabet, participated in such games from the beginning of the third century on.[5] The king of Sidon, Philocles, son of Rešephyaton-Apollodorus, who was a capable admiral of Ptolemy I and who gained for him, from 286 B.C.E. on, naval supremacy in the

[1] O. Mørkholm, *Antiochus IV of Syria*, Classica et Mediaevalia Diss. 7 (Copenhagen, 1966), pp. 115ff; A. H. M. Jones, *The Cities of the Eastern Roman Provinces* (2nd edn., Oxford, 1971), pp. 247ff.

[2] Cf. the *Hellēnogalatai* (Diod. v.32) and the *Gallograeci* (Livy XXXVIII.17.9) and the *mixhellēnes* among the Carthaginian mercenaries (Polyb. 1.67.7).

[3] XIV.5.24, 25 (C 678/9).

[4] Speyer, *JAC*, 10 (1967), 259f.

[5] Hengel, *Hellenismus*, p. 131 = ET 1, p. 71. The 'suffete' (*dikastēs*) Diotimus from Sidon was celebrated around 200 B.C.E. by a Greek verse inscription as victor in the Panhellenic Nemean chariot race in Argos.

eastern Mediterranean, is an example.[1] But the Phoenicians, who at least externally adopted Greek culture very quickly, had all along had a special relationship with the Greeks. The Strabo citation confirms that Hellenization depended largely on the behaviour of the ruling classes of a people. Strabo, living in the time of Augustus, could no longer acknowledge the traditional distinction. For him the designation Hellenes depended on the cultural status of the upper classes.

Hellenism and Hellenization in early Hellenistic times have a very strong political and social element. The philosophical, literary and religious aspects, which at first were of only secondary significance, were gradually given more weight. There are many statements, especially philosophical ones, which break out from the negative Greek–barbarian pattern, and which put emphasis on the common humanity, even the superiority of the barbarians. What we have here though is mostly the view of outsiders, and it gained ground only gradually. The influence of such views on the Hellenistic rulers and their Greco-Macedonian subjects must not be overrated. They would be influenced only by considerations of power politics and economics. The question of humanitarianism played a role only to the extent that royal philanthropy had a practical advantage.[2] Neither an Apollonius nor his agent Zenon, being wholly dominated by the profit motive, would have been very concerned with humanitarian problems. Such notions did, however, come into being, and, later in Roman times, when Stoic philosophy had become generally accepted, they gained a more important place. They were also used by Hellenistic Jewish and Christian apologists in their counter-attacks.

In the work of the sophist Antiphon the thought emerges that all men 'by nature', that is, 'biologically', are equal. Political equality was not yet claimed.[3] Such ideas were taken over by Cynics[4] and Stoics in the form of a 'concept of world citizenship', although at first it was totally unpolitical. It is no accident perhaps that the founder of the

[1] W. Peremans and E. van't Dack, *Prosopographia Ptolemaica VI*, Studia Hellenistica 17 (Louvain, 1968), pp. 95f, no. 15085.

[2] W. L. Westermann, 'The Ptolemies and the welfare of their subjects', *American Historical Review*, 43 (1937/8), 270–87. C. Préaux, *Les Grecs en Egypte après les archives Zenon* (Brussels, 1947).

[3] Antiphon in H. Diels and W. Kranz, *Die Fragmente der Vorsokratiker* (11th edn., Zurich–Berlin 1964), 2, pp. 352f, fr. 44B col. 2, l. 10: 'We are all by nature created the same in every respect, barbarians and Hellenes'. For this E. Schütrumpf, *Hermes*, 100 (1972), 20ff.

[4] Diogenes: Diogenes Laertius VI.63; cf. also Democritus in Diels and Kranz, *Fragmente*, 2, p. 194, fr. 247.

Stoics, Zeno of Kition, was himself Phoenician in origin, and was mocked by his opponents on that account. His opponent Epicurus was of the opinion 'that the Greeks alone could philosophize'.[1] Eratosthenes, the teacher of Ptolemy IV Philopator and director of the *mouseion*, had protested, under the inspiration of the Stoics, against the prevailing division into Greeks and barbarians. He was going against the advice given by Aristotle to Alexander on treating barbarians as slaves, and he extolled Alexander's conduct in judging men according to their qualities rather than their descent. Instead of dividing men into Greeks and barbarians, classification should depend on the measure of their *aretē* or their *kakia*.[2] Whether the not so successful foreign and home policies of his pupil were advanced by such considerations is questionable. Forced by his political plight, Philopator had to make concessions to the native population of Egypt, but in doing so created further difficulties for himself.

The statements and speculations of Greek scholars about the greater antiquity of Eastern cultures and the barbarian first inventors to whom the young Greek nation was heavily indebted, could make little impression on the élitist attitude of Greeks to whom the eastern world stood wide open. These opinions were furthermore confined to certain groups. In the early Academy the ancient wisdom of the oriental 'barbarians' was valued, but they remained, like Plato himself, conscious of Greek superiority.[3] The Cynics held before the Greeks the example of a supposed 'barbarian philosophy' with its extreme simplicity, and sought to rouse them to self-criticism.[4] We may note the oriental fantasies of a Ktesias,[5] or the scholastic utopia of Hecateus of Abdera, who saw the Egyptians as the oldest transmitters of culture, and who for the first time reported extensively and positively on the Jews, and who was the prototype for Euhemerus.[6] But these were more of sensational interest to the reading public than of political significance. Hecateus certainly did not influence the policies of the first

1 Zeno: M. Pohlenz, *Die Stoa* (Göttingen, 1959), 1, pp. 22f, 2, p. 14; Epicurus in Clement of Alexandria, *Stromata* 1.15.67 (GCS 52, p. 42 in Stählin rev. Früchtel).

2 Strabo 1.4.9 (C 66–7).

3 Cf. Pseudo Plato, *Epinomis* 986e–987d concerning the barbarian origin of astronomy and the concluding remark there: 'Whatever the Greeks may have taken over from the barbarians, they have improved'. S. O. Reverdin, 'Crise spirituelle et évasion' in *Grecs et barbares*, pp. 103ff, 106ff, cf. Jüthner, *Hellenen*, pp. 22ff.

4 Speyer, *JAC*, 10 (1967), 258ff, 267, 269ff, cf. also Philo, *quod omnis* 73ff, 94ff.

5 Reverdin, *Grecs et barbares*, 97ff; Diodorus 11.29.4 (in dependence on Ktesias) praises Chaldean philosophy in contrast to Greek.

6 W. Speyer, 'Hekataios', *Der kleine Pauly*, 2 (Stuttgart, 1967), cols. 980ff. For the Jews, see J. G. Gager, *Moses in Greco-Roman Paganism* (Nashville–New York, 1972), pp. 26–37.

Ptolemies in dealings with their first Egyptian subjects. On the other hand, first Jewish and then their Christian apologists obtained useful arguments from this literature and were able to use them against the contention that the Greeks were superior.[1]

The early Hellenistic period, especially the third century, was predominantly a time of decline of traditional religion and of enlightenment. Tyche, the goddess of chance, was the dominant deity, and she appeared later on many coins of Syrian cities in place of the local Astarte. The most encouraged religion of this period was the pseudo-religion of ruler worship, the divinization of the 'superman' endowed by Tyche with success.[2] At first oriental religions had only a slight attraction for the immigrant Greeks, who worshipped, if at all, their own gods in their traditional manner. With the decline of the Hellenistic monarchies religious interest increased, and astrology came to the fore. One exception was the cult of the Greco-Egyptian Sarapis, and following it the cult of Isis; these expanded in the third and second centuries owing to the encouragement of the Ptolemies. But Sarapis was represented as a Greek god with Egyptianizing traits; he found approval among Greeks and Greco-Egyptians, but not among the Egyptian populace.[3]

Against the complex and sometimes contradictory aspects of this background, it can be said that the initiative towards Hellenization, that is, for partial or total adoption of the Greek way of life, originated unilaterally from the Semitic and Egyptian natives who wished thereby to improve their social status and to participate in the prosperity and success of the Greeks. Thus Hellenization, that is, the acceptance of Greek language, education and way of life, was the individual achievement of individual orientals. The Greco-Macedonian ruling class had little interest in the Hellenization of barbarians, at least in the fourth and third centuries. They were one-sidedly interested in the maintenance of their power and social status, and in the optimal exploitation of the native labour force, though this did of course lead to collaboration and so a measure of contact. The possibility of full assimilation and equality of rights was only achieved in one generation by a few individual natives, and certain barriers, such as the attainment of civic rights in tradition-conscious cities, long remained insurmountable. The

1 K. Thraede, 'Erfinder', *RAC*, 5 (Stuttgart, 1962), cols. 1242ff, 1247ff, 1268ff. Here also belongs the motif of 'theft by the philosophers' which is known from the time of Philo on.

2 M. P. Nilsson, *Geschichte der Griechischen Religion*, 2 (Munich, 2nd edn., 1961), pp. 132–84, 200ff, 208ff.

3 Cf. Fraser, *Alexandria*, 3, p. 70, index s.v. Sarapis.

rigid barriers of the third century were somewhat moderated in the second and first centuries. But the contrasts remained down to Roman times and then became identified with the fundamental contrast between citizens of cities and the rural population. Basically the latter largely resisted Hellenization,[1] and finally gave rise to the Coptic and Syrian renaissance of late Roman and Byzantine times. Hellenistic culture remained always a city culture adopted by such orientals as wished to cross the barrier between Greek and barbarian and accept Hellenistic civilization with its many openings. This was so whether they were members of the native aristocracy or body of citizens, or natives who came into close contact with the Greeks as mercenaries, subordinate officials, labourers or slaves. For the Hellenized aristocracy of an oriental city, which legally possessed only the status of a *komē*, it was naturally a matter of the greatest interest to obtain through royal recognition the status of a *polis* with a constitution based on the Greek model.[2] In Egypt itself this was ruled out in advance, for the Ptolemies recognized as a *polis* only the established Naucratis, Alexandria and Ptolemais, newly founded by the Ptolemies themselves in upper Egypt. But in the Ptolemaic colonial areas the situation was substantially more favourable. The first cities to obtain this status, without being founded by the Macedonians, were the Phoenician coastal cities (see above, p. 178); this again is an indication of the special position of this seafaring people.

The first important step for individuals was to overcome the language barrier and be able to speak Greek fluently. The Greeks themselves seldom bothered to learn the language of their environment. Before the battle of Raphia Ptolemy IV Philopator exhorted his Egyptian phalanxes through an interpreter. Of the Ptolemies, Cleopatra VII, the last queen of the dynasty, is supposed to have been the first to master Egyptian. The Greek mother, who in the second century congratulated her son on mastering Egyptian, and consequently on finding in Alexandria a position as tutor in the family of an Egyptian doctor, was a very rare exception.[3]

The Greek language in the form of the Attic *koinē* achieved such significance because it was the world-wide bond which united all Greeks, transcending the boundaries of individual monarchies and extending from Bactria to Massilia. It was the Greek language, rather

[1] M. Rostovtzeff, *The Social and Economic History of the Roman Empire* (2nd edn., revised by P. M. Fraser, Oxford, 1957), 1, pp. 272ff for Syrians and Egyptians.

[2] Tcherikover, *Civilization*, pp. 26ff, 161ff.

[3] Rostovtzeff, *The Social and Economic History of the Hellenistic World* (Oxford, 1941), 2, p. 883, 3, p. 1545 n. 164 and Braunert, *Binnenwanderung*, pp. 72f.

than the political power of the fragmented and warring Greek states, that formed the ultimate basis of Hellenistic culture. That was why the victory of barbarian Romans and Parthians did not bring this culture to an end, for it lived on in both kingdoms, and indeed reached its zenith under the protection of the *pax Romana*. The famous saying of Isocrates, that 'he who shares in our *paideia* is Greek in a higher sense than he who only has common descent with us',[1] obviously understands *paideia* as primarily a correct command of Attic Greek and identifies 'those who speak Attic as the true Greeks'.[2] Accordingly, the verb *hellēnizein* means, not the acquisition of Greek culture, but 'to speak (and write) Greek correctly'.[3] Strabo calls the barbarians, who are beginning to speak Greek and thus still pronounce it incorrectly, *hoi eisagomenoi eis ton hellēnismon*.[4] These language barriers were at the same time social barriers, as is shown by the despairing lament of a (probably Semitic) assistant from Palestine, whom Zenon left behind in Jaffa after his Palestinian journey in 258 B.C.E. The promised salary was withheld from him, so that he had to run away to Syria, that is, to the interior, 'so that I die not from hunger'. Summoned back to Egypt, there also his vital keep was denied him,

> So in summer I am in need. [Jason] commanded that I should receive sour wine as wages. Now, they treat me contemptuously *because I am a barbarian*. I pray you now,...that you give them instructions, so that I may receive my due and that they pay me fully in future, so that I perish not from hunger, *for I have not mastered Greek correctly [hoti ouk epistamai hellēnizein]*.[5]

The complaint of an eminent Egyptian priest of Ammon sounds very similar; a Greek military colonist, Androbios, billeted on him, had flouted the law – 'he has scorned me because I am an Egyptian'.[6]

On the other hand, it is no accident that the rare noun *Hellēnismos*, with an extended sense which included the Greek way of life and

[1] *Panegyricus* 50. [2] Speyer, *JAC*, 10 (1967), 265; cf. Jüthner, *Hellenen*, pp. 34ff.

[3] H. G. Liddell and R. Scott, *A Greek-English Lexicon* (9th edn., Oxford, 1940), p. 536. The derived sense 'make Greek, Hellenize' appears for the first time as late as Libanius, *Or.* XI.103, who uses it to describe the city-founding policy of Seleucus I: 'he left no place which was suitable for it without founding there a city and constantly "Hellenized" the lands of the barbarians.' [4] XIV.2.28 (C 662).

[5] W. L. Westermann, C. W. Keyes and H. Liebesny, eds., *Zenon Papyri*, Columbia Papyri Greek Series, no. 4 (New York, 1940), 2, pp. 16ff, no. 66. For interpretation see C. Préaux, *ChE*, 40 (1965), 130 n. 1, against the editors.

[6] J. F. Oates, A. E. Samuel and C. Bradford Welles, *Yale Papyri in the Beinecke Rare Book and Manuscript Library*, 1, American Studies in Papyrology 2 (New Haven–Toronto, 1967), pp. 122ff, no. 46; cf. Rostovtzeff, *Social and Economic History of the Hellenistic World*, 3, p. 1421 n. 212.

culture, appears for the first time in a Hellenistic Jewish work. The unknown epitomator of the work of Jason of Cyrene, or else Jason himself, in a bitter polemic against Jason, son of Simon the Just, the high priest and leader of the Jewish reform party, blames him because on his initiative there had come about in Jerusalem 'a climax of Hellenization and an invasion of foreign ways'.[1] In a polemic reversal the Jewish Hellenists and their Seleucid accomplices are designated as barbarians and Jews who are faithful to the law as patriotic citizens.[2] Several times in 2 Maccabees we have for the first time the word *Ioudaismos*, standing in contrast to *Hellēnismos*, to designate the piety of those who lived according to the Law.[3] The verb *ioudaizein* occurs with *peritemnesthai*, 'to be circumcised', in the Greek version of the book of Esther as a translation of the *hithpaʿel* participle *mithyahᵃdîm* (root *yhd*), 'and many of the Gentiles became circumcised and adopted Jewish customs, for the fear of the Jews had fallen upon them'.[4] That is, the Jews, too, appear to have perceived in the new Greek way of life an aggressive civilization which threatened the distinctive tradition of their fathers. They set over against it their own tradition of the Law, which could also be aggressive, that is, missionarily active. The noteworthy feature of this controversy is that they tried to oppose this new, threatening civilization in its own language, literature and thought forms. We must not overlook the fact that in this controversy the Greek feeling of superiority based on the distinction between Greeks and barbarians was countered from the Jewish side by a consciousness of election which was unique in the ancient world, and which was manifested in the distinction between Israel and the peoples of the world. An example will illustrate this. Both Thales and Socrates, that is, the earliest as well as the most famous of Greek philosophers, are credited with saying the following: 'I thank Tyche that I was born a human and not a beast, a man and not a woman, a Greek and not a barbarian'.[5] The saying of R. Judah ben Ilai around 150 C.E. is very similar: 'Three praises must be uttered daily: Praised be God that he has not made me a woman! Praised be he that he has not made me an

[1] 2 Macc. 4:13, cf. 4:10, 15; 6:9: *metabainein epi ta hellēnika*; 11:24; 4 Macc. 8:8. Elsewhere *Hellēnismos*, as an *aretē logou*, means pure Greek style. See Diogenes of Babylon (*c.* 240–152 B.C.E.) *Stoicorum Veterum Fragmenta*, vol. 3, p. 214, no. 24 = Diog. Laert. VII.59 for the distinction between *Hellēnismos* and *barbarismos*.

[2] *Barbaroi*: 2 Macc. 2:21; (4:25); 10:4, cf. 5:22; 15:2 and Speyer, *JAC*, 10 (1967), 266f; *politai*: 2 Macc. 4:5; 5:6, 8, 23; 9:19; 14:8; 15:30. Cf. also *patris*: 4:1; 5:8, etc.

[3] 2 Macc. 2:21; 8:1; 14:38, cf. 4 Macc. 4:26.

[4] Esther 8:17 according to the LXX version. The L version has only *perietemonto*, see R. Hanhart, *Esther*, Septuaginta 8, 3 (Göttingen, 1966), pp. 196f.

[5] Diog. Laert. 1.33. Cf. Speyer, *JAC*, 10 (1967), 257.

ignorant man! Praised be he that he has not made me a Gentile, for "all gentiles are as nothing before him" (Isa. 40:17)'.[1] It is against the background of these almost identical and yet sharply opposed sayings, that we can understand the highly revolutionary nature of St Paul's statement: 'There is neither Jew nor Greek, there is neither slave nor free, there is neither male nor female; for you are all one in Christ Jesus' (Gal. 3:28). From this confrontation there arises a whole series of parallel phenomena: mixed marriages were frowned upon by proud Greek citizens, but even more so by Jews; and loyal adherence to the laws of the fathers, which was a mark of the true *polis*, formed the very basis of Jewish existence. If the sense of law and community (*to nomimon kai to politikon*)[2] was for Eratosthenes and others a characteristic of Hellenes, here too lay the strength of the Jewish people. It is no accident that, in Hellenistic Jewish literature from 3 Maccabees and the *Letter of Aristeas* on, the term *politeia* is used for the Torah, and the verb *politeuesthai* for life under the law: the reform attempt in Jerusalem led to 'the destruction of the *politeia* inherited from the fathers'.[3] Like the antitheticial usage of *Hellēnismos* and *Ioudaismos*, this also is a characteristic mode of speech in Hellenistic Judaism. It reveals, on the one hand, the inner affinity between Judaism and the Greek world and, on the other, the contrast. These two together characterize the political, intellectual and religious life of the Jewish Diaspora in its tension between assimilation and self-assertion. The question of the anti-Jewish Apion, 'If they are citizens, why do they not worship the same gods as the Alexandrians?'[4] could be raised in every Greek city in which a Jewish minority desired rights of citizenship. This is the cause of those difficulties to which the Jews were exposed not only in Alexandria and Syria, but also, even down to later republican times, in various cities in Asia Minor.[5] Josephus' reply that 'we form a single and united race' and intend to remain 'in the laws given to us at first',[6] would have been respected by any Greek, but must at the same time

[1] *T. ber.* 7.18 (Zuckermandel 16); par. *y. Ber.* 9, 2, 13b, ll. 57ff (Krotoschin). According to *b. Men.* 43b the tradition is ascribed to R. Meir. Cf. H. Strack and P. Billerbeck, *Kommentar zum Neuen Testament aus Talmud und Midrasch*, 3 (Munich, 1926), p. 611.

[2] Strabo 1.4.9 (C 67). According to the Greek view the barbarians had no *nomoi*, see Speyer, *JAC*, 10 (1967), 256.

[3] 2 Macc. 8:17; cf. H. Strathmann, 'Polis', *TWNT* 6, (Stuttgart, 1959), 5, pp. 525ff ET *TDNT* (1968), pp. 525–9; M. Hengel, 'Die Synagogeninschrift von Stobi', *ZNW*, 57 (1966), 179f.

[4] Jos. *C. Ap.* II.65, Tcherikover, *Civilization*, pp. 374ff.

[5] Cf. the petition of Ionian cities to Marcus Agrippa: 'if the Jews were to be kin to them, they should also reverence their gods', Jos. *Ant.* XII.126.

[6] Jos. *C. Ap.* II.66f. Cf. later Julian, *Ep.* 89a (J. Bidez and F. Cumont, eds. *Julian* I. *Epistulae, Leges* (Paris, 1922), 1, ch. 2. pp. 124; Loeb ed., *Works* 3, *Letter* 20, pp. 58–

have come into conflict with those city laws which included recognition of the official cults of the city. At this point a tradition-conscious Greek city could scarcely be tolerant.[1] The additional argument of the Jews in the Ionian cities that they (1) 'were born in the place' (*engeneis*) and (2) through their loyalty to their law did not interfere with other citizens,[2] afforded no way out of the basically religious dilemma. A genuine safeguard could only be provided by the supra-regional regulations of the Hellenistic kings and later the Roman Emperors. It is here that we find too one of the roots of anti-Judaism. Apollonius Molon of Rhodes at the beginning of the first century B.C.E. provides an example of this: he not only designated the Jews, on account of their behaviour in Greek cities, as *atheoi* and *misanthrōpoi*, but asserts them to be 'the most stupid of the barbarians' (*aphyestatous einai tōn barbarōn*), who had therefore 'produced no single invention of importance for life',[3] a reproach which Jewish apologists counter with their glorification of the patriarchs and Moses as 'the first inventors'. A little later Cicero repeats this defamation of Judaism as a *barbara superstitio*,[4] which then becomes a set topos which enters anti-Christian polemic also. The Jews in the Diaspora could on social grounds conform to so much of the language and way of life of this foreign civilization, that they themselves could claim full equality of civic rights, and yet, like the later Christians, had to remain in spite of this a 'theocratic' alien element,[5] a 'third nation' between Greeks and barbarians,[6] and, in order to maintain their position, they had to appeal to a higher law than that of the respective states in which they lived. Here lies the root of that inner strength which ancient Judaism displayed in the Greco-Roman world, and also of ancient anti-Judaism with its terrible consequences.[7]

61), who held up the fidelity of the Jews as an example to the Greeks, who 'forget the laws of the fathers'. He finds fault, however, with the Jews because they 'do not worship other gods', but their own God alone, though it is only a matter of different names.

1 E. Sandvoss, 'Asebie und Atheismus im klassischen Zeitalter der griechischen Polis', *Saeculum*, 19 (1968), 312–29.

2 Jos. *Ant.* XVI.59.

3 Jos. *C. Ap.* II.148.

4 *Pro Flacco* 28.67. Further examples in Speyer, *JAC*, 10 (1967), 262. Julian the apostate accused the Jews of having 'a miserable and barbaric form of legislation', see Cyril Alex. *C. Iul.* 7 (*PG* 76 (1863), col. 837 D).

5 Jos. *C.Ap.* II.165.

6 The concept appears for the first time in early Christian tradition, see the *Kerygma Petrou* in E. Hennecke and W. Schneemelcher, *Neutestamentliche Apokryphen*, 2 (Tübingen, 1964), p. 62, ET *New Testament Apocrypha*, 2 (London, 1965), p. 100 = Clem. Alex. *Strom.* VI.5.41 (GCS 52, ed. Stählin), cf. Ep. to Diognetus 1.

7 On anti-Judaism see R. Rémondon, 'Les Antisémites de Memphis', *ChE*, 35 (1960), 244–61; I. Yoyotte, 'L'Égypte ancienne et les origines de l'antijudaïsme', *RHR*, 163

THE ENCOUNTER BETWEEN JUDAISM AND HELLENISM IN THE DIASPORA

THE SOCIOLOGICAL PRESUPPOSITIONS: JEWS IN A GREEK-SPEAKING ENVIRONMENT

The milieu of Hellenistic mercenaries and military colonists brought Jews and Greeks most intensively together and compelled them to adapt themselves as well as they could to their environment. The Hellenistic kings retained not only a standing army in garrisons, but also established colonies of soldiers, especially on plots of land belonging to the king. In Egypt this occurred not so much in closed colonies, as scattered over the whole country. The mercenaries became peasant farmers, or else landowners who had their property worked by tenants. According to Pseudo-Hecateus and Josephus, Jewish and Samaritan auxiliaries served with Alexander's armies in Egypt and in Babylonia, and we have no grounds to mistrust in principle these statements.[1] In this, the king was only continuing an old tradition which had been widespread during the Saite dynasty and the Persian domination of Egypt. Perhaps some Jewish military colonies in Egypt were themselves taken over by the Macedonians. The Papyrus Cowley 81 in Aramaic, from around 310 B.C.E., mentions ten places between Migdal on the north-eastern frontiers of Egypt and Syene in the south in which Jews had settled. The papyrus throws light on the complex commercial activities of a Jewish large-scale merchant, Abihai, and includes numerous Jewish as well as Greek names, which indicates the contact between the two groups of people. In one case only does a Jew appear to have borne a Greek name, 'Haggai (the son of) *dyprs* [Diaphorus?]'.[2] After conquering Jerusalem (302 B.C.E.?), Ptolemy I Soter took a great number of Jewish captives to Egypt. Of these he is said to have enrolled 30,000 elite men into his army and settled them in colonies as cleruchs.[3] Again, those Jewish immigrants, reported by

(1963), 133–43; Gager, *Moses*, SBLMS 16 (Nashville–New York, 1972), p. 16 n. 4; D. Rokeah, 'Jews and their Law in the Pagan–Christian polemic in the Roman empire', *Tarbiz*, 40 (1970/71), 462–71 (in Hebrew); Fraser, *Alexandria*, see index under antisemitism, vol. 3, p. 7.

1 Jos. *C.Ap.* I.192ff; II.35, 42, 71f; *Ant.* XI.321, 339, 345; XII.8. Hengel, *Hellenismus*, p. 27 n. 83 = ET 2, p. 11 n. 84. Only the details given by Josephus about the *isopoliteia* granted by Alexander to Jewish military settlers in Alexandria are unhistorical. See Fraser, *Alexandria*, 1, pp. 54f.

2 According to the new edition by J. Harmatta, 'Irano-Aramaica', *Acta Antiqua*, 7 (1959), 337–409; see p. 338 col. A. l. 10.

3 Ps.-Arist. 13; see above, p. 50. According to Diod. XIX.85.4 Ptolemy I, after the battle of Gaza, arranged the distribution of 8,000 prisoners of war among the

Pseudo-Hecateus as having allegedly obtained a *politeia* of their own will, at least in part, have been Jewish mercenaries.[1] The Hellenization of Jewish garrison troops and cleruchs must have progressed, as far as language was concerned, relatively quickly. Only around twenty-five per cent of the names borne by Jewish military colonists in the papyri of the third century are Semitic; all the others are already Greek, and occasional double names indicate the process of transition.[2] In fact, the percentage is even smaller, for Jewish bearers of Greek names are known only through the by no means automatically appended *Ioudaios*. This speedy Hellenization process is connected with the fact that in the early Hellenistic period the cleruchs were not settled in closed ethnic groups, but were mixed up, and the garrisons were also a great mixture. In the second century Jewish mercenaries, who since the time of Ptolemy VI Philometor were grouped in independent units under their own commanders, had acquired great political significance. To some degree they had also organized themselves, as in Alexandria, into autonomous *politeumata* (see below, pp. 192f.). Consequently there occurs an increase in the proportion of Jewish names, a sign that, owing to their stronger political position in Egypt and in Palestine itself, national self-awareness had increased.[3] In Cyrenaica, where freedom-loving Greek inhabitants caused all sorts of difficulties for the Ptolemaic regime, the Ptolemies appear to have brought in Jewish mercenaries on a bigger scale.[4] They likewise organized themselves into *politeumata*, and later consciously formed a fourth force alongside Greek citizens, Libyans and *metoikoi*.[5] Even in Palestine itself there was in Ammanitis beyond the Jordan a mixed military colony of Jewish and Macedonian cavalry. A contract for the sale of a female slave in the early summer of 259 B.C.E. names as witnesses a Jewish cavalryman, the son of Ananias, and Greeks from Miletus, Athens, Colophon and

nomarchies of Egypt. They were probably settled as cleruchs; see F. Uebel, *Die Kleruchen Ägyptens under den ersten sechs Ptolemaërn*, Abhandlungen der Deutschen Akademie der Wissenschaften zu Berlin. Klasse für Sprachen, Literatur und Kunst 1968, 3, Berlin 1968, p. 349.

[1] Jos. *C.Ap.* I.189.

[2] V. A. Tcherikover and A. Fuks, *Corpus Papyrorum Judaicarum*, I (Cambridge, Mass., 1957), p. 148.

[3] *CPJ*, I, pp. 27f; M. Launey, *Recherches sur les armées hellénistiques*, Bibliothèque des écoles françaises d'Athènes et de Rome 169 (Paris, 1949/50), I, pp. 541–56; Uebel, *Kleruchen*, see index p. 420 under 'Ioudaios'.

[4] Jos. *C.Ap.* II.44; E. Will, 'La Cyrénaïque et les partages successifs de l'empire d'Alexandre', *Antiquité Classique* 29 (1960), 369ff; Hengel, *Hellenismus*, p. 28 = ET I, p. 16; S. Applebaum, *Greeks and Jews in Ancient Cyrene* (Jerusalem, 1969, in Hebrew).

[5] Strabo according to Josephus, *Ant.* XIV.115, see above, p. 172. For the *politeuma* of the Jews in Berenice, see *CIG*, 3, 5361 and 5362 supplemented in *SEG*, 16 (1959), pp. 243f., no. 931.

Aspendus.[1] The Jewish cleruchs, who here had to defend the boundaries of their lands against the Arabs, appear to have become extensively Hellenized. Later they fought as cavalry troops during the Maccabean uprising on the side of the orthodox against the Seleucids, but this may go back to their traditional pro-Ptolemaic attitude. Two of their officers, Dositheus and Sosipater, have Greek names.[2]

The Seleucids too made use of Jewish auxiliary troops. According to 2 Macc. 8:20 they played a crucial role in a battle between Antiochus I and the Galatians. Later, Antiochus III, around 210 B.C.E., settled 2,000 Jewish cleruchs from Babylonia with their families in Phrygia in order to pacify that unruly district.[3] In the second century, as the number of mercenaries from Greece, Thrace and Asia Minor declined owing to the economic and political decline of the Ptolemaic empire, the proportion of Semites clearly grew. The Jews, who, since the establishment of a military colony at Leontopolis by the High Priest Onias IV on his flight to Egypt, had been gaining ever greater political and military power in the Ptolemaic kingdom, and had attained positions in high command, now acquired a position which they were able to maintain until the Romans conquered the country after the battle of Actium.[4] They could only attain this position in a Hellenistic state because they were extensively Hellenized in language and manners. Contrary to the position e.g. in Asia Minor and Greece, the political position of the Jews in Egypt and Cyrenaica deteriorated significantly under Roman overlordship. This may provide one of the reasons for the suicidal uprising of 116–117 C.E., in which only the formerly Ptolemaic dominions of Egypt, Cyrenaica and Cyprus took part.

In addition to Jewish mercenaries and military colonists, the Jewish Diaspora was strengthened by Jewish slaves, peasants and craftsmen. Papyrus Cowley 81 is our only evidence of Jewish tradesmen in the early Hellenistic period. Obviously the Jews at that time were still predominantly an agricultural people. In Hellenistic times Syria and Palestine appear as important exporters of slaves, not least to Egypt, where the enslavement of free workers was forbidden by royal law and where slaves were thus in great demand. For the Greeks, it was a matter of course to employ household slaves, and they would not desist from this. 'It appears from the Zenon papyri that most of the slaves in

1 *CPJ*, 1, pp. 118ff, no. 1.

2 2 Macc. 12:19, 24, 35; Hengel, *Hellenismus*, pp. 502 = ET 1, p. 276.

3 Jos. *Ant.* XII.147–53, see above, p. 70.

4 Launey, *Recherches*, 1, pp. 89ff, 546ff; Tcherikover, *Civilization*, pp. 276f; Fraser, *Alexandria*, 1, pp. 55ff, 83f, 688ff.

Ptolemaic Egypt, including no doubt Alexandria, were Syrians.'[1] In the province of Syria and Phoenicia too Ptolemy II Philadelphus prohibited by law the enslavement of the semi-free rural population by the Ptolemaic military settlers and Greek landowners.[2] Despite strict controls, Greek tradesmen did sell Semitic slaves abroad while evading customs and without export licence.[3] Several times in the Zenon papyri slaves from Syria (*sōmata apo Syrias*) and Syrian villages are mentioned; for example, 'Syrians' worked either as slaves or as semi-free labourers in Egyptian vineyards. It is sometimes difficult to distinguish between the two groups.[4] In the household of the finance minister Apollonius we meet two female slaves called *Ioana* and *Anas*, that is, Joanna and Hannah. These may well have been Jewish. Zenon himself acquired several slaves in Palestine, of whom two Idumeans ran away and went back to their former masters. Four young Palestinian slaves, two of them probably Jews, were sent by the Jewish magnate Tobias to Apollonius.[5] It is quite understandable that such Semitic household slaves were quickly assimilated into their Greek environment. Evidence from the papyri is supplemented by that found in literature. Pseudo-Aristeas and Josephus, in dependence on Agatharchides, report that Ptolemy I Soter on conquering Jerusalem, as has already been mentioned, took most of the captives to Egypt as slaves. According to Pseudo-Aristeas they became the property of soldiers, but their freedom was bought by Ptolemy II Philadelphus.[6] Even if the details in the *Letter of Aristeas* are exaggerated, they must have a historical kernel. So it is unjustified to play off against these accounts the report by Hecateus that, at the suggestion of a High Priest Hezekiah, many Jews of their own free will emigrated to Egypt.[7] The one report does not exclude the other, and tendentious exaggerations are found in both.

The denunciation of Phoenician and Philistine slave-traders in Joel 3:4–8 (Heb. 4:4–8), which probably belongs to the fourth century B.C.E., shows that Jewish slaves had been sold into Greece and the

[1] Fraser, *Alexandria,* 1, p. 74; Tcherikover, *Civilization*, pp. 68f; Hengel, *Hellenismus*, pp. 79ff, 93f = ET 1, pp. 41ff, 48.

[2] *SB* 8008, see above p. 51.

[3] *PCZ* 59092.

[4] Rostovtzeff, *History*, 3, pp. 1365f n. 28, 1393f n. 119. C. Préaux, *L'économie royale des Lagides* (Brussels, 1939), pp. 303ff; Hengel, *Hellenismus*, p. 80 nn. 313 and 314 = ET 2, pp. 32f nn. 323, 324; W. Peremans, *Vreemdelingen en Egyptenaren in Vroeg-Ptolemaeisch Egypte* (Louvain, 1937), pp. 86f, 168.

[5] *CPJ*, 1, pp. 125ff, no. 4 = *SB* 6790.

[6] Ps.-Arist. 4, 12ff, 22ff; Jos. *Ant.* XII.7. Cf. *C.Ap.* 1.210.

[7] Against E. L. Abel, 'The myth of Jewish slavery in Ptolemaic Egypt', *REJ*, 12 (1968), 253–8.

Aegean (see above, p. 51). From the fourth century too comes a gravestone in Athens bearing the name Anna, which could be that of a Jewish slave girl. If so, it would be the earliest reference to Jews in Europe that we possess.[1] A little later an inscription from the early third century B.C.E. gives more information about the freeing of the Jew Moschus son of Moschion on account of an incubation dream he had in the temple of the god Amphiaraus. This Jewish slave 'in a strange land' (Joel 3:8, Heb. 4:8) had obviously been assimilated to the gentile environment.[2] In connection with the attack of Nicanor on the rebellious Jews we meet in 2 Macc. 8:11 Phoenician middlemen from the coastal region who hoped to trade in Jewish slaves. In the same period we find increasing reports of Jewish slaves being freed in Greece. A Jewish slave, whom his masters had simply called *Ioudaios* (*Ioudaios to genos Ioudaiōn*), was freed in Delphi in 163/162 B.C.E. To the same period, between 170 and 157/156, belongs the manumission of a Jewess Antigona and her daughters Theodora and Dorothea.[3] The names of both girls are unmistakably an acknowledgement of the God of Israel. It is certainly no accident that Dositheus occurs as the most frequent Greek name among Jews of the Diaspora; Theodotus and Theodorus were also commonly used. Dositheus, 'God gives', occurs almost exclusively among Jews.[4]

Occasional free Jewish labourers were also found alongside Jewish military colonists and slaves. In the Zenon archives in the middle of the third century B.C.E. there appear two Jewish vinedressers, Alexander and Samuel, who leased a vineyard of Zenon's, but without much luck; also a shepherd, a kennel-man and a brick-maker (or overseer), who would not work on the Sabbath.[5] Admittedly, such examples are not representative of Ptolemaic Egypt in general. They are confined to the activities of Zenon in the newly-established estate of Philadelphia in the Fayum, where a great number of those seeking work from various nationalities assembled because of its shortage of workers.[6] Yet, in addition we do have reports of Jewish farmers and shepherds from the third and second centuries, likewise from the Fayum. Philadelphus had newly opened up this district, and settled it not least with foreign immigrants. One village there had the name Samareia, presumably

[1] *IG*, II², 10678, cf. L. B. Urdahl, 'Jews in Attica', *Symbolae Osloenses*, 43 (1968), 48.

[2] M. Mitsos, ''Επιγραφαὶ ἐξ 'Αμφιαρείου', *Archaiologike Ephemeris* (1955), pp. 167–204.

[3] J. B. Frey, *Corpus Inscriptionum Judaicarum*, 1 (Rome, 1936), pp. 512ff, nos. 709/10.

[4] *CPJ*, 1, p. 29; see also 3, pp. 173f; and pp. 167–96 for Jewish prosopography in Egypt.

[5] *CPJ*, 1, pp. 134–43, nos. 9–14.

[6] Braunert *Binnenwanderung*, pp. 40ff.

because it was originally founded by Samaritans and Jews, although it later had a mixed population of Jews, Macedonians and Cilicians. In Samareia a Cilician officer even set up a gymnasium.[1] Jews and Greeks lived alongside one another as two specific ethnic groups in the village of Psenyris in the Fayum in the third century, but Egyptians are not mentioned there. Perhaps we are dealing here too with military colonists.[2]

In comparison with other occupations, it was the Jewish cleruchs that certainly enjoyed the highest living standard. They received portions of the king's land of various sizes, which they could pass on as an inheritance. Among them were officers, especially in the second century, several of whom controlled a considerable area of land.[3] Their economic activity is indicated by the relatively large number of private contracts, which were always in the Greek language. We are now touching upon that milieu in which Greek language and civilization were readily accepted in order to maintain and improve social status. The close contact between Jews and Greeks appears again in a second century list, supposedly of members of a military unit in which Jews and Macedonians were mixed.[4] Later Jewish members of such units could themselves be called 'Macedonians'. Even in Alexandria itself there was a brigade of Jewish Macedonians.[5] A great number of tax receipts on ostraca mainly from the second century B.C.E. show how Jews, Egyptians and Greeks (or Greco-Egyptians) lived together in Upper Egypt. Here we find some very rich Jewish tax farmers, such as Sambathaios, the farmer of ferry dues on the Nile; and again Simon, the son of Iazaros, who himself paid several talents in fisherman's taxes into the royal bank, and at the same time deposited grain as a collector of taxation, but was illiterate.[6] Since the last fact is specifically mentioned, it may be considered exceptional for a man in this position.

Our information about Alexandria in early Hellenistic times is very scanty. Josephus' assertion that Alexander settled Jewish mercenaries there and gave them the same rights as Macedonians must be rejected as unhistorical and tendentious, especially on the latter point (see above, p. 187 n. 1). On the other hand we cannot rule out the report of

[1] *CPJ*, 1, pp. 158ff, no. 22; pp. 171ff, no. 28; 3, p. 206; Hengel, *Hellenismus*, p. 29 n. 85 = ET 2, pp. 11f n. 27; Uebel, *Kleruchen*, pp. 188f.

[2] *CPJ*, 1, pp. 179f, no. 33.

[3] *CPJ*, 1, pp. 164f, no. 24 from 16 April, 174 B.C.E. Here two Jewish cavalry officers each own 80 *arourai* of land; cf. 1, pp. 13–16.

[4] *CPJ*, 1, pp. 175ff, nos. 30, 31 from the middle of the second century B.C.E.

[5] *CPJ*, 1, pp. 13ff. Cf. Jos. *C.Ap.* II.35ff.

[6] *CPJ*, 1, pp. 194ff. Sambathaios, nos. 51–60; Simon, nos. 61–3, 90, 107. Cf. 1, pp. 18f.

Pseudo-Hecateus that a high priest Ezekias emigrated from Judea to Alexandria, and obtained a royal decree for the Jews living there to be given a special status as an ethnic minority. Pseudo-Hecateus mentions in this context a *politeia gegrammenē* and emphasizes specifically that this Hezekiah 'was closely connected with us', which means that he had close contact with Greeks and that Greek customs were well-known to him.[1] Extensive legal autonomy, i.e. the formation of a *politeuma* of their own under the leadership of an 'ethnarch' or a 'genarch', which is attested by the Letter of Pseudo-Aristeas and the concentration in a particular quarter of the city was however only granted in the second century by the special favour of Ptolemy VI, who was friendly towards the Jews.[2] The fact that Jews and Macedonians, or Greeks, lived together in mixed military units and military colonies is supported by the Aramaic and Greek epitaphs of Jews found amongst Gentile tombs in the early Ptolemaic necropolis of Alexandria. Clermont-Ganneau conjectured that these were the tombs of mercenaries.[3] A further indication is found in the Tobiad romance found in Josephus. According to this the general tax-farmer in Jerusalem, Joseph, not only maintained a slave as his agent in Alexandria to manage his great wealth, but also had close connections with the Ptolemaic court.[4] It was the ambition of his brother Solymius to marry his daughter to a well-off Jew in Alexandria, exactly as later Marcus Alexander, son of the Jewish alabarch and nephew of Philo, married Berenice, daughter of Agrippa I.[5] For Jews in such influential positions, Greek education was a basic prerequisite. Since we thus find relatively rich Jewish tax-farmers even in Upper Egypt it can be assumed that there were still more rich Jewish businessmen in Alexandria; the lack of information about the Alexandrian Jewish community accounts for our lack of knowledge of them. The sources become more abundant only in Roman times. On the whole the Jews in Egypt, as in their homeland, were not very well-off but belonged rather to the lower and middle classes.[6] Josephus himself emphasized that the Jews were a nation of farmers rather than traders.[7]

The danger of total assimilation to the Greek world was strongest

[1] Jos. *C.Ap.* 1.189; Tcherikover, *Civilization*, p. 300.

[2] Fraser, *Alexandria*, 1, pp. 54ff, 83f. For the Jewish *politeuma* see Ps.-Arist. 310 = Jos. *Ant.* XII.108; for the *politeuma* in Berenice see p. 188, n. 5; M. Hengel, 'Proseuche und Synagoge', in *Tradition und Glaube. Festgabe für Karl Georg Kuhn* (Göttingen, 1971), p. 170 n. 57 (bibliography).

[3] *CRAIBL* (1907), 234–43, 375–80; J. B. Frey, *CIJ*, II, nos. 1424–31; Fraser, *Alexandria*, 1, p. 57; 2, p. 141 n. 165.

[4] Jos. *Ant.* XII.184, 200f.

[5] *Ant.* XII.187; cf. XIX.276f.

[6] Tcherikover, *Civilization*, pp. 338ff.

[7] *C.Ap.* 1.60. Cf. II.294.

among the upper classes. The single known example from early times is Dositheus son of Drimylus, who according to 3 Maccabees saved the life of King Ptolemy IV Philopator from a murderous attack by the renegade Theodotus before the battle of Raphia (see above, p. 67). 'He was in origin a Jew, but later fell away from the law and was estranged from the faith of his fathers'. In 240 B.C.E. he already probably held the position of *hypomnematographos*, i.e. he was one of the two heads of the royal secretariat. In 225/224 B.C.E. he accompanied Ptolemy III Euergetes on a journey in Egypt. In 222 B.C.E. he appears as a priest of Alexander and of the deified Ptolemies.[1] The course of his life can be compared with that of the Tobiad Joseph in Ptolemaic Judea; but the Diaspora Jew Dositheus in Alexandria assimilated totally to his Greek environment, whereas Joseph in Jerusalem remained, at least externally, loyal to Jewish tradition. It is instructive, however, to find that in the second half of the third century B.C.E. a Greek-educated Jewish apostate could attain to a high position in the Ptolemaic court, especially since this was still denied to Egyptians. A parallel case which occurs in Roman times was that of the apostate Tiberius Julius Alexander, another nephew of Philo and a brother of Marcus Alexander, who even attained the rank of prefect of Egypt. The only reference to a Jewish–Gentile mixed marriage in Ptolemaic times is not certain. In a petition to the king, one Helladote, daughter of Philonides, complains about her Jewish husband, whom 'she married [according to the law] of the Jewish community'. The text is rather uncertain and the wife's origin is unknown. If the supplementation offered is correct, it also contains the only mention of the Jewish law in the Egyptian papyri dealing with Jews.[2] This means that in external legal forms the Jews had adapted themselves totally to the Hellenistic law of their environment, as is testified by the papyri. Even the titles of the deified rulers were not omitted from official documents. And so the day-to-day working and commercial life of the Jewish settlers in Egypt was dominated not only by the language but by the law of the Greeks. The principle declared by the Babylonian teacher Mar Samuel in the third century C.E. was clearly in force here: 'The law of the state is the (valid) law.'[3]

[1] 3 Macc. 1:3; *CPJ*, 1, pp. 230ff, no. 127; A. Fuks, 'Dositheos son of Drimylos: A prosopographical note', *Journal of Juristic Papyrology*, 7/8 (1953/4), 205–9.

[2] *CPJ*, 1, pp. 236ff, no. 128. Tcherikover emphasizes, against F. Bozza, 'Il matrimonio nel diritto dei papiri dell'epoca tolemaica', *Aegyptus*, 14 (1934), 212ff, that this could refer to a Jewess. The papyrus is very fragmentary. Possibly also the 'Paeonian' Theodotos, son of Kassandros, *CPJ*, 1, pp. 158ff, no. 22, was the son of a Gentile father and a Jewish mother. Tcherikover supposes full Jewish extraction.

[3] *CPJ*, 1, pp. 32ff.

THE ADOPTION OF GREEK LANGUAGE AND CULTURE BY THE JEWISH DIASPORA IN PTOLEMAIC EGYPT

It is surprising how quickly the Jews in Ptolemaic Egypt abandoned their familiar Aramaic and adopted Greek. The number of documents in Aramaic and Hebrew from Hellenistic times is exceptionally small when compared with those in Greek.[1] Aramaic was probably still used in private life, for constant immigration from the homeland meant that Aramaic never totally died out in Egypt. Nevertheless Greek was the dominant official language, not only in dealings with the Hellenistic world but within the Jewish communities themselves. Jewish inscriptions, papyri and the new Hellenistic Jewish literature, including the Septuagint, provide overwhelming evidence of this fundamental change.[2] This triumph of the Greek language affected all social classes from the Jewish aristocracy in Alexandria down to day-labourers and slaves in the *chora*. We do have a very few references to Jewish illiterates,[3] but even these must have understood and spoken Greek. Demotic Egyptian did not interest the Jews, and there is no clear evidence that they learnt it.[4] This means that the attainment of a higher social status was sought by adopting the language of the new masters. Reference has already been made to the predominant use of Greek names among the Jewish military colonists as early as the third century (see above p. 188). How little they were narrow-minded is shown by the fact that about a third of these names were of pagan and theophorous character. Jews in Egypt appear with names like Apollonius, Artemidorus, Diosdotus, Demetrius, Dionysius, Diophantus, Heraclea, Heraclides, Hermeus, Hermias and so on.[5] Much favoured, as in Palestine too, was Simon, since the Semitic and Greek forms are

[1] See the inscriptions in the necropolis in Alexandria, above p. 193 n. 3; the early Ptolemaic P. Cowley 81, above p. 187 n. 2. Also from the same early period comes an Aramaic papyrus fragment with a list of oil sales to men with Greek names: E. Bresciani, 'Uno papiro aramaico di eta tolemaica', *Atti della Accademia nazionale dei Lincei,* 8 ser. 17 (1962), 258–64. Further instances of Aramaic in Hellenistic times in *CPJ*, 1, p. 30 n. 76. Add the inscription from the Temple in Abydus in M. Lidzbarski, *Ephemeris für Semitische Epigraphik*, 3 (1909–15), 103ff. The Nash papyrus with the Hebrew text of the Decalogue and of Deut. 6:4ff comes from a substantially later period and no doubt had the function of an amulet; see *CPJ*, 1, pp. 107f.

[2] *CPJ*, 1, pp. 30ff.

[3] *CPJ*, 1, pp. 190ff, no. 46, ll. 20f: a Jewish potter and his son, who together with three Egyptians leased a pottery in the Fayum; 1, p. 222, no. 107: the Jewish tax-farmer Simon the son of Iazaros in Upper Egypt (see above, p. 192).

[4] Our only evidence is that Jews very occasionally bore Egyptian names.

[5] See the prosopography of Jewish names in *CPJ*, 3, pp. 167ff; Hengel, *Hellenismus*, pp. 117f = ET 1, pp. 61ff.

very similar.[1] All this did not mean that there was a break with ancestral tradition. On the contrary, even Jewish worship, which was the spiritual focus of the Jewish community, adopted the Greek language as early as the first half of the third century. Those mercenaries and military colonists who were of good social standing probably played an important role in forming and organizing the Jewish communities. Because they were in constant close contact with the Greeks, they were also most dependent on the use of the Greek language. Other ethnic groups of soldiers also formed themselves into cultic communities with a common religion in the form of *politeumata* or *koina*.[2] Probably the Jews in Ptolemaic public employ were particularly interested in the introduction of the new language into divine service, as well as in the Greek translation of the Torah. This explains why the translation of the Law was promoted by Ptolemy II Philadelphus. This is the historical kernel of the *Letter of Aristeas*. The king, who was both prudent and wide-ranging in his interests, could not remain indifferent to the divine worship and the religious law of a specific group of his mercenaries amd military colonists.[3] It is thus understandable why the extant synagogue inscriptions from Ptolemaic times, which are entirely in Greek, almost all begin with a dedication to the Ptolemaic rulers. It is almost unthinkable that the new Jewish cult could be developed in Greek without the positive acquiscence, and even encouragement, of the Ptolemaic kings. In contrast to the numerous dedications in Gentile sanctuaries, the synagogue inscriptions do twice use the cultic title, but never include the designation 'theos'.[4] A certain analogy to all this is provided by the Hellenization of the worship of the Idumean god Qos-Apollo in the Idumean military colonies in the second and first centuries B.C.E., as attested by the inscriptions of the Idumean cultic communities in Hermopolis Magna and Memphis. Whereas however the Idumeans offered bloody sacrifices to Apollo-Qos 'according to the law of the fathers' even in a

[1] Hengel, *Hellenismus*, p. 120 n. 52 = ET 2, p. 46 n. 53. For Egypt, see *CPJ*, 1, p. 29; 3, pp. 191f.

[2] Launey, *Recherches*, 2, pp. 954ff, 959ff, 974ff, 1064ff.

[3] The initiative of Ptolemy II is wrongly interpreted as compulsory Hellenization by B. H. Stricker, *De brief van Aristeas. De Hellenistische codificaties der praehelleense godsdiensten* (Amsterdam, 1956); see the criticism of R. Hanhart, 'Fragen um die Entstehung der LXX', *VT*, 12 (1962), 156ff. Cf. however E. Bickerman, 'The Septuagint as a translation', *PAAJR*, 28 (1959), 8ff and S. Jellicoe, *The Septuagint and Modern Study* (Oxford, 1968), p. 55.

[4] N. Walter, *Der Thoraausleger Aristobulos*, TU 86 (Berlin, 1964), pp. 24f n. 23; Fraser, *Alexandria*, 2, p. 442n. 770.

foreign country and sang hymns 'in a foreign tongue',[1] the Jewish cult used a new and almost revolutionary form of worship in the Egyptian Diaspora. It became a purely verbal form of worship, with prayer (*proseuchē*), which probably included the singing of hymns, and a reading and exposition of the Law. This non-sacrificial service of the word, which had a strong ethical emphasis, must have made an impression of an almost philosophical character on the surrounding world. It is no accident, therefore, that early Greek informants like Theophrastus, Hecateus, Megasthenes, Clearchus of Soli and even Strabo (or perhaps his source Posidonius) describe the Jews and their lawgiver Moses as barbarian philosophers.[2] Jewish apologists down to Philo and Josephus take this up and maintain that the ethical monotheism proclaimed in the Jewish *proseuchai* was the true philosophical religion.[3] The new term for the building for divine service, *proseuchē*, is a clear reference to this new form of worship. The word itself is a new creation of the Septuagint.[4] The first *proseuchai*, that is, the very first Synagogues at all, figure in inscriptions from the time of Ptolemy III Euregetes (246–221 B.C.E.).[5] In the synagogue inscriptions the official designation of the God of Israel is *theos hypsistos*, and *interpretatio graeca* of the 'God of heaven' of the Persian period. This then becomes the official designation of the Jewish God in the whole later classical world.[6] As a term for God, *Kurios*, the Qere for the Tetragrammaton, used in Jewish worship, was not intelligible to the Greeks. The transcription of the divine name in the Septuagint as *Iao* was no more used in public in Egypt than in Palestine. Yet, just on that account, this (secret) divine name found its way into syncretistic Jewish magic.[7] Later, however, no doubt under Palestinian influence, *Iao* was replaced by the Tetragrammaton, written in either old Hebrew or

[1] *OGIS* 737; *PAP. Giss.* 99 in F. Zucker, *Doppelinschrift spätptolemäischer Zeit aus der Garnison von Hermopolis Magna*, Abhandlungen der Preussischen Akademie der Wissenschaften 1937, 6, Berlin 1938, p. 13; cf. U. Rappaport, 'Les Iduméens en Egypte', *Revue de Philologie* 3rd ser. 43 (1969), 73–82; Fraser, *Alexandria*, 1, pp. 280f; 2, pp. 438f.

[2] Hengel, *Hellenismus*, pp. 464ff = ET 1, pp. 255ff; Gager, *Moses*.

[3] Hengel, 'Proseuche', 162 n. 2.

[4] Hengel, 'Proseuche', 161f.

[5] *CIJ*, 1440 = *OGIS* 726 from Schedia near Alexandria; *CIJ* 1532 A (printed in *CPJ*, 3, p. 164) = *SB* 8939 from Arsinoe-Crocodilopolis in the Fayum.

[6] *Theos hypsistos: CIJ* 1433; 1443 (dedicated by the police officer Ptolemy and the Jews in Athribis); cf. also the inscriptions in Delos (*CIJ* 726–30) and the two prayers for vengeance from Rheneia, the cemetery island of Delos (*CIJ* 725). *Theos megas: CIJ* 1432 = *OGIS* 742; 1532 '*theos megas megas hypsistos*', the Jewish origin is not certain here. On the whole question, see Hengel, *Hellenismus*, pp. 544ff = ET 1, pp. 296f.

[7] R. Ganschinietz, 'Iao', *PW*, 9 (1914), cols. 698–721.

square script, or by the Qere *Kyrios*, though this first becomes common in the mss. only in the Christian period.[1]

The surprising literal translation of the Pentateuch attests that basically the Jews adhered faithfully to 'the law of the fathers'. The translators were men who had mastered the *koine* of early Hellenistic Egypt and who thus had received a good linguistic training. Presumably they had acquired, either from worship or from state and legal practice, a practical experience of translating. The Septuagint is devoid of all rhetorical finesse, and presents itself more as a solid 'craftsman-like' translation, such as we find in legal documents and contracts. It attains its unique linguistic character through its literal, though not slavish, translation. Whether a spoken Jewish Greek underlies it is still disputed.[2] We cannot speak of a Hellenistic philosophical influence.[3] The most significant interpretation is the translation of Yahweh's self-designation in Exod. 3:14, 'I am who I am', by *egō eimi ho ōn*: 'When the "Seventy" Platonized the Lord himself...they interpreted words, which, obscure in the original, called for some elucidation when rendered into Greek.'[4] Philo later saw in *ho ōn* the only adequate designation of God. There are, in addition, careful dilutions of offensive anthropomorphisms,[5] a very few slight allusions to Greek mythology,[6] modernization of the geographical world picture,[7] certain political bows to the Ptolemaic kings[8] and isolated legal adaptations of the Mosaic Law to current Hellenistic legal practice in

[1] Cf. S. Jellicoe, *The Septuagint and Modern Study* (Oxford, 1968), pp. 270ff. For the magical power of the divine name, cf. Artapanus, *FGrHist* 726 = Eusebius, *Praep. Evang.* IX.27.24f.

[2] E. Bickerman, 'The Septuagint as a translation', *PAAJR*, 28 (1959), 1–39; cf. H. S. Gehman, 'The Hebraic character of Septuagint Greek', *VT*, 1 (1951), 81–90; 3 (1953); also N. Turner, *Grammatical Insights into the New Testament* (Edinburgh, 1965), pp. 183ff on the problem of Jewish Greek. See also S. Daniel, *Recherches sur le vocabulaire du culte dans la Septante* (Paris, 1966), pp. 364ff, 382ff.

[3] J. Freudenthal, 'Are there traces of Greek philosophy in the LXX?', *JQR*, 2 (1890), 205–22; R. Marcus, 'Jewish and Greek elements in the LXX', in *Louis Ginzberg Jubilee Volume* (New York, 1945), 2, pp. 227–45.

[4] Bickerman, *PAAJR*, 28 (1959), 34f; cf. J. Whittaker, 'Moses Atticizing', *Phoenix*, 21 (1967), 196–201.

[5] Cf. Gen. 18:25; Ex. 4:16; 15:3; 24:10f; Num. 12:8; Deut. 14:23, etc. See C. T. Fritsch, *The Anti-anthropomorphisms of the Greek Pentateuch* (Philadelphia, 1943); cf. also H. M. Orlinsky, 'Studies in the Septuagint of the Book of Job', *HUCA*, 30 (1959), 153ff, especially on Job.

[6] Cf. the *gigantes*, Gen. 6:4; 10:8f etc.; the *seirēnes* in the translation of the prophets, Isa. 13:21; 34:13, etc.; H. A. Redpath, 'Mythological terms in the LXX', *AJT*, 9 (1905), 34f; H. Kaupel, 'Sirenen in der LXX', *BZ*, 23 (1935/6), 158–65.

[7] H. A. Redpath, 'The geography of the Septuagint, *AJT*, 7 (1903), 289–307.

[8] Bickerman, *PAAJR*, 28 (1959), 33f.

Egypt.[1] The conservative attitude of the translators favoured the growth of the legend, recorded in the *Letter of Aristeas*, that in origin the 72 translators were all Palestinian Jews. The author takes it as self-evident that these Palestinians had without exception had an excellent Greek education.[2] Religious controversies are indicated by the fact that the lascivious Canaanite nature-religion is in part described in concepts from the Dionysiac mysteries, a polemical tendency which was then taken further in Wisdom and Philo.[3] Exodus 22:27 – *theous ou kakologēseis* – is interpreted as a renunciation of polemic against foreign gods.[4] Their position as a minority made necessary a certain caution in dealing with the totally different religions around them. From the second century at the latest, an anti-Jewish attitude increased both among the Greek citizens of Alexandria and among the Egyptians of the Chora.[5] The Hellenizing tendency is markedly stronger in parts of the later translation of the prophetic books and the hagiographa, especially in Proverbs and Job. But corrections with a declared anti-Hellenistic trend also increase in number. This is the case when the Philistines are made Hellenes, when the book of Esther, probably translated in Jerusalem, makes Haman the Agagite a Macedonian.[6]

The notably Greek education of the authors, as well as the amalgamation of Jewish and Greek thought, becomes yet more evident in other Hellenistic Jewish writings than it is in the translation of the LXX. This shows the high degree of Hellenization among the intellectual leaders of the Jewish Diaspora in Egypt. 'The Jews as a whole were on a higher cultural level than the Egyptians, and, as the surviving works of Jewish–Greek literature of the third and second centuries show, the Greek culture which they acquired was of a superior quality.'[7]

Through the magpie-like Roman collector, Alexander Polyhistor

[1] E. Bickerman, 'Two legal interpretations of the Septuagint', *Revue internationale des droits de l'antiquité*, 3rd ser., 3 (1956), 81–104 for the re-interpretation given to *mohar*, 'bride price' by translating it *phernē*, 'dowry', and for the expansion of Exod. 22:4 in connection with field damage by cattle. Also the substitution of doctor's fees (*iatreia*) in Exod. 21:19 in cases of bodily injury and the omission of the distinction between the two Hebrew expressions for pledge, *ḥᵉbol* and *ʿᵃboth*, in favour of the single expression *enechyron* is in accordance with Greek legal thinking, see M. David, 'Deux anciens termes bibliques pour le gage', OTS 2 (1943), pp. 79–86.

[2] Ps.-Arist. 121. Cf. Hengel, *Hellenismus*, p. 111 = ET 1, p. 60.

[3] Num. 25:3, 5; Deut. 23:18. Cf. 1 Kings 15:12; Wisd. 12:14; 14:15.

[4] Philo, *Vit. Mos.* II.205; *Spec. Leg.* 1.53; Jos. *Ant.* IV.207; *C. Ap.* II.237.

[5] *CPJ*, 1, pp. 24f, 63f, 96f; Fraser, *Alexandria*, 1, pp. 88, 688f, 715f.

[6] Cf. Isa. 9:12; Jer. 26 (46):16; 27 (50):16: *machaira hellenikē* for *ḥereb yonah*; Esther 9:24 and E (16:) 10, 14; cf. *CPJ*, 1, p. 24 n. 61.

[7] Fraser, *Alexandria*, 1, p. 57.

(*circa* 105–after 49 B.C.E.), we have some fragments of Hellenistic Jewish writers from Ptolemaic times, probably all to be dated in the third and second centuries B.C.E. Unlike Palestinian literature, with the exception of Ben Sira, it is noticeable that they are neither anonymous nor pseudonymous, but are written under their authors' names. This means that, like the Greeks from the seventh or sixth centuries on, they had the concept of 'intellectual property', which scarcely existed yet in contemporary Palestine.[1] The traditional anonymous and pseudepigraphic literature was of course still found after this time in Egypt, but it was more popular in character and was restricted to certain forms taken over from the Palestinian homeland – the romance, the apocalypse and the book of wisdom. Although the themes of these new Hellenistic Jewish authors always served the purpose of glorifying their own sacred history, the literary form of their works was adapted to those of Greek literature. We find here a strictly 'scholarly' chronographic historical writing, which demonstrates the great antiquity of Jewish religion, and also, by the method of *aporiai kai lyseis*, resolves exegetical difficulties. An example is the chronographer Demetrius, who wrote in the time of Philopator (221–205/4 B.C.E.).[2] Artapanus, on the other hand, wrote an imaginative historical novel, making Joseph and Moses the first inventors; and he represented the Jewish lawgiver as Hermes-Thoth, or as Museus, the father of Orpheus, and so not only the discoverer of writing and literature, but even the founder of Egyptian (and indirectly also Greek) religion.[3] The tragedian Ezekiel describes the Exodus from Egypt in the form of a drama, and in the language of Aeschylus and Euripides. In contrast with the all-powerful Fate of the Greeks, it was according to him always the guiding hand of the God of Israel which directed the course of history.[4] It is quite possible that this drama was performed within the Jewish communities, especially since the synagogues often had large courtyards and the community in Berenice (Cyrenaica) even had an amphitheatre at its disposal.[5] Other writers, such as Theodotus the

[1] M. Hengel, 'Anonymität', p. 234.

[2] Text in A.-M. Denis, *Fragmenta pseudepigraphorum quae supersunt graeca* (Leiden, 1970), pp. 175ff. Cf. also his *Introduction aux pseudépigraphes grecs d'Ancien Testament* (Leiden, 1970), pp. 248ff; Hengel, 'Anonymität', p. 235; Fraser, *Alexandria*, 1, pp. 690ff; B. Z. Wacholder, 'Biblical chronology in the Hellenistic world chronicles', *HTR*, 61 (1968), 451–81, esp. 454ff.

[3] Denis, *Fragmenta*, pp. 186ff; *Introduction*, pp. 255ff; Hengel, 'Anonymität', 239ff; Fraser, *Alexandria*, 1, pp. 704ff.

[4] Denis, *Fragmenta*, pp. 207ff; *Introduction*, pp. 273ff; B. Snell, 'Ezechiels Moses-Drama', *Antike und Abendland*, 13 (1967), 150–64; also his (ed.) *Tragicorum Graecorum Fragmenta*, 1 (Göttingen, 1971), pp. 288–301, no. 128; Fraser, *Alexandria*, 1, pp. 707f.

[5] *CIG*, 8, 5361, for which Hengel, 'Proseuche', pp. 182, 178 n. 90.

Samaritan and Philo the Elder, describe the history of God's people, and of the holy cities of Shechem and Jerusalem, in the form of an epic in archaic hexameters.[1] The 'Jewish Sibyl' uses the same form.[2] These writings, dating *circa* 140 B.C.E. in their original form, are couched in the words of Homer and imitate political *vaticinia ex eventu*, such as are found e.g. in Lycophron's *Alexandra*.[3] They proclaim to the Greek world the coming judgement and kingdom of God, and at the same time offer an explanation of the meaning of world history as a whole. The author ascribes the whole work to a daughter-in-law of Noah, who later emigrated to Greece and was to be identified with the oldest Erythrean Sibyl. Here the classical form is employed for the purpose of anti-Hellenistic polemic: the theogony of Hesiod is 'demythologized' euhemeristically. The Titans and Olympic gods become primeval kings, who after the days of Noah brought war to the earth. The greatest poet of the Greeks, Homer, can be unmasked and shown to be a dangerous liar. This pseudepigraphic combination of Homeric speech forms and Jewish apocalyptic content had a tremendous influence. It was imitated again and again, right down to the Middle Ages, and its combination of world-history and salvation-history has, along with the book of Daniel, decisively moulded the western philosophy of history.[4] Alongside the Sibyl there were further 'apologetic' forgeries, which acknowledged the God of Israel, but in a Greek dress. To this class belong quotations from the Greek tragedians and comedians, supposed verses of Pythagoras, the didactic poem of Pseudo-Phocylides, the fragments of Pseudo-Hecateus and others.[5] The fragments of Aristobulus, preserved by Eusebius,[6] also have a philosophical and apologetic character. He supposedly worked as adviser on Jewish affairs to the pro-Jewish Philometor (180–145 B.C.E.). It is in him that we find the first attempts at an allegorical interpretation of objectionable verses in the Pentateuch, and the assertion that Pythagoras and Plato knew the Law of Moses, a thesis which Philo develops into a motif of theft by the Greeks. In setting out

1 Denis, *Fragmenta*, pp. 204ff, 203f; *Introduction*, pp. 272f, 270f.; Fraser, *Alexandria*, 1, p. 707.

2 Hengel, in *Pseudepigrapha*, 1, pp. 286ff; V. Nikiprowetzky, *La troisième Sibylle* (Paris, 1970).

3 He wrote after the battle of Cynoscephalae in 197 B.C.E., cf. S. Josifović, *PWSup*, 11 (1968), cols. 888–930 (esp. 925ff).

4 K. Löwith, *Meaning in History* (Chicago, 1949).

5 Denis, *Fragmenta*, pp. 149ff, 199ff; *Introduction*, pp. 215ff, 262ff; Hengel, in *Pseudepigrapha*, 1, pp. 296ff, 301ff.

6 Denis, *Fragmenta*, pp. 217ff; *Introduction*, pp. 277ff; N. Walter, *Der Thoraausleger Aristobulos*, TU 86 (Berlin, 1964); Hengel, *Hellenismus*, pp. 195ff = ET 1, pp. 163ff.; Fraser, *Alexandria*, 1, pp. 694ff. Cf. also 2 Macc. 1:10.

the foundations of the true Jewish philosophy, he cites not only a forged *Testament of Orpheus*[1] but also partly forged verses from Homer and Hesiod which emphasize the significance of the number 7, or of the seventh day, and also the beginning of the *Phainomena* of Aratus. Both the forged and the genuine classical verses are probably derived from an anthology of Jewish–Pythagorean origin. Divine Wisdom is identical with the number 7 and, as the primeval light, provides the 'noetic' framework of the world. For the first time we have here a fusion into one system of Old Testament revelation and Greek philosophical thinking, making the attempt at an intellectual synthesis. The aim of this early Jewish thinker was not assimilation, but a genuine response to the challenge met in superior Greek thought. It may be assumed that there existed, both before him and down to Philo, a Jewish philosophical school tradition in Alexandria.[2] The slightly later *Letter of Pseudo-Aristeas*[3] combines the most varied forms of Hellenistic literature to give an apologetic work which seems to take its stand on a double front. On the one hand, it defends Greek education and culture, as well as loyalty to the Ptolemaic royal house against the radical Jewish nationalism aroused by the Maccabean struggle. On the other, it is directed at those who despise the Jewish people and their law. This double stand was probably typical of the Greek-educated Jewish upper classes in Alexandria as a whole. The allegorical interpretation already begun by Aristobulus is developed further in the *Letter of Aristeas* in order to present an apology for the Law. In its outward form the work is a fictitious epistolary novel, in which a report of a journey, learned dialogue and, in particular, a royal symposium are incorporated, the latter furthermore including a 'mirror for the king'. Jason of Cyrene wrote an historical work dealing with the very recent past, namely the attempt at Hellenization and the Maccabean revolt, probably down to the death of Judas Maccabeus. It has a thoroughly scholarly character and belongs to a type of writing popular in Hellenistic times, a 'pathetic' (i.e. emotive) history.[4] An unknown epitomator then

1 Denis, *Fragmenta*, pp. 163ff; *Introduction*, pp. 230ff; Walter, *Aristobulos*, pp. 202ff.; Hengel, in *Pseudepigrapha*, 1, pp. 293f; it is found in many recensions. The oldest form is preserved in Ps.-Justin, *De monarchia*.

2 Walter, *Arisobulos*, pp. 141–9; W. Bousset, *Jüdisch-christlicher Schulbetrieb in Alexandria und Rom*, FRLANT 6 (Göttingen, 1915); M. J. Shroyer, 'Alexandrian Jewish literalists', *JBL*, 55 (1936), 261ff.

3 A. Pelletier, *Letter d'Aristée à Philocrate*, SC 89 (Paris, 1962); V. Tcherikover, 'The ideology of the letter of Aristeas', *HTR*, 51 (1958), 59–85; for the dating see E. van't Dack, 'La date de la lettre d'Aristée', *Antidorum W. Peremans* (Louvain, 1968), pp. 263–78; Fraser, *Alexandria*, 1, pp. 696ff; bibliography in S. P. Brock, C. T. Fritsch and S. Jellico, *A Classified Bibliography of the Septuagint*, ALGHJ 6 (Leiden, 1973), pp. 44ff.

4 Hengel, *Hellenismus*, pp. 176ff = ET 1, pp. 95ff; H. Cancik, *Mythische und historische Wahrheit*, SBS 48 (1970), pp. 108–26.

summarized the five books into the so-called second book of Maccabees.

The early Hellenistic Jewish writings from Alexandria exhibit a wide variety of literary forms and a very uniform tendency to glorify their own people, their God-guided history, their law and their truly philosophical religion. Their aim was not primarily to win over those of other faiths, but rather to satisfy the literary needs of the growing Jewish upper class in Alexandria itself. Traditional Jewish edificatory literature from Palestine no longer sufficed, although these too were translated into Greek one after another. The finest example of such activity in translating is the prologue written by the grandson of Ben Sira, who translated his Wisdom book into Greek.[1] Non-Jews hardly noticed these writings, any more than did the Septuagint.[2] The most likely exception in this respect would be the Sibylline books. Perhaps a still stronger influence might be attributed to the magical and astrological 'secret literature' of Jewish origin. To the classical world Moses was not only the great lawgiver but even more the arch-magician. Pseudepigraphic astrological books of Jewish origin were also in circulation.[3] But interest in Jewish literature outside Judaism itself grew for the first time in the period of the emperors, especially from the second century C.E. on, under Christian, Neopythagorean and Hermetic influence.

An extraordinarily rich intellectual life developed among the Jewish Diaspora in Egypt, especially in Alexandria. The upper classes, at least, as well as their knowledge of Greek, acquired a remarkably good education in rhetoric and philosophy. This meant that they gained admission to the educational institutions of the Greek world, to Greek

1 H. J. Cadbury, 'The grandson of Ben Sira', *HTR*, 48 (1955), 219–25; P. Auvray, 'Notes sur le prologue de l'Ecclésiastique', in *Mélanges A. Robert* (Paris, 1957), pp. 281–7.

2 Gager, *Moses;* Hengel, *in Pseudepigrapha* 1, pp. 307f. The supposed knowledge of the Septuagint of Isa. 14:12, etc. by Callimachus, and again of S. of S. 6:8–10 by Theocritus, as in Fraser, *Alexandria,* 1, pp. 584, 714, 716, 2, pp. 1,000 and 1,002 n. 255, is chronologically inconceivable. An acquaintance of Agatharchides with the LXX of Eccles. 12:8 is improbable. The motif of the spirit returning to the giver or to the place of origin is also found in Greek literature; Hengel, *Hellenismus*, p. 228 n. 132 = ET 2, p. 84 n. 134 on Eccles. 3:28.

3 Hengel, *Hellenismus*, pp. 427ff, 438ff = ET 1, pp. 236f, 242f; Gager, *Moses*, pp. 134ff; W. and H. G. Gundel, *Astrologumena*, Sudhoffs Archiv, Beiheft 6 (Wiesbaden, 1966), pp. 51–9. Hermippus (*c.* 220 B.C.E.), the disciple of Callimachus, who made Pythagoras, among others, an imitator of the Jews (line 21, Diodotus, Reinach *Textes* 3a) had, according to Vettius Valens II.28f (p. 96 ed. Kroll), known

schools, to the gymnasia and even more advanced education in rhetoric and philosophy. In Cyrenaica, as also in Asia Minor, Jewish names appear in the lists of ephebes.[1] Philo of Alexandria had a very broad education and was certainly not the only Jew who had behind him a comprehensive *enkyklios paideia*. Members of the Jewish Diaspora in Alexandria from as early as the third century B.C.E. had probably walked the same educational path. Hellenistic education was by no means restricted to a small circle in the Egyptian capital, as is shown by the numerous thoroughly Hellenized epitaphs and inscriptions from Leontopolis, which belong to the late Ptolemaic or early Roman period, on which, with few exceptions, only the names are indicative of Jewish tombs.[2] We hear in them of death-bringing Moira, the everlasting darkness of Hades and the gloomy descent to Lethe. For the Jewish official Abramos, who had been head of two Jewish *politeumata* and been renowned for his wisdom, the poet had only the timeless conventional wish: 'May the earth, the guardian of the dead, be light on you.'[3]

Despite this complete external Hellenization, which was not limited only to language and literary education, but included large parts of their way of life as well, the Jewish Diaspora did not assimilate unconditionally to its Hellenistic environment. Jews went through the obligatory training of the gymnasium; they learnt Homer and classical poetry, and pursued further studies in rhetoric and philosophy; they went to the theatre and the games; they had social contacts with non-Jews and even entered upon a successful career in the Ptolemaic civil service. But they did not accept Greek polytheistic religion. They kept the Sabbath, avoided unclean foods and attended worship in the synagogue, where more and more a polished didactic address in the style of the diatribe took its place alongside prayer and hymn and gave to the educated Jew the consciousness that he represented the true philosophy.[4] In a similarly many-sided educational milieu, Paul of Tarsus, the young Pharisee, developed his masterly rhetorical style, in

astrological books by the 'very remarkable Abraham', in which the horoscope for journeys was set out. Artapanus, the Samaritan anonymous and Eupolemus agree in making Abraham the transmitter or inventor of astrology.

1 Hengel, *Hellenismus*, p. 126 n. 83 = ET 2, p. 48 n. 84.

2 *CIJ*, 2, nos. 1451–1530 (with supplements no. 1530 A–D in *CPJ*, 3, pp. 162f).

3 *CPJ*, 3, p. 162, no. 1530 A; further L. Robert, *Hellenica*, 1 (Limoges, 1940), pp. 18–24.

4 Cf. H. Thyen, *Der Stil der jüdisch–hellenistischen Homilie*, FRLANT 65 (Göttingen, 1955); cf. above, p. 197.

which rabbinical exegesis and popular philosophy accompany an apocalyptic view of the world.

The limits within which movement was possible do vary. The Letter of Pseudo-Aristeas makes the courtier Aristeas provide the following explanation of Jewish belief: 'They worship the same god, the Lord and Creator of the Universe, as all other men, as we ourselves, O king, though we call him by different names, such as Zeus or Dis. This name was very appropriately bestowed upon him by our first ancestors, in order to signify that He through whom all things are endowed with life and come into being, is necessarily the ruler and lord of the universe.'[1] On the other hand, Aristobulus, in his version of the *Testament of Orpheus* and in his quotation from Aratus, replaces the name Zeus with *theos* and emphasizes explicitly: 'I have interpreted the passage as is necessary by removing the names "Dis" and "Zeus" which occur in the poems, since their meaning relates to God. This is why I have expressed them in this way....For all the philosophers agree that one must have pious views about God, and this is something which our philosophical school (*hairesis*) particularly insists on.'[2] Here we have indications of an inner-Jewish controversy about how far it is admissible to transfer the names of foreign gods to the true God. Greek and Roman attempts at the identification of the God of Israel with other gods, such as Dionysus, Sabazius or Jupiter,[3] show that this kind of critical delimitation was necessary. It is also shown by the fact that two Jews in Ptolemaic times set up two inscriptions in the temple of Pan at Redesieh in Apollinopolis Magna (Edfu) in Upper Egypt, in which they thanked God (*theou eulogia* and *eulogei ton theon*), one of them for deliverance from peril at sea.[4] It is quite possible that the fanatical Dionysus worshipper, Ptolemy IV Philopator, after his victory at Raphia, tried through pressure and promises to persuade Jews of the upper classes in Egypt to be initiated into the mysteries of Dionysus, for he himself regarded their god as a kind of Semitic Dionysus.[5] Some decades later radical Jewish reformers, working hand in hand with Antiochus IV and gentile military colonists, tried to transform the worship of Yahweh on Mount Zion into a cult of Zeus Olympius or

1 Ps.-Aristeas 16, cf. Jos. *Ant.* XII.22; C.Ap. II.168; the euhemeristic etymology of the name of Zeus in Sib. 3.141 is totally different. For the problem Hengel, *Hellenismus*, pp. 481ff. = ET 1, pp. 264ff.

2 Euseb. *Praep. Evang.* 13.12.7f (GCS 43, 2 p. 195 Mras).

3 Hengel, *Hellenismus*, pp. 473ff = ET 1, pp. 261ff.

4 *OGIS* 73, 74 (vol. 1, p. 125) = *CIJ*, 2, p. 445, no. 1537f.

5 3 Macc. 2:30; Hengel, *Hellenismus*, p. 480 = ET 1, p. 263; Fraser, *Alexandria*, 1, pp. 43ff, 202ff, 2, pp. 344ff.

Baal Shamem, since, for the outsider, it was basically a matter of just the same God of heaven.[1] Jews in the Diaspora as well as in the homeland, however, resisted this attempt in an overwhelming majority. The legend in 3 Maccabees attests, 'But the greater part stood firm with a noble courage and departed not from their religion.'[2] There is no real evidence of a Jewish–pagan syncretism in Egypt in pre-Roman Hellenistic times. The emergence of a 'Jewish gnosis', which is widely discussed today, was, in the present writer's opinion, only possible in the Roman period after the time of Philo. There is no evidence for it in Ptolemaic times.[3] Actual fusion between Jews and pagans occurred only in the field of magic and astrology, in which Egyptians, Jews and Greeks became increasingly interested from the second century B.C.E., and by which all classes of the population were affected.

THE HELLENIZATION OF THE DIASPORA OUTSIDE EGYPT

There is very little information about the early Hellenistic Diaspora outside Egypt and about its Hellenization. In late prophetic literature Joel 3:6f. (Heb. 4:6) has a polemic against the sale of Jewish slaves to the Greeks; and again in Isa. 11:11f. and especially in 66:19 there are references to Jewish emigration to the Aegean area of Greece and Asia Minor. These passages may come from the fourth century or the beginning of the third. Nothing more is heard about the fate of those 2,000 Babylonian Jews in Phrygia, whom Antiochus III during his *anabasis* to the eastern provinces (212–205 B.C.E.) settled there with their families in order to pacify the recently regained province.[4] A few years later this district came under the rule of the Attalids of Pergamum after the battle of Magnesia in 190 B.C.E.

Since we possess a large number of Jewish inscriptions of the Roman period from the interior of Asia Minor, from Phrygia and Lydia, it can be assumed that the foundation of the Diaspora in Asia Minor was laid

[1] E. Bickerman, *Der Gott der Makkabäer* (Berlin, 1937); Hengel, *Hellenismus*, pp. 515ff. = ET 1, pp. 283ff.

[2] 3 Macc. 2:32.

[3] With reference to the unending speculation about an alleged gnosis dating back to pre-Christian times, it should be noted that the word 'gnosis' does not figure at all in the comprehensive index to Fraser, *Alexandria*, which covers the entire range of sources dealing with ancient life in Alexandria as a whole. Our sources provide no ground for supposing the existence of any pre-Christian gnostic speculation in Alexandria, the place where gnosis has been supposed to have originated out of popular, syncretistic Platonism.

[4] Jos. *Ant.* XII.147–53; see above p. 70 n. 5.

by these cleruchs.[1] An epitaph from Hierapolis in Phrygia mentions the *katoikia* of the Jews who lived in Hierapolis. This uncommon term for a synagogue community may go back to the Jewish military colonists.[2] An early list of benefactors of the second century B.C.E. from Iasus in Ionia names one Nicetas son of Jason from Jerusalem (*Hierosolymitēs*), who donated a hundred drachmas for the festival of the Dionysia. Schürer rightly comments: 'This support of a heathen festival by a Jew reminds us of the analogous incidents in Jerusalem before the beginning of the Maccabean uprising'.[3] We do not know whether this Nicetas was still a real Jew nor whether his gift for the festival of Dionysus was offered of his own free will or under compulsion. It appears that in pre-Roman times the pressure exerted on Jews was heavier in the Greek cities on the western coast of Asia Minor than e.g. in Ptolemaic Egypt. In 13 B.C.E., in the presence of Marcus Agrippa, the Ionian states made the following demand upon the Jews living among them: 'if the Jews really belonged to them, they should also reverence their gods'.[4] A similar suggestion is made in the complaint by the rhetorician Apollonius Molon (Rhodian ambassador to Rome in 81 B.C.E.) that the Jews 'do not accept those who hold other conceptions of God'.[5] On the other hand, good relations between the new Jewish state and Rome following the successful war of independence against the Seleucids in Judea also brought benefits to the Jews in the Aegean and Asia Minor. This is shown, for example, by the decree of the Pergamenes in the time of Hyrcanus I, which refers to the friendship between Abraham and the ancestors of the Pergamenes. This is clearly a tendentious legend which reminds us of the relationship between Jews and Spartans (see below, pp. 219f.), and which perhaps originated among the Jewish military colonists who came to Magnesia during the rule of the Pergamene kingdom.[6] Again the Noah coin of Phrygian Apamea, which pictures him leaving the ark after the flood, may go back to a local Jewish legend of the Hellenistic period.[7] Letters written by a Roman consul in 142 or 139 B.C.E. for the benefit of the Jewish *ethnos* to a number of city states and territories in the Aegean and Asia Minor, and advising that fugitive Hellenistic Jews be handed over to Simon the high priest, prove that the Jews had

1 *CIJ* 2, nos. 750–80; cf. L. Robert, *Hellenica*, 11/12 (Paris, 1960), pp. 380–439; A. T. Kraabel, *Judaism in Western Asia Minor* (Dissertation, Harvard, 1968).

2 *CIJ*, 2, no. 775.

3 *CIJ*, 2, no. 749; E. Schürer, *Geschichte des jüdischen Volkes im Zeitalter Jesu Christi*, 3, (4th edn, Leipzig, 1909), pp. 16f.

4 Jos. *Ant.* XII.126.

5 *C.Ap.* II.258.

6 Jos. *Ant.* XIV.255.

7 B. V. Head, *Historia Numorum* (2nd edn., London, 1911, repr. 1963), pp. 666f.

spread over Asia Minor and the Aegean in the second half of the second century.[1] Slightly later, the earliest Synagogue yet excavated, in the transshipment port of Delos, indicates that a large and flourishing Jewish community lived there.[2] From roughly the same time come the two curse tablets from the cemetery island of Rheneia, which supplicate God to exact vengeance for the murder of two Jewish girls. These tablets, in addition to providing the first epigraphic evidence for the Septuagint, show that angels played a special role in the piety of these Diaspora Jews.[3]

Links between Jerusalem and Sparta appear to have existed in pre-Maccabean times. Only so can we explain why Jason, the son of Simon the Just, who inaugurated the Hellenizing reform after 175, following an abortive attempt at an uprising, fled first to Egypt and finally to Sparta, where he ended his days. The strange choice of this city arose from a belief in a kinship between the Jews and Lacedemonians.[4] From about the same period come the first Jewish epitaphs from Athens.[5] Jewish slaves can however be traced in Attica in the fourth and third centuries B.C.E. (see above, p. 191). From the first half of the third century, too, comes the report of Clearchus of Soli about an encounter between Aristotle and a Greek-educated Jew from Jerusalem who 'was a Greek not only in his language but also in his soul'. This encounter, which would have occurred around 340 B.C.E., is most probably to be dismissed as legendary. But it can be concluded from it that Clearchus, who came from Cyprus, had met such Greek-educated Jews in his own day.[6] This reflects the interest taken by the

[1] 1 Macc. 15:24. The following are mentioned: Caria, Pamphylia, Lycia, Halicarnassus, Myndos, Cnidus, Phaselis, Side, Amysos and the islands of Delos, Samos, Cos and Rhodes; cf. Tcherikover, *Civilization*, pp. 288f; A. Giovannini and H. Müller, 'Die Beziehungen zwischen Rom und den Juden im 2 Jh. v. Chr.', *Museum Helveticum*, 28 (1971), 156–71.

[2] *CIJ*, 1, nos. 725–31; A. Plassart in *Mélanges Holleaux* (Paris, 1913), pp. 201–5 = *RB*, 11 (1914), 523–34; Hengel, 'Die Synagogeninschrift von Stobi', *ZNW*, 57 (1966), 161 n. 53; 174 n. 97; P. Bruneau, *Recherches sur les cultes de Délos...*, Bibliothèque des écoles françaises d'Athènes et de Rome 217 (Paris, 1970), pp. 480–93. The synagogue was built on the site of a gymnasium, which had been abandoned after the sacking of Delos by Mithridates in 88 B.C.E.

[3] *CIJ*, 1, no. 725, cf. A. Deissmann, *Licht vom Osten* (4th edn., Tübingen, 1923), pp. 351–62, ET *Light from the Ancient East* (2nd edn, London, 1927), pp. 413–424: 'and notably the whole style of the prayer ...were adaptations to the Hellenic surrounding' (ET, p. 423). Cf. also that the later imperial-period inscription from Argos (*CIJ*, 1, no. 719).

[4] 2 Macc. 5:9; see below, pp. 219f.

[5] L. B. Urdahl, 'Jews in Attica', *Symbolae Osloenses*, 43 (1968), 39–56; cf. *IG* II², 12609 – the epitaph of one 'Simon Ananiou' (Urdahl, p. 46) from the second century B.C.E.

[6] Jos. *C.Ap.* 1.180 from the work *Peri Hypnou*, see F. Wehrli, *Die Schule des Aristoteles*, 3 (Basle, 1948), pp. 10f, 1 fr. 6 and the comment on pp. 47f: 'Clearchus's fiction

Aristotelian school in 'barbarian philosophy', an interest which is found again in the fragment of Theophrastus concerning the Jews and in Megasthenes. The Jews were thus associated with the Indian Brahmans.[1]

Under the rule of the Attalids in Asia Minor, where the Jews were much more in the minority, rather than in Egypt, there occurred mixed Jewish syncretistic cultures. In these e.g. the Phrygian Sabazius was identified with the *Kyrios Sabaoth* of the Jews. This would explain the strange report of Valerius Maximus that about 139 B.C.E. the praetor Cornelius Hispalus had expelled from Rome the Jews who wished to introduce the cult of *Iovis Sabazius*. However this report may be the result of a simple confusion of names.[2] The cult of *Zeus*, or *theos hypsistos*, is evidenced in Asia Minor, Macedonia, Thrace, Egypt and the kingdom of the Bosphorus; and in Roman Asia Minor in particular we find the worship of the *theos angelos*, who was to some extent identified with *Zeus hypsistos*.[3] But these cannot invariably be attributed to Jewish influence, although cross-linkages are probable.[4] It is striking, for example, that those *theos hypsistos* inscriptions which are clearly Jewish because they come from synagogues usually belong to the pre-Christian Hellenistic period, whereas the pagan cult of the 'highest god' first really flourished under the Roman empire. Another occasion for Jewish–pagan syncretism occurs in connection with Sabbath observance, which, despite polemic against it, seems often to have proved attractive to non-Jews.[5] Sporadic indications from

serves to give heightened honour to Greek religious teaching by means of a representative of the admired east'. Cf. Hengel, *Hellenismus*, pp. 467ff = ET 1, pp. 257f.

[1] W. Jaeger, *Diokles von Karystos* (Berlin, 1938), pp. 134ff; 'Greeks and Jews', *JR*, 18 (1938), 127–43 = *Scripta Minora*, 2 (Rome, 1960), pp. 169–83; L. Robert, 'De Delphes à l'Oxus, Inscriptions grecques nouvelles de la Bactriane', *CRAIBL* (1968), 443–54.

[2] Valerius Maximus 1.3.3. The account is found in the Epitome of Julius Paris and the shorter one of Nepotianus, which supplement each other; see Hengel, *Hellenismus*, pp. 478ff = ET 1, pp. 263f; W. Fauth, 'Sabazios', *Der Kleine Pauly*, vol. 4 (Munich, 1972), cols. 1479f. It is very improbable that the whole is an invention of Valerius Maximus, who aimed to please Tiberius with it, as held by S. Alessandrí, 'La presunta cacciata dei Giudei da Roma nel 139 a. Cr.', *SCO*, 17 (1968), 187–98.

[3] L. Robert, 'Reliefs votifs et cultes d'Anatolie', *Anatolia*, 3 (1958), pp. 115f., 120ff; cf. *Hellenica* 11/12 (1960), pp. 432ff; M. P. Nilsson, *Geschichte der Griechischen Religion*, 2 (2nd edn., Munich, 1961), pp. 540 n. 4; 577 n. 1.

[4] C. Roberts, T. C. Skeat and A. D. Nock, 'The Gild of Zeus Hypsistos', *HTR*, 29 (1936), 39–88; Hengel, *Hellenismus*, pp. 544ff = ET 1, pp. 296ff; G. Bertram, 'Hypsistos', *TWNT*, 8 (1969), 613ff, *TDNT*, 8 (1972), 614ff; C. Colpe, 'Hypsistos', *Der Kleine Pauly*, vol. 2 (Stuttgart 1967), cols. 1291f; Kraabel, *Judaism*.

[5] E. Lohse, 'Sabbaton', *TWNT*, 7 (1964), 17f, *TDNT* 7 (1971), 17f.

Phrygia testify to the cult of a *theos Sabathikos*. An inscription in verse calls him 'the greatest god' (*megistos hyparchōn*) 'who owns the world' (*tou katechontos ton kosmon*).[1] To the same Augustan period belong two inscriptions from Cilicia, which testify to a cultic community of Sabbatistai (*hetaireia tōn Sambatistōn*), who under the leadership of a *synagōgeus* worshipped a *theos Sabbatistēs*.[2] The 'Sambatheion' in Thyatira may however be a synagogue.[3] At the same time we find in Naucratis in Egypt a *synhodos Sambatikē*, where probably a similar cult was practised.[4] A clearly Jewish influence is to be seen in the *synhodos peri theon hypsiston* in Tanais at the mouth of the Don, where 'the worshippers of the highest god' (*sebomenoi theon hypsiston*) had formed themselves into a group. In other cities in this area however these 'god-fearers' were directly connected with the congregations of the Jewish synagogues.[5] These instances of syncretism continue specifically in Asia Minor, right down to the sect of the Hypsistarians in the fourth century C.E.[6] It is very likely that such Jewish–pagan syncretisms, which suddenly became prominent at the turn of the era, had already been formed in pre-Christian Hellenistic times. The place where this occurred should be sought in Asia Minor itself rather than in Egypt.

When dealing with these fringe groups, whose significance must not be overrated, it might be asked whether we are dealing with pagan associations which have been influenced by Judaism, or whether paganized Jews played the leading part. The former was most often probably the case. A Jew forsaking the Law was not likely to devote himself to a half-Jewish cult, but would prefer total assimilation to his Hellenistic environment. Diaspora Judaism outside Egypt too in Hellenistic times shows an astonishing power of resistance to any temptation to real assimilation, which would mean the abandonment of the essence of the Jewish faith with its obligation to the Law and to the one God. On the other hand, in e.g. Egypt, Cyrenaica, Asia Minor

[1] J. Keil and A. v. Premerstein, *Bericht über eine zweite Reise in Lydien*, Denkschriften der kaiserlichen Akademie der Wissenschaften in Wien 54 (Vienna, 1911), pp. 117f, no. 224; cf. also the Sabazius inscription, p. 113, no. 218.

[2] Schürer, *Geschichte*, 3, p. 562 n. 136; *OGIS* 573. For what follows see Tcherikover, 'The Sambathions' in *CPJ*, 3, pp. 43–56.

[3] *CIJ* 2, no. 752.

[4] *SB* 12, see Tcherikover, 'Sambathions', p. 47.

[5] E. Schürer, *Die Juden im bosporanischen Reiche und die Genossenschaften der sebomenoi theon hypsiston ebendaselbst*, Sitzungsberichte der königlich preussischen Akademie der Wissenschaften zu Berlin (Berlin, 1897), 1 pp. 200–25; E. R. Goodenough, 'The Bosporus inscriptions to the Most High God', *JQR*, n.s. 47 (1957), 221–44; M. Hengel, 'Proseuche und Synagoge' in *Tradition und Glaube* (Göttingen, 1971), pp. 173ff.

[6] Hengel, 'Proseuche', p. 179; B. Wyss, 'Zu Gregor von Nazianz', in *Phyllobolia, für Peter von der Mühll zum 60. Geburtstag*, edited by O. Gigon (Basle, p. 174) [1946].

and the Aegean, there were Diaspora communities which from pre-Maccabean times had possessed an independent tradition. These took a more liberal attitude towards Hellenistic culture than those communities which were first established after the time of the Maccabean revolt and came into being as a consequence of heavy immigration from Palestine, such as those in Rome and Italy. The role of Alexandria as the centre of operations for a Hellenistic Jewish education with a quite individual stamp has proved to be unique. A comparison of Jewish epitaphs from Leontopolis at the turn of the era with the numerous early common era Jewish inscriptions in Rome, as well as a comparison of Alexandrian Jewish literature down to Philo with the work produced in Rome by the Hellenized Palestinian Jew, Josephus, will illustrate the difference described.

It is strange that we know almost nothing about the early development of Diaspora Judaism in the area which had the largest share of the Jewish people in early common era times, namely Syria and Phoenicia. Josephus reports that Jews in Antioch, like those in Alexandria, had since the founding of the city possessed *isopoliteia*. But this is really only a matter of the special communal rights possessed by the Jews living there.[1] In the sources, the community first appears in the period of the Hellenistic reform. They were indignant about the assassination by Andronicus of the fugitive High Priest Onias III, who had sought sanctuary in the temple of Apollo and Artemis at Daphne.[2] They were obviously not scandalized that a Jewish high priest had sought asylum in a heathen temple. During the violent attempt at reform made in Jerusalem they were it appears not troubled. The anti-Jewish measures of the king and the radical reformers were confined to Palestine. Under 'the kings who followed Antiochus' the great synagogue in Antioch received as a royal gift some of the vessels which Antiochus had stolen from the Temple in Jerusalem. Josephus speaks in this connection of a *hieron*. After Jerusalem had more and more distanced itself from the kingdom of the Seleucids, possibly the attempt was made here, as at Leontopolis and at 'Araq el-Emir in east Jordan, to create a rival sanctuary.[3] Later the legend of the martyrdom of a Jewish mother and her seven sons was cherished among the community here. Possibly too, the treatise, heavily influenced by the Stoics, which is called 4 Maccabees, originated here.[4] But, unlike Alexandria, Antioch never gained an independent significance as a centre for Hellenistic Jewish

[1] Jos. *Ant.* XII.119–24; *Bell.* VII.44; *C.Ap.* II.39; cf. Tcherikover, *Civilization*, pp. 328f.

[2] 2 Macc. 4:35. [3] Jos. *Bell.* VII.44f; Hengel, *Hellenismus*, p. 499 = ET 1, p. 274.

[4] E. Bickerman, 'Les Maccabées de Malalas', *Byzantion*, 21 (1951), 63–83; R. Renehan, 'The Greek philosophic background of Fourth Maccabees', *Rheinisches Museum*, 115 (1972), 223–38.

culture and literature. The Seleucids never managed to make their capital an intellectual metropolis comparable to Alexandria. It can be assumed that the Hellenization of the Jews in Phoenicia and Syria made slower progress than in Egypt because the use of Aramaic by the broad mass of the population provided the Jews with a linguistic barrier. But, because of lack of sources, this can be no more than a presumption. The Canaanite spoken in the Phoenician cities however was close to Hebrew. By Roman times Greek had, however, taken over in this area too, at least in the larger cities and among the upper classes. This is also true for large parts of Palestine itself.[1] Because there were many ancient contacts between the Jewish heartland in Palestine, the Phoenician coastal cities and the Syrian metropolises in the north, like Damascus, Apamea and Antioch, the internal development of Judaism in Syria must always be treated in close association with that of the homeland itself.

THE INTERPENETRATION OF JUDAISM AND HELLENISM IN JEWISH PALESTINE IN THE PRE-MACCABEAN PERIOD

In the period after Alexander's conquest specifically in Palestine, the Jews came to know the Macedonians and Greeks not as a cultural force but for their absolute military and political supremacy. Even more than under Persian rule, they now became the passive objects of history and were exposed helplessly to the changing power-groupings in Syria and Palestine during the contests between the Diadochi. The fact that they are either not mentioned at all in the Greek sources of the period, or only in passing (as by Agatharchides and Hecateus of Abdera) only shows their political powerlessness. The revival of prophecy in the early apocalyptic of the anonymous author of Deutero-Zechariah[2] or of the Apocalypse of Isaiah, proves that now, under the impact of the horror of war and the hubris of the new overlords, there arose an intense expectation of God's intervention to deliver his people. Now,

[1] Cf. *CIJ*, 2, nos. 870–5, 877–81 and the numerous Greek inscriptions on Jewish tombs in Beth-shearim, which in part are due to Jews from Phoenician and Syrian cities; M. Schwabe and B. Lifshitz, *Beth Shearim* 2 (Jerusalem, 1967), nos. 136f, 147f, 164, 172, 199, etc; J. N. Sevenster, *Do you know Greek?* NovTSup 19 (Leiden, 1968); B. Lifshitz, 'Du nouveau sur l'hellénisation des Juifs en Palestine. A propos d'un livre récent', *Euphrosyne*, n.s. 4 (1970), 113–33; M. Treu, 'Die Bedeutung des Griechischen für die Juden im römischen Reich', *Kairos*, 15 (1973), 122–44.

[2] Cf. H. Gese, 'Anfang und Ende der Apokalyptik, dargestellt am Sacharjabuch', *ZTK*, 70 (1973), 20–49 (esp. 41ff).

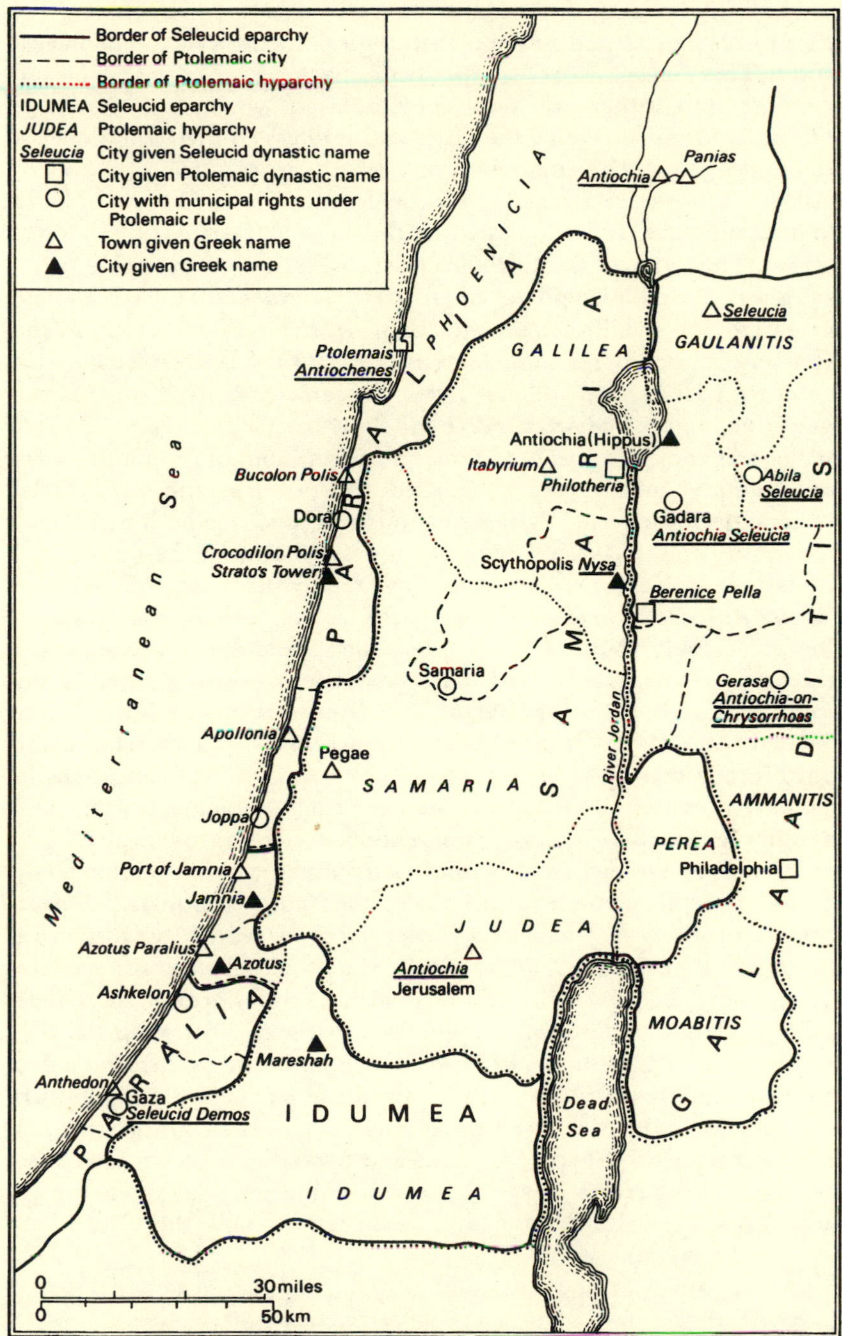

Fig. 1. The Greek cities in Palestine, 312 to 167 B.C.E.

instead of Assyria and Babylonia, the traditional enemies, the Greeks came to be represented as the eschatological enemies of the people of God.[1] This means that at the beginning we find not cultural encounter but rather polemical confrontation, which was thereafter continued in the image of the cruel and godless 'fourth kingdom' of later apocalyptic. The emigration of Jews to Egypt during the rule of Ptolemy I Soter reported as Pseudo-Hecateus was largely due to external pressure, as is suggested by the *Letter of Aristeas* (see above, p. 187). The work of the Chronicler demonstrates, on the other hand, that it was Macedonian power and fortress building and the large estate agriculture of the Ptolemies which made most impression;[2] at the same time, under increasingly harsher foreign rule they tended to paint their own past in ideal colours, and at the same time to strengthen the evaluative contrast between good and evil.

Whereas the destruction of Samaria and the founding of a Macedonian military colony greatly reduced the political and commercial superiority of their racially and religiously related northern neighbour (see above, pp. 40f.), the specifically Jewish district of the old Persian sub-satrapy of Yehud was in no way affected by the Greco-Macedonian military colonies founded in the coastal region and in east Jordan.[3] The great trade routes bypassed Jerusalem, and the eagerness with which the Phoenician coastal cities, at least outwardly, adopted the language and the way of life of the Greeks was not immediately imitated throughout the Jordan hill country. Later, at the end of the fourth century and the beginning of the third, political conditions in Palestine became stabilized, and the new ruler, Ptolemy I Soter, was carefully trying to bring military and commercial improvements to his newly-won Palestinian frontier-land. This policy was later followed by his no less brilliant son, Ptolemy II Philadelphus. Palestinian Judaism, which up to now had remained conservative for a start because of its geographical position, could no longer shut itself off from the spirit of the new age. The small size of the Jewish territory around Jerusalem and the relative poverty of the populace in comparison with the rich coastal cities of Phoenicia and Philistia should not hide it from us that in the various Jewish Wisdom schools in the land a lively intellectual life prevailed, which received its impulse not least from the growing Jewish Diaspora in Egypt, Babylonia and Syria. Since, as we have seen, the Jews who were in Egypt as military colonists, tradesmen, craftsmen, farmers or slaves, took over relatively quickly the Greek lan-

[1] Zech. 9:13; Dan. 7:7ff; 8:5ff; I Enoch 90:1ff; cf. also the allegory of the shepherd in Zech. 11:4ff.

[2] 2 Chron. 26:9–15; see above, p. 52.

[3] A. Alt, *Kleine Schriften zur Geschichte des Volkes Israel*, vol. 2 (Munich, 1953), pp. 396ff.

guage, and to some extent also the Greek way of life, their influence would work its way back to the homeland itself through the agency of returning emigrants.[1] Jewish literature of the fourth and third centuries as it is preserved to us fragmentarily in the latest works of the Old Testament canon and in the Apocrypha, exhibits a great variety in content and in literary form. It is by no means all religiously motivated, but exhibits in part a secular, 'belle-lettres' character.[2] Even if one must be cautious in attributing Hellenistic influence during this early period, we do find here an intellectual milieu which was open to stimulation and influence of many kinds: in particular certain tendencies in the development of Jewish wisdom, and also of apocalyptic, came about with a view to an encounter with Greek ideas.[3]

In the papyri which are connected with the journey undertaken in Palestine in 259 B.C.E. by Zenon, as agent of the finance minister Apollonius, we find numerous contacts between Greek officers, officials, traders and adventurers and the Semitic natives, Jews among them. The Ptolemaic government tried to administer its colony firmly and to exploit it commercially, as it did in Egypt itself. For this purpose they sent Greek agents and tax-gatherers to the remotest village. Whereas the native aristocracy no longer played any real part in Egypt, those in authority in the provinces were ready to work closely with the local upper classes, who were allowed to share in the revenues.[4] Consequently it was not a Greek, but a Jewish magnate, Tobias, who became commanding officer of the mixed Macedonian and Jewish military colony in Ammanitis in east Jordan. His family had ruled the district in Persian times and his ancestors had once caused great difficulties for Nehemiah.[5] According to Josephus he was a brother-in-law of the high priest. Zenon visited him at his castle in Ammanitis with a large retinue. Later he was in correspondence with Apollonius and the king in Alexandria, and treated them almost as he did his equals. In this correspondence he also turns out to be a very liberal Jew. Of course, he had the services of a Greek secretary. But, as commander of a Ptolemaic unit with Macedonian subordinates, he himself must have had a sufficient command of the Greek language both to speak and to write it.[6]

[1] Hengel, *Hellenismus*, pp. 30f = ET 1, pp. 17f.

[2] Morton Smith, in *Fischer Weltgeschichte*, vol. 5, *Griechen und Perser*, ed. H. Bengtson (Frankfurt, 1965), pp. 364ff; Hengel, *Hellenismus*, pp. 207ff = ET 1, pp. 113ff.

[3] *Hellenismus*, pp. 196ff, 453ff = ET 1, pp. 107ff, 247ff.

[4] Rostovtzeff, *Hellenistic World*, 1, pp. 263ff; Tcherikover, *Civilization*, pp. 64ff, 132ff.

[5] *CPJ*, 1, pp. 115ff, nos. 1–5; B. Mazar, 'The Tobiads', *IEJ*, 7 (1957), 137–45, 229–38; see also above, p. 58.

[6] V. Tcherikover, 'Palestine under the Ptolemies', *Mizraim*, 4/5 (1937), 37, 49f; Hengel, *Hellenismus*, pp. 110f, 486ff = ET 1, pp. 59, 267ff.

According to the novel of the Tobiads in Josephus, his son Joseph gained great political and economic importance in Jerusalem itself, probably under Ptolemy III Euergetes. He became not only *prostatēs*, that is, the representative of the Jewish people over against the Ptolemaic kingdom, but he successfully made a bid for the post of general tax-collector for the whole province of Syria and Phoenicia, since he had especially good relations with the royal house. Some Hellenistic cities which wished to offer resistance to the new tax-collector were subjugated by force. He maintained a permanent agent in Alexandria who administered his immense wealth, and, through numerous 'presents', maintained his connection with the court.[1] It is obvious that this Joseph was thoroughly Hellenized and also gave his sons a Greek upbringing.[2] His rapid success cannot otherwise be understood. His youngest son Hyrcanus later obtained the supreme command over the family estates in Ammanitis, including the military colony. His brothers on the other hand had great political influence in Jerusalem. Their descendants became the champions of the radical Hellenistic reform after the accession of Antiochus IV Epiphanes in 175 B.C.E. It was especially through the Tobiad family that a new and luxurious lifestyle found its way into the remote and backward city of Jerusalem. It was contradictory to the strict principles of ancient Israelite tradition, and is concisely and appropriately described by Ecclesiastes:

> Bread is made for laughter
> and wine gladdens life,
> and money answers everything.[3]

The gradual infiltration of Hellenistic culture can be seen also in the emergence of Greek names. In the third century numerous Greek names and Greco-Semitic double names occur in the Phoenician region. A motley mixture of Phoenician, Idumean, Jewish and Greek names occurs in a fully Hellenized milieu in the colony of Mareshah founded by Sidon in the middle of the third century. It lay only 40 km south-west of Jerusalem and was the capital of Idumea.[4] Shechem, where the Samaritans lived, probably also had a similar Sidonian colony. Fragments of inscriptions with Greek names have been found

[1] Jos. *Ant.* XII.160ff. See above, p. 69.

[2] Jos. *Bell.* 1.31f; *Ant.* XII.239f: The sons of Tobias supported the radical Menelaus. Cf. E. Schürer, G. Vermes and F. Millar, *The History of the Jewish People in the Age of Jesus Christ,* 1 (Edinburgh, 1973), pp. 149f, n. 30.

[3] Eccles. 10:19. Cf. Hengel, *Hellenismus*, pp. 92ff = ET 1, pp. 47ff.

[4] J. P. Peters and H. Thiersch, *Painted Tombs in the Necropolis of Marissa* (London, 1905); F.-M. Abel, 'Tombeaux récemment découverts à Marisa', *RB*, 34 (1925), 267–75; Hengel, *Hellenismus*, pp. 115ff = ET 1, pp. 62ff.

there too.[1] Goodenough's judgement on the epitaphs of Mareshah may also be true of Shechem, and even of much of Palestine at the transition from the third to the second century B.C.E.: 'It seems reasonable to suppose that we have here a picture of the sort of syncretizing Hellenization against which, as it affected Jews, the Maccabees revolted. Had syncretism gone on in this way among the Jews, Judaism would perhaps be now as little known as the other religions of the ancient Levant.'[2]

Greek names even occur among 'conservative' Jews in Palestine. The fathers of the ambassadors whom the Maccabees Jonathan and Simon sent to Sparta and Rome – and who were called Numenius son of Antiochus, Antipater son of Jason and Alexander son of Dorotheus – must have been born about the end of the third century and the beginning of the second.[3] The second son of the High Priest Simon the Just appears with the name Jason. He supplanted his conservative brother Onias III and in 175 became the promoter of the Hellenistic reform which wanted to change Jerusalem into a Greek *polis*. With royal permission, and also the general approval of the Jerusalem aristocracy, he built a gymnasium beside the Temple, and they allowed their sons to be educated there as ephebi.[4] Nevertheless, in a few years he had to give way before the yet more radical brothers, Menelaus, Lysimachus and Simon, from the priestly family of Bilga, who were closely associated with the Tobiads.[5] Another contemporary was the otherwise unknown Antigonus of Socho, who according to *M. Aboth* 1.3 had received the Torah from Simon the Just. The only two officers of the Maccabean cavalry troops from east Jordan who are mentioned by name, and who were probably from the cleruchy of Tobias and Hyrcanus, are called Dositheus and Sosipater.[6] John, from the priestly family of Haqqoz, who negotiated with Antiochus III around 200 B.C.E. (see above, p. 73), called his son Eupolemus. Under Judas Maccabeus he became the leader of the first mission to Rome, and it

[1] G. E. Wright, *Shechem* (New York, 1964), p. 183; Hengel, *Hellenismus*, p. 117 = ET 1, p. 62.

[2] E. R. Goodenough, *Jewish Symbols in the Greco-Roman Period*, 1 (New York, 1953), p. 74.

[3] 1 Macc. 12:16; 14:22, 24; 15:15. Cf. Jos. *Ant.* XIII.169; XIV.146. For this and what follows see Hengel, *Hellenismus*, pp. 119f = ET 1, p. 64.

[4] 2 Macc. 4:7ff; 1 Macc. 1:11ff; cf. Hengel, *Hellenismus*, pp. 135ff, 503ff = ET 1, pp. 73ff, 278ff.

[5] 2 Macc. 3:4; 4:23ff, 29, 39ff; see Hengel, *Hellenismus*, pp. 508ff = ET 1, pp. 279ff.

[6] 2 Macc. 12:19, 24, 35; see above, p. 189 and Hengel, *Hellenismus*, p. 502 = ET 1, p. 276.

was probably he who composed a history of the Jewish kings in Greek.[1] Later, under the Hasmoneans, this preference for Greek names and culture among the upper classes increased. Thus foreign names are found quite as frequently among the Maccabean opponents as among the advocates of Hellenistic reform. Among the 72 elders of the *Letter of Aristeas* too, who came to Alexandria to translate the Torah, there were many who bore Greek names such as Theodosius, Theodotus, Theophilus, Dositheus and Jason. For the author of the letter this was evidently quite natural.[2]

Even more important than the Greek names of individual translators is the fact that the author obviously takes it for granted that the 72 Jewish scholars from Palestine had 'not only mastered Jewish literature, but had also acquired a thorough knowledge of Greek'.[3] This means that the author considered that a perfect knowledge of the Greek language among educated Palestinian Jews in the middle of the second century was quite possible. Already in the first half of the third century B.C.E. Clearchus of Soli presumes a Greek education for Jews from Jerusalem.[4] For members of various Jewish missions, first to Antioch and then later to Sparta and Rome, a faultless mastery of the Greek language, both spoken and written, was one of the foundations of their success.[5]

This is likewise true of communication with Diaspora Judaism in Egypt, Asia Minor and the Aegean, where a knowledge of Aramaic had soon disappeared. If the Jerusalem Temple wished to retain and to develop its importance as the religious centre of the Judaism of the Hellenistic world, it had to keep in touch with these communities. The festival pilgrims who came from the west brought with them to Jerusalem their Greek mother-tongue.[6] The various documents in Greek from second-century Jerusalem, included by Josephus and in the books of Maccabees, indicate an experienced Greek diplomatic chancery in the Temple. Later the Hasmoneans tried quite deliberately to strengthen the religious and political influence of the Jerusalem sanctuary upon the Diaspora, and for this purpose encouraged the translation of Jewish literature into Greek.[7] We find the first slight traces of Greek linguistic influence in Ecclesiastes, in Ben Sira and in the lists of musical instruments in Daniel. In later Rabbinic Jewish

[1] 2 Macc. 4:11; cf. 1 Macc. 8:17; see below, p. 221 n. 3.

[2] Ps.-Aristeas 47–50.

[3] Ps.-Aristeas 121.

[4] Jos. *C.Ap.* 1.176–81; see above, p. 208 n. 6.

[5] 2 Macc. 4:5f; 14:4ff; 1 Macc. 8; 12:1ff; 14:16, etc.

[6] A good example from Roman times is the inscription of Theodotus, *CIJ*, 2, pp. 332–5, no. 1404; cf. for this Sevenster, *Greek*, pp. 131ff.

[7] Cf. 2 Macc. 2:14f; also the colophon of the Greek Book of Esther and on it E. J. Bickerman, 'The colophon of the Greek Book of Esther', *JBL*, 63 (1944), 339–62.

literature they are extremely numerous.[1] Literary Hebrew and Aramaic, such as we find e.g. in the books of the Qumran library, give the impression of a deliberately artificial and purist language when compared with the spoken idioms of later Talmudic literature. This suggests that the popular language had accepted loanwords at a considerably earlier stage, a situation that is now corroborated by the Aramaic copper scroll from Qumran.[2]

The establishment of a gymnasium with ephebes in Jerusalem in 175 B.C.E. would have been unthinkable, had not a knowledge of the Greek language, and partly also of Greek literature, been already widespread among the Jerusalem upper classes. This presupposes also the existence of a privately run Greek elementary school in the Jewish capital.[3]

A further indication of the penetration of Greek thought into the capital is the claim that there was a kinship between the Jews and Spartans through Abraham; this probably originated in pro-Greek circles in Jerusalem in the third century. It starts from a letter from the Spartan King Areus to the High Priest Onias II. Since King Areus I had fallen in the Chremonidean war at Corinth in 265 B.C.E., and the initiative concerning kinship could scarcely have originated with the Spartans, this letter may well be a forgery by Hellenistic Jews in the Jewish capital. In a similar way the Phoenicians appealed to their kinship with the Greeks through Cadmus; according to Hecateus the ancestors of the Greeks with the Daneans had, under the leadership of Cadmus, emigrated from Egypt at the same time that Moses set out for Palestine. According to the Jewish historian Cleodemus Malchus, Heracles married in Libya a granddaughter of Abraham. In Asia Minor the Pergamenes appealed to the former friendship of their ancestors with Abraham. While the Romans maintained that they were descended from fugitives from Troy, various cities in south-western Asia Minor made a claim to be Lacedemonian colonies. A letter of the Tyrians to Delphi preserved as an inscription calls the people of Delphi 'kinsmen'.[4] According to E. Bickerman these claims served as 'admission tickets into European culture',[5] that is, to the community of

[1] Dan. 3:5, 7, 10, 15; Hengel, *Hellenismus*, pp. 112ff = ET 1, pp. 60ff.

[2] Hengel, *Hellenismus*, p. 113 n. 23 = ET 2, pp. 43f n. 20.

[3] Hengel, *Hellenismus*, pp. 138ff = ET 1, pp. 74ff.

[4] 1 Macc. 12:6–23; 2 Macc. 5:9; Jos. *Ant.* XII.226f; XIII.167; older literature in R. Marcus, *Josephus*, vol. 7 (Loeb ed., 1943), p. 769; Hengel, *Hellenismus*, pp. 133f = ET 1, p. 72; B. Cardauns, 'Juden und Spartaner', *Hermes*, 95 (1967), 317–24; S. Schüller, 'Some problems connected with the supposed common ancestry of Jews and Spartans...', *JSS*, 1 (1956), 257–68; Schürer *et al.*, *History*, 1, pp. 184f n. 33.

[5] *PW*, 14 (1930), col. 786.

Hellenes. To this extent such theoretical reconstructions were already in the third century preparing the way ideologically for the transformation of Jerusalem into a Greek *polis* after 175 B.C.E. It is striking that even Jonathan the Maccabee, in his attempt to establish political relations with the Spartans, refers to this Hellenistic Jewish legend. It is clear from this that the Hasmoneans did not stop the process of Hellenization in Palestinian Judaism, but as soon as they came to power rather carried it further.[1] The fact that it was the kinship of the Jews with the Spartans especially which was stressed may have something to do with the conservative tendency in both peoples to cling to the law given to each by its respective lawgiver, Moses or Lycurgus, and their isolation from foreigners.

Higher literary Greek education also gradually won a foothold in Palestine. For example, two long inscriptions in faultless verse from about 200 B.C.E. have been found in Gaza and Sidon. The one from Gaza is an epitaph for two Ptolemaic officers and their dependants.[2] The one from Sidon is in honour of the suffete Diotimus for his victory in the Panhellenic Nemean chariot race in Argos. This poem emphasizes explicitly the mythological kinship between Argives, Thebans and Phoenicians.[3] A graffito from one of the tombs in Mareshah contains an elaborate erotic poem of the Locrian genre.[4] The fortress of Gadara in east Jordan seems to have been a nursery of Greek culture. Strabo, who confuses Gadara with Gazara (Gezer),[5] which became Jewish in Maccabean times, names four famous writers who came from this city which was so remote from all other centres of classical culture: 'Philodemus the Epicurean, Meleager, Menippus the satirist and Theodorus the rhetorician of our own days.'[6] Menippus was supposedly born towards the end of the fourth century and sold as a slave to Sinope in Pontus in Asia Minor. It might be concluded from this that he was not descended from new Greek immigrants, but from

[1] Cf. also the tombstone in Modein, 1 Macc. 13:25ff; Jos. *Ant.* XIII.210ff; C. Watzinger, *Denkmäler Palästinas*, 2 (Leipzig, 1935), pp. 22f and the tomb of Jason, L. Y. Rahmani *et al.*, *Atiqot*, 4 (1964).

[2] P. Roussel, 'Epitaphe de Gaza commémorant deux officiers de la garnison ptolémaîque', *Aegyptus*, 13 (1933), 145–51; W. Peek, *Griechische Grabgedichte* (Berlin, 1960), p. 112, no. 162. Probably a plague had claimed a number of victims in the family; cf. Hengel, *Hellenismus*, p. 26 n. 77 = ET 2, p. 10 n. 79.

[3] E. Bickerman, 'Sur une inscription grecque de Sidon', *Mélanges* R. *Dussaud* (Paris, 1939), 1, pp. 91–9; Hengel, *Hellenismus*, pp. 131f = ET 1, p. 71.

[4] W. Crönert, 'Das Lied von Marisa', *Rheinisches Museum*, NF 64 (1909), 433–48; Hengel, *Hellenismus*, p. 152 n. 185 = ET 2, p. 56 n. 192.

[5] Schürer *et al.*, *History*, 1, 191; cf. also the curse inscription, *CIJ* II, no. 1184.

[6] XVI.2.29 (C 759).

Syrians. This would be an example of how completely the Semites could already assimilate to Greek culture. Later he acquired the citizenship of Thebes. According to Diogenes Laertius, who calls him a Phoenician, he became a pupil of the cynic Metrocles. He was the creator of the polemical-cum-philosophical type of satire. A later Syrian, Lucian of Samosata, developed Greek satire further under the influence of Menippus. Meleager, the creator of the Greek Anthology, was born in the middle of the second century and received his education in Tyre, where the Phoenician school, important for Greek lyric, developed under Antipater of Sidon (*circa* 170–100 B.C.E.). Meleager himself calls his home city the 'Assyrian Attica', while a later epitaph gives it the honorific title *chrestomousia*.

In the second century B.C.E. important philosophers such as the Stoic Boethus of Sidon and the Epicurean Zeno of Sidon taught in the Phoenician cities. Meleager and the later Philodemus were both under the influence of the life-affirming spirit of Epicurus. Alongside Gadara, Ashkelon too developed in the second century into an intellectual centre which produced a succession of important philosophers and writers.[1] The intellectual development of Hellenistic Palestine did suffer a sharp blow from, first, the Jewish Hasmonean expansion, and then that of the Arabs and Itureans. Nearly all the Palestinian poets and philosophers emigrated to the west, especially to Italy. How far the lively intellectual milieu of the Phoenician cities and of some Greek colonies, like Gadara, had influence upon Jewish territory, must remain open. In any case the events during the Hellenistic reform show that the Hellenists of Jerusalem laid great value on good contacts specifically with the Phoenician cities as centres of Hellenistic culture. On the orders of Jason the high priest, citizens of the newly founded city of 'Antiocheia' in Jerusalem participated in the five-yearly games at Tyre initiated by Alexander. Nevertheless, they did not dare to hand over to the god the 300 drachmae which Jason the high priest had given to them to provide a sacrifice to the Tyrian Heracles-Melkart, but spent it in equipping ships.[2] Even the pro-Maccabean Jewish 'historian' Eupolemus relates proudly that Solomon once sent to King Suron of Tyre a golden pillar, which he erected 'in the Temple of Zeus', that is, of the Phoenician Baal Shamem. This reoprt is confirmed also by Tyrian historians.[3] For example, the Phoenician 'historians' Laitus and Menander report that Solomon married the daughter of the Phoenician king when King Menelaus of Sparta visited Tyre after the

[1] Hengel, *Hellenismus*, pp. 153–61 = ET 1, pp. 83–88.

[2] 2 Macc. 4:18ff; cf. 4:32, 39.

[3] Euseb. *Praep. Evang.* IX.34.18 = Jacoby, *FGrHist* 723 F 2; Hengel, *Hellenismus*, p. 173 = ET 1, p. 94; cf. Dius in Jos. *C.Ap.* I.112f.; Menander, in *C.Ap.* I.118;

conquest of Troy.[1] Such retouchings of national history opened up the possibility, on the one hand of stressing their links with the superior Greek culture, and on the other of showing the greater antiquity of their own tradition, which made them instructors of the Greeks. Of the same status is the statement of Meleager of Gadara that Homer was a Syrian 'as, according to the custom of his homeland, he never has the Achaeans eating fish, although the Hellespont is swarming with them'.[2]

Fragments from a Samaritan Jewish historical work of this type, probably originating in Palestine, which belongs to the period between the conquest of Palestine by the Seleucids and the outbreak of the Maccabean revolt, are preserved for us by Alexander Polyhistor. According to this Enoch, named Atlas by the Greeks, is said to have obtained the secrets of astrology from the angels and handed them on to posterity. Abraham, who 'surpassed all in nobility and wisdom', had then at God's command brought them to the west, and had instructed first of all the Phoenicians and only later the Egyptian priests of Heliopolis. The biblical sequence of the wanderings of Abraham is here consciously rearranged. As later in the Sibylline Oracles, the foreign gods are euhemeristically devalued, and through the motif of the *prōtos heuretēs* are made to minister to the greater glory of the Israelite people. The Samaritan origin of the work is shown by the stress upon 'the city sanctuary of Hargarizim' as the place where Abraham 'received gifts' from the priest–king Melchizedek.[3]

The spirit of the new era, and even direct influence of Greek thought, can be seen to some extent also in Hebrew Wisdom literature. This is especially true of the often puzzling book of Ecclesiastes, in which earlier scholars had already conjectured the influence of Greek philosophy. The work most probably originated in Jerusalem in the third century during the period of Ptolemaic rule, and to a degree breathes the spirit of the early Hellenistic *Aufklärung*.[4] Certain linguistic connections already show this. Favoured terms for destiny in

Theophilus in Euseb. *Praep. Evang.* IX.34.19 = Jacoby, *FGrHist* 733. The motif is already found in Herodotus II.44.2, see M. Hadas, *Hellenistic Culture*, pp. 95f, who sees in this reference a 'considerable latitudinarianism, or perhaps a tendency towards syncretism'.

1 Clem. Alex. *Strom.* I.114.2 and Tatian, *ad. Graec.* 37 = Jacoby, *FGrHist* 784 F 1 a,b.

2 Athen. IV.157b; cf. Hadas, *Culture*, p. 83.

3 Euseb. *Praep. Evang.* IX.17 and 18.2 = Jacoby, *FGrHist* 724; cf. Hengel, *Hellenismus*, pp. 162ff = ET 1, 88ff.; A.-M. Denis, *Introduction aux pseudépigraphes grecs d'Ancien Testament* (Leiden, 1970), p. 261.

4 Hengel, *Hellenismus*, pp. 210–40 = ET 1, pp. 115–30; R. Braun, *Kohelet und die frühhellenistische Popularphilosophie*, BZAW 130 (Berlin–New York, 1973).

Ecclesiastes, such as *miqreh*, 'fate of death' and *ḥeleq*, 'allotted portion' remind us of the Greek *moira* and *tyche*. A further Grecism has been found in the frequent phrase 'under the sun'. The characteristic concept of *hebhel*, 'nothingness', according to some, had a Greek equivalent in *typhos*. *'āsāh ṭôbh* corresponds to *eu prattein* or *eu dran*, and for *ṭôbh 'asher yapheh* there was the well-known *kalos kågathos* or *to kalon philon*.[1] Further, the stress on time as a concept of destiny has Greek parallels. In addition to this we have the impersonal concept of God, a reserve towards the cult and prayer, the complete absence of Jewish history and the law tradition, and above all the almost fatalistic concept that man's fate is determined and all that remains for him, as long as he is granted it, is to enjoy his lot. The invitation to *carpe diem*, and also the concept that after death 'the breath of man goes upwards', have a mass of Greek parallels.[2] A comparison with the Greek gnomic tradition shows that Ecclesiastes must have been conversant with it – whether from oral or literary tradition must remain open. Probably both were available. For nearly every verse parallels can be cited from Greek poetry and popular philosophy.[3] But it must be emphasized that Ecclesiastes combined in a highly original and artistically accomplished way these new impulses, which came from outside, with the traditional Jewish and oriental Wisdom teaching, which he criticised. It is thought that his offensive work, which broke with the old schema of a just, divine effected act-and-consequence system, and which must have aroused doubts concerning God's justice and goodness, was later edited and neutralised by a different hand.[4]

Another Wisdom teacher is Ben Sira, who lived a generation or two later than Ecclesiastes whose work he knew and used. In contrast to him he does not hide himself behind a puzzling pseudonym, but is the first author in Hebrew literature to give his name. This again is a sign of a new age.[5] The author consciously depicts himself as a 'sage' and 'scribe', who invites the young to his 'house of instruction' and consciously stands within the salvation-history tradition of Israel. Perhaps he was one of the Temple scribes who are mentioned in the edict of Antiochus III. Occasionally he makes a prophetic claim, and includes in his work as a scribe the interpretation of the prophetic books.[6] Still more central for him is the Torah, which God gave to Moses on Sinai and which he boldly identifies with that pre-existent

[1] Braun, *Kohelet*, pp. 44ff. [2] Hengel, *Hellenismus*, pp. 226ff = ET 1, pp. 123ff.

[3] See the survey in Braun, *Kohelet*, pp. 146ff, 158ff.

[4] K. Galling, *Prediger Salomo*, HAT 1, 18, 2nd edn. (Tübingen, 1969).

[5] Sir. 50:27, see Hengel, *Hellenismus*, p. 145 = ET 1, p. 79.

[6] Sir. 24:32f; 33:16–18; 38:34 to 39:8. Hengel, *Hellenismus*, pp. 246ff = ET 1, pp. 134f.

Wisdom which God has poured out on all his creation. This primeval and universal Wisdom had, at God's command, found itself a home on Mount Zion in Jerusalem. This mediatorial figure, which in its universality can be compared with the Platonic 'world-soul' or the Stoic 'logos', is here exclusively connected with Israel, God's chosen people, and with his sanctuary. In the hymn to Wisdom of chapter 24, which is the central point of his work, he has followed Prov. 8:22ff in taking over aretalogical forms, which are known to us from the Egyptian Isis aretalogies and which had perhaps been used in Palestine in honour of the Phoenician and Canaanite Astarte.[1] A marked characteristic, which fundamentally distinguishes him from Ecclesiastes, appears here. But he uses new Hellenistic forms and content in no lesser degree than does Ecclesiastes, though not to criticize the accepted religious tradition of Israel, but in order to defend it in the contemporary intellectual struggle. Therefore he inveighs against the transgressors and apostates, that is, the Hellenists of the Jewish upper classes, who wish to forsake the Law,[2] and against those who deny the freedom of the will and who blame God himself for their own failure, and above all against those who call in question the just recompense of God. With Stoic arguments he defends the purposefulness of the world, the righteousness and providence of God, that is, he seeks to outline a sort of 'popular philosophical' theodicy. The evil in the world is there for the just punishment of sinners, as was also stressed by Chrysippus.[3] He can describe God's relation to the world in almost pantheistic terms: 'and the sum of our words is: He is the all'.[4] On the one hand he takes up motifs from the social preaching of the prophets and protests against the exploitation of the poor by the rich landlords,[5] but, on the other, he is able to value wealth, is acquainted with Greek table manners, defends consulting physicians and extols the standing and political importance of the wise man, who travels abroad on errands to foreign countries.[6] Like Ecclesiastes, he knows Greek gnomic writing;[7] yet he does not glorify the wisdom and the heroes of

[1] 1:1–20; 24:1–34; cf. Hengel, *Hellenismus*, pp. 284ff = ET 1, pp. 158ff; J. Marböck, *Weisheit im Wandel*, BBB, 37 (Bonn, 1971).

[2] Sir. 41:8f.; 10:6–25; 16:4; Hengel, *Hellenismus*, pp. 270ff = ET 1, pp. 150ff.

[3] Sir. 39:24–34; Hengel, *Hellenismus*, pp. 256ff = ET 1, pp. 141ff; cf. Marböck, *Weisheit*, pp. 134ff; R. Pautrel, 'Ben Sira et le stoïcisme', *RSR*, 51 (1963), 535–49.

[4] Sir. 43:27. Cf. Marböck, *Weisheit*, p. 150 n. 13; p. 170 n. 46.

[5] Sir. 34:20–2; 13:2–5; 4:1ff, 8ff; 21:5; Hengel, *Hellenismus*, pp. 249ff = ET 1, pp. 136f; Tcherikover, *Civilization*, pp. 144ff.

[6] Sir. 10:27; 13:24; 25:3, etc; 31:12ff; 32:3ff; 34:9ff:38:1, 12 (but cf. the slightly earlier 2 Chron. 16:12); see Marböck, *Weisheit*, pp. 160ff.

[7] A wealth of parallels appear in T. Middendorp, *Die Stellung Jesu ben Siras zwischen Judentum und Hellenismus* (Leiden, 1973), pp. 7–34.

foreign people, but only the Torah and the great holy men of salvation-history from Adam and Enoch to his own contemporaries like the High Priest Simon the Just,[1] whose sons he warns against dissension.[2] The Hellenistic reform was already casting its shadows when he finished his work around 180 B.C.E. His eschatological prayer, with its petition for deliverance from the yoke of the heathen, shows clearly that he was very critical of Seleucid foreign rule. With the caution of the sage, he is able to conceal his criticism; the prayer also is built on an almost philosophically universal concept of God. It begins with the petition: 'Have mercy upon us, O Lord, God of all' and closes with 'and all who are on the earth will know that thou art the Lord, the God of the ages'.[3] The much debated question whether ben Sira was anti-Hellenist or pro-Hellenist is based on a false antithesis.[4] It must be evaluated against the complex historical situation in Judea in pre-Maccabean times. Moreover, a distinction must be made between a Hellenizing form and a basically anti-foreign attitude. He was religiously conservative, faithful to the Torah, a Jewish *sōphēr* who was nationalistic in outlook, but who, more than he himself was aware, was shaped by the spirit of his time, i.e. by Hellenistic ideas. Nevertheless, there can be no doubt that he was opposed to the Hellenistic reformers in the city, and that, if he lived through the events after 175 B.C.E., he certainly did not stand on the side of Jason, Menelaus, Alcimus or the Tobiads, but on the side of the Maccabees. He shows that spirit which we find again among the Sadducees, who were conservative, nationalist-thinking Jews and who bitterly opposed the Romans and resisted Herod's seizure of power.

Finally, we should consider the opposition movement of the Hasidim,[5] who shortly before or at the beginning of the Hellenistic reform formed themselves into an organization. Even, or rather, particularly in them, who stood in specially sharp opposition to the spirit of Hellenization, the influence of the new era is evident. This is true of the loose organizational form of their religious association,

[1] Sir. 44:1 to 50:24; T. Maertens, *L'Eloge des Pères, Ecclésiastique,* XLIV–L (Bruges, 1956); E. Bickerman, 'La chaîne de la tradition pharisienne', *RB,* 59 (1952), 44ff, Hengel, *Hellenismus*, pp. 248f = Et 1, pp. 135f.

[2] Sir. 50:23f (Hebrew text).

[3] Sir. 36:1–17, see above, p. 78.

[4] Middendorp, *Stellung* has recently tried to portray Ben Sira as an avowed 'Hellenist'. But even he has to concede that Ben Sira stood on the side of the High Priest Simon and opposed the Tobiads (pp. 167ff). Marböck, *Weisheit*, pp. 168ff is more cautious in his judgement.

[5] 1 Macc. 2:42; 7:13 and 2 Macc. 14:6. Cf. Hengel, *Hellenismus*, pp. 319ff = ET 1, pp. 175ff; Schürer *et al., History,* 1, p. 159.

which was later taken up again in the *yaḥad* (= *koinon*) of the Qumran Essenes and by the *ḥᵃbûrôt* of the Pharisees.[1] It appears also in many of their religious views which are mainly recorded in the apocalyptic writings which come from their circles. It would, therefore, be wrong to place the Hasidim, influenced as they were by apocalyptic, in conscious opposition to Jewish Wisdom or the Temple cult.[2] In reality the division amongst the people runs right through the priesthood and the Levites as well as through the class of scribes. A new phenomenon in the apocalyptic of the Hasidim was that it advanced the claim to special revelations of divine wisdom. The concept of 'secret' attained a central theological significance there.[3] Side by side with the Wisdom mediated through tradition, there went a 'higher wisdom', which was received through a *revelatio specialis*, through visions and dreams, through journeys to heaven and to hell, through angelic appearances and inspiration. The revelatory forms are the same as those in the Hellenistic world around, and men spoke to some extent the same 'religious *koine*'.[4] Jewish apocalyptic, which quickly spread through the Diaspora in the form of Sibylline Oracles, had its golden age from the second century B.C.E. on, and this runs parallel to the renewal of revelatory religion in the Hellenistic world, which began there somewhat later and only reached its climax in the time of the Empire from the second century C.E. on. A further important point was the development of an individual hope which transcended death, along with the concept of the judgement of the dead. In Palestine this expectation took the typically Jewish form of bodily resurrection from death. But at the same time, certainly under Greek influence, there developed alongside it the concept of the immortality of the soul, which was especially influential in the Diaspora. Both views could vary considerably, and could even be combined. The development of a hope beyond death is closely connected with the question of theodicy, which arose particularly as a consequence of persecutions. In Greece the

[1] Hengel, *Hellenismus*, pp. 447ff = ET 1, pp. 244ff; W. Tyloch, 'Les Thiases et la Communauté de Qumran', *Fourth World Congress of Jewish Studies. Papers*, 1 (Jerusalem, 1967), pp. 225–8.

[2] So, rather too one-sidedly, in the otherwise excellent book by O. Plöger, *Theokratie und Eschatologie*, WMANT 2 (Neukirchen Vluyn, 1956); ET *Theocracy and Eschatology* (Oxford, 1968). This is shown already by the significance of the Temple in the book of Daniel.

[3] So especially the Persian loan-word *raz* in Dan. 2:18f, 27–30, 47 and the Qumran writings and 1 Enoch 16:3; 38:3; 103:2; 104:12. Cf. Hengel, *Hellenismus*, p. 370 = ET 1, p. 202.

[4] Hengel, *Hellenismus*, pp. 381–94 = ET 1, pp. 210–18.

hope of immortality, the expectation of judgement after death and the concept of places where reward and punishment were meted out to the dead, were very much older. Influences from this direction on early Jewish apocalyptic are, therefore, not ruled out. This is especially true of the concept of astral immortality, and a future hope for wise teachers, such as is found at the end of the book of Daniel.[1]

Finally, mention must be made of the concept of the unity of world history, which is connected with the idea of a world empire, and which developed in the clash with the Hellenistic kingdoms. The imminent rule of God will soon bring an end to the overwhelming hubris of the world empire. The picture of four metals in descending order as symbols of world empires in the dream of Nebuchadrezzar is reminiscent of Hesiod's eras of four metals, which had a formative influence on the concept of history.[2] On the other hand, Jewish and Iranian apocalyptic has also influenced classical poetry. The clearest example of this is the fourth *Eclogue* of Virgil.[3]

The adoption of Hellenistic civilization, its language, literature and thought, by Judaism, as well as its opposition to it, is thus extremely rich in tensions and complex. The form it took in the Palestinian homeland was only partly different from that in the Diaspora; it spread through almost every class and group of the people and was concerned with political and economic spheres as well as with intellectual and religious. Individual classes and groups also reacted in different ways. The aristocracy proved to be the most open to this new way of life and education; but they were also most threatened by assimilation. But the wise man of the opposition, the Hasidean apocalyptist and the Hellenistic Jewish apologist, who wished to preserve undiluted their inheritance from their fathers, were in the political and intellectual battle not uninfluenced by the thought of the new era. Just by adopting and intensively reworking foreign ideas, ancient Judaism won the inner pull to withstand the strength of a seductive foreign culture, to preserve in a new language and in conjunction with new forms of thought and expression the religious heritage entrusted to them, and to

1 Dan. 12:2f; 1 Enoch 104:2; cf. T. F. Glasson, *Greek Influence on Jewish Eschatology* (London, 1961); Hengel, *Hellenismus*, pp. 357–69 = ET 1, pp. 196–202; G. W. E. Nickelsburg, *Resurrection, Immortality and Eternal Life in Intertestamental Judaism*, HTS 26 (Cambridge, Mass. 1972).

2 Hengel, *Hellenismus*, pp. 332ff = ET 1, pp. 182ff; Bodo Gatz, *Weltzeitalter, goldene Zeit und sinnverwandte Vorstellungen*, Spudasmata 16 (Hildesheim, 1967).

3 H.C. Gotoff, 'On the Eclogue of Virgil', *Philologus*, 111 (1967), 66–79; Gatz, *Weltzeitalter*, pp. 87ff.

remain true to their divine mission in history. Taken as a whole, the Judaism of the Hellenistic and Roman period, in the homeland as in the Diaspora, can be called Hellenistic Judaism.

(Editor's note: this chapter has also been published in an expanded form as M. Hengel, *Juden, Griechen und Barbaren*, SBS 76 (Stuttgart, 1976), ET *Jews, Greeks and Barbarians* (London, 1980), chs. 6–12.)

CHAPTER 6

THE MEN OF THE GREAT SYNAGOGUE (*circa* 400–170 B.C.E.)

The purpose of this chapter is to demonstrate the high probability of the following propositions:[1]

(1) That the Men of the Great Synagogue (Hebrew, *'anše keneset ha-gedolah*) constituted a tribunal, which was the supreme judicial authority of the Pharisees in its time.

(2) That the members of this tribunal and their followers considered it the body to which Deuteronomy 17:8ff referred in its command that a local judge or other authority in doubt as to the interpretation or application of the law should resort for guidance.

(3) That this tribunal was called into being by Ezra and Nehemiah, in an effort to offset the authority of the court consisting of the Temple priests and the lay aristocracy, which gave Nehemiah so much trouble.

(4) That the Great Synagogue claimed that its traditions derived from the prophets, and through them for Moses, having been revealed to him on Mount Sinai.

(5) That another theory regarding the Great Synagogue ultimately developed, denying that it alone possessed such traditions, but ascribing to it supreme judicial authority, as the legitimate heir to the pre-exilic tribunal of Jerusalem, established by the kings of the Davidic dynasty.

(6) That the rabbinic tradition, ascribing to this body the authority of Mishnah *Sanhedrin* 10.1, and the formulation of the central prayer of the Synagogue, as well as the most important home prayer, namely the Grace after the Meal, is authentic.

According to the prevailing rabbinic view, based on Mishnah *Aboth* 1.1, the Men of the Great Synagogue flourished between the time of the prophets and that of Simeon the Just, the high priest, who was a contemporary of Antiochus III of Syria.[2] They were the inter-

[1] The reader of this and the following chapters will, of course, observe that the writer's approach and conclusions are at variance with those of many distinguished scholars, for whom he has high regard and affection. They include, among others, such eminent figures as Professors Elias Bickerman, Sidney B. Hoenig, Jacob Neusner (whose own chapters dealing with related subjects appear in another volume), Morton Smith, and the late Solomon Zeitlin. The reader is, the editors believe, entitled to have before him varying opinions on these controversial subjects.

[2] See conclusive discussion of the date of Simeon the Just by George F. Moore, in *Jewish Studies in Memory of Israel Abrahams* (New York, 1927), pp. 348ff.

mediaries through whom the prophetic interpretation of the Mosaic Law, given to Moses by the Deity on Mount Sinai, reached the earliest identified Pharisaic teachers, Jose b. Joezer of Zeredah and Jose b. Johanan of Jerusalem. Simeon the Righteous himself is described as 'one of the last of the Men of the Great Synagogue' (but not necessarily the very last).

Outside the rabbinic tradition, the Great Synagogue is mentioned only once, in 1 Macc. 14:28, where we are told that 'a great synagogue[1] of priests, and people and princes of the nation, and the elders of the country,' formally ousted the Zadokide priests, who had presided over the Temple for seven centuries, ever since the time of King Solomon,[2] and replaced them with the Hasmoneans.

Great confusion has arisen about the nature and even the existence of the Great Synagogue, primarily because the Hebrew word *k^eneset* (Aramaic: *k^eništa*; Greek: *synagōgē*) generally signifies a congregation, an assembly of people to pray. It is difficult to understand how a congregation, even if called 'great', could serve as conduit of the teachings of the prophets to the heads of the Pharisaic schools; and it is even more difficult to understand how such a 'great synagogue' could legitimize the replacement of the ancient dynasty of Zadok, which had presided over the Temple for seven centuries, with the Hasmoneans, no matter what their merits might be.

But *k^eneset*, like its Aramaic equivalent, also signified 'tribunal'.[3] Thus the Hebrew phrase *anše k^eneset*, like its Aramaic equivalent, also signified 'tribunal'.[4] Thus the Hebrew phrase *anše k^eneset ha-g^edolah* is

[1] That the word *synagōgē* in this passage does not mean simply congregation or assembly, but a recognized tribunal, seems to have been recognized by I. Loew, (*Gesammelte Schriften*, 1 (Szegedin, 1889–1900), pp. 415ff), who calles it a 'synod'. However, his identification of Simeon the Just with Simeon, the Hasmonean, is surely a fantasy. How could Simeon the Hasmonean have been one of the teachers of Antigonus, himself the teacher of Jose b. Joezer, who died a martyr in the year 160 before the Common Era? As noted, a revolutionary change in regard to the high priesthood could have been made only by a recognized, authoritative tribunal. Flourishing many centuries before Montesquieu, the ancient Pharisees did not, of course, recognize the division of governmental powers. The supreme tribunal was at once the supreme court and the legislature, as well as to some extent the executive branch of the government. Thus, Mishnah *Sanhedrin* chapter 1, outlining the authority of the supreme court includes in it various functions, some of which we should describe as judicial, others as legislative, and still others as executive.

[2] See 1 Kings 2:26; 4:2.

[3] See L. Finkelstein, *Ha-Perušim w^e-'anše k^eneset ha-gdolah* (New York, 1950), p. 52. Cf. Mishnah *Makkoth* 3.2, and other passages there noted.

[4] That this tribunal was a Pharisaic court seems evident from the fact that the Pharisees held that their traditions derived from it. See further, below pp. 247ff., for the evidence offered by the decisions ascribed to the Men of the Great Synagogue. That

not to be rendered 'Men of the Great Synagogue' but 'Men of the Great Tribunal'. Furthermore *g^edolah* in this phrase has the same significance as *gadol* in the expression *Bet Din ha-Gadol*, often used in the Talmud for the supreme court. The *'anše k^eneset ha-g^edolah* thus turn out to be the members of the Pharisaic[1] supreme court. They were the court of the city of Jerusalem; and according to the Pharisaic interpretation of Deut. 17:8ff, a local court in doubt regarding an issue of law had to resort to it for guidance. Anyone disobeying its decisions was subject to capital punishment (Deut. 17:12).

A tribunal clothed with such jurisdiction might well replace the ancient high-priestly dynasty (which had become largely Hellenized) with another which had won Judea's independence from the Syrians, and was in fact Pharisaic in its outlook on the Law.[1] Being the supreme court, located in Jerusalem, its members chosen for their piety and learning rather than for social status, its decisions were held to be based on firm traditions from the prophets, who had received their interpretations of the Law through a chain of tradition going back to Moses himself, and through him, to the Deity.

For the sake of clarity, let us hereafter, then, render the term *'anše k^eneset ha-g^edolah*, 'members of the Great Tribunal'.

That this tribunal actually existed seems to be proven beyond doubt by a casual remark of a contemporary, preserved in *Aboth de* R. *Nathan* I, chapter 40, page 65a. (The text of the passage has been corrupted in all the manuscripts and editions. However, because the corruptions

Pharisaism existed long before the Maccabean era is evident from a number of texts, preserved as authoritative in rabbinic literature. See my discussion in *Conservative Judaism*, 23 (1969), 25ff, and now reprinted in L. Finkelstein, *Pharisaism in the Making* (New York, 1972), pp. 175ff. Pharisees are not mentioned by that name in the books of the Maccabees although, as will be seen (below, p. 260), one of their factions was very active in the revolt. The books of the Maccabees described them as *ḥasidim*, and, apparently, that was the name applied to them (as to others) in the pre-Maccabean age. The word *Perushim* was originally perjorative, meaning 'separatists', and occurs in the Talmudic works mainly in quotations of their opponents. They, of course, did not regard themselves as 'separatists' or sectarians; but as bearers of the authentic Mosaic tradition. Ultimately, they came to use the epithet, giving it the meaning of 'separatist from idol-worship' or from 'levitical impurity'. Neither in *Bell.* II.166 (see also ibid, 119) nor in *Ant.* XVIII.12 does Josephus suggest that they came into being in Hasmonean times, as is now the prevalent view. He describes them, in both passages, as already existing by the time under discussion. It can be shown that originally the Pharisees pronounced the Tetragrammaton in their synagogue prayers and benedictions, a practice which ceased in the latter part of the fourth or the middle of the third century B.C.E. See *Conservative Judaism*, 23 (1969), 27ff, now reprinted in Finkelstein, *Pharisaism*, pp. 175ff.

[1] For the Pharisaism of the Hasmonean family, see below, p. 260.

differ from one another, the original reading may be reconstructed with virtual certainty.)[1] According to it,

[1] See the readings cited in L. Finkelstein, *Mabo le-masekhtot Aboth ve-Aboth de* R. *Nathan* (New York, 1950), p. 171. The reading of the first edition of *Ab. d'*R.*N.* is supported by MS. Jewish Theological Seminary of America, and the citation in *Maḥzor Vitry*. The editor's proof reads: 'Any assembly which is for the purpose of a commandment *etc.* [thus in the text, omitting the difficult phrase "will endure"]. An assembly which was for the sake of a commandment was the *k'neset* of the Men of the Great [*sic.* Through a scribal confusion, the words "the Men of the Great Synagogue" were written out of order, becoming "the *k'neset* of the Men of the Great", which makes no sense at all.] One not for the sake of a commandment was the *k'neset* of the Generation of Division.' (This is also approximately the reading of MS. Jewish Theological Seminary of America.) *Maḥzor Vitry* (ed. S. Hurwitz, Nuremberg, 1923), p. 527, quotes the passage as follows: 'An assembly for the sake of a commandment was the assembly of the Men of the Great *K'neset*; one not for the sake of Heaven was the one of the Men of the Generation of the Division.'

However, MS. Epstein, as cited by Solomon Schechter, *Ab. d'*R.*N.*, offers the following text for the passage: 'Any assembly which is for the sake of Heaven will survive, and one which is not for the sake of Heaven will not survive. What is [an example of] an assembly for the sake of Heaven? For example [*sic*!] the *k'neset* of Israel before Mt. Sinai. And one not for the sake of Heaven? For example, the assembly of the Generation of Division.' MS. Oxford omits the whole first section of the text, reading only: 'Any assembly which is [corrected by the scribe or someone else to read 'which is not'] for the sake of Heaven, for example [*sic*!] the Men of the Generation of the Division.' In *Sefer Musar*, by R. Joseph b. Judah (ed. Z'eb Bacher, Berlin, 1911), p. 167, the passage is cited as follows: 'Any assembly which is for the sake of Heaven will endure: but one which is not for the sake of Heaven will not endure. What is an assembly for the sake of Heaven? For example [*sic*!] the *k'neset* of Israel before Mt. Sinai. And what is one not for the sake of Heaven? For example, [*sic*!] the assembly of the Generation of Division.' R. Menaḥem Meiri in his commentary on Mishnah *Aboth* 4.11 (*Bet habbḥirah'al Maseket Aboth*, Jerusalem, 1964) quotes simply: 'any assembly which is for the sake of Heaven was the assembly of Israel before Mt. Sinai. One not for the sake of Heaven was the assembly of the Generation of the Division.'

It seems obvious that all transmitters and copyists sought in some way to escape the impossible assertion that the Great Tribunal would endure, that is, last forever. Some copyists, like the one who wrote the MS. on which the editor's proof was based, simply omitted the difficult words, by writing instead the symbol for 'etc.' The copyists of MS. Epstein and MS. Oxford avoided the difficulty of substituting 'the *k'neset* of Israel before Mt. Sinai' for the Great Tribunal. But the word used for the assembly before Mt. Sinai would not be *k'neset* but *kenesiyah*, the word actually used in the citation by R. Menaḥem Meiri. The use of the word *k'neset* in that context in MS. Epstein and in the citation in *Sefer Musar* shows that the original text read, as MS. Jewish Theological Seminary of America and editor's proof suggest, "*anše k'neset ha-gdolah*'. In Mishnah *Aboth,* 4.11, R. Johanan ha-Sandlar, a disciple of R. Akiba, quoted the passage, limiting himself however merely to the first half of the statement. He said: 'Any assembly for the sake of Heaven will survive; but one not for the sake of Heaven will not survive.' Throughout this chapter and the next, I have followed the excellent translation of *Ab. d'*R.*N.* 1, by Professor Judah I.

An assembly (*kenesiyah*) for the sake of the Deity will endure; but one not for the sake of the Deity will not endure. What is [an example of] an assembly for the sake of the Deity? The assembly of the members of the Great Tribunal. And what is [an example of] an assembly not for the sake of the Deity? That is the assembly of the Generation of Division [that is, of the Tower of Babel].

(The author distinguishes carefully *kenesiyah*, meaning 'assembly', from *k^eneset*, which means 'tribunal'.)

Clearly, only a contemporary of the Great Tribunal could have suggested that it would 'endure', meaning, doubtless, endure forever. When his prediction turned out to be erroneous, the text was altered by transmitters and copyists, and has come down to us only in corrupted forms.

The remark in *Ab. d'R.N.* 1, however, needs further explanation. Why did the author feel called upon to assert that the Great Tribunal would endure? In what peril did it stand? And why did he contrast it, of all things, with the Generation of the Division, which was an *ad hoc* gathering of an entirely different type?

The durability of the Great Tribunal of the Pharisees had to be affirmed because of the opposition to it by the *Gerousia*, the leaders of the land, the high priests and their families, as well as their allies, the leaders of the lay clans – all constituting the aristocracy of the commonwealth. In contrast to these powerful men, the members of the Great Tribunal were socially obscure scholars, who earned their living by trade or as labourers. They had made a virtue of their anonymity, seeking neither recognition nor fame for themselves as individuals.[1]

In contrast to them were the Men of the Generation of the Division, who tried to build the tower of Babel, so as to 'get themselves a name' (Gen. 11:4). The author of the passage in *Ab. d'R.N.* was suggesting that a group of people who sought fame for themselves as individuals could not endure. Only a group for which personal anonymity, symbolic of personal selflessness, was a principle, would endure.

As observed, the general view of the Talmudic sages was that incorporated in Mishnah *Aboth* 1.1, and parallel passages, according to which the traditions of the Men of the Great Tribunal were authoritative because they were disciples of the prophets. According to the

Goldin, *The Fathers According to Rabbi Nathan* (New Haven, 1955); and I have benefited greatly, as the reader will see, from his learned notes. There is also a very good translation of *Ab. d'R.N.* II by Father Anthony J. Saldarini, S. J. (*The Fathers according to Rabbi Nathan, Abot de Rabbi Nathan, version B*, Leidein, 1975), which came into my hands too late for use in this work.

1 See discussion of the doctrine of anonymity among the men of the Great Tribunal in Finkelstein, *Ha-Perushim*, pp. 63ff; *Conservative Judaism*, 12 (1958), 1f; *Pharisaism*, pp. 187ff.

quotation of Mishnah *Aboth* in *Ab. d'R.N.*, they were, more specifically, disciples of the post-exilic prophets, Haggai, Zechariah and Malachi.

But, according to a dissenting opinion, the authority of the Great Tribunal derived from the fact that it was the successor to the royal tribunal of the Davidic dynasty. A passage, incorporating this notion, occurs in *Ab. d'R.N.* 1, chapter 1, page 1b. The passage contains a comment on the first part of the maxim of the Great Tribunal as recorded in Mishnah *Aboth* 1.2, 'Be gentle (*matun*) in argument (*din*)'.[1] *Ab. d'R.N.* 1 (chapter 1, page 1b) contains two interpretations of this passage. According to one, the word *matun* in the maxim means 'gentle'; and the word *din* means 'argument'. The passage in *Ab. d'R.N.* 1 reads: 'This teaches that one should be gentle in argument, for one who is gentle in argument is calm in argument.' That comment is followed by another, according to which, *matum* means 'slow', and *din* means 'judgement'. The comment therefore says: 'This teaches that one should take one's time in judgement; for one who takes one's time in judgement is calm in judgement. For thus we find that the Men of the Great Tribunal [took their time in judgement and] were deliberate in

[1] The word *matun* often has the meaning 'gentle' as in *Tosefta Shabbath* 7(8).24,25, ed. Lieberman, p. 29. According to this interpretation, the word *matun* is contrasted with proclivity to anger (*Ab. d'R.N.* 1, ch. 1, p. 2a). The word *din* in the maxim, accordingly, means 'argument' as in Mishnah *Pesaḥim* 6.2, and very frequently throughout Rabbinic literature. The original maxim was addressed to new members of the Tribunal, and to its immediate disciples.

The reading of *Ab. d'R.N.* 1 given here is reconstructed on the basis of the various texts of the book, all of which are corrupt (as often happens in that book); but which supplement one another. According to the witnesses of the 'Italo-French' family (see Finkelstein, *Mabo*, p. 126), the text reads: 'Be gentle in argument, this teaches that one should be gentle in argument; for one who is gentle in argument is calm in argument; for thus we find that the Men of the Great Tribunal were calm in argument, as it is said, "These also are proverbs of Solomon which the men of Hezekiah...copied out (Prov. 25:1)"'.

The witnesses belonging to the 'Spanish' family (Finkelstein, *Mabo*, p. 126) read 'Be *metunim* in judgement (*din*). This teaches that one should take one's time in judgement, for one who takes one's time in judgement is calm in judgement, as it is said, "These also are proverbs of Solomon which the men of Hezekiah...copied out" (Prov. 25:1). It was not that they copied out, but that they took their time'. (The root *'tq*, normally rendered 'copied out', is interpreted by these commentators to mean 'delayed'.)

According to this reading, the citation from Proverbs seems irrelevant; for the question arises, why the word for 'copied out' had the rare meaning 'took their time'? However, once one recognizes that each group of witnesses has suffered from an omission by *homoioteleuton*, the difficulty disappears. It seems clear that the original text of *Ab. d'R.N.* 1 included both variants, as shown in the reconstruction here given.

judgement, as it is said, "And these also are proverbs of Solomon which the Men of Hezekiah copied out" (Prov. 25:1). It is not that they copied out, but that they took their time.' (The words in brackets probably have to be added, although omitted in all texts.)

The author of the second comment obviously identified the 'men of Hezekiah' with the Great Synagogue of later times. According to his interpretation, the men of Hezekiah did not canonize the book of Proverbs, but postponed any decision about it. The decision to canonize it was taken only by their successors in the second commonwealth, centuries later.

It is easily demonstrable[1] that the first part of *Ab. d'R.N.* was composed by the Shammaitic school of the Pharisees, and their predecessors, consisting mainly of priests. These priests were provincials, who sought (for reasons which will presently become apparent) to convert their followers to Pharisaism. But they did not consider themselves bound by all the traditions of the Great Tribunal, most of which were congenial to Jerusalem's market-place, rather than to life in the provinces of Judea.

By adopting the view that the authority of the Great Pharisaic Tribunal derived from its status as the successor to that of the Davidic dynasty, the Pharisaic priests could recognize this tribunal as the supreme court of the land in regard to issues for which no precedent existed; and at the same time reject its claim as interpreter of the whole Pentateuchal Law, in matters concerning which they preserved local or family customs.

Thus, the priestly authorities to whom we owe most of the first part of *Ab. d'R.N.* in its present form, commenting on Mishnah *Aboth* (in an early version) did not consider gentleness in argument a virtue. On the contrary, it seemed to them a vice, indicating lack of conviction. However, they regarded deliberateness in judgement by a court important. Had the court of Hezekiah's time been hasty, it might have rejected the book of Proverbs as uncanonical. Mature reflection, over the centuries, showed that it was a sacred text. Hence their interpretation of the maxim of the Men of the Great Tribunal, as urging not gentleness in argument, but deliberateness in judgement.

Significantly, the authors of this comment in *Ab. d'R.N.* do not mention the books of Ecclesiastes and the Song of Songs. Perhaps, then, these books had not yet been composed in their time. Abba Saul (either the first one who flourished in the last generation of the Second Temple, or his namesake, the disciple of R. Akiba), discussed all three

[1] See Finkelstein, *Mabo*, pp. 51ff.

works; and concluded that the Men of the Great Tribunal had *interpreted* them, and thus made them appropriate for admission to the Canon.[1]

The explanation of the authority of the Tribunal as successor to the pre-exilic royal court seems to underlie also the record in 2 Chron. 19:5ff, which apparently sought to effect a compromise between the claim of the Pharisaic Great Tribunal to be the authorized interpreter of the Mosaic Law, and that of the priestly authorities in the Temple, who believed that the interpretation of the Law was their prerogative. In that passage, the Chronicler describes a judicial reform instituted by King Jehoshaphat. We are told that King Jehoshaphat appointed judges in all the cities of Judah, and he also appointed judges in Jerusalem, who included Levites, priests, and the heads of families in Israel. This court sat not in the Temple but in the city of Jerusalem.[2] Paraphrasing Deut. 17:8ff, the Chronicler tells how King Jehoshaphat gave his tribunal authority over 'any controversy [which] shall come to you from your brethren that dwell in the cities, between blood and blood, *between law and commandment, statutes and ordinances*, ye shall warn them that they may not be guilty toward the Lord' (2 Chron. 19:10). This plenary authority over all Jewish law is in sharp contrast with that described in the corresponding verse in Deuteronomy, which speaks only of cases 'between blood and blood, between judgement and judgement, between blow and blow', apparently confining the authority of the supreme tribunal to issues of civil and criminal law.[3]

According to the Chronicler, when headed by the lay leader for the house of Judah, the court had jurisdiction over all the king's matters, presumably problems of civil and criminal law. But when headed by the high priest, it had jurisdiction over 'all matters of the Lord', that is to say, all issues of ritual and religious law.

It is difficult to see what the purpose of the Chronicler's report could be, unless it was intended as a solution to the conflicting claims of the aristocratic tribunal of the Temple and the Pharisaic Great Tribunal of Jerusalem. The Chronicler, like the authors of the passage cited from *Ab. d'R.N.*, apparently held that the Pharisaic Great Tribunal was the legitimate successor of the royal tribunal of the first commonwealth.

[1] Abba Saul, also, held that the Men of the Great Tribunal of the Pharisees derived their legitimacy from the fact that they were successors of the pre-exilic royal tribunal of Jerusalem (see *Ab. d'R.N.* 1, 1, 1b).

[2] See 2 Chron. 19:8. According to the Masoretic text, the passage should be rendered 'and they returned to Jerusalem'. However, almost all modern commentators, changing slightly the punctuation of the verb, render it, 'And they *dwelt* in Jerusalem.'

[3] See discussion of the *baraita* interpreting this verse in L. Finkelstein, 'Baraita dᵉbet din šel liškat ha-gazit', *HUCA*, 32 (1961), Hebrew section, pp. 1ff.

According to him, this tribunal was created by King Jehoshaphat, in fulfilment of the command of Deut. 17:8ff. The Chronicler agreed with the Pharisaic claim that the central tribunal, to which all other courts had to turn when in doubt regarding the Law, was not the Temple court, but included erudite laymen, Levites and others, who resided in Jerusalem. But he suggested that this tribunal could render authoritative decisions in ritual matters only when the high priest presided over it.

The difference between the two conceptions of the authority of the Great Pharisaic Tribunal was fundamental. Both according to Deut. 17:8ff and the Chronicler, the central tribunal had authority to render decisions only when a local court, in doubt about the Law, turned to it. When local teachers or judges had local traditions, the central tribunal could not interfere.

But if the Great Tribunal of the Pharisees did, in fact, receive the interpretation of Mosaic Law held by the prophets, and going back to Moses himself, obviously its views were binding in every area of Jewish law. Local custom, in conflict with its traditions, would have to yield to it. How this difference of emphasis between the conception of the Great Tribunal affected the flow of events in later generations will presently become clear.

As A. Tcherikover has shown,[1] The body of lay leaders, closely allied with the high-priestly families, with whom Nehemiah so often had to quarrel (see Neh. 5:7, 13:11, and compare 7:5) was that which developed into the *gerousia* of Hellenistic times. (This court is often cited in rabbinic works as that of the 'Ancient Elders'.) Apparently in Nehemiah's times, as later, the heads of the priestly and lay clans constituted a tribunal, associated with the Temple, which rendered decisions regarding the Law. It was the tribunal which permitted the enslavement of children for unpaid debts of their parents (Neh. 5:7); authorized Tobiah the Ammonite to have an office in the Temple, using for that purpose the chamber previously set aside to store the tithes, heave-offerings, and Temple meal offerings (Neh. 13:11); permitted Tyrian peddlars to bring their wares to the gates of Jerusalem on the Sabbath for sale; and allowed even Judahites to sell their wine, grapes and figs on that day (Neh 13:15ff).

Probably it was to offset the power and authority of this group that Ezra and Nehemiah created the Great Tribunal, the genesis of which is described in Nehemiah chapters 9 and 10. Significantly, the document drawn up by this group includes several provisions, clearly designed to

[1] A. Tcherikover, 'Ha'im hayᵉta Yᵉrušalayim "polis" yᵉvanit biyme hapᵉrokuratorim', in *Eretz Israel*, 1 (Jerusalem, 1950–1), p. 99.

negate decisions of the council of the nobles, to whose actions Nehemiah took exception. Thus the new tribunal pledged its followers not to purchase goods from pagans on the Sabbath (Neh. 10:31), although the aristocratic council had permitted the practice (Neh. 13:15). It forbade intermarriage with pagans (Neh. 10:30), although the aristocratic council seems to have found no fault with such actions (Neh. 6:18).

It is particularly illuminating that some of the provisions of the document negate decisions not recorded in the name of the contemporary opponents of its authors, but in the name of priestly authorities of a later date. Doubtless these later priests had inherited their views from the early council of elders at the time of Nehemiah, and had not changed their practices, despite the provisions of the great document. Thus, the document pledged every follower of the Tribunal to give a third of a shekel each year for the maintenance of the public sacrifice (Neh. 10:32). That meant that all had an equal share in the public sacrifices. This view was apparently opposed in Nehemiah's time, as it was in a later age, by some aristocratic priests, who held that individuals who wished to do so might provide the cost of the public sacrifice. The subject became one of intense controversy between the Pharisees and Sadducees. The day when the Pharisees finally imposed their will on the Temple authorities in this regard, was declared a half-holiday.[1]

The document further required the tithe of all produce to be given to the Levites, who in turn would give a tithe of their tithe to the priests (Neh. 10:38). This provision, too, was rejected by the priests, who claimed that the whole tithe belonged to them. The issue was still a matter of controversy in the time of R. Akiba,[2] more than half a millennium after the promulgation of the document of Nehemiah chapter 10!

The document in Nehemiah chapter 10, incorporating the decisions of the council which Ezra and Nehemiah created, thus turns out to have been formulated in opposition to the priestly authorities. This conclusion confirms the tradition, according to which the framers of this document were the Men of the Great Tribunal, that is, early Pharisees, opponents of the contemporary priestly and aristocratic tribunal.

The Pharisaic interpretation of the Law rested on the exegesis of Deut. 17:8ff. The early Pharisees held that the 'place', mentioned in that

[1] See *Megillat Ta'anit*, ed. H. Lichtenstein, in *HUCA*, 8–9 (1931–32), 318, 323.

[2] *b. Yebamoth*, 86a.

verse, was the city of Jerusalem; hence its tribunal was the final authority to settle all disputes. But the Temple authorities, and their associates, the chiefs of the clans who were allied with them, held that 'the place' was the Temple. Since the tribunal consisting of the aristocratic priests and laymen, sat in the Temple courts, it, and not the Pharisaic tribunal of Jerusalem, had jurisdiction to decide cases concerning which the local courts were in doubt.

The issue involved more than the question of the jurisdiction of the tribunals. According to Deut. 16:7ff, the paschal lamb could be eaten only within 'the place' chosen. According to Deut. 14:23, the same rule applied to the second tithe. Long after the Great Tribunal had ceased to function, the Temple priests still insisted that both had to be consumed within the Temple courts.[1] Their opponents denied this, and held that

[1] The question of where the paschal lamb had to be eaten underlies a number of controversies between R. Eliezer the Shammaite, representing the priestly view in his day, and his colleagues, especially R. Joshua the Hillelite, representing the anti-priestly view of their day. Thus, Mishnah *Pesaḥim* 9.4 asserts that 'If the Paschal lamb was sacrificed when the majority of the community was impure [through contact with a corpse, and therefore permitted to offer it despite their impurity], even if other defiled persons, such as those suffering "from a flow", or women who had not been purified after childbirth, or women who were menstruating, ate its flesh [which was not permitted for them, for only defilement through contact with a corpse was set aside under the circumstances], they did not have to sacrifice a sin-offering for their transgression. R. Eliezer holds that they are also free from having to offer a sacrifice if they entered the Temple precincts.' See further *Tosefta Pesaḥim* 8.8, ed. Lieberman, p. 186. R. Eliezer's view is explicable only on the assumption that, according to him, the Paschal lamb had to be eaten in the Temple precincts. Therefore, the entrance of defiled persons into the Temple precincts, while unauthorized under the circumstances, did not subject them to the requirement of the sacrifice of a sin-offering. His colleagues, holding that the Paschal lamb could be eaten anywhere in Jerusalem, maintained that while the defiled persons were free from any penalty if they ate the meat of the Paschal lamb outside the Temple, they committed a serious transgression if they entered the Temple precincts. Therefore, they had to sacrifice a sin-offering for their guilt. Similarly, R. Eliezer held that Scripture, in freeing a person 'distant' from the place in which the Paschal lamb had to be sacrificed and eaten from any threat of punishment, referred to anyone outside the threshold of the Temple courts (Mishnah *Pesaḥim* 9.2), for the Paschal lamb had to be eaten within the Temple courts. R. Akiba held that such a person had to be outside the walls of Jerusalem. Significantly, the book of Jubilees (50:16) which reflects many priestly views, also held that the Paschal lamb had to be eaten within the Temple courts. Mishnah *Bikkurim* 2.2 provides that the slightest admixture of the First Fruits or the Second Tithe with other produce prevents the whole *from being eaten in Jerusalem*. The implication obviously is that the admixture had to be eaten in the Temple courts. (After the establishment of the Hasmonean state, and the vast increase of pilgrims, the ancient rule had to be relaxed even according to the priests, so that the second tithe was eaten throughout Jerusalem, according to all the authorities. Hence the difficulty commentators – ancient and modern – have found in their efforts to

both the Paschal lamb and the second tithe might be eaten anywhere in the city of Jerusalem. For, as far as they were concerned, 'the place' was the city of Jerusalem.

Other evidence of the conflict between the Temple tribunal and the Great Tribunal of the Pharisees will appear in the next chapter, in which further efforts to reach a compromise between the two institutions will be described.

Light is shed on the Pharisaic Tribunal by a study of Mishnah *Sanhedrin* 10:1, which Rab, the great Babylonian authority of the third century, ascribed to it.[1] As will be seen below, his ascription is confirmed by internal evidence of the text, which shows that in this instance, as in others,[2] Rab transmitted reliable traditions, which were perhaps commonplace in Palestine, but were unknown before his time in his native Babylonia, to which, in his maturity, he returned after a long absence in Palestine.

According to the passage of the Mishnah, 'all Israel have a share in the world to come.[3] But three kings and four commoners have no share in the world to come. The three kings are Jeroboam, Ahab, and Manasseh. The four commoners are Balaam, Doeg, Ahitophel and Gehazi'.

As the Talmud notes,[4] the inclusion of Balaam among those denied a portion in the future world implies the view that the pious Gentiles will share its bliss, a view cited in the name of R. Joshua, and apparently advocated by the Hillelites generally.

Clearly, the authors of this Mishnah also agreed with the views later held by the school of Hillel,[5] and more especially by R. Ishmael and

understand Mishnah *Bikkurim* 2.2. However, the passage clearly derives from pre-Maccabean or early Maccabean priestly sources. Thus understood, it represents no difficulty.)

The view that the second tithe had to be eaten in the Temple courts is also reflected in the book of Jubilees (32:10).

1 *b. Sanhedrin* 104b. See *Diqduqe Soferim*, ad loc., for the correct reading.

2 Cf. e.g. *b. Baba Bathra* 21a.

3 This passage is omitted from the text of the Mishnah following the Palestinian type. In Galilee it was apparently held that such a blanket assurance of immortality to all Israel was not desirable; for in this respect, as in others, the Galileans agreed with the Shammaites, that transgression had to be atoned for, and was punishable after death. See *Ab. d'R.N.* 1, 41, 67a.

4 *b. Sanh.* 105a.

5 *Ab. d'R.N.* 1, 41, 67a. According to that passage, the Hillelites held that the Middle Group, that is most of mankind, who are neither utterly wicked nor saintly, 'will not see Gehenna at all'. This view was reflected also in the assertion of R. Akiba that 'the world is judged with goodness *and not according to the majority of one's deeds*' (Mishnah *Aboth* 3.19). (In most editions the text has been corrupted to read 'And *everything* is according to the majority of one's deeds.' But the original text is preserved in some MSS.; see C. Taylor, *Sayings of the Jewish Fathers* (Cambridge, 1897) appendix, p. 152.)

his followers[1] that death atones for all transgressions; so that in general there is no punishment after death. Yet the seven people enumerated forfeited their share in the future life, although their transgressions seem to have been no worse than those of many others, like Cain, King Jehoiakim, and the kings of Israel in general. And since Balaam was not an Israelite, one may wonder at the omission from this list of Sennacherib, Nebuchadnezzar, Vespasian, and Titus, not to speak of Antiochus Epiphanes, and the Emperor Hadrian.

The trait common to the seven persons enumerated was that they not only committed serious transgressions, but led others into sin. This is explicitly stated in scripture of Jeroboam (1 Kings 14:16, 16:26; 2 Kings 17:21); Ahab (1 Kings 21:20), and Manasseh (2 Kings 21:9, 16). Balaam was blamed for the scheme of the Moabites to entrap the Israelites into sin at Baal Peor (Num. 31:16). Doeg was responsible for King Saul's order to destroy the priests of Nob (1 Sam. 22:9). Ahitophel was blamed for encouraging the rebellion of Absalom (compare 2 Sam. 15:31). Gehazi was blamed for profanation of the Name, and thus possibly leading Naaman into sin (2 Kings 5:21ff).

Evidently the authors of Mishnah *Sanhedrin* 10:1 held that while death atones for all transgressions one may personally commit, it does not atone for the sin of leading others, whether many or few, or even a single person, astray.[2] (The sin of 'profanation of the [Divine] Name'

See further discussion of the Hillelite norm against sacrificing a sin-offering which a person had set aside for that purpose before his death (*Sefer ha-Yobel l*'*Rabbi Ḥanok Albek*, Jerusalem, 1963, pp. 355ff). The Hillelites held that death having atoned for one's sin, atonement was no longer necessary, and therefore a sin-offering was no longer permitted. The Shammaites required the sacrifice to be offered.

[1] Cf. *Sifre* Numbers 112, p. 121, where according to R. Ishmael the passage in Num. 15:31 deals with the sin or idolatry. *Sifre* cites an anonymous view, according to which 'All those who die are forgiven for their transgression, through death', the standard Hillelite view. 'But', adds the anonymous authority, 'in this instance [it is not so, for Scripture says:] 'His iniquity shall be upon him (Num. 15:31);"' implying that even after death the iniquity remains with the spirit which must be punished. R. Ishmael takes issue with this anonymous authority. According to him, the passage means that the iniquity will be visited on the transgressor and not on his descendants.

[2] The severe attitude of the Sages toward one who caused others to transgress the law is reflected in other passages. So, for example, in *Seder 'Olam Rabbah* ch. 3 (ed. B. Ratner, Vilna, 1897, p. 9a; ed. A. Marx, Berlin, 1903, p. 9) it is asserted that the most sinful in Israel will be punished in the afterworld for twelve months, and thereafter be annihilated. 'But as for those who separate themselves from the community, like the sectarians, the Epicureans, the Boethusians, those who treat the festivals with contempt, those who deny the Resurrection, or say that the Torah is not revealed from Heaven, Gehenna will be sealed on them, and they will be subjected to torture for all eternities.' (See variant readings in the Marx edition; and the parallel passages noted by both editors.)

consists of acting in such a way as to lead others into transgression. Naaman had left Elisha with enormous respect for the prophet, and the Deity Whom he served, because Elisha had refused to accept any gifts from Naaman in return for curing him of leprosy. When Gahazi ran after Naaman, and asked for some gifts, he lessened Naaman's respect for the religion of Israel. Because profanation of the Name leads others into sin, it was held, apparently even by some Hillelites, to be beyond forgiveness even at the moment of death.)

The emphasis on the specific doctrine implied in the Mishnah and the remarkable omission from this list of Antiochus IV, suggest that the Mishnah was composed before his time, and was in fact directed at the Jewish Hellenists, whose sin consisted precisely in leading others into transgression. Moreover, the authors of the Mishnah took issue with 2 Chron. 33:12ff, according to which Manasseh repented his sin and was forgiven. Perhaps then, this Mishnah may rightly be held to have been composed at the same time as the final edition of the book of Chronicles or even earlier.

Internal evidence from Mishnah *Sanhedrin* 10.1 thus goes far to confirm the tradition of Rab, that it derived from the Men of the Great Tribunal, that is, the pre-Maccabean Pharisaic scholars.

Similarly, the persistent rabbinic tradition according to which the Men of the Great Tribunal formulated essential portions of the Jewish liturgy seems well founded. That they edited the original text of the Grace after Meals may be inferred from the fact that it is echoed in the book of Jubilees.[1] That they formulated the central prayer of the synagogue, the *'amidah*, in an early version, also seems highly probable.[2] One of the last paragraphs to be added to that prayer, if not the very last, was the petition for the frustration of the hopes of the *m^ešummadim*.[3] The word *m^ešummad*, which came to mean 'apostate',

[1] See *JQR*, N.S., 19 (1928–9), 219; citation from book of Jubilees 22:6–9.

[2] In *JQS* N.S., 16 (1925–26), pp. 1ff I followed the prevailing opinion that the *'amidah* was edited in the time of Rabban Gamaliel II. But on further consideration that view must be rejected. While Rabban Gamaliel II required every Jew to recite all eighteen benedictions (that is, paragraphs) of the daily *'amidah* on every weekday, his opponents, R. Joshua and R. Akiba also assumed the existence of an *'amidah*, consisting of eighteen benedictions. They disagreed with Rabban Gamaliel only in that R. Joshua held that one was permitted to recite a summary of the eighteen paragraphs; and R. Akiba held that one who knew the prayer by heart should say all eighteen, but others might recite only a summary (Mishnah *Berakoth* 4.3). Clearly, the existence of the weekday *'amidah* with its eighteen benedictions was presupposed by all three scholars. Apparently the text was not of recent origin in their time.

[3] According to *b. Berakoth* 28b–29a, Rabban Gamaliel II asked Samuel the Little to formulate a prayer against the *minim*. It is sometimes assumed that this prayer was the one for the frustration of the hope of the *m^ešummadim*. But this view must be rejected.

originally signified only Hellenist. Thus Alcimus, the high priest appointed by Antiochus IV in the effort to reach a compromise with the Hasmonean rebels, is described as a *m*e*šummad.*[1] The member of the priestly clan of Bilga, who insolently beat her shoe against the Temple altar, and on account of whose unspeakable behaviour the whole clan was penalized for many generations, is described as having become a *m*e*šummedet.*[2]

The Hellenists of those days were not idol-worshippers or necessarily transgressors of the Mosaic Law. The books of Maccabees, which denounce them vehemently, make no such accusation against them. The only specific charge made against them was that they underwent the difficult surgery necessary to conceal their circumcision, being ashamed to appear circumcised during their exercises in the gymnasium. Yet, it is not asserted that they failed to circumcise their children. Apparently, they considered concealment of the circumcision consistent with the letter of the Penteteuchal Law, if not with its spirit. It is highly significant in this regard that an animal slaughtered by a known Hellenist could be used for food, the assumption being that he had performed the ritual properly.[3]

What the pietists feared then was the *aspirations* of the Hellenists, that is the success of their efforts to extirpate not specific Jewish norms, but

The same record which reports that Samuel the Little, famous for his saintliness, was asked by Rabban Gamaliel to compose the prayer against the *minim*, also tells how Samuel the Little omitted it when he happened to lead the congregation in prayer somewhat later. Having done so, he looked about to see whether he was going to be asked to step aside and let someone else pray, in accordance with the rule that one omitting the prayer against *m*e*šummadim* must be removed from the pulpit, because he might either be a *m*e*šummad* or sympathize with them. But as no one said anything, he completed the prayer. (See *Yer. Berakoth* 5.3, 9c: *b. Ber.* 29a.) However, if the story meant that Samuel the Little omitted the benediction dealing with the *m*e*šummadim*, there certainly would have been an outcry from the congregation, for in that event his prayer would not have contained eighteen benedictions, as required by all scholars in his time. *Minim* in this passage must signify 'Christians' as it frequently does in Talmudic literature. Consequently, all texts of the Palestinian version of *'amidah* include a specific reference to *noṣrim* in this paragraph of the *'amidah*. The texts of the 'Babylonian' version include the word *minim*. The word was omitted, doubtless because of censorship in the printed text, and thus ceased to be said.

1 See *Midrash Tehillim* (ed. S. Buber, Vilna, 1891, repr. New York, 1947) 11.7, p. 52a.

2 *Tosefta Sukkah*, ed. Lieberman, p. 278.

3 *Tosefta Ḥullin* 1.1, E. Zuckermandel, p. 500. The *baraita* doubtless underlies the remark to the same effect quoted in the Babylonian academies, and which caused the scholars there much difficulty. It seemed to them impossible that the ritual slaughtering performed by a *m*e*šummad* should be considered satisfactory, for in Babylonia the word signified a person who had broken with Jewish law. The Talmud inevitably is forced to seek refuge in extremely difficult explanations (see *b. Ḥullin* 4b).

the general spirit of Jewish life. It was to these aspirations that the prayer addressed itself.

The Hellenists wanted to transform Jerusalem into a Greek *polis*, in which Greek fashions would prevail, including exercise in gymnasia, and a general adoption of Greek or Hellenistic manners, steps which the pietists feared would lead to the assimilation of the Jews and the disappearance of their faith.

The identification of the *mᵉšummadim* as Hellenists makes it virtually certain that the *ʿamidah* was edited in the years immediately preceding the Maccabean revolt. Surely this prayer was the work of a tribunal. That tribunal could not have been that of the Temple priests who were little concerned with the synagogue and its forms, and were probably under the control of the Hellenists when this prayer was added. Moreover, the official priesthood would hardly add to this prayer the petition it contains for the speedy overthrow of the Kingdom of Arrogance which could only refer to the Hellenistic monarchy.[1]

Thus it seems evident that the Men of the Great Tribunal constituted the supreme court of the Pharisees in pre-Maccabean times. The record according to which Simeon the Just was one of its last members seems justified. However, Mishnah *Aboth* 1.2 does not assert that he was its last surviving member. Perhaps then his disciple, Antigonus of Soko, was likewise one of its last members. And therefore, Jose b. Joezer of Seredah and Jose b. Johanan of Jerusalem, the heads of the Pharisaic schools in their time are described as having received the tradition 'from *them*',[2] that is, apparently, from both Simeon the Just and Antigonus of Soko; and perhaps from the Men of the Great Tribunal, as a whole.

Why this tribunal ceased to function as a unit, and thus virtually disappeared, must be considered in the next chapter.

1 The official priesthood was, after all, responsible to the government, and could hardly sponsor a denunciation of it, much less public petitions (for the *ʿamidah* in those days was recited *only* as a public prayer) for its downfall.

2 That seems to be the reading of all the texts of the Mishnah. I am indebted to Professor Elias Bickerman for drawing my attention to the importance and possible significance of this reading.

CHAPTER 7

PHARISAIC LEADERSHIP AFTER THE GREAT SYNAGOGUE (170 B.C.E.–135 C.E.)

The purpose of this chapter is to show that, contrary to the almost universally accepted view, there is no inconsistency between the rabbinic sources regarding the leaders of the Pharisees from the time of the Maccabean revolt and the non-rabbinic sources, such as the New Testament and Josephus. On the contrary, Josephus and the record in the New Testament supplement and confirm the rabbinic tradition with regard to these teachers.

It will be seen that of these teachers some were also heads of the contemporary Temple tribunal, which in the course of time came to be called the Sanhedrin; others were members of the Sanhedrin, but not its heads; still others were not even members of that body. But whatever their relation to the contemporary Sanhedrin might be, all were heads of the Pharisaic schools and tribunals, and indeed of Pharisaism as an organized movement.

Virtually all modern discussions regarding the Pharisees and Pharisaism are based on the premise that there existed only one form of Pharisaism. Doubtless this is because Josephus and the New Testament always speak of the Pharisees as a unit. Yet, as any student of the Talmud soon realizes, there were, in fact, two forms of Pharisaism, differing from each other on basic issues – the one, that which came to be known as the doctrine of the school of Shammai, the other, as that of the school of Hillel. While only about a score of issues are recorded as dividing the Pharisees from the Sadducees,[1] more than three hundred divided the Shammaites from the Hillelites. Nor were the issues between the two forms of Pharisaism confined to matters of ritual. Some concerned the laws of marriage, the criminal law, and the civil law. Logically, as the Talmud itself reminds us, the Hillelites should have considered children born of some marriages permitted, and even commanded, by Shammaitic law, illegitimate; and the Shammaites should have hesitated to marry into Hillelite families.[2] The disagree-

[1] See L. Finkelstein, *The Pharisees* (3rd edn., Philadelphia, 1962), 2, pp. 639ff.

[2] *Tosefta Yebamoth* 1.9, ed. Lieberman, p. 2, and parallel passages there noted.

ments of the factions regarding the laws of levitical purity should have prevented Shammaites from eating food prepared by Hillelites, and vice versa. Yet, each group recognized the legitimacy of the other's views.[1] Marriages were permitted between followers of the opposing schools; and they ate in each other's homes. Both traditions were considered authentic, each binding on its followers. How did this remarkable paradox of Pharisaism originate? Why does Josephus never allude to it?

Almost as difficult to understand is the record in the Mishnah[2] of five 'pairs' of scholars who were heads of the Pharisaic schools from the time of the Maccabean revolt onward. It can easily be shown that the first 'pair' flourished during the reign of Antiochus IV; and that the last 'pair' survived Herod.[3] The five 'pairs' thus led the Pharisaic movement for a period of about 170 years, an average tenure for each of 34 years. As it is hardly likely that anyone was appointed head of the Pharisees or his associate under the age of 40, the record seems to assume that the average lifespan of these sages was above 70. While such longevity for all of them is possible, it seems unlikely. Moreover, what does the Mishnah mean by saying that each 'pair' consisted of a *nasi* ('president') and an *'ab bet din* ('head of a court')? *Nasi*, or president, of what? And why did the Pharisees need two leaders in each period?

The difficulties in the way of understanding the traditions dealing with this period have led to astonishingly diverse interpretations of the sources; and no general consensus has yet been reached.

Many historians, some of them great scholars, still accept the account given by R. Jose (*Tosefta Ḥagigah* 2.9, ed. Lieberman, p. 383), and from him taken over in the Mishnah (*Sanhedrin* 11.2), as historical. They conclude that the Pharisaic *nasi* in each generation was the head of the national Sanhedrin, sitting in the Chamber of Hewn Stone in the Temple. Some of their opponents rely on the accounts in Josephus and the New Testament, which imply that the head of the Sanhedrin was the high priest. These scholars tend to reject the Pharisaic tradition as fiction. However, it seems clear that R. Jose's construction of the judicial system in the second commonwealth was theoretical. It was intended to indicate that the Sanhedrin was a Pharisaic institution. R. Jose developed his notion of the structure of the Judean judiciary to

[1] *Tosefta Yebamoth* 1.10, p. 3, and cf. the discussion by Prof. Saul Lieberman in *Tosefta Kifeshutah*, ad loc., pp. 7ff.

[2] Mishnah *Ḥagigah* 2.3ff.

[3] That Jose b. Joezer was a contemporary of Jodah the Maccabee is shown by the fact that he died about 160 B.C.E. That Shammai and Hillel survived the reign of Herod is obvious from the role which Shammai played in the revolt against Archelaus, see below, pp. 272ff.

show that before the time of Shammai and Hillel, there were no controversies about the Law. Everything was decided by majority vote of the Sanhedrin. He ascribed the emergence of the controversies between the schools to the 'disciples of Shammai and Hillel', who did not study 'as much as they should have', and therefore sometimes fell into error. The whole construction bears the stamp of apologetics, probably directed against contemporary sectarians, who, doubtless, like the Karaites of a later age,[1] asked how the Pharisees could claim that their tradition originated with Moses, when in fact, there were two Pharisaic traditions differing fundamentally from each other.

On the other hand, it will become evident in this discussion that during part of this period the Pharisaic *nasi* did sit at the head of the Sanhedrin. (This fact may have led R. Jose to argue that it was always so, although many passages in the Talmud show that it was not.)

Investigation into the problems involved in this chapter must begin with the rejection of the almost universally held, but quite untenable, view that the relation of the Pharisaic to the national judiciary of Judea remained unchanged throughout this period of turmoil, despite the violent political upheavals which marked it, as the early Hasmoneans gave way to the semi-Hellenized later ones; these to Herod and his family; they to the Roman procurators. Indeed a study of the rabbinic texts and of Josephus shows that important changes occurred in the relation of the Pharisaic leadership to the national government as time went on.

Another fact of great significance for understanding Pharisaism in this period, which has generally been overlooked, is the curious conformity of the doctrines of the later Hillelites with those ascribed to the Great Tribunal, and the apparent disagreement of the Shammaites with them.

As observed in the preceding chapter, one instance, remarked in the Talmud itself, is the agreement of the Mishnah *Sanhedrin* 10.1 (which the Talmud ascribes to the Men of the Great Tribunal) with the views of R. Joshua, who doubtless was (as often) articulating the doctrines of the whole Hillelite school.[2]

Another instance is that implied in the claim of the Pharisaic Great Tribunal to sole authority in interpretation of the Law. This claim could be justified only on the theory that the whole city of Jerusalem was 'the place which the Lord hath chosen'; for as has been shown in the preceding chapter,[3] the Pharisaic Great Tribunal, unlike the

[1] Cf. e.g., remarks of M. Margoliot, *Ha-Ḥilluqim šeben 'anše Mizraḥ u-bne Ereṣ Israel* (Jerusalem, 1938), p. 21.

[2] *b. Sanhedrin* 105a.

[3] See above, pp. 238ff.

patrician and high-priestly *gerousia*, did not meet in the Temple precincts. But that opinion was held in later times only in the school of Hillel. The Shammaites insisted that 'the place' was the Temple and its immediate environs.

We have already observed[1] the remarkable fact that as late as the time of R. Akiba priests, such as R. Eleazar b. Azariah (noted for his pro-Shammaite proclivities), demanded that the tithe of all produce be given to the priests, rather than to the Levites, as the Document of the Great Tribunal prescribed.

Some Shammaites, perhaps all of them, seem to have ignored the role of the Great Tribunal as the body through which the Mosaic interpretation of the Law was transmitted. When they cited ancient traditions in support of their views, they spoke of the 'pairs' having received them directly from the prophets.

Thus, R. Eliezer, the leading Shammaite of his day, quoting such a tradition, said, 'I have this tradition from Rabban Johanan b. Zakkai, who received it from the Pairs, and the Pairs from the Prophets, as a norm revealed to Moses on Mt. Sinai'.[2] A similar formula was used by a certain Nahum the scribe, the secretary of the contemporary Sanhedrin of the Chamber of Hewn Stones.[3] As secretary of the Sanhedrin of the Chamber of Hewn Stones, he was presumably a priest and probably a Shammaite; and, indeed, his failure to mention the Great Tribunal would itself suggest that his views coincided with those of R. Eliezer in a later age.

The failure of these stages to mention the Great Tribunal cannot be accidental. Clearly, both authorities held that the Pharisaic pairs, beginning with Jose b. Joezer of Zeredah and Jose b. Johanan of Jerusalem, had received traditions directly from the last prophets. Probably they held that the Great Tribunal of the Pharisees included prophets; but the tradition came from the prophets and not from the Tribunal, for not all of the decisions of the Tribunal were acceptable to the Shammaites.

Holding these views, Shammaitic scholars, including Shammai himself, often appealed to the authority of Haggai the prophet, as the source of their tradition. Thus Shammai asserted that he had received a tradition going back to Haggai, to the effect that 'a principal may be punished for crimes committed by his agent at his command'.[4]

R. Dosa b. Harkinas, an older contemporary of Rabban Gamaliel II,

[1] See above, p. 238.
[2] *Tosefta Yadaim* 2.16, ed. Zuckermandel, p. 583.
[3] Mishnah *Peah* 2.6.
[4] *b. Qiddušin* 43a.

and apparently a Shammaite, maintained that his views regarding the levirate marriage derived from Haggai.[1]

R. Eleazar b. R. Zadok, a pro-Shammaite priest, who flourished in the final generation of the Temple and survived it, maintained that his family preserved traditions going back to Haggai.[2]

In a much later age, R. Johanan, reflecting attitudes prevailing in his native Galilee, which was so much influenced by the Shammaites,[3] ascribed a tradition to Haggai, Zechariah, and Malachi.[4]

No wonder then that the maxim of the Great Tribunal, as it must be reconstructed on the basis of citations in *Ab. d'R.N.*, agrees with Hillelite attitudes rather than those of the Shammaites. As observed in the preceding chapter, the maxim originally was: 'Be gentle in argument, raise many disciples and make a hedge about your words.'[5]

Gentleness in argument was characteristic of the Hillelites, and not of the Shammaites. The type of retort given by Shammai himself in argument,[6] like those ascribed to R. Eliezer,[7] the leading Shammaite of his day, is never cited in the name of a Hillelite sage. Hillel warned his disciples that 'a person prone to anger cannot teach'.[8] While, doubtless, Shammai, like R. Eliezer, was ordinarily extremely courteous to everyone,[9] both considered patience in the academy weakness and wrong.

1 According to *Yer. Yebamoth* 1.6, 3a, he agreed with the Hillelites, regarding this law. That R. Dosa himself was a Shammaite is clear from the fact that, according to all accounts, he did not participate in the discussions of the academy of Rabban Johanan b. Zakkai, and did not even know all the visiting sages who came to interview him about the problem of the levirate marriage. According to both Talmuds, he reported that two other traditions of his derived from Haggai the prophet, one of which coincided with that reported by R. Eliezer in Mishnah *Yadaim* 4.3.

2 *Tosefta Kelim Baba Bathra* 2.3, ed. Zuckermandel, p. 592.

3 See Finkelstein *Pharisees*, pp. 7, 48, 49, 51.

4 *b. Ḥullin* 137b.

5 See above, p. 341 and Finkelstein, *Mabo*, p. 234, for the reconstruction of the original form of the maxim on the basis of the citations in *Ab. d'R.N.* I and II.

6 For Shammai's angry retort in an argument with Hillel, see *b. Shabbath* 17a.

7 For the language used by R. Eliezer in argument, see e.g. *b. Pesaḥim* 69a; *Sifra Tazria, pereq* 13.2, ed. Weiss 68b. R. Tarfon, who was famous for cursing his children in argument with his colleagues (cf. Mishnah *Ohaloth* 16.1, and many other passages) was a Shammaite in many of his attitudes (cf. *Akiba*, pp. 84ff). Rabban Gamaliel II, although a descendant of Hillel, tended to follow Shammaitic views (see *Akiba*, pp. 112ff); and was noted for his severity of discipline in the academy (see *Akiba*). His language in argument was usually Shammaitic.

8 Mishnah *Aboth* 2.5.

9 For Shammai's views, see Mishnah *Aboth* 1.15; for those of R. Eliezer, Mishnah *Aboth* 2.10. The inconsistency between the recorded practice of these scholars and their maxims suggests that they were probably harsh only in the academies, both in argument with their colleagues, and in relation to their disciples. Ordinarily, they treated equals with great courtesy, and considered this a virtue.

To raise many disciples would necessarily mean to open the doors of the academy to all applicants, and to encourage applicants, even among the poor, the humble, and the less competent, a position which *Ab. d'R.N.* ascribes to the Hillelites,[1] but which was rejected by the Shammaites.

To make a hedge about one's words meant, according to one interpretation preserved in *Ab. d'R.N., not* to add prohibitions to those actually found in Scripture.[2] This seems clearly to have been what the Men of the Great Tribunal had in mind. That apparently is one reason why in the recorded controversies between the Pharisees and the Sadducees, in which the question of rigour appears at all, the Pharisees almost always took the more lenient view. They permitted the use of light on the Sabbath, if a candle or lamp had been kindled before the Sabbath. They considered one who had been defiled free from impurity, in almost every respect, as soon as he had bathed. They declared a woman free from levitical impurity after childbirth during the time described as the days of her 'purification' (Lev. 12:1ff). They held that a master was not responsible for damages done by his slave without his consent. They were lenient in regard to punishment; rejected the *talio*; permitted one to carry utensils and other objects from one's home into a court, or even into a street on the Sabbath if the law of *'erub* had been followed. They rejected the Sadducean severities in all these matters, clearly refusing to accept them even as necessary additions to the written Law of the Pentateuch. However, a second interpretation, according to which 'making a hedge about one's words' signified precisely the opposite, namely to add restriction on restriction, is also cited in *Ab. d'R.N.*[3]

These interpretations cannot be reconciled; and doubtless emanate from different sources. Apparently, the first derived either from very early disciples of the Men of the Great Tribunal,[4] or from the school

[1] Ab. d'R.N. I, ch. 3, p. 7b.

[2] Cf. *Ab. d'R.N.* I, ch. 1; II, ch. 1, p. 2b. According to the interpretation given in *Ab. d'R.N.* I, ch. 1, if Adam had not added to the Divine prohibition against eating the fruit of the Tree of Knowledge, one of his own, namely not even to touch the Tree, Eve would not have committed the transgression.

[3] See *Ab. d'R.N.* I, ch. 2, p. 4bff and parallel passages in *Ab. d'R.N.* II.

[4] The interpretations of both the Hillelites and the Shammaites are cited in *Ab. d'R.N.* II, ch. 1, p. 2a. The passage reads: '*And make a hedge about your words.* A vineyard surrounded by a fence is not like one without a fence. [This teaches] that one should not make a fence higher than that which is to be protected, lest the fence fall and destroy the plants.' It is clear that the first explanation follows the view of the Shammaites; the second that of the Hillelites. The passage in *Ab. d'R.N.* I, ch. 3, 7b which reads as follows: 'And they made a hedge about their words; for the School of Shammai says, "One should not teach [the Torah] except to one who is wise, and meek, and a member of distinguished family and wealthy"; but the School of Hillel

of Hillel. The other, according to which the maxim recommended new restrictions, apparently derived from the Shammaitic school, as indeed can be shown from other passages.

Thus, several of the examples cited in *Ab. d'R.N.* of 'hedges about one's words', which were restrictions added to those of Scripture itself, were clearly rejected by the Hillelites.[1] It follows that according to the Hillelite interpretation, 'make a hedge about your words' meant not that one should add restrictions, but that one should avoid adding any.[2]

say, "One should teach anyone",' may refer to this difference between the Shammaites and Hillelites in their interpretation of the word 'hedge'. The Hillelites believed that they made a hedge for the command to 'raise many pupils' when they offered instruction to anyone, declining to exclude any prospective disciples. The Shammaites, interpreting 'hedge' in their way, thought that they were obeying the maxim, when they limited the number of disciples. (Schechter's emendation of the passage is thus unnecessary.) For other examples regarding Pharisaic law, see Finkelstein, *Pharisees*, pp. 641ff.

1 Otherwise it would be difficult to understand the inclusion in that portion of *Ab. d'R.N.* a view so contrary to its whole spirit, which is dominated by Shammaitic ideas (see L. Finkelstein, *Mabo le-masekhtot Aboth ve-Aboth de* R. *Nathan* (New York, 1950) pp. 17ff). Presumably, the earliest comments on the sayings of the Men of the Great Tribunal were made by their immediate disciples who dwelt in Jerusalem. These comments were supplemented by others deriving from provincial priests, who had adopted Pharisaism, but felt bound to interpret the sayings of the Men of the Great Tribunal and their disciples in harmony with their own attitudes toward life. To this extent, my remarks in *Mabo* (pp. 17ff) require amplification.

It is interesting to compare the views of the Shammaites about 'a hedge about one's words' with their tendency to approve stringent construction of the Law, when any doubt arose. See Mishnah *Zebaḥim* 8.10. The issue there was what was to be done if the blood of a sacrifice which had to be placed on all four corners of the altar had become mixed with blood which had to be poured only once, such as might happen if the blood of a whole-burnt offering was mixed with that of a firstling. R. Joshua held that the blood should be offered only in one dashing. R. Eliezer held that if one dashed the blood against the altar only once, one transgressed the rule against omission of a ritual. R. Joshua argued that if one dashed such blood on the four corners of the altar, one violated the rule against *adding* to the commands of the Torah. R. Joshua in his argument said, 'If you add to the commanded ritual, you have performed a prohibited action; if you simply dash the blood once, you have not performed a prohibited act'. This theory seems to underlie the whole attitude of the school of Hillel. To add severities to the Law was to perform a prohibited act; but the Shammaites did not distinguish between transgressions of omission and commission. Cf. Mishnah *Yadaim* 4.3, where the rule is set down that, 'The burden of proof falls on one who interprets the Law more stringently'.

2 Thus the rule is set down in *Ab. d'R.N.* that during her period of menstruation, a woman must refrain from the use of any cosmetics or trying to make herself attractive (*Ab. d'R.N.* I, ch. 2, p. 4b; *Ab. d'R.N.* II, ch. 3, p. 6b). This rule is emphatically rejected by R. Akiba, who doubtless was echoing the traditional Hillelite view (see *Sifra Mesora*, end 79c). The exegesis which held that although Moses was commanded to separate husbands from their wives only for two days before the Revelation (Exod. 19:10), he added one more day, according to his own

That the Hillelite interpretation of the maxim was correct is shown quite dramatically by the fact that the redactors of the Mishnah, living in Galilee, and sharing in some respects the outlook of the Shammaites, felt compelled to alter the language of the maxim, so that its final clause read: 'And make a hedge about the Torah.'[1]

The conclusion that the Hillelites adhered to the basic teachings of the early Pharisaic Great Tribunal in all respects, while the Shammaites opposed many of them, seems to follow also from a study of the *ʿamidah*, the central prayer of the Synagogue, which appears to have been edited by the Men of the Great Tribunal, as the Talmud repeatedly asserts.[2]

In this prayer, the first paragraph, following the introductory benedictions in praise of the Deity, is one for wisdom and understanding, that is to say wisdom and understanding which will help the petitioner love the Deity, understand the Torah, and adhere to Jewish worship. This view of learning and wisdom as a means to achieve

judgement, as a 'hedge' (*Ab. d'R.N.* I, ch. 2; *Ab. d'R.N.* II, ch. 2, p. 5a), is rejected in *Mekilta* Yithro, ch. 3, p. 211. (See also Mishnah *Shabbath* 9.3, the correct text of which is given by J. N. Epstein, *Mabo le-Nusaḥ ha-Mishnah* (Jerusalem, 5708 = 1948).) It seems apparent, as shown in Finkelstein, *Mabo*, pp. 23ff, that the examples of 'hedges' cited in *Ab. d'R.N.* which involved additional restrictions stemmed from the Shammaites.

[1] Mishnah *Aboth* 1.2. For the influence of the Shammaites in Galilee, see Finkelstein, *Pharisees*, pp. 54, 59.

[2] See above, pp. 242f; cf. *Yer. Berakoth* 2.4, 4d; *b. Berakoth* 17b. The view I expressed in my youth that the final redaction of the *ʿamidah* was made by Rabban Gamaliel II must be revised and the Talmudic tradition accepted. Cf. the discussion in *Conservative Judaism*, 23 (1969), pp. 26ff (reprinted in L. Finkelstein, *Pharisaism in the Making*, New York, 1972, pp. 175ff). The composers of the earliest paragraphs in the *ʿamidah* still propounded the Tetragrammaton both in the petition and in the doxology, in accordance with the practice which a very ancient *baraita* cited in *Tosefta Berakoth* 6 (7). 20, ed. Lieberman (Jerusalem, 1937), p. 39, and *Yer. Berakoth* 9.1, 11d, declared to be the practice of sages. Their successors, flourishing in times when the use of the Tetragrammaton in newly composed prayers was being discouraged, and yet unwilling to follow practices denounced in the ancient *baraita* as that of the mediocre, the ignorant, or the sectarian, replaced the Tetragrammaton at the beginning of the petition with the term 'our Father', a practice not condemned in the ancient norm. Later, it was felt that there was no need to insert any term of address to the Deity in individual paragraphs of the *ʿamidah*, since the whole prayer was addressed to Him. But all this development must have taken place before the Tetragrammaton was regularly replaced with the cypher now currently in use. This replacement occurred no later than the third or early part of the second century B.C.E., as is evident from the second and third books of Psalms, and the book of Daniel, where the Tetragrammaton is regularly replaced with the usual cypher. Thus it is impossible to accept the view that the *ʿamidah* was put into the form generally used in prayer after the Maccabean rebellion.

virtue was characteristic of the Hillelites, and not of the Shammaites.[1]

The petition for the frustration of the hope of the *m*ᵉ*šummadim*[2] or Hellenists is expressed with extraordinary mildness. It contains no malediction against them; only the frustration of their aspirations is asked. Such mildness suggests the type of thought characteristic of the later Hillelites, rather than the Shammaites. The prayer dealing with the Hellenists is immediately followed by one on behalf of the true proselytes[3] – a prayer which would hardly conform to the Shammaitic outlook on proselytism.

No wonder then that in the time of Rabban Gamaliel II, when the issue of the text of the *ʿamidah* to be used in private prayer was being discussed, R. Eliezer,[4] and his like-minded colleague, R. Simeon b. Nathaniel,[5] held that no fixed formula was even commendable. Their position was opposed to that of Rabban Gamaliel II, R. Joshua and R.

[1] Cf. *Sifre* Deut. 41, p. 85; *b. Qiddušin* 40a, *Yer. Pesaḥim* 3.7, 30b. The views ascribed in these passages to R. Akiba were those of the Hillelites generally, as is evident from many sayings of Hillel himself (see above, p. 251) R. Jose the Galilean and R. Tarfon who opposed R. Akiba at the conclave, described in these passages, frequently followed the views of the Shammaites.

[2] For the identification of the term *m*ᵉ*šummadim* as Hellenists, see above, p. 243.

[3] The difference between the Shammaite and Hillelite attitudes toward proselytes has been blurred by the efforts of later scholars to reconcile them. But it is clear from many passages that the Shammaites opposed proselytism, and considered proselytes below the descendants of Israelites both in social and legal status. The Hillelites rejected these views, considering proselytes the equals of descendants of Israelites in every respect. Thus Shammai, according to stories doubtless based on kernels of fact, rejected a number of applicants for proselytism, whom Hillel accepted (see *Ab. d'R.N.* I, ch. 15; II, ch. 29, 31a; *b. Shabbath* 31a). The rule that priests might not marry proselyte women, which has no basis in Scripture (see Lev. 21:7), was doubtless created by the Priests themselves, and thus was part of the Shammaitic tradition. Like other rules, which priests established for their tribe, this one was accepted as binding on them by later generations (see Maimonides, *Yad, 'Issure Bi'ah,* 18.3). It must be borne in mind that the word 'proselyte' in the context of these ancient laws meant not only a proselyte himself, but also his descendants. However, a descendant of an Israelite man by the proselyte wife had the status of any other Israelite, since status was determined by the male line. The rule that a proselyte might not be a member of the Sanhedrin doubtless stemmed from the Shammaitic priests, and cannot be reconciled with views expressed by R. Joshua, the spokesman of the Hillelites in his generation (see *Sifre* on Num. 78, p. 73), nor with the remarkable passage in *Yer. Horayoth* 1.4, 46a, which has greatly troubled the commentators. Because the descendant of any Israelite married to a proselyte woman had the status of any other Israelite, according to all groups, the discussion was unaffected by the record of the book of Ruth according to which the whole Davidic dynasty was descended from a proselyte woman (Ruth 4:17). Nor was the Shammaitic view inconsistent with the statement of *Sifre* Num. 78, p. 74, according to which Rahab was the ancestor of many priests and prophets.

[4] Mishnah *Berakoth* 4.4.

[5] Mishnah *Aboth* 2.13.

Akiba, who, while disagreeing with one another, were unanimous in their acceptance of the *ʿamidah*, formulated as authoritative centuries earlier by the Men of the Great Tribunal.

In general, as Professor Louis Ginzberg has brilliantly demonstrated,[1] the *halakah* of the Shammaites seems to reflect the mentality of the upper classes in Jerusalem. These were generally priestly or lay landowners; and it can be shown that other parts of the Shammaitic *halakah* reflect the mentality of wealthy provincials and priests.[2]

But there were, according to Josephus,[3] the very groups out of which Sadducaism sprang. Apparently, then, the Shammaites and the Sadducees had a common background, as well as a common outlook on many matters of ritual and law.

Thus, it appears that the intellectual and spiritual heirs of the Great Tribunal of the pre-Maccabean Pharisees were the Hillelites and their precursors. But in what event, the question arises, what was the origin of the Shammaites? Why were they accepted as legitimate Pharisees, while the Sadducees were rejected as heretics? And most especially, what was the relation of the Shammaites to the Great Tribunal of the Pharisees?

Unambiguous documentary evidence explaining these enigmas does not exist. We are therefore thrown back on conjecture to explain the established facts.

Probably, at some point in the history of the second commonwealth, a group of people, who normally might have been expected to share the Sadducean point of view, and whose ancestors had done so, rejected Sadducaism and associated themselves with the lowly Pharisees, accepting some of their doctrines, yet continuing to adhere to many of their ancestral customs in other matters. When could that have happened, and why? The change implies a major crisis in the history of the nation. What could it have been?

A crisis, which occurred during the second commonwealth, capable of producing such a revolution, was the rise of the Hellenistic movement in the third and at the beginning of the second century B.C.E.

It seems highly probable that as early as the middle of the third century B.C.E., the high priest, Onias, became concerned lest Hellenism of the people, stemming from Egypt (which ruled the country, and was even in prophetic times considered a peril to the purity of Israel's faith), should undermine loyalty to the Temple, and the Jewish tradition generally.

1 See his work, *On Jewish Law and Lore* (Philadelphia, 1955), pp. 77ff.

2 See Finkelstein, *Pharisees*, pp. 20f; 290f; 508ff.

3 Josephus, *Antiquitates Judaicae* XVIII.17.

In the light of these facts, historians[1] attach great significance to the story told in Josephus (*Antiquitates Judaicae* XII.158) of the refusal of the High Priest Onias, father of Simeon the Righteous, to pay the usual tribute to Ptolemy, and the intervention of the Tobiads who averted Ptolemy's threatened use of force, by paying the tax. They saw in the action of Onias an effort to turn from Egypt to Syria, hoping that Syria would prove culturally and religiously less dangerous, as a source of assimilation. The pro-Egyptian assimilationist Tobiads were apparently supported by the Hellenized *gerousia*.[2]

Joseph b. Tobiah went to Egypt, despite the objection of the high priest, paid the tribute, and brought about reconciliation between Judea and its overlords.

There thus lies hidden in the story told by Josephus about the Tobiads one about a conflict between the Hellenized *gerousia* and the high priest. The high priest was not removed by the Egyptian masters of the country, but Joseph b. Tobiah, becoming a tax-farmer for all Syria, was given a far more important office.

Probably, as part of the struggle between the high priest, Onias, and the Hellenized *gerousia*, Onias sought to limit its judicial authority.

This effort of the high priest is reflected in the otherwise inexplicable provisions found in *Sifre* Deuteronomy and parallel passages.[3] In its comment on Deut. 17:8ff, *Sifre* limits the authority of the central tribunal to specific cases. In doing so, *Sifre* clearly contradicts 2 Chron. 19:5ff, where the Deuteronomic passage is interpreted as giving the central tribunal jurisdiction over all aspects of Jewish religious Law. Quite apart from the strange inconsistency between the rabbinic exegesis and that of the book of Chronicles, the reason for the limitation imposed on the central tribunal is puzzling. If the central tribunal under discussion was considered to be that of the Pharisees, why should a rabbinic text have limited its jurisdiction? What was to be done when a local authority was in doubt about any other portion of such vast areas of Jewish Law as the ritual? If the central court under discussion was that of the Temple, why did the rabbinic authorities recognize that it had any jurisdiction? To make the problem even more complicated, it is evident (as will presently appear) that the authors of the Septuagint knew this passage of *Sifre*, and followed it – at least in part – in their translation.

[1] See V. Tcherikover, *Hellenistic Civilization and the Jews* (Philadelphia, 1959), pp. 129ff.

[2] Tcherikover, *Civilization*, pp. 132f. Especial significance seems to attach to the act of the 'people empowering Joseph' to act as *prostatēs*, in place of the high priest. See Jos. *Ant.* XII.164f. The assembly of the people in the Temple must refer to the *gerousia*. What other group would be called to gather in the Temple?

[3] *Sifre* Deut. 152, pp. 205ff; *b. Sanhedrin* 87a; *Yer. Sanhedrin* 11.3, 30a.

The enigma is resolved on the supposition that the High Priest Onias decided to limit the authority of the Temple tribunal or the *gerousia*. That body had become Hellenized to a great extent. Onias did not wish it to have authority over all Jewish religious life, and recoiled from the thought that local teachers and judges, in doubt about the ritual, might seek guidance from it.

Thus, probably in consultation with Pharisaic scholars, he developed the exegesis of Deut. 17:8ff, preserved in the passage in *Sifre*.

For example, the words 'between blow and blow', referring literally to physical injury of one person by another, are interpreted both in the Septuagint and in *Sifre* to mean 'between leprosy and leprosy'. Apparently, Onias wanted to deny the *gerousia* authority to decide questions regarding physical injury of one person by another. The reason was that the *gerousia*, like the Sadducees, interpreted the verse 'an eye for an eye' (Exod. 21:24) literally; and permitted only one able to pay a ransom, to escape the punishment of the *talio*. The Pharisaic tribunal considered such an interpretation of the verse discrimination against the poor, and held that only money payment was ever involved.[1] The interpretation of the passage in the Septuagint and in *Sifre* effectively removed such cases from the jurisdiction of the *gerousia*, giving it authority only to rule on cases of leprosy, regarding which its priestly members might be expected to be experts.

The words 'between blood and blood' in the biblical passage under discussion, certainly mean, literally, all issues involving charges of homicide. However, *Sifre* interprets them to mean 'between the blood of virginity,[2] menstrual blood, and that resulting from disease' (that is, a 'flow'). Why does *Sifre* reject the simple explanation of the words? Because, apparently, the *gerousia*, like the Sadducees, held that even one condemned to death could ransom his life, through money payment.[3]

1 See Finkelstein, *Pharisees*, pp. 720ff.

2 Accepting the reading *yaldut* (virginity) found in some texts, rather than the reading *yoledet* (a woman in childbirth), found in others. The latter seems clearly the result of a copyist's error who did not understand the unusual expression *yaldut*, and substituted the more familiar *yoledet*.

3 Apparently that was the reason underlying the Sadducean claim that false witnesses could not be condemned to death, unless the person against whom they had testified had already been executed. If he were still alive, although already condemned by the court, on the basis of their false testimony, the witnesses could not be condemned to death; they could claim that they merely wanted the defendant, against whom they testified, to pay a ransom. The Pharisees, who held that a person condemned to death could not free himself from the penalty by paying a ransom, held that if a court found that the witnesses had testified falsely and on the basis of their testimony had condemned the defendant to death the false witnesses had to suffer the penalty to which they sought to expose their victim, although he had been saved in time (Mishnah *Makkoth* 1.6; see discussion of the passage in *Sefer ha-Yobel likᵉbod Šalom*

The Pharisees denied that anyone condemned to death could escape the penalty in that way. Agreeing with them, Onias interpreted the words so as to give the Temple court jurisdiction only in cases in which it was necessary to decide whether blood found on a stained garment was virginal, menstrual, or the result of disease. The priest might be considered experts in such matters, as they were in regard to leprosy. The issue involved in the judgement might be one of ritual; for while the blood of virginity did not make one defiled, the others did.[1] But the question could be far more serious. According to *Sifre*, if, in the case of a newly married bride accused by her husband of not being a virgin (Deut. 22:13), a local court was unable to reach a decision regarding the blood found on the garment, it might take the issue to the *gerousia*. (The passage assumes that the words 'and they shall spread the garment before the elders of the city' [Deut. 22:17] are to be interpreted literally.[2] The wife's innocence was to be established by the fact that the garment was stained with blood of virginity.)

Finally, the phrase 'between judgement and judgement' was interpreted as giving the *gerousia* authority only to decide whether a litigated issue involved merely property, or the punishment with stripes, or capital punishment. The *gerousia* was not authorized to give a final decision with regard to the litigation itself concerning which a local court was in perplexity. The *gerousia* could decide only whether the litigation was one regarding property, to be settled by three judges, or one involving capital punishment, which required greater deliberation. Such issues might arise in the case of a person assaulting another on the Sabbath. The punishment for violation of the Sabbath was death;[3] but one who was exposed to this punishment was not under any further obligation to make payment for the injury he had caused.[4] Similarly,

Baron [being vol. 3 of *Salo Baron Jubilee Volumes*], Jerusalem, 1974, pp. 281ff). According to the express command of Scripture (Num. 35:31) ransom was not to be accepted from one guilty of homicide. How the Sadducees reconciled this attitude with the specific word of Scripture is difficult to understand. Perhaps they accepted ransom from an assassin only in some special cases. But the Sadducean judges did not hesitate to decide other matters differently from the explicit command of Scripture. (See Finkelstein, *Pharisees*, pp. 654ff.)

[1] See Mishnah *Niddah* 10.1; cf. Lev. 15:19ff; 15:25ff.

[2] See view of R. Eliezer b. Jacob (apparently the first), who frequently reflected Shammaitic views, in *Sifre* Deut. 237, p. 270. He was opposed by both R. Ishmael and R. Akiba, doubtless reflecting the views of the Hillelites. Cf. also the anonymous statement in *Sifre* Deut. 236, p. 258, where the passage is also interpreted literally. Anonymous statements in *Sifre* Deut. frequently reflect Shammaitic views (*Sefer Assa*, pp. 415ff). The view that the passage was to be interpreted literally is also ascribed to the Sadducees (see Finkelstein, *Pharisees*, pp. 730ff).

[3] Exod. 31:15.

[4] See Mishnah *Baba Qamma* 10.5, *et al.*

when a husband accused his wife of unfaithfulness, was he trying to have her executed as an adulteress, or simply to divorce her without any obligation to pay her dower?[1]

Moreover, it was held that the *gerousia* could not decide any cases, except those brought before it by local authorities, who were unsure of the law.[2] When the local authorities felt that they knew the Law, they could render decisions according to their own views or traditions. Thus Pharisaic judges who did not recognize the jurisdiction of the *gerousia* would not have to turn to it at all.

These interpretations of Deuteronomic Law could not have been made by the Men of the Great Tribunal, for they denied that the *gerousia* was meant in the passage at all. According to them, the authority for a local court or judge in doubt as to the Law, was, as suggested by the chronicler, the Great Tribunal itself, which was the court of the city of Jerusalem. The same view was apparently held by the son of Onias, the high priest, Simeon the Just, who became a member (and apparently the president) of the Great Tribunal. As will be seen presently, the rule set down in this passage of *Sifre* Deuteronomy was followed by Rabban Gamaliel I, about the year 40 C.E. and as already shown, it was known by the authors of the Septuagint, about 225 B.C.E. Thus, it necessarily originated with an authority who believed that Deuteronomy in this passage referred to the court sitting in the Temple; but who held that this court, as it had developed in his time, could not be permitted to be the final arbiter to decide issues concerning ritual, and some other issues. The evidence thus points unmistakably to the High Priest Onias, who presided over the Temple in the last decades of the third century B.C.E. as responsible for this exegesis.

The concern of Onias regarding the perils of Hellenization of the people is evident from other decisions which seem to have been made by him. It is demonstrable[3] that the earliest portion of the Passover

1 Cf. Mishnah *Soṭah* 4.1ff.

2 Deut. 17:8. Perhaps the word *mufla'* in *Sifre* Deut. 152, p. 205, and parallel passages, referred originally to a subject concerning which one is perplexed (rather than, as usually understood, to a person), in accordance with the literal interpretation of the verse. That is the sense in which the word occurs in Sirach 3:19 (20), ed. Segal, p. 16; and in the citation of that passage in *b. Ḥagigah* 13a and *Bereshit* R. ch. 8.2, p. 58. *Midrash Tannaim* 17.8, p. 102, puts the matter very clearly, asserting that the passage deals only with that which is 'covered'. Perhaps it was R. Jose who first interpreted the word *mufla'* to mean a particular person (*Tosefta Ḥagigah* 2.9, ed. Lieberman, p. 383 and parallel passages). See also remarks of Hanok Albeck on this passage in his edition of the Mishnah, *Šišah Sidre Mišna, seder nziqin* (Jerusalem–Tel Aviv, 1953–58), pp. 457f and the reference he gives.

3 See discussion of the origin of this part of the Passover *Haggadah* in *HTR*, 31 (1938), pp. 292ff (now reprinted in Finkelstein, *Pharisaism*, pp. 13ff). The thesis there presented, which seemed at the time daring to many critics, has now been rendered

Haggadah was made about his time (that is, the middle of the third century B.C.E.); and was evidently prepared under the authority of a high priest, and therefore presumably under his direction. One of the lessons this ancient text derives from the biblical passage which it discusses is that the Israelites in Egypt were careful to keep themselves 'distinguished' from their neighbours, that is, loyal to their ancestral traditions. It also stresses the fact that the Israelites went to Egypt only because of a divine command, and not of their own choice. This was apparently a message from Onias to the Egyptian pilgrims coming to Jerusalem for Passover. He implied that they, too, ought to remain in Palestine, if they could. If they could not, they should carefully preserve their ancestral traditions. How much more, then, was he likely to insist on adherence to the Jewish traditions, in every way, in Palestine itself.

One not accustomed to the manner in which judges deal with difficult texts commanding their respect, may wonder at the resort to this peculiar exegesis by the authors of the passage in *Sifre*, in order to achieve their purpose. However, the method is a commonplace of judicial adjustment to new situations of the Law as set down in a received text. The authors of the passage in *Sifre* may perhaps have been more radical than usual. But they sought support for their views in Scripture, and felt certain that their interpretation, no matter how novel, was correct.

When in 198 B.C.E. Antiochus III, supported by the High Priest Simeon the Just, and his followers among the Judeans, defeated Ptolemy V Epiphanes and became master of Palestine, a new era set in for Judea. In his gratitude to Simeon and his followers, Antiochus III made Jewish Law the law of the land for the Jews, as the king of Persia had done in the time of Ezra.[1] But who was to interpret this law? Simeon went back to the system envisioned in 2 Chron. 10:10–11, according to which the tribunal of the city of Jerusalem, when the high priest presided over it, was the authority to which everyone had to turn in religious matters. The tribunal of the city of Jerusalem, as distinct from that of the Temple, was the Great Tribunal of the Pharisees. Accordingly, Simeon became associated with this court, and inevitably its president.[2]

easier to accept through the discovery of the Judean scrolls, which show that *midrashim* of that character were quite common in the pre-Maccabean age.

[1] See, for example, Elias Bickerman in L. Finkelstein, *The Jews* (3rd edn., New York, 1960), p. 106.

[2] It is significant and instructive that in his maxim (Mishnah *Aboth* 1.3) he adopted the attitude of the Men of the Great Tribunal, later held only by the school of Hillel, but rejected by the Shammaites, placing study of Torah before worship.

According to the chronicler, the Great Tribunal of Jerusalem was also the supreme court in all civil questions, provided that in such matters it was headed by the prince for the house of Judah. How Simeon arranged for this appointment is unclear. Perhaps he and the Great Tribunal took it that since the monarchy was destroyed, and the high priest was the foremost citizen of the land, he could preside over the tribunal of Jerusalem also when it discussed matters of civil and criminal law. Or, some layman, who remains unknown, may have held this position.

Possibly it was at this time that the aristocratic family of Jose b. Joezer,[1] uncle of the future high priest, Alcimus, became Pharisees. It may be that the Hasmonean family, owners of a large estate in Modern, also adopted Pharisaism at this time.

(The Pharisaism of the Maccabees, though unmentioned in either book of the Maccabees or in Josephus, cannot really be doubted. Jonathan the Maccabee prayed for the souls of the dead [1 Macc. 12:43ff], apparently believing in the future world, and like the later Shammaites holding that the dead were in need of forgiveness for their sins. John Hyrcanus is described in the Talmud,[2] even by his detractors, as having been a Pharisee almost all his life. When insulted at a public banquet, he turned the question of the punishment to be inflicted on the guilty person over to the tribunal of the Pharisees.[3] Alexander Janneus performed the ceremony of the water-pouring during the festival of *Sukkot*.)[4]

Recognition by Simeon the high priest of the Pharisaic Great Tribunal as the authority to which 2 Chron. 19:5ff referred, meant that in a number of issues dividing the Pharisees from the Sadducees the

[1] For the wealth of Jose b. Joezer, see *b. Baba Bathra* 133b. That he was the uncle of Alcimus is asserted in *Midrash Tehillim* 11.7, p. 52a; and *Berešit* R. 65, 22, ed. J. Theodor and H. Albeck (Berlin, 1903–26), p. 742.

[2] *b. Berakoth* 29a.

[3] See Jos. *Ant.* XIII.288, 294, and *b. Qiddušin* 66a, where the Pharisees are called 'the Sages of Israel'. It is obvious from the context that the passage refers to the Pharisees.

[4] See Jos. *Ant.* XIII.372 and Mishnah *Sukkah* 4.9. The commentators on this passage of Josephus, and even historians, assume, because of the outbreak of the riot when the priest was believed to have performed the rite improperly, that Alexander Janneus was a Sadducee. But had he been a Sadducee, why did he perform the ceremony in the first place? It is apparent that he was following the Pharisaic ritual. Because of the distance between the altar and the mass of people crowding into the Temple courts, it was possible for evil-minded persons to spread the rumour, while he was performing the ritual, that he was pouring the water on his feet instead of on the altar. A riot ensued. One may presume that the persons initiating the rumour were enemies of the Hasmonean dynasty, possibly members of the former priestly dynasty of the Zadokides.

Pharisaic view would prevail. But, as no one was required to turn to the central court unless he was in doubt as to the Law, most of the ancient customs to which Sadducean families and local leaders had adhered could still be followed by them. Thus in regard to many ritual questions, the people remained divided – the neo-Pharisees following the customs of their ancestors, which they now insisted had come down by tradition from Moses himself, and the old Pharisees following their own customs.

Disputes about such issues are not therefore described as dividing the Pharisees from the Sadducees. The neo-Pharisaic customs ultimately came to be recorded as those of the school of Shammai, or were ascribed to individual Shammaitic or pro-Shammaitic scholars, like R. Eliezer.

The issues which are recorded as those about which the Pharisees and the Sadducees disagreed were those regarding which the Men of the Great Tribunal apparently insisted that all Pharisees – new as well as old – had to accept its view. While the Great Tribunal agreed that local traditions, inconsistent with the practices accepted by the Pharisees for generations, might also derive from the prophets, difference in matters which concerned the whole community was not possible, and in those instances inconsistencies and contradictory versions could not derive from the prophets. In regard to such issues the Pharisaic Great Tribunal could claim original jurisdiction and the right to impose its views on everyone.

There could obviously be only one calendar for the whole country. Hence all Pharisees agreed that the date of *Shabuot*, and therefore the date of the *ʿOmer* sacrifice on which it depended, had to be determined according to Pharisaic view.[1] Similarly, all Pharisees accepted the old Pharisaic principle that the public sacrifices had to be bought from funds to which all Jews contributed equally, the *sheqalim*.[2] The ceremony of the water libations on *Sukkot* was introduced in accordance with the Pharisaic contention that *Sukkot* was the season of Divine judgement regarding the rainfall; and the ritual was part of a ceremony required to assure adequate rains.[3]

The high priest had henceforth to perform the ritual of the incense offering on the Day of Atonement[4] in accordance with Pharisaic law;

[1] For the issues involved in this controversy, See Finkelstein, *Pharisees*, pp. 641ff.

[2] See above, p. 238 for the support of this view in the document of Nehemiah, ch. 10; and cf. Finkelstein, *Pharisees*, pp. 710ff.

[3] For the background of this controversy between Sadducees and Pharisees, see Finkelstein, *Pharisees*, pp. 700ff.

[4] For the issues underlying this controversy between the Pharisees and the Sadducees, see Finkelstein, *Pharisees*, pp. 654ff.

for the welfare of the whole community depended on the rituals of that day. While in other matters the priestly tradition established in the Temple continued to prevail, the Pharisaic Great Tribunal apparently succeeded in having its position concerning the preparation of the red heifer accepted, on the ground that the ceremony was conducted outside the Temple area; and that therefore the precedents established about it by priests of earlier generations were irrelevant.[1]

While theoretically capital punishment might be imposed by a local court, in practice this seems never to have happened. Not a single instance of capital punishment is recorded in either rabbinic or non-rabbinic works of the period as having been decided by a local tribunal. Thus, the views of the old Pharisees prevailed in every dispute concerning capital punishment, so long as the arrangement set up by Simeon the Righteous was followed.[2]

In regard to two issues involving ordinary litigation, we are told the Pharisees were unified, although the local courts probably had diverse precedents about them. One was the controversy regarding the division of inherited property between a surviving daughter and a granddaughter by a son. The Pharisees held that the granddaughter by a son received the whole property; the Sadducees held that it had to be divided equally.[3] The other involved the question of the responsibility of a master for depredations by his slave. The Sadducees held the master responsible for them, the Pharisees did not.[4] One must assume that in these instances, local courts, established in new communities and in doubt concerning the Law, turned to the central tribunal of the Pharisees for guidance. Because the Pharisees held that in these cases matters of principle were involved, the neo-Pharisees or proto-Shammaites were persuaded to follow the views of the old Pharisees, rather than the precedent established by the Zadokite courts of earlier times. The issue of the division of property between a surviving daughter and a granddaughter involved the question of whether the son who had died, leaving a daughter, could be said to exist. As the Pharisees believed in life after death, they could not agree that the dead son no longer existed; and that therefore the surviving granddaughter had to share the property with the daughter. This issue could not be referred

[1] The Temple ritual was conducted, in general, in accordance with the traditions of the priests; their court was, as it were, a local court which had authority over it. Hence the Temple rituals generally followed the principles advocated by the Shammaites generally. See Finkelstein, *Pharisees*, pp. 661ff, 687ff.

[2] That is except when, as will become apparent below, the Pharisees were deprived of judicial authority.

[3] See Finkelstein, *Pharisees*, pp. 694ff. [4] See Finkelstein, *Pharisees*, pp. 689ff.

back to the local court to decide according to the precedents established in its region.

Similarly, the Great Tribunal of the Pharisees could not agree that the issue of the responsibility of a master for the depredation by his slave should be decided on the basis of local precedent. The problem involved was whether a slave could be considered a sentient human being, and therefore himself responsible for his acts. The Pharisees held that he had to be held liable for them.

The neo-Pharisees accepted the doctrine of life after death, which Pharisaism had always considered a cornerstone of the faith.[1] Apparently, the neo-Pharisees also accepted the doctrine of the existence of immortal celestial beings,[2] although they hesitated to call them *mal'akim* (angels), but used for them only terms found in the prophets, such as *seraphim*. The neo-Pharisees further accepted the doctrine of Divine foreknowledge of all that will happen, and therefore agreed that man's actions are not entirely under his own control. But they insisted that man was free to make his own moral decisions.[3]

The use of fire on the Sabbath was, it would appear, considered not a mere matter of ritual difference between the Sadducees and the Pharisees. The Pharisees held that to refrain from the use of fire and artificial light on the Sabbath was to destroy the enjoyment of the day; and thus to deny one of the basic concepts of Scripture regarding the Sabbath, namely that it was blessed and holy. Simply to abstain from labour on the Sabbath might be to accept the notion that it was a day of ill-fortune – a concept not far removed from idolatry itself. Thus the issue of the Sabbath lights became one on which all Pharisees, new and old, agreed, in opposition to the Sadducees.[4]

The rule that 'sacred books defile the hands' is explained on quite practical grounds in the Talmud.[5] However its underlying theoretical

[1] See above, pp. 240f.

[2] The term *mal'akim* never occurs in the standard prayers in any version. But the *seraphim* are mentioned in the description of the celestial service at dawn. The omission of the word *mal'ak* in the prayer book, as well as in the Mishnah, can scarcely be accidental. See Finkelstein, *Pharisees*, pp. 160ff.

[3] See Finkelstein, *Pharisees*, pp. 195ff.

[4] For the issues involved in regard to the Sabbath lights, see Finkelstein, *Pharisees*, pp. 660ff.

[5] The Talmud maintains that the holy Scrolls were held to communicate defilement, to prevent priests from putting holy books and the heave-offering next to one another, causing injury to the scrolls, because mice might be attracted to the food, and thus come to destroy the scrolls (see *b. Shabbath* 14a). The ritual of washing one's hands after eating holy food, which was extended by the Pharisees into a requirement for washing them after every meal as well as before it, has never been satisfactorily explained. However it seems altogether probable that it is associated with the rule

concept seems to be that the Scrolls of the biblical works are as sacred as the priestly garments; and that therefore contact with them transmits some holiness to one's hands. Hence, according to Pharisaic notions, one's hands had to be rinsed after such contact. The Sadducean priests had refused to accept this doctrine, apparently holding that no sanctity attached to the Scrolls themselves. The Pharisees accepted the priestly view so far as the Scroll of the Pentateuch kept in the Temple was concerned;[1] for, being in the Temple, it was subject to the rules established by the priestly authorities of earlier ages; but they were united in their insistence that all other Scrolls of sacred books 'defiled the hands'.[2]

In addition, the Pharisees demanded recognition for two institutions which had been established long before their time, and had, according to them, been inherited from pre-exilic authorities, although they were not of Mosaic origin. These were the *ʿerub*, permitting one living in a court, containing also other homes, to perform a ceremony, which enabled residents to carry food and other objects from their homes into the courtyard on the Sabbath. The other was the rule requiring washing of one's hands before any meal, not only one consisting of holy food. The institution of the *ʿerub* was vital to life in the crowded quarter of Jerusalem where most of the Pharisaic traders and artisans dwelt.[3] There could be no unity between the neo-Pharisees and the old Pharisees unless the legitimacy of this institution were accepted by all, even those who did not need it because they lived in far more spacious and comfortable quarters.

Nor could the old Pharisees accept as authentic followers of their doctrine anyone who denied the rule that all food had to be kept undefiled, and that therefore one's hands had to be rinsed before eating any meal.[4]

Finally, of course, there was the central Pharisaic institution – the Synagogue and the prayer service, which all had to accept.

All three institutions became part of the common Pharisaic heritage, recognized by all, both old and new Pharisees.

In regard to virtually all the rest of the Law, the group now associated with the Pharisees adhered to its ancient customs and

requiring washing one's hands after performing any ritual in the Temple (see Finkelstein, *Pharisees*, pp. 719ff). That ritual was apparently based on the necessity for washing away particles of sacred material adhering to one's hands because of the ritual. That was also why the high priest on the Day of Atonement had to wash his hands after doffing his priestly garments. See however further below.

[1] Mishnah *Kelim* 15.6.

[2] *Loc. cit.*

[3] See Finkelstein, *Pharisees*, pp. 718ff.

[4] Finkelstein, *Pharisees*, pp. 718ff.

precedents. It maintained that just as the Men of the Great Tribunal claimed that they had a tradition from the prophets in support of their views, so the new Pharisees had their own traditions. Thus both groups accepted the doctrine of the oral law – but agreed that it had come down in two versions, both of which were authentic.

No matter how much the views of the two Pharisaic factions might diverge, they were united (and recognized themselves as united) by their common acceptance of the authority of the Pharisaic Great Tribunal in the *interpretation* of the Law. In this they were opposed to the Sadducees, who regarded the Temple court as the final arbiter in all interpretations of the Torah, and denied any authority whatever to the Great Tribunal. From the point of view of all Pharisees, this rejection of the authority of the Great Tribunal marked the Sadducees as heretics.

We can only surmise how in actual practice the Great Tribunal dealt with new situations requiring the application of traditions concerning which the two Pharisaic factions disagreed. We may assume that during the lifetime of Simeon the Just no serious problem was presented by the existence of opposing traditions regarding so many religious issues. After all, he was presumably head of the Pharisaic Great Tribunal as well as high priest. Under his guidance the Great Tribunal could decide each case as it arose in accordance with the traditions of the faction to which the questioners belonged.

How and why did the Pharisaic Great Tribunal cease to function? Simeon's successor, his son Onias, probably adhered to his father's policies. However, he was soon ousted from his post as high priest by his brother Jason, who purchased the office from the Syrian king, Antiochus IV, and obtained recognition of Jerusalem as a Hellenized *polis*. This action meant, in effect, that the proclamation of Antiochus III making Jewish Law the law of the land was nullified. With Jason as high priest all authority over problems of public concern reverted to the Hellenized *gerousia*, which doubtless supported him. The date of *Shabuot* and of the *'Omer* sacrifice was once more determined according to the anti-Pharisaic tradition. The *Sukkot* ceremonies which the Pharisees stressed were abandoned. Incense was offered by the high priest on the Day of Atonement in accordance with the views held by the opponents of the Great Tribunal. The vast area over which the Pharisaic Great Tribunal was to have jurisdiction was lost to it. On the other hand it could no longer function, as it had before the days of Simeon the Just, as a court to decide many matters of ritual for individuals adhering to Pharisaism; for Pharisaism was no longer uniform. In many issues involved in the area, which alone was left to

Pharisaic authorities, two opposing traditions now prevailed – that of the old Pharisees and that of the neo-Pharisees. A local Pharisaic tribunal, in doubt as to the application of the Law in any area of the Jewish religion subject to its decision, would turn not to the Great Tribunal as a whole, but either to its proto-Shammaitic or to its proto-Hillelite factional group. Thus the factional tribunals became important, for it was their guidance that was sought. The united Great Tribunal had no occasion to offer any decision.

That Pharisaism itself did not come to an end as a united group with the end of the Great Tribunal was probably due to a remarkable development in its history.

The transformation of Jerusalem into the Hellenized *polis*, another Antioch, not only involved the loss of any national authority by the Pharisaic sages, but threatened many Pharisees with economic ruin. For many years, probably generations, even under the high priests before Simeon and his father, the Pharisaic labourers and merchants had possessed a virtual monopoly over the manufacture of oil and wine, as well as their sale in Jerusalem. This was because the Pharisees, with their strict adherence to the Law, alone could be trusted to be levitically pure, and therefore not to defile products manufactured or sold by them. Farmers who did not themselves heed the laws of purity hired Pharisaic labourers to prepare their wine and oil to prevent their defilement.[1]

They had to do so, for much of the wine and oil in Judea was bought by the Temple authorities, both for use in connection with the public sacrifices, and for sale to private individuals, who needed wine and oil for their sacrifices.

While most pre-Maccabean Sadducean high priests and their allies might disapprove of the Pharisees, their sages and their Great Tribunal, they were meticulous adherents of the Law as they understood it. They were doubtless particularly careful not to violate the laws of levitical purity in the Temple lest the transgression nullify the effectiveness of the sacrifices, and bring harm to the whole community, as well as to themselves. Speaking of priests of this kind at a much later time, *Tosefta* reports that they were more concerned about the laws of impurity than about homicide.[2]

Thus the Temple authorities necessarily bought wine and oil needed at the Temple only from Pharisaic traders; and these were careful to

[1] This seems to be implied in Mishnah *Terumoth* 3.4, which discusses the right of labourers engaged in the manufacture of wine to set aside the heave-offering while they were still working, although others might not do so.

[2] *Tosefta Kippurim* 1.12, ed. S. Lieberman, p. 225, and parallel passages there noted.

buy their wine and oil only from Pharisaic farmers or from farmers who employed only Pharisaic labourers in the manufacture of the liquids.

Quite aside from the economic necessity forced on the farmer who was not a Pharisee to hire such labourers to keep his wine and oil levitically pure, in order to sell his products in Jerusalem, there was his conscience. The Judean farmer might not bother to preserve his own levitical purity; but he feared greatly causing defilement to the Temple and its sacrifices. To do so might bring calamity on the whole community. Thus the oil or wine manufactured by a Judean farmer could be accepted as pure by anyone, if the farmer knew that the wine or oil was to be used for the Temple service.[1] He might not observe the laws of levitical purity, and might defile his own food, but he would not defile the wine or oil to be used in the Temple.

But with Jerusalem a Greek *polis*, under the rule of assimilationist high priests, the old concern for the Law doubtless disappeared. The farmer no longer needed to employ Pharisees in the manufacture of wine and oil; and the Temple and pilgrims were no longer concerned to buy their supplies from Pharisaic dealers.

Apparently, to save themselves from utter ruin, the Pharisees at this time created an association, modelled after those common in Greece and in the Hellenistic world.[2] Its members ate only food prepared in their homes or in those of their comrades.[3] A farmer desiring to sell his produce in Jerusalem, and not wishing to lose much of his custom there, would have to become a Pharisee, or continue as before to hire Pharisaic labourers.[4] The Pharisaic trader of Jerusalem's market-place would not purchase the farmer's wine or oil under any other circumstances. Thus, while the Temple authorities might no longer heed the

1 Mishnah *Ḥagigah* 3.4.

2 The literature on these associations is extensive. For convenience, see M. Rostovtzeff, *The Social and Economic History of the Hellenistic World* (Oxford, 1941), index, s.v. Associations, and works cited by him; Paul Vinogradoff, *Outlines of Historical Jurisprudence* (London, 1920), 2, pp. 119ff; Erich Ziebarth, *Das griechische Vereinswesen* (Leipzig, 1896); Franz Poland, *Geschichte des grieschischen Vereinswesens* (Leipzig, 1909).

3 See Mishnah *Demai* 2.3.

4 See Mishnah *Terumoth* 3.4, which takes it for granted that a farmer who was an *'am ha-'areṣ* (i.e. was not meticulous in the observance of the laws of levitical purity) would hire Pharisees, who were meticulous, to manufacture his wine or oil. Therefore so long as the Temple was in existence, any Judean was trusted if he said that the wine or oil in his possession was fit for use in the Temple. Even after the destruction of the Temple, it could be assumed that the wine or oil was levitically pure so long as the workers were engaged in their labour. Even Gentiles frequently hired Jews to prepare wine so that Jews would be willing to purchase it (Mishnah *Abodah Zarah* 4.11), for otherwise Jews would not purchase wine manufactured by a Gentile.

laws of levitical purity, and many pilgrims, too, might defy these laws, there would still be sufficient reason for a farmer to hire Pharisaic labourers for his work.

The members of this Pharisaic association were called *ḥaberim*, a term generally synonymous in the Talmud with Pharisees.[1] Such Hellenistic associations usually had a president. The president of the Pharisaic association was called *nasi*, a term used also, as revealed in a surviving fragment, for the same office, by a Phoenician association for its president.[2] Apparently, this association was called *ha-k*e*neset*. Its members are therefore seometimes also referred to as *b*e*nē ha-k*e*neset*. They were not authoritative scholars; but like their colleagues, meticulous in their observance of the Law. Whether there was a difference in connotation between *ḥaberim* and *b*e*nē ha-k*e*neset* cannot be determined.[3]

Jose b. Joezer of Zeredah became the first *nasi* of this association.[4] But as Pharisaism now included two systems of interpretation of the law, it was necessary to have a separate tribunal for those adhering to the norms of the fraction not represented by him. The head of this tribunal was Jose b. Johanan of Jerusalem.

Not until the rise of the independent Hasmonean state under Simeon the Maccabee was there a need for a restoration of the Great Tribunal of all the Pharisees.

When Judas Maccabeus for a time, and somewhat later his brother, Jonathan, acted as high priests in the Temple, they seem to have consulted the tribunal of their faction when in doubt as to the correct ritual practice.[5] As is evident from some of their actions, such as

1 Cf. Mishnah *Demai* 2.3. In later times *ḥaber* came to be used for scholars; but that happened when the Pharisaic association had ceased to exist.

2 See Poland, *Geschichte*, p. 375.

3 See L. Finkelstein, *Ha-Perushim w*e*'anše k*e*neset ha-g*e*dolah* (New York, 1950), p. 83.

4 Mishnah *Ḥagigah* 2.2. In *Ha-Perushim*, pp. 22ff, I argued that the term *nasi* as used in Mishnah *Ḥagigah* 2.2 and elsewhere in the Talmud meant president of the Pharisaic tribunal, and not of the national judiciary. The term *nasi* occurs once in the Mishnah (*Nedarim* 5.5) as referring to the head of the state. Obviously Jose b. Joezer and his successors did not occupy this office. Under the Hasmoneans the head of state was the high priest; under the Herodians it was the king.

5 Hence the testimony of Jose b. Joezer regarding the laws of impurity (Mishnah *Eduyoth* 8.4). Jose b. Joezer testified that only a person who had himself been defiled through contact with a corpse was levitically impure according to biblical law and therefore had to offer a sacrifice if he entered the Temple precincts, having forgotten his impurity. The same view was held by the 'ancient elders', i.e. the *gerousia* before him (see *Sifra Ḥobah, pereq* 12.1, ed. Weiss, 22d). He also testified that the fluids of the Temple, i.e. those used for the libations, wine and oil, could not be defiled, according to biblical law (ibid.). He gave these opinions not in Hebrew, as was customary among the *Tannaim* and in all Temple conversations about the ritual (cf. Mishnah

Judas Maccabeus' praying for the dead,[1] their faction was that led by Jose ben Joezer; and indeed we find Jose b. Joezer giving them instructions regarding the rules guiding the Temple.[2]

It was apparently a rule of this Pharisaic association that when its president died he was not formally replaced so long as his colleague survived; it being held improper to appoint a new president of the association as a whole over the head of the surviving member of the pair. Thus, although Jose b. Joezer of Zeredah was executed about 160 B.C.E. by his nephew, Alcimus, his successor, Joshua b. Peraḥyah, apparently did not take office for a number of years, possibly not before Judea became an independent state under Simeon the Hasmonean in 142 B.C.E.

There is nothing in the decision taken by the first Pharisaic 'pair', or in the stories told of them, to suggest that the courts over which they presided had any function other than offering guidance in purely ritual matters to their followers. We hear, indeed, of incidents 'in the time of the Greeks', when a man was executed because he rode a horse on the Sabbath, and another was punished with stripes because he had sexual intercourse with his wife in public.[3] 'These decisions were not made because of the Law, but to prevent infraction of the Law.' If either of the Joses had been involved in the decisions, that would presumably have been recorded. Apparently these were military decisions made by a military tribunal consisting of zealots, who considered such conduct evidence of Hellenistic inclinations. We are also told of a 'court of the Hasmoneans' which decreed that an Israelite having sexual intercourse with a pagan woman violated at least two basic commandments; and if he was a priest, four.[4] Presumably, the rule was set up so that a transgressor would be punished separately for each violation. But again neither Jose is mentioned as a member of this Court. Possibly then this 'Hasmonean court' was also a military tribunal, determined to prevent rape of pagan women in the course of the wars.

But, as observed, a moment came when it was necessary to reconstitute the old Pharisaic Great Tribunal. This was when Simeon the Maccabee, having achieved virtual independence for Judea, desired to

Yoma 1.3; 3.1; 6.8; *Tamid* 1.4; 3.1, 2, 3; 5.1), but in Aramaic. Why? Apparently because he was not addressing his Pharisaic colleagues, but the Maccabean priests and their retainers, who did not know what the Temple regulations in such matters had been before its defilement by the Hellenists, and the conversation did not take place in the Temple courts, but outside them.

[1] 2 Macc. 12:43f.

[2] See p. 268 n. 5. It seems clear from Mishnah *Ḥagigah* 2.2 that Jose b. Joezer was the first leader of the faction ultimately led by Shammai.

[3] *b. Yebamoth* 90b.

[4] *b. Abodah Zarah* 36b.

have the displacement of the old Zadokide dynasty by himself and his descendants legitimized. To be generally accepted this decision could not emanate from the Temple tribunal, consisting now to a great extent of heads of families whom the Maccabean revolt had enriched, and who were therefore creatures of the Maccabees. The decision had to come from the scholars of Jerusalem, and be accepted as a decision of pious, learned men, who had no personal interest in the matter. It also had to be made by a court in which both Pharisaic factions were united. The Great Pharisaic Tribunal performed this function (1 Macc. 14:28ff), probably under the presidency of Joshua b. Peraḥyah, the successor of Jose b. Joezer as *nasi* of the Pharisaic association. (The inscription quoted in 1 Macc. 14:28ff speaks only of 'a great tribunal'. And while it mentions the merits of Simeon and Jonathan, it says nothing about the reason for the displacement of the former Zadokide dynasty, which had become Hellenistic. Obviously for the purpose it was intended to serve, to unite the whole nation under Simeon, pejorative remarks about the Zadokides would have been out of place and it would not have been appropriate for the Great Tribunal to use the opportunity to establish its authority to decide on the choice of the high priest).

It was to this re-established Great Tribunal that John Hyrcanus turned when his and his family's right to the high priesthood was challenged, both to investigate the claim and to punish the slanderer. However, when the Pharisaic court refused to condemn the culprit to death, but instead imposed the penalty of stripes, John Hyrcanus was infuriated.[1] In his anger he suppressed the Pharisaic courts, as well as, perhaps, their association.

When, after the death of Josua b. Peraḥyah and Nittai of Arbela, the Pharisees wanted to appoint Judah b. Tabbai as *nasi* of their association, despite the high priest's opposition, Judah fled the dangerous honour, seeking refuge in Alexandria,[2] where he remained for more than thirty years.[3]

However, when Queen Salome Alexandra, the widow of Alexander Janneus, ascended the throne of Judea in the year 76 B.C.E., she

[1] *b. Qiddušin* 66a; cf. Jos. *Ant.* XIII.294.

[2] See *Yer. Ḥagigah* 2.2, 77d. In *Ab. d'R.N.* I, ch. 10, 22a, Judah b. Tabbai is quoted as having said, 'Before I entered upon this high office [the *nasi* of the Pharisees], I would have liked to persecute anyone who proposed it to me even to the extent of [depriving him of] his livelihood. Now that I have entered upon it, if anyone tries to remove me, I will pour a kettle of hot water on him'. Cf. *Ab. d'R.N.* II, ch. 20, p. 22a. The statement confirms the story of his flight from the appointment, and of his reluctance to accept office even under Queen Salome.

[3] Apparently from before 109 B.C.E., the date of the death of John Hyrcanus, until 76 B.C.E., the date of the ascension of Queen Salome to the throne.

determined to win the Pharisaic leaders to her support.[1] Accordingly, she made Judah b. Tabbai and Simeon b. Sheṭaḥ heads of the Temple Tribunal, now called the Great Sanhedrin. The Pharisaic Great Tribunal was not re-established; but the two Pharisaic sages presided over the Temple court, which consisted overwhelmingly of heads of priestly and lay aristocratic families, precisely as had the Temple courts of pre-Maccabean times. But these new aristocrats were people who were pro-Hasmonean in every way.

Perhaps it was because of the nature of the office to which he was called that Judah b. Tabbai at first refused to accept even the invitation. However, he was persuaded.

Both he and Simon b. Sheṭaḥ, being untrained to power, did not recognize the necessary restraints of power. Thus the tribunal over which they presided rendered decisions which astonished later generations. One of these was the execution in one day of 80 women accused of witchcraft.[2]

How many other Pharisaic sages, if any, were members of the tribunal which rendered such amazing judgements, is unknown. However, a very interesting passage in *Tosefta* asserts that: 'Any Sanhedrin which includes two scholars able to carry on a discussion, while the rest can follow it, is fit to be a Sanhedrin. If there are three [able to carry on a discussion], it is moderately satisfactory (lit. *middle*, perhaps *average*). If there are four, it is a wise [Sanhedrin]'.[3]

No wonder that the astonishing decisions of Judah b. Tabbai and Simeon b. Sheṭaḥ were approved by their colleagues, who owed their offices not to erudition or qualifications as judges, but to wealth, and their pro-Hasmonean proclivities.

(Any doubt regarding the accuracy, in general, of the rabbinic tradition about the 'pairs' must be removed in the light of the astonishing candour of the rabbinic authorities about the activities of these judges. Not only did Simeon b. Sheṭaḥ execute 80 women for witchcraft, but either he or Judah b. Tabbai – the texts disagree about the identity of the scholar involved – executed a witness who had been shown to have testified falsely, although Pharisaic law permitted

[1] See Jos. *Ant.* XIII.405.

[2] There can be no doubt about the fact; for R. Eliezer and his colleagues referred to the incident centuries later (Mishnah *Sanhedrin* 6.7).

[3] *Tosefta Sanhedrin* 8.1, ed. Zuckermandel, p. 427. The passage seemed incomprehensible to the Babylonian authorities, who on the basis of *Tosefta Ḥagigah* 2.9, ed. Lieberman, p. 383, assumed that all the members of the Sanhedrin were fine scholars, able to carry on effective legal discussions. Accordingly, they changed the text completely (see *b. Sanhedrin* 17b). But the very strangeness of the rule set down in *Tosefta Sanhedrin* 8.1 is evidence of its accuracy.

neither witness to be punished, unless both were proven false.[1] It is clear that the tradition regarding the 'pairs' is quite accurate, but, of course, it has to be understood correctly.)

On the death of both members of the pair consisting of Judah b. Tabbai and Simeon b. Sheṭaḥ, they were succeeded by Shemaiah and Abtalion, whom Josephus calls Sameas and Pollio.[2] It is said that these scholars were descended from proselytes.[3] Perhaps their lack of distinguished ancestry made both of them particularly acceptable to the Hasmonean ruler who was subservient to Antipater, the father of Herod.

The members of this pair each had his factional court, which decided ritual questions, but seem to have presided also, as had Judah b. Tabbai and Simeon b. Sheṭaḥ before them, over the Temple tribunal. It was in the latter capacity that Sameas summoned Herod to answer for the execution of some Galileans while he was governor of that province. Herod appeared,[4] surrounded with a bodyguard, whose presence overwhelmed all the members of the tribunal, except Sameas and Pollio, with fear. Herod was thus never brought to trial. Nevertheless when he attained power as king, he executed all the members of the Temple court of Sanhedrin, with the exception of Sameas and Pollio, who had advised the people of Jerusalem not to resist him.[5]

But with the ascendancy of Herod the role of Sameas and Pollio as heads of the Temple tribunal, and indeed the tribunal itself, came to an end. Shemaiah and Abtalion were still heads of the Pharisaic courts; but the judicial authority was bestowed by Herod on his own creatures.

As heads of the Pharisaic factions, Sameas and Pollio were succeeded by Hillel and a certain Menahem; but Menahem was soon replaced with Shammai.[6] None of these scholars seem to have held any national judicial office. They were simply leaders of the Pharisees, Hillel as the president, Shammai as head of a factional court. Despite the comparatively large amount of information we have about these scholars, far more than about their predecessors, there is no hint that they possessed judicial authority of the kind exercised by Judah b. Tabbai and Simeon b. Sheṭaḥ in their time.

In the revolt against Archelaus,[7] the son and successor of Herod, the Shammaites took an active part, and they may indeed have been the

[1] See *Mekilta Mishpaṭim*, ch. 20, p. 327; and parallel passages there noted.
[2] Mishnah *Ḥagigah* 2.2; Jos. *Ant.* XIV.172–4.
[3] *b. Yoma* 71b.
[4] Jos. *Ant.* XIV.172–4.
[5] Jos. *Ant.* XIV.175–6.
[6] Mishnah *Ḥagigah* 2.2; *Ab. d'R.N.* II, ch. 22, 24a.
[7] For the story of this revolt, see Jos. *Ant.* XVII.215ff.

leaders of the movement. It was probably at this time of great patriotic and nationalist fervour that Hillel, the pacifist, was ousted from office as president of the Pharisaic association, and replaced by Shammai, who so dominated the joint Pharisaic Tribunal that he was able to bring about general acceptance of some Shammaitic ritual notions, as well as their political ones.[1] In fact, at one time, when they were in control of the Temple, the Shammaites tried to prevent Hillel from offering a sacrifice in accordance with the teachings of his faction.[2] No wonder that when the revolt was crushed the Shammaitic faction, as well as their factional court, were suppressed. Thus when Hillel died he was succeeded by Rabban Gamaliel I, his grandson, who had no associate.

By the time of Rabban Gamaliel I, the Temple tribunal had been re-established.[3] Herod, having executed the members of the old Temple tribunal (with the exception of Sameas and Pollio), had appointed various high priests who were loyal to him.

One of the high priests appointed by Herod was his father-in-law, Boethus. While the Hasmonean priests had followed the Pharisaic views in their conduct of the Temple, rather than those of their Zadokide predecessors, Boethus and his associates saw no need to do so. Thus the doctrines held by the high-priestly families before Onias and Simeon the Righteous had begun to make approaches to the Pharisees were revived. The followers of the revived Sadducean doctrine came to be known as Boethusians, and are generally so described in the Talmudic works. But there was no doctrinal division between the Sadducees and Boethusians.[4] The difference was simply

[1] See *b. Shabbath* 17a.

[2] *Tosefta Ḥagigah* 2.11, ed. S. Lieberman, p. 385 and parallel passages.

[3] Rabban Gamaliel I went to the Sanhedrin of the Chamber of Hewn Stone, which was the Temple tribunal of his time, to consult them about a question, specifically stated to be within its jurisdiction (see Mishnah *Peah* 2.6; and cf. *Sifre Deut.* 152, p. 206). That he was a member of the Sanhedrin but not its president is further implied in Acts 5:34. However, it appears from *Tosefta Sanhedrin* 2.6 (ed. Zuckermandel, pp. 416–17) that in his day the Pharisaic tribunal had the authority to determine the calendar, and even to add an intercalary month when necessary. That was not one of the prerogatives given the Temple court, according to *Sifre*, Deut. and parallel passages. But cf. *b. Sanhedrin* 87a.

[4] Cf. Mishnah *Menaḥot* 10.3; *Tosefta Sukkah* 3.1, ed. Lieberman, p. 366. Herod's penchant for priests descended from the ousted Zadokide dynasty and its followers is readily understood. One of the most important means he used to establish himself was to avoid giving the Hasmoneans or any of their followers important posts. The Boethusians were probably descended from the Zadokide and allied clans, who had retained their ancestral traditions, and followed them, despite the precedents set by the Hasmoneans and the teachings of the Pharisees.

that the Sadducees were descended from the ancient aristocratic families, while the Boethusians were, in general, the creatures of Herod and loyal to him and his successors.

Herod had doubtless enriched some priestly families. The heads of these families constituted the Temple tribunal. Rabban Gamaliel I, unlike Judah b. Tabbai, was not permitted to act as head of this Sanhedrin, but he seems to have been one of its members.[1]

After the destruction of the Temple R. Eleazar b. R. Zadok told how in his childhood he had witnessed the burning to death of the daughter of a priest, who had committed adultery.[2] His colleagues remarked that the Sanhedrin of that time was not learned in the Law.[3] Surely rabbinic scholars would not have dared assert that a Pharisaic tribunal of earlier times, over which Rabban Gamaliel I had presided, consisted of members ignorant of the Law. The tribunal which they condemned as ignorant was the Temple tribunal, of which Rabban Gamaliel I was probably one member, and which consisted overwhelmingly, like the Hellenistic *gerousia*, of heads of wealthy families. These were now heads of families enriched by Herod and his children.

After the death of Rabban Gamaliel I, he was succeeded by his son, Rabban Simeon b. Gamaliel I.[4] in Rabban Simeon's time the Pharisees re-established the bi-factional leadership of their group, so that Rabban Simeon b. Gamaliel I had an associate, namely Rabban Johanan b. Zakkai.[5] This 'pair' too did not preside over the Temple Sanhedrin, the head of which was now the high priest.[6]

1 See p. 273 n. 3.

2 Mishnah *Sanhedrin* 7.2.

3 Cf. the remark of Rab Joseph in *b. Sanhedrin* 52b.

4 That Rabban Simeon b. Gamaliel I was the *nasi* in his time is clearly stated in *b. Shabbath* 15a, and is also implied in Mishnah *Keritboth* 1.7, as well as in *Midrash Tannaim* 26.13, p. 176. That Rabban Johanan b. Zakkai was his *'Ab Bet-din* seems evident from his title *Rabban*, reserved after the time of the Rabban Gamaliel I (before whom no such title was apparently used) for the heads of the Pharisees. It is even more emphatically implied in *Midrash Tannaim* 26.13, where his name is coupled with that of Rabban Simeon b. Gamaliel I in the epistles calling on the various communities to separate the tithes. Apparently this letter was addressed to the Pharisaic groups.

5 See preceding note.

6 This seems evident from *Tosefta Parah* 3.8 ed. Zuckermandel, p. 632, where we are told that, to prevent the high priest from following the rule of the Sadducees in the preparation of the red heifer (see Finkelstein, *Pharisees*, pp. 661ff), Rabban Johanan b. Zakkai had to resort to violence. Apparently the high priest himself presided over this ceremony, in accordance with the teachings of *Sifre* Deut. 351, p. 408. In *Sifre* Deut. 152, p. 206, the reference to the ritual of the red heifer (which would be expected there on the basis of *Sifre* Deut. 351), is replaced by 'purification of the leper'. Apparently the older reading had given authority to the *gerousia*, with the high

Throughout this period, the influence of the Pharisaic tribunal among the Jews of the Diaspora had been considerable, and was probably growing. This influence may in fact be traced back to the times before the Maccabees, the days of Onias and Simeon the Righteous. Probably this influence derived from the contact of the Pharisees with the pilgrims who came to the Temple for Passover, and in lesser numbers for the other festivals. But it is also possible that Pharisaic emissaries travelled to nearby countries to communicate with the Jews dwelling there. Thus the authors of the Septuagint living in Alexandria generally followed the Pharisaic interpretation of Scripture, apparently as a matter of course.[1] This tendency included such matters as siding with the Pharisees in the explanation of the word *Šabbat* in Lev. 23:11 as meaning festival day, that is the first day of Passover rather than the weekly Sabbath. This fundamental Pharisaic view was bitterly opposed by the Temple priests; and it is revealing for the origin of the Septuagint that its authors followed the Pharisees rather than the Sadducees.[2]

When Judah b. Tabbai fled to Alexandria, apparently he found so ready a welcome there that he was reluctant to return to Jerusalem.

Alexandrian Jews (perhaps living in Jerusalem) turned to Hillel when they were unsure about the effect of some of their customs on the marriage law.[3] The fact that the Elders of Bathyra, who had immigrated from Babylonia, were persuaded to follow Hillel's interpretation of the law regarding the Paschal lamb, as soon as he said that it was based on a tradition stemming from Shemaiah and Abtalion,[4] further confirms the assumption that Pharisaic influence extended beyond the borders of Palestine. As already observed (above, p. 273), Rabban Gamaliel I wrote an epistle to the communities of the

priest at its head, over the ritual of the preparation of the red heifer; but later authorities denied them this prerogative. Cf. *Sifre* Num. 123, p. 151, and see also *Sifre Zutta* 19.3, p. 302. According to the tradition of the school of R. Ishmael, Rabban Johanan b. Zakkai *presided* over the preparation of the red heifer; and indeed his action may indicate that he considered himself to be presiding over it. His making the high priest unfit to perform the ritual, through an act of violence, was an assertion of the right of the Pharisaic tribunal in this matter.

1 See Z. Frankel, *Über den Einfluss der palästinischen Exegese auf die alexandrinische Hermeneutik* (Leipzig, 1851).

2 See Finkelstein, *Pharisees*, pp. 641ff; and see Septuagint to Lev. 23:15ff.

3 *b. Baba Meṣia* 104a.

4 *Yer. Pesaḥim* 6.1, 33a; *b. Pesaḥ* 66a. According to *Sifra Tazria, pereq* 9.15, ed. Weiss 67a, *Yer. Pesaḥim* 6.1, 33a, Hillel came to Palestine 'because of three issues'. It is often assumed that he came to find the answers to three questions; but it is also possible that he came to impose three Pharisaic views on the community, which, following the Temple tribunal, held otherwise.

Diaspora, announcing the addition of an intercalary month, when that occurred. Thus even before the events of the year 70 C.E., when the Temple was destroyed, the Pharisaic authorities had laid the foundations for the vast influence exerted on the Diaspora by the rabbinic scholars of later times.

The large number of pilgrims who came to Jerusalem from beyond the borders of Palestine for the various festivals, but particularly for Passover, reflected the influence of the Pharisees; for it was their Great Tribunal, as, in their time, the tribunal of the Hillelites, that sought to stimulate mass pilgrimages. The Temple priests did little to encourage them, and indeed preferred not to have crowds at the Sanctuary at any time.[1]

Josephus, in his interpretation of the Law, generally adopted the Shammaitic, rather than the Hillelite view.[2] He was a priest, and had studied in schools conducted by priests, who tended to be Shammaitically-minded. Perhaps he did not know the tradition of the Hillelites. But if he did, he would have found the explanation of two Pharisaic systems too complicated to explain to his pagan readers.

Thus a careful reading of the rabbinic texts shows that there is no conflict between them and the non-rabbinic sources regarding the role of the Pharisaic sages in the Sanhedrin. The belief that the two types of sources contradict one another is an error, arising from the view that in a stormy period of constant political upheaval the relation of the Pharisaic sages to the Temple tribunal, as well as the judicial authority of the Pharisaic sages, could possibly remain constant. The fact that each generation of Pharisees was guided by two scholars instead of one is accounted for by the division among the Pharisees from the time of the Maccabees onward. The assertion of the Mishnah that one member of each pair was a *nasi* was not a figment of rabbinic imagination, but reflected the reality of the organization of the Pharisaic association, established after the manner of other similar Hellenistic associations.

The long hiatus between the pair consisting of Joshua b. Peraḥyah and his colleague and the appointment of the succeeding pair, as well as the rule that no new *nasi* could be appointed while one of the pair was living, explain the extraordinary length of time during which the five pairs presided over the Pharisaic association.

[1] See Finkelstein, *Pharisees*, p. 707.

[2] This is obvious, for example, from the rule he set down that the verse 'an eye for an eye' is to be taken literally, except that the offender may pay ransom for his eye and thus escape bodily harm (*Ant.* IV.280; cf. the view of R. Eliezer in *b. Baba Qamma* 83b). The same rule is given in the name of R. Eliezer in *Mekilta Mišpaṭim*, ch. 8, p. 277.

It thus turns out from the discussion in the preceding chapter and this that the rabbinic tradition regarding the Great Tribunal of the Pharisees, as well as that describing the leadership of the Pharisaic factions after the time of the Great Tribunal, is quite consistent with what is told in the New Testament and Josephus, and is trustworthy when properly understood.

CHAPTER 8

ANTIOCHUS IV

For about twenty years the Jews of Palestine lived peacefully under the system of government established by Antiochus III after his conquest of the country in 200 B.C.E. (see above, chapter 2). Some of the leading families may for personal or traditional reasons have preferred the Ptolemaic rule, but to the majority it made no difference whether they were governed from Alexandria or Antioch. The son and successor of the conqueror, Seleucus IV (187–175 B.C.E.), continued, during the first part of his reign, his father's wise and tolerant policy and made contributions to the sacrifices in the Temple in Jerusalem. When troubles arose towards the end of Seleucus IV's reign, their causes must be sought in internal tension and strife between various factions or groups within the Jewish community. Already in the third century B.C.E. the antagonism between the rich and influential Tobiads and the Oniads, who held the office of high priest, had disclosed a serious disagreement within the leading Jewish circles as to the attitude towards the problems of co-existence with the surrounding peoples and a certain assimilation of the dominant Greek–Hellenistic culture (see chapter 2).

The first incident in this new series of quarrels among the Jews was the clash between the high priest, Onias III, and the *epistatēs* or financial administrator of the Temple, a certain Simon. As the latter was unable to secure the post of *agoranomos* or overseer of the market for himself on account of the high priest's opposition, he turned to the Seleucid governor of the province of Coele-Syria and Phoenicia, Apollonius, son of Menestheus, and revealed to him the existence of large funds in the Temple treasury, suggesting that the money might be appropriated by the Syrian king. Seleucus IV was naturally not averse to a suggestion that might help to alleviate the financial difficulties created by the war indemnity to Rome which the treaty of Apamea of 188 B.C.E. had imposed on the Seleucid kingdom. He soon dispatched his prime minister Heliodorus with instructions to confiscate the Temple treasure. The protests of Onias III, who pointed out that the money – 400 talents of silver and 200 talents of gold – belonged partly to widows and orphans, were of no avail. According to the legend, supernatural intervention was needed to avert the sacrilege. When Heliodorus entered the treasury he was whipped by two angels and had to be carried out. The opponents of the high priest were impudent enough to suggest that the scene had been carefully staged by him. However this may be, Heliodorus returned to Antioch without any money.

In spite of this abortive attempt on the Temple treasure, Simon still commanded a following among his compatriots and continued his campaign against the high priest, backed by the Seleucid governor of the province. The quarrel soon took a serious turn; political murder occurred in the city, and the Temple state of Judea was on the brink of civil war. Apparently Simon's faction was gaining ground. In this crisis, Onias III saw his only chance of maintaining authority in an appeal to the Seleucid king. Without royal intervention the re-establishment of peace in Jerusalem seemed impossible. Accordingly Onias III left the holy city for the royal court at Antioch in order to explain the situation to the king and implore his help. The discord of the Jewish factions had grown to such proportions that both parties now looked to their Greek overlords for a settlement of their disputes.

At this juncture, on 3 September 175 B.C.E., Seleucus IV died, murdered by Heliodorus, and after an interval of a few months his younger brother, Antiochus IV, who had lived as a hostage in Rome since 189 B.C.E. and had only recently been exchanged with a son of Seleucus IV, Demetrius (I), established himself on the Seleucid throne. At about the same time Simon, the *epistatēs* of the Temple, vanishes from history. However, his disappearance did not produce peace and order within the Jewish community. While Onias III was still in Antioch, waiting in order to obtain the king's help against his enemies, his brother Jason acquired the position of high priest for himself. During an interview with Antiochus IV he promised to pay a yearly tribute of 360 talents plus an additional 80 talents from other revenues.[1] Furthermore he offered to pay another 150 talents for permission to establish a *gymnasion* in Jerusalem, introduce the institution of *ephēbia* for the Jewish youth, and constitute a list of the 'Antiochenes in Jerusalem', which undoubtedly meant that the holy city of the Jews was to be refounded on the Greek pattern as a new Antiochia.

It is hardly surprising that Antiochus IV granted Jason's requests. Money is always a telling argument, and the king had every reason to

[1] 2 Macc. 4.8. It is not expressly stated that the figures cover a yearly tribute, but this is the most likely interpretation.

look with favour on a scheme which, without any expense to the royal treasury, purported to extend Greek culture to a section of his non-Greek subjects. It should be remembered that Antiochus IV had newly ascended the throne and had lived in Rome and Athens since 189 B.C.E. His knowledge of the state of affairs in Judea must have been derived from the reports of his officials and was presumably rather limited. More especially he can hardly have had any deep understanding of the peculiarities of the Jewish religion. And why should he mistrust Jason, who was a Jew of the best family and eager to introduce Hellenistic civilization among his compatriots? Jason's money and the general interest taken by Antiochus in Greek culture were sufficient motives for his decision to appoint Jason high priest. We have no reason to suppose that the Syrian king at this early date was already following a well-defined domestic policy aiming at the introduction of Greek culture throughout his realm.

After his return to Jerusalem, Jason set to work on the Hellenization of the holy city with the fervent energy of a convert. At the foot of the citadel he founded a *gymnasion*, where the youth of Jerusalem was instructed according to the Greek system of education. Even some priests neglected their duties in the Temple in order to throw the discus. Jason soon gave further proof of his liberal attitude. To the horror of the orthodox Jews he sent delegates in the name of the 'Antiochenes in Jerusalem' to the festival of Heracles in Tyre. The delegates brought 300 drachms of silver for offerings to the god, but moral scruples induced them to use the money for a less offensive purpose.

During Jason's tenure of office Antiochus IV visited Jerusalem, where he was received in great splendour, entering the city accompanied by torch-bearers and amid cheering crowds. However, in spite of his deference, Jason soon lost influence with the king. When in 172 or 171 B.C.E. he sent Menelaus, a brother of Onias III's opponent Simon, to Antioch in order to pay tribute and deal with various matters of administration, Menelaus seized the opportunity to insinuate himself into the favour of the king. On the promise that he would increase the tribute, he was recognized as high priest and returned to Jerusalem with a royal letter of appointment. Jason was deposed and fled to the country of the Ammonites beyond the Jordan.

Up to this point the Seleucid intervention in Judea had met with no organized opposition. From the silence of our sources it seems safe to conclude that the deposition of Onias III and the appointment of Jason had caused no serious troubles. Nor had the Hellenizing policy of Jason led to any disturbance of daily life in Judea, so far as we know.

The majority of the Jewish population undoubtedly looked with surprise and indignation on the 'Hellenizers' in the *palaestra*, but as long as they were left to live their own lives under the laws of the Torah, they did not react to the inherent challenge of the new way of life. Moreover, the number of Jews who sympathized with Jason and his policy of Hellenization must have been considerable, especially among leading circles in Jerusalem. Even from our biased sources it appears clearly that many Jews of the time, also among the priests, felt attracted by Hellenistic culture and were eager to acquire a formal Greek education in order to place themselves on an equal footing with the neighbouring peoples and overcome the isolation into which the orthodox followers of the Torah constrained themselves. To these people the strict Jewish separatism meant material and spiritual poverty to the whole nation.

The relative stability of the situation was changed with the appointment of Menelaus. He had belonged to the circle of 'Hellenizers' around Jason, but his position in Jewish society was quite different from that of his predecessor. While Jason had been of the best blood, a member of the hereditary family of high priests, Menelaus was not of the seed of Aaron.[1] As an upstart he did not automatically command the respect and loyalty of his compatriots. The Hellenizing Jews, who had always been a minority, were seriously weakened by this personal strife between their leaders, which split the party completely. Much influence seems still to have been wielded by the Tobiads who eventually supported Menelaus against Jason. Jason and his followers would have paid great attention to the rapidly deteriorating relations between Syria and Egypt, and with the Seleucid government backing Menelaus Jason must have pinned his hopes on an Egyptian intervention and re-conquest of Palestine.

Moreover, Menelaus had bought his position at a high price and soon found himself in financial difficulties. Most of the Temple funds had presumably been used by Jason to finance his various attempts to introduce Hellenistic institutions, and Menelaus most probably had to meet his obligations from other sources. The tribute to the king was nearly doubled, and when funds were lacking the only way to procure the money was a drastic increase of the taxes paid by the people, a measure which seldom makes its author popular. In this particular case the method proved insufficient. The money for the royal tribute was

[1] Josephus, *Antiquitates Judaicae* XII.238 (cf. XX.235) makes Menelaus a brother of Onias III and Jason and says that he was also called Onias. It can hardly be doubted that this tradition was invented in order to cover the fact that the high-priestly office had been defiled by a person of low origin.

not forthcoming, and after a short while Menelaus and Sostratus, the Seleucid official responsible for the collection of the royal taxes, were called to Antioch to explain the situation and render their accounts.

However, on their arrival in the capital, Menelaus and Sostratus found that Antiochus IV was conducting a small campaign in Cilicia and had left one of his friends, Andronicus, in charge of the government. Menelaus immediately resorted to bribery, offering the influential friend of the king some gold vessels from the Temple in Jerusalem. Other gold vessels from the same source were sold at Tyre and other cities to procure at least a part of the money to be paid to the king. The former high priest, Onias III, who was still detained in Antioch, somehow discovered the manipulations of Menelaus and was not slow to give vent to his indignation. Menelaus and Andronicus resolved to remove this dangerous witness, and after having lured Onias out of asylum in the temple of Daphne, Andronicus had him killed. According to Jewish tradition Antiochus resented the murder, and Andronicus, who had misused his authority, was condemned and executed, while Menelaus surprisingly enough escaped punishment.

During his absence from Jerusalem Menelaus had left his brother Lysimachus as his deputy. Lysimachus followed the precedent set by his brother and removed a great number of gold objects, vessels, and so on, from the Temple. When his sacrilegious acts became known in the city the population rose against him, and Lysimachus was killed in the street fighting which ensued. This was the first armed conflict between the Jewish people and the authority of the high priest appointed by Antiochus IV. The result of Menelaus' high-handed policy was that the opposition against him grew in force and gained the open adherence of the council of elders. Three members of the *gerousia* were sent to Tyre to lodge the complaints of the Jewish people against the high priest at the royal tribunal. In this crisis, Menelaus again resorted to bribery. When his cause seemed lost, he prevailed on Ptolemeus son of Dorymenes, the new *stratēgos* of Coele-Syria and Phoenicia, to influence the king in his favour. Consequently Menelaus was acquitted and the three Jewish delegates condemned to death. Menelaus was confirmed in his office and returned to Jerusalem as a 'great enemy of his compatriots'. The gap between the Hellenizing high priests, backed by royal authority, and the more conservative majority of the Jews had widened considerably and was not easily bridged.

Shortly after his interview with Menelaus, in the autumn of 170 B.C.E., Antiochus IV set out on his first expedition to Egypt, taking advantage of the opportunities for an attack which the feeble Egyptian government offered him. It is natural to assume that the opponents of

Menelaus in Judea became more openly pro-Egyptian with the outbreak of war between the two Hellenistic kingdoms, but for about a year our sources are silent as to what happened in Judea. In the autumn of 169 B.C.E., on his way back from Egypt, Antiochus IV visited Jerusalem for the second time. On this occasion he robbed the Temple of its treasures of gold and silver, including even the sacrificial instruments in his booty.[1] To the Jews this was an act of sheer plunder; but to Antiochus the matter may have looked quite different. Menelaus was still high priest, and from 2 Maccabees we know that he personally introduced the king into the Temple. As Menelaus had shown no hesitation in procuring money for the payment of tribute by selling the holy vessels already a year before, it seems most probable that he was also responsible for the confiscation of the Temple treasure in 169 B.C.E. What appeared to the Jews a sacrilege may have seemed to Antiochus IV to have been a legal administrative measure to recover the arrears of tribute, which Menelaus presumably still owed the royal treasury. The Syrian king returned to Antioch with 1,800 talents, a little less than three years' tribute according to his agreement with Menelaus.

We have no information as to what happened next in Jerusalem and Judea. A new clash between the Jews and the Seleucid authorities occurred in the late summer or early autumn of 168 B.C.E. During Antiochus' second campaign in Egypt it was rumoured in Judea that the Syrian king had died. This news called Jason, who must have been watching the situation carefully, back from his exile among the Ammonites. At the head of a small private army, a thousand strong, he launched an attack on Jerusalem and captured the city by surprise, while Menelaus took refuge with the Syrian garrison in the citadel. A general slaughter of Jason's opponents followed, and the monumental entrance gate to the Temple area was burnt in the confusion. Antiochus IV was on his way back from his humiliating interview with the Roman ambassador, Popilius Laenas, who had put an end to his plans of dominating Egypt, when he heard the news of Jason's *coup de main*. He inferred from the reports that Judea had rebelled against the royal authority, marched against Jerusalem with his army, and took the city by assault. The miserable inhabitants again saw soldiers plundering and murdering in the streets of their city. Jason had to withdraw for the second time beyond the Jordan. Menelaus was reinstated in his position as high priest. Antiochus IV soon returned to his capital, but in order

[1] 1 Macc. 1:20–3 relates the plundering of the Temple in 143 S.E. = 170/69 B.C.E., while 2 Macc. 5:15–16 connects it with Jason's attack in the following year.

to tighten his control over the agitated area he left the royal *epistatai* in Jerusalem and Samaria.

The repeated Seleucid intervention in Judea up to this date seems quite reasonable government. Antiochus IV undoubtedly felt entitled to depose and nominate high priests according to either his own will or the interest of the state, which amounted to much the same. And the personal rivalries between the leading Jews virtually provoked his intervention. That he tried to squeeze as much tribute as possible out of the candidates for the high-priestly office, and therefore conferred the dignity on the highest bidder, was quite understandable, even though the wisdom of the policy is, of course, highly questionable. Antiochus can hardly be blamed for permitting Jason and Menelaus to introduce Greek institutions into Jerusalem at their own request. As we have seen, a considerable number of the Jews among the upper classes welcomed the innovations, which purported to break down the barriers between the Jewish people and its neighbours. The confiscation of the Temple treasure in 169 B.C.E. was most probably an administrative measure to recover arrears of tribute. The intervention in the struggle between Menelaus and Jason was necessary in order to maintain peace and order in the province, and the Seleucid attack on Jerusalem in 168 B.C.E. was justified by the open rebellion of Jason against the central authority of the kingdom and by the necessity of keeping the vital frontier province against Egypt under firm control. However, the appointment of Menelaus was a political mistake, which can only be explained, if not excused, by the Syrian government's lack of understanding of the special position of the Jews. As the history of the Jews in antiquity shows, the Greeks, and also the Romans, always had great difficulty in grasping the realities of the Jewish way of life with its monotheistic religion, its strict adherence to the laws of the Torah, and worst of all, its absolute seclusion from the surrounding world. To the enlightened Greeks of the Hellenistic period this attitude implied a narrowness of mind which bordered on misanthropy and seemed tacitly to challenge the superiority of the Hellenistic culture, of which all Greeks were firmly convinced. The inability to understand often resulted in contempt and enmity. In this respect Antiochus IV was presumably neither worse nor better than the majority of the Greeks who entered into contact with the Jews. But in his case, his position as the secular overlord of the Jewish people made his lack of understanding disastrous.

In the summer or autumn of 167 B.C.E. Antiochus IV resolved to make a further attempt to settle the Jewish question in concert with Menelaus, who was undoubtedly the driving force behind the royal policy. A certain Apollonius was sent to Jerusalem. He entered the city without opposition and tried to win the inhabitants by issuing reassuring proclamations. Very soon, however, the intentions of the Syrian king became apparent. To ensure a lasting solution, the status of the Judean Temple state was completely transformed by a series of administrative measures. In the first place, the city walls of Jerusalem were razed to the ground. Then a part of the city was walled off from the rest, and in this quarter (the city of David, or the Akra) the Jewish adherents of the Hellenization policy were settled together with the Syrian and foreign soldiers. Here the official head of Judea, the high priest, also took up his residence. There can hardly be any doubt that the new settlement retained the organization of a Greek *polis*, and preserved the name of 'Antiochia in Jerusalem'. Presumably, participation in the administration and political life of Judea was restricted to the inhabitants of the city, while the rest of the country became dependent. In the eyes of the orthodox Jews this meant that they were deprived of their religious centre, that the holy city had become a 'colony of foreigners'. Apparently the razing of the city walls and the construction of the new quarter could not be accomplished without violence and bloodshed, and a part of the orthodox Jews preferred to leave Jerusalem altogether, their landed property being distributed among the new settlers.

Secondly, a new method of taxation seems to have been introduced at this time. The annual tribute, a fixed amount which was collected and paid by the high priest into the royal treasury, which Menelaus had found so difficult to provide, was replaced by a proportional land-tax levied directly on agricultural production and collected by royal agents. The new taxes are first mentioned in 153 B.C.E., under Demetrius I, whereas the tribute is not referred to explicitly after 170. But perhaps we have a clue to a more precise dating of the change in taxation. In 1 Maccabees the Seleucid official who was sent to Jeruslam in 167 B.C.E. is called *archōn phorologias*. This has been taken to be a mistranslation from Hebrew of the title *musarchēs*, which 2 Maccabees gives to Apollonius, but more probably it is a pun on his title, which gains its full effect if Apollonius in 167 B.C.E. was actually responsible for the introduction of the new taxation system. The direct taxes on agricultural products were undoubtedly most oppressive. In 153 B.C.E. the quotas levied as tax seem to have amounted to one-third of the production of grain and half the production of fruit. If these rates were introduced already under Antiochus IV, they can only be regarded as a punitive measure intended to curb the resistance to the king and his high priest.

Shortly after the introduction of these measures, which can be dated to the autumn of 167 B.C.E., the decisive blow was aimed at the orthodox Jews. A certain Atheneus brought to Jerusalem a royal decree containing regulations for the religious and social life of the inhabitants of Judea. According to the royal command, all specifically Jewish customs and rites were to be suppressed. The celebration of the Jewish festivals was forbidden, as well as the observance of the Sabbath. Circumcision was strictly prohibited and the scrolls of the Torah were to be confiscated and burnt. Transgressors were liable to capital punishment. The carrying into effect of the new enactments was entrusted to the provincial governor of Coele-Syria and Phoenicia, Ptolemeus, Dorymenes' son, in close co-operation with Menelaus.

The Seleucid officials, as well as the renegade high priest, set to work with enthusiasm. On 15 Chislev 145 S.E. (= *circa* December 167 B.C.E.) the daily sacrifices in the Temple of Jerusalem were suspended, and a heathen altar, the famous 'abomination of desolation', was built on or beside the great altar of Yahweh, which was thus desecrated in the eyes of the Jews. Ten days later the first heathen sacrifice took place there. A pig was slaughtered on the altar, because that animal was especially detestable to the Jews. At the same time the Temple was dedicated to Zeus Olympius, and a cult statue of the god was placed in the Temple together with statues of the king, whose birthday was to be celebrated by monthly sacrifices.[1] Other Greek cults, as for instance that of Dionysus, were also introduced in Jerusalem. Furthermore, pagan altars were constructed in the smaller towns and villages all over Judea, and here the Jews were compelled to sacrifice pigs to the new gods. The faithful, who wished to maintain the covenant with Yahweh, were persecuted, tortured, and put to death.

The religious persecution was not restricted to Judea. On the initiative of Ptolemeus commands were issued to the Greek or Hellenized cities of his province that the enactments of the king should be enforced against the Jews living there. An important document, preserved in Josephus, tells us what happened in Samaria. The royal officials here applied the new regulations to the Samaritans of Shechem, regarding them as Jews. The Samaritans responded by sending a petition to the king, pointing out that the custom of observing the Sabbath and the construction of their anonymous temple on Mount

[1] These measures were normal in Hellenistic ruler-worship and do not reveal anything about Antiochus' personal attitude to deification. Contrary to a widely help opinion, the king was *not* identified with Zeus, although he took a special interest in this deity. See O. Mørkholm, *Studies in the Coinage of Antiochus IV of Syria* (Copenhagen, 1963), pp. 58–61.

Gerizim were propitiatory measures introduced by their forefathers after a severe drought. They traced their origin from Sidon and styled themselves 'Sidonians in Shechem'. After these explanations they begged the king to instruct his officials to stop the persecution. In return they offered to dedicate their temple to Zeus, and pointed to the fact that, if they were left in peace, they would be better able to pay their taxes. After having consulted his friends, the king granted their requests and informed his local representatives, Apollonius and Nicanor, of his resolution. The royal letters were issued in 146 S.E. (167/6 B.C.E.), presumably in the spring of 166 B.C.E. In this way the Samaritans averted the danger of persecution.

Meanwhile religious persecution was raging throughout Judea; and it seems that the majority of the people bowed to the inevitable and complied with the king's order. However, a minority among the Jews preferred to leave their homes and go into the wilderness with their families in order not to defile themselves by obeying the royal decree. Naturally this passive resistance was regarded by the authorities as a form of rebellion. This *anachorēsis* of the peasants meant that land was left untilled and thus resulted in a diminution of the royal revenues. Consequently the fugitives were hunted down as far as possible and mercilessly killed. The task of the authorities was rendered easier by the fact that the orthodox Jews strictly observed the Sabbath and did nothing to defend themselves on Sabbath days. The persecutors were quick to take advantage of this 'superstition', with the result that the Jews abiding by the laws of the Torah were at the mercy of their enemies. On Sabbath days they were butchered like cattle, preferring not to depart an inch from the laws of the covenant. Judaism seemed doomed.

In this crisis a development of great importance took place. A movement of active resistance against the impious commands of the Syrian king grew up in Judea and found a leader in the priest Mattathias, of the family of Jehoiarib. The development of the Maccabean uprising will be dealt with in the following chapter, but a short account of the attitude of the Syrian government to this resistance movement during the last years of Antiochus IV's reign is necessary in order to arrive at a fair conclusion on the king's policy. A couple of minor engagements between Judas the Maccabee and two local Seleucid officials, Apollonius and Seron, during the summer of 166 B.C.E., ended with Jewish victories and undoubtedly strengthened the influence of the insurgents in Judea. However, the central administration in Antioch was hardly impressed, and in the spring of 165 B.C.E. Antiochus IV set out on an expedition to the eastern provinces of his kingdom, leaving the government of the western parts of the realm to a certain Lysias, a 'friend' of the king. For a time the problem of the Jewish uprising remained on a local level, but when in the summer of 165 B.C.E. an expeditionary force commanded by two trusted officers, Gorgias and Nicanor, and under the auspices of Ptolemeus, Dorymenes' son (the provincial governor) was defeated by Judas and his followers, the government in Antioch was bound to take notice.

The course of the subsequent events is difficult to establish with certainty. According to the sources at our disposal Lysias decided to intervene in person and led a Seleucid army against Judea (autumn 165 B.C.E. or winter 165/64 B.C.E.), only to be defeated by Judas. Some scholars, however, have felt very suspicious of this so-called 'first expedition' of Lysias and regard it as a duplication of his later expedition in 163 B.C.E. (see below, pp. 306–8) to which it has a striking similarity in many details. Also the chronology of the period becomes easier if we can discard this expedition as a fiction. The reason for the invention of the episode was obviously to remove the bad impression of a Jewish defeat at Beth-Zur in 163 B.C.E. by locating a fictitious victory at the same place two years earlier.

However this may be, in late 165 or early 164 B.C.E. Lysias apparently arrived at the conclusion that a military decision in Judea could only be achieved by an effort which was hardly worth while. He preferred negotiation. For the following development our source material consists of two valuable documents.[1] The first is a letter from Lysias to the Jews. Here the Seleucid vice-regent mentions his preliminary negotiations with two Jewish ambassadors, who had presented a petition containing the conditions of the Maccabean party for the establishment of peace and order. Some points Lysias had felt competent to concede immediately, while other questions, undoubtedly the more important, had been referred to the king, Antiochus IV, who was then far away in the east. Lysias requested the Jews to preserve their 'goodwill towards the State' and promised his assistance during the

[1] 2 Macc. 11:16–21 and 27–33. The same chapter contains two more documents, a letter from King Antiochus V to Lysias (22–6) and a letter from two Roman envoys to the Jews (34–8). In 2 Maccabees all four letters are referred to the time after Antiochus IV's death, although the date of letter 1 (Lysias to the Jews), 3 (King Antiochus to the Jews), and 4 (Roman envoys to the Jews) is given as year 148 S.E. = 165/4 B.C.E The authenticity of these letters has been much discussed, but most modern scholars accept them as genuine. In my opinion letter 4 is most likely spurious, while the first three are beyond suspicion. For two recent discussions see M. Zambelli, 'La composizione del secondo libro dei Maccabei', *Studi pubblicati dall' Istituto Italiano per la storia antica*, 16 (1965), 213–27, and O. Mørkholm, *Antiochus IV of Syria* (Copenhagen, 1966), pp. 162–5.

subsequent negotiations. Unfortunately the date of this important document is corrupt in our text. The year is correctly given as 148 S.E. (autumn 165/autumn 164 B.C.E.); but the name of the month, transmitted in the manuscripts in various variants – Dioskorinthios, Dioskorides, and Dioskoros – does not belong to the Macedonian calendar. Probably Dios, the first month of the Macedonian year and the only name which to some extent resembles the curious names in our manuscripts, is meant. As already mentioned, the first expedition of Lysias is presumably fictitious and thus does not prevent us from dating the letter to 24 Dios, or about the end of October 165 B.C.E.

According to the other letter at our disposal, the further negotiations with Antiochus IV were entrusted to Menelaus, the high priest, who presumably travelled east to meet the king. The choice of Menelaus clearly indicates that the Seleucid government did not intend to reverse its policy in Judea completely, but hoped to establish a *modus vivendi* between the Hellenizing Jews, who had maintained their loyalty to the king, and the Jewish insurgents. Lysias' plans were undoubtedly that the Maccabean rebels should return to their allegiance to the Syrian king on the assurance that they should not be punished for their rebellion and should be left free to perform their religious rites according to the Mosaic laws. On the other hand, Menelaus was to retain the office of high priest and his position as the representative of the central government. When peace was established, the direct intervention of Seleucid military forces would no longer be needed.

In accordance with this scheme, Antiochus IV issued his letter to the *gerousia* of the Jews and the rest of the people, proclaiming an amnesty for all rebels who returned to their place of residence and took up their previous occupation before the end of Xanthikos 148 S.E. (about March 164 B.C.E.). Furthermore, all Jews were allowed to 'use their expenditures and laws as previously', which presumably means that, besides religious freedom, the old system of taxation with a fixed annual tribute collected by the Jews themselves was re-established and the proportional land-tax from 167 B.C.E. abolished. With this letter, Antiochus IV sent Menelaus back to Judea with instructions to explain the new Seleucid policy to his compatriots and invite them to accept the royal amnesty. The letter of Antiochus IV is dated 15 Xanthikos 148 S.E., but the name of the month may well be wrong, as this dating would leave an incredibly short time, only a fortnight, between the proclamation of the amnesty and its termination.

In this way the Seleucid government hoped to promote peace between the various groups of the Jewish people; and the new governor of Coele-Syria and Phoenicia, Ptolemeus Macron, apparently did his best to make the Seleucid policy acceptable. The success of the new settlement, however, depended completely on the willingness of the Maccabean party to co-operate with their former enemies, more particularly with the high priest, Menelaus. It soon became apparent that the Maccabeans could not forget or forgive the terrible days of persecution, for which Menelaus was held responsible. They accepted the amnesty for the time being, but used the following period of Seleucid non-intervention to further their own political interests. As the victorious champion of the Jewish faith, Judas commanded an enormous prestige, and it can hardly be doubted that the majority of the Jewish people now looked to him for leadership. The withdrawal of direct help from the Seleucid government meant that the Hellenizing party among the Jews had lost its cause, and it is hardly surprising that the Maccabeans now looked forward to settling their account with the renegades. Consequently the insurgents did not return to ordinary civilian life, but kept their arms ready and preserved their military organization. During the summer of 164 B.C.E., most probably, Judas carried out a number of punitive expeditions against the neighbouring peoples in Idumea, the Jericho area, and Ammon, who had participated in the persecution of the Jews living among them. Emboldened by a series of successes he finally, towards the end of the year, felt strong enough to enter Jerusalem and restore the defiled Temple. At this time the Hellenizing party was apparently too weak to make the slightest attempt at opposition. On 25 Chislev 148 S.E. (December 164 B.C.E.), exactly three years after the first heathen sacrifice, the re-establishment of the cult of Yahweh was solemnly celebrated and the feast of Hanukka instituted to bear witness to posterity of the recovery of the Temple. Immediately afterwards Judas strengthened his position by fortifying Mount Sion and Beth-Zur and placing garrisons there. By these measures he brought to an end his preparations for the final reckoning with the Hellenizers.

About the same time as the rededication of the Temple of Jerusalem, Antiochus IV died in distant Persis. The foregoing analysis of events in Judea during his reign is admittedly written from the point of view of the Seleucid government, which naturally tended to regard the issue as political and economic and did not pay due attention to its religious aspect, which was the all-important factor to the orthodox Jews. This in itself was a grave mistake, which led to the failure of the Seleucid policy. As already stated, Antiochus IV can hardly be blamed for permitting the introduction of Greek culture among the Jews. His initial mistake was the appointment of Menelaus to the high-priestly office. The danger inherent in this decision ought soon to have been obvious to Antiochus IV and his government; but instead of removing Menelaus, the king continued his assistance to the unworthy high priest. The religious persecution of the Jews from 167 B.C.E. was a fatal blunder, and even though the policy of force was introduced and administered by Menelaus and Ptolemeus son of Dorymenes, the ultimate responsibility, of course, rests with the king. Undoubtedly the adoption of religious persecution as a means of solving the problems in Judea will always rank as one of Antiochus IV's greatest political mistakes. On the other hand, it must be admitted that, in the spring of 164 B.C.E., unfortunately rather too late, the Seleucid king did make a serious effort to redeem his errors by rescinding the decree concerning the persecution of the Jewish faith and proclaiming an amnesty for the rebels. Here Antiochus IV at last showed sound political judgement and demonstrated his flexibility by overturning his own former decisions, which events had proved wrong. That his attempt to establish an enduring co-existence of Hellenizers and orthodox Jews in Judea soon turned out to be a failure was mainly due to the uncompromising attitude of Judas and his followers, who regarded themselves as the only 'true Israel' and refused the proposed co-operation with the Hellenizers. Moreover, by lending force and authority to Menelaus during the persecution and thus interfering with what was essentially an inter-Jewish affair, the Seleucid government had become compromised for ever in the eyes of the orthodox Jews, and the lack of confidence was soon to lead to the resumption of hostilities.

ADDENDUM

My contribution reflects in the main my views as expressed in my dissertation of 1966. Since my manuscript was first submitted to the Press in 1970, much has been written on the subject, which has made me change my views on some details. I have profited especially from C. Habicht's introduction and commentary to 2 Maccabees in *Jüdische Schriften aus hellenistisch-römischer Zeit I* (Güterslöh, 1979, pp. 167–285). However, on all important points my interpretation is still valid, I believe (January 1983).

Dr Otto Mørkholm died on July 16, 1983.

CHAPTER 9

THE HASMONEAN REVOLT AND THE HASMONEAN DYNASTY

Great and sudden were the changes which the Hasmonean family brought to the character and religion of the Jews. Yet the members of the family never saw themselves as breaking with tradition. Their first revolutionary acts were in response to an unprecedented challenge, the persecution of the Jews by Antiochus IV, and they always took the patterns for their deeds from Scripture. To understand the changes which the Hasmoneans brought, we must consider what most believing Jews then seem to have taken for granted.

To judge by the surviving literature, all believing Jews then accepted as true the books of the Torah and the prophets. The teachings of the prophets kept pious Jews loyal to their God even after the disaster of 586 B.C.E. Their God had not been defeated when Jerusalem and the Temple were destroyed. Rather, their almighty God was punishing them for their sins when he placed them under foreign domination. Prophets taught the Jews that refusal to accept God's sentence upon them would bring catastrophic punishment, as when Zedekiah's refusal to accept the sentence of subjection to Babylonian rule had brought the destruction both of God's Temple and of Zedekiah's kingdom of Judah.[1]

The Jews in their long years of submission were indeed a peculiar people. There could be misguided hot-heads among them, but the *nation* never rebelled. Even the fall of Babylon did not end the sentence, though one might have thought so on reading Isaiah 40 to 66. Rather, instead of liberating Israel, God gave to Cyrus of Persia and his successors 'all the kingdoms of the earth',[2] and though independence and glory would eventually be restored to the Jews, it would come not by their own 'might and power' in rebellion, but only through the act of the 'spirit' of the Lord.[3]

Even in late 143 B.C.E., after the success of the Hasmonean revolt, the pious authorities in Jerusalem still believed that the persecutions

[1] Jer. 21, 24:1 to 25:29, 27:1 to 29:29, 30:1–17, 32:1–5, 38:17–23, 52:1–27; Ezek. 17; 2 Kings 24:18 to 25:21; 2 Chron. 36:11–21.

[2] 2 Chron. 36:22–3.

[3] Zech. 4:6.

brought upon the Jews by Antiochus IV were a punishment for the rebellion against the very same Antiochus perpetrated by the deposed High Priest Jason.[1] The unrebellious Jews were so loyal to their pagan masters that from the time of the Persian empire they were preferred as mercenary soldiers, particularly in troubled areas. The Jews' fealty could be shaken only under two sets of circumstances: a rival kingdom might seem to have a better claim to be the power chosen by God to impose servitude upon the Chosen People; thus the Jews passed from Ptolemaic to Seleucid rule in 201 B.C.E. Or again, the signs of the times might indicate that the sentence of servitude had been fully served. Even then, pious Jews might not rebel, for prophets had predicted that God might do all the fighting himself.[2]

In the reign of Antiochus IV Jews began to fight each other but still did not dare to rebel against the king. Pious Jews, from religious motives, rose, not against the king, but against the corrupt Hellenizing High Priest Menelaus and his followers. Even the deposed High Priest Jason carried out a coup against Menelaus at Jerusalem in 169 only after receiving a report that Antiochus IV had perished in Egypt. Perhaps Jason thought that the whole structure of pagan empires was crumbling as predicted in Daniel [2], or that the 'mandate of Heaven' was shifting from the Seleucids back to the Ptolemies. But Antiochus was alive; he had appointed Menelaus; and he was the protector of the Hellenizing Jews whom he had accepted as citizens of his 'Antiochene republic'. After several years of turbulence among the Jews he concluded in 167 B.C.E. that the Jews' religion was what made them a 'nation of rebels'. He proceeded to punish the rebels and sought to purge Judaism of its 'subversive' tendencies. As he saw it, he was removing the unwholesome hatred of foreigners and hatred of idolatry which evil teachers had brought into an originally admirable cult of the God of Heaven. Accordingly, he set up the 'Abomination of Desolation' on the Temple altar, as a representation of the deities of the cult of the God of Heaven, and he forbade the observance of the characteristic rituals and abstinences of Judaism.[3]

[1] 2 Macc. 1:7.

[2] Jewish soldiers: see B. Porten, *Archives from Elephantine* (Berkeley and Los Angeles, 1968); M. Hengel, *Judaism and Hellenism. Studies in their encounter in Palestine during the early Hellenistic period* (Philadelphia, 1974), I, pp. 15–18. Jewish loyalty: Jos. *Ant.* XI.316–19, 326 to 339; *Letter of Aristeas* 36 = Jos. *Ant.* XII.45, 119, 147–52; *C. Ap.* II.44. Prophets: Joel 2 to 3 (Heb. 4); Zech. 12:1–5, 14:1–11, and cf. 3:6.

[3] See J. A. Goldstein, *I Maccabees*, AB 41 (Garden City, N.Y., 1976), Introduction, part 6.

[See the different views of V. Tcherikover, 'Antiokiya biYᵉrušalayim', *Sefer ha-yobel lᵉY. Epstein* (1950), pp. 61–7, or *Hayᵉhudim ba-ʿolam ha-Yᵉwani wᵉha-Romi* (Tel Aviv, 1961), pp. 146–155; E. Bickerman, *Der Gott der Makkabäer* (Berlin, 1937); Hengel, *Hellenism*, I, pp. 277ff, Edd.]

The Jews faced a terrifying dilemma: their God would punish them severely for disobeying the Torah; their God would punish them severely for rebellion against the king; the king forbade them to obey the Torah, on pain of death. One course was clearly open to pious Jews: obey the Torah; do not rise in rebellion; and wait, meekly and bravely, to be killed by the king. Pious Jews, however, searched the Scriptures to find how their martyrdom might fit into God's plans of chastisement and redemption. Perhaps the helpless martyrdom of innocents might rouse God to take vengeance on the persecutors and bring a glorious redemption to the Chosen People.[1] Perhaps mass observance of the Sabbath might rouse God to rescue His servants.[2] Perhaps God would act soon, but in His own time, against the persecutors, and in fulfilment of Isaiah 26:19 He would resurrect the pious martyrs.[3]

Indeed, without the prospect of resurrection, such pious Jews faced extermination for no reward, whereas apostates could easily survive. There was no resurrection. The pious could easily have been wiped out, but for the audacity of the aged priest Mattathias, also called Hashmonay, and his family, whom we call the Hasmoneans. We learn of these events from surviving pieces of contemporary religious propaganda (Daniel 7 to 12, the *Testament of Moses*, and Enoch 85 to 90) and from two systematic histories written three-quarters of a century later, preserved in the first and second books of Maccabees. The authors of the two histories were bitter opponents, who lived during the reign of the Hasmonean King Alexander Janneus. Their bitter controversy allows us to use one as a check upon the other. In some cases we can show that the two authors drew on sources written by eye-witnesses of the events.[4] This fact and the evidence of the difficult and obscure propaganda of the time of the persecution and the Hasmonean revolts give us considerable assurance that the issues of the 160s are correctly reflected in the histories written in the 90s or 80s B.C.E.

The author of 1 Maccabees was an ardent partisan of the Hasmoneans. He believed that the Hasmonean dynasty was the stock to whom God had granted the privilege of bringing permanent victory to the Chosen People. Jason of Cyrene, the author of the lost work of which

[1] *Testament of Moses* 9:1 to 10:6 and 2 Macc. 7:6 and 8:3; the authors drew on Deut. 32:36, 42 to 43.

[2] 1 Macc 2:29–38 and 2 Macc. 6:11; the martyrs put their faith in Isa. 56:1–2, 58:11–14, and Jer. 17:19–27.

[3] Dan. 12:2.

[4] Contemporary religious propaganda: see Goldstein, *I Maccabees*, Introduction, part 2. Bitter controversy of the two historians and their date under Janneus: ibid., parts 1 and 4; J. A. Goldstein, *II Maccabees*, AB, 41A (Garden City, N.Y., 1983), Introduction, part 4. Eye-witness sources: ibid., Introduction, part 2.

the history in 2 Maccabees is an abridgement, approved of only one Hasmonean, Judas Maccabeus. As viewed by Jason, the others were incompetent and even wicked.

We know little of the antecedents of Mattathias. His father's name was John, his grandfather's Simeon, and perhaps his great-grandfather's was Hashmonay. Though Mattathias may have enjoyed some distinction in Jerusalem, his family had a home and a graveyard at the town of Modein. The family belonged to the priestly clan or course of Jehoiarib. In 1 Chronicles 24:7 Jehoiarib is listed as the first of the priestly courses, but some scholars have argued that the order of the courses there has been altered by pro-Hasmonean hands.[1]

Mattathias bore the additional identifying name, 'Hashmonay', just as his famous son Judas bore the additional identifying name, 'Maccabeus'.[2] Mattathias had five sons, John, Simon, Judas, Eleazar, and Jonathan. Mattathias found himself facing in his home town of Modein royal agents enforcing Antiochus' decrees and saw Jews willing to obey them by offering up an idolatrous sacrifice. The audacious priest did not wait for God, but in an act of zeal he slew an apostate and the king's agent, and thereupon he called upon other pious Jews to follow him into the mountains. There, with his followers, he carried on guerrilla warfare against the persecuting government and against Jews who collaborated with it.

How could Mattathias have been so audacious as to break with a Jewish belief which had been held for centuries? The author of 1 Maccabees, writing in the time of Mattathias' great-grandson, may well preserve Mattathias' own ideology. Mattathias could find no commandment in the Torah to justify his rebellion against the king. No true prophet, so far as he knew, had predicted the persecution or had given instructions that might be useful. Mattathias and his sons went beyond searching the Scriptures for prophecies; they sought *examples*. The author of 1 Maccabees presents Mattathias as viewing the crisis in his own time as similar to scale to the crisis which faced the zealous Phineas. As Phineas acted in zeal, so now should Mattathias. According to the author of 1 Maccabees, Phineas was not the only Israelite hero whose example was to be followed. Though it might be presumptuous for a Jewish subject of Antiochus IV to aspire to the glory of a Joseph, a Joshua, or of a David, we are told that Mattathias believed that even in his own time Jews might emulate those heroes.

Mattathias' revolutionary beliefs and the policies which flowed from them evoked violent opposition among many pious Jews. To Matta-

[1] See S. Loewenstamm, 'Yᵉhoyarib', *Enṣ. Miq.* 6, pp. 530–1.

[2] See Goldstein, *I Maccabees*, pp. 18–19.

thias' opponents, God's will required Jews to face martyrdom unflinchingly and forbade resistance to the king, and they condemned those of their fellows who joined the forces of the audacious priest.[1] All the more did they condemn Mattathias and his followers when Mattathias soon thereafter dared to legislate that Jews could fight to defend themselves on the Sabbath. Even David's legislation had been in clear harmony with the Torah and had touched nothing as fundamental as the Sabbath.[2] The bitter opposition of many of the pious to Mattathias' legislation can still be seen in the dogged insistence of Jason of Cyrene that the hero Judas Maccabeus never violated the Sabbath, and also in the insistence of the author of 1 Maccabees that Mattathias and his son Jonathan enjoyed divine favour *after* engaging in defensive warfare on the Sabbath.[3]

Mattathias conducted only a guerrilla campaign. He was old and died after about one year. His son Judas succeeded him. Judas was amazingly successful in rallying the militant pious Jews, badly split though they were by sectarian disputes. As long as he could pose as the defender of all Jewish sects against the persecutor, he could assemble a force of ten to eleven thousand men. He won an amazing series of victories and gained the admiration of circles otherwise hostile to the Hasmoneans, including the authors of 2 Maccabees and of 1 Enoch 90:9–19.

Judas and his growing band vanquished not merely local officials and their Jewish collaborators but even units of the royal army. Nevertheless, at first Judas and his men could not even hold villages. The guerrilla band struck from bases in the wilderness of Judea and Samaria. In Judas' first important victories he was reacting to government efforts to suppress him. The force stationed in the Akra, the citadel of Jerusalem on the hill north of the Temple mount,[4] had massacred pious Sabbath observers, but its function appears to have been to control Jerusalem and protect from Jewish zealots the Jews there who were obeying the king's decrees. The force was too small to suppress the Hasmonean band. Well-provisioned and confident that other Seleucid forces would deal with the problem, the people in the Akra at first saw no cause for alarm. The nearest commander with considerable military resources was Apollonius at Samaria.[5] He raised

[1] See Dan. 11:33–5, where the 'little help' is the Hasmonean guerrilla band.

[2] 1 Sam. 30:23–5; cf. Num. 31:25–7. [3] 2 Macc. 8:26–8; 1 Macc. 2:39–48, 9:43–73.

[4] See Goldstein, *I Maccabees*, note on 1:33–40.

[5] On the military aspects of the Hasmonean revolt see M. Avi-Yonah, 'The Hasmonean revolt and Judah Maccabee's war against the Syrian', in *The Hellenistic Age, Political History of Jewish Palestine from 332* B.C.E. *to 67* B.C.E., ed. A. Schalit (Ramat-Gan, 1972), pp. 147–82. [Edd.]

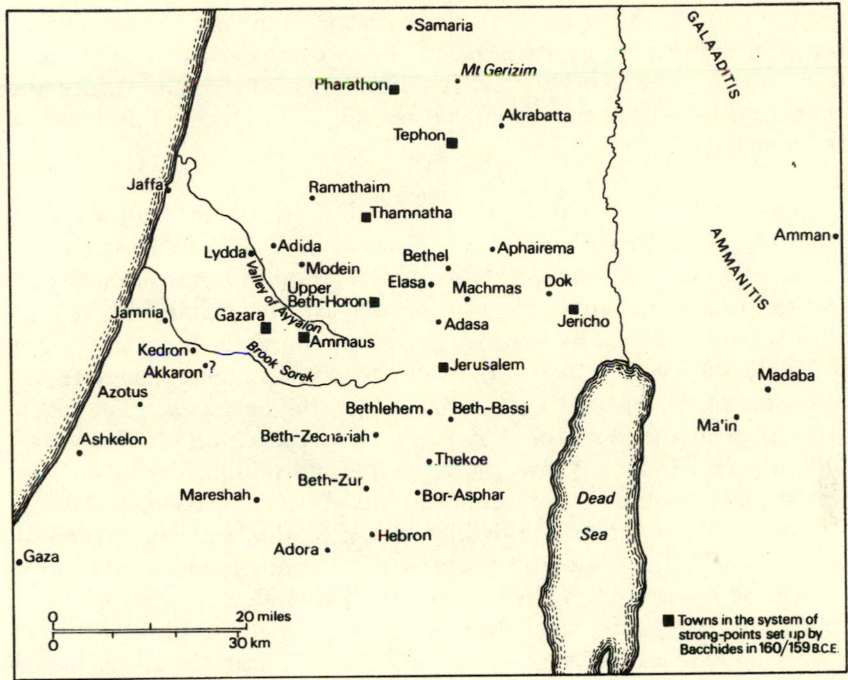

Fig. 1 Important places in Judea and her neighbours during the careers of Judas Maccabeus, Jonathan and Simon (160 to 134 B.C.E.). (Based on Plate IX in George E. Wright and Floyd V. Filson, The Westminster Historical Atlas to the Bible (Philadelphia, 1945).

a force from the local Gentiles, especially from the Greco-Macedonian inhabitants of the city of Samaria.[1] Judas met him in battle at a site now unknown. Apollonius' army was routed, and he himself fell. Next, Seron, commander of a large unit of the royal army, marched against Judas from somewhere in the north, only to be routed at the difficult pass of Beth-Horon.[2] Probably at this point Philip, commander of the garrison in the citadel of Jerusalem, sent an appeal for massive aid to Ptolemy, son of Dorymenes, governor of the huge province of Coele-Syria and Phoenicia, in which Judea lay.[3]

Earlier in his reign Antiochus IV had been careful not to allow a dangerously independent war-lord (such as Hyrcanus the Tobiad) or a dangerous rebellion (such as that of Jason the Oniad) to continue in

[1] Goldstein, *I Maccabees*, note on 3:10.

[2] See B. Bar-Kochva, 'Sēron and Cestius Gallus at Beith Ḥoron', *PEQ*, 108 (1976), 13–21. [Edd.]

[3] See Goldstein, *I Maccabees*, introductory note to 3:27–37.

regions close to the insecure border with the Ptolemaic empire. Surely the king did give some attention to the threats posed by the Hasmonean revolt. Nevertheless, Judas' force was still small. Antiochus appears to have been convinced that his subordinates could deal with it adequately.

The author of 1 Maccabees is probably wrong in thinking that religious revolts provoked by the policies of Antiochus IV had severely drained the imperial treasury. Nor did the king need to seek money to pay the indemnity imposed upon his dynasty by Rome, for he had already paid it in full. Rather, Antiochus' own grandiose projects were probably the cause which drove him to try squeezing the financial resources of the eastern regions claimed by the Seleucids.[1] The harsh experience in the reign of Antiochus II of the revolt of the satrap Molon (222–220 B.C.E.)[2] had shown that establishing order in the east was no task to entrust to a subordinate. Antiochus III had become Antiochus the Great through his Alexander-like feats in the east.[3] Antiochus IV thus chose to command the potentially lucrative eastern expedition himself, with half the imperial army. He made his little son Antiochus co-regent king of the west and appointed the minister Lysias guardian of the little co-regent, with authority to deal with the affairs of the west as long as the senior king should be absent.[4] To maintain order, Lysias received the other half of the imperial army. Surely such a force should have been able to cope with a guerrilla band of only 3,000 plus perhaps 3,000 reserves. Some Jews would even support the royal army. Nevertheless, the outcome proved contrary to the king's expectations.

At first the chief minister of the west may have left Judas' band to the provincial officials. The governor of Coele-Syria and Phoenicia entrusted the task of restoring order among the Jews to a strong force under the experienced commanders, Nicanor and Gorgias.[5] The expedition established its base at Ammaus (= Emmaus), a site well situated for moving along any of several routes into the mountainous territory haunted by Judas' band. Judas wisely avoided battle with the full Seleucid force. His men, living off the land, were not gravely threatened by static Seleucid forces at Ammaus and in the Akra. The full Seleucid force at Ammaus could move but slowly on the mountain

[1] Ibid., note on 3:29–30; Otto Mørkholm, *Antiochus IV of Syria* (Copenhagen, 1966), p. 65.

[2] See Edouard Will, *Histoire politique du monde hellénistique*, 2 (Nancy, 1967), pp. 11–17.

[3] Will, *Histoire*, 2, pp. 42–59.

[4] See Goldstein, *I Maccabees*, note on 3:32–3.

[5] Ibid., notes on 3:38.

roads, could hardly escape the notice of the hostile Jews in the hill-country, and would be vulnerable to ambushes. Meanwhile, the base at Ammaus could be more safely attacked. If the Seleucid troops should be divided in an attempt to run down Judas in a multi-pronged operation, the king's men risked losing in hostile territory the overwhelming numerical superiority needed to suppress guerrilla activity. Time favoured Judas. His survival would prove to pious Jews that God no longer condemned revolt against the king. The imperial government could well have feared that the Ptolemaic kingdom would take advantage of the situation. Whatever the reason, the commander, Gorgias, accepted the risk of trying to hunt down Judas. He took a force of 5,000 infantry and 1,000 cavalry, large enough to outnumber the Jewish rebels but small enough to move rapidly and perhaps to escape notice. With guides from the Akra, Gorgias had hopes of finding Judas' camp and taking it by surprise. Meanwhile the base-camp at Ammaus should be safe.

Judas frustrated the scheme. Somehow he got word of it. Though neither in First nor in Second Maccabees nor in Josephus is there a claim that a miracle occurred, a contemporary observer believed that an angel revealed Gorgias' plans to Judas (1 Enoch 90:14). Judas marched through the darkness to surprise Nicanor and the camp at Ammaus at daybreak. His men routed the superior Seleucid force, took and burned the camp, and in disciplined fashion faced about to meet Gorgias' returning column. Gorgias' men, on seeing the burning camp, panicked and fled into the coastal plain, leaving Judas' force free to take the rich spoils.

The brilliant victory convinced pious Jews that God was indeed with Judas. The king's agents no longer dared to go out from the Akra to enforce the decrees against the observance of the Torah and the Jews soon returned to open obedience to its commandments.[1] Strange as it seems, Judas' growing band made no effort to retake the Temple area or to attack the Akra. Many Jews believed that in accordance with the words of prophets God Himself would soon act in Jerusalem and purify His Temple: He might even cause a new Temple to descend from heaven. Meanwhile it would be presumptuous for mere flesh and blood to act. Judas and his men probably abstained even from entering Jerusalem.[2]

The chief minister of the west could no longer entrust to subordinates the dangerous rebellion in Judea. Lysias himself marched against the rebels with a large force. Since fighting uphill into the mountains of

[1] Ibid., note on 4:25; *Megillat Ta'anit* 24 Ab. [2] Goldstein, *I Maccabees*, pp. 273–4.

Judea had proved disastrous, Lysias took a downhill route into Judea, from the south, through the loyal territory of Idumea. Judas' band, now 10,000 strong, met Lysias in a bloody battle just inside Judea at Beth-Zur.[1] Probably neither side could truthfully claim a victory.

At this point many of Judas' pious supporters may have had misgivings about further resistance to the royal government. Would it not be better for the Jewish rebels to try to negotiate with Lysias, offering to stop fighting if Lysias would end the persecution? In addition, there were still Jews who saw no sign of the fulfilment of the words of the prophets and hence believed that God's sentence of subjection to foreign rulers still stood. Hard hit by the persecution, they now also faced the wrath of Judas and his men, whose presumption they viewed as impious. There were also Jews, including Menelaus, who had collaborated with the regime, willingly or unwillingly, and now faced the threat of pitiless punishment at the hands of the Hasmonean band. When Antiochus IV undertook to punish the Jews as a nation and sect of rebels, he had withdrawn recognition from their national organs. Now there still survived many members of what had been the Jewish council (*gerousia*) of elders. Along with the High Priest Menelaus these men probably were still viewed as *de facto* leaders of the nation by many Jews. Surely almost all members of this old élite must have been opposed to the Hasmonean guerrilla warfare, for otherwise the author of 1 Maccabees would have made much of their adherence to Judas' cause, just as he broadcast the adherence of the pietist Hasidim.

Before the battle of Beth-Zur Lysias had probably been confident he could suppress the Jewish rebels. His heavy losses showed him that the campaign would be long and costly, at a time when he could ill afford to be away from Antioch, for political rivals might try to seize control. Thus, if Jews sought to negotiate a settlement, he would be receptive.

The Hasmonean propagandist of 1 Maccabees is pleased to have recorded no negotiations between Judas and Lysias. In fact there probably were none. Jews, however, did negotiate with Lysias and succeeded in bringing an end to the persecution. Documents reflecting the negotiations survive, for Jason of Cyrene incorporated them into his work. Judas is not mentioned in the documents. The thought that heroic Judas took no part in the negotiations probably would have been incredible to Jason. In the letter of Lysias to the Jews (2 Macc. 11:16–21), Jason saw the names of two ambassadors, John and Absalom, and wrongly jumped to the conclusion that the ambassadors were sent by Judas.

[1] See Goldstein, *I Maccabees*, note on 4:29.

Rather, John and Absalom probably represented those militant pious rebels who were ready to break with Judas because of their misgivings over further resistance. They were among those who had just been facing Lysias in the field and had the power to offer an end to their own rebellion. Lysias gave a cordial response (2 Macc. 11:16–21) to the appeal presented by the ambassadors; he consented to some points and implied that he was passing others on to the king for his approval. The little co-regent at Antioch was a mere figurehead. Lysias was really sending the points in question to Antioch for approval by other powerful ministers.

Hitherto, Menelaus and the old élite, caught between the royal army and the rebels, had been unable to escape their predicament by negotiating a peace. Even if Menelaus gained a hearing from Lysias, what guarantee could he give the chief minister that the rebels would stop fighting? Now, however, it was clear that both Lysias and large numbers of the rebels were eager for peace. Moreover, surely Menelaus and the old élite did not like Lysias' negotiations with the rebels' ambassadors, authorities other than themselves. Now was the time for the high priest and the old élite to try both to re-establish their authority and to win the credit for ending the persecution.

Since Lysias had negotiated with the rebels, Menelaus did not go to him but went directly to the royal government at Antioch and was successful. A letter (2 Macc. 11:27–33) in the name of the little co-regent, addressed 'to the council of elders of the Jews and to the rest of the Jews', offered amnesty and an end to the persecution if they would lay down their arms by 27 March 164 B.C.E., fifteen days from the time the letter was written. The letter ignored Judas as well as the ambassadors John and Absalom and mentioned Menelaus as the Jews' spokesman.[1]

Since Judea was a compact country and the Jewish rebels were expectantly awaiting a reply from Antioch, we need not be surprised at the brief time allowed them for compliance. The fact that the address of the king's letter mentions the council of elders shows that the royal government again was recognizing that body. The regime, however, did not have to be generous otherwise with a rebel population ready to stop fighting: pious Jews henceforth would not be persecuted for failing to observe the imposed cult, but the Temple remained officially in the hands of the royal government; royal law still barred pious Jews from obeying those commands of the Torah which required that they

1 [For a different view of the authorship of the letter in 2 Macc. 11:27–33, as from Epiphanes, see M. Stern, *Ha-tᵉʿuda lᵉmered ha-ḥašmona'im* (Tel Aviv, 1965), pp. 57–70 (Edd.)]

punish as idolaters those who practised the imposed cult. Certainly the government did not have to restore to the Jews the privileged status of a nation (*ethnos*), and the Jews do not receive that title in the letters at 2 Macc. 11:16–21, 27–33.

For months the Hasmoneans had been enforcing observance of the Torah, and the royal armies had been unable to stop them. The Hasmoneans must have viewed the concessions in the king's letter as an ultimatum to lay down their arms in return for nothing beyond what they had already won. Indeed, the concessions were issued in the name of the little co-regent and could have been overruled by Antiochus IV at any time. Small wonder the Hasmonean party ignored so humiliating and insecure a charter! The Hasmonean propagandist who wrote 1 Maccabees does not mention it.

Other pious Jews, however, held a different view. In their eyes, Antiochus IV's persecutions could only have been a visitation sent by God. If now they were to be ended even temporarily, the fact was an act of God's mercy, to be welcomed as such. Accordingly, those Jews treasured the royal documents and made the anniversary of the arrival of the co-regent's proclamation an annual day of rejoicing.[1]

The peace of Lysias did break the coalition of pious Jews. Never again would Judas lead against a Seleucid army so large a force as he had against Lysias. The chief minister felt confident enough to withdraw from Judea without attempting to enforce the terms of the amnesty. Judas and his men retained their arms. The garrison of the Akra and pious Jews outside the Hasmonean party might well be able to prevent Judas' band from becoming again a menace to the regime.

Although the end of the persecution was surely welcomed by all pious Jews, it was embarrassing because none of the prophecies circulating among the faithful had predicted that the troubles would cease in so unspectacular a manner. Judgement should have first been visited upon Antiochus, and punishment upon the Gentiles and wicked Jews. The Seleucid empire should have been replaced by an eternal empire of the saints. There should have been a resurrection of the dead Jews, to reward the righteous and punish the wicked. A temple should have descended from heaven to replace the desecrated one built by men (1 Enoch 90:28–9). What now should be done about Jerusalem, the Temple, and the Temple service? Would it not be dangerous to restore the Temple before the predicted earthquake and natural upheavals? Would it not be presumptuous to resume services in a Temple which

1 On the peace negotiations, the participants on both sides, and the documents which resulted, see my notes on 2 Macc. 11:13–38 in my *II Maccabees*. There I establish that the document at 2 Macc. 11:23–6 is of early 163 B.C.E.

God himself was going to remove and replace? God Himself, the prophets said, would destroy all idols. Would it not be rash for mere flesh and blood even to destroy the Abomination of Desolation?

The writers of most of these prophecies had been so confident of their inspiration that they had set time-limits for their fulfilment. Prudence demanded that the Jews wait until the prophesied time-limits for the predicted miracles had passed. Daniel predicted great miracles for the beginning of the sabbatical year, in Tishri 164/3. Zechariah 14 contains a prediction of a great manifestation of God's power just before and during the festival of Tabernacles. Hence, Jews had to wait through the full festival of Tabernacles, including the Eighth Day of Solemn Assembly, through 15–22 Tishri. Other uncertainties imposed still further delay. Antiochus IV had made it impossible to intercalate the Jewish calendar, and now the Jewish calendar was probably two months out. What month would God regard as the month for performance of miracles? The month called 'Tishri' on the un-intercalated Jewish calendar? Or the astronomically correct Tishri, called 'Kislev' on the un-intercalated calendar? The only safe procedure was to wait through the astronomically correct Tishri, through the 'Festival of Tabernacles in the Month of Kislev'. From the first, the Hasmoneans may well have disbelieved the apocalypses and the pietist declarations that the fulfilment of Zechariah 14 was imminent. When all these pious hopes had been dashed, by 23 Kislev 164, Judas Maccabeus seems to have felt the appropriateness of dedicating a new Temple altar on the day of the monthly sacrifices which had profaned the old. He seems also to have wished to follow earlier precedents. Solomon had dedicated the altar of the first Temple by prolonging the autumn festival (of Tabernacles), adding to it days of dedication. How many days Solomon added is obscure because of textual difficulties which may have been present already in the Scriptures which lay before Judas. However, Moses and Zerubbabel in dedicating altars had held ceremonies for eight days, and so had Hezekiah in purifying the Temple. For Judas, two days of preparation, 23 and 24 Kislev, were sufficient for setting up a great eight-day celebration of the dedication of the new altar. Accordingly, Judas and his followers declared the 'Festival of Tabernacles in the Month of Kislev' to be prolonged through the two days of preparation and the eight days of dedication, producing a festival of eighteen days. The first eight, the doubtful days of Tabernacles and the Eighth Day of Solemn Assembly, had been days of frustrated expectation of the fulfilment of Zechariah 14. The two days of preparation were too insignificant to be remembered. But the last eight days were indeed the memorable Feast of Dedication (Hanukkah) and became an annual rite. The earliest attested name for Hanukkah is 'the Festival of Tabernacles in the Month of Kislev', a name which reflects the complex developments we have traced. No Jewish sect had any interest in recording the embarrassing and frustrating period of waiting for a miracle.[1]

Though the events which culminated in the Feast of Dedication perplexed the faithful, most Jews of the time surely believed they had entered a new age of miracles. At least prophecies of God's protection had been fulfilled, and reports circulated of miraculous apparitions.[2] The age of the Jews' servitude might not yet be over, but Judas could already dare to fortify the Temple mount against the men of the Akra and against any future effort of an arrogant king to overstep the limits of the power granted him by God by violating the Temple. Judas also fortified Beth-Zur in Judea against the traditional Idumean enemy.

Welcome as they were to the Jews, the evidences of renewed divine support brought down upon them the murderous wrath of neighbouring peoples. Some Gentiles were living on soil which had belonged to the kingdoms of Judah and Israel. All these neighbours were living on soil promised by the words of prophets to the Jews. Jews had made no secret of the promises, but as long as the Jews were clearly still under their God's sentence of servitude, the Gentiles felt secure. Now, however, the Jews over the border in Judea became a threat. The Chosen People surely would try to seize what God had promised them. Jews in Gentile-held territory were now viewed as a 'fifth column'. Innocent Jews living in Philistia, Phoenicia, Gilead, Edom, and Moab were in danger of being massacred. Only Judas' band was able and willing to protect them. However, now that the enemy was no longer the king, but Gentiles acting without royal sanction, Judas found pious Jews flocking to join his force.[3]

In a series of expeditions he was invariably victorious, though he did not always succeed in saving the menaced Jewish communities. Even when he failed to save the Jews of Jaffa and Jamnia, he was able to inflict severe punishment on the offending Gentile towns. In two areas the augmented Hasmonean band enjoyed dazzling success in rescuing

[1] On the events which culminated in the Feast of Dedication, see Goldstein, *I Maccabees*, note on 4:36–54.

[2] Zech. 9:8, 12:7–9; Joel 3:16–17 (Heb. 4:16–17); cf. Isa. 31:4–5, 37:35, 38:6. Miraculous apparitions: 2 Macc. 11:8–10, 1 Enoch 90:14–15.

[3] [For other considerations and reasons for the wars of Judah against the neighbouring Gentiles see U. Rappaport, 'He'arim ha-hellenisṭiyot wiYhudah šel 'ereṣ Yiśra'el bit^equfat ha-ḥašmona'im', *Meḥqarim muggašim l^eProf. B.Z.Katz* (Tel Aviv, 1967), pp. 219–30. [Edd.]

Jews. Judas' brother Simon led a force of 3,000 to Galilee and rescued the Jews there from enemies who had come from Ptolemais (Akko), Tyre, and Sidon. Judas, seconded by Jonathan, had even greater success leading a force of 8,000 to the rescue of Jews in 'Gilead', in what is today southernmost Syria. Far from conquering promised areas, the rescue forces found it miraculous enough that they were able to defeat their enemies while suffering minimal casualties themselves and then were able to evacuate the Jews of Galilee and Gilead to Judea. Also evacuated were the Jews of another area, probably the one near Caesarea called Narbatta.[1] These campaigns took place in the spring, while the streams were still running in southern Syria and before the Jewish Pentecost.

In this period the Jews suffered defeat only when Joseph and Azariah, left behind by Judas to hold the home front, disobeyed instructions and marched on Jamnia. They went into battle against Gorgias, governor of Idumea and lost 2,000 men. Joseph and Azariah may have been half-brothers of the heroic Hasmonean five.[2] In any case, the defeat was taken as demonstrating that the two were 'not of the stock through which God would bring victory to Israel'.[3]

After Pentecost came more campaigns, against Idumea and Azotus, not to rescue Jews, but to punish Gentiles. Priests not of the Hasmonean family again exposed themselves to danger and suffered heavy losses. The Hasmoneans and their supporters again saw the hand of God in the fact. Others saw the hand of God in the fact that Jews slain in the same campaign were found to be carrying under their tunics looted objects dedicated to idols, in violation of God's commandments.[4]

The wars with hostile neighbours had probably begun when the news of the death of Antiochus IV reached Jerusalem.[5] The exact date of the king's death is unknown. A cuneiform document lets us know that the news reached Babylon between 20 November and 18 December 164.[6] He died far away, in the Iranian regions claimed by him, at Tabai in the vicinity of Isfahan.[7] Though Jewish legend insisted that the king died after hearing the bitter news of the failure of his plans to crush the Jews, it is unlikely that the king heard of the dedication of the new Temple altar before his death.

1 Goldstein, *I Maccabees*, note on 5:23.
2 See my commentary on 2 Macc. 7:1.
3 1 Macc. 5:62.
4 1 Macc. 5:67, 2 Macc. 12:40.
5 Goldstein, *I Maccabees*, pp. 43, 293, 307.
6 A. J. Sachs and D. J. Wiseman, 'A Babylonian king list of the Hellenistic period', *Iraq*, 16 (1954), 202–4, 208–9.
7 See Goldstein, *I Maccabees*, notes to 6:4, *Babylonia*, and to 6:5, *Persis*.

On his deathbed, Antiochus IV appointed Philippos to replace Lysias as chief minister and guardian of the little co-regent, who now would become King Antiochus V in his own right. Lysias, however, kept control as chief minister of the new regime and forced Philippos to seek refuge in Ptolemaic Egypt. The new regime early in 163 B.C.E. attempted to conciliate the pious Jews. Again they were recognized as an *ethnos*; the Temple was restored to them as of right; the Hellenistic 'reform' was revoked and the Torah was declared to be binding on all Jews.[1] The pious had to decide how to respond to these concessions. They all probably believed that Antiochus IV had been slain by God. Was the wicked king's son now God's chosen ruler over the Jews? Or was the age of Jewish servitude over? The Hasmoneans seem never to have recognized the government of the little co-regent.[2] They may now have regarded his rule as king as illegitimate. However, they could not convince pious Jews who still looked for the prophesied miracles as signs of the age of Israel's liberation. Partisans of the Hasmoneans probably answered such doubts with suggestions that the victories in the wars against hostile neighbours were miraculous in scale. Some observers declared that they had seen miraculous apparitions. In any case, pious Jews could pursue an activist policy without directly rebelling against the king. The Akra still sheltered Jews whom the pious viewed as apostates worthy of expulsion if not of death. We hear that the garrison of the Akra had committed atrocities against pious Jews. One might reason that to attack the Akra was not quite the same as to rebel against the royal government. Perhaps the Hasmonean party so argued to convince pious doubters. They themselves cared little about such distinctions. To them, Antiochus V was not king over the Jews by the will of God. In late spring, 163 B.C.E., Judas was able to rally a large proportion of the Jews to besiege the Akra. Nevertheless, it would appear that some pious Jews joined the men of the Akra in protesting to the royal government against Judas' presumptuous act.[3]

The reaction of the government was predictable. Lysias had calculated that loyalists and pious Jews outside the Hasmonean party would be able to deal with Judas' force. Lysias perceived that his calculations were mistaken and took no chances. He brought overwhelming power against the Jewish rebels at the same time as he tried to win over the Jews without the use of force. Pious Jews objected strongly to

[1] On Philippos and his unsuccessful challenge to Lysias, see 1 Macc. 6:14–17, 2 Macc. 9:29, and Goldstein, *I Maccabees*, notes on 6:14–15, 55–6. On the concessions to the pious by the new regime, see 2 Macc. 11:23–6 and my notes to the passage in my *II Maccabees*.

[2] Goldstein, *I Maccabees*, note on 3:32–3.

[3] Goldstein, *I Maccabees*, notes on 6:18–24 and on 6:20.

Menelaus, the impious high priest maintained in power by the royal government. Lysias had Menelaus executed and sometime thereafter the regime appointed the pious Yaqim (called Alcimus in Greek) to the high-priesthood.[1] The regime thus passed over Onias IV, the pretender from the old Zadokite–Oniad high-priestly line. Onias IV thereupon emigrated to Egypt and eventually founded there a Jewish temple of his own.[2]

In Judea, the Seleucid army proved far too powerful for Judas' force, which had shrunk as a result of the defection of some of the pious. The royal troops besieged the Jewish garrison at Beth-Zur. Judas abandoned the siege of the Akra and marched to the rescue, but his men were defeated at Beth-Zechariah. His own brother Eleazar died a hero's death.[3]

Thereupon, Judas' force was driven back upon Jerusalem to face a siege on the Temple mount. Because it was the sabbatical year,[4] neither the garrison in Beth-Zur nor the force on the Temple mount had sufficient food. Hunger reduced the Jews at Beth-Zur to surrender. The royal army avoided the posture of persecutors. They allowed the vanquished to go home unmolested. Hunger also drove the bulk of the Jewish force on the Temple mount to take advantage of royal clemency and go home; perhaps even Judas did so.[5] Only a small force was left holding the stronghold on the Temple mount. To judge by Daniel 12:7, the last defenders may have called themselves the 'holy people', after Isaiah 62:12.

Unexpectedly, the besieged were rescued. The minister Philippos, left behind in charge at the Seleucid capital of Antioch, rebelled.[6] To meet the emergency, Lysias convinced the royal court and the army to make peace with the Jews.[7] On some points, however, the Seleucid regime did not yield. Hasmonean propaganda was to charge that Antiochus V violated his oath in destroying the fortifications of mount Zion. The Seleucid government also did nothing to remove from the Akra the Jewish sinners and the soldiers who protected them. The Hasmonean propagandist who wrote 1 Maccabees pointedly refrains from claiming that Judas negotiated so defective a settlement.

1 Ibid., p. 93 and notes on 6:63 and 7:16–17; my commentary on 2 Maccabees, note on 13:3–8.

2 Goldstein, *I Maccabees*, note on 6:63; 'The tales of the Tobiads', in *Christianity, Judaism and Other Greco-Roman Cults: Studies for Morton Smith at Sixty*, ed. Jacob Neusner, part 3 (Leiden, 1975), pp. 108–23.

3 B. Bar-Kochva, 'Qerev Bet-Zᵉkarya', *Zion* 39 (1974), 157–182. [Edd.]

4 Goldstein, *I Maccabees*, note on 6:20.

5 Ibid., note on 6:49–62.

6 Ibid., note on 6:55–6.

7 On the date, see Goldstein, *I Maccabees*, note on 6:63 and pp. 273–6.

The seer of 1 Enoch 90:31 had predicted that Judas, the great horned ram, would live to see God's miraculous vindication of the Jews. The surprising end of the siege of the Temple mount made it look as if Judas' survival was indeed part of God's plan.

The Seleucid policy of conciliation led to the removal of Menelaus and the appointment of Alcimus to the high priesthood. The evidence suggests that Alcimus was a pious priest who had refrained from rebellion even as he risked his life by refusing to participate in the cult imposed by Antiochus IV.[1] Though the Hasmonean party benefited from the peace, they recognized neither it nor the right of Alcimus to be high priest. If the age of Israel's subjection was over, Antiochus V had no right to appoint the high priest. And even if God still willed that Israel be subject to foreign rulers, the reign of the son of the monstrous persecutor might be illegitimate and brief (Isaiah 14:21). Lysias did prevail over the rebel Philippos at Antioch, but his own regime was doomed.

During the few remaining months of the reign of Antiochus V the Hasmonean party probably acted against Jews whom they viewed as sinners. The men of the Akra were safe behind its walls. Vulnerable were 'sinners' like the High Priest Alcimus, many of them pious opponents of the Hasmoneans. Their 'sin' probably consisted of collaboration with the 'illegitimate' regimes of the heinous persecutor and his son. Perhaps the shaky government of Lysias had decided to let the Jewish factions fight it out among themselves.

A more forceful Seleucid came and destroyed Lysias and the boy king. Demetrius I, son of Seleucus IV, had been kept as a hostage in Rome precisely because the Romans believed he would be a stronger ruler of the Seleucid empire than Antiochus V and his chief minister. As soon as Demetrius I had become king, the hard-pressed 'sinners' and the High Priest Alcimus appealed to him for aid against their opponents. Demetrius confirmed Alcimus as high priest and sent Bacchides, governor of Coele-Syria and Phoenicia, with troops to restore order. Bacchides, too, avoided the posture of a persecutor, though the Hasmonean party gave no credence to his pacific claims. Previously many pious Jews had hesitated to recognize Alcimus as high priest. Now, however, that he had been confirmed by a legitimate Seleucid king, they had to admit that Alcimus' priestly lineage and his piety were unimpeachable. After winning the trust of the pious, however, Alcimus or his protector Bacchides found it necessary to arrest and execute 70 of them, an act which contrasted ironically with

[1] See Goldstein, *I Maccabees*, note on 7:16–17.

the verses Alcimus had once written to mourn God's slaughtered saints (Psalm 79:2–3).[1]

Bacchides was determined to remove trouble-makers. He also arrested and executed persons whom the Hasmonean party regarded as collaborationists. Everywhere he acted to confirm the authority of Alcimus. Nothing as yet had dispelled the Hasmonean conviction that the age of servitude was over and that Demetrius' rule over the Jews was illegitimate. Judas and his followers in the countryside of Judea carried on a successful guerrilla campaign against Alcimus and his supporters, driving Alcimus to appeal again for royal aid.

The king sent the high official Nicanor with a strong force to pacify Judea. After a brief skirmish at Dessau, Nicanor turned to use diplomacy and even made friends with Judas. Alcimus immediately denounced this 'treason' to the king. To save his own skin, Nicanor had to try to capture Judas and suppress the Hasmonean band.[2] By executing pietists Bacchides had alienated pious Jews, so that their sympathies probably now were with Judas. But many of the pious still must have hesitated to regard the rule of Demetrius I as illegitimate. The king was not a persecutor, even if his agents had committed injustice. Hence in combat Judas at first had only the Hasmonean nuclear force of 3,000. In a battle at Kapharsalama the Hasmonean band defeated Nicanor. Surely the sympathies of the pious had made it possible for Judas and his men to survive and prosper. Hence Nicanor attempted to intimidate the pious; he threatened to destroy the Temple if Judas were not delivered into his hands. Nicanor marched out to Beth-Horon where he met reinforcements and conducted them back toward Jerusalem. At Adasa Judas blocked the road in front of the superior force, so confident was he of God's aid. In 1 Maccabees we are told that Nicanor was killed at the very beginning of the battle. The commander may have been an over-bold man, and his fall would go far to explain how Judas' outnumbered men were able to rout the enemy. Upon the rout of the Seleucid force, the sympathetic pious Jews of the countryside joined forces with the Hasmonean band in annihilating the survivors. The man who had threatened to destroy the Temple suffered condign punishment along with his army. Pious Jews saw a miracle in the victory, so like the triumphs of Jonathan and Gideon. Some claimed that Enoch himself had foretold Nicanor's defeat.[3]

The victory over Nicanor convinced Judas and many other pious

[1] See ibid.

[2] On the veracity of 2 Macc. 14:15–30, see Goldstein, *I Maccabees*, note on 7:27–30. The location of Dessau is unknown.

[3] 1 Enoch 90:19; cf. 1 Macc. 7:46 and 2 Macc. 15:16, 27–8.

Jews that the age of servitude was over. There were still reasons to hesitate. A sizeable minority of Jews probably still thought that the age of liberation had not yet come. The prophets had taught of the dreadful consequences of rebellion against a foreign king who ruled the Jews by the will of God. Even for the Hasmoneans and the majority the course was not clear. Should they do nothing themselves and wait for God to destroy the illegitimate empire of Demetrius I?[1] Should they, alone of mankind, join in God's work of destroying the wicked kingdom?[2] Would other nations become allies in God's work?[3] Surely the hostile neighbours of Judea would never be such allies. Alliances with the 'inhabitants of the land' were forbidden. Egypt was condemned by the prophets as a broken reed. Only distant peoples could be allies.[4] The Parthians, however, lay inaccessible across long reaches of Seleucid territory and were not yet an important power.[5] Rome was now the superpower in the Mediterranean world. No Graeco-Macedonian kingdom dared to clash with her. As seen through Jewish eyes, republican Rome, still puritanical, seemed to be almost Jewish.[6]

Accordingly, the official organs of the Jewish nation, perhaps prompted by Judas and the Hasmonean party, in 161 B.C.E. sent Eupolemus son of John of the priestly clan Hakkoz and Jason son of Eleazar on an embassy to Rome to establish ties of alliance.[7] The ambassadors succeeded. The Romans inscribed the name of the Jews in their list of friends and allies and made a treaty with the Jews. The text of the Roman reply and treaty is preserved in 1 Maccabees. It contains peculiar compromises and departures from regular Roman practice; all reflect the position of the Jews at the time.[8] Many Jews, perhaps the majority, were unwilling to risk outright rebellion against Demetrius unless Demetrius should commit wicked aggression against the Jews. Demetrius' troops occupied strong points on Jewish territory. Those many Jews could not bind themselves to observe the standard clause of a Roman treaty of alliance, whereby the ally was to refuse passage across his own territory to any power at war with Rome, for what if Rome should go to war with Demetrius? In their letter to the Jews, the

[1] Cf. Isa. 30:15.
[2] Cf. Isa. 63:5.
[3] Cf. Isa. 55:5.
[4] Cf. Josh. 9:6–22.
[5] See Mørkholm, *Antiochus IV*, pp. 172–90.
[6] See Goldstein, *I Maccabees*, note on 8:1–16.
[7] See ibid., note on 8:17–20.
[8] For a detailed discussion, see Goldstein, *I Maccabees*, notes on 1 Macc. 8:19–32. [On the foreign policy of the Hasmoneans see: T. Fischer, 'Zu den Beziehungen zwischen Rom und den Juden im 2. Jahrhundert v.Chr.'. *ZAW*, 86 (1974), 90–3; A. Giovannini and H. Müller, 'Die Beziehungen zwischen Rom und den Juden im 2. Jh. v.Chr.', *Museum Helveticum*, 28 (1971), 156–71; D. Timpe, 'Der römischer Vertrag mit den Juden von 161 v.Chr.', *Chiron*, 4 (1974), 133–52. Edd.]

Romans report that they have warned Demetrius not to oppress the Jews, but the warning in itself was a recognition of Demetrius' right to rule the Jews. Thus the Jewish ambassadors accepted a document which ran contrary to the Hasmonean view, that Seleucid rule over the Jews was no longer legitimate. The Roman document nowhere mentions Judas. Though the Hasmoneans may have originated the idea of establishing ties with Rome, the ambassadors represented a wider consensus, perhaps that of the Jewish council of elders.

Demetrius I was bold enough even to risk Rome's displeasure. If the Hasmonean party should attempt to deny legitimacy to the rule of Demetrius and to his appointment of the High Priest Alcimus, Rome would probably not help them, for the Romans might well view Alcimus as the legitimate head of the Jewish nation. Judas' band continued to resist Alcimus. Like his predecessors, Demetrius could not tolerate rebellion near the sensitive border with Ptolemaic Egypt. Again he sent Bacchides to pacify Judea, this time with half the élite infantry of the imperial army.

At first Judas was confident that God had ended Israel's servitude. 1 Enoch (90:31) had predicted that Judas would live to see God's miraculous triumph. However, even the 3,000-man nuclear Hasmonean force quailed at the size of Bacchides' army. All but 800 melted away from Judas' camp at Elasa. The Hasmonean historian implies that Judas' brothers and comrades urged him to withdraw and wait for a better day, but Judas saw such a course as beneath him. His tiny force fought bravely, but Judas was slain, and the survivors fled. Clearly he had been mistaken as to God's will!

Some Jews probably interpreted the words of Daniel 12:7, 'When the shattering of the power of the holy people comes to an end', to mean that when Judas should have been killed, the glorious triumph of God and Israel would come. The Hasmonean historian (1 Macc. 9:23) reflected bitterly that Judas' death led only to the flourishing of evildoers as Bacchides placed Alcimus and his supporters firmly in power, and a crop-failure made difficult even guerrilla resistance.[1] Members of the Hasmonean party were hunted down and punished. The surviving members of the party agreed to follow the leadership of Judas' brother Jonathan.

Bacchides tried to nip the new guerrilla movement in the bud, but Jonathan's band succeeded in escaping to the Judean desert where they established a stronghold by the water-hole Bor-Asphar.[2] Jonathan's

[1] See Goldstein, *I Maccabees*, note on 9:23–7.

[2] I supply the Hebrew word *Bōr* as part of the place-name, though the translator of 1 Maccabees has rendered it in Greek (*lakkou*).

band was not alone in defying Seleucid claims. The Nabatean Arabs stubbornly maintained their independence and had had friendly relations with the Hasmonean party already in the time of Judas. Now Jonathan sent his brother John to lead the non-combatants and the baggage from Bor-Asphar across the Jordan and southward to safekeeping among the Nabateans. Jonathan's band suffered a severe blow when the Arab Jambrites of Medaba captured the entire caravan. John was killed, and the loss was never retrieved, but Jonathan and his men had the satisfaction of wreaking vengeance upon the Jambrites; in their first military victory, Jonathan's band caught and massacred a rich Jambrite wedding procession. On withdrawing homeward, the band had a still more significant sign of divine favour. Bacchides tried to trap them in Transjordan on the Sabbath.[1] Jonathan and his men boldly fought off Bacchides' force and then plunged through the waters of the river to safety. Clearly God approved of the Hasmonean doctrine permitting self-defence on the Sabbath. Bacchides' force and the waters of the Jordan had not blocked Jonathan's band from returning to the Promised Land, just as Canaanite forces and the river waters had failed to stop Joshua's hosts. Jonathan was probably pleased when Bacchides established forts in Judea and Samaria and took hostages. Ultimately such measures would prove to be as ineffective against God's will as the fortifications of the Canaanites had been.

Divine displeasure soon appeared to fall upon an opponent of the Hasmoneans. Alcimus, following his own sectarian beliefs, sought to demolish a partition in the inner court of the Temple. At least the Hasmonean party viewed the partition as required by prophetic revelation.[2] In the course of the demolition, Alcimus suffered a paralytic stroke and died in helpless agony (May 159 B.C.E.).

Alcimus' high priesthood seems to have been the bone of contention. Jonathan and his men had learned from Judas' death in battle not to challenge the legitimacy of the rule of foreign king. Bacchides wisely judged that it was safe for him now to withdraw with his army from Judea. Wisely, he also left the high priesthood vacant. During the two quiet years (159–157 B.C.E.) that followed, Jonathan's band did not disperse. They probably did not stay at remote Bor-Asphar, since we are told that in their next time of peril they withdrew only to the more hospitable Beth-Basi, near Bethlehem. The continued existence of Jonathan's band in more settled areas of Judea or Samaria roused the apprehensions of anti-Hasmoneans who still had influence with the Seleucid government. With the approval of Bacchides they formed a

[1] See Goldstein, *I Maccabees*, note on 9:34–53. [2] See ibid., note on 9:54.

plot to take the band by surprise and arrest them. Bacchides is said to have set out with a large force, probably to deter any mass rising which might follow upon the arrests. However, the Hasmonean band found out, and the plot failed. Jonathan and his men took vengeance, killing about fifty of the conspirators.[1] To escape the superior force of Bacchides the Hasmonean band fled into the desert, this time only as far as the ruined stronghold of Beth-Basi. There they rebuilt the fortifications in time to face a siege by Bacchides. Jonathan was able to slip through the lines, leaving his brother Simon behind to command the defenders. Jonathan won the aid of nomad tribes.[2] Caught between nomad raiders outside and the defenders inside Beth-Basi, Bacchides suffered heavy losses and saw the defenders sally forth and burn his siege-works. Earlier Bacchides had sacrificed over-zealous loyalists in order to secure quiet in Judea. Now he did so again, executing the 'trouble-makers', and made peace with Jonathan. He returned the Jewish prisoners and withdrew from Judea. Evidently Bacchides had been given wide discretion by Demetrius. But Bacchides could bind only himself by oath to observe his agreement. He could not bind the king. The withdrawal of Bacchides left the Hasmonean band as the strongest military force in Judea. Jonathan still did not venture to take Jerusalem, but he moved to Machmas, famous for its associations with an earlier Jonathan. He and his followers saw his position as that of a latter-day judge, and he proceeded forcefully to 'wipe out the wicked from Israel' (from about 157 B.C.E.).

In 152 B.C.E. opportunities for greater things came to the judge. Alexander Balas, who claimed to be a son of Antiochus IV, landed at Ptolemais and was proclaimed king. The two claimants to the Seleucid throne began to bid against each other for the support of Jonathan and his party. Jonathan exploited the offers of both sides. From Demetrius' prompt bid he gained the legal right to raise troops and manufacture arms and the release of the hostages in the Akra, but not the removal of the garrison. The garrison of the Akra remained secure behind the walls, but now nothing could prevent Jonathan and his men from entering Jerusalem. The judge could pose as head of the entire nation and intimidate any opponents. Once inside Jerusalem, Jonathan followed the patterns of the kings of Judah and Nehemiah and rebuilt the walls of the city and the Temple mount.

Alexander Balas topped Demetrius' bid by appointing Jonathan to the long vacant high-priesthood and the order of the King's Friends. Jonathan entered upon the office during the festival of Tabernacles, in

[1] See ibid., note on 9:61.

[2] Ibid., note on 9:65–6.

October 152 B.C.E. Alexander and his partisans correctly judged Jonathan's favour to be the key factor. Demetrius made the mistake of trying to wean the Jews away from Alexander and Jonathan through sweeping concessions to the Jews and to an as yet unnamed high priest.[1] Jonathan's position among the Jews was already too strong, and pious Jews probably remembered with resentment the atrocities perpetrated by Demetrius' agents, Bacchides and Nicanor. The Jews did not participate in the decisive battle between the armies of the two kings, in which Demetrius fell (around midsummer 150 B.C.E.).

The Hasmoneans were probably among the Jews who believed in the truth of Daniel 2:43–4: when there should be a mixture by dynastic marriage between fragments of the Greco-Macedonian kingdom, the time for God's smashing of pagan empires would be near. Victorious Alexander Balas sought the hand of the daughter of Ptolemy VI of Egypt in marriage. Ptolemy consented to give him Cleopatra Thea. Jonathan and the Jews must have rejoiced over the signs of the times, though they now had the prudence to wait for God to act. With the wisdom of hindsight, the author of 1 Maccabees does not allude to Daniel 2:43–4, but he narrates the marriage in more detail than necessary. Clearly he viewed it as significant in the divine scheme. Alexander honoured Jonathan by inviting him to the wedding festivities at Ptolemais. Some Jews still opposed Jonathan. They brought a petition against him to King Alexander at Ptolemais, but the king responded by having Jonathan clothed in purple and paraded through the city accompanied by a herald proclaiming that petitions and suits against Jonathan were now forbidden. Jonathan received the rank of First Friend and the offices of *stratēgos* and *meridarchēs* of Judea.

The situation remained unchanged until Demetrius II, son of Demetrius I, landed in the Seleucid province of Cilicia in 147 B.C.E. and began to press his claims to the throne. Demetrius' efforts perturbed Alexander, but we hear nothing of their effects upon the Jews until early 145 B.C.E. By that time Apollonius, who had been governor of Coele-Syria for Alexander, deserted to Demetrius, who confirmed him in his office. Apollonius claimed Philistine descent and controlled much if not all of the coast of Palestine. Mockingly he challenged the mountain-dwelling Jews to risk battle in the plains where their ancestors had suffered defeat, implying that the Jews' God had no power there (compare 1 Kings 20:23–32). Jonathan with his brother

[1] See ibid., note on 10:22–45.

Simon vindicated the power of his God and advanced his sovereign's cause by occupying Jaffa and winning a smashing victory over Apollonius near Azotus.[1] Grateful Alexander promoted Jonathan to the rank of Kinsman of the King and gave him as his own heritage the old Philistine town of Ekron.[2]

Jonathan seems to have been loyal to Alexander, after the classical pattern of Jewish loyalty to the pagan rulers imposed by God, but he may well have believed that Daniel's prophecy (2:43–4) meant that the king's reign would be brief. Shortly after Jonathan's victory at Azotus, Ptolemy VI of Egypt marched into the Seleucid empire with a large army. Ptolemy probably claimed to be marching to aid Alexander against Demetrius II. If so, the claim may well have been true, but Ptolemy certainly intended to increase the power of his own kingdom, as once Antiochus IV had marched through Egypt posing as the defender of the interests of the very young Ptolemy VI. Ptolemy VI from the first may have intended to overthrow his incompetent son-in-law.[3] Jonathan could hardly read Ptolemy's mind. He piously obeyed Alexander's own commands that Ptolemy be welcomed. If Jonathan had any suspicion of the danger to his sovereign, he let events take their presumably God-given course. Ptolemy seized Antioch. Surely remembering what Antiochus IV had done to him in 169, Ptolemy had himself crowned king of the Seleucid empire, which he then granted to Demetrius II as 'vassal' king.[4] Alexander tried to resist, but in a battle north-east of Antioch he was routed. Ptolemy, however, was wounded in the head and died soon after, despite the efforts of his surgeons. Alexander fled to Arab territory nearby but the Arab chief Zabdiel beheaded him.[5] Upon Ptolemy's death, the Seleucid soldiers massacred some of the Ptolemaic troops and drove the rest out. Demetrius became sole king of the Seleucid empire.

Ptolemy VI had taken his daughter Cleopatra Thea, hitherto the wife of Alexander, and bestowed her on Demetrius. Thus again Jews who believed Daniel 2:42–3 could expect the imminent fall of pagan empires. Jonathan dared to besiege the Akra, but Demetrius forcefully summoned him to Ptolemais. Jonathan came, accompanied by enough Jewish notables to convince Demetrius that he was solidly backed by the Jewish nation. Jonathan was not ready to face the full might of the Seleucid empire, and Demetrius did not want war with the stubborn Jews. A compromise saved face for both sides. In return for lifting the

1 [See B. Bar-Kochva, 'Hellenistic warfare in Jonathan's campaign near Azotos', *Scripta Classica Israelica*, 2 (1975), 83–96. Edd.]

2 See Goldstein, *I Maccabees*, notes on 10:69–89.

3 Ibid., note on 11:1–11.

4 Ibid., note on 11:13.

5 Ibid., note on 11:16–17.

siege of the Akra,[1] Jonathan and the Jews gained most of the concessions once offered by Demetrius I, including the annexation to Judea of three toparchies of Samaria. By offering a single payment of 300 talents, Jonathan secured exemption from taxes for the enlarged Judea.

Throughout the rest of his career, Jonathan was probably under tension: he believed that the collapse of all pagan empires was imminent, wished to show his confidence in his God, but wished also to be prudent and not to act before God was ready.

When Demetrius faced a dangerous revolt of his discharged soldiers and of the citizens of Antioch, he sought Jonathan's aid, promising great rewards. As a loyal subject, Jonathan sent Jewish troops who quelled the rebels. Instead of showing gratitude, Demetrius sought to curb his dangerously powerful subject. Jonathan concluded he owed nothing to so faithless a sovereign but prudently waited for God's act of liberation. When shortly thereafter the military strong-man Diodotus-Tryphon raised up Alexander Balas' little son, Antiochus VI, as rival king, Jonathan turned himself and his nation into loyal subjects of the new regime. In return, he was promoted to high office. Jonathan and the Jews won brilliant victories for Antiochus over Demetrius' partisans. Once Jonathan narrowly escaped defeat. He snatched victory, it seemed, by offering up a timely prayer. If so, clearly God was with him! Accordingly he felt free to send an embassy to renew the alliance with Rome and establish friendly ties with Sparta.[2] He also dared to wall off the Akra from the rest of Jerusalem, threatening its inhabitants with starvation. Well could he do so, as a commander for Antiochus VI, since Demetrius had treated the men of the Akra as his own garrison.

Immediately after telling of the embassy to Rome and Sparta, Josephus says that the three sects, Pharisees, Sadducees, and Essenes, existed at that time. Josephus may have had information that Jonathan's presumption at this point had led one or more of the sects to oppose him. The 'wicked priest' of the Qumran texts may well have been Jonathan.[3] Josephus was a proud descendant of Jonathan and admired the sects.[4] He may have been unwilling to speak directly of their opposition to Jonathan.

According to 1 Maccabees, Diodotus-Tryphon plotted to do away

[1] Ibid., note on 11:22–9.

[2] On the diplomacy and on the authenticity of the documents quoted in 1 Macc. 12, see Goldstein, *I Maccabees*, introductory note to 12:1–38 and notes to 12:1–23.

[3] See J. T. Milik, *Ten Years of Discovery in the Wilderness of Judea*, SBT 26 (Naperville, Ill., 1959), pp. 64–72; and Goldstein, *I Maccabees*, Introduction, part 4, n. 21.

[4] See my article in *Studies for Morton Smith*, part 3, pp. 85–6.

with Jonathan because faithful Jonathan would have resisted his usurpation of the throne. But even contemporaries could hardly know what was in the strong man's mind. Probably, like Demetrius, Tryphon intended to curb and eliminate a dangerously powerful subject. When the wily Tryphon offered to surrender to Jonathan the important city of Ptolemais and other strong points, Jonathan probably thought God was acting upon Tryphon in fulfilment of prophecies.[1] With his usual caution, Jonathan took with him to Ptolemais a bodyguard of 1,000, but the hostile citizens there, acting for Tryphon, massacred the small contingent and took Jonathan prisoner.

Again Jewish hopes of imminent fulfilment of prophecy had been dashed. Would the hostile pagan neighbours, hitherto overawed by Jonathan's power, now jump to act as they had acted in the time of Judas? Many Jews must have felt panic as they reflected that Jonathan, too, was a 'violent son' of the people and had 'risen up to fulfil the vision and failed' (Daniel 11:14).

Simon's resolute leadership saw the Jews through the crisis. He was immediately accepted by the despairing Jews. Characteristically, he looked for no imminent fulfilments; God would act in his own time. Simon used his human military sagacity. He quickly secured Jaffa, which lay within his province as commander for Antiochus VI. Thus the Jews held a port through which they could call for the help of friendly Rome. Whenever Tryphon moved to enter the difficult mountains of Judea, Simon balked him.

Tryphon confronted Simon with a difficult choice when he offered to release Jonathan in return for 100 talents and two sons of Jonathan as hostages. Should Simon trust treacherous Tryphon? If he missed an opportunity to save Jonathan, he might be hated for supplanting his brother and leaving him in the hands of the enemy. Simon handed over the money and the sons, only to have Tryphon keep Jonathan.

Cut off from supplies by Jonathan's wall, the hard-pressed men of the Akra sent to Tryphon, begging him to march to their relief. Tryphon's effort was foiled by a rare (miraculous?) snowstorm (late 143 B.C.E.). Tryphon withdrew by way of Transjordan and somewhere in that area slew Jonathan. Simon recovered the body and placed it in the family cemetery at Modiin.

Tryphon's treachery far exceeded any of Demetrius II's misdeeds against the Jews. Pious Jews inferred that if God still willed that they be subjected to pagan rulers, the legitimate king must be Demetrius. Accordingly, the nation, not just the Hasmonean party, went over to

[1] See Isa. 49:7, 60:1–14.

Demetrius.[1] Except for Jaffa, the coastal plain and plateau, including Gazara, had long been held by the regime of Antiochus VI and Tryphon.[2] Now Simon felt free to besiege and take the troublesome royal stronghold of Gazara. Many supporters of Simon appear to have believed that neither of the two pretenders was a legitimate ruler over the Jews. These partisans now declared Simon to be high priest; other Jews refused to recognize the appointment unless it was ratified by a king. Contemporary documents reflect these events. The decree of the Jews in honour of Simon, dated in September 140 B.C.E., attests that the 'nation' appointed Simon high priest without waiting for Demetrius to act.[3] And the letter of the Jews of Jerusalem and Judea to the Jews of Ptolemaic Egypt, of late 143 B.C.E., does not mention Simon but is dated in the reign of Demetrius II, showing that the Jewish nation has abandoned the regime of Tryphon and Antiochus VI.[4]

Some Jews might still have adhered to Antiochus VI, but none accepted the tyrannical upstart Tryphon in 142 B.C.E. when he treacherously had the boy king slain and claimed to be king himself.[5] Tryphon made no pretence to be a Seleucid. Long before, pious Jews had sought Rome's aid against the injustices of Demetrius I even while they still acknowledged Seleucid sovereignty over them. Now most pious Jews probably supported Simon when he sought to renew the alliance with Rome. However, Simon's ambassador, Numenius, also secured from Rome for Simon a grant which was a threat to some of the pious: Rome asked many kingdoms and republics of the eastern Mediterranean area, perhaps all with sizeable Jewish communities, to extradite to Simon any fugitives from his rule.[6]

Such achievements stilled most Jewish opposition and (probably in October 142 B.C.E.) impelled Demetrius not only to confirm victorious Simon as high priest but also to grant the Jews practical independence, including exemption from taxes.[7] The Jews began counting an era of their own independence. A legal document would be dated: 'In the year one, when Simon was high priest and commander and the chief of the Jews.'

The Hasmonean party and many other Jews must have viewed the

[1] See Goldstein, *I Maccabees*, note on 13:34–42.

[2] 1 Macc. 11:60, 12:33–4, 13:12–20.

[3] 1 Macc. 14:35; see Goldstein, *I Maccabees*, notes on 13:34–42, 13:36, 14:34–6.

[4] 2 Macc. 1:7; see Elias Bickerman, 'Ein jüdischer Festbrief vom Jahre 124 v. Chr.', *ZNW*, 32 (1933), 233–54.

[5] The death of Antiochus VI preceded the fall of Demetrius II to the Parthians. See Goldstein, *I Maccabees*, note on 12:39–40.

[6] See ibid., notes on 14:14–24k.

[7] The date is derived from *Megillat Ta'anit* 3 Tishri. See Goldstein, *I Maccabees*, notes on 13:41 and 13:42.

event as of cosmic importance. The ode to Simon in 1 Maccabees 14:4–15 surely reflects the enthusiasm, as it echoes prophecies which seemed to be in the process of fulfilment. The remainder of Simon's reign was prosperous. Even so, some Jews had misgivings. The contemporary document at 1 Maccabees 14:27–49 confers great honour and power on Simon and his heirs after him, but it pointedly refrains from saying that Simon's career saw the liberation of the Jews!

Not all pious Jews outside the Hasmonean party compromised. The ancestors of the Essenes of Qumran hated him as the Cursed Man of Belial and were to rejoice over his death.[1] Simon surely refused to accept their interpretations of Jewish law and their Jewish calendar. Some sectarians may have insisted that Simon was not of the Zadokite line of priests and hence was ineligible to be high priest.[2]

Other pious Jews, however, soon thought they were seeing the fulfilment of God's promises. Simon found it easy to continue Jonathan's siege of the Akra. Jonathan had begun it as agent of Antiochus VI, acting against partisans of Demetrius II. By seeking Tryphon's aid, the besieged became enemies of Demetrius. As soon as the Jews became subjects of Demetrius, they were free to press the siege. So it was that the men of the Akra were starved into seeking a truce and were expelled from Jerusalem in June 141 B.C.E. Simon incorporated the Akra into the fortifications of the Temple mount and began to reside there himself with his retinue.[3]

Still more wondrous was the news of the day when Demetrius II was captured in battle by the army of the Parthian King Arsaces (between 142 and late 141 B.C.E.).[4] Surely here was a fulfilment of Isaiah 13:17 to 14:27 and Jeremiah 51:11 and a partial fulfilment of Daniel 2:41–4: the 'king of the Medes' had attacked and defeated the 'king of Assyria and Babylon' and captured the husband of the Ptolemaic princess Cleopatra Thea. Would not all pagan empires now yield to an empire of the Chosen People as predicted by Isaiah, Jeremiah, and Daniel?

Antiochus, brother of Demetrius II, seized the opportunity to rule the kingless Seleucid realm. Several months elapsed before he succeeded in taking power as Antiochus VII.[5] At the beginning of his

[1] See F. M. Cross, Jr., *The Ancient Library of Qumran* (Garden City, N.Y., 1961), pp. 144–52. Cross is probably wrong to identify the wicked priest with the cursed man; see Goldstein, *I Maccabees*, Introduction, part 4, n. 21.

[2] See *Cambridge History of Judaism*, vol. 3, chapter 5.

[3] In a future article I shall argue that the account at 1 Macc. 13:52 is correct, and that Josephus was misled by his own preconceptions and the vagueness of his sources to ascribe to Simon (*Bell.* 1.50; *Ant.* XIII.215–17) the drastic grading of the Akra hill, carried out by John Hyrcanus when he built the Baris.

[4] See Goldstein, *I Maccabees*, notes on 12:39–40 and 14:1–3.

[5] Ibid., note on 15:1–2.

enterprise he sought the support of Simon and the Jews against Tryphon. His letter confirmed the concessions of Demetrius and added to them the right to coin. The letter does not say what metals might be used. Coinage in silver was a mark of complete independence. Antiochus still claimed sovereignty over the Jews. Hence he probably conferred only the right to coin in bronze. Jewish scruples over making graven images may have held Simon back from using the new privilege. Antiochus was quick to revoke it when he established himself in power, so that there are no coins from Simon's high priesthood.[1]

Indeed, Antiochus VII soon felt free to dispense with the Jews' support and tried to curb their dangerous independent behaviour. He demanded the return of Jaffa, Gazara, and the Akra or else a payment of 500 talents for the taxes due from those cities plus 500 talents in damages. Simon, confident of God's support, replied that Jaffa, Gazara, and the Akra were parts of Israel's heritage. He offered to pay a token 100 talents for Jaffa and Gazara and for the rest was ready to defy Antiochus.

When Antiochus' commander Kendebaios established a base at Kedron in the Sorek valley and began to make punitive expeditions into Judea, the ageing Simon himself directed the counter-measures, though he entrusted the leadership in combat to his sons John and Judas. The old man even led his hesitant troops across a torrent.[2] In the battle not far from Modiin, the son routed Kendebaios. When Judas was wounded, John pressed the pursuit. In this battle Jewish cavalry appears for the first time. How did Simon convince his pious subjects that God allowed Jews to use horses, despite the frequent condemnations of them in Scripture?

Simon perished miserably through the treachery of his ambitious son-in-law, Ptolemy son of Abubos, commander at Jericho. Ptolemy plied Simon and his two sons, Judas and Mattathias, with drink and then murdered them at his castle of Dok by Jericho. He sent men to murder John, who was at Gazara. The Hasmoneans could find no way to fit the deaths into God's scheme, and the historian of 1 Maccabees tells the story so as to stress that Simon, the benefactor of the nation, fell to an ungrateful traitor whose first act thereafter was to bid for the support of Antiochus VIII by offering him the submission of the Jews. The historian is pleased to report that John foiled the attempt to kill him and succeeded Simon as high priest.

[1] See Baruch Kanael, 'Altjüdische Münzen', *Jahrbuch für Numismatik und Geldgeschichte*, 17 (1967), 165–6.

[2] See Goldstein, *I Maccabees*, note on 16:1–7.

Simon's thought-patterns can be seen in the elaborate monument he built over the family tomb. The architecture followed Hellenistic patterns but for a Jewish purpose. Within were displayed 'trophies', suits of armour mounted so as to look like a man wearing armour. In typical Hellenistic fashion these commemorated the great Hasmonean victories on land. Boldly Simon also displayed on pillars of the monument carvings of ships, the traditional Hellenistic design for celebrating a sea-victory. Clearly Simon expected that the Hasmoneans would yet dominate the seas, in fulfilment of Isaiah 42:10–13.

The ancestors of the Essenes of Qumran welcomed the death of the Cursed Man of Belial and his sons at Jericho; it fulfilled God's revealed will.[1] But the majority of Jews mourned Simon and supported his heir John and rejected the traitor Ptolemy.

Our good informant, the author of 1 Maccabees, gives us only one sentence on the high priesthood of John, also called Hyrcanus. The author lets us know that an account of John's mighty deeds and of the walls he built once existed in a chronicle of John's high priesthood. We, however, depend almost entirely on Josephus for our information on John. In both the *War* and the *Antiquities* Josephus' account is episodic, sketchy and vague and does not even mention John's wall-building. Clearly the chronicle of John's high priesthood was no longer available to Josephus. The problem of the sources of Josephus' accounts has yet to find a satisfactory solution and cannot be treated here in detail. Josephus' use of the pagan historian Nicolaus of Damascus has been greatly overestimated.[2]

Josephus' story of the early years of John's high priesthood bristles with difficulties. He has John seeking immediately to punish the murderer Ptolemy and besieging him in the fortress of Dagon near Jericho. He says that Ptolemy at first deterred John by torturing John's mother, whom he held prisoner, and that finally John had to give up the siege because of the advent of the sabbatical year. However, John's accession is fixed in February, 134 B.C.E., and though the dating of the sabbatical cycles is still a vexed question, the next sabbatical year probably began in early autumn, 129 B.C.E.[3] Josephus' narrative does not allow the siege to drag on for five and a half years, for he says that Antiochus VII invaded Judea in John's first year and forced John to

[1] See above, p. 319, n. 1.

[2] For a survey of the literature, see Ben Zion Wacholder, *Nicolaus of Damascus*, University of California Publications in History, 75 (Berkeley–Los Angeles, 1962), pp. 4–6, 54–64, and notes thereto; Emil Schürer, *The History of the Jewish People in the Age of Jesus Christ*, new English edition, rev. by Geza Vermes and Fergus Millar (Edinburgh, 1973), 1, pp. 30–2. I plan to treat Josephus' sources in a future study.

[3] See Goldstein, *I Maccabees*, Appendix 1, and note on 6:20.

acknowledge his overlordship and that thereafter John accompanied Antiochus on his expedition against the Parthians. Antiochus was killed in a winter battle with the Parthians, early in 129.[1]

Even if the sabbatical year could be dated in 134, Josephus' chronology would be improbable. Antiochus must have welcomed the death of unruly Simon and probably at first supported the murderer Ptolemy. Josephus himself says Antiochus invaded Judea in John's first year. John surely was aware of Antiochus' power. How could John have dared then to commit his forces to a siege near Jericho? Josephus reports that when John abandoned the siege, Ptolemy took refuge with Zeno Kotylas, 'tyrant' of Philadelphia (modern Amman). If Antiochus VII had been ruling, Ptolemy probably would have fled to *him*. And Antiochus put down the presumptuous 'tyrant' John, so the tyrant Zenon probably could gain power in Philadelphia only after the fall of Antiochus in 129.

Accordingly, we may guess that there was a Jewish tradition on John's thwarted vengeance which gave no dates. Josephus, or his source, wrongly guessed that pious, forceful John could not have delayed his vengeance and that Ptolemy could not have held his stronghold and John's mother for years. If so, the story of thwarted vengeance should be placed between the death of Antiochus VII early in 129 and the beginning of the sabbatical year in the autumn.

We may now reconstruct the history of John's high priesthood. John had the support of his people and prevailed in Jerusalem and Judea, but Ptolemy held Jericho and John's mother. The Jews knew Antiochus would be quick to march against them in support of Ptolemy. We have no information on the organs which made decisions for the Jewish nation at this time. By whatever process, the nation now decided to seek Rome's help. John may have won more solid support from the nation by renouncing some of the hereditary prerogatives granted to Simon, for the embassy to Rome went in the name of the Jews, not of John. The Jewish ambassadors brought the Romans the extravagant gift of a heavy golden shield, and the Senate granted the Jews full diplomatic support.[2] When the favourable Roman reply was filed in the archives at Jerusalem, John's officials still followed the system begun under Simon and dated the document 'in the month Panemos [= Sivan] in the ninth year [of the freedom of the Jews] when Hyrcanus was high priest and ethnarch' (May–June 134 B.C.E.).[3] John

[1] See Thomas Fischer, *Untersuchungen zum Partherkrieg Antiochos' VII.* (Diss. Tübingen; Tübingen 1970), pp. 29–48.

[2] Jos. *Ant.* XIV.145–8, as interpreted by Menahem Stern, ''Al ha-Yᵉḥasim ben Yᵉhuda wᵉRoma bime Yoḥanan Hurqanos', *Zion* 26 (1961), 1–6.

[3] See Goldstein, *I Maccabees*, note on 13:42.

was soon to give up the use of the dating-system as premature and presumptuous.

Roman diplomatic support was often effective, but Antiochus VII was the last Seleucid impetuous enough to defy Rome and knew that Roman force was far away. He was sure he could overcome John before the Romans intervened. The defenders of Jerusalem saw no divine purpose in Antiochus' attack and stoutly resisted his siege, which began before the November rains. The besieged suffered terribly, especially the non-combatants. Antiochus, however, showed respect for the God of the Jews. He granted a truce after months of siege for the festival of Tabernacles and sent a magnificent sacrifice to the Temple. The king probably saw the impracticality of trying to impose the hated Ptolemy on the fiercely resisting Jews. He was ready to compromise with Hyrcanus. Hyrcanus seized the opportunity for clemency. The besieged consented to hand over their arms. The Jews were to pay tribute to the king for Jaffa and the other towns bordering on Judea. At first the king demanded that a garrison of royal troops be stationed among the Jews. Josephus' narrative here mentions not John but the Jews: *they* refused to accept the garrison because it would involve their contact with Gentiles. Instead the king accepted their offer of hostages plus 500 talents of silver. The king also destroyed the circuit of the walls of Jerusalem.

If the terms specified that the Jews had to pay tribute for Jaffa and other border-towns, we may infer that the rest of the territory ruled by John remained tax-exempt. Antiochus could give such generous terms because he had just received hostages and probably also because he had the resource of Ptolemy son of Abubos. We may guess that Antiochus left Ptolemy in control of Jericho and that Ptolemy still held John's mother.

Submission to Antiochus meant that the Jews were no longer free of foreign domination, and probably at this point Jews stopped dating documents by the era of their own freedom and returned to the use of the Seleucid era. Antiochus appears soon to have shown consideration to his Jewish subjects by having a royal mint, probably at Ashkelon, strike bronze coins with types unobjectionable to Jews. Examples are known bearing dates from 180 to 183 S.E. (132/1–129/8 B.C.E.).[1]

The war and the payments to Antiochus VII left John's treasury empty. But he was able to recover financially without squeezing his hard-hit subjects. On opening an ancient tomb, he found a treasure of

[1] Numismatists long assumed that Jerusalem was the site of the mint (see Y. Meshorer, 'The beginning of Hasmonean coinage', *IEJ*, 24 (1974), 60), but see now U. Rappaport, 'Ašqelon umaṭbeoteha šel Yehuda', *Meḥqarim betoledot 'am Yiśra'el we'ereṣ Yiśra'el* (Haifa, 1979), vol. 4, pp. 77–85.

3,000 talents. Josephus reports that it was the tomb of David. The finding of so large a treasure in much-despoiled Jerusalem is surprising but not impossible. John used some of the money to hire a force of foreign mercenaries. If any Jews opposed this step, John probably replied that David himself had hired Philistine and 'Cretan' mercenaries.

Antiochus planned an ambitious expedition eastward, to recover territory lost to the Parthians as well as the person of his brother Demetrius II, a prisoner of the Parthian king since 140/39 B.C.E. Left behind in Judea, John might have rebelled. Antiochus followed a policy of caution and strength: he required John to accompany him with a force of Jews. In the course of the campaign the king respected the religious obligations of the Jewish soldiers. At first, in 131 B.C.E., Antiochus was so successful that he marched into Babylon and took the title 'the Great'. In the next year, he pushed farther east, into the Parthian heartland. Christian writers say that 'Hyrcanus' was an epithet acquired by John during Antiochus' campaigns (Hyrcania was a district along the south-eastern shore of the Caspian Sea). The name, however, is attested earlier among Jews, so that these authors are probably guessing. The source of their false inference was probably the lost account of Posidonius treating Antiochus' campaigns. The king did not come near Hyrcania until 130 B.C.E., so that we would then know that John was in eastern Iran early in 130.[1] It would appear that John was allowed to return to Judea, perhaps as a reward for distinguished service, for when Antiochus fell in battle in 129 B.C.E., John was not with him. According to Josephus, John *heard* of Antiochus' death and immediately proceeded to conquer territory bordering on Judea.

With Antiochus dead, John still faced the problem: was the time of Israel's subjection really past? Or was Simon's death God's judgement upon him for his presumption? John followed the Hasmonean pattern of striving for independence without taking irrevocable steps. It is debatable whether John ever issued even bronze coins in his own name.[2] He also continued to renounce hereditary prerogatives granted by the nation to Simon. When the Jews of Judea and Jerusalem

[1] See above, p. 322 n. 1.

[2] Meshorer, *IEJ*, 24 (1974), 59–61, and *Jewish Coins of the Second Temple Period* (Chicago, 1968), pp. 41–52; Richard S. Hanson, 'Toward a chronology of the Hasmonean coins', *BASOR*, 216 (December, 1974), 21–3. Uriel Rappaport presents arguments of some weight to show that John and his successor, Judas Arisobulus I, issued coins (vol. 1, pp. 35–8, and 'The emergence of Hasmonean coinage', *American Jewish Studies Review* 1 (1976), 171–86).

sent a letter in 124 to the Jews of Egypt, calling upon them to observe the festival on the twenty-fifth of Kislev which commemorated a *Hasmonean* victory, the letter contained no mention of John and was dated by the Seleucid era![1] John probably consented to these violations of the Jews' own decree.

John's first military act after Antiochus' death was probably to besiege Ptolemy son of Abubos in the fortress of Dagon near Jericho. Ptolemy, however, still held John's mother and perhaps two brothers as well. By torturing the mother before John's eyes, Ptolemy was able to hold out until the coming of the sabbatical year, in early autumn, 129. Josephus says that John was forced to lift the siege by the *coming* of the sabbatical year, not by a food shortage which the sabbatical year could have caused (contrast 1 Macc. 6:49, 53–4). Before the discovery of the Qumran texts, this fact was puzzling. Now we know that at least the Essenes of Qumran held warfare to be forbidden during the sabbatical year.[2] In his early reign, John followed a policy of foregoing prerogatives and of conciliating as many Jewish sects as possible. In accordance with this policy, John let the sabbatical year thwart his vengeance! Ptolemy killed his hostages and escaped to Zenon, tyrant of Philadelphia, and is not heard of thereafter.

John's aggressive policies went beyond domestic acts of vengeance. Even if God's decree of servitude still endured, perhaps it now required only token submission to the foreign ruler. The inept Demetrius II, released by the Parthian king, now reigned over the Seleucid empire. John judged that he could now embark on campaigns of conquest. John and his followers seem to have believed that Jewish expansion should fulfil Numbers 24:17–24, Isaiah 11:14, 15, 16 and 25:9–12, Jeremiah 30:18 to 31:15 and 48:1 to 49:22, Amos 9:12, Zephaniah 2:4–10, and Obadiah. Judas Maccabeus had already taken and destroyed Jazer in 'Moab' in fulfilment of Isaiah 16:8–9 and Jeremiah 48:32. According to Numbers 24:17 and Isaiah 25:9–12, Moab should be the first to be conquered in the time of God's salvation of Israel. In John's time Medaba appears to have been the most important city in the area which had been Moab. In his first act of conquest after the death of Antiochus VII, John took Medaba, though it fell only after a six-month siege. His next acquisition, the mysterious 'Samoga and its environs', also probably lay in Moab. If 'Samoga' is miswritten for 'Masoga' (Hebrew: *hmśgb*), John had begun to fulfil

[1] 2 Macc. 1:1–9; Bickerman, *ZNW*, 32 (1933), 233–54. The dating formula quoted in *b. Rosh ha-Shanah* 18b is probably of John Hyrcanus II; cf. the title of Hyrcanus II at Jos. *Ant.* XVI.163.

[2] 1QM 2:8–9; cf. Jub. 50:2–3, 12–13.

Isaiah 15:2 and Jeremiah 48:1 ('the fortress [*ha-miśgab*] is put to shame and broken down').[1]

Thereafter John took Shechem and mount Gerizim and destroyed the Samaritan temple (compare Jeremiah 31:4–21). He conquered Idumea, directly to the south of Judea. He confronted the conquered Idumeans (latter-day Edomites) with the choice: become Jews or leave the country.

John's conquest of Edom surely was taken as a fulfilment of Numbers 24:18, Amos 9:12, and Obadiah, but his forced conversion of those Idumeans who wished to remain in the land marked a new direction in Hasmonean policy toward pagan ethnic groups. Hitherto, Simon had expelled the inhabitants of Jaffa and Gazara and the Akra, without giving them the option of becoming Jews. Reasons of state rather than religion *might* explain all three of Simon's explusions. On the other hand, John is not reported to have either converted or expelled the inhabitants of conquered Moab. Moab was no part of the Promised Land, and conversion of Moabites was forbidden by Deuteronomy 23:3. John's conquest of Idumea, however, confronted pious Jews with a problem. Idumea had been part of the Promised Land. If Exodus 23:31–3 applied to the Idumeans, they could not be allowed to dwell in the land of Israel as Idumean idolaters. There was also the commandment at Deuteronomy 23:7, 'You shall not abhor an Edomite, for he is your brother.' It was probably in order to fulfil the two clashing commandments that John granted the Idumeans the option of becoming Jews. The conquered Idumeans could be allowed to live in the land of Israel as Jews who had abjured idolatry. Once the option had been devised for the Idumeans, it could be offered to other pagan peoples as the Hasmoneans reconquered more and more of the Promised Land.

In his wars of conquest John probably faced stout resistance. The bitterly hostile Idumeans surely knew that their liberty and their religion were at stake, and the Samaritans must have known that John intended to destroy their temple. The latest dated coins found in the excavations of Shechem were of 110. Perhaps John captured the city earlier and destroyed it only in or after 110.[2] There was a well-established Idumean *émigré* community in Egypt by 112 B.C.E.[3] There

[1] See Abraham Schalit, *König Herodes, der Mann und sein Werk's* (Berlin, 1969), p. 199 n. 186, and cf. Schalit's 'Die Eroberungen des Alexander Jannäus in Moab', *Theokratia,* 1 (1967/69), 3–50.

[2] See G. E. Wright, 'Schechem', *Encyclopaedia of Archaeological Excavations in the Holy Land*, vol. 4 (Oxford, 1978), pp. 1083–94.

[3] Uriel Rappaport, 'Les Iduméens en Égypte', *RPh,* 3rd series, 43 (1969), 73–82.

is no evidence to prevent us from following Josephus and from placing these conquests of John in the reign of Demetrius II.

Cleopatra II, at war with her brother Ptolemy VIII Euergetes II, offered the throne of Egypt in 129 B.C.E. to her son-in-law, Demetrius II. Against his inept Seleucid rival, Ptolemy VIII raised up Alexander Zebinas as a pretender to the throne of Syria. Alexander was ruling from Antioch by autumn, 128 B.C.E.,[1] and John established friendly relations with him. Neither Demetrius nor Alexander challenged John's inland conquests. Demetrius kept hold of Damascus, Ptolemais, and coastal Palestine until Alexander decisively defeated him at Damascus in 127/6 B.C.E. A document of Jewish diplomacy shows that Demetrius balked Jewish efforts to conquer westward and fulfil Isaiah 11:14 and Zephaniah 2:5–7. When John and the Jews found they could not win back Jaffa, Gazara, and Pegae and other territories lost to Antiochus VII, they sent an embassy to seek Roman aid. The Romans declared their friendship for the Jews and promised in the future to prevent such injuries to the Jews but took no action for the present. The letter of the Romans in reply to the embassy should be dated before Demetrius' final defeat.[2]

Alexander Zebinas was inept and fell by 123 B.C.E.[3] Antiochus VIII Grypus, son of Demetrius II, was a teenager. At first he shared rule with his mother, but even after her death in 121 B.C.E. we hear of no move by him to challenge John's Judea. From 114/113 B.C.E. Grypus had his hands full coping with the rival claimant to the Seleucid throne, his half-brother Antiochus IX Cyzicenus, son of Antiochus VII. Thus John was long left free to enjoy his enlarged territory and to attempt further expansion. If the conquests of Idumea and Samaritan Shechem and Gerizim were not yet finished, John completed them in those years. He also probably recovered Jaffa.

John and the Jews suffered a brief setback when Antiochus IX seized most if not all of the Seleucid empire in 114/113 B.C.E. By summer 112 B.C.E., coins of Antiochus IX were being minted in Ashkelon as well as in Ptolemais, Damascus, and Antioch.[4] Probably Cyzicenus held the entire coastal plain of Palestine. Hence we find the Roman senate granting the Jews' petitions 'that King Antiochus, son of Antiochus, shall do no more injury to the Jews and that he should restore anything taken from them, including fortresses, harbours, and territory', and

[1] Alfred R. Bellinger, 'The end of the Seleucids', *Transactions of the Connecticut Academy of Arts and Sciences,* 38 (1949), 61–3; Will, *Histoire,* 2, pp. 363–6.

[2] Jos. *Ant.* XIII.259–66, as interpreted by Stern, *Zion,* 26 (1961), 7–12.

[3] Will, *Histoire,* 2, pp. 365–6.

[4] Bellinger, 'Seleucids', 67, 87.

that he should withdraw his garrison from Jaffa. The Jews are even to be allowed to tax Seleucid goods exported through their harbours.[1]

Antiochus IX probably did not have to decide whether he was strong enough to defy the Romans. Antiochus VIII got support from Ptolemaic Egypt and took Antioch in summer 112 B.C.E. Antiochus IX held on to Sidon, Damascus, Ptolemais and Ashkelon.[2] In the course of the war of the brothers, John was able to recover the lost areas. In 111 B.C.E. coins of Antiochus IX ceased to be minted in Ashkelon. At the beginning of the Reign of Alexander Janneus (103 B.C.E.), in the coastal plain outside the Hasmonean realm there remained only Ptolemais, Gaza and Ashkelon.[3] If so, John fulfilled prophecies of conquests in Philistia.

Late in his reign, John took advantage of the war of the Seleucid brothers to conquer the city of Samaria. The *city* of Samaria had long been populated by Greek and Macedonian soldier–colonists, not by Samaritans.[4] Josephus reports that John's avowed aim was to punish the inhabitants for injuries they had perpetrated upon the people of Mareshah who were 'colonists and allies of the Jews'. The inhabitants are said to have acted in obedience to the kings of Syria. Josephus' report is probably correct. Though Samaria lay far from Mareshah, soldiers from Samaria, acting under royal orders, could well have attacked Mareshah. The people of Mareshah may still have been largely Phoenician. Like the rest of the inhabitants of Idumea, they probably were recent converts to Judaism.[5] As Phoenicians, they could be called 'allies'. As converts, they could be called 'colonists'.[6]

John's sons Antigonus and Aristobulus heavily besieged Samaria. In desperation, the inhabitants sought the help of Antiochus IX. However, John's sons routed him and pursued him as far as Scythopolis. Again the desperate inhabitants appealed to Antiochus IX, who came to the rescue with a force of 6,000 which he had obtained from Ptolemy IX Lathyrus. Josephus informs us that Cleopatra III of Egypt, who was then ruling jointly with her son Ptolemy IX, was so angry over the grant of soldiers that she almost deposed him. Thus we can get an approximate date for the campaign. Cleopatra III ruled jointly with Ptolemy IX from 116 B.C.E., but there were brief ruptures between her and the son she hated, beginning in late 110. She finally deposed him in

[1] Jos. *Ant.* XIV.247–55, as interpreted by Stern, *Zion* 26 (1961), 12–17.

[2] Bellinger, 'Seleucids', 87. [3] Jos. *Ant.* XIII.324; Schalit, *König Herodes*, pp. 198–9.

[4] See Goldstein, *I Maccabees*, note on 3:10.

[5] See M. Avi-Yonah, 'Mareshah', *Enṣ. Miq.* 5, p. 478. [See also M. Avi-Yonah, 'Šomᵉron u-Mareshah lᵉfi *Qadmoniot* XIII.275', *Yediot* 4 (1951–2), 29–31 [Edd.]

[6] See Goldstein, *I Maccabees*, note on 8:1–16 and note on 8:1.

October or November 107.[1] Thus, the long campaign against Samaria began between 111 and 107.

Antiochus IX tried to divert the besiegers by raids on Judea but suffered costly defeats. During one of these battles, John happened to be burning incense alone in the Temple, presumably on the Day of Atonement. He heard a voice saying that his sons had just defeated Antiochus. John went out and reported what he had heard to the assembled people, and his report soon proved to be true.[2] John's supporters must have begun to view him as a prophet. Antiochus may have deliberately attacked on the holy day. If so, John's sons were ready to defend themselves vigorously on the Day of Atonement.

After his defeats, Antiochus departed but left a force under Callimandrus and Epicrates to continue the war. The Jews defeated and killed Callimandrus. Epicrates failed to relieve Samaria and accepted bribes to betray Scythopolis and other points. 'Samaria-Wall' (a name for Samaria, the city, to distinguish it from the province?) fell on 25 Marheshvan.[3] John is said to have razed Samaria to the ground and even to have dug channels so that rain-water would eventually erase all trace of the ruins. In so doing he was probably trying to fulfil Micah 1:6, leaving it to God to send the rain to complete the erasure of the city.

Josephus says that John's successes and those of his sons roused against him the envy of the Jews. As an admirer of John, Josephus or his source could call the Jews' response 'envy'. Josephus may or may not be right in dating the rupture between the Pharisees and the Hasmoneans under John.[4] But he is correct in reporting that John had to fight rebellious Jews. At first John had given up prerogatives granted to the Hasmonean dynasty in the national decree of 140 B.C.E. in honour of Simon. Later, however, he felt justified in reasserting some of those prerogatives and in taking more. Simon and his heirs were to be chiefs and high priests of the Jews and to enjoy the other privileges 'until a true prophet shall arise'. John himself was a true

1 Hans Volkmann, 'Ptolemaios (30)', *PW*, 23 Part II (1959), 1740; Alan E. Samuel, *Ptolemaic Chronology* (Munich, 1962), pp. 148–51.

2 Jos. *Ant.* XIII.282–3; *b. Soṭa* 33a and parallels. Cf. Jos. *Bell.* 1.68–9.

3 *Megillat Ta'anit* 25 Marḥeshvan.

4 See Goldstein, *I Maccabees*, pp. 67–71. There, however, I put too much confidence in the rabbinic traditions. The early rabbinic authorities may have jumped to the conclusion that any tyrannical acts must be assigned to King Yannay, not to Yohanan the high priest. I shall return to the topic elsewhere and defend the historicity of the tradition at *b. Kidd.* 66a against the attacks of Y. Efron, 'Šim'on ben Šeṭaḥ weYannai ha-melek', *Sefer Zikkaron liGedalyahu 'Alon*, Tel Aviv 1970, pp. 78–92.

prophet! Though John did not assume the title 'king', many of his feats equalled those which the prophets had said would be accomplished by the coming king of Israel. Surely the 'spirit of the Lord' and the 'spirit of might' (Isaiah 11:2) rested upon John!

If such were the beliefs of John and his supporters, we can find an explanation for a strange phenomenon, the Greek names of John's sons. Though John could be friendly to Greeks, especially those far from Judea,[1] he was an ardent fulfiller of prophecies. Even the propaganda of his enemies does not accuse him of Hellenizing. But his sons bear Greek names in addition to their Hebrew names and perhaps even in preference to them, for Josephus most frequently uses the Greek names. From old Mattathias on, all Hasmoneans known to us bore the commonest Hebrew names. They also all bore the kind of additional names used to avert confusion when too many persons bear the same name.[2] The additional names of Mattathias and his sons are Semitic, not Greek. John's 'Hyrcanus' is Iranian and probably had long been naturalized among Jews.[3] Thus we need an explanation why John's sons have Greek additional names.

Josephus uses a peculiar formula to give the additional names of those sons, the Greek idiom *ho kai* ('alias') rather than the more usual *ho kaloumenos* ('called'). In the official styles of the Ptolemaic dynasty *ho kai* introduces a royal epithet only with Ptolemy X Alexander I (108/7–88 B.C.E.) who styled himself 'Ptolemy alias Alexander'.[4] Ptolemy X may have done so in order to outdo his brother and rival, Ptolemy IX Soter II, who bore the same cult-epithet as Ptolemy I. Ptolemy X took not merely a cult-epithet; he took the very name of Alexander the Great. The double names of John's sons, too, may have had a meaning in dynastic propaganda. John may have seen in the births of his sons fulfilments of prophecy. His sons were probably the first Hasmoneans to be born and named when the princely aspirations of the dynasty were openly proclaimed and widely accepted. John's son, Judas, could well have been destined to hold the sceptre of Jewish domination over the Gentiles in fulfilment of Genesis 49:10. Judas (= Judah) was a comman name, and there was nothing presumptuous in giving it to a son. But if John saw Genesis 49:8–12 as applying to his son and also called him 'Wonderful Counsellor' (*Pele'-Yō'ēṣ*), borrowing the messia-

[1] See Jos. *Ant.* XIV.149–55, 247–55, and Goldstein, *I Maccabees*, note on 12:5–23.

[2] See ibid., pp. 17–19.

[3] See Jacob Neusner, *A History of the Jews in Babylonia*, 1: *The Parthian Period* (2nd edn., Leiden, 1969), pp. 11–12 n. 2.

[4] Volkmann, 'Ptolemaios (31)', *PW*, 23 (1959), col. 1744.

[5] Cf. 1QH 3:5–12 and *Pss. Sol.* 8:20.

nic epithet from Isaiah 9:6 (Heb. 9:5),[1] many Jews would view it as intolerable. Greek 'Aristobulus' (best of counsellors') was an excellent substitute. Who could object to a Greek name already in use among Jews?[1] Later, Jews who found Janneus' use of the Hebrew title *melek* ('king') intolerable may have raised no objection to the use of the Greek equivalent *basileus* by Mattityah-Antigonus and by Herod.

John's second son bore the Greek name 'Antigonus' ('nobly[?]-born') and probably bore the Hebrew name 'Mattiyah' ('gift of the Lord').[2] The names may reflect 'to us a child is born, to us a son is given' in Isaiah 9:6. Even the names of John's third son may be derived from Isaiah 9:6. 'Janneus' is short for 'Jonathan' ('gift of the Lord'), and 'Alexander' may reflect 'mighty' (*gibbor*) in the same verse, for at Daniel 11:3 'mighty king' means Alexander. However, Janneus was only the third son, and John is reported to have disliked him. It seems more likely that Janneus himself took the name Alexander on his accession to proclaim that his future conquests, in fulfilment of prophecy, would surpass those of Alexander.

The words of Isaiah 9:7 could easily be interpreted to mean that the wonderful king would sit on the throne of David without being descended from David. John, if he was believed to be a prophet, could confirm that interpretation. Such presumptuous claims must have roused hostility. John also probably tried to settle disputes in Jewish Law through his claim to prophetic inspiration. He may have used his prophetic authority to enforce Pharisaic interpretations and also to justify his own abolitions of ancient rites, even of some prescribed in the Torah.[3] The *Testaments of the Twelve Patriarchs* contain propaganda of this time claiming such authority for the Hasmonean high priest,[4] and a text from Qumran bitterly denounces 'false prophets' and their teachings on Jewish Law.[5] John may be the 'false preacher' (*mtyp kzb*) of the Qumran texts.[6] Pharisees and other Jews may have joined with the Essenes in the revolt which came late in John's high priesthood, and Josephus could well name the rebels simply as 'the Jews'. John quelled the rebellion and died in peace in 104 B.C.E.

In the course of his prosperous reign, John carried out important building projects, especially fortifications. He rebuilt the walls of Jerusalem, breached or destroyed by Antiochus VII. In so doing, he extended the walled area to include the northern part of the western hill of old Jerusalem and made use both of his princely and of his prophetic

[1] See 2 Macc. 1:10 and Goldstein, *I Maccabees*, Appendix III.

[2] See Meshorer, *Jewish Coins*, p. 45.

[3] *M.M.Sh.*5.15 = *Soṭ* 9.10.

[4] *T. Levi* 8, 18:1–9; *T. Dan* 5:10–11.

[5] 1QH 4:16.

[6] Milik, *Discovery*, pp. 88–9.

authority.[1] John also built in Jerusalem the important fortress north of the temple called the Baris.[2] He may also have built the fortress Hyrcania (Khirbet Mird),[3] but Janneus may have done so and named it after his father.

Toward the end of his reign John was the outstanding example of a prince of a nation backed by Roman favour. Pergamum and Athens, seeking to curry favour with Rome, showed honour to John.[4] Such prestige let many Jews to believe that the glorious prophecies were being fulfilled.

John's successor was his son Judas Aristobulus I, perhaps also called 'wonderful counsellor' in Hebrew. Josephus' information on Judas' brief reign is very scanty. Josephus says that he was the first Hasmonean to establish a monarchy and take the title 'king'. Strabo, however, asserts that Alexander Janneus was the first to take the royal title.[5] Josephus is probably correct. Our conjecture about Judas' Greek name would support him. Most important, Josephus places Judas' assumption of the kingship in a chronological setting which seems to be based on an interpretation of the 70 weeks of years at Daniel 9:24–7: Judas became king 471 years and 3 months after the release from the Babylonian captivity.[6] If so, the 490 years from the time of Daniel's vision would end in 86 B.C.E., at the peak of the reign of Alexander Janneus. Josephus' source appears to have viewed Janneus as the last terrible tyrant to rule the Jews before the great redemption. Hence, though the chronology is schematic and visionary, the source was nearly contemporary with Judas, and its evidence is to be accepted.[7] Strabo knew of Judas[8] but was ignorant that he held the title king, perhaps because his reign was brief. The coins ascribed to him are rare and may belong rather to Aristobulus II.[9] Alexander Janneus assumed the royal title after first relinquishing it,[10] so Strabo could easily have made the mistake of thinking that Janneus was the first Hasmonean king.

On the other hand, Josephus strangely asserts that John, whose sons were mature men,[11] left his wife in control of Judea. Perhaps Josephus

[1] See Goldstein, *I Maccabees*, pp. 215–16.

[2] Jos. *Bell.* 1.75; *Ant.* XVIII.91. See above p. 319 n. 3.

[3] Earliest mention: Jos. *Ant.* XIII.417.

[4] See Goldstein, *I. Maccabees*, note on 12:5–23.

[5] *Geography*, XVI, 2.40 (C762).

[6] *Bell.* 1.70; in a future article I shall show that the figure of 481 years and 3 months at *Ant.* XIII.301 is a slip of the author or a scribal error.

[7] Against the view of Schalit, *König Herodes*, pp. 743–4.

[8] According to Jos. *Ant.* XIII.319.

[9] See p. 324 n. 2.

[10] See below, pp. 334–36.

[11] Even Janneus was about 22 at the time of his accession (Jos. *Ant.* XIII.404).

or his source confused John with Janneus. Janneus did indeed leave his wife in power, and Judas was reported to have caused his own mother's death. To supply a motive for the matricide, someone may have confused John with Janneus.[1]

A king of the Jews would be even more likely to try to fulfil prophecies than High Priest John had been. John had conquered Moab, Idumea, Samaria, and most of Philistia. If the boundaries of the Promised Land were to reach the Euphrates,[2] the next expansion should be northward and eastward. Pious Jews reading Zechariah 9:1–17 would think that anyone claiming to be king in Jerusalem would first have to make some conquests in the north. Accordingly, Judas is reported to have made conquests in the territory of the Itureans and to have forced the inhabitants who chose to remain there to become Jews, perhaps interpreting Zechariah 9:1 in the context of 9:7. These conquests probably lay in Galilee, since the main Iturean holdings were in the Lebanon and Antilibanus mountains and in the valley between them.[3] Scholars have been wrong to doubt the truth of the report.[4] Josephus accepts it from Strabo, who got it from the Greek historian Timagenes. Why would a Greek credit an ephemeral Jewish ruler with conquests he did not make? A king customarily received credit for the conquests of his subordinates, though he might have to put in a ceremonial presence at the moment of final victory.[5] Hence, even if Judas was too ill to take the field during most of his brief reign, he still could have been said to have conquered part of the Itureans and could have issued the decree compelling them to accept Judaism.

Judas received the epithet 'Philhellene'. His friendly relations with Greeks were probably similar to John's and may have been intended as a fulfilment of Zechariah 9:10: the king gives peaceful greetings to Greek Gentiles. Here would be another confirmation that Judas was a king. The hostile words against *Yawan* (usual meaning: 'Greece') at Zechariah 9:13 may have been taken by Judas as referring to the Seleucid empire.

Hostile Jews surely told the other stories in Josephus about Judas,

[1] On the ease with which John could have been confused with Janneus, see Goldstein, *I Maccabees*, pp. 67–70.

[2] Deut. 1:7, 11:24.

[3] Berndt Schaller, 'Ituraea', *Der kleine Pauly*, 2 (Stuttgart, 1967), col. 1492. Galilee is mentioned at Jos. *Bell.* 1.76.

[4] See Schalit, *König Herodes*, pp. 708–9.

[5] See 2 Sam. 12:26–7, 21:17; 1 Chron. 11:4–7; Simon received credit for taking Jaffa (1 Macc. 14:5) though he was not present when his subordinate occupied it (1 Macc. 13:11).

but they may be true. The king was cruel to his own family: he starved his mother to death in prison and imprisoned his brothers, except for Antigonus, whom he honoured. But jealous courtiers and the queen tricked Judas into having Antigonus killed at the time of the festival of Tabernacles. Judas soon died of disease, aggravated by remorse. An Essene named Judas is said to have predicted Antigonus' death. The sect had long since been hostile to the Hasmonean dynasty.

Upon the death of Judas, his wife Salina Alexandra[1] released all the imprisoned brothers and made Janneus, alias Alexander, king because he was the eldest survivor and had a 'good disposition' (*metriotēs*). Josephus knows that Janneus' queen bore the name Alexandra and was fourteen years older than Janneus,[2] and Eusebius attests that she bore the name Salina.[3] Clearly Janneus made a levirate marriage with his brother's widow, as required by Deuteronomy 25:5–6. His eldest surviving son bore the name 'Hyrcanus', not that of the dead king as might seem to be required by the literal meaning of Deuteronomy 25:6, but rabbinic interpretation takes the words differently and so may Janneus and the exegetes he followed.[4]

Janneus may be the first Hasmonean ruler who issued coins.[5] The coins give extremely important information. Josephus clearly believed that Janneus bore the title king and wore a diadem from the outset of his reign. Neither in Josephus nor in rabbinic tradition is there any hint that Janneus ever lacked or relinquished the royal title or renounced the wearing of a diadem. Plentiful and incontrovertible numismatic evidence shows that he relinquished both kingship and diadem and that late in his reign he bore the title king but did not wear a diadem.

There are coins of Janneus which originally bore on the obverse a flower (lily?) with the Hebrew legend *yhwntn hmlk* ('Yehonatan [= Jonathan] the king'), and on the reverse an anchor surrounded by a knotted diadem, with the Greek legend *Basileōs Alexandrou* ('of King Alexander'), but have been overstruck on the obverse with the Hebrew legend *yntn hkhn hgdl wḥbr hyhdym* ('Jonathan the high priest and the *ḥbr* of the Jews') and on the reverse with double cornucopias.[6] There are rare examples of the lily–anchor royal coins which have not been

[1] On the variants of the queen's name, see Schürer, *History*, I, pp. 229–30 n. 2. Was her Greek name 'Alexandra' a piece of dynastic propaganda, or a mere additional name?

[2] *Bell.* I.107ff; *Ant.* XIII.405ff. Ages: *Ant.* XIII.404 and 430.

[3] *Chronikon*, on the year of Abraham 1941; see also Schürer, *History*, I p. 229 n. 2.

[4] *b. Yebam.* 24a.

[5] See p. 324 n. 2.

[6] Meshorer, *Jewish Coins*, pp. 120–1, nos. 17 and 17A. I deliberately leave *ḥbr* untranslated. It *may* refer to the council of elders or Sanhedrin; see Marcus Jastrow, *A Dictionary of the Targumim, the Talmud Babli and Yerushalmi, and the Midrashic Literature* (New York, 1903), s.v. *ḥbr*. On the other hand, it may refer to the nation;

overstruck.[1] The lily–anchor coins are clear imitations of royal Seleucid issues struck for use by Jews, as one might expect of the first issue of coins by a young Jewish kingdom.[2] Furthermore, the types of the overstriking occur as the obverse and reverse of a common coin of Janneus.[3] Thus, coins signifying on both faces Janneus' royalty were overstruck with non-royal types on both faces and supplanted by non-royal coins. Clearly, Janneus at least for a time renounced the royal title and the diadem.

There are other abundant issues of King Janneus, on which his name stands with the royal title and on which a knotted diadem appears, and yet no overstruck examples of these issues have been found. Such are the beautiful coins bearing on the obverse an anchor surrounded by a knotted diadem and on the reverse a star with eight rays, as well as the wretched imitations of them.[4] Such also are the rare and poorly-preserved lead coins.[5] One may infer from the absence of overstruck examples that, after giving up the royal title and its prerogatives, Janneus later resumed them.

Finally, from late in Janneus' reign bearing dates from his twentieth and twenty-fifth years, come wretchedly-engraved coins which bear on the obverse an anchor inside a solid circle, with the legend *Basileōs Alexandrou*, and on the reverse a star with eight rays, with the Aramaic legend *mlk' 'lksndrws* ('King Alexander').[6] Similarly, on the legendless small denomination of Janneus, the anchor on the obverse is surrounded by a solid circle, not by a knotted diadem.[7] My analysis of the history of these numismatic motifs[8] shows that the use of a solid circle

see U. Rappaport, 'On the meaning of *Ḥeber ha-Yehudim*', *Meḥqarim bᵉtolᵉdot 'am Yiśra'el wᵉ'eres Yiśra'el* 3 (Haifa, 1974), pp. 59–67 (in Hebrew).

[1] Meshorer, *Jewish Coins*, p. 118, nos. 5 and 5A.

[2] Ibid., pp. 57–8, and *IEJ*, 24 (1974), 59–61. See also p. 323 n. 1. The cornucopiae on Janneus' high-priestly coins are also copied from a Seleucid numismatic motif, as is the palm tree (it is not the club of Herakles) on Janneus' high-priestly seal. see Percy Gardner, *the Seleucid Kings of Syria. A Catalogue of the Greek Coins in the British Museum*: (London, 1878; Bologna, 1963), p. 82, and N. Avigad, 'A Bulla of Jonathan the High Priest', *IEJ*, 25 (1975), 8–12, and 'A Bulla of King Jonathan', *IEJ*, 25 (1975), 245–6.

[3] Meshorer, *Jewish Coins*, p. 119, no. 12.

[4] Beautiful coins: Meshorer, *Jewish Coins*, p. 119, nos. 8, 8A. Meshorer informed me of the wretched imitations (and of other numismatic facts as well) in a letter to me of 9 June 1980.

[5] Meshorer, *Jewish Coins*, p. 118, nos. 7 and 7A; A. Kindler, 'Addendum to the dated coins of Alexander Janneus', *IEJ*, 18 (1968), 191.

[6] Meshorer, *Jewish Coins*, p. 119, no. 9. J. Naveh, 'Dated coins of Alexander Janneus', *IEJ*, 18 (1968), 20–5; Kindler, *IEJ*, 18 (1968), 188–91.

[7] Meshorer, *Jewish Coins*, p. 119, nos. 10 and 11.

[8] See my *II Maccabees*, Introduction, part 4.

instead of a knotted diadem must have been significant and intentional: in his late reign, Janneus bore the royal title but abandoned the non-Jewish practice of wearing a diadem. No overstruck examples of these diademless royal coins have been found. No later Hasmonean coins display diadems.[1]

My interpretation of these numismatic phenomena is confirmed by a strange feature of 1 Maccabees: at 1 Macc. 2:57 the Hasmonean propagandist portrays Mattathias as telling his descendants to aspire to be kings, yet at 1 Macc. 8:14 the propagandist condemns the wearing of a diadem! We thus have, preserved in literature, a reflection of the controversy which produced the numismatic phenomena. We also have a strong clue here to the date of the writing of 1 Maccabees. The wearing of a diadem was not an issue until a Hasmonean became king. The propagandist who wrote 1 Maccabees surely did not write in opposition to King Judas Aristobulus I, who never abandoned the diadem, or in opposition to King Janneus in his early reign, before he abandoned the royal title and the diadem, or in opposition to King Janneus after he resumed both. Probably the propagandist wrote during the period when Janneus abandoned the royal title and the diadem: he intended to encourage Janneus to resume the former but not the latter.[2]

Probably religious scruples drove King Janneus to refrain from coining in silver and gold.[3] Otherwise, Janneus throughout appears to have been a prisoner of the great hopes which the prophets had left in the minds of the Jews concerning the king who would reign after the end of the Age of Wrath. Judas had fulfilled some of those hopes in his brief reign. Judas' early death led some to think that the real fulfiller of the prophesies would be Janneus. The royal star-coins may well reflect such grandiose hopes. According to Numbers 24:17, 'A star will rise from Jacob...and smash the chiefs of Moab and plunder all the descendants of Seth.' All mankind are descendants of Seth! The Aramaic and Greek legends on the coins were probably for Gentiles to read: the Jewish Alexander would outdo the great Macedonian.

[1] Two seal impressions of Alexander Janneus are known, one bearing the legend *yntn khn gdl yršlm m* ('Jonathan high priest Jerusalem M') and the other *yhwntn mlk* ('Yehonatan King'). They, too, probably reflect the successive stages in Janneus' reign. See N. Avigad, *IEJ*, 25 (1975), 8–12, 245–6. For other views on the chronology of Janneus' coins, see Meshorer, *Jewish Coins*, pp. 57–9; B. Kanael, 'Altjüdische Münzen', *Jahrbuch für Numismatik und Geldgeschichte*, 17 (1967), 167–71; Schürer, *History*, 1, p. 604; M. D. McLean, 'The initial coinage of Alexander Jannaeus', *Museum Notes*, 26 (1981), 153–61.

[2] See also my *II Maccabees*, Introduction, part 4.

[3] See Hag. 2:8 and Deut. 17:17; cf. Isa. 2:7.

Janneus seems to have tried first to fulfil the prophecies of northward conquests at Zechariah 9:1–4. Josephus reports that as soon as he was securely in power he tried to conquer the Greco-Phoenician city of Ptolemais (all Phoenicians could be called Sidonians,[1] and Sidon is mentioned at Zechariah 9:2). Janneus never succeeded in taking it. At first the citizens of Ptolemais withstood him unaided. Then Ptolemy IX Lathyrus, who was ruling in Cyprus, landed with a strong army and diverted Janneus from Ptolemais. Janneus pretended to make an alliance with Lathyrus and thereby acquired the important city of Strato's Tower,[2] which Herod turned into Caesarea. However, Janneus also made offers to Lathyrus' mother, Cleopatra III. She had driven Lathyrus from Egypt, and when he learned of Janneus' intrigues, Lathyrus was furious. He attacked Judea, committed atrocities on Jewish towns and inflicted heavy casualties on Janneus' soldiers. Jews could see that God was not with them and their king! Jews in large numbers must have become violently opposed to Janneus.[3]

However, Janneus was rescued from his predicament by the army of Cleopatra III. The Egyptian queen could not let her hated son grow strong. Propaganda circulated among the Jews of Egypt in support of the Hasmonean cause. One piece, written in late 103 B.C.E., survives in the letter at 2 Maccabees 1:10 to 2:18. Cleopatra's commanders, Chelkias and Ananias, were Jews, sons of that priest Onias IV who had emigrated and founded a temple in Egypt. Now they might have pressed their claims to the high priesthood against the upstart Hasmoneans. Instead, they sympathized with the Jewish king. Chelkias fell in combat. Ananias defended Janneus' cause when Cleopatra thought to annex Judea. Cleopatra was induced to make an alliance with Janneus. The Jewish king may have allowed himself to accept alliance with Egypt (condemned by the prophets) thinking that now Egypt was no broken reed. Surely some Jews condemned the step.

Onias IV and his heirs were descended from Solomon's High Priest Zadok (= Sadduc). They and their supporters may well have been called 'Sadducees'. If so, only from this point in 102 B.C.E. could a Hasmonean prince join the party of the Sadducees.[4]

Cleopatra III took Ptolemais. Thereafter Janneus did not try to take the city. He probably felt, however, that he had to prove that he enjoyed God's favour by winning victories and fulfilling prophecies. If

[1] Sabatino Moscati, *The World of the Phoenicians* (New York and Washington, 1968), p. 4.

[2] See L. I. Levine, 'The Hasmonean conquest of Strato's Tower', *IEJ*, 24 (1974), 62–9.

[3] M. Stern, 'Ha-reqaᶜ ha-mᵉdini lᵉmilḥᵃmotaw šel Aleksander Yannai', *Tarbiz* 33 (1963–4), 325–336.

[4] See Goldstein, *I Maccabees*, pp. 548–9.

Phoenicia was closed to him, territory to the north-east lay open. In Gilead he took Gadara and Amathus, fulfilling Obadiah 19 and perhaps Zechariah 9:2, if Janneus believed that Amathus was Hamath. However, the local dynast at Amathus, Theodorus, counterattacked and killed 10,000 Jews and took rich spoils. Perhaps Janneus was hated by God? Undaunted, Janneus turned against Philistia. He took Raphia, Anthedon, and Gaza and destroyed Gaza. Thus he fulfilled most of Zephaniah 2:4–7. He spared Ashkelon, probably because it was under Ptolemaic protection.[1] Gaza fell to Janneus about 96 B.C.E., for Josephus says that about the same time Antiochus VIII was murdered.[2] Even so, the Jews suffered heavy casualties, especially at Gaza.[3]

The many Jews who viewed Janneus' assumption of royal prerogatives as rash and who believed he had flagrantly failed to fulfil prophecy now erupted in revolt. Josephus says the revolt began on the festival of Tabernacles. When Janneus was about to sacrifice, the people pelted him with citrons[4] and accused him of being unfit for the high priesthood, alleging that he was descended from a captive. Josephus says nothing of Janneus' royal claims and failures to fulfil prophecy, but Josephus is always extremely reluctant to speak to his Gentile audience about 'messianic' prophecies and about the failure of Jewish prophecies to be fulfilled. He does, however, say that when the people accused Janneus of being unfit for the high priesthood, they were 'adding insult to injury' (*prosexeloidorēsan*) and thus were not uttering their chief grievance.

Janneus first massacred 6,000 of the offenders and then built a wooden barrier around the altar and the inner sanctuary of the Temple to bar non-priests from access. In so modifying the architecture of the inner court of the Temple, Janneus was probably taking sides in a long-standing controversy among Jewish sects.[5] The step must have enraged his opponents.

For a time, the opposition was no match for Janneus' Jewish supporters and his Pisidian and Cilician mercenaries. If the opposition regarded his use of mercenaries as wicked, Janneus had only to remind them how David's Cherethites and Pelethites had helped him subdue the rebellious Israelite supporters of Absalom. Thus Janneus was strong enough to make conquests in Arab-held Moab and Gilead and to destroy Amathus.

1 See M. Stern, *Zion* 26 (1961), 20–1.

2 *Ant.* XIII.362–6; Bellinger, 'Seleucids', 72.

3 [For Janneus' foreign policy see U. Rappaport, 'La Judée et Rome pendant le règne d'Alexandre Jannée', *REJ,* 127 (1968), 329–45. Edd.]

4 The same incident may be reflected at *t.Sukk.* 3:16 and parallels.

5 See Goldstein, *I Maccabees*, note on 9:54.

But again God appeared to desert him as he lost an army to an ambush in his war with Obedas I, king of the Nabatean Arabs, near the Transjordanian village of Garada.[1] Again Janneus' failure provoked a mass Jewish uprising. The war dragged on for six years. Janneus' forces are said to have slain at least 40,000 Jews. To prevent the king of the Nabateans from taking advantage of the civil strife, Janneus had to cede to him his conquests in Moab and Gilead. When Janneus sought to conciliate his opponents, they told him to die! The bitter opposition even asked for the aid of the Seleucid Demetrius III Eucaerus (reigned 95–87 B.C.E.)[2] against their own king. They must have believed they were still living in the age of God's wrath. God was punishing His people by letting tyrannical Janneus rule them, but prophets had hinted that God would be more merciful if they should submit to the rule of foreign kings.[3]

The campaign was fought near Shechem, about 89 B.C.E. Demetrius tried to woo away Alexander's Greek mercenaries, and Alexander sought to win over some of his Jewish opponents; at first both failed. Alexander's mercenaries fought to the death for him, but Alexander lost the bloody battle. However, 6,000 of Demetrius' Jewish supporters rallied to the defeated Janneus! We may guess that some of the Jewish rebels viewed Janneus as totally wicked, but others only wanted to curb his 'tyrannical' presumption. Some Jews held that God willed that they be subject to foreign rule, but others may have believed that God would allow a properly humbled Jewish kingdom to exist in freedom. Demetrius' victory may have been so overwhelming that no prospect would be left for even a humble Jewish kingdom if Janneus were left to his fate. Demetrius had rivals to fight for the Seleucid throne.[4] After the heavy casualties suffered by his own forces, he could not risk more and withdrew, leaving the Jewish extremists to their fate. Janneus reduced them by siege at a place called 'Bemeselis'[5] or 'Bethome'[6] and then had 800 of them crucified at

[1] On the variants of the place-name in the manuscripts, see Schürer, *History*, I, p. 223 n. 17. On the conquests in Moab, see A. Schalit, 'Die Eroberungen des Alexander Jannäus in Moab', *Theokratia*, I (1967/69), 3–50.

[2] See Hans Volkmann, 'Demetrios 7', *Der kleine Pauly*, I (Stuttgart, 1964), col. 1466.

[3] See Jer. 21:3–11, Ezek. 17.

[4] Bellinger, 'Seleucids', 76–7.

[5] Jos. *Bell.* I.96.

[6] Jos. *Ant.* XIII.380. The two place-names are corrupt versions of a single original. The problem of what the original was has not been solved, but see Abraham Schalit, 'Der Schauplatz des letzten Kampfes zwischen den aufständischen Pharisäern und Alexander Jannäus', in *Josephus-Studien: Untersuchungen zu Josephus, dem antiken Judentum und dem Neuen Testament, Otto Michel zum 70. Geburtstag gewidmet*, ed. Otto Betz, Klaus Haacker and Martin Hengel (Göttingen, 1974), pp. 300–18.

Jerusalem.[1] While the crucified still lived, he had their wives and children slaughtered before their eyes as he himself looked on, carousing with his concubines. Eight thousand refugees fled into exile. Janneus' opponents thereafter referred to him as 'Thrakidas', a name common among the cruellest Hellenistic mercenaries.[2] However, for the rest of his reign Janneus was secure from domestic revolt.

Even then God did not let him pose as the prophesied king. Janneus' elaborate fortifications failed to protect Judea from invasion. Antiochus XII, in about 85 B.C.E., easily forced his way through the 'Maginot line' Janneus had constructed from Chapharsaba to Jaffa. Antiochus' objective, however, was not Judea but the Nabatean Arabs, who defeated and destroyed Antiochus and his army. Not long thereafter, the Nabatean king, Aretas III, became the strongest power in the area and at Damascus took the title 'king of Coele-Syria'. Aretas defeated Janneus deep in Jewish territory at Adida but withdrew after making a treaty. Aretas appears to have conceded to Janneus a limited area for expansion. Janneus stayed away from the caravan route through Philadelphia–Amman and Damascus and from other vital Nabatean interests.[3] But he captured Dium and 'Essa' (probably Essabon = Heshbon)[4] and Gaulana and Seleucia and Gamala to the north-east of

[1] The historicity of the crucifixion of 800 opponents of Janneus has been questioned. For its relation to Pesher Nahum, see Y. Yadin, 'Pesher Nahum (4Q pNahum) reconsidered', *IEJ*, 21 (1971), 1–12; and also D. Flusser, 'P^{e}rušim, Ṣ^{e}duqim w^{e}'Issiyim b^{e}Pešer Naḥum', *Sefer zikkaron liG^{e}dalyahu Alon, Meḥqarim b^{e}tol^{e}dot Yiśra'el uba-lašon ha'ivrit* (Tel Aviv, 1970), pp. 135–168 [Edd.].

[2] See M. Stern, 'Traqidas – l^{e}khinuyo šel Aleksander Yannai 'eṣel Yosephos W^{e}Sinqelos', *Tarbiz* 29 (1959–60), 207–9. [For Hellenistic anti-Jewish sources used by Josephus, see M. Stern, 'Niqola'os 'iš Dammešeq k^{e}maqor l^{e}tol^{e}dot Yiśra'el biyme bet Herodes ubet Ḥašmonai', *Ha-miqra w^{e}tol^{e}dot Yiśra'el. Meḥqarim ba-migra' ub^{e}sifrut y^{e}me bayit šeni, l^{e}zikro šel Y. Liver*, ed. B. Uffenheimer (Tel Aviv, 1971), pp. 375–394; Y. Baer, 'l^{e}signonah ha-hellenisṭi šel parašat Yannai Aleksandros 'eṣel Yosephos ul^{e}'inyan ha-ṣ^{e}liva b^{e}Pešer Naḥum", *Zion* 34 (1969), 39–42; D. Flusser, 'P^{e}rušim, Ṣ^{e}duqim w^{e}'Issiyim b^{e}Pešer Naḥum', *Sefer Zikkaron liG^{e}dalyahu Alon. Meḥqarim b^{e}tol^{e}dot Yiśra'el uba-lašon ha-'ivrit* (Tel Aviv, 1970), pp. 133–168 [Edd.].

[3] See Abraham Negev, 'The Nabateans and the Provincia Arabia', in *Aufstieg und Niedergang der römischen Welt*, II: *Principat*, ed. Hildegard Temporini and Wolfgang Hasse, 8 (Berlin and New York 1977), pp. 538–9; Nelson Glueck, *Deities and Dolphins* (New York, 1965), p. 361 and map on p. 362. Josephus (*Ant.* XIII.391) does not name the king ruling over the Nabateans at the time of the defeat and death of Antiochus XII; for conjectures as to the king's identity, see Schürer, *History*, I, pp. 577–8.

[4] The Latin at Jos. *Ant.* XIII.393 has *Essamon*. Georgius Syncellus (*Georgius Syncellus et Nicephorus Cp.*, ed. W. Dindorf (Corpus Scriptorum Historiae Byzantinae) Bonn, 1829, I, v. 235 (P. 295A), pp. 558–9) lists Esebon among Janneus' conquests as a Transjordanian city, separate from those in Ammon and Moab. 'Essa' can hardly be Gerasa, which lay on the main caravan route vital to the Nabateans. Though

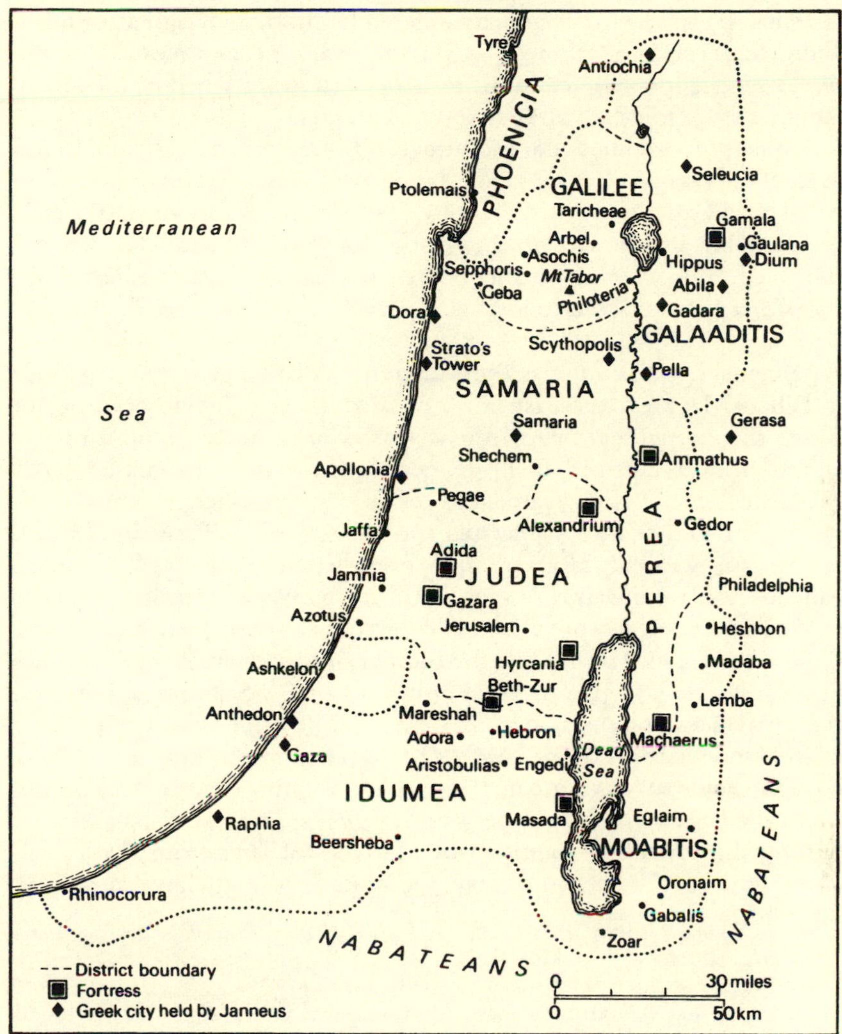

Fig. 2 The kingdom of Alexander Janneus, 103 to 76 B.C.E.

Judea. All lay in the direction of the promised Euphrates, but all were far to the south and west of land claimed by Aretas III. Janneus appears even to have recovered territory in Gilead and Moab. Josephus gives an inventory of the conquests of Janneus and his Hasmonean predecessors as of some three years before Janneus' death.[1]

Josephus said Janneus took Gerasa (at *Bell.* I.104), he corrected his error by omitting Gerasa from the list of Janneus' holdings at *Ant.* XIII.395–7.

[1] See Fig. 2, which draws on both Josephus and Syncellus.

In his last three years, Janneus suffered from the effects of alcoholism and malaria but continued to pursue wars of conquest. He was besieging the fort Ragaba in the territory of Gerasa when he died in 76 B.C.E. at the age of 49, after reigning 27 years.

Janneus left architectural monuments. Since coins of his were found in the excavations of Masada,[1] he is probably 'Jonathan the high priest'[2] and the 'early king'[3] who fortified that remote and nearly impregnable site. Jonathan, the brother of Judas Maccabeus, had not the need, the wealth, or the power to do so. Janneus also built the fortresses Alexandreion and Machaerus[4] and perhaps also Hyrcania.[5]

Janneus' reign saw literary productivity. A brilliant writer produced in Biblical Hebrew the first book of Maccabees as new Scripture, to prove the eternal legitimacy of the Hasmonean house as high priests and as princes destined to bring permanent victory to Israel.[6] Even excellent Greek works came out of Jerusalem, such as the Greek version of Esther by Lysimachus son of Ptolemy.[7] Pious and proud, hostile to 'wicked' idolaters but friendly to 'righteous' Gentiles, Janneus and Lysimachus saw no harm in the use of Greek.

We cannot reconstruct a complete history of those Jewish sects who opposed Janneus' claims to be the fulfiller of prophecy. At crucial times in his reign he was able to get the support of the Sadducees, but even they may have opposed him at others.[8] The Essenes seem to have called Janneus the 'lion of wrath' (*kpyr hḥrwn*) and to have hated him, though they may have gloated over his slaughter of Pharisees whom they called 'seekers after slippery things' (*dwšy ḥlqwt*), perhaps an ironic pun on the Pharisees' claims to be 'derivers of laws from the Torah' (*dwršy hlkwt*).[9] The fragmentary Qumran text may have meant to

1 See Y. Yadin, 'Masada,' *Encyclopedia of Archaeological Excavations in the Holy Land*, vol. III (Oxford, 1977), p. 816.

2 Jos. *Bell.* VII.285.

3 Ibid. IV.399.

4 Machaerus: Jos. *Bell.* VII.171. Queen Alexandra early in her reign used Machaerus and Alexandreion (Jos. *Ant.* XIII.417).

5 Jos. *Ant.* XIII.417; see above p. 325.

6 See Goldstein, *II Maccabees*, Introduction, Part 4, and 1 Macc. 5:62.

7 See E. J. Bickerman, 'The colophon of the Greek Book of Esther', *JBL*, 63 (1944), 339–62, and 'Notes on the Greek Book of Esther', *PAAJR*, 20 (1950), 101–33.

8 See Goldstein, *I Maccabees*, pp. 67–71 and appendix 3. The Sadducees' name suggests that they were partisans of the Zadokite line of high priests. Note also the tradition at *b. Soṭa* 22b, where Janneus anticipates that his wife might fear non-Pharisees as well as Pharisees.

9 See Y. Yadin, 'Pesher Nahum (4Q pNahum) reconsidered', *IEJ*, 21 (1971), 1–12; Joseph M. Baumgarten, 'Does *tlh* in the Temple Scroll refer to crucifixion?', *JBL*, 91 (1972), 472–81. Pun: Strugnell according to Milik, *Discovery*, p. 73 n. 1. Josephus says

stigmatize Janneus as a heretic (*kwpr*) when it called him 'lion' (*kpyr*),[1] and surely went on to predict a bad end for the king and his heirs.

Violent hatred existed between Janneus and the Pharisees. Strangely, Josephus does not name the Pharisees in his accounts of the civil strife during Janneus' reign. However, traditions preserved by the rabbis, the descendants of the Pharisees, reflect the same events as narrated by Josephus and let us know that the Pharisees were main targets of the king's wrath.[2] Josephus' reticence is due partly to his recognition that there was confusion in the traditions which lay before him: it was often impossible to distinguish a story about John Hyrcanus from one about Janneus.[3] Josephus says that the whole nation opposed Janneus. In so identifying the cause of the Pharisees with that of the whole nation, he may have been following a Pharisaic source. This part of his narrative is friendly to the Pharisees though elsewhere he draws on sources hostile to them.

Only in connection with Janneus' death do we find Josephus naming the Pharisees as active under Janneus. He has Janneus on his death-bed advising his apprehensive wife to seek security after his death by yielding some power to the Pharisees, whose influence over the Jewish masses would give her a safe reign. He is quoted as saying that his own struggles with the nation had been caused by the outrages he had perpetrated upon the Pharisees. This death-bed scene appears only in Josephus' later work, the *Antiquities*, not in his *War*. In later life, Josephus became more and more sympathetic to the Pharisees. The death-bed scene looks very much like Pharisaic propaganda. Did Josephus fabricate it to convince the Romans to back the Pharisees?[4] It is unlikely.

In composing the *War*, Josephus wrote at Rome, largely from memory and from his sentiments as a member of the priestly aristocracy which leaned toward the Sadducees. It can be shown that when Josephus departs in the *Antiquities* from the narrative given in the *War*, usually he had secured copies of sources previously unavailable to him at Rome.[5] There is a strong indication that Josephus drew on an

that Pharisees had a reputation for being the most accurate expositors of the laws (*Bell.* I.110; cf. *Ant.* XVII.149). Josephus' Greek expression may have translated a Hebrew דורש הלכות or דורש התורה.

1 See the Hebrew text of Ps. 34:10 (Heb. 34:11) and Jastrow, *Dictionary*, s.v. כפר.

2 *b.Kidd.* 66a; cf. *Sanh.* 107b, *Soṭa* 47a, and Scholia to *Megillat Ta'anit* 2 Shebat and 17 Adar.

3 See Goldstein, *I Maccabees*, pp. 67–70.

4 So believes Morton Smith, 'Palestinian Judaism in the first century', in *Israel: Its Role in Civilization*, ed. Moshe Davis (New York, 1956), pp. 67–81.

5 See Goldstein, *I Maccabees*, pp. 60–1. I plan to treat this subject in detail in a future work.

earlier source here. Both in the *War* and in the *Antiquities* his portrayal of the Pharisees is linked to his portrayal of Janneus' successor, Queen Alexandra. In the *War* he portrays Alexandra favourably, except for calling her gullible and dominated by the Pharisees. He treats her far more unfavourably in the *Antiquities*. In the *War* he praises her strict religiosity; in the *Antiquities* that religiosity is but part of her subservience to the Pharisees. The case of the anti-Pharisaic opposition Josephus puts far more eloquently in the *Antiquities*. His final judgement there on Alexandra is that she was absolutely unscrupulous, with no thought for the future, and sowed the seed for the downfall of the Hasmonean dynasty, even though she maintained peace during her reign. He adds that she 'expressed the same opinions as those who were hostile to her dynasty' or perhaps (if we emend the text) 'lent the weight of her own authority to those who were hostile to her dynasty'.[1] In the immediate context, friends of the dynasty oppose the Pharisees, so 'those hostile' here must be the Pharisees. If Josephus had fabricated the death-bed scene as propaganda for the Pharisees, he would also have excluded from his account attacks on them and the queen who favoured them. Rather, Josephus took from previously existing sources both the seemingly pro-Pharisaic story of Janneus' last words and funeral and the anti-Pharisaic account of Alexandra's reign. As a member of the priestly aristocracy, who late in life became a fervent Pharisee, Josephus could easily draw on such opposing traditions.

Forceful Queen Alexandra kept political power in her own hands. Her elder son, John Hyrcanus II, was pliant, in contrast to his vigorous younger brother Judas Aristobulus II. The Queen was glad to let Hyrcanus succeed his father as high priest only. For rule of Israel by a queen there was only the inauspicious precedent of Athaliah.[2] Rule by a queen when there were male heirs past the age of infancy was absolutely unprecedented. Sectarian opposition to the royal claims of the dynasty may have led to the strange arrangement. A queen could not fulfil glorious prophesies about a king. She could preserve for the dynasty the royal title without rousing opposition. Meanwhile, her son and heir would keep the high priesthood in the family. The situation under Queen Alexandra may be reflected in the numerous well-minted coins which display the Hebrew legend 'John the high priest and the *ḥbr* of the Jews' beneath a conspicuous Greek letter alpha which may well stand for 'Alexandra'.[3] The alpha on these coins is quite different

[1] *Ant.* XIII.431.

[2] 2 Kings 11.

[3] Meshorer, *Jewish Coins*, p. 121, no. 19. On *ḥbr*, see above, p. 334 n. 6.

from the alpha or monogram combining alpha and pi on other coins of John Hyrcanus II.[1] Those other coins have the letter or monogram not on the most important side, the one bearing the high priest's name but rather on the 'reverse'; on those other coins, the letter or monogram is far less conspicuous and probably refers to Antipater. Finally, the inconspicuous alpha on the reverse appears on coins which bear the legend 'John the high priest, chief [of the?] *ḥbr* of the Jews'.[2] The new title 'chief' (*r'š*) probably reflects the grant by Julius Caesar of the title 'ethnarch' to Hyrcanus II in 47.[3]

Indeed, the Hebrew word 'king' (*mlk*) disappears forever from Hasmonean coinage, as if the dynasty feared to offend their subjects by using the word of the prophecies. Even vigorous Aristobulus II on his coins (if, indeed, they are his) styles himself only 'Judah high priest'.[4] The coins of the last Hasmonean to reign, Mattityah Antigonus (40–37) have the royal title only in Greek.[5] Perhaps he called himself 'king' in Greek to intimidate the Greeks whom Pompey in 63 B.C.E. had freed from Jewish rule, but we may guess that he used Greek because the royal title in Hebrew would have provoked pious opposition.

As long as Queen Alexandra was vigorous, she dominated her sons, maintained internal peace, and followed her pious inclinations to carry out the programmes of the Pharisees. Rabbinic literature names the leading sage of the period as Simeon ben Sheṭaḥ.[6] Some Sadducees perished in a purge, but the sect as a whole remained loyal to the dynasty. In rabbinic tradition, her reign was a golden age in which the crops were exceptionally bountiful.[7] Though Janneus fell short of David's achievements, the surrounding peoples had been overawed, as in the reigns of David and Solomon. The queen held hostages for the good behaviour of neighbouring rulers. Only once in her reign is she reported to have sent an army in a direction which might suggest an attempt to expand toward the borders promised by the Torah and the prophets: she sent her son Aristobulus on an expedition to protect

1 Meshorer, *Jewish Coins*, p. 122, nos. 20, 20A, 21A and 23.

2 Ibid., no. 23.

3 Ibid., p. 46; Jos. *Ant.* XIV.190–8; on the question whether Hyrcanus I or Hyrcanus II issued the various types of coins bearing the legend 'John the high priest', see the references cited in p. 324 n. 2.

4 Meshorer, *Jewish Coins*, pp. 123–9; on the question of which Aristobulus issued the coins see the references cited in p. 324 n. 2.

5 Ibid., pp. 124–6.

6 That Simeon ben Sheṭaḥ was not brother-in-law of Janneus has been postulated by Y. Efron, 'Šim'on ben Šeṭaḥ wᵉYannai ha-melek', *Sefer zikkaron liGᵉdalyahu 'Alon, Meḥqarim bᵉtolᵉdot Yiśra'el uba-lašon ha-'ivrit*, Tel Aviv 1970, pp. 132–69.

7 Sifra *Bᵉḥuqqotay* 1:1; *b. Ta'an.* 23a (note the version quoted in the Tosafot to *Sabb.* 16b); Lev. R. 35:10.

Damascus from the Iturean Arab chief, Ptolemy son of Mennaios, whose realm was centred in the Vale of Lebanon. Was she imitating David's protection of Toi, king of Hamath?[1] The expedition returned home after accomplishing nothing significant. Other signs suggested that the age of fulfilment had not yet come. King Tigranes of Armenia suddenly grew into a power menacing Judea. He conquered much of Syria and besieged Ptolemais. A Jewish embassy purchased his favour, but Tigranes soon proved to be no match for Rome and ceased to menace Judea. Alexandra may have refrained from expansion thereafter to avoid provoking Rome.

Alexandra grew old and feeble. The vigorous and soldierly Aristobulus had been the spokesman for the supporters of his father, men who had bitterly opposed the Pharisees. Now he and they feared that the queen's death and the accession of the weak Hyrcanus would leave them at the mercy of the Pharisees. When Alexandra fell ill, Aristobulus easily won over the garrisons of twenty-two forts where Janneus' old supporters had been stationed. In the forts he found money to hire a formidable army from the neighbourhood. The dying Alexandra had only enough strength to order that Aristobulus' wife and children be put under arrest in the fortress Baris, north of the Temple. She also authorized Hyrcanus and the elders to act as they saw fit, and then she died (in 67 B.C.E.), at the age of 73, after a reign of nine years. Hyrcanus bore the title 'king' in her last months.[2]

Soon after her death. Alexandra's sons and their supporters went into battle near Jericho. Many of Hyrcanus' soldiers deserted to Aristobulus, and his side was routed. Hyrcanus still controlled the Baris with Aristobulus' wife and children. From the Baris Hyrcanus proposed a peaceful solution: Aristobulus was to be king and high priest[3] while Hyrcanus should live without taking part in public affairs but still enjoying his other possessions and privileges. The pact was solemnly concluded in the Temple, and the two brothers exchanged residences.

Did Aristobulus II aspire to fulfil the prophecies of a wondrous king? He had scant opportunity to act upon such aspirations in his brief

[1] 2 Sam. 8:10.

[2] Jos. *Bell.* I.120, *Ant.* XIII.430. Josephus dates Hyrcanus' accession as king in Olympiad 167, year 3, in the consulship of Quintus Hortensius and Quintus Metellus Creticus. The date is probably equivalent to 69/8 B.C.E., not to the 70/69 B.C.E. suggested by some scholars, for a survey of Josephus' Olympiad dates indicates that he usually followed the 'Polybian' system. See Elias Bickerman, *Chronology of the Ancient World* (Ithaca, N.Y., 1968), p. 76. I shall survey Josephus' dates in a future article.

[3] High priest, too; see Jos. *Ant.* XIV.42, 97, and XX.243–4.

and troubled reign. The coins of 'Yehudah high priest', even if they are his, do not display the royal title and bear only Hebrew legends. Hyrcanus, however, was later to accuse him of raids against neighbouring peoples and of piracy.[1] If the accusations are true, they could reflect such aspirations.[2]

Left to himself, Hyrcanus probably would have done nothing to disturb the settlement. Among his supporters, however, was the formidable Antipater, a man descended from converted Idumeans. Antipater's father, Antipas, had governed Idumea for Janneus and Alexandra. Antipater had reason to fear and hate Aristobulus and plied the reluctant Hyrcanus with suggestions that Aristobulus wished to kill him and that he should seek refuge with Aretas III, king of the Nabatean Arabs. Finally he persuaded Hyrcanus, who first sent him to Aretas to gain assurances of safety. Then Hyrcanus and Antipater fled from Jerusalem to Petra, the Nabatean capital. There Antipater importuned Aretas to back Hyrcanus' cause with armed force. Hyrcanus offered to return to the Nabateans Janneus' conquests in Moab. Aretas consented and marched with an army of 50,000 and defeated Aristobulus in battle. Aristobulus fled to the fortified Temple, where the Nabateans and Hyrcanus' Jewish supporters besieged him. During the siege the famous saint Honi (Onias) was asked to curse Aristobulus and his faction. Instead, Honi prayed to God to grant to neither side what it asked against the other. Furious bystanders thereupon stoned him to death.

Aristobulus and the priests in the Temple carried on the sacrificial cult despite the siege. At first they paid exorbitant prices to the besiegers for the necessary animals. Ultimately the besiegers took the money and refused to supply animals. According to one report, they even sent up a pig. Pious Jewish observers ascribed a subsequent earthquake and storms and famine to God's wrath over the atrocity.[3]

The remainder of the story is soon told. The invincible Roman legions under Pompey were now in Syria. Pompey's legate, Scaurus, confronted embassies from both brothers and sided with the more able Aristobulus. The threat of Roman force drove the Nabateans to withdraw and allowed Aristobulus to turn the tables as he inflicted a heavy defeat on their retreating army. However, cleverer than Scaurus was Pompey, who soon came into the region and, unlike Scaurus, delayed making a final decision. When at last he gave the disputants a hearing at Damasucs, not only Hyrcanus and Aristobulus came to press

[1] Jos. *Ant.* XIV.43; cf. Diodorus XL.2.2.

[2] See Goldstein, *I Maccabees*, note on 13:29–30.

[3] Jos. *Ant.* XIV.25–8; *b. Soṭa* 49b, *Menaḥ*. 64b.

their claims, but also a delegation of 200 leading men who posed as spokesmen for the nation.[1] That delegation charged that although they were accustomed to obey the priests of God and though Hyrcanus and Aristobulus were of priestly descent, the two had no legitimate right to rule, since both aspired to establish a tyranny. The principle of the illegitimacy of tyrants was accepted in the Greco-Roman world and could also be derived from Jewish sources.[2] In the version of the story preserved by Diodorus, the anti-Hasmonean spokesmen for the nation objected to the use by both brothers of the title 'king'. Romans would tend to sympathize, for Romans long abhorred the institution of kingship.[3]

Hyrcanus charged that Aristobulus had deprived him by force of his rights as first-born to the kingship and the high priesthood. To the charges of the spokesmen for the nation, Aristobulus replied that he acquired the royal office through no revolutionary act of tyranny, but by legitimate inheritance from his father. To the charges of Hyrcanus he replied that Hyrcanus' own ineptitude had lost him his prerogatives. Aristobulus claimed to have acted for fear outsiders might seize power from Hyrcanus' feeble grasp.

Pompey still wished to put off his decision until he should be sure of the submission of the Nabateans. Pompey may have rebuked Hyrcanus and his followers,[4] but Aristobulus had good reason to fear that Pompey would decide in favour of the elder brother. Roman policy for generations had favoured weaker claimants to disputed thrones, especially in the Seleucid empire.[5] Aristobulus might have lost out even had his diplomacy been better. As it was, he had insufficient strength to resist Rome. His inconsistent behaviour revealed his hostile suspicions and antagonized Pompey, who took the force he intended to use against the Nabateans, and other troops at his disposal, and marched against Aristobulus. Aristobulus soon surrendered, but his partisans in Jerusalem continued to resist on his behalf, seizing the heavily fortified Temple. Hyrcanus' faction opened Jerusalem to Pompey's troops and co-operated with them, but the siege of the Temple dragged on for three months. Even under siege, Aristobulus' supporters strictly observed the Sabbath, to the point of not attacking the Romans, who built siege-works and brought up siege-engines on

[1] Jos. *Ant.* XIV.40–6; Diodorus XL.2.2.

[2] Polybius VI.3.9–10; 4.2, 6, 8; 7.6 to 8.2; Livy 1.49, 59.8–11; Cicero, *De re publica,* II.25.45 to 27.49; Deut. 17:20; 2 Sam. 12:1–12; 1 Kings 12:1–24; 2 Kings 9 and 10; 2 Chron. 10; Jer. 22:13–19; Ezek. 45:7–10, 46:16–18.

[3] See Hugh Last in *The Cambridge Ancient History*, 7 (Cambridge, 1928), p. 395.

[4] Diodorus XL.2.2.

[5] See Will, *Histoire,* 2, pp. 303–60.

the Sabbaths. The Temple fell on the Day of Atonement.[1] On the authority of pagan authors, Josephus says that large numbers of Jews and priests were cut down as they steadfastly pursued the rituals of the day. Twelve thousand Jews fell to the Romans and their Jewish supporters or took their own lives. Pompey himself dared to enter the Holy of Holies, though he refrained from plundering the rich treasures of the Temple.

Pompey restored the high priesthood to Hyrcanus. Once again, Jerusalem and the Jews were subjected to tribute. Pompey freed from Judea the great Hasmonean conquests, including the coastal areas and Samaria, Galilee, and Transjordan. The whole area once subject to Hasmonean Judea was placed under the control of the Roman governor of Syria. Pompey returned to Rome, taking with him as prisoners Aristobulus and his family, including his two sons and his two daughters. *En route* the elder son, Alexander, escaped.

These events must have stunned those Jews who believed that the age of God's wrath had ended forever with the heroic Hasmonean liberation of Israel. Now, contrary to the promises at Isaiah 52:1 and Zechariah 9:8, unclean and uncircumcised foreigners and tax-gatherers marched through the Holy Land. Even the sober Josephus in telling the story uses language drawn from Lamentations.[2] The author of the *Psalms of Solomon*, a contemporary of the events, sees them as punishment for the sins of the generation[3] and especially of the Hasmo-

1 The date should not be questioned. If the day had not already been a fast day, a fast would have been established on the anniversary of so great a disaster. Because of chronological problems, some scholars have rejected the date as the error of a pagan author who confused the Sabbath with a fast day. See Schürer, *History*, I, pp. 239–40 n. 23. Josephus can hardly have allowed so gross an error to stand. Josephus dates the fall in Olympiad 179 (64–60 B.C.E.), without giving the year within the Olympiad. He also dates it in the consulship of Antionius and Cicero (63 B.C.E.). The Day of Atonement, 63 B.C.E., fits both dates. Some scholars hold that if the year number has been omitted from an Olympiad date, the author meant the first year of the Olympiad, and Olympiad 179, year 1, ran from midsummer 64 B.C.E. to midsummer 63 B.C.E. and did not contain the Day of Atonement, 63 B.C.E. Since, however, Josephus followed the 'Polybian' system, in which the Olympiad year was equated with the Roman consular year which began within it (see above, n. 2 on p. 346) the Day of Atonement, 63 B.C.E., would indeed be placed in Olympiad 179, year 1. Strabo does confuse the Sabbath with a fast day (*Geography* XVI.2.40, C 763), and Josephus could have read Strabo. But Strabo there does not date the fall of the Temple, but speaks of the use Pompey made of the defenders' scruples against violating the Sabbath. Only Dio Cassius (XXVII.16) says that Jerusalem fell on the Sabbath.

2 With *Ant*. XIV.74, cf. Lam. 1:1; with *Ant*. XIV.77, cf. Lam. 5:2; with *Ant*. XIV.78, cf. Lam. 5:8. Perhaps Josephus alludes to Lam. 4:20 at *Ant*. XIV.79.

3 *Pss. Sol.* 1; 2:3, 7–19; 8; 9; 17:14–22.

neans,[1] even as he condemns the impious Pompey and gloats over his ignominious death.[2] In the *Psalms of Solomon* we can see the rising hopes that God will raise again the extinct or hidden dynasty of David to redeem Israel.[3] Pious Jews who rejected the royal claims of Janneus and his sons found it natural to assert the claims of the dynasty of David. The Hasmoneans probably did their utmost to suppress such challenges to the legitimacy of their rule. Nevertheless the mass of Jews may have been slow to accept anti-Hasmonean 'messianic' preaching of the coming glory of David's stock. The faith in a Davidic Messiah is conspicuous by its absence from the literature earlier than the *Psalms of Solomon*. Second Maccabees is an abridgement of the anti-Hasmonean polemic work which Jason of Cyrene wrote in the middle of Janneus' reign, but it contains no trace of the messianic hope. Mention of the Davidic dynasty is also conspicuous by its absence from the fragment preserved at *b. Qiddushin* 66a. There only Janneus' claims to the high priesthood, not those to the kingship, are in dispute, and even his claims to the high priesthood are declared to be just. Only at sectarian I Enoch 90:37 (by spiritual ancestors of the Essenes) is there a Davidic Messiah figure in a text of this age.

The inconsistencies in our sources as to the nature of the Hasmonean kingship probably reflect the clashing Jewish points of view. Jewish opposition may well have caused the banishment of the word 'king' from Hasmonean coins, at least in Hebrew. The anti-Hasmonean interpolation in the *Testament of Moses* describes the dynasty as 'imperious kings' who 'shall be called priests of the Highest God'. Does the writer mean that, though kings, they shall have in Hebrew only the title 'priest of the Highest God'? Hyrcanus II is known to have borne that title.[4] Qumran texts and 1 Enoch 91–104 never use the title 'king' in alluding to Hasmoneans. The kings in 1 Enoch 37–71 are probably not Hasmoneans. Josephus, however, records that Aristobulus II and even Hyrcanus II were regarded as kings by their subjects.[5] Did some Jews use as a royal title only the Greek *basileus* or the Aramaic *malkā*? Rabbinic tradition unhesitatingly speaks in Hebrew of the Hasmonean *kings*,[6] and even the writer of the *Psalms of Solomon*, though regarding the Hasmonean dynasty as illegitimate, calls their rule a 'kingdom'.[7]

The Greek additional names and the Greek coin legends and the

1 Ibid. 8:16–17; 17:5–13, 22.
2 *Pss. Sol.* 2.
3 Ibid. 17:21–51.
4 Jos. *Ant.* XVI.163; *b. Rosh. Hash.* 18b.
5 *Ant.* XIV.4–6; 97; 157, 165, 172.
6 See Gedaliahu Alon, *Meḥqarim b^etol^edot Yiśra'el*, I (Tel Aviv, 1957), pp. 17–18.
7 17:6.

parallels between Hasmonean expansionism and the practices of Hellenistic dynasties have led modern writers to say that the later Hasmoneans were heavily Hellenized and for that reason incurred the opposition of pious Jews. No ancient text says so, though the Apocrypha and Pseudepigrapha and rabbinic literature teem with attacks on those who ape the Gentiles. The Hasmoneans were like the rest of the Jews. Jews did not hesitate to adopt Greek techniques and institutions if they did not conflict with Jewish beliefs. The Greek additional names, the coin legends, and the expansionism, as we have seen, may all reflect Jewish interests. Both the Hasmoneans and their bitter Jewish opponents were men of zeal, who fought to fulfil the words of the Torah and the prophets.

CHAPTER 10

JEWISH LITERATURE IN HEBREW AND ARAMAIC IN THE GREEK ERA

The Hellenistic period begins in Palestine with the arrival of Alexander the Great in 332 B.C.E. The appearance of the Macedonian conqueror did not, however, change things overnight, and certainly not in the sphere of Jewish literature. Such literature continued to be written in Hebrew or Aramaic, though Greek influence may be detected in it here and there. The Greek language gained ground only slowly in Palestine. Palestine came to be encircled by a ring of Greek cities, for it was mainly on the edges of Jewish territory, on the coast and to the east of Jordan, that the conquering Greeks established, one by one, their settlements. Gaza, which was devastated during Alexander's conquest, must have been one of the first cities to be rebuilt on the pattern of a Hellenistic town.[1] At Samaria, which now became Sebaste, a Macedonian garrison was established on the orders of Alexander himself. Perdiccas was the founder of the Greek city of Gerasa in the Transjordan. He was undoubtedly one of the first of Alexander's followers to settle a Macedonian population in Palestine. Dion and Pella were presumably founded at this same period. The object of implanting these Macedonian colonies was partly to ensure the loyalty of the local inhabitants and partly to reward the soldiers with grants of land.

But it was mainly during the century from 300–200 B.C.E., when the country was under the control of the Ptolemies, that Greek cities came to flourish in Palestine. In this period there originated Ptolemais (Akko), Philoteria on the shore of lake Tiberias, Scythopolis (Beth Shean) and Philadelphia (Amman) to name only a few. At least thirty cities, on any reckoning, were established in Palestine during the Hellenistic period on the orders of the Macedonian kings.[2] The Hellenization of Palestine meant the introduction of a Greek-speaking population made up not only of Macedonians but doubtless also of

[1] Arrian II.27.7.

[2] V. Tcherikover, *Hellenistic Civilization and the Jews* (Philadelphia, 1959), p. 105.

people of Egyptian origin. This is shown by the Zenon papyri which reveal the existence of commercial links between the two countries.[1] These foreigners introduced Greek customs into the social life of Palestine. They introduced gymnasia, where the *ephēboi* daily displayed their nude bodies, stadia, hippodromes and theatres which drew citizens of all social classes. There are no texts to give us precise information about the diffusion of Greek customs among Palestinian Jews in the fourth and third centuries B.C.E., but the first book of Maccabees tells us how the Hellenizing Jews constructed a gymnasium in Jerusalem at the beginning of the Seleucid occupation.

In those days [under Antiochus Epiphanes] lawless men came forth from Israel, and misled many, saying, 'Let us go and make a covenant with the gentiles round about us, for since we separated from them many evils have come upon us.' This proposal pleased them, and some of the people eagerly went to the king. He authorized them to observe the ordinances of the gentiles. So they built a gymnasium in Jerusalem, according to gentile custom.[2]

Although we have no documentary evidence of it from Palestine itself there are grounds for believing that alongside the gymnasia Greek schools were founded, for Greek culture and customs could hardly become widespread without the spread of knowledge of the Greek language. Marrou has written:

Wherever the Greeks settled in the villages of the Fayum, where the Ptolemies organized a military colonization, in Babylon, in far-off Susiana – one of their first tasks was to set up their own institutions, their educational establishments – their primary schools and gymnasiums. For education was a matter of primary importance to them. They were isolated in a foreign land, and their chief concern was to enable their sons, despite the influence of the surroundings, to preserve the distinguishing marks of the Hellenic character – the thing they clung to more than anything else.[3]

But even though Greek was the language of all cultivated men in the lands bordering the eastern Mediterranean, and even though the civilization of which it was the vehicle might have a powerful attraction for educated Jews, the sacred writers of Palestine continued to write in Hebrew, or even in Aramaic, throughout the third century B.C.E. So

1 V. Tcherikover and A. Fuks, *Corpus Papyrorum Judaicarum* (Cambridge, Mass, 1957–64), I, p. 115.
2 I Macc. 1:11–14.
3 H.-I. Marrou, *Histoire de l'éducation dans l'Antiquité* (Paris, 1948), p. 157; ET *A History of Education in Antiquity* (London, 1956), p. 99.

lively was the ancestral tongue that even at this period of intensive Hellenization it could still produce a poetic masterpiece in the Song of Songs; serious historical works such as Chronicles and Ezra–Nehemiah; and a work of religious edification like the book of Esther. Though some of the midrashic stories in the first part of Daniel circulated in Aramaic, doubtless because they originated in Babylon, the difficult and composite Deutero-Zechariah, which contains echoes of Alexander's conquest of Palestine, is written in Hebrew. And the second part of Daniel, which was written, it may be supposed, by one of the Hasideans who supported the Maccabees in their critical hour of resistance to Hellenism, could be written in nothing but the old sacred tongue. It was also in Hebrew that Ecclesiastes and Ecclesiasticus were composed, the latter being the last great compilation of Wisdom materials to be made on Palestinian soil. In Hebrew, again, the Essenes of Qumran drew up the greater part of their writings: hymns, rules, commentaries on the Bible, apocalyptic works like *The War of the Sons of Light against the Sons of Darkness*, and more besides. All this leads us to conclude that the Hellenization of Palestine had had the effect of giving the old sacred language a new lease of life. Greek was to be used for the production of sacred writings only in the Diaspora, especially in Egypt, for the sake of Jews who knew no Hebrew.

SONG OF SONGS

Renan, recognizing the secular character of the Song of Songs, arrived at the conclusion that it was a love song which had strayed into the canon by mistake. He wrote:

> By a strange miracle (thanks to a species of contempt in regard to which criticism could not afford to be very severe, since she has preserved to us what is the most curious, perhaps, work of the monuments of antiquity) an entire book, the work of moments of forgetfulness, when the people of God allowed their infinite hopes to slumber, has come down to us.[1]

This quotation neatly poses the problem of the nature and meaning of the Song of Songs, which, whatever Renan's opinion of it, has in fact come down to us as part of the Hebrew canon of Scripture. It belongs to the third great section of the canon, the *Kethubim*, and by the Jews it is reckoned as one of the five Megilloth (the others being Ruth, Ecclesiastes, Lamentations and Esther) which are used in the liturgies of particular festivals. It is placed between Ruth and Ecclesiastes, and

[1] E. Renan, *Le Cantique des Cantiques, traduit de l'hébreu avec une étude sur le plan, l'âge et le caractère du poème* (Paris, 1860), p. iv; ET *The Song of Songs* (London, 1896), p. xix.

since the sixth century C.E.[1] the Song of Songs has been read at the feast of Passover because of its descriptions of springtime and its allusion in 1:9 to the Exodus from Egypt. But the inclusion of the Song of Songs in the canon raised problems for the rabbis at an early date, by reason of the book's singular and apparently secular nature. So amenable was it to secular use that, if we are to believe Rabbi Akiba (died in 135 C.E.), it was sung in the taverns as a common drinking song. 'He who sings the Song of Songs in the taverns,' he says, 'will have no portion in the world to come.'[2] There are rumblings of doubt which issue in discussions as to whether the Song of Songs does or does not 'defile the hands', that is, whether it is to be considered as sacred Scripture. There is a passage in the Mishnah where the opinions of several rabbis on this point are reported. In spite of this Rabbi Akiba solemnly declares:

No man in Israel ever disputed about the Song of Songs [that he should say] that it does not render the hands unclean, for all the ages are not worth the day on which the Song of Songs was given to Israel; for all the Writings (*Ketubim*) are holy, but the Song of Songs is the Holy of Holies. And if aught was in dispute the dispute was about Ecclesiastes alone.[3]

These discussions about the 'holiness' of the Song of Songs give us every reason to believe that if it had not already been canonized by the first century C.E., not only would the rabbis not have gone to so much trouble to justify it, but it would quite simply have been rejected by the Synagogue.

Today, as in the rabbinic era, the book still presents plenty of problems. These problems relate to its composition, its structure and literary type, its date and its interpretation. It is these various questions which we shall in turn examine. The book sings of the love of a man for a woman – of the lover for his beloved – from the first line to the last. At first sight it does not look like an organic literary work but a collection of small literary units, about thirty of them, which follow each other with no strong logical connection holding them together other than their common theme of love. The structure attributed to this writing largely depends on what view is held of the nature of the work as a whole. If it is seen as a drama in the proper sense of the word, it will

1 The custom of reciting the Song of Songs at Passover is mentioned in the tractate *Sopherim* 14, 3, which dates from the sixth century. Cf. I. Elbogen, *Der jüdische Gottesdienst in seiner geschichtlichen Entwicklung,* 3rd edn. (Frankfurt, 1931; repr. Hildesheim, 1967), p. 185.

2 Tosephta *Sanh.* XII.10; cf. *b. Sanh.* 101a; H. L. Strack and P. Billerbeck, *Kommentar zum Neuen Testament aus Talmud und Midrasch,* I (Munich, 1922), p. 516.

3 H. Danby, *The Mishnah*, Yadaim 3.5 (Oxford, 1933), p. 782.

be natural to look for acts and scenes. If it is viewed as an historical allegory, then some chronological progression will be sought in it. If one regards it as a simple love poem, either in the ordinary or the symbolic sense, then one will find in it the different stages of a burgeoning love, or variations on the theme of mutual longing, expressed, in either case, in the sort of rich symbolism that only an eastern imagination could employ. But the possibility that the Song of Songs is a drama in the proper sense should be ruled out. It is difficult to detect in the writing any progression or any development. But in any case this Greek species of literature is never met with in Jewish circles.[1] Drama as a literary genre was unknown among the Jews since it was thought of as pagan and irreligious.[2] Nevertheless it must be noted that two manuscripts of the Septuagint, codices Alexandrinus and Sinaiticus, have notes at the head of certain passages indicating particular speakers, the bridegroom and the bride. These are mentioned, in all, seven times.[3] This would seem to show that the copyist was treating the work as a drama even at that early date. But the composition of the Song of Songs is best explained if it is recalled how in ancient Egypt love poetry was arranged. The pieces are set out as songs in dialogue, making up a coherent drama, a lyric romance, but one in which it does not appear to have been felt necessary to indicate who – lover or beloved – should pronounce which couplets.[4] It is in fact the romantic literature of Egypt with which the Song of Songs offers most parallels.[5] Written as it is in a refined, educated style, it by no means gives the impression of being a collection of popular wedding songs, as some authors have maintained.[6]

The interpretation of this little book is much debated. There are those who espouse a symbolic interpretation. The Song of Songs, in

[1] One of the last essays in support of the dramatic theory is that of G. Pouget and J. Guitton, *Le Cantique des Cantiques* (Paris, 1934). One of the earliest supporters of the idea seems to have been Origen (*PG* 13 (1862), col. 61).

[2] H. H. Rowley, 'The interpretation of the Son gof Songs', *The Servant of the Lord and other essays on the Old Testament* (London, 1952), p. 205; 2nd edn. (Oxford, 1985), pp. 214f.

[3] The text of these rubrics will be found at the end of the edition of the Septuagint published by A. Rahlfs, *Septuaginta id est Vetus Testamentum graece iuxta LXX interpretes* (Stuttgart, 1935), 2, p. 270.

[4] P. Gilbert, *La poesie égyptienne* (Brussels, 1949), p. 77; J. Winandy, *Le Cantique des Cantiques, poème d'amour mué en écrit de sagesse* (Maredsous, 1960), pp. 68–9.

[5] The most important study of the non-biblical parallels to the Song of Songs is that of R. Tournay, in A. Robert and R. Tournay, *Le Cantique des Cantiques* (Paris, 1963), pp. 339–426. For the Egyptian literature see S. Schott, *Les Chants d'Amour de l'Egypte ancienne* (Paris, 1956); see also Gilbert, *La poesie* and *ANET*.

[6] Winandy, *Le Cantique*, pp. 43–4.

their view, has in mind the love of Yahweh for Israel, on the lines of the marriage analogies of the prophets. This line of exegesis, widespread among Christians, was already established in Judaism, but it cannot be traced back to the earliest period; neither is it consistently adhered to. 4 Ezra, written at the end of the first century C.E.,[1] contains what looks at first sight like the earliest example of Jewish exegesis on these lines. However, it may not really be so. In this Jewish pseudepigraphical writing Israel is a lily preferred before all other flowers (5:24), the dove, named from among all created birds (5:26), the bride (7:26). But the author of 4 Ezra could simply be alluding to the book of Hosea, which contains the same similes or symbols.[2] Likewise, even though there are some traces of allegorical exegesis in one passage of the Mishnah,[3] the same passage exhibits alongside it a naturalistic understanding of the Song of Songs, for it says that the young girls of Jerusalem used to go twice a year to dance in the vineyards and invite the young men to marriage, singing the words of Prov. 31:30–1 and S. of S. 3:11. Yet this same passage from the Song of Songs was understood by Simeon ben Gamaliel (*circa* 140 C.E.) as referring to the gift of the Law and the rebuilding of the Temple. At about the same period, according to the testimony of Mekilta on Exod. 15:2, Rabbi Akiba was interpreting several passages of the Song of Songs as referring allegorically to Yahweh.[4] Of this allegorical exegesis we may perhaps already have some foreshadowing in the New Testament.[5] But however widespread the symbolic interpretation may be, all this evidence for it is late by comparison with the date of composition of the Song of Songs itself. Furthermore, the argument from parallel passages in the prophets, which some have advanced in order to support their thesis that the book speaks of the love of Yahweh for Israel, is not a convincing one. These parallels are apparent rather than real, and are not close enough to be of any value as evidence.[6] Finally, if the hypothesis were correct that the Song of Songs was written as an allegory, the author would be obliged to lift the allegorical veil for us at least now and again. This never happens. Nowhere in the Song of

[1] 4 Ezra (2 Esdras) 5:24–6. Cf. A. Robert and R. Tournay, *Le Cantique des Cantiques*, EBib (Paris, 1963), pp. 43–4.

[2] For the bride, cf. Hos. 2; the lily, Hos. 14:5; the dove, Hos. 7:11, 11:11.

[3] Mishnah, *Ta'anith* 4.8.

[4] J. Bonsirven, 'Exégèse allégorique chez les Rabbins Tannaïtes', *RSR*, 24 (1934), 38–9, and P. Benoît, 'Rabbi Aqiba ben Joseph sage et héros du Judaïsme', *RB*, 54 (1947), 77.

[5] M. Cambe, 'L'influence du Cantique des cantiques sur le Nouveau Testament', *Revue Thomiste*, 62 (1962), 5–26.

[6] J.-P. Audet, 'Le sens du Cantique des Cantiques', *RB*, 62 (1955), 206ff.

Songs is Yahweh spoken of; or at least, to be more precise, he only appears fortuitously in a stereotyped expression in which love is described as a 'flame of Yahweh'.[1] The other partner in the allegory, Israel herself, is not named either, and nowhere is there any reference to the covenant or to prostitution as there is in the prophets. We must therefore regard the Song of Songs as a song of human love written in a language that is clear enough for there to be no need to torture our minds to read symbols into it. The author sings with delicacy of real love, never descending to the purely erotic. Everything is fresh and poetic, and it has rightly been called a masterpiece of pure poetry.

For dating the work the only criteria available to us are linguistic ones. Aramaisms are found, which seem to demand a late date, but also some rare and exotic words. Some have even suggested that the word *'appiryon*, 'palanquin',[2] is a borrowing of the Greek φορεῖον, but this is not certain, for the term could as readily be connected with the old Persian *ūpariyana*.[3] Furthermore, if the word were a Greek borrowing, the presence of this foreign technical term in the Song of Songs would not by itself establish the composition of the book in the Greek period. It would be better to draw attention to the fact that the Song of Songs bears the marks of a learned literature, in spite of its appearance of spontaneity and freshness. It is reminiscent of those poets who wrote in Greek at Alexandria in the third century, such as Theocritus with his *Idylls* or Callimachus and his *Epigrams*. The most striking of the literary fashions which were then in vogue in Egypt was the presentation of love and music in a pastoral setting, as if the life of shepherds, simple country-dwellers, were somehow more propitious than that of other men.[4] True, the Song of Songs is more like the Egyptian love poems than it is like the *Idylls* of Theocritus of the *Epigrams* of Callimachus, but one could easily envisage the author borrowing from these latter not only the basic idea for the work itself, but also particular methods and characteristics, such as their way of making geographical or historical allusions, and the pastoral setting and artificial style.[5] This is not to say that some of the love songs might not have had their own history behind them and go back to the sacred marriage literature celebrating the divine loves of Dumuzi (Tammuz) and Inanna (Ishtar).[6]

[1] S. of S. 8:6. [2] S. of S. 3:9.

[3] L. Koehler and W. Baumgartner, *Hebräisches und aramäisches Lexicon zum Alten Testament*, 3rd edn., I (Leiden, 1967), p. 78. F. Rundgren, "appirjôn, Tragsessel, "Sänfte", *ZAW*, 74 (1962), 70–2.

[4] P. H. E. Legrand, *Bucoliques grecs, Théocrite* (Paris, 1925), 1, p. 3.

[5] Winandy, *Le Cantique*, pp. 44–5.

[6] H. Schmökel, *Heilige Hochzeit und Hoheslied* (Wiesbaden, 1956); T. Meek, in Wilfred H. Schoff, *The Song of Songs: A Symposium* (Philadelphia, 1924), pp. 48–9; S. N.

To sum up, it seems best to us to date the work in the Greek period,[1] rather than the Persian era where several authors place it.[2]

ECCLESIASTES

Of the two Wisdom books from the Greek period which are preserved wholly or partly in Hebrew Qoheleth (Ecclesiastes) is the older. But whereas the 'Wisdom of Jesus ben Sira' bears the name of an author, the book of Ecclesiastes is anonymous. However, its author is referred to at least once (1.12) by the mysterious title 'Qoheleth', a name which has been explained in a variety of ways. Some suggest that the sage is representing himself as 'the assembly' (*qahal*), or as 'a man of the assembly', that is, a member of the public.[3] Others observe that the word *qoheleth* belongs to a class of Hebrew nouns of feminine form which commonly denotes persons of particular function, for example, *has-sophereth*, 'the scribe'.[4] This observation has led to a number of different interpretations: 'president of the assembly', as in the Greek translation 'Ἐκκλησιάστης; or even, 'the one who speaks before the assembly', 'the preacher', which is an explanation given as early as Midrash Rabbah and which was retained by Luther, who called the book *Der Prediger*. But there is nothing in the book to suggest that its author has any responsibility in connection with the religious assembly. Even more difficult to sustain is the opinion of those who make *qoheleth* the 'collector of sayings'. For one thing, the word *qahal* only refers to a collection of persons, not of things, and for another, there is nothing in the book to support the theory that this was his role.[5] This mysterious title must hide someone who had a prominent place in an assembly (*qahal*), but what is most likely is that it was an assembly of the wise. But it would be a mistake to see the noun *qoheleth*, because of its feminine form, as an epithet for wisdom personified, because in the passages where the term appears[6] it is construed as masculine. Besides, we have already observed that some titles of functions or

Kramer, *The Sacred Marriage Rite. Aspects of Faith, Myth and Ritual in Ancient Sumer* (Bloomington, Ind., 1969), pp. 85–106.

[1] In support of dating during the Greek period may be cited L. Krinetzki, *Das hohe Lied* (Dusseldorf, 1964), p. 42.

[2] W. Rudolph, *Das Buch Ruth. Das hohe Lied. Die Klagelieder* (Gütersloh, 1962), p. 111.

[3] R. Pautrel, *L'Ecclésiaste*, BJ (3rd edn., Paris, 1958), p. 9.

[4] Neh. 7:57, Ezra 2.55.

[5] A list of the various opinions held in ancient times will be found in C. G. Ginsburg, [*The Song of Songs and*] *Coheleth (commonly called the book of Ecclesiastes), with a commentary historical and critical* (London, 1861; repr. New York, 1970), pp. 3–9.

[6] Eccles. 1:2, 12; 7:27, 12:8, 9, 10.

offices are given feminine form quite regularly.[1] Ecclesiastes is casting himself in the role of a king in Jerusalem, and the book's title, more exactly, makes him the son of David, that is, Solomon.[2] Is it sufficient explanation to say that Solomon is the model of the wise king? If this were the case the author would surely have put the name 'Solomon' directly in the work's title. But he does not. The book insists throughout that he is a king in Jerusalem, which shows that he is following a literary convention like the one which was current in Egypt, where didactic or moralistic works were put into the mouth of a king. So we have, for example, 'The instruction of the king for his son Merikare', 'The instruction of king Amenemhet for his son', and so on.[3]

The book of Ecclesiastes poses a number of problems which are far from being resolved. The problems of its composition and of its teaching are specially difficult.

Ecclesiastes is a man of original mind and is not content to repeat the ideas already arrived at by his predecessors. He intends to see for himself, to ponder and to draw his own conclusions, 'till I might see what was good for the sons of men to do under heaven during the few days of their life'.[4] Enquiry, reflection, the giving of a verdict, these are the three stages of the author's thought, an author whose distinctive work is like no other book in the Old Testament. One could almost believe it to be by a modern analytical thinker. His lucid investigation is dotted with characteristic phrases, such as: 'I saw' or 'I have seen';[5] 'moreover, I saw...';[6] 'again I saw';[7] 'I have also seen';[8] 'all this I observed'.[9] Having meditated on the data of experience, a process which he indicates by such phrases as: 'I applied my mind to know',[10] he is led to formulate a judgement based on experience and on reason. Hence such expressions as: 'I found' or 'I have found';[11] 'I perceived', 'I know'.[12] But what does he discover through this process of analysis? He discovers that 'all is vanity', or even 'vanity of vanities', that is, absolute vanity, total vanity, vanity supreme. The Hebrew word used here is *hebel*, which means 'vanity', 'breath', and indicates the inconstant, fleeting, empty nature of the things of this world. 'Vanity of vanities, says the Preacher, vanity of vanities! All is vanity.' This sombre verdict recurs like a bitter chorus,[13] and the word 'vanity' itself

[1] E. Podechard, *L'Ecclésiaste*, EBib (Paris, 1912), p. 133.
[2] 1:1, 12, 16.
[3] P. Humbert, *Recherches sur les sources égyptiennes de la littérature sapientiale d'Israël* (Neuchatel, 1929), pp. 107–8.
[4] 2:3.
[5] 1:14; 2:13, 24; 3:10, 22; 4:4, 15; 5:13, 18; 7:15.
[6] 3:16.
[7] 9:11.
[8] 9:13.
[9] 8:9.
[10] 1:17; 7:25; 8:9, 16; 9:1.
[11] 7:27–9.
[12] 2:14; 3:12, 14; 7:25; 8:17.
[13] 1:2; 12:8.

figures 31 times in the work as a whole. Life is vain and rolls inexorably on in an unending cycle in which all things, ruled by a stern determinism, continually begin again, until things seem weary with the perpetual new beginnings.[1] There is therefore nothing to hope for, because everything has already happened: 'There is nothing new under the sun'.[2] Man cannot claim to improve on what his predecessors did,[3] and he makes the harshness of his condition even worse by his activities, his daily busy-ness: 'For all his days are full of pain, and his work is a vexation'.[4] In addition, experience contradicts the categorical assertion of the traditional Wisdom, which says that God renders to every man according to his works.[5] Ecclesiastes feels bound to declare that there are in this world no sanctions, no rewards or punishments for acts good or evil: 'there is a righteous man who perishes in his righteousness, and there is a wicked man who prolongs his life in his evil-doing'.[6] But nevertheless he does not deny the doctrine of retribution in this life, to which he remains firmly attached[7] and, by contrast with Job, he does not take issue with God.

If nothing in the facts of the case corresponds with the teachings of the wise, is it credible that when the edifice erected by the wise collapses Wisdom herself should survive? Nothing is less certain. For Wisdom is neither respected, nor indeed always recognized by men,[8] and besides, human wisdom is of brief duration, shallow, and, far from being a guarantee of comfort, brings only increased misery to its devotee: 'for in much wisdom is much vexation, and he who increases knowledge increases sorrow'.[9] There need be no doubt that what we have here is a sharp criticism of the author's wise colleagues who extolled the joys of both the search for Wisdom and its possession.[10] And then there is death, the conclusion of our life, the thought of which obsesses Ecclesiastes. In Sheol all is finished, all activity is excluded; all conscious life, all relations with the world of the living brought to an end. Thus 'a living dog is better than a dead lion'. So what is there left for man? There is misery and resignation. And yet, instead of falling into a despairing pessimism, Ecclesiastes, among the ruins that he creates as he prosecutes his case against complacent happiness, commends to man the little joys of day to day: the pleasures of the table, the affection of a wife one loves. Even the chorus of 'all is vanity' is paralleled in his book by another: 'Go, eat your bread with enjoyment, and drink your wine with a merry heart; for God has already approved

[1] 1:5–8.
[2] 1:9–10.
[3] 1:15.
[4] 2:23.
[5] Prov. 24:12.
[6] Eccles. 7:15.
[7] 8:12–13; 11:9; 12:14.
[8] 9:15–16.
[9] 1:18.
[10] Sir. 4:12; 6:28; 14:20–7.

what you do. Let your garments be always white; let not oil be lacking on your head. Enjoy life with the wife whom you love, all the days of your vain life which he has given you under the sun.'[1] It has not yet been given to this wise disputant to envisage a transcendent eschatology, although he is a convinced Yahwist who believes in providence[2] and who fully recognizes the distinction between good and evil.[3]

Such is the teaching that Ecclesiastes has left us in his book; a book in which it is not easy to discover any satisfying structure, in spite of numerous attempts to find one.[4] The work abounds in discordant themes, and the complexity of its teaching is not unrelated to its literary complexity. The theory has been advanced that an original *Urschrift* has been added to by later authors. One exponent of this view is Podechard.[5] It has been noted that in the epilogue (12:9–14) the title Ecclesiastes is ascribed to the author twice (12:9–10), although he only styles himself so on one other occasion. Accordingly, the epilogue has been identified as an editorial addition by someone other than Ecclesiastes himself, a disciple perhaps. But some go further than this. Amongst the first person material of the confessions of Ecclesiastes, the material claimed to have made up the original writing, can be detected reflections in third person form. These look like insertions of material from the Wisdom schools.[6] On these grounds some have been led to postulate, besides the original work and that of the epilogue-writer, additions by two principal hands, those of a pious *ḥasid* and those of a wise man, a *ḥakam*. The additions of the *ḥasid* were meant to correct Ecclesiastes' rather daring assertions about retribution, to make them conform better with traditional teaching.[7] Other additions have been introduced by a wise man who retouched the work in the interests of traditional Wisdom.[8] But recent writers are more inclined to allow unity of authorship. It is pointed out that the Wisdom writings are not necessarily systematic compositions. Nothing is easier than to make interpolations into a collection of maxims, but nothing is harder to

[1] Eccles. 9:7–9.

[2] 3:11, 14–15; 8:17; 11:5.

[3] 3:16; 4:1; 5:6; 7:15; 8:10–14; 9:2. See H.-P. Müller, 'Wie sprach Qohälät von Gott?', *VT*, 18 (1968), 507–21.

[4] For the most recent attempts see A. G. Wright, 'The Riddle of the Sphinx: the structure of the Book of Qoheleth', *CBQ*, 30 (1968), 313–34, and O. E. Glasser, *Le procès du bonheur par Qohelet*, LD 61 (Paris, 1970).

[5] *L'Ecclésiaste*, pp. 156–70.

[6] 1:15, 18; 2:16; 4:5–6, 9–12; 5:9; 7:1–9, 26; 9:4b; 10:8–20; 11:1–6.

[7] The following passages have been attributed to a pious author: 2:26a, b; 3:17; 7:26b; 8:2b, 5–8, 11–13; 11:9c; 12:1a, 13–14.

[8] Podechard attributes the following to the *ḥakam*: 4:5, 9–12; 5:2, 6a; 6:7; 7:1–12, 18–22; 8:1, 2a, 3–4.

prove than diversity of origins.[1] Might not the presence of contradictory observations and the somewhat chaotic order suggest the work of a sage with a unique attitude to study? Might he not have felt entitled to contradict himself, precisely because he had difficulty in finding a coherent solution to the mysteries of human existence and of individual retribution?[2]

Some have attempted to discover foreign influences in this apparently unorthodox book. Before much was known about oriental literature the main interest was in the influence on Ecclesiastes of Greek thought. A surprise affinity was noticed with Greek pessimism, gnomism and popular philosophy, though not such as to countenance talk of direct borrowing.[3] Another group of exegetes, by contrast, stressed possible parallels between Ecclesiastes, on the one hand, and sometimes the Egyptian world,[4] sometimes the Mesopotamian,[5] and sometimes the Phoenician,[6] on the other. The hypothesis of a Phoenician origin was maintained primarily on the grounds of linguistic comparisons. But up to the present no one has found among Phoenician or Ugaritic writings any pessimistic literature of a sort to corroborate the theory. The fact that so many different influences can be appealed to is itself evidence that Ecclesiastes belongs to an era when many varied ideologies were coming together. Such was the Hellenistic age. Can we be more exact about the date? Nothing in the book makes it necessary to bring its date down beyond the beginning of the Seleucid era. In any case, the absence of any allusions to the persecution under Antiochus Epiphanes forbids us to put it in that period, or to bring its date any lower than the middle of the second century B.C.E. As it happens, a fragment of a document from Qumran, written in a very beautiful hand, which makes it one of the Essene sect's best-looking manuscripts, has to be dated earlier than 150 B.C.E.[7] The use of words of Persian origin and the presence of numerous Aramaisms[8] oblige us

1 A. M. Dubarle, *Les sages d'Israël* (Paris, 1946), p. 97.

2 For this opinion, see A. Barucq, *Le Libre de l'Ecclésiaste*, VS (Paris, 1968), p. 30, and H. Lusseau in *Introduction critique à l'Ancien Testament*, ed. H. Cazelles (Paris, 1973), p. 629.

3 This question has recently been raised again by R. Brain, *Kohelet und die frühhellenistiche Popularphilosophie*, BZAW 130 (Berlin, 1973).

4 P. Humbert, *Recherches*, pp. 106–24.

5 O. Loretz, *Qohelet und der alte Orient* (Freiburg, 1964), pp. 135–216; A. F. Rainer, 'A study of Ecclesiastes', *CTM*, 35 (1954), 148–57.

6 M. J. Dahood, 'Canaanite–Phoenician influence in Qoheleth', *Bib*, 33 (1952), 30–52, 191–221; 'The Phoenician Background of Qoheleth', 47 (1966), 264–82.

7 J. Muilenburg, 'A Qoheleth Scroll from Qumran', *BASOR*, 135 (1954), 20–8.

8 The thesis put forward by H. L. Ginsberg, *Studies in Koheleth* (New York, 1950), pp. 16–30, that the book was written in Aramaic, has not found favour.

to regard Ecclesiastes as a work of late Hebrew literature. But since Ben Sira exhibits a number of points of contact with Ecclesiastes, which would indicate that he knew and used Ecclesiastes' work, Ecclesiastes must be placed before 200 B.C.E., the date at which Ben Sira wrote.[1] We might therefore locate Ecclesiastes about the middle of the third century and, as to its geographical location, in Palestine, and, more particularly, in Jerusalem where the schools of the wise met.

ESTHER

The book of Esther is of a very different kind, even though Wisdom elements have been recognized in it.[2] Its contents are well known. Hadassah, or Esther, a young Jewish girl, becomes the wife of Ahasuerus, that is, Xerxes, and queen of Persia. When the grand vizier Haman orders a general massacre of the Jews, Esther manages to save her people, thanks to the advice of her cousin and guardian Mordecai. On Adar 13, the very date when the Jews are due to be executed, what happens is quite the reverse. With royal permission the Jews massacre 75,000 of their enemies. Esther even obtains from the king, as a privilege for her compatriots who live in Susa, permission to continue the massacre into the second day. In memory of this event Mordecai (who has succeeded Haman as grand vizier) institutes a regular celebration, the feast of Purim.

This book posed in the past, and still poses, numerous problems. Its canonicity was not at first accepted, either by Jews or Christians. No copy of the book has yet been found at Qumran, and the Qumran sect, furthermore, did not celebrate the feast of Purim.[3] It is the only book of the Palestinian rabbinic canon which has not been found in the Dead Sea caves.[4] Besides this, in rabbinic Judaism it was not received into the canon without question. The first allusion to anything reported in the book of Esther is found in the second book of Maccabees, which mentions a 'Mordecai's Day', as the day after the celebration of the victory over Nicanor.[5] The canons of Melito, Athanasius and Gregory of Nazianzus omit the book of Esther, whilst Amphilochus and Nicephorus are doubtful about its canonicity. According to the

[1] Podechard, *L'Ecclésiaste*, pp. 55–65.

[2] S. Talmon, '"Wisdom" in the Book of Esther', *VT*, 13 (1963), 419–55.

[3] J. T. Milik, 'Le travail d'édition des manuscrits de Désert du Juda', *Volume du Congrès, Strasbourg 1956*, VTSup 4 (Leiden, 1957), p. 25.

[4] P. W. Skehan, 'The Biblical Scrolls from Qumran and the text of the Old Testament', *BA*, 28 (1965), 87–90; also 'The Scrolls and the Old Testament text', in D. N. Freedman and J. Greenfield, *New Directions in Biblical Archaeology* (New York, 1969), p. 111.

[5] 2 Macc. 15:36.

Babylonian Talmud, *Megillat* 7a, Mar Samuel around the year 230 C.E. again cast doubt on Esther's canonicity. The book, in his judgement, 'was composed to be recited, but not to be written'. This proves that the Synagogue did not accept the book as sacred Scripture on the same level as the rest.[1] The absence of any mention of the divine name, and indeed of religious elements in general, in addition to the hatred it displays for the Gentile world, account for these hesitations over canonizing it.

The date of composition of the work is also a problem. The book tells a story set in the time of the Persian King Xerxes, but it is clear that it was not written during the reign of that king, for he is spoken of in the past: it was 'in those days when King Ahasuerus sat on his royal throne'.[2] Numerous anachronistic details, both archeological and of other kinds, show that the author was not living in the period in which the events he describes are placed. External evidence gives us certain limits for the date of composition of the work. The great literary opus of Chronicles–Ezra–Nehemiah, which recounts the history of the beginning of the Persian period, including the reign of Xerxes,[3] does not mention any of the events described in the book of Esther. Ben Sira, when he celebrates the achievements of Israel,[4] does not include that of Esther, the heroine of our book. The colophon at the end of the Greek translation of Esther is the first witness to the book's existence and claims that it was taken to Egypt in the fourth year of the reign of Ptolemy and Cleopatra. Among the numerous Ptolemies who were associated with Cleopatras there are two who might be the one referred to: Ptolemy Lathyrus in 114 and Ptolemy XII, the brother of the illustrious Cleopatra, in 48.[5] The book of Esther already existed, therefore, in Greek translation, perhaps by 114 or at least by 48 B.C.E. This datum fits well enough with the reference to a 'Mordecai's Day', which is nothing other than the feast of Purim, in 2 Maccabees, for 2 Maccabees is to be dated at about the end of the second century B.C.E. (see p. 463). In favour of a date in the Greek period linguistic and archeological evidence can also be appealed to. As far as language is concerned, much has been made of the presence in the book of Persian and Elamite words. Their presence reflects a political and cultural situation which only existed after the resurgence of the Elamites which took place in the time of Antiochus IV (175–163 B.C.E.) and continued

1 D. Barthélemy, *Les devanciers d'Aquila*, VTSup 10 (Leiden, 1963), p. 158.

2 Esther 1:2, cf. 10:1–3.

3 Ezra 4:6.

4 Sir. 44–9.

5 E. J. Bickerman, 'The colophon of the Greek Book of Esther', *JBL*, 63 (1944), 339–62, suggests the year 78–77 B.C.E., under Ptolemy XII and Cleopatra V.

until 140 B.C.E. On the other hand, the absence of Greek words from the book of Esther must be noted, for it is rather odd for a book composed during the Greek period. In the archeological sphere arguments have been based on the fact that in the book of Esther the Apadana (the palace) at Susa housed both the court and the administrative offices under one roof, and this was a situation which only existed during the time of Antiochus III (223–187 B.C.E.).[1]

But the author of Esther could have known Elamite or Persian names from his sources, and it has not been shown that the local colour and the topographical information about the palace at Susa reflect first hand knowledge.[2] The language of the book, which is quite similar to that of Ecclesiastes, Chronicles and Daniel, in any case speaks in favour of a date of writing close to that of these latest inclusions in the Palestinian canon. It has even been suggested that one of the complaints which Haman brought against the Jews, that their laws were different from those of all other peoples,[3] could be an allusion to the persecution under Antiochus Epiphanes. It is true that Antiochus was the first of Israel's overlords to impose a unity of outlook on all his subjects by getting them to renounce their own religious laws.[4] But the mass of second-century Hebrew documents which have emerged from Qumran now permit linguistic comparisons with Esther and it has to be admitted that the language of the latter has practically nothing in common with that of the Qumran writings.[5] This observation, in conjunction with the lack of Greek words (which, by contrast, we do find in Daniel), obliges us to take the date of Esther back at least to the beginning of the third century B.C.E., or even earlier, to the beginning of the Greek period; though we must not make it too early, for there is still some distance between the writing of Esther and the events which it reports.

Within this framework we must consider the historicity of Esther. The story contains a number of improbabilities which militate against calling it historical. We may mention that, amongst other things, the banquet provided by the king for his various administrative officers lasted 'a hundred and eighty days,' which is hardly likely (1:1–4). Queen Vashti's refusal to obey the king is odd (1:12); odd, too, is the description of how the king writes to every nation in its own language,

[1] F. Altheim and R. Stiehl, *Die aramäische Sprache unter den Achaimeniden* (Frankfurt, 1963), 1, pp. 203–13.

[2] H. Bardtke, *Das Buch Esther*, KAT 17:5 (Gütersloh, 1963), p. 249 n. 20.

[3] Esther 3:8.

[4] A. Lods, *Histoire de la littérature hébraïque et juive depuis les origines jusqu à' la ruine de l'Etat juif* (135 *après J.C.*) (Paris, 1950), p. 799.

[5] C. A. Moore, *Esther*, AB 7B (Garden City, 1971), p. lvii.

giving the injunction that every man is to be master in his own house (1:22). Apart from the basic unlikelihood of this happening at all, we know from elsewhere that the official language was imperial Aramaic. Neither is it altogether probable that the king should give high positions of state to people who were not Persians, as he is said to have done to Mordecai (6:10, 8:2, 10:3). Besides these improbabilities some well-known historical errors have been pointed out. Whereas Herodotus mentions that there were twenty satrapies in the Persian empire the book of Esther makes it 'one hundred and twenty-seven' (1:1). More serious still is the fact that according to Herodotus,[1] Xerxes' queen was Amestris, although in our Jewish book Esther held that title between the king's seventh and twelfth years (2:16, 3:7). Finally, the artificial scheme of the book, which deals in opposites and contrasts, Jews and pagans, Vashti and Esther, Haman's hanging and the installation of Mordecai as vizier, the massacre of the Gentiles and the anti-Jewish pogrom, suggests a work of fiction. The book has even been described as an historical novel,[2] but this description does not seem a happy one for the Hebrew version of Esther. It would be more appropriate, by contrast, to the Greek Esther, which does make use of some features of the Greek romance.[3] But even though a fiction, the story of Esther was not invented in a vacuum. There is doubtless some historical happening underlying it, something which took place at the court at Susa, though it is difficult to determine what this was.[4] There is also, in addition, the celebration of the feast of Purim. The origins of this festival have been much debated. A Greek origin, a Persian one and a Babylonian one have all been proposed; the latter evidently finding most favour.[5] But the origin of the festival doubtless pre-dates the story which provides its justification.[6] The story is a legend, in the proper, etymological sense of that word, and illustrates to some degree a fact often asserted in the history of religions, that the rite precedes the

[1] VII.114; IX.112.

[2] O. Eissfeldt, *The Old Testament, an Introduction*, ET (Oxford, 1965), p. 507.

[3] H. Cazelles, 'Note sur la composition du rouleau d'Esther', *Lex tua veritas*, Festschrift für Hubert Junker (Trier, 1961), pp. 19ff.

[4] Marduk is the name of an official mentioned in an Aramaic letter from the fifth century B.C.E. Cf. G. R. Driver, *Aramaic Documents of the Fifth Century BC* (Oxford, 1957), p. 56. In a text from Borsippa Marduka is the name of a functionary at the court of Darius I. Cf. Altheim and Stiehl, *Die aramäische Sprache*, pp. 195–219.

[5] A summary of opinions on this point will be found in Lods, *Histoire*, pp. 801–4. See also V. Christian, 'Zur Herkunft des Purim-Festes', *Alttestamentliche Studien Friedrich Nötscher zum 60. Geburtstag gewidmet* (Bonn, 1950), pp. 33–7; J. Lewy, 'Old Assyrian *puru'um* and *pūrum*', *Revue Hittite et Asianique*, 5 (1939), 117–24; A. Bea, 'De origine vocis פור (Est. 3, 7; 9, 24 etc.)', *Bib*, 21 (1940), 198f.)

[6] See H. Malter, 'Purim', *Jewish Encyclopedia*, 10 (New York, 1905), pp. 274–8.

myth. The feast of Purim displays the characteristics of a spring festival at which the New Year is celebrated. It is the feast at which the lot is cast and the fate determined for the coming year. It resembles in this respect the Babylonian Akitu festival[1] and the Jewish Rosh ha-Shanah.[2]

If this is the *Sitz im Leben* of the book of Esther it brings us to the question of its literary composition, and with regard to this problem scholars have taken up a variety of positions. Some begin with the observation that there are doublets in the book: the two banquets (1:3, 5); two lists of seven names (1:10, 14); the 'second harem' (2:14); the second gathering of the candidates (2:19); the two discussions between Haman and his friends (5:14, 6:13), and so on. And they conclude that we have here two stories which have been combined. One is characterized as liturgical and centres around Esther, the other centres round Mordecai and is said to be of historical type.[3] Others, instead of two sources, find three of midrashic origin; a Vashti story, which could have been a harem story originally; a story of Mordecai, which concerned court intrigues; and finally the story of Esther, a young Jewess who, after becoming the king's favourite, prevented a certain persecution of her people.[4] It is towards this opinion that the present writer inclines.[5] The text of Esther has therefore quite a history behind it, and one of the later landmarks in that history is the addition of the apocryphal sections to the Greek Esther. These additions represent orthodox corrections to the Hebrew book. The Hebrew book itself seemed to be too secular and too liberal to be included as it stood in the religious heritage of Judaism.[6] But already in the Hebrew book the presence of God in the events of Jewish history may be detected like a watermark, in spite of the absence of any specific mention of the divine name in the text.

THE WORK OF THE CHRONICLER

The work of the Chronicler consists of the books of Ezra–Nehemiah and the books of Chronicles. These were the last to be given their

1 S. A. Pallis, *The Babylonian Akitu Festival* (Copenhagen, 1926), pp. 183f.
2 A. Michel, 'Nouvel An. Dans le Judaïsme', *DBSup* 6 (1960) cols. 612ff.
3 Cazelles, 'Notes', pp. 26ff.
4 This is Bardtke's view (*Esther*, pp. 248–52), recently accepted by Moore, *Esther*, p. li.
5 See M. Delcor and A. Lefèvre in *Introduction critique à l'Ancien Testament*, ed. H. Cazelles (Paris, 1973), pp. 734–7.
6 W. H. Brownlee, 'Le livre grec d'Esther et la royauté divine. Corrections orthodoxes au livre d'Esther', *RB*, 73 (1966), 161–85. See also Delcor and Lefèvre, *Introduction*, pp. 734–7.

position in the Hebrew canon, which does not necessarily mean that they were the last to be written. The books of Chronicles are entitled in the Hebrew Bible 'Acts' or, literally, 'Things of the Days' (or 'of the Years') and make up part of the collection called 'The Writings' (*kethubim*). Because of their late inclusion in the canon the books of Chronicles appear rather curiously after Ezra–Nehemiah, though Ezra–Nehemiah deals with the post-exilic period whereas Chronicles covers the history of the period up to the exile. The ancient versions re-established the chronological order by placing the books of Chronicles after the books of Kings and before Ezra–Nehemiah. In any case, Chronicles and Ezra–Nehemiah are closely connected with each other. The end of 2 Chronicles contains the first lines of Cyrus' edict, a document which is referred to and quoted in its entirety at the beginning of Ezra. Why then has this great historical work, attributed to a single (anonymous) author whom we call the Chronicler, been cut in two, one half becoming Ezra–Nehemiah and the other the two books of Chronicles? We must reply that it does not appear to have been an accident but a pre-meditated act. The books of Chronicles, in fact, present for a second time, and from a different point of view, the material of the historical books, Samuel and Kings. To this extent they are more or less redundant. It was doubtless for this reason that their acceptance into the canon was delayed until the synod of Jamnia, and that they were left out when Ezra–Nehemiah was first taken in, for Ezra–Nehemiah constituted an original work on the post-exilic period and had nothing corresponding to it in Jewish history-writing.

THE BOOKS OF EZRA–NEHEMIAH

One of the peculiarities of the books of Ezra–Nehemiah is that a number of official documents have been incorporated into them. This bears witness to a feeling for documentation and a taste for rigorous precision in historical matters on the part of authors and readers at this period. These rather novel departures afford a contrast with the historiography of the preceding period, represented by the Deuteronomic history as contained in the books of Samuel and Kings. Whatever might be said, on other accounts, about the value of the materials, we find there no more than one or two lists, such as the list of David's warriors or Solomon's officials; nothing in the shape of documents drawn from archives. In chronological order the catalogue of documents quoted in Ezra–Nehemiah is as follows: (1) The edict of Cyrus authorizing the return of the Jewish exiles and ordering the rebuilding of the Temple (text in Hebrew).[1] (2) A list in Hebrew of those repatriated with Zerubbabel and Joshua.[2] (3) A copy of a report in Aramaic sent to King Darius I by Tattenai, governor of the province of Beyond the River (Abar Nahara) concerning the rebuilding of the Jerusalem Temple.[3] (4) King Darius' reply in Aramaic, giving instructions that the work of rebuilding the Temple should continue at his expense and referring to an edict of Cyrus. The edict is quoted, but in a different form from the one listed in this catalogue under (1).[4] (5) A report in Aramaic sent by Rehum, governor of Samaria, to Artaxerxes, denouncing the returned exiles for undertaking the rebuilding of the walls of Jerusalem.[5] (6) The king's reply, in Aramaic, requiring the work to stop.[6] (7) An edict of Artaxerxes sent to Ezra, officially establishing Mosaic Law and ritual in Judah and Jerusalem; recognizing the Jerusalem Temple as a legitimate centre of Jewish worship, to be supported at the expense of the Persian treasury; and recognizing Ezra as the religious leader of Palestine.[7] (8) A list of Ezra's companions.[8]

Many critics have denied the historical value of the Aramaic documents contained in Ezra chapters 4 to 6. It has been alleged that the Jewish redactor invented them in their entirety. Apart from the fact that their contents are so favourable to the Jews, they imply that a Persian king wrote not in Persian but in Aramaic, a suggestion which once seemed strange to the critics. In fact, none of these arguments can now stand. We know that imperial Aramaic was used as a diplomatic language by the Persian kings, as is shown particularly by the Aramaic papyri found at Elephantine[9] and the letters, also in Aramaic, emanating from the Persian satrap of Egypt.[10] Both these collections of documents come from a period quite close to that of our biblical texts. Besides this, the liberal policies of the Achemenid kings towards conquered peoples are today an established historical fact, and is therefore nothing surprising about their liberality in the particular case of the Jews.

THE EDICT OF CYRUS

The specific question of the historicity of Cyrus' edict must be examined separately. This document has been preserved in three different places: at the end of the book of Chronicles[11] and at the

[1] Ezra 1:2–4. [2] Ezra 2; Neh. 7:6–73. [3] Ezra 5:6–17.
[4] Ezra 6:1–12. [5] Ezra 4:9–16. [6] Ezra 4:17–22.
[7] Ezra 7:11–26. [8] Ezra 8:1–14.
[9] A. Cowley, *Aramaic Papyri of the Fifth Century BC* (Oxford, 1923).
[10] G. R. Driver, *Aramaic Documents of the Fifth Century BC* (Oxford, 1957).
[11] 2 Chron. 36:23.

beginning of the book of Ezra[1] it is repeated in identical form and in the Hebrew language, whereas on the third occasion, in the same book of Ezra, it appears in a quite different form and in Aramaic.[2] By this decree Cyrus authorizes the return of the exiles to Palestine and the rebuilding of the Temple at Jerusalem. Two essential questions arise with regard to the document. Are the events described authentic? And if they are, which of the two forms of the document is closest to the original edict?

Late nineteenth century critics were not much impressed by the alleged decrees (or for that matter by any of the documents contained in Ezra–Nehemiah). For its rehabilitation it had to await the work of Eduard Meyer on the origins of Judaism. Meyer overcame the suspicion in which the document had been held by the learned world.[3] As it was, several ancient authors, as well as more modern ones, had complained about the improbability of the facts. Was it likely that Cyrus, at the head of a great empire and having just seized control of Babylon (538/7), should have interested himself in the tiny nation of the Jews? Was it not even less likely that an original edict should not only have allowed the Jews exiled in Babylon to return to their own country but should have restored to them the cultic objects of precious metal which had been looted by Nebuchadnezzar, and, moreover, have permitted the restoration of the Temple at imperial expense?[4] Some critics went further; pushing to the limits their distrust of the facts as the chronicler stated them, they maintained that what we were dealing with here was literary fiction. The Chronicler was trying to turn into historical reality the dreams of Deutero-Isaiah, who had seen in Cyrus not only the liberator of the Jews but the restorer of the Temple at Jerusalem.[5] It was for this reason that he wished to begin his description of the return of the tribes of Judah and Benjamin with an edict of Cyrus, dated in the first year of his reign (538), in which the king invited the Jews to return to Jerusalem and ordered his Babylonian subjects to give them their co-operation. Among the more recent representatives of this point of view may be cited the names of Hölscher,[6] Torrey[7] and Pfeiffer.[8]

This radical criticism of the Cyrus edict is exaggerated. Even if it is

[1] Ezra 1:2–4. [2] Ezra 6:3–5.
[3] E. Meyer, *Die Entstehung des Judenthums* (Halle an der Saale, 1896).
[4] Ezra 6:4–5. [5] Isa. 44:28.
[6] G. Hölscher, *Geschichte der israelitischen und jüdischen Religion* (Giessen, 1922), pp. 138–41.
[7] C. C. Torrey, *Ezra Studies* (Chicago, 1910; repr. New York, 1970), pp. 145ff.
[8] R. H. Pfeiffer, *Introduction to the Old Testament*, rev. edn. (New York, 1948), pp. 821ff.

conceded that the Hebrew version of the document, as it is preserved by the chronicler, is giving us a Jewish presentation of the facts – a presentation which we owe to the redactor himself – it nevertheless remains that the Aramaic text, both in form and content, affords us proofs of its authenticity. The religious policies of the Achemenid ruler as they are witnessed to in this document correspond quite well with what we know of them from elsewhere. There are a number of inscriptions which give us information about how Cyrus behaved with regard to the sanctuaries of Mesopotamia. On the cylinder which Rawlinson found at Babylon and which is preserved in the British Museum we read the following words, put into the mouth of Cyrus:

I returned to (these) sacred cities on the other side of the Tigris, the sanctuaries of which have been ruins for a long time, the images which (used) to live therein and established for them permanent sanctuaries. I (also) gathered all their (former) inhabitants and returned (to them) their habitations. Furthermore, I resettled upon the command of Marduk, the great lord, all the gods of Sumer and Akkad whom Nabonidus had brought into Babylon to the anger of the lord of the gods, unharmed, in their (former) chapels, the places which make them happy.

May all the gods whom I have resettled in their sacred cities ask daily Bel and Nebo for a long life for me and may they recommend me (to him); to Marduk, my lord, they may say this: 'Cyrus, the king who worships you, and Cambyses his son....' (the text is destroyed beyond this point).[1]

The Nabonidus Chronicle enables us to give more precision to the preceding text as to the date of the events described. We learn from it that when Gobryas, the governor of Gutium, had entered Babylon without a blow being struck, the area of the city where the sanctuary Esagila was situated was so well protected by the troops that the ceremonies inside the temple were able to continue uninterrupted. 'From the month of Kislimu [December 539] to the month of Addaru [March 538], the gods of Akkad which Nabonidus had made come down to Babylon...returned to their sacred cities'.[2] In view of this, when the book of Ezra places the edict in 'the first year of Cyrus' (meaning by this not the first year of his reign over the Persians, which would take it back to the year 559, but the first year of his domination of the ancient Babylonian empire (539/8)), it is in agreement, on this point, with the Nabonidus Chronicle. Cyrus, whether acting in a spirit of toleration or from political motives, had everything to gain by encouraging his new subjects to forget the impious upheavals caused by Nabonidus, a half-mad king who had dethroned Marduk in favour

[1] J. B. Pritchard, *Ancient Near Eastern Texts Relating to the Old Testament* (Princeton, 1950; 3rd edn. 1969), p. 316.

[2] Pritchard, *Texts*, p. 306.

of the god Sin and had uprooted from their sanctuaries many divinities.

In view of all this a high degree of historical probability must be allowed to the Cyrus decree as presented by the book of Ezra in its Aramaic form.[1] If this document indicates the dimensions which the Temple in Jerusalem is to have, and is explicit about the materials to be used in its construction (stone and timber) there is nothing improbable in that. There is no reason why Cyrus should not have consulted some Jewish expert about these specifications, since what was being planned was a replacement for Solomon's Temple, on the same site and of comparable dimensions.

As far as costs are concerned, the edict does not say that these are to be paid by the Persian king himself. It says that appropriations should be made from the revenues of the province of Judah to cover the expenses incurred in rebuilding the sanctuary.[2] The Jews themselves, in fact, were to pay for the work. The charges were to be set against the imposed royal tribute. It may be noted that there is no contradiction here between the book of Ezra and the book of Haggai at this particular point. When the prophet accuses the Jews of self-centredness and greed,[3] the accusations would make no sense if the king himself had made available the money for the rebuilding. But everything becomes clear if we understand that it was the Jews who, because of their poverty and selfishness, had not collected a sufficient sum to do the job properly.

On the other hand, we must reject as partly unauthentic the proclamation of Cyrus as it is drawn up in Hebrew,[4] because it contains turns of phrase which are characteristic of Jewish religious language, though they do, it is true, run parallel to similar expressions which appear in Achemenid inscriptions. It must be admitted, therefore, that in the Hebrew version of the edict we have a reworking of an authentic Persian document which the chronicler has reworded.[5]

These Persian government documents, as they originally were, have been inserted into a framework provided by the memoirs of Ezra and Nehemiah. The Ezra memoirs may be isolated from chapters 8, 9 and 10, if attention is paid to the chronological data. From the information given it may be deduced that Ezra stayed in Jerusalem for about a year, having been sent on a mission there by the Persian king. His report, intended for the Persian authorities, extends over chapters 7 to 10 of

[1] Ezra 6:1–5.
[2] Ezra 6:8.
[3] Hag. 1:2–6.
[4] Ezra 1:2–4 and 2 Chron. 36:23.
[5] R. de Vaux, 'Les décrets de Cyrus et de Darius sur la reconstruction du temple', *Bible et Orient* (Paris, 1967), pp. 112–13; ET *The Bible and the Ancient Near East* (London, 1972), pp. 94–6.

the book of Ezra, which concerns mainly the regulation of cultic practice and the suppression of mixed marriages, that is marriages between Jews and foreigners. But the question arises whether what we are pleased to call the Ezra memoirs are entirely Ezra's work, or whether the actual memoirs of Ezra merely lie behind them as source material which the Chronicler has used. This latter theory seems to be supported by the alternation between passages in the first person,[1] where Ezra speaks for himself, and passages in the third person.[2] In the Nehemiah memoirs we have an homogeneous and coherent account, in which Nehemiah tells in the first person of his mission to Jerusalem. This covers chapters 1 to 7 of the book of Nehemiah. There is very little trace in these chapters of later redactional activity. They are concerned with Nehemiah's activities in connection with the rebuilding of the city walls and the restoration of the Jewish community.

The memoirs of Ezra and Nehemiah, dealing as they do with the respective missions of these two leaders to Jerusalem, raise a difficult problem concerning the chronological order of the two men. From the existing order of the books of Ezra and Nehemiah we might seem justified in assuming that Ezra preceded Nehemiah and that the two both lived in the reign of the same king, generally identified as Artaxerxes I. This view has been held by some very reputable scholars, such as Kittel and de Vaux.[3] But in recent years many equally reputable exegetes have maintained the contrary, that Nehemiah preceded Ezra.[4] On this latter view it is argued that Ezra came to Jerusalem in 398, in the seventh year of Artaxerxes II, whereas Nehemiah undertook his first mission in 445, under Artaxerxes I. On this hypothesis the order of the book of Ezra–Nehemiah, which places Ezra first, is due to the Chronicler, who wished to give precedence to a priest–scribe over a layman. Nehemiah's first mission in 445 had as its aim the rebuilding of the wall of Jerusalem. He returned to the holy city in 443 and undertook a series of reforming measures which he legitimated by appealing to Deuteronomy. In 398 Ezra was given full powers by the Persian king, who had just lost control of Egypt, to unite the two elements in the Jewish population; that is, the old-established population governed from Samaria, and the returned exiles from Babylon. He promulgated a national law which included

1 Ezra 7:27 to 9:15. 2 Ezra 7:1–26; 10:1–44.

3 R. Kittel, *Geschichte des Volkes Israel* (Stuttgart, 1927–29), 1, pp. 610ff; R. de Vaux, 'Israel, histoire d' ', *DBSup*, 4 (1949), cols. 765f.

4 H. H. Rowley, 'Nehemiah's mission and its background', *BJRL*, 37 (1954–5), 529–61 (reprinted in H. H. Rowley, *Men of God* (Edinburgh, 1963), pp. 211–45); H. Cazelles, 'La mission d'Esdras', *VT*, 4 (1954), 113–40, and many others.

Deuteronomy, the established law of the country, and the Priestly Code, which was that of the returned exiles.

THE BOOKS OF CHRONICLES

The title of these two books goes back to St Jerome who designated them the 'chronicum totius divinae historiae'. This description of them corresponds closely with the Hebrew title, 'Acts of the Days'. But for some centuries the title 'Chronicles' was slow to win acceptance, the Fathers preferring to use the one given by the Septuagint, 'Paralipomena'; that is, 'things left aside', 'omitted', as against the 'things passed on'. The Septuagint's title for the work passed into the Vulgate, but Luther brought back into favour Jerome's designation, and in our time it has become the accepted one. The Septuagint translators evidently understood our two books to be dealing with matters left out by the earlier books, by the books of Kings in particular. This conception of the books raises at the outset two problems: first, what is the relation between the books of Chronicles and the great Deuteronomistic work preserved in the books of Samuel and Kings? Second, what other sources did the Chronicler have available to him?

The period covered by the book of Chronicles is vast: it stretches from the creation to the beginning of the exile. One complete section (1 Chron. 1–9), covering the period from Adam to David, consists mainly of genealogies, whose purpose is to give universal significance to the anticipated Davidic kingdom. For this reason considerable space is given to David (1 Chron. 10–29), of whom the Chronicler's own peculiar theology prompts him to give us an idealized picture, as we shall see. He also manages to leave some important things out,[1] and his silences are eloquent. Nothing is said of the king's adultery, or his act of murder; neither is there any mention of the bloody dramas of his old age. As well as omissions, there are some significant changes. It is not God who urges David to take a census, but Satan.[2] It seems to the author unworthy of his hero that he should carry away the idols of the defeated Philistines (2 Sam. 5:21). He prefers to record that 'David gave command, and they were burned' (1 Chron. 14:12), in accordance with the prescription of Deuteronomy (Deut. 7:5). Solomon, too, has a good deal of space devoted to him in the Chronicler's work (2 Chron. 1–9). But the modifications which the author has made to his portrait are

[1] A useful tool, indicating at sight where the chronicler is, and where he is not, following earlier histories, is P. Vannutelli's *Libri Synoptici Veteris Testamenti seu Librorum Regum et Chronicorum loci paralleli*, 2 vols. (Rome, 1931–4).

[2] Cf. 1 Chron. 21:1 and 2 Sam. 24:1.

even more audacious. To give only two examples: according to the book of Kings, Solomon was obliged to give 'twenty cities in the land of Galilee' to the king of Tyre, to pay for the deliveries of timber and gold used in the construction of the Temple (1 Kings 9:10ff). The Chronicler thinks this fact unworthy of the memory of a great king. He has therefore omitted it and substituted quite a different tradition. 'Solomon rebuilt the cities which Huram had given to him, and settled the people of Israel in them' (2 Chron. 8:1). The king's presence at Gibeon for the purpose of offering sacrifice (1 Kings 3:3–4) was bound to shock the Chronicler, holding as he did that there was only one legitimate sanctuary. This has led him to explain that at Gibeon was situated the 'tent of meeting' which Moses had had constructed in the wilderness (2 Chron. 1:3). It is also noteworthy that he omits from the latter part of his history, which deals with the kings of Judah (2 Chron. 10–36), everything which concerns the history of the northern kingdom, a kingdom which 'has been in rebellion against the house of David to this day' (2 Chron. 10:19).[1] The northern kingdom only makes an appearance to be an instrument of Judah's punishment when she does wrong (25:17–24, 2 Chron. 28:9–15), or to act as an agent tempting her to go astray (2 Chron. 18:1–27, 20:37). Another point about which the Chronicler has been most careful is to eliminate from Nathan's prophecy everything which might seem a bad omen for the future of the dynasty. The divine threats which the second book of Samuel includes in this context have disappeared from the Chronicler's account: 'When he commits iniquity, I will chasten him with the rod of men, with the stripes of the sons of men' (2 Sam. 7:14).[2]

These facts prompt us to raise a question: what was the Chronicler trying to do in relation to the Deuteronomic historical work? In the first place, the books of Chronicles are trying to show how Yahweh prepared for and brought into being the dynasty of David, whose mission was to establish the kingdom of God on earth. For that reason, God entered into an eternal covenant with the dynasty, and guaranteed its permanence. David and Solomon instituted a theocratic kingdom in Israel. David's kingdom is the kingdom of God and the king is Yahweh's lieutenant, Yahweh himself being the kingdom's true head. The Chronicler actually expresses this in so many words through the mouth of the queen of Sheba when she comes to visit Solomon: 'Blessed be the Lord your God, who has delighted in you and set you on his throne as king for the Lord your God!' (2 Chron. 9:8). In

[1] G. Wilda, *Das Königsbild des chronistischen Geschichtswerkes* (thesis, Bonn, 1959).

[2] H. van den Bussche, *Le texte de la prophétie de Nathan* (Louvain, 1948).

addition, Chronicles can say, 'The kingdom of the Lord' is 'in the hand of the sons of David' (2 Chron. 13:8).[1] From this it may be understood that the books of Chronicles cannot be regarded as a simple restatement or amplification of the material which has come down to us in Samuel and Kings.

Neither are they 'paralipomena', giving us what the books of Samuel and Kings omit. In order to support the theory which he wishes to establish, that is, that the theocracy was founded in Israel and took shape under the dynasty of David, the chronicler looks at his principal sources, the books of Samuel and Kings, and others, afresh from that point of view. This method of adapting and making use of existing sources in the interests of a particular thesis is reminiscent of Midrash.[2] But others prefer to see Chronicles as a work of exposition, a sort of commentary on, or interpretation of, earlier historical works.[3] In the last resort these come to the same thing. There is another solution which the great majority of historians, prompted by the large number of sources which the chronicler cites, have opted for. (For the enumeration of these sources see below.) They reckon that the writings referred to are not ones which the chronicler himself has made use of as separate sources, but that they were already combined into a single work, distinct from the books of Samuel and Kings, which has been called the Midrash on the Book of Kings, borrowing the title from a document which the chronicler himself cites (2 Chron. 24:27).[4]

What are these sources?[5] Apart from the canonical texts already mentioned, the books of Samuel and Kings and the Pentateuch, the Chronicler himself refers explicitly, in a manner that is not common among ancient historians, to the documents he employed. Some are historical, others prophetic in type. The historical sources are as follows:

The Book of the Kings of Judah and Israel (2 Chron. 16:11, 25:26 etc.)
The Book of the Kings of Israel and Judah (2 Chron. 27:7, 35:27 etc.)
The Book of the Kings of Israel (1 Chron. 9:1; 2 Chron. 20:34)

1 A. Noordtzij, 'Les intentions du Chroniste', *RB*, 49 (1940), 161–8, and A.-M. Brunet, 'La théologie du chroniste. Théocratie et messianisme', *Sacra Pagina* (ed. J. Coppens *et al.*, Gembloux 1959), 1, pp. 384–97.

2 H. Lusseau, in H. Cazelles ed. *Introduction critique à l'Ancien Testament* (Paris, 1973), pp. 670–1.

3 Cf. T. Willi, *Die Chronik als Auslegung. Untersuchungen zur literarischen Gestaltung der historischen Überlieferung Israels* (Göttingen, 1972), pp. 48ff.

4 F. Michaeli, *Les livres des Chroniques, d'Esdras et de Néhémie* (Neuchâtel, 1967), p. 11.

5 A.-M. Brunet, 'Le Chroniste et ses sources', *RB*, 60 (1953), 481–508; *RB*, 61 (1954), 394–86.

The Chronicles of the Kings of Israel (2 Chron. 33:18)
The Midrash on the Book of Kings (2 Chron. 24:27)
The Chronicles of King David (1 Chron. 27:24)

And the prophetic sources:

The Words (or Chronicles) of Samuel the Seer (1 Chron. 29:29)
The Words (or Chronicles) of Gad the Seer (1 Chron. 29:29)
The Words (or Chronicles) of Nathan the Prophet (1 Chron. 29:29)
The Prophecy of Ahijah the Shilonite (2 Chron. 9:29)
The Visions of Iddo the Seer (2 Chron. 9:29)
The Words (or Chronicles) of Shemaiah the Prophet (2 Chron. 12:15)
The Words (or Chronicles) of Iddo the Seer (2 Chron. 12:15)
The Midrash of the Prophet Iddo (2 Chron. 13:22)
The rest of the Words (or Acts) of Uzziah which Isaiah wrote (2 Chron. 26:22)
The Vision of the Prophet Isaiah (2 Chron. 32:32)
The Words (or Chronicles) of the Seers (2 Chron. 33:19)
Jeremiah's Lament for Josiah (2 Chron. 35:25)

Not one of these writings is known to us from elsewhere. In these circumstances, what historical value ought we to attach to the book of Chronicles? For several reasons circumspection is advisable.

(1) Given the particular theological viewpoint which he holds, we may say with certainty that it was not the Chronicler's intention to produce an historical work in the modern sense of the word. He was not trying, primarily, to reconstruct events with the rigour and precision that would be expected of a secular historian.

(2) It is difficult to establish to what extent the Chronicler himself has elaborated on his documentary sources. Where he is presenting us with material that is demonstrably not from Samuel or Kings it is not easy to tell whether he is reproducing otherwise unknown sources or supplying the material himself. There are some who maximize the Chronicler's own creativity, and there are others who ascribe all the differences between the Chronicler and the books of Samuel–Kings to other historical documents which the Chronicler has used. But this question can only be settled by making an individual study of each instance.

(3) There are aspects of the Chronicler's work which from a strictly historical point of view look rather suspicious. The statistics which he quotes are manifestly exaggerated: Abijah's 400,000 men and the 800,000 'picked mighty warriors' whom Jeroboam put in the field against him (2 Chron. 13:3); Asa's 580,000 men, and the million of Zerah the Cushite (2 Chron. 14:7f) and so on. Then there is Abijah's speech (2 Chron. 13:4–12), which is not so much a real appeal as a sermon, and

a sermon, at that, aimed at the Samaritans who, at the time when the Chronicler was writing, had already split off from the Jews.[1]

(4) On the other hand, several pieces of information given to us by the Chronicler are worthy of consideration. They are even corroborated sometimes by extra-biblical sources. Among these are the list of cities fortified by Rehoboam (2 Chron. 11:5–12a) and by Uzziah (26:6, 15); Jotham's building projects (27:3b–4); details concerning the funeral rites of Asa (2 Chron. 16:14) and Hezekiah (32:33); more exact information about how Ahaziah was assassinated by Jehu (22:7–9), and about the death of Josiah at Megiddo (35:20–5). The tradition about how Manasseh became tributary and prisoner of the Assyrians (33:11) is confirmed by cuneiform documents.[2] The period of prosperity and military success which the chronicler ascribes to the reign of Jotham fits in very well with what we know of Judah at that time (2 Chron. 27:3–6) for it agrees with Isa. 2:7–16. Finally, the details about Hezekiah's tunnel (2 Chron. 32:30) are fuller than those reported in 2 Kings (20:20). Historian's attitudes to the historicity of the book of Chronicles are therefore much more nuanced than they were, let us say, in the days of Wellhausen. For Wellhausen, history as the chronicler presents it is not history as it really happened, but history as the Chronicler thinks it ought to have happened.[3]

Can we establish with exactitude the date of the Chronicler's work?[4] To this question we can only return a negative answer, as is the case with many other books of the Old Testament. All we can do is to argue from the evidence offered by the books of Ezra–Nehemiah and Chronicles to arrive at a rough idea of the date. The priestly genealogy in Neh. 12:11–22 goes as far as a certain Jaddua, who was contemporary with Darius the Persian. Now according to the Jewish historian Josephus this Jaddua is to be identified as the high priest at the time of the Macedonian conquest,[5] in which case Darius the Persian must be Darius III (Codomannus) who was defeated by Alexander the Great. Assuming that the Chronicler himself put the work into its final form, this gives us an indication of the date of writing which fits quite well with what we can deduce from the books of Ezra–Nehemiah. At all

[1] M. Delcor, 'Hinweise auf das samaritanische Schisma im Alten Testament', *ZAW*, 74 (1962), 282–5.

[2] L. Randinelli, *Il libro delle Cronache*, La Sacra Bibbia (Turin, 1966), p. 473.

[3] J. Wellhausen, *Prolegomena zur Geschichte Israels* 6th edn. (Berlin, 1905), pp. 165–223; ET *Prolegomena to the History of Israel* (Edinburgh, 1885), pp. 171–227.

[4] A. C. Welch, *The Work of the Chronicler, its Purpose and Date* (Oxford, 1939); Martin Noth, *Überlieferungsgeschichtliche Studien* (Halle 1943, Tübingen, 1957), pp. 150–61.

[5] *Antiquities* XI.322.

events, a writing which gives an account of the exile can only be dated after that event. The Chronicler's language, too, bears witness to a fairly late date.[1] The Chronicler can only have written after Darius I, since he reckons in *darics* (and in an account relating to the reign of David, at that!) (1 Chron. 29:7). This anachronism gives him away. But we are not necessarily, therefore, in the Persian period, for Cyrus, like all the other Achemenid kings, is expressly called 'king of Persia', which suggests that the empire was already in Greek hands. Finally, the genealogy of the family of David is followed up, it would appear, as far as the eleventh generation after Zerubbabel (1 Chron. 3:17–24). If we count only twenty years to a generation this brings us to about the year 300, or even down to about 250 B.C.E. It is equally possible that the speech of Abijah (2 Chron. 13:4–12) has in mind the Samaritan schism which had already been made final.[2] In any case, the Chronicler wrote before 157, because it was at this date that Eupolemus made use of the book of Chronicles in Greek translation. All in all, we may place the Chronicler's work between 300 and 200 B.C.E.[3] The Chronicler is an anonymous author, and at all events cannot be identified with Ezra, as Albright, in accordance with Jewish tradition, maintained.[4] He is to be looked for among the Levites, and in the setting of the Temple, for this is exactly where his ideas place him.[5]

DEUTERO-ZECHARIAH

Chapters 9 to 14 of the book of Zechariah are generally ascribed to an author or authors distinct for the writer of the first eight chapters of the book. These chapters present extreme difficulties, both with regard to their date and the question of their literary unity. Up to the seventeenth century there was no problem concerning the authenticity of Zech. 9 to 14. Jewish and Christian tradition had never thought of these chapters as having any other author than the prophet Zechariah, a prophet about whom, in any case, almost nothing is known. It was Joseph Mede (1586–1638), Fellow and Greek Lecturer at Christ's College, Cambridge, who was the first to attribute to chapters 9, 10 and 11 a pre-exilic origin. He did this in order to explain the citation in Matt. 27:9,

1 A. Kropat, *Die Syntax des Autors der Chronik* (Giessen, 1909).

2 W. Rudolph, *Chronikbücker*, HAT 1, 21 (Tübingen, 1955), p. 238.

3 Noth, *Studien*, p. 155.

4 W. F. Albright, 'The biblical period', in *The Jews, their history, culture and religion*, ed. L. Finkelstein (New York, 1949), 1, p. 54.

5 R. Mosis, *Untersuchungen zur Theologie des chronistischen Geschichtswerkes* (Freiburg, 1973).

'Et acceperunt triginta argenteos', which the Vulgate attributes to Jeremiah.[1] More than two hundred years before Astruc raised the problem of the Pentateuch, Mede raised that of Deutero–Zechariah. It is not our business to consider here the history of the interpretation of the book between Mede and the present day,[2] but to indicate the reasons which have led us to place it in the Greek period. There is a certain measure of agreement that it is to be located in the period after the arrival of Alexander the Great in Palestine. The introduction to the book (9:1–8) is a landmark for the dating of the work, which constitutes, as we shall see, a coherent whole. These verses describe the lightning advance of Alexander along the Palestinian coast after the battle of Issus in 332. The author attaches great importance to the city of Tyre, whose resounding fall spread panic among the cities of the Philistine coast: Ashkelon, Gaza and Ekron. The prophet envisages the introduction of Philistines and bastards into the holy nation. Now much of our information about Alexander's campaign, as it has been preserved by Arrian, fits quite well with Deutero–Zechariah's description. Elliger and the present author have independently arrived at the same conclusions.[3] The only conceivable objection would be that the scheme of invasion in Deutero–Zechariah might be fitted equally well into another period of history. It might relate, for example, to the time of Tiglath-Pileser III who campaigned in the same area, first in 738 and then between 734 and 732, when he subdued Philistia, Gaza receiving special mention on that occasion.[4] However, it is known that at that time Tyre was not ill-treated, and that by contrast, Damascus and the area around it were subjugated with great ferocity. This is not in accord with Zech. 9:1, which makes Damascus a place of rest for Yahweh. According to the Greek hypothesis the mention of a return of captives in 9:12 implies that the author was writing in the aftermath of a serious deportation. This would be the deportation of 312, when, after the capture of Jerusalem by Ptolemy I (Soter) a considerable number of prisoners left for exile in Egypt. Chapter 10 presupposes no different historical situation; it draws out the theme of a return of captives which

[1] J. Mede, *Dissertationum ecclesiasticarum Triga....quibus accedunt fragmenta sacra ad Mt. 27.9* (London, 1653).

[2] For an outline of the history of exegesis of Deutero–Zechariah see the present author's introduction to the subject in A. Deissler and M. Delcor, *Les Petits Prophètes*, La Sainte Bible, 7, Part 1 (Paris, 1964), pp. 545–7. For further details, B. Otzen, *Studien über Deuterosacharia*, Acta Theologica Danica 6 (Copenhagen, 1964), pp. 11–34.

[3] K. Elliger, 'Ein Zeugnis aus der jüdischen Gemeinde im Alexanderjahr 332 v. Chr.', *ZAW*, 62 (1949–50), 63–115; M. Delcor, 'Les allusions à Alexandre le Grand dans Zach. IX.1–8', *VT*, 1 (1951), 110–24.

[4] Otzen, *Studien*, pp. 62–123.

was first broached in chapter 9. The allegory of the shepherds (11:14) speaks of 'annulling the brotherhood between Judah and Israel', which must be understood as a reference to the Samaritan schism, which took place, according to scholarly opinion, at the end of the Persian period or the beginning of that of the Greeks. The date of composition of chapter 11 is therefore later than the Samaritan schism, which is spoken of as a past event.[1] Chapters 12 to 14, because of their more specifically apocalyptic character, offer fewer precise historical allusions. The beginning of chapter 14, verses 1–2, describing the severe blow which has fallen on Jerusalem, half of whose inhabitants have been taken away into exile, accords very well with what we are told by the *Letter of Aristeas*[2] and by the Jewish historian Josephus,[3] who speak of enormous numbers (100,000 for Palestine as a whole) deported by Ptolemy I (Soter). The description of the territory which the Jews are to occupy, which excludes the Samaritan lands from consideration (14:10), and the exclusion of Canaanites (by which, again, the Samaritans are to be understood) from the Temple in Zech. 14:21, provide additional evidence prompting us to date these chapters in the period after the schism. The mention of Javan in 9:13, although it does not necessarily refer to the Greece of Alexander, presupposes that we are already well into the Greek period. Finally, the frequent references to Egypt, which is several times taken to task, are readily understandable after the death of Alexander, since Palestine was under the yoke of the Ptolemies from that time until 217 (9:11, 10:10–11, 14:18–19). In conclusion, we may say that the events of 312 must have had a considerable psychological impact on the Jews who remained in Judah and Jerusalem, who would appear to be the originators of our little book. The book would then be a book of consolation, composed by an anonymous author, someone who was very familiar with the Scriptures. This would also help to explain the messianic promises which are in evidence in these chapters.

We have so far spoken as if the literary unity of these chapters was not in question. This is not in fact the case. Numerous critics, struck by the apparent lack of unity, have drawn the quite natural conclusion that they are the work of several different authors. Some have thought of separating chapters 9 to 11 from chapters 12 to 14, seeing the two sections as not so much the work of two different authors as two series of collections.[4] Whereas chapters 9 to 11 are composed almost entirely

[1] Delcor, *ZAW*, 74 (1962), 281–91.

[2] A. Pelletier, *Lettre d'Aristée à Philocrate*, SC 89 (Paris, 1962), p. 109.

[3] *Ant.* XII.7. See also F.-M. Abel, "Aṣal dans Zacharie XIV, 5', *RB*, 45 (1936), 385–400.

[4] This view is still represented in two current works on Old Testament introduction, O. Eissfeldt, *Introduction* (Oxford, 1965), p. 440, and E. Sellin and G. Fohrer (ET G. Fohrer, *Introduction to the Old Testament*, London, 1970), pp. 465–8.

of poetry and present us with prophecies having some links with history, chapters 12 to 14 are in prose and are exclusively eschatological in content, presenting no historical connections.[1] But, as we have indicated above, it cannot be said of the beginning of chapter 14 that it has no point of attachment to history. Of course, even if we show that the whole of Zech. 9 to 14 is correctly dated in the Greek period this does not by itself establish unity of authorship. Nevertheless, this conclusion does seem to follow from some other considerations.

It may be observed that in each part of the literary collection which it is convenient to call Deutero–Zechariah special use is made of Ezekiel, Trito-Isaiah, Jeremiah and Joel. This has been described as the author's 'anthological style'. In his method of using these sources he displays the same liberty from one end of the book to the other. He is no slave to the text: though he grasps the spirit of it, he is quite free with the letter.[2] It must be admitted that this interesting technique of using earlier sacred authors still does not oblige us to postulate unity of authorship. One could, with an effort, imagine several redactors all employing comparable literary methods. But in the case before us this does not seem to be the best hypothesis. Finally, it has been observed that these chapters exhibit a well-marked and systematic outline.[3] Now this overall structure could be the work of a final author–redactor organizing older material. But it must be stated that this unity is rather theological than literary, for it is to be observed that the work revolves round the central figure of the Messiah. We must now be more exact about the nature of this messianism and where it fits into post-exilic literature. If our interpretation of chapter 9 is correct we have there a description of the coming of Alexander from the area of the Levant, followed directly by a description of the messianic king. It is clear from this that the latter is regarded as a national hero ('your king', 9:9), a genuine descendant of David and Solomon. The emphasis which our author places on his specifically Jewish character is intended to illustrate the idea that salvation comes from the Jews. We are thus a long way, a very long way, as we shall see, from the messianism of the Servant Songs. Practically all trace of a national or royal Messiah is missing from the Servant Songs, except perhaps in Isa. 53:2, where his national or royal characteristics are not, however, emphasized, but are simply alluded to in an echo of Isa. 11:1. These differences would

[1] This view is maintained notably by K. Elliger, *Das Buch der zwölf kleine Propheten*, ATD 25 (Göttingen, 1956), pp. 143–4.

[2] M. Delcor, 'Les sources du Deutéro-Zacharie et ses procédés d'emprunt', *RB*, 59 (1952), 385–411.

[3] P. Lamarche, *Zacharie 9–14. Structure littéraire et messianisme*, EBib (Paris, 1961).

appear to make rather improbable any dependence of our author on the Servant Songs, as has sometimes been maintained.[1] If pressed, one might allow (as many critics do) that there is a certain correspondence between the pierced one of Zech. 12:10 and the slaughtered servant of Isa. 53, in the obvious sense that in both cases someone is put to death, but this is far from arguing the direct dependence of the one on the other.[2] But even allowing that there were such dependence, it would then be rather surprising that there is no allusion whatever in Zechariah to the redemptive death of the pierced one, an idea so clearly expressed in Isa. 53:10–11. How could this silence be explained if the Servant Songs had really influenced our author?

After the long pause which followed the years of the restoration, messianic expectation was revived, we have said, by the arrival of Alexander the Great on Palestinian soil. It is important to understand what the biblical writer is trying to do. He is setting up in contrast to Alexander, whose resounding conquests had dazzled some of the Jews, an authentically Jewish Messiah, riding on a Palestinian mount, like David, and of a peaceful disposition, like Solomon. This renaissance in the Greek period of the idea of a Davidic Messiah came after its long eclipse during the Persian era; an era in which many Jewish writings make no reference at all to an individual Messiah. Joel and Malachi, for example, are both quite silent on the subject. For the latter, at all events, if the Messiah is not absent altogether his role is very ill-defined (Mal. 4:5–6). This eclipse of messianic expectations in the Persian period is readily understandable. Nehemiah, who was sent by Artaxerxes to be governor of Judah, had the full backing of the Persian king and he succeeded in harnessing national aspirations to such good effect that his enemies accused him of encouraging the prophets to proclaim that 'there is a king in Judah' (Neh. 6:7). Whatever may be said of these accusations it is certain that at this period Nehemiah took the place of a king, even though he was not explicitly given that title.

In the Greek period the Chronicler too revived the messianic hope by placing David at the centre of his work, making of him a genuine religious reformer and cult organizer, in short, a new Moses. The presentation which the Chronicler gives us of David in the past corresponds quite closely with the presentation which Deutero-Zechariah offers us of the future messiah, though admittedly there are slight differences.

[1] Lamarche, *Zacharie 9–14*, pp. 139–47. See also the criticism of Delcor, *Les Petits Prophètes*, p. 553.

[2] M. Delcor, 'Un problème de critique textuelle et d'exégèse, Zach. xii, 10: *et aspicient ad me quem confixerunt*', *RB*, 58 (1951), 189–99.

CHAPTER 11

JEWISH–GREEK LITERATURE OF THE GREEK PERIOD

The origin of Jewish–Greek literature can be traced back to the translation of the Hebrew Torah (the Pentateuch) into Greek, the so-called Septuagint. This is the source which nourished the greater part of the literary production of the Hellenistic Jews. Originally the legend of the 70 (or 72) translators who were said to have rendered the Hebrew Bible into Greek in the reign of Ptolemy II Philadelphus (285–246 B.C.E.)[1] – whence too the name 'Septuagint' – referred only to the Torah, the first and properly speaking the canonical part of the Hebrew Bible, or rather its Greek version. This traditional story contains at least a core of truth: shortly after 300 B.C.E. the Jews of the Diaspora, especially in Egypt, felt the need for a Greek translation of their Holy Scripture, because obviously only a minority of Jews in that Greek-speaking environment were still capable of reading and understanding Hebrew. However, some scholars are inclined to follow the legendary narrative of the Pseudo-Aristeas letter. The Ptolemaic kings may be supposed to have had a certain interest in the literature of the peoples incorporated into their kingdom (the Jews of Palestine being subjected to the Ptolemaic reign in the third century B.C.E.), so that the initiative for the translation of the Pentateuch might have come from the Ptolemaic court itself.[2]

The literary critic may well conclude that the Greek of the Septuagint, and to some extent the language of subsequent Jewish–Greek literature as well, was rather 'uncouth' and in places 'quite unintelligible', so that it must have at times appeared somewhat 'ridiculous' to a cultured Greek reader.[3] To be sure, this sort of judgement appears in

[1] The Pseudo-Aristeas letter (of about 120 or 100 B.C.E.) offers a more complex version of the legend; an older form of the tradition may be found in Aristobulus F3 (Eusebius, *Praeparatio Evangelica* XIII.12.2).

[2] See esp. E. Bickerman, 'The Septuagint as a translation' (1959), in idem, *Studies in Jewish and Christian History*, AGJU 9, 1 (Leiden, 1976), pp. 167–200, esp. pp. 171–5. For further details about the Septuagint and the scholarly problems relative to it, see Chapter 15.

[3] This was how E. R. Bevan once characterized the language of the Septuagint, in *The Cambridge Ancient History*, vol. 9 (Cambridge, 1932), p. 430.

a different light once we become more familiar with the colloquial language of the Hellenistic period, especially beyond the shores of the Greek mother country – a language which was made more accessible to us through the papyrus discoveries, particularly those unearthed in Egypt. At all events, one should acknowledge the epoch-making achievement which the translation of such an extensive work from a Semitic into the Greek language represented. It is a noble testimony to the intellectual and linguistic capacities of the Hellenistic Jews of Egypt (or, as the Septuagint legend would have it, of Jerusalem). The grandson of Jesus ben Sira, who translated the 'sayings' of his grandfather into Greek after 130 B.C.E., reveals in his prologue that he is fully aware of the difficulty of producing an accurate translation.

> You are asked to read with goodwill and close attention and to exercise tolerance wherever – despite all the pains taken over the translation – we appear to have rendered certain expressions rather infelicitously. For if something is first said in Hebrew and is then translated into a foreign tongue, the meaning undergoes a slight change. And not only this book but also the Law itself, the Prophetic books and the other scriptures reveal not inconsiderable discrepancies if one compares them with the original.[1]

For the rest we should bear in mind that the need for a Greek translation of the Hebrew Bible was felt not only in Egypt and in other areas of the Diaspora but also in the Palestinian homeland itself.[2] The few surviving examples of Jewish–Greek literature from Palestine, above all the historian Eupolemus, are based on the Septuagint; so too the scroll of the Dodekapropheton discovered in 1957 in the Nahal Hever near Qumran and a few other fragments from the Qumran caves 4 and 7 attest the use of Greek biblical texts among the Jews of Palestine.

BIBLICAL EXEGESIS AND RELIGIOUS OR PHILOSOPHICAL LITERATURE

Normally the Jewish–Greek writers whose books survive only in fragments are grouped together under the heading 'historians'.[3] But this designation is appropriate only to a small minority of the authors

[1] Sir., Prologue, 5–7.

[2] On the subject of Hellenism in Palestine during the Maccabean and post-Maccabean period, see above all V. Tcherikover, *Hellenistic Civilization and the Jews* (Philadelphia, 1959), ch. 1, and M. Hengel, *Judentum und Hellenismus*, WUNT 10 (Tübingen, 1969); 2nd edn., 1973), ET *Judaism and Hellenism*, London, 1974.

[3] Most of the relevant fragments, except for those of Aristobulus, are preserved only in quotations used by the Greco-Roman writer Alexander Polyhistor (around the middle of the first century B.C.E.) from whose book 'On the Jews' Clement of Alexandria and, to a greater extent, Eusebius of Caesarea in turn made excerpts.

concerned – indeed, to be precise, only to the Palestinian Eupolemus mentioned above. The other fragmentary writings are in part in the nature of narrative fiction, in part they are poetic compositions in metric form, and in part they represent other, quite different genres. In each case they furnish an insight into the diverse forms in which the Hellenistic Jews strove to get to grips with the biblical heritage and to make it their own under the alien conditions of Hellenistic culture.

Thus the oldest of the writers known to us by name, *Demetrius*, is in point of fact an exegete. In a fragment preserved in Clement of Alexandria,[1] the text of which is somewhat unreliable in its detail, Demetrius indicates that he lived in the reign of the fourth Ptolemy, that is, Ptolemy IV Philopator (221–204 B.C.E.). For he gives the interval between the Babylonian Exile of the Jews – which was obviously the point his own account had reached – and his own day and age as 338 or presumably, to be more correct, 438 years. At the same time the fact that Demetrius invokes the age of Ptolemy at all points to Alexandria as the locale of his activity.

According to Clement's evidence, it seems as if the book was entitled 'Concerning the Kings in Judea'. However, this does not accord with the principal group of fragments which have come down to us from Alexander Polyhistor (and after him Eusebius). These fragments suggest something very different from a history of the Judean monarchy.[2] As far as we can see, Demetrius deals primarily with exegetical problems, such as obviously exercised the minds of attentive Bible readers among the Alexandrian Jews when they perused the books of Genesis and Exodus. In the most extensive fragment (F2) he considers at considerable length the question of how according to the information given in the Bible in Genesis 29:31 to 30:24 Jacob could have had eleven sons and a daughter within the space of his second period of service under Laban, a span of seven years (Gen. 29:30).[3] Thus he works out a precisely calculated explanation, according to which the children are born at the shortest practicable intervals of ten months, first to Leah, then to the two maidservants, finally to Rachel and again to Leah, some of the half-brothers or the baby girl thereby being born at the same time. Similarly in other parts of the text, Demetrius repeatedly displays his interest in testing the correlation between the chronological and the genealogical information given in the biblical narrative.[4] In this way he erects on the basis of the

[1] *FGrHist* 722, F 6: Clemens Alex. *Stromateis* I.141.1–2.

[2] F 1: Euseb. *Praep. Evang.* IX.19.4; F 2: ibid. 21.1–19; F 3: ibid. 29.1–3; F 4: ibid. 29.15; F 5: ibid. 29.16d.

[3] In F 2: Euseb. *Praep. Evang.* IX.21.3–5.

[4] F 2: Euseb. *Praep. Evang.* IX.21.11f and 16–19; F 3: ibid. 29.1–3.

Septuagint text the framework of a chronological scheme which ranged from Adam up to the Exodus from Egypt and which clearly continued to exert its influence well into early Christian chronography.

Nevertheless Demetrius is not really a chronographer but an interpreter of the Bible. This can be seen in other questions that he tackles: why did Joseph, after he had attained high office and standing in Egypt, wait nine years before summoning his father?[1] Why does Joseph, when his brothers come to him with Benjamin, place a fivefold portion of food before his youngest brother (Gen. 43:34)?[2] How can Moses and Zipporah be alive at the same time when one belongs to the seventh generation after Abraham, the other to the sixth? And why should Zipporah be called a 'Cushite' by Aaron and Miriam (Num. 12:1)?[3] Finally, how did the Israelites suddenly come to be armed after the journey through the Red Sea (Exod. 17:8ff)?[4]

Problems of this kind were thus being discussed by the Jews of Alexandria; and the manner in which Demetrius attempts to solve them testifies to the sober, realistic attitude of mind of these particular readers of the Scriptures. At the same time we can perceive echoes of the Hellenistic concern with Homer, the 'classical' text of Greek literature. The literary form of the *aporiai* (or *zētēmata*) *kai lyseis* (problems and solutions) which had emerged by this period is reflected in Demetrius even down to matters of style.

The whole task of interpretation is orientated towards the Greek text of the Septuagint; it is thus our earliest direct evidence for the use of the latter. Nowhere is there any suggestion that Demetrius was conscious of interpreting a translated text. To him and his contemporaries the Torah is self-evidently a Greek book. And the way in which they read it similarly displays a Greek spirit, though of course they do not on that account renounce their faith in the God of Israel.

In this context the small fragment of an exegete called *Aristeas* deserves mention because in its own way it is similar to what we know of Demetrius' book.[5] We cannot deduce anything as to its dating and place of origin from the brief text available. But the very fact that this fragment too was handed down by Alexander Polyhistor is proof that it originated about 100 B.C.E. or shortly after.

The fragment deals with the identity of Job. Aristead identifies him with the Jobab who is named in Genesis 36:33, thus making him an

[1] F 2: Euseb. *Praep. Evang.* IX.21.13.
[2] F 2: ibid. 21.14–15.
[3] F 3: Euseb. *Praep. Evang.* IX.29.2 and 3.
[4] F 5: Euseb. *Praep. Evang.* IX.29.16d.
[5] In Euseb. *Praep. Evang.* IX.25.1–4. The exegete Aristeas should not be confused with the author of the Pseudepigraphic *Letter to Philocrates*.

Edomite, indeed a direct son of Esau. This identification, together with further details, makes it certain that Aristeas too was working from the Septuagint; the very form of the names in Hebrew would have prevented an association of one with the other. For the rest the fragment consists mostly of a terse summary of the narrative framework of the book of Job, in the course of which the four friends of Job are mentioned by name. What is interesting is that the addendum to the Septuagint translation of the book of Job contains the same information as our fragment; moreover verbal echoes make it clear that one is a literary borrowing from the other. The apocryphal 'Testament of Job', incidentally, is likewise based on the identification of Job with Jobab.

The most important of the Alexandrian Jewish exegetes before Philo was undoubtedly *Aristobulus*. Admittedly the text of the Torah interested him in a different way from Demetrius: he devoted his attention, not to the pragmatic historical questions raised by the stories concerning the patriarchs, but to the theological or philosophical aspects of Moses' 'law-giving' (for Aristobulus they amount to the same thing). No title for this work has come down to us; a few fragments are preserved by Clement of Alexandria and more extensive sections by Eusebius.[1] Several times in his book Aristobulus addresses 'King Ptolemy' and specifically refers to him as the successor of Ptolemy Philadelphus.[2] According to the ancient and, to my mind, correct version in Clement, the ruler in question is Ptolemy VI Philometor. This would take us back to the period around 175–150 B.C.E. and indicate a writer who, perhaps as one of the scholars of the Mouseion at Alexandria, had gained for himself at least literary access to the court of the Ptolemies. The letter of 2 Macc. 1:10 to 2:18, forged about 60 B.C.E.,[3] even describes him as the king's 'tutor' (1:10).[4]

[1] F 1: Euseb. *Historia Ecclesiastica* VII.32.16–18; F 2: Euseb. *Praep. Evang.* VIII.10.1–17; F 3: Euseb. *Praep. Evang.* XIII.12.1–2; F 4: ibid. 12.3–8; F 5: ibid. 12.9–16 – the quotations of Clement are included within those of Eusebius, so do not need to be listed separately.

[2] F 3: Euseb. *Praep. Evang.* XIII.12.2; see also F 2: Euseb. *Praep. Evang.* VIII.10.1 and 7.

[3] Some scholars think the letter of 2 Macc. 1:10 to 2:18 is genuine (originating from the year 163 B.C.E.): B. Z. Wacholder, 'The letter from Judah Maccabee to Aristobulus: Is 2 Maccabees 1:10b–2:18 authentic?' *HUCA*, 49 (1978), 89–133. For the traditional view see E. Bickerman, 'Ein jüdischer Festbrief vom Jahre 124 v.Chr.' *ZNW*, 32 (1933), 233–54, also in idem, *Studies in Jewish and Christian History*, AGJU 9, 2 (Leiden, 1980), pp. 136–58, esp. pp. 136f.

[4] The misgivings voiced by several scholars around 1900 concerning the historicity of Aristobulus and the authenticity of the fragments handed down under his name have now been disposed of. See N. Walter, *Der Thoraausleger Aristobulos*, TU 86 (Berlin, 1964).

Clement and Eusebius call Aristobulus a 'peripatetic'. This is correct in so far as he certainly thought of himself as a philosopher, not of course as a representative of Aristotelian teaching but as a disciple of Moses. The latter, as the 'giver of the Law', was for him the founder of true philosophy. Any 'correct' insights that occur in Greek thinkers like Pythagoras, Socrates and Plato,[1] or in the peripatetic school alluded to by Aristobulus himself[2] or in the great poets (he mentions Homer, Hesiod, Orpheus, Linus and Aratus) are joyfully noted by Aristobulus as parallels to the utterances of Moses. He even surmises that Plato or Pythagoras was dependent on an ancient translation of the Torah into Greek.[3] But such theses do not encompass the main burden of Aristobulus' thought as is sometimes claimed: rather, they were first pushed into the foreground by Eusebius.

If one views Aristobulus in terms of the history of philosphy, one cannot but demur at Clement's judgement and conclude that he was influenced above all by the Stoa. He shares, as does Philo later, the same kind of physical-cum-theological thinking. Unlike the Stoa, he does believe the cosmos to be indubitably the creation of God; there is no question of the universe being ultimately identical with the divine. Human reason is capable of perceiving the uniform law (*logos*) underlying the whole of nature and therein the workings of God in His creation. Thus too man is able to hear the voice of divine wisdom which proclaims itself in the cosmic *logos* and to obey it in his own life.[4] In accordance with the importance of the Sabbath for Judaism, the number seven plays a special role in all this as a symbol of the cosmic order; in this respect Aristobulus may be linking up with Pythagorean speculation about the significance of numbers.

The longest of the surviving fragments is concerned with the proper understanding of the Torah,[5] above all those utterances which were not readily comprehensible to a philosophically schooled Hellenist, whether he was a Jew or not. There is particular concern with the correct interpretation of the anthropomorphic statements about God, such as the references to God's 'hands', His 'arm', His 'standing' and His 'descending'. Here Aristobulus strives for explanations which can be vindicated both *vis-à-vis* the biblical text and before the spirit of Greek philosophy. He resorts to the allegorical interpretation of Homeric mythology that was practised by the Stoa, and explicitly justifies its application to the Bible. Ostensibly this justification is

[1] F 4: Euseb. *Praep. Evang.* XIII.12.4.
[2] F 5: Euseb. *Praep. Evang.* XIII.12.10.
[3] F 3: Euseb. *Praep. Evang.* XIII.12.1; F 2: Eusebius, *Praep. Evang.* VIII.10.4.
[4] F 4: Euseb. *Praep. Evang.* XIII.12.3–8 and F 5: ibid. 12.9–16.
[5] F 2: Euseb. *Praep. Evang.* VIII.10.1–17.

directed at the king, but implicitly it is also addressed to the forum of his co-religionists, whose comprehension of the text he sought to facilitate by means which were obviously not common in his day and must have been regarded with some degree of suspicion:

I would therefore beg you to consider the true meaning of the commentary and to retain the proper conception of God and not to lapse into a mythical and anthropomorphic (conception of the) existence (of God). For frequently when our law-giver Moses, in order to express what he (really) wants to say, uses words which refer to other things – that is, things that have a visible substance – he thus gives utterance to essential truths and to the nature of important things...I desire now to examine the individual designations (and to elucidate them) to the best of my ability. But if I should be wide of the mark and fail to convince (you), then do not impute absurd statements to the law-giver but rather blame me for being unable to elucidate his meaning properly.[1]

Aristobulus then explains: when the Bible speaks of God's 'arm', it means His power; God's 'standing' is an expression for His constancy, that is, the permanence of the world and its laws. It is more difficult for Aristobulus to explain how God 'descends' on Sinai (Exod. 19:18 etc.). Clearly he refuses to abandon the idea of God's direct self-revelation in connection with the giving of the Torah to Moses.[2] Philo's concept of a mediating hypostasis between God and man, for example, the *logos*, is obviously still alien to him. Yet this very problem of God's self-revelation on Sinai must have called particularly strongly for a solution along the lines of a hypostasis.

Thus Aristobulus is a pioneer of the allegorical interpretation of the Bible which later, especially with Philo, established itself as the prime method of understanding the text at a deeper level. We should note, however, that for Aristobulus the allegorical approach is merely a device to facilitate the comprehension of biblical passages whose literal meaning creates ideological difficulties for the philosophically schooled reader. As a hermeneutic technique, the allegorical method performs for him a still completely subordinate function, whereas in Philo it emerges as a totally independent method of exegesis. In a tentative way, but conscious of the difficulties, Aristobulus initiates the process of reflection on biblical hermeneutics which proves to be necessary whenever an established tradition enters a new intellectual ambience.

Around 120 or 100 B.C.E. we find this process being continued in the

[1] F 2: Euseb. *Praep. Evang.* VIII.10.2–3 and 6.
[2] F 2: Euseb. *Praep. Evang.* VIII.10.7–17.

pseudepigraphic *Letter of Aristeas to Philocrates.*[1] The author, in the guise of a Greek official at the Ptolemaic court, offers his readers not only the legendary account of the origins of the Greek translation of the Torah, the Septuagint legend (incidentally, not yet in as miraculous a version as will occur later in Philo and in early Christian literature); above all he provides for the Gentile reader guidance for the proper understanding of this holy book. For Pseudo-Aristeas any sentence of the Torah which does not possess a specific religious or ethical meaning must be interpreted allegorically. If for instance the ironically detached reader should ask why the Torah declares certain animals to be unclean and forbids eating them, the author explains that there is no question here of mice or weasels and similar fauna being singled out for special attention (§144); the issue is rather the proper form of divine worship, in contrast to the animal worship cultivated by the Egyptians, and likewise the proper mode of human existence. The permitted beasts and fowl are symbols of gentleness and purity, while the animals called 'unclean' by Moses are wild and vicious and represent corresponding modes of human conduct. What matters, therefore, is not whether one abstains from or consumes certain kinds of meat, but whether one adopts the appropriate principles of ethical behaviour (§§128–71). The allegorical method is here being applied above all as a means of providing an ethical interpretation of biblical statements.

The pseudonymous author lays altogether great store by an ethos of kindness, reason and piety. Almost half his 'letter' (§§184–300) is devoted to the depiction of (invented) table talk between the Ptolemaic king and his guests, the self-same 72 Jewish scholars from Jerusalem, before they are allowed to set about the Torah translation. In the course of seven evenings all the Jewish dinner guests in succession have to answer philosophical or moral questions put to them by the king. Thus with tedious discursiveness (which finally the author himself becomes aware of: §295), and in the manner of a textbook on good government, there unfolds the panorama of a humane ethic that is as enlightened as it is devout. We shall quote only the seventy-second and final section:

(The King) then asked the very last one: what is the most important (factor) in kingship? And he answered: that the subjects should live in perpetual peace and be granted swift judgements in legal disputes. But this the ruler achieves if he hates evil, loves good and considers it a great deed to save a human life; just as you too regard injustice as the worst evil of all and have won immortal fame

[1] The common designation of this booklet is a 'letter', but there is neither letter-type introduction nor signature; the book rather pretends to be a literary narrative of the (presumably non-Jewish) author, determined to entertain and instruct his friend (f. §§1 and 322).

through your just conduct of affairs, since God vouchsafes you a pure mind untainted by any evil. (§§291f)

The 'long drawn-out, joyful applause' of all those present, which then ensues (§293), as on previous occasions, shows the author's underlying principal aim. He wants to demonstrate that the Jews have attained the highest level of development, philosophically and ethically, and that, without having to give up their distinctiveness, they deserve to be acknowledged as an equal member of the Hellenistic family of nations. Whereas in the case of Aristobulus we see above all a reflection of internal debate among the Jews about the proper understanding of the Bible in terms of Greek thinking, the author of the Pseudo-Aristeas letter is exercised by the question of the intellectual recognition of the Jews on the part of their Greek environment.

As is likewise clear from other writings which we now intend to mention briefly, a humane ethic rooted in religious principles provided the most appropriate meeting point between Jews and those of their Greek fellow-citizens who were schooled in popular philosophy.

The anthology of aphorisms on matters of practical piety which *Jesus ben Sira* composed in Hebrew about 180 B.C.E. is discussed in chapter 12. His grandson, who moved from Palestine to Alexandria around 132 B.C.E., considered his grandfather's book sufficiently important – even in his new milieu – to translate it into Greek (see above, p. 386). He himself, or a later Jewish–Greek copyist, there added further maxims which are lacking in the Syriac translation and in those portions of the Hebrew text that have come to light since the beginning of this century, especially at Masada in 1964.[1] These additions revolve above all around the idea that the whole of man's capacity for good springs from God. The fear of God as the foundation of practical wisdom, and both awe and wisdom as gifts of God[2] – such is the core of Israelite–Jewish teaching even in the Hellenistic period. This is what is meant by conduct according to the Law which the grandson of ben Sira (at the end of his prologue), together with Pseudo-Aristeas (§127 etc.), extol as the supreme fulfilment of human life.

The pseudonymous *Wisdom of Solomon* also rests on this foundation. But this book, unlike the proverbs and sayings of ben Sira, does not present a collection of individual maxims in a fairly loose sequence but

[1] Y. Yadin, *The Ben Sira Scroll from Masada* (Jerusalem, 1965). The fragments contain the Hebrew text of Sir. 39:27 to 43:30.

[2] Sir. 1.12 and 17, each one with a gloss.

rather a composition divided into three logically connected parts with a clearly recognizable and developing theme.

The first section (chs. 1 to 5) depicts the ultimate victory of the righteous over the evil-doers who now appear to have the upper hand. In the second part (chs. 6 to 9) 'Solomon' urges all rulers to strive for wisdom and relates how he himself was vouchsafed it as a gift from God. Then he praises its great value and its all-pervading power; his prayer for wisdom concludes this section. The third and final part (chs. 10 to 19) depicts the rule of Wisdom in the history of Israel from Adam to the Exodus from Egypt; an interpolation (chs. 13 to 15) speaks of the folly of idolatrous practices, especially the animal cult favoured by the Egyptians.

Content and style alike indicate that the author was a Hellenistic Jew from Alexandria, probably writing in the first century B.C.E. (at all events in the first century C.E.). His choice of vocabulary puts us in mind not only of the Septuagint but also of the language of Hellenistic popular philosophy. Only the first section with its small number of Hebraisms and its consistently applied *parallelismus membrorum* suggests the possibility of a Hebrew original, a question on which even today scholarly opinion is still divided. But even this part is completely permeated with the Hellenistic spirit; it teaches a peculiar hybrid doctrine, combining apocalyptic hope of resurrection and the Platonic conception of the eternity of the soul. The contemporary targets of this section appear to have been those Jews who had turned their backs on the faith of their fathers and joined the ranks of those who were making life difficult in some respects for the Alexandrian Jews. To them and to the faithful the author wants to show the sublimity of a Hellenistically interpreted Judaism; he encourages the readers on his own side to persevere steadfastly in the hope of being compensated in the life to come. Hence in the second section he urges them to entrust themselves to the leadership of wisdom which will conduct them to every virtue (as defined by the Stoics). The third part then shows how such trust has frequently been vindicated in the course of Jewish history, especially during the tribulations of the Israelites in Egypt; by contrast the Egyptian religion is subjected to corrosive prophetic scorn.[1] In this way, for all his claim to supra-historical validity, the author pursues quite immediate and concrete aims in his exhortation and encouragement to his contemporaries and fellow Jews.

A didactic poem composed in quite a different form is that known by

[1] Wisd. 13–15 belongs to the tradition of prophetic texts such as Jer. 2:26–8 and 10:1–5 and Deutero-Isaiah 44:9–20; see also *Jubilees* 12:1–14; *Apocalypse of Abraham*, 5–7 and the story *Bel and the Dragon* (additions to Daniel).

the pseudonym of the Greek aphorist *Phocylides* of Miletus. This poem remains closer to the biblical tradition of aphoristic literature with a universal appeal. It was probably written by a Hellenistic Jew in Egypt during the first century C.E. In 230 lines of often not very elegant hexameters, which try to imitate the Homeric style, the author offers a compendium of Jewish–Greek ethical teaching. Although no overall structure is apparent, the maxims dwell on the issues of piety, righteousness, the proper kind of neighbourly love, moderation, frugality and the family. What strikes us is that all the doctrinal observances strictly characteristic of Judaism are avoided. Indeed at the end (line 228) the author adopts an explicitly 'enlightened' attitude towards ritualistic detail, with the aphorism: 'Purification rites signify a purification of the soul, not of the body'. Obviously only those ethical rules are incorporated into the poem which could command assent from cultured Gentiles and which would not give the lie to the chosen pseudonym.

In the light of all this, of course, the question has repeatedly been raised whether it is justifiable to attribute the poem to a Jewish author at all, as Jakob Bernays set out to do in 1856. Yet that is beyond dispute – not only because the aphorisms in general are strongly reminiscent of the language of the Septuagint and stand in close proximity to certain sections of the maxims of ben Sira, Pseudo-Aristeas and the *Hypothetica* of Philo; but also above all because two chapters which furnish the core of the ethical teaching of the Torah (Lev. 19 and Deut. 27:15–26) also inform the whole of this particular poem. Thus in the opening section (1.8) we find a principle reminiscent of Lev. 19:2–3: 'Honour first God, then after Him your parents'. However, Jewish authorship is also indicated by links with the traditions articulated in early Christian texts (the *Didascalia Apostolorum* and book 2 of the *Oracula Sybillina*, the latter of which took over a large section of these aphorisms).

If one asks what is the aim of this didactic poem, one ought not to assume that it was written for a missionary or propagandistic purpose. After all it lacks any commendation of Judaism or of specifically Jewish ideas and ethical values. Nor, for this same reason, can it have been intended as an apologia for Judaism *vis-à-vis* a gentile readership. Rather, the author seems to be addressing himself to his fellow Jews. He wants to show them, through the mouth of the Greek aphorist, that the ethical values of their fathers, as laid down in the Torah, bear comparison with the highest Greek standards. He thus tries to restore the self-respect of those Jews of the Diaspora who were susceptible to alien cultural influences, some of whom like Tiberius Julius Alexander, the nephew of Philo,[1] were flirting with the possibility of renouncing Judaism: the heritage of your fathers, he argues, is on a par with the Greek ethical tradition; thus you will gain nothing by turning to paganism; on the contrary you would only surrender the advantages of belonging to your own nation. In addition one might also consider the possibility that the poem was intended for the classroom as an exercise in style and as an elementary lesson in ethics. In fact it was used for such purposes in the Middle Ages and even into the modern period.

A particularly characteristic example of the religious and philosophical literature of the Hellenistic Jews is the treatise 'On pious Reason as the Tamer of Passions', the so-called *Fourth Book of the Maccabees*, that has come down to us in a few Bible manuscripts and in part too among the works of Josephus.

The anonymous author, presumably writing in the last half century B.C.E. or in the first century C.E. in Alexandria or in some other centre of Hellenistic culture, strives for a comprehensive discussion of this theme. First we get a somewhat dry philosophical or academic contemplation of it (chs. 1 to 3); then he cites examples of Jewish martyrs of the Maccabean period and narrates their history with a sometimes agonizing vividness and with a highly-charged religious commentary (chs. 4 to 17). Through their steadfastness and loyalty to the Torah, which they maintained to the point of death despite grievous suffering, the priest Eleazar, the seven Maccabean brothers and their mother are said to have demonstrated the power of reason over natural desire (a Stoic thesis, it should be noted). What their story shows far more clearly, however, is the superiority of the spirit of self-sacrifice, sustained by an unswerving faith, over tyrannical secular power (17:2 and 8 to 16). A book which begins as a philosophical treatise (1:1–12) ends as an open exhortation to the 'descendants of Abraham', the 'Israelites' (ch. 18) to demonstrate similar fidelity to the Law.

J. Freudenthal (see bibliography, p. 685) described the treatise as a homily specifically meant to be preached in the synagogue;[2] others think of it as a more literary conception and point to the stylistic influence of the later diatribes with their pronouncedly didactic treatises. At all events the book is an eloquent testimony to the way in which Jewish piety and Hellenistic, especially Stoic, thinking, could be

[1] Josephus, *Antiquitates Judaicae* XX.100.

[2] Three other Synagogue homilies from the Hellenistic Diaspora, surviving only in Armenian translation, under the pseudonym of Philo, are now accessible in German translation: F. Siegert, *Drei hellenistisch-jüdische Predigten*, 1, WUNT 20 (Tübingen, 1980).

intimately fused in certain circles of the Diaspora, though in such a manner that ultimately the Jewish substance still breaks through the Hellenistic form.

HISTORIOGRAPHY

One writer who was concerned to depict a period of Israelite–Jewish history was, to judge by the surviving fragments, *Eupolemus*. This author must be identical with the Eupolemus whom 1 Maccabees (8:17f; see also 2 Macc. 4:11) names as one of the envoys sent by Judas Maccabeus to Rome in 160 B.C.E. in order to negotiate a Jewish–Roman friendship treaty. This identification is consistent with the information supplied in fragment 5,[1] according to which Eupolemus carried his chronological calculations down as far as 158 B.C.E., in other words down to the fifth year of the reign of Demetrius (I Soter). Eupolemus thus lived and worked in Palestine and was at least a sympathizer with the Maccabean movement. This is also interesting from the point of view of literary history, for it emerges in passing that the Septuagint translation, on which Eupolemus' account undoubtedly rests, was by this time being used as a matter of course even in Palestine and that therefore even there a fervent devotion to the Torah did not yet necessarily entail a renunciation of Hellenism (2 Macc. 4:13). On the other hand certain details of the fragments reveal that Eupolemus was, of course, also familiar with Hebrew.

Eupolemus' book clearly bore the title *On the Kings of Judea*,[2] which from a retrospective point of view meant also the rulers of the whole of Israel, David and Solomon. For the surviving text deals above all with these two kings. An introduction appears to have made only brief mention of Moses and Joshua and the 'Judges' – or at least Samuel; not even Saul is discussed in any detail.[3] The account does not grow more discursive until it gets to David. But even here his political and military deeds are quickly dismissed. The narrative does not become detailed until Eupolemus begins to describe the plan of the Temple building.[4] His special interest in the Temple is very plain in the main part of the surviving text, the story of Solomon. Here, unless Alexander Polyhistor, the author responsible for making the excerpts, has given us the wrong impression, Eupolemus speaks almost exclusively of Solomon's efforts to erect and complete the Temple, in which connection he includes a detailed description of the building.[5] Eupolemus also

[1] Clem. Alex. *Strom.* 1.141.4. [2] Clem. Alex. *Strom.* 1.153.4 (cf. ibid. 141.1 and 4).

[3] F 1: Euseb. *Praep. Evang.* IX.26.1 and F 2: ibid. 30:1–2.

[4] F 2: Euseb. *Praep. Evang.* IX.30.3–8.

[5] F 2: Euseb. *Praep. Evang.* IX.31.1 to 34.17.

interpolated into his account the texts of fictitious correspondence between Solomon and a (legendary) Pharaoh Vaphres, and between Solomon and King Suron (Hiram) of Tyre[1] on the subject of the despatch and payment of foreign workers for the building of the Temple. A further fragment[2] refers briefly to the dispute between King 'Jonachim'[3] of Judah and the prophet Jeremiah, to the capture and pillage of Jerusalem by Nebuchadnezzar and to Jeremiah's taking the Ark of the Covenant and the Tablets of the Law to a place of safety.

The main part of the surviving text reveals Eupolemus' enthusiasm for the greatness and splendour of the Temple of Solomon. This doubtless reflects the joy of the Jews who had remained faithful to the Temple at the reconsecration in 164 B.C.E. of the (post-exilic) Temple after its desecration by Antiochus IV Epiphanes.

All in all, Eupolemus stands before us as the oldest of the Jewish historians known to us by name who provides in Greek an outline of the history of his people. It must remain an open question whether he was here addressing himself to educated Greek-speaking members of his own nation, or whether he had Gentile readers in mind. We do not detect any apologetic note in his fragments, nor is there any hint of a missionary tendency, unless one is inclined to term his effusive glorification of the Temple an apologia. At all events such tendencies are far more pronounced in the works of his great successor and fellow-Palestinian Josephus, who in his account of Jewish history was clearly concerned to win the sympathy and understanding of a Greco-Roman audience.

As is well known, the Maccabean period also inspired historians to write about the immediate past and even their own day. I make only a passing reference to this point since the books in question are discussed in other parts of the present work. Yet the supposition should be noted that Eupolemus also wrote a history of the Maccabean uprising and that the First Book of the Maccabees, which was written in Hebrew towards the end of the second century B.C.E., drew on this account by Eupolemus for its information about Judas Maccabeus. But this is of course no more than a hypothesis.

The Second Book of the Maccabees, on the other hand, is presented to us as the epitome of a five-volume work on the Maccabean struggle by a certain Jason of Cyrene (2 Macc. 2:19–32). The very epithet, together with the marked influence of Greek culture that he betrays,

[1] This correspondence is based on 1 Kings 5 or 2 Chron. 2.

[2] F 4: Euseb. *Praep. Evang.* IX.39.2–5.

[3] Under this name Eupolemus mistakenly identifies the two kings Jehoiakim and Jehoiachin (2 Kings 23:36 to 24:16).

tells us that Jason was a Jew of the Diaspora from Cyrene. Nowadays there is an increasing tendency to regard him as a contemporary, even – in the view of some – an eyewitness of the events which he describes and which take us down to 160 B.C.E.;[1] certain historical improbabilities can doubtless be laid at the door of the later epitomator. If this assumption is correct, Jason would also be a direct contemporary of Eupolemus (which might explain the allusion in 2 Macc. 4:11).

His writing is influenced by the spirit of the highly-charged historiography of the Hellenistic tradition; this influence can be seen in his strongly didactic presentation and in his predilection for legendary embellishment. Jason unhesitatingly narrates miraculous events and shows supernatural beings taking a direct hand in affairs. On the other hand, the work bears the stamp of Hasidean piety: the events surrounding the Temple, which God protects again and again in a wondrous manner, and at the outset the figure of the sole legitimate High Priest Onias III, stand at the centre of attention, while interest in the patriotic aspect of the Maccabean struggle recedes completely. Thus Jason is at once a witness to the effective Hellenization of Jewish literature and to the fundamental distrust of that same 'Hellenism': he coined this term with a pejorative sense (2 Macc. 4:13).

Among historiographical literature as it was understood in the Hellenistic period one should also include the fragments of an anonymous Samaritan ('Pseudo-Eupolemus') and of Cleodemus Malchus, in which biblical accounts of primeval or ancient history are mingled in a singular manner with pagan mythology. But the Samaritan and the Jewish author align themselves with a recognizable literary genre to be found among other nations which had recently come into close contact with Greek culture, such as the Babylonians, the Phoenicians, the Egyptians and so on; we have examples in the works of the Babylonian Berossus or of the Egyptian Manetho. Their aim is to trace their national history as far back as possible and to expound its connection with the history of other peoples. So here myth and history blend indiscriminately with one another, a process which was facilitated by the widespread euhemeristic notion that the gods of mythology were in fact originally human beings of outstanding excellence.

A fragment of the book by the *anonymous Samaritan* has been handed down to us – presumably in error – under the name of Eupolemus (hence the frequently used designation *Pseudo-Eupolemus*). He shows

[1] See Tcherikover, *Civilization*, pp. 381–90, and Hengel, *Hellenismus*, pp. 176–83; ET 1, pp. 95–9.

himself to be a Samaritan by the way in which he transfers the story of Abraham and Melchizedek (Gen. 14) to Gerizim and reveals a strong affinity towards Phoenicia. His book may have been composed in an earlier, pre-Maccabean period – at all events, it must have been before the destruction of the Temple on Gerizim by John Hyrcanus (129 B.C.E.) The surviving fragment[1] reveals the author's attempt to bring together Greek and especially Babylonian mythology, interpreted euhemeristically, and biblical pre-history by dint of identifying biblical with pagan names. He thus has Bel (Kronos) in place of Noah in the genealogy; he identifies the Greek Atlas – because of his connection with astrology – with Enoch. For the rest the surviving text glorifies above all the figure of Abraham, who is said to have brought the wisdom of Babylon first to Phoenicia and only then from there to Egypt, and to have introduced the true religion. In the case of several of the points mentioned the author reveals his familiarity with Palestinian traditions about Abraham and Enoch (compare the Book of Jubilees and the Apocalypse of Abraham, together with the Ethiopic Apocalypse of Enoch); on the other hand it is equally clear that the anonymous writer was conversant with Greek (Herodotus) and Babylonian–Greek literature (Berossus).

The other author mentioned above, *Cleodemus Malchus*, of whose book only a short fragment survives,[2] combines biblical traditions and pagan mythology in a similar manner. However, the mythological traditions that he adduces point to Hellenistic North Africa (Libya or Mauretania). Cleodemus establishes a kinship between two grandsons of Abraham and Keturah (Gen. 25:4; for Epher Cleodemus writes Apheras and Iaphras, whence he derives the name Africa) and Hercules. The two descendants of Abraham aid Hercules during his campaign against the Libyan giant Anteus; Hercules marries the daughter of Apheras, and from this union issues the Libyan tribe known as the Sophakes, who are thus counted among the direct descendants of Abraham. By showing the alleged blood relationship between his own people and their host nation, Cleodemus, who was obviously a Jew belonging to the Libyan or Carthaginian Diaspora about 100 B.C.E., attempts to include the Jews as equal members of the Mediterranean community, that is, the *oikumenē* – let us remember the similar claim in 1 Macc. 12:5–23 that a bond of kinship exists between Jews and Spartans.

[1] F 1: Euseb. *Praep. Evang.* IX.17.2–9. To this can be added a small F 2 (Euseb. *Praep. Evang.* IX.18.2b), which repeats very briefly the contents of the first.

[2] F 1: Jos. *Ant.* 1.239–41 (and on the basis of this Euseb. *Praep. Evang.* IX.20.2–4).

NARRATIVE FICTION

The book of an author called *Artapanus*, of which three fragments survive,[1] one of them in a quite extensive form, is quite different in character from the works discussed hitherto. Here we probably have to do with a Jewish author from Egypt, again writing about 100 B.C.E.

The book titles, which Alexander Polyhistor mentions in his excerpts, namely 'Concerning the Jews' or again 'Judaica', could hardly represent the original titles. At all events, to judge by the fragments, the book seems to have been less a depiction of Jewish history than a fictionalized biography of Moses. Abraham and Joseph were probably given only a brief mention at the beginning, with reference to their relations with Egypt;[2] from this point of view the other patriarchs could be overlooked.

In the main part of the text Artapanus tells of Moses' career in Egypt, depicting him in the characteristically Hellenistic fashion as a hero, indeed even as a *theios anēr*.[3] We hear of the adoption of the boy Moses by Princess Merris and of his royal upbringing, his important inventions and institutions in the fields of technology, government, culture and religion; we hear of various perils to which he was exposed in consequence of Pharaoh's envy but from which he always emerged triumphant. Likewise in the ensuing, freely adapted, version of the events surrounding the deliverance of the Israelites out of Egypt, the glorious character of Moses occupies the foreground. On one occasion he shows himself superior to Pharaoh: when asked which God sends him, Moses whispers God's name in Pharaoh's ear, whereupon Pharaoh collapses unconscious but is revived again by Moses. The story breaks off after the crossing of the Red Sea; there follows only a kind of personal description of Moses. The events on Sinai or the contents of the Torah as revealed through Moses are of no interest to the author.

What is strange in a Jewish writer is the manner in which Artapanus deals with Egyptian religion. On several occasions Moses takes an active part in the establishment of animal cults. Yet Artapanus does not thereby seek to legitimize Egyptian religion and place it on a par with the Jewish faith. Rather he views it quite contemptuously as a simple means of manipulating more easily the ignorant Egyptian masses.[4] The background to Artapanus' work, as in the case of other writers, is

[1] F 1: Euseb. *Praep. Evang.* IX.18.1; F 2: ibid. 23.1–4; F 3: ibid. 27.1–37.

[2] F 1 and F 2.

[3] See F 3: Euseb. *Praep. Evang.* IX.27.6, where Moses is also identified with (Thoth-) Hermes.

[4] F 3: Euseb. *Praep. Evang.* IX.27.4f.

the euhemeristic interpretation of religions, according to which the (pagan) cults are human institutions and the divinities originally human beings of great excellence. Naturally Artapanus sees the Jewish religion and the God who sends Moses in quite a different light. It is therefore all the more surprising to observe how far he has in effect become assimilated to his Egyptian–Hellenistic milieu in his interpretation of the religious element; hence rationalistic enlightenment and notions of magical powers (as in the episode about the effect of pronouncing God's name) stand naîvely side by side.

Artapanus' interest in things Egyptian doubtless gives us a clue as to his origins. But it seems questionable whether he really knew the Egyptian cults from first-hand experience. All the details he mentions could easily have been drawn from Hellenistic literature about Egypt, such as the *Aigyptiaka* of Hecateus of Abdera. We should not attribute a missionary purpose to him. Rather, Artapanus wishes to show the importance and superiority of Moses – and thus indirectly of Judaism as such – and in this way perhaps to counteract a deprecatory attitude towards the Jews, possibly even to refute particular calumnies. But in the first instance he doubtless has in mind the need of a Jewish–Greek readership to be diverted and entertained.

Among the works of narrative fiction we must also include a book of Jewish origin ascribed to an author mentioned in the last paragraph: Hecateus of Abdera (*Pseudo-Hecateus I*).[1] This too probably originated towards the end of the second century B.C.E. in the Egyptian Diaspora. In accordance with the author's fictitious identity, 'Hecateus' relates his experiences among the Jews, for example, on the campaigns of Alexander the Great and Ptolemy I, and imparts his knowledge of them which he claims to have derived from a certain Ezekias, a high priest. In this guise he voices several tributes to the size and beauty of Judea and Jerusalem, and to the faithfulness of the Jews to their Law for which they are ready to endure suffering. An anecdote at the end of the surviving text tells how during one campaign it was decided to elucidate which route to take next by having recourse to augury, and how the Jewish soldier Mosollamus fearlessly demonstrated the absurdity of such divination by shooting down the bird.

The aim of this little book is clear: the unprejudiced voice of a well-known Greek author was to sing the praises of the Jews and at the same

[1] Quoted in Josephus, *Contra Apionem* I.183b–205 and in II.43 – to be distinguished from Pseudo-Hecateus II ('On Abraham and the Egyptians'), a book mentioned by Josephus in *Ant.* I.159 and by Clement of Alexandria in *Strom.* V.113–1 (on this point, see p. 407 n. 3).

time recall the good relationship which once existed between Alexander the Great and the early Ptolemies on the one hand, and the Jews in their service on the other; as a result the writer presumably hoped to combat a deterioration of this relationship in his own day. The purpose is thus in several respects similar to that of the roughly contemporary Pseudo-Aristeas letter discussed above (pp. 392f).

In this context we must at least mention in passing the so-called *Third Book of the Maccabees*. As is already widely known, this has nothing to do with the history of the Maccabees but tells of the persecution of the Jews of Alexandria under Ptolemy VII Euergetes (known as Physcon) and of the divine retribution visited upon the persecutors. Written in Alexandria perhaps towards the end of the first century B.C.E., this book too tries in its own way to make clear the need for harmony and understanding between the Greek and Jewish communities in Alexandria.

Finally, a small book which has survived in its entirety deserves our attention: in literary terms it can properly be described as a romance or a 'spiritual novella'[1] and its purpose was doubtless a missionary one. We refer to the anonymous work called *Joseph and Asenath*, which was probably composed around the turn of the millennium in the Egyptian Diaspora and is written in a Greek saturated with the language of the Septuagint.[2]

The story develops the biblical statement (Gen. 41:45) that Joseph took to wife in Egypt the woman Asenath, daughter of an Egyptian high priest, into a charming *novella* of love and conversion which combines motifs from Hellenistic erotic fiction with those of Jewish *novellas* of spiritual import (Esther, Judith, Tobit). The beautiful but proud daughter of the priest is deaf to all suitors. However, her pride dissolves when she catches sight of Joseph visiting her father. Full of inward restlessness she renounces her idols and in utter solitude does penance in sackcloth and ashes for seven days. On the eighth day, in answer to her humble prayer, one of the archangels appears in her chamber, raises her up, strengthens her with a heavenly honeycomb – one might say a combination of manna with nectar and ambrosia – and prepares Asenath for the arrival of Joseph her bridegroom. The latter

[1] Thus C. Burchard, *Untersuchungen zu Joseph und Aseneth*, WUNT 8 (Tübingen, 1965), p. 106.

[2] The question of how far the transmitted text has been modified by Christian revisers remains unresolved. Against Burchard's view (see previous note) there is T. Holtz, 'Christliche Interpolationen in "Joseph und Aseneth"', *NTS*, 14 (1967–68), 482–97.

too had been told by the angel that Asenath was the bride destined for him by God, and so there are no further obstacles to the wedding. Later the marriage is once again imperilled because of a plot contrived by Pharaoh's son out of jealousy. But divine intervention and Asenath's magnanimity bring everything to a happy conclusion.

On the one hand the story disposes of the problem of how Joseph could marry a pagan – a woman, moreover, who was to become the mother of two Israelite tribes. It is shown that the marriage was preceded by a genuine conversion on her part. In this way, on the other hand, the story also commends and glorifies conversion to Judaism as the proper fulfilment of human life: Asenath becomes the mother of all future proselytes. Yet this praise of Judaism is not directed at any particular wing of the faith such as the Essenes of Therapeutae, as some scholars have maintained; the peculiarities of, for instance, the ritual practices of these groups play no part here. Rather, the readers of this little tale are presented with a devout, open-minded Judaism characterized by loving-kindness, forgiveness and a profound spirituality.

POETIC LITERATURE

Jewish–Greek writers also tried to establish links with the great poetic tradition of Greece. A few samples from epic and dramatic works have come down to us, again mediated exclusively by Alexander Polyhistor; they too thus belong to the period around (or before) 100 B.C.E., though it is impossible to be more precise about the dating.

The epic poet *Philo* composed his poem 'On Jerusalem' in the tradition of city epics, a favourite genre in Hellenistic times. The three short fragments that have survived[1] cannot indeed give us a proper impression of the overall plan of the work which is said, perhaps erroneously, to have had at least fourteen volumes.[2] The fragments relate that it was Abraham who introduced circumcision, they tell of his sacrifice of Isaac, and of Joseph's reign in Egypt, and finally refer to two swimming baths in Jerusalem. The contents of the first fragment may be connected with Jerusalem in so far as Philo presumably equates the mountain in the land of Moriah (Gen. 22) with the Temple mount

[1] F 1–3: Euseb. *Praep. Evang.* IX.20, 24, 37. The epic poet Philo ought certainly not to be identified with his namesake, the author of a 'History of the Judean Kings' whose work we know only from two references and whom Josephus (*C.Ap.* 1.218) calls 'Philo the Elder' (see also Clem. Al. *Strom.* 1.141.3).

[2] F 2: Euseb. *Praep. Evang.* IX.24.1.

(2 Chron. 3.1); but the relevance of the Joseph fragment to Jerusalem is not at all clear. The poet uses a deliberately obscure, barely comprehensible language and spices his hexameters with obsolete or unusual vocabulary. Whether he wrote his epic in Jerusalem or in somewhere like Alexandria must remain open. The highly wrought artificial form may well suggest Alexandria; after all Pseudo-Aristeas too extolled the glory of Jerusalem from an Alexandrian point of view (Pseudo-Aristeas §§83–91).

The other epic poet, *Theodotus*, wrote his verse in plainer hexameters: a fragment of 47 lines has survived under the title 'Concerning the Jews'.[1] However, we must surely regard the poem as an epic about Shechem. For it seems to have opened with a description of the location of Shechem; only then does there appear to have been, by way of an introduction, a brief mention of Jacob's sojourn with Laban, his marriage and the birth of his children; thereafter the poem concentrated mainly on telling the story of Hamor and Dinah and the vengeance of the brothers Simeon and Levi on the inhabitants of Shechem (Gen. 34). Since the poem concentrates on Shechem, scholars formerly supposed the author Theodotus to be a Samaritan who through his epic aimed to glorify the centre of the sacrificial cult of his people. But the tendency of his writing is not in favour of the inhabitants of Shechem but of the sons of Jacob, who overcame Hamor and his people; their killing of the Shechemites is justified by reference to a divine oracle. Therefore recently some scholars have seen Theodotus as a Jewish author who by his poetry sought to justify the Hasmonean conquest of Samaria and the destruction of the temple on Mount Gerizim in 129–109 B.C.E.[2]

The poet *Ezekiel* tried to work up the Exodus from Egypt into a drama in the style of classical tragedy.[3] Two hundred and sixty nine iambic trimeters have come down to us. After a historical retrospect placed in the mouth of Moses, the action begins in Midian (which Ezekiel calls 'Libya'); it tells of the marriage to Zipporah, then of the confrontation with God in the episode of the burning bush, and of the mission entrusted to Moses to deliver Israel. In the prologue the voice of God speaks of the ten plagues. One fragment gives more detailed instructions about the Passover; the last two extant passages tell (in the form of a herald's report) of the crossing of the Red Sea and of the

[1] Euseb. *Praep. Evang.* IX.22.1–11.

[2] See for instance J. J. Collins, 'The epic of Theodotus and the Hellenism of the Hasmoneans', *HTR*, 73 (1980), 91–104.

[3] Euseb. *Praep. Evang.* IX.28.1–4; 29.4–16.

destruction of the Egyptian pursuers, and of the discovery of the oasis of Elim.

Thus as far as we can see Ezekiel does not always select episodes according to their dramatic force, presumably because the most exciting scenes would have been difficult to depict in the theatre; he prefers to use monologues for retrospective or anticipatory statements, together with the reports of messengers. We must ask ourselves, however, whether the author ever thought seriously in terms of a theatrical presentation of his work or whether, with due regard for dramaturgical laws, this is not primarily a literary composition. We do know that Philo occasionally visited the theatre;[1] but it is difficult to imagine a theatre run exclusively for the Jews.

But even if we view his work as a purely literary composition, Ezekiel obviously had a hard struggle to reconcile his given material with his chosen form. Doubtless this is also connected with the fact that as a devout Jew Ezekiel could not bring the real mover of the action, the God of Israel, on to the stage in person; consequently his dramatic scenes necessarily lack dynamism.

Ezekiel follows the text of the Septuagint closely and consistently. But he combines with this a remarkable familiarity with the Greek tragedians, especially Euripides, which enables him repeatedly to weave original tragic phrases into his text without creating an impression of being out for artificial effects. The formal skill here displayed by Ezekiel is at the same time a mirror of his intentions. By choosing a Greek literary form that had to be taken seriously, he seeks to preserve the religious tradition of his forefathers for his co-religionists who were imbued with a Hellenistic culture, and at the same time to make it attractive in literary terms to sympathetic non-Jewish readers.[2]

The instances of metric verse which we must now discuss ought to be seen not so much as tokens of the poetic spirit of the Hellenistic Jews but rather as attempts at an apologia, attempts to vindicate certain basic assumptions of Judaism through the ostensible testimony of famous Greek poets.

First of all there is a group of hexameters under the venerable names

[1] In *Omn. prob. lib.* 141 Philo reports that he attended a performance of Euripides.

[2] This leaves open, of course, the question of whether these attempts made any impact on non-Jewish readers; see on this point V. Tcherikover, 'Jewish apologetic literature reconsidered', *Eos,* 48, 3 (1956 = *Symbolae* R. *Taubenschlag dedicatae* (Wroclaw–Warsaw, 1957), 3, 169–93). The lines are preserved only in early Christian writings; see the next two notes.

of *Homer, Hesiod* and *Linus*; lines which Aristobulus cited as evidence for the cosmic significance of the number seven[1] and which must therefore have been extant as early as the first half of the second century B.C.E. Some of them are genuine, more or less unchanged Homeric lines; for the rest, it is not absolutely clear whether they are of Jewish origin or whether they stem from a Pythagorean collection which had been put together in order to aid speculation about the theory of numbers. A Jew like Aristobulus would have selected from an anthology of this kind those lines which seemed to him to underline the importance of the Sabbath.

There is no connection between these 'Sabbath verses' and a *gnomologion* of *dramatic lines* under the names of great Greek tragedians and comedy writers such as Aeschylus, Sophocles and Euripides, Menander, Diphilus and Philemon.[2] This ostensible anthology of quotations which probably originated in the first century B.C.E. or C.E. was obviously designed as an organic whole and attributes to the Greek poets what are essentially Jewish ideas, in particular the doctrine of the one God and the impossibility of creating an image in His likeness – the latter notion in conjunction with a polemic against graven images; furthermore, the doctrine of the end of the world and of retribution in the life to come for good and evil deeds on earth. A quotation from this gnomologion appears to have been cited in a flimsily attested (second) pseudo-Hecatean work 'On Abraham and the Egyptians'.[3] However, it is unjustifiable to ascribe the whole gnomologion to this Pseudo-Hecateus II on such slender grounds.

There are thematic and probably also chronological affinities between this gnomologion and the *pseudo-Orphic poem* which purports to be the last testament of the singer Orpheus, addressed to his son and disciple Museus. The original version proclaims the unity of God as the creator and ruler of the world and commends the reader to trust devoutly in him.[4] The first revised version speaks in addition of Abraham as the first man to perceive the true nature of the invisible God;[5] a second revision seems to have taught how God could be

[1] Aristobulus, F 5: Euseb. *Praep. Evang.* XIII.12.13–16. On what follows see N. Walter, *Der Thoraausleger Aristobulos*, TU 86 (Berlin, 1964), pp. 75–8 and 150–71.

[2] Preserved in the pseudo-Justinian writings *De monarchia dei* (2–4) and *Cohortatio ad Graecos* (15), also in Clem. Alex. *Protrepticus* 74 and *Strom.* V.113–33. See Walter, *Aristobulos*, pp. 172–201.

[3] Clem. Alex. *Strom.* V.113.1; see Jos. *Ant.* I.159 (cf. p. 402 n. 1).

[4] Transmitted in *De monarchia* 2 and *Cohortatio ad Graecos* 15, fragments also in Clem. Alex. *Protr.* 74 and *Strom.* V *passim*.

[5] This version too is cited by Clem. Alex. (*Strom.* V.123f).

recognized in his creation,[1] while a still later version introduced the Torah, which was mediated by Moses, as the means of coming to know God.[2] Finally an anonymous Christian writer of the fifth century C.E. strove to concoct a composite version out of all the versions of the poem known to him.[3] Thus in its complicated history the poem reflects the constant struggle of Hellenistic Jewish writers to solve the problem of how one could attain authentic knowledge of God. Precisely because of the immutable principle that God was essentially unknowable and impossible to depict in images, fresh statements were constantly demanded as to how one could say anything significant about this God as the creator and disposer of human destinies.

Finally in this section on pseudepigraphic poetic writings, we must not forget the Jewish sections of the *Sibylline Oracles*, that remarkable Hellenization of Jewish apocalyptic thinking, whose oldest parts (in the third book of *Sib.Or.*) were composed in Egypt under the reign of Ptolemy VIII Euergetes II Physcon (170–164 and 145–117 B.C.E.). The reader will find further details of these in chapter 12.

At the end of this brief survey of Jewish–Greek literature before Philo and Josephus, we must remember that we would know nothing about a substantial proportion of the relatively colourful palette of Jewish writing in Greek, were it not for the collector's zeal of the Greco-Roman author Alexander Polyhistor (about the middle of the last century B.C.E.) and later the great learning of men like Clement of Alexandria and especially Eusebius of Caesarea, who preserved for us, at least in fragmentary form, many of the works discussed here. How many more literary monuments may have simply disappeared without trace! But enough has survived to give us a vivid impression of the manifold ways in which Jewish authors of the second and first centuries B.C.E. engaged with the rich Hellenistic culture of their age. The literature that we have examined shows that the Greek-speaking Jews of these two centuries were able to derive from their intensive exposure to the Greek spirit and Greek culture the impulse to create their own cultural achievements in ways that were originally alien to them but which they succeeded in assimilating to their own faith and philosophy.

[1] This Stoic-type revision has been reconstructed by literary critics; it is not directly attested. See next note.

[2] Attested in Euseb. *Praep. Evang.* XIII.12.5 within an Aristobulus fragment; yet it is improbable that this late version was really an original part of the text of Aristobulus. On this point and on the history of how the pseudo-Orphic poem was handed down, see Walter, *Aristobulos*, pp. 103–15 and 202–61.

[3] The 'Tübinger Theosophie' edited by K. Buresch, *Klaros* (Leipzig, 1889) and also by H. Erbse, *Fragmente griechischer Theosophien* (Hamburg, 1941), §56.

CHAPTER 12

THE APOCRYPHA AND PSEUDEPIGRAPHA OF THE HELLENISTIC PERIOD

THE DEUTEROCANONICAL OR APOCRYPHAL BOOKS

It is important at the very outset to define some terms, for the lack of agreement over terminology between Catholic and Protestant works on this subject invites confusion. The books which Catholics customarily call 'deuterocanonical' correspond, or very nearly correspond, to what Protestants call the apocryphal books. The term 'deuterocanonical' is contrasted with 'protocanonical'. Now the protocanonical books are identical with those of the Hebrew Bible of Palestinian Judaism, and are the only ones which the Protestants officially accept. The deuterocanonical books appear in the Greek version of the Bible, the Septuagint. These two ancient collections of sacred writings, the one preserved in Hebrew, the other handed down in Greek, differ appreciably from one another. Apart from differences in the order of the books, and often quite important textual variants, the Septuagint is not a simple reproduction in Greek of the Hebrew Old Testament. It contains several writings which do not appear in the Hebrew canon at all, and these are the ones which the Catholics call deuterocanonical. The adjectives 'protocanonical' and 'deuterocanonical' applied to the Scriptures were not used before the sixteenth century, and are generally believed to have been invented by Sixtus of Siena (1520–1569) in his *Bibliotheca Sacra* of 1566. Catholics recognize seven deuterocanonical books: Judith, Tobit, 1 and 2 Maccabees, Wisdom, Ecclesiasticus and Baruch. To these must be added the Greek portions of Esther and the Greek additions to Daniel, i.e., the Prayer of Azariah and the Song of the Three Young Men (called in the older English versions the Song of the Three Holy Children), the story of Susanna and the story of Bel and the Dragon. The Protestants include in the Apocrypha, as well as these deuterocanonical works recognized by Catholics, the Prayer of Manasseh, the Third Book of Esdras (called 1 Esdras in the English Apocrypha), and sometimes also the Fourth Book of Esdras (or 4 Ezra; in the English Apocrypha this appears as chapters 3 to 14 of 2 Esdras), and 3 and 4 Maccabees. To clarify the differences of usage further it should be added that in Catholic terminology the canonical Ezra is called 1 Esdras and the canonical Nehemiah is 2 Esdras.

The reformers thought of the apocryphal books as edifying and at first continued to print them in an appendix to their Bibles, though there was not always exact agreement as to which books should be included. In this they were following the practice of the fathers, for those fathers who omitted the deuterocanonical works from their lists of sacred writings still continued to commend them to the faithful to be read for edification, continued to quote them and make use of them in their writings, and went so far as to defend them against attacks by heretics. Origen and Epiphanius both took this stand, and so did Jerome, notwithstanding his staunch defence of the *veritas hebraica*. Such, therefore, was the standing of the apocryphal books in the early Church. St Augustine made it his business to champion the canonicity of the new books. He was followed by numerous fathers and by the councils of Hippo (393) and Carthage (397), and his view prevailed practically everywhere until the Reformation.

Neither the Protestant nor the Catholic designation is at all satisfactory. To speak of deuterocanonical and protocanonical works suggests that there once existed two canons. Now originally there existed nothing of the kind. There never were two closed and distinct canons, one for the Palestinian Jews, one for the Hellenistic Jews. In the beginning only the Torah was regarded as binding and there was a duty to read it in its entirety in the synagogues. This is why among the Alexandrian Jews the Torah alone had been officially translated into Greek. The Greek-speaking Jews living in Egypt and elsewhere did not receive from their fellow-Jews of Palestine a closed canon, or for that matter, any canon at all in the modern sense of the word. What they did, in fact, was to complete the collection that had been handed down to them in a way they considered appropriate, and the Jews saw no reason to take exception to the additions which the Septuagint made. If arguments did go on between the two branches of Judaism, they concerned the Greek translation of numerous passages of the Hebrew text which the Palestinian Jews alleged that the translators had got wrong. It should be added that the discovery of the Qumran manuscripts has significantly modified the ideas that had hitherto been held about the history of the canon. The Qumran documents show that there were Jewish circles where ideas about the canon were entertained which were very different from those of official Pharisaic Judaism. The Psalms scroll from cave 11, for example, contains non-canonical Psalms mixed with canonical ones, and shows the Psalter to have been a section of the canon which was particularly open.[1] The fixing of the Hebrew canon only took place as a result of the work of the Jewish scholars of Jamnia between 85 and 100 C.E.

In addition, for certain deuterocanonical books the problem arises of what their original language was, Hebrew or Aramaic. When we consider the original language of the writings there is less difference between the Palestinian and Alexandrian canons than appears at first sight. This question of the original language of the deuterocanonical writings is one that already engaged the attention of Jerome, anxious as he was to follow throughout the *veritas hebraica*.

As for the description 'apocryphal books', even though it is an ancient one going back at least as far as St Cyril of Jerusalem (*Catechetical Lectures* IV.33, 35), it is no happier a designation than 'deuterocanonical'. As applied to literature, the adjective ἀπόκρυφα (contrasted with κανονικά) has more than one meaning. A book may be called 'apocryphal', that is, 'hidden', either because it is deemed to have been hidden deliberately or because its origin is hidden, that is, unknown. In the first case, a book may be hidden because what it contains is of exceptional worth and ought only to be made known to those of more perfect knowledge, i.e. the wise among the people. Such books are more or less esoteric, as for example those used by the gnostics, like the Gospel of Thomas, or the books of Zarathushtra. According to Clement of Alexandria (*Stromateis* 1.15.69) the reading of the latter was reserved to themselves by the disciples of a certain Prodicus. Apocryphal books of this type correspond more or less to those called by the rabbis the *sepharim ḥiṣonim*, 'the outside books', that is, the books outside the canon.

But a book could also be 'hidden' because it was of inferior value, either because of the material state of the copy or because of what it contained. If a book was dirty or damaged and for this reason could no longer be used in the Synagogue it was hidden (*ganaz*), in fact buried, and the special hiding place for books was given the name of *Genizah*. The best known Genizah is that of the synagogue at El-Fusṭaṭ in old Cairo, where many thousands of fragments of Hebrew manuscripts were discovered. Alternatively, if a book's content was suspect it met the same fate as one which had suffered physical damage.

[1] F. M. Cross, 'The history of the biblical text in the light of discoveries in the Judaean desert', *HTR*, 57 (1964), 281–99, distinguishes three major recensions of the Old Testament around the beginning of the Christian era: the Egyptian text (the Septuagint and some texts from Qumran), the Palestinian text, and the Babylonian, which became the Masoretic text. On the history of the fixation of the Hebrew canon, see F. M. Cross in vol. 3 of this series.

In some cases, finally, books whose origin was unknown came to be treated as apocryphal and were made use of by the heretics, who exploited the belief in ancient sacred books. From this arose the notion of apocryphal books as books which had been falsified, and this pejorative sense was the one which the word 'apocryphal' eventually assumed. For all these reasons, the use of the word 'apocrypha' to describe an entire group of biblical books would seem nowadays to be quite improper. To this it must be added that the Protestant use of the word 'apocrypha' leads to confusion in another direction, since Catholics use the very same word to designate those works which Protestants call pseudepigrapha.

What is to be understood by a 'pseudepigraphical book'? In Protestant usage the pseudepigraphical books are those which are outside the canon of Scripture and which are ascribed to spurious authors. These include, for example, the *Testaments of the Twelve Patriarchs*, which are credited to the twelve Patriarchs themselves; the *Testament of Abraham*, ascribed to Abraham; and the *Apocalypse of Baruch*, ostensibly written by Baruch. The literary device of pseudepigraphy or pseudonymity has been employed in many literatures,[1] and in the area that concerns us at the moment there are examples of it in the very midst of the canonical literature of the Old Testament. Various Wisdom books, for example, are attributed to Solomon, although that king of Israel had nothing to do with their composition. Several different explanations have been offered for the pseudonymity of the works under discussion. In the case of the pseudonymous apocalypses, such as that of Daniel, the risk of persecution has been advanced as a reason for the author to hide his real identity. But if this were the motive, anonymity would have been sufficient. Some have sought the explanation in the appeal that these alleged recipients of revelation, with their great antiquity, would have had for Jewish readers. It has also been argued that the authority of the Torah was such that it was difficult to put forward new revelations which did not appear in the Law unless they were ascribed to prestigious figures of the past. This last explanation is not unconvincing. As far as the canonical book of Daniel is concerned, Rowley proposed what seems to be a plausible solution. Daniel was chosen as the figure who received and wrote down the visions in order to indicate that they came from the same anonymous author or authors who produced the Daniel

[1] J. A. Sint, *Pseudonymität im Altertum* (Innsbruck, 1960); W. Speyer, *Die literarische Fälschung im heidnischen und christlichen Altertum. Ein Versuch ihrer Deutung* (Munich, 1971).

stories.[1] In favour of this explanation of Rowley's I might add that the affinity between the literary genres of midrash and apocalyptic would make it all the easier to attribute them to a single fictitious author, Daniel. It was only among Daniel's apocalyptic imitators that pseudonymity became a somewhat artificial device. It must further be remembered that the description 'Old Testament Pseudepigrapha' is an especially badly chosen one because it cannot be restricted to the extra-canonical books. A number of canonical books in the Old Testament itself are pseudepigraphical. To employ such terminology is to risk confusing works of very different periods and to imply that they make up a single corpus of literature, which is not the case. The expression 'apocrypha and pseudepigrapha of the Old Testament' has been popularized in the realm of biblical scholarship by the well-known collections of Kautzsch[2] and Charles.[3] But it is necessary to combat this usage.

What are we to say of the term 'inter-testamental literature'?[4] This is a term which is made use of especially in the English-speaking world and was introduced for the very reason that it avoids the difficulties indicated above. It is a much better description that the two preceding ones, offering a certain advantage from the historical point of view especially. It is meant to remind us that there is not really any literary gap between Malachi, the last book of the Hebrew Bible, and Matthew, the first book of the New Testament corpus. An entire literature, in fact, came into being during the Hellenistic and Roman periods which has not been universally recognized as holy scripture.[5] But to speak of the literature of the inter-testamental period is to take up a decisively Christian standpoint, for none but Christians allow the existence of two testaments. This description is therefore unusable for anyone looking at the subject from a purely Jewish angle, even though the rabbinic world did not know the literature concerned, or gave it a hostile reception. It is worth pointing out that even from the point of view of

[1] H. H. Rowley, *The Relevance of Apocalyptic*, 3rd edn. (London, 1963); M. Delcor, *Le libre de Daniel* (Paris, 1971), p. 26.

[2] E. Kautzsch, *Die Apokryphen und Pseudepigraphen des Alten Testaments* (2 vols., Tübingen, 1900).

[3] R. H. Charles (ed.), *The Apocrypha and Pseudepigrapha of the Old Testament* (2 vols., Oxford, 1913).

[4] A recent small book by D. S. Russell is entitled, *Between the Testaments* (London, 1960), and R. H. Charles, as early as 1914, published his *Religious Development between the Old and the New Testament* (London–New York–Toronto, 1914).

[5] A new edition of these writings which is in process of publication in German under the direction of W. G. Kümmel has retained a purely historical title: *Jüdische Schriften aus hellenistisch-römischer Zeit* (Gütersloh, 1973–).

chronology the term is not entirely appropriate, for some of these writings are earlier than certain books of the Apocrypha, whilst others are later than the last book of the New Testament.

It is understandable, therefore, why P. Riessler, attempting to avoid the drawbacks of the accepted terms, should have chosen a somewhat imprecise title for his book which appeared in German in 1928: 'Ancient Jewish writings outside the Bible'.[1] Similar arguments operated to produce the title of a collection of recent studies devoted to the subject at the biblical conference at Louvain in 1969 and edited by W. C. van Unnik: 'Jewish literature between Tenakh and Mishnah.'[2] 'Tenakh' is the Jewish acronym for the Hebrew Bible, which is composed of *Torah, Nebi'im* and *Kethubim*. The literature which is here being studied, therefore, is that which is situated between the Hebrew Bible and the Mishnah, the collection of Jewish legal material compiled by Rabbi Judah the Prince I (135–200 C.E.). This means that it covers a period of about three hundred years, namely the last two pre-Christian centuries and the first century of the common era. It seems to us likewise that the best description of this body of literature is that which designates it by the period of its production, that is, the Hellenistic and Roman periods.

From the literary point of view these writings are far from being a unity. In the so-called 'deuterocanonical' collection a number of different literary genres may be distinguished: the teachings of Wisdom writers, edifying stories of midrashic type, and several varieties of historical accounts. The 'deuterocanonical' or 'apocryphal' writings reflect a similar variety of literary types to the *Kethubim* or hagiographa, and have in common their late date. The 'pseudepigrapha', for their part, are not a homogeneous unity either. Though it is often difficult to classify them, it is nevertheless possible to pick out from this group some books which belong to the testamentary literature, some which are of apocalyptic type, and some which are midrashic or haggadic. All these writings are marked in general by a certain lack of spontaneity, and by a high degree of textual fluidity, a feature which they have in common with the hagiographical writings; for these latter, too, often appear in diverse recensions, longer or shorter, and have been subjected to numerous re-workings. Thus one often finds oneself dealing with a fluctuating text whose original is difficult to establish or to date.

[1] P. Riessler, *Altjüdisches Schrifttum ausserhalb der Bibel* (Heidelberg, 1928; repr. Darmstadt, 1966).

[2] W. C. van Unnik (ed.), *La littérature juivre entre Tenach et Mischna. quelques problèmes*, RechBib 9 (Leiden, 1974).

But from the point of view of Christian doctrine these writings are in general of the highest importance, for they prepare the way for the New Testament period.

ECCLESIASTICUS OR SIRACH (THE WISDOM OF JESUS BEN SIRA)

THE TITLE

In Greek the book of Ecclesiasticus bears the title: 'Wisdom of Jesus son of Sirach'. The author's name is thus given to us at the outset. Ecclesiasticus is practically unique in biblical literature in that the author mentions himself by his own name at the end of his work, adding that he comes from Jerusalem (50:27). A variant in some Greek manuscripts makes him a priest. The Hebrew text does not call him Jesus but 'Simon, son of Jesus, son of Eleazar, son of Sira' (50:27) which constitutes a small divergence from the Greek. The Latin name Ecclesiasticus, which has been in use since the time of Cyprian, has not yet been satisfactorily explained. It probably alludes to the use of the book in the moral catechesis of the Church.

THE TEXT AND THE HISTORY OF THE BOOK

For a long time the text of Ecclesiasticus was known only in Greek. But St Jerome had seen a Hebrew text of the book, though he did not himself make a new translation of it into Latin. Because of the low esteem in which he held the deuterocanonical works he was content to transcribe the Old Latin text without changing it. In the tenth century Saadya Gaon still knew a Hebrew text, but the Hebrew Ben Sira was eventually lost until there were discovered, in 1896 to 1900 in the Genizah of a synagogue in Old Cairo, portions of five Hebrew manuscripts of Ecclesiasticus, totalling about two-thirds of the book in all. The manuscripts dated from the eleventh or twelfth centuries. Since that time our knowledge of the Hebrew text of Ben Sira has grown further. Two fragments of the work were among the finds from Qumran cave 2. The ms. was dated on paleographical grounds to the second half of the first century B.C.E. Qumran cave 11 provided a fragment of the same book (51:13ff). Y. Yadin, too, discovered, during the excavations at Masada, some Hebrew fragments whose text is basically the same as that of the Cairo manuscripts. Again on paleographical grounds, this fragmentary copy is dated between 100 and 70

B.C.E.; it is therefore the oldest manuscript of the book which we possess.[1]

The prologue to the Greek version says explicitly that the book had been translated from Hebrew into Greek by Ben Sira's grandson for the use of the Alexandrian Jews among whom he was living. He dates his activity in the thirty-eighth year of Ptolemy VII Euergetes (170–116 B.C.E.). It was therefore about 132 B.C.E. that the author's grandson translated the work. The question of the authenticity of the Hebrew text has been debated ever since the Cairo Genizah fragments were found. Though many scholars have accepted its originality a number of others have cast doubt upon it, claiming that the Hebrew is a re-translation from the Greek, from Syriac, or even from Persian. Recent discoveries and the work which they have prompted militate in favour of authenticity. The successive stages in the history of the text may be envisaged as follows: in the first quarter of the second century B.C.E. Ben Sira wrote his book in Palestine, in Hebrew. Around 132 his grandson made a Greek translation. At the same time copies were circulating in Palestine, where the work commended itself especially to the Qumran sect, the Essenes, probably because of its mention of the Zadokite priests. At the Synod of Jamnia, at the end of the first century C.E., the rabbis excluded Ecclesiasticus from the canon and only a few copies of it in Hebrew remained in circulation. It was from one Hebrew manuscript that the Syriac translation was made, by a Christian, in the second century C.E. At the end of the eighth century the Hebrew text of Ben Sira was discovered in a cave near Jericho, doubtless one of those same caves, in the neighbourhood of Khirbet Qumran, where the scrolls were discovered from 1947 onwards. The Karaites who rediscovered the Hebrew manuscript of Ben Sira made several copies of it. It is possible that, because of the bad state of preservation of the manuscript and the difficulty of reading it, they re-translated from the Syriac some passages lacking in the Hebrew text.[2]

CONTENT

Ben Sira's work by its very nature lends itself to such upheavals. It is an unordered collection of sayings on very diverse subjects. The Greek

[1] Cf. Y. Yadin, *The Ben Sira Scroll from Masada with introduction, emendations and commentary* (Jerusalem, 1965).

[2] Cf. A. A. di Lella, *The Hebrew Text of Sirach* (The Hague, 1966), pp. 150–1; M. Delcor, 'Le texte hébreu du Cantique de Siracide li, 13 et ss. et les anciennes versions', *Textus,* 6 (1968), 27–47. Cf. also H. P. Rüger, *Text und Textform in hebräischen Sirach*, BZAW 112 (Berlin, 1970).

sprinkled the work with subtitles (1:1; 18:30; 20:27; 23:7; 24:1; 30:1, 14, 16; 32:1; 33:25; 44:1; 51:1), but these headings usually relate only to the short passages which follow them and do not constitute a real structuring of the book. Only the title in 44:1, 'Hymn to the fathers', also occurs in the Hebrew text, and it does refer to an important block of material (44 to 50). Clearer subdivisions are marked by two short epilogues (24:28–32 and 33:16–18) analogous to the final epilogue (50:27–9, 51:13–30). This suggests that a shorter original book has been expanded in successive stages.

In the body of the book a number of *poems in praise of Wisdom or of God the Creator* serve at the same time to divide the book and to bind together the shorter collections of which it is composed. A hymn to Wisdom opens the series (1:1–10), and the hymn is extended by a group of sayings concerning wisdom and the fear of God (1:11–30). Next come the basic elements of growth in wisdom. Courage, founded on patience and trust, is necessary for entry upon a career as a wise man (chapter 2). The first steps are in filial piety (3:1–16); respect for all that is beyond a beginner's capabilities (3:17–27); and the doing of works of charity, which 'rubs the corners' off the apprentice wise man and makes him lovable to men and to God (3:28 to 4:10). This brings us to a hymn in praise of Wisdom, who exalts her sons to glory by passing them through disciplinary tests (4:11–19).

In the following collection of sayings the disciple learns to *discern what is truly good*; shame both good and bad; the difference between confidence and presumption; the benefits and dangers of friendship (4:20 to 6:17). A new invitation to the reader to subject himself to the instruction of the wise, in courage and modesty, and in the fear of God (6:18–37), opens a collection of sayings which introduce the disciple to the great world and to social life (7:1 to 14:19). All the components of human society are examined; family life and working life; priests and poor; the old in their decline, and the dead; the irascible, the fools, all the different human temperaments; women, friends, powerful men and princes. The teacher derives lessons from all these, to point his disciple to that difficult middle way in the use of this world's goods, for in death we have neither honours nor riches. But it is not the thought of death so much as the fear of God which has the last word in this section. The praise of the wise man who fears God (14:20 to 15:10), and a series of thoughts on man's place before God (15:11 to 16:21), are rounded off by a hymn to the Creator (16:22 to 18:14).

In the pleasant, rather free collection which follows there comes through as the dominant theme a double warning against excesses of the tongue on the one hand and the temptations of covetousness on the other (18:15 to 23:27). After a prayer for the grace of self-mastery (23:1–6) the series ends with warnings against the misuse of speech (23:7–15), and against adultery (23:16–27). In imitation of Proverbs 1 to 9, where a hymn in praise of Wisdom follows warnings against adultery (Prov. 7 to 8), the collection finishes with a poem in which Wisdom sings her own praise (24:1–29).

In the *epilogue* of 24:30–34 the teacher encourages his pupil to draw deeply, as he himself has done, from the fountains of Wisdom. Thus the manual of the apprentice wise man comes to a close. In its apparent disorder it is possible to trace a progressive initiation into the study and practice of wisdom.

A *first supplement* (25:1 to 33:18) ends with a similar though shorter epilogue (33:16–18). The main interest is in the fear of God. Some themes recur insistently: women (25:1, 12–26; 26:1–18); conversations (27:4–24) and disputes (28:8–26); duties to one's neighbour (29:1–20); domestic peace, rooted in moderation (29:21 to 32:24).

The *last supplement* is a kind of testament of the teacher. Thoughts of death form the framework of it (33:19–23 and 41:1–13) and come to the surface more than once in the body of it. The legacy the wise man leaves is his long experience, which is not confined within the limits of his own people (34:9 to 36:17). He has learnt much from his contact with men (36:18 to 37:26), always preserving that moderation which is so vital to health (37:27 to 38:23). All trades and professions are worthy of honour, for all render service to society, but the part of the wise man is better than all the others (38:24 to 39:11). This thought fills the old teacher with exaltation (39:12–15) and he sings a hymn to the Lord in whose works Wisdom is revealed (39:16–35). From this there is a natural transition to the praise of God in creation (42:15 to 43:33), and to the praise of those who, by the wisdom granted to them by God, carry on his work (44 to 50). Throughout Ben Sira's book, though by our standards it is not well ordered, a continuous motion, like a series of waves, carries the reader, or rather the disciple, from the practice of wisdom to the contemplation of God, of God exhibited in his well ordered works, in the world and in mankind.

SOURCES AND LITERARY GENRE

Ben Sira makes his appearance as the last of the wise. He implies this himself through the images he uses. He describes himself as the gleaner who comes after the grape-gatherers, or as the grape-gatherer who tops up the winepress (33:16). What he has to offer is what he has found among the wise who preceded him and among the prophets whose teachings he ponders (39:1). Indeed, though actual quotations from the Old Testament are very rare in Ecclesiasticus,[1] there are many reminiscences, not only of Proverbs, but also of the prophets and the Psalms. Ben Sira employs what has been called an anthological style, a shared subject leading to a shared vocabulary. He has been nourished on the Bible and meditates on it constantly, but he seems also to have been influenced by stoicism,[2] which is not surprising in an author who prides himself on being widely travelled (34:11). It is also recognized that he has made extensive use of the *Wisdom of Ahikar*.[3] Ecclesiasticus is not merely, as Schürer has put it, 'a non-canonical doublet of the canonical Proverbs'.[4] Ben Sira, when he pictures the learned man pouring forth his words of wisdom (39:6), is presenting himself as rather like the scribe in the gospel, who brings out from his treasure things both new and old (Matt. 13:52). Ben Sira is not only the last of the wise men, he is the first of the scribes (*sopher*), for he is above all a man of the book (*sepher*), which he studies in order to search out (*darash*) the 'Law' (32:15), the Law and Wisdom being identified (6:37). The scribe invites his disciples to resort to him and to lodge in his school, which he calls 'the house of study' (*beth midrash*) (51:23). An activity concerned entirely with the sacred books (*midrash*) is thus mentioned here for the first time in Scripture.

The prologue to Ecclesiasticus describes the book as a work 'pertaining to instruction and wisdom'. We thus expect to find in it the classical literary forms of Wisdom writing. The basic component of Ben Sira's work is the *mashal*. Accordingly, as Jerome informs us, the book was known among the Jews as *Meshalim*, 'Proverbs'. A *mashal* may be a simple maxim or proverb, in the usual sense of that word (4:20–31; 9:10–18), or it may be a more extended unit, such as Proverbs chapters 1, 9, or 25 to 27. Such longer units are found in Ecclesiasticus in chapters 1; 4:11–19; 6:18–37. Sometimes a series of sayings is connected by the repetition of a single expression, for example, 'the fear of God' (1:11–30). There is also the numerical *mashal* which puts its observations in a progressive list (25:7–11). Ben Sira also combines the two techniques and produces what one might call a second order numerical *mashal* (40:18–27). He knows, too, how to produce a pen portrait, such as that of the scribe, which is then contrasted with those

1 J. G. Snaith, 'Biblical quotations in the Hebrew of Ecclesiasticus', *JTS*, n.s. 18 (1967), 1–12.

2 R. Pautrel, 'Ben Sira et le stoïcisme', *RSR*, 51 (1963), 535–49.

3 F. Nau, *Histoire et Sagesse d'Ahiqar l'assyrien* (Paris, 1907), pp. 60–3.

4 E. Schürer, *The History of the Jewish people in the time of Christ*, vol. 3 I (Edinburgh, 1986), pp. 188–9.

of the workmen (38:25 to 39:11). But he lacks the mastery of the classical Hebrew writers (Prov. 5:7; compare Sirach 23:16–27). His eulogies of Wisdom (1:1–10; 24:1–22) are inferior to his models (Job 28, Prov. 8). On the other hand, he comes into his own with a fine gallery of historical portraits (44 to 50). For Ben Sira, exhortation is paramount, and his exhortations achieve a certain warmth, in strong contrast to the impersonal tone of the older proverbs (Prov. 10 to 22). He likes to take the stage in person (24:30–4; 33:16–18; 39:12–16; 51:13–22) in the manner of the Wisdom Psalms (Pss. 34 and 37, among others). Embedded in his work are several complete hymns, and hymnic passages and songs of thanksgiving (16:18–19; 39:12–16; 42:15 to 43:33; 50:22–4). He also writes lamentations (22:27 to 23:6). These passages are interesting since they are evidence of the later development of the literary genres which appear in the psalter.

In short, what the author has aimed at producing is a biblical book, exhibiting all the literary characteristics of such a work. And this he has achieved, even though from a literary standpoint he falls short of his predecessors.

THE TEACHING OF THE BOOK

Ben Sira's work is a faithful mirror of the traditional theology of his time. To put it in perspective we must stress that the book was produced before the great conflicts of the Maccabean era, when in Palestine itself Judaism and Hellenism clashed head on. The book was able, therefore, to play a part in forming the characters of those who then took their stand against the dangerous attractions of a triumphant Greek culture. One of the central ideas in Ben Sira's teaching is that of the fear of the Lord (φόβος Κυρίου). The concept appears persistently on nearly every page.[1] In his very first chapter the author asserts that the beginning of wisdom is to fear God (1:14). It is a glory, an honour and a joy (1:12). The fear of God is rewarded with long life (1:12). It proceeds from an absolute trust in God (2:8); it shows itself in obedience and faithfulness to the commandments (2:15), and in respect for parents (3:7). But the fear of God makes its demands: it requires great sacrifices, for the service of God may begin with much testing (2:1–6). It must be said that the courage of Ben Sira's disciples in the face of the persecutions brought on by Antiochus IV Epiphanes

[1] For a complete list of the occurrences of this expression in the Greek, Syriac and Hebrew witnesses to the text, see the table in J. Haspecker, *Gottesfurcht bei Jesus Sirach. Ihre religiöse Struktur und ihre literarische und doktrinäre Bedeutung* (Rome, 1967), pp. 48–9.

demonstrates the efficacy of his teaching. They had learnt from him a pride in their faith and a contempt for death. Nevertheless, his book is not by any means simply a reaction against Greek paganism; on the contrary. In Ben Sira's time such an attitude would doubtless have been premature.

THE INFLUENCE OF BEN SIRA AND HIS LIMITATIONS

After the collapse of Jewish religious institutions in 70 C.E., and the disappearance of the Sadducees, who had been up to that time the backbone of Judaism, the Synod of Jamnia carried out a purge of the Scriptures, and the work of this decent, upright man did not escape it. The Talmud justifies the rejection of the book, listing its faults as misogyny, epicureanism and misanthropy. Rabbi Akiba, according to the Jerusalem Talmud, reckoned it among the 'outside books' (*s^epharim ḥiṣonim*), the works of the *minim*, that is, the heretics. Though it was thus under suspicion in classical Judaism the book was highly regarded among the Essenes of Qumran, and by their spiritual heirs, the Karaites. The latter claimed a connection with Zadok the priest, who is known from some of the Qumran texts and is mentioned in the Hebrew of Sirach 51:12.[1] Attention has also been drawn to certain affinities between Ecclesiasticus and the Qumran texts.[2]

In spite of being treated with suspicion, Ben Sira's book nevertheless exercised a great influence over rabbinic Judaism. It is generally maintained that the doctrine of the 'evil inclination', which the Tannaim regarded as a component of sinful human personality, is already found in Sirach 15:14.[3] Quotations and frequent echoes of the book have been found in the Talmud, in the midrashic commentaries on the Bible and in the works of well-known medieval Jewish authors. Jewish liturgy, as well as Christian, has made use of it.[4] The pseudepigraphical literature (*Slavonic Enoch* and the *Psalms of Solomon*) reflect knowledge of it. Clement of Alexandria quotes it so frequently that his works are as important for the establishment of its text as the biblical manuscripts themselves.

However, Ben Sira has his limitations. As far as the afterlife and

1 Cf. J. Trinquet, 'Les liens "sadocites" de l'écrit de Damas, des manuscrits de la Mer Morte et de l'Ecclésiastique', *VT*, 1 (1951), 287–92.

2 Cf. M. R. Lehmann, 'Ben Sira and the Qumran literature', *RevQ*, 3 (1961–2), 103–16; J. Carmignac, 'Les rapports entre l'Ecclésiastique et Qumrân', *RevQ*, 3 (1961–2), 209–18.

3 For a contrary opinion see J. Hadot, *Penchant mauvais et volonté libre dans la Sagesse de Ben Sira (L'Ecclésiastique)* (Brussels, 1970).

4 Cf. C. Roth, 'Ecclesiasticus in the synagogue service', *JBL*, 71 (1952), 171–8.

human destiny are concerned he attains to no certainty at all. The blessings of which he speaks are terrestrial ones, and they are promised to the pious man or to his children. We have to wait for the Maccabean crisis before the problem of death is answered by the promise of the martyrs' resurrection. Nor does Ben Sira recognize any place in the plan of salvation for the Davidic Messiah.[1] He has sometimes been criticized for identifying Wisdom too closely with the Law. However, in this respect he hardly does more than continue a line of thought initiated by Deut. 4:5–8 and carried on by the prophets (Isa. 2:3 and 51:4) and the psalmists (Pss. 19, 119 etc.). According to this strand of thinking the Law is a manifestation of the word of God, which governs both the harmony of the world and the conduct of men.[2] This is the same line of development which leads to the *logos* theology of St John's gospel.[3]

In spite of his limitations, Christian readers may none the less feel at home with Ben Sira. To sum up, 'his charm lies in the good-natured way in which he approaches every problem and finds moderate but sound solutions, in conformity with the religion of his fathers'.[4]

ETHIOPIC ENOCH, OR THE ENOCHIC CORPUS

The book of Enoch is very badly named, for it does not consist of a single book but an entire corpus. This corpus includes within it works of various dates whose only common feature is that they ostensibly record revelations made to the antediluvian patriarch, Enoch.

Until a relatively short time ago all that was known of this literature was an Ethiopic version, containing the whole corpus, and a Greek and a Latin version, only preserved in part. Fragments in Aramaic and Hebrew were discovered among the manuscripts at Qumran. A very small Coptic fragment has also been found, covering the section 93:3–8.[5] Bruce in 1773 brought back three copies of Ethiopic manuscripts of Enoch from Ethiopia but they were left for some time in the libraries before being published. The first published partial translation, into

[1] Cf. A. Caquot, 'Ben Sira et le Messianisme', *Semitica,* 12 (1966), 43–68.

[2] Cf. A. Robert, 'Le sens du mot Loi dans le Ps. cxix (Vulg. cxviii)', *RB,* 46 (1937), 182–206.

[3] Cf. C. Spicq, 'Le Siracide et la structure littéraire du prologue de S. Jean', *Mémorial Lagrange* (Paris, 1940), pp. 183–95.

[4] Cf. H. Duesberg and I. Fransen, *Les Scribes inspirés: Introduction aux livres sapientiaux de la Bible* (Maredsous, 1966), p. 657.

[5] S. Donadoni, 'Un frammento della versione copta del "Libro di Enoch"', *AcOr,* 25 (1960), 197ff.

Latin, was brought out by Silvestre de Sacy in 1800, on the basis of the Paris manuscript.[1] The first edition of the Ethiopic text was produced by R. Laurence in 1838 on the basis of the manuscript brought back by Bruce and kept in the Bodleian library in Oxford.[2] Dillmann used five manuscripts in his edition of 1851.[3] Flemming's edition which appeared in 1902 lists twenty-six manuscripts.[4] That of Charles refers to twenty-three, although his translation lists twenty-nine.[5] Most of these date from the seventeenth and eighteenth centuries, the oldest being from the sixteenth century.[6] The book of Enoch often appears in manuscripts with the Ethiopic Bible.

The Ethiopic text is of course a translation, probably from Greek. In fact, many unintelligible passages in the Ethiopic text are explicable as renderings of a misread Greek exemplar. But the Greek text which underlies the Ethiopic is not itself the original, for the original was Semitic, either Hebrew or Aramaic. The extant Greek text is fragmentary and is primarily preserved in quotations from it made by George Syncellus in his *Chronography*. Several editions of these quotations have been produced.[7] There is also a fragment in the Vatican library.[8] At the end of last century in Egypt two quite considerable papyrus fragments of Enoch were discovered in a tomb, during the excavations of the necropolis at Akhmim-Panopolis,[9] but the text is of poor quality. It comes from the sixth century.[10] A significant portion of the Greek text was found among the papyri acquired by Chester Beatty and the University of Michigan.[11] It contains the closing chapters of the

[1] A. I. Silvestre de Sacy, 'Notice du Livre d'Hénoch', *Magasin Encyclopédique*, Year 6, vol. 1 (1800), 382ff. This Latin translation was reproduced by R. Laurence, *The Book of Enoch the Prophet* (Oxford, 1821), pp. 169–180.

[2] R. Laurence, *Libri Henochi Prophetae Versio Aethiopica* (Oxford, 1838), p. xv.

[3] A. Dillmann, *Liber Henoch Aethiopice* (Leipzig, 1851).

[4] J. Flemming, *Das Buch Henoch. Äthiopischer Text*, TU 7 (Leipzig, 1902).

[5] R. H. Charles, *The Ethiopic Version of the Book of Enoch, edited from twenty-three manuscripts together with the fragmentary Greek and Latin Versions* (Oxford, 1906); R. H. Charles, *The Book of Enoch or 1 Enoch translated from the Editor's Ethiopic Text* (Oxford, 1912), pp. xxi–xxiv.

[6] Cf. now M. A. Knibb, *The Ethiopic Book of Enoch. A new edition in the light of the Aramaic Dead Sea Fragments*, 2 vols. (Oxford, 1978).

[7] H. B. Swete, *The Old Testament in Greek* (3 vols., Cambridge, 1899): vol. 3, pp. 788–809 and appendix pp. 897–9; J. Flemming and L. Radermacher, *Das Buch Henoch* (Leipzig, 1901); Charles, *Enoch...translated*, pp. 273–305.

[8] A. Mai, ed. *Nova Patrum Bibliotheca*, 2 (Rome, 1844).

[9] U. Bouriant, *Fragments grecs du Libre d'Hénoch* (Paris, 1892); A. Lods, *L'Evangile et l'Apocalypse de Pierre. Le Texte grec du Libre d'Enoch* (Paris, 1893).

[10] F. G. Kenyon, *The Palaeography of Greek Papyri* (Oxford, 1899), p. 119.

[11] C. Bonner and H. C. Youtie, *The Last Chapters of Enoch in Greek*, SD 8 (London, 1937).

work (97:6 to 104 and 106 to 107). It lacks chapters 105 and 108. The Greek version of Enoch always quotes the Bible in the Hebrew form of the text, never in its Septuagintal form. The chronology of the patriarchs does not follow that given in the Greek Bible, but that found in the Samaritan Pentateuch. A number of Hebrew words which were not understood by the translator have been transcribed into Greek. Everything therefore seems to indicate that the original of Enoch was written in Hebrew. However, we shall return to this problem later.

The Latin version is found in a fragment discovered in the British Museum by James. It consists of a very imperfect rendering of Enoch 106:1–18. It was published by its discoverer in 1893.[1] It was known that several Latin authors such as Tertullian, Hilary and Priscillian quote passages of Enoch, but it was wondered whether they might not be taking their citations from a Greek text. The discovery of the Latin fragment corroborates the theory that a Latin version of Enoch did exist.

One of the problems which arises in connection with this book is that of its original language. Writers on the subject have acknowledged that it must have been written in either Hebrew or Aramaic. The earliest defender of a Hebrew original was the French scholar J. Halévy.[2] Schmidt on the other hand maintained that the original was Aramaic.[3] As for Charles, he supposed that, like the book of Daniel, it was written partly in Hebrew and partly in Aramaic.[4] At first sight, the Qumran discoveries seem to favour this last theory. Aramaic fragments were recovered from cave 4 which represent every section of the book except the section called 'the Similitudes'.[5] By contrast, only two fragments in Hebrew have been found, in cave 1, and these cover Enoch 8:4 to 9:4 and 9:1–4 respectively.[6] M. Black thinks however that Enoch was originally composed in Aramaic, and that if a Hebrew

[1] M. R. James, *Apocrypha Anecdota. A collection of thirteen apocryphal books and fragments*, TextsS 2, no. 3 (Cambridge, 1893), pp. 146–50.

[2] J. Halévy, 'Recherches sur la langue de la rédaction primitive du Livre d'Enoch', *JA*, 108–9 (1876), 325–95.

[3] N. Schmidt, 'The original language of the parables of Enoch', in *Old Testament and Semitic Studies, in memory of W. R. Harper* (Chicago, 1908), vol. 2, pp. 329–49.

[4] Charles, *Enoch...translated*, p. lvii.

[5] For the details of the Aramaic passages of Enoch which have been identified, see M. Black, 'The fragments of the Aramaic Enoch from Qumran', in *La Littérature juive*, ed. van Unnik (Leiden, 1974), pp. 17–18; J. T. Milik, *The Books of Enoch: Aramaic Fragments of Qumran Cave 4* (Oxford, 1976).

[6] D. Barthélemy and J. T. Milik, *Qumran Cave 1*. DJD 1 (Oxford, 1955), pp. 84 and 153.

version existed it was a secondary version, based on the Aramaic. As for the Ethiopic text, which alone was known until recently to contain the whole corpus, according to the same author it is dependent on the Greek, which in turn is a translation from the Aramaic.[1]

The book of Enoch, as we have said, is a corpus of revelations of various dates, attributed to the biblical Enoch (Gen. 5:24). What made it all the easier for apocalyptic writers to choose this particular figure from the past to play the role of mediator of visions was that he is said to have been 'taken' to be with God, because of his sanctity, whereas the other patriarchs underwent the experience of death. It seems, moreover, that Enoch is the biblical counterpart of the seventh antediluvian king, Enmeduranki, king of Sippar, to whom Shamash and Adad revealed divine secrets and to whom they delivered the tablets of the gods. This Enmeduranki went on to teach the mysteries to his sons.[2] Ben Sira, writing about 190 B.C.E., bears witness to an analogous tradition about Enoch, calling him 'a sign of knowledge to all generations' (Sirach 44:16b – Hebrew only). Similarly, the book of Jubilees says of him: 'he was the first...who learnt...knowledge and wisdom' (Jub. 4:17).

The Enochic corpus is made up of five sections which form a sort of Pentateuch.

(1) *Chapters 1 to 36* have come down to us in a form which is composite and has suffered many alterations. This section has sometimes been called 'The Book of the Watchers' and its most notable feature is its account of the fall of the angels (6 to 16).[3] The angels entered into marriages with the daughters of men, to whom they revealed all kinds of supernatural knowledge, such as the preparation of potions and spells, the knowledge of metals and the techniques of working them, astrology, and many other secrets besides. But these unions had dire consequences, for the issue of the mixed marriages between mortals and immortals was a race of giants, who began to slaughter animals and men. This situation provoked divine punishment, set out in a fourfold sentence. The giants were to devour each other. The angels, their fathers, were to be bound in the valleys of the earth for 70 generations, whilst Azazel himself, the chief of the angels, who was responsible for

1 Black, 'Fragments', pp. 22f.

2 P. Grelot, 'La légende d'Hénoch dans les Apocryphes et dans la Bible: origine et signification', *RSR*, 46 (1958), 5–26 and 181–210.

3 J. T. Milik, 'Problèmes de la littérature hénochique à la lumière des fragments araméens de Qumrân', *HTR*, 64 (1971), 343–54. The title 'Book of the Watchers' is given to the Ethiopic collection on the basis of the Greek title *peri tōn egrēgorōn* given by Syncellus.

the divulging of the secrets, was to be buried in a desert. In the fourth sentence, which in its present form seems to be incomplete, God announces the flood which is to be the punishment of the guilty men. In these chapters the author attributes to the myth of the fall of the angels (6 to 16) the same function as the Apocalypse of Ezra and St Paul later attribute to the sin of Adam. They are seen as the origin of the evil present in the world. In Enoch it is said quite explicitly (10:8): 'To him (Azazel) ascribe all sin'. The doctrinal importance which the fall of angels has acquired in Enoch is manifest when his account is compared with the one in Genesis (Gen. 6:1–4). In Genesis the story of the union between the *b^ene 'elohim*, the sons of God, and the daughters of men is introduced at this point, it appears, simply to explain how the giants, about whom extraordinary stories were told, acquired their stature and their strength.[1]

The Book of the Watchers is represented by five manuscripts from cave 4 at Qumran. Jubilees 4:21–2 briefly summarizes the Book of the Watchers, mentioning both the part dealing with angelology (Enoch 6 to 16) and the section concerned with cosmography (Enoch 17 to 36).[2] According to Milik[3] this portion of the Enoch literature dates from the middle of the third century B.C.E. and its author is likely to have been a Judean engaged in the perfume and spice trade, judging by his interest in Jerusalem and in the spice and perfume producing countries (Enoch 26 to 32).[4]

(2) *Chapters 37 to 71* constitute the section known as the book of Similitudes or the book of Parables. This part of the work (which should more accurately be called the Second Vision of Enoch, following the opening words of the collection) comprises three parables, that is, three units of teaching. The first deals with the righteous, the angels and the secrets of astronomy (38 to 44). The second parable (45 to 57) is a revelation concerning the messianic judgement upon righteous and sinners. The third parable consists of teaching about the eternal felicity of the elect and the fate of the righteous and elect ones who have betrayed their trust (58 to 69). The last two chapters of this section describe Enoch's assumption into heaven, and how he is allowed to contemplate 'the Ancient of Days'. The collection of parables is not

[1] A. Lods, *Histoire de la littérature hébraïque et juive, des origines à la ruine de l'Etat juif (135 ap. J.C.)* (Paris, 1950), p. 862.

[2] Milik, *HTR*, 64 (1971), 345.

[3] Ibid., 347.

[4] J. T. Milik, 'Hénoch au pays des aromates (ch. XXVII à XXXII). Fragments araméens de la grotte 4 de Qumrân', *RB*, 65 (1958), 70–7; P. Grelot, 'La géographie mythique d'Hénoch et ses sources orientales', *RB*, 65 (1958), 33–69.

homogeneous. It appears to contain remnants of an apocalypse of Noah, into whose mouth is put a series of revelations (60 to 68). This apocalypse of Noah was originally an independent work.[1] The Book of Similitudes is marked by a number of characteristics peculiar to itself. God is very often called 'the Lord of Spirits', a title rarely found elsewhere. It does appear in 2 Macc. 3:23f and also at Qumran, in the Hymns (10.8).[2] In the third parable appears the figure of the Son of Man and the Elect One, whose name has been named before 'the Lord of Spirits' (ch. 46; 48.2). The Son of Man, whose title is evidently borrowed from the book of Daniel (Dan. 7), is a symbolic figure, and refers to an individual. He is chosen by the Lord of the Spirits and is pre-existent (48:2–6). But he also fulfils a universal eschatological role and all judgement is committed to him (69:27). There is no other book in Judaism in which the Son of Man is credited with such a position and such dignity as in the Similitudes of Enoch.[3] It is therefore not surprising that, primarily for theological reasons, the problem of the origin of the Similitudes has been keenly debated. Earlier writers often reached their opinion on *a priori* dogmatic grounds, based on the fact that Enoch was quoted in the epistle of Jude. They therefore maintained either that the Similitudes are of Christian origin, or even that the entire book of Enoch is a Christian compilation. More recent writers have reacted against these extreme conclusions. It is observed that there are no allusions, even of the most veiled kind, to the person of Jesus, or to the specific events of his death and resurrection. A Christian could hardly have failed to mention these.[4] For this reason it has been maintained by numerous scholars that the Similitudes are of Jewish origin.[5] However, a new factor has entered the discussion, for among the thousands of Aramaic fragments discovered at Qumran, virtually all the sections of Enoch are represented except the Simili-

[1] Lods, *Histoire*, p. 877.

[2] M. Delcor, ed. *Les Hymnes de Qumran (Hodayot). Texte hébreu, introduction, traduction, commentaire* (Paris, 1962), pp. 225f.

[3] The problem of the Son of Man in Enoch has given rise to a substantial literature, of which we can mention here only a few titles: E. Sjöberg, *Der Menschensohn im äthiopischen Henochbuch* (Lund, 1946); N. Messel, *Der Menschensohn in den Bilderreden des Henoch*, BZAW 35 (Giessen, 1922); T. W. Manson, 'The Son of Man in Daniel, Enoch and the Gospels', *BJRL*, 32 (1949–50), 178ff; F. H. Borsch, *The Son of Man in Myth and History*, New Testament Library (London, 1967), pp. 145–56.

[4] See already on this subject the observations of E. Schürer, *The Jewish People in the Time of Jesus Christ* (Edinburgh, 1885–1891), div. II, vol. 3, p. 68; Lods, *Histoire*, p. 880.

[5] M. Delcor, 'Le milieu d'origine et le développement de l'apocalyptique juive', in *La littérature juive*, ed. van Unnik (Leiden, 1974), p. 111.

tudes. From this, some have concluded that the book of Similitudes did not exist at Qumran and must therefore have had a Christian origin. The book of Giants which has been identified at Qumran would then have occupied the place of the book of Similitudes, which did not exist in the Jewish corpus of Enochic literature. Milik is explicit on this subject:

> It seems to me quite certain that (the Similitudes) did not exist in the pre-Christian period in any Aramaic, Hebrew or Greek text, since no Semitic or Greek fragment of it has been recovered from the very rich finds of manuscripts in the Qumran caves. It is therefore a Greek Christian composition (its use of the Septuagint text has already been mentioned) which has clearly been inspired by the New Testament books, and especially by the gospels, starting with their titles for the pre-existent messiah, 'Son of Man' (Matt. 9:6, 10:23 etc.) and 'The Elect' (Luke 23:35).[1]

He goes on to argue from the fact that the book of Similitudes is not quoted anywhere between the first and the fourth centuries that it is not *early* Christian. It must be remarked, in criticism of this extreme position, that the absence of the book of Similitudes from the Qumran fragments allows us to conclude, at most, that the book was not used by the Qumran community. It is necessary to remind ourselves again that the argument from silence has to be used with care. Dupont-Sommer is very conscious of this when he writes: 'Today, as before the Qumran discoveries, the question of the origin of the book of the 'Similitudes' must be examined essentially by means of internal criteria'.[2]

What are we to make of the arguments for Essene authorship which some scholars have advanced? One fact seems at first sight to be strongly against any such theory, namely, the application to the Messiah of the title 'Son of Man'. Never, to our knowledge, has anyone yet encountered a mention of the Son of Man among the Qumran writings. This is very surprising if the book of Similitudes, which uses the title freely, is of Essene origin. On the contrary, its teaching about the Son of Man would connect the Similitudes most naturally with the Hasidean work which makes up the second half of the book of Daniel. This is the first writing to make use of the Son of Man title, though it is true that in Daniel the title is used in a collective sense.[3] But it is only right to point out that in the Similitudes the title 'Son of Man' not only

[1] Milik, *HTR*, 64 (1971), 375, translated.

[2] A. Dupont-Sommer, *Les écrits esséniens découverts près de la Mer Morte* (Paris, 1959), pp. 310f.; ET *The Essene Writings from Qumran* (Oxford, 1961), p. 300.

[3] M. Delcor, *Le libre de Daniel* (Paris, 1971), pp. 17–19.

signifies quite indisputably an individual, but by comparison with Daniel's use of the term it has been reworked and enriched to a singular degree. This leads us to think that the book of Similitudes is quite distant in time from the second half of Daniel and that it does not emanate from the Hasidean movement.

In favour of the Essene hypothesis we may note several points of contact with the Qumran writings which do not seem to be entirely fortuitous. These comprise both verbal and theological similarities. We have already mentioned above that the title 'Lord of Spirits', occurring constantly in the Similitudes but rare elsewhere, does appear at least once in a hymn from Qumran. We may note, too, the 'garments of glory' in which the elect are clothed in I Enoch 62:15 and IQS 4.8, and the binding in chains of the evil angels, which is mentioned in I Enoch 69:28, Qumran Hymn 3.18 and the book of Mysteries. This last text is particularly close in thought to that of Enoch.[1] A close study of the Similitudes would without doubt enable us to lengthen this list of points of contact between the Similitudes and the Qumran documents. Though these contacts do not allow us to conclude with certainty that the work is of Essene origin, they are at least evidence of Essene influence upon it. If we accept the theory of Jewish origin, the Similitudes are to be dated either in the time of Alexander Janneus, between 103 and 76 B.C.E., or during the period of the first Roman governors.

(3) The third section of the book, the book of the Luminaries of Heaven, or Astronomical Book (72 to 82), looks like a treatise on astronomy. Enmeduranki, who is usually considered to be the Babylonian prototype of Enoch, had been initiated into the mysteries of the heavens and the earth.[2] We are not therefore surprised to find astronomical data occupying such a large space in the books attributed to Enoch. It is also possible that the name 'Enoch' itself, being derived from a Semitic root meaning 'to understand', 'to be wise', may have encouraged legends attributing to him great knowledge of astronomy. Astronomy was, in the ancient world, *the* science, *par excellence*. It is worth noting that in this book the author is arguing in favour not of a lunar year, but of a solar year of 364 days. This calendar is known to be of sacerdotal origin and to have been respected in Qumranian circles. Now the Astronomical Book accuses the sinners of error 'in the

[1] Delcor, 'Le milieu d'origine', p. 112: Milik, *The Books of Enoch. Aramaic Fragments of Qumran Cave 4* (Oxford, 1976), pp. 89ff.

[2] P. Dhorme, *Choix de textes religieux assyro-babyloniens* (Paris, 1907), pp. 141–7. Dhorme expresses reservations about the parallel between Enoch and Enmeduranki. (*Recueil E. Dhorme, Etudes bibliques et orientales*, Paris, 1951, pp. 26f.)

reckoning of all their days' (82:4), and of failure to observe the order of the stars and the calendar (80:7). The Qumran documents reveal the same preoccupation with the calendar and these discussions in the Enoch literature therefore give the impression that they come from the same circles. Enoch's astronomical knowledge is presented as originating in heaven, for it is revealed through the angel Uriel, 'Light of God' (75:3). It is interesting to see how far the apocalyptic astronomers were behind contemporary Greek science, which rests not on revelation but on observation. It is equally curious that the 365-day year which was in use among surrounding peoples was not accepted in the Jewish circles which produced this work.[1] This would indicate that the traditions concerning the calendar were preserved within a closed community, which is exactly what the Qumran community was.

(4) *The dream visions* (83 to 90) make up the fourth part of the Enochic corpus. They take the form of a history of the Chosen People from the Creation onwards. The Israelites are symbolized by bulls, and then, from Jacob onwards, by sheep, lambs and rams. Israel's enemies are represented by elephants, camels, donkeys and by all sorts of animals, even birds of prey. Thus the book is sometimes known as the 'Vision of Animals'. From I Enoch 90:6 onwards the author is recounting events which to him are contemporary. He deals with the origin of the Hasidean party (90:6–7); with the murder of the High Priest Onias in the summer of 170 (90:8); and with the exploits of the Maccabees (90:9). In 90:13–15 the author describes how the battle of Beth-Zur was won by Judas, thanks to the intervention of a heavenly horseman. This is in line with the tradition reported in 2 Macc. 11:1–12. The dream visions would have been composed during the year 164 B.C.E., some weeks or months after the battle of Beth-Zur.[2] The author believes that the eschatological judgement is imminent (90:31).

(5) *The Apocalypse of Weeks* (91 and 93). Some distinguish these two chapters as a separate work, though others include them in the epistle of Enoch (91 to 108). However that may be, the text of this apocalypse is in disorder. Chapter 91:12–17 must be read following 93:3–10, as is confirmed by the Aramaic text from Qumran cave 4. The apocalypse divides the history of the world into ten 'weeks'. During the tenth week the great eternal judgement will take place, in which God will execute vengeance amongst the angels (91:15). It is difficult to date this apocalypse since sufficiently explicit historical details are lacking.

(6) *The Epistle of Enoch* (92 and 94 to 105). This title is known from the

[1] O. Neugebauer, 'Notes on Ethiopic astronomy', *Orientalia*, n.s. 33 (1964), 58–61, is very critical of the astronomical knowledge displayed in this book.

[2] Milik, *HTR*, 64 (1971), 359.

Chester Beatty and Michigan Greek papyrus. In the Greek text chapters 105 and 108 are missing, which supports Charles' theory that they never formed part of the original epistle. The central theme is the contrast between the rich, who are identified with the sinners, and the poor, who are the persecuted righteous. The sinners are accused of idolatry (99:6–9; 104:9), which implies that the author has in mind Gentiles rather than Jews. For this reason it seems to some scholars difficult to accept the suggestion that the author was a Pharisee criticizing the Sadducees. Such scholars suggest instead that the situation which best fits the composition of the Enochic collection is the setting of a rich and prosperous Hellenistic city where the Jews were discriminated against.[1] But several passages militate against this theory, indicating that the sinners were in fact Jews who had forsaken 'the fountain of life', that is, the Law (96:6), and who had altered the words of uprightness and transformed themselves into what they were not, that is, they had apostatized (99:2). Furthermore, these Jews refuse to believe some of the doctrines which the books of Enoch are trying to inculcate, and in particular the idea that there are heavenly tablets on which the sins of men are recorded in advance (98:6–7; 104:7). Moreover they deny that there are rewards and punishments after death (102:6–8, 11). It is thus fairly easy to recognize these Jews as the Sadducees, who, as we know, refused to believe in destiny (εἱμαρμένη) and believed that the soul disappears at death.[2] This entire section looks like the work of a Hasidean, that is a pious man, a Pharisee, or perhaps an Essene, who lived at the time of Alexander Janneus, or at all events, at a time when the Sadducees, that is to say the Hasmoneans, were in power.[3]

(7) *Chapters 106 to 107* do not come from the same hand as 91 to 105, although they too appear in the Greek text. They have sometimes been called the Noachic fragment because they belong to an apocalypse of Noah which is no longer extant. Their principal topic is the theme of the miraculous birth of Noah (106). The final chapter, 108, does not belong to the preceding section. It is generally agreed that it was added by an editor to strengthen the faith of the righteous for whom the messianic kingdom was slow in coming. The chapter appears to be altogether Essene in tone. It has a high regard for asceticism, despises gold and silver (108:8–10), and its author believes in the immortality of

[1] Ibid., 361.

[2] Josephus, *Bellum Judaicum* II.164–6; *Antiquitates Judaicae* XVIII.16–17. J. Le Moyne, *Les Sadducéens*, EB (Paris, 1972), pp. 37f.

[3] H. H. Rowley, *The Relevance of Apocalyptic* 3rd edn. (London, 1963), p. 59; Charles, *Book of Enoch*, pp. liiff.

the soul (108:11–14).[1] To this we should add that the eschatological glorification of the righteous in light, in Enoch 108:12, recalls the words of the psalmist in one of the Qumran hymns (1QH 11:14), 'I will be resplendent in sevenfold light'.

It will be apparent that the Enochic corpus contains materials of diverse dates and perhaps also of diverse origins. It is readily understandable, therefore, why the teachings, particularly on the hereafter, which are expressed in one part are not always entirely homogeneous with those which appear in others.[2]

THE BOOK OF JUBILEES

Until comparatively recently the text of the book of Jubilees was known in its entirely only in the Ethiopic version. It was published for the first time by Dillmann in 1859, the text being established on the basis of the only two Ethiopic manuscripts then known, the manuscripts C and D. In 1895 R. H. Charles published a fresh edition of the Ethiopic version because new Ethiopic manuscripts had by that time been discovered. A sixteenth-century manuscript from the British Museum was made the basis of the edition, though it was not the oldest available. Quite apart from the fact that this edition by Charles left a good deal to be desired, it is today unobtainable. A new edition is therefore proposed, manuscripts now being to hand which were unknown to Dillmann or to Charles, who only made use of four.[3]

The Ethiopic version is based on a Greek text, which itself is only a translation of a Semitic original. That a Greek text does underlie the Ethiopic is shown by the presence in the Ethiopic of Greek words, and especially proper names which have been transcribed in their Greek form.

Numerous fragments of the Greek text itself are known to us through quotations by the Greek fathers and other church writers, such as Justin, Origen, Diodore of Antioch, Isidore of Pelusium, Epiphanius, Syncellus, and others. These quotations have been conveniently reassembled by A.-M. Denis, with an English translation of them borrowed from Charles.

A Latin version containing about a quarter of the book was discovered by Ceriani in the Ambrosian Library at Milan and published

[1] Charles, *Book of Enoch*, p. 271.

[2] P. Grelot, 'L'Eschatologie des Esséniens et le livre d'Hénoch', *RevQ*, 1 (1958–9), 113–31.

[3] W. Baars and R. Zuurmond, 'The project for a new edition of the Ethiopic Book of Jubilees', *JSS*, 9 (1964), 67–74.

by him in 1861. The Latin text was re-edited by Rönsch in 1874. The Latin is of great interest from the text-critical point of view, in spite of being corrupt in places. It is acknowledged fairly generally that the Latin text, like the Ethiopic, was made from the Greek. Some of the corruptions are explicable by the fact that the Greek has been misunderstood. In 38:13 the words *et posuerunt jugum timoris super ipsis* make very little sense compared with the Ethiopic, which reads 'yoke of servitude'. This suggests that the Greek had ζυγὸν δουλείας, which the Latin translator read as ζυγὸν δειλίας. The Latin translation was most probably made in Egypt by a Palestinian Jew.

Charles suspected the existence of a Syriac version of *Jubilees*. Fragments of such a version were discovered by Tisserant contained in an anonymous chronicle published by the patriarch Raḥmani in 1904.[1] Each Syriac fragment is reproduced by Tisserant with a French translation, and, opposite, the French translation of the corresponding Ethiopic. The translations of the Ethiopic are taken from a translation by F. Martin which unfortunately remains unpublished.[2] Tisserant concludes that the Syriac translator worked directly from an original in Hebrew, without reference to an intermediate Greek translation.[3]

The reader will realize from this that the text's various editors had suspected the existence of a Hebrew original, but this had never been actually proved. Happily this theory was verified by the discovery in the Qumran caves of several Hebrew fragments of Jubilees. Some of these fragments, the ones found in Cave 4, have not yet been published.[4] The very presence of Jubilees at Qumran raises the question of the circles in which it originated. But before dealing with this problem we must first see what kind of book it is and say something about its contents.

One of the titles which the book bore among the Greeks was 'the Little Genesis' (ἡ λεπτὴ Γένεσις). The book does indeed claim to be a revelation given by God to Moses, through an angelic intermediary, about the history of the world from the creation down to Moses' own time. It is ostensibly a new history covering both the origins of the

[1] I. E. Rahmani, *Chronicum civile et ecclesiasticum anonymi auctoris* (Charfé, Lebanon, 1904).

[2] E. Tisserant, 'Fragments syriaques du livre des Jubilés', *RB*, 30 (1921), 55–86, 206–232; republished in *Recueil Cardinal Eugène Tisserant Ab Oriente et Occidente* (Louvain, 1955), vol. 1, pp. 25–87.

[3] Tisserant, *RB*, 30 (1921), 230–2.

[4] A provisional account of the known Hebrew fragments will be found in A.-M. Denis, *Introduction aux Pseudépigraphes grecs d'Ancien Testament* (Leiden, 1970), pp. 157–8; J. C. VanderKam, *Textual and Historical Studies in the Book of Jubilees* (Missoula, 1977), pp. 8–88.

world and the patriarchal period, and it does effectively constitute a new book of Genesis. This vast compilation would be in danger of being just a motley collection of diverse traditions if it were not that its rigid chronological framework, dividing time into weeks of years and into jubilees, confers on it a certain unity. From the literary point of view it is presented as an apocalypse, since some passages envisage the coming of a new world, after a covenant has been made with God. But Jubilees also has something of the character of a testament. It includes the spiritual testaments of several patriarchs, including Noah (7:20ff), Abraham (20 to 22), Isaac (36), and even Rebecca (35).[1] But because Jubilees is developing traditions which have the book of Genesis as their starting point it also has something of midrash in it. In this respect it has similarities with the Genesis Apocryphon from Qumran, though there are differences too.[2]

We turn now to the question of the circles in which Jubilees originated. Since the discovery of the Dead Sea Scrolls it does not seem possible any longer to maintain its Pharisaic origin.[3] Everything points instead to the Essenes.[4] It had already been observed that the Damascus Rule (CD 16.3–4), several copies of which have also been found at Qumran, expressly alluded to the book of Jubilees, and this demonstrated at least the esteem in which the Essenes held it.[5] But that is not all. Jubilees makes use of the solar calendar which is exactly the calendar, sacerdotal in origin, that was in use at Qumran.[6] The use of their special calendar evidently obliged the Qumran group to lead a religious life totally at variance with that of the Pharisees and Sadducees, and drove them at length to abandon the sacrificial cult at the Jerusalem Temple.[7] This is just what we are told the Essenes did. It must further be added that the book of Jubilees contains in embryo every specific element of the teaching of the Dead Sea community: the

[1] M. Testuz, *Les idées religieuses du livre des Jubilés* (Geneva–Paris, 1960), p. 11.

[2] N. Avigad and Y. Yadin, *A Genesis Apocryphon* (Jerusalem, 1956), pp. 24–5. The similarities lie especially in the geographical notions which the two writings share, the same chronology underlying them, and the same persons who figure in both.

[3] The book has been attributed to the Pharisees by the following authors: A. Dillmann, H. Rönsch, W. Bousset, E. Schürer and R. H. Charles.

[4] The attribution of the book to the Essenes was suggested as early as 1855 by A. Jellinek, by F.-M. Lagrange and recently by K. Berger.

[5] C. Rabin, *The Zadokite Documents* (Oxford, 1954; 2nd edn., 1958). The Damascus Document, or Zadokite Document, speaks explicitly of 'the Book of the Divisions of the Times, according to their Jubilees and Weeks'.

[6] A. Jaubert, 'Le calendrier des Jubilés et de la secte de Qumrân: ses origines bibliques', *VT*, 3 (1953), 250–64.

[7] On this point see A. Jaubert, *La notion d'alliance dans le Judaïsme aux abords de l'ère chrétienne*, Patristica Sorbonensia 6 (Paris, 1963), p. 97.

importance of destiny; the place held by angelology; the horror of defilement, which implies an overriding ideal of physical and moral purity – to name only some. In fact the words 'defilement', 'impurity', 'abomination', 'fornication' recur like a leitmotif in innumerable passages of Jubilees. There are also numerous similarities between Jubilees and the Qumran writings. Nevertheless, it does not appear that the author of the book of Jubilees as a whole felt any rooted hostility towards the official priesthood in Jerusalem. The very precise rules concerning the sacrifices in the sanctuary (50:10–11) would make no sense if the members of the community which produced the book had no access to the Temple. For this reason it has been thought that Jubilees dates from a period when the separation from the Temple had not yet taken place. This conclusion is strengthened by the feeling one gets in reading Jubilees that no written law has yet been promulgated for the governing of a closed community, and that the members are still participating in national life.[1]

If we wish to define more closely the date of composition of the book of Jubilees, what further evidence have we on which to proceed? We observe in Jubilees a powerful detestation of the Gentiles, and especially of Philistines, who are to be devoted to extermination at the hands of the 'righteous nation'. Now it is known that Jonathan Maccabeus ravaged Philistia (1 Macc. 10:84; 11:61) and that John Hyrcanus captured and burnt Ashdod. What is more, the description of the massacre at Shechem (Jub. 30) could be an allusion to the destruction of Samaria by the same Hasmonean prince around 110 B.C.E. The allusion in Jub. 38:14 to the yoke of servitude placed on Edom by Israel would fit into the same historical context, for John Hyrcanus conquered Idumea in about the year 125.[2] It has also been emphasized that Levi is called 'priest of the Most High God' (Jub. 32:1), a title which was borne exclusively by the Maccabees.[3] The *terminus a quo* for the date of composition of Jubilees could not be earlier than 153 B.C.E., the date at which Jonathan took over the high-priesthood. Other, earlier dates, going back as far as the fifth to the third centuries B.C.E., have been proposed by some scholars, but these suggestions have not met with favour.[4]

Scholars have up to now argued as if the whole book of Jubilees was

[1] On this point see Jaubert, *La notion*, p. 94, and Testuz, *Les idées religieuses*, p. 187.

[2] R. H. Charles, 'The Book of Jubilees', in *APOT*, 2, p. 6.

[3] Josephus, *Antiquitates Judaicae* XVI.163.

[4] S. Zeitlin, 'The Book of Jubilees, its character and its significance', *JQR*, n.s. 30 (1939–40), 1–31; W. F. Albright, *From the Stone Age to Christianity: Monotheism and the Historical Process* (Baltimore, 1940), pp. 266f.

composed at the same period. But this assumption has recently been challenged. The challenge has serious consequences, especially for our assessment of the book's eschatology. The angelic discourse in 2:1 to 50:4 has been ascribed to one major author, who lived at the end of the third century B.C.E. or the beginning of the second. He was particularly concerned about the practice of astrology (8:3ff and 11:9ff), about idolatry (11:4, 16; 12:1–5, 16–20), the neglect of circumcision (15:11ff), marriage with non-Israelites (20:4–5) and other such failings. A second edition of the work, it is argued, came into being with the addition to it of a new introduction (1:4b–26), and of one or two other verses (1:29; 23:21). These additions would reflect the Maccabean struggles and would date from 166–160 B.C.E. Finally, at a third stage, 1:27–8 was added. This could not be from the same hand as added 1:4b–26 because, in the longer addition, Moses is given the order to write down what is to happen during the weeks and jubilees to come, whereas in the two verses (1:27–8) it is the angel who has to write what will happen up to the time when the sanctuary is established. The redactor of the pericope relating to the sanctuary will have lived at Qumran during the reigns of Simon and of John Hyrcanus. He would be, effectively, a third author.[1]

In respect of its teachings the book of Jubilees affords great interest. Of the resurrection there is no mention at all. Quite the contrary: it is said of the righteous that their bones shall rest in the earth, while their spirits will have much joy (23:31). The author greatly exalts the house of Levi. To the descendants of Levi is promised an authority which is both civil and religious (31:14ff). The angelology of Jubilees is more developed that that of the book of Job, but we do not yet find in it angels who have names and individuality, as we do in Daniel or in 1 Enoch (Ethiopic Enoch).[2]

THE TESTAMENTARY LITERATURE

Literature in testamentary form is well represented among the pseudepigrapha. As many as seven works fall within this category: the *Testaments of the Twelve Patriarchs*, the *Testaments of Abraham, Isaac* and *Jacob*, the *Testament of Job*, the *Testament of Solomon* and the *Testament of Moses* (this last is commonly known as the *Assumption of Moses*), following the titles given by Paul Riessler in his collection of non-

[1] G. L. Davenport, *The Eschatology of the Book of Jubilees*, SPV 21 (Leiden, 1971), pp. 10–18.

[2] Testuz, *Les idées religieuses*, pp. 75–80.

biblical Jewish writings.[1] The testaments generally deal with the last moments of some biblical character and the account of these last moments is interspersed with discourses and descriptions of visions. Before dying, the patriarch or other figure calls together his children, reminds them of some of the events of his life, and stresses one fault to be avoided and one quality to be imitated. This category of literature has its roots deep in the Old Testament. Jacob in the book of Genesis addresses a farewell discourse to his sons (Gen. 49). He dies after blessing them and commanding them to bury him in the tomb of his fathers. Deuteronomy itself has sometimes been thought of as a farewell address made to the people by Moses after the Exodus.[2] He goes up Mount Nebo to die. First he recalls the wilderness period (chapters 1 to 3), then he exhorts his listeners to obey the Law (chapters 4ff). His addresses are interspersed with pressing exhortations to keep the precepts of the Lord. Then, having installed Joshua in his place (chapter 31), he pronounces blessings before dying (chapter 33).

The apocryphal or deuterocanonical literature has preserved the last words of certain people. Mattathias on his deathbed gives counsel to his sons (1 Macc. 2:49–70). The Jewish martyrs, on the point of drawing their last breath, address those who torture them and give encouragement to one another (2 Macc. 6 to 7).

In the pseudepigraphical literature, too, farewell discourses are found. In Ethiopic Enoch (91:1–19) Methuselah calls together all the sons of Enoch for Enoch to make known to them what is to happen to them in eternity. Enoch invites them to live in righteousness and reveals to them what has been called 'the Apocalypse of Weeks' (chapter 93). In Slavonic Enoch or the Book of the Secrets of Enoch, Enoch admonishes his children before being taken up to heaven; then, coming back once more to earth, he gathers together the members of his family and the elders of the people and addresses them before his final assumption (chapters 38ff; 57ff in the edition of Forbes, *APOT* 2). It has been said that the book of Jubilees is the best illustration of Judaism's predilection for farewell discourses.[3] Jubilees contains not only the last words of Abraham to his children and grandchildren before his death, but also his final instructions to Isaac and Jacob (chapters 20 to 22).

Testamentary literature continues into the New Testament. Among

[1] Riessler, *Altjüdisches Schrifttum ausserhalb der Bibel* (Heidelberg, 1928; repr. Darmstadt, 1966).

[2] J. Munck, 'Discours d'adieu dans le Nouveau Testament et dans la littérature biblique', *Mélanges Goguel, Aux sources de la tradition chrétienne* (Paris, 1950), p. 156.

[3] Munck, 'Discours', p. 158.

the most important examples of the farewell discourse may be cited that addressed by Jesus to his disciples before his Passion, in Luke 22:31–8 and John 13 to 17.

The *Testaments of the Twelve Patriarchs* constitutes the most considerable collection, and one of the oldest collections, of testamentary literature. Because of its importance, it is the one to which we shall devote most attention.

This work presents each of the sons of Jacob in turn, each of them ostensibly giving his final commands to his descendants before he dies. Each testament is composed according to an identical formula. Taking the form of a haggadic midrash based on the book of Genesis, it recounts happenings from the life of the patriarch, bringing out some defect or quality characteristic of him. The discourses have a strongly didactic character. Then the patriarch makes predictions concerning Israel's future, almost always emphasizing Levi's precedence over the other tribes. The death and burial of the patriarch are recounted at the end of the testament. What we have here is a literary genre of mixed type, which partakes at the same time of the nature of haggadah, moral exhortation and apocalypse.

The book has been preserved in Greek and in various oriental languages; preserved in some cases in its entirety, in others only partially. The Greek text of the *Testaments of the Twelve Patriarchs* was edited by Charles on the basis of nine manuscripts, which he grouped into two recensions, α and β. The α recension, which is represented by three manuscripts, is marred, in Charles opinion, by some omissions, but contains fewer Christian interpolations than β. The β recension is represented by six manuscripts. Charles preferred the α recension to the β one (though his reasons for doing so were not by any means adequate) and he tried to show that the main divergences between the two groups of manuscripts went back to two different recensions of the Hebrew. Charles, moreover, produced an eclectic text, making use of all the material available to him, and provided his edition with such a complicated textual apparatus that it is difficult to gain from it an accurate idea of what the original Greek text was. M. de Jonge edited the Greek text on the basis of the Cambridge manuscript, with all the faults that it contains. The variants of the different manuscripts are reported in the critical apparatus. This minor edition is meant primarily to assist specialists in using Charles's edition. It is not intended to replace Charles altogether.

Burchard devoted a study to the manuscript tradition of the Armenian text of the *Testaments of the Twelve Patriarchs*, a version to which Charles attached exaggerated importance in reconstructing the original text. Charles reckoned that the Armenian version contained relatively few Christian interpolations. Burchard enumerates 45 manuscripts and 5 printed editions, though Charles knew only 12 manuscripts and made use of just 9 of them. Burchard's conclusion is that the interest of the Armenian version lies principally in its early date, whence its importance as a witness to the text.[1] At Qumran some fragments in Aramaic of the *Testament of Levi* have been discovered. They add to our existing holdings of twelfth-century fragments from the Cairo Genizah, now preserved in the Bodleian Library at Oxford and the University Library at Cambridge. The Qumran fragments represent a longer text than the received Greek text of the *Testament of Levi*, but they agree with a long and clumsily inserted addition made in a tenth-century Greek manuscript from Mount Athos. This addition is found at *Testament of Levi* 18:2, after the word ἡμερῶν. It is valuable because it demonstrates that there existed a Greek translation of the Aramaic text of Levi.[2] A Hebrew text of the *Testament of Naphtali* has also been recognized among the Qumran finds. It is longer than the Greek version of the *Testament of Naphtali*.[3] We already had a late Hebrew text of *Naphtali* which differs considerably from the Greek, and which exhibits a deep hostility to Joseph. One gains the impression that in the *Testaments of Levi* and *Naphtali* the Greek text is condensing the Semitic text of Qumran. Up to now we have not found at Qumran Semitic texts of any of the remainder of the Testaments, but there are good reasons for asserting that the community knew the testaments of Reuben, Simeon, Levi, Judah, Zebulun, Dan, Naphtali, Gad, Asher, Joseph and Benjamin, as is shown by the numerous parallels in the Damascus Document which are cited in Rabin's edition.[4]

From what circles do the Testaments emanate? Continuing debates have gone on among scholars concerning this question, without any agreement being reached. Before the Qumran discoveries were made, most scholars agreed with Charles that the Testaments were a Jewish work with Christian interpolations. This view was advanced as early as 1698 by Grabe, the first editor of the Testaments.[5] Some more

[1] C. Burchard, 'Zur armenischen Überlieferung der Testamente der zwölf Patriarchen', in W. Eltester, ed., *Studien zu den Testamenten der zwölf Patriarchen*, BZNW 36 (Berlin, 1969), p. 28; M. de Jonge ed., *Studies on the Testaments of the Twelve Patriarchs. Text and Interpretation* (Leiden, 1975), pp. 120–139.

[2] J. T. Milik, 'Le Testament de Lévi en araméen. Fragment de la grotte 4 de Qumrân', *RB*, 62 (1955), 405.

[3] J. T. Milik, *Dix ans de découvertes dans le désert de Judah* (Paris, 1957), p. 32; ET p. 34.

[4] Rabin, *Zadokite Documents*.

[5] J. E. Grabe, *Spicilegium SS Patrum, ut et haereticorum* (Oxford, 1698), vol. 1, pp. 134, 138, 140.

precisely asserted that the Christian redaction was the work of a group who took a profound interest in Jewish non-biblical writings. These they judged to be the Jewish Christian circles of the first century, but not the heretical Jewish Christian groups of the following period. The Testaments would then be the oldest interpolated Jewish writings which concerned themselves with the future of Israel and the salvation of the heathen.[1] Since the discovery of the Dead Sea Scrolls the problem has been taken up again by a number of scholars. According to some, the Testaments are a Christian work by a Christian author who was making use of Jewish materials. They are the work of a compiler, not an interpolator. De Jonge[2], who at one time maintained this position, publicly abandoned it in 1969 at the *Journées bibliques de Louvain*. J. T. Milik, however another supporter of the theory, has not apparently done so.[3] According to Philonenko on the other hand the *Testament of Levi*, to which were added the *Testaments of Judah* and *Naphtali*, passed through the hands of a final Essene redactor who made a shorter version of them. The other Testaments were added to this nucleus and a final redactor, again an Essene, expanded the text of some of the Testaments. For Philonenko, most of what Charles regarded as Christian interpolations are the work of a second Essene redactor, and passages where Charles saw christological glosses are interpreted as relating to the Teacher of Righteousness spoken of in the Qumran documents.[4] These theories have attracted hardly any adherents.[5] There is thus a tendency to revert to the earlier theory of Christian interpolations into a Jewish writing, particularly in respect of christology, though in the light of the Qumran documents there is more hesitancy about the number and extent of such interpolations.[6] The question of the origin of the Testaments is complex, and this is true whether we are speaking of the Semitic originals or of the Greek version. Even if it were proved that the Christianizing tendency was manifest in the earliest Greek manuscripts, we should not be entitled to conclude that these elements were part of the primitive Semitic work. Writings such as the Testaments, it has been rightly observed, tend by

[1] J. Jervell, 'Ein Interpolator interpoliert. Zu der christlichen Bearbeitung der Testamente der zwölf Patriarchen', in Eltester, ed., *Studien*, pp. 30–61.

[2] M. de Jonge, *The Testaments of the Twelve Patriarchs. A study of their text, composition and origin* (Assen, 1953).

[3] Milik, *Dix ans*, p. 32.

[4] M. Philonenko, *Les interpolations chrétiennes des Testaments des douze Patriarches et les manuscrits de Qumrân* (Paris, 1960).

[5] See the review by M.-E. Boismard in *RB*, 68 (1961), 419–23; also F.-B. Braun, 'Les Testaments des xii Patriarches et le problème de leur origine', *RB*, 67 (1960), 543.

[6] Jervell, 'Ein Interpolator'.

their very nature, as well as by the tastes and habits current in their natural environment, to give rise from the start not merely to families of manuscripts with a pure line of descent, but, what is something quite different, to definite recensions, with different degrees of admixture with alien material and different pretensions. Often it is only at a much later stage that these kinds of writings come to be treated with more respect and in their transmission are able to give rise to true textual families, each relatively stable and concerned for its legitimacy. But in fact this is because by then they are living merely a diminished life, the somewhat lethargic life of the library, and most often outside the circles where they were produced and where they first found favour. To draw far-reaching literary conclusions from a disputed solution of the relations between manuscript families in the case of a work like the Testaments, with all the hazards of attempting to establish the critical priority of one over another, and when the earliest witnesses do not go back earlier than the tenth century, is not much more reliable as asking an old man with a bad memory for his recollections of his infancy and youth. It would be better to try other approaches.[1]

We turn therefore to internal criticism of the Greek text. Now there are a number of important affinities between the Testaments and the Qumran texts. The following are some of the most significant:

(1) Common to the Qumran texts and the Testaments is the expectation of two Messiahs, the one priestly, the Messiah of Aaron, the other Davidic, the Messiah of Israel, and the subjection of the latter to the former.[2]

(2) Noteworthy, too, is the prominence in the Testaments of teaching on the two spirits, the spirit of good and the spirit of evil, which pull a man in opposing directions. This is a central teaching at Qumran in the Community Rule (3:13 to 4:26).

(3) We may observe that in the Testaments the personification of evil is called Beliar, the equivalent of some of the Qumran documents.

(4) The Testaments mention the star and sceptre which are to arise out of Jacob, in accordance with Balaam's prophecy.[3] This prophecy is used several times in the Essene texts and seems to belong to an Essene collection of testimonia.[4]

1 J.-P. Audet, *La Didachè. Instructions des apôtres*, EB (Paris, 1958), p. 161 n. 1.

2 R. Eppel, *Le piétisme juif dans les Testaments des douze patriarches* (Paris, 1930), pp. 97–105; G. R. Beasley-Murray, 'The two messiahs in the Testaments of the Twelve Patriarchs', *JTS*, 48 (1947), 1–12; A. S. van der Woude, *Die Messianischen Vorstellungen der Gemeinde von Qumran* (Assen, 1957), pp. 190–216; K. G. Kuhn, 'The two messiahs of Aaron and Israel', in *The Scrolls and the New Testament*, ed. K. Stendahl (New York, 1957), pp. 54–64.

3 *Test. Jud.* 24:1–5; *Test. Levi* 18:3.

4 CD 8:18–21; IQM 11:6; IQSb 5:27; 4QFlor.

(5) Both sets of writings make use of Jubilees and I Enoch.

(6) There are many points of similarity in linguistic usage.[1]

Such specific and distinctive parallels oblige us to envisage some real relationship between the Testaments and the Qumran texts, although there are also certain divergences which ought not to be minimized. But we may deduce that the Testaments, because of the kind of literature they are, were bound to contain deposits of different date and origin. It is also necessary to bear in mind that the Qumran texts are spread out over several centuries and reveal within themselves a development of thought. Taking account of these facts, scholars incline more and more to the opinion that the oldest elements in the *Testaments of the Twelve Patriarchs* are Essene in substance.[2] Thomas, however, maintains that in their present form the Testaments have no place at all either in the Hasmonean milieu or in that of Qumran. He argues that since a central place is occupied by Joseph, who was the patron and symbol of the Egyptian diaspora, the Testaments are addressed to Egyptian Judaism. The composition of the book is then to be placed between 168 and 63 B.C.E., and the original is likely to have been in Hebrew or Aramaic.[3] Attempts have been made to outline the history of the text of the Testaments, and Becker has distinguished three stages in its development. The basic work appeared in the third or second century B.C.E. The second stage extended as far as the first century C.E. Eventually, in a third stage, the Christian community brought the teaching of the Testaments up to date by making additions to it. This was at the beginning of the second century C.E. The first two stages of the history of the text belong to Hellenistic Judaism and took place in Egypt.[4] The existence of the third stage in the history of the text is something about which scholars often enough agree, but apart from that, and for the dating of the earlier two, we are reduced to mere hypotheses. The literary problem of how the collection of the twelve Testaments was formed is likewise debated. Whereas some think that

[1] On all this see M.-A. Chevallier, *L'Esprit et le Messie dans le bas-judaïsme et le Nouveau Testament*, Études d'histoire et de philosophie religieuses 49 (Paris, 1958), pp. 116–20.

[2] A. Dupont-Sommer, *Les écrits esséniens découverts près de la Mer Morte* (Bibliothèque historique, Paris, 1959), pp. 313–18; ET *The Essene Writings from Qumran* (Oxford, 1961), pp. 301–5; van der Woude, *Die Messianischen Vorstellungen*, p. 215. F.-M. Braun is more nuanced in his opinion but inclines against Essene origin: *RB*, 67 (1960), 547–9.

[3] J. Thomas, 'Aktuelles im Zeugnis der Zwölf Väter', in Eltester, *Studien*, pp. 62–148.

[4] J. Becker, *Untersuchungen zur Entstehungsgeschichte der Testamente der zwölf Patriarchen*, AGJU 8 (Leiden, 1970), p. 376; A. Hultgård, *L'eschatologie des Testaments des Douze Patriarches* (Uppsala, 1982), vol. 2, pp. 227ff.

the *Testament of Levi* was the first to be composed, Rengstorf suggests that at the basis of the Testaments was a work concerning Joseph or a *Testament of Joseph*. To this primitive nucleus the *Testaments of Levi* and *Judah* were then, he argues, added. The nine others will then have followed.[1] Equally debatable is the nature of the original Semitic language. Some argue that it was Hebrew,[2] others Aramaic.[3]

JUDITH

THE TEXTUAL TRADITION

The Greek text of Judith is classified into four or five manuscript families.[4] The ordinary text is represented by the great uncials, Alexandrinus, Vaticanus and Sinaiticus. We also possess a Lucianic text, and a text (found in MSS. f (583) and k (58)) to which the Vetus Latina is related.[5] It is generally agreed that the Greek text is a translation from a Semitic original, which some hold to have been Aramaic, though the majority of scholars believe it was Hebrew. The more recent versions (Latin, Syriac) are wholly dependent on the Greek. The Vulgate represents a revision by St Jerome, made with the help of an Aramaic text. The Vulgate text is notably shorter than the others, but since Jerome made his translation somewhat hurriedly and without much concern for accuracy (J. P. Migne, *PL* 29 (1846), cols. 37–40) we cannot depend on the vulgate to reconstruct the Aramaic text, which is now irrecoverable. But there do exist several Hebrew texts of Judith, which have recently been edited and studied by A. M. Dubarle. These texts are in close agreement with each other and with the Vulgate. It has been claimed that these Hebrew manuscripts represent the original text of Judith, but in fact what they contain seems to be a translation from the Vulgate, intended to make Jews of the Middle Ages familiar with an ancient tradition of their people. This is shown by the Hebrew transcriptions of Latin proper names.

1 K. H. Rengstorf, 'Herkunft und Sinn der Patriarchen-reden in den Testamenten der zwölf Patriarchen', in *La littérature juive*, ed. van Unnik, pp. 44ff.

2 R. H. Charles, *The Testaments of the Twelve Patriarchs translated*...(London, 1908), p. xlvii. The Aramaic fragments would on this view also derive from a Hebrew original. Cf. P. Grelot, 'Notes sur le Testament araméen de Lévi (Fragment de la Bodleian Library, colonne a)', *RB*, 63 (1956), 391–406.

3 Van der Woude, *Die Messianischen Vorstellungen*, p. 192.

4 Cf. J. Schwartz, 'Un fragment grec du livre de Judith', *RB*, 53 (1946), 534–7.

5 On the Old Latin, see M. Bogaert, 'La version latine du livre de Judith dans la première Bible d'Alcala', *Revue Bénédictine*, 78 (1968), 7–32 and 181–212; 'Un témoin liturgique de la vieille version latine du livre de Judith', ibid., 77 (1967), 7–26.

THE DATE OF COMPOSITION AND THE BOOK'S LITERARY TYPE

The dating of Judith raises difficult problems. It is hazardous to argue from its historical allusions, for on the subject of history the book contains manifest errors. The reign of Nebuchadnezzar, who is called king of the Assyrians, is placed shortly after the return from exile, the Temple having already been rebuilt. Now we know that Nineveh was destroyed in 612; that the Assyrian empire disappeared in 610; that Nebuchadnezzar reigned in Babylon from 604 to 562, and that he destroyed Jerusalem and its Temple. We know also that Cyrus, having crushed the power of Nebuchadnezzar's successors, put an end to the exile in 538, but that the Temple was not rebuilt until 515 in the reign of Darius. Thus it is preferable to date the book of Judith by attempting to date the institutions to which it refers, and by looking for a setting in which religious policies are known which were in line with the attitude to the Jews which Nebuchadnezzar in the book displays. Even on that basis we can only date the Greek translation, because a translator may misrepresent political and religious institutions by employing a technical vocabulary reflecting the institutions of his own time rather than those of the original author.[1]

There are, to begin with, some typically Persian touches: 'to prepare earth and water' (2:7); 'the God of Heaven' (5:8); the ἀκινάκης, a Persian sword (13:6); the mention of the Persians as invaders (16:10) and the names of Holophernes and Bagoas. For these reasons some have wished to place Judith in the Persian period. The *Chronicle* of Eusebius, in the version of Jerome, suggests the reign of Cambyses, and St Augustine accepted this date. Sulpicius Severus, around 420 C.E., places the Judith episode in the reign of Artaxerxes Ochus. This Artaxerxes, according to Eusebius' *Chronicle*, deported Jews to Hyrcania, doubtless on the occasion of his Egyptian campaign. But the Holophernes of whom Diodorus speaks did not die miserably. He returned, with honours heaped upon him, to his satrapy in Cappadocia, with the expectation that his descendants would take the title of king. If the story of Judith has a historical basis in this period, it must be based on some very minor incident.

As well as the Persian features in Judith we also find some Greek ones. There is the mention of the *gerousia* (11:14; 15:8) and the use of garlands (3:7; 15:13). Above all, the religious policies attributed in Judith to the invader (destruction of local shrines – 3:8; 4:1 – attempt to

[1] Cf. M. Delcor, 'Le livre de Judith et l'époque grecque', in *Klio*, 49 (1967), 152ff.

destroy the Jerusalem Temple and its altar – 9:8), presuppose neither the Achemenid period nor, for that matter, the Seleucid period in general. The allusions to a King Nebuchadnezzar who was treated as a god (3:8; 6:2) fit closely what the Bible says of Antiochus Epiphanes, especially if we regard the name Nebuchadnezzar as merely a cipher. Finally, there is some literary dependence of Judith (3:8) on the Septuagint of Daniel 3:2, 4, 7, 96, 97 (LXX numbering). We are obliged, therefore, to date the book of Judith later than the Septuagint version of Daniel (c. 145 B.C.E.).

It is quite evident that in the modern sense of the word 'history' the book of Judith is history only in outward appearance. The author of the Greek book seems to have made use of a story from the Achemenid period, which he has adapted, after a fashion, to the Seleucid period in which he was living. He has not taken much care to avoid anachronisms, and they remain here and there in the work, evidence of one of the re-workings to which the text of Judith has been subjected over the centuries. If one wishes to grasp the religious message of the book one must not stumble over the anachronisms, which the author himself did not feel to be such. One has to try to understand the author's own point of view, which is assuredly not that of a modern historian. In a given framework (we suppose a Seleucid one), he has developed characters of the Seleucid period, or even of the Achemenid period. But the object is to give embodiment to his conviction that the God of Israel is present with his people when they suffer for him and fight his battles, and that the Jews will triumph over their enemies.

To characterize the literary genre of the work is quite difficult. It displays at one and the same time elements of midrash and of apocalyptic.[1] It is from this latter genre, certainly, that the book draws some of the literary techniques it uses, such as the use of cryptography, which is a similar device to pseudonymity. Nebuchadnezzar, presented as typical of the enemies of Jerusalem, stands for Antiochus IV (Epiphanes); Nineveh represents Antioch; Bethulia is an unknown place, but its very name, meaning 'house of God', is sufficiently evocative. Judith, 'Jewess', represents the Israelite people, personified as a woman.

The narrator has composed a book which is pleasant to read, and in which he displays some artistry. He knows how to husband his effects. He takes his time in setting the scene, and Judith does not actually appear until chapter 8. The action builds up slowly and progressively. The author first of all describes the distant preparations. Then the plans

[1] E. Haag, *Studien zum Buche Judity* (Trier, 1963), p. 125, in a similar way describes this writing as a free parabolic historical description.

become more imminent, until we reach the point at which the tragedy is precipitated. As the geographical stage contracts, the drama intensifies, the forces of evil join together to press upon the little people of God. The reader must try to forget the too familiar dénouement in order to sense the anguish as the vice tightens.

CONTENTS

When the curtain rises the stage is occupied by a Nebuchadnezzar who is much larger than life (chapter 1). Opposing him, and rivalling him in stature, is Arphaxad, who has built a city with walls of fabulous thickness. Against such an adversary Nebuchadnezzar calls to arms the forces of the entire world, from Elam and Persia, and as far as the borders of Egypt and Ethiopia. The whole of the west rejects his call. With his eastern troops alone Nebuchadnezzar overthrows Ecbatana like a house of cards. The victory is celebrated on the spot with a feast lasting 120 days; but the peoples of the west, among whom Jerusalem and Samaria are numbered as very small members, can only wait with apprehension.

Events develop slowly. As they do, Nebuchadnezzar himself remains at first in the lofty isolation that befits a god (3:8). It is Holophernes who is given the task of taking vengeance on the rebels (2:1–3). The immense army gathers and is accoutred at Nineveh. Then it advances remorselessly towards the west. In one bound it reaches the frontiers of Japhet, the shores of Ionia. Suddenly it turns its march southwards. Syria and Damascus are laid waste; the whole of the coast, from Tyre to Gaza, submits. The army takes the road for Egypt. It is already in the plain of Esdraelon, but in order to reach the coastal road the troops must cross the hills which join the mountains of Samaria to the Carmel promontory. Their assemblage in the plain takes a whole month (3:9–10).

We have now reached the place at which the action begins. The invading tide is at the foot of the mountains which defend the access to Jerusalem. The narrator gives us a month's respite for the tragedy of the situation to sink in. In the face of this conquering army is a poor little people, barely escaped from the prison of their captivity (4:3). The high priest sends to the battle front the order to seize the passes into the hills, especially the one commanded by Bethulia. At the same time, by fasting and solemn prayers, supplication is made to the Lord not to deliver the house of Israel to the ungodly (4:4–15).

This resistance drives Holophernes to fury. But our skilful narrator does not bring on the attack hastily. Holophernes calls together the rulers of the neighbouring countries to tell them about the local situation. An Ammonite, Achior, explains what it is that makes Israel different from all the other peoples. Their history shows them to be invincible as long as they remain faithful to their God. The rest of the assembled council sneers, and Holophernes replies: 'There is no god but Nebuchadnezzar' (6:2). Achior is taken through the lines and left to join the Jews, that he may share the fate of this invincible people. In Bethulia Achior makes known the intentions and the anger of Holophernes. For the besieged, as for the reader, Achior's intervention is not without point. It makes clear what is really at stake in this struggle. It is not just a matter of army against army; it is God and Nebuchadnezzar who are face to face. Some see here an apocalyptic theme, similar to that of Ezek. 38 to 39, and of the Qumran document, the 'War of the Sons of Light against the Sons of Darkness'.

Eventually Holophernes mounts the attack (7:1–3). The people of Bethulia are besieged within their walls (7:4–5). On the advice of his Ammonite and Moabite allies, who know the country, the impetuous general defers his final assault. He seizes control of the spring below the city and the besieged have no choice but to surrender or to die of thirst. Within the city the leaders are prepared to hold out, but the people are of Ecclesiastes' opinion, that a living dog is better than a dead lion. They would rather live as slaves than see themselves and their children die of hunger and thirst. The city's chief ruler secures with great difficulty a delay of five days. Who knows whether in that time the Lord might not display his power on his people's behalf? Nebuchadnezzar had taken five years to subdue Ecbatana. God had five days to overthrow the power of his victorious army.

It is at this point that the heroine takes the stage. Judith has been for some years a widow. In spite of her wealth she lives a life of prayer and fasting. As with Daniel and his friends, the rigour of her religious observance has only made her beauty the more striking (8:1–8). She summons the elders of the city and reproaches them for treating God like a mere man by giving him an ultimatum. He is entitled to an unreserved confidence, whether it pleases him to chastise or save. The duty of the citizens of Bethulia is to sacrifice themselves for the defence of the hinterland and the Holy City. Uzziah, the chief ruler of the city, replies that in five days there is time for God to send rain to refill the cisterns. Judith's answer is that it is no use waiting for a miracle. Let her leave the city with her servant, and within the five days that have been set Uzziah will see what God can do by a woman's hand (8:9–36).

It is *the hand of God* which accomplishes everything. In fact the theme of the hand of God plays an important part in the chapters concerning

Judith. The author seems to be drawing a deliberate parallel between what the hand of God did when it acted through the hand of Moses, and what the hand of God does when it acts through that of Judith.[1] Before going into action the heroine addresses a fervent prayer to the God of her father Simeon (chapter 9). On the mountains where the patriarch took revenge on those who seduced his sister, a seducer of Israel raises his sacrilegious hand: may God help his servant to seduce the seducer and to overthrow him. Then, with deliberation, Judith goes into action. She observes the rituals of feminine seduction no less scrupulously than she does the rites of the Law (10:1–5). Thus armed, she goes out to face the enemy. From the outposts to the general's tent her beauty opens up the way (10:6–23).

Taken into the presence of her countrymen's enemy, she beguiles him as much by the charm of her conversation as by her beauty (chapter 11). But in the midst of the heathen she remains faithful to God. Every night she goes to the spring outside the camp. After her ritual ablutions she offers to God a pure prayer. During the day she never touches heathen food, but eats from the provisions which she has brought with her and which are prepared by her servant. Three days are spent thus in waiting (12:1–9). At last, on the fourth day, the prey is ensnared. Holophernes is disgusted with himself for having allowed Judith to impose on him such restraint (12:10–12). He invites her to a banquet. Calmly, as always, she accepts his invitation. Eventually she is left alone with the old warrior, and he is dead drunk. One last prayer to the God of Israel to give her strength and, with the sword that hangs from the bed post, she cuts off Holophernes' head. As on previous nights, she is allowed to leave the camp. She goes straight to Bethulia, with Holophernes' head in her servant's food bag (13:1–10).

The night is spent in thanksgiving. Uzziah blesses the sagacious and resourceful woman and the God who has guided her actions. Achior, overcome by the sight of Holophernes' head, confesses his faith in the God of Israel and is circumcised there and then. When the fifth day dawns, it shines on Israel's triumph. The besieging army is routed and flees. Israelites gather from all parts to despoil the enemy. The high priest comes in person from Jerusalem to bless the heroine: 'You are the glory of Jerusalem' (15:9). The new Deborah chants a victory song, which is also a hymn of thanksgiving, and the procession journeys to Jerusalem to make an offering in the Temple from the spoils of the enemy camp (16:18–20).

Judith lived for a long time afterwards, rich and famous, but

[1] Cf. P. W. Skehan, 'The hand of Judith', *CBQ*, 25 (1963), 94–109.

refusing all who made her offers of marriage. And Israel lived at peace until her death, and for long afterwards (16:21–5).

THE THEOLOGY AND MORALITY OF THE BOOK

Moralists have condemned Judith's action. To achieve a good end, the liberation of her people, she employed evil means, lies and seduction. To criticize in this way is to forget that the book of Judith is not an ethical case study; it is not even a work of edification. It is a theological statement. To his enemies, as to his servants, God applies the *lex talionis*. Judith is an instrument of justice in his hand. It is appropriate that he who would have seduced Israel into the ways of idolatry should himself be seduced and beguiled. The key to the book is in Judith's prayer (chapter 9). Conversely, those who are faithful *to* God may count on the faithfulness *of* God. Judith plays the part of a prophetess. It is God who puts the words into her mouth. Judith is a model of observance of the Law and of confidence in God. Those who behave like her may count on *God's protection*. Conversely, the pride which elevates itself even against God himself leads those who behave like Holophernes into degradation and the most despicable vices. Thus do they come to their deserved and lamentable end. The *just judgements of God* are not carried out by the fires of heaven; they are manifested in the ordinary consequences of human conduct. The author even takes care to show by the example of Achior that though salvation comes from Israel, no one is excluded from it.

Skill allied with courage, prudence in counsel with calmness and determination in execution, these are the qualities which, enhanced by a beauty which shines through her speech as well as her appearance, make of Judith a perfect example of the Jewish humanistic ideal. Christians too have never ceased to admire her, not least because her chastity in widowhood has seemed to them a foreshadowing of the Christian ideal of virginity.

ADDITIONS TO THE BOOKS OF ESTHER AND DANIEL

ADDITIONS TO ESTHER

The book of Esther, after it appeared in Hebrew, enjoyed great popularity and wide distribution.[1] For this reason people continued to

1 It does not seem to have been read at Qumran, for no trace of it has been found there. But in any case, it is known that the feast of Purim was not celebrated by the Dead Sea community.

embroider the basic story. There are three Aramaic targums of Esther. The last of these, a very literal one, appears only in the Paris polyglot Bible. The other two, which are reproduced in the rabbinic Bibles, include expansions which went on growing over the years. We also know of a whole series of midrashim, emanating from the medieval period. Finally, there are what it is agreed to call the Greek 'Additions' found in the Septuagint, which are the only expansions which here concern us. Before Jerome's time the form of the story which was in common use, in Latin as well as in the Greek, was a longer one than that contained in the Hebrew book. When Jerome translated the Hebrew recension he placed in an appendix the main sections of the story which did not appear in his Hebrew, but which had up to that time been acknowledged. Detached in this way from their contexts these additions (10:4 to 16:24) become very difficult to make use of. They are to be found in their right place in the editions of the Septuagint but the editors have never adopted a uniform system of reference. Below is a catalogue of the additions, with the mode of reference in three columns: first, that of the Vulgate; second, that of Swete (followed by the large edition of the Cambridge Septuagint and by Hanhart in the Göttingen edition, 1966); third, that of Rahlfs (followed by the Jerusalem Bible).

	Vulgate	Swete	Rahlfs
(1) Mordecai's dream	11:2–12	A 1–11	1:1*a–b*
(2) Plot against Ahasuerus	12:1–6	A 12–17	1:1*m–r*
(3) Edict of extermination of the Jews	13:1–7	B 1–7	3:13*a–g*
(4) Mordecai's prayer	13:8–18	C 1–11	4:17*a–i*
(5) Esther's prayer	14:1–19	C 12–30	4:17*k–z*
(6) Mordecai's appeal to Esther	15:1–3	4:8	
(7) Ahasuerus' reception of Esther	15:4–19	D 1–16	5:1*a–2b*
(8) Edict of rehabilitation of the Jews	16:1–24	E 1–24	8:12*a–x*
(9) Interpretation of the initial dream	10:4–13	F 1–10	10:3*a–k*
(10) The translation taken to Egypt	11:1	F 11	10:3*l*

DATE

It is difficult to assign the additions to one single date. They are written in different styles and may emanate from a variety of authors. It is probable that A, C, D and F developed gradually and received their existing form after being handed down orally for some years. The two edicts (B and E) are from a different hand from the four additions already mentioned, which have strongly marked Hebraic characteristics. They exhibit some similarities with 2 Maccabees. It is generally agreed that the entire body of additions was composed directly in Greek rather than being translated from a Semitic original.[1] The Hebrew text of Esther in its present form is consistent, and, taken as a whole, intelligible. The additions contradict the Masoretic text at more than one point, and the disagreement is sufficient to show that they were not made for the Hebrew text. Thus, 12:1–6 is already included in 2:21–3, with some irreconcilable variations. The edicts duplicate the summaries (3:13 and 8:11–12), and the tenor of the second edict (16:1–24) does not correspond to its summary (8:11–12). It is therefore not really accurate to speak of 'additions' at all: there are two different editions of Esther, one in Hebrew and one in Greek.

THE RELATIONSHIP BETWEEN THE TWO EDITIONS

Interpreters are divided on the question of the relative priority of the Greek and Hebrew texts. Some allege that the Hebrew text represents an abridgement of a Semitic original from which the Greek translation was made. This opinion was common in earlier times, being held especially by many Catholics who held to the canonicity of the Greek text, and in more recent years it received the support of Torrey, who also maintained the Greek text's priority. In Torrey's view the Greek was a translation of an Aramaic original which antedated the Hebrew.[2] But the majority of writers reckon that the Hebrew text represents the original.[3] This view was voiced as early as Bellarmine. Another author, beginning with this *shorter text*, composed a *longer recension*, which is what lies behind the Greek text. This hypothesis is much more closely in line with the 'midrashic' development so well known in later Jewish literature.

THE HISTORY OF THE GREEK TEXT

The problem of the history of the text of Esther is itself very complicated. The Greek text is actually preserved in three quite different forms. The common text is represented by the great uncials (Alexandrinus, Vaticanus, Sinaiticus and Venetus). This common text was in use as early as Josephus (*Antiquities* XI) and seems to represent a compromise between the original Greek text and the Hebrew. Accord-

[1] See, most recently R. Hanhart, *Esther* (Göttingen, 1966), p. 96.

[2] C. C. Torrey, 'The older book of Esther', *HTR*, 37 (1944), 1–40.

[3] Among others H. Cazelles, 'Note sur la composition du rouleau d'Esther', in *Lux tua Veritas*, Festschrift H. Junker (Trier, 1961), p. 20.

ing to a note in the colophon to Esther (11:1) in the text of the Septuagint, this recension was the work of one Lysimachus of Jerusalem, which was brought to Egypt in the fourth year of Ptolemy and Cleopatra. This probably means Ptolemy XII and Cleopatra V, and so the year is 78/77 B.C.E.[1] The Lucianic text, printed on the lower half of the page by Hanhart, is preserved in four minuscules. According to Moore, this is not a late recension of the Septuagint but a separate Greek translation. It was made, he argues, from a Hebrew text which did not correspond either to the Masoretic or to the text from which the Septuagint itself was translated.[2] The text to which the Old Latin bears witness seems to be the oldest of the three, and is as noteworthy for its coherence as for its important omissions (the omissions include especially 5:19; 9:1–2; 11:1; 12:1–6). J. Schildenberger regards it as a witness to the most primitive Greek rendering.[3] It would not be surprising if this suggestion were correct, especially if one remembers that for the books of Tobit and Maccabees the Old Latin does represent just such a witness to the oldest Greek text.

LITERARY GENRE AND PURPOSE

The literary genre of the supplements (or rather, of the Greek edition) is the same as that of the Hebrew original. It is history, but history treated freely for didactic purposes. It uses some of the techniques of the Greek romance. It uses dreams, for example, rather as Heliodorus uses them in his *Aethiopica*. The new developments which our Hellenistic Jewish author introduces are well described by Jerome: 'He improvises as one does in a school exercise, to bring out the feelings of those who are subjected to injustice, or of those who inflict injustice on others' (*PL* 28 (1845), cols. 1433f).

To what are these amplifications to be attributed? It is not sufficient to say that contact with the Greek world had predisposed the Jews to rhetorical embellishments. The author has deeper motives. In the Hebrew form of the story God is never mentioned. Someone has felt the urge therefore to introduce a more religious colour into the work. Hence the addition of prayers and of reflective passages in which God is the subject of the reflections. The author of the additions has also wished to make the book more humane, by suppressing features which show too much hostility to pagans (9:5–19). In total, however, the

[1] E. Bickerman, 'The colophon of the Greek book of Esther', *JBL*, 63 (1944), 339–62.

[2] C. A. Moore, 'A Greek witness to a different Hebrew text of Esther', *ZAW*, 79 (1967), 351–8.

[3] J. Schildenberger, *Das Buch Esther* HSAT 4.3 (Bonn, 1941), p. 245.

doctrinal contribution of the deuterocanonical expansions is not particularly great.

ADDITIONS TO DANIEL

The Greek Bible contains, as well as the twelve chapters of the Semitic Daniel, chapters 13 and 14 (which the Vulgate also reproduces) and in addition the Prayer of Azarias and the Song of the Three Young Men (3:24–90). We thus have two sets of additions, the one external to the book, the other internal. For the external additions the order in the Greek text is as follows: the Story of Susanna comes first, followed by the text of Daniel proper, and the whole is rounded off by the story of Bel and the Dragon. These additions have been attached to the book of Daniel because their contents marked them out as part of the Daniel cycle. In the Story of Susanna Daniel intervenes to save a young woman from the consequences of a miscarriage of justice, whilst in Bel and the Dragon the same person reveals to the king the deceptions of the priests of Bel. The text which we now possess has come down to us in two versions: that of the Septuagint, and that attributed to Theodotion. There are quite considerable differences between them.

ADDITIONS TO CHAPTER 3

The Prayer of Azarias (3:26–45)

There is nothing in the text itself which relates this prayer directly to the situation of the three young men who had been thrown into the furnace. It is properly a communal lamentation, and consists simply of an acknowledgement of the sins of the people as a whole. It is therefore fairly generally agreed that what we are dealing with is an independent composition, originally written in Hebrew, which has been taken over and put into the mouth of Azariah when he had just been thrown into the furnace, or was just about to be thrown in. We are thus dealing with a case similar to that of the psalm of Jonah (Jonah 2:3–9) which was inserted into the text afterwards.

This prayer is of the same type as the prayer of Daniel (9:4–19). It is made up of standard and well-known phrases of the sort regularly found in communal laments, and widely distributed in the Psalms and elsewhere (compare Jer. 14:7–10; Ezra 9:6–15; Neh. 1:5–11). But there are some more specific phrases, such as the allusion to the fact that sacrifices have ceased (verse 38), which seem to point to the Maccabean period. In verses 30 to 40 the idea is expressed that personal expiation may take the place of ritual offerings. The offering of one's self in expiatory sacrifice is an idea that acquires all the more force if we compare the words of the young martyr in 2 Macc. 7:37f.

The Song of the Three Young Men (3:51–90)

This song falls into three parts. After a single verse of introduction (verse 51) come praises addressed directly to God and beginning with the formula: 'Blessed art thou...' (verses 51 to 56). This is a formula beloved of Jewish prayer but rare in the Hebrew Bible (Ps. 119:12 and 1 Chron. 29:10). All creatures are invited to praise the Lord, each separate appeal being introduced by the injunction, 'Bless' (verses 57 to 87). Finally there follow the praises of the three young men themselves (verses 88 to 90). The literary genre of the text is that of the hymn, but the introduction into it of a response, derived from liturgy, after the invitation to bless (verses 57 to 87) gives it the character of a litany. If one looks for analogous forms there is something similar in Ps. 136 (compare Pss. 106:1 and 107:1). Critics generally reckon the original of the song to be Semitic, and probably Hebrew.

The narrative of verses 46 to 50, which appears in both the Greek and the Syriac traditions, is partly superfluous, for it refers again to the fate of the executioners. Besides this, in the Septuagint verse 46 adds gratuitous elaboration, for it distinguishes the men whose job it was to throw the three into the furnace from those who were feeding the fire. On the other hand, the mention of the actions of the angel, who comes to the rescue of the three Jews in the furnace, really is necessary, for in the Aramaic text, at verse 25 (28), LXX 92 (95), all that is mentioned is the presence of a divine being accompanying the three young men, without any attempt to make clear what he was doing there. We are simply left to assume that he took beneficial action. Verses 46 to 50 give the impression of a rather clumsy padding out of the story by a redactor. The verses, moreover, differ in the two Greek versions, the Septuagint and Theodotion. An Aramaic fragment of Daniel found in cave 1 at Qumran agrees with the Masoretic tradition, for it lacks the Song of the Three Young Men.[1]

SUSANNA (CHAPTER 13)

The text of Susanna, like that of Daniel, is known in its Septuagint version from a single manuscript. This represents the short text of the

[1] Cf. D. Barthélemy and J. T. Milik, *Qumran Cave 1*. DJD 1 (Oxford, 1955), p. 151.

Greek tradition. Theodotion's text is decidedly longer and there are a number of differences between it and the Septuagint. It seems that Theodotion expanded and re-worked the Septuagint text by making use of certain oral traditions which were current in Jewish circles.

The story of Susanna may be divided up thus: (1) introduction (verses 1 to 4), which describes Susanna's family background and her home in Babylon; (2) the elders' passion for Susanna (verses 5 to 18); (3) the elders' attempted seduction of Susanna (verses 19 to 27); (4) Susanna's judgement by the elders and her condemnation to death (verses 28 to 43); (5) Daniel's intervention and his judgement (verses 44 to 59); (6) conclusion (verses 63 to 64).

The story of Susanna is a piece of fiction, historical in appearance but in nothing else. Julius Africanus (*circa* 220 C.E.) already doubted the historicity of this chapter. But the facts it relates, of seduction, perjury and miscarriage of justice, are not improbable in themselves, for they are found at all times. The author of the story has, it appears, taken the Bible as his point of departure. He has found in Jer. 29:21–3 the information that there were among the Judean exiles in Babylon two people who are described as false prophets, and who committed adultery with their neighbours' wives, and who were condemned to be burnt by the king of Babylon. Taking his cue from this text the author has created the whole story from his imagination. The story thus has the character of a midrash inspired by Jeremiah's letter to the exiles. Scholars do not agree what the story of Susanna is meant to teach. But at least we may draw from it the idea that Providence does not abandon one who is falsely accused. The story must have been put into its final form at a date later than the book of Daniel itself. Critics do not agree about the language in which it was originally composed, whether Greek or Hebrew.[1]

BEL AND THE DRAGON

The author of the story of Bel and the dragon found his model in Daniel chapter 6. He has added a sarcastic note to it. The date of composition of these episodes may therefore be put at the end of the second century B.C.E. or even at the beginning of the first century B.C.E. The original was perhaps written in Aramaic. In spite of the polemical tone of the stories there is nothing to indicate that they were written at a time when Jews were being fiercely persecuted. The Jewish author concerns himself solely with idolatry, a theme which appears in

[1] C. A. Moore, *Daniel, Esther and Jeremiah*, pp. 81–4.

prophetic preaching at periods as far apart as those of Jeremiah, Deutero-Isaiah, Baruch and so on. In order to ridicule the crude idolatry of the pagans the author proceeds in two stages. He wishes to show first that the images of the gods do not eat. Then he demonstrates that if the serpent-god of Babylon does eat, he is for that very reason not a god, but is, *ipso facto*, a mortal just like any other living being. It cannot be said that this apologetic really goes very far.

THE BOOKS OF MACCABEES

NAME AND TEXTUAL TRADITION

There are four books of Maccabees, but only the first two have anything to do with the Maccabean movement and only these two are classed as deuterocanonical by the Catholic church. They owe their title to the nickname of Judas, the principal hero of the struggle against Antiochus Epiphanes (1 Macc. 5:34). The name was subsequently taken over by other members of the family, and even by his successors. The derivation of the name is disputed. Some see it as derived from the word *maqqaba*, 'hammer', and compare it with the name applied to Charles Martel. This would be appropriate for the man who is said to have struck down the horn of impiety (1 Macc. 2:48; compare Zech. 2:1–4). But the name may also be explained as deriving from the Hebrew *maqqabyahu*, meaning 'appointed by Yahweh', which would be a reference to the choice of Judas as commander-in-chief (1 Macc. 2:66). To give the name to the four books of Maccabees towards the end of the second century involved an extension of its meaning. In the usage of the church the name Maccabees is also given to the seven martyred brothers (2 Macc. 7), who are the only Old Testament saints to be mentioned in the Latin rite.

The original text of 1 Maccabees was in Hebrew, and St Jerome had seen a copy of it in that language. No fragment of the book, either in Hebrew or Aramaic, has been found in the Qumran caves. But there is nothing remarkable about that, if one recalls for a moment the antagonism which must have existed between the Maccabean rulers of Jerusalem, who were deeply compromised by Hellenism, and the rigidly observant community on the shores of the Dead Sea. Neither did Pharisaic Judaism preserve the Hebrew text of 1 Maccabees. Josephus, himself a Pharisee, reflects the prevailing Jewish opinion of his time when he fails to count the books of Maccabees among the sacred scriptures (*Contra Apionem* 1.38–41). Origen reproduces in Greek characters the primitive title of 1 Maccabees, σαρβηθ σαβαναιελ, a title whose meaning is difficult to establish with certainty (Eusebius, *Historia Ecclesiastica* VI.25).

The second book of Maccabees was undoubtedly composed in Greek. In the manuscripts of the Septuagint the books of the Maccabees are represented in a variety of combinations.[1] Codex Alexandrinus (fifth century) has four books of Maccabees, while Sinaiticus (fourth century) exhibits only the first and the fourth books, and Vaticanus (fourth century) knows none at all. The Old Latin version is acquainted with the first and second books only. This version goes back to about the year 200, for it is cited as early as Cyprian. The Old Latin was translated from Greek manuscripts which often embody an older and better text that any which could be reconstructed on the basis of the Greek uncials alone.[2] The Vulgate has preserved this version, for Jerome had no desire to emend it. But the translation was revised at a later date, so thoroughly that it is only a poor witness to the original text.

I MACCABEES

Content

The story which 1 Maccabees tells covers a forty-year period, 175–134 B.C.E., from the time when Antiochus IV ascended the throne of Syria up to the death of Simon, the last surviving brother of Judas Maccabeus. It is the history of the first generation of the Hasmoneans. It unfolds in chronological order. After an introduction which describes the situation before the revolt began (chapters 1 to 2), it goes on to deal with the three phases of Jewish resistance, in which the rebels were led successively by Judas (3:1 to 9:22), Jonathan (9:23 to 12:53) and Simon (13 to 16).

The historian is an artist, skilled in composition. His introduction is a diptych in which the progress of impiety (chapter 1) is balanced by the growth of resistance (chapter 2). On the one hand, Hellenism, personified in Alexander, puts forth a creeping shoot of impiety which flourishes so well that eventually the Abomination is installed on the

[1] Cf. W. Kappler, *Maccabaeorum Liber I* (Göttingen, 1936); R. Hanhart, *Maccabaeorum Liber II* (Göttingen, 1959).

[2] D. de Bruyne, *Les anciennes traductions latines des Machabées*, Analecta Maredsolana, 4 (Maredsous, 1932); 'Notes de philologie Biblique', *RB*, 30 (1921), 405–9; 'Le texte grec des deux premiers livres des Machabées', *RB*, 31 (1922), 31–54; 'Le texte grec du deuxième libre des Machabées', *RB*, 39 (1930), 503–19; A. Wilmart, review of D. de Bruyne and B. Sodar, *Les anciennes traductions latines des Machabées*, *RB*, 42 (1933), 263–9.

altar at Jerusalem; the Wrath bears down on Israel. On the other side, Judaism incarnates itself in Mattathias, the head of the Hasmonean house. He raises the standard of resistance. He organizes the resistance. And when he dies, the testament which he leaves his sons is a fiery exhortation to struggle to the death for the people and the Law. Faithful Jews will stem the tide of Wrath. Mattathias's sons fall, one by one, in the breach, each in his turn having led the struggle in accordance with his own temperament and his own methods.

Judas is the warrior hero. He kindles in his troops an irresistible fervour from the religious flame which burns in his exhortations and his prayers before combat (3:18–22, 58–9; 4:8–11, 30–3; 7:41–2). Having defeated the Syrian armies, he returns in triumph to Jerusalem, where he purifies the Temple (chapters 3 to 4). Thence he extends his power to the remotest ends of the country, being available everywhere to help his persecuted countrymen (chapter 5). Antiochus dies miserably on an expedition far away (6:1–16). Judas pursues the struggle against his successors, Eupator (6:17–63) and Demetrius (chapter 7), culminating in his brilliant victory over Nicanor. The two feasts of the Rededication and of the day of Nicanor (4:59 and 7:49), preserve the memory of his exploits for posterity. The narrator inserts documents bearing on Judas's diplomatic activities (chapter 8), and finally recounts his glorious death in desperate combat (9:1–22).

Jonathan lacks the heroic grandeur of his brother. More adept at fierce guerrilla fighting than at open war, he is above all an astute politician. Thanks to these talents he is able to 'judge' Israel in peace for about seven years (9:23–73). When the title to the Seleucid throne is in dispute between Demetrius and Alexander Balas, the shrewd Jonathan gets them bidding against each other for his support, and so successfully that honours are showered on him from both sides, culminating in the sovereign high priesthood of Jerusalem and the court title of King's Friend. When Demetrius is killed in battle, Jonathan, for a consideration, obtains the purple from Alexander, together with the titles *stratēgos* and *meridarchēs* (10:1–66). After reigning for five years Alexander is supplanted by his cousin, Demetrius II, and for the next fifteen years the throne of Antioch is in dispute between two, and sometimes even three, contenders. This embroiled situation was the sort that suited Jonathan's diplomacy exactly. He managed to preserve his privileged position and even to have his brother Simon nominated as *stratēgos* of the coastal province. We thus arrive at the ironical situation in which the brothers of Judas, now officials of the king, govern the whole territory of Palestine on behalf of Antiochus' successors. Shrewd diplomacy renews the old relationship with Sparta. The two brothers consolidate their position by furnishing the country with fortified positions (10:66 to 12:38). How could such a crafty operator as Jonathan allow himself to be caught by a trick of Trypho's? But he does so, and is taken prisoner, soon to be put to death (12:39–53; 13:23).

Simon did not wait for Jonathan's death to take the situation in hand. Fighting and negotiating at the same time, he could not succeed in saving his brother, but he drove Trypho from the country and resumed relations with Demetrius II, who recognized him as head of the Jewish nation (13:1–42). This event marks the beginning of a new era, the era of liberation: 'the people began to write in their documents and contracts, "In the first year of Simon..."' (year 170 of the Greeks = 142 B.C.E.: 13:42). Though just as brave and as shrewd as his brothers, Simon knew better than they the virtue of clemency. This was how he obtained at little cost the last surrender of the islands of resistance, in particular the celebrated Akra of Jerusalem (13:43–53). The author of 1 Maccabees is not afraid to use messianic language in eulogizing the saviour of his country (14:1–15). Sparta, Rome and Antioch vie with each other in acknowledging the sovereignty of Simon, ethnarch of the Jews (14:16 to 15:24). A short-lived quarrel with Antiochus VII, who reigned during the captivity of his brother Demetrius II, gives Simon's sons the opportunity to demonstrate their valour (16:1–10). The renowned old man meets his end at a banquet, at the hands of an undistinguished rival. But the book closes with the introduction of his son John, who is to become the father of the Hasmonean kings.

The book's conclusion is modelled on the formula with which the books of Kings close their account of each reign. The form of this conclusion implies that the author was writing after the death of John Hyrcanus, which occurred in 104 B.C.E., after he had exercised the high-priesthood for more than thirty years. His sons, Aristobulus I (104–103 B.C.E.) and Alexander Janneus (103–76 B.C.E.) both took the title of 'king'. It was doubtless during the reign of the latter that 1 Maccabees was written, to the glory of the ancestors of the dynasty.

Sources

The sources of 1 Maccabees are of two kinds. The author draws first of all on personal reminiscences, especially when dealing with the exploits of Judas. But he also appeals to written documents, which he was able to consult in the official archives of the treasury (see 1 Macc. 14:49). He made use in fact of numerous letters; some from the Roman senate, some from the Seleucid kings, and addressed variously to Judas, Jonathan and Simon. Critical opinion with regard to these documents has not always been agreed, but the more closely one studies Hellenistic epistolography the more convincing the case for their authenticity seems. In the Temple archives, whose origin goes back to the time of Nehemiah (see 2 Macc. 2:13), the author was also able to consult the priestly annals (cf. 1 Macc. 14:49; 16:24).

In addition to these documents the author made use of a pagan source, which told the history of the Seleucid kingdom and established its chronology. Just because of this documentation the historian who wrote 1 Maccabees deserves particular credit. As history, 1 Maccabees has a real superiority over 2 Maccabees, even though some writers do prefer to follow 2 Maccabees on the order of events (Starcky). Nevertheless, on one important point the author of 1 Maccabees has his own bias. His political sympathies are on the side of the Hasmonean dynasty, whose defender he is. Thus, as Josephus and the Jewish nationalists do, he exaggerates the size of their forces (see 5:45; 7:46). His undisguised admiration for Judas prompts him, for example, to explain away the defeat at Jamnia by the disobedience of the Jews to the Maccabean leader's advice (5:55–62). Correspondingly, he fails to do full justice to the Seleucids.

Authorship and date

All that we know of the author has to be deduced from the work itself. The knowledge of Palestinian topography which he displays together with his descriptions of events, which for part of the time give the impression of being eyewitness accounts, argue that the author was resident in Palestine, probably in Jerusalem. Perhaps we may deduce from the fact that he had access to the Temple archives that he was of Sadducean extraction. His book was composed before 63 B.C.E., for on that date Pompey took Jerusalem and aroused among the Jews an explosion of hatred towards the Romans. After that date no ardent nationalist such as the author of 1 Maccabees could have sung the praises of the Romans, as he does in 1 Macc. 8. The last lines of the book (16:23f.) if they were not added by an editor other than the author himself, must have been written after 104, the date of John Hyracanus' death. It makes sense that at that date the author, speaking of the family tomb of the Hasmoneans, erected at Modein in 142 B.C.E., can say that 'it remains to this day' (13:30). It is therefore possible to place 1 Maccabees somewhere around the year 100 B.C.E.

Literary genre and chronology

The author has imitated the literary forms of the earlier historical books (Judges, Samuel and Kings). He probably saw himself as writing a sequel to the history of the Chronicler, showing that God was in control of history in the Seleucid period just as he had been in earlier ages. The events which he describes succeed each other without a great deal of connection being made between them. The author is not interested in the causal chain of events. In spite of this, his work constitutes a unity, because the whole is dominated by a specific concept, that of the opposition between Israel and the nations. Within each of his accounts he displays the art of composition which he has learnt from the Hellenistic writers. It is an art which is marked by a certain sobriety, though under the sobriety enthusiasm shines through. But, as with the older historical books, poetry is mixed with the prose accounts in the shape of hymns of thanksgiving, songs of lamentation (1:24–8, 36–40), eulogy of the Maccabean leaders (3:1–9; 14:4–15), and also the leaders' speeches (2:7–13).

The chronological framework of the events of the Maccabean era is that of the Greek Seleucid era which began in the year 312. In 1 Maccabees about thirty or so events are explicitly dated. This should enable us to date with precision a series of events which cover, in total, half a century (180–130 B.C.E.). But the chronological problems raised by the two books of Maccabees are complex, owing to a double system of reckoning the Seleucid era, the one autumnal, reckoning from a beginning in September–October 312 B.C.E., the other the vernal system, reckoning from March–April, 311 B.C.E. From this arise some significant discrepancies in dating. For instance, the death of Antiochus is dated after the feast of the Dedication in 1 Macc. 6:17, and before it in 2 Maccabees. The discovery of a cuneiform tablet in the British Museum which fixes the date of the king's death in October 164 B.C.E. has recently confirmed the chronology of 2 Maccabees, for the feast of the Dedication was celebrated in mid-December 164 B.C.E. (1 Macc. 4:52).[1]

Teaching

The religious views of the author are those of the older historians and are impregnated with Deuteronomic theology: 'Keep the Law and you

[1] Cf. J. Schaumberger, 'Die neue Seleukiden-Liste BM 35603 und die makkabäische Chronologie', *Bib*, 36 (1955), pp. 423–35.

shall possess the land.' The Law is the centre of everything.[1] It is the Law that divides men into two camps. The struggle is not between the Seleucids and the Hasmoneans. It is not even between the pagan kingdoms and the Jewish state. It is between those who observe the Law and those who oppose it. Mattathias' sons have no hesitation in dealing with heathen powers when that helps to guarantee the observance of the Law. But although it is right to depend on the covenantal promises, that does not mean falling back on a quietist fatalism. The author has no word of praise for those who allowed themselves to be slaughtered rather than infringe the Sabbath rest. It is much better to fight for the right to keep the Law. The author goes yet further, and approves imposing respect for religious prescriptions by force (2:39–48). The supreme glory is to die under arms in defence of the Law (2:64). This history thus exalts human values at the same time as spiritual ones. Faith engenders heroism. Devotion to the fatherland is inseparable from devotion to the one God.

More specifically political aims are discernible in the work. When John Hyrcanus and his sons clashed with the strict observers of the Law, the Pharisees, it was very useful to be able to recall that the Hasmonean dynasty owed its elevation precisely to its zeal for that very Law. The pro-Hasmonean bias, perceptible throughout, is sometimes emphasized with no false reticence (5:62). By contrast, the Hasideans, the spiritual ancestors of the Pharisees, though intensely devoted to the Law, are not always very practical in the way they show that devotion (7:8–18). These features of the book are discreet hints to the Pharisees that support of the Hasmoneans would perhaps be the best way to serve the Law's interests.

This heroic history in spite of everything leaves the reader unsatisfied. For a start, it seems a little excessive when we find that the author's religious feelings actually prohibit him from pronouncing the name of God at all. But the predominance of the Law and the silence of the prophets are not without dangers either. The enthusiasm for possession of the land is in danger of placing limitations on the universality of the hope. The eulogy of Simon in messianic terms indicates the same danger. To sum up, even for the Chosen People, the union of politics and religion is not without its dangers of confusion. Mattathias could never have imagined that his sons would reach the point where they solicited titles and offices in their own state from pagan kings, to say nothing of the high priesthood itself. The decline became even

[1] Cf. B. Renaud, 'La loi et les lois dans les livres des Maccabées', *RB*, 68 (1961), 39–67; A. Penna, 'Διαθήκη e συνθήκη nei libri dei Maccabei', *Bib*, 46 (1965), 149–80.

more marked later, when Hyrcanus' sons took the title of king. We know that eventually the dynasty placed on the throne of Jerusalem Herod the Idumean. It was a singular end for a movement of such pure beginnings.

2 MACCABEES

The author and the date of composition

We do not know the identity of the author of 2 Maccabees. We only know that he abridged a work in five volumes written by Jason of Cyrene (see 2 Macc. 2:23). Of Jason of Cyrene himself we know nothing more. Doubtless he was a member of the Jewish community in Cyrenaica. Perhaps he put together a work which followed a purely historical order, and the epitomator substituted a more theological plan. Jason's work must have covered more ground than the book of 2 Maccabees as it now stands, because it told the story of Judas Maccabeus and his brothers (2:19), while 2 Maccabees does not even complete the story of Judas himself. The period covered by the book runs from the year 175 B.C.E., from before the outbreak of the persecution, down to Judas' victory over Nicanor in 160 B.C.E. Jason's work must thus have been much fuller than that of 2 Maccabees, for the epitomator has made a selection from his stories and anecdotes (ἐπιτομή, 2:26, 28). But in making this selection he has not always managed his transitions very skilfully. Ocassionally he introduces people not previously named (for example, Bacchides and Timothy) as if they were already known to the reader. It is usually argued that Jason must have written his book shortly after Nicanor's death in 160 B.C.E. This would be a plausible suggestion if it were not for the fact that 2 Maccabees tells us explicitly (2:19) that Jason composed a history which related to Judas Maccabeus *and his brothers*. The work of the anonymous epitomator, which, be it noted, betrays no influence at all from 1 Maccabees, must be placed towards the end of the second century B.C.E., but earlier than 1 Maccabees.

The Festal Letters

By way of a foreword (1:1 to 2:18) the book includes two letters from the Jews at Jerusalem. The first is addressed to the Jews in Egypt and is dated in December 124. It recalls how, in a letter written twenty years earlier, the writers sent news of their deliverance from tribulation. They invite the Jews in Egypt to celebrate with them the feast of the

Dedication. There is, it appears, a discreet allusion in this letter to the temple at Leontopolis (1:4) which was built by Onias IV in about 152 B.C.E.[1]

The second letter is also addressed to the Jews in Egypt by those of Jerusalem. It is not dated, but it is considerably earlier than the first letter. It was written a little before the dedication of the Temple in 164 B.C.E. The Jerusalem Jews invite those of Egypt to celebrate this feast with them also. The letter recalls the death of Antiochus IV, the Jews' persecutor, and then tells a long story about the miraculous events which marked the restoration of the Temple under Nehemiah. This is recounted in order to enhance the importance of the feast of Dedication of the writers' own day. There is no adequate reason for suspecting the authenticity of these letters as a whole. They were evidently written in Hebrew, or perhaps more likely, Aramaic, and translated into Greek by the epitomator.[2] He has placed them at the beginning of his work where they occupy the position of a preface. The purpose of these letters is clearly indicated (1:9, 18; 2:16). They represent an attempt to involve the Egyptian Jews in celebrating the feast of the Purification of the Temple which was instituted by Judas Maccabeus.

Contents

The author's work proper follows the two letters with a preface in which he explains his intentions and his method (2:19–32). He has with great labour simplified the bulky work of Jason, which was very full of statistics. He has attempted to make of it a readable account, for the benefit of educated people. With this purpose in mind he has been obliged to take some liberties with his source; all the more because it is not his aim to write a history in the technical sense of that word. Alone among biblical writers, the author himself defines for us what literary category he sees his work belonging to. The work develops in five scenes, in which the centre of the stage is occupied throughout by the Temple. Under a pious high priest such as Onias the sanctity of the Temple is inviolable. Heliodorus discovers this to his cost (chapter 3).

When the high priesthood becomes the prey of pro-Hellenistic schemers, Jason and Menelaus, the wrath of God weighs heavily on Israel, the Temple is despoiled, and profaned by impure sacrifices. The

[1] Cf. M. Delcor, 'Le temple d'Onias en Egypte', *RB*, 75 (1968), 188–203.

[2] Cf. E. Bickerman, 'Ein jüdischer Festbrief', *ZNW*, 32 (1933), 233–54; C. C. Torrey, 'The letters prefixed to Second Maccabees', *JAOS*, 60 (1940), 119–50. Torrey attempted to reconstruct the Aramaic text of these letters. Cf. also F.-M. Abel, 'Les lettres préliminaires du second livre des Maccabées', *RB*, 53 (1946), 513–33.

sacrifice of their lives which faithful Jews offer him is an expiation which averts the wrath of the Almighty (chapters 4 to 7).

'The wrath of the Lord had turned to mercy.' Judas turns the tables on the pagans. Antiochus dies, acknowledging the hand of the Lord which strikes him down. Judas purifies the Temple (8:1 to 10:9).

Under the administration of Lysias, who governs on Eupator's behalf, Judas fights a war on all fronts, against the royal armies, against the Hellenized cities, and against the pagan peoples around. He thereby secures recognition of their freedom of worship. Lysias even has sacrifices offered in the Temple and directs the neighbouring cities not to molest the Jews (10:10 to 13:26). The scheming Menelaus is put to death.

Under Demetrius, who has killed Lysias and Eupator, a new claimant, Alcimus, attempts with the king's support to seize the high-priesthood. The commander-in-chief of the royal armies, Nicanor, blasphemes against the Temple. He is defeated and killed by Judas. His head is cut off and publicly displayed in full view of the Temple, and the people sing: 'Blessed is he who has kept his own place undefiled.' A festival is instituted to act as an annual reminder of this victory (14:1 to 15:37).

Finally the author, as a good rhetorician, takes leave of his readers with a commendation of his work, couched in terms of customary modesty (15:38–9).

Literary genre

Each scene is composed in the oratorical manner. The style is designed to be moving and persuasive. With Onias we savour the peace of regular service in the Temple. We share his anguish when the holy place is threatened. Then at last we taste with him the joy of triumph when the chastened Heliodorus acknowledges the sanctity of the God who dwells there. In the second discourse we trace the progress of impiety, and the parallel progress of the wrath of God, from Jason to Menelaus, from the pillage of the Temple to its profanation. In contrast, the death of the martyrs, which is to avert the divine anger, leaves the reader with a feeling of hope. In the three last discourses Judas grows in stature, while his adversaries collapse: Epiphanes, Lysias, Eupator, and finally Nicanor, each of them demonstrating in his own way the glory of the Almighty which is manifested in the Temple. Everything converges on the glory of God who has made His dwelling in Jerusalem (3:38, 7:37; 10:7; 13:23; 15:34).

The author pleads his cause like an advocate. He knows how to pick out and present effectively those episodes which evoke deeply held feelings. His style is designed to arouse the emotions. Everything about him speaks of the orator: the cutting epithets; the biting remarks; the striving for effect; the ample, not to say bombastic, style. What we have in 2 Maccabees is a kind of writing, widespread in Hellenistic literature, which has rightly been called *histoire pathétique*, 'history with feeling'.

When we look at the book in this light we are in a better position to appreciate the author's positive achievements. He sets himself to bring out the meaning and religious significance of events, but he does not concern himself with detailed precision as a scrupulous historian would feel obliged to do. Chronological ordering has had to give way before the demands of oratorical composition. The orator, as he tells his story, is entitled to pick out and to magnify the significant features. Thus 'the help which comes from heaven' (1 Macc. 16:3) takes the form in 2 Maccabees of manifestations of heavenly beings (3:24–6; 10:29–30; 11:8; compare 12:22; 15:11–16). Such 'epiphanies', that is, appearances of gods coming to the aid of the combatants, were common in the Hellenistic type of 'pathetic history' which Jason of Cyrene was imitating. The Jewish author has modified the form of it in conformity with his belief in a Providence which governs the world through the medium of angels. It is from Jason that our biblical author has derived these stories.

In spite of taking oratorical liberties, what our author has produced in 2 Maccabees remains a *historical work*. His pleading has weight in so far as the facts he presents are historical, and events as they happened and events as he presents them are not allowed to get too far apart. In fact putting his work alongside 1 Maccabees enables us to check the accuracy of his documentation (see the table of comparisons between the two works on p. 469). The documents only found in the second book (letters and edicts: 9:19–27; 11:16–38) appear with the same guarantees of authenticity as those in the first book. The festal letter at the beginning of 2 Maccabees (1:1–9) is very much what one would expect of the Jerusalem scribes. The long memorandum which accompanies it (1:10 to 2:18) has the characteristic marks of a haggadic construction. The author knows just what he is doing, and when he deals with the death of Antiochus he is careful to give us a more exact account (chapter 9; compare 1:13–17). On two important points 2 Maccabees happily supplements the too scanty data offered us by 1 Maccabees. First, the part played by the high priests in the moves towards Hellenization (2 Macc. 4) gives us a better explanation of the origins of the conflict than anything we are offered in 1 Maccabees. Second, the terms concluded with Lysias (2 Macc. 11) put the purification of the Temple into a more probable historical context.

Teaching

It is especially from the religious point of view that the second book of Maccabees surpasses the first. For the author of 2 Maccabees observance of the Law and the pursuit of political aims are not so readily confused. The struggle is between Judaism (the word appears in 2 Maccabees for the first time: 2:21; 8:1; 14:38) and Hellenism (4:13). The opposition between the two is total. Any compromise can lead only to disaster (4:7–17), and there is no question of accepting the high priesthood at the hands of a pagan king (11:2–3).

The absolute quality of Jewish religion springs from its *sanctity*. The holy Law (6:23, 28) cannot be transgressed, even in the interests of legitimate self-defence (5:25; 6:6; 15:3). The holy Lord of all holiness (14:36) cannot allow any defilement in the holy land, in the holy city, in his holy dwelling, or amongst his holy people. The sword of Judas is holy too; it comes from God (15:16). And the reader is not surprised to find the heavenly hosts taking part in the struggle.

The issue in the struggle is in fact one not of this world. It could be said that what Judas is working for is the coming of the kingdom of the saints, of which Daniel speaks. The enjoyment of the good things God has promised is transferred to another world by belief in the resurrection (7:14, 36). But, while awaiting the achievement of this, all the saints work together for the coming of the kingdom. Prayer, ritual sacrifice, and the willing sacrifice of one's own life acquire a significance which is not limited to the present generation (7:32–8; 12:39–45; 15:11–16). Judaism of this kind is in no danger of being diverted into becoming a political movement, for it has transcended worldly values.

One feature alone must suffice to indicate the distance which separates the two books of Maccabees, and that is their attitude to the *martyrs*. For in 1 Maccabees their death is simply a result of the divine wrath which bears down on Israel (1:64). It is armed resistance, the sword of Judas, that turns away that wrath (3:8). For 2 Maccabees the trials which are endured are certainly a punishment, but the willing acceptance of these trials is an expiation which itself will avert the wrath of God, and if Judas wins victories it is because the sacrifices have won acceptance (2 Macc. 7:36; 8:5).

Influence

Josephus has four accounts in common with 2 Maccabees which are not found in 1 Maccabees: the intrigues concerning the high-priesthood which prompted Syrian intervention; the consecration to Jupiter by the Syrians of the temple at Gerizim; the execution of Menelaus at Beroea; and lastly, the landing of Demetrius Soter at Tripolis. But this is not a matter of borrowings from 2 Maccabees, for Josephus cannot have known 2 Maccabees, any more than he can have known the work of Jason of Cyrene. On the other hand, Josephus makes very free use of 1 Maccabees. Philo of Alexandria seems to have known 2 Maccabees, which is understandable enough in view of its Egyptian origins. A little later, the fourth book of Maccabees offers us a treatise on the martyrs which is inspired by 2 Maccabees.[1]

In the New Testament, the author of the epistle to the Hebrews (11:35) must have known what is said of the martyrs in 2 Maccabees 6. Among the church fathers quotations from 2 Maccabees appear from the third century onwards. The cult of the seven martyred brothers appears in Antioch in the fourth century. St John Chrysostom delivered two homilies in their honour.[2]

Rabbinic literature was but little concerned to keep alive the memory of the Maccabees and their exploits. *Megillat Ta'anit* preserves a calendar containing some feasts commemorating events of the Maccabean period, the most notable of these being Hanukkah, which celebrates the purification and rededication of the Temple. It does this however without mentioning the part played by Judas and his brothers. The rabbinic silence about this family can be explained by the strong opposition of the Pharisees towards the Hasmoneans. This opposition began under John Hyrcanus and reached its climax under Alexander Janneus, who had many of the Pharisees crucified.

Table of comparisons between 1 and 2 Maccabees

The table below gives the correspondences between 1 and 2 Maccabees. It will be sufficient to show what liberties 2 Maccabees has taken with the chronological order.

[1] Cf. A. Dupont-Sommer, *Le Quatrième livre des Maccabées* (Paris, 1939).

[2] Cf. *PG*, 50 (1862), cols. 617–26; cf. H. Delehaye, *Origine du culte des martyrs* (2nd edn., Brussels, 1933), pp. 201–2.

Events	1 Maccabees	2 Maccabees
Accession of Antiochus IV Epiphanes (September 175 B.C.E.)		
Hellenism in Jerusalem	1:10–15	4
Plundering of the Temple (169 B.C.E.)	1:16–28	5:1–20
The governors' misdeeds	1:29–32	5:21–6
The Akra as a fortress of Hellenism	1:33–40	
Enforced Hellenization	1:41–55	6:1–9
The Abomination set up on the altar	1:54, 59	
Massacre of the faithful	1:56–63	6:10–11
The divine wrath	1:64	6:12–17
Eleazar; the seven martyr brothers		6:18 to 7:42
Resistance by Mattathias and his sons	2:1–28	cf. 5:27
Massacre of those who observe the Sabbath	2:29–38	cf. 5:25; 6:11
Resistance is organized	2:39–48	
Testament of Mattathias, and his death	2:49–70	
Judas begins his campaign	3:1–26	8:1–7
Antiochus goes east; Lysias regent	3:27–37	cf. 10:10–13
Judas defeats Nicanor and Gorgias at Emmaus	3:38 to 4:25	8:8–29, 34–6
Summary of other campaigns		8:30–3
First campaign by Lysias	4:26–35	11:1–12
Negotiations; toleration		11:13–21, 27–38
Purification of the Temple, re-dedication	4:36–61	10:1–8
Battles with neighbouring peoples	5:1–67	10:14–23; 12:1–45
Timothy killed at Gazara		10:24–38
Death of Antiochus (*circa* December 164 B.C.E.)	6:1–16	9; cf. 1:13–17
Eupator's edict of pacification		11:22–6
Lysias remains regent	6:17	10:9–11
Attack by Judas upon the Akra	6:18–27	
Lysias' second campaign	6:28–54	13:1–22
Peace agreed; Lysias withdraws	6:55–63	13:23–6
Demetrius seizes the crown (*circa* November 162 B.C.E.)	7:1–4	14:1–2
Intrigues by Alcimus and Bacchides	7:5–25	14:3–4
New offensive by Alcimus and Nicanor	7:26–32	14:5–30
Nicanor's blasphemy against the Temple	7:33–8	14:31–6
The heroism of Razis		14:37–46
Nicanor's day	7:39–49	15

Dates are indicated only where they can be checked by secular sources. The events recorded by 2 Maccabees alone (in italics) are out of sequence and impossible to date.

THE LETTER OF JEREMIAH

THE TEXTUAL TRADITION

The *Letter* is preserved in Greek and is placed in the Septuagint after Lamentations, at least in the majority of the Greek manuscripts and in the Syro-Hexaplar. But in some Greek manuscripts, in the Peshitta and the Vetus Latina it comes immediately after Baruch and counts as chapter 6 of that work. It is known that the text of the Vulgate is the same as that of the Old Latin, because Jerome did not think it worthwhile to make a new Latin version of Baruch or of the *Letter of Jeremiah*.[1] The great Greek uncials which contain the *Letter of Jeremiah* (Alexandrinus, Vaticanus, Marchalianus, etc.) present us with no important variant between them. Generally speaking, the Syriac is a very free translation of the Greek, whereas the Syro-Hexaplar and the Vetus Latina follow it very closely.

THE ORIGINAL TEXT

In the quality of its Greek style the *Letter* rises above the general level of Septuagint books, though it is not written in such pure Greek as the book of Wisdom. For a long time, therefore, the prevailing opinion, expecially among Protestant scholars, has been that the author was a Hellenistic Jew of Alexandria. But since the publication of Ball's study there is a tendency now to allow that the original was Hebrew.[2] In addition to Semitisms in the work, which could, just conceivably, be explained as 'Septuagintisms', Ball has drawn attention to real anomalies which can only be errors of translation. The most obvious is in verse 71 where the idols are dressed 'in purple and marble', whereas what is evidently behind the phrase is the well-known formula found in the Parable of Dives and Lazarus, 'clothed in purple and fine linen' (Luke 16:19). What has happened is that the word *šeš*, which means 'costly white cloth' (Prov. 31:22), has been confused with its homonym, meaning 'alabaster' or 'marble' (S. of S. 5:15).

DATE OF COMPOSITION

The date of the book's composition is difficult to establish, but a study of the sources which have inspired the *Letter of Jeremiah* furnishes us

[1] *Prol. in Jer.*, *PL* 24 (1845), col. 680.

[2] See C. J. Ball, 'Epistle of Jeremy', *APOT*, 1, pp. 596–611.

with a *terminus a quo*. In fact, this letter, which is a real satire on idolatry, makes use of similar passages from the prophetic tradition, and especially of Isa. 44:9–20, which has as its background the Babylonian situation. This latter text puts forward a number of arguments. The idol-makers are nothing. The gods are useless and ineffective; they put their worshippers to shame, for they have no understanding. But the similarities between the *Letter* and Jer. 10:1–16 (a passage which is an addition to the authentic words of Jeremiah) are even more obvious. In fact, Jer. 10:1–16 is the immediate model for the *Letter*. Throughout, however, the author is not solely dependent on his biblical sources, for he has been able to observe for himself the gods of Babylon, their priests, the cult which centred on them, and the psychology of the believers. But he is not speaking about classical Babylon in the period of its splendour. The Babylon he describes is the later Babylon, probably the Babylon which Alexander the Great had seen with his own eyes. Older forms of worship were coming back into favour. Alexander had rebuilt the Esagila, which had been destroyed by Xerxes, and the Seleucids followed his lead in this work of restoration. Indeed, our knowledge of the ceremonies of the Babylon New Year Festival is derived from a ritual text of the Greek period. It would therefore seem necessary to date the *Letter of Jeremiah* in this period of renewal of the cult of idols, and certainly before the composition of 2 Macc. 2:1, which probably contains an allusion to the *Letter*.

LITERARY GENRE

This writing, which purports to be a letter sent by Jeremiah to those about to be carried away captive into Babylon, is not, in spite of its title, a genuine letter. Notwithstanding its opening declaration (vs. 1), which attributes it to the great prophet, it has nothing to do with Jeremiah and remains anonymous. St Jerome was not far wide of the mark when he described the *Letter* as a pseudepigraph.[1] This 'letter' is in fact a satirical dissertation put together in no very methodical fashion. The author simply puts down one after the other his thoughts concerning the nothingness and powerlessness of idols. His aim is to encourage the Israelites to remain faithful to the religion of the true God.

From the point of view of teaching, the work presents us with nothing new over and above what we find in its prophetic sources or in Ps. 115:4–8 = 135:15–18. Later, the book of Wisdom was to take up and expand the same theme (Wisd. 13 to 15).

[1] *Prol. in Jer.*, *PL* 24 (1845), col. 680.

TOBIT

THE TEXTUAL TRADITION

Until recent years we had access to this book only through the Greek, Syriac and Latin versions. The Latin showed evidence of repeated overworking, the final state of the revision being represented by the Vulgate. The Greek version, which is the most important, and the one from which the others were derived, is preserved in two forms. The first recension is that of Alexandrinus, Vaticanus and the minuscules, the watered-down 'received text', which has lost its more picturesque features in the cause of edification. The second is that of Sinaiticus, which is a longer, more lively text, reflecting the primitive text much better. This second recension served as the basis for the older Latin versions. The principal texts (of Vaticanus, Sinaiticus and the Old Latin) were published in full in the great critical edition of the Septuagint, the Cambridge edition, in 1940.

Scholars had long agreed in seeing behind the Greek version a Semitic original, either Hebrew or Aramaic. But now among the Qumran documents we have just these Semitic versions, in the shape of fragments of four Aramaic manuscripts of Tobit and one Hebrew one.[1] The text of these fragments is in agreement with the long Greek recension of Sinaiticus and of the Vetus Latina. As had already been suspected, the shorter text turns out to be the work of a Hellenistic redactor.[2]

The Hebrew and Aramaic texts which were known before the Qumran discoveries were made represent only a translation back from the Greek version. This is particularly the case with the Aramaic Tobit discovered in the Bodleian library at Oxford and published by Neubauer in 1878.[3] The Qumran texts may represent the original Tobit, but it is still necessary to decide whether the book was written in Hebrew or Aramaic. Jerome had no very high regard for Tobit. He did, however, take on the task of translating it into Latin (as he explains in his introduction to Tobit) in response to the requests of Bishop Chromatius and Bishop Heliodorus. For this purpose he procured an

[1] For details of the passages contained in these fragments, see J. T. Milik, 'La patrie de Tobie', *RB*, 73 (1966), 522.

[2] Cf. P. W. Skehan, 'The Scrolls and the Old Testament Text', in *New Directions in Biblical Archaeology*, ed. D. N. Freedman and J. C. Greenfield (New York, 1969), p. 111.

[3] Cf. A. Neubauer, *The Book of Tobit: A Chaldee Text from a Unique MS. in the Bodleian Library* (Oxford, 1878).

Aramaic exemplar. Since he did not know the language, a Jewish interpreter translated it for him into Hebrew, whereupon Jerome himself dictated it in Latin to a secretary. He completed the whole work very rapidly, and without taking any great trouble, in a single day (*PL*, 29 (1846), cols. 23–6).

CONTENTS

In spite of their differences in points of detail, all the recensions of the book of Tobit are in agreement about the story as a whole. By way of introduction the aged Tobit gives us an account of his life's joys and sorrows down to the period in which the story proper begins. Tobit is an Israelite of the tribe of Naphtali. Already, even while living in his native land, he was almost the only one still faithfully keeping the Law. Having been deported to Nineveh, with his wife Anna and his son Tobias, he remains faithful in spite of all temptations, until the day when his scruples draw down on him the almost blasphemous insults of his wife. Ruined and blind, abandoned by everyone, he turns to God and asks him, in a humble and penitent prayer, to let him depart from this evil world in which he no longer has anything to hope for (1:3 to 3:6).

Now at that very hour, the narrator goes on, in Ecbatana, Sarah, the daughter of Raguel, was listening to the insults of her servant, who was mocking her for her misfortune. She had attempted to marry, successively, seven husbands, and seen each of them in turn die. A jealous demon, Asmodeus, had killed each of them before they could approach her. She too appeals to God with a cry of distress, asking the Lord to put an end either to her days or to her humiliation (3:7–15).

The double prayer is granted, and God sends his angel Raphael to take charge of the situation (3:16–17).

The leading character is the young Tobias. His father gives him much good advice (so that chapter 4 becomes a little collection of proverbs on the subject of good works) and then sends him to recover a sizeable sum of money left on deposit with a certain Gabael in a remote part of Media (5:1–3). It is then that Raphael appears, using the name Azarias, and offers to go with the young man and show him the way (5:4–22). The angel is far more than a guide; he teaches Tobias how to meet the dangers facing him. He also teaches him remedies for his father's blindness and to counteract the spells of the demons. Azarias praises the charms of Tobias' cousin Sarah and suggests that he should ask for her hand in marriage (chapter 6). Having arrived at Ecbatana Tobias is very pressing in his request to marry his cousin, and, to the great amazement of her parents, the wedding night passes without untoward incident. Fourteen days of festivities are not too many to celebrate the wedding of the happy couple. In the interval Azarias goes himself to recover the money and brings Gabael (chapter 7 to 8). Meanwhile, in Nineveh, Anna and Tobit are worried that their son has not returned. So Tobias hastens his departure and begins the return journey with his wife, all the while being led by the angel. The joy at Tobias' return is at its height when Tobias restores his father's sight, with the help of the remedy which Raphael has taught him. The renewed rejoicings are prolonged still further in a feast of welcome for the bride and bridegroom (chapters 10 to 11).

All that remains is for the actors to take their leave. Raphael reveals his true identity before disappearing, though not without giving yet more teaching on good works in some proverbs. He ends by inviting his listeners to give thanks to Providence (chapter 12). Tobit hastens to fulfil this injunction in a hymn which spreads itself in prophetic descriptions of the future glory of Jerusalem (chapter 13). The old man's end is like that of the patriarchs. On his deathbed he unveils the future to his son, and recommends to him again the duties of filial piety, the practice of good works and the fear of God (14:1–11). Tobias, having fulfilled his last duties, first to his father and afterwards to his mother, moves to Ecbatana to undertake there the same care for the old age of his parents-in-law. He himself eventually dies, full of days, having had the satisfaction of seeing the deathbed prophecies of his father realized (14:12–15).

LITERARY GENRE

The Greek manuscripts vary in the place which they give to the group of books comprising Tobit, Judith and Esther, doubtless because they were unsure to what literary category they properly belonged. Whereas in Sinaiticus they come immediately after the great historical books, Vaticanus has them following the Wisdom books. We shall assess its literary genre more successfully if we begin by asking what the author of this book was hoping to achieve. In the case of Tobit, the author is trying to convince his readers that God never abandons a pious man. If such a man remains faithful under testing, not only will God restore him but he will compensate him for what he has suffered. Throughout the book the author exhorts his fellow countrymen to obey the law. For even if they live in the Diaspora God will not fail to protect them, as long as, in spite of the difficulties of their peculiar position, they remain faithful to him.

If the book of Tobit is in its intention a didactic work we should not be surprised to find it a piece of fiction, a kind of short story, which happens to have borrowed from history such names of kings as Shalmaneser (1:2), Sennacherib (1:15) and Esarhaddon (1:21), and from geography some rather vague facts. The author, in composing his account, has sought inspiration in the stories of Genesis; in particular, the story of Joseph and that of the mission of Abraham's servant (Gen. 24), have provided him with models. Like the stories of the patriarchs, that of Tobit contains numerous benedictions, exchanged in greeting or farewell (for example, 9:6; 11:17). Prayers, whether appeals for assistance (3:11; 8:5–7) or songs of thanksgiving (8:15–19; 11:14–15; 12:6; 13:1–18) all begin with the formula of blessing which has been standard in Jewish prayer down to our own day. The book closes with a similar formula, and the author expresses the hope that some day all nations will unite their voices with those of Jerusalem to bless the Lord (14:7). It will be observed, nevertheless, that Sarah's prayer is more personal than that of Tobit (3:1–6, 11–15), for the latter is full of the traditional formulae of liturgical prayer (Ezra 9; Neh. 1 and 9; Dan. 9:4–20).

The fact that there are to be found in the book medical prescriptions for curing Tobit's blindness, and even two collections of proverbs (4:3–19; 12:6–10), is sufficient to indicate that it has connections with the Wisdom writings (compare Sirach 38:3–8; 39:3). Both its form and its content place it ultimately in the category of Wisdom literature. It is of the essence of this kind of writing that it transmits moral and religious teaching in an attractive literary form. The problem of the historicity of the story, which so preoccupied ancient commentators, is therefore, when we consider the book in proper perspective, very much a secondary one. The purpose of the author was not to satisfy the curiosity of historians, but to produce a didactic work. He has succeeded perfectly, and has composed a little masterpiece, in which he shows himself to be a master of the arts of story-telling and of accurate portrayal of character (such as the character of Azarias–Raphael). Everything in the book contributes to its captivating charm which rejoices the heart with its tale of well-doing in the sight of God.

TEACHING

The question of rewards and punishments in the world to come had not yet been raised when Tobit was written. It is in this world that a man may expect happiness, in accordance with the blessing promised to Abraham. And happiness consists in producing descendants who will possess the land (4:12) and in living a long time to see this happy posterity (12:9). On *angelology* the book is, by contrast, more original. Good and evil angels play an important part in it. The names Asmodeus and Raphael are meaningful: the one kills, the other heals. The efficacy attributed to the fumigation which drives Asmodeus away speaks of a medical science which is not far removed from magic and the use of spells. But what is brought out most strongly is that the Destroyer has power only over those who transgress the Law. According to the prescriptions of the Law Sarah, as an heiress, ought to marry within her own family (Num. 27:9–11; 36:1–12), and God punishes with death those who violate the *laws of marriage* (Lev. 20). In the setting of Jewish belief, Asmodeus (whose name is Persian) appears therefore as the instrument of divine justice. Raphael, for his part, is one of the good angels. He is one of the seven who stand before God (12:15) and present to him the prayers of men and their good works (12:13). The angels descend, if the need arises, into the human sphere to help those whose requests God has granted (3:17; 12:14, 18). They take on human form so as not to be recognized (5:4ff) and act as guardian angels, accompanying the virtuous and protecting them (5:17, 21).

The book emphasizes the value of charitable acts, especially the giving of alms (1:17; 2:2–4; 4:7–11) and piety towards the dead (4:4; 14:12–13). In the book of Tobit scrupulous respect for all manner of legal prescriptions is advocated, from the making of pilgrimages to Jerusalem at the great annual feasts (1:6; 5:13) to abstinence from forbidden foods (1:10–12). But there is nothing rigid about this legalism, for it is prompted by genuine charity to the poor and the dispossessed.

EXTRA-BIBLICAL SOURCES, DATE AND AUTHORSHIP

One of Tobit's acknowledged sources is the *Wisdom of Ahikar*, the story of whom is summarized in 14:10. The book makes Ahikar Tobit's nephew and the treasurer of Esarhaddon and his predecessor Sennacherib (1:22; 2:10; 11:18). There are also, here and there, verbal reminiscences of the *Wisdom of Ahikar*.[1]

It is generally agreed nowadays that the story of Ahikar comes from Babylon. In fact, Ahikar's name has recently been identified by J. van Dijk among texts found during excavations at Warka: 'Aba-enlil-dari whom the Aḫlamu call Aḫikar'.[2] The *Wisdom of Ahikar* was a very

[1] Cf. F. Nau, *Histoire et Sagesse d'Ahiqar l'Assyrien* (Paris, 1909), pp. 58ff.

[2] Cf. J. van Dijk, 'Warka', *AfO*, 20 (1963), 217.

popular work of ancient Near Eastern literature. It has been preserved in Aramaic among the Elephantine papyri, in a copy dating from the fifth century but in a very bad state of preservation.[1] The book takes the form of a story in which are set collections of proverbs; but the fusion of the two elements, story and proverbs, is not as well done as in the book of Tobit. Ahikar, who is in favour at the court, first of Sennacherib and then of Esarhaddon, is slandered by his adopted son Nadan, who is over-eager to take his place. He is condemned to death, but is saved by his executioners, who keep him in hiding. When the king expresses regret at having lost such a counsellor, Ahikar is restored to him alive. He extricates Esarhaddon from great embarrassment, and Nadan dies of chagrin.[2] Everything suggests that we should place Tobit and Ahikar together in the same literary category. A curious variation in the title of Ahikar is instructive. The Syriac version of it, which is dated well into the Christian era, is entitled 'Proverbs or story of Ahikar', whereas the old title of the Aramaic papyrus is simply 'Proverbs of Ahikar'. The ancient authors did not have the same illusions about the historical value of this type of literature as the later copyists had. Another possible source of Tobit is the Egyptian treatise called the *Tractate of Khons*, which tells how a princess in Ecbatana was delivered from a demon by one of the Egyptian gods.

It is difficult to establish with certainty where the book of Tobit was composed.[3] What has just been said about the possible sources of the work would suggest Egypt as the place of origin, if the problem of the original language of the book, probably Aramaic, did not raise a difficulty. The fact is that the Jews of Egypt habitually wrote in Greek. They were certainly doing so at the time when Tobit was written. It is very generally held that the date of composition is earlier than the Maccabean period and that it should be placed about 200 B.C.E. Some would even like to push back the date as far back as 300 B.C.E.[4] Tobit is cited as early as Polycarp's letter to the Ephesians, but it was not commented on by the fathers.

[1] Cf. A. Cowley, *Aramaic Papyri of the Fifth Century B.C.* (Oxford, 1923), pp. 212ff. The proverbs contained in this papyrus are translated into French by P. Grelot in *RB*, 68 (1961), 178–94.

[2] A French translation of the Syriac versions will be found in Nau, *Histoire*.

[3] The attempt has recently been made to show it to be a Samaritan work, composed either in the capital of this Persian and Macedonian province, or even at Shechem. Cf. Milik, *RB*, 73 (1966), 530.

[4] Cf. J. Lebram, 'Die Weltreiche in der jüdischen Apokalyptik. Bemerkungen zu Tobit (14, 4–7), *ZAW*, 76 (1964), 328–31.

WISDOM

THE TITLE

The manuscripts of the Greek Bible give this book the title of Wisdom of Solomon, which at the very outset raises the question of authorship. In fact, as is proved by its demonstrably late date, this is just another example of a device that was widespread in antiquity, the attaching of a prestigious name to an anonymous work in order to give it greater authority. Solomon, as the wise man *par excellence*, has attributed to him a number of works, such as the Song of Songs, the book of Proverbs and the Psalms of Solomon. The Vulgate entitles the work simply *Sapientia*, as if to suggest its unparalleled standing among the books of Wisdom literature. It is indeed the richest in ideas, the closest to the New Testament and the most carefully composed. As W. O. E. Oesterley observed, the book was certainly looked upon in the early Church as one of the most important of the books which are reckoned as deuterocanonical. Reminiscences of the book of Wisdom are found in some New Testament writings, notably in the Fourth Gospel and in St Paul's letters.[1] The church fathers made use of it (the Didache, Clement of Rome, the Shepherd of Hermas, Tatian, Ireneus and Hippolytus of Rome). The Muratorian Canon is open to the interpretation that it regards Wisdom as canonical, while Jerome later rejected it, admitting into the canon only books that were written in Hebrew.

THE AUTHOR

The book of Wisdom is written in Greek, and in a Greek which does not look like that of a man translating from a Semitic original. The author writes with a measure of spontaneity and uses alliteration, assonance and paronomasia in a way which would be very difficult for a translator. Though there are Semitisms in the work, they are due to the influence of the Septuagint. The author was an anonymous Jew, and the efforts of commentators to penetrate the secret of his identity have not met with much success. Various names have been suggested: Philo Judeus (St Jerome), Aristobulus the friend of Ptolemy Philometor, Jesus ben Sira (St Augustine) or even Apollos, St Paul's fellow worker.

The emphasis in the book on things Egyptian prompts us to think of someone living in Alexandria, perhaps a teacher in one of the Jewish schools of the metropolis. At any rate, he was someone well acquainted

[1] Cf. C. Romaniuk, 'Le livre de la Sagesse dans le Nouveau Testament', *NTS*, 14 (1967–68), 498–514.

with Greek culture. But he cannot be identified with Philo, although this is an ancient opinion and one which has been revived in our own time. Philo's teaching, his methods of exegesis, his language and his style are too different from those of the book of Wisdom. The composition of the work can be dated in the first half of the first century B.C.E. It was certainly written before Philo and before the New Testament books, but after the publication of the Septuagint translation of the Prophets and the Writings.

COMPOSITION

The book of Wisdom has a well-defined structure,[1] in which respect it contrasts with the Wisdom books preserved in Hebrew, such as the book of Proverbs. It comprises three sections. Section 1 contrasts the way of Wisdom with the way of the impious (chapters 1 to 5). Section 2 deals with Wisdom herself (chapters 6 to 9); and section 3 describes how the works of Wisdom are exhibited in the course of history (chapters 10 to 19). Several scholars have held that the book of Wisdom is the work of more than one author. As many as three have been suggested. Marked differences of tone and style are claimed between the first and the last sections of the work. There is no reference in chapters 11 to 19 to wisdom and immortality, unlike the earlier sections. And there are a striking number of linguistic differences between the sections, especially in the vocabulary and in the choice of particles. However, the majority of critics defend unity of authorship, for there is a genuine homogeneity in the vocabulary as well as in the ideas. The stylistic differences between one section and another can be explained by the fact that the book was not written all at one time, and by the literary influence of the sources from which the writer drew his inspiration. The first chapters (1 to 5) are based principally on the prophets, and their style is quite a Hebraizing one. Chapters 6 to 9, which make use, along with the book of Proverbs, of scraps of Greek philosophy, are less clearly influenced by biblical style. The last chapters (10 to 19), where the history of Israel is described in terms very remote from those of the canonical sources, are in a style very different from that of the Old Testament.

WISDOM AND THE IMPIOUS

At the outset, in a hortatory appeal (1:1–15), the author calls upon the kings, addressing them man to man, which is not surprising, since it is

[1] Cf. A. G. Wright, 'The structure of the Book of Wisdom', *Bib*, 48 (1967), 165–84; J. M. Reese, 'Plan and structure of the Book of Wisdom', *CBQ*, 27 (1965), 391–9.

supposed to be Solomon who is speaking. Thereafter he seems to lose sight of his audience of monarchs, save that he recalls it in odd moments now and again. He has in fact turned to address the impious, whom he threatens with divine punishment. 'For wisdom is a kindly spirit, and will not free a blasphemer from the guilt of his words' (1:6). *Coming from God, Wisdom is presented in effect as a spirit which becomes more internal to man than he is himself.* Wisdom's job is to keep a man in the way which leads to God. Deviations from the way can lead only to death. Now God did not make death, but created everything for life. The impious, for their part, treat death as a friend to whom they are fit to belong (1:16). In chapter 2 the author sets out the views of the impious in a long discourse. In it all belief in life after death is denied. 'For our allotted time is the passing of a shadow, and there is no return from our death, because it is sealed up and no one turns back' (2:5). In these circumstances we have to enjoy the good things of life (2:6–9). The wicked pursue the just with hatred and mockery (2:10–20). 'They did not know the secret purposes of God, nor hope for the wages of holiness, nor discern the prize for blameless souls' (2:22), whereas God created man for immortality and made him in the image of his own nature.

There is no self-defence of the righteous corresponding to this speech by the wicked. It is the author himself who defends the cause of the righteous. The death of the righteous is only an apparent death (3:1–4). They are in the hand of God, and God's *judgement* will make plain their glory. *They will shine like stars* and judge the nations (3:7–9). The ungodly will be punished in their offspring (3:10–12). Much better to have no children than to have ungodly children, for the childlessness of the righteous will bear fruit when the judgement comes (3:13–15), whilst the posterity of adulterers are bound to come to a grievous end (3:16–19). Childlessness with virtue is crowned with triumph in eternity (4:1–2), whereas the posterity of the ungodly will come to nothing (4:3–6). What does long life matter? Ripeness of age is measured by virtue, not by mere numbers of years. The early death of the righteous is a blessing, because 'being perfected in a short time, he fulfilled long years'. Thus the Lord 'took him quickly from the midst of wickedness' (4:7–15). As for the ungodly who live a long time, they will become 'an outrage among the dead for ever' (4:16–20).

The judgement will therefore at last reaveal *true values*. The righteous will stand before the judgement with great confidence (5:1) while the ungodly will come trembling, forced to acknowledge their error concerning the fate of the righteous (5:2–13). Their speech of confession (5:4–13) stands in contrast to the long opening discourse (2:1–20). The righteous are destined to reign for ever with the Lord (5:15–16), while the divine spirit becomes a tempest which will overwhelm the wicked (5:17–23).

WISDOM: ITS ORIGINS, ITS ESSENCE, ITS ACTIVITY AND THE MEANS OF ACQUIRING IT

Wisdom has led the righteous to true royalty. Solomon makes an easy transition from this to his exposition of *royal Wisdom* (chapters 6 to 9). He begins by warning the kings to think of the severe judgement which awaits them (6:1–11). Then he excites the desire for Wisdom in his noble audience by depicting her most desirable characteristics (6:12–25). She goes before those who seek her, conducting them to the throne of God, to reign there for ever. Being of a generous nature, Solomon has no greater joy than to share with everyone the treasure which he himself received as a gift. In order to convey the advantages of Wisdom he embarks on a description of his own experience.

He begins by recalling that he is by nature a man like any other (7:1–6). That he has become wise is a gift from God, given in answer to his prayer (7:7). He valued Wisdom above all things (7:8–10), and he was not deceived, because she has brought him all good things along with her (7:11–14). In his discourse he expatiates on the qualities which give Wisdom such value. She teaches knowledge of all creation (7:15–20), and is the unifying principle of all that exists (7:22–4). More precisely, *in the creation she is the emanation of beauty and of the power of God.* She thus makes pleasing to the Creator the creatures in whom he is found, especially the soul of man (7:25 to 8:1). Also Solomon has sought out and loved Wisdom, who is the sole object beloved of God himself (8:2–3). He has sought her all the more because she brings with her all other benefits, riches and virtue, skill and knowledge which is imperishable (8:4–13). She assists the king when he takes counsel concerning the government of men; she is with him still to refresh him in his moments of leisure (8:14–16). Knowing all this, Solomon also knows that, though he is so well endowed, wisdom is over and above his natural endowments. He could obtain her only by prayer (8:17–21). Solomon's prayer (chapter 9) is the culmination of the whole essay on Wisdom which we have had up to this point (chapters 6 to 8). It gathers together all the main points which have so far been made. It is also the spiritual high-water mark of the book.

THE WORKS OF WISDOM

The closing words of the prayer evoke Wisdom's role as saviour (9:18). The rest of the book shows us the outworking of that role. Wisdom saved the patriarchs, from Adam to Joseph, among all dangers to both body and soul. But those who strayed from her, such as Cain and the men of Sodom, drew down cataclysms on the earth (10:1–14). It was also Wisdom which saved the Chosen People by means of its servant Moses, and made their enemies perish (10:15–21). This whole history is entirely transparent to one who has read Genesis and Exodus, though recounted without a single proper name being mentioned.

The subject of the nation's salvation is then taken up and developed at length. A series of seven scenes contrasts the two modes of God's action. Salutary trials assist, by his grace, the spiritual development of his children, while by similar trials the ungodly are brought to their destruction. Seven plagues are in this way brought into the picture: thirst (11:2–14), hunger (16:1–4), the bites of animals (16:5–14), hail (contrasted to manna) (16:15–29), darkness (17:1 to 18:4), sudden death (18:5–25) and drowning (19:1–12).

Such conduct on God's part might seem to be lacking in generosity or justice, so a double digression inserted between the first two scenes answers this objection. God showed mercy even to the heathen nations (11:15 to 12:27). The idolators are themselves solely responsible for their own destruction, for in making creatures into gods they made all the creation their enemy (11:15–16). The long excursus against idolatry stresses that pagans who have been led astray by vanity are responsible for their own acts (chapters 13 to 15).[1] It is their own folly which has led to the withdrawal from them of the blessing which God placed on every creature (15:19).

At the end of the book the same idea is taken up again but from another angle (19:13–22). The various elements of creation make up a harmonious system, but a system which works to the detriment of those who become alienated from the divine order, at the same time as it works to the joy and glory of God's people.

LITERARY GENRES

Though the book of Wisdom makes use of a variety of literary genres, the work as a whole has been defined as a didactic exhortation, a protreptic, which is a category of literature that was widespread in the

[1] M. Gilbert, *La critique des dieux dans le livre de la Sagesse (Sg 13–15)* (Rome, 1923).

Hellenistic world.[1] The protreptic was not a formal treatise on abstract philosophical problems, but an appeal to pursue philosophy as a source of life. It was aimed particularly at students, reminding them of the impact that knowledge was bound to have on their moral progress.

The third section of Wisdom (chapters 10 to 19), which has sometimes been called the *Book of History*, is considered by many scholars either to be a midrash or to belong to the midrashic genre. Not all interpreters indeed are in agreement about how this term is to be understood, but to simplify matters we may quote the definition of A. Robert: 'the word "midrash" may be applied to all attempts to elucidate the meaning of scripture which are undertaken in the light of the whole Bible, and aim at giving contemporary value to the biblical text by means of procedures deriving, for the most part, from the oriental imagination'.[2]

The author of this third section alludes to the subject of Israel's origins, the Exodus, and especially the plagues of Egypt. A detailed comparison of his account with those of Genesis and Exodus reveals with what freedom and daring he makes use of the pentateuchal texts, filling the gaps in traditional stories, suppressing anything which would get in the way of his exposition and embellishing other aspects to suit the needs of his thesis, which is to point to Wisdom's action in history. In some instances (compare 10:21), these midrashic traditions take as their point of departure the Targums, the scriptural paraphrases such as were used in the Synagogues of Palestine or Alexandria.[3] However, there are some scholars who refuse to ascribe these chapters of Wisdom to the category of midrash at all. They prefer to class them with the συγκρίσεις, 'comparisons' which are common to the Attic orators and the later Greek historians.[4] We never do in fact find in Jewish midrash any arrangement of biblical events in the artificial form of the σύγκρισις.

Chapters 1:1 to 6:11 and 6:17–20 have been classed as eschatology by Fichtner.[5] It is undeniably true that this part of the book deals with the subject of eschatology. But in order to expound his eschatology the author uses the diatribe, a literary form which attained its fullest development in the third century B.C.E. In lively and colourful

[1] Cf. J. M. Reese, *Hellenistic Influence on the Book of Wisdom and its Consequences* (Rome, 1970), pp. 117–18.

[2] A. Robert, *Le Cantique des cantiques* (Paris, 1951), p. 11.

[3] Cf. P. Grelot, 'Sagesse 10,21 et le Targum de l'Exode', *Bib*, 42 (1961), 49–60.

[4] Cf. Reese, *Hellenistic Influence*, pp. 98ff.

[5] J. Fichtner, *Die altorientalische Weisheit in ihrer israelitisch-jüdischen Ausprägung*, BZAW 62 (Giessen, 1933).

language the author attempts both to defend his position and to win adherents (compare Reese).

THE BOOK OF WISDOM AND HELLENISM

The book of Wisdom, originating as it did in Alexandria, appears at the confluence of two streams, the streams of Jewish tradition and Greek culture. But the extent of Hellenistic influence upon it is a question which we still have to decide.[1] As far as style is concerned, the author remains faithful to the technique of parallelism, especially antithetical parallelism, which is dear to the Hebrew genius. Chapters 1 to 5 and 10 to 19 are built up entirely on the basis of this stylistic device. But he has learnt from the Greeks the art of making transitions from one subject to another, and he handles the Greek language well. With regard to his vocabulary, the author uses 335 words (which amounts to nearly twenty per cent of his total vocabulary) which occur nowhere else in the books of the Old Testament canon, though the subjects he is dealing with do occur. This demonstrates that in his terminology he stands some way from the Septuagint.

Even where he does use the vocabulary of the Greek Old Testament he employs some words in new senses. For example, ἄβυσσος (Wisd. 10:19) is used as an adjective in the sense of 'bottomless', rather than of the 'abyss' as we use the word. There are instances where the author uses, in parallel with a biblical word, a Hellenistic one which never appears in the Septuagint. In the description of the divine Wisdom he employs four terms which were common in the Hellenistic religious vocabulary: ἀμάραντος, 'unfading' (6:12), ἀπαύγασμα, 'effulgence' (7:26), ἀπόρροια, 'emanation' (7:25), πάρεδρος, 'attendant' or 'coadjutor' (9:4). The influence of Greek philosphical vocabulary on the book has long been recognized, especially the language of Stoicism. This technical language is used to express ideas which had long been part of the Israelites' religious thinking: προνοία, 'providence' (14:3), διοικεῖν, 'to order' (8:1; 12:18; 15:1), στοιχεῖα, 'elements' (7:17; 19:18), συνέχειν, 'to hold together (1:7), τεχνῖτις, 'fashioner' (7:22; 8:6).

Epicurus' influence is observable in the use of the word ἀφθαρσία, 'incorruptibility'; for the true nature of God, for this philospher, is his incorruptibility, his impassibility. We observe in this author also a certain familiarity with astronomy and the main themes of astrology. But we must note nevertheless that he has not completely assimilated

[1] Cf. J. M. Reese. In his *Hellenistic Influence*, he has made a special study of this aspect of the book.

the insights of the philosophers. All this would make excellent sense if the work was intended to be read by Jewish students preparing themselves for life in the metropolis of Alexandria. The author is trying to show them that they need neither be swallowed up by Hellenism nor despise it (Reese).

TEACHING

The teaching is that of the Old Testament, even though it is given a Hellenized dress because of the milieu in which the book was written and in which its first readers lived. But in addition the author stresses the idea of a blessed immortality in God's presence, which is the reward that Wisdom confers on the righteous (2:23; 3:1; 3:15; 6:19). This idea was an absolutely new one as expressed, and the term Wisdom uses, ἀθανασία, 'immortality', appears here for the first time anywhere in the Old Testament. Greek philosophy had provided pseudo-Solomon with a precise vocabulary, which allowed him to express clearly a doctrine towards which Israel's nascent speculative thought was already feeling its way.[1] At the same time we observe that the idea of the resurrection of the body is passed over in silence, although Israel had already formulated a clear notion of it in the Maccabean period (Dan. 12:2–3; 2 Macc. 7).[2] Numerous scholars have thought that the author of Wisdom was trying by his silence to avoid coming into conflict with the Greeks (cf. Acts 17:32).[3]

Though offered in the form of a new synthesis, the teaching of the book of Wisdom is profoundly traditional in substance, for we find gathered together in it elements which existed already in dispersed form in the prophetic and Wisdom books. But the author is widely acquainted with his people's scriptures, and sometimes makes use of traditions found also in apocryphal works or the writings of Qumran. For example, 2:24, which deals with the temptation of man by the devil, makes a double allusion, to the seduction of the primal couple by the serpent (compare Genesis) and to the malice of a party of demons who attack men (cf. *The Community Rule*, IQS 3.20–4).[4]

[1] Cf. M. Delcor, 'L'immortalité de l'âme dans le livre de la Sagesse et dans les documents de Qumran', *NRT*, 77 (1955), 614–30.

[2] On this point, cf. P. Grelot, 'L'eschatologie de la Sagesse et les apocalypses juives', in *Mémorial Albert Gelin: A la Rencontre de Dieu* (Le Puy, 1961), pp. 165–78.

[3] But cf. P. Beauchamp, 'Le salut corporel des justes et la conclusion du livre de la Sagesse', *Bib*, 45 (1964), 491–526.

[4] Cf. A. M. Dubarle, 'La tentation diabolique dans le livre de la Sagesse', in *Mélanges Eugène Tisserant*, Studi e Testi, 1 (Rome, 1964), pp. 187–95.

At the period when the author of Wisdom was writing there was a flood of different doctrines of salvation. Salvation was sought by some in the mystery religions, by others in gnosis. Pseudo-Solomon invites the reader to seek after God (1:1), and promises that he will find God if only he takes the divine Wisdom as his spouse (8:2). It is only in this way, by uniting himself with her, that man will be initiated into the divine secrets (8:4) and will obtain immortality (8:13). The author also teaches a truth which both Greeks and Jews found it hard to accept, that wisdom cannot be acquired by man's own strength. *Enkrateia* is a *grace* which must be asked of God (8:19–21). Before ever it becomes a human virtue justice must in the first place be a gift of God. But what, in the last resort, is Wisdom? She is nothing less than God himself communicating himself to his spiritual creation. She is the breath of the power of God, a pure emanation of the glory of the Almighty (7:25). She appears throughout the ages in holy souls, making them *friends of God* (7:27). In fact, Wisdom enters into the soul that opens itself to her, and leads it in the ways of God's service, until it arrives at eternal life in God's presence (8:9–21; chapter 10). It will be seen that we are here very close to the New Testament. Paul and John use the same formulae when they speak of the Spirit of God diffusing His love in men's hearts, to make them pleasing to God and to make all the virtues in them (Rom. 5:5). It has been claimed furthermore that the apostle Paul was familiar with the thought-world of Wisdom (Windisch[1]). Windisch even stressed the dependence of Paul's christology on the Wisdom writings, and especially on Pseudo-Solomon. There are various pieces of evidence to support this contention: for example, the designation of Christ as the image of God (εἰκών) (Col. 1:15; Wisd. 7:26); an echo, or a very probable echo, of Wisdom 7:24 in Col. 1:17 (τὰ πάντα ἐν αὐτῷ συνέστηκεν); and the role assigned to Christ in the creation and upholding of the world. Thus did the author of Wisdom prepare the minds of men, Christians would say, as far as it was possible to do so, to receive the relevation of the Trinity.

THE SIBYLLINE ORACLES

The collection of Sibylline Oracles comprised originally some fifteen books and various fragments. Three books (IX, X and XV) are completely lost, and there are lacunae in several of those which have survived. What remains constitutes a considerable amount of literature, but most of it is of relatively late date. We are interested here only in books III, IV

[1] Cited by C. Larcher, *Etudes sur le livre de la Sagesse* (Paris, 1969), p. 17.

and v, which are the oldest. Of these three we will deal in detail only with book III.

Σίβυλλα appears at first as a proper name and its etymology remains much disputed. The earliest writers knew only one Sibyl, as is attested by Heraclitus of Ephesus (whom Plutarch cites),[1] Aristophanes, Plato and Aristotle. Homer and Hesiod, in common with all the Greek writers before the sixth century, know nothing of her existence. It has been concluded that divination through the mediation of the Sibyl must have come into being during the interval which separates Hesiod from Heraclitus.[2] The Sibyls seem to have been modelled on the 'pythonesses' who prophesied at Delphi, but whereas the Pythons of Apollo's oracle were women who really existed, the Sibyls were imaginary beings comparable to the Muses or the nymphs. Furthermore the multiplication of legends which associated them with a variety of localities in the known world transformed the word 'Sibyl' from a proper name into a generic term for all sorts of prophetesses. Several Greek Sibyls are known, one of the most famous being the Sibyl of Erythrea. There were also the Italian Sibyls, including the Sibyl of Cumae immortalized by Virgil.[3] It was she, it is said, who sold to Tarquin the Elder the three famous books which were destroyed in the burning of the Capitol in 83 B.C.E. Finally, there were oriental Sibyls, including the Libyan or Egyptian Sibyl, the Persian Sibyl and the Babylonian (Chaldean or Hebrew) Sibyl. This last is of particular interest to us here since the author of the third book attributes his work to the Babylonian Sibyl. In connection with this book problems of its composition, its literary genre, its date and its milieu are raised.

The third book comprises 829 hexameters and is divided into four main sections. After a prologue (1–96), which is a discourse about God, follows a great historical panorama which traces history from the tower of Babel to the Roman empire (97–294). Verses 295–488 comprise a set of oracles against the nations. The last section (489–829) contains, as well as oracles against the nations, some eschatological oracles. Although the book contains disparate, even contradictory elements, which indicates an artificial collection, it cannot be said that it is entirely chaotic. The overall impression is of a certain unity, and it looks as if some effort has been made to put it into order. It has been said that

1 Plutarch, 'The oracles at Delphi', *Moralia*, vol. 5 Loeb Classical Library edition (1936), pp. 272–3.

2 V. Nikiprowetzky, *La Troisième Sibylle* (Paris, 1970), p. 8.

3 *Eclogues* iv.4f. And see the commentary by J. Carcopino, *Virgile et le mystère de la IVème Eclogue* (Paris, 1943).

there is more order in the book of the Sibyl than in some of the canonical prophets.[1]

Before suggesting a date for the composition of the third book it is important to decide to what literary category it belongs. Its connections, in fact, are with apocalyptic. One of the rules of apocalyptic writing is that the work must be attributed to some celebrated figure of a bygone age. In Palestine Daniel, Enoch and Moses were obvious choices. In Alexandria, where the Jews had been introduced to Greek literature and where they were attempting to exercise intellectual and moral influence over the pagans, they appealed instead to Greek philosophers and moralists of repute. Aristobulus makes use of spurious citations from Homer, Hesiod and others. But in addition to philosophers they assumed also the mask of the Sibyls. Given the fact that a number of writings were circulating under their name it was easy to put into circulation others in which Jews could get a hearing for ideas which were close to their hearts. Thus there came into being Sibylline oracles of Jewish origin, real works of propaganda aimed at Greek readers. Thus, it has been said, the Alexandrian form taken by apocalyptic literature was 'sibyllism'.[2] Indeed, 'sibyllism' came into being in Alexandria about the same time as apocalyptic originated in Palestine. It is generally recognized that the third book constitutes the oldest section of the oracles, that it is of Jewish composition, and that it contains few Christian glosses. It announces on several occasions that idolatry will come to an end for the period 'when there shall reign over Egypt a new king, the seventh of his race, from the empire of the Hellenes' (191–3; 316–18; 608–16). It is generally reckoned that the seventh Egyptian king is either Ptolemy VI Philometor (181–145 B.C.E.) (this counts Alexander the Great as the first Greek sovereign of Egypt) or, more likely, leaving Alexander the Great out of the reckoning, Ptolemy VIII Physcon, who was first coopted onto the throne by his brother from 170–164, and who reigned alone from 145–116 B.C.E. Into this period fits the mention of the invasion of Egypt by a great king of Asia (i.e. Antiochus Epiphanes in 171–168 B.C.E.).[3] We should therefore have to place the redaction of the third book around 140 B.C.E. This dating, which has been discussed elsewhere,[4] depends

[1] Nikiprowetzky, *La Troisième Sibylle*, p. 70. But see J. J. Collins, *The Sibylline Oracles of Egyptian Judaism* (Missoula, 1974), pp. 21–22.

[2] E. Renan, *Les Evangiles et la seconde génération chrétienne* (Paris, 1877), p. 162.

[3] A. Hilgenfeld, *Die jüdische Apokalyptik und ihre geschichtliche Entwicklung* (Jena, 1857; repr. 1966), p. 85.

[4] Nikiprowetzky, *La Troisième Sibylle*, pp. 197ff.

on assuming unity of authorship, an assumption disputed by some scholars.[1]

The question of the circles in which the book originated is one which has never ceased to interest scholars even before the Qumran discoveries were made, some writers had already established a connection either with Essenism in general or with the Therapeutae in particular, not only for the third book but for the Sibylline Oracles as a whole.[2] Though the Sibylline collection had also been observed to have affinities with the Enochic corpus, the book of Jubilees, and the Testaments of the Twelve Patriarchs, it was claimed in the contrary sense that none of the rites alluded to in the Sibylline Oracles reflected anything that was contrary to the Old Testament or to traditional Judaism. Further, we do not find in the third book a description of the way of life of the Therapeutae as in Philo's *De Vita Contemplativa*. Scholars have therefore argued that the collection we are dealing with was concerned with wider matters than the beliefs of the Therapeutae and was meant for a wider audience than that sect would have provided.[3] What is in any case certain is that the Sibylline Oracles were repudiated by Judaism, and that for two main reasons. In the first place, the figure of the Sibyl was too closely connected with paganism. In the second place, the Oracles were discredited along with the rest when apocalyptic literature fell rapidly into disfavour. The Jews became disillusioned with apocalyptic literature as a whole when the end of the world did not take place within the time scale which the apocalyptists had reckoned on.

It is agreed that the third book originated in Egypt, and one can best place the Babylonian Sibyl, her pagan exterior masking Jewish apologetic, among Greek-educated Alexandrian Jews. There are many pieces of evidence to support this picture: the book's familiarity with the language of Homer, its euhemerism, its syncretistic assimilation of Greek mythology and the biblical stories, its allusions to animal cults. Egyptian animal worship could well be reflected in the following verses of the prologue: 'You neither revere God nor are in awe of him, but you vainly go astray, bowing down before serpents, sacrificing to cats, to dumb idols, to effigies of men made of stone' (3.29–31). In order to affirm and to defend the unity and sovereignty of God the Sibyllists mercilessly attacked pagan idolatry, an idolatry which many of the

[1] H. H. Rowley, *Darius the Mede and the Four World Empires in the Book of Daniel* (2nd edn., Cardiff, 1959), pp. 115ff; J. Geffcken, *Komposition und Entstehungszeit der Oracula Sibyllina* (Leipzig, 1902), pp. 1–17.

[2] Renan, *Les Evangiles*, p. 168.

[3] Nikiprowetzky, *La Troisième Sibylle*, p. 265.

Greeks themselves already repudiated. Ceaselessly the authors of our present work insist on the doctrine of the one God, who created all things and maintains all things in being, and who is also judge of the world.

As far as the cult is concerned, though the third book is orthodox with regard to the Temple and animal sacrifice (573–9), the fourth book, which can perhaps be dated to about 80 C.E., rejects temples, altars and bloody sacrifices (4.27–8) and could reflect more clearly Essene teaching.[1]

THE THIRD BOOK OF ESDRAS OR THE GREEK EZRA

The book's very title leads to serious confusion. In most of the manuscripts of the Greek Bible (manuscripts A, B and a large number of minuscules) the book that we call 3 Esdras appears as First Esdras and the book of Ezra-Nehemiah as Second Esdras. In fact in the Hebrew Bible the books of Ezra and Nehemiah originally formed only one book. Baba Bathra says explicitly: 'This is the order of the hagiographa;... Esther, Ezra, Chronicles...Ezra wrote his own book and continued the genealogies of Chronicles down to his own time'.[2] The title 1 Esdras given to the book in the Apocrypha is explained by the fact that its record of events begins at an earlier point than that of the canonical Ezra. The title 3 Esdras is that of Latin Bibles since Jerome, because they call the canonical books of Ezra and Nehemiah 1 and 2 Esdras.

III Esdras or the Greek Ezra is clearly a composite work whose contents, with the exception of one important passage, are found also in the canonical books of Chronicles, Ezra and Nehemiah. Here follows a brief analysis. The book falls into three parts:

(1) Chapter 1 of the Greek Ezra repeats the two final chapters of Chronicles (2 Chron. 35 to 36), which deal with the end of the reign of Josiah from the great Passover which he celebrated, with the reigns of his three sons and the fall of Jerusalem.

(2) Chapters 2:1 to 9:36 repeat the whole of the material in the canonical Ezra, but with one transposition. The letters exchanged during the reign of Artaxerxes on the subject of Jewish rebuilding

[1] This is the view taken by A. Peretti, 'Echi di dottrine esseniche negli oracoli sibillini giudaici', *La Parola del Passato*, 17 (1962), 247–95. But it is strongly attacked by Nikiprowetzky in his article, 'Réflexions sur quelques problèmes du quatrième et du cinquième livres des Oracles Sibyllins', *HUCA*, 43 (1972), 35ff.

[2] *b. Baba Bathra*, 14b–15a.

(Ezra 4:7–24) are transferred to a point before Ezra chapters 2 and 3, which deal with the returned exiles and the rebuilding of the altar. In this section, 3:1 to 5:6, a genuinely original addition is found concerning the story of the three pages. We shall return to this below.

(3) The book ends with the opening verses of the account of the promulgation of the Law by Ezra, verses which are found in Neh. 7:74 to 8:12. But very oddly the account ends abruptly in the middle of a sentence (9:37–55).

Let us now turn to the original part of the book, which is unparalleled elsewhere in the Old Testament, that is, 3:1 to 5:6. King Darius, it tells us, gave a great banquet and invited all his servants. After the meal, Darius retired to sleep while his three bodyguards, or pages (σωματοφύλακες) kept watch. They made a wager together: 'Let each of us state which one thing is strongest; and to him whose statement seems wisest, Darius the king will give rich gifts and magnificent honours'. Each writes his answer and puts it under Darius' pillow. Darius, on waking, calls together the great men of Persia and Media to hear the pages' answers. The first page had written: 'Wine is strongest'; the second, 'The king is strongest'; the third, 'Women are strongest, but truth is victor over all things.' The third page, Zerubbabel, was given the king's verdict, and the king offered him whatever he desired. He recalled Darius' vow when he ascended the throne, that he would rebuild Jerusalem and restore the sacred vessels of the Temple which had been carried away to Babylon. Darius fulfilled his promise and gave to the winning page an escort to conduct him back to Jerusalem with the returning exiles. Various favours of an exceptional kind are granted to the Jews.

In this section there is clearly nothing historical at all. We can detect in it implausibilities, and contradictions with what is said elsewhere in the book. The story shares some of the characteristics both of the philosophical story and of haggada.[1] One of the possible sources of the narrative has been discovered in the Egyptian Wisdom literature.[2] In the maxims of Ptaḥḥotep, known from papyri which date back to about 2000 B.C.E., we find sayings of the type: 'Truth is great; it endures; it is firmly established',[3] and 'there is strength in truth; it

[1] Lods, *Histoire*, p. 952.

[2] P. Humbert, 'Le troisième livre d'Esdras', in his *Recherches sur les sources égyptiennes de la littérature sapientiale d'Israël*, Mémoires de l'Université de Neuchâtel, 7 (Neuchâtel, 1929), pp. 148–51.

[3] Z. Žába, *Les Maximes de Ptaḥḥotep* (Československá Akademie Věd, Prague, 1956, p. 74, ll. 88, 97), Žaba's translation is however a little different from Humbert's, for what we have reported as being said of truth is in Žaba's translation said of justice.

endures'. Similarly , in the Eloquent Peasant, dating from the same period, we have the words: 'Practice truth, for it is great, it is powerful, it endures'.[1] The similarity of these sayings to the words of the Greek Ezra, 'Great is truth, and strongest of all' (4:41), is striking. The rivalry between the three pages is a theme common to oriental folklore, whether Greek or Egyptian. One of the most significant parallels which has been cited to the Greek Ezra is found in the story of Setmé Khamois.[2] A king of Ethiopia overheard three magicians, subjects of his, discussing what would be the best evil spell to cast upon Egypt, the traditional enemy. One of them won the competition and put his plan into effect.[3]

Leaving aside the problems concerning the origin of the story of the three pages, three essential questions arise with regard to the Greek Ezra as a whole: its historicity, the aim of its author, and the book's canonicity.

The Greek Ezra claims to be a historical source of the same standing as other historical books of the Bible. In fact the historian Josephus made use of it, for he follows its order of events.[4] But it inspires little confidence by reason of its lack of chronology, or rather, because the chronology it does display is backwards. It mentions Persian kings in the order: Cyrus, Artaxerxes, Darius, Cyrus, Darius, Artaxerxes. Quite apart from this confusion, contradictions abound. A significant example is that according to 5:68–71 it was in the time of Cyrus that Zerubbabel rebuilt the Temple. Yet in the story of the three pages Zerubbabel is quite young when he obtains permission to go to Jerusalem, and this is in the reign of Darius (4:47). In yet a third passage (5:5) a son of Zerubbabel is a member of the party which returns to Jerusalem in the reign of Darius. It will be apparent from this why it is that the majority of critics attach no historical value whatever to this work. The most recent commentator on the book, however, reckons that in spite of its being relegated to the Apocrypha it does contain some important historical facts; for example, it bears witness that the Edomites burnt the Temple (4:45) and draws a clear distinction between Zerubbabel and Sheshbazzar (6:18).[5]

The aim which the author set himself when composing this work is

[1] Cited by Humbert, 'Le troisième livre', p. 149.

[2] Lods, *Histoire*, pp. 952–3.

[3] G. Maspéro, *Les contes populaires de l'Egypte ancienne* (Paris, 1957), pp, 47ff.

[4] *Ant.* XI.1–158. The problem of the relations between Josephus and Greek Ezra has been studied at length by K.-F. Pohlmann, in his *Studien zum dritten Esra* (Göttingen, 1970) pp. 74–126. He concludes that Josephus is dependent on Greek Ezra.

[5] J. M. Myers, *I and II Esdras*, AB 42 (Garden City, N.Y., 1974), p. 15.

not easy to establish with certainty. Scholars have attempted to detect a basic theme controlling the collection and selection of the material. Some conclude that the author meant to construct a history of the Temple, from the last days when it was in use before the Exile, up to the re-establishment of the cult after the return. Others see no one dominant idea which might reveal the author's intentions.[1] Sometimes they emphasize the important part which Ezra himself, called 'high priest' (*archiereus*), plays in the book. He is mentioned nearly twenty times. It is noticed at the same time that the part played by Nehemiah is minimized in comparison with that of Ezra.[2] But perhaps it is better to see in this literary collection a rearranged fragment of a translation of the larger work, Chronicles-Ezra-Nehemiah.[3] It would have been preserved for the sake of the story of the three pages, which constitutes a genuinely original tradition. The date of the book is difficult to establish with exactness. It is earlier than Josephus, who made use of it, and on the other hand it is later than Daniel and Esther which have provided some of its inspiration. For instance, the fact that the Persian empire was divided into 127 provinces 'from India to Ethiopia' is mentioned both in the Greek Ezra (3:2) and in Esther 1:1 and 8:9. And here and there commentators note reminiscences of Daniel, especially in the story of the three pages.

The Greek Ezra seems to have originated in the Greek-speaking Jewish community in Egypt, where the compiler probably knew the maxims of Ptaḥḥotep and other similar writings mentioned above.

There is a problem regarding the canonicity of the book. The fathers of the Church knew the book from quite an early period and made use of it frequently. Clement of Alexandria, Origen, Cyprian and Augustine, to name only a few, all show knowledge of it. But St Jerome's severe judgement was fatal to it, and the Latin church followed his lead.[4] The Council of Florence (1442) and later that of Trent (1546) rejected it as uncanonical. Protestants have been no less severe than the Catholics. Some have tried to question the judgement of the Council of Trent in pronouncing against its canonicity. R. H. Charles, writing about the Tridentine decree concerning the canonical scriptures, expressed himself as follows: 'This decree of the Council of Trent was

[1] Lods, *Histoire*, p. 954.

[2] Myers, *I and II Esdras*, p. 9.

[3] C. C. Torrey, 'A revised view of First Esdras', in *Louis Ginzberg Jubilee Volume* (New York, 1945), p. 395. Torrey concludes that the Greek Ezra is 'merely a piece of the oldest Greek version of the Chronicler's work'. For earlier, and different, views see C. C. Torrey, *Ezra Studies* (Chicago, 1910), p. 18.

[4] The question of canonicity has been well treated by J. B. Frey in his article 'Apocryphes' in *DBSup* 1 (1928), cols. 432–41.

ratified by fifty-three prelates "among whom there was not one German, not one scholar distinguished by historical learning, not one who was fitted by special study for the examination of a subject in which the truth could only be determined by the voice of antiquity."'[1] But whatever may be said of the expertise of the bishops who ratified the decree, it is surely not regrettable that this book, whose purpose and religious value are so little apparent, was not counted among the canonical writings.

THE THIRD BOOK OF MACCABEES

The name 'Third Book of Maccabees' which this book bears is entirely inappropriate, for it has nothing at all to do with the Maccabees. Its title is to be explained solely by the position it occupies in the manuscripts of the Septuagint, where it follows Maccabees 1 and 2. The book begins with an account of the battle of Raphia, in which Ptolemy IV Philopator routed Antiochus III, the Great, in 217 B.C.E. After his victory Ptolemy visited Jerusalem, where, in spite of lively protests, he was determined to enter the sanctuary (1:6–29). According to 3 Maccabees Simon the High Priest at this point addressed himself to prayer, in order to obtain from the Lord the result that the Temple would not be profaned by this pagan (2:1–20), and Ptolemy was thereupon punished by a miraculous intervention of God (2:21–4). Furious at this setback, he returned to Egypt and swore that he would take revenge on the Egyptian Jews. He decreed that they should be deprived of their citizenship unless they subscribed to the cult of Dionysus (2:25–33). In addition, he gave orders that all Jews found in his territory should be arrested and sent as prisoners to Alexandria (chapter 3). He had them collected in a hippodrome near Alexandria with the intention of using drunken elephants to trample them to death (chapter 4), but suddenly he forgot his plan and postponed it to the following day (5:1–22). He changed his mind once more before finally deciding to put his scheme into operation (5:23–51). On the intervention of an old priest Eleazar, and in response to his prayer, two angels appeared who frightened the elephants so much that they turned against the Egyptian soldiers and killed many of them (6:1–21). The king then became the protector of the Jews (6:22–9), who massacred those of their fellow Jews who had apostatized during the persecution. They held a seven-day celebration of their deliverance, which is repeated annually (6:30–40).

[1] *APOT*, I, p. x.

Two basic problems arise in connection with this work: the problem of its date and origin, and the problem of its historicity.

As to the question of date, we must have recourse first of all to internal criticism. Although the book has really nothing to do with the Maccabees, many of its leading ideas can be paralleled in 2 Maccabees. The experience of Ptolemy in 3 Maccabees is similar to that of Heliodorus who wished to enter the Temple treasury (2 Macc. 3:22–31), and that of Antiochus in 2 Macc. 9:4. Other features of 2 Maccabees are also common to 3 Maccabees, for example, the miraculous visions which occur in 2 Macc. 3:25 and 10:29; the emphasis placed on the sanctity of the Jerusalem Temple and on the prayers which the priests offer to God for its defence (2 Macc. 3:15–22; 8:2–4; 14:34–6); the prominence of feasts which commemorate acts of deliverance (2 Macc. 10:6; 15:36), and the central role played by a pious and aged man called Eleazar (2 Macc. 6:18).

Numerous similarities of style and language between the two books have also been pointed out.[1] Emmet, however, argues that in spite of some striking resemblances, there are differences which prevent us from attributing both works to a single author. The style of 2 Maccabees, he shows, is closer to that of Polybius than is that of 3 Maccabees. It is, moreover, difficult to establish any direct literary dependence between the two books.

Similarities have also been noted between 3 Maccabees and the *Letter of Aristeas*. These similarities concern ideas, style, and language.

Both 3 Maccabees and the *Letter of Aristeas* delight in glorifying the Jews, particularly in the eyes of the Hellenistic world. In each of them a King Ptolemy is featured who recognizes the protection which God accords the Jews (*Aristeas* 16; 19; 37). We also find in both books an emphasis on the beauty and inviolability of the Temple at Jerusalem. Both include official letters, and both give prominence to a priest called Eleazar (*Aristeas* 22; 29; 33; 41). From the point of view of language, the similarities are chiefly concerned with the use of a technical and official style. The observations about the style are also corroborated by the papyri, a fact which suggests that 3 Maccabees belongs to the Ptolemaic period and not the Roman.[2] The connections of 3 Maccabees with 2 Maccabees and with the *Letter of Aristeas*, both of them works which can be dated, broadly speaking, around the year 100 B.C.E.,[3] provide us with an indication of approximate date. We cannot, in any case, take back the date of 3 Maccabees earlier than the Song of

[1] Cf. Emmet, in *APOT*, 2, pp. 156–7.

[2] Ibid., p. 157.

[3] On these two works see pp. 463–69 and 497–500.

the Three Young Men in the furnace (LXX) to which we apparently have an allusion in 6:6. The Song of the Three Young Men, though difficult to date, is likely to be from the last quarter of the second century B.C.E.[1]

The book gives the appearance of being an apologetic work, and has seemingly been written primarily for the Jews themselves, to give them encouragement in facing persecution, but it by no means loses sight of the fact that it might have a Greek audience as well. It presents the Jews as very loyal supporters of the Ptolemies, in which it is reminiscent of certain Christian apologists who go out of their way to show that Christians are the Emperor's best citizens. The book belongs to orthodox Alexandrian circles rather than to any kind of heterodox setting.

What are we to say of the historicity of the work? Or perhaps we should rather ask: is there any real event at the basis of the fantastic story which 3 Maccabees tells? What is said of the battle of Raphia, not far from Gaza, in which Ptolemy Philopator and Antiochus III met, is in general agreement with what is reported by Polybius on the same subject in Book 5 of his history (82–6). But it has been questioned whether the differences which are apparent between Polybius and 3 Maccabees derive from the use by the author of 3 Maccabees or another source of information, perhaps the memoirs of Ptolemy of Megalopolis. In fact the latter, who was one of Polybius' fellow-countrymen, did write an account of the reign of Ptolemy Philopator which was by no means in the king's favour. The unflattering picture of his court and the changeable nature of the king's character, as well as certain details of the battle of Raphia which are not found in Polybius, may be derived from Ptolemy of Megalopolis.

But apart from this historical kernel, the rest of the story of 3 Maccabees is legendary, as is especially obvious if we compare some of the data it gives us with the facts provided in Josephus' *Contra Apionem*.[2] Some of the actions with 3 Maccabees attributes to Ptolemy IV Philopator Josephus attributes to Ptolemy III Euergetes or to Physcon. After Philometor's death the Alexandrian Jews took Cleopatra's part against her brother Ptolemy Physcon. The latter, says Josephus, to take revenge on the Jews, gave them over to elephants which had previously been made drunk. But, Josephus goes on, the result was exactly the reverse of what the king had hoped, for the animals turned on their own friends and many of them were killed.

[1] C. Kuhl, *Die drei Männer im Feuer (Daniel Kapitel 3 und seine Zusätze)*, BZAW 55 (Giessen, 1930).

[2] Josephus, *Contra Apionem* II.48–55.

Furthermore it is said that an apparition appeared to Ptolemy Physcon, forbidding him to harm the Jewish people. This divine intervention in the Jews' favour is the basis of a feast celebrated in Alexandria. Josephus also reports that Ptolemy III Euergetes journeyed to Jerusalem in order to offer sacrifice after a victory. He emphasizes the services rendered by the Jewish generals Onias and Dositheus and he mentions the intercession which the king's concubine, Ithaca or Irene, made to Physcon on the Jews' behalf. It is clear that Josephus' story is more credible than the manifestly legendary one of 3 Maccabees, which teems with miracles. What the author of 3 Maccabees has done is to combine elements drawn from a variety of sources in order to glorify the Jewish nation. Thus we may say, in summary, that the Third Book of Maccabees is a haggadic story with an apologetic aim.

THE LETTER OF ARISTEAS

In antiquity the *Letter of Aristeas* enjoyed an extraordinary popularity on account of the information which it offered concerning the origin of the Greek translation of the Jewish Law. It was because of the story which this letter tells for the first time that the Greek version as a whole acquired the title 'Septuagint'. Aristeas, a high official of the court of Ptolemy II Philadelphus (285/3–246 B.C.E.), is writing to his brother Philocrates to tell him of a mission to Eleazar the high priest of Jerusalem with which he has been charged. Demetrius of Phalerum, the king's librarian, had been given large funds to increase the number of manuscripts in the collection at Alexandria from two hundred thousand to five hundred thousand. Among those which the library lacked was a translation of the Jewish Law, 'which, being divine, is full of wisdom and infallible'. Aristeas travels to Jerusalem, carrying with him rich presents, to request Eleazar to appoint 72 men, six from each tribe, who are to determine the best text of the Law and make a translation of it into Greek. These 72 representatives are installed on the Isle of Pharos to get on with their work, which is completed in 72 days. When the translation is finished it is submitted to the Alexandrian Jewish community for approval. They vouch for its absolute accuracy and invoke a curse on anyone who allows any change whatever to be made in it. The king has the work read to him and admires it greatly, at the same time expressing astonishment that no Greek historian or poet has even mentioned such an important book.

The manuscript tradition is now represented by more than twenty manuscripts containing either the whole text of the *Letter of Aristeas* or significant extracts from it. These span the eleventh to the sixteenth centuries, and the earliest of them is Laurentianus 44, preserved at Florence. In all these manuscripts the text of the *Letter* is found alongside the Catena on the Octateuch, a vast compilation probably made by Procopius of Gaza. One tradition of the *Letter* is shown us by Josephus, who quotes most of it,[1] and by Eusebius of Caesarea.[2]

Two essential problems arise in connection with the *Letter of Aristeas*, its date of composition and its historical value.

As far as the date of the writing is concerned, one assertion may be made to begin with: this letter was not composed until long after the time of Ptolemy II. One or two pieces of evidence are sufficient to establish this. In §182 the words appear: 'For this arrangement had been made by the king, and it is an arrangement which you see maintained to this day'. Further, the disgrace of Demetrius of Phalerum makes impossible his alleged collaboration with Ptolemy II, for Ptolemy II sent him into exile at the very beginning of his reign. The anachronism is thus a flagrant one. In fact the Museum and Library at Alexandria were founded under Ptolemy I Soter at the suggestion of Demetrius of Phalerum. If Aristeas prefers to speak of Ptolemy II Philadelphus rather than Ptolemy I Soter it is because the former stood in higher repute than the latter and therefore suited his apologetic purpose better.

But the precise date of composition is still a question about which scholars are divided. Three principal theories have been advanced; one puts the *Letter of Aristeas* about the year 200 B.C.E. (E. Schürer); one places it between 96 and 93 B.C.E. (P. Wendland); and a third assigns it to a date in Tiberius' reign or later, after 33 C.E. (H. Willrich, H. Grätz). The main argument in favour of a date around 200 B.C.E. is based on the reference by the Jewish philosopher Aristobulus (170–150 B.C.E.) to the translation of the Septuagint. Aristobulus' statement is quoted by Eusebius of Caesarea in his *Praeparatio Evangelica*.[3] But the external evidence bearing on Aristobulus is not very convincing, and the contents of the surviving fragments of this author's own works give rise to the gravest suspicions.[4] Thus the early date proposed for the *Letter of Aristeas* lacks firm support. Wendland's dating proposal begins from the passage in §115 of the *Letter*, which states that the

[1] Jos. Ant. XII.12–118. Cf. the study by A. Pelletier, *Flavius Josèphe adaptateur de la Lettre d'Aristée* (Paris, 1962).

[2] Eusebius of Caesarea, *Praeparatio Evangelica* VIII.2–5, 9 and IX.38 (Mras edition).

[3] *Praep. Evang.* XIII.12.

[4] J. G. Février, *La date, la composition et les sources de la lettre d'Aristée à Philocrate* (Paris, 1925), pp. 8–11. See also A.-M. Denis, *Introduction aux Pseudépigraphes grecs d'Ancient Testament* (Leiden, 1970), pp. 281–3.

ports of Ashkelon, Jaffa, Gaza and Ptolemais are in the hands of the Jews. While Jaffa was conquered in about 140 B.C.E., Gaza was only taken and destroyed by Alexander Janneus in 96 B.C.E. It must therefore have been after the latter date that the *Letter of Aristeas* was composed. But since Ashkelon and Ptolemais never were at any time part of Jewish territory, and it is manifest that when the author speaks of them he is in error, it may reasonably be asked whether the mention of Gaza as a Jewish port might not be equally erroneous.

A date later than the year 70 B.C.E. cannot be maintained in view of the absence of definite allusions to the Roman occupation. In fact it seems to us difficult to place the work in the Herodian period or later. Arguments which have been advanced for placing the *Letter* in the first century C.E. are based on passages which some scholars regard as interpolations.[1] The theory of a date of composition after 33 C.E. would make very difficult the use of the *Letter* by Josephus, for when Josephus wrote the reputation of the work would scarcely have time to become sufficiently established. A date in the region of 100 B.C.E. would seem to fit well, for the *Letter* has derived some of its information from Hecateus of Abdera (§31), or more precisely, from the Pseudo-Hecateus who wrote at a date later than 128 B.C.E.[2]

The discussion of the date of the *Letter of Aristeas* itself raises the question of authorship. It is necessary to distinguish between what the author makes himself out to be and what he was in reality. Aristeas wishes to be thought a pagan, a Hellenistic Greek. Speaking of the Jews he says, 'They worship the same God...as all other men, as we ourselves, O king, though we call him by different names, such as Zeus...' (16) He represents himself as a high official of the Alexandrian court, writing to his brother Philocrates, who is also a pagan. In reality the author is certainly a Jew, as is shown by the great knowledge he displays of things Jewish, and by his enthusiasm for the Jewish cause. He is an Alexandrian, for he is well informed about the customs of the Ptolemaic court. He disguises himself as a pagan in order to write an apologetic work. His book, devoted to the glorification of the Jewish law, would have had much less authority in the pagan world if he had not hidden his Jewish identity. The description 'letter' which the work bears was not given to it until a late date. It is found for the first time in a fourteenth century manuscript preserved at Paris.[3] Neither Josephus nor Eusebius ever refers to it as a letter, but as a book or treatise.

The historical value of the *Letter of Aristeas* is therefore extremely

[1] Février, *La date*, p. 30.
[2] Lods, *Histoire*, p. 900.
[3] S. Jellicoe, *The Septuagint and Modern Study* (Oxford, 1968).

problematical. Commentators have drawn attention to the glaring anachronisms in the book.[1] The main account which it contains, namely, of the translation of the Septuagint, is manifestly legendary.[2] There is nowadays no longer any doubt that the Greek version was prepared, not at the demand of the Ptolemaic king, but to meet the needs of the Greek-speaking Jewish communities in Egypt who did not understand Hebrew. It is equally clear that the translation was not made by Palestinian Jews, but by Jews of Alexandria who knew the language spoken in Egypt. This is proved by the linguistic parallels between the Septuagint and the Egyptian papyri. The number of translators who worked for the 72 days is also legendary. But the *Letter* does contain a certain number of elements of value. The Pentateuch, that is, the Jewish Law, forms a separate corpus within the Greek Bible. The version of the Torah approved by the Alexandrian Jewish community is represented as a standard text, to which no addition, revision or omission ought to be made. But this Greek translation of the Pentateuch was not the first: it is a revised version. This seems to be the sense we can deduce from a difficult passage in the letter: 'The books of the Law of the Jews (with some few others) are lacking, for they read them in Hebrew characters and pronunciation, and they have been written' (or, according to another possible translation of σεσήμανται, 'have been translated' or 'interpreted') 'carelessly, and do not represent the original text, as I am informed by those who know' (§30). For my own part, I incline to the translation of this phrase which interprets the 'carelessness' as applying to the making of the Greek versions and not to the writing of the Hebrew texts. For on any view, what interests the author of this *Letter* is not carelessly written Hebrew exemplars but inaccurate Greek versions, which have necessitated the production of a new Greek translation.[3]

JOSEPH AND ASENATH

The book of *Joseph and Asenath* or the Confession and Prayer of Asenath has been known for a long time.[4] The apocryphal story of the

[1] Charles, *APOT*, 2, pp. 83–4.

[2] So first Humfrey Hody, *Contra historiam Aristeae de LXX interpretibus dissertatio* (Oxford, 1684).

[3] P. E. Kahle, *The Cairo Geniza* (London, 1947), pp. 135–6; 2nd edn. (Oxford, 1959), pp. 213–14. But see the observations of Jellicoe, *Septuagint*, pp. 59ff and p. 51, and of D. W. Gooding, 'Aristeas and Septuagint origins: a review of recent studies', *VT*, 13 (1963), 357–79.

[4] Asenath is the name given to Joseph's wife in the Hebrew Bible. The form of the name found in the Septuagint and in the Greek text of our apocryphon is 'Ασεννεθ.

marriage of Jacob's son, Joseph, to Asenath, daughter of Potiphera, is preserved in a Latin version in the *Speculum historiale* of Vincent of Beauvais (*circa* 1260). It was translated into French in the fourteenth century, into German in 1539, and in the eighteenth century even into Icelandic. J. A. Fabricius in 1723 published the Greek text of this work on the basis of MS. Baroccio 148 in the Bodleian Library at Oxford.[1] Batiffol edited the Greek text again in 1889, but this time on the basis of four manuscripts.[2] Since then Burchard has enumerated sixteen Greek manuscripts which he has classified into four families.[3] Burchard makes some very severe criticisms of Batiffol's edition, which is neither critical nor always very exact in its transcriptions. The same goes for Istrin's edition of 1898. Philonenko, who is dependent on the work of Burchard on *Joseph and Asenath*, has attempted to produce a critical edition.[4] Apart from the Latin versions, which have been known for a long time,[5] there are other versions too. The Ethiopic version is no longer extant, but the Syriac survives in two manuscripts. The Syriac dates from the sixth century and is a translation from Greek. It is incorporated into a large compilation which is ascribed to Zacharias the Rhetor.[6] Seventeen manuscripts of an Armenian translation are in existence. An edition of the Armenian text was published in 1885 at Venice by the Mechitarist Benedictines.[7] A partial French version of it was published by Carrière.[8] A Slavonic version is known, which exists in two manuscripts, and there exist also a Romanian version and a modern Greek one. The Slavonic version presupposes a Greek original. Neither the Slavonic, the Romanian nor the modern Greek are of importance for establishing the original text.[9]

The number and variety of translations shows the wide geographical

[1] J. A. Fabricius, *Codicis Pseudepigraphi Beteris Testamenti Volumen alterum* (Hamburg, 1723), pp. 85–102.

[2] P. Batiffol, *Studia patristica*, Etudes d'ancienne littérature chrétienne, fasc. 1 (Paris, 1889), pp. 89–118.

[3] C. Burchard, *Untersuchungen zu Joseph und Aseneth*, WUNT 8 (Tübingen, 1965), pp. 2–24.

[4] M. Philonenko, *Joseph et Aséneth* (Leiden, 1968).

[5] Burchard, *Untersuchungen*, pp. 35–7.

[6] First edited by J. P. N. Land, in *Anecdota Syriaca* (Leiden, 1870). It may be found now in an edition, with translation, by E. W. Brooks in the CSCO (Scriptores Syri, vols. 38 and 41, Louvain, 1919–24; repr. 1953).

[7] Burchard, *Untersuchungen*, pp. 25–34.

[8] A. Carrière, 'Une version arménienne de l'histoire d'Aséneth', in *Nouveaux mélanges orientaux*, Publications de l'Ecole des Langues Orientàles vivantes, 2nd ser., 19 (Paris, 1886), pp. 471–511: Armenian text pp. 490–8, French tr. pp. 499–511.

[9] Burchard, *Untersuchungen*, pp. 37–8.

distribution of this writing and its great popularity. It doubtless owed this popularity to its subject matter.

The book recounts, in twenty-nine short chapters, the meeting between Joseph and Asenath. Both of them were of great beauty, and love sprang up between them at their first encounter. The book goes on to tell of the repentance and conversion of the Egyptian pagan Asenath and the marriage of the two young people. It tells also of the jealousy of the pharaoh's son, who was himself in love with Asenath, and of the abortive plot against Joseph in which the sons of Bilhah and Zilpah were implicated. Finally, the book recounts the death of the pharaoh's son and eventually of the pharaoh himself, whom Joseph succeeds on the throne. This romance, which has something of the character of an idyll, expresses through its heroes a great genuineness and freshness of feeling. For this reason it has been asked whether it may not be a Christian work. Batiffol, its first editor, defended this theory and his opinion was for a long time taken very seriously. In his view the Jewish story was really a cloak for a Christian allegory. Joseph was undoubtedly a figure of Christ, and Asenath stood either for the Church, or for the soul of the Christian, or for a consecrated virgin, or even for virginity itself. But serious objections must be advanced against this theory, which may be summarized as follows: (1) There is no christology whatever in *Joseph and Asenath*, which would be very strange in a Christian work. (2) No clearly Christian interpolations or revisions, such as are found in the *Testaments of the Twelve Patriarchs* or the *Ascension of Isaiah*, can be shown to be present. (3) There are no quotations from the New Testament and no certain allusions to it.[1]

The book is in fact a Jewish work, as the majority of modern scholars recognize. But modern scholars are not always in agreement about the circles in which it originated. Following Riessler, some have sought to treat *Joseph and Asenath* as an Essene work, citing as evidence the prayer of Asenath facing the sun, the eulogy of virginity and the participation in a sacred meal.[2] But there are definite discrepancies between the book and some Essene practices. For example, the Essenes shunned the use of oil for anointing.[3]

To circumvent these difficulties, several scholars attribute *Joseph and Asenath* to the Therapeutae, who had some characteristics in common

[1] For details see M. Delcor, 'Un roman d'amour d'origine thérapeute: Le Livre de Joseph et Asénath', *BLE*, 63 (1962), 5–13.

[2] P. Riessler, 'Joseph und Asenath. Eine altjüdische Erzählung', *Theologische Quartalschrift*, 103 (1922), 1–22 and 145–83.

[3] *Bell.* II.123.

with the Essenes but also were in several respects different.[1] In particular, they were less misogynistic that the Essenes, and they anounted their bodies with oil on the seventh day.[2] According to others, this book, which is certainly of Egyptian origin, is simply written by Egyptian Jews and is aimed at leading the pagan world to the Jewish faith. It is, in fact, a missionary work; hence its theme.

Philonenko goes so far as to see the work as an apologia in favour of mixed marriages, meant to be read by both Jews and Egyptians.[3] But these last theories are not without difficulties. In the first place, the Jews were hardly missionaries. In the second place, a defence of mixed marriages, even on the condition that the pagan partner accept conversion, is scarcely consonant with the struggle which Judaism at all periods put up on this very issue.

As for the date of composition, the two suggestions generally made are either the beginning of the second century C.E., or the first century B.C.E.[4] We should place the book at all events earlier than 30 B.C.E. when Caesar Octavian entered Egypt and conquered Alexandria. This was the date at which Egypt lost her independence. But we have no allusion at all to the Romans in *Joseph and Asenath*, and we may take it as certain, therefore, that Egypt was still an independent power.

(Editor's note: some sections of this chapter have also appeared in French in H. Cazelles ed., *Introduction critique à l' Ancien Testament* (Paris, 1973).

[1] K. G. Kuhn, 'The Lord's Supper and the communal meal at Qumran', in K. Stendahl, *The Scrolls and the New Testament* (New York, 1957), p. 76; P. Geoltrain, 'Le traité de la vie contemplative', *Semitica,* 10 (1960), 26–7; Delcor, *BLE,* 63 (1962), 22–6.

[2] Philo, *De Vita Contemplativa* 36.

[3] Philonenko, *Joseph et Aséneth*, p. 106.

[4] There is a summary of opinions in A.-M. Denis, *Introduction*, p. 47.

CHAPTER 13

THE BOOK OF DANIEL

It is clear that the book of Daniel falls into two quite different parts: Daniel A, chapters 1–6, the book of court stories, and Daniel B, chapters 7 to 12, the book of apocalypses. Because the historical background of B is, as was first pointed out by the neo-Platonist philosopher Porphyry (*circa* 260 C.E.) – whom Jerome quotes in order to polemize against him – unmistakably the period when the Seleucid King Antiochus IV Epiphanes (175–163 B.C.E.) first persecuted and then outlawed Judaism, the prevailing critical opinion in the late nineteenth and early twentieth centuries, of which S. R. Driver's commentary entitled *The Book of Daniel* (first printed in 1900 and repeatedly reprinted) is a good representative, was that the entire book was produced during that period, though it was admitted that what we have dubbed Daniel A made use of older traditions. During the first half of the twentieth century, however, an impressive number of reputable scholars insisted that there was not the slightest reflection of, let alone allusion to, the Epiphanian situation in Daniel A without benefit of midrash, and therefore assigned a pre-Epiphanian date to it. During the third quarter of our century, however, there has been a retreat to the older critical view.[1] That the reaction is a retrogression

[1] The retreat came about mainly under the spell of H. H. Rowley. It can be drastically illustrated by the contrast between Aage Bentzen, *Daniel* (1st edn., Tübingen, 1937) and *Daniel* (2nd edn., HAT 1, 19, Tübingen, 1952), and between O. Eissfeldt, *Einleitung in das Alte Testament* (1st edn. Tübingen, 1934), and *Einleitung in das Alte Testament* (2nd edn., Tübingen, 1956, 3rd edn. 1964; ET 1965), followed by G. Fohrer's completely rewritten revision of E. Sellin's *Einleitung in das Alte Testament* (Heidelberg, 1965; ET Nashville, 1968). Fohrer (ET p. 473, lines 7 to 5 from foot) represents Ginsberg's views inaccurately. Ginsberg assigns not chs. 1–12 but chs. 7–12 to four authors, for he does not assign ch. 8 to the same author as chs. 10–12. Despite the evidence that ch. 2 underwent literary expansion decades before the end of the third century B.C.E. (see below), Fohrer denies that chs. 1–6 ever existed as 'a pre-Maccabean book'. Gratifyingly, however, he also denies that they betray 'any basic enmity toward the pagan state and its ruler' (Fohrer, ET, p. 475 top). Notable holdouts against this reaction have been E. Bickerman, *Four Strange Books of the Bible* (New York, 1967), pp. 51–138, and H. L. Ginsberg, most recently in *EncJud*, vol. 5, cols. 1277–89.

will, it is hoped, become clear from the following exposition. [There is considerable agreement between it and the commentary of L. F. Hartman and A. A. Di Lella, *The Book of Daniel*, AB 23 (Garden City, 1978) (who have adopted many of the present author's previously published views), but it was already in the editorial hopper when their volume came out.]

DANIEL A, CHAPTERS 1 to 6

Chapter 1

King Nebuchadnezzar of Babylon, on an expedition to Jerusalem – corresponding to that of 2 Kings 24:10–16 but wrongly dated – took back with him not only some of the Temple vessels, which he deposited in his own Temple in Babylon, but also several boys of good family, handsome looks, and promising intellect. He charged his grand vizier with the task, to be completed in three years, of rearing them and educating them in 'booklore and the Chaldean tongue' (1:4) in order to qualify them for the king's service. Four of these boys, Daniel, Hananiah, Mishael, and Azariah – whom the grand vizier furnished with Babylonian names (only two of which can be plausibly identified as such) in the same way as Joseph was furnished with an Egyptian name according to Gen. 41:45 – took measures to avoid eating the excellent but non-kosher rations which, not from malice but from ignorance, had been assigned to them. After a trial period of ten days had satisfied him that these youths on a straight diet of raw vegetable fare thrived even better than the others did on the prescribed rations, the inferior official whom the grand vizier had charged with delivering them was persuaded to keep the dainty royal food and drink for himself and to substitute the raw vegetable products.

Chapter 2

The four young men came to the king's attention even before they completed their term of study. The king – again like Joseph's pharaoh – had a dream which became a problem. He summoned the 'graduate' sages of every variety and demanded that they tell him both what he had dreamed and what it signified. This test they naturally flunked, and the king in a rage decreed the slaughter of all the sages of Babylon. When Daniel and his companions learned that, in spite of their 'undergraduate' status, the decree included them, Daniel inquired of the king's captain of the guard, who had been commissioned to perpetrate the slaughter, what the cause of the decree was; and on being enlightened, he requested a period of grace in which to come up with the solution. He then told his companions how matters stood and urged them to pray to 'the God of Heaven' (which is how the Jews later identified their God for the benefit of their Persian rulers, but hardly – and among themselves! – under the Babylonians) for the solution of the mystery. The solution was revealed to Daniel in a vision of the night. After thanking the God of his fathers, he proceeded to the captain of the guard, and told him that the massacre of the sages was unnecessary: if the captain would but usher Daniel into the king's presence, he would tell him both dream and interpretation. The captain complied with Daniel's request and announced to the king: 'I have found a man of the community of captives from Judah who can answer Your Majesty's questions.' As little affected with Judeophobia as his captain of the guard, Nebuchadnezzar merely asked Daniel if he really could. Daniel took the opportunity to explain that he could indeed – but not because he was smarter than everybody else, but because the God who had made the king have that dream so as to reveal to him the future course of events, had revealed both the dream and its interpretation to Daniel for the same purpose. So Daniel related the dream and interpreted it, and Nebuchadnezzar (who, according to the retrogressive exegesis that has – but certainly not for much longer – become dominant again, is meant to remind the Jewish reader of the time around 166 B.C.E. of the ruthless Macedonian who was at that moment holding court in Apamea or in Antioch) prostrated himself before Daniel and ordered oblations to be offered to him, asserting that 'Your [plural, that is the Jews'] God is God of gods and Lord of kings (or kingships) and revealer of secrets, since you were able to solve this mystery'. And he not only showered Daniel with many rich gifts but invested him with supreme authority over the province of Babylon and also made him chief prefect of all the sages of Babylon. At Daniel's request, however, the king transferred the supreme administrative office to Daniel's three companions, leaving him only with the 'academic' one which, however, gave him a seat in 'the king's gate'.

We shall return to the dream and its interpretation in order to discover their true background.

Chapter 3

Daniel's three companions, as high administrative officials, become, like the high official Ahikar before them and the high official Mordecai after them, targets of the intrigues of rivals. Nebuchadnezzar, like the capricious (but not 'anti-Semitic') sovereigns of ancient and medieval popular tales, has a colossal statue erected in the plain of Dura and summons all the various kinds of officials to its inauguration (verses 2 to 3 – in which 'sages', like private citizens, are *not* mentioned). As they are standing before it, a herald proclaims aloud, 'Take note, O peoples, nations and tongues [that is, all present, no matter of what ethinic or linguistic group]: when you hear the sound of...and of every sort of musical instrument, you are to fall prone and prostrate yourselves. Anyone who disobeys will be thrown into the furnace of blazing fire.' Everybody obeyed but the three Jewish officials, who were reported to the king, with specification of name and nationality, by some 'Chaldean men'. That the latter were themselves officials is obvious from the fact that they were present and that they knew the exact nationality, names, and offices of the culprits. The Jews are cited by Nebuchadnezzar and given another chance: next time the band plays, they either prostrate themselves to the image or into the furnace they go. They tell him in advance that they will on no account worship his gods. So Nebuchadnezzar orders some stout fellows to perform the execution. Shadrach, Meshach, and Abed-nego are flung into the fiery furnace fully clothed and bound. But though the fierce heat slays the executioners, Nebuchadnezzar presently jumps to his feet because he sees not three but four men, one of whom looks like a divine being, walking in the flames unbound. He approaches the gate of the furnace close enough to shout: 'Shadrach, Meshach, and Abed-nego, servants of the Supreme God! Come out here!' They do, and everybody is astonished to find that not even their clothing has been damaged. The alleged Antiochus symbol thereupon praises their God and decrees death for anybody who speaks disrespectfully of him, and he promotes them even higher in the province of Babylon.

Chapter 4[1]

This is a circular letter whose author is Nebuchadnezzar, the monarch who is supposed to remind the persecuted Jews of the Seleucid monster. However, its stated purpose is to make known 'to all the peoples, nations, and tongues that dwell everywhere on earth' his own marvellous experiences at the hands of 'the Supreme God', whom he praises lyrically at the beginning and at the end of his epistle and perhaps even more so in an outburst of his which he reports near the

[1] According to the chapter division of the English versions; according to the less logical division of Hebrew editions, 3:31–3 and chapter 4.

end (4:34–5, Hebrew Bibles 4:31–2). What happened was that he had a dream, which this time he did not ask his sages to guess but related to them. None of them was able to interpret it until at the end 'Daniel, also called Belteshazzar,' appeared before him. On hearing the dream, Daniel first stood aghast for a while; but when the king graciously encouraged him, he said (verse 19: Hebrew Bible v. 16), 'My lord, may the dream be for your enemies and its interpretation for your foes!' For it portended a period of seven years during which the king was to be afflicted with an insanity, feeding on grass like an ox (an echo of Job 40:15) and getting soaked by the rain of heaven, so that he might learn the lesson that 'the Most High rules over the dominion of men and gives it to whomever he wishes'. However, his kingship would be preserved for Nebuchadnezzar and restored to him when he had learned his lesson. Daniel advises the king to spend any period of grace that may be granted him atoning for his sins (which apparently consist only of smugness) with charitable deeds. But Nebuchadnezzar's hubris is such that, though his good fortune holds for another year, he evidently fails to take advantage of it, so that the seven years of madness follow. Then he recovers and is reinstated as world-king, but he is now so filled with an awareness that there is One higher than he that he is moved to disseminate all over the world an account of his conversion and how it came about. (N.B. The sense of the last clause of Dan. 4:33 (Heb. 4:30), as emended by me in F. Rosenthal and others, *An Aramaic Handbook* (Wiesbaden, 1967), p. 31 footnote, is 'until his hair had grown like a *goat's* and his nails like an eagle's (claws)'. Correct Hartman and Di Lella, p. 173, accordingly.)

Chapter 5

'King' Belshazzar (who in real history was a son of Nabonidus, the last king of Chaldean Babylon, but was never himself king) makes a banquet for his 1,000 grandees. Under the influence of the wine, he orders the Jerusalem Temple vessels (see p. 505, on chapter 1) produced, and has his wives and concubines as well as his 1,000 grandees (but no Jews!) drink from them with him and hymn the gods of gold, silver, copper, iron, stone and wood. To his horror, a hand appears on the wall opposite the lampstand and writes something on the plaster of the palace wall. He shouts for all the wizards, astrologers and soothsayers to be summoned and offers to anyone who can read and interpret the writing the privilege of clothing himself in purple and wearing a gold chain on his neck in addition to the office of 'third ruler of the realm'. They are all nonplussed. But the queen mother, roused by the commotion, enters the hall and informs the king that there is still in his realm a genius whom his 'father' Nebuchadnezzar made chief of all magicians, wizards, etc., a Jew named Daniel whom Nebuchadnezzar renamed Belteshazzar. She advises him to summon this man. He does so, and repeats to Daniel the offer he made to the others. Daniel first makes bold to tell the king that instead of so impiously desecrating the vessels of the God of Heaven he should have learned a lesson from the experience of Nebuchadnezzar that is related in the previous chapter, but then he reads and interprets the writing. Alt may well have hit upon the truth with his surmise that the Aramaic words for 'mina, mina, shekel, half-mina, half-mina' were represented on the wall (as in the Elephantine papyri) by their initials, and that Daniel was so smart as not only to recognize that they were initials but also to interpret the full words that they represented according to their root meanings, which portended the imminent passage of the Chaldean empire into the hands of the Medes and the Persians. Belshazzar immediately bestowed the promised reward upon the bringer of these shocking tidings! That the recipient had earned it was proved that very night. The Chaldean Belshazzar was killed, and his empire passed on to 'Darius the Mede'.

Chapter 6

We are told at the outset (6:1, English versions 5:31) that Darius was 62 years old on his accession, implying that he only reigned for some eight years. And we are told at the conclusion that 'Daniel prospered in the reign of Darius, and in the reign of Cyrus the Persian', implying that Darius was the only Median world-ruler. Having found Daniel in the office of a sort of triumvir (5:29), he kept him on in an analogous one. Above the 120 (Septuagint: 127, compare Esther 1:1) 'satraps' among whom he distributed the government of his entire realm, he appointed three presidents, one of whom was Daniel, and decreed that the satraps should report not to himself but to these presidents, so that 'the king should not be bothered'.[1] And Daniel so distinguished himself that the king planned to make him grand vizier; so now it was his turn to be intrigued against.[2] The two other presidents and the satraps conferred on means to bring about Daniel's downfall, but they found his record so clean that they saw no alternative to bringing his religiosity into conflict with the law. So they went in a body to the king and told him

[1] It has been demonstrated that that is the true sense of the final clause in 6:3, EVV 6:2; see H. L. Ginsberg, 'Lexicographical Notes', in B. Hartmann *et al., Hebräische Wortforschung*, SVT 16 (Leiden, 1967), p. 81.

[2] Cf. pp. 506f., on chapter 3.

that, after mature deliberation, all the high administrative officials had decided that the good of the realm required a decree that for a period of thirty days no person, under pain of being thrown into the lions' den, was allowed to address any petition to any god or man other than the king – a baroque notion which Bickerman plausibly explains as inspired by a Jewish misunderstanding of a Babylonian superstition that food offerings made to one's personal god during the month of Tebet (and the accompanying petitions) were unlucky. As might be expected of a king who so thoroughly conformed to the popular stereotype of a Persian king (or a medieval caliph) by arranging to have the satraps' reports addressed to the presidents 'so that the king might not be bothered', Darius draws up the required document without asking for any explanations. An orthodox Jew faced by such a decree would either have abstained from all prayer or prayed only in secret until the thirty day period was over. But then there would have been no story. So Daniel's reaction had to be as odd as the decree itself: he prays on his knees three times a day in his upper chamber, before open windows facing Jerusalem. The conspirators came gleefully to the king and informed him that his decree was being flouted by Daniel. Darius was utterly dismayed, and strove in vain until sunset to save him. But the officials sternly reminded him that under Medo-Persian law a decree once issued could not be rescinded, and he had no choice but to order Daniel cast into the lion pit. After expressing to Daniel the hope that the God whom he worships so constantly will save him, the king departs for a supperless evening and sleepless night in his palace. At the crack of dawn, he hurries to the edge of the pit and calls in a broken voice, 'O Daniel, servant of the living God! Has the God whom you worship so constantly been able to save you from the lions?' And what is his joy to hear Daniel's voice and be reassured! He promptly orders Daniel pulled up and his accusers cast down, and to these the beasts give short shrift. Darius issues a decree that Daniel's God must be treated with awe and reverence throughout his realm, and Daniel continues to serve with distinction as vizier to Darius the Mede and to Cyrus the Persian. The faithful will agree with Rowley that Darius is 'held up to obloquy' for the very same thing as Antiochus Epiphanes: the unregenerate will remain unable to see that he is held up to anything but admiration.

If all these tales emphatically do not reflect the persecution of Judaism by Antiochus Epiphanes, they on the other hand, in addition to being composed in a post-Persian Aramaic and even containing three Greek loanwords (*kitharis, psaltērin* [vulgar for *psaltērion*], and *sumphōnia*: 3:5, 7, 10, 15), betray too great an ignorance of Babylonian and Persian history to be pre-Hellenistic. We have seen that they make of Belshazzar a son of Nebuchadnezzar and a king, though he was neither, and that they insert 'Darius the Mede' between the Chaldean world-empire and the Persian, though the Median kingdom came to an end even before the Chaldean and though none of its kings was named Darius. Just in which phase of Hellenistic history Daniel A arose can be determined by a closer examination of chapter 2.

First of all, there is no excuse of refusing to recognize that 'and the toes' in 2:41 and the whole of 2:42–3 represents a later stratum than the rest of the chapter. For not only do they introduce and interpret features not included in the narration of the dream (which might conceivably be an 'afterthought' of the writer of the body of the chapter), but verse 43 pointedly corrects verse 41a*b*–b's interpretation of a feature which *was* included in the narration of the dream. It therefore behoves us to consider first verses 31 to 45 apart from this additional matter. In the dream, then, Nebuchadnezzar sees facing him a colossal statue with a head of pure gold, a chest and arms of silver, a belly and thighs of copper, legs of iron, and feet part iron and part tiling. As he looks, a stone comes rolling unpropelled by any human force ('hands') and strikes the feet of iron and tiling. Thereupon all of the five substances named crumble to dust and are carried off by the wind. The stone, on the other hand, becomes a great mountain, filling all the earth. All this is interpreted as follows. The golden head represents the grandeur of Nebuchadnezzar himself (the continuation, however, implies that his Chaldean successors are included), and the silver chest and arms, the copper belly and thighs, and the iron legs three succeeding empires, of which the last will be the most powerful. The iron feet with tiling, however, indicate that it will be a divided kingdom; yet its iron component will lend it toughness. As for the intervention of the stone and what follows in its wake, verses 44 to 45 read as follows: 'And in the days of those kings (or kingdoms) the God of Heaven will raise up a kingdom which shall never be destroyed, and whose kingship shall never be left to any other people. It shall smash and annihilate all those kingdoms and shall itself endure forever (45), *inasmuch as you saw* that a stone rolled from the mountain unpropelled by hands and smashed the iron, the copper, the tiling, the silver, and the gold, etc.' In other words, the circumstance that in the dream it is only the impact of the stone on the feet that causes the upper parts of the statue to crumble and vanish, means that the first three kingdoms will survive as petty kingdoms, even after their loss of world hegemony, until the moment when the fourth is liquidated. This, then, is not an unwarranted notion that only originated with some twentieth-century scribbler but the opinion of the biblical author. We must therefore look for a period when there was not only a residual Persian kingdom in the shape of the principality of Persis (in the territory of the modern Iranian province of Fars) and a residual Media in the shape of the principality of Atropatene, which Strabo also refers to as 'Atropatian Media' (on the western shore of the Caspian sea, today divided between Soviet and Iranian Azerbaijan), but also a residual Babylonian kingdom in the shape of the territory of Seleucus I while it was still centred on Babylon (310 to *circa* 301 B.C.E.) and could be regarded as forming no part of the 'Greek kingdom' which was a bone of contention among Ptolemy, (Demetrius son of) Antigonus, Cassander, and Lysimachus. The added word in verse 41 and the two added verses 42 to 43, then, add the feature that the toes of the statue – instead of consisting like the feet proper of both iron and tiling – were some of them all iron and some of them all tiling, and infer from it that a part of the fourth kingdom will be all tough and a part of it all fragile. The interpolator then goes on to contradict the inference of verse 41 from the combination of the two substances in the feet; for he insists that this feature signifies (not that both parts of the fourth kingdom will be partly tough, but merely) that the two parts will make an abortive attempt to fuse the two royal lines biologically, thereby dating verses 42 to 43 shortly after the events of 252–246 B.C.E. In those years, the Seleucid Antiochus II put away his wife Laodice and took instead Berenice, daughter of Ptolemy II, who bore him a son. But the latter perished along with his mother – and with his father too – when Antiochus became reconciled with Laodice. As a result, Berenice's brother Prolemy III invaded the Seleucid dominions in 246, penetrating all the way to Babylon, from which he brought back the statues of Egyptian gods that had been carried off thither by the Persian King Cambyses in 525. Ptolemy III annexed some coastal areas permanently, and left the Seleucid kingdom so crippled that the enormous satrapy of Media revolted and Seleucid Asia Minor became an independent kingdom. By thus making the house of Seleucus a part of the divided Greek kingdom, our interpolator – perhaps a better term would be reviser – contradicts verses 44 to 45, according to which a residual Babylonian kingdom is to survive until the final dénouement of history (unless he was under the impression that Molon, the revolting satrap of Media, also controlled Babylonia). But then, how many interpolators are wholly consistent?

DANIEL B, CHAPTERS 7 to 12

What we have here are not more courtier tales but apocalypses, four of them in fact: Apocalypse I, Apocalypse II, Apocalypse III, and Apocalypse IV – with the authors of III and IV, in addition to composing each a revelation of his own, interpolating those of their predecessors. All four of these revelations purport to be the work of Daniel, the hero of the third-person narratives of Daniel A.

Apocalypse IV is perhaps the easiest to understand because, being the last, it is uninterpolated by later apocalyptists. The apocalyptist's own complete apocalypse is enshrined in chapter 9, of whose 27 verses, however, only 10, namely verses 1 to 3, 21 to 27, are by him. For verses 4 to 20, which might be expected to give the exact wording of the prayer in which Daniel asked enlightenment on the meaning of Jeremiah's puzzling sentence of Jerusalem to 70 years' ruin (Jer. 25:11, 29:10), do nothing of the sort; they are a prayer on behalf of the whole community, which does not petition God for any exegesis of Scripture but confesses (in a tone reminiscent of the famous self-flagellating pericope Ezra 9:6 to 15; compare Neh. 9:15–37) that it has richly deserved all that it has suffered, which has been no more than it had been warned against in no ambiguous terms by its prophets and already in the teaching of Moses. The prayer entreats the Lord to have mercy on his city and on his people for the sake of his name, which once for all he associated with them. Incidentally, this prayer is the only piece of original – and very inspiring – Hebrew in the book of Daniel. (For just like the Hebrew of 1:1–2:4a, that of 8–9:3 and 9:21 to 12:12 is translated from Aramaic. But in the case of chapters 8 and 10 to 12, intelligibility has been impaired to a far greater extent by the translator's very imperfect understanding of the allusions, the strangeness of which in his original, outside of chapter 9, was aggravated by the working over of earlier by later apocalyptists that has already been mentioned.) And 9:20, by awkwardly duplicating verse 21a, shows that verses 4–20 are interpolated. In 9:21ff, then, the angel Gabriel appears to Daniel and supplies an exposition of the Jeremianic prediction that has caused Daniel so much grief. Not 70 literal years but 70 weeks of years of expiation through suffering were decreed for Israel and its holy city. During the first 7 weeks (all but the last of which have already elapsed, Dan. 9:21), Jerusalem was to be desolate and without a priest–prince; during the next 62 weeks, it shall stand rebuilt. But then the priest–prince (concretely, probably Onias III) shall be cut off, and a final week of persecution shall ensue. For the second half of that septennium sacrifice and oblation shall be idle, with an abomination of desolation on 'their stand' (in 9:27 read *kannâm* for *kᵉnap*) that is, on their altar, and finally the decreed judgement (a phrase borrowed from Isa. 10:23; 28:22) shall be poured down upon the (abomination of) desolation.

Apocalyptist IV repeats this term of half a septennium in the form 'a period, two periods, and half' in his interpolations at 7:25 and 12:7. Clearly, he is writing, on the one hand, after the abolition of the sacrificial cult in the Jerusalem sanctuary and 'the erection of the abomination of desolation [that is, a stone symbolizing the presence of a heathen deity] upon the altar' (1 Macc. 1:54) on the fifteenth day of Chislev – that is, near the end – of the year 167 B.C.E. On the other hand, our author clearly antedates the date on which he anticipates the final dénouement of history, which is some time in the first half of the year 163. A more exact *terminus post quem* can be inferred from the allusion, by the same man, to Epiphanes' defeating three kings in an interpolation at Dan. 7:24, which will be considered presently.

Whereas Apocalypse II (chapter 8 minus interpolations) and Apocalypse III (chapter 10 to 12 minus interpolations) date, like Apocalypse IV, from after the crowning tragedy of December 167 B.C.E., the same is not true of Apocalypse I (chapter 7 minus interpolations). Unlike IV, which has just been described, and III, which likewise dispenses with any vision of symbols, Apocalypse I is – like the dreams, or portents, and interpretations in chapters 2, 4, and 5 – an account of symbols and their interpretation. But in Apocalypse I the symbols are seen not by a king but by Daniel himself, and they are interpreted for him by an angel. Daniel dreams that he sees arising from 'the Great Sea' (vaguely identical with the Great Deep, which is the opposite pole of Heaven, Gen. 49:25; Deut. 33:13) four great beasts, and later 'one like a human being coming with the clouds of heaven' who in the end is given dominion over all nations. The *angelus interpres* explains to Daniel that the beasts represent 'four kingdoms that will arise from the earth' (7:17) while the 'one like a human being, coming with the clouds of heaven' represents 'saints of the Most High' or 'a people of saints of the Most High'. The resemblance of this to Daniel's interpretation of Nebuchadnezzar's dream in chapter 2 as portending four monarchies and a fifth, is obvious, and it is the obvious explanation of Apocalyptist I's choice of Daniel as his spokesman. At the same time, it is, critically speaking, a mortal sin to shut one's eyes to the differences. To begin with, chapter 2, in contrast to modern professors, attributes absolutely no moral significance to the relative values of the four or five substances of which the statue consists, and obviously harbours no – as one might say – 'urgent' animosity against any of the four kingdoms. Chapter 7, in contrast, says both of the fourth beast in the symbolism and of the fourth kingdom in the interpretation that, following a divine judgement, it will be annihilated, whereas all other entities will merely be stripped of their dominion and will come under the rule of the fifth monarchy (7:11b–14, 26–7). Moreover, the fourth kingdom of chapter 2 is not identical with that of chapter 7. In the former, it is simply the Macedonian empire of some fifteen years after the death of Alexander the Great – which, as we saw, is not even conceived of (in the primary stratum) as including Seleucus' Babylonia; in the latter, on the other hand, it is the Seleucid kingdom, and the Seleucid kingdom alone. For practically everybody, today, identifies its last king as Antiochus Epiphanes, whether one counts eleven kings or only ten (in view of the obvious fact that verse 8 – which for one thing differs dialectally from the rest of the chapter by employing for 'behold' twice the word *'ᵃlū* as against the *'ᵃrū* of verses 2, 5, 6, 7, and 13 – with its eleventh horn, is secondary and with it all other references to an eleventh horn and/or an eleventh king). The first king is in any case Alexander the Great; see now the Akkadian list of Seleucid kings that has been published in recent years.[1] The end of the sentence referring to 'Philip, the brother of Alexander', is broken away, but it may well have stated that he was prevented from succeeding Alexander by his mental incapacity. It is in any case followed by a statement to the effect that for some years there was no king in the country and by a defective statement about Antigonus (perhaps to the effect that he for a time held dominion over Babylon illegitimately). There follows 'Alexander, the (posthumous) son of Alexander, with 6 (legitimate) years. Year 7 is the first year (of Seleucus), etc.'. So, too, Berossus obviously counts only one reign between those of Alexander I and Seleucus I.[2] Now, by this system Antiochus IV is the tenth sovereign of the Alexandro-Seleucid kingdom. Whether the interpolator who speaks of an eleventh horn and an eleventh king knew of a different system, which made Antiochus the eleventh in the series, is irrelevant; in any case, he is an interpolator. Bickerman's refusal to face this fact forces him to impose an unnatural interpretation upon both verse 25b*a* and verse 25b*b*. In 25b*a*, 'and he (the last king) will think to change *seasons* and *law*' is made to mean – not (despite the remarkable terminological contacts with 1 Macc. 1:44ff) that the king himself will command Jerusalem and the towns of Judah to follow the *laws* of the heathen, to put a stop to burnt offering,

[1] See the Akkadian Seleucid king list in *ANET*, p. 567.

[2] In support of this assertion, H. L. Ginsberg, *Studies in Daniel* (New York, 1948), p. 74 n. 59, refers to P. Schnabel, *Berossos* (Leipzig, 1923), p. 5ff, cited by W. Baumgartner, *TRu*, Neue Folge, 11 (1939), 204.

sacrifice and libation, to profane Sabbaths and festivals and *to 'alter'* (Greek *allaxai) every statute* – but merely that the king will support the 'Reformed Pontiffs' of Jerusalem who, Bickerman[1] supposes (without a semblance of 'proof') devised certain calendar reforms. And in verse 25b*b*, the 'season, (two) seasons and half a season' (that is, the semi-septennium) for which the 'saints of the Most High' will be delivered into the king's hands is made to date, not as everywhere else (8:13–14; 9:27b; 12:7, 11, 12), from the king's outright proscription of Judaism but from earlier, namely, from 'between the fall of 169 and the end of 167'. This last phrase should be noted very carefully. It means that Bickerman is unable to escape the overall impression from chapter 7 that it dates – as the present writer has always insisted – from before the outright proscription of Judaism, and that he is only driven to imposing his forced exegesis upon verse 25b*a* by his refusal to recognize the existence of a secondary stratum in the chapter![2] As was pointed out above, the entire system of septennia originated with Apocalyptist IV, the author of chapter 9.[3] Much less serious is the fact that Bickerman's dating of the secondary, as well as the primary, clauses before 'the end of 167' compels him to assume that the Judean writer was aware, and could assume that his readers were aware, that from 'the fall of 170' on, the Ptolemaic kingship was vested, officially, in Ptolemy VI, Ptolemy VII, and their sister and spouse Cleopatra II. But surely even with such knowledge a Judean might continue to think of Cleopatra as not really a 'king' in her own right, 11:25ff. And since in addition all the clauses in question in chapter 7 are decidedly secondary, the old explanation (of Porphyry) that the interpolator (who is identical with the author of chapter 9, Apocalypse IV) wrote after Epiphanes' defeat of King Artaxias of Armenia in the summer of 165, and that the three kings whom Epiphanes 'humbled' were Ptolemy VI, Ptolemy VII, and Artaxias, remains the more probable one. It is the same with Bickerman's insistence on retaining – on the strength of representations on two Achemenid (but not Hellenistic!) objects in the British Museum of lions standing or walking on their hind legs without anything to lean on, more blatantly unrealistic than a horse doing a 'flying gallop' – the existing snag in verses 4 to 5. That the writer could have known such representations (from museums?) is, of course, a (*bare*) *possibility*; but that he had, in the Syria–Palestine of the second century B.C.E. observed erect bears – wild or tame (for example, trained

[1] *Four Strange Books*, p. 106.

[2] In *Four Strange Books*, pp. 51ff.

[3] On the 'short' semi-septennium of 8:14; see my cautious suggestion, *Studies in Daniel*, p. 77, lines 3ff.

to 'dance' standing or walking on two feet) – in real life is *a very strong probability*. Consequently, the decisive consideration must be that the spectacle of a lion, at first winged, being stood upright on its hind feet and equipped with a human mind after its wings have been torn off and it has been annihilated, and again the spectacle of the Syrian brown bear (which, like all bears other than the polar bear and the American grizzly – to our author surely unknown – feeds mostly on roots, buds, berries, insects and carrion) being characterized by a phenomenal gluttony for meat rather than the lion, and so many incongruities – that all these are too high a price to pay for the preservation of the received order of the clauses.[1]

While, therefore, Bickerman in 1967[2] assigns chapter 7 to the same *terminus ante quem* – late autumn 167 – as we did in 1948, obviously we could not have based it on verses 24b to 25 (see above) which are interpolated and reflect the outlawing of Judaism at the end of 167. But we have always argued that the main text on the one hand precludes the outright outlawing of Judaism precisely by the absence of any allusion either to it or to the specific wickedness of the last king. On the other hand – by the violence of its hatred for the Seleucid kingdom and by the prediction of its utter annihilation, following a trial by the divine Judge, in the lifetime of its present sovereign – the text does presuppose some or all of the hateful measures that preceded the outlawing of Judaism: to wit, the treating of the high priesthood as merchandise to be bartered, the encouragement of Hellenization, the settling of pagans on the Akra and the making of Jerusalem an appendage of the Akra.

Next in time to Apocalypse I (the original core of chapter 7) is Apocalypse II (the original core of chapter 8). Like Apocalyptist I, Apocalyptist II makes Daniel his spokesman. But the revelation that Daniel receives here is designated not a dream (Aramaic *ḥelem*) but a vision (Hebrew *ḥazon*). The reason for this is that in Hab. 2:2–3 the prophet is commanded to set the prophecy – which is there called *ḥazon* (the same word that is employed in the sense of 'vision' in Daniel 8) – down in writing so that, since time is destined to elapse until it is fulfilled, anyone who desponds may be comforted by reading it. Apocalypse II's use of the same word, albeit in a slightly different sense, is somewhat similarly motivated: this message refers to a period so many generations later than Daniel that it is of no interest to his contemporaries, and therefore he is told not merely to record it in

[1] See *Studies in Daniel*, pp. 11–18, with the pertinent notes at the back of the volume. [It is gratifying to note that they have in substance been followed in Hartman and Di Lella, *The Book of Daniel*, (Garden City, 1978), pp. 200–20.]

[2] *Four Strange Books*, pp. 51ff.

writing (though that is implied) but to hide it away (Dan. 8:26b) – no doubt to be rediscovered when it becomes relevant. In this vision, as in the preceding dream, kingdoms are represented by animals: the two Iranian monarchies, namely, the Median and the Persian, by a ram with two horns, and the Hellenic ones by a he-goat with at first one horn, representing the empire of Alexander, and then four horns, representing the four succession monarchies. From one of these four horns a scion branches off, meaning that a certain king arises. He reaches out in every direction and even toward the 'host of heaven', and he knocks down some of the stars, which he tramples. (Since Daniel's *angelus interpres* does not explain this, we may surmise that it means that the king will commit sacrilege against some of the gods of the nations.) More, he reaches out against 'the Commander of the host' and 'takes the Constant [the daily morning and evening sacrifice] away from him', and 'places offence upon the stand of the Constant' (verse 12, reading the Aramaic form *wᶜtintin* for the Masoretic text's *tinnāten* and moving *mkwn* from the end of 11 to follow *ᶜl* in verse 12). 'But', as the interpreting angel adds in verse 25 (end), 'he shall be broken by no (human) hand.' The entire chapter comprises only 27 verses, and if one deducts 18–19, which are from the hand of Apocalyptist III (the author of chapters 10 to 12), and verses 13 to 14, 16, 23*ab*, 26a, 27b, which are from the hand of Apocalyptist IV (the author of chapter 9) – barely 21. The gist of these is the very thing we missed in Apocalypse I (the main text of chapter 7), namely prediction of the outlawing of Judaism and the paganization of the Temple, and an execration of the last king. Clearly, those final outrages intervened between Apocalypse I and Apocalypse II, and the sole purpose of the latter was to assure the reader that they too had been predicted long before. Why had the prediction not turned up earlier? Because Daniel had been ordered to hide it away (8:26b), as being of no relevance to *his* contemporaries – but only to the contemporaries of the real author of chapter 8! As Apocalypse III puts it (12:4), 'As for you, Daniel, hide the words away and seal up the book until the season of the appointed time, when the masses will seek (?) and knowledge will increase').

For whereas Apocalyptist II wrote in the shock of the days immediately following the measures that culminated in the erection of the abomination of desolation upon the altar of the Jerusalem Temple, Apocalyptist III wrote when the new decree had been in force for about a year and the situation gave no promise of changing in a hurry. This difference explains for one thing the contrast between the brevity of Apocalypse II and the verbosity of Apocalypse III; for the latter Apocalyptist had to convince himself and his readers that everything was going according to a preconceived divine plan. And it explains for another thing why Apocalypse III varies Apocalypse II's application of Hab. 2:3. Whereas II employs the word *ḥāzōn* not (like Habukkuk) in its more common, derived sense of 'prediction' but in its less common, etymological sense of 'vision', III adopts a derived sense akin to that in which Habakkuk uses it, but with stress on God's foreordainment rather than on the prophet's prediction. For the sense of 10:14 is: 'I have come to inform you what is destined to befall your people at the end of the present age, for more events are foreordained for the present age'. And 11:14b[1] surely means 'will attempt *to stop* [Gen. 29:35, 30:9; 2 Kings 13:18; Nahum 2:9] the march of *foreordained* events, but they shall fail'. Accordingly, the end of 11:27 means, 'for there is yet a phase to the period', and similarly the end of 11:35 (reading *qēṣ* before *lammōʿēd*).

Apocalypse III, even before Apocalypse IV (see above) dispenses with a dream or vision of symbols that comes to Daniel spontaneously, and instead has Daniel pray for three weeks, during which he practises self-mortification, for enlightenment about the future of his people. At the end of that period an angel, described in somewhat Ezekielic terms, appears and explains that Daniel's petition was received favourably the very first day, but that he, the angel, was busy holding the 'prince' (i.e. the angel viceroy) of Persia in check (and will presently have to contend with the 'prince' of Greece). At last, Michael, one of the leading 'princes', stepped in to relieve him for a spell, and he is now taking advantage of the respite to come and instruct Daniel. Thus, every nation has its angelic protector; indeed, the arch-'prince' Michael is the special protector of Israel (12:1). Of course, the idea of the nations being assigned to angelic viceroys is inspired by Deut. 32:8: 'When the Most High gave nations their homes/and set the divisions of man,/he marked off the territories of peoples/according to the number of the children of God' (the reading of the LXX and a Hebrew fragment from Qumran). To be sure, Apocalyptist III, in line with the surprising autonomy which we have just seen him confer on the other viceroys, departs from his source in also assigning such a viceroy to

[1] This meaning was first proposed by me for the predicate in *Studies in Daniel*, p. 79, line 4. Bevan's emendation of the subject to *ubone pirṣe ʿammᵉka*, 'and those who [desire to] repair the breaches of your people' (A. A. Bevan, *A Short Commentary on the Book of Daniel*, London, 1892, ad loc.) founders before the fact that both the masses of the Jews and their elders sided with Antiochus III (cf. Dan. 11:14a: 'And at that time the many [= the Jewish masses] will rise against the king of the south') and rendered him very valuable assistance, which he handsomely rewarded, whereas the leaders of the pro-Ptolemaic party had to migrate to Egypt. See E. Bickerman, *Studies in Jewish and Christian History*, 2 (Leiden, 1980), pp. 44ff.

Israel, for his source goes on to stress (Deut. 32:9) that Israel is distinguished from the other nations by having a *direct* relationship with YHWH: 'But YHWH's people is his own portion, Jacob his own allotment.' As for Apocalypse III's use of 'prince (*śr*) and 'princes' (*śrym*), it represents a deliberate softening of the more original 'children' (*bny*) of the Septuagint and the Qumran fragment of Deut. 32:8, while the masoretic reading *bny yśr'l* 'children of Israel' is a conflation of the original and the softened readings.

In previewing the history of the Near East from the present moment down to the climax of history, Daniel's angelic informant reveals an astonishingly good knowledge of the wars and marriages between the Houses of Seleucus and Lagus, for which Apocalyptist III may have been able to draw on a written account (perhaps produced when either Antiochus III or Antiochus IV was at the height of his power). On the other hand, his knowledge of Persian history is poor. The supposed date of the revelation we are dealing with was the third year of Cyrus of Persia (10:1), and the angel says, 'Now, three more kings of Persia are going to arise.... The fourth one shall...' (11:2). Like most critical writers, Bickerman accepts the view of Jerome that '*the* fourth' means '*a* fourth' and assumes that the biblical author had read Herodotus and so knew about Cambyses and even Smerdis, and that he shared the Greek view that Alexander's annihilation of the Persian empire was in revenge for Xerxes' famous invasion of Greece, so that he would feel justified in leaping from Cyrus, Smerdis, Cambyses, Darius, and Xerxes straight to Alexander. However, there can be no doubt that Montgomery[1] was right in insisting on the natural meaning of '*the* fourth' and that our writer's only source of Persian history was Scripture, which furnished him with only four names of Persian kings (it so happens that all of them are listed, and in the right historical order, in Ezra 4:4–7). We have pointed out elsewhere[2] that the identical number is hinted at by the four heads (the 'four' before 'wings' means the same thing, but it may be intrusive) of Daniel 7:6 (as are also the 'scriptural' numbers of Chaldean and Median emperors in verses 4 to 5, when the clauses are rearranged as they must be).

For Apocalyptist III was nothing if not steeped in Scripture. We have already seen his use of Hab. 2:3 and Deut. 32:8–9. It should therefore come as no surprise that as soon as he comes to the Seleucids' penetration of Coele-Syria, he should equate the Seleucid kingdom with Assyria. Thus he applies the phrase 'swirling through', which

[1] J. A. Montgomery, *A Critical and Exegetical Commentary on the Book of Daniel*, ICC (New York, 1927), ad loc.
[2] *Studies in Daniel*, p. 19.

Isaiah uses of the Euphrates as symbols of Assyria (Isa. 8:8), both to the actual assault of Antiochus III (Daniel 11:10) and to the anticipated counterattack of Antiochus IV against the anticipated invasion of Coele-Syria by 'the king of the South' (11:40). It is also only natural that he should expect Antiochus IV to retain the upper hand over the Jews 'until the indignation has spent itself, the decreed (destruction) having been wrought – 11:36; compare Isa. 10:23–27 (26:20–1) – and eventually to meet his just fate in Judea, 11:45; compare Isa. 14:24–27. In passing, at Dan. 11:30 he applies Num. 24:24 to the events of the year 168: ships coming from Kittim (here, Italy) shall oppress the Assyrians (i.e. order the Seleucid forces to withdraw from Egypt), and the latter shall oppress the Hebrews. It may well be because he found all that ammunition in Isaiah that he also conceived the idea that his own party of loyal resisters – who sought and found comfort in the study of the Scriptures and 'justified the masses' both by encouraging them to keep faith and by suffering martyrdom – were none other than the masses–justifying Suffering Servant of Isaiah 53:11*ac*. In any case, it is because the pericope about the Suffering Servant opens with: 'Indeed my servant shall prosper (*yaśkil*), he shall be exalted and raised to great heights' (Isa. 52:13) that he (1) names his party 'the *maśkilim*', which can mean both 'the Enlightened' and 'the Enlighteners', and (2) predicts that 'the *maśkilim* shall shine with a splendour like that of the heavens; the Justifiers of the Masses, like the stars for evermore' (Dan. 12:3).

His designation of the opposing party, the active paganizers, as 'the wicked' (12:10) or 'the wicked of the Covenant' (11:32) is apparently inspired by Isa. 53:9; and the designation of their fate, namely, 'eternal horror' (*dir'ōn*, Dan. 12:2) unquestionably by Isa. 66:24: 'Their worms shall not die nor their fire be quenched; they shall be a horror (*dērā'ōn*, in the reading of the 'Orientals' *dir'ōn*) to all flesh'. For of course the very idea that 'many of those that sleep beneath the dust shall awake' (Dan. 12:2) is inspired by Isa. 26:19: 'Oh, let your dead revive! Let corpses arise! Awake and shout for joy, you who dwell in the dust!'

Like Apocalypse II, Apocalypse III has the angel instruct Daniel to conceal the extremely long-term prediction until it becomes actual (12:4), and since it goes without saying that Daniel is to be one of those who are resurrected for eternal glory, the angel concludes, 'You, meanwhile, go to your rest, to arise for the lot that is in store for you in the time of the age'.

It is no doubt because this conclusion of Apocalypse III sounds so final that the author of Apocalypse IV, who, as has already been stated, is the author of chapter 9, preferred not to place his message after that of Apocalypse III but assigned it to a date and position between Apocalypse II and Apocalypse III. It has been noted that Apocalyptist IV's original contribution is the scheme of septennia, and that he interpolates the last semi-septennium into the apocalypses of his three predecessors. In the case of Apocalypse II and Apocalypse III, his interpolation involves an apparent direct contradiction. Thus in 8:15 Daniel prays for an explanation of the *ḥāzōn*, by which he means the antics of the ram and the he-goat (8:1–12), whereupon a manlike figure materializes and introduces his explanation with, 'Pay attention, mortal, for the *ḥāzōn* relates to a remote period' (verse 17), and concludes with (verse 26b) 'as for you, conceal the *ḥāzōn*, since it is for a long term'. But in between, Daniel is reported to catch sight of two divine beings and to overhear an exchange of question and answer between them (verses 13 to 14, in verse 14 read 'to him' for 'to me'), and then he hears a human voice instruct Gabriel to interpret (not the *ḥāzōn* but) the *mar'ē* to Daniel. What the *mar'ē* is, is clear from verse 26a, 'and the *mar'ē* about the mornings and the evenings that was *uttered*', which can only refer to the aforementioned audition of verses 13 to 14; and although Daniel has received a full exposition of the *ḥāzōn*, he reports (verse 27b), 'I wondered about the *mar'ē* and could not understand it'. Clearly, *mar'ē* must mean something like 'statement' or 'declaration'. So, too, after the *angelus revelator* (to Daniel, he is not an *angelus interpres* in any sense) of chapters 10 to 12 has revealed at length what history has in store (12:4), he concludes: 'As for you, Daniel, keep the words secret and hide the book until the appointed season, when the masses shall seek and knowledge shall increase'. But then Daniel notices two more heavenly beings who address to Daniel's *angelus revelator* a question analogous to those of the first holy being of 8:13–14 and receive an answer similar to that given by the second holy being. And to Daniel's request for the *'ḥryt* (read *'aḥᵃrīt*) of that answer, his *angelus revelator* replies that it is to remain (not just hidden away but) inherently mysterious and unintelligible until D-day (12:5ff). Obviously, *'aḥᵃrīt* here means something very similar to *mar'ē* in the verses just cited from chapter 8.

This is a suitable juncture at which to cite some proofs for the assertion that the Hebrew portions of Daniel (apart from 9:4–20, as previously explained) are translated from an Aramaic original. *Mar'ē* in the sense of 'statement or declaration' (though its proper meaning is 'spectacle') is most naturally explained as an inept rendering of an Aramaic *'aḥᵃwāyā* 'telling' literally 'showing'; and our *'aḥărīt* clearly goes back to the construct state of the same Aramaic word, to be translated 'explanation of' as in 5:12. Another example is the description of Seleucus IV – who inherited from Antiochus III the crippled kingdom, staggering under an enormous burden of reparations, to which the Romans had reduced his realm – as (11:20) *maʿᵃbîr nōgēś heder malkût*. The current interpretation of this is too stilted to be probable. It is actually a rendering of an Aramaic original *mhʿdy šlṭn wyqr mlkw* (but the position, and even the presence, of the conjuction *w* is a matter of doubt), meaning 'one stripped of dominion and the majesty of kingship'. For the first two of the four words, see Dan. 7:12a; for the last three, see 7:14aα. The translator's mistake was that he took *mhʿdy* as an active instead of a passive participle and assigned to *šolṭān* the sense of 'magistrate' or 'ruler' which it has sometimes (and in which it has, through Arabic and Turkish mediation, found its way into English as *sultan*) but does not have here, where it was intended in its commoner sense of 'dominion'. (That 'magistrate' or 'ruler' is a legitimate sense of the Hebrew *nōgēś* is proved by Isa. 3:12; 60:17b.) For our third example, it may be recalled that the phrase '(to set up) the abomination of desolation', Dan 9:27b*b*; 11:31; 12:11, occurs in the identical historical context in 1 Macc. 1:54. It would therefore not be surprising to find in close proximity to it another phrase from the same context in 1 Macc. 1. Actually, in the aforementioned verse, Dan. 11:31, we find the clause 'and they will profane the sanctuary, *hammāʿōz*', which is strongly reminiscent of the phrase 'and to defile sanctuary and saints', 1 Macc. 1:46, except that *hammaʿoz*, which earlier in chapter 11 is encountered repeatedly in the sense of 'fortress' or 'stronghold' (11:7, 10, 19), seems rather remote in meaning from 'saints'. But the two words look very much alike in Aramaic, in which 'fortress' is *ḥsn* and 'saints' *ḥsyn*,[1] and '*the* fortress' is *ḥsn*' and '*the* saints' *ḥsy*'. Another passage in which the translator has thus blundered into writing 'fortresses' for 'saints' is the first sentence in 11:39. Here the *author* evidently wanted to say, 'And he (Antiochus Epiphanes) will *bring over* to the citadel of the saints (i.e. the Akra of Jerusalem) a people *ʿam* of an alien god'. Then why did the *translator* write 'and he will make' instead of 'he will bring over'? Because in Aramaic the latter, *wyʿbr* (read *wyaʿbar*), is practically indistinguishable, graphically, from *wyʿbd* (read *wyeʿbed*), which means 'and he will make'.

[1] See Syriac *ḥasyā* 'sanctus', C. Brockelmann, *Lexicon Syriacum* (2nd edn., Göttingen, 1928), p. 245b, and the numerous other words from the same root that follow. The presumable Aramaic original of the phrase in Dan. 11:31 is therefore *wyhpswn (m)qdš wḥsyn*.

CHAPTER 14

THE MATRIX OF APOCALYPTIC

The Jewish writings gathered under the headings 'apocrypha' and 'pseudepigrapha' are broadly heterogeneous, as indicated by Professor Delcor in chapter 12. This heterogeneity is due in part to the wide diversity of literary genres utilized by the various writers represented in these ancient works. On a deeper level, however, it reflects a social and religious matrix of great complexity, characterized by divergent streams, diverse foreign and domestic influences, and differing responses to those influences. We shall briefly consider the major apocryphal and pseudepigraphical writings of the last centuries B.C.E. with attention to their social and religious setting. And while conceding the great diversity of these works, we shall suggest that they fall into two general categories which reflect opposing tendencies within post-exilic Judaism.

Diversity existed within Israelite religion from early times, as seen for example in divisions caused by the introduction of monarchy, the role of the cult, the claims of rival priestly families, the separate kingdoms of Judah and Israel, and the relation of Yahwism to other religions. Over the sweep of the pre-exilic period, however, a centripetal force was exerted by the concept of a central cult and the ideal of one people in covenant with Yahweh. This force is manifested, for example, by the way in which even northern prophetic traditions were assimilated to a central Temple ideology in the Deuteronomistic history.

This centripetal force was dealt a stunning blow in the events culminating in 587/6: the Temple was destroyed, and nationhood was lost. Not only were the institutions thereby lost which had contributed a unifying quality to Jewish religious experience; more profoundly, the central theologumenon upon which Yahwism was based was threatened: Zion, the mountain elected by Yahweh, had been violated by worshippers of Marduk, which seemed to thow into question the status of Israel's election, and the binding authority of her institutions. The onset of a centrifugal tendency was immediate, recorded concretely and permanently by the Diaspora, and left its marks in the literature by the diversity of religious expression contained within the apocrypha and pseudepigrapha.

The blow to the heart of Yahwism occasioned by the futile death of the David *redivivus*, Josiah, and the destruction of the Temple is expressed by haunting cries of doubt and despair during the early sixth century: 'Yahweh will not do good, nor will he do ill' (Zeph. 1:12; compare Ezek. 8:12; 18:25; Isa. 57:1). Certain exiles in Egypt expressed doubts which threatened to deny Yahwism its central claim of effectiveness within the concrete realities of history: so long as they were faithful in their worship of the Assyrian Queen of Heaven, 'we had plenty of food, and prospered, and saw no evil. But since we left off burning incense to the queen of heaven, and pouring out libations to her, we have lacked everything and have been consumed by the sword and by famine' (Jer. 44:17–18).

It is not surprising that this threat of religious and social anomie evoked divergent answers, for the cohesive effects of Temple and national autonomy were lost. These answers fall to one side or the other along a continuum that will serve as our key in the classification of the Jewish writings of the Hellenistic and Roman periods as we proceed to describe the social matrix within which those writings arose. On one side of the continuum fall the writings of hierocratic circles dedicated to the preservation of institutional and doctrinal structures which maintained continuity with the past. On the other side we find the writings of visionaries who viewed the events of the early sixth century as proof of Yahweh's displeasure with the structures of the pre-exilic period, leading them to yearn for divine acts of intervention which would inaugurate a new order of things. That the position adopted by a specific party or individual was intimately related to that party's or individual's relation to the governing offices should come as no surprise, for in all periods of history those in power tend to favour existing structures as offering the best answers for the future, whereas the disenfranchised dream of the dawn of a new order in which their vindication would be accomplished.

First, in turning attention to hierocratic circles advocating continuity with structures of the past, we recognize the culmination of the Temple-centred theology of the pre-exilic period in the Deuteronomic Law and the history constructed upon that base (Dtr[1]). Though the events of 609 and 587 called into question the very heart of the Deuteronomistic theology, Zadokite priestly circles, dedicated to the Temple structures over which they had presided in the pre-exilic period, did not respond to the crisis by abandoning those structures, but by rewriting certain sections of the Deuteronomistic history so as to reduce the contradictions between its theology and the shocking events of history. Josiah's death and the destruction of the Temple were reconciled with the doctrine of retribution by accentuating the depravity of Manasseh: so great was his sin that it required Yahweh's judgement on Zion, Josiah's righteousness and reform efforts notwithstanding.[1]

The same bridge of continuity between Zadokite structures of the pre-exilic period and restoration plans for the future was constructed by Ezekiel. In spite of his harsh indictments on the sins of the people (including Temple personnel), Ezekiel assured his audience that the reconstituted community would be built upon the institutional and official structures of the first Temple. It was his programme (Ezek. 40 to 48) which served as the blueprint for Zerubbabel and Joshua in their activities of rebuilding the Temple. Their prophetic supporters, Haggai and Zechariah, urged the people on to redoubled efforts in the building project, for re-establishment of the Zadokite Temple structures of the past held the key to a future of blessing as God's elect people.

This ideology of continuity with the religious norms of the past was given its definitive formulation in the final, priestly edition of the Pentateuch. Moreover, the hierocratic structures of the post-exilic period were given legitimacy in relation to those norms through the reformulation of Israel's history in the Chronicler's work. With these two monumental writings, a textual basis was established for a Law- and temple-centred religious community. In Israel's distant past all norms for the full life as God's people had been given. What was required, therefore, was obedience to the statutes and ordinances of the Torah, a theme which the original Deuteronomic Law did not tire of reformulating,[2] and which remains throughout the post-exilic period the cardinal principle of the hierocratic group advocating continuity with the past.

Before tracing the further extension to the hierocratic tendency down through the post-exilic period, we turn to give brief accounting of the other side of the continuum, involving visionaries interpreting the events of 609 and 587 as proof of Yahweh's displeasure with the structures of the past, and awaiting restoration only on the other side of

[1] Cf. F. M. Cross, Jr., *Canaanite Myth and Hebrew Epic* (Cambridge, Mass., 1973), pp. 274–89.

[2] 'You shall therefore keep all the commandment which I command you this day, that you may be strong, and go in and take possession of the land which you are going over to possess, and that you may live long in the land which the Lord swore to your fathers to give to them and to their descendants, a land flowing with milk and honey' (Deut. 11:8–9; cf. 4:1, 5, 14; 6:1; 8:1).

a mighty divine intervention inaugurating a new order. The seeds of this view were already planted in the eschatology of eighth and seventh century prophecy, where there developed a tendency to view Israel's past as a history of rebelliousness, answerable only by divine judgement. 'Woe unto you that desire the day of the Lord!' It 'is darkness, and not light' (Amos 5:18). 'So will I break this people and this city, as one breaks a potter's vessel, so that it can never be mended' (Jer. 19:11a). Jeremiah was unable to hold out hope within existing structures; a radically new beginning was necessary (Jer. 31:31–4). This view is formulated climactically by Second Isaiah, who, in standing on the other side of the catastrophe, awaits restoration not as a renewal of the old structures, but as a new creative act of Yahweh. In a most unorthodox way, this anonymous prophet diverts attention away from the old forms: 'Remember not the former things, nor consider the things of old. Behold, I am doing a new thing; now it springs forth, do you not perceive it?' (Isa. 43:18–19a).

A pessimistic view of Israel's past, and a belief that only a radical new beginning inaugurated by divine intervention would set reality back on a redemptive track: these twin principles define the response of a visionary tendency discernible throughout the post-exilic period. In recurrent periods of duress, whether caused by internal conflict or enemy attack, visionaries would condemn existing institutions and leaders as dominated by evil, and would describe in apocalyptic terms a new era which could arrive only after God had dealt ruthlessly with the powers of this world, and had re-established the oppressed remnant to positions of honour.

The lines between hierocratic leaders defending existing Temple and sacrificial structures on the basis of a past revelation and protesting visionaries dreaming of judgement on those very structures and a new order predicated on reversal would be drawn repeatedly during the post-exilic period. Though this dichotomy does not answer the background questions of every apocryphal and pseudepigraphical writing, it does add a good measure of clarity to the complex matrix within which these writings arose.

In tracing several of the most critical periods of tension between the visionary and hierocratic tendencies, we shall recognize the inadequacy of categories like 'canonical', 'apocryphal', and 'pseudepigraphical'. For the history of that tension is recorded in writings which do not fit into such classifications. Indeed, the first example of this tension involves a struggle between visionaries and dissident priests (whose oracles come to expression in Isaiah 56 to 66 and Zechariah 9 to 14) and Zadokite restoration groups drawing upon the programme of Ezekiel

40 to 48 and sponsered by the prophets Haggai and Zechariah.[1] Within this sixth century struggle, the major themes of both tendencies receive their basic formulation.

Of great importance for the further development of both tendencies was the victory of the Zadokite party over the visionary critics in the late sixth century. This victory was assured in large part by the alliance maintained between the Zadokites and their Persian sponsors.[2] With the authority of community rule vested solely in the high priest, we enter the fifth century, a period of consolidation of the hierocratic position. Though the books of Malachi and Joel, together with Isaiah 24 to 27, Zechariah 9 to 14, and Ezekiel 38 to 39, indicate that the visionary perspective did not lack proponents in the late sixth and fifth centuries, it was increasingly forced underground. Indeed, the missions of Nehemiah and Ezra, again sponsored by the Persians, were apparently intended to eliminate factional strife. The effect was a tightening up of the structures and laws prescribed by the Torah, that is, the reinforcement of the hierocratic posture. Though the fourth century is a period lacking in historical documentation, what materials are available suggest a community, in the environs of Jerusalem at least, which is firmly under the norm of the decretal with which Ezra was sent to the Jews under the commission of the Persian King 'the law of your God, which is in your hand' (Ezra 7:14, which probably refers to the Pentateuch).

The monumental product culminating this period of normalcy under the Torah is the early second century B.C.E. book of Ecclesiasticus (the Wisdom of Jesus Ben Sira), which therefore stands as the first example from the apocrypha of the Temple-centred circles advocating continuity with the past. Here the disciple sits at the feet of the wise teacher, and learns how the great heritage of the Torah relates to each facet of life. The ideal is a well-ordered life, founded on the principles articulated by the sages of old, and optimistic in the belief that the godly life will be richly rewarded. The twin principles of apocalypticism, pessimism *vis-à-vis* the structures of this world and the fervent hope of divine intervention and reversal, are totally lacking.

Arising also within hierocratic circles, but now in the wake of the Seleucid take-over and oppression in the first half of the second

[1] For a description of this first encounter between these tendencies as the setting within which Jewish apocalypticism was born, see P. D. Hanson, *The Dawn of Apocalyptic* (Philadelphia, 2nd edn., 1979) and *The People Called* (San Francisco, 1986).

[2] Where over zealous hierocrats stepped out of line, they were apparently disposed of by the Persians, as suggested by the disappearance of Zerubbabel.

century, is the book of 1 Maccabees (*circa* 100 B.C.E.). The Law and the Temple are in the centre of the stage throughout this work. Historical threats and setbacks do not call the traditional structures into question, but increase the resolve to defend them, with full trust that God takes the side of the defenders of the Law. This fidelity to the Law does not lead to the type of pure extremism characterizing the legal piety of apocalyptic circles. Faithful to the example set by the early hierocrats of the Persian period, compromises with the Romans or any other power were willingly made in the name of expedience. The political idealism of prophetic and later apocalyptic thought is thus totally absent (1 Macc. 14:41 notwithstanding), as are the other characteristic traits of the visionary tendency. Moreover, Maccabean kingship and the transfer of the priestly office to the Hasmoneans are defended as natural developments out of ancient patterns. It should come as no surprise that this book is found neither at Qumran nor among the writings of the Pharisees (try to imagine the praise heaped upon the Romans in 1 Maccabees 8 being sung at Qumran!).

A whole group of writings from the period after the Seleucid persecutions is characterized by fidelity to the Torah and orthodoxy in regard to Temple praxis, but is open in varying degrees to Hellenistic forms of expression. In contrast to Sirach and 1 Maccabees, this group of writings stands at a greater distance from Sadducean thought, and in closer relation to the milieu of the Pharisees, sometimes explicitly defending their doctrines (for example, resurrection) against the criticism of the Sadducees (compare 2 Maccabees and the Psalms of Solomon). In Diaspora writings like the Wisdom of Solomon and the Sibylline Oracles, a deep borrowing not only of the literary forms but of the philosophical concepts of Hellenism is in evidence, betraying origins in a Jewish piety which, while holding firmly to the Law of Moses, desired to make that law intelligible to the Greeks (compare Eupolemus' identification of Moses with the Muses or Hermes). It is in this same spirit of apologia that the Greek Additions to Esther were written. Jewish piety combined with certain pagan motifs also characterize two other narrative works, Tobit, and Joseph and Asenath. Finally, mention should also be made of 3 Maccabees, an apologia defending loyalty to orthodox belief in the face of persecution.

This brief description cannot characterize every writing belonging to this group, nor enumerate the unique features distinguishing even the works cited. It has sought only to describe in general terms the milieu within which originated our first group of writings from this period, the milieu of a Jewish piety standing in unbroken continuity with an authoritative Torah which is accepted as the guide to community life and Temple praxis. It is at the same time a piety which is practical rather than utopian or extreme in its relating Judaism to foreign powers and influences, for its orientation is not eschatological, but pragmatic. This is the customary attitude of those holding positions of leadership and esteem within circles subservient to the Jerusalem Temple cult, whether those circles be located geographically in Egypt, Babylon, or the environs of Jerusalem.

We turn now to consider the second group of writings, that falling on the opposite side of the continuum. In sharp contrast to writings coming from circles standing in *continuity with* the traditions stemming from Ezra are those which are characterized in the first instance by a *break with* the traditions of the sacrificial cult of the Jerusalem Temple. In studying these writings, one recognizes again the familiar line of confrontation between champions of the structures of the past, and those disenfranchised from those structures who focus their hopes on a new order of reality. As in the case of the writings categorized under circles faithful to the Temple cult, so too diversity in detail characterizes the various writings which we categorize as protest documents. More significant than differences, however, are the lines of connection uniting them, for they involve major teachings and practices, and once again testify to provenance within a common religious milieu.

Here significant new light has been shed by discoveries in the Judean desert, especially at Qumran, which have led to the recognition of a common sectarian community behind several of the previously known pseudepigraphs as well as the sectarian writings of Qumran themselves. For example, in place of the calendar of the Jerusalem Temple we find a solar calendar of 364 days underlying Jubilees, 1 Enoch, and the Qumran community documents. Clearly a cultic system had been developed which was irreconcilably at variance with the Jerusalem sacrificial system. Since the hostility toward the Temple manifested, for example, by 1 Enoch and the Testament of Levi, is absent from the book of Jubilees, it seems apparent that Jubilees records an early chapter in the development of the protest group, before its final break with the Temple in the latter part of the second century B.C.E., whereas 1 Enoch and the Testament of Levi represent later developments.

The Temple Scroll, edited by Y. Yadin,[1] offers an alternative Temple plan to that in Jerusalem. Here we see the specific blueprints of a Zadokite priesthood, excluded from the Temple hierarchy, but awaiting Yahweh's day of vindication when it would be returned to

[1] *The Temple Scroll*, ed. Y. Yadin, 3 vols. (Jerusalem, 1977).

power, with rebuilding plans in hand. The situation is closely parallel to that of the late sixth century visionaries, except that the Zadokite party which was in power in 520 is now among the disenfranchised, clear indication that it is not party affiliation, but status in relation to institutional structures which determines an individual group's position along the continuum extending from subservience to traditional structures to protest against them.

In the place of the promulgation of the received structures we therefore find harsh condemnation of Temple and priesthood as the common theme unifying this group of writings. Here we shall offer several further examples. In the *Testament of Levi* a harsh attack on the defilement of the Jerusalem priesthood is followed by the eschatological promise of a new priesthood, free from sin (chapters 14 to 19). In 1 Enoch 6 to 11, an ancient myth of the rebellion of angelic beings is utilized to describe the entire created order as fallen and the Temple antidote for defilement (the Yom Kippur rite) as totally ineffectual; this is followed by a description of Yahweh's end-time intervention to establish a new creation in which the 'plant of righteousness' (the pure community) would be restored to a position of honour and power within a healed and sanctified order. In the Apocalypse of Weeks (1 Enoch 93 and 91:12–17) we find the familiar pattern of this literature: pessimism regarding the present fallen order followed by the eschatological anticipation of God's inauguration of a new order in which evil will be cleansed from the earth and the 'plant of righteousness' will be established forever. In the countdown of events through the ten weeks, we discern the same mentality which informs the War Scroll found among Qumran manuscripts.

The protest documents which we have discussed stem in the main part from the second and first centuries B.C.E. What was the nature of the interrelationship between Temple and protest tendencies which made that period one of such productivity? Chief among the causes of tension between these tendencies, and indeed catalyst of the final break of the Essene group from the Temple community, was the Hasmonean takeover of the Temple priesthood, which development to be sure was intertwined with the troubled events of the time involving Seleucid persecution, Ptolemaic intrigue, and Roman interference. Even as the visionary group of the sixth century found itself excluded by the Zadokite party's domination of the restoration Temple, the circles producing the writings in our second group found themselves excluded by the Hasmonean party's rise to power. Within this situation the self-identity of the two conflicting groups was established not on the basis of family genealogy, but on the basis of spiritual ancestry. The disenfranchised Zadokites of Qumran identified with the disfranchised Levites and disciples of Second Isaiah of the sixth century, whereas the Hasmoneans identified with a line of priestly tradition formerly transmitted by the house of Zadok! In both, obedience to the Torah remains; but in the latter case it is a Torah ensconced within a Temple hierarchy, in the former a Torah absorbed into an apocalyptic sectarian consciousness envisioning bold new divine acts of judgement on existing Temple structures. It is no accident, therefore, that the metaphors of new creation, second exodus, and cosmic conflict taken from Second Isaiah by the visionaries of the sixth century were reapplied by the Essenes to their situation. Even as the Hasmoneans perpetuate a position reaching back to Ezra, the Chronicler, and the Jerusalem priests of the Josianic Era, so too a common visionary perspective can be traced all the way from the sixth to the first century B.C.E., borne by apocalyptic circles protesting the exclusiveness of temple structures, and anticipating vindication of their cause not within existing structures but in a new order to be introduced by God through cataclysmic judgement and the creation of a new order supplanting the old.

While recognizing distinct lines of continuity running through these two tendencies over a period of six centuries, this general reconstruction must not be allowed to obscure the peculiarities of individual writings. Within the Temple group we have discussed the traces of two distinct parties, the Sadducees and the Pharisees, and similar differences exist within the protest group, as can be seen in differing positions taken on messianic expectations, angelology, and the apocalyptic timetable. Moreover, it remains unclear how a writing like the Testament of Moses relates to the Essene group centring around Qumran. Could it reflect the piety of a rural synagogue? While it shares characteristics of the Qumran secratian writings (hatred of the Hasmoneans, attack on the Pharisees, a sectarian desire to avoid the defilement of those not following 'the truth of God'), it does not fit the teachings of the Qumran sect in other features. There were obviously groups and sub-groups among the apocalyptic protest movements as well, some of them documented by historians like Josephus, others leaving their traces no doubt only in anonymous and pseudonymous documents.

It should also be noted that writings from the Hellenistic and Roman periods may also fall at a point on the continuum which actually mediates between the extremes. The most notable example is Daniel, which shares the vision of the inbreaking of a new order with the writings considered above, but which stems from a period in the history of the *ḥᵃsîdîm* which antedates the division of that movement into two branches, one accepting the Temple structures even after they came under the patronage of the Hasmoneans, the other moving into a posture of radical protest and withdrawal.

In spite of these strictures, however, the fact remains that the writings of the apocrypha and pseudepigrapha coming out of the last centuries B.C.E. can be understood properly only when the complex social and religious matrix from which they stem is grasped. And one aspect of that matrix is the tension which existed between two tendencies, one hierocratic in nature and dedicated to the preservation of structures of the past, the other visionary in perspective and yearning for reversal and the inauguration of a new order of reality.

CHAPTER 15

THE SEPTUAGINT AND ITS HEBREW TEXT

By about 200 B.C.E. the Jewish community of Alexandria had become large and sophisticated enough to require a translation of its Hebrew Bible into its current vernacular, Greek; the Septuagint translation of the Torah was the result.

JUDAISM IN ALEXANDRIA: HALAKAH AND THE HEBREW LANGUAGE

Ever since Jews had begun to settle in Egypt in increasing numbers, whether because pro-Babylonian forces in Judah from about 600 B.C.E. had made it necessary for them to emigrate or because subsequent social–political conditions at home had made flight desirable, the growing community had adjusted itself extraordinarily well to the pagan environment. A significant portion of the Jewish population had retained its loyalties and ties – especially the religious – with Judah at the same time as it adopted many of the more meaningful aspects of the gentile society in which it dwelt and flourished. Thus the Alexandria Jewish community sent tithes and made pilgrimages to the Temple in Jerusalem and acknowledged the religious authority in Jerusalem as theirs also.

One of the most radical changes that had taken place in the homeland was the belief that the spirit of prophecy, since Malachi, had ascended to heaven and that until God let it descend again it was only those who were learned in His written Law who were authorized to speak in His name. 1 Macc. 4:42–6 (see also, for example, 9:27 and 14:4) put it this way:[1] [Judah] chose blameless priests devoted to the Law, and they cleansed the Sanctuary...they tore down the altar, and stored the stones

[1] The translations offered in this chapter derive from various sources, e.g. the New Jewish Version of the Bible (NJV; 1962ff), the Revised Standard Version (RSV), the Jewish Apocryphal Literature (Dropsie College ed.), the translations of the *Letter of Aristeas* by Thackeray and by Meecham, and my own variations on them; but I have not introduced anything radical in the translation of any word or phrase without drawing specific attention to it.

on the Temple Mount, in a suitable place, until a prophet should come to decide what to do with them.' *Yoma* 9b expressed it as follows: 'after the last of the prophets, Haggai, Zechariah, and Malachi died, the Holy Spirit departed from Israel (*nistalqah rúaḥ ha-qódesh mi-yisra'el...*'[1] For after the priestly group acquired supremacy in post-exilic Judah, the status of anyone who claimed that he received revelation, and hence authority, directly from God – in other words, one who claimed to be imparting prophecy in the manner of the old-fashioned prophets – was drastically diminished and finally abrogated. Henceforth it was the established and growing priestly bureaucracy, deriving its authority from the received Law of Moses, that comprehended and executed the will of God. Subsequently, the Judean community entered a new stage, in the Hellenistic period, when the theocratic state was replaced by a commonwealth and when the Torah constitution was reinterpreted by the liberalizing Pharisees in accordance with the new conditions. From now on it was the halakah as the Pharisees comprehended it, it was the Torah of Moses as the Pharisees interpreted it and applied it in their attempts to introduce changes in Judea's social structure, that prevailed; nomocracy had set in. It is this phase of Judaism, the emphasis on halakah and on the authority of those who were learned in halakah, that is reflected in and even dominates the *Letter of Aristeas*.[2]

The forbears of the Jews of Alexandria had been at home in Hebrew and/or Aramaic, the latter, for example, being the language of the Elephantine papyri of the sixth-fifth centuries B.C.E.; but Alexander's conquest of Egypt and the social forces unleashed in its wake resulted *inter alia* in the decreased use of Hebrew and Aramaic and in the rapid adoption of the national language of the country, Greek. In

1 This belief, namely, the role of the Law (*halakah*) and the cessation of prophecy, is evident already from a careful reading of the three verses that came to be attached to the end of Malachi (4:4–6; Heb. 3:22–4): 'Be mindful of the Law of my servant Moses, whom I charged at Horeb with laws and rules for all Israel. Lo, I am going to send the prophet Elijah to you before the great and awesome day of the Lord comes', where it is clearly the precepts and regulations of the Law (*torat Mosheh ʿabdi...ḥuqqim u-mishpaṭim*) that are pre-eminent and where Elijah, one of God's spokesmen of old – not a new, prophetic successor to Malachi – will return to bring His message to His people and work His will among them.

It may be noted that in the rabbinic literature (e.g. *Tosefta Yadayim* 2.13), the phrase *mi-kan wᵉ-'elekh* ('from then on') came to be used technically to indicate: when prophecy ceased in Israel. See in general, E. E. Urback, 'When did prophecy cease?', *Tarbiz*, 17 (1945–46), 1–11 (in Hebrew), though the argument is uneven.

2 For an analysis of this phenomenon, see the references to S. Zeitlin and E. Rivkin in H. M. Orlinsky, 'The Septuagint as Holy Writ and the philosophy of the translators', *HUCA*, 46 (1975), 100 n. 14.

fine, the Jewish community of Alexandria had become Hellenized.

The religious basis of Jewish life, in Alexandria no less than in Judah, remained God's Torah to Moses and Israel; and the only correct understanding of the Torah, in both communities, was that provided by the halakists, the learned interpreters of the Law. As long as the Jews of Alexandria read and understood the Torah in Hebrew, there was no problem; but the situation changed when the original became less than comprehensible to a constantly growing number of them. The need for a version of the Torah – a thoroughly reliable and acceptable version, naturally – that the Jewish population could read directly, became urgent. In this historical setting, the main reason for the composition of the *Letter of Aristeas* becomes clear.[1]

THE LETTER OF ARISTEAS AND THE ORIGIN OF THE SEPTUAGINT

The *Letter*, from which most of our information about the origin and the making of the Septuagint derives, is said by its purported author, Aristeas, to have been written 'to my dear brother (or simply: friend) Philocrates', telling him how Demetrius, head of the famous library in Alexandria, persuaded Ptolemy II Philadelphus (285–246 B.C.E.) to send a delegation to the High Priest Eleazar in Jerusalem with a letter requesting that he appoint six elders from each of the twelve tribes, 'elders of exemplary life who possess skill in the Law and ability to translate' (§39), for the purpose of translating the Hebrew Torah into Greek. The translation was to be deposited in the royal library.

Eleazar, the *Letter* continues to relate, in the presence of 'our entire

[1] The parallel between nineteenth–twentieth century American Jewry and third–second century B.C.E. Alexandrian Jewry, so far as Bible translation is concerned, is striking. For tens and, later on, hundreds of thousands of Jews of Central and Eastern Europe who came to the New World found increasingly that they had to give up the languages of their homeland (German, Hungarian, Yiddish, Russian, etc.) for the national language of their adopted country, English, and that their knowledge of Hebrew suffered in more or less equal proportion. Loyal as they were to the Bible from which their religious beliefs and authority derived, a reliable version of the Bible in English became imperative – first Lesser (1845; Harkavy, 1916), then the Jewish version of 1916, and now NJV (1962ff); see, e.g., H. M. Orlinsky, 'Wanted: a new English Translation of the Bible for the Jewish people' and 'Jewish biblical scholarship in America' (respectively chapters 18 and 16 in *Essays in Biblical Culture and Bible Translation* (New York, 1974), pp. 349–62 [with reference there to M. L. Margolis, *The Story of Bible Translations* (Philadelphia, 1922)] and 287–332 *passim*).

people' and with their consent, complied enthusiastically with the unprecedented royal request. He appointed 72 elders, all of them pious and learned in the Law and in worldly wisdom, and sent them off, with appropriate gifts 'and the precious parchments in which the Law was inscribed in Jewish letters with writings of gold, the material being wonderfully worked and the joinings of the leaves being made imperceptible' (§176). After a royal banquet that lasted seven days, the elders were taken across 'the breakwater, seven stades long, to the island [of Pharos]', to a magnificently appointed and secluded mansion by the seashore. There, in precisely 72 days, the elders accomplished the mission they had been chosen for (§§ 301–7). And,

> When the work [of translation] was completed, Demetrius assembled the Jewish people at the place where the translation had been made, and read it aloud[1] to the entire gathering. These received a great ovation from the community...When the rolls had been read aloud, the priests and the elders of the translators and some of the corporate body and the leaders of the people rose up and said,[2] 'Inasmuch as the translation has been well and piously made and is in every respect accurate, it is right that it should remain in its present form and that no revision of any sort take place.' And when all had assented to what had been said, they bade that an imprecation be pronounced, according to their custom, upon any who should revise the text by adding or transposing anything whatever in what had been written down, or by making any excision; and in this they did well, so that the work might be preserved imperishable and unchanged forever (§§ 308–11).

Subsequently the translation was read out to the king and he made obeisance and gave orders 'that great care be taken of the books and that they be watched over reverently' (§ 317). He sent them off with gifts – including gifts for Eleazar – and a standing invitation to return at their pleasure (§ 321).

THE TERM 'SEPTUAGINT'

A word about the term 'Septuagint' (frequently abbreviated to LXX), derivative of Greek *hebdomēkonta* by way of Latin *septuaginta* – all meaning 'seventy'. (So too, for example, early Jewish usage: *targum ha-*

[1] Or 'read it out'. On this meaning of the Greek term *paranagignōskō* and its use elsewhere (e.g. §§ 43, 299, and 312 of the *Letter*; 2 Macc. 8:23; 3 Macc. 1:12) – as of shorter *anagignōskō* (e.g. § 310; 1 Macc. 10:7; Luke 4:16; 1 Thess. 5:27) – see n. 9a (with its reference to Meecham, etc.) in Orlinsky, *HUCA*, 46 (1975), 91f.

[2] On the Hebraism in Greek *stántes...eipon* (lit., 'standing up...they said') for the corresponding Hebrew phrase *wa-yaqúmu...wa-yomru*, which is idiomatically to be rendered 'they proceeded to say' or 'thereupon they said', see Orlinsky, *HUCA*, 46 (1975), 101, n. 15.

šibʿim 'the Translation of the Seventy.') It has been generally assumed that these Greek and Latin terms for 'seventy' for the Old Greek translation of first the Torah, and then of the whole Bible and whatever other books in circulation were regarded as sacred and divinely inspired, are but round numbers, convenient shorter forms of the fuller *hebdomḗkonta kaì dúo* and *septuaginta et duo* (Heb. *shibʿim u-shnayim*), 'seventy-two', the fuller expression being less suited to popular, oral usage.[1]

In his article on 'Septuagint' (*IDB*, 4 [1962], p. 273), J. W. Wevers proposed that the term was

> apparently a shortened form of the title *Intepretatio secundum* (or *iuxta*) *septuaginta seniores*. The term...'seventy' is based on the ancient tradition (Exod. 24:1, 9) that seventy elders accompanied Moses up the Mount...whereupon God gave the tables of the law to Moses. It was only fitting that seventy elders should in turn be responsible for translating the Torah into Greek. Aristeas increased the number to seventy-two in order to make six times twelve (tribes).

The sources, however, do not support any of the above explanations; instead, they indicate another explanation. The earliest source for the origin of the Septuagint, the *Letter of Aristeas* makes it clear that 72 elders – six from each of the twelve tribes – made the translation. All ancient statements about the Septuagint (including the early rabbinic and patristic data) derive from this source and none contradicts it.[2]

[1] Thus, for example, F. Buhl, *Canon and Text of the Old Testament* (Edinburgh, 1892), p. 115: 'for seventy is simply a round number for seventy-two'; and H. B. Swete, *An Introduction to the Old Testament in Greek* (2nd edn., Cambridge, 1914), while admitting (p. 10) that 'All forms of the name point back to a common source...the pseudonymous letter [of Aristeas]...', is nevertheless content with the misleading statement (p. 9): 'the translation was attributed by Alexandrian tradition to seventy or seventy-two Jewish elders'. The bald assertion in S. Talmon, 'The Old Testament text' (in *The Cambridge History of the Bible,* 1, 1970, ed. P. R. Ackroyd and C. F. Evans), p. 167, 'The pseudepigraphic *Letter of Aristeas* credits King Ptolemy II...with having inaugurated the translation of the Pentateuch in to Greek by seventy [*sic*!] sages', has nothing to commend it.

[2] By now it should hardly be necessary more than to note in passing that the well-known statement in the post-talmudic 'Tractate of the Scribes' (*Massekhet Soferim*), 1. 7, (*maʿaśeh) bᵉ-he/bahᵃmiššah zᵉqenim (še-katᵉbu...)*, '[It happened] that five elders [translated from the Torah into Greek for King Ptolemy...]', derives from nothing more than a scribal corruption; a scribe misread a reading *bᵉ-ha-zᵉqenim* ('the elders') as *bᵉhe zᵉqenim* ('the five elders'; the letter *he* being construed as representing the number 'five'), a misreading that may have derived from the common expression 'five elders' in the rabbinic literature and the 'five' books of Moses. This explanation accords well with the 72 elders and the 72 cells in the statement immediately following in the Tractate (1.8): 'Again, it happened once that King Ptolemy assembled seventy-two elders and put them in seventy-two separate cells; and without telling them why he had assembled them, he went into each one and told them to translate the Torah of their teacher Moses...' In this connection it should also be noted that the phrase 'five

That 'seventy' is not simply a 'round number' for 'seventy-two' seems clear from the fact that no pertinent examples or parallels of this kind have been cited in any of the Hellenistic, Roman, or Jewish records known to us.[1]

On the other hand, while the number 'seventy-two', deriving from Aristeas, is original, the widespread use of the number 'seventy' because of such pertinent contexts as the seventy elders at Sinai (Exod. 24:1, 9), the seventy elders co-opted by God to help Moses in administering the Law (Num. 11:16), the seventy members of the Sanhedrin, and the seventy apostles of Jesus (Luke 10:1, 17 – where, it should be noted, some ancient sources offer 'seventy-two'), could readily have influenced the use of the number 'seventy' *in connection with the Septuagint* to the point where it became a popular alternate term for 'seventy-two' – without, however, contradicting in the least the original number, or the account, in Aristeas. This is borne out, for example, in Josephus (*Antiquities* XII); after mentioning, specifically, no less than three times 'six elders from each tribe' (XII.39, 49, 56), Josephus proceeds immediately (XII.57; cf. XII.86) with the statement: 'But I have not thought it necessary to report the names of the seventy [*sic*!] elders who were sent by Eleazar and brought the Law, their names being set down at the end of the letter'.[2]

elders' is lacking in the important Munich manuscript of *Soferim*, and that the corresponding passage in the related post-talmudic 'Tractate of the Torah Scroll' (*Massekhet Sefer Torah*), reads 'seventy elders'.

The corruption in *Massekhet Soferim* was best discussed already by A. Berliner, *Targum Onkelos*, Part II (1884), pp. 76–80; other data on the readings in the two tractates mentioned above may be found in the editions of M. Higger, pp. 101f. in *Soferim* (New York 1937) (or on pp. 12f. in J. Muller's ed.; New York, 1878) and on p. כב in *Sefer Torah* (in M. Higger, *Seven Minor Tractates* שבע מסכתות קטנות; New York, 1933).

[1] Cf. in general. M. Steinschneider, 'Die kanonische Zahl der muhammedanischen Secten und die Symbolik der Zahl 70–73, aus jüdischen und muhammedanisch-arabischen Quellen nachgewiesen,' *ZDMG*, 4 (1850), 145–70.

[2] R. Marcus has missed the point in his comment on Josephus' 'seventy (elders)' (Loeb edn. of Josephus, vol. 7, p. 31 n. b on XII.57): 'Josephus carelessly forgets that there were 6 from each of the 12 tribes'. Josephus was no more careless or forgetful than were the rabbis and Church fathers who in the same breath can talk of the 72 translators, and the 72 cells (or 36 cells, one for every two translators), and the 72 days it took to achieve the translation, and yet refer to the translators, and their product, as the 'Seventy'; some of the references may be found on p. 14 of H. B. Swete, *Introduction to the Old Testament in Greek* (Cambridge, 1902, 2nd revised edn., 1914, ed. R. Ottley; reissued 1968).

It is hardly likely that Josephus' 'seventy (elders)' gave rise to the 'familiar designation of the Alexandrian version...as οἱ ἑβδομήκοντα or ό [= 70] (although οβ [= 72] also occurs in the MSS.), in Latin *Septuaginta*' (so Marcus, *Josephus*, 'possibly'); the term 'seventy' as used here by Josephus would already indicate familiarity and popular usage – apart from the fact that the rabbinic use of the term

In fine, 'seventy' for 'seventy-two' is not a round number, any more than it is a precise number; it is a popular number (and term) only for the Old Greek translation, because of the widespread use of the number 'seventy' in readily connected contexts.

THE AUTHENTICITY AND PURPOSE OF THE LETTER OF ARISTEAS: THE SEPTUAGINT AS HOLY WRIT

Not much need be said at this stage of research about the authenticity of the events, personal names, and other details presented in the *Letter*; rather, it is their significance that deserves close study. Put concretely: it may be readily conceded that the twelve tribes of Israel no longer existed as such in the third–second centuries B.C.E.; what must be determined, then, is why the author of the *Letter* made such prominent use of this non-existent institution.

Up to the end of the seventeenth century the *Letter* was generally accepted as reliable; but this attitude changed drastically after Humfrey Hody published in 1684 his treatise *Contra Historiam Aristeae de LXX interpretibus dissertatio*.[1] This acute and comprehensive analysis set the tone for virtually all serious publications on the subject during the two and half centuries that followed. Thus, for example, it was the opinion of Swete (*Introduction* (1914), p. 15) that 'the great majority of modern scholars, and perhaps all living experts, recognize the unhistorical character of much of the story of Aristeas'.[2] More recently, however, Sidney Jellicoe has put the matter in proper perspective ('Prolego-

'seventy' hardly derives from Josephus. The number 70 (like 5, 10, and the like) is a round number; but it is not a round number for any specific number (such as for 72), any more than 10 is a round number for 12, or 5 for 7; and the like.

On the way in which the numbers 70 and 72 in relation to each other – not, however, as round but as specific numbers! – came to be employed by the rabbis and in early Christianity, see J. M. Baumgarten, 'The duodecimal courts of Qumran, Revelation, and the Sanhedrin', *JBL*, 95 (1976), 68 (n. 29), and 76 (nn. 64–6).

[1] This study was subsequently incorporated as part of the larger volume, *De Bibliorum textibus originalibus, versionibus Graecis, et Latina vulgate libri iv* (Oxford, 1705).

[2] F. P. W. Buhl put it well for the preceding generation (*Canon and Text*, Edinburgh, 1892, p. 113), '...there prevails at this day general agreement to this extent, that no one entertains the idea of accepting the story [of the *Letter*] as credible in all its details. As the author himself quite evidently was a Jew writing under a heathen mask, there is also much in his book which is clearly pure invention *in majorem gloriam Judaeorum*. On the other hand, among the most distinguished investigators there still prevails a difference of opinion with regard to the question, whether the whole is a purely fictitious romance, or whether a historical core lies hidden under the legendary form...'.

menon', p. xxiv): 'Removed from the microscope of the historical critic (though a historical kernel is generally conceded as discernible), the document in modern times has found its proper *mise-en-scène* in the wider corpus of Jewish–Hellenistic literature, and concern has centred upon such questions as its nature and purpose, its intended audience, and its ideology.'[1]

The Jewish–Hellenistic literature, that is, the literary compositions by Jews in the Greek language, has long been made, and to a considerable extent still is, something of a stepchild in the scholarly study of the intertestamental period, and the *Letter of Aristeas* is no exception. That is to say, this is a genre of literature in which, broadly put, the specialist in the Jewish aspects of that literature is less than equally competent in the non-Jewish aspects (Hellenistic, Roman, or Christian), and where the reverse is even more prevalent, with the specialist in the non-Jewish aspects hardly ever at home in the Jewish data and their interpretation. And given the anti-Jewish atmosphere permeating already in eighteenth–nineteenth centuries in such an outstanding centre of scholarly research as Germany – the situation in England, for example, was only relatively better – it is small wonder that the Jewish–Hellenistic literature composed in post-biblical Hebrew and Aramaic has not fared well in scholarly circles.

So far as the *Letter of Aristeas* is concerned, the fact that it was widely regarded – and essentially still is – as unhistorical, is one thing; but far more importantly, it has been branded, as put by such an eminent and influential authority as Emil Schürer, 'Jewish propaganda in pagan disguise...directed to the pagan reader, in order to make propaganda for Judaism among the Gentiles.'[2] One could easily fill a page with the names of scholars who have shared this view; it will suffice here to cite

[1] In a review (*Crozer Quarterly*, 29 (1952), 201–5) of M. Hadas, *Aristeas to Philocrates*, I presented eight arguments in favour of the proposition that the *Letter* was composed early in the second century B.C.E., certainly prior to the successful Maccabean revolt against Syria, Ptolemaic Egypt's notable rival in the Near East. I know of no cogent evidence against this dating. S. Jellico has now made available a fine survey of Aristeas in general, in *The Septuagint and Modern Study* (Oxford, 1968), ch. 2 (pp. 29–58).

[2] The specific reference to Schürer's *Geschichte*, from which this quotation derives, as well as to J. Gutman, R. Tramontano, and R. H. Pfeiffer cited in the sentence immediately following, may all be found on p. 59 of V. Tcherikover's study of 'The ideology of the Letter of Aristeas', *HTR* 51 (1958), 59–85 (reprinted in *Studies in the Septuagint: Origins, Recensions, and Interpretations*, ed. S. Jellicoe, New York, 1974, pp. 181–207).

Already in 1947, in criticizing the section on 'Die hellenistisch–jüdische Litteratur' by Otto Stählin in W. von Christ's *Geschichte der griechischen Litteratur* (6th edn., Munich, 1920, ed. W. Schmid; vol. 2, 1, pp. 535–656), I noted that it was 'the direct continuation of the work and spririt of Schürer...(who) himself was guilty of "anti-

but three out of the eight mentioned by V. Tcherikover on the first page of his study of 'The Ideology of the Letter of Aristeas'. To J. Gutman (1928), the *Letter* reflected 'an inner need of the educated Jew, which at the same time served as 'a strong means for making Jewish propaganda in the Greek world'; to R. Tramontano (1931), the *Letter* manifested 'an apologetic and propagandistic tendency'; and to R. H. Pfeiffer (1949). 'This fanciful story of the origin of the Septuagint is merely a pretext for defending Judaism against its heathen denigrators, for extolling its nobility and reasonableness, and for striving to convert Greek speaking Gentiles to it'.

It would now seem clear that the basic reason for composing the *Letter* in the first place was the desire to accord the Septuagint version of the Torah the same sanctity and authority long held by the Hebrew original – in a word, to certify the divine origin of the Septuagint, to declare it canonical. The argument for this view may be conveniently summarized as follows:

(1) In the Bible, the expression for 'to canonize', to designate a document as official and binding, as divinely inspired, is the Hebrew phrase 'to read aloud to (lit. in the ears/hearing of) the people' (*qara'...be-'ozne ha-'am*), usually followed by an expression of consent by the assembly. Thus, for example, at the great event at Mount Sinai (Exod. 24:3–7),

Moses went and repeated to all the people all the commands and all the rules of the Lord; and all the people answered with one voice: 'All the things that the Lord has commanded we will do!'...Then he took the document [Heb. *sefer*, traditional 'book'] of the covenant and read it aloud to the people [*wa-yiqra' be-'ozne ha-'am*]. And they said, 'All that the Lord has spoken we will faithfully do!'

And when Neh. 8:1–6 tells of the formal designation of the Torah as Sacred Scripture (fifth century B.C.E.), the text reads:

All the people gathered as one man into the square in front of the Water Gate and asked the scribe Ezra to bring the document of the Torah of Moses...the priest Ezra brought the Torah before the assembly...and read from it... from early morning until noon in the presence of the men and women...and [in] the hearing of all the people...Ezra then blessed the Lord...and all the people replied, 'Amen, Amen!'...[1]

Jewish propaganda under a scholarly mask"'. See H. M. Orlinsky, p. 161 (n. 23) of 'Current progress and problems in Septuagint research', ch. 8 (pp. 144–61) in *The Study of the Bible Today and Tomorrow* (Chicago, 1947), ed. H. R. Willoughby.

[1] The text here is somewhat conflated and, in spots, corrupt. The rendering of the official translations (e.g. RSV), 'and the ears of all the people were attentive (Jerusalem Bible, NEB: "all the people listened attentively") to the book of the law', conceals the fact that the Hebrew phrase is hardly Hebraic; contrast, for example,

This biblical expression and procedure for the act of canonization were employed also by Aristeas to indicate that the Septuagint, exactly as the Hebrew Torah, was canonized. As put in §§ 308–11, 'When the work of translation was completed, Demetrius assembled the Jewish people...and read it aloud to the entire gathering...And when all had assented...'

(2) The Bible adjured the Israelites to preserve the divine Hebrew text that contained God's laws to them as His covenanted people; as put in Deut. 4:1–2: 'And now, O Israel, give heed to the laws and regulations which I am instructing you to observe...you shall not add anything to what I command you or take anything away from it.' This is precisely what the *Letter* tells us (§ 310), immediately following on the description of the act of canonization:

Inasmuch as the translation has been well and piously made...it should remain in its present form and no revision of any sort take place. And when all had assented...to what had been said, they bade that an imprecation be pronounced, according to their custom, upon any who should revise the text by adding or transposing anything in what had been written down, or by making any excision.

(3) The Torah was canonized at the very spot – Mount Sinai – that it was offered by God through Moses to His people (Exod. 24:1ff; compare 19:1ff). In line with our proposition, then, it should come as no surprise that the act of canonization for the Septuagint is said in the *Letter* to have taken place precisely where the 72 divinely-inspired translators of the Torah offered their version (§ 308): 'When the work of translation was completed, Demetrius assembled the Jewish people at the place (*eis ton topon*) where the translation had been made, and read it aloud to the entire gathering.' This constitutes a strong argument in favour of our theory, for the natural site for such a gathering and event was clearly Alexandria and not the island of Pharos – apart from the problems of transportation and geography; compare even the brief description in § 301:

'oznekha-qaššébet twice earlier in the same book (lines 6, 11) – where the official translations render exactly as in our verse (without *qaššebet*!). It may be noted here that the comment by L. W. Batten, *The Books of Ezra and Nehemiah*, ICC (Edinburgh, 1913), on Neh. 8:2 (p. 353), '...The assembly was composed of men, women, and children, a condition emphasized in this section because it was unusual in Jewish practice', would have read differently had the act of canonization been recognized.

For the additional biblical instances of the phrase 'to read aloud to all the people' in connection with canonization, and a fuller treatment of the subject, see Orlinsky, 'The canonization of the Bible and the exclusion of the Apocrypha', ch. 15 in *Essays*, pp. 257ff.

Demetrius took the men [namely, the seventy-two translators] with him and crossed the breakwater, seven stades long, [from Alexandria] to the island [of Pharos]; there he crossed over the bridge and proceeded to the northerly parts. There he called a meeting in a house (or: mansion) built by the seashore, magnificently appointed and in a secluded location, and bade the men carry out the work of translation.

I do not know how else this incident is to be explained in the context; the author of the *Letter* had a very important point to make, and he did whatever he could to make it.[1]

(4) Not only startling but even incredible is the assertion early in the *Letter* (§ 32) that a committee of 72 elders, six from each of Israel's twelve tribes, co-operated in the making of the Septuagint. For everyone knew at the time – the Bible itself was a source for this – that the tribes, at least ten of them, had ceased to exist half-a-millennium previously! Why, when he could have readily credited one man, even if fictitiously, with translating what one man, Moses, was credited with writing, did the author of the *Letter* resort to rather obvious fiction in crediting the Septuagint to representatives of the long extinct tribes of Israel?[2]

There can be only one reasonable explanation for this remarkable phenomenon. When Moses received from God on Mount Sinai what Jewish tradition came to identify as the Torah (Exod. 24:3–7),

Moses went and repeated to all the people all the commands and all the rules of the Lord; and all the people answered with one voice: 'All the things that the Lord has commanded we will do!'...Early in the morning, he set up an altar at the foot of the Mount, with twelve pillars for the twelve tribes of Israel...Then he took the document of the covenant and read it aloud to the people.

The reason that the author of the *Letter* involved the twelve tribes of Israel in the translation of the Torah was that it was the twelve tribes of Israel that were involved in the revelation of the Torah in the first place.[3]

In this connection it should be noted that when King Ptolemy's letter reached the High Priest Eleazar, the latter is said to have replied (§§ 42–6): 'When we received your letter...we assembled our entire

[1] Of course when 'at the place' is explained (e.g. by Hadas) as 'Surely somehow connected with the festival on Pharos of which Philo speaks' (p. 221, on § 308; cf. also his comment on p. 218 on § 301, with further reference to pp. 24–5), it is only Philo, not Aristeas, that is being explained.

[2] On the number of authors and of translators per biblical book, see Orlinsky, *HUCA*, 46 (1975), 89ff (and n. 2), 107 (n. 25).

[3] On the use of the terms 'first', 'second', 'third', etc., instead of 'Reuben', 'Simeon', etc., for the twelve tribes, see Orlinsky, 'Septuagint', 99. Numerous references to the number 'twelve' in relation to or deriving from the twelve tribes of Israel may be found in Baumgarten, *JBL*, 95 (1976), 59–78.

people and read it aloud to them...we straightway offered sacrifices ...and the entire multitude prayed...And in the presence of all we selected elders good and true.' In other words, following the example at Sinai, all the Jews of Judea participated in the authorization of the making of the Septuagint.

(5) The role of the elders is significant. In the biblical account of the Revelation at Sinai, the elders constituted mere witnesses to the event; their role was quite passive. In the *Letter*, on the other hand, the qualities of the elders are praised – even by Hellenistic standards – beyond the usual literary conventions. There is good reason for this; the elders in the *Letter* were not mere witnesses to the event of the translation, they were the actual authors of the event; they personally brought the Greek Torah into being! And for that – not because of the desire or need to impress non-Jews with the greatness of the Law and its Jewish interpreters, or because current Hellenistic style demanded it – they are described as the most learned in God's Law, and (but only secondarily) in worldly (that is, Greek) wisdom too. Divinely inspired and learned in the Law, they came as close as was possible to being facsimiles of Moses the Lawgiver. Divine inspiration – as understood in the post-Malachi (Ezra–Nehemiah) period – was theirs in the highest possible degree.[1]

(6) The role of the priests, as well as that of the elders, in the Revelation at Sinai is duplicated by Aristeas in his description of the making of the Septuagint; that is to say, since the distinction between the two groups and their precise roles at Sinai are unclear in the biblical accounts, just so are they in Aristeas' account of the translation.[2] One

[1] Philo, in common with the earlier rabbis, understood very well Aristeas' description of the role of the elders as translators when he referred to them 'as it were possessed and under inspiration' and 'as prophets' (cf. *On Moses*, Book 2, §§ 36, 40, in F. H. Colson's edition and translation of *Philo*, vol. 6, in the Loeb Classical Library series). On the lavish praise of the translators in the *Letter* and elsewhere in Jewish circles – in contrast to the Jewish downgrading, and even rejection, of the translation after the Roman destruction of Judean sovereignty and the increasingly rapid growth of Christianity – see Orlinsky, 'The Septuagint as Holy Writ', nn. 12 and 13 on pp. 97–9. In this connection, W. Schwarz's 'Discussions on the origin of the Septuagint', constituting ch. 2 of his *Principles and Problems of Biblical Translation* (Cambridge, 1955), is worth reading; it has been reprinted conveniently in *Studies in the Septuagint*, ed. S. Jellicoe.

[2] This fact seems to have escaped notice hitherto. The problem as reflected in the biblical account (Exod. 19:6 [priests], 19:7 [elders], 19:22–4 [priests]; 24:1ff [elders; and note that 'young (apprentice?) Israelites', not priests, offered up the sacrifices, 24:5]) and in the Aristean *vis-à-vis* the biblical account, has been noted on pp. 100–1 of Orlinsky, *HUCA*, 46 (1975). It must be kept in mind that the author of the *Letter* could not well designate as priests the elders of the twelve (non-Levi) tribes; also, that the documentary theory and the matter of editorial redaction and compilation did not enter into the picture in those days.

has but to read carefully Exod. 19:5–8 and §§ 184 and 310 to appreciate the problem that confronted the author of the *Letter* and his solution of it.

(7) The act of canonization that took place at Sinai was accompanied by sacrifices (Exod. 24:4ff; and compare the ritual purification in Exod. 19), and in the light of our hypothesis one would expect a similar procedure for the Septuagint.

But how could sacrifices be offered in Egypt, outside the Holy Land? The author of the *Letter* solved this difficulty simply and cleverly; he tells us that when King Ptolemy's letter reached the High Priest Eleazar in Jerusalem, Eleazar responded to it as follows (§§ 42–6):

When we received you letter we rejoiced greatly because of your resolution and your goodly plan, and we assembled our entire people and read it aloud to them, in order that they might know the piety you cherish for our God...You too have vouchsafed our countrymen great and unforgettable benefits in many ways. We have therefore straightway offered sacrifices on your behalf...and the entire multitude prayed that your affairs might always turn out as you desire... and that the copy of the holy Law might come about to your advantage and carefully executed. And in the presence of all we selected elders good and true, six from each tribe, with whom we have sent [a copy of] the Law.[1]

But after the translation had been made and canonized, the Alexandrian Jewish community could only give the translators 'a great ovation' (§ 308); and from the king they received high commendation and bountiful gifts (§§ 312ff).[2]

(8) It is no accident that it was the high priest himself who played the central role in deciding that the Septuagint translation should be made,

[1] The great banquet that the king gave in honour of the elders–translators before the work of translation began, constituting a major portion of the *Letter* (§§ 187–292), was opened by a prayer offered by 'Eleazar the eldest of the priests who had come with us [from Jerusalem]' §§ 184–6). This banquet hardly served as a substitute–parallel for sacrifice but rather derived from the Hellenistic environment of the Jews. On Eleazar, see below.

[2] The king also 'made obeisance and gave orders that great care be taken of the books [viz., the new Greek version of the Torah] and that they be watched over reverently' (§ 317). Most scholars believe that the obeisance was made to the new Greek version (cf. § 179, 'It was right, my God-fearing friends, first to pay homage to those treasures for whose sake I summoned you...'); but the author may have intended a more general use to include God: 'When they had uncovered the rolls and had unrolled the parchments, the king paused for a long while, and after making obeisance some seven times said, "I thank you, friends, and him that sent you still more, but most of all I thank God whose (holy) words these are"' (§ 177). Or compare, for example § 42 (Eleazar to Ptolemy), '...in order that they might know the piety you cherish for our God'. For Josephus on this point, see § 114 in his *Antiquities*, Book XII and Marcus' comment (note g) in the Loeb edition, vol. 7, p. 57.

who picked the 72 elders who were to make the translation, and who selected and sent the copy of the Hebrew Torah from which the translation was to be made (§§ 41–6). For it was the high priest, Aaron, who was associated with Moses in the Revelation at Sinai (Exod. 19:24; 24:1ff). This much has long been noted, if not always sufficiently appreciated.[1]

But what has been overlooked is that this specific connection of the high priest in Jerusalem with the high priest at Sinai – more than a millennium apart – was actually carried a step farther, rather a significant step, by the author of the *Letter*. I refer to the name given by the author to the high priest in Jerusalem, Eleazar. Out of all the names that Aristeas had at his disposal for the high priest in Jerusalem, why did he choose that of Eleazar? On our hypothesis – that Aristeas' primary motive in composing the *Letter* was to promote the Greek translation within the Jewish community as divinely inspired – the choice of name was not fortuitous.

For Eleazar, third son of Aaron (Exod. 6:23; Num. 3:2)[2] after serving as 'head chieftain of the Levites...in charge of those attending the duties of the sanctuary' (Num. 3:32), succeeded Aaron as high priest (Num. 20:25–8; Deut. 10:6) – in fact, Moses himself, at the express command of God, invested Eleazar on Mount Hor with Aaron's own garments (Num. 20:25–8) – and he occupied that exalted office not only under Moses but also under Joshua; he even participated with Joshua and the tribal heads in allotting territory to the Israelites in Canaan (Josh. 14:1). In every way he could think of, even in choosing a name for the high priest, the author of the *Letter* made the Septuagint *nomos* the equivalent of the Hebrew *torah*.

In this he succeeded very well indeed. The Jewish community

[1] Some of the matters discussed above have been dealt with especially by Tcherikover, *HTR*, 51 (1958), 59–85, and I have stated elsewhere (*HUCA*, 46 (1975) 93 n. 8) that 'I accept fully his overall explanation: "...the Septuagint translation...is Aristeas' main subject in the Letter. He makes every effort to prove the sanctity of the translation". However...Tcherikover overlooked the several specific points of contact between the *canonization* of the Septuagint and that of the Torah, constituting Aristeas' proof that the Septuagint was as divinely revealed as the Hebrew original'. My comment also applies to G. Howard, 'The *Letter of Aristeas* and diaspora judaism', *JTS*, N.S., 22 (1971), 337–48 (especially 340ff).

[2] It may be recalled that Aaron's first two sons, Nadab and Abihu, who were present with the 'seventy elders' (= a total of 72 in all – not including Moses and Aaron) at the Revelation at Sinai (Exod. 24:1, 9), were said to have been utterly rejected by God for good cause (Lev. 10:1ff), and that the line of Eleazar, which included Zadok, dominated thereafter. On the name Eleazar in the *Letter*, and the names Eleazar and Elisha among the 72 translators, see Orlinsky, *HUCA*, 46, (1975), 101–2 and the notes there.

outside Judea, wherever Greek was the vernacular, adopted the Greek version as thoroughly authoritative. It became the Bible of Diaspora Jewry and its official history of biblical Israel to such an extent that when Christianity began to develop within its midst and then grew in numbers and influence outside of and in opposition to it, it was natural for Christians to regard and use the Greek Bible as Judeans and other Jews regarded and used the Hebrew original. Had Christianity developed such that it continued to remain within the Jewish fold, the Septuagint would have continued as *the* Bible for those Jewries in the Diaspora (parallel to the Targum and the Hebrew original for others) to whom Greek was the mother tongue.

THE PHILOSOPHY OF THE SEPTUAGINT TRANSLATORS

One could hardly dare claim divine inspiration for a translation of the Hebrew Torah that tended to be free or paraphrastic, that tended to combine two verses into one, that was disposed to leave out from the Hebrew – or add to it – a word or phrase that perverted the plain meaning of the Hebrew; and the like. One did not deal lightly with the text of God's Holy Law. So that, whatever were the philosophies of translation that prevailed in the Hellenistic world in general and in Alexandria in particular in the third and second centuries B.C.E.,[1] it is the tendency toward literal, word-for-word rendering that pervaded the Septuagint translation of the Torah.[2] The fact that the literal rendering not infrequently made up a no-sense sentence is beside the point;[3] interpretation – even if in the form of eisegesis rather than exegesis – took care of that.

But precisely because the Septuagint translators were bound by the word-for-word philosophy of translation – and unable to resort to footnotes of any kind – they are generally more trustworthy than perhaps the majority of modern translators, who have (even if unwit-

[1] S. P. Brock and R. Hanhart are among the few who have dealt with this aspect of Septuagint research; see Orlinsky, *HUCA*, 46 (1975), p. 103 n. 18.

[2] Of course this statement is a generalization; each biblical book requires independent study and specifically appropriate description. In his study of *Syntactical Evidence of Semitic Sources in Greek Documents*, SBLSCS 3 (Missoula, 1974) p. 2 n. 1, R. A. Martin put it this way, 'Even a cursory study of the Septuagint will reveal that the translators share a common characteristic – whether they are skilled or relatively inept at their task, they tend to translate word for word'.

[3] On pp. 103ff of 'The Septuagint as Holy Writ', *HUCA*, 46 (1975) I have dealt with Gen. 15:2–3 and 1:1–3 in this connection, and in n. 22 I have cited a number of other cases to the point.

tingly) more often than is realized misled their readers into believing that they knew exactly what the Hebrew text means.

For to translate the Hebrew text faithfully, even word for word, is one thing; it is gratuitous, however, to assume that the translator always, and necessarily, understood the text literally. Indeed, one has but to think of the amount and the several kinds of hermeneutics employed by the ancient interpreters of the Bible to realize that the plain meaning of the text was not easily permitted to stand in the way of anyone's interests. So that such generalizations as 'every translation is a commentary' and '*traduttore traditore*' have no meaning when the Hebrew text of the Torah is turned into 'pony' or 'crib' Greek (or English).

Thus, the fact that the Septuagint translators reproduce faithfully the anthropomorphisms and anthropopathisms of their Hebrew text should not cause the modern scholar to jump to the conclusion that they therefore believed and mean to convey to their readers, that God, in the manner of man, had hands and feet, eyes and ears, nose and lips, mouth and heart, and the rest; or that God was vexed, when He did not fume or rage; or that He was envious and cruel – any more than we today would attribute to modern translators, from Tyndale–Luther on, the belief that God had human qualities simply because, after the manner of the Septuagint, they reproduced the pertinent phrases literally ('in the eyes of God', etc.). Nor did the Septuagint translators, any more than their modern counterparts, worry that their readers might get anthropomorphic notions, for they were translating in the service of their religion and of their fellow Jews, not for apologetic or missionary purposes *vis-à-vis* the pagan community.[1]

Within the framework of faithful translation, much variation is possible. The translator of Joshua reproduced his Hebrew text faithfully, even if he frequently avoided mechanical verbalism. Thus in 4:24 he rendered *lᵉmáʿan dáʿath (kol-ʿamme ha-'áreṣ) 'et-yad* YHWH *(ki ḥᵃzaqah hi')* by *(hópōs gnôsin pánta tà éthnē tês gês hóti) hē dúnamis toũ kuríou (ischurá estin);* thereby not only did he do full justice to the Hebrew idiom *yadaʿ ...'eth...ki hi'* (avoiding the literal 'know...the hand/might ...that it is'; compare, for example, Gen. 1:4) but he recognized, correctly, that the Hebrew author did not mean that it was the 'hand' but the 'might' of God that the whole world would acknowledge as great. Or compare, for example, Josh. 7:7 – where God is not the object and where the idiomatic use of *yad* was similarly recognized; *latet ('otánu) bᵉyad (ha-*

[1] For the literature on this subject, see Orlinsky, *HUCA*, 46 (1975), pp. 106f and nn. 23–5. The statement by E. Tov ('Septuagint', § A, *2b, IDBSup* (1976), p. 810), 'Other theological trends reveal themselves in...anti-anthropomorphic renditions', is too general and vague.

'emori)/paradoũnai (autòn) tō (Amorraiō). By the same token, the Septuagint did not omit (*wa-yélek y^ehoshú^a'*) *'elaw* (*wa-yó'mer lo*) in 5:13 (as asserted by Margolis[1]) but reproduced the Hebrew phrase *wa-yélek...'el* idiomatically and correctly as 'approaching (Joshua said to him)', instead of literal 'went...to'.[2] The Greek word used here, *prosérchomai*, usually represents a Hebrew word for 'approach, come forward' (*niggash; qarab*).

The translator of Job will render variously not only an elusive word such as *tushiyyah* (for example, by 'assistance' in Job 6:13 and 'strength' in 12:16) but also such common words as *'áwen, ḥéreb, ma'as*, and *naqi'* – at the same time that he followed the principle of faithful translation.[3] This principle may be further observed, for example, by the recognition of the translator's use of *apobainō* 'to become' (Heb. *hayah l^e-*) as distinct from *epibainō* 'to set upon, attack, mount', a word with which it has been confused both by ancient scribes and modern textual critics.[4]

All the book of Exodus is rendered closely; yet so regular is the use of *aulē* for Heb. *ḥaṣer* – not only in Exodus but throughout the Bible – that one is taken by surprise when one notes four times in chapters 38 to 40 the word *skēnē* as the correspondent. But further study reveals the fact that there is more than ample independent evidence, noted already in 1862 by J. Popper, that chapters 36 to 40 in the preserved Septuagint text are the product of a translator other than the one who was responsible for the parallel section (chapters 25ff) and the rest of the book.[5] Similarly, it has been demonstrated that the translator of Isa. 36 to 39 was someone other than that of chapters 1 to 35 and 40 to 66.[6]

[1] M. L. Margolis, *The Book of Joshua in Greek*, parts 1–4 (Paris, 1931–38).

[2] On Joshua, see H. M. Orlinsky, 'The Hebrew *Vorlage* of the Septuagint of the book of Joshua', *Rome Congress Volume 1969*, VTSup, 17, pp. 186–95, and the literature cited there, including the reference to Margolis, *The Book of Joshua in Greek*. On Gen. 1:4, see Orlinsky, *Notes on the ...Torah*, p. 56, ad loc.

[3] H. M. Orlinsky, 'Studies in the Septuagint of the book of Job', *HUCA*, 29 (1958), 270f.

[4] H. M. Orlinsky, 'Studies in the Septuagint of the book of Job', *HUCA*, 33 (1962), 129–32.

[5] In more than 350 occurrences in the Bible (including Exodus, chapters 18, 25 to 31, 33, 35, and 37 to 40) *skēnē* represents Heb. *'óhel* or *mishkan*; only in Exod. 38:16 (37:14), 38:31 (39:8/9), 39:40 (19), and 40:8 (6) – and in Gen. 25:16 – was it employed for Heb. *ḥaṣer*. See H. M. Orlinsky, '*Ḥāṣēr* in the Old Testament', *JAOS*, 59 (1939), 35f; and now also the detailed study by D. W. Gooding, *The Account of the Tabernacle: Translation and Textual Problems of the Greek Exodus* (Cambridge, 1959) – whose thesis *vis-à-vis* Popper I cannot follow – and the (generally overlooked) detailed study by A. H. Finn, 'The Tabernacle chapters', *JTS*, 16 (1915), 449–82.

[6] See M. S. Hurwitz, 'The Septuagint of Isaiah 36–39 in relation to that of 1–35, 40–66', *HUCA*, 28 (1957), 75–83; note there e.g., the avoidance of anthropomorphisms, cf. the summary chart on p. 81, as against the procedure in the rest of the book. See also the reference in p. 544 n. 2 to the literature on the two-translator theory.

One should not be led by the generalizing descriptions of the character of the Septuagint translation of individual Books into assuming that while some translators rendered their Hebrew text faithfully, others played fast and loose with their *Vorlage*. When Swete asserted that 'The Pentateuch is on the whole a close and serviceable translation; the Psalms and more especially the Book of Isaiah shew obvious signs of incompetence. The translator of Job was perhaps more familiar with Greek pagan literature than with Semitic poetry; the translator of Daniel indulges at times in a Midrashic paraphrase. The version of Judges...the Greek of Ecclesiastes',[1] he was presenting 'evidence in favour of a plurality of translators' of the Septuagint of the Bible as a whole.[2]

Once it is recognized that the Septuagint was made by Jews for Jews and that its philosophy of translation was basically that of verbal equivalence, it is incumbent upon the modern textual critic, translator, or commentator to approach the Septuagint with the utmost respect – indeed, with far greater respect than in dealing with the received (so-called Masoretic) Hebrew text. For the latter came into being piecemeal and over a long period of many centuries, and experienced many changes at different hands under varied circumstances and influences; moreover, the Hebrew text itself was never officially fixed (see below, pp. 557ff).

In contrast, the Septuagint translation of each book was made, for the most part – that is, excepting such portions of a book as Exod. 36 to 40, Isa. 36 to 39, and excesses in the preserved Hebrew text over the shorter versions from which the Septuagint of Joshua, Samuel, Jeremiah, and Job derived (see below) – from a single, complete Hebrew book, and it did not experience the process of redaction, in its various forms, by several hands over an extended period. It had but a single source, namely, the Hebrew text, before the translators; and it had essentially but a single milieu – allowing for Judean influence – namely, Hellenistic Jewish Alexandria.[3] Our preserved Hebrew text,

[1] *Introduction*, pp. 315f, 'The Septuagint as a version'.

[2] The descriptions offered here by Swete are in need of very considerable revision. Thus the term 'incompetence' has no meaning for the Septuagint translation of Psalms and Isaiah. The translator of Job knew poetry as well as any Septuagint translator did; the fact that he had an extremely difficult Hebrew text to translate and employed his considerable knowledge of Greek pagan literature in performing his task (cf. his knowledge of Theophrastus, *Enquiry into Plants*; Orlinsky, *HUCA*, 33 [1962], 133, § 8) ought, surely, not to be held against him!

[3] It is difficult not only to prove but even to justify, in the milieu of Judean Jewish society of the last two centuries B.C.E., the statement by Barthélemy (*IDBSup*, 1976, p. 879a), '...it is equally probable that the Greek translation of the Psalter was made in Palestine. As for the Greek version of Samuel and Kings, there is no difficulty in holding that it was brought from Palestine to Alexandria toward the beginning of the second century B.C....'. Who in Judea at that time needed a Greek translation of Scripture and who made such translations for export?

on the other hand, had a number of sources deriving from several milieux, some of them quite beyond recovery.

Finally, it must be kept in mind that when a redactor dealt with the Hebrew documents at his disposal, they were not yet canonical books; they were documents that were not yet Holy Writ. The Septuagint translators, in contrast, were dealing with books that were canonical, or that had acquired the kind of authority that only their widespread knowledge and use could provide. Consequently, scholars should never have treated the text of the Septuagint as cavalierly as the received Hebrew text; that is, they should not have dismissed the Septuagint – apart from the usual scribal corruptions, conflations, adaptations, and the like, that such documents come to experience – as an unreliable witness to the Hebrew text of the biblical book from which it derived.[1]

Scholars like J. Wellhausen and S. R. Driver in the late nineteenth and early twentieth centuries recognized the nature and value of the Septuagint for the textual criticism of the Hebrew Bible. However, circumstances after World War I favoured those scholars whose attitude toward the Septuagint *vis-à-vis* the received Hebrew text was less than positive; so that the negative attitude of an A. Dillmann and the conservative attitude of such an authority as M. L. Margolis came to prevail.[2]

THE SEPTUAGINT AND THE DEAD SEA SCROLLS

It remained for the discovery of the Dead Sea Scrolls in the mid-twentieth century to force scholars to turn back to the Septuagint as a reliable witness to the Hebrew text whence it derived. It is true that too much uncritical enthusiasm was expressed for the Septuagint text of Isaiah and its alleged derivation from a Hebrew text virtually identical with that of the first, complete Isaiah Scroll (designated IQIsa[a]) when it was made public first in part and then in whole. By now it is clear that

[1] It cannot be emphasized too strongly that it is only the Hebrew books (not even their order beyond the Torah, i.e., the order of the books that came to constitute the Prophets and the Writings) that were canonized, not the Hebrew text of these books. The Hebrew text of the Bible was never canonized or fixed. By the same token, the definite article 'the' has no meaning in the common phrase 'the masoretic text'; nor does the term 'masoretic' have any meaning in this phrase as scholars use it. (See below.)

[2] See H. M. Orlinsky, 'Whither biblical research?', *JBL*, 90 (1971), 1–14 (= chapter 11 in *Essays*, pp. 200–17); *HUCA*, 46 (1975), 108ff. and the notes there. (See also below.)

where the text of the Scroll differed from the preserved Hebrew text, the Septuagint regularly agreed with the latter – apart from the fact that it is only rarely that the Scroll offered a more original reading than that preserved in the received Hebrew text or in the Hebrew *Vorlage* of the Septuagint.[1]

But the complete Isaiah Scroll aside, it is the Samuel and Jeremiah fragments among the Scrolls that have had by far the greatest effect upon scholarship. Already the ancients were aware that the Septuagint text of Jeremiah was about one eighth shorter than the received Hebrew,[2] and that, in addition, the sequence of the text was different.[3] In the case of Samuel words, phrases and sentences are sometimes lacking in the received Hebrew but present in the Septuagint translation, and vice versa. In Joshua, there is a 'plus' in the received Hebrew text, though in less drastic form. The Greek Job, on the other hand, offers even less in quantity of text *vis-à-vis* the Hebrew, no less than one-sixth less; but the sequence of the texts – unlike the case in Jeremiah – is the same.

For such ancient worthies as Origen and St Jerome, the problem was readily resolved: since for them the *veritas* was the *Hebraica*, the

[1] See, e.g. M. Burrows, *The Dead Sea Scrolls* (London, 1955), pp. 301ff; *More Light on the Dead Sea Scrolls* (London, 1958), pp. 146ff; H. M. Orlinsky, 'The textual criticism of the Old Testament', ch. 5 in *The Bible and the Ancient Near East: Essays in Honor of W. F. Albright*, ed. G. E. Wright (New York, 1965), pp. 140–69; article 'Textual criticism, OT' by J. A. Thompson in *IDBSup* (1976), pp. 886–91; Barthélemy, ibid., pp. 878–84.

[2] In his *Letter to Africanus*, after commenting on the Septuagint and Hebrew of Job, Origen continues (§ 4), 'But why should I enumerate all the instances I collected with so much labour, to prove that the difference between our copies and those of the Jews did not escape me? In Jeremiah I noticed many instances, and indeed in that book I found much transposition and variation in the readings of the prophecies.' For a useful survey of the work done to date on the Septuagint–Hebrew of Jeremiah, see J. G. Janzen, *Studies in the Text of Jeremiah* (Cambridge, Mass., 1973), Introduction, pp. 1–9. On the history of the treatment of Job in the matter of the quantitative difference between the Septuagint and the received Hebrew text, see H. M. Orlinsky, 'Studies in the Septuagint of the Book of Job', Ch. 1, 'An analytical survey of previous studies', *HUCA*, 28 (1957), 53–74.

[3] Beyond 1:1 to 25:13, the Hebrew order that came to be designated 25:15 to 45:5 corresponds to chs. 32–51 in the Septuagint, with chs. 44 to 49 in the Hebrew corresponding variously to chs. 51, 26, 29, 31, 30, and 25:14 to 26:1 in the Septuagint. Chapters 50 to 51 in the Hebrew = 27 to 28 in the Greek, and both texts end with the same ch. 52. There are also occasionally differences in the sentence order within a chapter (cf. below p. 556 and n. 2). These differences can be seen at a glance in Swete, *Introduction*, p. 233 (cf. pp. 241f), or on p. 147 of J. Ziegler's edition of the Göttingen Septuagint, *Jeremias* (vol. xv) (Göttingen, 1957), or at the back of the four page *Explanatio signorum* in A. Rahlfs' two-volume edition of *Septuaginta* (Göttingen, 1935).

Septuagint had to be accommodated to it. In his many-columned Bible, the Hexapla,[1] Origen filled the 'minuses' in the Greek from other Greek translations (for example, in Job it was Theodotion), marking the insertions by symbols, while St Jerome made his definite Vulgate translation of the Bible directly from the Hebrew text.

The modern critical scholar cannot do this. Quite properly, he ought to look upon the received Hebrew text of the Bible as he would upon any ancient document, but he must regard the Septuagint as a most respectful and faithful translation of the text because the translator considered it sacred. All too often, however, modern scholars have failed to put themselves in the position of the kind of ancient Jew who, knowledgeable enough in Hebrew and Greek, had undertaken to translate the book of Joshua or Samuel or Jeremiah or Job into Greek. The Hebrew text from which he will translate is for him a sacred text, one that speaks to him and to his Jewish community directly and with the utmost authority. It is the word of God!

It is scarcely conceivable that with this attitude and motivation, the translator would proceed to alter or delete whenever he was so moved words and phrases – as he is alleged to have done in Joshua and especially in Samuel – and entire sentences and sections – as in Jeremiah and Job – and even alter the order of chapters and verses of his sacred Hebrew text – as in Jeremiah. Put more bluntly: the modern scholar has no right to assume *a priori* that the Septuagint translator manipulated his Hebrew text, when – in point of fact – it is the opposite assumption that would be valid, namely, that unless and until a case is made for regarding the Septuagint translation of any book as an unreliable witness to the Hebrew text, the translator must be regarded as a faithful reproducer of that text.

A few cases in point. When Swete asserted that the Septuagint translator of Gen. 31:46ff 're-arranged [his Hebrew Text] with the view of giving greater consistency to the narrative', and that in Gen. 35:16ff. 'The transposition in G appears to be due to a desire to locate Eder...between Bethel and Bethlehem',[2] not only was he guilty of gratuitous assumption but he did not ask himself what there was at

[1] See Orlinsky, 'An analytic survey', *HUCA*, 28 (1957), 53ff (and the notes there), 73f. The articles mentioned there 'The columnar order of the Hexapla' and 'Origen's Tetrapla – a scholarly fiction?'), as well as J. A. Emerton's 'The purpose of the second column of the Hexapla' and S. P. Brock's 'Origen's aim as a textual critic of the Old Testament', are now conveniently reproduced as a group in *Studies in the Septuagint*, ed. S. Jellicoe (New York, 1974), § III, ii, pp. 343–91. See also S. Jellicoe, *The Septuagint and Modern Study* (New York, 1968), ch. 5, 'Origen and the Hexapla', pp. 100–33.

[2] *Introduction*, p. 234.

stake for the translator that he had to shift verse 21 to verse 16 and to alter the text in the process (for example, to delete the initial 'And they journeyed' in verse 16)? How much more likely – disregarding for the moment the faithfulness of the Septuagint translation of Genesis generally – that a purely accidental corruption involving 'Bethel' in verses 15 and 16 and initial 'And they/he journeyed' in verses 16 and 21 is involved here, whether in our received Hebrew text or in the Hebrew *Vorlage* of the Septuagint.

In Deut. 31:1, the discovery of a Dead Sea Scroll fragment with the reading *waykal Mosheh l^{e}dabber 'et kol (ha-d^{e}* [*barim ha-'éleh*]...) has helped to prove that Septuagint 'And Moses finished (*sunetélesen*) speaking all [these words]' was not a correction of the received *wa-yélek Mosheh waydabber 'et (ha-d^{e}barim ha-'éleh*...) to accord, perhaps, with 32:45, but the literal rendering of the reading in its Hebrew *Vorlage*: the originality of that reading, as against that of our received text, is something to be argued separately.

The 'minuses' in the Septuagint of Joshua – 'minus' only *vis-à-vis* the received Hebrew text – are a very good case in point. The expression *Mosheh 'ébed YHWH* occurs seventeen times in the book, but the phrase *'ébed YHWH* is lacking in the Septuagint four times (1:1, 15; 12:6; 22:4); the word *'^{a}ron*, with *(ha-)b^{e}rit* and/or *YHWH*, occurring twenty-nine times in the received Hebrew text, is absent six times in the Greek (4:5; 6:4, 6 [*bis*], 7; 7:6); out of the thirteen times that the phrase *'éber ha-yarden* is found in the Hebrew text, it is lacking once in the Greek (1:14 – actually, all three words *Mosheh b^{e}'éber ha-yarden* are absent). In all these instances – as well as in those that involve such other words as *zeh/ha-zeh, gadol, torah* and *miṣráyim* – Margolis, in his monumental attempt to achieve 'the nearest approach to the Greek original as it left the hands of the translator(s)', was content with the sweeping 'explanatory' comment: 'G omits'.

But this comment was only an assertion that had never been demonstrated, one that – even if it came from so erudite a scholar as Margolis – failed to do justice to the Septuagint translator of his sacred Hebrew text in the first place, and which failed to derive from an objective study of the character of the Septuagint translation of Joshua in the second place; neither did Margolis study these 'pluses' in the Hebrew text to see whether they were the kind that could be attributed to glossator–revisers or redactors of the Hebrew text, whether in Joshua or elsewhere in the Bible. Put differently, Margolis' characterization of the Septuagint translation of Joshua was justified neither *a priori* nor *a posteriori*. In point of fact, there had appeared already in 1914 an excellent study by S. Holmes of *Joshua: The Hebrew and Greek Texts*; but the negative attitude of Dillmann played an important role in the neglect of this fine monograph, a neglect that the work of Margolis did nothing to lessen.[1]

No scroll fragments of Joshua and Job have as yet come to light to help prove the integrity of the Septuagint translators of these books *vis-à-vis* the longer preserved Hebrew text; the student of the book of Jeremiah, on the other hand, has been more fortunate. As indicated above (p. 553 n. 3) ch. 10 in Jeremiah coincides in the Septuagint and preserved Hebrew in chapter sequence; but the verse order in the Greek is 5a, 9, 5b, 11 – with verses 6 to 8 and 10 altogether lacking – as against verses 5 to 11 in the Hebrew. A recently discovered Dead Sea Scroll fragment of Jeremiah has confirmed the verse order of the Septuagint. Consequently, it has been easier than it would have been otherwise for Janzen's meticulous *Studies in the Greek–Hebrew Text of Jeremiah* to receive favourable reaction.[2] His overall conclusions that '...in the overwhelming majority of instances the shorter Greek text is superior, while the longer Masoretic text is to be explained as being due to secondary expansion...' (p. 86), and that 'In view of the clear character of M [= the Masoretic text] as heavily expanded, of G [= the Old Greek text, as critically reconstructed] or its *Vorlage* as frequently defective by haplography, and of the lack of clear and cogent evidence for abridgement by the translator, this latter hypothesis ought to be abandoned once and for all' (pp. 114f), are thoroughly justified.[3] By

[1] Margolis, *Joshua*, parts i–iv (1931–38); part v (covering 19:38 to the end) and the all-important Introduction have never appeared. See Orlinsky, 'Margolis' work in the Septuagint', in *Max Leopold Margolis: Scholar and Teacher*, ed. R. Gordis, 3 (Philadelphia, 5712–1952), pp. 34–44; and '*Vorlage*' in *VTSup*, 17 (1969).

In 1939, '*Ḥāṣēr* in the Old Testament', *JAOS*, 59 (1939), § 3, 34f., I argued that the early corruption of original (*wᵉ-'et-malkāh wᵉ-'et-kol-) ḥᵉṣeréha* in Josh. 10:39 – so the Septuagint (whose *kṓmē* represents *ḥaṣer* in its Hebrew *Vorlage*) – into the preserved *'aréha* helped to prove that, 'against Margolis,...the translator did not omit these words in v. 37, for they did not exist there as yet; they came in [in the preserved Hebrew text] only after *ḥᵉṣēréha* of v. 39 had become corrupted into *'āréha* in the post-Septuagint Square Script...'.

[2] On 10:1–11, see Janzen, *Jeremiah*, pp. 121f and 132. Correct in Rahlfs' edition of *Septuaginta* the verse numbers '9, 5, 11' to '5a, 9, 5b, 11' (with 5a replacing his 9, which, in turn, should be shifted to *argúrion* [*prosblētón*] in the next line).

[3] It is a pity that Janzen has suppressed mention of the studies mentioned above, depriving the reader of a broader and more correct view of the research done and results achieved in this specific field. Limiting himself as he does to citing essentially only the works of his fellow students and his mentor, and those who agree with them, the matter has become something of an academic *la ronde*, indeed a circle as difficult to break out of as into (cf. the description of the same circle in D. F. Morgan's review of P. D. Miller, *The Divine Warrior in Early Israel*, *JBL*, 95 (1976), 475). Uncited, for example, is the discovery that there is rabbinic evidence that a

and large, this conclusion holds true of the Greek–Hebrew of the book of Job.

THE HEBREW TEXT (*VORLAGE*) OF THE SEPTUAGINT

The term 'the Masoretic text' has been avoided in this essay, and the term 'the received (or traditional, or preserved) Hebrew text' has been used instead. It is still insufficiently realized that:

> There never was, and there never can be, a single fixed masoretic text of the Bible! It is utter futility and pursuit of a mirage to go seeking to recover what never was ...any editor of the Hebrew text of the Bible who claims that his edition is based upon ...'*the* Masorah' is employing an expression that is utterly without meaning; he has, in reality, simply reproduced a form of the preserved, or traditional, or received Hebrew text (*textus receptus*), a form whose provenance – especially in the period preceding the invention of printing – is generally unknown to us...All that an editor can claim with justification is that he has reproduced the text of a single manuscript, be it Aleppo (Hebrew University Bible Project), or Leningrad B 19a (*Biblia Hebraica*[3, 4]), or British Museum Or 2626-27-28 (Snaith), and the like...At the same time, it cannot be emphasized too strongly that none of these manuscripts or of the printed editions based on them has any greater merit or 'masoretic' authority than most of the many other editions of the Bible, than, say, the van der Hooght, Hahn, Letteris, Baer, Rabbinic, and Ginsburg Bibles.[1]

By the same token, scholars have usually assumed that just as the books of the Bible were canonized, so was the Hebrew text of the books; expressions such as the 'official' or 'standard' or 'stabilized' Hebrew text are the norm. Bu this scholarly assumption, whether it be fiction or simply unproved or unprovable, has little practical value.

Hebrew text-type close to that of the Samuel Dead Sea Scroll fragments and the Septuagint *Vorlage* was known at least as late as the fourth century; cf. H. M. Orlinsky, 'The Masoretic text: a critical evaluation', Prolegomenon to KTAV reissue of C. D. Ginsburg, *Introduction to the Massoretico-Critical Edition of the Hebrew Bible* (New York, 1966), pp. XXII–XXIII.

1 Quoted from pp. XVIII, XXIII–XXIV, and XXXVI of Orlinsky, 'Masoretic text'; and see L. R. Bailey's clear note on 'Textus Receptus' in *IDBSup*, p. 895. While agreeing with my main point, M. Goshen-Gottstein, in the 'Introduction' (Hebrew and English) to the Makor reissue (Jerusalem, 1972) of the Bomberg–Ibn Adonijah edition (Venice, 1525) of *Biblia Rabbinica*, has obfuscated the problem to the point where discussion is unprofitable; contrast, for example, the clear and forthright assertion by Barthélemy (*IDBSup*, 1976, p. 883a): 'Perhaps it should be said that there has never existed a complete MS of the Bible that presented an entirely unified Masoretic tradition.'

Thus when such books as Joshua and Samuel and Jeremiah were canonized as part of the second division, the Prophets – and already Ben Sira (ch. 46 and 49:4–7 – part of the notable section, ch. 44 to 49, that begins with 'Let us now praise famous men') knew them as such, *circa* 200 B.C.E.[1] – there is no evidence that the Hebrew text of these books had been fixed and/or were 'on file' in some such central, official place as the Temple. For it is unlikely that the Jews who undertook to translate these books into Greek would not have made serious efforts to obtain a copy of the official text. This is no idle assertion. For the author of the *Letter of Aristeas* made it a special point that the Hebrew text that was to be used for the Greek translation in Alexandria was brought from Jerusalem, and that the high Priest Eleazar himself gave it to the elders–translators to take with them; nothing is said at the end of the *Letter* as to its fate, though it may be surmised that it accompanied the translators back to the homeland. Regardless of the degree of veracity of this particular aspect of the *Letter*, the idea behind the story is the fact that an acceptable translation could derive only from an acceptable Hebrew text, one that had the blessings of the head of the Jewish people.[2]

It may even be possible to cite a biblical passage that points to a fixed or official text of a canonical book of the Bible in the days of the First or Second Temple; and by the same token, a relatively early rabbinic passage may be quoted to the same effect. Thus Deut. 4:1–2, while specifically mentioning 'the laws and rules' (*ḥuqqim...mishpaṭim*) to which nothing was to be added and from which nothing was to be

[1] On the bipartite division of the Bible at the time (the Law and the Prophets), a division that became tripartite in Judea (but not in Egypt and hence not in Christianity either) only toward the end of the first century C.E., see Orlinsky, 'The canonization of the Bible and the exclusion of the Apocrypha', in *Essays*, ch. 15, pp. 263ff; and the abstract of the paper read at the 1976 meeting of the International Organization for Septuagint and Cognate Studies (in conjunction with the Society of Biblical Literature), 'Some observations on Josephus' 22 books of the Hebrew Bible and related matters' (p. 38 of *SBLASP*, ed. G. W. MacRae).

[2] From the *Letter of Aristeas* no one would know that there were Hebrew MSS. of the Torah in circulation in Alexandria; all mention of the Hebrew Torah, including the king's awe of them, revolves about the copy that the High Priest Eleazar sent along with the 72 elders to Egypt; cf. §§ 3 ('for it [viz. the Law] exists among them [viz. the Jews of Judea; cf. §§ 10–11] written on parchments in Hebrew characters'), 30, 38, 46, 176ff. It may be noted that nothing is said in the *Letter* about the return of the Hebrew Torah to Jerusalem, though the safe return of the elders–translators is specified several times (§§ 46, 123; and cf. 172 and 318ff); the statement of Josephus (*Antiquitates Judaica* XII.56), 'We have also chosen six elders from each tribe and have sent them along with the Law. And it will be the part of your piety and uprightness to send back the Law when it has been translated, together with those who are bringing it, in safety,' has no basis in Aristeas.

subtracted, could well imply that the very text of these commandments was to be kept unchanged. Indeed, in this connection the phrase 'do not add to...or subtract from...' was something of a formula, conventionally invoked.[1] It was essentially no different, for example, from the injunction 'to protect the poor, the widow, and the fatherless', also common in the ancient Near East and in Biblical Israel; protocol, deriving from harsh reality, required that these formulas be invoked.[2]

The practical import and consequences, however, were something else again. For the fact remains that different texts of the books of Joshua, Samuel, Jeremiah, and Job, for example, were simultaneously in circulation, none of them any longer – if any ever were – identifiable as official, and all of them having experienced or still in the process of experiencing change, some more than others. But the data go beyond the period of the Second Temple, even the last two or three centuries of its existence.

In many scores of instances, the fragmentary remains of Aquila's translation – 'slave to the Hebrew letter' is how Origen put it – manifest readings different from those of the preserved Hebrew text, and this in the late first to early second centuries C.E.[3] But apart from translations and versions of the Bible, for example, the Samaritan, the Targums, the Peshitta, and the Vulgate, such tannaitic works as the *Mechilta*, *Sifra*, and *Sifre*,[4] the Gemara, the Kethib-Qere

[1] Compare, for example, Deut. 13:1, Jer. 26:2, Prov. 30:6 and Rev. 22:18–19 – all cited by S. R. Driver, *Deuteronomy* ICC (1895), at Deut. 4:1; and compare Josephus, *Contra Apionem* 1.42.

[2] Cf. F. C. Fensham, 'Widow, orphan, and the poor in ancient Near Eastern legal and wisdom literature', *JNES*, 21 (1962), 129–39, reproduced in *Studies in Ancient Israelite Wisdom*, ed. J. L. Crenshaw (New York, 1976), pp. 161–71.

[3] Swete, *Introduction*, pp. 31–42, still offers a good survey of Aquila, now supplemented by Jellicoe, *Septuagint*, pp. 76–83. The standard work on Aquila is J. Reider's dissertation under Margolis, *Prolegomena to a Greek–Hebrew and Hebrew–Greek Index to Aquila* (1916; reprinted from *JQR*, n.s. 4 (1913–14), 321–56, 577–620; n.s. 7 (1916–17), 287–366) – now completed and revised by N. Turner, *An Index to Aquila*, VTSup, 12 (1966); but see the important caveats and data in the reviews by J. Barr, *JSS*, 12 (1967), 296–304, a review of J. Reider, *An Index to Aquila*, completed and revised by N. Turner (Leiden, 1966); R. Hanhart, *ThRev* 64 (1968), 391–4, a review of Reider, *Index to Aquila*; and E. Tov, *Textus*, 8 (1973), 164–74, 'Some corrections to Reider–Turner's Index to Aquila'.

[4] S. Rosenfeld, *Mishpaḥat Sofrim* (Wilna, 1883), has compiled a number of the variants in these tannaitic midrashic and related works; see also V. Aptowitzer, *Das Schriftwort in der rabbinischen Literatur*, covering Joshua, Judges, and Samuel (1906–15), reissued by KTAV (1970) with a useful prolegomenon by S. Loewinger. In the light of these preserved texts, it is not easy to accept the assertion by Talmon 'The Old Testament text', p. 159 – and cf., for example, pp. 165f, 'The third phase...'; 'During the period [of the final phases of the canonization of the Old Testament

system,[1] and even liturgical compositions and grammatical works of the late first millennium, not to mention manuscripts of the Hebrew Bible of the second millennium – all these offer the discriminating textual critic quotations from the Hebrew text that differ from our preserved Hebrew text and that are readily demonstrable as deriving from actual biblical texts in circulation and not from faulty memory or carelessness.

In Num. 34:2, the received Hebrew text reads (*'el-)ha-'áreṣ (kᵉnáʿan)*; but the Sifre reads *'éreṣ*, the reading designated as a Sebir and preserved in four Hebrew manuscripts listed by Kennicott. Again, whereas the received text of 2 Kings 3:15 reads (*...wa-tᵉhi ʿalaw) yad (YHWH)*, the eleventh-century grammarian Ibn Janaḥ quotes the passage as *rúaḥ*,[2] the reading not only of more than a score of Kennicott and de Rossi manuscripts but also of the Targum (*rúaḥ nᵉbu'ah min qᵃdam YY*). Or when the Babylonian Talmud, *Berakot* 54b, cites Josh. 10:11 as (*wayhi bᵉnusam) mippᵉne bᵉne Yiśra'el*, as against the preserved *mippᵉne Yiśra'el*, the Septuagint also reads *bᵉne*, and so do two de Rossi MSS.[3] As a final case in point, it will be recalled (p. 556 n. 3) that at least as late as the fourth century a biblical text of Samuel was known in which the phrase *wa-yélek 'Elqanah 'aḥᵃre 'ishto* (in connection with 1 Sam. 1 to 2) was present – a reading that is no longer preserved in any of the three Hebrew texts of Samuel (the received, the Septuagint *Vorlage*, and the Qumran fragments) but fully authenticated by them.

In all these cases, it is not a question which reading an editor would select for his 'Masoretic' text, or even which reading is the 'original'; it

books]...the Jewish scribes and sages decided on, and carried out, the minute fixation of the consonantal text of the scriptures in the original Hebrew tongue' – especially in the light of what the author himself wrote on pp. 161f.; but limitation of space precludes detailed analysis.

[1] Early in the second half of the first millennium C.E., when the Kethib–Qere system came into being, more than a thousand variant readings were still to be found in MSS. in current use that could not be reconciled by vocalization. Thus whereas all four forms, יושבים, ישבם, יושבם, and ישבים, could be vocalized with the identical signs (*ḥolem, shwa*, and *ḥireq*), justlike all *matres lectionis* and silent letters (e.g., מְצָתִי without the *alef*, in Num. 11:11), variants such as הוצא/היצא (Gen. 8:17) could not; those in the last mentioned category became members of the Kethib–Qere system. Cf. H. M. Orlinsky, 'The origin of the Kethib–Qere system: a new approach', *Oxford Congress volume*, VTSup, 7 (1959), pp. 184–92 (= pp. 407–15 in *The Canon and Masorah of the Hebrew Bible: An Introductory Reader*, ed. S. Z. Leiman (New York 1974)); also the article 'Qere–Kethibh (QK)' by G. E. Weil in *IDBSup*, pp. 716–23. It may be observed that the argument is not affected if the Kethib–Qere system is the product of men who corrected rather than compiled readings found in their mauscripts.

[2] In *Sefer Ha-Riqmah*, ed. M. Wilensky, 1, p. 67, line 10.

[3] See Orlinsky, 'The Masoretic text' pp. xx ff.

is rather a matter of realizing that any such term as a 'fixed' or 'official' or 'stabilized' Hebrew text of the Bible – if ever there really were such a text in existence – is meaningless in the face of the reality of divergent readings and texts from pre-Septuagint times to well into the Middle Ages.[1] So that any attempt to take at its face value the rabbinic statement that there were three copies of the Torah on deposit in the Temple loses all relevance for our purpose.[2]

It is still too early to reconstruct with reasonable confidence the geographical history of the Hebrew texts of the Bible during the days of the Second Temple, especially the Hellenistic and Roman period; the matter revolves about the career of these texts in Babylonia, Judea, and Egypt. However, this aspect is outside the scope of this essay – except that it may be noted that the Hebrew texts used by the Alexandrian Septuagint translators ought not be labelled automatically 'Egyptian' texts unless other evidence can be adduced; for these texts – compare pp. 536f. above for the statement in Aristeas about the Judean origin of the text of the Torah brought by the translators to Alexandria – are far more likely Judean than Egyptian in origin.[3]

[1] Under the heading 'Pre-Tannaitic evidence: the emergence of the Textus Receptus', four articles, by M. H. Segal, M. Greenberg, W. F. Albright, and F. M. Cross, Jr. (nos. 14–17, pp. 285–348) have been reproduced in Leiman, ed., *The Canon and Masorah of the Hebrew Bible*. From first to last (compare, for example, Segal, 'We may plausibly conjecture...', p. 285; Albright, 'we know far too little to be dogmatic ...There are, of course, other possibilities' pp. 332f; Cross, 'If we put together all evidence now at hand, woven together, to be sure, with occasional skeins of speculation, I believe that the ... promulgation [*sic*!] of the new, standard recension evidently took place sometime near the mid-first century A.D.,' pp. 346–8) they are characterized far more by conjecture and speculation than by the kind of specific source data on which one can build with confidence. See also n. 5 below.

Passing mention may be made here of A. Mirsky, 'Biblical variants in medieval Hebrew poetry', *Textus*, 3 (1963), 159–62 – with reference in nn. 1–5 to other 'Lists of such readings', and S. Esh, 'Variant readings in mediaeval Hebrew commentaries ...(Rashbam)', *Textus*, 5 (1966), 84–92.

[2] The articles by J. Z. Lauterbach, S. Talmon, and S. Zeitlin reproduced as nos. 21–3 (pp. 416–72) in Leiman, ed. *The Canon and Masorah of the Hebrew Bible*, deal with the matter, as do L. Blau, *Studien zum althebräischen Buchwesen* (Strasbourg, 1902), pp. 101ff – against whom Lauterback argued, largely in vain – and H. M. Orlinsky (in connection with Kethib–Qere; no. 20, pp. 407–15).

[3] Barthélemy put it this way (*IDBSup*, pp. 878f.), 'Drawing on his expert knowledge of the unpublished fragments from Cave IV, Cross proposed a theory of "local texts"....[This] theory...has been favourably received by some...but sharply criticized by others...To this [theory] it may be objected that we know practically nothing about the literary vitality – or lack of it – in Babylonian Judaism during the period from Ezra to Hillel. Neither are we any better informed on any alleged literary competence in Hebrew on the part of Egyptian Jews of the same period...We cannot...automatically qualify as Egyptian every Hebrew *Vorlage* of a book of the

Finally, mention must be made of the textual criticism of the Hebrew and Septuagint texts of the Bible. In pre-World War I and pre-archeology days, the work of J. Wellhausen[1] and S. R. Driver[2] manifested the highest quality of achievement in this area of research. The same high standard may be seen in the publications of M. L. Margolis, for example, 'The scope and methodology of Biblical philology'[3] – a masterly study of Job 3:3 – and in the commentaries of J. A. Montgomery (in the ICC series) on *Daniel*[4] and *Kings*;[5] the tradition is continued by H. M. Orlinsky, a student of theirs.[6] A clear and useful survey of 'Textual criticism, O(ld) T(estament)' is now offered by J. A. Thompson in *IDBSup* (1976), pp. 886a–891b, with considerable bibliography, in connection with which one may read H. M. Orlinsky, 'Whither biblical research?'[7]

[This chapter was originally submitted in Feb. 1977.]

LXX. A further objection...' Nor does Talmon – even if unwittingly – offer any comfort to Cross and his followers; cf. his assertion (Leiman, ed., *The Canon and Masorah of the Hebrew Bible*, p. 159). 'For the preceding phases (prior to *c.* 300 B.C.E.) in the history of the (Old Testament) text woefully little historical evidence is available, and none of it is contemporary. Any account of the development of the text...in the Persian period, not to mention the periods of the Babylonian Exile or of the First Temple, must perforce rely upon conjecture and, at best, upon deductions and analogies derived from later literature and later manuscripts.' And see now the searching critique by D. W. Gooding, 'An appeal for a stricter terminology in the textual criticism of the Old Testament', *JSS*, 21 (1976), 15–25, in which some of the inner confusion and contradictory statements in Cross' arguments and historical reconstructions are pointed out.

1 *Der Text der Bücher Samuelis* (Göttingen, 1871).

2 *Inter alia, Notes on the Hebrew Text ... of the Books of Samuel* (2nd edn., Oxford, 1913).

3 *JQR*, n.s. 1 (1910–11), 5–41.

4 1927, see, e.g., § III, 'Ancient Versions', pp. 24–57 of the Introduction.

5 1951, ed. H. S. Gehman.

6 Cf. 'Studies in the Septuagint of the Book of Job', chs. 1–5, *HUCA*, 28 (1957), 53–74; 29 (1958), 229–71; 30 (1959), 153–67; 32 (1961), 239–68; 33 (1962), 119–51; 35 (1964), 57–78; 36 (1965), 37–47.

7 *JBL*, 90 (1971), 1–14 (= ch. 11 in *Essays*, pp. 200–17). E. Würthwein, *The Text of the Old Testament* (Oxford, 1957), dealing largely with the critical apparatus in R. Kittel's ed. of *Biblia Hebraica* (3rd edn., Stuttgart, 1929), is more misleading than helpful (see the review by H. M. Orlinsky, *JSS* 4, (1959), 149–51; but cf. ed. 2, Grand Rapids, 1979). R. W. Klein's more recent guide to the *Textual Criticism of the Old Testament*, etc. (Philadelphia, 1974) would have been much more useful and representative had it not been limited to so great an extent by the views and data of his mentor (cf. p. 556 n. 3). See now D. W. Gooding's severe critique of Cross and Klein, along the same lines, 'A recent popularisation of Professor F. M. Cross' theories of the text of the Old Testament', *Tyndale Bulletin* 26 (1975), 113–32; and A. Pietersma's rejection of the theory of Cross and his students in the matter of 'Proto-Lucian and the Greek Psalter', *VT*, 28 (1978), 66–72, with reference also to Genesis and Deuteronomy.

CHAPTER 16

THE TARGUMIM

In the Jewish world of the Diaspora (and also in Palestine), historical and linguistic conditions had, as early as the third century B.C.E., led to the translation of the Bible into Greek. Similar reasons explain the origin of Targums. The problems posed in this connection, however, are considerably greater and more complex than for the LXX.

The word *targum* signifies 'translation' and derives from the verb *tirgem* meaning 'to translate', 'to explain', or 'to read out' (compare Ezra 4:7); it is a denominative of *turgeman* (= interpreter) to which an Akkadian origin is generally attributed.[1] In rabbinic usage *tirgem* is employed to designate a version translated from the Hebrew into any language whatever (*y. Kidd* 1.59a; *y. Meg.* 1.71c), but *targum* is used only for a translation of the Bible into Aramaic or for the Aramaic passages of the Old Testament (*Yad.* 4.5). The professional Synagogue translator was called *turgeman* or *meturgeman* (*Meg.* 4.4). As a literary genre Targum is distinct from Midrash in that it is primarily a translation and not a commentary and, in its strictest definition, a translation intended for the liturgy of the Synagogue.

We now possess Targums of all the books of the Bible, with the exception of Ezra–Nehemiah and Daniel. Until recently the most commonly accepted opinion was that these were late productions, distributed between the fourth and fifth centuries C.E. and the Middle Ages. It was conceded that the institution of Targum itself was pre-Christian; but because of the prohibition upon putting into writing the oral tradition, the texts themselves could not have been anterior to the first writings of rabbinic Judaism (about 200 C.E.). Recent studies, and particularly the Qumran discoveries, compel a revision of this point of view. Targumic activities, and even the writing down of Targums, precede the Christian era and, although the greater part of our texts may have made their appearance only at a later period, the certainty that the bulk of their content is more ancient permits us to consider the

[1] C. Rabin suggests a borrowing from the Hittite *tarkummāi-*, *tarkummiya-* = to announce, explain, translate; 'Hittite words in Hebrew', *Orientalia*, n.s. 32 (1963), 134–6.

problem of the Targums here as a whole, leaving the more important recensions to be considered in detail later. Our primary aim is to summarize the problems and the viewpoints, often contradictory, to which they have given rise.

ORIGIN AND *SITZ IM LEBEN*

The origin of the Targum is to be explained by a double necessity: that of promoting a knowledge of the Torah among the people and, consequently, that of expounding this knowledge in a language known to all.

The greater part of the institutions of Judaism are incomprehensible without reference to the shock of the Exile. Since, according to the prophets and the theology of Deuteronomy, infidelity to Yahweh was the ultimate cause of misfortune, the new guides of Israel sought to promote that knowledge and scrupulous observance of the Law which had become the constituent element of the post-Exilic community. The Synagogue,[1] whose origin probably goes back to the time of the Exile, as much a place of teaching as of worship, took on at this time the pre-eminent role it has kept in the development and survival of Judaism.

In this new climate the linguistic factor was to be similarly decisive.[2] Since before the Exile, knowledge of Aramaic must have been fairly widespread among the upper classes of Judea, on account of the necessary relations with the Aramaic-speaking peoples of the east. From the end of the seventh century B.C.E. this language became a sort of lingua franca, utilized in the relations between the peoples of the Near East. At a later date it even became the official language of the Persian empire. In the time of Hezekiah (716–687 B.C.E.) we note that, if certain sections of the population understood Aramaic, the people themselves used only Hebrew (2 Kings 18:26–8 = Isa. 36:11–13). But before long the situation was in some degree reversed; the Jews of the Babylonian Diaspora were obliged to learn the dominant language, Aramaic, which, in the space of a few generations, was to supplant Hebrew in common usage. We may thus suppose that in Babylon a certain degree of activity in biblical translation developed as from those distant times; regrettably, we have no reliable knowledge of this matter. The Talmud notes that God chose Babylon as the place of exile for his people because of the kinship between the two languages, Hebrew and Aramaic (*b. Pesaḥ.* 87b). But Hebrew, as the language of worship and of the sacred literature, certainly continued to be used.

[1] Cf. chapter 6 above, and vol. 3, chapter 5.

[2] Cf. chapter 3 above, and vol. 1, chapter 6.

In Palestine, after the return from the Exile, the situation developed by degrees towards an increased preponderance of Aramaic dialects. We learn from Neh. 13:24 that the 'language of Judah' was in peril, retreating before the inroads of other languages. Coins, inscriptions and jar-seals show that the process was well under way in the fourth century B.C.E. Hebrew ceased to be the ordinary language of the people and today there are those who even maintain that from about 500 B.C.E. it had completely disappeared as a spoken language.[1] It must nevertheless be borne in mind that the writings of the post-Exilic prophets were in Hebrew, as were almost all the later books of the Old Testament. Ben Sira wrote in Hebrew (*circa* 180 B.C.E.), as did the sectarians of Qumran; but in these instances we are dealing with learned men, and their Hebrew is already markedly different from that of the period before the Exile. These arguments are not decisive as regards the language spoken by the people, above all since in the Orient the spoken and the written language may diverge in the same country. The bilingual character of Ezra and of Daniel presupposes among the Jews a measure of familiarity with both Hebrew and Aramaic.

The literature of the desert of Judea has thrown new light on this area: it demonstrates the permanence of Hebrew as a living language *in Judea* until after the second Revolt (132–135 C.E.). Hebrew, in its 'Mishnaic' form, lived on as a learned language in the academies of Galilee, whilst fundamental texts such as the Targum and the Palestinian Talmud were written in Galilean Aramaic, which thus found itself, from the third century C.E., raised to the level of a literary language.

How, in face of the established fact of the survival of Hebrew as a spoken language down to the second century C.E., are we to explain the emergence of the Targum? The traditional solution remains tenable: because of the steadily reduced comprehension of the Hebrew of the Bible. In all the provinces, even in Judea, Aramaic was dominant; 'Mishnaic' Hebrew was very different from that of the scriptures, if we are to judge from good manuscripts of Jewish literature, not 'retouched' (like our present editions) according to the conventions of Biblical Hebrew or, still more, from the texts of Qumran or Murabba'at.[2] Classical Hebrew texts called for a version in a modern language, of which the most usual was Aramaic.

On the other hand, the Targum was a necessity even for those who

[1] Cf. K. Beyer, *Althebräische Grammatik* (Göttingen, 1969), p. 14.

[2] Cf. J. T. Milik, *Les 'petites grottes' de Qumrân*, DJD 3 (Oxford, 1962), pp. 221–35; E. Y. Kutscher, *A History of the Hebrew Language* (Jerusalem, 1982), pp. 115–20; J. A. Emerton, 'The problem of vernacular Hebrew in the first century A.D. and the language of Jesus', *JTS*, n.s. 24 (1973), 1–23 (with bibliography).

could still, more or less, comprehend the biblical texts. These were often difficult; to translate them in the presence of the people was not enough. They still had to be *interpreted*. The Targum gave the traditional interpretation, placing the text within the people's grasp, explaining it and drawing all the practical conclusions relevant to life. Translation and homiletic commentary must, in ancient times, often have been on an equal footing; but on this point we are able only to make conjectures.

The famous scene in Neh. 8 clearly illustrates the two factors which explain the development of Targum: concern with the teaching of the Torah and the impact of linguistic conditions. In this narrative Jewish tradition is unanimous in seeing the origin of the Targum (compare *Meg.* 3a). Does this scene of a public reading of the Torah along with commentaries (verses 8, 9) draw its inspiration from an already existing tradition, or rather did it serve as a model for the subsequent liturgy? It is difficult to provide an answer. In it we see Ezra, the priest–scribe, reading from the Law, 'translating (*m^{e}poraš*) and providing its meaning'. The meaning of *m^{e}poraš* is controversial, some maintaining that at that point in time a translation was not called for. However, in his commentary W. Rudolph adopts the opinion of H. H. Schaeder who understands this as a translation into Aramaic.[1] This term indicates the practice of the chancelleries of the Persian empire of translating an Aramaic document, on the spot, into the language of the country or *vice versa*. Be that as it may, we may suppose that a certain kind of translation went hand-in-hand with this conscious effort to put the Torah within the grasp of the people.

The *oral* Targum was developed principally in relation to the liturgy of Synagogue readings, and thus must be as ancient as the readings themselves. This *Sitz im Leben* is basic to an attempt to work out what the ancient Targum must have been. In fact, at the period of the text's *redaction* in its present form, new elements were active which modified its nature. Unfortunately, reconstructions of the pre-Christian Jewish liturgy remain conjectural.

We are certain that at the time of the New Testament the convention of the Sabbath readings of the Torah and the prophets was well established (Luke 4; Acts 13:14–15; 15:21). Flavius Josephus (*Contra Apionem* II.175) dates back to Moses himself a weekly reading of the Torah, a tradition perpetuated in the rabbinic writings (*y. Meg.* 4.1 75a). In the times of Josephus there were probably not yet any fixed readings (save, perhaps, at festivals), nor was there any *lectio continua*

[1] W. Rudolph, *Esra und Nehemia*, HAT 1, 20 (Tübingen, 1949), p. 149.

(which made its appearance only at the beginning of the second century C.E.). The origin of a triennial (in Palestine) or an annual (in Babylon) cycle of readings of the Torah came later (the end of the second century or the beginning of the third century C.E.). The very existence of a regular festive synagogal service before 70 C.E. is problematical; probably it appeared at a later date, filling the role of the festive worship of the Temple.[1] The prophetic reading (*haphtarah*) was freely chosen, but certain pericopes were probably fairly soon imposed on account of their affinity with the text of the Torah (*parashah*) previously read (compare *b. Meg.* 29b).[2]

It is only with the Mishnah (*Meg.* 4)[3] that we have precise details on the liturgy of the readings. Each reader was assisted by a translator (*meturgeman*) who provided from memory (that is without recourse to the text) the Aramaic version of every verse of the Torah – after every third verse in the case of the prophets. We find a reflection of this classical scene in the Targum itself which presents Aaron as the *Turgeman* (N) or the *meturgeman* (O) of Moses in his mission to the Pharaoh (Exod. 4:16). Certain passages were read in Hebrew (Gen. 35:22; Exod. 32:21–5; 2 Sam. 11:2–17; 13), but not translated for reasons strictly 'targumic' – the intention of saying nothing which might dishonour the ancestors (4.10).[4] As for the Torah, it was forbidden to 'skip' a passage, although for the prophets this point was conceded. These details recall to mind an important fact – dating from an early period – concerning the Jewish attitude to the Scriptures: the diminishing hierarchy established between Torah, prophetic writings and hagiographa. This was to be manifested also in the history of the appearance of the various Targums, as in the manner in which each of them stood with more or less liberty in relation to the text to be translated.

Rabbinic prescriptions forbade the translator to set eyes on the

[1] We summarize here the conclusions of C. Perrot, *La lecture de la Bible dans la Synagogue – Les anciennes lectures palestiniennes du Shabbat et des fêtes* (Hildesheim, 1973).

[2] Care should be taken in making use of the lists of readings published by A. Büchler, based on manuscripts from the Cairo Genizah. See Perrot, *La lecture* and B. Z. Wacholder's *Prolegomenon* to the re-edition of J. Mann's *The Bible as Read and Preached in the Old Synagogue* (New York, 1971), pp. xi–lxxii.

[3] It is difficult to assign a precise date to this chapter. Note, however, that it is concerned with anonymous *mishnayoth* which, usually, points to a considerable antiquity, and that the greater part of the texts are indeed anterior to their redaction by Yehuda ha-Nasi; cf. C. Albeck, *Einführung in die Mischna*, Studia Judaica 6 (Berlin, 1971), pp. 94–129.

[4] Cf. P. S. Alexander, 'The Rabbinic lists of forbidden Targumim', *JJS*, 27 (1976), 177–91.

biblical scroll and, above all, himself to make use of any written text whatever; 'That which has been expressed orally [must be transmitted] orally and that which has been expressed in writing [must be transmitted] in writing' (*y. Meg.* 4.1 74d). This oft-repeated adage (*b. Git.* 60b; *Tem.* 14b) was valid only for the ***public*** usage of texts of the oral tradition. It is striking that the Talmud contains no mention whatever of a written Mishnah;[1] but we must perhaps consider the interdiction upon putting the oral tradition into writing as purely legendary, in as far as the pre-rabbinic period is concerned.[2] This applies as much to the transmission of *halakah* (regulative material) as to the *haggadah* (illustrative material), and thus also to the Targum. This leads us to a problem as important as it is intricate.

WHEN WERE THE TARGUMS WRITTEN DOWN?

Whereas the ancient practice of the oral Targum was not in doubt, the not long since current opinion was that our written Targums could not be anterior to the Talmudic period. Nevertheless, in the first edition of his *Gottesdienstlichen Vorträge der Juden* (1832), L. Zunz pointed out that the Jews of the Greek Diaspora had not hesitated to translate the Scriptures; one might suppose that where Aramaic had become the language of the people, in Palestine and Babylonia, they must as quickly have done likewise and that 'written Aramaic translations of most of the biblical books did certainly exist under the Hasmoneans'.[3] Thus he formulated an intuition which was to be confirmed, more than a hundred years later, by the discoveries of Qumran.

In 1956 Bedouin discovered in Cave 11 extensive fragments of a Targum of Job (11Qtg Job).[4] This comprises 17:14 to 42:9–11, found on the remains of 38 columns, the last ten of which contain many entire verses, the lower part of the scroll being lost. The writing is of the square type called 'Herodian' (37 B.C.E. to 70 C.E.), and the copy itself

[1] S. Lieberman, *Hellenism in Jewish Palestine* (New York, 1962), p. 87.

[2] Cf. R. Meyer in *TWNT*, 9 (1973) pp. 34–5; ET *TDNT*, 9 (1974), p. 34; H. L. Strack and G. Stemberger, *Einleitung in Talmud und Midrasch*, 7th rev. edn. (Munich, 1982), pp. 41–54 (with recent bibliography).

[3] Second edition (Frankfurt am Main, 1892), p. 65. C. Rabin has suggested that it was the targumic activity in Palestine which might have stimulated the composition of the LXX: 'The translation process and the character of the Septuagint', *Textus*, 6 (1968), 20.

[4] See Fig. 1. J. P. M. van der Ploeg and A. S. van der Woude, *Le Targum de Job de la grotte XI de Qumrân* (Leiden, 1971); M. Sokoloff, *The Targum to Job from Qumran Cave XI* (Ramat-Gan, 1974); J. A. Fitzmyer and D. J. Harrington, *A Manual of Palestinian Aramaic Texts* (Rome, 1978), pp. 10–46 (bibliography, pp. 195–7).

Fig. 1 Fragment from the Targum of Job. (Plate from p. 129 of J. P. M. van der Ploeg and A. S. van der Woude, *Le Targum de Job de la Grotte XI de Qumrân* (Leiden, 1971), reproduced by permission of E. J. Brill, Leiden)

dates from the middle of the first century of our era. The language appears to be more ancient than that of the *Genesis Apocryphon* (1 QapGen) dated by E. Y. Kutscher in the first century B.C.E.,[1] and closer to the Aramaic of Daniel. The editors question whether the redaction of this Targum might not be shown to go back to 'the latter part of the second century B.C.E.'[2] Thus we may have here the most ancient targumic text at present known, which 'definitely proves that there were written targums in the time of Jesus Christ, and that they probably existed already in about the year 100 B.C.E.'[3] This text contains nothing 'heterodox, nothing to point to known teachings of the Essenes, nothing indeed which would betray the document's Qumranian origin, except that it was found in 11Q'.[4]

What we have here is a Targum of a simple type, without the long paraphrases customary in Palestinian Targums, adding only an occasional few words, so that the text is scarcely longer than the original Hebrew. It is not a translation in the modern sense but precisely the type of *interpretation* which characterizes the Targums as a genre.

Similarly, in Cave 4 there were found two small fragments of another Targum of Job (4QtgJob). They are in poor condition and contain no more than a few words of Job 4:16 to 5:4. The same sections of the text are not reproduced, and it is impossible to state whether these belonged to a different recension. However, these meagre fragments, edited by J. T. Milik,[5] proved at least that written Targums were not altogether unusual.

These discoveries confirm a rabbinic tradition mentioned in the two Talmuds (*y. Sabb.*16.1.15c; *b. Sabb.* 115a). We are told that one day a Targum of Job (*spr 'ywb ktwb trgwm*) was brought to Rabban Gamaliel the Elder, grandson of Hillel, which he had walled up in the masonry of the Temple, then still under construction. This did not prevent his grandson, Gamaliel II, from still being able to read a copy in Tiberias at

1 E. Y. Kutscher, 'The language of the Genesis Apocryphon', in *Aspects of the Dead Sea Scrolls*', Scripta Hierosolymitana, 4, part 1 (Jerusalem, 1957), p. 22. Cf. S. A. Kaufman, 'The Job Targum from Qumran', *JAOS*, 93 (1973), 317–27; T. Muraoka, 'The Aramaic of the Old Targum of Job from Qumran Cave XI', *JTS*, 25 (1974), 425–43.

2 *Le Targum de Job*, p. 4.

3 Ibid. p. 8.

4 Ibid. p. 7. Nevertheless the first study of the Targum of Job comes down in favour of an Essene origin, Job even being presented as a type of the 'Teacher of Righteousness': E. W. Tuinstra, *Hermeneutische Aspecten van de Targum van Job uit Grot XI van Qumrān* (Diss. Groningen, 1970), p. 109. We have not been convinced by the arguments advanced.

5 R. de Vaux and J. T. Milik, *Qumrân Grotte 4: I Archéologie; II Tefillin, Mezuzot et Targums (4Q 128–4Q 157)*, DJD 6 (Oxford, 1977), p. 90 (= 4 Q157).

the end of the first century, according to *t. Sabb.* 13. The reason for Gamaliel's act of censorship is surely not that this was a *written* Targum; it may be that it contained some tendentious interpretations, and we might well think of a version similar to the one found in Qumran.

It may well be that at the end of Job 42:17b in the LXX too there is an allusion to an Aramaic version of the book: Οὗτος ἑρμηνεύεται ἐκ τῆς Συριακῆς βίβλου. The interpretation of this addendum is, however, much disputed. It has led some authors to suppose that it was the books not publicly read in the Synagogue which were the first to benefit by a written translation. The data are insufficient to bear out such a conclusion. At all events it is striking that in the Targum of Job we have the Targum of a text whose liturgical use is not attested. Why, then, this version? We know that certain passages of Job were read in the presence of the high priest on the night of Kippur, or passages (according to *Yoma* 1.6) of Ezra or of Daniel. A. Berliner suggests that the high priests of the time had some problems in understanding the difficult Hebrew of Job – especially during the nocturnal vigil.[1] On the other hand it should not be forgotten that there is a tradition attributing the composition of the book to Moses himself (*b. Bath.* 14b). The esteem accorded to this book might thus have contributed to the production of the Aramaic version.

The character of the Targum of Job, the uncertainty as to its ultimate provenance and its usage, might lead one to conclude that no useful conclusions can be drawn from it regarding the bulk of the more ancient Targums. Nevertheless, certain writers have suggested that the Aramaic texts of Qumran and in particular the Targums, might have an origin outside of the community: they might thus bear witness for a far wider mass of the Palestinian Jewish community.[2] But it would be odd if they had a written translation of Job before that of the Torah.

Now some fragments of a Targum of Leviticus from Cave 4 of Qumran (4QtgLev) provide proof of the existence of a written Aramaic version (at least partial) of the Torah at about the beginning of the Christian era.[3] There survive only a few words of Lev. 16:12–15, 18–21 dealing with the ritual of Kippur. The translation is extremely literal but it contains an interesting rendering of *kappōret* (propitiatory or mercy seat) as *ksy'*, 'covering'. From such a text, which scarcely

1 A. Berliner, *Targum Onkelos* (Berlin, 1884), p. 90.

2 S. Segert, 'Die Sprachenfragen in der Qumrāngemeinschaft', in *Qumrān-Probleme*, ed. H. Bardtke (Berlin, 1963), p. 322.

3 R. de Vaux and J. T. Milik, *Qumrân Grotte 4*, pp. 86–9 (= 4Q 156). Cf. J. A. Fitzmyer, 'The Targum of Leviticus from Qumran Cave 4', *Maarav*, 1 (1978), 5–23.

provides a significant sample, we can draw no conclusion concerning the nature – literal or paraphrastic – of the ancient Targums of the Pentateuch; here, too, the other recensions are literal, the biblical text calling for no explanation. Nevertheless the fragments of the Targum of Job incline one to believe that the ancient Targums did not confine themselves to a servile fidelity to the Hebrew.[1]

Among the mass of the Qumran manuscripts, the harvest of targumic material is certainly poor, even if we take into consideration that 1QApGen (which, properly speaking, is neither Targum nor Midrash), in retelling the story of Gen. 14, might have been inspired by a Targum. 'This may be due', J. T. Milik writes, 'to the fact that such translations were little needed in the highly educated milieu of the Essene Community.'[2] It is all the more significant that it should be precisely in this milieu that they have been found! However, it is probable that the early Targum was intended above all for a popular audience, to which it aimed to make fully accessible the text of the Scripture.

All the targumic fragments of Qumran are written in Imperial Aramaic (*reichsaramäisch*), a developed form of which is to be found in the Babylonian Targum of the Pentateuch (Onkelos). These discoveries permit us, at least in part, to recognize an element of truth in K. Beyer's affirmation: 'When Hebrew died out in the sixth century B.C.E. an Aramaic translation of the Old Testament became needed, and was undoubtedly undertaken as early as the fourth century B.C.E., naturally in Imperial Aramaic.'[3] Similar conclusions have been obtained in other ways. Sheldon R. Isenberg, in a Harvard dissertation (1968), has studied more than a dozen biblical variants of which all the ancient versions, or the greater part of them, are at one in disagreeing with the Masoretic text. He has demonstrated in particular that the Palestinian Targum contains elements going back 'to the Old Palestine text-type current in Palestine from the fifth century B.C.E. to no later than the first half of the first century C.E.'[4] As a matter of fact A. Baumstark and

[1] This translation of the ritual of a festival is reminiscent of the Elephantine Passover Papyrus (419 B.C.E.) which is also concerned with the formal side of a liturgical celebration and which may be 'the first written trace of a Targum of the Pentateuch, very limited in its objective, concerned exclusively with the halakah': P. Grelot, 'Le papyrus pascal d'Eléphantine: essai de restauration'. *VT,* 17 (1967), 207.

[2] J. T. Milik, *Ten Years of Discovery in the Wilderness of Judaea*, SBT 26 (London, 1959), p. 31.

[3] K. Beyer, 'Der reichsaramäische Einschlag in der ältesten syrischen Literatur', *ZDMG,* 116 (1966), 252.

[4] S. R. Isenberg, 'An anti-Sadducee polemic in the Palestinian Targum tradition', *HTR,* 63 (1970), 438.

P. Kahle have long since put forward the hypothesis of a dependence of the Syriac version (*Peshitta*) on the Jewish Targums of the Pentateuch, which would suggest that they were committed to writing before the middle of the first century C.E.

There are those authors who, on the contrary, think of a relationship between Onkelos and Peshitta. But, in either case, since in the last analysis Onkelos rests upon a Palestinian source, the existence of a Palestinian Targum of the Pentateuch seems to be confirmed. To the affinities of vocabulary, identities of interpretation, and so on, we may thus now add, in favour of a relation of dependence between Palestinian Targum and Peshitta, the use of a similar *Vorlage* anterior to the Masoretic recension. A significant example is Gen. 4:8 in which Targum, LXX, Peshitta and Samaritan add, 'Let us go out into the field'. The Targum has thus been made on the basis of a Hebrew text of the proto-Masoretic type, at a date anterior to the middle of the first century of our era. In his dissertation Isenberg has examined more than a dozen targumic variants pointing back to the same type of text.[1]

Other arguments in favour of Targums having been put into writing at an early date gain weight in view of the discoveries of Qumran. It has been thought, for example, that in writing *The Antiquities of the Jews* Josephus made use of the Aramaic sources and even, at times, directly of a Targum.[2] It should not be forgotten that Aramaic was his mother-tongue, and that he first wrote *The Jewish War* in that language (Preface 1, §3). Account has also been taken of certain texts of the New Testament; thus Eph. 4:8, of which the reading 'he gave gifts unto men' tallies with the Targum of Psalm 68:19, or again Matt. 27:46 and parallels. The Jannes and Jambres of 2 Tim. 3:8 are unknown to the Old Testament, but their names are to be found in this form in the Targum of Exodus 1:15 and 7:11. Luke 6:36 has a striking parallel in the Targum of Leviticus 22:28: 'My people, children of Israel, as I am merciful [*rḥmn*] in heaven, so shall you be merciful on earth.'[3] The Targum of Genesis 49:25: 'Blessed are the breasts that have given thee suck and the womb wherein thou hast rested', is so similar to Luke 11:27 that one might believe one had found in the Targum a gospel citation, were this not quite impossible. Nevertheless these accords do not necessarily suppose the use of the same *texts*, but may be explained by simple coincidence or by common oral exegetic tradition. However,

[1] Cf. S. R. Isenberg, 'On the Jewish–Palestinian origins of the Peshitta to the Pentateuch', *JBL*, 90 (1971), 69–81.

[2] S. Rappaport, *Agada und Exegese bei Flavius Josephus* (Frankfurt am Main, 1930), pp. xx–xxiv.

[3] On this text see M. McNamara, *Targum and Testament* (Shannon, 1972), p. 118.

the large number of connections drawn between the Palestinian Targum and the New Testament incline one not to be too hasty in casting aside, at least as a working hypothesis, the possibility of actual dependence on a common stock.[1] In this matter of the date at which written Targums made their appearance, thought has often too precipitately been given to the idea of the redaction of *fixed* and *official* texts, as was to happen later in Babylon in the case of Onkelos, but never, as we shall see, came about in Palestine. In this connection the judgement of G. Dalman,[2] confusing the problem of redaction with that of the very existence of Targum, has seriously influenced the attitude of scholars for half a century. An oral targumic tradition surely preceded the appearance of the written evidence we possess.

If the rarity of ancient documents imposes the necessity of drawing only cautious conclusions, it is necessary also to beware of applying to the ancient period conclusions drawn from the nature of Targums, official or otherwise, written at a later date. The story of Gamaliel proves that certain ancient texts had been suppressed. It is all the more striking that certain Targums, even in the form in which we know them today after centuries of transmission, have been useful in clarifying the Qumran texts. Thus W. H. Brownlee could conclude, perhaps a trifle over-optimistically, from a comparison between 1QpHab and T Habakkuk: 'The frequent dependence of 1QpHab upon the Targum indicates that the Targumic text had taken definite shape by the middle of the First Century B.C.'[3] C. Rabin has put forward a suggestion which deserves detailed study: 'It might be argued that the nearest literary form to the interpretative Targumim is the Qumran *pesher*.'[4] What is more, the *pesher* genre (text plus commentary) might reflect the use in the Synagogue of a paraphrase translation of previously read Hebrew verses.

It is plain that targumic activity was not confined to Palestine – it must also have developed in a parallel manner in Babylon according to particular principles and methods, the impact of which we recognize in the formation of the Targum Onkelos and of its Masorah.[5] But we lack documents to illustrate in a precise fashion this intense activity which

[1] J. T. Forestell, *Targumic Traditions and the New Testament. An Annotated Bibliography with a New Testament Index*, SBL Aramaic Studies 4 (Chico, California, 1979).

[2] G. Dalman, *Grammatik des jüdisch–palästinischen Aramäisch* (Leipzig, 1905), p. 12.

[3] W. H. Brownlee, 'The Habakkuk Midrash and the Targum of Jonathan', *JJS*, 7 (1956), 184. This judgement is accepted by P. Kahle in *The Cairo Geniza*, 2nd edn. (Oxford, 1959), p. 196.

[4] Rabin, *Textus*, 6 (1968), 17 n. 58.

[5] G. E. Weil, 'La Massorah Magna du Targum du Pentateuque', *Textus*, 4 (1964), 30–54; 'La Massorah', *REJ*, 131 (1972), 5–102.

led up to that of the illustrious Babylonian academies which is better known.

EXTANT TARGUMS

The written Targums are the *terminus ad quem* of a long period of development and are one of the literary forms in which the results of a long period of study (in Hebrew *midrash*) of the Scriptures have been condensed. A preliminary remark is here imperative: if for the ancient period the liturgical *Sitz im Leben* and the fact of the oral transmission of Targums are the most important factors for understanding their nature, what matters now is the tendency of the compilers – and their greater or lesser ability – to include within the limits of a version the greatest possible number of elements of that exegetical tradition, both halakic and haggadic. Each Targum will have its own method, sometimes making use of a single word, of an evocative allusion to a known Midrash, elsewhere a more extensive paraphrase, traditionally recalled by the verse in question. The boundary between Targum-translation and commentary-Midrash will often be blurred. We shall indicate here only those characteristics of the recensions which can take us back to the more ancient period with which we have been concerned. What we call the Palestinian Targum represents not a unified recension but a mass of exegetical traditions, only part of which was to be condensed into a multiplicity of currents of traditions and finally of recensions.

TARGUMS TO THE PENTATEUCH

The Onkelos Targum (O), which it would be more correct to call the *Babylonian Targum*, is the official version of the Torah which won pride of place in Jewish tradition, in the wake of *Talmud Babli*. The name Onkelos has its origin in *b. Meg.* 3a; but the parallel passage of the Jerusalem Talmud (*y. Meg.* 1.8.71c) shows that here we have a confusion with Aquila, the author of a Greek version of the second century C.E. The only Targum, apart from those of the Prophets, to have had a controlled and unified redaction, it sets forth a canonical interpretation of the Torah in accordance with the decisions of the Babylonian academies, whose doctrine came in practice to impose itself on the entire Jewish world. The Talmud calls it 'our Targum' (*Kidd.* 49a).

Onkelos is the result of a precise and systematic revision and the fruit of the discussion of academies such as those of Sura and Nehardea.

Endowed with a Masorah which illustrated the divergencies of readings between the two schools, it must at a fairly early date have known a fixed consonantal form, since Nehardea was destroyed in 259. The lists of Hebrew–Aramaic equivalents tended by degrees rigorously to fix the text; the redaction of Onkelos was carried on in Babylon down to the fourth–fifth century. It is there that it will have been provided with the supralinear vocalization which can still be discerned under the corrections (of Tiberian inspiration) of certain manuscripts such as Vat. Ebr. 448, or again in the Sabbioneta edition of 1557 (the original manuscript of which has been lost), taken up again by A. Berliner in 1884. The minuteness of researches attested by the Masorah, its almost flawless fidelity to the Masoretic text and its agreement with the official interpretation explain the canonical status of Onkelos.

Onkelos was written down in a developed form of *reichsaramäisch* which in Babylon had acquired certain oriental characteristics. Affinities with the Aramaic of Qumran, and with the Samaritan dialect,[1] and above all the similarity of certain paraphrases to those of the Palestinian Targum[2] permit the inference that Onkelos is Palestinian in origin and was already committed to writing, at least in part, when it was brought to Babylon, probably after the second Jewish revolt (135 C.E.).[3] Some scholars have used the expression 'Proto-Onkelos' apropos of 4 QtgLev. It is at all events clear that Onkelos reflects the teachings of the Tannaim (doctors of the first–second centuries C.E.) and above all the literalist methods of exegesis of the school of Akiba (compare Gen. 3:22; Exod. 20:24).[4] Concern to preserve in the version the closest possible fidelity to the Hebrew led to the suppression of some paraphrases, preserved in the Palestinian Targum, which are necessary for an understanding of the abridged text of Onkelos (compare Gen. 3:15, 22; 22:14; Deut. 1:1...). But a multitude of halakic and haggadic aggenda have remained; Onkelos is indeed sometimes paraphrastic

[1] See A. Díez Macho, 'La lengua hablada por Jesucristo', *Oriens Antiquus*, 2 (1963), 105. For Qumran, cf. E. Y. Kutscher, 'Genesis Apocryphon', 10.

[2] I have provided a long, though incomplete, list in *Introduction à la littérature targumique* (Rome, 1966), p. 86.

[3] Cf. S. A. Kaufman, 'Job Targum', 327 ('The final Palestinian form of Targums Onkelos and Jonathan must...date between 70 A.D. and the fall of Bar-Kochba'); A. Tal (Rosenthal), *The Language of the Targum of the Former Prophets and its Position within the Aramaic Dialects* (Tel-Aviv, 1975), p. x ('The compilation of this section of TJ (= Targum Jonathan) is not to be dated later than the crushing of Bar-Kochba revolt'); J. Greenfield, 'Aramaic', in *IDBSup*. (Nashville, 1976), p. 40.

[4] Cf. Berliner, *Targum Onkelos*, pp. 107–8; A. E. Silverstone, *Aquila and Onkelos* (Manchester, 1931), pp. 107–22.

whilst the Palestinian Targum gives a literal version (Gen. 43:15; Exod. 22:30; 23:18; Deut. 16:2; 24:16; 33:26). It has preserved the messianic exegesis of Gen. 49:10 and Num. 24:17 and certain of its interpretations, such as that of Exod. 4:25–6 which sees an expiatory significance in the blood of circumcision, accord with a pre-Christian Palestinian interpretation.[1]

It is the encounter of the Palestinian teachers, fleeing from Roman persecution, with the more literalist traditions of Babylonia, which explains the development of a Targum like Onkelos, a 'definitive and academic redaction, executed in a scholarly Aramaic on the basis of older texts'.[2] This version was to return to Palestine after the Arab conquest and progressively to supplant the ancient Palestinian Targum. But to some extent it underwent the influence of the Masoretic schools of Tiberias, and it was under this form that it was transmitted in Judaism. Manuscript study should before long make possible the discovery of the pure and ancient form of the version, typical of Babylon.

The supremacy of Onkelos caused the diverse recensions of the ancient Palestinian Targum, whose halakah was no longer up to date, to fall by degrees into desuetude. They were scarcely any longer recopied, or only fragmentarily; this explains the tormented history of the Palestinian Targum, of which today we possess only two complete manuscripts in two different recensions.

The *Palestinian Targums* of the Pentateuch represent the ramifications of a form of oral Targum which never knew an official, unified recension. Even within one given recension the variations are important.[3] Thus it is utopian to expect ever to get back to an *Urtext* of the Palestinian Targum: each version must be judged on its relation with the Hebrew original and not by reference to a targumic prototype. It is improbable that the Jews had had a standard Targum before the fixation of the Hebrew text, about the beginning of the second century C.E. Our targumic recensions correspond, therefore, to an epoch in which an oral tradition, the content of which is often pre-Christian, was progressively put into writing in an Aramaic dialect still in use among the people. But to exactly which region and which epoch do they

[1] Cf. G. Vermes, *Scripture and Tradition in Judaism* (Leiden, 1961), pp. 178–92. See also his article, 'Haggadah in the Onkelos Targum', *JSS*, 8 (1963), 159–69 and the list of haggadic addenda in Onkelos given by Berliner, *Targum Onkelos*, pp. 224–45.

[2] G. E. Weil, *REJ*, 131 (1972), 45.

[3] This was made clear when the Cairo fragments published by P. Kahle provided several versions of a single passage: compare, e.g. Gen. 38 and 43 in manuscripts D and E.

belong? This is a thorny problem.[1] Reduced to writing, at first only fragmentarily, following interpretations which readily became traditional – thanks, partly, to the memorization imposed upon the *meturgeman* – the Targum of the Torah was probably fairly soon completed. But all these recensions still wait for definite clarification of their confused history.

The Palestinian Targum is known in two forms, one *complete* in the Targum known as *Pseudo-Jonathan* (because of an erroneous reading of TJ = Targum Jerushalmi) and in the recension of *Codex Neofiti* 1 (N) of the Vatican Library; the other, very *incomplete*, is represented by some 850 verses included as marginal variants in various manuscripts, especially in those of Onkelos. They were published for the first time in the Rabbinic Bible of D. Bomberg in 1517 and are commonly called the *Fragmentary Targum* or *Targum Yerushalmi* II (TJ II), as distinct from Pseudo-Jonathan which is called *Targum Yerushalmi* I (TJ I). Much discussion has gone on – and continues – regarding the origin of Targum Yerushalmi II. Sometimes, the paraphrase covers entire chapters (especially in Deut.), at other times all that remains is one or two words or a midrash on a verse. The material of this miscellaneous collection often agrees with that of one or another of the other recensions. These fragments are sometimes to be found transcribed, one after another, in manuscripts (such as the MS. *Hebr.* 110 of the Bibliothèque Nationale in Paris, or *Vat. Ebr.* 440), or inserted beside the corresponding text of Onkelos (as in the *Codex 1* of Leipzig). Some remains of the Palestinian Targum found in the Cairo Geniza and published in 1930 by P. Kahle incontestably go back to *complete* recensions and should not be incorporated under the term *Fragmentary Targum*.

Pseudo-Jonathan is less a translation than a paraphrase which constantly incorporates halakic and haggadic data. In its language and interpretation it has been much influenced by Onkelos – but this influence could have come about partially before the formation of Onkelos as we now know it. *Lectiones conflatae* often combine the readings of the Palestinian Targum and Onkelos, and it is a matter of debate whether the basic text is a Palestinian text influenced by Onkelos, or a Targum Onkelos filled out with Palestinian traditions. The contribution made by Tanaitic midrashim is so important that, for correct interpretation, it must always be read 'in parallel' with the Midrash. The final redaction is post-Talmudic. Exod. 26:9 mentions

[1] Cf. J. A. Fitzmyer, 'The languages of Palestine in the first century A.D.', *CBQ*, 32 (1970), 501–31; A. Díez Macho, 'Le Targum palestinien', *Revue des Sciences religieuses*, 47 (1973), 169–231.

the six *sedarim* of the Mishnah and Gen. 21:21 gives the names of the wife and daughter of Muhammad, Adisha and Fatima. But, on the other hand, the marks of a high antiquity for some of the material in Pseudo-Jonathan are not lacking, such as the prayer for John Hyrcanus the high priest (Deut. 33:11) of which R. Meyer has made use to clarify the ancient history of the Qumran sectaries.[1] Used in a critical way, it furnishes a mass of information on an ancient Jewish tradition, as is proved by the numerous passages which are not in accord with the halakah. The text of Pseudo-Jonathan, which lacks only some fifteen verses, is known in only two recensions – a manuscript (British Library Add. 27031) published by M. Ginsburger (Berlin, 1903) and D. Rieder (Jerusalem, 1974)[2] and the text of the *edito princeps* of Venice (1591), made use of in the Polyglots and Rabbinic Bibles, the original manuscript of which is, however, lost.

It is the *Geniza Fragments* of Cairo which contain the Palestinian Targum in its most ancient form, as yet uninfluenced by Onkelos. They were written by scribes who still spoke Aramaic. Soon after the publication of P. Kahle's edition (*Masoreten des Westens II*, Stuttgart, 1930), A. Marmorstein was able to demonstrate the antiquity and the interest of the traditions they preserve.[3] They have done much to reverse the thesis of the priority of Onkelos over the recensions of the Palestinian Targum, sustained by many since G. Dalman. At the same time they have made it possible to recognize in Neofiti 1 an authentic Palestinian Targum.

Neofiti 1 is a practically complete recension of a family of the Palestinian Targum very close to the Cairo fragments and the fragmentary Targum. This manuscript of 447 parchment folios, catalogued in the Vatican as an Onkelos Targum, was identified in 1956 by A. Díez Macho of the University of Barcelona. The date of composition he has put forward (second century C.E.) has been contested, but to pronounce with certainty we must await the results of further studies and the careful dating of all the elements of this mixed version. The great

1 R. Meyer, '"Elia" und "Ahab" (Tg. Ps-Jon. zu Deut. 33:11)', in *Abraham unser Vater*, Festschrift für O. Michel (Leiden, 1963), pp. 356–68. On the interpretation of this text, see the reservations put forward by B. Schaller in *JSJ*, 3 (1972), 52–60.

2 Publication followed in 1984 of the text of Pseudo-Jonathan and a Concordance by E. G. Clarke of Toronto.

3 A. Marmorstein, 'Einige vorläufige Bemerkungen zu den neuentdeckten Fragmenten des jerusalemischen (palästinensischen) Targums', *ZAW*, 49 (1931), 231–42. Various other fragments from the Geniza have since been published. A new edition by M. L. Klein of all the fragments so far identified is in the press. Cf. M. L. Klein, 'Nine fragments of Palestinian Targum to the Pentateuch from the Cairo Genizah (Additions to MS A)', *HUCA*, 50 (1979), 149–64.

antiquity of the bulk of this recension seems to us beyond doubt.[1] Neofiti 1 sometimes reflects a pre-Masoretic *Vorlage*, offers a halakah anterior to that of the Tannaitic midrashim and, at all events, has none of the addenda which oblige us to ascribe a relatively late date to the final redaction of Pseudo-Jonathan. It has nevertheless undergone in the course of transmission the influence of Onkelos, as it has that of rabbinic vocabulary and exegesis.

The interest of the multiple marginal variants lies in the fact that they bear witness to the existence of other recensions and confirm variants already known; they often manifest surprising agreement with the Cairo Geniza fragments[2] and there is no reason to doubt their authenticity and take them for mere scribal corrections.

The rabbinic citations in the ancient Midrashim prove that a text comparable to Neofiti 1 (and not Onkelos) was known to the Palestinian Tannaim, and we may well ask, in view of the uniformity of certain translations (such as that of 'a land flowing in milk and honey'), whether Neofiti 1 is not a quasi-official recension representing the exegesis most commonly accepted in Palestine in the second–third centuries C.E. As regards the Aramaic of Neofiti 1, once purged of the influence of Onkelos and of the mistakes of copyists, it might restore to us a form of Aramaic spoken at a fairly early date. Neofiti 1 also provides the possibility of sorting out that which is original and ancient in *Pseudo-Jonathan*, that which is Palestinian in Onkelos, and of posing within a wider framework the problem of the relations between the Peshitta and the ancient Palestinian Targum. The later date of the copy of the manuscript (1504) no doubt explains the fact that it has been transmitted in a rather careless fashion; at least 26 whole verses are missing, and about 154 verses are distorted by the omissions of scribes or the erasures of the censor Andrea de Monte (died 1584).[3] These, however, are easily restored, thanks to parallel recensions.

[1] See the series of *Introductions* in the *editio princeps* by A. Díez Macho, *Neophyti 1. Targum Palestinense Ms de la Biblioteca Vaticana*, 6 vols. (Barcelona–Madrid, 1968–79); R. Le Déaut, *Targum du Pentateuque*, Tome I *Genèse* (SC 245) (Paris, 1978), pp. 38–41; M. Kasher, *Torah Shelemah* (Jerusalem, 1974), volume 24 (Aramaic Versions of the Bible. A Comprehensive Study of Onkelos, Jonathan, Jerusalem Targums and the full Jerusalem Targum of the Vatican Manuscript Neofiti 1).

[2] E. G. Clarke, 'The Neofiti 1 marginal glosses and the fragmentary Targum witnesses to Gen. VI–IX', *VT*, 22 (1972), 257–65; R. Le Déaut, 'Lévitique XXII 26–XXIII 44 dans le Targum palestinien. De l'importance des gloses du *codex Neofiti 1*', *VT*, 18 (1968), 458–71; S. Lund and J. Foster, *Variant Versions of Targumic Traditions within Codex Neofiti 1*, SBL Aramaic Studies 2 (Missoula, 1977).

[3] Cf. R. Le Déaut, 'Jalons pour une histoire d'un manuscrit du Targum palestinien (Neofiti 1)', *Bib*, 48 (1967), 509–33.

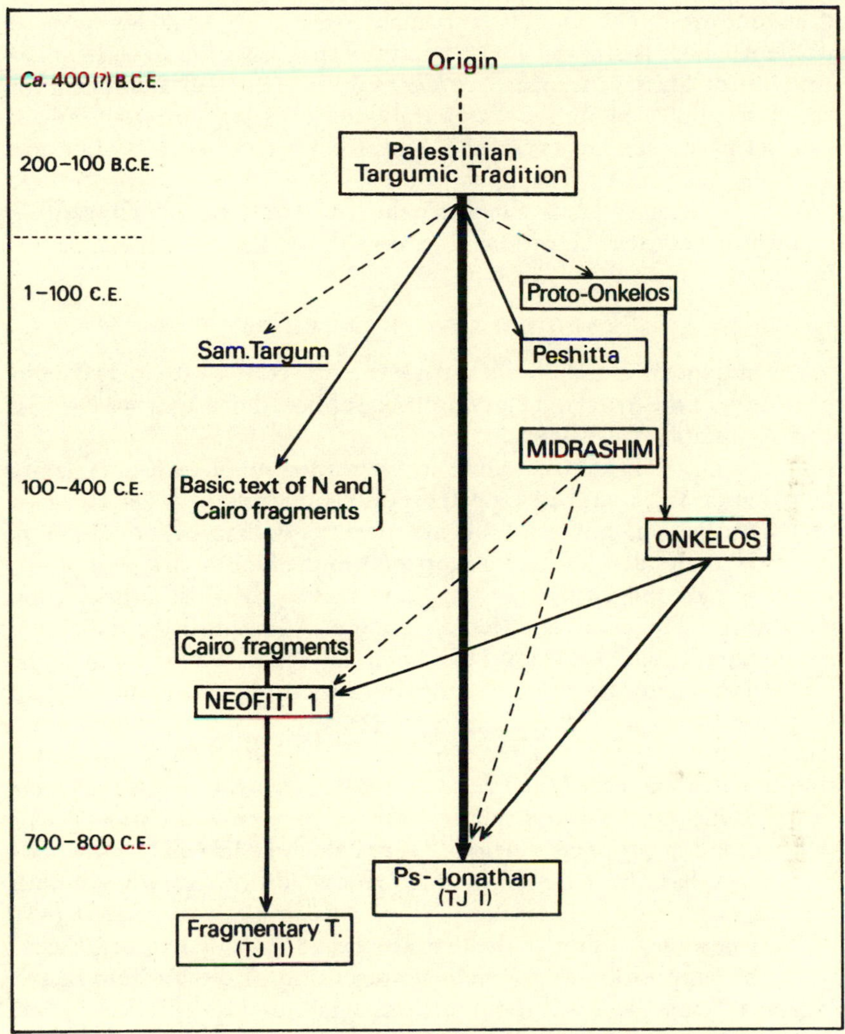

Fig. 2 Aramaic versions of the Torah.

It is necessary, finally, to mention the *Samaritan Targum* of the Pentateuch. What is in question here is a literal version, but one which has never known a *textus receptus*, the recensions varying among themselves as we have seen in the case of the Palestinian Targum. As is shown by the Graecisms, the affinity with expressions from the New Testament, the Palestinian Targum and Marqah, a Samaritan writer of the fourth century, the committal to writing goes back to the fourth–

fifth centuries. The linguistic coincidences with Onkelos pose a problem which is still debated; it may be that what we have here are survivals of literary Aramaic (*reichsaramäisch*). The Samaritan Targum was first published in the Paris Polyglot of 1645 (after a Vatican manuscript copied in 1514) and was followed in that of London (1657).[1]

A provisional schema of the principal relations which can be established between the various Targums of the Pentateuch is given in Fig. 2.

TARGUMS TO THE PROPHETS

Since readings from the Prophets took their place at a very early date in the liturgy of the Synagogue, it might be supposed that they were given an interpretation in Aramaic.

The official Targum, according to the testimony of *b. Meg.* 3a, bears the name of Jonathan ben Uzziel, a famous disciple of Hillel (*circa* 50 C.E.). Here again, however, we are dealing with a misnomer; it is suggested that it derives from a supposed connection with Theodotion, the author of the Greek version. The history of this Targum, the uniformity of its characteristics, its style and its language, make it a perfect parallel with Onkelos. Palestinian in origin, it too was brought to Babylon where, after centuries of revision, it must have received its definitive form towards the seventh century. It is less literal than Onkelos; we note too that the version of the *Latter Prophets* is more paraphrastic than that of the *Former Prophets* – above all in view of their greater difficulty. Tradition places this Targum in a tradition going back to the last prophets Haggai, Zachariah,and Malachi (*b. Meg.* 3a). A. Sperber has already published a critical edition in two volumes (Leiden, 1959, 1962).

The Palestinian origin of the text attributed to Jonathan ben Uzziel led to the supposition of a *Palestinian* recension of the Targum of the Prophets. Some Jewish authors such as Rashi or David Kimchi cited passages from it as *Targum Yerushalmi*; other passages were copied out in the margins of such manuscripts as the *Codex Reuchlinianus* (written in 1106) published by P. de Lagarde in his *Prophetae Chaldaice* (1872).[2]

[1] A. Tal has provided the first critical edition in two volumes: Part I: *Genesis, Exodus* (Tel-Aviv, 1980); Part II: *Leviticus, Numeri, Deuteronomium* (Tel-Aviv, 1981). A detailed *Introduction* appeared in 1983. Cf. my review in *Bib*, 65 (1984), 270–73.

[2] These variants were subjected to detailed study by W. Bacher, 'Kritische Untersuchungen zum Prophetentargum', *ZDMG*, 28 (1874), 1–72. Among them 80 are introduced as being *Targum Yerushalmi*. On the nature of these texts cf. R. Kasher, 'The Targumic additions to the *Haphtara* for the Sabbath of Hanukka', *Tarbiz*, 45 (1975–6), 27–45.

P. Grelot and A. Díez Macho[1] have recently recognized various other fragments of a Palestinian recension of a Targum of the Prophets. There are probably still others among the ancient *Maḥzorim* (such as Isa. 10:32 to 11:11 and Hab. 2:20 to 3:19 in *Maḥzor Vitry*, pp. 168–71) or among the prophetic quotations scattered throughout the Palestinian Targums (compare Targum S. of S. 1:1 citing Isa. 30:29). One can easily understand the interest of a Palestinian recension unrevised by the Babylonian authorities, especially for an understanding of the ancient messianic interpretation of certain prophetic oracles.[2] Some chapters (for example, Isa. 53) have undergone a radical adaptation to later rabbinic ideas. Nevertheless the Targum of the Prophets has retained a fair number of messianic interpretations (compare 2 Sam. 23:4; Isa. 4:3; 13:12; 40:31; Hos. 6:2; Mic. 5:1), also found in the Haggada.[3]

TARGUMS TO THE HAGIOGRAPHA

Although we possess versions of the Hagiographa (and even, in the case of *Esther*, three recensions), none of them has had the benefit of official recognition. In fact, apart from the *Megilloth* (from a date which it is difficult to determine with any precision) they were not read in the Synagogue. Each Targum has its own character, its own special history and its particular problems. As language and traditions indicate, all are Palestinian in origin, but their dates of composition range at least from the fourth to the seventh centuries C.E. Even though we find ourselves here face to face with ancient traditions, the bulk of this material indicates a period other than that which we are considering here.

The late date of the redaction has permitted a considerable influence of the language and ideas proper to Babylonian sources. Let us note merely that the Targum of Job has very little in common with that of Qumran and probably with that condemned by Rabban Gamaliel. It has many affinities with that of Psalms and, like the latter, it often contains a double or even a triple version of the same verse. The surprising similarity between the Targum of Proverbs and the Syriac translation has not yet been satisfactorily explained. A Targum of

1 'Un nuevo Targum a los Profetas', *EstBib*, 15 (1956), 287–95; 'Un segundo fragmento del Targum Palestinense a los Profetas', *Bib*, 39 (1958), 198–205; P. Grelot, 'Une tosephta targoumique sur Zacharie II, 14–15', *RB*, 73 (1966), 197–211; 'Deux tosephtas targoumiques inédites sur Isaïe LXVI', *RB*, 79 (1972), 511–43.

2 P. Grelot, 'L'exégèse messianique d'Isaïe LXIII, 1–6', *RB*, 70 (1963), 371–80.

3 P. Humbert, *Le Messie dans le Targum des Prophètes* (Lausanne, 1911); P. Churgin, *Targum Jonathan to the Prophets* (New Haven, 1927), pp. 93–110.

Chronicles first came to light only with the edition of M. F. Beck (Augsburg, 1680–83), and we have published a hitherto unknown text of this Targum (1971) based upon *Cod. Vat. Urb. Ebr. 1*. The Targums of the Hagiographa are to be found in a convenient form in de Lagarde's *Hagiographa Chaldaice* (Leipzig, 1873) or in A. Sperber's edition (Leiden, 1968) – which, however, lacks Job, Psalms and Proberbs.

THE TARGUMIC METHOD

Targum is often referred to as if it were a uniform body of works; Targum is in fact a generic term covering numerous recensions, each one of which must be evaluated with its own appropriate methods. Nevertheless, there exist common characteristics which permit us to describe here some general tendencies.

A problem still debated is that of establishing the course of development taken in the history of biblical versions. Was the development from the paraphrastic to the literal, or from the literal style towards amplification? Solid arguments may be found for either positions, particularly when all the versions are taken into account. Onkelos is certainly a reduction from a Targum of a more elaborate form. On the other hand, the Targums of Qumran and the case of LXX seem to show that in ancient times the written Targum was intended to be no more than a translation, including only the minimum of addenda necessary to the comprehension of the text. But what about the oral paraphrase, more or less improvised, the character of which must have varied enormously with the competence of the translator and the nature of his audience?

It is impossible to pronounce upon the most ancient form of the Targum during the period of principally oral transmission. To take the length of a paraphrase as a criterion for deciding upon a date, ancient or more recent, is entirely arbitrary. It may well be that the attempts at a revision in the Greek, attested by the ancient recensions of the LXX in Palestine,[1] reveal a reaction against the excesses of biblical paraphrase. At all events, the later rabbinic reaction, and the precise rules imposed upon the translator (*Meg.* 4.4) are to be explained by the existence of real abuses in this matter. We wonder, however, whether the first written Targums were not rather 'guides to translation', closely following the original and at the same time leaving to the extempore

[1] D. Barthélemy, *Les devanciers d'Aquila* (Leiden, 1963). If the *Letter of Aristeas* is in answer to criticism of the LXX, the movement towards literalness might well be ancient; cf. S. P. Brock, 'The phenomenon of the Septuagint', in *The Witness of Tradition*, OTS 17 (1972), p. 24.

efforts of the *meturgeman* the developments he drew from a fund of oral tradition. As regards the ancient period we can draw no sure conclusions from Targums written at a later date, which meet peculiar needs and belong to an epoch when an age-old tradition of biblical interpretation has been distilled. This was also the time in which the *Midrashim* were collected in writing, and the Targums often represent a partial fusion of two literary genres, Midrash and Targum.

All translation implies an interpretation, a seeking-out of the meaning and the significance of the text, in the broad sense a midrash.[1] An ancient version such as the Targum will not hesitate to go beyond the text so as clearly to bring out its implications, working in the halakic and the haggadic interpretation given by tradition to the passage. The text is transmitted along with its commonly received exegesis, and some authors – who would have it they are translators – like those of the Greek Bible – have frequently transmitted the sense given by current exegesis rather than that of the original. How could they have done otherwise in the numerous cases in which the sense of the original was not plain?[2]

The technique of Targum may be summed up in terms of a double concern for *making a text immediately comprehensible* – and not merely translating it – and making it *alive and immediately relevant* to the listeners in the congregation of a Synagogue – a concern for explanation and actualization which is also the fundamental principle of midrashic activity. The presuppositions of targumic exegesis are precisely those of Midrash, and are already to be seen at work in the development and the transmission of the text of the Bible itself.[3]

To ensure immediate comprehension, the Targum does not hesitate to modify the syntax of the original, to replace an interrogative with an affirmative (Targum of Jeremiah 18:14, 11 QtgJob 34:13), or to make use of direct speech and the second person so as to enliven the text (11 QtgJob 38:8). Where clarity demands, subjects and complements are supplied – and sometimes, to establish the connection between two episodes, a whole story. The Bible being conceived as a *unity*, these connections are thought of as necessary; but at times they modify the

[1] Cf. *CHJ*, vol. 4, ch. 9. Certain phenomena mentioned further on appertain to the context of any translation. They become *targumisms* because they arise spontaneously in the ancient liturgical versions.

[2] Cf. M. H. Goshen-Gottstein, 'Theory and practice of textual criticism', *Textus*, 3, (1963), 130–58.

[3] Cf. I. Heinemann, *The Methods of the Haggadah* (Hebrew) (3rd edn., Jerusalem, 1970); I. L. Seeligmann, 'Voraussetzungen der Midraschexegese', *Congress Volume, Copenhagen 1953*, VTSup, 1 (Leiden, 1953), pp. 150–81.

sense of a passage by virtue of its being interpreted in terms of a different context. Thus it is that the revolt of Korah is linked with the regulation concerning fringes (Num. 15 to 16; compare Pseudo-Philo 16) and the episode of Peor with the story of Balaam (Num. 24 to 25; cf. Rev. 2:14).

Obscure words and formulae are interpreted, uncommon terms are rendered in more simple words, especially in the case of *hapax legomena* (e.g. 11 QtgJob 21:20; 40:12; 41:14). A single term may replace many corresponding Hebrew terms; thus, in 11 QtgJob, *'ḥd* (to take) translates at least five different terms, and *ḥṭ'* (to sin) translates four verbs in the original. A precise sense is given to unduly vague terms (*ksp* = silver is rendered by *zuz* = a silver coin in 11 QtgJob 27:16), or to terms lending themselves to different interpretations – in 11 QtgJob 33:24 the word *šḥt* (grave or corruption) is translated as *ḥb*[*l'*] which demands the sense of corruption (compare Acts 2:27). Sometimes two terms make the sense of a single word more explicit, as in 11 QtgJob 30:15 ('my welfare...my dignity'); 39:20 ('terror and fear'); 42:2 ('strength and wisdom').

Concern for clarity leads to the giving of the real meaning of a metaphor or of an allegory (compare Targum of Isa. 5) or of a parable (Targum of 2 Chron. 25:18); comparisons and images are expressed in concrete language, as are metonymies – 'earth and heaven' become '*the inhabitants* of the earth' (Targum of Genesis 41:47 Onkelos) and '*the angels* upon high' (Targum of 2 Chronicles 16:31).

Questions which might arise in the minds of listeners receive an answer in the translation itself. The Targum explains the origin of Noah's vine after the flood (Gen. 9:20), and whence came the Egyptian in the camp of the Israelites (Lev. 24:10), how Noah could be aware of what happened whilst he was asleep (Gen. 9:24) and how the baker could know that Joseph had rightly interpreted his colleague's (the butler's) dream (Gen. 40:16). Lacunae and contradictions, real and apparent, are eliminated; for the Bible, as a sacred book, cannot contain errors. Thus it is that it could not really say (Gen. 4:26) that Enosh was able to invoke the name of Yahweh, which was not revealed until long after his time (Exod. 3:15). Every passage which might run the risk of being misunderstood at once receives a clear and 'orthodox' interpretation (for example, Gen. 3:22; 20:13). Each version, in its own way, escapes from the implication, insupportable for a theology of divine omniscience, implicit in Gen. 4:14, that it is possible to hide oneself from the face of God.

This touches upon the essential aspect, that of the *actualization* and the adaptation of the text. This must reflect the religious conceptions of the people, and correspond to its developed ideas, in particular as regards the divinity. Hence the concern to avoid not only unduly anthropomorphic formulae, but still more all that might prejudice the transcendence of God and the infinite respect which is his due. This use of substitutes and periphrases to avoid the pronunciation of the divine Name is well known: thus *Memra* (Word), (*Kabod*) (Glory), *Shekinah* (Presence), locutions such as 'before Y' or 'in the presence of Y' (*qdm* or *mn qdm*), the use of the passive in place of the active, and so on. As yet, in respect of the ancient period, no wholly convincing history has been written of these usages, which are widely attested in the texts we possess, but which must have undergone constant revision in the light of rabbinic theology.

As regards the ancestors and the people of Israel, an analogous tendency leads to a 'retouching' of compromising or inglorious formulae and episodes, as in the cases of Abraham, Moses and Aaron. Consider the story of David and Bathsheba, passed over in embarrassed silence in Chronicles which, however, retains a formula ('David remained at Jerusalem': 1 Chr. 20:1) which is meaningful only in so far as it introduces the episode in question (2 Sam. 11:1).

Actualization leads to the inclusion in the version of the conceptions of the milieu and the epoch concerning messianism, eschatology, angelology, the cult of the Torah, concerning the facts and the personages of biblical history, whose image is constantly retouched – often diversely, according to the diverse currents of Judaism. Thus the Targum becomes a valuable source for the history of religious ideas. In this way, a good knowledge of the development of Jewish religion makes it possible, also, to determine the approximate date of the appearance of certain traditions and therefore to date the redaction of the relevant targumic passages.

Concretely, the concern with actualization will lead to 'sociological' adaptations (by readjustment to contemporary customs and institutions), or readjustments of a geographical or historical sort (compare LXX with Isa. 9:11 where 'Syria and the Greeks' replaces 'Aram and the Philistines'). This logical and natural process (to be found already in the transmission into Akkadian of the Sumerian epics) went on down to the last redaction of the Targums. Accretions and modifications of this kind, therefore, can serve only to date the precise context in which they were inserted and not the basic text.

Paraenetic or horatory actualization is expressed by the insertion of brief exhortations (compare Exod. 20), exclamations (Exod. 32:19;

Num. 11:7), and by all the artifices of a pious rhetoric aimed at drawing attention to the Law and promoting its practice.[1]

In these elaborations of the text, the targumist does not proceed in an arbitrary fashion but in accordance with recognized principles such as that of the unity of the Scriptures, implying that the Bible must be explained, first and foremost, in terms of the Bible. This may be manifested in the use of quotations, allusions and parallel passages, recognized as such by the presence even of a single word, and by the making explicit of texts by means of historical references. In this way the elliptical text of Isa. 43:12 is clarified by a reference to Abraham, to Exodus and to the handing down of the Law. A supposedly literal text such as Onkelos does not hesitate to resort to frequent borrowings of parallel passages to complete a too laconic text. The interpreter plainly has no notion of the long history of the development of a text and utilizes it uncritically, although we know that the development of institutions accounts for the contradictions we recognize, for example, in ritual and legislation.

Targumic (and midrashic) procedures were to develop in terms both of techniques and of rules (such as the seven rules attributed to Hillel). But they seem already to take their bearings from certain of these – the antiquity of which is confirmed by the use made of them by the sectaries of Qumran,[2] and, it would seem, by the translators of the Greek Bible.[3] D. Daube and S. Lieberman have, on the other hand, suggested an origin of the rabbinic rules in comparable techniques of the Hellenistic world. The Qumran Targum of Job furnishes examples of exegesis founded on the permutation of consonants (21:20; 39:23; 41:14) and even an example of the technique called *'al tiqré* (do not read...but...) which leads to a double version at 29:7: '...the *mornings* at the city *gates*', the Hebrew *ša'ar* (gate) being read also as *šaḥar* (dawn; compare LXX ὄρθριος).

We may lump together all these phenomena attested in the biblical versions, of which we have mentioned only a few under the name *Targumism*, a tendency incorporating all the mutations, more or less conscious and spontaneous, which occur in the (above all popular)

[1] A. Geiger has nicely summed up the targumic characteristics by the three words *Erklärung* (explanation), *Erweiterung* (amplification), *Ermahnung* (exhortation): *Urschrift und Übersetzungen der Bibel* (Breslau, 1857; 2nd ed. Frankfurt am Main, 1928), p. 452. A good example is Targum of Deuteronomy 1:1.

[2] W. H. Brownlee, 'Biblical interpretation among the sectaries of the Dead Sea Scrolls', *BA*, 14 (1951), 54–76; E. Slomovic, 'Toward an understanding of the exegesis in the Dead Sea Scrolls', *RevQ*, 7 (1969–71), 3–15.

[3] Cf. L. Prijs, *Jüdische Tradition in der Septuaginta* (Leiden, 1948).

translation of the Scriptures, destined to be read and *understood* in a liturgical assembly, and which may equally be manifested in other aspects of the use of biblical texts. The concrete results of this tendency may be called *targumisms*.[1] Of the diverse tendencies, to expansion, to explanation, to adaptation, the most constant is the process of actualization, common to Targum and Midrash, which prevents the Bible from becoming mummified. It might be described as the projection of a problematical present on the facts of the past and of the profound meaning of the past upon present conditions.

CONCLUSION

The Targum, the first link between Scripture and its tradition, constitutes a precious source for understanding not only ancient Jewish hermeneutics (often very remote from our search for the literal sense) and the conduct of the interpreter in relation to the sacred text, but also a mass of information on Jewish ideas from the beginnings of the Christian era down to the talmudic period. The Targum was the Bible of the Jewish people (a *Volksibibel* according to Rendel Harris), and it was upon it that they relied for their understanding of the sacred text. In it we clearly see at work procedures which were already manifested in the final stages of the redaction of the Old Testament. It is from this standpoint they can render the greatest services and not too exclusively that of textual criticism: with them we may in fact consistently expect to find exegetical preoccupations which touch upon the original text but do not necessarily presuppose a different *Vorlage*. Each case must be carefully considered. The advisability of caution in the use of the LXX is, *a fortiori*, as valid for the Targums.[2] Nevertheless they have made a considerable contribution to the history of the formation of the canonical Hebrew text and of the recensions which preceded it.

In face of the extreme anarchy revealed by the manuscripts, the most urgent task for targumic studies is to assemble the material and publish good critical editions, such as those projected by the *Madrid Polyglot*.[3] The use of Targums could then be placed on a more certain basis, as much for textual criticism as for linguistic studies – for which it is

[1] R. Le Déaut, 'Un phénomène spontané de l'herméneutique juive ancienne: le "targumisme"', *Bib*, 52 (1971), 505–25.

[2] R. Le Déaut, 'Critique textuelle et exégèse – Exode XXII 12 dans la Septante et le Targum', *VT*, 22 (1972), 164–75; E. Tov, *The Text-Critical Use of the Septuagint in Biblical Research*, Jerusalem Biblical Studies 3 (Jerusalem, 1981).

[3] A. Díez Macho, *Biblia Polyglotta Matritensia*, Series IV, *Targum palaestinense in Pentateuchum, Numeri* (Madrid, 1977); *Exodus, Leviticus, Deuteronomium* (Madrid, 1980).

necessary to write grammars and up-to-date lexicons for the diverse varieties of Aramaic attested in the Targum. In this respect the solid studies made on the Aramaic of Qumran represent an excellent point of departure and comparison.[1]

We should also apply to the targumic traditions and their redactions the modern methods of form-criticism and redaction-criticism, so as to identify the strictly targumic genre (as opposed to that which is midrashic), to date the diverse strata of these traditions and thus reconstitute the history of their transmission and their development.

The study of Targum is indispensable for that of the Midrash itself: if it is true that there was a long period of biblical interpretation before the need arose for translation, it remains no less possible that the appearance of the midrashic phenomenon in the Bible is contemporary with the first interpretative versions. Midrash and Targum will soon go hand-in-hand, at times even becoming fused in such a way as to be henceforth inextricable. But the pride of place taken by Scripture and its interpretation among all the activities in the life and in the history of the Jewish people, notably in the formation and development of its different sects and movements, all of which take the Scripture as their point of reference, oblige the historian to investigate these sources, hitherto too often neglected, with new techniques – techniques which have been tested in other sectors of modern research.

[1] Cf. J. A. Fitzmyer, *The Genesis Apocryphon of Qumran Cave 1: A Commentary* (2nd edn., Rome, 1971); J. A. Fitzmyer and D. J. Harrington, *A Manual of Palestinian Aramaic Texts* (Rome, 1978).

CHAPTER 17

THE SAMARITANS

THE SAMARITAN HERESY

Jewish and Christian writings of the Roman period bear witness to the existence of a sizeable non-Jewish yet allegedly Israelite sect in the territory of Samaria. The centre of the religious life of this community was Mount Gerizim and the cities and villages adjacent to it, although its constituents were also to be found elsewhere in Palestine and in a diaspora in the Mediterranean world which extended as far as Rome.[1] These 'Samaritans' claimed to be the descendants of the old Israelite tribes of Ephraim, Manasseh, and Levi, and contended that they had faithfully worshipped the ancestral Hebrew God in their spiritual centre at Gerizim from the time of the Israelite conquest of Canaan to that very day. Their community had had, or so they claimed, a continuous and unbroken history throughout this long period. They further maintained that the true centre of Israelite worship had always been, and always should be, at Mount Gerizim. They thus viewed the religion of the descendants of the tribe of Judah, which had Jerusalem as its spiritual centre, as an aberration of the classical Yahwistic faith. Essentially, what the Samaritan community claimed for itself was what the Jewish community claimed for itself: that it was the Israel of God constituted by the Mosaic legislation and sustained by obedience to its precepts. Ultimately, the issue which separated Samaritans and Jews was the question of the true holy place, Jerusalem or Shechem. Neither community was inclined to grant to the other any consideration which might represent acquiescence in the contention between these mutally antithetical positions.

The Jewish community responded to the Samaritan claim by maintaining that the Samaritans were not *ethnically* what they claimed to be. Rather than being the surviving remnant of the old Joseph tribes, these people were, it was claimed, descendants of the colonists who had

[1] On the Samaritan Diaspora, see especially J. A. Montgomery, *The Samaritans, the Earliest Jewish Sect: their History, Theology and Literature* (Philadelphia, 1907), pp. 148–53; Yishaq Ben-Zvi, *Sēfer ha-šōm'rōnīm* (Tel Aviv, 1935), pp. 133–45.

been settled in northern Palestine by the Assyrians in the late eighth century B.C.E. The Jewish account of that settlement, found in 2 Kings 17:24–41, contains a severe indictment of those colonists for their syncretistic religious practices, half-pagan, half-Yahwistic. The Samaritans were consequently called the *Kûtîm* by the Pharisees (so too Josephus, *Antiquities* IX.288, and *passim*) after *Kûtâh*, one of the five Mesopotamian cities from which the colonists were said to have been brought. *Kûtâh* was a city otherwise known to have been a centre of the worship of the Babylonian god Nergal. The insinuation in the use of this untoward sobriquet was clar: Samaritanism was no more Israelite religion than were the Samaritans the descendants of Israelites. Even the use of the term 'Samaritans' (*šōmᵉronîm*) by the Jews in reference to these people (the Samaritans do not appear to have used the term for themselves) appears to have carried a negative connotation. The only place in the Jewish scriptures in which the term is employed as an ethnic designation is in 2 Kings 17:29, where it is used for the racially mixed and religiously syncretistic northern Palestinian population of the late eighth century. Although the epithet *Kûtîm* may have served as a useful anti-sectarian polemic to undercut the Samaritan claim for legitimacy, the use of the term for the contemporary religious community in Samaria was certainly less than fair. That the Pharisees in fact thought more highly of Samaritan religious practice than this opprobrium might suggest is indicated by a number of halakic traditions in which Samaritan practices are mentioned.[1] From these it would appear that the Samaritans were as orthodox as they maintained. Some Pharisaic teachers even went so far as to commend them for the scrupulousness of their religious observances.[2] None the less, the Pharisaic claim concerning Samaritan origins provided the Jews with a decided advantage over the Samaritans in their long-standing quarrel. It moved the centre of discussion from the issue of whether Samaritan religion was true Israelite religion to the question of whether the Samaritans were truly Israelites. This obviated the necessity of matching the claims of Judah against the claims of Joseph, which would have opened to debate those very theological presuppositions which had become axiomatic in the religious foundations of the second Jewish

[1] See *b. Qiddûšin* 76a; *Berākôt* 46b; *Gittin* 10a; *Ḥullin* 46a; cf. also Montgomery, *Samaritans*, pp. 167–82.

[2] So Rabbi Simeon ben Gamaleil: 'Whatever precepts the *Kûtîm* have adopted, they are very strict in the observance thereof, more so than the Israelites.' (*b. Qiddûšin* 76a.) Cf. also the opening lines of the extra-Talmudic tractate *Kûtîm*: 'The usages of the Samaritans are in part like those of the Gentiles, in part like those of Israel, but mostly like Israel' (Montgomery, *Samaritans*, p. 197).

commonwealth, something which the religious leaders of Jerusalem would have wished to avoid.

Early Christian attitudes toward the Samaritans appear to have been more ambivalent. At least one New Testament writer regarded them as being other than 'the house of Israel', although in a category somewhere between Jews and Gentiles (Matthew 10:5–6). Other New Testament writers were, however, more favourably disposed towards the people of Samaria, as is evidenced by such tests as the parable of the good Samaritan (Luke 10:25–37), the story of the Samaritan who was the only thankful leper out of ten who were cleansed (Luke 17:11–19), and the account of Jesus' revelation of his vocation to the Samaritan woman at Jacob's well (John 4:1–42). Inasmuch as these favourable reports contrast with the animus expressed toward the Samaritans in much Jewish writing,[1] it is tempting to attribute these to some peculiar Christian attraction to these people. It would not be difficult to find reasons for this, given the success of the Christian mission in Samaria (so Luke–Acts), and given the fact that the early church found itself in an adversary relationship with the Jewish leaders, in particular the Pharisees, analogous to that of the Samaritans (so John's gospel). It is likely, however, that the early church was no more or no less ambivalent towards the Samaritans than was the Jewish community of that time. Such value judgements as were levelled against the Samaritans, whether affirmative or negative, were usually related to particular religious issues or concerns. When judged by their fidelity to the Torah and their scrupulousness in religious observance, the Samaritans could not be faulted by the Jews. When judged by religious values such as compassion, thankfulness, and faith they received a good report by Christians. It was, however, on the issue of the holy place of Israelite worship that Samaritanism received its ultimate testing. For those within the Jewish tradition for whom the Jerusalem mystique was an essential part of their religious faith, for whom the understanding that true Israelite religion was inextricably related to the belief that Jerusalem was the spiritual centre, Samaritanism as a religion which claimed to be truly Israelite could only be regarded as an arch-heresy. It is one of the ironies of religious history that a religion will be abusive towards its heretics, while maintaining high levels of tolerance for others.

[1] This animus is particularly pronounced in almost every treatment of the Samaritans by Josephus. In addition to representing them as foreigners in origin and reprobates in practice, he accuses them also of considerable mischief. Compare *Antiquities* XVIII.30. The extra-Talmudic tractate *Kûtîm* is a catalogue of rabbinic objections to Samaritans (Montgomery, *Samaritans*, pp. 196–203).

The Samaritan 'heresy' was, of course, deeply rooted in Israelite history, a fact of which the Jews were aware and which caused them no little embarrassment in their relations with the Samaritans. The Hebrew God had been worshipped at Shechem and Gerizim long before a cultic centre had been established for his worship in Jerusalem. In fact, he had been worshipped at a number of sanctuaries in Palestine, north and south, throughout the monarchal period. The Jews did not deny this, but maintained, through the sacred writings they developed and canonized, that in the history of God's dealings with Israel Jerusalem had *become* the chosen holy place to the *exclusion* of other cultic centres. The Samaritans, however, refused to accept the sancity of those writings through which this Jewish claim was maintained. They accepted only the Torah as Scripture, and that in a distinctively sectarian redaction in which the primacy of the Gerizim sanctuary was maintained. For the Jews, then, the seriousness of the Samaritan claim was not simply that it promoted a cultic centre which was a rival to Jerusalem. There was nothing new in this. Rival sanctuaries had existed in pre-exilic times, and they existed as well in post-exilic times. More than that, Samaritanism promoted a theological view of Israelite history which was inimical to the Jewish understanding, for it maintained that the people of Samaria and not the Jews were heirs to the sacred traditions of ancient Israel. The view of sacred history entertained by Jerusalem was aptly stated by the Chronicler, in particular in his account of the history of the post-exilic Jewish community. Although this writer did not use the term Judaism, it was nonetheless about *Judaism* that he was writing in his history. It was his contention that the religion of Israel had been expressed most faithfully in ancient times in Jerusalem, and that it was transmitted in its true form by the exiles of the tribe of Judah who returned from Babylonia to rebuild Jerusalem and its Temple. It was the Jewish community which was heir to the Torah and the sacred traditions of old Israel, and it was to this community that the future of the Israelite faith belonged. Samaritanism as a Jewish heresy had had its origins among those Palestinians who refused to acknowledge the position which the Chronicler had expounded. Although the chronicler had made a strong appeal in his writing for what had been called 'the maintenance of the unity of Judaism under the hegemony of Jerusalem',[1] this proved to be an elusive goal. The centre was not able to hold all of the extant elements of the Israelite–Jewish tradition within its orbit.

[1] R. J. Coggins, 'The Old Testament and Samaritan origins', *ASTI*, 6 (1967–8), 46.

The historical process which eventually brought the Samaritan religious community into being may be traced ultimately to the rift which developed in the late sixth century B.C.E. between the people of Samaria and the returning Jews of the Babylonian exile. Judging from our sources (Ezra–Nehemiah, 1 Esdras) this rift was initiated and intensified by the policies of certain Jewish leaders (from Zerubbabel to Ezra) which tended to exclude significant elements of the native Palestinian population from participation in the spiritual life of the second Jewish commonwealth. The policies of the leaders in Samaria (in particular, those of Sanballat the Horonite in the time of Nehemiah) must also be said, however, to have contributed to the intensification of antipathies between the two communities. The initial incident in the chain of strained relations between Jews and Samaritans in the early Persian period was the rebuff by Zerubbabel of those Samaritan Yahwists who offered their assistance in the rebuilding of the Jerusalem Temple (Ezra 4:1–5). These people were identified as descendants of the Assyrian colonists. The sources do not indicate if courtesies were extended by the returning Jews to Palestinians of native Israelite stock who had not participated in the Exile to Babylonia or the earlier Assyrian exile. Evidently not. The leadership of the post-exilic Jewish community appears to have been limited to those who had participated in the Babylonian Exile, and the people of the land were regarded in general as ethnically and religiously suspect. The contempt of the returnees for the native Palestinian population led to the harassment of the Judeans by their neighbours, the initial seriousness or pettiness of which is difficult to assess. These hostilities become more serious in the time of Nehemiah, when the Samaritan governor Sanballat was in league with Tobiah of Ammon and Geshem of the Arab Qedarite confederacy in efforts to frustrate the reconstruction of the Jewish state. Sanballat's political motivations are quite clear. He was opposed to the development of an economic–political centre in southern Palestine which would have rivalled his own in Samaria, and he was able to muster support in Transjordania and Qedar from those who shared this concern. His opposition to Nehemiah could only have served to intensify the suspicions of the Jews concerning the good will of their neighbours to the north. Likewise, the policies of Ezra must have had a debilitating effect upon Samaritan attitudes towards the Jews. Ezra's attempts to consolidate Judaism through ethnic purification (that is, the outlawing of mixed marriages) were in a sense a continuation of that policy of exclusion first expressed in the time of Zerubbabel.

Although the nature of Samaritan–Jewish relations during the

Persian period might have caused the two societies to regard one another as aliens, there was one important factor which related the two communities, albeit tenuously. There were many in the territory of Samaria who were, as were the Jews, worshippers of the ancestral Israelite God. Many of these were, to be sure, descendants of proselytes to that religion, and the nature of their religious expression was probably syncretistic and, by Judean standards, corrupt. But there were others in Samaria of native Iraelite stock, and very likely many worshippers of the Hebrew God whose practices were as much in accord with classical Yahwistic norms as were those of the Jews. The refusal of the Jewish community to allow the Samaritans to participate in the spiritual life of their society did not cause the Yahwists of Samaria to regard themselves as other than Israelite, and they would scarcely have shared the view of their compatriots to the south that the future of the Israelite faith belonged to the returning exile of Judah. It is not surprising, then, that the Yahwists of Samaria were to build in time their own temple for the maintenance of their religious life apart from the Israelitic community of Judah. The available evidence indicates that the Samaritan temple was built on Mount Gerizim early in the Hellenistic period, at about the same time that the Samaritans took up residence at the site of the ancient Israelite city of Shechem. The Samaritans were to occupy that site until its destruction by John Hyrcanus, around 107 B.C.E. The time of the Samaritan residence at Shechem proved to be one of the most creative periods in the history of the Samaritan people, indeed, the formative period in the history of that community as a religious sect.

THE SAMARITANS AT SHECHEM, 332–107 B.C.E.

FROM THE BUILDING OF THE SAMARITAN TEMPLE TO ANTIOCHUS IV

The date of the building of the Samaritan temple on Mount Gerizim was for many years a subject of considerable debate. This was due to the fact that the only literary source giving an account of its construction (Josephus, *Antiquities* XI.302–25) appeared to many to contain serious chronological difficulties. It is now evident that these difficulties are not as serious as had been thought, and that Josephus is a more reliable witness than many had credited him with being. Josephus dated the construction of the Samaritan temple in the time of Alexander the Great, around 332 B.C.E. The problem in accepting his testimony at face value arose from the nature of the story which he related to provide the background for that event. The story seemed to many to be a variant of a story contained in the Bible of an incident which occurred more that three-quarters of a century before the time of Alexander. According to Josephus, the Samaritan governor Sanballat sought permission from Alexander to build a temple for the vocational benefit of his son-in-law Manasseh, a member of the high-priestly family of Jerusalem (identified as the brother of Jaddua, high priest in Jerusalem). Manasseh had been expelled from Jerusalem because of his marriage to Sanballat's daughter Nicaso, and the Samaritan governor hoped to save his daughter's marriage by building a temple at which Manasseh could function as high priest (*Antiquities* XI.302–8). The memoirs of Nehemiah also contain an account of the expulsion of a priest from Jerusalem, who was said to have been the son-in-law of Sanballat the Horonite (Nehemiah 13:28). The biblical account does not identify the priest by name, but claims that he was one of the sons of Joiada, nephew of the High Priest Eliashib. The Bible says nothing about the building of a Samaritan temple as a result of the incident. Although a few scholars were willing to entertain the idea that these were two separate incidents of intermarriage, involving two distinct Sanballats and two different sons-in-law (the identification of the son-in-law is not the same in the two accounts), most were inclined to think that Josephus had been guilty of an anachronism. It was argued that he had either alluded to an incident which had occurred in the Persian period (the intermarriage and the building of the temple) and incorrectly placed it in the Greek period, or had correctly recorded an event of the Greek period (the building of the temple) and incorrectly associated it with an incident from the Persian period (the intermarriage). Scholarly opinion was about equally divided between these two points of view, but lacking external data to test these hypotheses it was difficult to determine if either position were correct. It has only been in recent times that sufficient external data have become available to resolve the problem raised by Josephus and to enable a proper assessment of his account.

Recently discovered archeological data from the late Persian and Hellenistic periods relating to the Samaritans, Shechem, and Mount Gerizim now indicate that Josephus was most certainly correct in his contention that the Samaritan temple was built in the time of Alexander the Great. There are also data which strongly suggest that he was correct in maintaining that the leader of the Samaritan community at that time bore the name Sanballat (although he could not have been Sanballat the Horonite, the contemporary of Nehemiah). Inasmuch as there is no *a priori* reason why intermarriage between the ruling houses of Samaria and Jerusalem could not have occurred twice within 75 years, there is no reason to maintain that the story in *Antiquities* XI.302–8 must be an anachronistic reference to Nehemiah 13:28. It could just as easily be an account of a separate incident, in which some details are coincidentally similar. It would appear that it was not Josephus but his interpreters who confused the two accounts. This now seems evident on the basis of the following data.

(1) *The Aramaic Papyri from the Wadi Daliyeh*: the recently discovered papyri from the Wadi Daliyeh provide historical data from that period of Palestinian history for which Josephus had few sources (the fourth century to the time of Alexander), and about which little had been known from practically any other source. From these it is learned that there had been a Sanballat who was the father of one Hananiah, governor of Samaria in 354 B.C.E. This Sanballat could not have been Nehemiah's contemporary, for it is known from the Elephantine papyri that Sanballat the Horonite had been succeeded by his sons Delaiah and Shelemiah in the last decade of the fifth century. He could not have been the Sanballat known from Josephus' account who was the contemporary of Alexander the Great, although the chronological situation is such that he could have been his grandfather. This is the first evidence outside Josephus that the name of the illustrious (or notorious) Samaritan governor of Nehemiah's time was perpetuated in subsequent generations. Although these papyri do not give direct evidence of a Sanballat who ruled in Samaria at the time of Alexander's invasion of Palestine, they do provide evidence that papponymy was practised in that ruling house, and they provide a chronological sequence into which a Sanballat III would fit in Alexander's time.[1]

(2) *Excavations at Tel Balatah*: from the excavations of the ancient biblical city of Shechem, it is known that this site was rebuilt in the late fourth century B.C.E. after having been virtually abandoned for nearly two hundred years. This rebuilding was an extensive work involving the refortification of the city and the construction of major public buildings. The rebuilding of Shechem, of what had been in ancient times a major Israelite city with a significant religious and political history, coincided with the rebuilding of ancient Samaria as a Greek city after the suppression of a revolt there by Alexander's general, Perdiccas. It is evident that Shechem was rebuilt by refugees from Samaria. These people were to remain in control of Shechem until the time of its destruction by John Hyrcanus in 107 B.C.E. The develop-

[1] See F. M. Cross, 'The discovery of the Samaria papyri', *BA*, 26, (1963), 110–21.

ment of a cultural–political base at Shechem, adjacent to Mount Gerizim, would have been the natural corollary of the erection of a temple on the sacred mountain. It is now known that this activity was initiated at the beginning of the Hellenistic period, not surprisingly at about the same time Josephus claims the Samaritan temple was built.

(3) *Excavations at Tell er-Ras*: excavations of a Hadrianic temple of the Roman period at er-Ras on Mount Gerizim indicate that this sanctuary had been built upon the foundations of an older temple. The earlier sacred building had been a structure of about twenty metres square and eight metres in height. Pottery finds indicate that this temple dates from the Hellenistic period. There is every reason to think that this is none other than the temple which served the cultic needs of the Samaritan community at Shechem from the time of Alexander the Great to John Hyrcanus (following Josephus).

More details are known of Samaritan history during the last third of the fourth century B.C.E. than of any subsequent period of the Samaritan incumbency at Shechem, thanks not only to Josephus, but to the newer archeological data which may be collated with his account. From these, the following historical reconstruction may be offered: not long before the invasion of the Near East by Alexander the Great, the Persian king, Darius (III), appointed Sanballat (III) as governor in Samaria. Although Josephus states that Sanballat was sent to Samaria, being of the same ethnic background as the people (the *Kûtîm*) he was to govern, it is likely that he was a native-born Palestinian (but with Josephus, of non-Israelite stock) of the ruling family appointed to that position. In order to establish good relations with the south, and perhaps also to promote Samaritan hegemony, Sanballat arranged a marriage between his daughter Nicaso and Manasseh, the brother of Jaddua, the high priest in Jerusalem. The Jerusalem priesthood was, however, disturbed by the marriage, being fearful that this would be a dangerous precedent in regard to intermarriage with non-Jews. They consequently informed Manasseh that he would have to relinquish his priestly prerogatives or divorce his Samaritan wife. Faced with these alternatives, Manasseh informed his father-in-law that he would choose the priesthood. According to Josephus, it was this situation which prompted Sanballat to seek permission from the political authorities to build a temple on Mount Gerizim, it being his intention to provide a sanctuary at which his son-in-law could function as high priest. There is no reason to doubt that this was the precipitating factor in the construction of the Samaritan temple, but there is also no reason to maintain that this was the only motivation for its erection. It would have been politically advantageous for Sanballat to strengthen the loyalties of his people to the Samaritan region by providing them with their own sanctuary, and the Yahwists in Samaria had become increasingly uncomfortable over the years in their relations with Jerusalem. Sanballat first sought authorization for the building of his temple from Darius, but while arrangements were being made the political situation was disrupted by the military incursion into Asia by Alexander. When it became evident that Palestine would come under the control of the Macedonians, Sanballat then found it necessary to deal with Alexander rather than Darius. According to Josephus, the Samaritan governor shifted his allegiance, offering Alexander the use of 8,000 troops in the siege of Tyre, and asking in exchange permission to build the Gerizim temple (*Antiquities* XI.313–25). It was on the basis of this approval that the Samaritan temple was finally built.

This account is preserved in Josephus, being the first of three separate stories concerning Alexander in Palestine. The second account (*Antiquities* XI.326–39) deals with Alexander and Jerusalem, and the third account is again concerned with the Samaritans (XI.340–5). The second of the two Samaritan–Alexander stories differs considerably from the first. In the latter, relations between Alexander and the Samaritans (identified as being from Shechem) are represented as being completely negative. That Josephus was dependent upon three distinct sources in his treatment of Alexander in Palestine is evident and generally acknowledged. It has also been suggested that the first of his three sources was a legend of Samaritan origin, associating the foundations of the Samaritan temple with the illustrious Macedonian hero.[1] This may well have been the case. Such a story would have been useful to Samaritans living under Hellenistic rule, especially those in Alexandria. The legend may also have had currency at Shechem during the Hellenization of the Gerizim sanctuary in the time of Antiochus IV (see p. 605). That the Samaritan legend had some historical basis now seems evident from what is known from Balatah and er-Ras of the cultural and religious renascence of the Samaritan community at Shechem in the Hellenistic period.

The concord between the Samaritans and their Hellenistic conquerors was, however, short-lived. Sanballat died during the second month of Alexander's siege of Gaza (so *Antiquities* XI.325), and his successors proved less skilful in their dealings with the Macedonians. Indeed, a situation arose which resulted in severe punitive measures against the people of Samaria, concerning which a few details are known from

[1] So Büchler. See R. Marcus, *Josephus* vol. 6 (Loeb Classical Library), Cambridge, Mass., 1937), pp. 530–2.

classical writers and from the archeological data associated with the recovery of the papyri of Wadi Daliyeh. According to the Latin historian Quintus Curtius, after Alexander had subdued Palestine and marched into Egypt he left an official named Andromachus in charge of Coele-Syria. During his absence an insurrection is said to have occurred, in which the people of Samaria reportedly burned the prefect alive. The cause of the revolt and other details concerning it are unknown. Upon returning from Egypt, Alexander appointed Menon to succeed the murdered Andromachus, and took steps to suppress the revolt.[1] To this information, Eusebius and Syncellus add that Macedonians were settled in Samaria by Alexander, although in another context Eusebius states that the Greek colony was established by Alexander's general, Perdiccas.[2] The rebuilding of Samaria as a Greek city is known also from the excavations of that site. The severity of the reprisals against the Samaritans is indicated by what is now known to have happened to some of the refugees who fled from that city. A group of Samaritan noblemen and their families, perhaps as many as 300, hastily departed from Samaria, taking with them only a few personal possessions. They sought temporary refuge in a cave in the Wadi Daliyeh in the Jordan valley north of Jericho. Their flight proved of no avail. They were pursued by the Macedonians and put to death to the last woman and child. Josephus did not know of this event, although he was in possession of one source (the so-called third source in his account of Alexander in Palestine) which knew of negative relations between the Samaritans and Alexander. His source adds to our general knowledge the information that some Samaritans were deported to Egypt by Alexander for service in the Thebaid (*Antiquities* XI.345). From elsewhere in Josephus' writing (*Against Apion* II.43) it is also learned that the district of Samaria was given to the Jews as an administrative territory free of tribute by Alexander. Josephus cites Hecateus (Pseudo-Hecateus?) as his source for this information, who notes that this was done out of consideration to the Jews *for their loyalty*. If this tradition is historically accurate, the people of Jerusalem remained aloof from the revolt against Andromachus which was centred in Samaria, and to their own benefit.

The Samaritan Yahwists who had exercised political authority and cultural leadership in Samaria for a considerably long period now

[1] Curtius Rufus, *History of Alexander* IV.8.9–11; Eusebius, *Chronicon* II.223–9, ed. Aucker (II.114–18, ed. Schoene); for the Syncellus sources see the texts cited by R. Marcus, 'Alexander the Great and the Jews', in *Josephus*, vol. 6 (Loeb Classical Library), Cambridge, Mass., 1937), pp. 523–5.

[2] R. Marcus, *Josephus*, vol. 6, pp. 523–5.

found themselves in dire straits. Exiles as they were from their home city, and with no prospects of assistance or succour from Jerusalem, their only hope was in the establishment of a new place of residence. The suggestion that Shechem was repopulated by the disenfranchised Yahwists from Samaria at this particular time, and for this particular reason, provides the best explanation for the renascence of that abandoned site. This situation was not without parallel in the ancient eastern Mediterranean world. As Elias Bickerman has noted, 'It often happened that when a Greek colony was established, native villages under its control formed a union around an ancestral sanctuary.'[1] It was apparently after such a pattern that the Samaritans organized themselves at Shechem and Mount Gerizim.

Not a great deal is known of the Samaritan community during the period from the death of Alexander to the time of Seleucid hegemony over Palestine, *circa* 200 B.C.E. From Josephus (*Antiquities* XII.5–10, following Agatharchides of Cnidus), it is learned that a number of Samaritans as well as Jews were settled in Egypt following Ptolemy I's victory at Gaza in 312, and that those Shechemites maintained a high degree of loyalty to the Gerizim temple. This loyalty, in fact, resulted in hostilities between Jews and Samaritans in Egypt, with each group maintaining that offerings for sacrifices be directed to its respective sanctuary. This issue was to remain a point of contention between the two groups in the Diaspora, judging from the account of a Samaritan–Jewish debate at a later time, during the reign of Ptolemy Philometor (*Antiquities* XIII.74–9). Relations between these two groups in Egypt may, in fact, have been one of the more important factors in the development of strong animosities and hostilities between Shechem and Jerusalem. While it would have been possible for Jews and Samaritans to live peacably in their respective provinces in Palestine, the situation would have been different in Egypt. When Samaritans and Jews lived in the same communities in the Diaspora, it was necessary to defend primary allegiances to the authorities from whom privileges were requested. When a boon for one was a loss for the other, trouble was sure to follow. In returning to their respective homelands, Samaritans and Jews would have brought back those mutual antipathies and resentments which they first experienced in the Diaspora.

The first record of open hostility between the Shechemites and the people of Jerusalem is contained in Josephus, *Antiquities* XII.154–6, and is dated to the time of Ptolemy V (Epiphanes) and Antiochus III (the Great), around 200 B.C.E. According to Josephus, the Jews were

[1] E. Bickerman, *From Ezra to the Last of the Maccabees* (New York, 1962), pp. 43–4.

harassed by the Samaritans at that time, through the despoiling of Jewish land and the taking of Jews as slaves. The historian mentions no provocative activities which might have prompted such acts, but suggests that the Samaritans took advantage of a situation in which the Jews found themselves out of favour with Ptolemy due to the avarice of the high priest Onias. This Onias is identified by Josephus as the son of Simon I (whom he incorrectly identified as Simon the Just) and the father of Simon II (whom most scholars today, following the work of G. F. Moore and S. Zeitlin, identify as Simon the Just). This writer has argued elsewhere that this particular incident of anti-Judaic activity by the Samaritans should be placed in the time of Simon II (the Just), rather than Onias, and that it was related to the Samaritan–Jewish hostilities of Simon's time known from the scholion on the Day of Gerizim in the *Megillat Ta'anit*.[1] According to the latter tradition, the people of Shechem sought to despoil the Jerusalem Temple, but were foiled by Simon the Just, with the result that the mischief was turned back upon the Samaritans and the day (the 21st of Kislev) was declared a festival day for Jews, the 'Day of Gerizim', on which mourning was prohibited. Simon is said to have received the assistance of Alexander the Great (an obvious anachronistic confusion with *Antiochus* the Great) in his great accomplishment. A doublet of the tradition of Simon the Just's meeting with Alexander (i.e. Antiochus) appears in *Yoma* 69a, and this story may also have served as the model of Josephus' account of the meeting of Jaddua and Alexander (*Antiquities* XI.326–39). The traditions concerning Samaritan–Jewish hostilities in the time of Simon the Just provide some clarification for Ben Sira's well-known invective against the 'foolish people (*gôy nābāl*) dwelling in Shechem' (Sirach 50:25–6). Ben Sira's denunciation of the Shechemites follows his laudatory hymn on Simon, and is probably to be understood as arising from his hatred of those people who had caused Simon so much trouble.

Simon's difficulties with the Samaritans appear to have been related to the larger political issues of that day, in particular to the alignment of loyalties in Palestine with either the Seleucids or the Ptolemies. V. Tcherikover has demonstrated that prior to the capitulation of Jerusalem to Antiochus III, the politics of that city had been dominated by a pro-Seleucid party, made up of the priestly aristocracy (including Simon the Just) and the majority of the wealthy and influential Tobiad family.[2] The Tobiad family, however, was engaged at that time in a major dispute between Hyrcanus, son and successor of the famous tax-

[1] J. D. Purvis, 'Ben Sira' and the foolish people of Shechem', *JNES*, 24 (1965), 90–2.

[2] V. Tcherikover, *Hellenistic Civilization and the Jews* (Philadelphia, 1959), pp. 81–9.

farmer Joseph, and his brothers. That this was no mere family quarrel is indicated by Josephus, who states that Jerusalem was divided into two camps, with the majority, including Simon the Just, siding with the elder brothers against Hyrcanus (*Antiquities* XII.228–36). As a result of this situation, Hyrcanus was driven to the Transjordanian area where he built, or rebuilt, the ancestral estate at ʻAraq el-Emir. The political dimensions of this dispute have been astutely assessed by S. Zeitlin: the Jerusalem branch of the Tobiad family was pro-Seleucid; the Transjordanian branch was pro-Ptolemaic.[1] When the gates of Jerusalem were opened to Antiochus III by Simon the Just, around 198 B.C.E., the people of Jerusalem were amply rewarded for their loyalty. Those who had been sympathetic to the Ptolemies did not fare as well. Hyrcanus, for example, fearing Antiochus, took his own life. It thus becomes clear why the Samaritans were suppressed by Antiochus III (following the scholion in *Megillat Taʻanit*). They had sided with the Transjordanian branch of the Tobiad family against the Tobiads of Jerusalem, and paid heavily for what was interpreted as a pro-Ptolemaic policy. The Samaritans had been allied with the Tobiads at a much earlier time, when Sanballat the Horonite and Tobiah the Ammonite had been in league against the Judean governor Nehemiah. That cordial relations between this family and the Samaritans had continued down to the Hellenistic period is evident from the fact that Joseph the Tobiad, the father of Hyrcanus, was financed at the beginning of his career by 'his friends in Samaria' (so Josephus, *Antiquities* XII.168). Cultural and religious sympathies between the Shechemites and the Tobiads of Araq el-Emir would also have been encouraged by the fact that both communities maintained temples at their respective centres. The Samaritan–Transjordanian Tobiad alliance of Simon's time proved, however, to be no more and indeed less helpful for the Samaritans against the Jews than the earlier alliance in the time of Nehemiah. The extent of the suppression of the Samaritans with the shift in political hegemony in Palestine to the Seleucids is indicated by the fact that the people of Shechem made no attempt to resist Seleucid cultural and political domination during the time of Antiochus IV.

FROM ANTIOCHUS IV TO JOHN HYRCANUS

It is evident from Samaritan as well as Jewish sources that the community at Shechem was affected by the Hellenizing activities which

[1] S. Zeitlin, *The Rise and Fall of the Judaean State* (Philadelphia, 1968), I, pp. 69–70.

occurred in Palestine during the reign of Antiochus IV. The Jewish sources do not indicate that the Hellenization of Shechem was as severe or as radical as the Hellenization of Jerusalem, and there is no record of persecution of the Samaritans by Antiochus, or of a subsequent revolt such as occurred among the Jews. According to Jason of Cyrene, Antiochus appointed a governor named Andronicus at Gerizim (2 Maccabees 5:23), and later sent an Athenian (or Antiochian) named Geron to enforce Hellenistic practices and to rename the sanctuary there the Temple of Hospitable Zeus (*Diòs Xeniou*) (2 Maccabees 6:1–2). This was the same person who was said to have been sent to Jerusalem to force the Jews to abandon their ancestral laws and to rename the Jewish sanctuary the Temple of Olympian Zeus (*Diòs Olympiou*). Although Jason claimed that the ensuing situation in Jerusalem was abominable by traditional Jewish standards, he was silent on the situation at Gerizim. To this writer, then, Hellenization was impressed upon the Samaritans, just as it was also forced upon the Jews, with the significant difference that the Jews resisted. Josephus, on the other hand, maintained that the Hellenization of Shechem was not the result of an externally impressed policy, but was rather a situation which the Samaritans sought for their own benefit (that is, to avoid the misfortunes which had come upon the Jews who had resisted Hellenization). To support this claim, Josephus cited a letter allegedly written by the Samaritans to Antiochus, in which they agreed to live by Greek customs and asked that their unnamed temple be named the Temple of Hellenic Zeus (*Diòs Hellēniou*) (*Antiquities* XII.257–64). It is evident that Josephus was not the author of this document, for there is a significant contradiction between his précis of the communication and the letter itself. Josephus reports that the Samaritans represented themselves as colonists from the Medes and Persians (following his earlier account of Samaritan origins), whereas the letter claims that the Samaritans were of Sidonian origin. Nor was the letter as self-damning as Josephus intimated. In it, the Samaritans simply stated that they were a people distinct from the Jews in ethnic background and custom (although similarities existed in regard to Sabbath observance and temple worship) and that they wished to be acquitted of any charges of which the Jews were guilty. It is likely that Josephus' source at this point was in fact a document of Samaritan origin, and that if it did not represent the opinion of all Samaritans it at least reflected the viewpoint of a Hellenistic party in Shechem.[1]

[1] Following Zeitlin, *Judaean State*, p. 93, and M. Delcor, 'Vom Sichem der hellenistischen Epoche zum Sychar des Neuen Testamentes', *ZDPV*, 78 (1962), 34–48. For an alternative point of view, see E. Bickerman, 'Un document relatif à la persécution

The situation in Shechem in regard to Hellenization may perhaps best be understood by the analogy of the situation which is known to have pertained in Jerusalem. The Jews themselves were divided on the issue of Hellenization, as is indicated by the existence of a party in Jerusalem sympathetic with Greek customs. It is evident that the Hellenistic party there played a significant role in the development of the situation which led to the Maccabean revolt, although the extent of its activity is a matter of scholarly dispute. The Samaritan letter preserved in Josephus may be taken to represent the position of the Hellenistic party in Shechem, which was evidently more successful in promoting an acceptable *détente* between Hellenistic and Hebraic traditions than was its opposite number in Jerusalem. Whether the majority of the Samaritans were sympathetic with the Hellenizers in Shechem or not, the adoption of their policies enabled the community to avoid the difficult and desperate situation in which the Jews found themselves on the eve of the Maccabean revolt. From the Samaritan letter in Josephus it is even possible to identify the Hellenistic party in Shechem by name. The authors of the letter identified themselves as 'the *Sidonians* in Shechem' (*hoi en Sikímois Sidōnioi*). The use of this epithet has prompted some scholars to suggest that there existed a semi-Greek Phoenician colony at Shechem, similar to that which is known to have existed at Mareshah. There is, however, no archeological evidence from Tell Balatah which would support this view. It is more likely that the term was a self-adopted nickname through which the Hellenists identified themselves with Phoenician culture. That the Hellenizing Samaritans called themselves Sidonians is evident also from the Greek fragments of the Samaritan writer Pseudo-Eupolemus, cited by Alexander Polyhistor and preserved in Eusebius.[1] This writer, who skilfully fused biblical and pagan traditions by such identifications as Noah–Belus–Kronos, Nimrod–Belus, and Enoch–Atlas, referred repeatedly to Canaan as Phoenicia and stressed the pre-eminence of Babylonian and Phoenician culture over Egyptian. The work of Pseudo-Eupolemus is important also in providing a clue to the understanding of the nature of Hellenization in Shechem, if not elsewhere in Palestine. If Pseudo-Eupolemus was representative of the movement as a whole, Hellenization was not a complete adoption of Greek culture with the loss of Israelite traditions, but a blending of the

d'Antiochos IV Epiphane', *RHR*, 115 (1937), 188–223. See also A. Schalit, 'Die Denkschrift der Samaritaner an König Antiochos Epiphanes zu Beginn der grossen Verfolgung der jüdischen Religion im Jahre 167 v. chr.', *ASTI*, 8 (1970–71), 131–83.

1 Eusebius, *Praeparatio Evangelica* IX.17–18.

two. This may be seen in Pseudo-Eupolemus' exegesis of Genesis.[1] His perspective was certainly cosmopolitan, but his work was that of the interpretation of the Israelite tradition. There may have been, on the other hand, Samaritan Hellenists who had a more cavalier regard for their Israelite heritage. Such would not be surprising, given the mixed ethnic and religious background of northern Palestine.

It is difficult to assess the long-range effect of the Hellenization of this time upon Samaritan culture. Pagan elements which may have entered the cultus were eventually expunged. Samaritan theological writings of the fourth century C.E. and later reveal the influence of Greek philosophy, but this may have been due to contemporary influences rather than to a residue of Hellenistic thought from an earlier period. In time, Samaritanism became parochial rather than cosmopolitan in its exposition of the Israelite religious tradition. Pagan mythological elements may have survived in Samaritan sectarian movements of the Roman period, to be rejected, however, by mainline Samaritan religious thought. But if the Hellenization of Shechem did not greatly affect the future development of Samaritanism, it certainly adversely affected Jewish attitudes towards the Samaritans. Josephus in particular was piqued that the people of Shechem avoided the misfortunes which fell upon the Jews for their resistance of Hellenization. The acquiescence of the Shechemites to Hellenism, with the concurrent strengthening of parochial Judaism in Jerusalem, would certainly have been a major contributing factor to the Jewish understanding that the Samaritans were pagans rather than Israelites. This impression proved to be difficult to eradicate, even with the later strengthening of classical Israelite traditions among the Samaritans. H. Kippenberg is probably correct in suggesting that the traditions found in Josephus and rabbinic literature concerning the pagan antecedents of Samaritanism were derived from Jewish reaction to this episode in Samaritan history.[2]

The Jewish historical sources are silent on the people of Shechem from the time of the Maccabean revolt to the time of John Hyrcanus. The religious reforms which occurred among the Jews following that revolt are not said to have extended to Gerizim, and the region of Samaria is not mentioned in connection with the military exploits of Judas. Although Judas was engaged in Transjordania, and Simon in the Galilee, the Maccabees bypassed Samaria, perhaps because of the

[1] B. Z. Wacholder, 'Pseudo-Eupolemus' two Greek fragments on the life of Abraham', *HUCA*, 34 (1963), 112–13.

[2] H. G. Kippenberg, *Garizim und Synagoge*, RGVV 30 (Berlin, 1971), p. 85. For an alternative view, see R. J. Coggins, *Samaritans and Jews: The Origins of Samaritanism Reconsidered* (Oxford, 1975), pp. 98–9.

strength of its capital city. Evidently Shechem was of no concern to them, even though the character of their battles had the dimensions of a religious war. It was not until late in the second century B.C.E. that a member of the Hasmonean family took steps to deal with Shechem and its sanctuary, and that for political as well as religious reasons. In 129 B.C.E., following the death of the Syrian ruler Antiochus VII (Sidetes), John Hyrcanus initiated a major military campaign. He captured the Syrian cities Medeba and Samoga, and then pillaged Shechem and Mount Gerizim, destroying the Samaritan temple in 128 B.C.E. He then marched to the south, where he subdued the Idumeans, forcing them to accept circumcision and to adopt the customs and ordinances of the Jews.[1] Not long afterward (*circa* 107 B.C.E.) he besieged Samaria, taking the city and destroying it after one year.[2] From archeological data at Tell Balatah it is evident that the final and complete destruction of Shechem also occurred at this time.

It is not difficult to determine the political reasons for Hyrcanus' military activities in Samaria and Idumea. Jewish control of territories outside of Judea had been one of the major issues of contention between Hyrcanus' father Simon and Antiochus VII. Simon had been commanded by Sidetes to deliver up large sums of money for controlling these regions. Simon had been willing to do this for Joppa and Gazara, but he refused to do so for those territories which he declared to be of 'our ancestral heritage' (1 Maccabees 15:28–36). When Simon was murdered in Jericho, a city populated by Idumeans and outside Judean jurisdiction, the resolution of this issue fell to Hyrcanus. With the death of Sidetes, Hyrcanus moved quickly to establish Judean hegemony, in particular in those areas which his father had declared to belong to Judah. These lands would certainly have included the three districts of Samaria, Aphairema, Lydda, and Rathamin, which were confirmed as Judean possessions by Demetrius II in the time of Jonathan (so 1 Maccabees 10:30, 38; 11:34), and which Josephus claimed had been earlier given to the Jews by Alexander the Great (*C. Apionem* II.43). Territory in the south under Idumean jurisdiction would also have belonged to that land for which Hyrcanus' father had claimed right of possession by ancestral heritage. The religious dimensions of Hyrcanus' military activities may be seen in the destruction of the Samaritan temple and in the forced conversion of the Idumeans. Not only were those territories to be Judean but their inhabitants were to be Jews. The people of Samaria and Idumea were to be brought into that ethnic–spiritual family which was centred in Jerusalem and its

[1] *Ant.* XIII.254–8; cf. *Bell.* I.62–3. [2] *Ant.* XIII.275–81; cf. *Bell.* I.64–5.

Temple. His ambitions for Samaria were, of course, not realized. Although the region was to remain under Judean political control, the people of Samaria refused to be brought under Judean spiritual hegemony. Rather than embracing that form of Judaism which had Jerusalem as its centre, the Samaritans continued to maintain an alternative non-Judean religious system.

Some scholars have maintained that revulsion towards the excessive bloodshed of Hyrcanus, especially in Samaria, may have been one of the contributing factors in his rift with the Pharisaic party (*Antiquities* XIII.288–98). Such hardly appears to have been the case.[1] The Torah had not prohibited offensive warfare against idolaters (with whom the Shechemites would have been categorized, rightly or wrongly, along with the residents of Samaria), and the Judaization of the Palestinian population would most likely have met with Pharisaic approval. Indeed positive reaction to Hyrcanus' humbling of Shechem is indicated in a number of Jewish literary sources of the Hellenistic period. The approval of Hyrcanus' destruction of Shechem is most certainly reflected in the extended account of Simeon and Levi's conquest of that city (following Genesis 34) in the book of Jubilees (30:1–26) as well as in the subsequent account of Jacob's battle against seven Amorite kings in the vale of Shechem (39:1–11; compare *Testament of Judah* 3–7). More striking yet is the reference to the Sword of Simeon against the Shechemites in the prayer of Judith, by which the Jewish maiden strengthened herself for her righteous bloody deed (Judith 9:1–4, compare also 5:16). The slaughter of the Shechemites by Hyrcanus may also be reflected in the locale chosen as the site for Judith's slaughter of Holophernes. Although the identification of Bethulia is not clear, it may have been a pseudonym for Shechem.[2] If it was not Shechem, it was a city somewhere in the territory of Samaria, and the story carries the ironic element of a Jewish victory over a pagan king in a territory notorious for its earlier hostility to Jerusalem. Such a view would have been impossible to entertain if it had not been for Hyrcanus' subjection of this region to Jewish control. Perhaps the strongest approbation of Hyrcanus' conquest of Shechem is reflected in the reference to the Genesis 34 incident in the *Testament of Levi* 7:1–3: 'By thee will the Lord despoil the Canaanites, and will give this land to thee and to thy seed after thee. For from this day forward shall Shechem be called a city of imbeciles (*pólis asynétōn*); for as a man mocks a fool so did we mock them'.

[1] Following V. Tcherikover against V. Aptowitzer. See *Hellenistic Civilization*, p. 256.

[2] So C. C. Torrey, *The Apocryphal Literature* (New Haven, 1945), pp. 91–3.

With the destruction of the sanctuary and the devastation of Shechem by the Hasmonean ruler Hyrcanus, the Samaritans found themselves in a situation very much like their earlier predicament in the later fourth century when they had been expelled from Samaria. On that earlier occasion they had been forced to re-evaluate their status when they were deprived by the Macedonians of political and cultural leadership of the territory of Samaria. They were now faced with a more serious crisis which necessitated defining more clearly their relationship with Jerusalem as well as clarifying their own self-understanding. This was no easy task, for it necessitated substantiating the legitimacy of their independent and distinctive existence apart from Judaism, and there was little in their immediate past of which they could be justifiably proud. The Samaritans responded to this crisis by reaffirming their ancestral Yahwistic faith and by maintaining that their understanding and practice of this faith was in accord with classical Israelite traditions. Not only was their faith the true expression of the ancient Mosaic faith, but Judaism had erred and departed from this faith in transferring its centre from Shechem to Jerusalem. It was the community of Shechem, persecuted by the Jews, and deprived of the opportunity of offering sacrifices on the Holy Mountain, which represented the remnant of the true Israel. The vehicle by which this claim was affirmed and promoted was the distinctively sectarian edition of the Pentateuch promulgated by the Samaritans. It was in this document that the disfranchised priests of Shechem maintained that God had commanded the Israelites to build an altar on Mount Gerizim and to worship only at the place which he had chosen. The command to worship specifically on Mount Gerizim was documented by interpolating lengthy passages from Deuteronomy 27:2, 3a, 4–7, and 11:30 (with the reading Gerizim rather than Ebal in 27:4) at the end of the Ten Commandments in Exodus 20 and Deuteronomy 5. The affirmation that God had already chosen his place of worship (that is, Shechem rather than the late-comer Jerusalem) when Moses gave the Torah was substantiated by the omission of the *yod*-prefix in the twenty-one occurrences of the Deuteronomic phrase 'the place which the hand of thy God will choose'. The omission of the letter changed the tense of the verb from imperfect to perfect: God had already chosen the place. It was none other than Shechem.

Until recently, it had been assumed that the Samaritan Pentateuch as a sectarian monument was a literary product contemporaneous with the construction of the Samaritan temple. It is now evident that this sectarian redaction of the Pentateuch was produced at a much later time, in the late Hasmonean period, roughly contemporaneous with the destruction of that temple.[1] This is evident from three factors: (1) The script in which the Samaritan Pentateuch is written is a distinctive Samaritan form of the paleo-Hebrew writing which eventually fell out of use among Jews but which was revived from time to time down to the second century C.E. From the comparative typological analysis of the Samaritan and Jewish paleo-Hebrew scripts it is evident that the Samaritan script began its independent development from the Jewish paleo-Hebrew in the early first century B.C.E. The script of the Samaritan Pentateuch is not an ancient variety of the paleo-Hebrew writing, but a sectarian script which developed from the paleo-Hebrew of the Hasmonean period. (2) The orthography of the Samaritan Pentateuch is the standard full orthography characteristic of Hebrew writing of the Hasmonean period, which contrasts with the restricted orthography of the Pentateuchal text of both the earlier Greek and the later rabbinic periods. (3) The textual tradition of the Pentateuch used by the Samaritans was one of three textual types now known to have been in use during the Hasmonean period, and which is known to have completed its development as a distinct text-type during that time. The Samaritan Pentateuch could not have been produced prior to the Hasmonean period. It now appears that this sectarian monument was an expression of the response which the Samaritans made to the abusive and repressive measures of John Hyrcanus. The response provided a rationale for the authentic autonomy of the sect, and gave the community a *raison d'être* sufficient to assure its existence from that time to the present day.

In addition to the promulgation of a canonical sectarian edition of the Pentateuch, the Samaritan community would also have felt the need to produce other literature by which its claim for legitimacy could be maintained. Indeed, an abundance of such writings exists, although these are for the most part medieval and modern texts of Aramaic, Hebrew, and Arabic works. Some of the Aramaic literature of the community can be dated to the fourth century C.E., but none with certainty earlier than this time. The determination of which Samaritan traditions in these writings belong to the earlier life of the sect can be made only with great difficulty, and with some caution and reserve. There is good reason, however, for maintaining that medieval Samaritan texts attesting to the genealogy of the Samaritan high priesthood are derived from very old traditions in the history of the sect, going

[1] As is argued by this writer, in *The Samaritan Pentateuch and the Origin of the Samaritan Sect*, HSM 2 (Cambridge, Mass., 1968), pp. 16–87. See also R. Pummer, 'The present state of Samaritan studies: I', *JSS*, 21 (1976), 42–7; and the article by C. D. Mantel in *Bar Ilan, Sefer Ha-Shanah* 7–8 (1970), 162–74.

back perhaps to the Hellenistic period.[1] Just as it was important for the sect to substantiate the primacy of the sacred place, it would also have been important for the religious leaders of that centre to authenticate their priestly legitimacy. This was accomplished through the production of a priestly genealogy in which the legitimacy of a distinct high-priestly succession was authenticated through Eleazar and Phinehas, without recourse to suggesting (as does Josephus) that the Samaritan priesthood was a collateral branch of the Zadokite priesthood in Jerusalem. The Samaritan claim for a legitimate priestly succession independent of Jerusalem would, of course, have been an embarrassment to the Jews. The Zadokite priesthood had failed in Jerusalem and the accession to the high-priestly office by the Hasmoneans was viewed by many Jews as an illegitimate usurpation. The Samaritans could of course have achieved similar results (if embarrassment alone were the motive) by accepting the claim (which was probably true) that their priesthood was derived from the Zadokites in Jerusalem. It was their desire, however, to dissociate themselves from Jerusalem, and to maintain that their cult (place and priests) was derived from the old cultus of Shechem. The synagogue came to replace the destroyed temple as the institutional base of Samaritanism. The development of Samaritanism following the destruction of its temple did not, however, proceed along the same lines as the later reconstruction of Judaism following the destruction of its temple. The Samaritan priesthood continued to be active and to fulfil necessary religious functions within the community. The Passover, for example, remained as a sacrificial rite, over which the high priest presided, and the priests officiated at pilgrimage rites on Mount Gerizim. It is evident from later Samaritan writings that tensions eventually developed between lay and priestly elements within the community and that differences of opinion were held in regard to the relative importance of Gerizim rites and synagogue worship. These tensions were undoubtedly of importance in the development of sectarian movements in Samaritanism during the Roman period.[2]

The Samaritans had come to Shechem at the beginning of the Hellenistic period as a people of mixed ethnic and religious background. When they left that site in the early first century B.C.E., eventually to reside in Neapolis and its environs, it was as a religious community with a very clear self-understanding. During the period of

[1] So Kippenberg, *Garizim*, pp. 60–8. On Samaritan sectarianism during the Roman period, see especially S. J. Isser, *The Dositheans: A Samaritan Sect in Late Antiquity* (Leiden, 1976).

[2] So J. Bowman, 'Pilgrimage to Mount Gerizim', *Eretz Israel* (1964), 17–28.

their incumbency at Shechem their relations with the Jewish community of Jerusalem had deteriorated until it finally became evident that the rupture between them would never be healed. The Samaritans had built a temple which they had regarded as legitimate, by traditional Israelite standards if not by the canons of the cultus of Jerusalem. The destruction of that temple in 128 B.C.E., and the ravaging of their city, was an indication that they would never be accepted on their own terms by their compatriots in Judah. Yet they steadfastly maintained the legitimacy of their autonomy and the authenticity of their expression of the Israelite religious tradition. They substantiated this claim in the promulgation of a distinctively sectarian edition of the Pentateuch. Although there was much in their heritage (from religious syncretism at an early period to Hellenization in the more recent past) which caused many Jews to regard them with suspicion and disdain, they had come to regard themselves not simply as a part of the Israelite nation, but as the true remnant of the ancient Israelite faith. Conversely, they regarded the Jews as a deviant and apostate part of the Israelite nation which had departed from the true faith of which they were the representatives. It was not they who were schismatics from Judaism (as Josephus was to maintain); it was the Jews of Jerusalem who were schismatics from the house of Israel, the spiritual heirs of the schism which had been initiated in ancient times when Eli had removed the sanctuary from Shechem to Shiloh. The authentic adherents of the Mosaic religion were to be found at Mount Gerizim.

CHAPTER 18

THE GROWTH OF ANTI-JUDAISM OR THE GREEK ATTITUDE TOWARDS THE JEWS

The first clear evidence of the Greeks beginning to notice the Jewish people, and the Jewish way of life, comes from the last two decades of the fourth century B.C.E. This new awareness was one of the direct results of the eastern world being thrown open to the enquiring spirit of the Greeks, in the wake of Alexander the Great's victorious expedition (Phoenicia and Syria were conquered in 332 B.C.E.). That huge expansion of human and geographical horizons prompted a new departure in Greek ethnographic studies, which had been enriched, since their first flowering in the period of colonial expansion, by developments in philosophical and theoretical thought. Cultural history, science and religion provided perspectives by which the endless mass of newly available fact could be accommodated in theories based on precise concepts, and judged by carefully formulated canons of interpretation. It is in this context that we should consider the awakening of interest in the Jews and their customs. To establish the chronological sequence in which the first Greek authors reflected and wrote about the Jews is difficult, if not impossible, not only because of our fragmentary knowledge of their works, and because our only clues come from brief excerpts, but also because it is difficult to date the works themselves with any precision. Besides, the need to establish such a chronological priority is obviated, or at any rate greatly diminished, when we consider that these first Greek authors wrote about the Jews quite independently of each other – a fact which seems fairly well established. Theophrastus, Clearchus of Soli, Hecateus of Abdera and Megasthenes appear to us as original, independent witnesses of the Greek discovery of the Jewish world, and they are all the more important for that. The coincidences and the divergences in their accounts indicate on the one hand an interesting similarity of reaction to the novelty of their subject, on the other hand the diversity of their sources of information and points of view.

The information is still uncertain and sometimes mistaken. Although the purely geographical data seem reliable by and large, we must wait a little longer for the distinctions between the various peoples of the Syrian and Phoenician regions to emerge, so that the characteristics of each race may be correctly attributed. Information about those geographical regions, subject of course to exaggeration and distortion could have reached Greece and Asia Minor for some time beforehand, brought by travellers and merchants. The character of these accounts must have been casual and fragmented.[1] In the age of Alexander, earlier accounts were supplemented by those of the soldiers returning from the expedition. They obviously had ample opportunities to establish closer contact with the various peoples of the area, but their reflections on this experience would be dictated by curiosity or casual observation, rather than a scientific spirit of research. Interest in the Eastern world had always been an important feature of Greek historical writing, from Hecateus of Miletus to Herodotus, Ctesias and the historians of the fourth century B.C.E. It is not necessary to dwell here on the influence of Eastern philosophy, science, and religious and historical traditions on the critical thought of the Greeks: it is enough to remember that this influence seems to have grown more important during the fourth century, as can be seen from Plato's later works and the early Aristotle. So, at the end of the fourth century B.C.E., there was a strong predisposition in the Greek world to accept and assimilate those new data which recent historical developments had brought to the notice of historians and philosophers alike.

Information on certain aspects of the physical geography of Palestine had, of course, been available for some time before this. Aristotle mentions the peculiar properties of a Palestinian lake, whose salty waters prevent men and animals from drowning, but also prevent fish from living there.[2] This fact, however, is given with an air of incredulity which would be quite inconceivable after 332 B.C.E.[3] Theophrastus, in his *Historia plantarum*, gives information in several places about the palm-trees, aromatic plants and incense of Syria, and gives the precise geographical locations where these may be found in Coele-Syria, the great valley which runs from the source of the Orontes to the gulf of Aqaba.[4] It is possible that he got this information from veterans of Alexander's expedition (the date-palm was an important

[1] See appendix 1, p. 654.

[2] Aristotle, *Meteorologica* II.3.359a. M. Stern, *Greek and Latin Authors on Jews and Judaism I* (Jerusalem, 1974), pp. 6–7.

[3] See appendix 2, p. 655.

[4] E. Bickerman, 'La Coelé-Syrie. Notes de géographie historique', *RB*, 54 (1947), 256–7.

element in the army's logistics), but the theory advanced by J. Bernays is equally plausible, that a botanist like Theophrastus could have collected data on such important plants well before the Macedonian king's expedition. In any case, we may suppose that Theophrastus' account of the Jewish people, which we will discuss later, derives from a similar source.[1]

The Greek authors' delay in 'discovering' Judaism was a source of worry and irritation to the Jews in the Hellenistic age, who soon found themselves arguing that their civilization was older, and therefore superior, to that of the Greeks. The author of the *Letter of Aristeas*, towards the close of the second century B.C.E., attempting to prove the perfect compatability of Judaism with the surrounding Greek culture, and to explain the origins of the Greek translation of the Pentateuch, attributes to Demetrius of Phalerum a quotation from Hecateus of Abdera, in which it is suggested that the sacred majesty of the doctrines contained the Mosaic Law had inhibited writers, poets and historians from mentioning them.[2] This idea is repeated at the end of the *Letter*, where the same Demetrius, answering a direct query of King Ptolemy II, cites from his own experience the cases of Theopompus and Theodectes, who wished to insert passages from Scripture in their own works, but were prevented from divulging sacred truths to common men by grave illnesses sent by God.[3] These passages show that it had not been possible to find any references to the Jews in Greek literature before the Hellenistic age. Much later, Flavius Josephus, in his *Contra Apionem* (whose correct title is 'On the Antiquity of the Jewish People'), following the tradition of earlier pro-Jewish polemical writings, returns to the problem of the Greeks' failure to mention the Jews, which in the meantime had become a well-established argument against the Jewish claim to antiquity.[4] Josephus makes the valid point that there could not have been direct contact between the Greeks and the Jews, since the latter did not live along the coast, nor did they engage in commerce like the Egyptians, the Phoenicians and other seafaring nations.[5] Equally forceful is the parallel he draws with the Romans, awareness of whom among the Greeks came comparatively late (Josephus, of course, is not referring to the Sicilian and Italiot historians) and also his comparison of the Jews with the peoples of the

[1] W. Pötscher (ed.), *Theophrastos*, περὶ εὐσεβείας, Philosophia Antiqua 11 (Leiden, 1964), p. 123 n. 1.

[2] *Aristeas* 31.

[3] *Aristeas* 312–16. Theodectes fr.17 Nauck (Strabo xv.1.24, C 695) shows a knowledge of the Ethiopians: E. Diehl, *PW*, 2nd ser., 5 (1934) s.v. Theodektes, col. 1726.

[4] Josephus, *Contra Apionem* 1.2.

[5] Jos. *C.Ap.* 1.60–5.

western world, who were insufficiently known and incompetently described even by famous historians.[1] Passing on to the later period, however, Josephus strives to convince the reader that the Greek historians suppressed all mention of the Jews out of sheer malice, and cites the case of Hieronymus of Cardia, who wrote nothing about the Jews in his book, even though he had occasion to do so.[2] In fact Hieronymus, who wrote about the Dead Sea and placed it in the land of the Nabateans,[3] probably had no clear knowledge of the various peoples of that region.

The undoubted silence of Greek writers on the subject of the Jews before the age of Alexander did not prevent Josephus, and others before him, from pointing out several passages in classical Greek authors where real or imagined references to the Jews could be found. This was done in the case of Herodotus, and also of the epic poet Choerilus.[4] In a passage of his *Histories*,[5] Herodotus refers to the Egyptian origin of the inhabitants of Colchis, and among other pieces of evidence he adduces the practice of circumcision, which is found only among the Egyptians, the inhabitants of Colchis, and the Ethiopians. He goes on to mention that the Phoenicians and the 'Syrians of Palestine' (Σύροι οἱ ἐν τῇ Παλαιστίνῃ) have adopted this practice in imitation of the Egyptians. But if we compare this passage with another section of the *Histories*,[6] where Palestine is the name given to the coastal region of Syria, stretching down as far as Egypt, some doubt arises whether Herodotus intended this as a precise reference to the Jewish people. It must be remembered, however, that this identification seems much older than Josephus or his source, and probably dates back to Hecateus of Abdera. In the Egyptian section of the first book of Diodorus, which in all probability is the work of Hecateus, the same practice is attributed quite definitely to Colchis and Judea alike, both being described as colonies of Egypt.[7] The next example in Josephus' text comprises five verses by the poet Choerilus from his description of Xerxes' Persian troops going on an expedition against Greece.[8]

1 Jos. *C.Ap.* 1.66–8.

2 Jos. *C.Ap.* 1.213–14; cf. Philo, *de vita Mos.* 1.2.

3 F. Jacoby, *FGrHist* 154 F 5, cf. II D, p. 546.

4 Jos. *C.Ap.* 1.168–71; 172–4.

5 Herodotus, *Histories* II.104.1–3; Stern, *Authors* I, pp. 1–4.

6 Herod. *Hist.* VII.89; in III.5 Palestine reaches as far as the territory of Κάδυτις, in all probability Gaza.

7 Diodorus 1.28.2–3; the statement is repeated at 1.55.4–5; in the apparatus of the Vogel edition the parenthesis καθάπερ καὶ παρὰ τοις 'Ιουδαίοις is indicated as 'suspectum'.

8 G. Kinkel, *Epicorum Graecorum Fragmenta* I (Leipzig, 1878), p. 268, fr. 4; Jacoby, *FGrHist* 696 F 33–4 (the verses quoted at 34e).

Josephus identifies as Jews the people described there, who speak the Phoenician language and live in the Solymoi mountains beside a great lake. They are distinguished by their close-cropped hair and wear hoods made out of the hide of horses' heads. Josephus' identification is ingenious, but for various reasons unacceptable.[1] It is obvious that the principal reason for identifying these people with the Jews was the similarity between the name of their mountains and Jerusalem. Other alleged references to Jews in Greek classical authors are based on even weaker premises, and are sometimes quite simply misreadings.[2] They only serve to show how doggedly every possible reference was ferreted out.

The first Greek author who, as far as we know, spoke of the Jews with real interest was the peripatetic philosopher Theophrastus. But the passage which interests us is not the quotation reproduced by Josephus from Theophrastus' 'Laws' where he sees a detail about the laws of the Tyrians as a reference to a Hebrew word (*Qorban*) and a Jewish institution.[3] Rather, J. Bernays discovered an important fragment from Theophrastus in Porphyry's *De Abstinentia*, which is the source of Eusebius' reference.[4] While Eusebius correctly opens his discussion of Greek authors on the Jews with this very passage, the original statement by Theophrastus seems to have escaped the notice of the Jewish researchers, who ransacked the texts of Greek authors for references to their own people. This is a very odd omission, especially as we have seen, and will continue to see, examples of real or supposed references dug out of quite unimportant writers. One cannot help suspecting that Theophrastus' account was deliberately ignored, because it stated that the Jews had performed human sacrifices. The passage certainly escaped the notice of the anti-Jewish controversial-

[1] See appendix 3, p. 655.

[2] For the quotations from Hellanicus and Philochorus in Ps.-Justin, *Cohortatio ad Graecos* 9 (F. Jacoby, *FGrHist.* 328 F 92b) see Jacoby, *FGrHist* IIIb Supplement vol. II (Leiden, 1954), p. 278 n. 1.

[3] Jos. *C.Ap.* 1.166–7; Stern, *Authors* I, p. 12. For Qorban cf. V. Taylor, *The Gospel according to St. Mark* (London, 1952), pp. 341–2. Theophrastus wrote a book entitled Ἀκίχαρος, which must have dealt with the well-known story of Ahikar, cf. Diogenes Laertius v.50; M. Hengel, 'Anonymität, Pseudepigraphie und "Literarische Fälschung" in der jüdisch-hellenistichen Literatur', *Pseudepigrapha*, 1 (Geneva, 1972), p. 259 and n. 2.

[4] Porphyry, *De Abstin.* II.26–28.4 (fr. 13 in Pötscher, *Theophrastos*, pp. 172ff); Eusebius, *Praeparatio Evangelica* IX.2; J. Bernays, *Theophrastos' Schrift über die Frömmigkeit* (Berlin, 1866), pp. 109ff.; Stern, *Authors* I, pp. 10–12. The editor of Porphyry, Nauck, indicated the mention of Jews in Porphyry's text as 'suspectum'; but he was wrong: Porphyry, *De l'abstinence*, II (Paris, 1979), pp. 58–67. Cf. A. Momigliano, *Alien Wisdom* (Cambridge, 1974), pp. 74ff.

ists, who would have been glad of so eminent an authority as Theophrastus to bolster up their case. When the charge that the Jews offered human sacrifices finally emerged in the second century B.C.E., it came from quite different sources. Theophrastus' comment, which is included in a general survey of the history of civilization, had no bearing on the later allegations.

Theophrastus traces the evolution of sacrificial practices: the first offerings consisted of the fruits of the soil, which were the food of men. When the fruits failed to grow, men resorted to cannibalism on the one hand, human sacrifices on the other. These were later replaced by sacrifices of animals, which eventually became the food of men in their turn. In this context Theophrastus mentions the Jews, who are geographically classified as part of the Syrian nation: they still perform holocausts, that is to say, they do not eat the flesh of their victims, who are sacrificed, covered in wine and honey, during the night (to hide this horrible deed from the all-seeing eye of God). When they perform this ritual, they fast on the intervening days, and during the sacrificial period, being a nation of philosophers, they speak together of the deity, looking to the stars at night and invoking God in their prayers. They are supposed to have been the first people to offer up human and animal sacrifices, compelled by necessity rather than greed.

The question whether Theophrastus' account corresponds to the truth is much less important than the picture which it paints of the Jews. Their religious outlook, manifesting itself principally in the observation of the order and movement of the stars (obviously seen as proof of the existence of God, who is sought in the skies) appeared to Theophrastus very close to the Greek philosophical tradition, and the Jews are firmly classified as philosophers (ἅτε φιλόσοφοι τὸ γένος ὄντες). The fact of their monotheism is not yet stated, but this concept is implicit in his account. The sacrificial practices are quite marginal to Theophrastus' description. His reference to human sacrifices, which it is clear from the context he considers a thing of the past, may be explained in various ways, but it is probable that the philosopher was simply told by his informant about these ancient customs. It seems superfluous to search here for a precise allusion to the episode of Abraham and Isaac. As Theophrastus remarks slightly later that human sacrifices were still being offered in his own lifetime in Arcadia, to Zeus Lykaios,[1] and in Carthage, it may be that, since he classifies the Jews among the Syrian nation, he is simply attributing to them a custom

[1] M. P. Nilsson, *Geschichte der griechischen Religion* 1 (Munich, 1941), pp. 372ff, 2 (Munich, 1950), pp. 241–2.

which was well known and still very much alive among the Phoenicians of Carthage.

The origin of Theophrastus' information is a very important historical problem, which goes far beyond the normal scope of the criticism of sources. The most widely-held theory is that of W. Jaeger, who maintains that Theophrastus, both in his treatise 'On Stones' (where he quotes from official Egyptian documents) and in his treatise 'On Piety' (from which our fragment is taken) based himself on Hecateus of Abdera's 'Egyptian History', where similar documentation is used. This theory, however, runs into chronological difficulties. The treatise 'On Piety' can be dated to 319–314 B.C.E.; 'On Stones' was written about 315–314 B.C.E., while Hecateus' work is either contemporary or, more probably, later. Besides, Hecateus' information is intrinsically different and shows a clear divergence in geographical and cultural slant. Theophrastus' account, as in his botanical books, comes directly from people who saw the Jews in Palestine and were struck by their customs. How much of his material comes from his informant and how much is due to his own personal elaboration cannot be precisely determined, but it is clear that the information is presented as part of an enquiry into cultural and religious history, and it is significant that this is the context of the first certain reference to Judaism in Greek literature, reflecting the new direction of Greek ethnographic studies. It is equally significant that this interpretation is not an isolated case.

A fragment of the treatise 'On Sleep' by Clearchus of Soli narrates a curious episode in the life of Aristotle, who was the author's teacher. Aristotle had been in Asia Minor for some time after Plato's death, and this story is told in his own words. At that time he encountered a Jew from Coele-Syria. The Jews are descendants of the Indian philosophers, and just as philosophers in India are called Kalanoi, we are told, so in Syria they are known as Jews, from the name of the region where they live. Their city has a very difficult name: Hierusaleme. This Jew had come down to the coastal area of Asia Minor, and he was a Greek not only in language but also in spirit. He arranged a meeting with Aristotle and other philosophers of his school, in order to put their wisdom to the test. But having contacts with many sages, it was the Jew who gave some of his wisdom to Aristotle and his followers, rather than the other way around. Clearchus further reports that Aristotle found the Jew admirable for his resistance (καρτερία) and his temperance (σωφροσύνη).[1]

[1] Jos. *C.Ap.* 1.175–82 = F. Wehrli, *Die Schule des Aristoteles*, 3, *Klearchos* (Basle, 1948), fr. 6, comment on p. 45; Stern, *Authors* I, pp. 49–52.

We cannot tell whether this fragment should be linked to another passage from the same work by Clearchus,[1] which tells of an experiment performed before Aristotle by a magician, who drew the soul out of a sleeping young man, thus convincing the philosopher that the soul is separate from the body. At any rate it seems likely that Josephus cut short his quotation from Clearchus at a point where the sequel would have contained material which went against the drift of his argument. The unreliability of this anecdote from Clearchus need not concern us much (although the presence of Jews in Asia Minor towards the middle of the fourth century B.C.E. may be supported by the mention of Sepharad, identified with Sardis, in Obadiah 20).[2] But the setting in which Clearchus places the Jews is highly significant. They are presented as the caste of philosophers in Syria—though they are also defined in geographical terms—and they are compared to the caste of Indian philosophers: indeed the Jews are said to be their descendants. Clearchus is recalling a tradition by which the Indian philosophers were called Kalanoi, in a misunderstanding or generalization of the name of the 'philosopher' Kalanos, whose encounter with Alexander had made a considerable impression on the Greeks, being reported in the very earliest histories of the Macedonian king's exploits. What Clearchus and his source probably had in mind was the caste of Gymnosophistai in India, whom Clearchus believed to be descendants of the Magi: in the passage from Diogenes Laertius where his opinion is recorded, it is also mentioned that some people trace the ancestry of the Jews back to the Magi.[3] That is obviously another ancient tradition which saw the Jews in the same perspective. The importance of the passage from Clearchus would appear to lie precisely in this profile of the Jews, which confirms the philosophical and cultural context in which the newly-identified race was examined by the Greeks. And if the wise Jew is described by Aristotle–Clearchus as a Greek in mind and language, then it seems that the traditional Greek search for wisdom in the East is combined with some kind of meeting between the Greek and Jewish civilizations, a meeting which was seen as a mutual exchange and discovery of affinities.

With Clearchus, too, we must face the problem of his source of information. The most widely-held theory, that he was following Megasthenes' analogous description of a meeting between Greek and Indian sages, was already quite difficult to sustain because, even

[1] Wehrli, fr. 7.

[2] *EncJud*, 14 (1971), col. 1164.

[3] Diogenes Laertius 1.9 (prol.) = Wehrli, *Schule*, 3, p. 13, fr. 13; cf. T. Reinach, *Textes d'auteurs grecs et romains relatifs au judaïsme* (Paris, 1895; repr. Hildesheim, 1963), p. 175, no. 98.

considering the poor credibility assigned to Clearchus, one had to suppose that he had misread or distorted Megasthenes' report. But the recent discovery in Bactriana of a Greek inscription, with an accurate transcription of Delphic proverbs made by one Clearchus, and the certain identification of this Clearchus with Clearchus of Soli, proves that our Clearchus must have travelled, probably in the first decade of the third century B.C.E., in those countries which had recently been opened up to the curiosity of the Greeks.[1] His information must therefore be considered independent of the writings of Megasthenes, and the encounter which he describes must derive from independent reflection on things which he saw personally, and which he understood with a certain amount of inevitable confusion.

Megasthenes' opinion is more complex in a certain way, because the brief fragment about the Jews, which comes from his 'Indian History', bears witness to the combination of an ethnographic interest in problems of history and religion with the philosophical or scientific spirit of enquiry into the origins of civilization. Megasthenes, in fact, says that 'all the opinions expressed by the ancients about nature may also be found in philosophers outside Greece: some expounded in India by the Brahmins, others in Syria by those people known as Jews'.[2] The traditional theme of the non-Greek origin of wisdom both in philosophy and in science (one need only recall Herodotus) is here extended, albeit without any alleged priority and rather as an example of coincidence, to the Indians and the Jews. Megasthenes' treatment of the Jews does not appear to have gone beyond a simple comparison, whereas his discussion of Indian thought was fully articulated, as we can see from the fragments,[3] and formed part of a vast interpretation of the history of civilization. But it is interesting none the less that a writer with direct knowledge of Indian society and civilization (even though his account contains some strange exaggerations) should also present the theme of the Jews as a class of philosophers comparable to the Brahmins. Megasthenes was a contemporary of King Seleucus I Nicator of Syria; he had served as his ambassador to the Indian King Sandrakottos; his knowledge of the Jews can have been little more than superficial. His 'Indian History' seems to date from about 290 B.C.E.

Thus, from the evidence of Theophrastus, Clearchus and Megas-

[1] L. Robert, 'De Delphes à l'Oxus. Inscriptions grecques nouvelles de la Bactriane', *CRAIBL* (1968), 416–57.

[2] Jacoby, *FGrHist,* 715 F 3 (= Clemens Alexandrinus, *Stromateis* 1.72.4); Reinach, *Textes*, p. 13, no. 8; Stern, *Authors* I, pp. 45–6.

[3] Jacoby, *FGrHist,* 715 F 33–4.

thenes we find that the Greeks' first impression of the Jews, whom they met in their own country, was of a people of philosophers whose heritage of wisdom was comparable and similar to their own. The ethnographic comments on the Jews are part of a religious and philosophical context, and the comparison with the best-known Indian thinkers may have been designed to illustrate a social fact which was not easily understandable at the time. In these early fragments we find no trace of concern or acquaintance with the history of the Jewish people. The confusion of the Jews with the surrounding Syrian population may explain this strange omission. Theophrastus presents his data in the course of an anthropological reconstruction, which can stand without reference to the separate identity of the Jewish people. And it is noteworthy that even later on, both in the friendly and hostile accounts of Judaism, the actual history of the race is unknown and ignored, except in so far as it impinges on Egyptian history. It is obvious that quotations from Berossus, or any of the Tyrian historians, are used by Josephus simply, or at least mainly, to confirm the antiquity of the Jewish race by foreign testimony,[1] even though the Chaldean historian, writing about the fortunes of his own country and the conquests of his king, had occasion to mention Judea and the Jews quite frequently in the course of his narrative.[2] (Berossus seems to have been very little read outside the Jewish, and later the Christian world.) Greek historiography, interested mainly in politics and institutions, is on the whole ignorant of the Jews and their history right up to the Roman era (with the possible exception of local or third-rate authors),[3] while on the other hand there is a growing interest in certain aspects of Jewish life and customs, on the part of minor historians concerned with propaganda or polemics. The initial cultural and religious image of Judaism does not disappear completely from later writings: in fact, it was the indirect source of several attempts at imaginative reconstruction. Hermippus, towards the end of the third century B.C.E., was probably the first writer to see Pythagoras as a descendant of the Jewish philosophical tradition – a new idea which

[1] Chronicles of Tyre are quoted for exactly this purpose by Jos. *C.Ap.* 1.106–11 (Jacoby, *FGrHist*, 794 F 1c), together with the historians Dios (*C.Ap.* 1.112–15; *FGrHist* 785 F 1) and Menander of Ephesus (*C.Ap.* 1.117–27; *FGrHist* 783 F 1) on the subject of the relations between Solomon and Hiram I, king of Tyre.

[2] Jos. *C.Ap.* 1.131–42 (*FGrHist* 680 F 8a); *C.Ap.* 1.145–53 (*FGrHist* 680 F 9a). Berossus is quoted frequently by Josephus in the *Antiquitates Judaicae*; it is doubtful whether in the fragment reproduced in *Ant.* 1.158 (*FGrHist* 680 F 6) Berossus was really referring to Abraham, although it seems that Pseudo-Eupolemus already interpreted the passage in this way.

[3] Jos. *C.Ap.* 1.216.

was later developed in various directions.[1] And since Hermippus, a pupil of Callimachus, must have worked in Alexandria, he could well have been influenced personally by Jewish theories, which were possibly current in Alexandria already at that time. The philosophical–cultural profile recurs in those writers of the first century B.C.E. who were relatively free from polemical considerations. It was taken up in somewhat superficial fashion by the Hellenistic Jewish writers, still trying to establish the chronological primacy of their people and their faith. They were prompted by Greek practice to invest figures from their ancient history with ideal qualities of philosophical wisdom, scientific knowledge, and inventiveness in the arts and technology. But when the author of the *Letter of Aristeas* imagines the discussions of monarchy that were supposed to have taken place between Ptolemy II and the 72 Jewish sages, he was returning more or less consciously to the philosophical image of the Jews which had prevailed among the first Greek writers.

The picture of Judaism drawn by Hecateus of Abdera is quite different from anything we have so far examined, although chronologically speaking the author is close to Theophrastus. A fundamental feature of Hecateus' account is its partial concentration on the Jews of the Alexandrian Diaspora, and all his information is coloured by this new slant in the point of view. Hecateus is the first exponent of that distortion in describing the Jewish world which grew up, so to speak, from the barriers in Egyptian and Greco-Alexandrian society. Our information on the Jews from the third century B.C.E. onwards, in so far as it derives from Greek sources, is all conditioned to a greater or lesser extent by this original distortion, which also seriously affected Hellenistic Jewish literature, forcing it into a defensive, self-justifying mould. The growth and development of anti-Jewish themes is directly related to the co-existence of Greek and Jewish communities in Egypt, especially in Alexandria. This co-existence, all the more significant for being set in the peculiar cultural and historical context of Egypt, heavily conditioned the themes and attitudes of Hellenistic Jewish

[1] Jos. *C.Ap.* 1.162–5; Origen, *C. Celsum* 1.15; Reinach, *Textes*, pp. 39–40, nos. 14–15; Stern, *Authors* I, pp. 25–6. That Euhemerus had really spoken of the Jews (Jos. *C.Ap.* 1.216) is doubtful, cf. G. Vallauri, *Evemero di Messene* (Turin, 1956), p. 55, whereas the exploitation of euhemeristic theories in the Jewish polemic against the pagan gods is understandable: *Aristeas* 136–7. For a supposed reference to Moses in the Pythagorean *Ocellus Lucanus* 46: R. Harder, *Ocellus Lucanus. Text und Kommentar* (Berlin, 1926), pp. 128–32; W. Burkert, in *Pseudepigrapha* I (Geneva, 1972), pp. 48–9; Stern, *Authors* I, pp. 54, 133.

writing as well. In studying the texts from both sides, the principal danger is that of projecting on to the earliest writings the themes and more especially the tones which developed and intensified with the passage of time.

Information concerning the Jews was included in Hecateus of Abdera's 'Egyptian History'.[1] It seems probable that this work was composed between 312 and 305 B.C.E. An earlier dating (320–315) is less acceptable, although its supporters (O. Murray and others) feel that some of the work's central themes are more easily explained within the context of the first phase of Ptolemaic rule in Egypt, when a policy of conciliation with Egyptian culture and traditions was still in vogue, and Ptolemy I's Greek tendencies in cultural and political matters had not yet become clear-cut. These themes are: the idealized description of the rule of the ancient pharoahs; the unmistakeable presence of Egyptian nationalist elements, arising from the author's priestly sources; the ambiguous meaning of the implied comparison of the conquests of King Sesostris and those of Alexander, which puts the Egyptian king in the better light; the description of priestly power outweighing royal power, which must have been rather embarrassing in the Ptolemaic setting. The significance of Hecateus' book is certainly unclear. On the one hand, there is evidence of some royal patronage, but the opposite view, that it is aimed against the Ptolemies, has been put forward by E. Schwartz and S. K. Eddy. It has also been suggested that the 'Egyptian History' was a piece of propaganda, promoting a certain idea of Egypt in Greek public opinion, and that the works of Megasthenes and Berossus should be seen as replies on behalf of India and Babylon. In any case, the explanation of Hecateus' ideological or political significance has little bearing on his account of the Jews. But it is important to note that Egyptian history is presented in this work according to the schemata of the new Greek ethnography.

A far more serious and fundamental task is to determine the consistency and authenticity of the information about the Jews which has come down to us under the name of Hecateus. A large fragment from book XL of Diodorus has been passed down to us by Photius.[2]

[1] The fragments of Hecateus are collected in Jacoby, *FGrHist* 264 (commentary at IIIa, pp. 29–87). The generally-held theory of the possibility of reconstructing the outlines of Hecateus' work from the first book of Diodorus has been called in question, apparently incorrectly, by W. Spoerri, *Späthellenistiche Berichte über Welt, Kultur und Götter* (Basle, 1959): A. Burton, *Diodorus Siculus, Book I. A Commentary* (Leiden, 1972), pp. 1–34.

[2] Jacoby, *FGrHist* 264 F 6 (Diodorus XL.3); Reinach, *Textes*, pp. 14ff, no. 9; Stern, *Authors* I, pp. 26–35.

The account is actually attributed to Hecateus of Miletus, but this is certainly a mistake by Diodorus, and it really comes from Hecateus of Abdera. A description of the origins, political institutions and religious customs of the Jews is inserted by Diodorus into book XL, on the occasion of Pompey's wars in Judea in 63 B.C.E. Diodorus must have taken this account from Hecateus' Egyptian narrative, which he follows in his own book I, transferring it to a position better suited to his requirements.

Extensive fragments from a work by Hecateus entitled 'On the Jews' are reproduced by Josephus in *Contra Apionem*.[1] A mention of Hecateus from the *Letter of Aristeas*, quoted in a letter supposedly by Demetrius of Phalerum, probably refers to the same work.[2] Lastly, a book by Hecateus entitled 'On Abraham and the Egyptians' is cited by Clement of Alexandria.[3] But as this contains fake verses from classical Greek poets, it is obviously counterfeit.

Any consideration of authenticity must involve the treatise 'On the Jews', and the doubts expressed on this score take as their point of departure a statement by Philo of Byblus, a writer from the time of Hadrian. Philo was uncertain about Hecateus' authorship of this work, and added that if it really were by Hecateus, then he must have been seduced by the Jews' persuasiveness, and have joined their sect.[4] Philo's remarks must be considered in the anti-Jewish climate of his times; the work which he wrote 'On the Jews', from which the above-mentioned passage is taken, may itself have been anti-Jewish in tone. The pro-Jewish attitude, which surprised Philo in Hecateus' treatise, is also present, on the other hand, in the fragment from Diodorus, if we consider it apart from the later polemics against the Jews. It must be

[1] Jos. *C.Ap.* I.186–205 (Jacoby, *FGrHist* 264, (Faelschungen) F 21); *C.Ap.* II.42–7 (Jacoby, *FGrHist* 264 F 22); Reinach, *Textes*, pp. 227ff; Stern, *Authors* I, pp. 35–44.

[2] *Aristeas* 31, cf. 313; Reinach, *Textes*, p. 235.

[3] Clemens Alex. *Strom.* V.14, 113ff. The reference in Josephus, *Ant.* I.159 is probably to the work 'On the Jews'.

[4] Jacoby, *FGrHist* 790 F 9 (= Origen, *C. Cels.* I.15). The non-authenticity of the fragment from Hecateus in *Contra Apionem* has been maintained in recent studies by Jacoby, *FGrHist* IIIa, pp. 61–74; B. Schaller, 'Hekataios von Abdera über die Juden', *ZNW*, 54 (1963), 15–31; Hengel, in *Pseudepigrapha* I, pp. 301–3. Its authenticity has been defended by H. Lewy, 'Hekataios von Abdera περὶ Ἰουδαίων', *ZNW*, 31 (1932), 117–32; J. G. Gager, 'Pseudo-Hecataeus again', *ZNW*, 60 (1969), 130–9. H. Lewy and J. G. Gager have, in my opinion, furnished convincing explanations of the undoubted internal difficulties in the passage. Gager has also reminded us of an important archeological and numismatic piece of evidence for the historicity of the Hezekiah who is mentioned in *C.Ap.* I.187 (for the hypothesis that this personage was modelled on Onias, who founded the temple at Leontopolis see O. Murray, 'Aristeas and Ptolemaic kingship', *JTS*, n.s., 18 (1967), 342 n. 4).

observed that Diodorus' fragment and the one reproduced by Josephus come from different parts of Hecateus' writings, and also that Josephus must have known the fragment, which he quoted, already excerpted from the 'Egyptian History' and with its own particular title. The fragment in *Contra Apionem* is logically and chronologically situated after the battle of Gaza in 312 B.C.E., in which Ptolemy I defeated Demetrius I Poliorcetes, and to which Hecateus seems to have been an eye-witness. The rest of the fragment is completely taken up by a series of statements and reflections about the Jews of Palestine, many of whom were said, after the battle, to have moved to Egypt, drawn by Ptolemy's benevolence and humanity. This information about the Palestinian Jews is derived partly from a personage of considerable importance in priestly circles (Hezekiah, who followed the king into Egypt), and partly from the author's personal knowledge acquired more or less directly on the spot (although his description of Jerusalem is not drawn from personal observation).

The origin of Diodorus' fragment in book XL is completely different. Although we cannot be quite certain, in all probability Hecateus was writing about the Jews in that section of his Egyptian history which dealt with the great Egyptian colonization, found in Diodorus 1.28.2. The colonization which concerned the Jews was of a special type, because Hecateus says that, in the wake of an oubreak of pestilence, the Egyptians, convinced that the scourge was divinely ordained on account of the presence in the country of foreigners who practised different cults, drove all foreigners out of Egypt. The most worthy of these came to Greece with Danaos and Cadmos, while the majority made their way to Judea. On the basis of information which he certainly obtained from Egyptian priestly sources (and which we will find later on in other authors, developed in greater detail and then distorted), telling of a great expulsion of foreigners from Egypt, the Greek historian weaves together on the one hand the Greek tradition which named Danaos and Cadmos as the carriers who bore the inventions of Egyptian civilization into Greece, and on the other hand the Jewish traditions of Exodus and other parts of the Pentateuch, which he probably heard from Jewish priestly sources in Alexandria. (The existence of a Greek translation of the Pentateuch, earlier than the Septuagint, which Aristobulus postulated in the second century B.C.E. in order to explain the Mosaic origins of the Platonic constitution, is a superfluous theory.)

Later in Diodorus' selections from Hecateus we meet the figure of Moses, represented in the Greek style as the man who conquers the land, founds cities, establishes the Temple, institutes the cult, organizes the constitution and government of his people. The taboo against representing the divinity is, according to Hecateus, the consequence of identifying God, the lord of the universe, with the sky (we have seen a similar idea in Theophrastus). The priestly class forms a capable élite, invested not only with religious duties but also with judicial functions and political power. The law-giver had planned and organized the military education of young people, and promoted the necessary virtues. Territorial conquests had made possible the allocation of equal plots of land, with larger plots only for the priests. The system of non-transferable land tenure was intended to keep the population at a high level. The laws governing marriages and funerals were different from those of other peoples. Hecateus concluded that in the aftermath of Persian and Macedonian domination, the Jews had been compelled to make considerable modifications to their traditional institutions.

It is quite possible to compare and substantiate Hecateus' description with passages from Scripture. At one point, in fact, where Hecateus says 'at the end of the laws it is written that Moses, having heard these things from God, transmits them to the Jews', it has even been suggested that he had direct knowledge of the biblical text (in a translation earlier than the Septuagint?), but it is more likely that Hecateus is repeating, not quite literally, a formula which he had heard from his Jewish informant. There are inaccuracies, as when his insistence on the predominant power of the priests is accompanied by the statement that the Jews never had kings. This is not his mistake: the age of the kings had been deliberately left out of Jewish history by Hecateus' source.

In any case it is quite clear that the attitudes and tone of this fragment are entirely Greek. The themes which Hecateus brings out correspond to the interests of Greek ethnography in his day: institutional, political and religious problems predominate. The progression of Moses' work is presented quite differently from the scriptural account, and repeats the typical schema of Greek foundations. It is obvious that this is a highly idealized representation of the Jewish world, and equally obvious that it is congruent with the description of Egyptian society, with its monarchy dominated and supported by priestly power. More debatable is the opinion, put foward by W. Jaeger, that the Mosaic Law, the structure of Jewish society and the virtues which presided over it, are for Hecateus the embodiment of the Platonic ideal in politics and education. Others (O. Murray) have suggested an ideal Spartan model. But there can be no doubt that Hecateus' tone, in this fragment from Diodorus, is highly favourable and sympathetic towards the Jews. And it is, therefore, on the basis of this observation that we must judge that passage from the fragment which has been interpreted as a note of disapproval, or as an indication of anti-Jewish attitudes. Hecateus says that 'as a consequence of having been driven out (of Egypt), Moses introduced a way of life which was to a certain extent misanthropic and hostile to foreigners'.[1] This sentence follows as a corollary to the statement that the Jewish sacrificial rites and way of life were different from those of other peoples (the same idea recurs later in §9 of the fragment, in connection with the laws for marriages and funerals). Taken in its context, Hecateus' remark is not at all negative, and serves to explain the peculiarity of certain religious and social customs. Hecateus notes an ethnographic peculiarity, without adding any value judgement. The misanthropic reserve of the Jews must have caused all the more amazement as the idea, if not of the oneness of the human race, at least of the universality of law outweighing the differences between the laws of individual peoples, was gaining ground in Greek philosophy and ethnography.[2] However, the Jewish misanthropic reserve is actually justified by Hecateus, when he refers to the injuries which had previously been suffered. A very different justification was later advanced by the Jewish author of the *Letter of Aristeas*, who had to answer precise anti-Jewish accusations.[3]

Hecateus' remark arose from direct observation, and is explained by a setting in which the Jews were thrown together with other peoples at close quarters, where differences in religious and social customs and their misanthropic way of life must necessarily impinge on their neighbours: Alexandria, the capital where different peoples had gathered together and where the presence of Jewish elements from the earliest period of the city is well attested.[4] This is where Hecateus must have made his observations and obtained his information. In the fragment from Hecateus in *Contra Apionem*, this theme does not recur, for obvious reasons; instead, the attachment of the Jews to their customs, despite the scorn of neighbours and foreigners and the outrages committed by the kings and Persian satraps, is emphasized. So, too, Hecateus' remark about the peculiar Jewish way of life may be

[1] Diod. XL.3.4: διὰ γὰρ τὴν ἰδίαν ξενηλασίαν ἀπάνθρωπόν τινα καὶ μισόξενον βίον εἰσηγήσατο.

[2] H. C. Baldry, *The Unity of Mankind in Greek Though* (Cambridge, 1966), pp. 141ff.

[3] *Aristeas* 141–2.

[4] V. Tcherikover, *Hellenistic Civilization and the Jews* (Philadelphia, 1959), pp. 55–6; *CPJ*, 1, pp. 1–2; E. L. Abel, 'The myth of Jewish slavery in Ptolemaic Egypt', *REJ*, 127 (1968), 253–8.

explained in the context of his ethnographic portrait of the Jews, which is very sympathetic if not exactly idealized, and drawn from the Alexandrian experience and information derived from that quarter. The anti-Jewish polemic does not begin with Hecateus, but what does begin with Hecateus, in the literary and historiographical sphere, is the dangerous correlation of the Jewish world with Egypt. The fragment in *Contra Apionem* is set in a new historiographical context; it has an occasional character in the aftermath of the Syrian war of 312 B.C.E., and it refers particularly to the Palestinian Jews and their territory.

The description of the Jews in Hecateus presents some points of contact with the fragment from Theophrastus, notably where the Jewish divinity seems to be identified or sought in the skies. But apart from this the authors offer no further coincidences, which is quite understandable when we consider how different are their criteria of observation and how geographically distant their points of view. There is no possibility of either of them following the other's account, and this hypothesis is also rejected by the chronological data.

The 'Egyptian History' of Hecateus was a work in the Greek style, following the tastes and interests of the times. The *Aegyptiaca* or 'Egyptian History' of Manetho is totally different. This author was an Egyptian high priest, probably in the temple of Heliopolis, who had already reached an important position in the court of Ptolemy I, and who had been partly responsible for introducing the cult of Serapis.[1] His historical opus, apparently dedicated to Ptolemy Philadelphus (and therefore dating from after 285 B.C.E.), was probably designed to play the same role as Berossus' histories of Chaldea and Babylon, that is, to inform the Greek public by means of qualified representatives of local cultures, about the most ancient phases of the history of those countries which had recently come into the Greek orbit. It is reasonable to doubt whether this aim was achieved, since neither Manetho nor Berossus seem to have been known to Greek and Roman historians, but notwithstanding this, the political intention of the authors, and of the patrons who commissioned these histories, remains the same. Manetho had at his disposal the material from the priestly archives and official Egyptian documents. Those sources which Herodotus, and indeed Hecateus, could use only indirectly and therefore with errors and misinterpretations (Manetho was critical of Herodotus) were available to the Egyptian priest for consultation at first hand. This documentation was essential above all for establishing a precise chronological

Laqueur, *PW*, vol. 14, 1930, s.v. Manetho cols. 1060–3; Jacoby, *FGrHist* 609 T 1–14; W. G. Waddell, *Manetho* (Loeb Classical Library; London–Cambridge, Mass., 1940), pp. vii–xiv; Stern, *Authors*, pp. 62–86.

framework, within which the history of the pharaonic dynasties could be situated. Besides this official documentary material, Manetho drew perhaps most heavily on the heritage of traditional, anonymous popular tales, which were often legendary; but he distinguishes this material conscientiously from that based on official sources.[1] The legendary material, in so far as it has come down to us, has kept its typical Egyptian colouring, and it is not easy to extract the basic historical facts, which are buried in a rich texture of fiction and serious anachronisms.

Manetho comes into the question of the relations between the Greek and Jewish worlds, because some episodes from his 'History' have been compared, or even identified, with episodes from Jewish history. To derive these comparisons or identifications, the text of Manetho has been subjected to manipulation and distortion from the very earliest times, so that the original meaning of the historical text has been disfigured. Reconstructing the original is made all the more difficult by the fact that our tradition, which derives essentially from Flavius Josephus, first met those passages from Manetho which were concerned (or so it was thought) with Jewish history, shorn of their context and already manipulated and confused. On the other hand, Manetho's text was exploited for controversial ends both by the Jews and their enemies, so that contradictions were created which cannot necessarily be resolved simply by eliminating one or other of the two tendencies. In this state of affairs, the reconstruction of the original text and of Manetho's genuine opinions is a difficult and controversial task. Although any interpretation must for obvious reasons remain inconclusive, the best and most plausible reconstruction would appear to be the one proposed by F. Jacoby. Jacoby's interpretation brings with it one grave and fundamental consequence: Manetho did not mention the Jews at all in his work.[2]

The episodes from Manetho's 'History' which furnished material for Jewish and anti-Jewish distortion were two: the story of the 'shepherds' and the story of the 'polluted'. Manetho tells in the second book of his History about an invasion of Egypt by an unknown people from

1 Jos. *C.Ap.* 1.105; 228–9; 287; E. Meyer, *Geschichte des Altertums,* 2 1 (3rd edn., Basle, 1953), pp. 420–6.

2 Jacoby, *FGrHist* 609 F 8, 9, 10 (with important annotations included in the critical apparatus; the use of different typefaces and parentheses all helps to explain the editor's views). Jacoby reaches conclusions which are broadly similar to those of E. Meyer, *Aegyptische Chronologie* (Berlin, 1904), pp. 71ff (French tr. *Chronologie égyptienne* (Paris, 1912), pp. 103ff), of Laqueur, *PW*, s.v. Manetho cols. 1064–80, of Heinemann, *PWSup* 5 (1931) 'Antisemitismus' col. 26. Manetho is the first anti-Jewish writer according to Tcherikover, *Hellenistic Civilization*, pp. 361–4.

the East, who conquered the land and ruled it harshly for a long time. The city of Avaris became the conquerors' centre of power, and it was here that the 'shepherds' took refuge when their dominion was threatened by the opposition of the Theban kings and a rebellion of the Egyptian people. From Avaris, following a treaty, the 'shepherds' (who were known as the 'prisoners' in another copy of Manetho's History) left Egypt for Syria, and when they reached Judea they stopped and founded the city of Jerusalem. It is obvious that this passage from Manetho refers to the period when Egypt was ruled by the Hyksos.[1]

The second episode is much more complicated.[2] Manetho himself declared that it was not derived from the sacred books. The historian tells (restricting ourselves to the essentials) that during the reign of a certain King Amenophis, the desire to rid the country of lepers and polluted people (and there were some priests among the lepers) led firstly to their being forced to work in the stone caves, and then to their being given the city of Avaris, which according to the theological tradition was dedicated to the god Typhon. Here the lepers and polluted people, under the guidance of a priest named Osarseph, unleashed a rebellion. Their leader was said to have overthrown the religious traditions and the customs of Egypt and to have established new customs and practices. Then he called on the 'shepherds' for aid, and they came to Avaris. King Amenophis retired to Ethiopia for thirteen years, with many Egyptians and the sacred animals. Meanwhile the 'shepherds' and the 'polluted' established a cruel, sacrilegious regime in Egypt, destroying temples and killing sacred animals. At last Amenophis and his son Ramses were said to have returned from Ethiopia to launch a counter-attack; they defeated the 'shepherds' and the 'polluted', killed many of them and drove the others into Syria.

It is not clear whether this story, which is rich in imaginative colouring, refers to any precise historical facts. It has been suggested that the story combines and confuses two historical events which were chronologically quite distinct: a Syrian invasion at the time of the Pharaoh Merneptah, which was reversed by a campaign of Rameses III, and the religious revolution of Amenophis IV (E. Meyer).[3] It is certain, at any rate, that the theme of Manetho's story, which I have summarized, its constituent elements and its narrative technique are all

[1] Jos. *C.Ap.* 1.74–92 (*FGrHist* 609 F 8).

[2] Jos. *C.Ap.* 1.223–53 (*FGrHist* 609 F 10).

[3] There is a different reconstruction in P. Montet, *Le drame d'Avaris. Essai sur la pénétration des Sémites en Égypte* (Paris, 1941), pp. 173ff. Cf. R. Weill, *Les Hyksôs et la restauration nationale dans la tradition égyptienne et dans l'histoire* (Paris, 1914).

in the purest Egyptian tradition, probably from the period of the New Empire, but with some elements from a later era (J. Yoyotte).

According to the reconstruction of Manetho's text proposed by F. Jacoby, the Jews had as yet no part in this narrative or in its themes, or at least not in any explicit manner, although Manetho's text, where it spoke of the foundation of Jerusalem by the 'shepherds', did provide one very important clue. The correlation of the two episodes from Manetho with Jewish history is therefore a later development, in all probability. It has been maintained with considerable acumen by J. Yoyette that the Jews had already been inserted into this Egyptian tradition of a war against invaders from the East, before Manetho and the Hellenistic age. According to this theory, anti-Jewish feeling dates back to the Persian age, and to the part played by Jewish troops (for example at Elephantine) in the final phase of Achemenid rule towards the end of the fifth century B.C.E., when they remained faithful to the Persian king during the Egyptian rebellion. This is undoubtedly an ingenious theory, but on the one hand it has to overestimate the importance of the Elephantine colony, generalize the local conflict with the Egyptian priests, and magnify the extent of Jewish nationalism at the time, while on the other hand it has to push the date of the original story behind Manetho's account too far back, dating it to the period of the Achemenids. Neither must we forget the fact that Jewish soldiers had been brought to Egypt while there were Egyptian kings. It is true that a local xenophobic tradition lies behind Hecateus' account of the foreigners being driven out of Egypt, but this tradition is still at a rather vague stage compared with Manetho's story, and such a feature of Hecateus' account cannot be ascribed solely to the intervention of a Greek interpretation.

The connection of Manetho's account with the Jews is a later development, and Manetho is in no way responsible for the insertion anti-Jewish elements into his 'History'. This connection presupposes at least three factors: Manetho's own text with the report of Jerusalem being founded by the 'shepherds'; the necessity for the Jews who lived in Egypt in the third century B.C.E., in a particular political and social context, to explain their presence in Egypt and Egyptian history in relation to their own traditions of Genesis and Exodus; the diffision of the Jewish version of Exodus, strongly anti-Egyptian in tone, which resulted from the Greek translation of the Pentateuch (although something of it was known already before that, naturally).[1]

[1] Tcherikover, *Hellenistic Civilization*, p. 531 n. 79.

The causes which led to the Greek translation of the Pentateuch are not clear. The ancient tradition maintained that the translation was commissioned by King Ptolemy Philadelphus (285–246 B.C.E.), on the grounds that the royal library would have been incomplete without a copy of the Jewish laws, or else as a gesture of goodwill towards the Jews of Egypt and of his other territories;[1] but more probably because the Pentateuch was a source for the history and customs of the Jewish subjects of the Egyptian king. A comparison with the histories composed under royal patronage by Berossus and Manetho, and an analysis of the meaning and practical commitment of such a translation, make the ancient explanation of a royal decision appear most plausible (E. Bickerman). In any case, the Greek translation spread a wider knowledge of the history of the Israelites, particularly the Egyptian phase, and it also facilitated comparison with the Egyptian version of the same facts, now available in Manetho, although at first this was done only in Jewish circles. We are certain of the existence of a Graeco-Jewish school in Alexandria at the end of the third century B.C.E., which was interested mainly in problems of chronology. In Manetho's account the Jews found an excellent opportunity to identify themselves with the 'shepherds', who ruled Egypt for a long time and then left the country honourably, to go and found Jerusalem. But working on the same text of Manetho, which incidentally implicated those same 'shepherds' in the rebellion of the 'polluted', the Jews' adversaries, no doubt irritated by the biblical version of the Jewish Exodus from Egypt, had little trouble in finding a new identity for the Jews, casting them this time in the role of the 'polluted' and the lepers, who were driven out by Amenophis. The rebel priest Osarseph, naturally, was cast as Moses.

In other words the sojourn of the ancient Jews in Egypt, and especially the Exodus, became bones of contention, not only in the cultural and historiographical fields, between the Jews and the Egyptians (even Alexander the Great was caught up in the controversy).[2] It is hard to say who first started misreading, and then distorting, Manetho's text according to their own interests. Perhaps indeed the identification of the Jews with the 'shepherds' came about in good faith, towards the end of the third century B.C.E., although it seems

[1] *Aristeas* 10, 30, 38: E. Bickerman, 'The Septuagint as a translation', *PAAJR*, 28 (1959), 1–11, repr. in *Studies in Christian and Jewish History* I (Leiden, 1976), pp. 167–200.

[2] Jos. *C.Ap.* II.6; Philo, *de vita Mos.* I, 25; Tertullian, *Adversus Marcionem* II.20; I. Lévy, 'La dispute entre les Égyptiens et les Juifs devant Alexandre', *REJ*, 63 (1912), 211–15.

certain that even the chronology of Manetho's first two books was tampered with, in order to find parallels with biblical chronology.[1] The Jewish Hellenistic writers certainly concentrated their attention on the problem of the Jews in Egypt.

The historical–cultural conflict takes on a new dimension in the political and social framework of Egypt from the third century B.C.E. onwards, and in the context of relations between Jews and Greeks in Alexandria. The concentration of power in the hands of the Graeco-Macedonian ruling class, and the distinction of the two cultures, Greek and Egyptian, which although they influenced each other remained essentially strangers, characterized the Ptolemaic regime from the very start. After the middle of the third century B.C.E., the weakening of the central power enhanced the first tentative stirrings of anti-Hellenic opposition, linked to priestly circles and the lower classes. Manifestations of cultural and religious nationalism blended with social upheavals caused by food shortages, and with outbreaks of genuine revolution. A popular 'literature', coming perhaps from priestly sources and often apocalyptic in tone, contrasted the present with the golden age of the great pharaohs of the past, and encouraged xenophobic feelings. The deterioration of the kingdom's position is apparent most of all during the second century B.C.E., as for example from its diminished capacity to engage in foreign policy (C. Préaux, W. Peremans, S. K. Eddy). It is not always easy to make out the position of the Jews in this context, scattered as they were all over Egypt. One very significant feature, however, was their participation in the army, from which the Egyptians were excluded (recruitment for the Syrian war, which ended with the victory at Raphia, provoked a nationalist revival among the native soldiers, causing them to rebel). The Jews had already served as mercenaries in the Egyptian armies of the last native kings, and then later under the Persians, always distinguishing themselves by their faithfulness. According to the *Letter of Aristeas*, Ptolemy I had enrolled 30,000 Jews, chosen from among the prisoners taken in the Syrian wars, and had distributed them in various garrisons around the country. Well paid and highly trustworthy, they served to keep the native population at bay, and the natives apparently retaliated against them from time to time.[2] When Flavius Josephus and Philo speak of the traditional hostility to the Jews among Egyptians, they are referring not only to the distant past, but also to the Ptolemaic period. This factor was of course useful to later generations of Jewish controversialists in distinguishing the Jews from the mass of Egyptians

[1] M. B. Rowton, 'Manetho's date for Ramesses II', *JEA*, 34 (1948), 67.

[2] *Aristeas* 13–14; 36–7.

in the eyes of the Greeks and Romans.[1] The conflict between Jews and Egyptians had its roots, therefore, in hard political reality, and the quarrels about history are merely a reflection of this conflict. Anti-Judaism in its origins is an Egyptian phenomenon, and it remained such for a long period of time. The Jewish–Egyptian controversy takes on greater importance when it transcends its local setting and combines with other hostile elements in the Greek polemic. Hostility among the Greeks had its origins in Alexandria in the third century B.C.E., when Hecateus already had occasion to mention the different way of life and the misanthropic reserve of the Jews. However, it was during the second century B.C.E., with the increasing political and military importance of Jews in the kingdom, that the Greek anti-Jewish polemic acquired consistency, and was then fused with hostile elements which had grown up in the Syrian camp, following the revolt of the Maccabees.

The fundamental reason for the emergence of anti-Semitism has been correctly isolated by V. Tcherikover in the clash between the religious, political, administrative, economic and cultural organism which formed the basis of Greek (and classical) social co-existence, that is to say, the *polis*, and the religious and political organization of the Jewish communities of the Diaspora, founded on total adherence to the traditional laws and special customs of the Jewish people, which were, as a rule, guaranteed by special privileges granted by the Hellenistic kings, and later by the Roman government. So the ethnic Jewish community lives side by side with the Greek community in the same city, and enjoys the advantages of Greek civic life, in which indeed it is anxious to play a part. But it cannot renounce its own traditions and obligations, which means that it does not take its fair share of the city's burdens, nor of course can it recognize the religious foundations of Greek city life. There must have been daily causes for annoyance, arising from the Greeks' inability to understand such an attitude, and the Jews' inability to stop themselves.[2] Thus the phenomenon of anti-Judaism can be readily explained in an urban society where social life is organized on the basis of the *polis*. In Egypt, for example, anti-Jewish manifestations are quite comprehensible in Alexandria (and also in Memphis, for example, in the first half of the first century B.C.E.). In the country areas, where the Jews were also quite numerous, anti-Jewish

1 Jos. *C.Ap.* I.223–6; II.69–70; Philo, *In Flaccum* 17; 29; A. Pelletier, *Philon, In Flaccum* (Paris, 1967), pp. 170–1; V. A. Tcherikover, 'The decline of the Jewish Diaspora in Egypt in the Roman period', *JJS*, 14 (1963), 8–9.

2 Tcherikover, *Hellenistic Civilization*, pp. 371–7.

outbreaks are much smaller in scale, late to develop, and inspired rather by political reasons of a general nature.

In Alexandria the confrontation between Greeks and Jews must have been present from the start, and as we can infer from Hecateus' observations, must have given rise above all to curiosity. The Greeks must have had no idea what the Jews were like, with their way of life, their history, their customs. If they did begin to learn something about them subsequently, this information came through an Egyptian filter and was therefore hostile in tone. On the other hand the Jewish community was in good standing with the Ptolemaic kings, since it was useful to them, and it is possible that the Jews enjoyed a special 'charter' of privileges from the time of Ptolemy I (if we may interpret thus an ambiguous passage from Hecateus in Flavius Josephus).[1]

The Jewish community in Alexandria, in the course of the third century B.C.E., found itself having to defend its own identity and history in the face of the generally hostile traditions of Egyptian history, and also having to establish its own historical tradition on an equal footing, in competition with the much better known traditions of Egypt and Greece. This defence of history and traditions also meant the need consciously to reinforce its total commitment to the Law and traditional customs, against the threat of assimilation into a Greek culture. The emergence of a Jewish literature in Alexandria, at the end of the third century B.C.E., does not betoken a missionary or apologetic campaign directed towards Greek readers, but rather an internal need of the Jewish community itself, since it aims to strengthen the Jews' own consciousness of their religion and nationality. (Later, Josephus asked himself whether there had been a Jewish tradition of spreading a knowledge of the Law among the Gentiles, but all he could quote in support of this hypothesis was Ptolemy II and the Greek translation of the Pentateuch.)[2] However, the new Jewish literature cannot be understood unless its subject-matter is compared to the historical and cultural themes of Greek (and Egyptian) opposition to Judaism, as these are known to us from later apologetic works (especially the anti-Jewish accusations reported in *Contra Apionem*), but which must be considered as much earlier, since they already provoke a response from Jewish writers in the third and second centuries B.C.E. Only in this context are these authors comprehensible. It now appears that Hellenistic Jewish literature, answering the needs of the Jewish community, provided in a Greek literary form the necessary materials and argu-

[1] Jos. *C.Ap.* 1.189: Tcherikover, *CPJ*, 1, p. 7 n. 18; other interpretations are also possible.

[2] Jos. *Ant.* 1.9–11.

ments for defending Jewish identity, and at the same time for proving through historical arguments the Jews' right to coexist in the Hellenic world; so that literature, although it remained unknown to Greek contemporaries, played a very important practical role in the political and cultural controversy from the third century B.C.E. onwards. However, Jewish culture, by acting in this way, ended up by consciously venturing into the territory of Greek culture.

The first task for Jewish scholarly research in Alexandria was to insert Jewish history into the framework of Greek, Egyptian and oriental history. This was made all the more urgent because of the existing works of historical chronology by Manetho, Berossus and Eratosthenes. The last-named had, in Alexandria itself, laid the foundations for a chronology of Greek history.[1] The Jewish chronological enquiry, which has its first exponent at the end of the third century B.C.E. in Demetrius (who takes his place in the tradition of Alexandrian studies in chronology and chronography, and possibly sees himself as a counterpart of Manetho), intended to establish the greatest possible antiquity for the origin of its own people in comparison to the other chronological systems, and thus to demonstrate the priority of the Jewish Law, which could not be based on previous models, and of the Jewish system of organized social life. It also exploited a Greek idea, often applied to Sparta, and argued that the Law must be good because of the continuity and unswerving perseverance in its application.[2] From chronological exercises of this type, many logical developments were promoted in Alexandria and elsewhere. One could argue, as Aristobulus did, that Pythagoras, Socrates and Plato all derived their ideas from Moses:[3] this assertion picked up a statement which Hermippus had just put into circulation concerning Pythagoras, and thus the attempt was made to insert Jewish culture into the history of Greek culture, in the shape of a primary source. It may be that this theory played on the tradition of Greek sages visiting Egypt. After all, Eratosthenes had already suggested that ethnic controversies could be solved by a positive evaluation of quite independent civilizations.[4]

[1] B. Z. Wacholder, 'Biblical chronology in the Hellenistic world chronicle', *HTR*, 61 (1968), 451–81; 'How long did Abram stay in Egypt?', *HUCA*, 35 (1964), 43–56; *EncJud*, 5 (1971), s.v. Demetrius, 1490–1; E. J. Bickerman, 'The Jewish Historian Demetrius', in *Studies* 2 (Leiden, 1980), pp. 347–58.

[2] Jos. *C.Ap.* II.152–3.

[3] The fragments of Aristobulus in M. Black and A.-M. Denis (edd.), *Fragmenta Pseudepigraphorum quae supersunt graeca, una cum historicorum et auctorum judaeorum hellenistarum fragmentis*, PVTG 3 (Leiden, 1970), pp. 217ff. Cf. N. Walter, *Der Thoraausleger Aristobulos* (Berlin, 1964).

[4] Strabo 1.4.9 (C 66).

A Samaritan writer like Pseudo-Eupolemus who was an exponent of a Hellenized Palestinian tradition, writing towards the first half of the second century B.C.E., could happily describe Abraham as a scientist and philosopher who taught astrology to the Phoenicians and Egyptians, thus blending biblical, Greek and Babylonian traditions.[1] Josephus was quick to pick up this idea,[2] since the figure of Abraham as a wise inventor allowed him to refute vigorously the typical Greek allegation, which was already in circulation in the second century B.C.E. and frequently repeated thereafter, that the Jews had produced no men worthy of admiration or famous for their wisdom and inventions.[3] This charge was already well known to the author of the *Letter of Aristeas*, who attacked all those inventors who had done nothing but combine elements which were already present in creation.[4] The message of this description of Abraham was all the more controversial, in that teaching the Egyptians meant, at one remove, teaching the Greeks, who from Herodotus to Hecateus of Abdera had always been ready to concede priority to the Egyptians in the history of civilization.

This idea reverberated in Eupolemus' writings and reached paradoxical heights in Artapanus. Eupolemus, who is probably the personage sent to Rome in 166 B.C.E. by Judas Maccabeus,[5] declared that Moses was the first sage and invented the alphabet for the Jews, from whom it passed to the Phoenicians and then at last to the Greeks. He knew of an exchange of letters on an equal footing between Solomon and an Egyptian pharaoh, and also with the king of Tyre.[6] To praise Solomon's power was a sign of political awareness after the Maccabees' struggle. The story told by Artapanus is so strange that it has been suggested that it was a romance.[7] In the first fragment Abraham instructs the Egyptians in astrology; in the second fragment it is Abraham's descendant Joseph's turn to come to Egypt: he is nominated as governor of the country by the king, and improves the state of

[1] Jacoby, *FGrHist* 724; B. Z. Wacholder, 'Pseudo-Eupolemus' two Greek fragments on the life of Abraham', *HUCA*, 34 (1963), 83–113; N. Walter, 'Zu Pseudo-Eupolemos', *Klio*, 43–5 (1965), 282–90; M. Hengel, *Judentum und Hellenismus* (Tübingen, 1973), pp. 162ff; ET *Judaism and Hellenism* (London, 1974), I, pp. 88–92.

[2] Jos. *Ant*. I.165–8; L. H. Feldman, 'Abraham the Greek Philosopher in Josephus', *TAPA*, 99 (1968), 143–56.

[3] Jos. *C.Ap*. II.135; 148. For the continuity of a tradition free from modificatory inventions: *C.Ap*. II.182–3.

[4] *Aristeas* 136–7.

[5] I Macc. 8:17; Jacoby, *FGrHist* 723 T I.

[6] *FGrHist* 723 F 2; Hengel, *Hellenismus* (Tübingen, 1973), pp. 169ff.; ET I, pp. 92–5.

[7] *FGrHist* 726; I. Lévy, 'Moïse en Ethiopie', *REJ*, 53 (1907), 201–11.

agriculture, which had previously been very disturbed on account of the bad distribution of land, and because the strong were oppressing the weak. He starts by making a new division of the land and establishing frontiers, assigns special holdings to the priests, invents a system of measurements, and marries the daughter of a priest of Heliopolis; his father and brothers come to Egypt and found temples there. At his death, Joseph can truly be described as lord of Egypt. In the third fragment there is a long discussion of Moses, who is identified with the personage known to the Greeks as Museus. Moses is said to have been Orpheus' teacher, and to have given mankind very useful inventions, including ships, machinery for lifting stones, Egyptian weapons, hydraulic and warlike engines, and philosophy. He divided the country into *nomoi*, laid down for everyone which divinity was to be adored, and invented the sacred alphabet for priests. Among the deities were sacred animals. Finally, he assigned special lands to the priests. In this way, he won the people's hearts and the superior esteem of the priests, who identified him with the god Hermes (Thoth). It is of no importance to follow the further history of Moses in Egypt and the Exodus.

Even admitting that Artapanus' narrative is extravagant, all the same it does not seem to derive purely from a conciliatory or syncretistic attitude, which has led some people to suggest that it derives from the circle of the temple at Leontopolis.[1] Jewish superiority is asserted in the spheres of religion, thought and politics, to the ridiculous extent of crediting Moses with the introduction of the cult of animals, which was a strong point in the Jewish polemic against the Egyptians. The whole argument is a reaction to anti-Jewish tendencies, if not writings. The political setting is obvious: the allusion to agrarian unrest cannot but refer to the grave situation in the Egyptian countryside, and the peasants' revolts of the second century B.C.E. One statement which Artapanus makes is particularly interesting: he says at one point that 'Moses had done all these things to lend greater stability to the monarchy' of the pharaoh.[2] This is possibly an allusion to the military support which the Jews of Leontopolis lent to the Ptolemaic kings in the second half of the second century B.C.E.[3] It could also be a reply to those charges of disloyal feelings towards the state which were contained both in the Greek reworking of Esther (written towards the first decades of the first century B.C.E.) and in 3 Maccabees where they

[1] Hengel, *Pseudepigrapha* I (Geneva, 1972), p. 239; he speaks justifiably of a Mosaic aretalogy.
[2] *FGrHist* 726 F 3, 5.
[3] Tcherikover, *Hellenistic Civilization*, pp. 281ff.

are refuted.[1] In the edict of Artaxerxes against the Jews in the Greek Esther, as well as the usual allegations that the Jews have peculiar laws and customs, different from other peoples, and that they are anti-social, a new accusation is added: they are disobedient to the king and disturb the public peace. These accusations, purely political in character, are explained by the dynastic struggles in Egypt in the second and first centuries B.C.E., when the political and military commitment of the Jews was very deep and naturally controversial. On a more general level, remembering the revolt of the Maccabees, such an accusation could be seen as a normal consequence of Jewish exclusiveness, which it was easy to present as injurious to the state in order to undermine the policy of royal privileges. It is not for nothing that the author of the *Letter of Aristeas* advances purely philosophical and moral explanations for Jewish exclusiveness, and interprets the much-criticized dietary regulations in an allegorical manner.[2] At the same time the general tone of this little work is full of respect for the king, and it tries to show that the Ptolemaic policies are perfectly acceptable to the Jews.[3]

The general subject-matter of this Hellenistic Jewish literature is substantially nationalist in the Palestinian authors, and anti-Egyptian as well in the Alexandrian authors. In so far as it claims chronological priority and therefore inventions for ancient Jewish figures, it also appears anti-Greek in tone, although this cannot be said to have been the main objective. All the same, it allows us to catch a glimpse of a complex of anti-Jewish themes which are much more substantial than the banal, ridiculous accusations which we have seen, although the latter also gain much wider diffusion because they are now embodied in striking formulae of propaganda. Although this controversy with its attendant literature seems important to us, it did not spread at the time beyond the local confines of Egypt, and, as we shall see, of Syria and Palestine. The Greeks carried on in complete ignorance of the Jews and their history. Greek historiography in the second century B.C.E., starting with Polybius, had much more serious problems to handle, as for instance the Romans' expansionism towards Greece, the Greek-controlled orient, and the west.

Polybius refers to the Jews in relation to the progress of the Syrian war in 201–200 B.C.E., when the Egyptian general Scopas temporarily

[1] E. J. Bickerman, *Four Strange Books of the Bible* (New York, 1967), pp. 227ff.

[2] *Aristeas* 140ff.

[3] O. Murray, 'Aristeas and Ptolemaic kingship', *JTS*, n.s., 18 (1967), 337–71; according to G. Howard, the demonstration is directed towards Palestinian Judaism: 'The *Letter of Aristeas* and Diaspora Judaism', *JTS*, n.s., 22 (1971), 337–48.

conquered Judea. Soon afterwards, defeated by Antiochus, he had to retire, and 'the Jews who live around the temple known as Hierosolyma' surrendered to the Syrian king. The formula used to define Jerusalem and the Jews is administratively correct. Polybius added that he was reserving for a later occasion the other things which he had to say about this, and especially about the magnificence of the Temple.[1] What the later occasion was to be, we can only guess: probably the sack of 168 or the events of 167 B.C.E., connected with the new cult of Zeus Olympios introduced by Antiochus IV.[2] It is not necessary to suppose that Polybius had seen the city for himself. In any case, this description did not pass into later tradition (which is all the more strange since the passages quoted from Polybius are alluded to by Flavius Josephus),[3] and so we do not know how Polybius dealt with the revolt of the Maccabees. Very brief descriptions of the city, probably in connection with the warlike deeds of Antiochus IV Epiphanes or Antiochus VII Sidetes, were given by two almost unknown historians, Timochares and Xenophon.[4] A fragment falsely attributed to the geographer Polemon of Ilium spoke of an Egyptian army which was driven from the country and established itself 'in the Palestine which is known as Syria' under the rule of Apis, son of Phoroneus. This must be interpreted as an attempt to fuse Greek and oriental mythical traditions.[5] More important is the passage from Agatharchides of Cnidus, a prominent historian in the middle of the second century B.C.E.,[6] who told how Ptolemy's capture of Jerusalem in 320 B.C.E. was accomplished on a Saturday, the day which the inhabitants set aside for prayer and rest. The narrative is accompanied by moralizing comments: the Jews' attitude is senseless, their Law is obviously bad and superstitious. However, since the author feels it necessary to explain about 'those people known as Jews, who live in a city which is exceptionally well protected, which the inhabitants of that place call Hierosolyma', and so on, we may infer that the average reader knew

[1] Polybius XVI.39.1 and 3 (Stern, *Authors* I, pp. 113–5); F. W. Walbank, *A Historical Commentary on Polybius,* 2 (Oxford, 1967), pp. 546–7; E. Bickerman, 'Une proclamation Séleucide relative au temple de Jerusalem', *Syria,* 25 (1946–48), 84, repr. in *Studies* 2, pp. 86–104.

[2] P. Pédech, *La méthode historique de Polybe* (Paris, 1964), p. 562 n. 276.

[3] Cf. *C.Ap.* II.83–4.

[4] Jacoby, *FGrHist* 165 (II B, commentary p. 595); *FGrHist* 849; Reinach, *Textes*, pp. 53–4, nos. 22, 23; Stern, *Authors*, I, pp. 134–5, 137–8.

[5] Reinach, *Textes*, p. 41, no. 15; K. Deichgräber, *PW* 21, 1952, s.v. Polemon (9), col. 1302–4; Stern, *Authors*, I, pp. 102–3.

[6] Jacoby, *FGrHist* 86 F 20a (= Jos. *C.Ap.* I.205), 20b (= Jos. *Ant.* XII.5); Stern, *Authors* I, pp. 106–9.

nothing about the Jews. This appears to be the first reference in a historical work to the Sabbath controversy. The episode may have had a certain importance as an example, because Pompey was able to capture the city in 63 B.C.E. by taking advantage of the Sabbath,[1] and the same was said of Herod and Titus.[2]

The uninterested silence of Greek historiography about Jewish history is confirmed by the fact that the chronographical field of study remained exclusively Greek for a long period. 'Works such as those of Berossus, Manetho, and Jewish attempts at history remained in the long run without much influence'.[3] Lists of Eastern kings were first taken into consideration by Pseudo-Apollodorus, Castor and Alexander Polyhistor. The latter was also to be the compiler who sought to bring Jewish history to the attention of the Roman world.

Another hotbed of anti-Judaism of a strictly political kind gew up around the middle of the second century B.C.E. in the Seleucid kingdom, following the revolt of the Maccabees. Seleucid propaganda is responsible for circulating charges of infamy against the Jews, drawing on anti-Jewish material from Egyptian sources, and wilfully distorting Jewish traditions and customs, as well as indulging in sheer invention.

The rumour about the Jews worshipping a donkey's head (or, in later versions, a whole donkey), was encouraged by the difficulty for the average Greek or Egyptian in understanding how the Jewish god could exist without being in any way depicted.[4] The charge of atheism against the Jews derives from the same cause. The origin of the rumour about the donkey almost certainly lies in the equation of the Jews with the lepers and polluted of Avaris. The god of Avaris, Typhon or Set, who was the god of evil, was represented by a donkey's head.[5] On this Egyptian base is superimposed, in the first half of the second century B.C.E., a strange story told by a pupil of Eratosthenes, the historian Mnaseas from Patara in Lycia, and known to us through Josephus, but dating to a much earlier period.[6] The story concerns the capture by an

1 Strabo XVI.2.40 (C 763); Jos. *Ant.* XIV.63–6; Cassius Dio XXXVII.16.

2 Plutarch, *de superstitione* 8 (Reinach, *Textes*, p. 136, no. 66); Cass. Dio XLIX.22; LXV.7.

3 Jacoby, *FGrHist* IIB p. 719 (Commentary on 244).

4 Plutarch, *Quaestiones conviviales* IV.5 (Reinach, *Textes*, pp. 142ff, no. 69; Stern, *Authors* I, pp. 550–62.)

5 Tcherikover, *Hellenistic Civilization*, pp. 365–6.

6 Jos. *C.Ap.* II.112–14 (Reinach, *Textes*, p. 49, no. 19; Stern, *Authors* I, pp. 99–101); Laqueur, *PW* 15, 1932, s.v. Mnaseas (6), cols. 2250–2. The fragment comes from the work 'On Asia'. Müller's fragment 32 (= Athen. VIII.346d) refers to the goddess-queen Atargatis (*Dea Syria*) and to the prohibition against eating fish.

Idumean of the image of an enemy god (a donkey's head). This story had been jeeringly applied to the Jews, and Seleucid propaganda adopted it for its own ends. Thence it passed into anti-Jewish propaganda from the first century B.C.E. onwards. Posidonius records the story, told in a manner less than totally hostile, that Antiochus Epiphanes, entering the Temple in the year 168, had found that a statue of a bearded man, holding a book and seated on a donkey, was honoured there.[1] This obviously refers to Moses.

More serious and insidious was the charge of ritual murder which was levelled against the Jews, with a great wealth of detail, by anti-Jewish literature from the first century B.C.E. onwards, but which goes back to Seleucid propaganda. This story too was connected to the violation of the Temple by Antiochus Epiphanes. He was supposed to have found a Greek there, captured in Judea and fattened up prior to being slaughtered. This sacrifice was said to happen every year: the Jews tasted the victim's entrails and swore eternal enmity to the Greeks.[2] This narration, clearly Greek in tone, combines several diverse elements: the classical theme of a conspiracy founded on an oath of hatred, linked to a human sacrifice; and the ancient ethnographical tradition of the annual slaughter, on a fixed day, of a human being. In Seleucid propaganda this accusation against the Jews served a dual purpose: it reinforced the ideas of exclusiveness and hostility to foreigners which had been established in Egyptian anti-Jewish stories, and it also excused Antiochus from the possible charge of sacrilege for having sacked the Temple of Jerusalem in 168 B.C.E.[3] Subsequently, in 167, the Temple was desecrated and the traditional customs and ceremonies of Jewish worship were forbidden.[4] Discredit and ridicule were heaped on these ceremonies, and this was certainly the starting-point for the hostile propaganda against those features of Jewish life which seemed particularly susceptible to jokes and crude parody (circumcision, the Sabbath, dietary prescriptions: the *Letter of Aristeas* was to attempt to give an allegorical and moral interpretation to the Mosaic prescriptions of purity).[5] In its accusation of ritual murder,

[1] Jacoby, *FGrHist* 87 F 109.

[2] Jos. *C.Ap.* II.91–6 (from Apion); cf. E. Bickerman, 'Ritualmord und Eselskult', *MGWJ*, 71 (1927), 171–87, 255–64. A different opinion in A. Jacoby, 'Der angebliche Eselskult der Juden und Christen', *ARW*, 25 (1927), 281–2.

[3] Bickerman, *MGWJ*, 71 (1927); Tcherikover, *Hellenistic Civilization*, pp. 366–7 would date this legend in the Roman era, Apion being the first to put it in a literary form.

[4] 1 Macc. 1:41–53; 2 Macc. 6:1; R. de Vaux, 'Les sacrifices de porcs en Palestine et dans l'Ancien Orient', *Von Ugarit nach Qumran*, Festschrift Eissfeldt, BZAW 77 (Berlin, 1958), pp. 250–65.

[5] *Aristeas* 142–69.

Seleucid propaganda was probably building on existing pretexts, perhaps exploiting Scriptural references to human sacrifices in Israel,[1] and linking them to the anti-Greek feelings which grew up during the persecution of Antiochus Epiphanes. This charge was destined to make a huge impression, and to have a wide circulation even after the persecution stopped. (Later, the Alexandrian author of the *Wisdom of Solomon*, who echoes passages from Greek tragedy in his writings, was to reproach the Canaanites, who were the previous inhabitants of Judea, with child sacrifices, cannibalism and other barbarous rites signifying religious mysteries.)[2] The *Letter of Aristeas* implicitly rejects charges of exclusivism and anti-social behaviour when it says that the Law commands that all men be treated justly, and that justice is the basis of social co-existence between men.[3] After all, the author of this little work presents himself as a pagan convinced of the superiority of the Jewish God. In the same perspective should be considered the theory, dating from the time of the Maccabees and possibly deriving from Cyrenaican circles, that the Jews and the Spartans are related through Abraham,[4] and the story of an ancient friendship, in the time of Abraham, between Jews and Greeks of Pergamum.[5] The Jewish colony in Rome was said to have carried on proselytizing activities towards the middle of the second century B.C.E., and they were driven out of the city for this in 139 B.C.E., along with Chaldean soothsayers.[6] However, according to Posidonius, in 134 B.C.E. the counsellors of King Antiochus Sidetes advised the king to destroy the Jews, for they alone among all peoples refused all relations with other races, and saw everyone as their enemy; their forebears, impious and cursed by the gods, had been driven out of Egypt.[7] The counsellors repeated the legend of the lepers and the polluted, and of the Jews' hatred of all mankind, sanctioned by their very laws, which forbade them to share their table with a Gentile or give any sign of benevolence. These are the same charges which the *Letter of Aristeas* rebuts in the name of justice, the basis of human co-existence. The counsellors' appeal to the example of Antiochus Epiphanes confirms the role played by Seleucid propa-

[1] R. de Vaux, *Studies in Old Testament Sacrifices* (Cardiff, 1964), pp. 52–90.

[2] Wis. 12:3–7; D. Gill, 'The Greek sources of Wisdom XII.3–7', *VT*, 15 (1965), 383–6.

[3] *Aristeas* 168–9.

[4] 1 Macc. 12:19–23; B. Cardauns, 'Juden und Spartaner. Zur hellenistisch-jüdischen Literatur', *Hermes*, 95 (1967), 317–24; Hengel, *Hellenismus*, pp. 133f, ET I, p. 72.

[5] Jos. *Ant.* XIV.247–55.

[6] Valerius Maximus 1.3.3; a different view in S. Alessandrí, 'La presunta cacciata dei Giudei da Roma nel 139 a. Cr.', *SCO*, 17 (1968), 187–98.

[7] Jacoby, *FGrHist* 87 F 109.

ganda in spreading these accusations, where the anti-Jewish traditions of Egypt were taken up and developed.

All the evidence tends to show that by the second half of the second century B.C.E. the anti-Jewish controversy had entered an acute phase, which prepared the ground for the emergence in the next century of the first unmistakable libels against the Jews. This new phase must have been encouraged by a hardening of postures within the Jewish Diaspora, due to the presence of the Hasmonean state, which could not but be reflected in the practical attitudes of the Jews towards the Greek world, intent now on strengthening their own self-consciousness by accentuating all differences and distances.

The first publication which directly attacked the Jewish people was that of Apollonios Molon.[1] This writer was a politically and culturally influential figure in Rhodes during the first decades of the first century B.C.E. He had been to Rome as an ambassador in the year 81 B.C.E. after the Mithridatic war. A master of rhetoric and grammar, his audience at Rhodes included Cicero, who had already heard him in Rome and praised him highly, as well as Caesar and other prominent Romans. We do not know why he wrote a polemical historical work 'Against the Jews', but it is not difficult to imagine that he was influenced by the Greek experience of living with the Jews in the cities of Asia Minor, if not indeed at Rhodes itself, where the privileges granted by the Roman government to the Jewish communities were already in force.[2]

His treatment was undoubtedly insidious, because the hostile criticisms were not bunched together but were scattered thinly through the historical content.[3] The fact that this appears to have been the only anti-Jewish work exploited by Alexander Polyhistor suggests that it was the best available text in 63 B.C.E. Josephus combats it strongly in his *Contra Apionem*, along with Apion's more recent work, and one has the impression that Apollonios was on a higher level than the Egyptian historian. Apollonios traced a history of the Jewish people after the Flood; he spoke of Abraham and his descendants, one branch of whom had settled in Arabia, while another branch were ancestors of Joseph and Moses.[4] He spoke of the expulsion from Egypt and gave a date different from that proposed by Manetho, and from the other date which was later suggested by Lysimachus (the reign of Bocchoris):[5] it

[1] Jacoby, *FGrHist* 728; Stern, *Authors* I, pp. 150–6.

[2] J. Juster, *Les Juifs dans l'Empire Romain* (Paris, 1914), 1, pp. 188ff, 213ff.

[3] Jos. *C.Ap.* II.148 = *FGrHist* 728 T 3a.

[4] *FGrHist* 728 F 1 = Euseb. *Praep. Evang.* IX.19.

[5] Jos. *C.Ap.* II.16 = *FGrHist* 728 F 2.

could be that he was not referring to the identification of the Jews with the 'polluted'. Moses was probably accused of charlatanry, and his laws were said to be contrary to justice and truth.[1] Apollonios accused the Jews of atheism and misanthropy, of not wishing to associate with other peoples with different customs and religious beliefs; he charged them with laziness (the Sabbath problem again), but also with desperate rashness (because of the Maccabees' revolt?); and he revived the charge that the Jews had not co-operated in the progress of human civilization.[2] It seems that Apollonios' tone was far from the sharpest edges of the controversy, and that his work did not include the most outrageous charges against the Jews, which were also the most ridiculously factitious and grotesque.

We cannot tell whether Apollonios' little treatise had any influence in Roman quarters, although it is possible that Varro's demonstrable knowledge of the Jewish religion could have come partly from this source. In Jewish circles, quite a lot of importance seems to have been rightly attributed to Apollonios' attack, as can be seen, for instance, from the reaction of Flavius Josephus. One could probably identify a counterblast to Apollonios' account in the source of Strabo's excursus on the Jews.[3] This passage has usually been attributed to Posidonius, mainly because of a certain coincidence which it presents with Posidonius' religious ideas, as these are known to us from other sources. Furthermore, later in the same passage of Strabo, Posidonius is quoted in connection with the Dead Sea. Thus, in Jacoby's collection, Strabo's excursus is printed among the fragments from Posidonius.[4] It was not clear to what part of Posidonius' writings the excursus had originally belonged (Strabo apparently knew of it only through an intermediate source). Jacoby inclined to the opinion that it was brought into the account of the capture of Jerusalem by Antiochus Sidetes in 134 B.C.E.: as we have seen, another fragment which certainly comes from Posidonius treated of this episode, and reported the anti-Jewish advice of the royal counsellors.[5] A less probable source would be the monograph dedicated by Posidonius to Pompey: in this case, the occasion would be the conquest of 63 B.C.E.[6]

The attribution itself is uncertain. The tone of Strabo's excursus is clearly pro-Jewish. But Posidonius appears in Josephus among the

1 Jos. *C.Ap.* II.145 = *FGrHist* 728 F 3a.
2 Jos. *C.Ap.* II.148 = *FGrHist* 728 F 3 a; II.258 = *FGrHist* 728 F 3b.
3 Strabo XVI.2.34–9 (C 760–2); Stern, *Authors* I pp. 159–62.
4 Jacoby, *FGrHist* 87 F 70; commentary in II C, pp. 196–9.
5 Jacoby, *FGrHist* 87 F 109.
6 Jacoby, *FGrHis* IIIa, p. 47.

anti-Jewish historians, along with Apollonios Molon.[1] Although it is very probable that Josephus was referring to the events of 134 B.C.E., it does seem rather unlikely that he could have been unaware that Posidonius in fact held opposite views, as would be the case if Strabo's excursus came from him. A more likely theory is that Strabo followed the text, or at any rate the ideas, of a Hellenized Jew who had some knowledge of Posidonius' theories.[2]

The contents of Strabo's chapters, in summary, are as follows. Moses, a priest of Lower Egypt, disapproving of the Egyptian cult of animals, and also of the Greeks' anthropomorphic worship, and believing in one single Godhead, incapable of being represented because coextensive with the heavens, the universe and all Creation, left Egypt with a large following and came into Judea. His teaching was that the deity must not be represented, but should be honoured without a temple, in a sacred enclosure with a suitable altar. Only those who had lived with wisdom and justice should expect to receive blessings, gifts and signs from God. (From a parenthesis which is not well connected with the context, it appears that the deity manifests himself in dreams; but it is suspected that this sentence is a comment by Strabo himself.) Quite a few sensible people followed Moses. He led them to the place where Jerusalem now stands, a very rocky area, although supplied with water, and therefore not desired by other people or worth fighting a war over. The territory nearby and for some way is also rocky, sterile and without water. Instead of arms he put forward as defences sacrifices and his deity, declaring his intention of finding a suitable place for them, and promising to establish a worship and ritual which would not afflict its devotees with expenses, divine inspirations or similar nonsense. Honoured by his own people, he established an unusual kind of government, and all the neighbouring peoples came to him naturally out of fellowship and because of his promises for the future. This state of affairs lasted with his successors for some time. Then superstitious people occupied the supreme priesthood, and these were followed by tyrants. From superstition arose the prescriptions of dietary purity, and male and female circumcision was established along with other rules of the same sort. The tyrannical power gave rise to policies of violence and depredation in both their own and other countries, while others, by agreement with the ruling clique, stole other people's property and overran much of Syria and Phoenicia. There

[1] Jos. *C.Ap.* II.79 = *FGrHist* 87 F 69.

[2] A. D. Nock, 'Posidonius', *JRS*, 49 (1959), 1–15 (repr. in *Essays on Religion and the Ancient World* (Oxford, 1972), 2, pp. 853–76); J. G. Gager, *Moses in Graeco-Roman Paganism* (Nashville–New York, 1972), pp. 38ff.

remained however a sense of respect and reverence for the Temple itself, which was not seen as the seat of tyranny.

The following two chapters seem rather to be comments and comparisons made by Strabo himself:[1] they recall legislators who claimed divine origins for the rules which they laid down, in order to increase their authority, and all the more so when this happened with the prophets, whose commandments are valid even after their death.

In its portrayal of Moses, Strabo's account does not follow the Greek ethnographic model as used by Hecateus, but retraces in part the outlines of the Egyptian narrative, distilling them from the mass of accusation and slander. Moses is an Egyptian priest, he disapproves of the cult of animals and idols (but wreaks no destruction), he leaves the country voluntarily with many respectable folk (instead of being driven out with a horde of lepers and 'polluted' people). Other elements then come in. The country to which he goes is not the one described in the *Letter of Aristeas* as a paradise of fertility: it is sterile and stony. But his simple religious laws and his government attracted the neighbouring peoples (instead of isolating the Jews; their enemies said that the worst people among their neighbours joined them).[2] Thus far, this tradition is able to vindicate the origins of the Jewish people, the present Moses as a priest driven by religious motives and lofty ideals, and to defend the justice of his laws and their relation to the outside world. The movement from contemporary historical reality is made without recourse to strained interpretations or allegory, but rather with dignified respect. The idea of decadence in religion and religious institutions (and the pantheistic account of Jewish monotheism) need not necessarily derive from Posidonius. This theme was widespread in Greek and Jewish circles in the first century B.C.E., and anyway it was already present in Hecateus. Strabo's tradition recognizes that superstition has cramped an original religious freedom with a host of ritual requirements. Implicitly it seems to admit the negative consequences of these isolatory prescriptions. Superstition in the high priesthood chronologically precedes the advent of tyranny, by which is undoubtedly meant the regime of the Hasmoneans. We are faced here with a complex tradition which shares the objections to the expansionist policies of the Hasmoneans, at least from John Hyrcanus onwards, to the violent conversion to Judaism of neighbouring populations, and to the pillaging and confiscation of enemy property by the Jewish aristocracy, especially in the time of Alexander Janneus. Some of these notes may

[1] Strabo XVI.2.38–9 (C 161–2).

[2] Tacitus, *Histories* V.5.

also be heard in certain lamentations from the book of Enoch.[1] On the other hand, the theory that superstition had added new restrictions to the Mosaic Law seems to agree with certain criticisms made against the Pharisees, as these are known to us through Josephus.[2] The idea of distinguishing between ancient laws and recent institutions of a worse kind was also present in the anti-Jewish tradition.[3]

In any case, the tradition which we are discussing, faced with hostile criticism of some considerable weight, as in the case of Apollonios Molon, re-emphasized the purity of the origins of Judaism, and indicated the causes of decadence, which were fundamentally political.

The year 63 B.C.E. is fundamental not just to the political history of Judea, on account of Pompey's conquest, but also for the knowledge which the Romans acquired of the Jews and their history. The good relations which had been established in the course of the second century B.C.E. between Rome and the Hasmoneans[4] had not prevented the expulsion of the Jews in 139, and turned out to be nothing but a diplomatic device, which produced no visible consequences in the first half of the first century B.C.E. Pompey's conquest in the year 63 is at the root of at least two historical works on the Jews, probably designed to furnish the Romans with facts and information about the new people with whom they had come in direct contact, and many representatives of whom had arrived in Rome as slaves. Nothing is known of the 'Jewish History' in six books by Teucer of Cyzicus;[5] but we are well informed on the treatise 'On the Jews' by Cornelius Alexander Polyhistor.[6] This must have been an anthology, similar to other works of history and ethnography by the same author, which were intended to introduce the Romans to peoples and literatures of which they knew little or nothing, and which had just come into their political orbit. His treatise 'On the Jews' must certainly have fulfilled its task of popular information, but on a literary level it is never quoted before Clement of Alexandria.[7] Thereafter, it was used extensively by Eusebius of Caesarea in his *Praeparatio Evangelica*. It is very odd that Josephus had

[1] Tcherikover, *Hellenistic Civilization*, pp. 258ff; cf. Trogus, *Prol.* 39; Justin XL.2.

[2] Jos. *Ant.* XIII.297. Cf. E. Bickerman, *Der Gott der Makkabäer* (Berlin, 1937), p. 130; Hengel, *Hellenismus*, pp. 469–71; ET I, pp. 258f.

[3] Tacitus, *Hist.* V.5.

[4] A. Giovannini and H. Müller, 'Die Beziehungen zwischen Rom und den Juden im 2. Jh. v.Chr.', *Museum Helveticum*, 28 (1971), 156–71.

[5] Jacoby, *FGrHist* 274; Stern, *Authors* I, pp. 165–6.

[6] Jacoby, *FGrHist* 273 F 19a–b; cf. F 101, 102(?), 121, commentary in III A, pp. 248ff; Stern, *Authors* I, pp. 159–62.

[7] Clem. Alex. *Strom.* I.130.3.

no knowledge of it. The latter historian does quote from Polyhistor a passage by the historian Cleodemus Malchus on the descendants of Abraham, especially concerning Africa and a possible relationship with Heracles (an allusion to the Phoenician colonization of Africa, and a preface to the theory of a Jewish–Spartan relationship?), but it seems likely that his source in this was the 'Libyka' by Polyhistor, not the work 'On the Jews'.[1] Josephus himself shows that he had no knowledge of the Hellenistic Jewish literature which Polyhistor used.[2]

Polyhistor expounded Jewish history by combining extracts from other authors, and we cannot tell whether he added his own linking material between the various extracts. If we accept the use that Eusebius made of it, we must say that the work was a mosaic of quotations arranged according to chronology and not according to author. Eusebius used this work up as far as the Babylonian captivity, but Polyhistor certainly brought the narrative up to 63 B.C.E. Going by Eusebius, one must conclude that the authors which Polyhistor used were all Jewish with the exception of Apollonios Molon and Timochares: we owe to him our knowledge of Hellenistic Jewish literature from the third to the first century B.C.E. Apollonios was undoubtedly an anti-Jewish author. It is probable that Polyhistor knew others, although the story of the two sons of Semiramis, Iouda and Idoumaia, which probably presupposes the union of the two territories under John Hyrcanus (126 B.C.E.), does not seem to be an argument in this direction.[3] Besides, in this work on Rome he manages to mention that a Jewish woman, Moso, had written the Law of the Jews.[4] It is certain that despite his knowledge of anti-Jewish traditions, Polyhistor practically never exploited them in his work, just as he refrained from using non-Jewish traditions. It is unlikely that this conclusion arises solely from the knowledge that we have of his work through Eusebius, given the arrangement of the material. It may be that he used anti-Jewish sources for the more recent period, although it is not clear what these might be unless he drew on Seleucid propaganda. Nor does it seem likely that he would have described the Jews to the Romans, who were their allies in the Maccabean period, in hostile terms. Perhaps, in order to justify the Roman intervention, he may have given a harsh judgement on the last Hasmonean kings. In any case, for the origins of the Jewish people he steered clear of the Egyptian anti-Jewish traditions: and that was the most controversial subject of all. Given this

[1] Jos. *Ant.* 1.240 = *FGrHist* 273 F 102; 727 F 1.

[2] Jos. *C.Ap.* 1.218; Jacoby, *FGrHist* IIIa, p. 269.

[3] Jacoby, *FGrHist* 273 F 121.

[4] Jacoby, *FGrHist* 273 F 70.

state of affairs it does not seem that Polyhistor was just an objective or neutral anthologist: as far as we know he was pro-Jewish.

We still do not know how Polyhistor came to know of such obscure figures as the Jewish–Hellenistic writers. As these writers were Judean and Samaritan, it has been suggested that Polyhistor was drawing on a manuscript collection which bore witness to the controversy between the two groups, and which he used without noticing its polemical character. This hypothetical collection, of Alexandrian origin, would date from the period of Ptolemy Philometor (according to Freudenthal), or Ptolemy Physcon (according to Susemihl).[1] But the basis of this theory, an Egyptian journey by Polyhistor,[2] remains dubious, all the more so because he also quoted obscure authors in his other historical and ethnographic works. Jewish and Samaritan documents must have been available in Rome after 63 B.C.E.[3]

Polyhistor's work must have spread a certain knowledge of Judaism among educated Romans. Judging from the references in Roman writers from the end of first century B.C.E., one might also remark that they are rather familiar with the commonplaces of the anti-Jewish controversy.

This controversy had not by any means abated, and indeed took on a new lease of life after the Roman conquest of Egypt (30 B.C.E.). To the second half of the first century B.C.E. probably belongs Lysimachus, whose 'Jewish History' includes an anti-Jewish version of the Exodus.[4] Lysimachus' narrative brings further proof that the genuine tradition of Manetho has nothing precise to say against the Jews. For Lysimachus calmly shifts the expulsion of the 'polluted', with its attendant identification of the Jews, into a completely new historical context: the reign of King Bocchoris, whom he seems to have dated some 1,700 years before his own period.[5] The reign of Bocchoris was later given as the date of the Exodus by Apion, who furnished the date of the seventh Olympiad (752–749), and by Tacitus, who quoted in this regard the consensus of *plurimi auctores*.[6] For Lysimachus, of course,

[1] J. Freudenthal, *Alexander Polyhistor* (Breslau, 1875), pp. 102–3; F. Susemihl, *Geschichte der griechischen Literatur in der Alexandrinerzeit* 2 (Leipzig, 1892), p. 361 n. 76 and p. 655; Jacoby, *FGrHist* IIIa, p. 253. Cf. Jos. *Ant.* XIII.75–9.

[2] It is supposed to be proved by the eyewitness character of F 5.

[3] B. Z. Wacholder, 'Greek authors in Herod's Library', *Studies in Bibliography and Booklore,* 5 (1961), 102–9.

[4] F. Jacoby, *FGrHist* 621; Stern, *Authors* I, pp. 383–6. The identification with the paradoxographer of the same name should be discarded: Jacoby, *FGrHist* IIIB. Kommentar, Text, pp. 165ff; Gager, *Moses*, pp. 118–20.

[5] Jos. *C.Ap.* II.16 = *FGrHist* 621 F 2.

[6] Apion: Jacoby, *FGrHist* 616 F 4a (= Jos. *C.Ap.* II.15–17); Tacitus, *Hist.* V.3.

the leader of the 'polluted' is Moses. King Bocchoris is a historical character: he was a king of the fourteenth dynasty, and reigned from 720 to 715 B.C.E. Under his reign occurred an Ethiopian conquest of Egypt, and the king himself came to a tragic end.[1] The king is remembered in the Greek tradition too, with widely differing characterizations: sometimes he is a wise ruler, sometimes a cruel king who slights the gods.[2] He had a role to play in Egyptian apocalyptic literature, which linked his reign with the famous 'prophecy of the lamb', which is known to us through the Greek tradition,[3] but mainly from a demotic text of the year 4–5 C.E.[4] in this fragmentary demotic papyrus there is a mention of Assyria (Iowar), source of the many ills which plague the country. It is possible that the version of the episode in Pseudo-Plutarch is based on Manetho, but in any case it seems that the 'prophecy of the lamb', which concerned the reign of Bocchoris, was current at the beginning of the Christian Era, and that might be enough to explain why writers from this period or slightly later (Lysimachus, Apion, Tacitus' source) fastened the story of the 'polluted' on to this king, rather than follow the tradition of Manetho, who incidentally was to find a follower in Chaeremon, another writer of Egyptian history.[5]

The case of Lysimachus lends itself to the formulation of final conclusions, being almost symbolic in character. Until the middle of the first century B.C.E., and in some cases even later, the Greek and Roman view of Judaism continued essentially to pass through the filter of Egyptian history, that is to say, through a hostile tradition. Direct knowledge of biblical texts is lacking, and the solitary quotation by the writer 'On the Sublime' is the exception which proves the rule; that quotation may be explained by a more or less direct derivation from a Jewish source.[6] There were in practice no works dedicated to the history of Judea, and Polyhistor's anthology does not seem to have attracted many readers. The initial Greek interest in the religious-political *bios* of the Jews, when this was first discovered, quickly dwindled away, only to be revived in the middle of the first century B.C.E. by a few students of religious history such as Varro. Hecateus'

[1] E. Drioton and J. Vandier, *Les peuples de l'Orient Mediterranéen*, 2: *L'Égypte* (3rd edn., Paris, 1952), pp. 544–5.

[2] Diod. 1.65.1; 79.1; 94.5; Aelian, *De natura animalium* XI.II.

[3] Ael. *NA* XII.3; Pseudo-Plutarch, *de prov. Alex* 21 ed. Crusius (Leipzig, 1887).

[4] C. C. McCrown, 'Hebrew and Egyptian apocalyptic literature' *HTR*, 18 (1925), 392–7; E. Bresciani, *Letteratura e poesia dell'antico Egitto* (Turin, 1969), pp. 561–2.

[5] Jacoby, *FGrHist* 618 F 1.

[6] *De sublim*. IX.9; Hengel, *Hellenismus*, p. 473; ET I, p. 260.

account, inserted in a context of Egyptian history, was however to be used by Diodorus. There remained the polemical works on both sides. The one by Apollonios must have reached a wide readership; later a pro-Jewish work came down to Strabo, though we do not know exactly how. There were also the commonplaces that hostile propaganda had put into circulation and which, like all slanders, had taken root and prospered. Greek and Egyptian propaganda in Alexandria soon had a fresh opportunity to thrive with the establishment of Roman government in Egypt, and the new political, administrative and social problems which this provoked in the former capital city. That propaganda was a prime source for historiography when the Jewish revolt of 66 C.E. threw Judea suddenly and violently into the forefront of Roman politics. But the roots of anti-Judaism in the imperial age go deep down into the preceding Hellenistic age.

APPENDIX I

Alcaeus' fragment 50 in E. Diehl (ed), *Anthologia lyrica graeca* (*vol.* 1, Leipzig, 1925) (= 350 Voigt, Amsterdam, 1971) hints at mercenary service by Alcaeus' brother, Antimenidas, with the Babylonians towards the end of the seventh century and at the beginning of the sixth B.C.E. (D. L. Page, *Sappho and Alcaeus* (Oxford, 1955), pp. 223–4; M. M. Austin, *Greece and Egypt in the Archaic Age*, Proc. Cambridge Phil. Soc. Supplement 2 (Cambridge, 1970), pp. 15–17). The fragment reports the killing of a gigantic warrior by Antimenidas, and it has been connected with a scholion to Alcaeus (*Oxyrhynchus Papyri*, ed. B. P. Grenfell and A. S. Hunt (London, 1898ff), vol. II (1915), 1360, fr. 13), which seems to contain the name either of Jerusalem or of its inhabitants 'Ιεροσυ̣[. The supplement of the text is not certain (S. Mazzarino, 'Per la storia di Lesbo nel VI secolo a.C.', *Athenaeum*, n.s., 21 (1943), 76) and in any case it is unwise to read into fr. 50 an episode of the siege of Jerusalem by Nebuchadnezzar (S. Luria, 'Die Belagerung von Jerusalem bei Alkaios', *Acta Antiqua,* 8 (1960), 265–6). However, it should be remembered that in another fragment by Alcaeus (82 Diehl = 48 Voigt) the reference to 'Ασκάλωνα is firmly attested. This fragment can be linked with the conquest of the town, now certainly dated in 604 B.C.E. (J. D. Quinn, 'Alcaeus 48 (B16) and the Fall of Ascalon (604 B.C.)', *BASOR,* 164 (1961), 19–20). Cf. now Stern, *Authors* 3 (Jerusalem, 1984), pp. 1–4.

APPENDIX 2

Aristotle is one of the very few authors between Herodotus and the Augustan age who use the name Παλαιστίνη (cf. Meteorol. 2, 3, 359 a, 17): E. Bickerman, 'La Coelé-Syrie. Notes de géographie historique', *RB*, 54 (1947), 260. In the Ps.-Aristotelian *De Plantis* 2.2, 824a, 26 the passage in the *Meteorologica* is repeated in substantially the same form except that the lake is called ἡ νεκρὰ θάλασσα. This name is only attested from Pausanias v.7.4 on. However we come across it in Justin xxxvi.3.6, who may have found it in the earlier Pompeius Trogus: F.-M. Abel, *Géographie de la Palestine* (Paris, 1938), 1, pp. 498ff. Very important is Diod. xix.98–100.3 (told of Demetrius Poliorcetes, 312 B.C.E.).

APPENDIX 3

It should be noted, first of all, that the identification of the people attested in Choerilus as the Jews, proposed by Josephus, clashes to a certain degree with the previous interpretation of Herodotus 11.104, 1–3. If 'the Syrians from Palestine' are the Jews, the same people is named in Herod. vii.89 in connection with Xerxes' fleet and in completely different context. In any case the identification of the inhabitants of the Solymoi Mountains or of the Solymoi as the Jews was rather common, as can be seen from the pro-Jewish additions to Manetho or from Tacitus, *Histories* v.2, where Homer is referred to.

Choerilus' assumption is certainly based on Herodotus. The passage which the poet took as his source, in Herodotus' list of the Persian troops, is beyond doubt the description of οἱ ἐκ τῆς 'Ασίης Αἰθίοπες in Herod. vii.70. The historian distinguishes them from their Libyan homonyms because of their language and because of the different type of hair (they have straight hair, perhaps because it is cut short, while other Ethiopians have woolly hair); moreover they wear skin taken from horses' foreheads as headgear. According to Choerilus their hair was shaven, in a similar way perhaps to the hair of the Arabs described in Herod. iii.8. As is well known, in Lev. 19:27 the cutting of hair is forbidden. The detail of the 'Phoenician' language, attributed to them by Choerilus, seems likely to have originated too from the statement of Herodotus that the eastern Ethiopians differed on this point from African Ethiopians. Choerilus seems to have been well versed in the languages of the East (R. Drews, 'Herodotus' other *logoi*', *AJP*, 91 (1970), 181–91; according to Reinach, *Textes*, p. 6 n. 1, this verse could have been interpolated). He must have had not difficulty in attributing a 'Phoenician' language to the Eastern Ethiopians (it is not easy to decide what he meant by 'Phoenician'). The detail too of the Solymoi mountains can be explained, as has already been shown, by the fact that they are referred to in connection with the Ethiopians in a passage in Homer, *Odyssey* v.282–3. On his way back from the Ethiopians Poseidon looks down from the mountains of the Solymoi, and sees Odysseus sailing on the sea. In Homer the mountains would be rather a long way away from the Ethiopians, but, given a certain poetic licence, Choerilus could have maintained the connection, especially as these mountains were not precisely located. According to Herod. I.173, Σόλυμοι was the old name for the Lycian Μιλύαι, who are mentioned in Xerxes' army at VII.77 wearing skin headgear. The 'famous Solymoi' of Homer, *Iliad* VI.184, are situated in Lycia or nearby. In Strabo XIII.4.16 (C 630) the Καβαλεῖς are called Σόλυμοι, and a hill with the same name existed above Termessus, where a lake too is attested: cf. Strabo XIV.3.9–10 (C 666–7). But it seems very doubtful whether the Solymoi mountains can be identified as the hill near Termessus: Ruge, *PW* 2nd ser., 3 (1929), cols. 988f., s.v. Σόλυμα, τά; G. Huxley, 'Choirilos of Samos', *GRBS,* 10 (1969), 12–29. F. Dornseiff, *Echtheitsfragen antik-griechischer Literatur* (Berlin, 1939), pp. 66–7, considered Choerilus older than Herodotus and accepted the interpretation given by Josephus as perfectly right, while, in his opinion, there had been a misunderstanding on Herodotus' part (cf. R. Lehmann-Nitsche, 'König Midas hat Eselsohren', *Zeitschrift für Ethnologie,* 68 (1936), 297–8). This theory, which was not generally accepted, was based on his attribution (Dornseiff, *Echtheitsfragen*, pp. 52–65) of Diodorus' chapters on the Jews to Hecateus of Milethus. Cf. now Stern, *Authors* 3, pp. 5–7.

BIBLIOGRAPHIES

GENERAL BIBLIOGRAPHY ON THE HELLENISTIC PERIOD

For earlier work see *The Cambridge Ancient History*, vol. 7: *The Hellenistic Monarchies and the Rise of Rome*, edited by S. A. Cook, F. E. Adcock, and M. P. Charlesworth (Cambridge, 1928), p. 867.

More recent bibliographies include:

Delling, G. *Bibliographie zur jüdisch-hellenistischen und intertestamentarischen Literatur 1900–1970*. TU 106. 2nd edn. Berlin, 1975.

Hengel, M. *Judentum und Hellenismus. Studien zu ihrer Begegnung unter besonderer Berücksichtigung Palästinas bis zur Mitte des 2. Jh.s.v. Chr.* WUNT 10. Tübingen, 1969; 2nd edn. 1973 (bibliography). ET: *Judaism and Hellenism. Studies in their Encounter in Palestine during the Early Hellenistic Period.* Philadelphia, 1974. Vol. 2, pp. 217–66.

Rappaport, U. *Bibliography of Works on Jewish History in the Hellenistic and Roman Periods, 1971–1975*. Jerusalem, 1976.

Abel, F.-M. *Histoire de la Palestine depuis la conquête d'Alexandre jusqu'à l'invasion arabe*. 2 vols. EBib. Paris, 1952.

Alon, G. *Jews, Judaism and the Classical World*. Jerusalem, 1977.

Altheim, F. *Der hellenisierte Orient*. Baden-Baden, 1969.

Applebaum, S. *Jews and Greeks in Ancient Cyrene*. SJLA 28. Leiden, 1979.

Avi-Yonah, M. *Hellenism and the East. Contacts and Interrelations from Alexander to the Roman Conquest*. In Hebrew. Jerusalem, 1978.

Baer, Y. F. *Israel among the Nations*. In Hebrew. Jerusalem, 1955.

Bagnall, R. S. *The Administration of the Ptolemaic Possessions outside Egypt*. Columbia Studies in the Classical Tradition 4. Leiden, 1976.

Bar-Kochva, B. *The Seleucid Army*. Cambridge, 1976.

Baron, S. W. *A Social and Religious History of the Jews*. Vols. 1 and 2. 2nd edn. Philadelphia, 1952.

Bengtson, H. *Die Strategie in der hellenistischen Zeit*. 3 vols. MBPAR 26, 32, 36. Munich, 1937–52.

Griechische Geschichte von den Anfängen bis in die römische Kaiserzeit. HAW 3.4. 4th edn. Munich, 1969.

Ben-Sasson, H. H. (ed.). *History of the Jewish People*, vol. 1: *The Ancient Times*. In Hebrew. Tel Aviv, 1969. ET: Cambridge, Mass., 1976.

Bevan, E. R. *The House of Ptolemy*. London, 1927.

Bickerman, E. J. *Der Gott der Makkabäer*. Berlin, 1937; ET *The God of the Maccabees*. SJLA, 32. Leiden, 1979.

Institutions des Séleucides. Paris, 1938.
From Ezra to the Last of the Maccabees. New York, 1962.
Studies in Jewish and Christian History. 2 vols. AGJU 9.1, 2. Leiden, 1976–80.
Box, G. H. *Judaism in the Greek Period*. Clarendon Bible. Oxford, 1932.
Bury, J. B., Cook, S. A. and Adcock, F. E. (eds.). *The Cambridge Ancient History*. Vols. 6–9. Cambridge, 1927–32.
Cary, M. *A History of the Greek World, 323–146 B.C.* London, 1951
Colledge, M. A. R. *The Parthians*. Ancient Peoples and Places 59. London, 1967.
Eddy, S. K. *The King is Dead. Studies in the Near Eastern Resistance to Hellenism, 334–31 B.C.* Lincoln, Nebraska, 1961.
Fraser, P. M. *Ptolemaic Alexandria*. 3 vols. Oxford, 1972.
Frey, J.-B. *Corpus Inscriptionum Iudaicarum*. 2 vols. Rome, 1936–52.
Freyne, S. *Galilee from Alexander the Great to Hadrian, 323 B.C.E. to 135 C.E.* Notre Dame, 1980.
Grimal, P. *Der Hellenismus und der Aufstieg Roms*. Fischer Weltgeschichte, vol. 6. Frankfurt, 1965; ET *Hellenism and the Rise of Rome*. London, 1968.
Gruen, E. S. *The Hellenistic World and the Coming of Rome*. 2 vols. Berkeley, 1984.
Hadas, M. *Hellenistic Culture, Fusion and Diffusion*. New York, 1959.
Hayes, J. H. and Miller, J. M. (eds.). *Israelite and Judaean History*. OTL. Philadelphia, 1977.
Hengel, M. *Judentum und Hellenismus. Studien zu ihrer Begegnung unter besonderer Berücksichtigung Palästinas bis zur Mitte des 2. Jh.s.v. Chr.* WUNT 10. Tübingen, 1969; 2nd edn., 1973. ET: *Judaism and Hellenism. Studies in their Encounter in Palestine during the Early Hellenistic Period*. 2 vols. Philadelphia, 1974.
Juden, Griechen und Barbaren. SBS 76. Stuttgart, 1976. ET: *Jews, Greeks and Barbarians*. Philadelphia, 1980.
Jones, A. H. M. *The Cities of the Eastern Roman Provinces*. 2nd edn. Oxford, 1971.
Kahrstedt, U. *Syrische Territorien in hellenistischer Zeit*. AGG, NF 19, 2. Berlin, 1926.
Kasher, A. *The Jews in Hellenistic and Roman Egypt*. In Hebrew. Tel. Aviv, 1978.
Klauser, T. and Dölger, F. J. (eds.). *Reallexikon für Antike und Christentum*. Multiple vols. Stuttgart, 1950ff.
Klausner, J. *History of the Second Temple*. In Hebrew. Vols. 1–5. 6th edn. Jerusalem, 1963.
Kolbe, W. *Beiträge zur syrischen und jüdischen Geschichte*. BWANT 2.10. Stuttgart, 1926.
Lieberman, S. *Greek in Jewish Palestine*. New York, 1942.
Hellenism in Jewish Palestine. 2nd edn. New York, 1962.
Texts and Studies. New York, 1974.
Maehler, H. and Strocka, V. M. *Das ptolemäische Aegypten*. Mainz, 1978.
Meyer, E. *Die Entstehung des Judenthums*. Halle an der Saale, 1896.
Momigliano, A. *Alien Wisdom. The Limits of Hellenization*. Cambridge, 1975.
Hochkulturen im Hellenismus. Die Begegnung der Griechen mit Kelten, Römern, Juden und Persern. Munich, 1979.
Mørkholm, O. *Antiochus IV of Syria*. Classica et Mediaevalia Dissertations 8. Copenhagen, 1966.
Nilsson, M. P. *Geschichte der griechischen Religion*, vol. 2: *Die hellenistische und römische Zeit*. HAW 5. 2, 2. 3rd edn. Munich, 1974.
Noth, M. *Geschichte Israels*. Rev. edn. Göttingen, 1954. ET: *History of Israel*. Rev. edn. London–New York, 1960.

Oesterley, W. O. E. *The Jews and Judaism during the Greek Period: The Background of Christianity*. London, 1941.

Oesterley, W. O. E. and Robinson, T. H. *A History of Israel*. Vol. 2. London, 1932.

Paulys Real-encyclopädie der classischen Altertumswissenschaft. New edn. by G. Wissowa, W. Kroll, *et al.* Stuttgart, 1893–1963; 2nd ser., 1914–1972; Supplement, 1903–78, index 1980.

Peters, F. E. *The Harvest of Hellenism: A History of the Near East from Alexander the Great to the Triumph of Christianity*. New York, 1970.

Préaux, C. *Le monde hellénistique I–II*. Paris, 1978.

Rappaport, U. *A History of the Jewish People in the Period of the Second Temple*. In Hebrew, 2nd edn. Tel Aviv, 1976.

Ringel, J. *Césarée de Palestine. Étude historique et archéologique*. Paris, 1975.

Rostovtzeff, M. *The Social and Economic History of the Hellenistic World*. 3 vols. Oxford, 1941.

Roth, C. and Wigoder, J. (eds.). *Encyclopaedia Judaica*. 16 vols. Jerusalem–New York, 1971–2.

Russell, D. S. *The Jews from Alexander to Herod*. New Clarendon Bible. Oxford, 1967.

Schalit, A. (ed.). *The World History of the Jewish People*, vol. 6: *The Hellenistic Age*. Jerusalem, 1972.

Schlatter, A. *Geschichte Israels von Alexander dem Grossen bis Hadrian*. 3rd edn. Stuttgart, 1925; repr. Stuttgart, 1977.

Schürer, Emil. *The History of the Jewish People in the Age of Jesus Christ (175 B.C.–A.D. 135)*, rev. and ed. Geza Vermes, Fergus Millar, and Matthew Black. Vols. 1–3. Edinburgh, 1973–87.

Sevenster, J. *The Roots of Pagan Anti-Semitism in the Ancient World*. NovTSup 41. Leiden, 1975.

Simon, M. and Benoit, A. *Le judaïsme et le christianisme antiquite*. Nouvelle Clio 10. Paris, 1968.

Smith, M. *Palestinian Parties and Politics that Shaped the Old Testament*. New York, 1971.

Stern, M. *Greek and Latin Authors on Jews and Judaism*, vol. 1: *From Herodotus to Plutarch*. Jerusalem, 1974.

Stone, M. E. *Scriptures, Sects, and Visions*. Philadelphia, 1980.

Tarn, W. W. and Griffith, G. T. *Hellenistic Civilization*. 3rd edn. London, 1952.

Tcherikover, V. *Hellenistic Civilization and the Jews*. Philadelphia, 1959.

Tcherikover, V. and Fuks, A. *Corpus Papyrorum Judaicarum*. 3 vols. Cambridge, Mass., 1957–64.

Temporini, H. and Haase, W. (eds.). *Aufstieg und Niedergang der römischen Welt. Geschichte und Kultur Roms im Spiegel der neueren Forschung*. Parts 1 and 2; numerous vols. Berlin–New York, 1972ff.

Toynbee, A. *Hellenism, the History of a Civilization*. Oxford, 1959.

Will, E. *Histoire politique du monde hellénistique (323–30 av. J.-C.)*. 2 vols. Annales de l'Est 30, 32. Nancy, 1966–67.

Le monde grec et l'orient. Vol. 2. Paris, 1975.

Zeitlin, S. *The Rise and Fall of the Judean State*. Vol. 1. Philadelphia, 1962.

CHAPTER 1. THE ARCHEOLOGY OF HELLENISTIC PALESTINE

General Works

Abel, F.-M. and Starcky, J. *Les Livres des Maccabées*, BJ. 3rd edn. Paris, 1961.

Albright, W. F., *The Archaeology of Palestine*. Harmondsworth, 1949; rev. edn. 1960.

Avi-Yonah, M. *Ten Years of Archaeology in Israel*. Jerusalem, 1958.

Barrois, A.-G. *Manuel d'Archéologie biblique*. 2 vols. Paris, 1939, 1952.

Bliss, F. J. and Macalister, R. A. S. *Excavations in Palestine*. London, 1902.

du Buit, M. *Archéologie du peuple d'Israël*. Paris, 1960.

Goodenough, E. R. *Jewish Symbols in the Greco-Roman Period*. Vols. 1 to 13. Bollingen Series 37. New York, 1953–68.

Kenyon, K. M. *Archaeology in the Holy Land*. 4th edn. London, 1979.

Macalister, R. A. S. *A Century of Excavations in Palestine*. London, 1925.

Rostovtzeff, M. *The Social and Economic History of the Hellenistic World*. 3 vols. Oxford, 1941.

Watzinger, C. *Denkmäler Palästinas*. 2 vols. Leipzig, 1933–35.

Yeivin, S. *A Decade of Archaeology in Israel 1948–1958*. Publications de l'Institut historique et archéologique néderlandais de Stamboul, 8. Istanbul, 1960.

Fortifications

Amiran, R. and Eitan, A. 'Excavations in the courtyard of the Citadel, Jerusalem, 1968–1969 (preliminary report)', *IEJ*, 20 (1970), 9–17.

Avi-Yonah, M. 'Excavations in Jerusalem. Review and evaluation', in *Jerusalem Revealed*, ed. Y. Yadin, pp. 21–4. Jerusalem, 1975.

Bliss, F. J. *Excavations at Jerusalem, 1894–1897*. London, 1898.

Crowfoot, J. W., Crowfoot, G. M. and Kenyon, K. M. *Samaria-Sebaste, Reports of the Joint Expedition in 1931–1933*. 3 vols. London, 1942–57.

Crowfoot, J. W. and Fitzgerald, G. M. 'Excavations in the Tyropoeon Valley, Jerusalem 1927', *PEFA*, 5 (1927).

Elgavish, J. *The Excavations of Shikmona. A Seleucian Garrison Camp from Hasmonean Times*. Haifa, 1972.

Johns, C. N. 'The Citadel, Jerusalem. A summary of work since 1934', *QDAP*, 14 (1950), 121–90.

Kaplan, J. 'Exploration archéologique de Tel-Aviv–Jaffa', *RB*, 62 (1955), 92–9.

Kelso, J. L. and Baramki, D. C. 'Excavations at New Testament Jericho and Khirbet en-Nitla', *AASOR*, 29–30 (1949–51: pubd. 1955).

Kenyon, K. M. *Jerusalem. Excavating 3000 Years of History*. London, 1967.

Launey, M. *Recherches sur les armées hellénistiques*. Bibliothèque des écoles françaises d'Athènes et de Rome, 169. 2 vols. Paris, 1949–50.

Macalister, R. A. S. 'Excavations on the Hill of Ophel, Jerusalem, 1923–25', *PEFA*, 4 (1926).

Mazar, B., Dothan, M. and Dunayevsky, I. 'En-Gedi. The first and second seasons of excavations 1961–1962', *'Atiqot*, English series 5. 1966.

Reisner, G. A., Fisher, C. S., *et al. Harvard Excavations at Samaria 1908 to 1910*. 2 vols. Cambridge, Mass., 1924.

Sellers, O. R. *The Citadel of Beth-Zur*. Philadelphia, 1933.

Sellers, O. R., Funk, R. W., McKenzie, J. L., Lapp, P. and N. 'The 1957 excavation at Beth-Zur', *AASOR*, 38 (1968).

Sinclair, L. A. 'An archaeological study of Gibeah (Tell el-Fûl)', *AASOR*, 34/35 (1954–56: pubd. 1960).

Tsafrir, Y. 'The location of the Seleucid Akra in Jerusalem', in *Jerusalem Revealed*, ed. Y. Yadin, pp. 85–6. Jerusalem, 1975.

Vincent, L. H. *Jérusalem de l'Ancien Testament*. Recherches d'Archéologie et d'Histoire. 3 vols. Paris, 1954–56.

Weill, R. *La Cité de David. Compte-rendu des fouilles exécutées à Jérusalem, sur le site de la ville primitive*. Paris, 1920.

Winter, F. E. *Greek Fortifications*. Toronto, 1971.

Wright, G. E. *Shechem, the Biography of a Biblical City*. London–New York, 1964.

Dwelling places

Avigad, N. 'Excavations in the Jewish quarter of the Old City, 1969–1971', in *Jerusalem Revealed*, ed. Y. Yadin, pp. 41–51. Jerusalem, 1975.

Macalister, R. A. S. *The Excavation of Gezer*. 3 vols. London, 1912.

Martin, R. *L'Urbanisme dans la Grèce antique*. Paris, 1956.

Netzer, E. 'Notes and news: Jericho', *IEJ*, 23 (1973), 260.

'The Hasmonean and Herodian winter palaces at Jericho', *IEJ*, 25 (1975), 89–100.

Weinberg, S. S. 'Tel Anafa', *IEJ*, 19 (1969), 250–2.

'Tel Anafa – A problem-oriented excavation', *MUSE, Annual of the Museum of Art and Archaeology*, University of Missouri-Colombia, 3 (1969), 16–23.

'Tel Anafa: the Hellenistic town', *IEJ*, 21 (1971), 86–109.

'Tel Anafa: the second season', *MUSE*, 4 (1970), 15–24.

'Tel Anafa: the third season', *MUSE*, 5 (1971), 8–16.

'Tel Anafa – 1972: the fourth season', *MUSE*, 6 (1972), 8–18.

'Excavations at Tel Anafa, 1973', *MUSE*, 8 (1974), 14–28.

Tombs

Abel, F.-M. 'Tombeaux récemment découverts à Marisa', *RB*, 34 (1925), 267–75.

Avigad, N. 'Aramaic inscriptions in the tomb of Jason', *IEJ*, 17 (1967), 101–11.

'The architecture of Jerusalem in the second Temple period', in *Jerusalem Revealed*, ed. Y. Yadin, pp. 14–20. Jerusalem, 1975.

Benoit, P. 'L'inscription grecque du tombeau de Jason', *IEJ*, 17 (1967), 112–13.

Parrot, A. *Golgotha et Saint-Sépulcre*. Cahiers d'Archéologie Biblique, 6. Neuchâtel, 1955.

Peters, J. P. and Thiersch, H. *Painted Tombs in the Necropolis of Marissa (Marêshah)*. London, 1905.

Rahmani, L. Y. 'Jason's tomb', *IEJ*, 17 (1967), 61–100.

Cultic monuments

Aharoni, Y. *Beer-Sheva I*. Tel-Aviv, 1973.

'Trial excavation in the "solar shrine" at Lachish', *IEJ*, 18 (1968), 157–69, 254–5.

Amy, R. 'Temples à escaliers', *Syria,* 27 (1950), 82–136.
Avigad, N. 'Excavations at Makmish 1958. Preliminary report', *IEJ,* 10 (1960), 90–6.
Avi-Yonah, M. 'Mount Carmel and the God of Baalbek', *IEJ,* 2 (1952), 118–24.
'Syrian Gods at Ptolemais-Accho', *IEJ,* 9 (1959), 1–12.
Brett, M. J. B. 'The Qaṣr el-ʿAbd: a proposed reconstruction', *BASOR,* 171 (1963), 39–45.
Bull, R. J. 'The two temples at Tell er-Ras on Mount Gerizim in occupied Jordan', *AJA,* 74 (1970), 189–90.
Butler, H. C. 'Ancient architecture in Syria. Section A: Southern Syria', in *Publications of the Princeton University Archaeological expeditions to Syria in 1904–05...,* Division 2, Part 1, pp. 1–25. Leiden, 1919.
Dunand, M. 'Byblos, Sidon, Jérusalem. Monuments apparentés des temps achéménides', *Congress Volume, Rome 1968.* VTSup 17, pp. 64–70. Leiden, 1969.
Dupont-Sommer, A. 'Les autels à encens de Lakish', *Mélanges Isidore Lévy,* pp. 135–52. Paris, 1953.
Hill, D. K. 'The animal fountain of 'Arâq el-Emîr', *BASOR,* 171 (1963), 45–55.
Irby, C. L. and Mangles, J. *Travels in Egypt and Nubia, Syria and the Holy Land, including a journey round the Dead Sea and through the country east of Jordan.* London, 1844.
Landau, Y. H. 'A Greek inscription from Acre', *IEJ,* 11 (1961), 118–26.
Laperrousaz, E.-M. 'A-t-on dégagé l'angle sud-est du "Temple de Salomon"?', *Syria,* 50 (1973), 355–99.
Lapp, P. W. 'Soundings at 'Arâq el-Emîr (Jordan)' *BASOR,* 165 (1962), 16–34.
'The second and third campaigns at 'Arâq el-Emir', *BASOR,* 171 (1963), 8–39.
Mazar, B. 'The Tobiads', *IEJ,* 7 (1957), 137–45; 229–38.
Saulcy, F. de *Voyage en Terre Sainte,* vol. 1, pp. 211–35. Paris, 1865.
Tufnell, O. *Lachish III, The Iron Age.* Oxford, 1953.
de Vogüe, M. *Le Temple de Jérusalem. Monographie du Haram ech-Chérif, suivie d'un essai sur la topographie de la ville-sainte.* Paris, 1864.

Pottery

Dothan, M. 'Ashdod II–III. The second and third seasons of excavations 1963, 1965', *'Atiqot,* English series, 9–10. Jerusalem, 1971.
Dothan, M. and Freedman, D. N. 'Ashdod 1, the first season of excavations 1962', *'Atiqot,* English series, 7. Jerusalem, 1967.
Grace, V. 'Stamped amphora handles found in 1931–32. (The American excavations in the Athenian Agora – Fourth Report)', *Hesperia,* 3 (1934), 197–310.
Lapp, N. R. 'Pottery from some Hellenistic loci at Balâtah (Shechem)', *BASOR,* 175 (1964), 14–26.
Lapp, P. W. *Palestinian Ceramic Chronology 200 B.C.–A.D. 70.* ASOR, Publications of the Jerusalem School, Archaeology, Vol. 3. New Haven, 1961.
Zayadin, F. 'Early Hellenistic pottery from the theater excavations at Samaria', *Annual of the Department of Antiquities of Jordan,* 11 (1966), 53–64.

CHAPTER 2 THE POLITICAL AND SOCIAL HISTORY OF PALESTINE FROM ALEXANDER TO ANTIOCHUS III

Primary literature

Inscriptions and papyri

Edgar, C. C. *Zenon Papyri*, 1. Catalogue général des antiquités égyptiennes du Musée du Caire 79, nos. 59001–139. Cairo, 1925.

Lenger, M.-T. *Corpus des Ordonnances des Ptolémées*. Académie royale de Belgique. Classes des lettres, mémoires 57, 1. Brussels, 1964.

Tcherikover, V. A. and Fuks, A. *Corpus Papyrorum Judaicarum*, 3 vols. Cambridge, Mass., 1957–64.

Welles, C. B. *Royal Correspondence in the Hellenistic Period*. New Haven–London, 1934.

Westermann, W. L., Keyes, C. W. and Liebesny, H. *Zenon Papyri*, 2. Columbia Papyri Greek Series, 4. New York, 1940.

Individual texts and further epigraphical and papyrological material are *passim*.

Literary sources

Appian, *Syr.* 1, 5, 50, 52–4, 57, 65.

Arrian, *Anabasis* II.11, 13, 15–27; III.6, 16.

Curtius Rufus III.12, 13; IV.1–6, 8; X.10.

Diodorus XVII.40–9, 52; XVIII.3, 6, 28, 39, 43, 73; XIX.57–9, 61, 69, 79–86, 93–100; XX.47, 73–6, 113; XXI. fr. 1, 5.

Eusebius, *Chronica*: GCS 20, pp. 117f, 197–203 *passim*. *Chron. d. Hieronymus*: GCS 47, pp. 123–38 *passim*.

Jerome, *In Danielem*: CC 75 A, pp. 899–913 *passim*.

Josephus, *Antiquitates Judaicae* XI.302–47; XII.1–9, 129–46, 154–326; *C. Apion.* I.184–9, 192, 194, 200, 209–11; II.43, 48.

Justin, *Epitome* XI.10; XIII.4; XV.I; XVIII.3, 4; XXX.1; XXXI.1.

Plutarch, *De fortuna Alexandri* 24, 25, 29; *Demetrius* 5–7, 19, 31–3.

Polybius V.34, 40, 42, 43, 45, 46, 48, 49, 55, 57–71, 79–87, 107; VIII.19; XIV.12; XVI.18, 19, 22a, 27, 39; XVIII.49, 51; XXVIII.1, 20.

Daniel 11

3 Maccabees 1, 2

Pseudo-Aristeas

Further passages from the Hebrew Old Testament and other ancient literature are *passim*.

Secondary literature

Abel, F.-M. *Histoire de la Palestine depuis la conquête d'Alexandre jusq'à l'invasion arabe*. EBib. 2 vols. Paris, 1952.

Géographie de la Palestine. EBib. 2 vols. 1933–8; 3rd edn. Paris, 1967.

'Alexandre le Grand en Syrie et en Palestine', *RB*, 43 (1934), 528–45; *RB*, 44 (1935), 42–61.

'La Syrie et la Palestine au temps de Ptolémée 1er Soter', *RB*, 44 (1935), 559–81.

Bagnall, R. S. *The Administration of the Ptolemaic Possessions Outside Egypt*. Columbia Studies in the Classical Tradition 4. Leiden, 1976.

Bengtson, H. *Die Strategie in der hellenistischen Zeit*. Vols. 1–3. MBPAR 26, 32, 36. Munich, 1937–52; repr. 1964–67.

Griechische Geschichte von den Anfängen bis in die römische Kaiserzeit. HAW 3.4. 4th edn. Munich, 1969.

Berve, H. *Das Alexanderreich auf prosopagraphischer Grundlage*. 2 vols. Munich, 1926.

Bickerman, E. J. *Der Gott der Makkabäer*. Berlin, 1937; ET *The God of the Maccabees*. SJLA 32. Leiden, 1979.

Institutions des Séleucides. Bibliothèque archéologique et historique 26. Paris, 1938.

Chronology of the Ancient World. London, 1968.

'La Coele-Syrie. Notes de Géographie historique', *RB*, 54 (1947), 256–68.

Delcor, M. *Le livre de Daniel*. SB. Paris, 1971.

Hengel, M. *Judentum und Hellenismus*. WUNT 10. 2nd edn. Tübingen, 1973. ET *see* p. 658.

Juden, Griechen und Barbaren. SBS 76. Stuttgart, 1976. ET *see* p. 658.

Die Zeloten. AGJU 1. Leiden, 1961.

Jones, A. H. M. *The Cities of the Eastern Roman Provinces*. 2nd edn. Oxford, 1971.

Kahrstedt, U. *Syrische Territorien in hellenistischer Zeit*. AGG, NF 19, 2. Berlin, 1926.

Kippenberg, H. G. *Garizim und Synagoge*. RGVV 30. Berlin–New York, 1971.

Mørkholm, O. *Antiochus IV of Syria*. Classica et Mediaevalia Dissertations 8. Copenhagen, 1966.

Niese, B. *Geschichte der griechischen und makedonischen Staaten*. Vols. 1–3. Gotha, 1893–1903; repr. Darmstadt, 1963.

Peters, J. P. and Thiersch, H. *Painted Tombs in teh Necropolis of Marissa*. London, 1905.

Pfister, F. *Eine jüdische Gründungsgeschichte Alexandrias*. SAH, 1914, p. 11.

Alexander der Grosse in den Offenbarungen der Griechen, Juden, Mohammedaner und Christen. Abhandlungen der Deutschen Akademie der Wissenschaften zu Berlin, 1956, Schriften der Sektion für Altertumswissenschaft 3, Berlin 1956.

Préaux, C. *L'économie royale des Lagides*. Brussels, 1939.

Rostovtzeff, M. *Dura-Europos and its Art*. Oxford, 1938.

The Social and Economic History of the Hellenistic World. Vols. 1–3. Oxford, 1941.

Schalit, A. *König Herodes*. Studia Judaica 4. Berlin, 1969.

(ed.). *The World History of the Jewish People*. 6: *The Hellenistic Age*. Jerusalem, 1972.

Schmitt, H. H. *Untersuchungen zur Geschichte Antiochos' des Grossen und seiner Zeit*. Historia, Einzelschriften 6. Wiesbaden, 1964.

Schürer, E. *Geschichte des jüdischen Volkes im Zeitalter Jesu Christi*. Vols. 1–3 and index. 4th edn. Leipzig, 1901–11; repr. Hildesheim, 1964.

Schürer, E., Vermes, G. and Millar, F. *The History of the Jewish People in the Age of Jesus Christ*. Vol. 1. Edinburgh, 1973.

Seibert, J. *Untersuchungen zur Geschichte Ptolemaios' I*. MBPAR 56. Munich, 1969.

Alexander der Grosse. Erträge der Forschung 10. Darmstadt, 1972.

Sellers, O. R. 'Coins of the 1960 excavation at Shechem', *BA*, 25 (1962), 87–96.

Smith, M. *Palestinian Parties and Politics that Shaped the Old Testament*. New York, 1971.

Tcherikover, V. *Die hellenistischen Städtegründungen von Alexander dem Grossen bis auf die Römerzeit*. Philologus Supplement, 19, 1. Leipzig, 1927.

Hellenistic Civilization and the Jews. Philadelphia, 1959.

'Palestine under the Ptolemies', *Mizraim*, 4/5 (1937), 7–90.

Thissen, H.-J. *Studien zum Raphiadekret*. Beiträge zur klassischen Philologie 23. Meisenheim am Glan, 1966.

Weinberg, S. S. 'Tel Anafa: the Hellenistic town', *IEJ*, 21 (1971), 86–109.

Welten, P. *Geschichte und Geschichtsdarstellung in den Chronikbüchern.* WMANT 42. Neukirchen-Vluyn, 1973.

Will, E. *Histoire politique du monde hellénistique (323–30 av. J.-C.).* Annales de l'Est 30, 32. 2 vols. Nancy, 1966–67.

CHAPTER 3 HEBREW, ARAMAIC AND GREEK IN THE HELLENISTIC AGE

Hebrew

Kutscher, E. Y. *Ha-lašon wᵉha-reqaʿ ha-lᵉšoni šel mᵉgillat Yᵉšaʿyahu ha-šᵉlema mi-mᵉgillot yam ha-melaḥ.* Jerusalem, 1959. ET: *The Language and Linguistic Background of the Isaiah Scroll (1QIsaᵃ).* Studies on the Texts of the Desert of Judah 6. Leiden, 1974.

'The language of the Hebrew and Aramaic letters of Bar Kosiba and his contemporaries. 2: The Hebrew letters', *Leš,* 26 (1962), 7–23. (In Hebrew.)

'Mišnisches Hebraîsch', *Rocznik Orientalistyczny,* 28 (1964–5), 35–48.

'Hebrew language. Dead Sea Scrolls; Mishnaic' *EncJud* vol. 16, cols. 1583–1607. Jerusalem, 1971.

Rabin, C. 'Hebrew'. Sections on the second Temple period and Mishnaic Hebrew, *Current Trends in Linguistics,* 6, 316–24. The Hague, 1970.

Scripta Hierosolymitana. Vol. 4: *Aspects of the Dead Sea Scrolls.* Jerusalem 1958: articles by Goshen-Gottstein, 'Linguistic structure and tradition in the Qumran documents'; Rabin, 'The historical background of Qumran Hebrew'; Ben-Hayyim, 'Traditions in the Hebrew language, with special reference to the Dead Sea Scrolls'.

Aramaic

Fitzmyer, J. A. *The Genesis Apocryphon of Qumran Cave 1.* 2nd edn. Biblica et Orientalia, 18a. Rome, 1971.

Kutscher, E. Y. 'The language of the Genesis Apocryphon', in *Scripta Hierosolymitana.* Vol. 4: *Aspects of the Dead Sea Scrolls*, pp. 1–36. Jerusalem, 1958.

'The language of the Hebrew and Aramaic letters of Bar Kosiba and his contemporaries. 1: The Aramaic letters', *Leš,* 25 (1961), 119–33. (In Hebrew.)

'Aramaic', in *Current Trends in Linguistics,* 6, 347–412. The Hague, 1970.

'Aramaic', *EncJud*, vol. 3, cols. 259–87. Jerusalem, 1971.

Greek

Barr, J. *The Typology of Literalism in Ancient Biblical Translations.* AGG. 11. pp. 275–325. Göttingen, 1979.

Brock, S. P., 'The phenomenon of the Septuagint', *The Witness of Tradition*, ed. A. S. van der Woude, OTS, 17 (1972), pp. 11–36.

Debrunner, A. *Geschichte der griechischen Sprache.* Vol. 2. Sammlung Göschen 114. Berlin, 1954.

Hengel, M. *Judaism and Hellenism.* 2 vols. London–Philadelphia, 1974.

Jellicoe, S. *The Septuagint and Modern Study.* Oxford, 1968.

Leon, H. J. *The Jews of Ancient Rome*. Philadelphia, 1960.
Lieberman, S. *Greek in Jewish Palestine*. Philadelphia, 1942.
Rabin, C. 'The translation process and the character of the Septuagint', *Textus*, 6 (1968), 1–26.
Sevenster, J. N. *Do You Know Greek?* NovT Sup 19. Leiden, 1968.
Swete, H. B. *An Introduction to the Old Testament in Greek*. Cambridge, 1900; 2nd edn. 1914.
Tcherikover, V. A. *Hellenistic Civilization and the Jews*. Philadelphia, 1959.
Tcherikover, V. A. and Fuks, A. *Corpus Papyrorum Judaicarum*. Vol. 1: 1957; vol. 2; 1960; vol. 3: 1964. Cambridge, Mass.

CHAPTER 4 THE DIASPORA IN THE HELLENISTIC AGE

Sources

Old Testament, Jewish and Christian sources

Die Apokryphen und Pseudepigraphen des Alten Testaments, ed. E. Kautzsch. 2 vols. Tübingen, 1900; repr. Darmstadt, 1960.
Aramaic Papyri of the Fifth Century B.C., ed. A. Cowley. Oxford, 1923; repr. Osnabrück, 1967.
Aristeas, Letter of: Aristeasbrief, ed. N. Meisner, Jüdische Schriften aus hellenistisch–römischer Zeit, 2.1. pp. 35–87. Gütersloh, 1973.
Lettre d'Aristée à Philocrate, ed. A. Pelletier. SC 89. Paris, 1962.
Aristobulus, ed. N. Walter. Jüdische Schriften aus hellenistisch–römischer Zeit, 3.2, pp. 261–79. Gütersloh, 1975.
Charles, R. H. (ed.). *the Apocrypha and Pseudepigrapha of the Old Testament in English*. 2 vols. Oxford, 1913.
Clement of Alexandria. Vol. 1, ed. O. Stählin, Leipzig, 1936. Vol. 2. ed. O. Stählin and L. Früchtel, 3rd edn., Berlin, 1960. Vol. 3, ed. O. Stählin and L. Früchtel, 2nd edn., Berlin, 1970. GCS 12, 15, 17.
Corpus Inscriptionum Judaicarum, ed. J. B. Frey. Vol. 1, Rome–Paris, 1936; vol. 2, Rome, 1952.
Corpus Papyrorum Judaicarum. Vols. 1, 2: ed. V. A. Tcherikover and A. Fuks. Cambridge, Mass., 1957, 1960; vol. 3: ed. V. A. Tcherikover, A. Fuks and M. Stern. Cambridge, Mass., 1964.
Daniel, ed. J. Ziegler. *Susanna, Daniel, Bel et Draco*. Septuaginta, Societas Litterarum Gottingensis 16.2. Göttingen, 1954.
Eusebius, *Praeparatio Evangelica*, ed. K. Mras. 2 vols.: GCS 43, 1.2. Berlin, 1954, 1956.
Fragmente jüdisch-hellenisticher Historiker, ed. N. Walter. Jüdische Schriften aus hellenistisch-römischer Zeit, 1.2. Gütersloh, 1976.
Josephus, Flavius, *Opera*, ed. B. Niese. Vols. 1 to 5. 2nd edn. Berlin, 1955.
De bello Judaico – Der jüdische Krieg, ed. M. Michel and O. Bauernfeind. Darmstadt: vol. 1:1959; vol. 2, 1, 1963; vols. 2, 2; 3, 1969.
Maccabaeorum Liber 1, ed. W. Kappler. Septuaginta, Societas Litterarum Gottingensis, vol. 9.1. Göttingen, 1936; 2nd edn. 1968.
Maccabaeorum Libri 2, 3, ed. W. Kappler and R. Hanhart. Septuaginta, Societas Litterarum Gottingensis, vol. 9.2, 3 Göttingen, 1959–60.

2. *Makkabäerbuch*, ed. C. Habicht, Jüdische Schriften aus hellenistisch-römischer Zeit, 1.3. Gütersloh, 1976.

Megillat Ta'anit. Die Fastenrolle, ed. H. Lichtenstein. *HUCA*, 8–9 (1931–32), 257–351.

Philo: Colson, F. H. and Whitaker, G. H. (trans.). *Philo*. 10 vols. Loeb Classical Library. Cambridge, Mass. 1929ff.

Philo Supplement, Questions and Answers on Genesis/Exodus, English translation by R. Marcus. 2 vols. The Loeb Classical Library. Cambridge, Mass., 1953.

Philonis Alexandrini Opera Quae Supersunt, eds. L. Cohn and P. Wendland. 7 vols. Berlin, 1896–1930.

Philo von Alexandria: Die Werke in deutscher Übersetzung, ed. L. Cohn, I. Heinemann, M. Adler and W. Theiler. 4 vols. 2nd edn. Berlin, 1962.

Rahlfs, A. *Septuaginta*. 2 vols. Stuttgart, 1935.

Reinach, T. (ed. and transl.). *Textes d'Auteurs Grecs et Romains relatifs au Judaîsme*. Paris, 1895. Repr. Hildesheim, 1963.

Sapientia Jesu Filii Sirach, ed. J. Ziegler. Septuaginta, Societas Litterarum Gottingensis, vol. 12.2 Göttingen, 1965.

Sapientia Salomonis, ed. J. Ziegler. Septuaginta, Societas Litterarum Gottingensis, vol. 12.1. Göttingen, 1962.

Sibylline Oracles: *Die Oracula Sibyllina*, J. Geffcken, ed. GCS 8. Leipzig, 1902.

Stern, M. *Greek and Latin Authors on Jews and Judaism*. Vol. 1: *From Herodotus to Plutarch*. Jerusalem, 1974.

Talmud Babli. Vols. 1–12. Wilna, 1895–1908.

The Babylonian Talmud. English Translation, ed. J. Epstein. London, 1935–48.

Graeco-Roman secular writers

Arrian: *Arrianus*, ed. A. G. Roos. 2 vols. Leipzig, 1907, 1928.

Cicero: *Ciceronis Scripta Quae Manserunt Omnia*, ed. F. Marx, E. Strobel, W. Trillitzch and K. F. Kumaniecki. Leipzig, 1914ff.

Corpus Inscriptionum Graecarum, ed. A. Boeckhius. 4 vols. Berlin, 1825–77.

Curtius Rufus, *Historiae Alexandri Magni*, ed. E. Hedicke. Leipzig, 1919.

Diodorus Siculus: *Diodorus Siculus*, ed. C. H. Oldfather *et al.* 12 vols. The Loeb Classical Library, London, 1933–67.

Die Fragmente der griechischen Historiker, ed. F. Jacoby, 3 vols., with commentary volumes. Leiden, 1935ff.

Inscriptiones Graecae. Preussische Akademie der Wissenschaften. Berlin, 1873ff.

Plutarch, *De Alexandri magni fortuna aut virtute*, libri 2, in: Plutarch, *Moralia*, ed. F. C. Babbitt. Vol. 4, pp. 382–487. The Loeb Classical Library, London–Cambridge, Mass., 1936.

Plutarch, *Alexander*, in: Plutarch, *Lives*, ed. B. Perrin. Vol. 7, pp. 224–439. The Loeb Classical Library. London–New York, 1918.

Strabo: *Strabonis Geographica*. Vol. 4, ed. W. Aly. Bonn, 1957.

Supplementum Epigraphicum Graecum, ed. J. J. E. Hondius *et al.* Leiden, 1923ff.

Tacitus, *Histories*, ed. G. G. Ramsey. London, 1915.

Secondary literature

Altheim, F. *Weltgeschichte Asiens im griechischen Zeitalter*. 2 vols. Halle, 1947–8.

Applebaum, S. *Greeks and Jews in Ancient Cyrene*. In Hebrew. N.p., 1969.

'The legal status of the Jewish communities in the Diaspora', in: *The Jewish People in the First Century*, vol. 1, pp. 420–63. Edited by S. Safrai and M. Stern. Assen, 1974.

'The organization of the Jewish communities in the Diaspora', in: *The Jewish People in the First Century*, vol. 1, pp. 464–503. Edited by S. Safrai and M. Stern. Assen, 1974.

'The social and economic status of the Jews in the Diaspora', in: *The Jewish People in the First Century*, vol. 2, pp. 701–27. Edited by S. Safrai and M. Stern. Assen, 1976.

Askowith, D. *The Toleration of the Jews under Julius Caesar and Augustus*. New York, 1915.

Avigad, N. 'Excavations at Beth She'arim, 1954', *IEJ*, 5 (1955), 205–39.

Barag, D. 'The effects of the Tennes rebellion on Palestine', *BASOR*, 183 (1966), 6–12.

Baron, S. W. *A Social and Religious History of the Jews*. 2nd edn. vols. 1 and 2. Philadelphia, 1952.

Bengtson, H. *Greichische Geschichte von den Anfängen bis in die römische Kaiserzeit*. HAW 3–4. 4th edn. Munich, 1969.

Herrschergestalten des Hellenismus. Munich, 1975.

Bevan, E. R. *The House of Seleucus*. 2 vols. London, 1902; repr. 1966.

A History of Egypt under the Ptolemaic Dynasty. London, 1927; repr. as *The House of Ptolemy*. Chicago, 1968.

Bickerman, E. *From Ezra to the Last of the Maccabees: Foundations of Post-Biblical Judaism*. New York, 1947.

'La Charte Séleucide de Jérusalem'. *REJ*, 100 (1935), 4–35.

Bouché-Leclerq, A. *Histoire des Lagides*. 3 vols. Paris, 1903ff.

Histoire des Séleucides. 2 vols. Paris, 1913ff.

Braude, W. G. *Jewish Proselyting in the First Five Centureis of the Common Era*. Brown University Studies 6. Providence, R. I. 1940.

Brücklmeier, M. *Beiträge zur rechtlichen Stellung der Juden im römischen Reich*. Theological dissertation. Münster, 1939.

Burr, V. *Tiberius Julius Alexander*. Antiquitas 1, 1. Bonn, 1955.

Collins, J. J. 'The court-tales in Daniel and the development of apocalyptic', *JBL*, 94 (1975), 218–34.

Davies, W. D. *The Gospel and the Land: Early Christianity and Jewish Territorial Doctrine*. Berkeley, 1974.

'The Jewish state in the Hellenistic world', in: *Peake's Commentary on the Bible*, new edn. pp. 686–92. Ed. M. Black. London, 1962.

Delling, G. *Bibliographie zur jüdisch–hellenistischen und intertestamentarischen Literatur, 1900–1965*. TU 106. Berlin, 1969.

Denis, A.-M. *Fragmenta Pseudepigraphorum quae supersunt Graeca una cum historicorum et auctorum Iudaeorum hellenistarum fragmentis*. PVTG 3b. Leiden, 1970.

Introduction aux Pseudépigraphes Grecs d'Ancien Testament. SVTP 1. Leiden, 1970.

Eissfeldt, O. *Einleitung in das Alte Testament*. 3rd edn. Tübingen, 1964. ET: *The Old Testament*. Oxford, 1965.

Fox, R. L. *Alexander the Great*. London, 1973. German translation: Düsseldorf, 1974.

Fraser, P. M. *Ptolemaic Alexandria*. 3 vols. Oxford, 1972.

Geraty, L. A. *Third Century B.C. Ostraca from Khirbet el Kom*. Ph.D. Dissertation, Harvard Divinity School, 1972.

Goldstein, J. A. 'The tales of the Tobiads', *Christianity, Judaism and other Graeco-Roman Cults. Studies for Morton Smith at Sixty*, ed. J. Neusner. Part 3: *Judaism before 70*, pp. 85–123. SJLA 12.3. Leiden, 1975.

Goodenough, E. R. *Jewish Symbols in the Greco-Roman Period.* 13 vols. New York, 1952–68.

Harmatta, J. 'Irano-Aramaica (Zur Geschichte des frühhellenistischen Judentums in Ägypten)', *Acta Antiqua,* 7 (1959), 337–409.

Hegermann, H. 'Das griechischsprechende Judentum', *Literatur und Religion des Frühjudentums,* ed. J. Maier and J. Schreiner, pp. 328–52. Gütersloh-Würzburg, 1973.

'Das hellenistische Judentum', *Umwelt des Urchristentums,* ed. J. Leipoldt and W. Grundmann. Vol. 1, pp. 292–345. Berlin, 1975.

Hengel, M. *Judentum und Hellenismus.* WUNT 10, 2nd edn. Tübingen, 1973. ET: *Judaism and Hellenism.* 2 vols. London, 1974.

Juden, Griechen und Barbaren. Aspekte der Hellenisierung des Judentums in vorchristlicher Zeit. SBS 76. Stuttgart, 1976. ET: *Jews, Greeks and Barbarians.* London, 1980.

'Proseuche und Synagoge. Jüdische Gemeinde, Gotteshaus und Gottesdienst in der Diaspora und in Palästina', *Tradition und Glaube,* Festgabe für K. G. Kuhn, ed. G. Jeremias, H.-W. Kuhn and H. Stegemann, pp. 157–84. Göttingen, 1971.

Humphreys, W. L. 'A life-style for Diaspora: a study of the tales of Esther and Daniel', *JBL,* 92 (1973), 211–23.

Jacobs, J. 'Tribes, lost ten', *Jewish Encyclopedia,* vol. 12, pp. 249–53. New York, 1906.

Jones, A. H. M. *The Greek City from Alexander to Justinian.* Oxford, 1940.

Kaerst, J. *Geschichte des Hellenismus.* Leipzig, vol. 1, 3rd edn. 1927, vol. 2, 1926; repr. Darmstadt, 1968.

Kahle, P. E. *The Cairo Geniza.* 2nd edn. Oxford, 1959.

Kornemann, E. *Weltgeschichte des Mittelmeer-raumes, von Philipp II. von Makedonien bis Muhammed,* ed. H. Bengtson. Munich, 2 vols. 1948–9, repr. 1967.

Kraeling, C. H. 'The Jewish community at Antioch', *JBL,* 51 (1932), 130–60.

Krauss, S. *Synagogale Altertümer.* Berlin–Vienna, 1922; repr. Hildesheim, 1966.

Kuhn, K. G. and Stegemann, H. 'Proselyten', *PWSup* 9, cols. 1248–83. Stuttgart, 1962.

Kuhn, K. G. 'προσήλυτος', *TWNT,* 6 (1959), pp. 727–45; *TDNT,* 6 (1968), pp. 727–44.

Launey, M. *Recherches sur les armées hellénistiques.* 2 vols. Paris, 1949–50.

Lifshitz, B. *Donateurs et Fondateurs dans les Synagogues Juives.* Cahiers de la Revue Biblique, no. 7. Paris, 1967.

Liver, J. 'The half-shekel offering in biblical and post-biblical literature', *HTR,* 56 (1963), 173–98.

Lohse, E. 'σάββατον κτλ.', *TWNT,* 7 (1964), pp. 1–35; *TDNT,* 7 (1971), 1–35.

Maier, J. *Geschichte der jüdischen Religion,* pp. 10–91. Berlin–New York, 1922.

Das Judentum, pp. 160–200. Munich, 1973.

McCown, C. C. 'The density of population in ancient Palestine', *JBL,* 66 (1947), 425–36.

Moehring, H. R. 'The *Acta pro Judaeis* in the *Antiquities* of Flavius Josephus', *Christianity, Judaism and other Graeco-Roman Cults. Studies for Morton Smith at Sixty,* ed. J. Neusner. Part 3: *Judaism before 70,* pp. 124–58 SJLA 12. 3. Leiden, 1975.

Nilsson, M. P. *Geschichte der griechischen Religion,* vol. 2: *Die hellenistische und römische Zeit.* 2nd edn. Munich, 1961. 5.2.

Olshausen, E. 'Zeuxis', *PW,* 2nd ser., 10 (1972), cols. 381–5.

Parsons, E. A. *The Alexandrian Library.* Amsterdam–London, 1952.

Pfister, F. *Eine jüdische Gründungsgeschichte Alexandrias. Mit einem Anhang über Alexanders Besuch in Jerusalem*. SAH, 1914, 11. Heidelberg, 1914.

Roberts, C., Skeat, T. C. and Nock, A. D. 'The Gild of Zeus Hypsistos', *HTR*, 29 (1936), 39–88.

Rostovtzeff, M. *The Social and Economic History of the Hellenistic World*. 3 vols. Oxford, 1941, 1972.

Roux, J. and G. 'Un Décret du politeuma des Juifs de Béréniké en Cyrenaîque', *REG*, 62 (1949), 281–96.

Russell, D. S. *The Jews from Alexander to Herod*. New Clarendon Bible. London, 1967.

Ruppel, W. 'Politeuma: Bedeutungsgeschichte eines staatsrechtlichen Terminus', *Philologus*, 82 (1927), 268–312, 433–54.

Schachermeyr, F. *Alexander der Grosse. Das Problem seiner Persönlichkeit und seines Wirkens*. SAW 285. Vienna, 1973.

Schalit, A. 'The letter of Antiochus III to Zeuxis regarding the establishment of Jewish military colonies in Phrygia and Lydia', *JQR*, n.s. 50 (1960), 289–318.

Schmidt, K. L. 'διασπορά', *TWNT* 2 (1935), pp. 98–104; *TDNT*, 2 (1964), pp. 98–104.

Schneider, C. *Kulturgeschichte des Hellenismus*. Munich: vol. 1, 1967; vol. 2, 1969.

Schrage, W. 'συναγωγή', *TWNT*, 7 (1964), pp. 798–839; *TDNT*, 7 (1971), pp. 798–841.

Schubart, W. 'Alexandria', *RAC*, 1, 271–83. Stuttgart, 1950.

Schürer, E. *Geschichte des jüdischen Volkes im Zeitalter Jesu Christi*. Leipzig: vol. 1, 5th edn., 1920; vol. 2, 4th edn., 1907; vol. 3, 4th edn., 1909.

History of the Jewish People in the Age of Jesus Christ. A new English version revised and edited by G. Vermes, F. Millar *et al.*, vol. 1. Edinburgh, 1973.

Seibert, J. *Untersuchungen zur Geschichte Ptolemaios'* I. MBPAR 56. Munich, 1969.

Alexander der Grosse. Erträge der Forschung, 10. Darmstadt, 1972.

Siegert, F. 'Gottesfürchtige und Sympathisanten', *JSJ*, 4 (1973), 109–64.

Simon, M. *Verus Israel*. Paris, 1948; 2nd edn. 1964.

Smallwood, E. M. *The Jews Under Roman Rule*, SJLA 20. Leiden, 1976.

Smith, M. *Palestinian Parties and Politics that Shaped the Old Testament*. New York, 1971.

Snaith, N. H. *The Jews from Cyrus to Herod*. Wallington, 1949.

Strathmann, H. 'πόλις, πολίτευμα', *TWNT*, 6 (1959), pp. 516–35; *TDNT*, 6 (1968) pp. 516–35.

Sukenik, E. L. *Ancient Synagogues in Palestine and Greece*. Schweich Lectures 1930. London, 1934.

Tarn, W. W. *Alexander the Great*. 2 vols. Cambridge, 1948; German translation: Darmstadt, 1963.

Hellenistic Civilization, revised by the author and G. T. Griffith. 3rd edn. London, 1959; German translation: *Die Kultur der hellenistischen Welt*, Darmstadt, 1966.

Tcherikover, V. *Hellenistic Civilisation and the Jews*. Philadelphia, 1959.

'The Hellenistic environment', *The Hellenistic Age: Political History of Jewish Palestine from 332* B.C.E. *to 67* B.C.E., ed. A. Schalit. The World History of the Jewish People, First Series, vol. 6, pp. 5–50. Jerusalem, 1972.

Vidmann, L. *Isis und Sarapis bei den Griechen und Römern*. RGVV 29. Berlin, 1970.

Volkmann, H. 'Ptolemaios, II: Die Dynastie der Ptolemäer in Ägypten', *PW*, 23 (1959), cols. 1600–1761.

Walter, N. *Der Thoraausleger Aristobulos*. TU 86. Berlin, 1964.

Will, E. *Histoire politique du Monde hellénistique (323–30 a.v. J.-C.)* 2 vols. Annales de l'Est 30, 32. Nancy, 1966f.

Wolff, H. J. *Das Justizwesen der Ptolemäer*. MBPAR 44. 2nd edn. Munich, 1970.

CHAPTER 5 THE INTERPRETATION OF JUDAISM AND HELLENISM IN THE PRE-MACCABEAN PERIOD

Primary sources

Inscriptions and papyri

Frey, J.-B. *Corpus Inscriptionum Iudaicarum*, 2 vols. Rome, 1936/52.

Tcherikover, V. A., Fuks, A. and Stern, M. *Corpus Papyrorum Judaicarum*. 3 vols. Cambridge, Mass., 1957–64.

Individual texts and further epigraphical and papyrological material are *passim*.

Literary sources

Qoheleth; Sirach; 1 to 3 Maccabees; Pseudo-Aristeas; Sibylline Oracles 3 to 5; Josephus, *Antiquitates Judaicae, Bellum Judaicum, Contra Apionem*.

Denis, A.-M. *Fragmenta Pseudepigraphorum quae supersunt Graeca*. PVTG 3. Leiden, 1970.

Reinach, T. *Textes d'auteurs grecs et romains relatifs au Judaïsme*. Paris, 1895, repr. Hildesheim, 1963.

Stern, M. *Greek and Latin Authors on Jews and Judaism*, 1. Jerusalem, 1974.

Individual passages and texts and further material from the Old Testament Hebrew and other ancient literature are *passim*.

Secondary literature

Bickerman, E. J. 'The Septuagint as a translation', *PAAJR*, 28 (1959), 1–39.

Braun, R. *Kohelet und die frühhellenistische Popularphilosphie*. BZAW 130. Berlin–New York, 1973.

Braunert, H., *Binnenwanderung*. Bonner historische Forschungen, 26. Bonn, 1964.

Deissmann, A. *Licht vom Osten*. 4th edn. Tübingen, 1923; ET *Light from the Ancient East*. 2nd edn. London, 1910.

Denis, A.-M. *Introduction aux pseudépigraphes grecs d'Ancien Testament*. SVTP 1. Leiden, 1970.

Feldman, L. H. 'The orthodoxy of the Jews in Hellenistic Egypt', *Jewish Social Studies*, 22 (1960), 215–37.

Fraser, P. M. *Ptolemaic Alexandria*. 3 vols. Oxford, 1972.

Gager, J. G. *Moses in Greco-Roman Paganism*. SBLMS 16. Nashville–New York, 1972.

Hadas, M. *Hellenistic Culture. Fusion and Diffusion*. New York, 1959.

Harmatta, J. 'Irano-Aramaica (Zur Geschichte des frühhellenistischen Judentums in Ägypten)' *Acta Antiqua*, 7 (1959), 337–409.

Hengel, M. *Judentum und Hellenismus*. WUNT 10. 2nd edn. Tübingen, 1973; ET see p. 658.

Juden, Griechen und Barbaren. SBS 76. Stuttgart, 1976; ET see p. 658.

'Die Synagogeninschrift von Stobi', *ZNW*, 57 (1966), 145–83.

'Proseuche und Synagoge. Jüdische Gemeinde, Gotteshaus und Gottesdienst in der

Diaspora und in Palästina', in : *Tradition und Glaube. Festgabe für K. G. Kuhn*, pp. 157–84. Göttingen, 1971.

'Anonymität, Pseudepigraphie und "Literarische Fälschung" in der jüdisch-hellenistischen Literatur', in: *Pseudepigrapha* 1, pp. 229–308. Entretiens sur l'antiquité classique 18. Geneva, 1972.

'Zwischen Jesus und Paulus. Die "Hellenisten", die "Sieben" und Stephanus (Apg 6, 1–15; 7, 54–8, 3)', *ZTK*, 72 (1975), 151–206.

Jüthner, J. *Hellenen und Barbaren*. Das Erbe der Alten, NF 8. Leipzig, 1923.

Launey, M. *Recherches sur les armées hellénistiques*. 2 vols. Bibliothèque des Écoles françaises d'Athènes et de Rome, 169, Paris, 1949–50.

Marböck, J. *Weisheit im Wandel*. BBB 37. Bonn, 1971.

Middendorp, T. *Die Stellung Jesu ben Siras zwischen Judentum und Hellenismus*. Leiden, 1973.

Peremans, W. *Vreemdelingen en Egyptenaren in vroeg–Ptolemaeisch Egypte*. Louvain, 1937.

Préaux, C. *L'économie royale des Lagides*. Brussels, 1939.

Les Grecs en Égypt d'après les archives de Zénon. Brussels, 1947.

Rostovtzeff, M. *The Social and Economic History of the Hellenistic World*. 3 vols. Oxford, 1941.

Schürer, E. *Geschichte des jüdischen Volkes im Zeitalter Jesu Christi*. 3 vols and index. 4th edn. Leipzig, 1901–11.

Schürer, E., Vermes, G. and Millar, F. *The History of the Jewish People in the Age of Jesus Christ*, 1. Edinburgh, 1973.

Sevenster, J. N. *Do You Know Greek?* NovT Sup 19. Leiden, 1968.

Speyer, W. 'Barbar A,B', *JAC*, 10 (1967), 251–67.

Tarn, W. W. and Griffith, G. T. *Hellenistic Civilization*. 3rd edn. London, 1952.

Tcherikover, V. *Hellenistic Civilization and the Jews*. Philadelphia, 1959.

Treu, K. 'Die Bedeutung des Griechischen für die Juden im römischen Reich', *Kairos*, 15 (1973), 123–44.

Uebel, F. *Die Kleruchen Ägyptens unter den ersten sechs Ptolemäern*, Abhandlungen der deutschen Akademie der Wissenschaften zu Berlin, Klasse für Sprachen, Literatur und Kunst 1968, 3. Berlin, 1968.

Vatin, C. *Recherches sur le mariage et la condition de la femme mariée à l'époque hellénistique*. Bibliothèque des Écoles française d'Athènes et de Rome, 216. Paris, 1970.

Walter, N. *Der Thoraausleger Aristobulos*. TU 86. Berlin, 1964.

CHAPTER 6 THE MEN OF THE GREAT SYNAGOGUE

Sources

The Bible

Charles, R. H. *Apocrypha and Pseudepigrapha of the Old Testament*. 2 vols. Oxford, 1913.

Mishna, ed. C. Albeck. Jerusalem, 1953–59.

The Mishnah on which the Palestinian Talmud rests, ed. W. H. Lowe. Cambridge, 1883.

Mekilta, ed. H. S. Horovitz and I. A. Rabin. Frankfurt-am-Main, 1931; repr. Jerusalem, 1960.

Mekilta of R. *Simeon*, ed. J. N. Epstein and E. Z. Melammed. Jerusalem, 1955.

Sifra, ed. I. H. Weiss. J. Schlossberg. Vienna, 1862.

Sifre on Numbers, and *Sifre Zutta*, ed. H. S. Horovitz. Leipzig, 1917; repr. Jerusalem, 1966.

Sifre on Deuteronomy, ed. Louis Finkelstein. Berlin, 1939; repr. New York, 1969.

Midrasch Tannaim zum Deuteronomium, ed. D. Z. Hoffmann. 2. Parts. Berlin, 1908–9.

Talmud, Babylonian, ed. brothers and widow Romm. Vilna, *ca* 1870–86. Repr. New York, 1919 and often.

Talmud, Jerusalem, Venice, 1522–23(?).

Talmud: *Aboth d'R. Nathan*, ed. S. Schechter. Vienna, 1887.

Tosefta, ed. M. S. Zuckermandel. Pasewalk, 1877–82; reproduced with supplement by S. Lieberman. Jerusalem, 1937.

Tosefta Berakoth, ed. S. Lieberman, Jerusalem 1937.

Tosefta, ed. S. Lieberman. New York. *Z'ra'im*, 1955; *Mo'ed*, 1962; *Našim*, 2 parts, 1967–73.

General

Albright, W. F. *From the Stone Age to Christianity*, pp. 267, 273. Baltimore, 1940.

Bacher, W. 'Synagogue, the Great', *Jewish Encyclopedia*, pp. 640ff. New York, vol. 11, 1905.

Tradition und Tradenten in den Schulen Palästinas und Babyloniens, pp. 47f. Leipzig, 1914.

Baron, S. W. *A Social and Religious History of the Jews*, vol. 1, pp. 162, 367, 397; vol. 3, p. 41 n. 24. Philadelphia, 1952ff.

Bickerman, E. ' "Viri Magnae Congregationis" ', *RB*, 55 (1948), 397ff.

Bloch, M. A. *Ša'are Torat ha-Taqqanot*, 1, pp. 107–273. Brno, 1879.

Bondi, J. 'Simon der Gerechte', *Jahrbuch der jüdisch-literarischen Gesellschaft*, 5, (1907), pp. 245ff.

Brüll, J. *M'bo ha-Mišna*, 2 vols. Vol. I, pp. 3ff. Frankfurt, 1876–85.

Elbogen, I. *Der jüdische Gottesdienst in seiner geschichtlichen Entwicklung*, pp. 240, 552. 2nd edn., Frankfurt, 1924.

Englander, H. 'The men of the Great Synagogue', *Hebrew Union College Jubilee Volume*, pp. 325ff. Cincinnati, 1925.

Finkelstein, L. *Akiba, Scholar, Saint and Martyr*, pp. 34, 293. New York, 1935.

Ha-p'rušim w'anše k'neset hagdola. New York, 1950.

The Pharisees, pp. 576ff, 661. Philadelphia, 1938; 3rd edn, 1962.

Foerster, W. 'Der Ursprung des Pharisäismus', *ZNW*, 34 (1935), 46ff.

Frankel, Z. *Darke ha-Mišna*, pp. 3ff. Leipzig, 1859.

Funk, S. 'Die Männer der Grossen Versammlung und die Gerichtshöfe im nachexilischen Judentum', *MGWJ*, 55 (1911), 33–42.

Ginzberg, L. *Legends of the Jews*, 6, p. 445 n. 49; p. 447 n. 56; p. 449 n. 58; also p. 368 n. 89. Philadelphia, 1928.

Perušim w'-ḥiddušim biYrušalmi, 1, pp. 327ff. New York, 1945.

Guttmann, J. 'Anše K'neset Ha-G'dolah', *Hašiloah*, 21 (1909), 313ff.

Halevy, T. *Dorot ha-Rišonim*, 3, pp. 94aff. Frankfurt, 1905–6.

Hoffmann, D. 'Über die Männer der "Grossen Versammlung"', *Magazin für die Wissenschaft des Judenthums*, 10 (1883), 45–63.

Kaufmann, Y. *Tol'dot ha-'emunah ha-yisra'elit*, 8, pp. 329ff. Tel Aviv, 1956.

Krauss, S. 'The Great Synod', *JQR*, 10 (1898), 347–77.

Krochmal, N. *Moreh N'buke ha-z'man*, vov, 1851; ed. S. Ravidovitz, p. 56. Berlin, 1924; repr. London–Waltham, Mass., 1961.

Leszynsky, R. *Die Sadduzäer*, pp. 130ff. Frankfurt, 1912.

Loew, I. *Gesammelte Schriften*, 1, pp. 399–449. Szegedin, 1889–1900.
Mantel, H. 'The nature of the Great Synagogue', *HTR*, 60 (1967), 69–91.
Moore, G. F. 'The rise of normative Judaism, 1. To the reorganization at Jamnia', *HTR*, 17 (1924), 325ff.
Judaism in the First Two Centuries of the Christian Era, pp. 7ff. Cambridge, Mass., 1930.
'Simeon the Righteous', *Jewish Studies in Memory of Israel Abrahams*, pp. 145ff. New York, 1927.
Sperber, D. 'Synagogue, the Great', *EncJud*, vol. 15, cols. 629–31. Jerusalem, 1971.
Strack, H. L. *Einleitung in Talmud und Midrasch*, p. 7. 5th revd. edn. Munich, 1921; ET *Introduction to the Talmud and Midrash*, pp. 9f. Philadelphia, 1931.
Talmudi (pseudonym), 'Ha-Talmud', *Hašiloah*, 7 (1901), 481ff.
Tschernowitz, C. *Tolᵉdot ha-halakah*, 3, pp. 50ff. New York, 1950.
Urback, E. E. *The Sages*, pp. 121, 132, 567–9, 609. Trans. from Hebrew. Jerusalem, 1975.
Weiss, I. H. *Dor Dor wᵉdoršaw*, 1, pp. 84ff. Berlin, 1871.
Yavetz, Z. *Tolᵉdot Yisra'el*, 3, pp. 148ff; 4, pp. 10ff. Tel Aviv, 1934.
Zeitlin, S. 'Šimeon ha-Ṣaddiq ū-kᵉneset ha-gᵉdolah', *Ner Maʿarabi*, 2 (1924–25), 137ff.

CHAPTER 7 THE PHARISAIC LEADERS AFTER THE GREAT SYNAGOGUE

Abrahams, I. 'Sanhedrin', in J. Hastings, *Encyclopedia of Religion and Ethics*, 11, Edinburgh, 1920, pp. 184–5.
Albeck, C. 'Ha-Sanhedrin u-nᵉśi'ah̠', *Zion*, 8 (1942–43), 165–78.
Altschüler, M. *Ma'ᵃmarim*. Vienna, 1895.
Bickerman, E. ''Al ha-Sanhedrin', *Zion*, 3 (1938), 356–9.
Büchler, A. *Das Synedrion in Jerusalem und das grosse Beth-Din in der Quaderkammer des Jerusalemischen Tempels*. Vienna, 1902.
Cohn, H. H. 'Reflections on the trial of Jesus', *Judaism*, 20 (1971), 10–23.
Efron, Y. 'Ha-Sanhedrin wᵉha-Gᵉrousia biyme ha-bayit hašeni', *World Congress of Jewish Studies*, 1–2 (1965), pp. 89–93.
Finkelstein, L. 'Ha-nᵉsiut sanhedrin bᵉYisrael', *Ha-Tekufah*, 30–1 (1946).
Finkelstein, L. *Ha-pᵉrušim wᵉ' anše kᵉneset ha-gᵉdolah*, pp. 1ff. New York, 1950.
Flusser, D. 'A literary approach to the trial of Jesus', *Judaism*, 20 (1971), 32–6.
Ginzberg, L. 'The significance of the Halachah for Jewish history', in *On Jewish Law and Lore*, pp. 77–124. Philadelphia, 1955; this ch. trd. from the Hebrew publ. in 1931.
Graetz, H. 'Die erste Meinungsverschiedenheit in der halachischen Gesetzgebung', *MGWJ*, 18 (1869), 20–32.
Greenwald, L. *L'tolᵉdot ha-Sanhedrin bᵉYisrael*. New York, 1950.
Ha-Levi, A. A. 'Ha-maḥloqet ha-rišonah', *Tarbiẓ*, 28 (1958–59), 154–7.
Herzog, I. 'He'arot historiyot bᵉhilkot Sanhedrin', *Sinai*, 3 (1938–39), 1, parts 1–2, pp. 24–9; parts 3–4, pp. 393–6.
Hoenig, S. B. *The Great Sanhedrin*. Philadelphia, 1953.
'Sof ha-Sanhedrin ha-gᵉdolah biyme bayit ha-šeni', *Horeb*, 3 (1936), 169–75.
'Synedrion in the Attic orators, the Ptolemaic papyri and its adaption by Josephus, the Gospels and the Tannaim', *JQR*, N.S. 37 (1946), 179–87.
Hoffmann, D. *Der Oberste Gerichtshof in der Stadt der Heiligtums*. Berlin, 1878; ET 'The

highest court in the city of the sanctuary' in *The First Mishnah and the Controversies of the Tannaim*, New York, 1972.
'Die Präsidentur im Synedrium', *Magazin für die Wissenschaft des Judenthums*, 5 (1878), 94–9.
Kook, S. H. 'He'arah b^e'inyane Sanhedrin', *Sinai*, 3 (1939–40), part 7, 94–5.
Kuenen, A. 'Über die Zusammensetzung des Sanhedrin', *Gesammelte Abhandlungen zur biblischen Wissenschaft*, pp. 49–81. Freiburg im Breisgau, 1894.
Lauterbach, J. Z. 'Sanhedrin', *Jewish Encyclopedia* vol. 11, pp. 41–4. New York, 1905.
Levy, J. 'Die Presidentur im Synhedrium', *MGWJ*, 4 (1855), 266–74.
Mantel, H., *Studies in the History of the Sanhedrin*, Harvard Semitic Series 17. Cambridge, Mass. 1961.
'Sanhedrin', *EncJud*, vol. 14, cols. 836–9. Jerusalem, 1972.
Moore, G. F. *Judaism*. 3 vols. Cambridge, 1927. See index under 'Sanhedrin'.
Reifmann, J. *Sanhedrin*. Berdichev, 1888.
Sachs, S. 'Ueber die Zeit der Entstehung des Synhedrins', *Zeitschrift für die religiösen Interessen des Judenthums*, 2 (1845), 301–12.
Schneider, G. 'Jesus vor dem Synedrium', *Bibel und Leben*, 2 (1970), 1–15.
Schreier, S. 'L^{e}tol^{e}dot ha-Sanhedrin ha-g^{e}dolah BiY^{e}rušalayim', *Ha-šiloaḥ*, 31 (1914–15), 404–15.
Schürer, E. *Geschichte des jüdischen Volkes im Zeitalter Jesu Christi*, 4th edn., vol. 2, pp. 373ff. Leipzig, 1907.
'Review of A. Büchler, *Synedrion*', *TLZ*, 28 (1903), 345–8.
Schwarz, A. 'Die Erste halachische Controverse', *MGWJ*, 37 (1893), 164–9; 201–6.
Sidon, A. 'Die Controverse der Synedrialhaupter', *Gedenkbuch an David Kaufman*, pp. 358ff. Breslau, 1900.
Taubes, H. Z. *Ha-Nasi ba-Sanhedrin ha-G^{e}dolah*. Vienna, 1925.
Tschernowitz, C. *Tol^{e}dot ha-halakah*, 4, pp. 101ff. New York, 1950.
Valentin, P. 'Les comparutions de Jésus devant le Sanhédrin', *RSR*, 59 (1971), 230–6.
Weiss, A. 'Liš^e'elat ṭib ha-bet din šel šib'im w^e'eḥad', *Louis Ginzberg Jubilee Volume*, Hebrew section, pp. 189–216. New York, 1946.
Wolfson, H. A. 'Synedrion in Greek Jewish Literature and Philo', *JQR*, N.S. 36 (1945–46), 303–6.
Zeitlin, S. *The Rise and Fall of the Judaean State*, 1, pp. 202ff. Philadelphia, 1962.
'The political Synedrion and the religious Sanhedrin', *JQR*, N.S. 36 (1945–46), 109–40.
'The Semikah controversy between the Zugoth', *JQR*, N.S. 7 (1916–17), 499–517.
'The titles High Priest and the nasi of the Sanhedrin', *JQR*, N.S. 48 (1957–58), 1–5.
Who Crucified Jesus?, pp. 68–84. 4th edn., New York, 1964.
Zucker, H. *Studien zur jüdischen Selbstverwaltung im Altertum*, pp. 91ff. Berlin, 1936.
Zuri, J. S. *Tol^{e}dot ha-mišpat ha-ṣibburi ḥa-'ibri*. 3 vols. Paris, 1931–38.

CHAPTER 8 ANTIOCHUS IV

Abel, F.-M. *Les Livres des Maccabées*. EBib. Paris, 1949.
'Antiochus Epiphane', *Vivre et penser*, 1 (1941), 231–54.
Abel, F.-M. and Starcky, J. *Les Livres des Maccabées*. 3rd edn. BJ. Paris, 1961.
Bevan, E. R. 'A note on Antiochos Epiphanes', *JHS*, 20 (1900), 26–30.

Bickerman, E. *Der Gott der Makkabäer*. Berlin, 1937; ET *The God of the Maccabees*. SJLA 32. Leiden, 1917.

Institutions des Séleucides. Paris, 1938.

'Un document relatif à la persécution d'Antiochos IV Epiphane', *RHR*, 115 (1937), 188–223.

Dagut, M. B. 'II Maccabees and the death of Antiochus IV Epiphanes', *JBL*, 72 (1953), 149–57.

Dancy, J. C. *I Maccabees: A Commentary*. Oxford, 1954.

Galling, K. 'Judäa, Galiläa und der Osten im Jahre 164/3 v. Chr.', *PJ*, 36 (1940), 43–77.

Hengel, M. *Judentum und Hellenismus*. WUNT 10. Tübingen, 1969; ed. 2 1973, ET see p. 658.

Hof, P. van't. *Bijdrage tot de Kennis van Antiochus IV Epiphanes*. Dissertation. Amsterdam, 1955.

Kolbe, W. *Beiträge zur syrischen und jüdischen Geschichte*. BWANT n.f. 10. Berlin, 1926.

Laqueur, R. 'Griechische Urkunden in der jüdisch–hellenistischen Literatur', *Historische Zeitschrift*, 136 (1927), 229–52.

Jansen, H. L. 'Die Politik Antiochos' des IV.', *Skrifter utg. av det Norske Videnskaps-Akademi i Oslo* 2. Hist.-filos. Klasse. no. 3. Oslo, 1943.

Mago, U. *Antioco IV Epifane, Re di Siria*. Sassari, 1907.

Meyer, E. *Ursprung und Anfänge des Christentums*, 2. Berlin, 1921.

Mittwoch, A. 'Tribute and land-tax in Seleucid Judaea', *Bib* 36 (1955), 352–61.

Mørkholm, O. *Antiochus IV of Syria*. Classica et Mediaevalia dissertation. 8. Copenhagen, 1966.

'Studies in the coinage of Antiochus IV of Syria', *Historisk-filosofiske meddelelser* 40, 3 (1963).

Nagel, G. 'Révolte et réforme à Jérusalem (169–166 avant J.-C)', *Recueil de la Faculté de Théologie de Genève*, 8 (1942), 5–22.

Niese, B. *Geschichte der griechischen und makedonischen Staaten seit der Schlacht bei Chaeronea*, 1–3. Gotha, 1893–1903.

Kiritik der beiden Makkabäerbücher. Berlin, 1900.

Plöger, O. 'Die Feldzüge der Seleukiden gegen den Makkabäer Judas', *ZDPV*, 74 (1958), 158–88.

Reuter, F. *Beiträge zur Beurteilung des Königs Antiochos Epiphanes*. Dissertation. Münster, 1938.

Rowley, H. H. 'Menelaus and the Abomination of Desolation', *Studia orientalia J. Pedersen dicata*, pp. 303–15. Copenhagen, 1953.

Schaumberger, J. 'Die neue Seleukiden-Liste BM 35603 und die makkabäische Chronologie', *Bib*, 36 (1955), 423–35.

Schunk, K. D. *Die Quellen des I und II Makkabäerbuches*. Dissertation. Halle, 1954.

Tcherikover, V. *Hellenistic Civilization and the Jews*. Philadelphia, 1959.

Willrich, H. *Urkundenfälschung in der hellenistisch–jüdischen Literatur*. FRLANT n.f. 21. Göttingen, 1924.

Zambelli, M. 'La composizione del secondo libro dei Maccabei', *Studi pubblicati dall' Istituto Italiano per la storia antica*, 16 (1965), 195–299.

Zeitlin, S. *The Rise and Fall of the Judaean State*. vol. 1 Philadelphia, 1962.

CHAPTER 9 THE HASMONEAN REVOLT AND THE HASMONEAN DYNASTY

General

Comprehensive bibliographies

Very full bibliographies can be found in the following:

Hengel, M. *Judaism and Hellenism*. 2 vols. Philadelphia, 1974.

Schürer, E. *The History of the Jewish People in the Age of Jesus Christ*, I. New English edition. Revised by G. Vermes and F. Millar. Edinburgh, 1973.

Texts and Commentaries

Abel, F.-M. *Les Livres des Maccabées*. EBib. Paris, 1949.

Abel, F.-M. and Starcky, J. *Les Libres des Maccabées*. 3rd edn. BJ. Paris, 1961.

Charles, R. H. *The Apocrypha and Pseudepigrapha of the Old Testament*. 2 vols. Oxford, 1913.

Enoch. See Charles, and bibliography to ch. 12.

Eusebius. *Eusebii Pamphili Chronici Canones Latine vertit, adauxit, ad sua tempora produxit S. Eusebius Hieronymus*, ed. J. K. Fotheringham. London, 1923.

Chronicorum libri duo, ed. A. Schoene. Berlin, 1875–76.

Eusebius Werke, vol. 7: *Die Chronik des Hieronymus*, ed. R. Helm. GCS 47. Berlin, 1956.

Goldstein, J. A. *I Maccabees*. AB 41. Garden City, 1976.

II Maccabees. AB 41A. Garden City, 1983.

Grimm, C. L. W. *Das erste Buch der Maccabäer*. Dritte Lieferung of *Kurzgefasstes exegetisches Handbuch zu den Apokryphen des Alten Testamentes*, ed. Otto F. Fritsche. Leipzig, 1853.

Das zweite, dritte und vierte Buch der Maccabäer. Vierte Lieferung of *Kurzgefasstes exegetisches Handbuch zu den Apokryphen des Alten Testamentes*. Leipzig, 1857.

Josephus, *Flavii Iosephi opera*, ed. B. Niese. Berlin, 1887–95.

Josephus with an English Translation, 1 to 10, ed. H. St J. Thackeray, R. Marcus, A. Wikgren and L. H. Feldman. The Loeb Classical Library. London–Cambridge, Mass., 1926–65.

1 Maccabees. See bibliography to ch. 12.

2 Maccabees. See bibliography to ch. 12.

Megillat Taʿanit. Lichtenstein, H. 'Die Fastenrolle', *HUCA*, 8–9 (1931–32), 257–351.

Psalms of Solomon. See *APOT*.

Reinach, T. *Textes d'auteurs grecs et romains relatifs au Judaïsme*. Paris, 1895; repr. Hildesheim, 1963.

Sachs, A. J. and Wiseman, D. J. 'A Babylonian king list of the Hellenistic period', *Iraq*, 16 (1954), 202–12.

Stern, M. *Greek and Latin Authors on Jews and Judaism*. 3 vols, Jerusalem–Leiden, 1974–84.

Ha-teʿudot lᵉmered ha-ḥašmonaʾim. The Documents on the History of the Hasmonaean Revolt. Tel Aviv, 1965.

'Ha-re-qaʿ ha-mᵉdini lᵉmilḥᵃmotaw šel Aleksander Yannai', *Tarbiz* 33 (1964), 325–336.

Syncellus, Georgius. *Georgius Syncellus et Nicephorus Cp.*, ed. W. Dindorf. Corpus scriptorum historiae Byzantinae, 12–13. Bonn, 1829.

Testament of Moses. See *APOT*.

Other works

Abel, F.-M. *Géographie de la Palestine*. EB. Paris, 1933–38.
'Topographie des campagnes machabéennes', *RB*, 32 (1923), 495–521; 33 (1924), 201–17, 317–87; 34 (1925), 194–216; 35 (1926), 206–22, 510–33.
Aharoni, Y. and Avi-Yonah, M. *The Macmillan Bible Atlas*. New York–London, 1968.
Alon, G. *Meḥqarim b'-toledot Yiśra'el. Studies of Jewish History*. 2 vols. Tel Aviv, 1957, 1958.
Avi-Yonah, M. *The Holy Land*. Grand Rapids, Mich., 1966.
Baron, S. W. *A Social and Religious History of the Jews*. 2nd edn., revised and enlarged. Vols. 1–2. New York, 1952.
Bengtson, H. *Griechische Geschichte*. 4th edn. HAW 3.4 Munich, 1969.
Grundriss der römischen Geschichte. HAW 3.5.1. Munich, 1967.
Bevan, E. R. *The House of Seleucus*. 2 vols. London, 1902.
Bickerman, E. *Institutions des Séleucides*. Paris, 1938.
Chronology of the Ancient World. Ithaca, N.Y., 1968.
'Une question dauthenticité: les privilèges juifs'. *Annaire de l'Institut de Philologie et d'Histoire orientales et slaves*, 13 (1953), 11–34.
Bouché-Leclercq, A. *Histoire des Lagides*. Paris, 1903–7.
Histoire des Séleucides. Paris, 1913–14.
Cross, F. M., Jr. *The Ancient Library of Qumran*. Garden City, N.Y., 1961.
Debevoise, N. C. *A Political History of Parthia*. Chicago, 1938.
Derenbourg, J. *Essai sur l'histoire et la géographie de la Palestine*. Paris, 1867; repr. Farnborough, 1971.
Dussaud, R. *La pénétration des Arabes en Syrie avant l'Islam*. Paris, 1955.
Eddy, S. K. *The King is Dead*. Lincoln, Neb., 1961.
Encyclopedia of Archaeological Excavations in the Holy Land, ed. M. Avi-Yonah. 4 vols. Oxford, 1975–8.
Gardner, P. *The Seleucid Kings of Syria. British Museum, Department of Coins and Medals: Catalogue of Greek Coins*. London, 1878; repr. Bologna, 1963.
Geiger, A. *Urschrift und Übersetzungen der Bibel*. Breslau, 1857; 2nd edn. Frankfurt am Main, 1928.
Glueck, N. *Deities and Dolphins*. New York, 1965.
Goldstein, J. A. 'The tales of the Tobiads', in: *Christianity, Judaism and Other Greco-Roman Cults: Studies for Morton Smith at Sixty*, ed. J. Neusner, part III, pp. 85–123. SJLA 12. Leiden, 1975.
Graetz, H. *Geschichte der Juden*. 5th edn. Vol. 3. Leipzig, 1905.
Hengel, M. See p. 658: General bibliography.
Hill, G. F. *Catalogue of the Greek Coins of Palestine. British Museum, Department of Coins and Medals: Catalogue of Greek Coins*. London, 1914; repr. Bologna, 1965.
Hölscher, G. 'Josephus (2)', *PW*, 9 (1916), cols. 1934–2000.
Jepsen, A. and Hanhart, R. *Untersuchungen zur israelitisch-jüdischen Chronologie*. BZAW 88. Berlin, 1964.
Kanael, B. 'Altjüdische Münzen', *Jahrbuch für Numismatik und Geldgeschichte*, 17 (1967), pp. 157–298.
Klausner, J. *Historiah šel habbayit haššeni*. Vol. 3. Jerusalem, 1950.
The Messianic Idea in Israel. New York, 1955.
Kolbe, W. *Beiträge zur syrischen und jüdischen Geschichte*. BWANT, II.10. Stuttgart, 1926.

Kugler, F. X. *Von Moses bis Paulus*. Münster, 1922.

Le Rider, G. *Suse sous les Séleucides et les Parthes*. Mémoires de la Mission archéologique en Iran 38. Paris, 1965.

Meyer, E. *Ursprung und Anfänge des Christentums*. 3 vols. Stuttgart–Berlin, 1921–23.

Milik, J. T. *Ten years of Discovery in the Wilderness of Judaea*. SBT 26. Naperville, Ill., 1959.

Moscati, S. *The World of the Phoenicians*. New York–Washington, 1968.

Nickelsburg, G. W. E. *Resurrection, Immortality, and Eternal Life in Intertestamental Judaism*. HTS 26. Cambridge, Mass, 1972.

Nickelsburg, G. W. E. (ed). *Studies on the Testament of Moses*. SBLSCS 4. Missoula, Montana, 1973.

Parker, R. A. and Dubberstein, W. H. *Babylonian Chronology, 626 B.C.–A.D. 75*. Brown University Studies 19. Providence, 1956.

Rostovtzeff, M. *The Social and Economic History of the Hellenistic World*. 2nd edn. Oxford, 1953.

Samuel, A. E. *Ptolemaic Chronology*. MBPAR 43. Munich, 1962.

Schalit, A. (ed.). *The Hellenistic Age*. Vol. 6 of *The World History of the Jewish People*, first series: *Ancient Times*. Jerusalem, 1972.

Schürer, E. See p. 659: General bibliography.

Geschichte des jüdischen Volkes im Zeitalter Jesu Christi. 4th edn. 3 vols. and index. Leipzig, 1901–11.

Sepher Yerushalayim. Ed. M. Avi-Yonah. Tel Aviv, 1956.

Tcherikover, V. A. *Hellenistic Civilization and the Jews*. Philadelphia, 1959.

Thackeray, H. St J. *Josephus, the Man and the Historian*. New York, 1929.

Volkmann, H. 'Ptolemaios (24–31)', *PW*, 23 (1959), cols. 1702–47.

Wacholder, B. Z. *Nicolaus of Damascus*. University of California Publications in History 75. Berkeley–Los Angeles, 1962.

Will, E. *Histoire politique du monde hellénistique*. Annales de l'Est 32. Vol. 2. Nancy, 1967.

Early Hasmoneans: Mattathias, Judas, Jonathan, and Simon

Bickerman, E. *Der Gott der Makkabäer*. Berlin, 1937; ET, *The God of the Maccabees*. SJLA 32. Leiden, 1979.

'Makkabäerbücher', *PW*, 14 (1930), cols. 779–800.

'Ein jüdischer Festbrief vom Jahre 124 v. Chr.', *ZNW*, 32 (1933), 233–54.

Bunge, J. G. *Untersuchungen zum zweiten Makkabäerbuch: Quellenkritische, literarische, chronologische und historische Untersuchungen zum zweiten Makkabäerbuch als Quelle syrisch-palästinensischer Geschichte im 2 Jh. v. Chr*. Dissertation. Bonn, 1971.

Fischer, T. 'Zu Tryphon', *Chiron*, 2 (1972), 201–13.

Seleukiden und Makkabäer. Bochum, 1980.

Graetz, H. *Geschichte der Juden*. 3rd edn. Vol. 2, second half. Leipzig, n.d.

Laqueur, R. 'Griechische Urkunden in der jüdisch-hellenistischen Literatur', *Historische Zeitschrift*, 136 (1927), 229–52.

Møkholm, O. *Antiochus IV of Syria*. Classica et Mediaevalia Dissertation 8. Copenhagen, 1966.

Niese, B. 'Eine Urkunde aus der Makkabäerzeit', in: *Orientalische Studien Theodor Nöldeke zum siebzigsten Geburtstag...gewidmet*, ed. C. Bezold, pp. 817–29. Giessen, 1906.

Otto, W. *Zur Geschichte der Zeit des 6. Ptolemäers*. Abhandlungen der Bayerischen Akademie der Wissenschaften, Philosophisch-historische Abteilung N.F. 11. (Munich, 1934).

Schaumberger, J. 'Die neue Seleukiden-Liste BM 35603 und die makkabäische Chronologie', *Bib*, 36 (1955), 423–35.

Volkmann, H. 'Demetrios I. und Alexander I. von Syrien', *Klio*, 19 (1925), 373–412.

Later Hasmoneans: John Hyrcanus I, Judas Aristobulus I, Alexander Janneus, Salome Alexandra, John Hyrcanus II and Judas Aristobulus II

Avigad, N. 'A bulla of Jonathan the High Priest', *IEJ*, 25 (1975), 8–12.

Baumgarten, J. M. 'Does *tlh* in the Temple Scroll refer to crucifixion?', *JBL*, 91 (1972), 472–81.

Bellinger, A. R. 'The end of the Seleucids', *Transactions of the Connecticut Academy of Arts and Sciences*, 38 (1949), 51–102.

Bickerman, E. J. 'Ein jüdischer Festbrief vom Jahre 124 v.Chr.', *ZNW*, 32 (1933), 233–54.

'The colophon of the Greek book of Esther', *JBL*, 63 (1944), 339–62.

'Notes on the Greek book of Esther', *PAAJR*, 20 (1950), 101–33.

Fischer, T. *Untersuchungen zum Partherkrieg Antiochos' VII*. Dissertation. Tübingen, 1970.

Kindler, A. 'Addendum to the dated coins of Alexander Jannaeus', *IEJ*, 18 (1968), 188–91.

Levine, L. I. 'The Hasmonaean conquest of Strato's tower', *IEJ*, 24 (1974), 62–9.

Meshorer, Y. *Jewish Coins of the Second Temple Period*. Chicago, 1968.

'The beginning of Hasmonaean coinage', *IEJ*, 24 (1974), 59–61.

Naveh, H. 'Dated coins of Alexander Janneus', *IEJ*, 18 (1968), 20–5.

Otto, W. and Bengtson, H. *Zur Geschichte des Niederganges des Ptolemäerreiches*. Abhandlungen der Bayerischen Akademie der Wissenschaften, Philosophisch–historische Abteilung, N.F., 17 (1938).

Rappaport, U. 'Les Iduméens en Egypte', *RPh*, 3rd series, 43 (1969), 73–82.

Schalit, A. *König Herodes, der Mann und sein Werk*. Studia Judaica 4. Berlin, 1969.

'Die Eroberungen des Alexander Jannäus in Moab', *Theokratia*, 1 (1967–69), 3–50.

Smith, Morton, 'Palestinian Judaism in the first century', *Israel: Its Role in Civilization*, ed. M. Davis. New York, 1956.

Stern, M. 'Traqidas-lᵉkhinuyo šel Aleksander Yannay 'eṣel Yosephos wᵉSinqelos' ('Thrakidas–surname of Alexander Yannai in Josephus and Syncellus'), *Tarbiz*, 29 (1959–60), 207–9.

''Al ha-yᵉḥasim beyn Yᵉhudah wᵉRomi bimey Yoḥanan Hurqanos' ('The relations between Judea and Rome during the rule of John Hyrcanus'), *Zion*, 26 (1961), 1–22.

Yadin, Y. 'Pesher Nahum (4Q pNahum) reconsidered', *IEJ*, 21 (1971), 1–12.

CHAPTER 10 JEWISH LITERATURE IN HEBREW AND ARAMAIC IN THE GREEK PERIOD

The Song of Songs

Audet, J.-P. 'Le sens du Cantique des Cantiques', *RB*, 62 (1955), 197–221.
Feuillet, A. *Le Cantique des Cantiques*. LD 10. Paris, 1953.
Gerleman, G. *Das hohe Lied*. BKAT 18/2. Neukirchen, 1963.
Ginsburg, C. D. *The Song of Songs*. London, 1857; repr. New York, 1970.
Gordis, R. *The Song of Songs*. New York, 1954.
Joüon, P. *Le Cantique des Cantiques*. Paris, 1909.
Krinetzki, L. *Das hohe Lied. Kommentar zu Gestalt und Kerygma eines alttestamentarischen Liebesliedes*. Kommentare und Beiträge zum Alten und Neuen Testament. Düsseldorf, 1964.
Loretz, O. *Das althebräische Liebeslied, Untersuchungen zur Stichometrie und Redaktionsgeschichte des Hohenliedes und des 45. Psalms*. AOAT 14/1. Neukirchen, 1971.
Lys, D. *Le plus beau chant de la création*. LD 51. Paris, 1969.
Nolli, G. *Cantico dei Cantici*. La Sacra Bibbia. Turin, 1967.
Pope, M. H. *Song of Songs. A new translation with Introduction and Commentary*. AB 7C. Garden City, 1979.
Pouget, G. and Guitton, J. *Le Cantique des Cantiques*. EBib. Paris, 1934; ET *The Canticle of Canticles*. New York, 1948.
Renan, E. *Le Cantique des Cantiques, traduit de l'hébreu avec une étude sur le plan, l'age et le caractère du poème*. Paris, 1860; ET *The Song of Songs*. London 1896.
Robert, A. and Tournay, R. *Le Cantique des Cantiques*. EBib. Paris, 1963.
Rowley, H. H. 'The interpretation of the Song of Songs', in: *The Servant of the Lord and other Essays on the Old Testament*, pp. 189–234. London, 1952, pp. 195–245. 2nd edn. Oxford, 1965.
Rudolph, W. *Das Buch Ruth. Das hohe Lied. Die Klagelieder*. KAT 17.1–3 Gütersloh, 1962.
Schmökel, H. *Heilige Hochzeit und Hoheslied*. Abhandlungen für die Kunde des Morgenlandes 32. Wiesbaden, 1956.
Schott, S. *Les chants d'amour de l'Egypte ancienne*. L'Orient ancien illustré, 9. Paris, 1956.
Tournay, R. J. *Quand Dieu parle aux hommes le langage de l'amour*. Cahiers de la Revue Biblique 21. Paris, 1982.
Vajda, G. *Le commentaire d'Ezra de Gérone sur le Cantique des Cantiques*. Pardês: études et textes de mystique juive. Paris, 1969.
Vulliaud, P. *Le Cantique des Cantiques d'après la tradition juive*. Paris, 1925.
Winandy, J. *Le Cantique des Cantiques, poème d'amour mué en écrit de sagesse*. Bible et vie chrétienne. Maredsous, 1960.
Würthwein, E. *Ruth, Das Hohelied, Esther*. HAT 1, 18. Tübingen, 1969.

Ecclesiastes

Barton, G. A. *The Book of Ecclesiastes*. ICC. Edinburgh, 1908.
Barucq, A. *Le Livre de l'Ecclésiaste*. VS. Paris, 1968.
'Qohéleth', *DBSup* 9 (1979), cols. 609–74.
Braun, R. *Kohelet und die frühhellenistische Popularphilosophie*. BZAW 130. Berlin, 1973.
Castellino, G. R. 'Qohelet and his Wisdom', *CBQ*, 30 (1968), 15–28.

Dahood, M. 'Canaanite–Phoenician influence in Qoheleth', *Bib*, 33 (1952), 30–52, 191–221; cf. *Gregorianum*, 43 (1962), 55–79, and *Bib*, 47 (1966), 264–82.
Di Fonzo, L. *Ecclesiaste*. La Sacra Bibbia. Turin, 1967.
Duesberg, H. and Fransen, I. *Les scribes inspirés*, pp. 537–92. Maredsous, 1966.
Ellermeier, F. *Qohelet. Untersuchungen zum Buche Qohelet*. Herzberg, 1967–70.
Galling, K. *Der Prediger*. HAT 1, 18. Tübingen, 1969.
Gese, H. 'Die Krisis der Weisheit bei Kohelet', *Les sagesses du Proche-Orient Ancien, Colloque de Strasbourg*, pp. 139–51. Paris, 1966.
Ginsberg, H. L. *Studies in Koheleth*. New York, 1950.
Ginsburg, C. D. *Coheleth (commonly called the book of Ecclesiastes), with a commentary, historical and cricital*. London, 1861; repr. New York, 1970 as *The Song of Songs and Coheleth*.
Glasser, O. E. *Le procès du bonheur par Qohelet*. LD 61. Paris, 1970.
Gordis, R. *Kohelet–The Man and His World*. 3rd edn. New York, 1968.
Hertzberg, H. W. *Der Prediger*. KAT 17.4. Gütersloh, 1963.
Humbert, P. *Recherches sur les sources égyptiennes de la littérature sapientiale d'Israël*. Mémoires de l'Université de Neuchâtel, 7, pp. 107–24. Neuchâtel, 1929.
Lauha, A. *Kohelet*. BKAT 19. Neukirchen–Vluyn, 1978.
Lohfink, N. *Kohelet*. Die neue EB. Würzburg, 1980.
Lys, D. *L'Ecclésiaste ou Que vaut la vie? Traduction, Introduction générale, Commentaire de 1, 1 à 4, 3*. Paris, 1977.
Loretz, O. *Qohelet und der alte Orient. Untersuchungen zu Stil und theologischer Thematik des Buches Qohelet*. Freiburg, 1964.
Muilenburg, J. 'A Qoheleth Scroll from Qumran', *BASOR*, 135 (1954), 20–28.
Neher, A. *Notes sur Qohéléth (L'Ecclésiaste)*. Paris, 1951.
Pedersen, J. *Scepticisme israélite*. Cahiers de la Revue d'Histoire et de Philosophie religieuses. Paris, 1931.
Podechard, E. *L'Ecclésiaste*. EBib. Paris, 1912.
Renan, E. *L'Ecclésiaste*. Paris, 1882.
Wright, A. G. 'The riddle of the Sphinx: the structure of the book of Qoheleth', *CBQ* 30, (1968), 313–34.
Zimmerli, W. *Das Buch des Predigers, Salomo*. ATD 16.1. Göttingen, 1962.
Zimmermann, F. *The Inner World of Qohelet*. New York, 1973.

Esther

Bardtke, H. *Das Buch Esther*, KAT 17, 5. Gütersloh, 1963.
Berg, S. B. *The Book of Esther: Motifs, Themes and Structure*. SBLDS 44. Missoula, 1979.
Bickerman, E. *Four Strange Books of the Bible*. New York, 1967.
'The colophon of the Greek book of Esther', *JBL*, 63 (1944), 339–62.
Brownlee, W. H. 'Le livre grec d'Esther et la royauté divine. Corrections orthodoxes au livre d'Esther', *RB*, 73 (1966), 161–85.
Cazelles, H. 'Notes sur la composition du rouleau d'Esther', H. Gross and F. Mussner edd., *Lex tua veritas. Festschrift für Hubert Junker*, pp. 17–29. Trier, 1961.
Dommershausen, W. *Die Estherrolle*. Stuttgarter biblische Monographien 6. Stuttgart, 1968.
Gaster, T. H. *Purim and Hanukkah in Eastern and Western Traditions*. New York, 1950.
Gerleman, G. *Esther*. BKAT 21/1. Neukirchen-Vluyn, 1970.
Moore, C. A. *Esther*. AB7B. Garden City, 1971.

Paton, L. B. *The Book of Esther*. ICC. Edinburgh, 1908.
Ringgren, K. V. H. and Weiser, A. *Das Hohelied, Klagelieder, Das Buch Esther*. ATD 16.2. Göttingen, 1958.
Würthwein, E. *Die fünf Megillot, Ruth, das Hohelied, Esther*. HAT I, 18. Tübingen, 1969.

The books of Ezra–Nehemiah

Galling, K. *Die Bücher der Chronik, Esra, Nehemia*. ATD 12, Göttingen, 1954.
Gilbert, M. 'La place de la Loi dans la prière de Néhémie 9', in *De la Tôrah au Messie*, Mélanges Henri Cazelles, pp. 307–16. Paris, 1981.
Kellermann, U. *Nehemia: Quellen, Überlieferung und Geschichte*. BZAW 102. Berlin, 1967.
Michaeli, F. *Les Livres des Chroniques, d'Esdras et de Néhémie*. CAT 16. Neuchatel, 1967.
Mowinckel, S. *Studien zu dem Buche Esra–Nehemia*. Vol. 2. Oslo, 1964–66.
Noth, M. *Überlieferungsgeschichtliche Studien*, pp. 110–80. Halle an der Saale, 1943; 2nd edn. Tübingen, 1957.
Rowley, H. H. 'The chronological order of Ezra and Nehemiah', *The Servant of the Lord and other essays on the Old Testament*, pp. 129–59. London, 1952; pp. 135–68. Oxford, 1965.
'Nehemiah's mission and its background', *BJRL*, 37 (1955), 528–61; repr. in H. H. Rowley, *Men of God*, pp. 211–45. Edinburgh, 1963.
Rudolph, W. *Esra und Nehemia samt 3 Esra*. HAT, 1, 20. Tübingen, 1949.
Schneider, H. *Die Bücher Esra und Nehemia*. HSAT IV, 2. Bonn, 1959.
Torrey, C. C. *Ezra Studies*. Chicago, 1910; reprinted, New York, 1970.
Vaux, R. de 'Les décrets de Cyrus et de Darius sur la reconstruction du Temple', *Bible et Orient*, pp. 112–13. Paris, 1967; ET *The Bible and the Ancient Near East*, pp. 94–6. London, 1972.

Bea, A. 'Neuere Arbeiten zum Problem der Chronikbücher', *Bib*, 22 (1941), 46–58.
Brunet, A.-M. 'Le Chroniste et ses sources', *RB*, 60 (1953), 481–508; 61 (1954), 349–86.
'La théologie du Chroniste. Théocratie et messianisme' *Sacra Pagina*. ed. J. Coppens *et al*. 2 vols. Vol. 1, pp. 384–97. Gemblaux, 1959.
Cazelles, H. *Les Libres des Chroniques*. BJ. Paris, 1954; 3rd edn. 1961.
Carmignac, J. 'Les devanciers de S. Jérôme. Une traduction latine de la recension καιγε dans le second Livre des Chroniques', in *Mélanges Dominique Barthélemy*, ed. P. Casetti *et al*. pp. 31–50. OBO 38. Freiburg–Göttingen, 1981.
Curtis, E. L. and Madsen, A. A. *A Critical and Exegetical Commentary on the Books of Chronicles*. ICC. Edinburgh, 1910.
Galling, K. *Die Bücher der Chronik, Esra, Nehemia*. ATD 12. Göttingen, 1954.
Kropat, A. *Die Syntax des Autors der Chronik*. BZAW 16. Giessen, 1909.
Michaeli, F. *Les Livres des Chroniques, d'Esdras et de Néhémie*. CAT 16. Neuchâtel, 1967.
Mosis, R. *Untersuchungen zur Theologie des Chronistischen Geschichtswerkes*. Freiburger Theologische Studien, 92. Freiburg, 1973.
Myers, J. M. *The Books of Chronicles: Ezra, Nehemiah*. AB 12, 13, 14 Garden City, 1965.
Noth, M. *Überlieferungsgeschichtliche Studien*. Halle an der Saale, 1943; Tübingen, 1957.
Rad, G. von *Das Geschichtsbild des Chronistischen Werkes*. BWANT 54. Stuttgart, 1930.
Randinelli, L. *Il libro delle Chronache*. La Sacra Bibbia. Turin, 1966.
Rudolph, W. *Chronikbücher*, HAT, 1, 21. Tübingen, 1955.
Welch, A. C. *The Work of the Chronicler, its purpose and date*. Oxford, 1939.
Willi, T. *Die Chronik als Auslegung. Untersuchungen zur literarischen Gestaltung der historischen Überlieferung Israels*. FRLANT 106. Göttingen, 1972.

Deutero-Zechariah

Chary, T. *Aggée, Zacharie, Malachie*. SB. Paris, 1969.

Delcor, M. *Les Petits Prophètes*. BPC 8, part 2. Paris, 1964.

'Un problème de critique textuelle et d'exégèse, Zach. XII.10, '*et aspicient ad me quaem confixerunt*', *RB*, 58 (1951), 189–99.

'Les sources du Deutéro-Zacharie et ses procédés d'emprunt', *RB*, 59 (1952), 385–411.

'Hinweise auf das samaritanische Schisma im Alten Testament', *ZAW*, 74 (1962), 281–91.

Elliger, K. *Das Buch der zwölf kleinen Propheten*. ATD 25. Göttingen, 1949, 5th edn. 1964.

'Ein Zeugnis aus der jüdischen Gemeinde im Alexanderjahr 332 v. Chr.', *ZAW*, 62 (1949–50), 63–115.

Jansma, T. *Inquiry into the Hebrew Text and the Ancient Versions of Zechariah ix–xiv*. Leiden, 1949.

Lacocque, A. *Zacharie 9–14*. CAT 11c. Neuchâtel–Paris, 1981.

Lamarche, P. *Zacharie 9–14. Structure littéraire et Messianisme*. EBib. Paris, 1961.

Otzen, B. *Studien über Deuterosacharja*. Acta Theologica Danica 6. Copenhagen, 1964.

Saebø, M. *Sacharja 9–14, Untersuchungen von Text und Form*. WMANT 34. Neukirchen, 1969.

Willi-Plein, I. *Prophetie am Ende. Untersuchungen zu Sacharja 9–14*. BBB 42. Bonn, 1974.

CHAPTER 11 JEWISH–GREEK LITERATURE OF THE GREEK PERIOD

Editions and translations of the texts

General

Greek texts

Denis, A.-M. (ed.). *Fragmenta Pseudepigraphorum quae supersunt Graeca una cum historicorum et auctorum Judaeorum Hellenistarum fragmentis*, pp. 149–228. PVTG 3b. Leiden, 1970.

Jacoby, F. (ed.). *Die Fragmente der griechischen Historiker*. Vol. 3, C 2, pp. 666–98. Leiden, 1958.

Stearns, W. N. (ed.). *Fragments from Graeco-Jewish Writers*. Chicago, 1908. Unreliable; with English translation.

English and German translations

Charles, R. H. (ed.). *The Apocrypha and Pseudepigrapha of the Old Testament*. 2 vols. Oxford, 1913, repr. 1963. A selection containing only some works dealt with in chapter 11.

Charlesworth, J. H. (ed.). *The Pseudepigrapha of the Old Testament*. 2 vols. Garden City/N.Y., 1983–5. Comprehensive collection of relevant writings, in English translation with short introductions.

Kautzsch, E. (ed.). *Die Apokryphen und Pseudepigraphen des Alten Testaments*. 2 vols. Tübingen, 1898–1900, repr. 1921 and Darmstadt, 1962. A selection similar to that of Charles, in German translation.

Kümmel, W. G. (ed.). *Jüdische Schriften aus hellenistisch-römischer Zeit*. Gütersloh, 1974ff. Published in fascicles, not yet finished; German translation of all relevant writings, with introductions, short notes and bibliographies.

Riessler, P. *Altjüdisches Schrifttum ausserhalb der Bibel*. Heidelberg, 1928, repr. 1966. Comprehensive, but not always reliable German translation; now more and more outdated by the collection by Kümmel.

On individual texts (in order of discussion)

Wendland, P. (ed.). *Aristeae ad Philocratem epistula*. Bibliotheca Teubneriana. Leipzig, 1900.

Hadas, M. *Aristeas to Philocrates*. Jewish Apocryphal Literature. New York, 1951. With English translation.

Pelletier, A. *Lettre d'Aristée à Philocrate*. SC 89. Paris, 1962. With French translation.

Sapientia Jesu Filii Sirach, ed. J. Ziegler. Septuaginta ed. auctoritate Societatis Litterarum Gottingensis, vol. 12.2. Göttingen, 1965.

Sapientia Salomonis, ed. J. Ziegler. Septuaginta ed. auctoritate Societatis Litterarum Gottingensis, vol. 12.1. Göttingen, 1962.

(Pseudo-Phocylides:) *Theognis. Ps.-Pythagoras. Ps.-Phocylides. Chares* (etc.), ed. D. Young. Bibliotheca Teubneriana. Leipzig, 1961; 2nd edn. 1971.

Maccabaeorum liber I, ed. W. Kappler. Septuaginta ed. auctoritate Societatis Litterarum Gottingensis, vol. 9.1. Göttingen, 1936; 2nd edn. 1968.

Maccabaeorum liber II, ed. W. Kappler and R. Hanhart. Septuaginta ed. auctoritate Societatis Litterarum Gottingensis, vol. 9.2. Göttingen, 1959; 2nd edn. 1976.

Maccabaeorum liber III, ed. R. Hanhart. Septuaginta ed. auctoritate Societatis Litterarum Gottingensis, vol. 9.3. Göttingen, 1960.

Le livre de la Prière d'Aséneth, ed. P. Batiffol. Studia Patristica 1. 1–2. Paris, 1889–90.

Joseph et Aséneth, ed. M. Philonenko. SPB 13. Leiden, 1968. With French translation.

Wieneke, J. *Ezechielis Judaei poetae Alexandrini fabulae quae inscribitur* ΕΞΑΓΩΓΗ *fragmenta*. Diss. phil. Münster, 1931. With detailed commentary.

Snell, B. (ed.). *Tragicorum Graecorum Fragmenta,* 1, pp. 288–301. Göttingen, 1971. (For Ezekiel the tragedian.)

General studies and selected monographs

Burchard, C. *Untersuchungen zu Joseph und Aseneth*. WUNT 8. Tübingen, 1965.

Charlesworth, J. H. *The Pseudepigrapha and Modern Research*. SBLSCS 7. Missoula, 1976; 2nd edn. 1981.

Dalbert, P. *Die Theologie der hellenistisch-jüdischen Missions-Literatur unter Ausschluss von Philo und Josephus*. TF 4. Hamburg–Volksdorf, 1954.

Delling, G. *Bibliographie zur jüdisch-hellenistischen und intertestamentarischen Literatur 1900–1970*. TU 106² 2nd edn. Berlin, 1975.

Denis, A.-M. *Introduction aux Pseudépigraphes grecs d'Ancien Testament*. SVTP 1. Leiden, 1970.

Eissfeldt, O. *Einleitung in das Alte Testament*, pp. 773–864. 3rd edn. Tübingen, 1964. ET: *The Old Testament: An Introduction*. pp. 571–637. New York–Oxford, 1965.

Freudenthal, J. *Die Flavius Josephus beigelegte Schrift Ueber die Herrschaft der Vernunft (IV. Makkabäerbuch)*. Breslau, 1869.

Alexander Polyhistor und die von ihm erhaltenen Reste jüdäischer und samaritanischer

Geschichtswerke, 1–2, Hellenistische Studien, 1–2. Jahresberichte des jüdisch-theologischen Seminars 'Fraenkel'scher Stiftung', Breslau, 1874–75.
Gutman, Y. *The Beginnings of Jewish Hellenistic Literature*, 1–2. (In Hebrew.) Jerusalem, 1958–63.
Hadas, M. *Hellenistic Culture. Fusion and Diffusion*. New York, 1959. German translation: *Hellenistische Kultur. Werden und Wirkung*. Stuttgart, 1963.
Hegermann, H. 'Griechische-jüdisches Schrifttum', in: J. Maier and J. Schreiner (eds.), *Literatur und Religion des Frühjudentums*, pp. 163–80. Gütersloh–Würzburg, 1973.
Hengel, M. *Judentum und Hellenismus. Studien zu ihrer Begegnung unter besonderer Berücksichtigung Palästinas bis zur Mitte des 2. Jh. v. Chr.* WUNT 10. Tübingen, 1969; 2nd edn. 1973; ET *Judaism and Hellenism*, London 1974.
'Anonymität, Pseudepigraphie und "Literarische Fälschung" in der jüdisch-hellenistischen Literatur', in K. von Fritz (ed.), *Pseudepigrapha* 1, pp. 229–329. Entretiens sur l'Antiquité Classique 18. Geneva, 1972.
Horst, P. W. van der. *The Sentences of Pseudo-Phocylides*. SVTP 4. Leiden, 1978.
Küchler, M. *Frühjüdische Weisheitstraditionen*. OBO 26. Freiburg–Göttingen, 1979.
Schürer, E. *Geschichte des jüdischen Volkes im Zeitalter Jesu Christi*, vol. 3, pp. 420–633. 4th edn., Leipzig, 1909; repr. Hildesheim, 1964. ET: *The History of the Jewish People in the Age of Jesus Christ* (175 *B.C.–A.D. 135*). A new English version revised and edited by G. Vermes, F. Millar (and M. Black), 1–3. Edinburgh, 1973–87.
Tcherikover, V. *Hellenistic Civilization and the Jews*. Philadelphia, 1959.
'Jewish apologetic literature reconsidered', *Eos*, 48, 3 (1956) (= Symbolae R. Taubenschlag dedicatae, III), 169–93. Wroclaw–Warsaw, 1957.
Wacholder, B. Z. *Eupolemus. A Study of Judaeo-Greek Literature*. Monographs of the Hebrew Union College 3. Cincinnati, 1974.
Walter, N. *Der Thoraausleger Aristobulos. Untersuchungen zu seinen Fragmenten und zu pseudepigraphischen Resten der jüdisch-hellenistischen Literatur*. TU 86. Berlin, 1964.
Untersuchungen zu den Fragmenten der jüdisch-hellenistischen Historiker. Diss. theol. (Habilitationsschrift). Halle, 1968 (typescript).

CHAPTER 12 THE APOCRYPHA AND PSEUDEPIGRAPHA OF THE HELLENISTIC PERIOD

The deuterocanonical or apocryphal books

General bibliography

André, L. E. T. *Les Apocryphes de l'Ancien Testament*. Florence, 1903.
Charles, R. H. (ed.). *The Apocrypha and Pseudepigrapha of the Old Testament*. 2 vols. 1. *Apocrypha*. Oxford, 1913.
Charlesworth, J. H. *The Pseudepigrapha and Modern Research*. Missoula, 1976; revd. ed., *The Pseudepigrapha and Modern Research with a Supplement*. SBLSCS 7 Chico, California, 1981.
Delling, G. *Bibliographie zur jüdisch-hellenistichen und intertestamentarischen Literatur 1900–1970*. TU 106² Berlin, 1975.
Denis, A.-M. *Introduction aux Pseudépigraphes grecs d'ancien Testament*. SUTP 1. Leiden, 1970.
Díez Macho, A. *Apocrifos del Antiguo Testamento*. 4 vols. Madrid, 1982–83.

Hengel, M. *Judentum und Hellenismus*. WUNT 10. Tübingen, 1969, 2nd edn. 1973. ET: *Judaism and Hellenism*. London, 1974.

Kautzsch, E. *Die Apokryphen und Pseudepigraphen der Alten Testaments*. 2 vols. 1: *Die Apokvyphen*. Tübingen, 1900.

Metzger, B. M. *An Introduction to the Apocrypha*. New York–Oxford, 1957.

Nickelsburg, G. W. E. *Jewish Literature between the Bible and the Mishnah*. London, 1981.

Oesterley, W. O. E. *An Introduction to the Books of the Apocrypha*. London, 1935.

Pfeiffer, R. H. *History of New Testament Times with an Introduction to the Apocrypha*. New York, 1949.

Sacchi, P. *Apocrifi dell'Antico Testamento*. Classici delle Religioni, 2. La religione ebraica. Turin, 1981.

Szekely, S. *Bibliotheca Apocrypha. Introductio historico-critica in libros apocryphos utriusque Testamenti cum explicatione argumenti et doctrinae*. Vol. 1: *Introductio generalis, sibyllae et Apocrypha Vet. Test. Antiqua*. Freiburg-im-Breisgau, 1913.

Tcherikover, V. *Hellenistic Civilization and the Jews*. Philadelphia, 1959.

Torrey, C. C. *The Apocryphal Literature, a Brief Introduction*. Yale, 1945.

Turdeanu, E. *Apocryphes slaves et roumains de l'Ancien Testament*. SVTP 5. Leiden, 1981.

Wicks, H. J. *The Doctrine of God in the Jewish Apocryphal and Apocalyptic Literature*. London, 1915; repr. New York, 1971.

Ecclesiasticus or Sirach (The Wisdom of Jesus ben Sira)

Introductions, translations and commentaries

Barthélemy, D. and Rickenbacher, O. edd. *Konkordanz zum hebräischen Sirach mit syrisch-hebräischem Index*. Göttingen, 1973.

Ben-Ḥayyim, Z. (ed.) *The Book of Ben Sira. Text, Concordance and Analysis of the Vocabulary*. Jerusalem, 1973.

Box, G. H. and Oesterley, W. O. E., *APOT*, vol. 1, pp. 268–517.

Crenshaw, J. L. (ed.) *Studies in Ancient Israelite Wisdom*. New York, 1976.

Old Testament Wisdom. An Introduction. London, 1982.

di Lella, A. A. *The Hebrew Text of Sirach: A Text-critical and Historical Study*. Studies in Classical Literature, 1. The Hague, 1966.

Dubarle, A. M. *Les Sages d'Israël*, pp. 147–85. Paris, 1946.

Duesberg, H. and Auvray, P. *Le Livre de l'Écclésiastique*. BJ. Paris, 1953.

Duesberg, H. and Fransen, I. *Les Scribes inspirés: Introduction aux livres sapientiaux de la Bible*, pp. 597–711. Maredsous, 1966.

Ecclesiastico, La Sacra Bibbia. Turin, 1966.

Gilbert, M. (ed.) *La Sagesse de l'Ancien Testament*. Gembloux–Leuven, 1979.

Hadot, J. *Penchant mauvais et volonté libre dans la Sagesse de Ben Sira (L'Ecclésiastique)*. Brussels, 1970.

Hamp, V. *Sirach*. EB13. Würzburg, 1951.

Haspecker, J. *Gottesfurcht bei Jesus Sirach. Ihre religiöse Struktur und ihre literarische und doktrinäre Bedeutung*. AnBib 30. Rome, 1967.

Lévi, I. *L'Ecclésiastique ou la Sagesse de Jésus, fils de Sira*. Bibliothèque de l'Ecole des Hautes Etudes. Sciences religieuses, 10.1, 2. Paris, 1898–1901.

Marböck, J. *Weisheit im Wandel. Untersuchungen zur Weisheitstheologie bei Ben Sira*. BBB 37. Bonn, 1971.

Middendorp, T. *Die Stellung Jesu Ben Siras zwischen Judentum und Hellenismus*. Leiden, 1973.

Peters, N. *Das Buch Jesus-Sirach oder Ecclesiasticus*. Exegetisches Handbuch zum Alten Testament 21. Münster, 1913.

Prato, G. L. *Il problema della teodicea in Ben Sira*. AnBib 65. Rome, 1975.

Rickenbacher, O. *Weisheitsperikopen bei Ben Sira*. OBO 1. Freiburg–Göttingen, 1973.

Rüger, H. P. *Text und Textform im Hebräischen Sirach*. BZAW 112. Berlin, 1970.

Schechter, S. and Taylor, C. *The Wisdom of Ben Sira. Portions of the Book Ecclesiasticus*. (Hebrew Text with an English translation). Cambridge, 1899.

Smend, R. *Die Weisheit des Jesus Sirach*. 2 vols. Berlin, 1906.

Spicq, C. *Les Livres Sapientaux*. BPC 6. Paris, 1951.

Vattioni, F. *Ecclesiastico*. Pubblicazioni del Seminario di Semitistica. Testi 1. Naples, 1968. (Hebrew, Greek, Latin and Syriac texts).

Winter, M. M. *A Concordance to the Peshitta Version of Ben Sira*. Monographs of the Peshitta Institute, Leiden 2. Leiden, 1976.

Yadin, Y. *The Ben Sira Scroll from Masada, with introduction, emendations and commentary*. Jerusalem, 1965.

Ziegler, J. *Sapientia Jesu filii Sirach*. Septuaginta ed. auctoritate Societatis Litterarum Gottingensis, vol. 12.2. Göttingen, 1965. Critical edition of the Greek text.

Ethiopic Enoch or the Enochic Corpus

Texts

Ethiopic

Charles, R. H. *The Ethiopic Version of the Book of Enoch, edited from twenty-three mss together with the fragmentary Greek and Latin Versions*. Anecdota Oxoniensia, Semitic series xi. Oxford, 1906.

Flemming, J. *Das Buch Henoch. Äthiopischer Text*. TU 7. Leipzig, 1902.

Knibb, M. A. *The Ethiopic Book of Enoch. A new edition in the light of Aramaic Dead Sea Fragments*. 2 vols. Oxford, 1978.

Greek

Black, M. *Apocalypsis Henochi graece*. PVTG 3. Leiden, 1970.

Bonner, C. and Youtie, H. C. *The Last Chapters of Enoch in Greek*. SD 8. London, 1937.

Flemming, J. and Radermacher, L. *Das Buch Henoch*. GCS 5. Leipzig, 1901.

Latin

James, M. R. *Apocrypha Anecdota. A Collection of thirteen apocryphal books and fragments*. TextsS 2, no. 3, pp. 146–50. Cambridge, 1893.

Coptic

Donadoni, S. 'Un frammento della versione copta del "Libro di Enoch"', *AcOr*, 25 (1960), 197–202.

Translations

English

Charles, R. H. *The Book of Enoch or 1 Enoch translated from the Editor's Ethiopic Text.* Oxford, 1912.

'1 Enoch'. *APOT*, vol. 2, pp. 163–281.

The Book of Enoch. Translation of Early Documents, ser. 1: Palestinian Jewish Texts (Pre-Rabbinic). London, 1917.

French

Martin, F. *Le livre d'Hénoch.* Documents pour l'étude de la Bible. Paris, 1906.

German

Beer, G. 'Das Buch Henoch', *APAT*, vol. 2, pp. 217–310.

Riessler, P. *Altjüdisches Schrifttum ausserhalb der Bibel*, pp. 355–451. Heidelberg, 1928; repr. 1966.

Italian

Sacchi, P. *Apocrifi dell'Antico Testamento*, pp. 415–723. Turin, 1981.

Spanish

Coniente, F. and Pinero, A. in A. Díez Macho, *Apocrifos del Antiguo Testamento*, vol. 4. Madrid, 1983.

Aramaic

Milik, J. T. *The Books of Enoch, Aramaic Fragments of Qumran Cave 4.* Oxford, 1976.

Theisohn, J. *Der auserwählte Richter. Untersuchungen zum traditionsgeschichtlichen Ort des Menschensohngestalt der Bilderreden des Äthiopischen Henoch.* SUNT 12. Göttingen, 1975.

Principal studies

Caquot, A. 'Remarques sur les ch. 70 et 71 du livre éthiopien d'Hénoch' in *Apocalypses et théologie de l'espérance*, pp. 111–22. Paris, 1977.

Casey, M. 'The use of the term "Son of Man" in the Similitudes of Enoch', *JSJ*, 7 (1976), 11–29.

Charlesworth, J. H. 'The SNTS Pseudepigrapha seminars at Tübingen and Paris on the book of Enoch', *NTS*, 25 (1979), 315–23.

Delcor, M. 'Le mythe de la chute des anges et de l'origine des géants comme explication du mal dans le monde dans l'apocalyptique juive. Histoire des traditions', *RHR* 190 (1976), 3–53.

'Le livre des Paraboles d'Hénoch Ethiopien. Le problème de son origine à la lumière des découvertes récentes', *EstBib*, 38 (1979–80), 5–33.

Dexinger, F. *Henochs Zehnwochenapokalypse und offene Probleme der Apokalyptikforschung.* SPB 29. Leiden, 1977.

Dimant, D. 'I Enoch 6–11: A methodological perspective', in *Society of Biblical Literature 1978 Seminar Papers*, 1: 323–39. Ed. P. J. Achtemeier. Missoula, 1978.

Fitzmyer, J. A. 'Implications of the new Enoch literature from Qumran', *Theological Studies*, 38 (1977), 332–45.

Grelot, P. 'La légende d'Hénoch dans les Apocryphes et dans la Bible. Origine et signification', *RSR*, 46 (1958), 5–26, 181–210.

'La géographie mythique d'Hénoch et ses sources orientales', *RB*, 65 (1958), 33–69.

'L'eschatologie des Esséniens et le livre d'Hénoch', *RevQ*, 1 (1958–59), 113–31.

Hanson, P. D. 'Rebellion in heaven, Azazel and euhemeristic heroes in I Enoch 6–11' *JBL*, 96 (1977), 195–233.

Hartman, L. *Asking for a Meaning. A Study of 1 Enoch 1–5*. Coniectanea Biblica, NTS 12. Lund, 1979.

Hindley, J. C. 'Towards a date for the Similitudes of Enoch. An historical approach', *NTS*, 14 (1968), 551–65.

Messel, N. *Der Menschensohn in den Bilderreden des Henoch*. BZAW 35. Giessen, 1922.

Milik, J. T. 'Problèmes de la littérature hénochique à la lumière des fragments araméens de Qumrân', *HTR*, 64 (1971), 333–78.

'Tarfan et Qumran, Livre des Géants juif et manichéen', *Tradition und Glaube. Das frühe Christentum in seiner Umwelt*, Festgabe K. G. Kuhn, pp. 117–27. Göttingen, 1971.

'Ecrits préesséniens de Qumran: d'Enoch à Omram', in M. Delcor (ed.), *Qumrân: sa pieté, sa théologie et son milieu*, BETL 46. pp. 91–106. Paris–Louvain, 1978.

Müller, K. 'Menschensohn und Messias', *BZ*, NF 16 (1972) 161–87; NF 17 (1973), 52–66.

Müller, U. B. *Messias und Menschensohn in jüdischen Apokalypsen und in der Offenbarung des Johannes*. Studien zum neuen Testament 6. Gütersloh, 1972.

Nickelsburg, G. W. E. 'Enoch 97–104: A study of Greek and Ethiopic texts', in Stone, M. E. (ed.), *Supplementary Volume to Sion*, pp. 90–156. Jerusalem, 1976.

'Apocalyptic and myth in I Enoch 6–11', *JBL*, 96 (1977), 383–405.

Sacchi, P. 'Il "Libro dei Vigilanti" e l'apocalittica', *Henoch*, 1 (1979), 42–92.

Sjöberg, E. *Der Menschensohn im äthiopischen Henochbuch*. Lund, 1946.

Suter, D. W. *Tradition and Composition in the Parables of Enoch*. SBLDS 47. Missoula, 1979.

Theisohn, J. *Der auserwählte Richter: Untersuchungen zum traditionsgeschichtlichen Ort der Menschensohngestalt der Bilderreden des Äthiopischen Henoch*. SUNT 12. Göttingen, 1975.

Ullendorf, E. 'An Aramaic Vorlage of the Ethiopic text of Enoch', in *Is Biblical Hebrew a Language?*, *Studies in Semitic Languages and Civilizations*, pp. 172–80. Wiesbaden, 1977.

Wacker, M.-T. *Weltordnung und Gericht: Studien zu 1 Henoch 22*. Forschungen zur Bibel 45. Würzburg, 1982.

The Book of Jubilees

Editions of the text

Hebrew fragments

Barthélemy, D. and Milik, J. T. *Qumran Cave 1*. DJD 1, pp. 82–4. Oxford, 1955.

Baillet, M., Milik, J. T. and Vaux R. de *Les 'Petites grottes' de Qumrân*. DJD 3, pp. 77–9. Oxford, 1962.

Deichgräber, R. 'Fragmente einer Jubiläen-Handschrift aus Höhle 3 von Qumran', *RevQ*, 5 (1964–6), 415–22.

Milik, J. T. 'Le travail d'édition des fragments manuscrits de Qumrân', *RB*, 63 (1956), 60.

van der Woude, A. S. 'Fragmente des Buches Jubiläen aus Qumran Höhle XI (11 Q Jub)', in *Tradition und Glaube. Das frühe Christentum in seiner Umwelt*, Festgabe K. G. Kuhn, pp. 140–6. Göttingen, 1971.

Syriac fragments

Tisserant, E. 'Fragments syriaques du livres des Jubilés', *RB*, 30 (1921), 55–86, 206–32.

Greek fragments

Denis, A.-M. *Fragmenta pseudepigraphorum quae supersunt graeca*. PVTG 3, pp. 70–104. Leiden, 1970.

Latin fragments

Ceriani, A. M. *Monumenta sacra et profana ex codicibus praesertim bibliothecae Ambrosianae*, vol. 1, fasc. 1, pp. 15–62. Milan, 1861.

Charles, R. H. *The Ethiopic Version of the Hebrew Book of Jubilees*. Anecdota Oxoniensia. Oxford, 1895.

Rönsch, H. *Das Buch der Jubiläen oder die kleine Genesis unter Beifügung des revidirten Textes der in der Ambrosiana aufgefundenen lateinischen Fragmente*, pp. 10–211. Leipzig, 1874.

Ethiopic texts

Charles, R. H. *The Ethiopic Version of the Hebrew Book of Jubilees*. Anecdota Oxoniensia. Oxford, 1895.

Dillmann, A. *Liber Jubilaeorum...aethiopice, ad duorum librorum manuscriptorum fidem*. Kiel, 1859.

English translations

G. H. Schodde, 'The Book of Jubilees, translated from the Ethiopic' in *Bibliotheca Sacra*, 42 (1885), 629–45 and 43 (1886), 57–72, 356–71, 455–86, 727–45.

Charles, R. H. *The Book of Jubilees or the Little Genesis translated from the Ethiopic text*. Translations of Early Documents, series 1: Palestinian Jewish Texts (Pre-rabbinic). London, 1917.

'The Book of Jubilees'. *APOT*, vol. 2, pp. 11–82.

German translations

Berger, K. *Das Buch der Jubiläen*. Jüdische Schriften aus hellenistisch-römischer Zeit, 2.3. Gütersloh, 1981.

Littmann, E. 'Das Buch der Jubiläen'. *APAT*, vol. 2, pp. 31–119.

Riessler, P. *Altjüdisches Schrifttum ausserhalb der Bibel*, pp. 539–666. Heidelberg, 1928; repr. 1966.

Italian translation

Sacchi, P. *Apocrifi dell' Antico Testamento*, pp. 181–411. Turin, 1981.

Spanish translation

Corriente, F. and Pinero, H. in A. Díez Macho, *Apocrifos del Antiguo Testamento*, vol. 2. Madrid, 1983.

Studies

Albeck, C. *Das Buch der Jubiläen und die Halacha*. Berlin, 1930.

Baillet, M. 'Remarques sur le manuscrit du Livre des Jubilés de la grotte 3 de Qumran', *RevQ*, 5 (1964–66), 423–33.

Büchler, A. 'Studies in the book of Jubilees', *REJ*, 82 (1926), 253–74.

'Traces des idées et des coutumes hellénistiques dans le Livre des Jubilés', *REJ*, 89 (1930), 321–48.

Caquot, A. 'Les enfants aux cheveux blancs (Remarques sur Jubilés xxiii, 25)', *RHR*, 177 (1970), 131–2.

Cazelles, H. and Vogt, E. 'Sur les origines du calendrier des Jubilés', *Bib*, 43 (1962), 202–16.

Davenport, G. L. *The Eschatology of the Book of Jubilees*. SPB 20. Leiden, 1971.

Jaubert, A. *La date de la Cène*, pp. 13–30. Paris, 1957. ET: *The Date of the Last Supper*, pp. 15–30. Staten Island, N.Y. 1965.

'Le calendrier des Jubilés et de la secte de Qumrân: ses origines bibliques', *VT*, 3 (1953), 250–64.

'Le calendrier des Jubilés et les jours liturgiques de la semaine', *VT*, 7 (1957), 35–61.

Martin, F. 'Le livre des Jubilés: but et procédés de l'auteur. Ses doctrines', *RB*, 20 (n.s. 8) (1911), 321–44, 502–33.

Milik, J. T. 'Recherches sur la version grecque du livre des Jubilés', *RB*, 78 (1971), 545–57.

Morgenstern, J. 'The calendar of the Book of Jubilees, its origin and its character', *VT* 5 (1955), 34–76.

Rowley, H. H. 'Criteria for the dating of Jubilees', *JQR*, n.s. 36 (1945–46), 183–7.

Steck, O. H. 'Die Aufnahme von Genesis 1 in Jubiläen 2 und 4. Esra 6', *JSJ*, 8 (1977), 154–82.

Testuz, M. *Les idées religieuses du livre des Jubilés*. Geneva–Paris, 1960.

van der Kam, J. C. *Textual and Historical Studies in the Book of Jubilees*. HSM 14. Missoula, 1977.

Wiesenberg, E. 'The Jubilee of Jubilees', *RevQ*, 3 (1961–2), 3–40.

The Testaments of the Twelve Patriarchs

Editions of the Greek Text

Charles, R. H. *The Greek Versions of the Testaments of the Twleve Patriarchs, edited from nine MSS, together with the variants of the Armenian and Slavonic versions and some Hebrew fragments*. Oxford, 1908.

De Jonge, M. *Testamenta XII Patriarcharum edited according to Cambridge University Library MS Ff. 1.24 fol. 203a–262b. PVTG* 1, Leiden, 1964.

Editions of the Testament of Levi in Aramaic

The Cambridge Fragments have been edited by:

Pass. H. L. and Arendzen, J. 'Fragment of an Aramaic text of the Testament of Levi', *JQR*, 12 (1900), 651–61.

The Bodleian Library fragments have been edited by:

Charles, R. H. and Cowley, A. 'An early source of the Testaments of the Patriarchs', *JQR*, 19 (1907), 566–83.

Grelot, P. 'Notes sur le Testament araméen de Lévi (Fragment de la Bodleian Library, colonne a)', *RB*, 63 (1956), 391–406.

Both the Oxford and the Cambridge fragments were re-edited by Charles in his Greek edition of the Testaments, Appendix III, pp. 245–56.

The Qumran fragments have been edited by:

Hultgård, A. *L'eschatologie des Testaments des Douze Patriarches*. 1. *Interprétation des textes*. Acta Universitatis Upsaliensis, Historia Religionum 6. Uppsala, 1977.

Milik, J. T. *Qumran Cave 1*, DJD 1. no. 21, pp. 87–91. Oxford, 1955.

'Le Testament de Lévi en araméen. Fragment de la grotte 4 de Qumrân', *RB*, 62 (1955), 398–406.

Editions of the Testament of Naphtali in Hebrew

Gaster, M. 'The Hebrew Text of one of the Testaments of the Twelve Patriarchs' *Proceedings of the Society of Biblical Archaeology*, 16 (1893–94), 33–49, 109–117.

The text was re-edited by Charles in his edition of the Greek text, Appendix II, pp. 239–44.

Milik has drawn attention to a Hebrew text of Naphtali at Qumran which is longer than that of the Greek Testament:

Milik, J. T. *Dix ans de découvertes dans le désert de Judah*, p. 32. Paris, 1957; ET *Ten Years of Discovery in the Wilderness of Judaea*. SBT 26. p. 34. London, 1959.

Other versions:

Armenian

Josepheanz, H. S. *Treasury of ancient and recent fathers. Non-canonical writings of the Old Testament*. In Armenian. Vol. 1, pp. 27–51. Venice, 1896.

The text has been translated by:

Issaverdens, J. *The Uncanonical Writings of the Old Testament. The Testaments of the Twelve Patriarchs*, pp. 271–358. Venice, 1901.

Stone, M. E. *The Testament of Levi. A first study of the Armenian manuscripts of the*

Testaments of the XII Patriarchs in the convent of St. James, Jerusalem. Jerusalem, 1969.
The Armenian Version of the Testament of Joseph. SBL Texts and Translations 6. Missoula, 1975.

Syriac

A Syriac fragment has been identified by:

Wright, W. *Catalogue of Syriac MSS. in the British Museum*, Part 2 (= vol. 2) p. 997 (Add. 17, 193). 3 vols. London, 1870–72.

Old Slavonic

Tichonravov, N. *Pamyatmiki otrečennoj russkoj literatury* (= Monuments of Russian apocryphal literature) vol. 1, pp. 96–232. St Petersburg, 1863.
Turdeanu, E. 'Les Testaments des Douze Patriarches en slave', *JSJ*, 1 (1970), 148–84.

English translations

Charles, R. H. 'The Testaments of the XII Patriarchs', *APOT*, vol. 2, pp. 296–367.
Charles, R. H. *The Testaments of the Twelve Patriarchs*. Translations of Early Documents, Series 1, Palestinian and Jewish Texts (Pre-Rabbinic). London, 1917.

German translations

Becker, J. *Die Testamente der zwölf Patriarchen*. Jüdische Schriften aus hellenistisch-römischer Zeit, 3.1. Gütersloh, 1974.
Kautzsch, E. and Schnapp, F., *APAT*, vol. 2, pp. 458–506.
Riessler, P. *Altjüdisches Schriftum ausserhalb der Bibel*, pp. 1149–250. Heidelberg, 1928; repr. 1966.

Italian translation

Sacchi, P. *Apocrifi dell'Antico Testamento*, pp. 727–948. Turin, 1981.

Commentaries and principal studies

Becker, J. *Untersuchungen zur Entstehungsgeschichte der Testamente der zwölf Patriarchen*. AGJU 8. Leiden, 1970.
Braun, F. M. 'Les Testaments des Douze Patriarches et les problèmes de leur origine', *RB*, 67 (1960), 516–49.
Burchard, C., Jervell, J. and Thomas, J. *Studien zu den Testamenten der zwölf Patriarchen*. BZNW 36. Berlin, 1969.
Charles, R. H. *The Testaments of the Twelve Patriarchs translated from the editor's Greek text and edited, with introduction, notes and indices*. London, 1908.
Cortès, E. *Los Discursos de Adiós de Gn 49 a Jn 13–17; Pistas para la historia de un género literario en la antigua literatura judía*. Barcelona, 1976.
Jonge, M. de *The Testaments of the Twelve Patriarchs. A study of their text, composition and origin*. van Gorcum's Theologische Bibliothek, 25. Assen, 1953.
(ed.) *Studies on the Testaments of the Twelve Patriarchs: text and interpretation*. SVTP 3. Leiden, 1975.

Eppel, R. *Le piétisme juif dans les Testaments des douze patriarches*. Etudes d'Histoire et de Philosophie religieuses publiées par la Faculté de Théologie protestante de l'Université de Strasbourg 22. Paris, 1930.

Hollander, H. W. *Joseph as Ethical Model in the Testaments of the Twelve Patriarchs*. SVTP 6. Leiden, 1981.

Hultgård, A. *L'Eschatologie des Testaments des Douze Patriarches*. 1. *Interprétation des textes*. Acta Universitatis Upsaliensis, Historia Religionum 6. Uppsala, 1977.

Kuhn, K. G. 'Die beiden Messias Aarons und Israels', *NTS*, 1 (1954–5), 168–79.

Nickelsburg, G. W. E. *Studies on the Testament of Joseph*. SBLSCS 5. Missoula, 1976.

Nordheim, E. von *Die Lehre der Alten*. 1. *Das Testament als Literaturgattung im Judentum der hellenistisch-römischer Zeit*. ALGHJ 13. Leiden, 1980.

Philonenko, M. *Les interpolations chrétiennes des Testaments des Douze Patriarches et les manuscrits de Qumrân*. Cahiers de la Revue d'Histoire et de Philosophie religieuses 35. Paris, 1960.

Rengstorf, K. H. 'Herkunft und Sinn der Patriarchen-Reden in den Testamenten der zwölf Patriarchen', in *La littérature juive entre Tenach et Mischna, quelques problèmes*, ed. W. C. van Unnik, pp. 29–47. Semaine biblique de Louvain, 1969. Recherches bibliques, 9. Leiden, 1974.

Slingerland, H. D. *The Testaments of the Twelve Patriarchs: A Critical History of Research*. SBLMS 21. Missoula, 1977.

Stone, M. E. 'New evidence for the Armenian version of the Testaments of the Twelve Patriarchs', *RB* (1977), 94–107.

Turdeanu, E. 'Les Testaments des douze patriarches en slave', in *Apocryphes slaves et roumains de l'Ancien Testament*, pp. 239–75. SVTP 5. Leiden, 1981.

Judith

Introductions, translations and commentaries

Barucq, A. *Judith, Esther*. BJ. Paris, 1952.

Brunner, G. *Der Nabuchodonosor des Buches Judith*. Berlin, 1940; 2nd edn. Berlin, 1959.

Cowley, A. E., *APOT* vol. 1, pp. 242–267.

Delcor, M. 'Le livre de Judith et l'époque grecque', *Klio*, 49 (1967), 151–79.

Dubarle, A. *Judith: formes et sens des diverses traditions*. 2 vols. AnBib 24. Rome, 1966.

Enslin, M. S. and Zeitlin, S. *The Book of Judith. Greek text with an English translation, commentary and critical notes*. Jewish Apocryphal Literature 7. Leiden–Philadelphia, 1972.

Haag, E. *Studien zum Buche Judith*. Trierer Theologische Studien 16. Trier, 1963.

Lefèvre, A. 'Judith', *DBSup, vol.* 4 (1949), cols. 1315–21.

Miller, A. *Judith*. HSAT 4.3. Bonn, 1940.

Osty, E. and Trinquet, J. *La Bible*. Recontre edition. Lausanne, 1970ff.

Priero, G. *Giuditta*. La Sacra Bibbia. Turin, 1959.

Stummer, F. *Geographie des Buches Judith*. Bibelwissenschaftliche Reihe 3. Stuttgart, 1947.

Stummer, F. *Das Buch Judit*. EB 11, Würzburg, 1950.

Torrey, C. C. 'The surroundings of Bethilia', in *Florilegium Melchior de Vogüe* pp. 599–605. Paris, 1909.

Additions to the books of Esther and Daniel

See the books of Esther and Daniel. For Esther may be added:

Gregg, J. A. F. 'The additions to Esther', *APOT* vol. 1, pp. 665–684.

Roiron, F.-X. 'Les parties deutérocanoniques du Livre d'Esther', *RSR*, 6 (1916), 3–16.

For Daniel may be added:

Baumgartner, W. 'Susanna. Die Geschichte einer Legende', im *Zum Alten Testament und seiner Umwelt*, pp. 42–67. Leiden, 1959.

Davies, T. W. 'Bel and the dragon', *APOT* vol. 1, pp. 652–664.

Delcor, M. *Le livre de Daniel*, SB. pp. 260–72. Paris, 1971.

Kay, D. M. 'Susanna', *APOT* vol. 1, pp. 638–651.

Moore, C. A. *Daniel, Esther and Jeremiah. The Additions*. AB 44. Garden City, 1977.

Milik, J. T. 'Daniel et Susanne à Qumran?' in *De la Tôrah au Messie, Mélanges Henri Cazelles*, ed. M. Carrez *et al.* pp. 337–59. Paris, 1981.

The Books of Maccabees

Introductions, translations and commentaries

Abel, F.-M. *Les livres des Maccabées*. EBib. Paris, 1949.

Abel, F.-M. and Starcky, J. *Les Livres des Maccabées*. BJ. 3rd edn Paris, 1961.

Bévenot, H. *Die beiden Makkabäerbücher*. HSAT 4, 4. Bonn, 1931.

Bickerman, E. *Die Makkabäer*. Berlin, 1935.

Der Gott der Makkabäer. Berlin, 1937; ET The God of the Maccabees. SJLA 32. Leiden, 1979.

Institutions des Séleucides. Paris, 1938.

Four Strange Books of the Bible. New York, 1967.

'Makkabäerbücher', in *PW*, 14, cols. 779–797. Stuttgart, 1928.

'Héliodore au temple de Jérusalem', *Annuaire de l'Institut de Philologie et d'Histoire orientales et slaves de l'Université de Bruxelles*, 7 (1939–44), 5–40.

Breitenstein, U. *Beobachtungen zu Sprache, Stil und Gedankengut des Vierten Makkabäerbuchs*. Basle–Stuttgart, 1976.

Dancy, J. C. *A Commentary on 1 Maccabees*. Oxford, 1954.

Dhorme, E. in *La Bible. L'Ancient Testament*. Bibliothèque de la Pléiade, vol. 1. Paris, 1956.

Goldstein, J. A. *I Maccabees. A new translation with Introduction*. AB 41. Garden City, 1979.

Grandclaudon, M. *Les livres des Maccabées*. BPC 8.2. Paris, 1951.

Hadas, M. *The Third and Fourth Books of Maccabees*. Jewish Apocryphal Literature. New York, 1953.

Jaubert, A. *La notion d'alliance dans le judaïsme aux abords de l'ère chrétienne*. Patristica Sorbonensia 6. pp. 69–88. Paris, 1963.

Lefèvre, A. *Maccabees (livres 1 et 2)*. *DBSup*, vol. 5, cols. 597–612. Paris, 1957.

'Maccabées (Livre de)'. *DTC, Tables Générals*, Pt. 2, 1967, cols. 3047–51.

McEleney, N. J., in *JBC*.

Moffatt, J. '2 Maccabees', *APOT* vol. 1, pp. 125–154.

Nickelsburg, G. W. E. *Resurrection, Immortality and Eternal Life in Intertestamental Judaism*. HTS 26. Cambridge, Mass., 1972.

Oesterley, W. O. E. 'I Maccabees', *APOT* vol. 1, pp. 59–124.

Osty, E., *La Bible*. Rencontre edition. Lausanne, 1972.
Penna, A. *Libri dei Maccabei*. La Sacra Bibbia. Turin, 1953.
Schötz, D. *Das erste und zweite Buch der Makkabäer*, EB 3. Würzburg, 1948.

The letter of Jeremiah

Text in J. Ziegler, *Ieremias-Baruch-Threni. Epistula Ieremiae*. Göttingen, 1957.
Baars, W. 'Two Palestinian Syriac texts identified as parts of the Epistle of Jeremy', *VT*, 11 (1961), 77–81.
Ball, C. J. 'Epistle of Jeremy', *APOT*, vol. 1, pp. 596–611.
Robert, A. 'Jérémie (La Lettre de)', *DBSup*, vol. 4 (1949), cols. 849–57.

Tobit

Introductions, translations and commentaries

Clamer, A. 'Tobie (Livre de)', *DTC* 15 (1946), cols. 1153–76.
Fritzsche, O. *Die Bücher Tobit und Judith*. Kurzgefasstes exegetisches Handbuch zu den Apocryphen des Alten Testament. Leipzig, 1853.
De Vine, C. F. in *CCHS* (ed. 1).
Deselaers, P. *Das Buch Tobit. Studien zu seiner Entstehung, Komposition und Theologie*. OBO 43. Freiburg–Göttingen, 1982.
Dumm, R. *JBC*. vol. 1, pp. 620–4. London, 1968.
Guillaumont, A. in *La Bible. Ancien Testament*. Bibliothèque de la Pléiade. vol. 2. Paris, 1959.
Greenfield, J. C. 'Aḥiqar in the book of Tobit', in *De la Tôrah au Messie, Mélanges Henri Cazelles*, pp. 329–36. Paris, 1981.
Lamparter, H. *Weisheit Salomos, Tobias, Judith, Baruch (Die Apokryphen II)*. Stuttgart, 1972.
Löhr, M. 'Das Buch Tobit'. *APAT*, vol. 1, pp. 135–47.
Miller, A. *Tobit*. HSAT 4.3. Bonn, 1940.
Osty, E. *La Bible*. Rencontre edition. Lausanne, 1970ff.
Pautrel, R. and Lefebvre, M. 'Trois textes de Tobie sur Raphaël', *RSR*, 39 (1951–52), 115–24.
Pautrel, R. *Tobie*. 2nd rev. ed. BJ. Paris, 1959.
Poulssen, N. *Tobit*. De Boecken van het Oude Testament. Roermond, 1968.
Priero, G. *Tobia*. La Sacra Bibbia. Turin, 1953.
Schumpp, M. M. *Das Buch Tobias*. Exegetisches Handbuch zum Alten Testament 11. Münster, 1933.
Simpson, D. C. 'Tobit', *APOT* vol. 1, pp. 174–241.
Stummer, F. *Das Buch Tobit*. EB 11. Würzburg, 1950.
Zimmermann, F. *The Book of Tobit*. Jewish Apocryphal Literature. New York, 1958.

Wisdom

Introductions, translations, commentaries

Beauchamp, P. 'Epouser la Sagesse – ou n'épouser qu'elle? Une énigme du Livre de la Sagesse', in M. Gilbert (ed.), *La Sagesse de l'Ancien Testament*, pp. 347–69. Gembloux–Leuven, 1979.

Bigot, L. 'Sagesse (Livre de la)', *DTC*, vol. 14 (1939), cols. 703–44.
Dubarle, A. M. *Les Sages d'Israël*. Paris, 1969.
Duesberg, H. and Fransen, L. *Les scribes inspirés*, pp. 753–865. Maredsous, 1966.
Fichtner, J. *Weisheit Salomos*. HAT 2, 6. Tübingen, 1938.
Fischer, J. in *Das Hohe Lied, Rut und Das Bucher Weisheit*. EB. Würzburg, 1950.
Gilbert, M. *La critique des dieux dans le Livre de la Sagesse (Sg 13–15)*. AnBib 53. Rome, 1973.
Guillaumont, A. in *La Bible, l'Ancient Testament*. Bibliothèque de la Pléiade. vol. 2. Paris, 1959.
Heinisch, P. *Das Buch der Weisheit*. Exegetisches Handbuch zum Alten Testament 24. Münster, 1912.
Holmes, S. *APOT*, vol. 1, pp. 518–568.
Larcher, C. *Etudes sur le livre de la Sagesse*. EBib. Paris, 1969.
Le livre de la Sagesse. EBib. Paris, 1983.
Lattey, C. *CCHS*.
Osty, E. *Le Livre de la Sagesse*. 2nd rev. edn. BJ. Paris, 1957.
Reese, J. M. *Hellenistic Influences on the Book of Wisdom and its Consequences*. AnBib 41. Rome, 1970.
Schütz, R. *Les idées eschatologiques du livre de la Sagesse*. Paris, 1935.
Weber, J. J. *Les Livres Sapientaux*. BPC 6. Paris, 1946.
Winston, D. *The Wisdom of Solomon*. AB 43. Garden City, 1979.
Ziener, G. *Die theologische Begriffssprache im Buche der Weisheit*. BBB 11. Bonn, 1956.

The Sibylline Oracles

Editions of the texts

Alexandre, C. *Oracula Sibyllina, Textu ad codices manuscriptos recognitos...* 2 vols. Paris, vol. 1, 1841–3. vol. 2, 1856.
Geffcken, J. *Die Oracula Sibyllina*. GCS 8. Leipzig, 1902.
Kurfess, A. *Sibyllinische Weissagungen. Urtext und Übersetzung*. Munich, 1951.

Translations

English

Lanchester, H. C. O. 'The Sibylline oracles', *APOT*, vol. 2, pp. 368–406.

German

Blass, F. 'Die Sibyllinischen Orakel', *APAT*, vol. 2, pp. 177–217.
Geffcken, J. translation of Or. Sib. 3.1–45 and 63–92 in E. Hennecke, *Neutestamentlichen Apokryphen in deutscher Übersetzung und mit Einleitungen herausgegeben*, pp. 363–92, 2nd edn. pp. 399–422. Tübingen, 1904; 2nd edn. 1924.
Kurfess, A. *Sibyllinische Weissagungen. Urtext und Übersetzung*. Munich, 1951.
Riessler, P. 'Sibyllinische Orakel', *Altjüdisches Schrifttum ausserhalb der Bibel*, pp. 1014–45, and 1326–8. Heidelberg, 1928; repr. 1966.

French

Champier, S. and Robertet, S. *Oracles de la Sibylle*. Paris, 1702–3.
Nikiprowetzky, V. *La Troisième Sibylle* (translation of the third Sibylline), pp. 293–331. Etudes juives 9. Paris, 1970.

Spanish

Suárez de la Torre, E. 'Oraculos Sibilinos', in A. Díez Macho (ed.), *Apocrifos del Antiguo Testamento* 3. In preparation.

Principal Studies

Collins, J. *The Sibylline Oracles of Egyptian Judaism*. SBLDS 13. Missoula, 1974.
Flusser, D. 'The four empires in the fourth Sibyl and the book of Daniel', *Israel Oriental Studies*, 2 (1972), 148–75.
Geffcken, J. *Komposition und Entstehungszeit der Oracula Sibyllina*. TU 23.1. Leipzig, 1902.
Nikiprowetzky, V. *La Troisième Sibylle*. Etudes juives 9. Paris, 1970.
Rzach, A. 'Sibyllen', in *PW*, 2nd ser., 2 (1923), cols. 2073–103.
'Sibyllinischen Orakel', *PW*, 2nd ser., 2 (1923), cols. 2103–83.

The Third Book of Esdras or the Greek Ezra

Greek Text

See the editions of the Septuagint by Swete and Rahlfs, where the book appears under the title of 'First Book of Esdras'.

Latin Text

The Vulgate of the Greek Ezra is printed in all Latin Bibles in an appendix.

Syriac Text

Lagarde, P. de *Libri Veteris Testamenti apocryphi Syriace*. Leipzig, 1861.
Walton, B. *Biblia Sacra Polyglotta*. Vol. 4. pp. 1–29. London, 1657.

Ethiopic Text

Dillmann, A. *Biblia Veteris Testamenti Aethiopica*. Vol. 4. Berlin, 1894.

Translations

English

Cook, S. A. *APOT*, vol. 1, pp. 1–58.
Myers, J. M. *I and II Esdras, Introduction, Translation and Commentary*. AB 42. Garden City, 1974.

German

Guthe, H. *APAT*, vol. 1, pp. 1–23.
Rudolph, *Esra und Nehemia samt 3 Esra*. HAT 1, 20. Tübingen, 1949.

French

Migne, J. P. *Dictionnaire des Apocryphes.* Troisième et dernière Encyclopédie Théologique, 23–4. Vol. 1, cols. 513–70. Paris, 1856.

Principal Studies

Humbert, P. 'Le troisième livre d'Esdras', *Recherches sur les sources égyptiennes de la littérature sapientiale d'Israël.* Mémoires de l'Université de Neuchâtel. 7, pp. 148–51. Neuchâtel, 1929.

Kellermann, U. 'Das III. Esrabuch und die Nehemiahüberlieferung', *Nehemiah: Quellen, Überlieferung und Geschichte*, pp. 128–33. BZAW 102. Berlin, 1967.

Mowinckel, S. *Studien zu dem Buche Ezra–Nehemia*, vol. 1, pp. 1–28; vol. 3, pp. 10–11. Oslo, 1964–65.

Pohlmann, K.-F. *Studien zum dritten Esra. Ein Beitrag zur Frage nach dem ursprünglichen Schluss des chronistischen Geschichtswerkes.* FRLANT 104. Göttingen, 1970.

Torrey, C. C. *Ezra Studies.* Chicago, 1910; repr. New York, 1970.

The Third Book of Maccabees

Text

Hanhart, R. *Maccabaeorum Liber III.* Septuaginta Vetus Testamentum graecum auctoritate Societatis Litterarum Gottingensis editum, vol. 9.3. Göttingen, 1960.

The text is also to be found in the editions of the Septuagint by Rahlfs and Swete.

Translations

German

Kautzsch, E. *APAT*, vol. 1, pp. 119–35.

Riessler, P. *Altjüdisches Schrifttum ausserhalb der Bibel*, pp. 682–99. Heidelberg, 1928; repr. 1966.

English

Emmet, C. W. *APOT*, vol. 1, pp. 155–73.

Emmet, C. W. *The Third Book of Maccabees.* Translations of Early Documents. Series II. Hellenistic–Jewish Texts. London, 1918.

Hadas, M. *The Third and Fourth Books of Maccabees.* Jewish Apocryphal Literature 3. New York, 1953.

Hebrew

Kahana, A. *Ha-sepharim ha-ḥiṣonim*, vol. 2. pp. 237–57. 2nd edn., Tel Aviv, 1956.

Principal Studies

Hadas, M. 'III Maccabees and Greek romance', *Review of Religion*, 13 (1949), 155–62.

Jesi, F. 'Notes sur l'édit dionysiaque de Ptolémée IV Philopator', *JNES*, 15 (1956), 236–40.

Lévy, I. 'Ptolémée Lathyre et les Juifs', *HUCA*, 23 (1950–51), pt. 2, 127–36.

Moreau, J. 'Le troisième livre des Maccabées', *ChE* 31 (1941), 111–22.
Tracy, S. 'III Maccabees and Pseudo-Aristeas', *Yale Classical Studies*, 1 (1928), 241–52.
Willrich, H. 'Der historische Kern des III. Makkabaeerbuches', *Hermes*, 39 (1904), 244–58.

The Letter of Aristeas

Text

Pelletier, A. *Lettre d'Aristée à Philocrate*. SC 89, Paris, 1962.
Thackeray, H. St J. 'The Letter of Aristeas'. Appendix to H. B. Swete, *An Introduction to the Old Testament in Greek*, pp. 531–606. 2nd edn. Cambridge, 1914.

Translations

German

Meisner, N. *Aristeasbrief*. Jüdische Schriften aus hellenistisch-römischer Zeit, 2.1. pp. 35–85. Gütersloh, 1973.
Riessler, P. *Altjüdisches Schrifttum ausserhalb der Bibel*, pp. 193–233. Heidelberg, 1928; repr. 1966.
Wendland, P. *APAT*, vol. 2, pp. 1–31.

English

Andrews, H. T. *APOT*, vol. 2, pp. 83–122.
Hadas, M. *Aristeas to Philocrates*. Jewish Apocryphal Literature. New York, 1951.

French

Pelletier, A. *Lettre d'Aristée à Philocrate*. SC 89, Paris, 1962.

Italian

Tramontano, R. *La Lettera di Aristea a Filocrate*, Naples, 1931.

Modern Hebrew

Kahana, A. *Ha-sepharim ha-ḥiṣonim* vol. 2, pp. 21–71. 2nd edn. Tel Aviv, 1956.

Principal Studies

Bickerman, E. 'Zur Datierung des Pseudo-Aristeas', *ZNW*, 29 (1930), 280–98.
Février, J. G. *La date, la composition et les sources de la lettre d'Aristée à Philocrate*. Bibliothèque de l'Ecole des Hautes Etudes – sciences historiques et philologiques, 242. Paris, 1924.
Gooding, D. W. 'Aristeas and Septuagint origins: a review of recent studies', *VT*, 13 (1963), 357–79.
Jellicoe, S. 'The occasion and purpose of the Letter of Aristeas: a re-examination', *NTS*, 12 (1965–6), 144–50.
Kahle, P. E. *The Cairo Geniza*, pp. 132ff. London, 1947; pp. 209–14. 2nd edn., Oxford 1959.

Meecham, H. G. *The Letter of Aristeas. A linguistic study with special reference to the Greek Bible*. Manchester 1935.

Mendels, D. '"On kingship" in "the Temple Scroll" and the ideological *Vorlage* of the seven banquets in the "Letter of Aristeas to Philocrates"', *Aegyptus*, 59 (1979), 127–36.

Pelletier, A. *Flavius Josèphe, adaptateur de la lettre d'Aristée. Une réaction atticasante contra le Koiné*. Etudes et commentaires 45. Paris, 1962.

Vincent, H. 'Jérusalem d'après la lettre d'Aristée', *RB* 17 (n.s. 5) (1908), 520–32; 18 (n.s. 6) (1909), 555–75.

Zuntz, G. 'Aristeas studies, I: "The seven banquets"; II: Aristeas on the translation of the Torah', *JSS*, 4 (1959), 21–36, 109–26.

Joseph and Asenath

Greek text

Batiffol, P. *Studia patristica*. Etudes d'ancienne littérature chrétienne, fasc. 1–2, pp. 39–87. Paris, 1889–90.

Philonenko, M. *Joseph et Asénath. Introduction, texte critique. Traduction et notes*. SPB 13, pp. 128ff. Leiden, 1968.

Syriac text

Brooks, E. W. *Historia ecclesiastica Zachariae Rhetori volgo adscripta*, 1. CSCO, 83. Scriptores syri III, 5, vol. 38, pp. 13–55. Louvain, 1919. repr. 1953.

Translations and commentaries

Brooks, E. W. *Joseph and Asenath. The Confession and Prayer of Asenath Daughter of Pentephres the Priest*. Translations of Early Documents series II, Hellenistic–Jewish Texts. London, 1918.

Philonenko, M. *Joseph et Aséneth*. SPB 13. Leiden, 1968.

Riessler, P. *Altjüdisches Schrifttum ausserhalb der Bibel*. pp. 497–538. Heidelberg, 1928; repr. 1966.

Studies

Aptowitzer, V. 'Asenath, the wife of Joseph. A haggadic literary–historical study', *HUCA*, 1 (1924), 239–306.

Berger, K. 'Jüdisch-hellenistische Missionsliteratur und apokryphe Apostelakten', *Kairos*, 17 (1975), 232–48.

Burchard, C. *Untersuchungen zu Joseph und Aseneth*. WUNT 8. Tübingen, 1965.

'Joseph et Aséneth, Questions actuelles', in: *La littérature juive entre Tenach et Mischna*, ed. W. C. van Unnik, pp. 77–100. Leiden, 1974.

'Joseph und Aseneth neugriechisch', *NTS*, 24 (1977), 68–84.

'Ein vorläufiger griechischer Text von Joseph und Aseneth', *Dielheimer Blätter zum Alten Testament*, 14 (1979), 2–53.

'Joseph und Aseneth 25–29 armenisch', *JSJ*, 10 (1979), 1–10.

Delcor, M. 'Un roman d'amour d'origine thérapeute: le Livre de Joseph et Asénath', *BLE*, 63 (1962), 3–27.

Delling, G. 'Einwirkungen der Sprache der Septuaginta in "Joseph und Aseneth"', *JSJ*, 9 (1978), 29–56.

Holtz, T. 'Christliche Interpolationen in "Joseph und Aseneth", *NTS*, 14 (1967–8), 482–97.

Kuhn, K. G. 'The Lord's Supper and the communal meal at Qumran', in K. Stendahl (ed.), *The Scrolls and the New Testament*, pp. 65–93. New York, 1957.

Philonenko, M. 'Joseph et Aséneth: Questions actuelles', in W. C. van Unnik (ed.), *La littérature juive entre Tenach et Mischna*, pp. 73–6. Leiden, 1974.

Sänger, D. *Antikes Judentum und die Mysterien. Religionsgeschichtliche Untersuchungen zu Joseph und Aseneth*. WUNT 2.5. Tübingen, 1980.

'Bekehrung und Exodus. Zum jüdischen Traditionshintergrund von "Joseph und Aseneth"', *JSJ*, 10 (1979), 11–36.

Stehly, R. 'Une citation des Upanishads dans Joseph et Aséneth', *RHPR*, 55 (1975), 209–13.

CHAPTER 13 THE BOOK OF DANIEL

Alt, A. 'Zur Menetekel-Inschrift', *VT*, 4 (1954), 303–5.

Baumgartner, W. *Das Buch Daniel*. Giessen, 1926.

'Neues keilschriftliches Material zum Buche Daniel?', *ZAW*, 44 (1926), 38–56.

'Das Aramäische im Buche Daniel', *ZAW*, 45 (1927), 81–133; repr. in *Zum Alten Testament und seiner Umwelt* (Leiden, 1959), pp. 68–123.

'Ein Vierteljahrhundert Danielforschung', *TRu*, N. F. 11 (1939), 59–83, 125–44, 201–28.

Beek, M. A. *Das Daniel-buch. Sein historischer Hintergrund und seine literarische Entwicklung*. Leiden, 1935.

Behrmann, G. *Das Buch Daniel*. HKAT. Göttingen, 1849.

Bentzen, A. *Daniel*. HAT 1, 19. 2nd edn. Tübingen, 1952.

Bevan, A. A. *A Short Commentary on the Book of Daniel*. London, 1892.

Bickerman, E. J. *Four Strange Books of the Bible*. New York, 1967.

Brekelmans, C. H. W. 'The saints of the Most High and their kingdom' *kaph-he. 1940–1965*, ed. P. A. H. de Boer, OTS, 14 (1965), pp. 305–29.

Bruce, F. F. 'The book of Daniel and the Qumran community', *Neotestamentica et Semitica, Studies in honour of Matthew Black*, ed. E. E. Ellis and M. Wilcox. pp. 221–35. Edinburgh, 1969.

Caquot, A. 'Les quatre bêtes et le 'Fils d'homme' (Daniel 7)', *Semitica*, 17 (1967), 37–71.

Charles, R. H. *A Critical and Exegetic Commentary on the Book of Daniel*. Oxford, 1929.

Collins, J. J. 'The Son of Man and the saints of the Most High in the book of Daniel', *JBL*, 93 (1974), 50–66.

Coppens, J. 'Le fils d'homme danièlique et les relectures de *Dan*. vii, 13 dans les apocryphes et les écrits du Nouveau Testament, *ETL*, 37 (1961), 5–51.

'Le chapitre VII de Daniel', *ETL*, 39 (1963), 87–113.

'La vision danièlique du Fils d'Homme', *VT*, 19 (1969), 171–82.

Delcor, M. 'Les sources du chapitre VII de Daniel', *VT*, 18 (1968), 290–312.

Le Livre de Daniel. SB. Paris, 1971.

Dequeker, L. 'Daniel VII et les Saints du Très-Haut', *ETL*, 36 (1960), 353–92.

Dexinger, F. *Das Buch Daniel und seine Probleme*. SBS 36. Stuttgart, 1959.

Driver, G. R. 'The Aramaic of the book of Daniel', *JBL*, 45 (1926), 110–19.

Driver, S. R. *The Book of Daniel.* Cambridge Bible for Schools and Colleges. Cambridge, 1900.

Eissfeldt, O. 'Daniels und seiner drei Gefährten Laufbahn im babylonischen, medischen und persischen Dienst', *ZAW*, 72 (1960), 134–48.

The Old Testament: An Introduction, pp. 512–29. Oxford, 1965.

Emerton, J. A. 'The origin of the Son of Man imagery', *JTS*, n.s. 9 (1958), 225–42.

Gadd, C. J. 'The Harran inscriptions of Nabonidus', *Anatolian Studies*, 8 (1958), 35–92.

Gall, A. von *Die Einheitlichkeit des Buches Daniel.* Giessen, 1895.

Gammie, J. G. 'The Classification, stages of growth, and changing intentions in the book of Daniel', *JBL*, 95 (1976), 191–204.

Ginsberg, H. L. *Studies in Daniel.* Texts and Studies of the Jewish Theological Seminary of America 14. New York, 1948.

'The oldest interpretation of the Suffering Servant', *VT*, 3 (1953), 400–4.

'The composition of the book of Daniel', *VT*, 4 (1954), 246–75.

'Daniel' *EncJud*, vol. 5, cols. 1274–5, 1277–89. Jerusalem, 1971.

Goettsberger, J. *Das Buch Daniel.* HSAT 8.2. Bonn, 1928.

Gruenthaner, M. J. 'The four empires of Daniel', *CBQ*, 8 (1946), 72–82, 201–12.

Haller, M. 'Das Alter von Daniel 7', *TSK*, 93 (1920–21), 83–7.

Hammer, R. *The Book of Daniel.* Cambridge Bible Commentary. New York–Cambridge, 1976.

Hanhart, R. 'Die Heiligen des Höchsten', *Hebräische Wortforschung, Festschrift W. Baumgartner.* VTSup, 16, (1967), pp. 90–101.

Hartman.

Heaton, E. W. *The Book of Daniel.* Torch Bible Commentary. London, 1956.

Hitzig, F. *Das Buch Daniel.* Kurzgefasstes exegetisches Handbuch zum Alten Testament. Leipzig, 1850.

Hölscher, G. 'Die Entstehung des Buches Daniel', *TSK*, 92 (1919), 113–38.

Hoonacker, A. van 'L'historiographie du livre de Daniel', *Muséon*, 44 (1931), 169–76.

Jeffrey, A. and Kennedy, G. *The Book of Daniel.* IB 6. Nashville, 1956.

Jepsen, A. 'Bemerkungen zum Danielbuch', *VT*, 11 (1961), 386–91.

Junker, H. *Untersuchungen über literarische und exegetische Probleme des Buches Daniel.* Rome, 1932.

Koch, K. 'Die Weltreiche im Danielbuch', *TLZ*, 85 (1960), 829–32.

'Spätisraelitisches Geschichtsdenken am Beispiel des buches Daniel', *Historische Zeitschrift*, 193 (1961), 1–32.

Kruse, H. 'Compositio libri Danielis et idea Filii Hominis', *Verbum Domini*, 37 (1959), 147–61.

Linder, J. *Commentarius in librum Daniel.* Cursus Scripturae Sacrae II. Commentarii in Vetus Testamentum 23. Paris, 1939.

Marti, K. *Das Buch Daniel.* Kurzer Hand-Commentar zum Alten Testament 18. Tübingen, 1901.

Meinhold, J. *Die Composition des Buches Daniel.* Munich, 1889.

Mertens, A. *Das Buch Daniel im Lichte der Texte vom Toten Meer.* Stuttgarter Biblische Monographien 22. Würzburg–Stuttgart, 1971.

Möller, W. *Der Prophet Daniel.* Zwickau, 1940 (repr. out of *Einleitung in das Alte Testament*, Zwickau, 1934).

Montgomery, J. A. *A Critical and Exegetical Commentary on the Book of Daniel.* ICC. Edinburgh, 1927.

Morgenstern, J. 'The Son of Man of Daniel 7, 13f. A new interpretation', *JBL*, 80 (1961), 65–77.

Nelis, J. T. *Daniel.* De Bocken van het Oude Testament, XI.2. Roermond, 1954.

Noth, M. 'Zur Komposition des Buches Daniel', *TSK*, 98/99 (1926), 143–63.

Das Geschichtsverständnis der alttestamentlichen Apokalyptik. Köln–Opladen, 1954 = *Gesammelte Studien zum Alten Testament*, pp. 248–73. 2nd edn. Munich, 1960; ET *The Laws in the Pentateuch*, pp. 194–214. Edinburgh, 1966.

Plöger, O. *Theokratie und Eschatologie.* 2nd edn. Neukirchen Kreis Moers, 1962: ET *Theocracy and Eschatology.* Richmond, 1968.

Das Buch Daniel, KAT 18. Gütersloh, 1965.

Porteous, N. W. *Das Danielbuch.* ATD 23. Göttingen, 1962; in English; *Daniel. A Commentary.* OTL. London, 1965.

Rosenthal, F. *et al. An Aramaic Handbook.* Wiesbaden, 1967. Pertinent sections by H. L. Ginsberg: Part I/1, pp. 23–39 (text); Part I/2, pp. 16–41 (glossary).

Rowley, H. H. 'The bilingual problem of Daniel', *ZAW*, 50 (1932), 256–68.

'Early Aramaic dialects and the book of Daniel', *JRAS*, 2 (1933), 777–805.

Darius the Mede and the Four World Empires in the Book of Daniel. 2nd edn. Cardiff, 1950.

'The unity of the book of Daniel', *HUCA*, 23 (1950/51), pt. I, 233–73; repr. in *The Servant of the Lord*, pp. 235–68. London, 1952; pp. 247–80. 2nd edn. Oxford, 1965.

'The composition of the book of Daniel', *VT*, 5 (1955), 272–6.

Sellin, E. and Rost, L. *Einleitung in das Alte Testament.* 9th edn. Heidelberg, 1959.

Sellin, E. and Fohrer, G. *Einleitung in das Alte Testament.* 10th edn. Heidelberg, 1965. ET as by G. Fohrer: *Introduction to the Old Testament.* Nashville, 1968.

Stevenson, W. B. 'The identification of the Four Kingdoms of the book of Daniel', *Transactions of the Glasgow University Oriental Society*, 7 (1934–35), 4–8.

Thilo, M. *Die Chronologie des Danielbuches.* Bonn, 1926.

Torrey, C. C. 'Notes on the Aramaic part of Daniel', *Transactions of the Connecticut Academy*, 15 (1909), 241–82.

Towner, W. S. 'The poetic passages of Daniel 1–6', *CBQ*, 31 (1969), 317–26.

Young, E. J. *The Prophecy of Daniel, a Commentary.* Grand Rapids, 1949.

The Messianic Prophecies of Daniel. Exegetica, ser. 1 Pt. 6. Delft, 1954.

Zevit, Z. 'The structure and individual elements of Daniel 7', *ZAW*, 80 (1968), 385–96.

Zimmermann F. 'The Aramaic original of Daniel 8–12', *JBL*, 57 (1938), 255–72.

'Some verses in Daniel in the light of a translation hypothesis', *JBL*, 58 (1939), 349–54.

'Hebrew translation in Daniel', *JQR*, 51 (1960–61), 158–208.

CHAPTER 14 THE ORIGINS OF APOCALYPTIC

Ackroyd, P. R. *Exile and Restoration.* OTL. Philadelphia, 1968.

Berry, G. R. 'The apocalyptic literature of the Old Testament', *JBL*, 62 (1943), 9–16.

Collins, J. J. 'Apocalyptic eschatology as the transcendence of death', *CBQ*, 36 (1974), 21–43.

Cross, F. M. 'New directions in the study of Apocalyptic', *JTC*, 6 (1969), 157–65.

Frost, S. B. *Old Testament Apocalyptic: Its Origin and Growth.* London, 1952.

Gese, H. 'Anfang und Ende der Apokalyptik, dargestellt am Sacharjabuch', *ZTK*, 70

(1973), 20–49; repr. in *Von Sinai zum Zion*. Beiträge zur Evangelischen Theologie 64. pp. 202–23. Munich, 1974.

Hanson, P. D. *The Dawn of Apocalyptic: The Historical and Sociological Roots of Jewish Apocalyptic Eschatology*. Philadelphia, 1975; 2nd edn. 1979.

'Jewish Apocalyptic against its Near Eastern environment', *RB*, 78 (1971), 31–58.

'Old Testament Apocalyptic reexamined', *Int*, 25 (1971), 454–79.

'Apocalypticism', in *IDBSup* pp. 28–34. Nashville, 1976.

'Prolegomena to the study of Jewish Apocalyptic', *Magnalia Dei: The Mighty Acts of God, Essays on the Bible and Archaeology in Memory of G. Ernest Wright*, eds. F. M. Cross, W. E. Lemke and P. D. Miller, pp. 389–413. Garden City, New York, 1976.

Koch, K. *The Rediscovery of Apocalyptic*. SBT, 2nd series, 22. London, 1972.

Ladd, G. E. 'Why not prophetic-apocalyptic?', *JBL*, 76 (1957), 192–200.

North, R. 'Prophecy to apocalyptic via Zechariah', *Congress Volume Uppsala 1971*. VTSup, 22 (1972), pp. 47–71.

Osten-Sacken, P. von der *Die Apokalyptik in ihrem Verhältnis zu Prophetie und Weisheit*. Theologische Existenz heute 157. Munich, 1969.

Plöger, O. *Theocracy and Eschatology*. Richmond, 1968.

Rowley, H. H. *The Relevance of Apocalyptic*. 3rd edn. New York, 1963.

Russell, D. S. *The Method and Message of Jewish Apocalyptic*. OTL. Philadelphia, 1964.

Schmidt, J. M. *Die jüdische Apokalyptik. Die Geschichte ihrer Erforschung von dem Anfängen bis zu den Textfunden von Qumran*. Neukirchen–Vluyn, 1969.

Schmithals, W. *The Apocalyptic Movement: Introduction and Interpretation*. Nashville, 1975.

Schreiner, J. *Alttestamentlich-jüdische Apokalyptik. Eine Einführung*. Biblische Handbibliothek 6. Munich, 1969.

Vawter, B. 'Apocalyptic: its relation to prophecy', *CBQ*, 22 (1960), 33–46.

CHAPTER 15 THE SEPTUAGINT AND ITS HEBREW TEXT

The literature on the Septuagint, the Hebrew texts from which the various books of the Bible were translated into Greek, the relationship between the Septuagint translation, its Hebrew *Vorlagen*, and the preserved (so-called Masoretic) Hebrew text, the history of the Septuagint text and its use in the making of other translations of the Bible and on commentaries on the Bible, is very considerable, widely scattered, and frequently not readily accessible.

Much of the older literature was used and cited by H. B. Swete in his still very useful *Introduction to the Old Testament in Greek* (Cambridge, 1902; 2nd, revised ed. by R. R. Ottley, 1914 – reissued 1968). A significant amount of updating of Swete was achieved by S. Jellicoe in *The Septuagint and Modern Study* (New York, 1968). Two additional compilations dealing with the Septuagint have appeared in recent years: *A Classified Bibliography of the Septuagint*, ALGHJ 6 (1972), prepared by S. P. Brock, C. T. Fritsch and S. Jellicoe (cf. the review by E. Tov, *VT*, 25 (1975), 803–9); and a considerable collection of significant *Studies in the Septuagint: Origins, Recensions, and Interpretations* (New York, 1974; 609 pp.), selected (and with a valuable 50-page prolegomenon) by S. Jellicoe.

Since it was founded in 1968, the International Organization for Septuagint and Cognate Studies (IOSCS) has been helpful through its *Bulletin* (no. 9 appeared in 1976, ed. G. Howard) and other publications (in the series, *Septuagint and Cognate Studies*, in co-operation with the Society of Biblical Literature and Scholars Press), in informing the interested public of the state and direction of research in matters Septuagintal.

Several surveys of Septuagint and related research are worth consulting. H. M. Orlinsky, 'Current progress and problems in Septuagint research' (1947), P. Katz (W. P. M. Walters), 'Septuagintal studies in the mid-century: their links with the past and their present tendencies' (1956), and G. Howard, 'The Septuagint: a review of recent studies' (1970), are conveniently grouped in *Studies in the Septuagint* (1974), ed. S. Jellicoe (under 'Surveys of Septuagint studies', respectively pp. 3–20, 21–53, and 54–64). In this connection the bibliographical data compiled by J. W. Wevers in his 'Septuaginta-Forschungen' (*TRu*, N.F., 22 (1954), 85–138, 171–90) are very useful; also his article on 'Septuagint' in *IDB*, 4 (1962). Limitation of space prevented the most recent survey, 'Septuagint, §A: contribution to OT scholarship' by E. Tov in *IDBSup* (1976), pp. 807–11, from being even more useful than it is; thus the subsection on 'Theological exegesis' requires drastic revision and elaboration.

For the specific attempt to get back to the original text of the Septuagint ('as it left the hands of the translators'), the Proto- (or Ur-)Septuagint – a project that is more feasible than that involving the 'original' Hebrew text of the books of the Bible, a text that for such books as Samuel and Jeremiah never existed – a number of studies are available. Those by H. M. Orlinsky, 'On the present state of Proto-Septuagint studies' (1941), P. Katz, 'Septuagint studies in the mid-century §4', (1956), and J. W. Wevers, 'Proto-Septuagint studies' (1964), may be found on pp. 78–109, 50–3 (with further reference on p. 52 n. 2, to two earlier essays), and pp. 138–57 of *Studies in the Septuagint*, ed. S. Jellicoe.

A new phase of this area of research has been opened up since the 1950s by the discovery of the Dead Sea Scrolls and, though only secondarily as yet, of several ancient fragments of Septuagint texts of the intertestamental period (chiefly bits of the Pentateuch), a phase that is very promising indeed. However, while numerous studies have appeared, it is still too early for a clear picture of this aspect of Septuagint research to emerge. The reason for this is twofold. (1) Too many of the studies have been written on the basis of other studies that derive from still unpublished material, and the writers frequently belong to a single school. (2) The vast territory and many centuries involved – the entire Fertile Crescent and the east Mediterranean part of Europe, and the period from about 600 B.C.E. to the second to third centuries C.E. – is such that while the complete picture consists of many hundreds of peices, only a few score of them have become available so far, and it is not possible to connect more than a few of them at a time and to relate these groups of connected pieces to one another. The jigsaw puzzle is still in the process of emerging meaningfully both in outline and in detail. This is evident from the survey articles on 'Text, Hebrew, history of' by D. Barthélemy and 'Septuagint, §B: Earliest Greek versions ("Old Greek")' by R. A. Kraft, respectively pp. 878ff and 818ff in *IDBSup* (1976), and even – though unintentionally – from K. G. O'Connell's article on 'Greek versions (minor)', pp. 377–81.

Basic to the further research in every area of Septuagint are reliable editions of the text. Towards the end of the nineteenth century, a portable (three normal-sized volumes) relatively inexpensive edition of one manuscript of the Septuagint, Codex Vaticanus, was published under the editorship of H. B. Swete by Cambridge University Press (*The Old Testament in Greek*, 1887–94; rev. ed., 1895–99); widely used in its time, this has been replaced by a more accurate and less expensive two-volume edition by A. Rahlfs (*Septuaginta*, Göttingen, 1935). Both editions, it should be added, provided the reader with variant readings from several other uncial manuscripts (chiefly Codex Alexandrinus and Codex Sinaiticus); see ch. 6 'Printed texts of the Septuagint', in Swete's *Introduction*, pp. 171–94.

In March 1883, Cambridge University announced in its *Reporter* that it planned to issue an elaborate edition of the Septuagint (including the Apocrypha) that would contain the readings of all the important Greek manuscripts, of the more important versions, and of the quotations made by Philo and Josephus and the more significant ecclesiastical writers (Church Fathers). Nine volumes appeared from 1906 to 1940; but this edition, regretfully, will hardly be resumed. A generally similar kind of project was planned also by the Göttingen Septuagint Commission, spurred on – as was the Cambridge University project – by the keen work of the great orientalist, Paul de Lagarde. Initiated by R. Smend and J. Wellhausen, the Septuaginta-Unternehmen of the Göttingen Academy sponsored the preliminary work by Lagarde's disciple, A. Rahlfs. The volumes that have appeared in this series are excellent examples of what a critical edition of the Septuagint text of a biblical book should be. The main editor for the Prophets and related books was J. Ziegler, who between 1939 and 1965 produced Isaiah, Jeremiah–Baruch–Lamentations–Epistle of Jeremiah, Ezekiel, Daniel–Susannah–Bel and the Dragon, the Minor Prophets, the Wisdom of Solomon, and Ecclesiasticus (Isaiah, Ezekiel, and the Minor Prophets appeared in revised form in 1967). R. Hanhart has been responsible for 2 Maccabees (with W. Kappler, who produced 1 Maccabees in 1936) and 3 Maccabees, 1 Esdras, and Esther, and is currently working on the book of Judith (to be followed by Tobit, and perhaps Ezra and Nehemiah). J. W. Wevers, following on his model critical edition of *Genesis* and the companion volume, *Text History of the Greek Genesis* (both 1974), has been assigned the rest of the Pentateuch; the critical edition of Deuteronomy and its companion volume are to appear shortly, to be followed by Numbers and the remaining two books (Exodus and Leviticus).

Special mention might be made in this connection of M. L. Margolis' edition (all in autograph!) of *The Book of Joshua in Greek*, parts 1–4 (Paris, 1931–38); the rest of the book and the Introduction were lost. The subtitle indicates the purpose and scope of this monumental work: *According to the Critically Restored Text. with an Apparatus Containing the Variants of the Principal Recensions and of the Individual Witnesses* (cf. H. M. Orlinsky, 'Margolis' work in the Septuagint', pp. 34–44 in *Max Leopold Margolis: Scholar and Teacher* [5712–1952], with reference there also to the related work by J. A. Montgomery). Finally, P. Walters' study of *The Text of the Septuagint: Its Corruptions and their Emendations*, posthumously worked up and edited by D. W. Gooding (Cambridge, 1973), should be noted.

CHAPTER 16 THE TARGUMIM

Editions and translations

The majority of the Targums are to be found in the Paris (1645) and the London (1653–57) Polyglots, along with their Latin versions, and in the Rabbinic Bibles (London Polyglot reprinted Graz, 1964–65).

Berliner, A. *Targum Onkelos*. Berlin, 1884; reprinted Jerusalem, 1968–69.

Díez Macho, A. *Neophyti 1. Targum Palestinense MS de la Biblioteca Vaticana*. Madrid–Barcelona: vol. 1 (Génesis) 1968; vol. 2 (Éxodo) 1970; vol. 3 (Levítico) 1971); vol.

4 (Números) 1974; vol. 5 (Deuteronomio) 1978; vol. 6 (Apéndices) 1979. These volumes contain a long introduction, Spanish, French and English translations, and a list of rabbinic parallels.

Biblia Polyglotta Matritensia, Series IV, *Targum Palaestinense in Pentateuchum, Numeri*, Madrid, 1977; *Exodus, Leviticus, Deuteronomium*, Madrid, 1980. Aramaic texts of Neofiti, Fragmentary Targum and Pseudo–Jonathan (and Spanish version of Pseudo-Jon.)

Etheridge, J. W. *The Targums of Onkelos and Jonathan ben Uzziel on the Pentateuch with the Fragments of the Jerusalem Targum from the Chaldee*. London, 1862–65; reprinted New York, 1968. English translation only.

Ginsburger, M. *Das Fragmententhargum*. Berlin, 1899; reprinted Jerusalem, 1966.

Pseudo-Jonathan (Thargum Jonathan ben Usiël zum Pentateuch) nach der Londoner Handschrift (Brit.Mus. Add 27031). Berlin, 1903; reprinted Jerusalem, 1966.

Grossfield, B. *The Targum to the Five Megilloth, edited with an Introduction*. New York, 1973 (translation only).

Kahle, P. *Masoreten des Westens* 2. BWANT 3.14. Stuttgart, 1930.

Klein, M. L. *The Fragment-Targums of the Pentateuch According to their Extant Sources*. 2 vols. AnBib 76. Rome, 1980. Text and translation.

de Lagarde, P. *Prophetae Chaldaice*. Leipzig, 1872; reprinted Osnabrück, 1967.

Hagiographa Chaldaice, Leipzig, 1873; reprinted Osnabrück, 1967.

Le Déaut, R. *Targum du Pentateuque*. 5 vols. SC 245, 256, 261, 271, 282. Paris, 1978–81. French translation only.

Le Déaut, R. and Robert, J. *Targum des Chroniques*. 2 vols. AnBib 51. Rome, 1971. Text and French translation.

Levine, E. *The Aramaic Version of Ruth*. AnBib 58. Rome, 1973. Text and translation.

Merx, A. ed. *Chrestomathia Targumica*. Berlin, 1888.

Mulder, M. J. *De targum op het Hooglied*. Exegetica n.s. 4. Amsterdam, 1975. Translation and commentary.

van der Ploeg, J. P. M. and van der Woude, A. S. *Le Targum de Job de la grotte XI de Qumrân*. Leiden, 1971.

Rieder, D. *Pseudo-Jonathan. Targum Jonathan ben Uziel on the Pentateuch*. Jerusalem, 1974. Text only.

Pseudo-Jonathan. 2 vols., with Hebrew version, notes and parallels. Jerusalem, 1984–5.

Sokoloff, M. *The Targum to Job from Qumran Cave XI*. Ramat-Gan, 1974.

Sperber, A. *The Bible in Aramaic*. 1. *The Pentateuch According to Targum Onkelos*. Leiden, 1959, 2. *The Former Prophets According to Targum Jonathan*. Leiden, 1959, 3. *The Latter Prophets According to Targum Jonathan*. Leiden, 1962, 4a. *The Hagiographa. Transition from Translation to Midrash*. Leiden, 1968.

Stenning, J. F. *The Targum of Isaiah*. Oxford, 1949. Text and translation.

General introductions

Bacher, W. 'Targum', in *The Jewish Encyclopedia*, vol. 12, pp. 57–63. New York–London, 1906.

Bowker, J. *The Targums and Rabbinic Literature*. Cambridge, 1969.

Díez Macho, A. 'Targum', in *Enciclopedia de la Biblia*, vol. 6, cols. 865–81. Barcelona, 1963.

El Targum. Introducción a las traducciones aramaicas de la Biblia. Barcelona, 1972; reprinted Madrid, 1979.

Geiger, A. *Urschrift und Übersetzungen der Bibel in ihrer Abhängigkeit von der innern Entwickelung des Judenthums*. Breslau, 1857; 2nd edn. Frankfurt am Main, 1928.

Grossfield, B. 'Bible: Aramaic: the Targumim' *EncJud*, vol. 4, cols. 841–51. Jerusalem, 1972.

Kahle, P. E. *The Cairo Geniza*. London, 1947; 2nd edn. Oxford, 1959.

Le Déaut, R. *Introduction à la littérature targumique*. Rome, 1966.

McNamara, M. *Targum and Testament*. Shannon, 1972.

'Targums', in *IDBSup* pp. 857–61. Nashville, 1976.

Schäfer, P. 'Bibelübersetzungen II. Targumim', in *Theologische Realenzyclopädie*, vol. 6, pp. 216–28. Berlin–New York, 1980.

Schürer, E., Vermes, G. and Millar, F. *The History of the Jewish People*, vol. 1, pp. 99–114. Edinburgh, 1973 (with extensive Bibliography).

Zunz, L. *Die gottesdienstlichen Vorträge der Juden*. Berlin, 1832; 2nd edn. Frankfurt am Main, 1892; reprinted Hildesheim, 1966. In Hebrew, *Ha-dērāšôt bᵉYisrā'el*, ed. C. Albeck, with supplementary notes, Jerusalem, 1954/1974.

Special studies

Churgin P. *Targum Jonathan to the Prophets*. New Haven, 1927; reprinted New York, 1971.

The Targum to Hagiographa. In Hebrew. New York, 1945.

Heinemann, J. *Aggadah and its Development*. In Hebrew. Jerusalem, 1974.

Klein, M. L. *Anthropomorphisms and Anthropopathisms in the Targumim of the Pentateuch*. In Hebrew. Jerusalem, 1982.

Komlosh, Y. *The Bible in the Light of the Aramaic Translations*. In Hebrew. Bar-Ilan University, Series of Research Monographs 12. Tel-Aviv, 1973. Good bibliography.

Le Déaut, R. *La nuit pascale*. AnBib 22. Rome, 1963; reprinted 1980.

'The current state of Targumic studies', *Biblical Theology Bulletin*, 4 (1974), 3–32.

The Message of the New Testament and the Aramaic Bible (Targum). Subsidia Biblica 5. Rome, 1982.

McNamara, M. *The New Testament and the Palestinian Targum to the Pentateuch*. AnBib 27. Rome, 1966; reprinted 1978.

Muñoz Leon, D. *Dios-Palabra. Memrá en los Targumim del Pentateuco*. Granada, 1974.

Gloria de la Shekiná en los Targumim del Pentateuco. Madrid, 1977.

Petuchowski, J. J. and Fleischer, E. (ed). *Studies in Aggadah, Targum and Jewish Liturgy in Memory of Joseph Heinemann*. Jerusalem, 1981.

Shinan, A. *The Aggadah in the Aramaic Targums to the Pentateuch*. In Hebrew. 2 vols. Jerusalem, 1979.

Vermes, G. *Scripture and Tradition in Judaism*. SPB 4. Leiden, 1961; corrected reprint 1973.

Post-Biblical Jewish Studies. SJLA 8. Leiden, 1975.

'Bible and Midrash: early Old Testament exegesis', in P. R. Ackroyd and C. F. Evans, edd. *The Cambridge History of the Bible*, vol. 1, pp. 199–231, Cambridge, 1970.

Weiss, R. *The Aramaic Targum of Job*. In Hebrew, with English summaries. Tel Aviv, 1979.

Bibliographies

Forestell, J. T. *Targumic Traditions and the New Testament. An Annotated Bibliography with a New Testament Index*, SBL Aramaic Studies 4. Chicgo, 1979.

Grossfeld, B. *A Bibliography of Targum Literature*. 2 volumes: Bibliographica Judaica 3 and 8. New York, 1972 and 1977.

Nickels, P. *Targum and New Testament – A Bibliography together with a New Testament Index*. Scripta Pontificii Instituti Biblici 117. Rome, 1967.

CHAPTER 17 THE SAMARITANS

Sources

Charles, R. H. ed. *APOT*.

Gall, A. von *Der hebraische Pentateuch der Samaritaner*. 5 vols. Giessen, 1914–18.

Gifford, E. H. ed. and tr. *Eusebii Pamphili Evangelicae Praeparationis Libri xv*. 4 vols. Oxford, 1903.

Lichtenstein, H. 'Die Fastenrolle, eine Untersuchung zur jüdisch-hellenistischen Geschichte, *mglt tʿnyt*', *HUCA*, 8–9 (1931–32), 257–351.

Marcus, R. *Josephus*. Vols. 6–7. Loeb Classical Library. Cambridge, Mass., 1937–43.

The Samaritan heresy

Including general works on the Samaritans

Ben-Zvi, Y. *Sefer ha-šomᵉronim: tolᵉdotehem, mošabotehem, datam wᵉsifrutam*. Tel Aviv, 1935, reprinted Jerusalem, 1970, ed. S. Talmon.

Coggins, R. J. *Samaritans and Jews: The Origins of Samaritanism Reconsidered*. Growing Points in Theology. Oxford, 1975.

'The Old Testament and Samaritan origins', *ASTI*, 6 (1967–8), 35–48.

Gaster, M. *The Samaritans: Their History, Doctrine, and Literature*. Schweich Lectures. London, 1925.

Isser, S. J. *The Dositheans: A Samaritan Sect in Late Antiquity*. SJLA 17. Leiden, 1976.

Macdonald, J. *The Theology of the Samaritans*. The New Testament Library. London, 1964.

Montgomery, J. A. *The Samaritans, the Earliest Jewish Sect: their History, Theology, and Literature*. Philadelphia, 1907.

Pummer, R. 'The present state of Samaritan studies: I', *JSS*, 21 (1976), 39–61.

The Samaritans at Shechem

From the building of the Samaritan Temple to Antiochus IV

Bickerman, E. *From Ezra to the Last of the Maccabees*. New York, 1962.

Bull, R. J. 'The excavation of Tell er-Ras on Mt. Gerizim', *BA*, 31 (1968), 58–72.

Bull, R. J. and Campbell, E. F., Jr., 'The sixth campaign at Balâṭah (Shechem)', *BASOR*, 190 (1968), 2–41.

Bull, R. J. and Wright, G. E. 'Newly discovered temples on Mt. Gerizim in Jordan', *HTR*, 58 (1965), 234–7.

Cross, F. M., Jr., 'The discovery of the Samaria papyri', *BA*, 26 (1963), 110–21.

'Aspects of Samaritan and Jewish history in late Persian and Hellenistic times', *HTR*, 59 (1966), 201–11.

Marcus, R. *Josephus*. Vol. 6. Loeb Classical Library, Cambridge, Mass. 1937.

Purvis, J. D. 'Ben Sira and the foolish people of Shechem', *JNES*, 24 (1965), 88–94.

Rowley, H. H. 'The Samaritan schism in legend and history', in *Israel's Prophetic Heritage: Essays in Honor of James Muilenburg*, eds. B. W. Anderson and W. Harrelson, pp. 208–22. New York, 1962.

'Sanballat and the Samaritan Temple', in *Men of God: Studies in Old Testament History and Prophecy*, pp. 246–76. London, 1963.

Tcherikover, V. *Hellenistic Civilization and the Jews*. Philadelphia, 1959.

Wright, G. E. 'The Samaritans at Shechem', in *Shechem: The Biography of a Biblical City*, pp. 170–84. New York, 1965.

Zeitlin, S. *The Rise and Fall of the Judaean State*. Vol 1. Philadelphia, 1962.

Bickerman, E. 'Un document relatif à la persécution d'Antiochos IV Epiphane', *RHR*, 115 (1937), 188–223.

Bowman, J. 'Pilgrimage to Mt. Gerizim', *Eretz Israel*. (1964, *L. A. Mayer Memorial volume*), pp. 17–28.

Delcor, M. 'Vom Sichem der hellenistischen Epoche zum Sychar des Neuen Testaments', *ZDPV*, 78 (1962), 34–48.

Kippenberg, H. G. *Garizim und Synagoge: Traditionsgeschichtliche Untersuchungen zur samaritanischen Religion der aramaischen Periode*. RGVV 30. Berlin, 1971.

Lapp, P. W. and Lapp, N. L. *Discoveries in the Wâdi ed-Dâliyeh*. AASOR 41. Cambridge, Mass., 1974.

Mantel, H. D. 'The secession of the Samaritans' (in Hebrew) *Sefer Ha-Shanah, Bar Ilan University*, 7–8 (1970), 162–77.

Purvis, J. D. *The Samaritan Pentateuch and the Origin of the Samaritan Sect*. HSM 2. Cambridge, Mass., 1968.

'Samaritan Pentateuch', *IDBSup*. pp. 772–5. Nashville, 1976.

Schalit, A. 'Die Denkschrift der Samaritanern an König Antiochos Epiphanes zu Beginn der grossen Verfolgung der jüdischen Religion im Jahre 167 v. chr.', *ASTI*, 8 (1970–71), 131–83.

Torrey, C. C. *The Apocryphal Literature*. New Haven, 1945.

Wacholder, B. Z. 'Pseudo-Eupolemus' two Greek fragments on the life of Abraham', *HUCA*, 34 (1963), 83–113.

CHAPTER 18 THE GROWTH OF ANTI-JUDAISM OR THE GREEK ATTITUDE TOWARDS THE JEWS

General works

Abel, F.-M. *Géographie de la Palestine*. EBib. 2 vols. Paris, 1933–8.

Adriani, M. 'Note sull' antisemitismo antico', *Studi e Materiali di Storia delle Religioni*, 36 (1965), 63–98.

Bickerman, E. J. 'The historical foundations of post-biblical Judaism', in *The Jews. Their History, Culture and Religion*, ed. L. Finkelstein, 3rd edn. Vol. 1, pp. 70–114. New York, 1955.

Böhl, F. M. T. de Liagre 'Die Juden im Urteil der griechischen und römischen Schriftsteller', *Theologische Tijdschrift*, 48 (1914), 371–89; 473–98, repr. in *Opera minora*, pp. 111–33; 485ff Groningen, 1953.

Davis, S. *Race-relations in Ancient Egypt: Greek, Egyptian, Hebrew, Roman*. 2nd edn. London, 1951.

Drioton, E. and Vandier, J. *Les peuples de l'Orient méditerranéen* 2. *L'Egypte*, 3rd edn. Paris, 1952.

Eddy, S. K. *The King is Dead. Studies in the Near Eastern Resistance to Hellenism 334–31 B.C.* Lincoln, Nebraska, 1961.

Fraser, P. M. *Ptolemaic Alexandria*. 3 vols. Oxford, 1972.

Gager, J. G. *Moses in Greco-Roman Paganism*. SBLMS 16. Nashville–New York, 1972.

Hengel, M. *Judentum und Hellenismus, Studien zu ihrer Begegnung unter besonderer Berücksichtigung Palästinas bis zur Mitte des 2. Jh.s.v. Chr.* WUNT 10. 2nd edn. Tübingen, 1973. ET: *Judaism and Hellenism*. London, 1974.

Juster, J. *Les Juifs dans l'empire Romain*. 2 vols. Paris, 1914; reprinted New York, n.d.

Lagrange, M.-J. *Le Judaïsme avant Jésus-Christ*. EBib. Paris, 1931.

Meyer, E. *Geschichte des Altertums*. 2, 1–2. 3rd edn. Basle, 1953.

Ursprung und Anfänge des Christentums, 1–2. 4th–5th edn. Stuttgart, 1924–25. 3. 1st–3rd edn. Stuttgart, 1923.

Radin, M. *The Jews among the Greeks and Romans*. Philadelphia, 1915.

Rostovtzeff, M. *The Social and Economic History of the Hellenistic World*. 3 vols. Oxford, 1941.

Schürer, E. *Geschichte des jüdischen Volkes im Zeitalter Jesu Christi*, 3. 4th edn. Leipzig, 1909.

Stähelin, F. *Der Antisemitismus des Altertums*. Basle, 1905.

Stern, M. (ed.), *Greek and Latin authors on Jews and Judaism*. Vol. 1: *From Herodotus to Plutarch*. Jerusalem, 1974.

Susemihl, F. *Geschichte der griechischen Literature in der Alexandrinerzeit*. 2 vols. Leipzig, 1891–92; reprinted Hildesheim, 1965.

Tcherikover, V. *Hellenistic Civilization and the Jews*. Philadelphia, 1959.

Tcherikover, V. and Fuks, A. and Stern, M. *Corpus Papyrorum Judaicarum*, 1, pp. 1–47. Cambridge, Mass., 1957.

Textes d'auteurs grecs et latins relatifs au Judaïsme. Revised, translated and annotated by T. Reinach. Paris, 1895, reprinted Hildesheim, 1963.

Willrich, H. *Juden und Griechen vor der makkabäischen Erhebung*. Göttingen, 1895. *Judaica*. Göttingen, 1900.

Greek authors on the Jews

Abel, E. L. 'The myth of Jewish slavery in Ptolemaic Egypt', *REJ*, 127 (1968), 253–8.

Austin, M. M. *Greece and Egypt in the Archaic Age*. Proceedings of the Cambridge Philological Society, Supplement 2. Cambridge, 1970.

Baldry, H. C. *The Unity of Mankind in Greek Thought*. Cambridge, 1966.

Bérard, J. 'Les Hyksôs et la légende d'Io. Recherches sur la periode prémycénienne', *Syria*, 29 (1952), 1–43.

Bernays, J. *Theophrastos' Schrift Über Frömmigkeit*. Berlin, 1866.

Bickerman, E. 'La Coelé-Syrie. Notes de géographie historique', *RB*, 54 (1947), 256–68.

Bidez, J. and Cumont, F. *Les mages hellénisés.* 2 vols. Paris, 1938. pp. 240–2: 'Hécatée sur les Juifs et Démocrite'.

Burton, A. *Diodorus Siculus, Book I. A commentary.* Leiden, 1972.

Cole, A. T. *Democritus and the Sources of Greek Anthropology.* Cleveland, 1967.

Dihle, A. 'Zur hellenistichen Ethnographie', *Grecs et Barbares*, pp. 202–32. Entretiens sur l'Antiquité Classique, 8. Geneva, 1962.

Eichholz, D. E. *Theophrastus, De lapidibus.* Oxford, 1965.

Festugière, A.-J. 'Grecs et sages orientaux', *RHR*, 130 (1945), 29–41.

Froidefond, C. *Le mirage égyptien dans la littérature grecque d'Homère à Aristote.* Paris, 1971.

Gager, J. G. 'Pseudo-Hecataeus again', *ZNW*, 60 (1969), 130–9.

Huxley, G. 'Choirilos of Samos', *GRBS*, 10 (1969), 12–29.

Jaeger, W. 'Greeks and Jews. The first records of Jewish religion and civilization', *JR*, 18 (1938), 127–43, repr. in *Scripta Minora* 2, pp. 169–83. Rome, 1960.

Diokles von Karystos, pp. 134–53. Berlin, 1938, reprinted 1963: 'Theophrast und der älteste griechische Bericht über die Juden'.

Katzenstein, H. J. 'Is there any synchronism between the reigns of Hiram and Solomon?', *JNES*, 24 (1965), 116–17.

Levy, I. *La légende de Pythagore de Grèce en Palestine.* Paris, 1927.

Recherches esséniennes et pythagoriciennes. Geneva–Paris, 1965. Cf. V. Nikiprowetzky, *REJ*, 125 (1966), 313–52.

Lewy, H. 'Hekataios von Abdera Περὶ 'Ιουδαίων', *ZNW*, 31 (1932), 117–32.

'Aristotle and the Jewish sage according to Clearchus of Soli', *HTR*, 31 (1938), 205–35.

Luria, S. 'Die Belagerung von Jerusalem bei Alkaios', *Acta Antiqua* 8 (1960), 265–6.

Meyer, E. *Aegyptische Chronologie.* Berlin, 1904; *Chronologie égyptienne.* French tr.: Paris, 1912.

Momigliano, A. 'Intorno al *Contro Apione*', *Rivista di Filologia* N.S., 9 (1931), 485–503.

Montet, P. 'Le roi Amenophis et les Impurs', *Révue des Etudes anciennes*, 42 (1940), 263–9.

Le drame d'Avaris. Essai sur la pénétration des Sémites en Egypte. Paris, 1941.

Murray, O. 'Hecataeus of Abdera and pharaonic kingship', *JEA*, 56 (1970), 141–71.

Pötscher, W. ed. *Theophrastos*, Περὶ Εὐσεβείας. Philosophia Antiqua 11. Leiden, 1964.

Robert, L. 'De Delphes à l'Oxus. Inscriptiones grecques nouvelles de la Bactriane', *CRAIBL*, (1968), 416–57. Reprinted in P. Barnard, ed. *Fouilles d'Aî Khamoun.* Paris, 1973.

Rowton, M. B. 'Manetho's date for Ramesses II', *JEA*, 34 (1948), 57–74.

Schaller, B. 'Hekataios von Abdera über die Juden', *ZNW*, 54 (1963), 15–31.

Schwartz, E. 'Hekataios von Teos', *Rheinisches Museum*, NF 40 (1885), 223–62.

Schwartz, J. 'Les conquérants perses et la littérature égyptienne', *BIFAO*, 48 (1949), 65–80.

'Le "cycle de Petoubastis" et les commentaires égyptiens de l'Exode', *BIFAO*, 49 (1950), 67–83.

Spoerri, W. *Späthellenistische Berichte über Welt, Kultur und Götter.* Schweizerische Beiträge zur Altertumswissenschaft 9. Basle, 1959.

Stern, M. and Murray, O. 'Hecataeus of Abdera and Theophrastus on Jews and Egyptians', *JEA*, 59 (1973), 159–68.

Troiani, L. 'Sui frammenti di Manetone nel primo libro del *Contra Apionem* di Flavio Giuseppe', *SCO*, 24 (1975), 97–126.

Vallauri, G. *Evemero di Messene-testimonianze e frammenti*. Turin, 1956.

Vaux, R. de *Studies in Old Testament Sacrifice*, pp. 52–90. Cardiff, 1964.

Waddell, W. G. ed. *Manetho*. Loeb Classical Library. London–Cambridge, Mass., 1940.

Weill, R. *Les Hyksôs et la restauration nationale dans la tradition égyptienne at dans l'histoire*. Paris, 1914.

West, M. L. *Early Greek Philosophy and the Orient*. Oxford, 1971.

Yoyotte, J. 'L'Egypte ancienne et les origines de l'antijudaïsme', *RHR*, 163 (1963), 133–43.

Jews and Egypt in the third to second centuries B.C.E.

Bickerman, E. 'The Septuagint as a translation', *PAAJR*, 28 (1959), 1–39.

Black, M. and Denis, A.-M. (eds.). *Fragmenta Pseudepigraphorum quae supersunt Graeca, una cum historicorum et auctorum Judaeorum hellenistarum fragmentis*. PVTG 3. Leiden, 1971.

Denis, A.-M. *Introduction aux Pseudépigraphes Grecs d'Ancien Testament*. SVTP 1. Leiden, 1970.

Feldman, L. H. 'Abraham the Greek Philosopher in Josephus', *TAPA*, 99 (1968), 143–56.

Freudenthal, J. *Alexander Polyhistor und die von ihm erhaltenen Reste judäischer und samaritanischer Geschichtswerke*. Hellenistische Studien, 1–2. Breslau, 1874–75.

Kraeling, E. G. *The Brooklyn Museum Aramaic Papyri. New Documents of the Fifth Century B.C. from the Jewish Colony at Elephantine*. New Haven, 1953, reprinted 1969.

Lévi, I. 'La dispute entre les Egyptiens et les Juifs devant Alexandre', *REJ*, 63 (1912), 211–15.

Lévy, I. 'Moïse en Ethiopie', *REJ*, 53 (1907), 201–11.

Marcus, R. 'Alexander the Great and the Jews', *Josephus*, vol. 6, pp. 512–32, appendix C. London–Cambridge, Mass., 1937.

Montet, P. *L'Egypte et la Bible*. Cahiers d'Archéologie Biblique 11. Neuchâtel, 1959.

Peremans, W. 'Egyptiens et étrangers dans l'Egypte ptolémaïque', *Grecs et Barbares*. Entretiens sur l'Antiquité Classique, 8, pp. 123–55. Geneva, 1962.

Pfister, F. *Alexander der Grosse in den Offenbarungen der Griechen, Juden, Mohammedaner und Christen*, pp. 24–35. Deutsche Akademie der Wissenschaften zu Berlin, Schriften der Sektion für Altertumswissenschaft 3. Berlin, 1956.

Porten, B. *Archives from Elephantine. The life of an ancient Jewish military colony*. Berkeley–Los Angeles, 1968.

Préaux, C. 'Esquisse d'une histoire des révolutions égyptiennes sous les Lagides', *ChE*, 22 (1936), 522–52.

Tcherikover, V. 'Jewish apologetic literature reconsidered', *Eos*, 48, 3 (1956) [1956] = Symbolae R. Taubenschlag dedicatae, 3), 169–93.

'The decline of the Jewish Diaspora in Egypt in the Roman period', *JJS*, 14 (1963), 1–32.

Wacholder, B. Z. 'Pseudo-Eupolemus: two Greek fragments on the life of Abraham', *HUCA*, 34 (1963), 83–113.

'How long did Abram stay in Egypt?', *HUCA*, 35 (1964), 43–56.

'Biblical chronology in the Hellenistic World Chronicles', *HTR*, 61 (1968), 451–81.

Walter, N. *Der Thoraausleger Aristobulos*. TU 86. Berlin, 1964.
'Zu Pseudo-Eupolemos', *Klio*, 43–5 (1965), 282–90.

Anti-Judaism in the II–I cent. B.C.E.

Alessandrí, S. 'La presunta cacciata dei Giudei da Roma nel 139 a.Cr.', *SCO*, 17 (1968), 187–98.

Alföldi, A. '*Redeunt Saturnia regna*. II: An iconographical pattern heralding the return of the Golden Age in or around 139 B.C.', *Chiron*, 3 (1973), 131–42.

Bickerman, E. J. 'Ritualmord und Eselskult. Ein Beitrag zur Geschichte antiker Publizistik', *MGWJ*, 71 (1927), 171–87, 255–64.
'Un document relatif à la persécution d'Antiochos IV Epiphane', *RHR*, 115 (1937), 188–223.
Der Gott der Makkabäer. Berlin, 1937; ET *The God of the Maccabees*. SJLA 32. Leiden, 1979.
'Héliodore au Temple de Jérusalem, *Annuaire de l'Institut de Philologie et d'Histoire orientales et slaves*, 7 (1939–44), pp. 5–40.
Four Strange Books of the Bible. New York, 1967.

Bresciani, E. *Letteratura e poesia dell' Antico Egitto*. Turin, 1969.

Cardauns, B. 'Juden und Spartaner. Zur hellenistisch-jüdischen Literatur', *Hermes*, 95 (1967), 317–24.

de Vaux, R. 'Les sacrifices de porcs en Palestine et dans l'Ancien Testament', *Von Ugarit nach Qumran*. Festschrift Eissfeldt, pp. 250–65. BZAW 77. Berlin, 1958.

Giovannini, A. and Müller, H. 'Die Beziehungen zwischen Rom und den Juden im 2. Jh.v.Chr.', *Museum Helveticum*, 28 (1971), 156–71.

Gill, D. 'The Greek sources of Wisdom XII 3–7', *VT*, 15 (1965), 383–6.

Harder, R. *Ocellus Lucanus. Text und Kommentar*. Berlin, 1926.

Hengel, M. 'Anonymität, Pseudepigraphie und "Literarische Fälschung" in der jüdisch-hellenistischen Literatur', *Pseudepigrapha* I. 231–308. Entretiens sur l'Antiquité Classique, 18. Geneva, 1972.

Howard, G. 'The *letter of Aristeas* and Diaspora Judaism', *JTS*, N.S. 22 (1971), 337–48.

Jacoby, A. 'Der angebliche Eselskult der Juden und Christen', *ARW*, 25 (1927), 265–82.

McCown, C. C. 'Hebrew and Egyptian apocalyptic literature', *HTR*, 18 (1925), 357–411.

Momigliano, A. *Prime linee di storia della tradizione maccabaica*. Turin, 1931; reprinted Amsterdam, 1968.

Murray, O. 'Aristeas and Ptolemaic kingship', *JTS*, N.S., 18 (1967), 337–71.

Nikiprowetzky, V. *La Troisième Sibylle*. Etudes juives 9. Paris–La Hague, 1970.

Nock, A. D. 'Posidonius', *JRS*, 49 (1959), 1–15; repr. in *Essays on Religion and the Ancient World* 2, pp. 354ff. Oxford, 1972.

Parente, F. 'La *lettera di Aristea* come fonte per la storia del giudaismo alessandrino durante la prima metà del I sec. a.C.' *Annali Scuola Normale Superiore Pisa*, Classe Lettere, ser. 3, 2 (1972), 177–237; 517–67.

Pédech, P. *La méthode historique de Polybe*. Collection d'études anciennes. Paris, 1964.

Peremans, W. 'Diodore de Sicile et Agatharchide de Cnide', *Historia*, 16 (1967), 432–55.

Wacholder, B. Z. 'Greek authors in Herod's library', *Studies in Bibliography and Booklore*, 5 (1961), 102–9.

CHRONOLOGICAL TABLE[1]

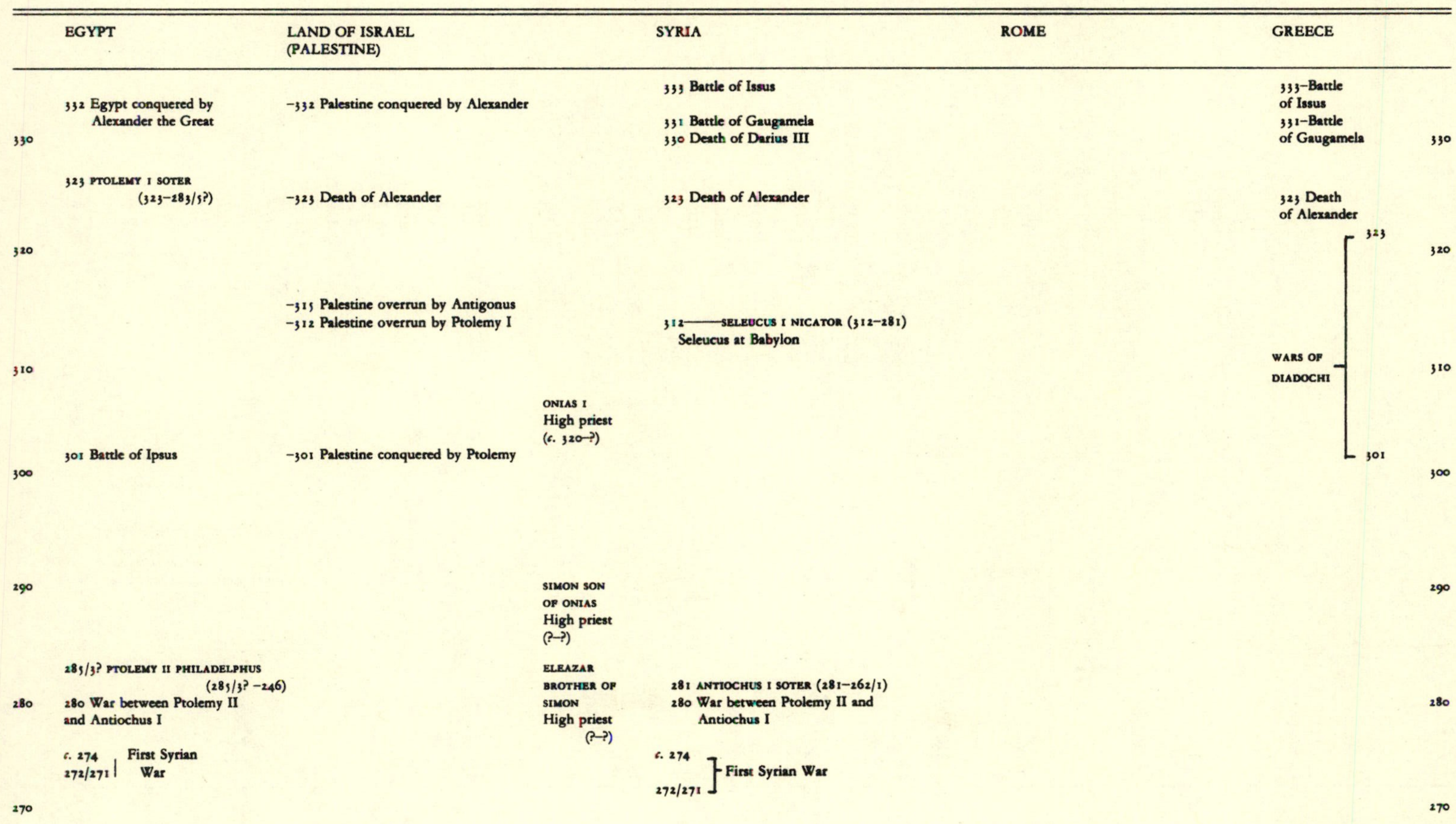

	EGYPT	LAND OF ISRAEL (PALESTINE)		SYRIA	ROME	GREECE	
				333 Battle of Issus		333–Battle of Issus	
	332 Egypt conquered by Alexander the Great	–332 Palestine conquered by Alexander		331 Battle of Gaugamela		331–Battle of Gaugamela	
330				330 Death of Darius III			330
	323 PTOLEMY I SOTER (323–283/5?)	–323 Death of Alexander		323 Death of Alexander		323 Death of Alexander	
320						323	320
		–315 Palestine overrun by Antigonus –312 Palestine overrun by Ptolemy I		312——SELEUCUS I NICATOR (312–281) Seleucus at Babylon			
310						WARS OF DIADOCHI	310
			ONIAS I High priest (c. 320–?)				
	301 Battle of Ipsus	–301 Palestine conquered by Ptolemy				301	
300							300
290			SIMON SON OF ONIAS High priest (?–?)				290
	285/3? PTOLEMY II PHILADELPHUS (285/3? –246)		ELEAZAR BROTHER OF SIMON High priest (?–?)	281 ANTIOCHUS I SOTER (281–262/1)			
280	280 War between Ptolemy II and Antiochus I			280 War between Ptolemy II and Antiochus I			280
	c. 274 – 272/271 First Syrian War			c. 274 – 272/271 First Syrian War			
270							270

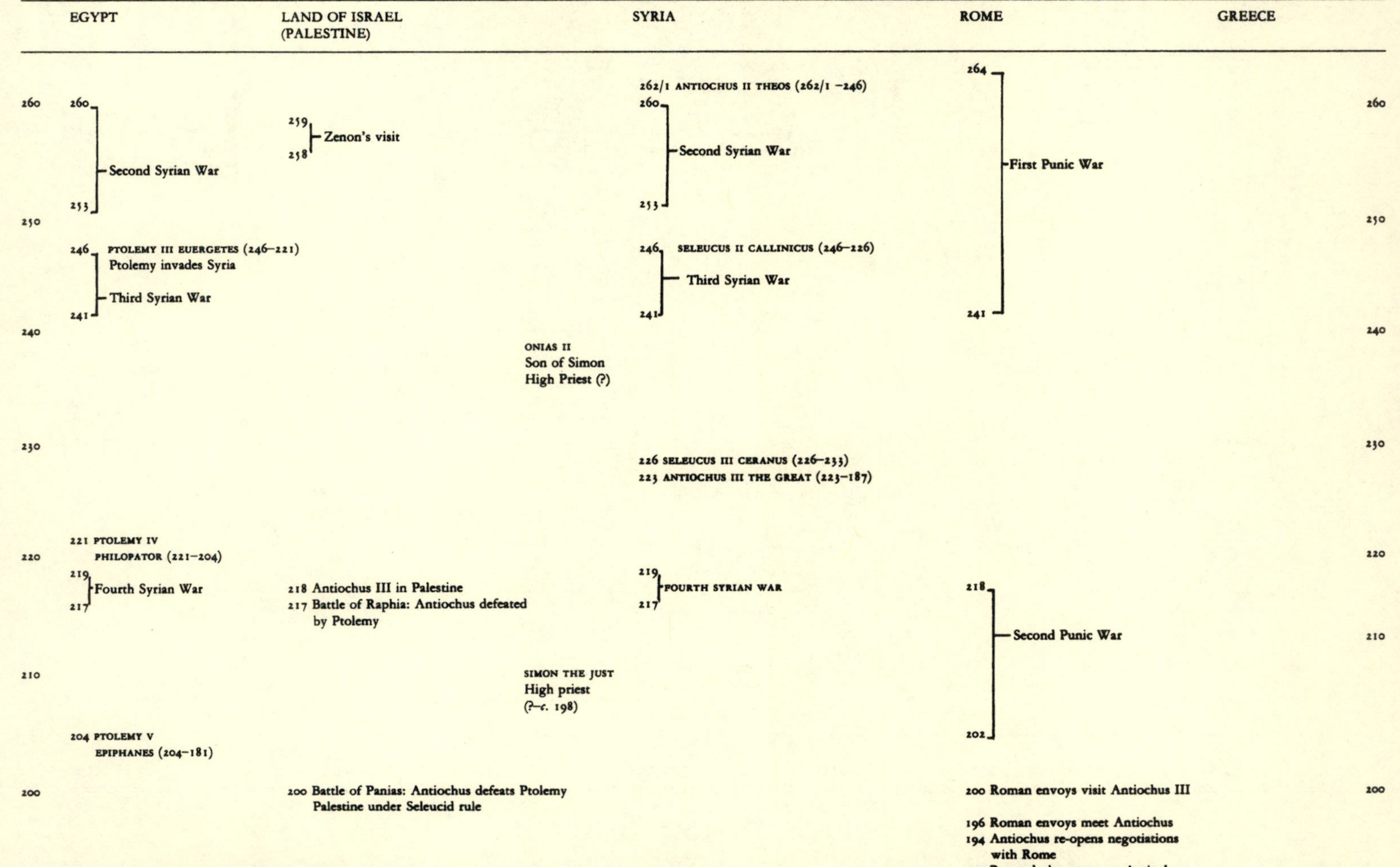

	EGYPT	LAND OF ISRAEL (PALESTINE)	SYRIA	ROME	GREECE	
				264 First Punic War (264–241)		
			262/1 ANTIOCHUS II THEOS (262/1 –246)			
260	260–253 Second Syrian War	259–258 Zenon's visit	260–253 Second Syrian War			260
250						250
	246 PTOLEMY III EUERGETES (246–221) Ptolemy invades Syria		246 SELEUCUS II CALLINICUS (246–226)			
	246–241 Third Syrian War		246–241 Third Syrian War	241		
240		ONIAS II Son of Simon High Priest (?)				240
230						230
			226 SELEUCUS III CERANUS (226–233)			
			223 ANTIOCHUS III THE GREAT (223–187)			
	221 PTOLEMY IV PHILOPATOR (221–204)					
220						220
	219–217 Fourth Syrian War	218 Antiochus III in Palestine	219–217 FOURTH SYRIAN WAR	218 Second Punic War (218–202)		
		217 Battle of Raphia: Antiochus defeated by Ptolemy				210
210		SIMON THE JUST High priest (?–c. 198)				
	204 PTOLEMY V EPIPHANES (204–181)			202		
200		200 Battle of Panias: Antiochus defeats Ptolemy Palestine under Seleucid rule		200 Roman envoys visit Antiochus III		200
				196 Roman envoys meet Antiochus		
				194 Antiochus re-opens negotiations with Rome		
				192 Rome declares war on Antiochus		

190				190 Battle of Magnesia: Antiochus defeated by Rome	190 Battle of Magnesia: Antiochus defeated by Rome	190
			ONIAS III High priest	187 SELEUCUS IV PHILOPATOR (187–175)		
	181——PTOLEMY VI PHILOMETOR (181–145)					
180						180
		175/4 Onias III deposed by Antiochus IV Epiphanes		175 ANTIOCHUS IV EPIPHANES (175–164)		
			JASON High priest			
170	170–170/69 Antiochus IV invades Egypt	c. 170 Onias III killed by Menelaus		170–169 First campaign against Egypt		170
	168–65? Temple of Leontopolis founded	169 Jason seizes Jerusalem. Antiochus suppresses revolt and loots Temple		168 Second campaign against Egypt	168 Romans halt Seleucid invasion of Egypt	
		167/6 Maccabean revolt.	MENELAUS High priest			
	PTOLEMY VIII (Brother of of Ptolemy VI) co-regent 170–164 Ptolemy VIII sole ruler 164–163	166 Mattathias dies. *Judas* takes over. 164 Rededication of Temple		164 ANTIOCHUS V EUPATOR (164–162)	164 Romans invaded in negotiations between Syria and Palestine	
			ONIAS IV High priest	162 DEMETRIUS I SOTER (162–150)	163/62 Second commission sent to East	
		161 Treaty concluded with Rome	ALCIMUS High priest 160/59		161 Treaty with Maccabees	
160		160 Battle of Eleasa: Judas killed; Jonathan assumes leadership				160
		157 Treaty between Jonathan and Bacchides: Syrians withdraw	INTER-SACERDOTAL			
		152 Jonathan named high priest by Alexander Balas				
150		150 Jonathan named military and civil governor		150 ALEXANDER BALAS (150–145)	149–146 Third Punic War	150
	PTOLEMY VII 145 Ptolemy VIII defeats Alexander Balas PTOLEMY VIII PHYSCON (145–116)		JONATHAN High priest	145 Civil war between; DEMETRIUS II NICATOR (145–138) ANTIOCHUS VI (145–142?) DIODOTUS TRYPHON (142 138)		
		143 Treaty renewed with Rome Jonathan murdered by Tryphon 142/1 Demetrius recognizes Jewish freedom 141 Simon captures citadel	143		c. 143 Treaty between Romans and Maccabeans renewed c. 142–139 Treaty again renewed	
140		140 Simon confirmed as high priest, commander and ethnarch	SIMON High priest		139 Expulsion of Jews from Rome?	140
				139/8 Parthians capture Demetrius ANTIOCHUS VII SIDETES (139/8–129)		

	EGYPT	LAND OF ISRAEL (PALESTINE)	SYRIA	ROME	GREECE	
	131	134 Simon assassinated Antiochus VII invades and besieges Jerusalem 135 John Hycanus comes to terms with Antiochus VII. Judea temporarily under Seleucid domination	134	134 Jews appeal to Rome: Antiochus III ignores decree sent from Rome		
130	Civil war between — Ptolemy and wife, Cleopatra II	129/8? Samaritan temple destroyed. Antiochus dies: Judea is *de facto* free 128 Campaign in Transjordan 126 104 Expansion into Samaria and Idumea	130 Campaign against Parthians 129 DEMETRIUS II NICATOR (second reign: 129–126/5) 126/5 Civil war between: SELEUCUS V (125) ALEXANDER ZEBINAS (128–122?) ANTIOCHUS VIII GRYPUS (125–113) 123 Antiochus defeats Alexander ANTIOCHUS VIII GRYPUS (123/2–113)			130
120	118 116 PTOLEMY IX LATHYRUS (116–108/7, 88–80)	JOHN HYRCANUS High priest	113 Antiochus VIII deposed ANTIOCHUS IX CYZICENUS (113–95) 111 Divided kingdom ANTIOCHUS VIII: Greater Syria ANTIOCHUS IX: Coele-Syria			120
110	108—PTOLEMY X ALEXANDER (108/7–88)	? John Hyrcanus breaks with Pharisees 104? Aristobulus conquers Galilee ARISTOBULUS I 104 103		*c.* 108 Jews appeal to Rome; *Senatus consultum* passed directing Antiochus IX to cease action against Jews		110
100	94 Civil War: Pharisees revolt against Alexander Janneus		96 Death of Antiochus VIII 95 Antiochus IX defeated Civil Wars (95–83) between the son of Antiochus IX: ANTIOCHUS X EUSEBES PHILOPATOR and the sons of Antiochus VII: SELEUCUS VI ANTIOCHUS XI PHILIP DEMETRIUS III EUCAERUS ANTIOCHUS XII			100
90	88 Civil war ends when many defect to Alexander Janneus in order to repel the invasion of Demetrius III of Syria	ALEXANDER JANNEUS High priest and king	83 Tigranes, King of Armenta, takes Syria TIGRANES (83–69)			90
80	PTOLEMY XI AULETES (80 51)					80

Date	Events	Rulers	Seleucid/Syria	Rome	Date
70		SALOME ALEXANDRA: Queen HYRCANUS I High priest	69 Lucullus defeats Tigranes		70
	67 Outbreak of Civil War Hyrcanus abdicates to Aristobulus 65 Hyrcanus and Aretas the Nuabatean besiege Aristobulus. Romans halt siege	ARISTOBULUS High priest 63	64 Pompey takes possession of Syria Seleucid rule comes to an end	66 Final defeat of Mithridates 65 Roman army in Palestine 64 Pompey annexes Syria 63 Pompey besieges Jerusalem; Jerusalem falls; end of Hasmonean rule	
63	63 Pompey besieges Temple; Jerusalem falls				63

[1] Strict accuracy in dating is not always possible. Question marks in the chart indicate uncertainties.

INDEX